3/9/12 Gale

W9-AAE-537

Newsmakers®

ISSN 0899-0417

Newsmakers®

The People Behind Today's Headlines

Laura Avery

Project Editor

2012
Cumulation

Includes Indexes from
1985 through 2012

GALE
CENGAGE Learning

Detroit • New York • San Francisco • New Haven, Conn • Waterville, Maine • London

Newsmakers 2012, Cumulation

Project Editor: Laura Avery

Editorial Support Services: Emmanuel T. Barrido

Rights Acquisition and Management: Margaret Chamberlain-Gaston

Imaging: John Watkins

Composition and Electronic Capture: Amy Darga

Manufacturing: Cynde Lentz

For product information and technology assistance, contact us at **Gale Customer Support, 1-800-877-4253.** For permission to use material from this text or product, submit all requests online at **www.cengage.com/permissions.** Further permissions questions can be emailed to **permissionrequest@cengage.com**

While every effort has been made to ensure the reliability of the information presented in this publication, Gale, a part of Cengage Learning, does not guarantee the accuracy of the data contained herein. Gale accepts no payment for listing; and inclusion in the publication of any organization, agency, institution, publication, service, or individual does not imply endorsement of the editors or publisher. Errors brought to the attention of the publisher and verified to the satisfaction of the publisher will be corrected in future editions.

EDITORIAL DATA PRIVACY POLICY. Does this publication contain information about you as an individual? If so, for more information about our editorial data privacy policies, please see our Privacy Statement at www.gale.cengage.com.

Gale
27500 Drake Rd.
Farmington Hills, MI 48331-3535

ISBN-13: 978-1-4144-4881-7
ISBN-10: 1-4144-4881-3

ISSN 0899-0417

This title is also available as an e-book.
ISBN-13: 978-1-4144-5337-8
ISBN-10: 1-4144-5337-X
Contact your Gale, Cengage Learning sales representative for ordering information.

Printed in the United States of America
1 2 3 4 5 6 7 16 15 14 13 12

Contents

Obituaries

Introduction

Newsmakers provides informative profiles of the world's most interesting people in a crisp, concise, contemporary format. Make *Newsmakers* the first place you look for biographical information on the people making today's headlines.

Important Features

- **Attractive, modern page design** pleases the eye while making it easy to locate the information you need.

- **Coverage of all the newsmakers** you want to know about: people in business, education, technology, law, politics, religion, entertainment, labor, sports, medicine, and other fields.

- **Clearly labeled data sections** allow quick access to vital personal statistics, career information, major awards, and mailing addresses.

- **Informative sidelights essays** include the kind of in-depth analysis you're looking for.

- **Sources for additional information** provide lists of books, magazines, newspapers, and internet sites where you can find out even more about *Newsmakers* listees.

- **Enlightening photographs** are specially selected to further enhance your knowledge of the subject.

- **Separate obituaries section** provides you with concise profiles of recently deceased newsmakers.

- **Publication schedule and price** fit your budget. *Newsmakers* is published in three paperback issues per year, each containing approximately 50 entries, and a hardcover cumulation, containing approximately 200 entries (those from the preceding three paperback issues plus an additional 50 entries), *all at a price you can afford!*

- And much, much more!

Indexes Provide Easy Access

Familiar and indispensable: The *Newsmakers* indexes! You can easily locate entries in a variety of ways through our four versatile, comprehensive indexes. The Nationality, Occupation, and Subject Indexes list names from the current year's *Newsmakers* issues. These are cumulated in the annual hardbound volume to include all names from the entire *Contemporary Newsmakers* and *Newsmakers* series. The Newsmakers Index is cumulated in all issues as well as the hardbound annuals to provide concise coverage of the entire series.

- **Nationality Index**—Names of newsmakers are arranged alphabetically under their respective nationalities.

- **Occupation Index**—Names are listed alphabetically under broad occupational categories.

- **Subject Index**—Includes key subjects, topical issues, company names, products, organizations, etc., that are discussed in *Newsmakers*. Under each subject heading are listed names of newsmakers associated with that topic. So the unique Subject Index provides access to the information in *Newsmakers* even when readers are unable to connect a name with a particular topic. This index also invites browsing, allowing *Newsmakers* users to discover topics they may wish to explore further.

- **Cumulative Newsmakers Index**—Listee names, along with birth and death dates, when available, are arranged alphabetically followed by the year and issue number in which their entries appear.

Available in Electronic Formats

Licensing. *Newsmakers* is available for licensing. The complete database is provided in a fielded format and is deliverable on such media as disk or CD-ROM. For more information, contact Gale's Business Development Group at 1-800-877-4253, or visit our website at http://www.gale.cengage.com/bizdev.

Online. *Newsmakers* is available online as part of the Gale Biographies (GALBIO) database accessible through LexisNexis, P.O. Box 933, Dayton, OH 45401-0933; phone: (937) 865-6800, toll-free: 800-227-4908.

Suggestions Are Appreciated

The editors welcome your comments and suggestions. In fact, many popular *Newsmakers* features were implemented as a result of readers' suggestions. We will continue to shape the series to best meet the needs of the greatest number of users. Send comments or suggestions to:

The Editor
Newsmakers
Gale
27500 Drake Rd.
Farmington Hills, MI 48331-3535

Or, call toll-free at 1-800-877-4253

Trace Adkins

Singer and songwriter

Born Tracy Darrell Adkins, January 13, 1962, in Springhill, LA; married first wife (divorced); married second wife, Julie (divorced, c. 1994); married Rhonda Forlaw (a publicist), May 11, 1997; children: Tarah, Sarah (from first marriage), Mackenzie, Brianna, Trinity (from third marriage). *Education:* Attended Louisiana Tech University.

Addresses: *Contact*—P.O. Box 121889, Nashville, TN 37212. *Web site*—http://www.traceadkins.com/wired/.

Career

Sang with gospel quartet, c. 1979-91; worked on offshore oil rigs and oil fields as a derrick-man, c. early 1990s; sang on the honky tonk circuit, c. early to mid-1990s; signed with Capitol Nashville, 1995; released debut album *Dreamin' Out Loud,* 1996; appeared as guest on multiple episodes of *Politically Incorrect,* c. late 1990s-2002; *Greatest Hits Collection, Vol. 1,* debuted at number one on the country album charts, 2003; appeared as guest on *Hollywood Squares,* 2003-04; provided a voice characterization for *King of the Hill* (animated), FOX, 2003-05, 2007; appeared on *Yes, Dear,* CBS, 2004; competed on reality show *Celebrity Apprentice,* NBC, 2008; guest starred on *The Young and the Restless,* CBS, 2008; appeared in films *Trailer Park of Terror* and *An American Carol,* 2008; signed with Toby Keith's label Show Dog Nashville, 2010; released first album on Show Dog, *Cowboy's Back in Town,* 2010.

Awards: People's Choice Ark-La-Tex Award for male gospel vocalist of the year, 1980; award for best new male vocalist, Academy of Country Music, 1997; award for male star of tomorrow, TNN (The Nashville Network)/Music City News, 1997, 1998.

Sidelights

While country music star Trace Adkins is perhaps best known for hit singles like "Honky Tonk Badonkadonk," his career spanned at least two decades and many popular albums. Beginning with his well-received 1996 debut *Dreamin' Out Loud,* Adkins put out successful record after successful record and had hits with nearly every album. Adkins' distinctive baritone voice, tall stature, and everyman outlook also contributed to his achievements. John Rose, the vice president of sales for Capitol Nashville, told Doug Reece of *Billboard,* "Trace comes from the world of oil rigs and honky-tonks, and that's why his songs come across as real and convincing as they do."

Born on January 13, 1962, in Springhill, Louisiana, Adkins was exposed to country music from an early age. His grandfather was a bass singer and two uncles were recording artists in their own right in gospel and boogie-woogie piano. Adkins attended a high school in Sarepta, Louisiana, where he began singing bass in a gospel quartet while still a student. Of this time in his life, he told John Wooley of the *Tulsa World*, "I was a little shy then, and I think that if I hadn't had the chance to get up and sing in a quartet, where it wasn't just me singing, I might not be here today. It helped me get over my stage fright, and to get some confidence in myself."

Adkins continued his education at Louisiana Tech University. There, he studied petroleum technology, played football for a time, took two semesters of voice training, and continued to sing gospel with the quartet until he was 23 years old. After Adkins left college, he spent the next few years working on offshore oil rigs and oil fields as a derrick-man. Deciding on a career in music, he began playing honky tonks in Louisiana, New Mexico, Mississippi, Texas, and Tennessee, and educating himself on music with stints living in Dallas and Nashville. He had been exposed to country his entire life, at home, on the car radio, and everywhere else, though gospel predominated at church.

After playing what Adkins called combat country in these venues for several years, he had his big break when he met an executive with Capitol Records, Scott Hendricks. Adkins told Mario Tarradell of the *Dallas Morning News*, "I met Scott Hendricks ... at the baggage claim at the airport. I was introduced to him as a singer, told him I was playing a little gig outside of town. He came out to see me. I played my first set, and he went up on stage and said, 'I'll give you a record deal.' My knees buckled and I went, 'For ten years, I've been waiting on this. Where in the hell have you been?'" Adkins signed to Capitol Nashville in October of 1995 and released his debut album, *Dreamin' Out Loud*, in 1996.

Adkins had success from the first. While *Dreamin' Out Loud* received mixed reviews, critics saw much potential. As Teresa Gubbins wrote in the *Dallas Morning News:* "Not only is he an impressive sight in his wide-brimmed black hat and dark overcoat draped over a hulking 6-foot-6-inch frame, but he's got one of those whiskey-barrel voices, dark and deep enough to rattle your insides. His vocal delivery carries his hit single, the contemplative 'There's a Girl in Texas,' and lends the album a brooding atmosphere."

Dreamin' Out Loud reached the top ten on the album charts, sold a million copies, and was certified platinum. The album produced several hit singles, including "There's a Girl in Texas," which was a top 20 hit on the country music charts, "Every Light in the House" which reached number three on the same charts, and a cover of Wilson Pickett's "634-5789." In 1997, he had his first number-one hit with "(This Ain't) No Thinkin' Thing," which also came from that album. Adkins toured continuously in support of the album, telling Frank Roberts of the *Virginian-Pilot*, "I leave the stage a sweaty mess. I give all I got—give folks their money's worth. The show is high energy and a lot of fun."

Adkins followed up *Dreamin' Out Loud* with 1997's *Big Time*, also produced by Hendricks. Critics responded positively to this album as well, noting that the singer had increased confidence and was becoming a noteworthy country artist. Adkins was also happier with his sophomore album as well, telling the *Dallas Morning News'* Tarradell that "It's lot more me." Adkins also stated: "For me, the relaxed atmosphere and being more comfortable in the studio comes across in terms of expressiveness and creativity on the second one."

However, the new country-oriented *Big Time* did not produce the hit singles that *Dreamin' Out Loud* did, though critics praised songs on the album like his recording of the gospel song "Wayfaring Stranger." While it was eventually certified gold, its lack of success was blamed on the marketing at Capitol which focused primarily on its biggest star, Garth Brooks, to the detriment of other artists like Adkins. In the late 1990s, Adkins career further suffered as Capitol Nashville underwent a shakeup that saw Hendricks replaced as president by Pat Quigley. It took more than two years for his next album to come out, but Adkins' career eventually rebounded.

Adkins released his third album, *More ...*, in 1999. It produced several hits, including the top 50 country hit "Don't Lie" and the top ten hit "More." The singer was happy with *More ...*, in part because his label gave him the freedom to do the album the way he wanted to within a reasonable budget. Because of a messy ankle fracture caused by stepping into a hole on his Tennessee-based farm, Adkins had to take off several months from touring.

More label turmoil, including the replacement of Quigley with another president, Mike Dungan, contributed to another two-year break between albums. Adkins released his fourth album, the rock-edged *Chrome*, in 2001, with the full support of Dungan and the backing of Capitol Nashville; however, its sales suffered because it was released shortly after the terrorist attacks of September 11, 2001. Despite this setback, the album went gold and produced the hit single "I'm Tryin'," in 2001, and "Chrome," in 2003. Critics found the album diverse, with Deborah Evans Price of *Billboard* noting, "it's Adkins' deep, resonant voice that takes center stage on this collection of songs."

Adkins' career and life saw highs and lows in 2003. He had some of the strongest sales of his career to date for his *Greatest Hits Collection, Vol. 1,* which debuted at number one on the country album charts and produced a top 15 hit with the new track "Then They Do." He was inducted into the Grand Ole Opry and was honored with the Trace Adkins Chrome 300 NASCAR Busch Series race in Nashville. But Adkins also checked himself into a rehabilitation center to address his addiction to alcohol. Adkins had been struggling with a drinking problem for years and was arrested for drunk driving in July of 2001. He embraced sobriety after being in rehab.

By the end of 2003, Adkins had released a new studio album, the well-received *Comin' On Strong.* This album was also number one the week it was released and produced hit singles like "Hot Mama." Critics like Mandy Davis in the *St. Louis Post-Dispatch* called it one of his "most well-rounded albums."

In 2005, Adkins continued his string of successful releases with *Songs About Me.* The album debuted at number one on the country charts and number eleven on the *Billboard* 200 album charts. *Songs About Me* featured the smash hit single "Honky Tonk Badonkadonk." Because of the strength of that single and other hit singles like "Songs About Me," the album sold two million copies. Writing about the album in *Billboard,* Deborah Evans Price commented, "Adkins has delivered a solid album buoyed by strong songs and personality-packed performances."

Riding a crest of success, Adkins stretched his musical wings on his next album, *Dangerous Man,* released in 2006. "Ain't No Woman Like You" was an R&B track while others were driving, anthemic, and fun as many of his most popular tracks had been. Some critics labeled the album a retread of his massive hit "Honky Tonk Badonkadonk," while others embraced Adkins' attempts to move beyond cookie cutter country. Adkins followed *Dangerous Man* with another compilation, *American Man: Greatest Hits, Vol. II,* which produced the number-one country single "You're Gonna Miss This." He also published the nonfiction, semi-autobiographical, opinion-filled book *A Personal Stand: Observations and Opinions from a Freethinking Roughneck.* Both were put out in 2007.

In 2008, Adkins' public profile rose with his appearance on the competitive reality show on NBC, *Celebrity Apprentice.* He lost in the final episode to British talk show host and tabloid editor Piers Morgan. It was not Adkins' first time on television. He had previously been known for his multiple appearances on the talk show *Politically Incorrect* in the late 1990s and early 2000s until the show ended its run in 2002. He appeared on numerous other late night talk shows, and various other programs like the syndicated game show *Hollywood Squares.* He contributed his voice to a character on multiple episodes of the animated FOX series *King of the Hill,* and appeared on the CBS situation comedy *Yes, Dear,* and the CBS soap opera *The Young and the Restless.* In addition, he acted in such films as *Trailer Park of Terror* and *American Carol.*

Of his acting and related appearances, Adkins told Beth Harris of the Associated Press State & Local Wire, "I'd like to do some more of the acting stuff. I'm at a point in my life and my career, I'm at such a beautiful place, if something doesn't sound like fun to me I probably won't do it. It's a luxury to pick and choose the projects you want to be a part of." Adkins' appearance on *Celebrity Apprentice* was not his only highlight of 2008. That year, he also released his tenth album for Capitol Nashville, *X.* Generally well received, the diverse album had a hit with the serious ballad "Muddy Water" and "You're Gonna Miss This."

After *X,* Adkins left the financially struggling Capitol Nashville for a new label, Show Dog Nashville, owned by country music star Toby Keith. His first album with the label was released in 2010: *Cowboy's Back in Town.* The album was also co-produced by Adkins and emphasized humor and positiveness in its tracks, though tender moments abounded. *Cowboy's Back in Town* produced such hits as "This Ain't No Love Song."

Outside of music, Adkins was interested in Civil War history. The interest began when he was 14 years old through his grandfather. His grandfather's grandfather fought with the 31st Louisiana Infantry in that war. Adkins' interest in Civil War history extended to attending battle re-enactments.

Making music, however, was Adkins' true passion. Explaining his music, Adkins told Nancy Gordon of the Bloomington, Illinois *Pantagraph,* that his song lyrics were all about "pain and sex." He added, "That's life, man. I'm a roughneck, and I won't try to hide it." Fellow country music star Blake Shelton told Chris Talbott of the Associated Press of Adkins, "He's one of the coolest, biggest … guys in entertainment. He just has this huge presence."

Selected discography

Dreamin' Out Loud, Capitol Nashville, 1996.
Big Time, Capitol Nashville, 1997.
More ..., Capitol Nashville, 1999.
Chrome, Capitol/EMI Records, 2001.
Greatest Hits Collection, Vol. 1, Capitol/EMI Records, 2003.
Comin' on Strong, Liberty, 2003.
Songs About Me, Capitol Nashville, 2005.
Dangerous Man, EMI Music Distribution, 2006.
American Man: Greatest Hits, Vol. II, 2007.
X, Capitol Nashville, 2008.
Cowboy's Back in Town, Show Dog Nashville, 2010.

Selected writings

A Personal Stand: Observations and Opinions from a Freethinking Roughneck, Villard (New York City), 2007.

Sources

Periodicals

Associated Press, August 14, 2006; December 6, 2007; November 24, 2008; August 17, 2010; August 19, 2010.
Associated Press State & Local Wire, April 10, 2008.
Associated Press Worldstream, October 11, 2001.

Billboard, February 22, 1997, p. 10; November 1, 1997; October 16, 1999; October 6, 2001, p. 51; November 29, 2003, p. 36; April 16, 2005, p. 40; April 12, 2008, p. 55; November 22, 2008; July 24, 2010.
Charlotte Observer (NC), August 1, 2003, p. 13E.
Chicago Sun-Times, June 25, 2004, p. 3.
Dallas Morning News, July 7, 1996, p. 8C; January 16, 1998, p. 55.
Knoxville News-Sentinel (TN), June 18, 2009.
Pantagraph (Bloomington, IL), February 4, 2000, p. D2.
Press Enterprise (Riverside, CA), May 2, 2008, p. D1.
Sherbrooke Record (Quebec, Canada), September 8, 2006, p. 15.
Spokesman Review (Spokane, WA), January 16, 2004, p. 4.
State Journal-Register (Springfield, IL), June 13, 2002, p. 15.
St. Louis Post-Dispatch (MO), December 4, 2003, p. F3.
Telegram & Gazette (MA), August 11, 1998, p. C5.
Times Union (Albany, NY), March 13, 2008, p. P18.
Tulsa World, July 19, 1996, p. 3.
Virginian-Pilot (Norfolk, VA), June 19, 1997, p. E4.

Online

"Trace Adkins: Artist Main," Country Music Television, http://www.cmt.com/artists/az/adkins_trace/artist.jhtml (February 26, 2011).
"Trace Adkins," Internet Movie Database, http://www.imdb.com/name/nm0012081/ (February 26, 2011).

—A. Petruso

Akon

Singer, songwriter, and producer

Born Aliaune Damala Thiam, April 30, 1973, in St. Louis, MO; son of Mor (a percussionist) and Kiné (a dancer) Thiam; married; children: four.

Addresses: *Record company*—Universal Motown, 1755 Broadway, New York, NY 10107. *Web site*—http://www.akononline.com.

Career

Signed with Universal, 2003; released *Trouble,* 2004; produced other artists' tracks, 2005—; released *Konvicted,* 2006; released *Freedom,* 2008; released *Akonic,* 2010.

Awards: Favorite Soul/R&B Male Artist, American Music Awards, 2007.

Sidelights

R&B singer, rapper, songwriter, and music producer Akon built a successful music career during the early 21st century based on his diverse musical style that incorporates elements of pop and world music into a mainstream urban sound. His exploration of music purportedly started during a three-year stint in prison, with the behind-bars anthems providing the basis for Akon's slow-building 2004 debut, *Trouble.* "His voice represents the world," commented artist Wyclef Jean to Laura Checkoway of *Vibe.* "No matter what he's talking about, the hustle is in him.... His voice is the world. It defines no area. You can hear it in London, Brook-

lyn, Atlanta, Africa." With two platinum-selling albums, a slew of high-charting singles, and a handful of Grammy Award nominations under his belt, Akon has the distinction of being the first artist to hold the number-one and number-two slots on the *Billboard* 200 not once but twice. Akon has also become a frequent collaborator and influential tastemaker, helping give other artists such as Lady Gaga a break in the music industry. He is nearly as well-known for his much-discussed criminal past that he has stated included drug dealing and serving as the ringleader of a nationwide automobile theft ring. Although the veracity of these claims has been disputed, unquestionably Akon has encountered legal troubles throughout his career; in 2008, he pled guilty to minor charges relating to an incident at a concert in which he threw a fan off the stage.

Akon was born Aliaune Damala Thiam in St. Louis, Missouri, to Senegalese parents Mor Thiam, a noted percussionist, and Kiné Thiam, a dancer. Although the family lived primarily in Africa, Akon's parents had traveled to the United States for his birth to guarantee that their son would have U.S. citizenship. The artist has declined to confirm his actual birth date, and estimates have suggested years as recent as 1981; however, court documents published on the Smoking Gun Web site list Akon's birth date as April 30, 1973. After his birth, Akon and his family returned to Africa, and the artist spent the next several years growing up in Dakar, Senegal. When Akon was seven, the Thiam family settled in Jersey City, New Jersey, so that their children could attend school in the United States. Because of his parents' involvement with music and entertainment, Akon was exposed to a variety of sounds from an early age. He met artists including Michael Jackson and James Brown, and developed a love for diverse musical styles ranging from rock to R&B to soul. Nevertheless, the transition from Africa to his new homeland was a difficult one for the young boy. Speaking to C. Bottomley in an interview on VH1.com, Akon recalled, "I used to get picked on because I was from Africa. I had nappy hair and my clothes were cultural. So people reacted to me in an ignorant way because they didn't know my culture. My whole thing was, if you're going to be ignorant to me I'm going to be ignorant to you. It got to the point where I was fighting every day at school."

During his teen years, Akon developed a passion for hip-hop music even as he became involved in the world of crime. The artist claimed to have operated a test question and marijuana sales ring out of his high school locker, and even for a time to have rented out his gun for $100 a day. Wanting to make more money, Akon began stealing cars and selling them to local drug dealers. In about 1993, Akon left New Jersey for Atlanta, Georgia; accounts differ on whether this happened after he dropped out of high school, was expelled from high school, or graduated from high school with a basketball scholarship to a Georgia college. Regardless of the impetus, by the mid-1990s the artist had settled in the Atlanta area, began writing songs, and even signed a contract with Elektra/East West Records that ultimately did not result in a release. Akon then turned more seriously to crime, reputedly becoming the head of a nationwide car theft ring that specialized in high-end automobiles. After a dramatic confrontation with the police, he was sentenced to three years in prison.

However, Akon's official version of his life story has been strongly disputed by the Smoking Gun. In 2008, the Web site collected and published information culled from a series of police records and other documents that contradicted the artist's accepted back story. The investigation found that Akon had in fact been charged in September of 1998 with handgun possession and receiving stolen property and then arrested a few months later while driving a stolen car. However, the jail time resulting from these charges had spanned five months rather than three years. A subsequent weapons possessions charge in New Jersey ended in probation rather than prison. "This guy is so phony. He's an arrogant

SOB," former FBI agent Peter McFarlane, who examined a fraudulent vehicle title to the stolen BMW Akon was found driving, told the Smoking Gun. Police detective R. L. Brewer, the arresting officer in the incident, told the Web site, "I don't think he had any role besides [wanting] to drive a high-dollar vehicle. And I say this because we didn't link him to any other cars."

The Smoking Gun's findings led the Web site and other commentators to conclude that Akon had embellished or, in some cases, entirely fabricated his past in order to establish his bona fides among a hip-hop community that may consider street toughness and a criminal background a symbol of authenticity. The artist dismissed the allegations, however, telling Chris Harris of MTV News that, "Everyone's entitled to their own opinions.... The Konvict movement is keeping me out of jail. It's nothing I want to glorify or go back to.... To try to discredit an artist, it makes no sense to me."

Regardless of how Akon actually spent the time period between 1999 and 2002, he certainly dedicated part of it to writing songs. In 2003, Akon's demo made its way to a music executive at Universal, and the artist signed a recording contract with that label. In 2004, Akon released his debut album, *Trouble*, on Universal Records. Drawing lyrical inspiration from the artist's time in prison—particularly on hit singles "Lonely" and "Locked Up"—the album combined musical influences ranging from rap to reggae to R&B to West African rhythms to create Akon's uniquely blended sound. Calling the album "surprisingly strong," *New York Times* reviewer Kelefa Sanneh observed that "Akon moves deftly from hard-knock stories to dance-floor sleaze to inspirational ballads." Propelled by the popularity of its prison-anthem singles, *Trouble* climbed to number eleven on the *Billboard* R&B Albums chart and eventually went platinum.

Akon's cross-genre notoriety continued to rise thanks to appearances and production work for other hip-hop and pop artists. A 2005 collaboration with rapper Young Jeezy, "Soul Survivor," proved a massive hit. Another pair of collaborations contributed to the great success of Akon's sophomore effort, *Konvicted*, released in 2006. Inaugural single "Smack That," featuring Eminem, and follow-up track "I Wanna Love You" with Snoop Dogg both became chart hits, and *Konvicted* itself eventually achieved double-platinum sales. "These songs seem both homemade and grand," commented Sanneh in a *New York Times* review of *Konvicted*. Sanneh continued, "you picture Akon holed up in a New Jersey basement, cranking out potential hits." In a review for *Allmusic,* Andy Keller observed that "Akon ... tends to go with what suits him best: bragging and seducing while delivering like-sounding hooks in his unique voice."

After the success of *Konvicted,* Akon began to turn his attention to other creative endeavors. He formed two record labels, Konvict Musik and Kon Live Records, and began work on a clothing line, also called Konvict. One of the artists that Akon signed to his Kon Live label was flamboyant singer Lady Gaga, who went on to become a global pop superstar. Akon has also dabbled in producing, helming tracks for other artists, including Gwen Stefani and Chamillionaire.

In 2007, the artist generated discussion over his behavior rather than his music. In the spring of that year, he was videotaped simulating sex with a young woman during a performance at a club in the Caribbean nation of Trinidad; reports later revealed that the woman was underage, despite the club's stated policy of admitting only of-age patrons. "I want to sincerely apologize for the embarrassment and any pain I've caused to the young woman who joined me onstage, her family and the Trinidad community for the events at my concert," Akon said in a statement quoted in a *New York Times* article by Jeff Leeds. As a result of the ensuing scandal, cell phone company Verizon ended its promotional affiliation with the performer, removing him from its ads and pulling its sponsorship dollars from the Gwen Stefani tour on which he was the opening act.

Soon thereafter, Akon was again in the news for his actions. At a June performance at a stadium in Fishkill, New York, the artist was videotaped reacting strongly after a fan threw something at him onstage. After asking the crowd to identify the culprit, Akon had a teenage boy brought on to the stage. He then picked up the fan, placed him on his shoulders, and threw him back into the crowd. The boy landed on another fan, who then claimed that she suffered a concussion. Because of the injury the second fan sustained, Akon was charged with endangering a minor—a misdemeanor offense—and a count of second-degree harassment. "It was never Akon's intention to violate the law," commented his lawyer Benjamin Brafman in a statement quoted in the *New York Times.* "This unfortunate incident was a spontaneous reaction during a live concert that Akon deeply regrets." Although the artist had initially pled not guilty, he changed his plea when the case finally went to trial in December of 2008 and was sentenced to pay a small fine and perform 65 hours of community service.

Legal troubles did not prevent Akon from continuing to write and record music, and his third album *Freedom* hit shelves in late 2008. A poppier, dancier effort than his preceding records, *Freedom* drew upon European club influences to create a sound strikingly different than Akon's previous rap-R&B hybrid. Although the album cracked the top three of the *Billboard* R&B Albums chart and produced three moderately successful singles, it failed to excite either critics or fans in the same way that Akon's first two releases had. *Entertainment Weekly*'s Simon Vozick-Levinson complained of the album's "boring retreads," while *Rolling Stone*'s Jody Rosen shrugged off the album's sounds as "closer to early Peter Gabriel than to 2008 hip-hop."

The following year, Akon began work on a fourth studio effort tentatively titled *Stadium;* however, the recording experienced several delays and no new material appeared until mid-2010. The effort's first formal single, "Angel," was released in September of 2010 to noticeably less commercial success than most of Akon's earlier tracks; the song peaked at number three on the *Billboard* Mainstream Top 40 chart and failed to break into the upper half of the Hot 100. Lacking the support of a hit single, Akon's much-delayed and retitled fourth album *Akonic* dropped in November of 2010 to practically no notice. During the spring of 2011, Akon returned to the road with fellow crooner Usher.

Selected discography

Trouble, Universal Records, 2004.
Konvicted, Universal Records, 2006.
Freedom, Universal Records, 2008.
Akonic, Universal Records, 2010.

Sources

Books

Contemporary Black Biography, vol. 68, Gale, 2009, pp. 1-3.
Contemporary Musicians, vol. 61, Gale, 2008, pp. 12-13.

Periodicals

Entertainment Weekly, December 5, 2008.
New York Times, July 14, 2004; November 13, 2006; May 10, 2007; December 4, 2007; December 18, 2008, p. C2.

Rolling Stone, November 27, 2008.
Vibe, April 2007, p. 90.

Online

"Akon: Biography," *Allmusic,* http://allmusic.com/artist/akon-p535592/biography (March 7, 2011).
"Akon Responds to *Smoking Gun* Report that He Fabricated His Criminal Past: 'It Only Helps Me,'" MTV News, http://www.mtv.com/news/articles/1587614/akon-addresses-report-that-fabricated-his-criminal-past.jhtml (March 7, 2011).
"Akon's Con Job," Smoking Gun, http://www.thesmokinggun.com/documents/crime/akons-con-job (March 7, 2011).

"Akon: Trouble No More," VH1, http://www.vh1.com/artists/interview/1501105/05022005.tif/akon.jhtml (March 7, 2011).
"Chart Beat," *Billboard,* http://www.billboard.com/bbcom/search/google/article_display.jsp?vnu_content_id=10035678.tif11#/bbcom/search/google/article_display.jsp?vnu_content_id=10035678.tif11 (March 7, 2011).
"Konvicted," *Allmusic,* http://allmusic.com/album/konvicted-r932394 (March 7, 2011).

—Vanessa E. Vaughn

Yael Alkalay

Founder of Red Flower

Born c. 1969; married. *Education:* Boston University, bachelor's degree; Columbia University, M.B.A., 1997.

Addresses: *Office*—Red Flower Boutique, 13 Prince St., New York, NY 10012. *Web site*—http://www. redflower.com.

Career

Worked as creative director for Shiseido, early and mid-1990s; worked in cosmetics product development for Calvin Klein, mid-1990s; launched Red Flower, 1999.

Sidelights

Personal-care entrepreneur Yael Alkalay is best known as the founder of Red Flower, an environmentally and socially conscious line of candles, teas, toiletries, and beauty products. Drawing on her personal heritage and professional cosmetics industry background, Alkalay began her company in the late 1990s with seed money provided by a Columbia University venture capital fund for the school's business graduate students. Red Flower grew quickly, and within a decade Alkalay's offerings had expanded to encompass several scent lines that reflected the founder's respect for nature and the traditional personal care practices of various cultures. "Being connected to real things that are true and lasting is a unique feeling," she told Christine Muhlke of *Vanity Fair.* "You can't invent a thousand years of experience." All of the products from

this earth-friendly company are certified organic and are fully biodegradable. Red Flower has further worked to support environmental efforts by partnering with the Blue Project to help protect threatened coral reefs in the Bahamas.

Born around 1969, Alkalay grew up in the city of New Bedford on the southern coast of Massachusetts; however, her family background reflects a much more international heritage. Her grandfather was a dermatologist who emigrated from communist Bulgaria to Israel in 1954, and her family on one side traces its roots to fifteenth century Spanish Jews who settled in the more welcoming climate of Ottoman Turkey. On the other side, Alkalay is descended from native Argentineans; her parents met in Israel. This diverse background and its history of geographic upheaval have left a mark on the entrepreneur. She considers a rare family heirloom—a handful of Turkish gold coins that were part of her grandmother's dowry—a personal good luck charm and reaffirmation of her own identity. "I reach in my pocket to feel them sometimes," she told David Colman of the *New York Times,* "and it's like, 'Am I still all there?'"

As a child, Alkalay became acquainted with botanical products created by her farmer mother as foods, beverages, and personal care products. After completing high school, Alkalay enrolled at Boston University, where she continued her education in botany, culture, and perfume making. During this time, she visited Japan. After completing her degree, she took a job in that country as the creative director of cosmetics company Shiseido, barely escaping the 1995 subway nerve gas attack that affected thousands of Tokyo commuters—oddly enough, because of an unplanned return home to collect the forgotten pile of gold coins, which she had developed the habit of keeping with her at all times.

In about 1996, Alkalay left her position with Shiseido to return to the United States. She settled in New York City and began pursuing graduate studies at Columbia University, completing a master's degree in business administration in 1997. Alkalay also continued to work in the beauty industry, holding a position in product development for Calvin Klein's cosmetics arm for a time in the late 1990s. However, she soon decided to strike out on her own and began planning the launch of her own candle, tea, and personal care products line, Red Flower. Drawing on her own love of travel, diverse heritage, and experiences in Japan, Alkalay focused on creating a line that infused exotic scents into natural, environmentally friendly products. The result was a line that aimed "to create beauty that is founded on emotional connectivity, optimism, rich aesthetic principles, an environmental mission, and deep health," explained the entrepreneur to Laura Katzenberg of *Vanity Fair.*

In order to finance the start-up company, Alkalay relied on a grant of $250,000 from the Columbia University Eugene Lang Entrepreneurial Fund, a then-recently created venture capital fund specifically designed to support business initiatives by Columbia business students. This funding proved valuable not only in monetary terms, but also in educational ones; after a test run selling products in museum stores, Alkalay decided that Red Flower needed to widen its distribution in order to truly succeed. "I think a typical venture capital fund wouldn't give you the opportunity to learn on someone else's dollar," the entrepreneur commented to Jane Hodges of *Fortune* of the experience in 1998. Alkalay put her early findings to use, launching the Red Flower line formally in 1999 through placement in high-end retailers such as the department store Barney's New York. Red Flower grew quickly, making sales of about $700,000 in 2000 and achieving distribution in some 45 outlets in addition to opening its own branded brick-and-mortar store by 2001. Red Flower cultivated its sense of responsible luxury through careful product selection and partnering; an early herbal tea, for example, was sold with an accompanying sterling silver straw. "'It's like tasting beauty," Alkalay characterized the rose- and lavender-infused teas in a *New York Times* spot. The company continued to grow steadily over the next decade, expanding to add new scents and products such as certified organic perfumes scented with natural flower extracts.

The inspiration for Red Flower's natural scents has come largely from Alkalay's life and interests. For example, Wanderlust, a 2008 product line featured in luxury hotels and spas, stemmed from the entrepreneur's passion for her adopted hometown of New York. "It is the best city in the world to be aimless in. I often feel captivated in a dreamlike state as I walk through parts of the city," she explained to Katzenberg in the same *Vanity Fair* piece. A trip to Finland provided both unique ingredients and a renewed sense of vigor that informed other Red Flower products. Speaking of her experience heating and then chilling herself through the traditional Finnish sauna cycle in *Town & Country,* Alkalay recalled, "By round 15, I had found my life force. Everything about me felt better, and my skin glowed." Other Red Flower products contain exotic scents evocative of Alkalay's familial ties to Turkey and Argentina.

Toward the end of the 2000s, Alkalay affirmed Red Flower's commitment to environmental causes by partnering with the Blue Project. Founded in 2007, the Blue Project works to identify and protect delicate coral reef sites in the Bahamas. Red Flower contributed part of its proceeds from the sale of its Ocean scented product line to the Blue Project, joining other corporate sponsors such as American Express and JetBlue along with environmental groups including the Nature Conservancy and the Kerzner Marine Foundation.

Sources

Periodicals

Crain's New York Business, August 6, 2001, p. 20.
Fortune, October 26, 1998, p. 70.
New York Times, December 19, 1999; February 20, 2005.
Town & Country, May 2008.
Vanity Fair, May 2005, p. 108.

Online

Blue Project Official Web Site, http://www.blueproject.com (March 2, 2011).
"Red Flower Power," *Vanity Fair,* http://www.vanityfair.com/online/daily/2008/09/red-flower.html (March 2, 2011).

—*Vanessa E. Vaughn*

Sunny Anderson

© Tom Briglia/FilmMagic/Getty Images

Television personality and chef

Born April 9, 1975, in Ft. Sill, OK; daughter of Thomas (a retired U.S. Army colonel) Anderson.

Addresses: *Home*—Brooklyn, NY. *Office*—Food Network, 75 Ninth Ave., New York, NY 10011. *Web site*—http://www.sunnyanderson.com/.

Career

Served in the U.S. Air Force, 1993-97, and reached the rank of senior airman; announcer and host, Armed Forces Radio and the Air Force News Agency's Hometown News Service; disc jockey, WYLD-FM (New Orleans, LA), WJWZ-FM (Montgomery, AL), WDTJ-FM (Detroit, MI), and WHQT-FM (New York, NY); founder of catering company, Sunny's Delicious Dishes, 2003; made first appearance on a Food Network show as a guest on *Emeril Live,* October 2005; food and lifestyle editor, *Hip Hop Weekly* magazine, 2006-07; co-host, *Gotta Get It,* Food Network, 2007; host, *Cooking for Real* and *How'd That Get on My Plate?*, Food Network, 2008—.

Sidelights

Sunny Anderson hosts two shows for the Food Network, *Cooking for Real* and *How'd That Get on My Plate?* The former disc jockey credits the U.S. Air Force for providing her with her broadcast training, but acknowledges her family for instilling in her a love of preparing and sharing food with others. "Every day I wake up and say thank you,"

she said in an interview with Matthew Bates for the U.S. Air Force publication *Airman.* "I still can't believe where I am and how lucky I've been."

Anderson was born in the hospital of a U.S. Army base at Fort Sill, Oklahoma, on April 9, 1975. Her father Thomas was an army colonel who moved his family several times, including a stint in Germany, but always brought them back home during the summer months for visits to both sets of grandparents. Her father's parents had a farm in Elloree, South Carolina, and Anderson's visits there would later serve her well in preparation for her land-to-table informational show, *How'd That Get on My Plate?* "I loved being on the farm because my granddad had pigs," she told Phil Sarata, a journalist with the *Times & Democrat* of Orangeburg, South Carolina. "The best part was getting up in the morning. Whatever was left after we ate breakfast went into the slop bucket. I wouldn't gain as much weight because I was trying to sneak out and feed the pigs."

Anderson's family settled for a time in Charleston, then San Antonio, Texas, where she graduated from high school and decided to enlist in the U.S. Air Force. After basic training she was deployed to South Korea, leaving home for good on the day before Thanksgiving of 1993. Immersion into military life was not an especially tough challenge for her, but she missed her mother's cooking dearly. "I realized I didn't want to eat at the mess hall," she told Sarata. "My culinary school tuition was my phone bill to my mom, who was calling me with recipes and ingredients."

In the Air Force, Anderson found her niche in broadcasting, hosting a show on the Armed Forces Radio network and then traveling for a job with the Air Force News Agency and its Hometown News Service, which films short videos of service members sending greetings to their family back home for broadcast on local television stations. She served four years in the Air Force, reaching the rank of senior airman, and then went to work for various urban adult-contemporary radio stations. She spent some time at WYLD-FM in New Orleans, was on the air at WJWZ-FM in Montgomery, Alabama, and even moved to Detroit when she was hired by WDTJ-FM. In 2001, she landed one of the most highly sought-after jobs in the urban-music radio format when she arrived at HOT 97 in New York City. Known more formally by its call letters WQHT-FM, HOT 97 touted itself with the slogan "Where Hip-Hop Lives," and Anderson was present during a tumultuous period in the station's history at its studio on Hudson Street in the West Village. In February of 2001 the studio address was the site of an altercation between rappers Lil' Kim and Foxy Brown, and four years later was host to another shooting, this one involving parties allied with 50 Cent and 50's former ally, Jayceon (the Game) Taylor.

As DJ Sunny, Anderson was one of a handful of female personalities at HOT 97. She interviewed Sean "P. Diddy" Combs and other stars, while the station's executives spent lavishly to court major names to their side in an ongoing rivalry with another leading New York radio station. Anderson remained above the internal and even on-air drama at the station—one of her colleagues, for example, derided their HOT 97 boss as "Benson," a reference to the 1980s sitcom about an African-American butler—but the free-wheeling social whirl did lead her to her second career. "One summer, my boss and all these executives went to a house out in the Hamptons that the radio station had," she told Bates in the *Airman* interview. "I brought my mac and cheese, my chicken, a lot of standout dishes." Within days her bosses started doling out catering jobs to her for station events, and she eventually had to set up her own catering company and hire staffers to help out.

Anderson ran Sunny's Delicious Dishes out of Jersey City, New Jersey, after 2003 and still held on to her HOT 97 show. She sometimes talked about cooking or recipes on the air, and that led to an invitation to appear as a guest on *Emeril Live*, the top-rated Food Network show hosted by Emeril Lagasse. That was in October of 2005, and the show's producer told her she did an exceptional job in front of the cameras. Anderson left the radio station to concentrate on building her company, working as a food and lifestyle editor for *Hip Hop Weekly* magazine before the Food Network hired her as co-host of a gadget and appliance show, *Gotta Get It*, in April of 2007. Exactly a year later, her own show, *Cooking for Real*, debuted on the Food Network. Anderson, noted Janet K. Keeler of the *St. Petersburg Times*, "does not have the professional food chops of some of her older colleagues, several of whom are veteran chefs and restaurateurs. But when the camera comes on, so does she."

Anderson regularly turns up on NBC's *The Today Show* and *Good Morning America* on ABC for cooking segments. Her other Food Network show, which also debuted in 2008, is the informative *How'd That Get on My Plate?* in which Anderson and a camera crew visit dairy farms, produce- and fish-processing plants, and even apiaries (a bee yard). She has sponsorship deals with Kimberly-Clark's Viva paper-towel brand and Kenmore, the major appliance maker. As a former servicewoman, Anderson relishes on-air opportunities to promote efforts to support U.S. troops serving overseas and their families back home. "You know, you learn a lot of intangibles in the military, things like duty, honor, integrity, and confidence," she said in the *Airman* interview. "I've taken these with me throughout my life and they've helped me get where I am today."

Sources

Periodicals

Airman, January-February 2011, p. 30.
St. Petersburg Times, March 10, 2010, p. 1E.
Times & Democrat (Orangeburg, SC), October 18, 2009.
USA Today, December 16, 2010, p. 11B.

Online

"Sunny Anderson," Food Network, http://www.foodnetwork.com/sunny-anderson/bio/index.html (November 26, 2011).

—*Carol Brennan*

Lamberto Andreotti

**Chief Executive Officer of
Bristol-Myers Squibb**

Born c. 1952, in Rome, Italy; son of Giulio (a politician) and Livia Danese Andreotti. *Education:* Sapienza University Rome, bachelor's degree; Massachusetts Institute of Technology, M.S., c. 1977.

Addresses: *Office*—Bristol-Myers Squibb Co., 345 Park Ave., New York, NY 10154.

Career

Joined Farmitalia-Carlo Erba SpA, late 1970s; stayed with the company after it merged into Pharmacia and then Upjohn; senior corporate vice president for Italian operations and worldwide oncology, Upjohn, until 1998; vice president and general manager for Italy and European Oncology in the Worldwide Medicines Group, Bristol-Myers Squibb, 1998-2000, then president for its European divisions, 2000-02, senior vice president for BMS pharmaceutical divisions in Europe and Asia-Pacific, 2002-05, president of newly combined U.S. and global divisions, 2005-07, executive vice president and chief operating officer for the Worldwide Pharmaceuticals, 2007-08, executive vice president and chief operating officer, 2008-09, appointed to BMS board of directors, 2009, president and chief operating officer, 2009-10, chief executive officer, 2010—.

Sidelights

Lamberto Andreotti advanced through senior management ranks to become chief executive officer of Bristol-Myers Squibb (BMS) in 2010. The decade prior to his promotion was a period of enormous difficulties for the pharmaceutical giant as it weathered several legal and financial scandals. Andreotti remained on board through several management shakeups and helped refocus company resources on finding a new generation of top-selling drugs like Plavix, the blood-clot preventative. "I want integrity. Our DNA has been restructured to do the right things," he told Andrew Jack of the *Financial Times.* "If it doesn't come naturally, it comes through our processes."

Born in the early 1950s, Andreotti is the son of one of Italy's most famous political figures, seven-time prime minister Giulio Andreotti. The senior Andreotti was leader of the Christian Democratic Party for decades and held numerous cabinet posts before ascending to his first term as prime minister in February of 1972. Later that year the journalist William Murray visited the Andreotti home for a lengthy profile on the politician that ran in the *New York Times Magazine.* "That he has so far been able to produce a working government is an extraordinary achievement," Murray wrote, and called him "the most interesting, perhaps the most talented democratic political leader to rise to power in Italy since Alcide De Gasperi," the founder of the Christian Democrats. The *New York Times Magazine* article featured a photograph of the new prime minister at home with his four children and wife, Livia Danese. The informal portrait showed Andreotti as a young adult next to brother Stefano; sisters Marilena and Serena flank their seated father.

Andreotti was likely working on his engineering degree at the Sapienza University of Rome when the photograph was taken. He went on to earn a master's degree in civil engineering from the Massachusetts Institute of Technology with a 1977 master's thesis that bore the title *Coordinating Construction Projects: Modern Organisation Theory Applied to Project Managements*. For the next two decades, Andreotti held a variety of positions in the pharmaceutical business: he was with the Milan-based Farmitalia-Carlo Erba SpA, which was acquired by a larger company, Sweden's Pharmacia, in the early 1990s. Pharmacia, in turn, was merged into Upjohn in 1995. In his final years with the company Andreotti served as senior corporate vice president for Italian operations and worldwide oncology. Both companies later became part of Pfizer Incorporated.

Andreotti joined BMS in the spring of 1998 as vice president and general manager for Italy and European Oncology in the Worldwide Medicines Group. Like Farmitalia and Pharmacia, the company had a long and distinguished history of scientific advances. The original Bristol-Myers company mass-produced ether for surgical procedures in the early decades of the twentieth century and made several popular consumer products, including the hairstyling aid Vitalis for Men and Mum deodorant. In the late 1950s Bristol-Myers bought hair-color company Clairol and Mead Johnson, the maker of the infant formula Enfamil. In a curious corporate footnote, Bristol-Myers even entered the moviemaking business for a time, financing several box-office hits of the 1970s, including *The Taking of Pelham One Two Three* and *The Stepford Wives* through the now-defunct Palomar Pictures. In 1989, Bristol-Myers merged with a Brooklyn-based maker of pharmaceuticals, Squibb, which had scored significant profits with mass-market penicillin and a successful anti-tuberculosis drug after World War II.

Andreotti rose to the post of president for the European divisions in 2000 at BMS, which operated in a crowded, competitive, and highly regulated industry. Over the next few years, the U.S.-headquartered company was rocked by a series of scandals: senior corporate executives were accused of falsifying accounting statements to show better sales figures, which boosted the stock trading price and earnings forecasts of the publicly traded company, and several U.S. states filed suit against BMS' U.S. division for keeping a generic form of the cancer drug Taxol off the market. The U.S. Department of Justice, the Federal Trade Commission, and the U.S. Securities and Exchange Commission all stepped into the fray, examining the company's practices and imposing stiff fines and compliance orders. Chief executive officer James Dolan was forced to resign in 2006 as part of a court-mandated management overhaul.

Andreotti was not implicated in these troubles. In late 2002 he took over as senior vice president for BMS pharmaceutical divisions in Europe and Asia-Pacific, and three years later was named president of newly combined U.S. and global divisions at BMS. "There couldn't be a better moment to assume worldwide responsibility for the pharmaceutical business of Bristol-Myers Squibb," he told Neal M. Bellucci in *R & D Directions* at the time. "I have the exciting task of continuing the positive momentum created by our key growth drivers, and launching several promising new products, assuming approval, that address serious diseases and conditions."

In May of 2007, Andreotti was named an executive vice president and chief operating officer for the Worldwide Pharmaceuticals division of BMS. He was promoted to the exact same titles, only for the larger BMS itself, a year later, and in March of 2009 was given a seat on the board of directors and named company president as well as chief operating officer. Twelve months later, BMS announced that Andreotti would be the next chief executive officer effective May 4, succeeding James M. Cornelius, who stayed on as board chair.

Andreotti took over a company that posted revenues of $18.8 billion in 2009. BMS' strongest sellers included Plavix and Coumadin, another anticoagulant that was originally developed as a rat poison, and it was working on a new one, Apixaban, with Pfizer. Andreotti also oversaw the acquisition of smaller biotechnology firms that had made significant advances in cutting-edge medical research. One of them was ZymoGenetics, a maker of hepatitis C drugs, which became part of the BMS family in September of 2010. Though BMS was not even in the top ten among big pharma companies according to sales and revenues—companies like Johnson & Johnson, Sanofi-Aventis, and GlaxoSmithKline dominate those rankings—Andreotti's company had managed to weather some tough crises during the past decade. "This is the company with the most significant changes in the industry in the last few years," he said in a *Financial Times* interview with Andrew Jack. "In 2007, we were at the point where we had good products and good people but very ugly finances."

Sources

Periodicals

Financial Times, October 11, 2010, p. 17.
New York Times Magazine, November 19, 1972, p. 44.
R & D Directions, November-December 2005, p. 55.
Times (London, England), March 19, 2009.

Online

"Lamberto Andreotti al Vertice di Bristol," Il Sole 24 Ore, http://www.ilsole24ore.com/art/SoleOn Line4/Finanza 0.000000e+00%20Mercati/2010/03/andreotti-vertice-bristol_PRN.shtml (February 15, 2011).

"Lamberto Andreotti," Bristol-Myers Squibb, http://www.bms.com/ourcompany/leadership/Pages/lamberto_andreotti_bio.aspx(February 15, 2011).

"Lamberto Andreotti," *Forbes,* http://people.forbes.com/profile/lamberto-andreotti/13402 (February 15, 2011).

—Carol Brennan

Carmelo Anthony

Jerritt Clark/Getty Images

Professional basketball player

Born Carmelo Kyam Anthony, May 29, 1984, in New York, NY; son of Carmelo and Mary (a housekeeper) Anthony; married LaLa Vazquez, July 10, 2010; children: Kiyan (son). *Education:* Attended Syracuse University, 2002-03.

Addresses: *Office*—c/o New York Knicks, 2 Penn Plaza, 14th Fl., New York, NY 10121. *Web site*—http://www.thisismelo.com/.

Career

Played college basketball at Syracuse University, 2002-03; drafted by the Denver Nuggets, National Basketball Association (NBA), 2003; played for Denver Nuggets, 2003-11; played for the U.S. Olympic basketball team, 2004, 2008; suspended for 15 games for physical altercation, 2006; traded to New York Knicks, NBA, 2011; played for New York Knicks, 2011—.

Awards: Most Outstanding Player at the Final Four, National Collegiate Athletics Association (NCAA), 2003; Western Conference Rookie of the Month, National Basketball Association, November 2003-April 2004 (six times); Bronze Medal (with others) in men's basketball, Summer Olympics, Athens, Greece, 2004; Male Athlete of the Year, USA Basketball, 2006; Western Conference Play of the Month, National Basketball Association, March 2006, April 2007; Western Conference All-Star, National Basketball Association, 2007, 2008; Gold Medal (with others) in men's basketball, Summer Olympics, Beijing, China, 2008.

Sidelights

A 6'8" small forward, Carmelo Anthony is considered one of the best scorers in the NBA (National Basketball Association). Known by the nickname "Melo," he won an NCAA (National Collegiate Athletics Association) championship with Syracuse University, then was a top draft pick for the Denver Nuggets and won medals in two Olympic games. Though a consistent shooter and superb clutch player, Anthony's greatness could not overcome his loss of enthusiasm for playing for Denver. After months of trying to force a trade, Anthony got his way and was traded to the Knicks in the spring of 2011 where he hoped to win a championship. Of Anthony's strengths as a player, Will Leitch wrote in *New York Magazine*, "Carmelo is one of the most accomplished scorers in NBA history, and advanced statistical metrics consistently confirm what fans have known for years: When the score is tied in the final seconds, there's no one in the game you want to have the ball more than Carmelo."

Born on May 29, 1984, in New York City, he was the son of Carmelo and Mary Anthony. His basketball-playing father died of cancer when Anthony was two years old. Anthony was the youngest of four children, and his mother worked in housekeeping at the University of Baltimore to support her family. Raised in the Red Hook West housing projects in Brooklyn and in west Baltimore, he grew up in an area where murder and drug deals were common. Anthony's mother played basketball growing up in South Carolina, and wanted her children to go to college. None of her kids achieved this goal until Anthony, who looked to his mother for everything, enrolled at Syracuse University. As he told David Kindred of the *Sporting News*, "My mom was my inspiration, she was my mom and my dad." Anthony shared his mother's gift for basketball, learned to play hard on the streets, and used it to better his life.

Recognized as one of the best high school basketball players in the United States, Anthony completed his senior year of high school at Virginia's Oak Hill Academy, a basketball powerhouse. In February of 2002, Anthony and his high school team played against one of the most highly regarded high school players of his era, Ohio junior LeBron James. Though flashy, buzzed-about James scored 36 points for his less-talented team, Anthony scored 34 to lead Oak Hill to a 72-66 victory. Observers noted that James was living out aspects of an NBA lifestyle while only in high school and Anthony was more humble and low key. Oak Hill coach Steve Smith told the Syracuse *Post-Standard*, "For all the attention he's got, Carmelo is very level headed. Carmelo doesn't have an entourage. He doesn't look like a heavyweight fighter when he walks into the hotel or the gym."

While jumping right to the NBA was an option for Anthony that he considered, he took the ACT three times to earn a score that made him eligible to play at his chosen college, Syracuse University. His freshman year was his only year with the Orangemen, but he found the transition from high school to college basketball easy. Anthony went on to average 22.5 points and nine rebounds per game in the 29 games he played that season. He scored in double figures every game. Other coaches lauded Anthony's skills, with University of Missouri head coach Quin Snyder telling Kevin Tatum of the *Philadelphia Inquirer* "He's as good a player as I've ever seen in college. I don't know who's better." St. John's coach Mike Jarvis told Tatum, "There aren't many players in the country, offensively, better than him. If there are, I'd love to see them, and I'd certainly love to have them."

There were many reasons for the praise heaped on Anthony, including his ability to create his own shot, being hard to defend, ability to control a game,

easygoing personality, sense of humor, and leadership skills. Of the way he became the Syracuse team leader, he told Jack Carey of *USA Today*, "It has just kind of evolved over time. When I came in, I knew and my teammates knew that [senior guard] Kueth Duany was the leader. Then we started doing good things, and I started playing really well, and the team just started looking me as a leader. I have no problem taking over that role. Leadership is something I was born with."

Syracuse had a 26-5 record for the year and earned a trip to the NCAA. During the college basketball tournament, Anthony continued to shine as the Orangeman defeated the University of Texas in the semifinals. In that game, he scored a career-high 33 points as well as 14 rebounds. Anthony and the Orangeman made it to the finals against the University of Kansas, and won the national championship by defeating Kansas 81-78. Controlling the first half with dominance, Anthony scored 20 points and had 10 rebounds in the victory, which marked the first time Syracuse had ever won the national title. For this effort, he was named Most Outstanding Player at the Final Four, only the third time a freshman was given the honor.

Of his freshman year, Anthony told Mike DeCourcy of the *Sporting News*, "Coming to Syracuse and losing the first game, and then going from unranked to the No. 1 team? I don't regret anything. I thought we were one year away. We shocked everybody. To be a part of this and be the national champions, there's no feeling like that. Something I always wanted to do was play on a stage like this." During the tournament run, Anthony would not say if he was returning for his sophomore year, but it became evident that he was a top pick for the professional draft.

After season's end, Anthony decided to enter the NBA draft. He told Mike Waters of the Syracuse *Post-Standard*, "I have to move on. We won a national championship. I don't want to make it sound bad, but there's really nothing more I could get out of college. I came here for a year, and I'm still going to get my degree." Experts predicted that Anthony would be a top-three pick and sign a three-year contract worth about $10 to $12 million. These predictions proved correct when he was drafted by the Denver Nuggets in the first round with the third overall pick in the 2003 NBA draft and signed a $10 million contract. (James was drafted first by the Cleveland Cavaliers.)

As an NBA rookie, Anthony continued to shine while playing for what was then one of the worst teams in the NBA. Though some observers had concerns about the pressure placed on him to succeed and become the savior of the Denver sports scene, Anthony rose to the occasion early on. He said all the right things, telling Lacy J. Banks of the *Chicago Sun-Times*, "All I care about is winning. I've been on winning teams all my life. I'm not saying we're not going to lose games this season. But I'm a winner, and I'm going to go out there and do what I have to do to make us a winning team." While Denver did not turn into an instant championship team, the Nuggets did make their first playoff appearance in nine years. Anthony had an excellent rookie year, averaging 21 points and 6.1 rebounds per game to help get them there. He was also the six-time Western Conference rookie of the month, winning consistently from November 2003 to April 2004.

Honors continued to come Anthony's way after his rookie year. He was selected to play for the United States in men's basketball at the summer Olympics in Athens, Greece, in 2004. Though the team was considered a disappointment for only winning a bronze medal, Anthony set a record for the United States by scoring 35 points in a preliminary round game against Italy. Twenty-nine of those points came in the second half. Returning to the NBA for his second year, Anthony continued to play well, and had the support of a mentor, veteran Bryon Russell. With Russell's help, Anthony shook off the loss of his shooting touch in the first few weeks of the 2004-05 season to play better for a few months.

However, by the spring of 2005, Anthony was not playing well with his accuracy from the field declining and other numbers nose diving as well. His attitude on the court was sometimes nonchalant. Denver's coach, George Karl, benched him on occasion, a move that made Anthony brood. Karl wanted Anthony to prove himself, something that happened slowly over the next few years. While in 2004-05, Anthony averaged 20.8 points and 5.7 rebounds per game, his numbers greatly improved in 2005-06 when he averaged 26.5 points per game. He was named the Western Conference player of the month for March 2006. During the summer of 2006, Anthony was arguably the best player on the U.S. team that competed in world championships. He also signed a five-year, $80 million contract with Denver.

In December of 2006, Anthony's reputation was damaged by an on-the-court altercation just days after he opened a youth center that he spent $1.5 million to build in Baltimore. Though he was leading the league in scoring before the December game with the New York Knicks, he was suspended for 15 games after sucker punching Knick Mardy Col-

lins in retaliation for Collins' committing a fragrant foul on J. R. Smith. While Anthony immediately took responsibility for his actions in the matter and apologized, NBA Commission David Stern took a dim view of the incident and handed down the harsh sentence on Anthony and other players involved in the brawl. Despite the suspension, Anthony was the player of the month in April 2007, was a Western Conference All-Star, and had a career high average of 28.9 points and 6.0 rebounds per game.

Anthony continued to play at a high level for Denver over the next few years, though some seasons were better than others. In the 2007-08 season, he averaged 25.7 points and 7.4 rebounds per game, and was a Western Conference All-Star. During the summer of 2008, Anthony again played for the United States in the Summer Olympics, winning a gold medal with his teammates in Beijing. During the Olympic tournament, Anthony averaged 11.5 points and 4.3 rebounds per game, playing an average of more than 19 minutes per game. Back in the NBA, his numbers went down in 2008-09 when he averaged 22.8 points and 6.8 rebounds per game, though had streaks where he was hot and helped carry the team to victory.

Early in the 2009-10 season, Anthony played like a man possessed to improve on those numbers. One reason he succeeded in this goal was he took part in intensive summer workouts with fitness guru Gunnar Peterson and the Nuggets' training staff. His body fat went from 8.6 to 7 percent, while his weight dropped from 240 to 228. In early November 2009, Anthony was averaging 32 points per game and had two back-to-back games with 40 points; the team was 5-0. He finished the season averaging 28.2 points and 6.6 rebounds per game.

During the summer of 2010, Anthony demanded a trade from the Nuggets to one of several teams, including New York Knicks, Chicago Bulls, and New Jersey Nets. He had been reportedly unhappy in Denver for months, and wanted to be traded to a more high-profile team that had a chance of contending for the championship trophy. Denver seemed to have a blockbuster deal in place in September of 2010 that would have sent Anthony to the Nets, but it fell apart when the Nets ended talks. Anthony continued to play for the Nuggets in 2010 and into early 2011, but publicly stated that he would not sign a contract extension with the team. He told Marc Berman of the *New York Post*, "They want to sit down and talk, but my thing is it's way beyond this year. It ain't got nothing to do with the new GM, president, the players. For me, it's a time for change."

Despite the turmoil, Anthony's numbers stayed consistent. He averaged 26.3 points and 6.7 rebounds per game while playing with Denver that year. By February of 2011, he was even publicly stating a willingness to consider signing an extension with the Nuggets if they did not trade him. Within two weeks, however, a trade was made and Anthony went to the Knicks with Chauncey Billups for four players, three draft picks, and six million dollars after Anthony signed a three-year, $65 million contract extension with Denver that was agreed to as part of the trade. Anthony was expected to lead the Knicks to a championship. He immediately helped the team, averaging 26.3 points and 6.7 rebounds per game in the 27 games he played with the Knicks.

The trade contributed to the Knicks making the post-season for the first time since 2000, despite inconsistencies as Anthony and Billups were integrated into the lineup. Though the Knicks lost in the first round, winning a championship remained Anthony's goal. Speculating on what would that look like for New York City, he told *New York Magazine*'s Leitch, "Winning the championship here, for these fans, in this city, that would be amazing. Man, can you imagine the parade?" He added to Steve Serby of the *New York Post*, "The sky's the limit, man."

Sources

Periodicals

BusinessWorld, March 16, 2005, p. 23.
Chicago Sun-Times, November 11, 2003, p. 105.
Daily News (NY), December 29, 2008, p. 56; September 29, 2010, p. 62; February 10, 2011, p. 62.
Denver Post, October 5, 2003, p. CC-1; February 15, 2004, p. C-1; November 17, 2004, p. D-1.
Newsday (NY), February 24, 2011, p. A59.
New York Magazine, April 25, 2011.
New York Post, October 29, 2010, p. 87; April 25, 2011, p. 67.
New York Times, December 18, 2006, p. D1; February 23, 2011, p. B10.
Philadelphia Inquirer, March 26, 2003, p. E4.
Post-Standard (Syracuse, NY), February 11, 2002, p. D4; April 25, 2003, p. A1.
South Florida Sun-Sentinel (Fort Lauderdale, FL), November 5, 2009.
Sporting News, April 14, 2003, p. 12; April 14, 2003, p. 60.
Times Union (Albany, NY), December 19, 2006, p. C1.
USA Today, April 7, 2003, p. 8C.

Online

"Carmelo Anthony Bio Page," NBA, http://www.nba.com/playerfile/carmelo_anthony/bio.html (May 29, 2011).
"Carmelo Anthony Career Stats Page," NBA, http://www.nba.com/playerfile/carmelo_anthony/career_stats.html (May 29, 2011).
"Carmelo Anthony," ESPN, http://espn.go.com/nba/player/_/id/1975/carmelo-anthony (May 29, 2011).
"LaLa Vazquez, Carmelo Anthony Say 'I Do,'" *US Weekly*, http://www.usmagazine.com/stylebeauty/news/lala-vazquez-carmelo-anthony-say-i-do-2010107 (June 10, 2011).

—A. Petruso

Arcade Fire

Rock group

Group formed in 2003 in Montreal, Quebec, Canada; members include Will Butler (born October 6, 1982, in Woodlands, TX), bass, guitar; Win Butler (born April 14, 1980, in Woodlands, TX; married Régine Chassagne, 2003), vocals, guitar; Régine Chassagne (born August 18, 1977, in Saint-Lambert,

Quebec, Canada), vocals, piano, accordion; Jeremy Gara, drums, guitar, keyboard; Tim Kingsbury, bass; Sarah Neufeld (born August 27, 1979, Vancouver Island, British Columbia, Canada), violin; Richard Reed Parry, guitar, keyboards, accordion.

Addresses: *Record company*—Merge Records, 409 E. Chapel Hill, Durham, NC 27701. *Web site*—http://www.arcadefire.com.

Career

Formed in Montreal, Quebec, Canada, 2003; released debut album, *Funeral*, 2004; released *Neon Bible*, 2007; released *The Suburbs*, 2010.

Awards: June award for songwriter of the year, Canadian Academy of Recording Arts and Sciences, for "Wake Up," "Rebellion (Lies)," and "Neighborhood #3 (Power Out)," 2006; Juno Award for alternative album of the year, Canadian Academy of Recording Arts and Sciences, for *Neon Bible*, 2008; Grammy Award for album of the year, National Academy of Recording Arts and Sciences, for *The Suburbs*, 2010; Juno Awards for group of the year and songwriter of the year, Canadian Academy of Recording Arts and Sciences, 2011; Juno awards for album of the year and alternative album of the year, Canadian Academy of Recording Arts and Sciences, both for *The Suburbs*, 2011; Shockwaves *NME* Award for best album, *NME*, for *The Suburbs*, 2011; Brit Award for best international album, British Phonographic Industry, for *The Suburbs*, 2011; Brit Award for best international group, British Phonographic Industry, 2011.

Sidelights

Grammy-award-winning Canadian indie rock group Arcade Fire became one of the critically esteemed musical outfits of the early twenty-first century following the release of its 2004 debut, *Funeral*. Centered on the performances of husband-and-wife team Win Butler and Régine Chassagne, the group enriches its sound both in the studio and on the road with a wide array of instrumentalists. This lush yet driving sound won Arcade Fire critical and popular notice, and garnered them influential fans such as rock icon David Bowie and Talking Heads' singer David Byrne. The group became a staple on the festival circuit, performing at such high-profile events as Lollapalooza and Coachella. Sophomore effort *Neon Bible*, recorded in a converted Montreal-area church, appeared to equally great acclaim in 2007. That album soared to the number-two position on the *Billboard* 200, establishing Arcade Fire as a veritable crossover sensation.

Extensive touring preceded the release of Arcade Fire's chart-topping third full-length release, *The Suburbs*, in 2010. An exploration of theme related to growing up in suburban North America, that album went on to garner the band numerous awards, including a Grammy for Album of the Year and four Juno Awards—the Canadian Grammy equivalent—for Group of the Year, Songwriter of the Year, Album of the Year, and Alternative Album of the Year.

Arcade Fire first formed in Montreal, Quebec, Canada in 2003 as the project of Texas native Win Butler and Canadian singer Régine Chassagne. While attending Montreal's McGill University, Butler noticed Chassagne performing jazz standards at a Montreal art exhibit, and, enamored by her vocal skills, persuaded her to begin a songwriting partnership with him. Soon, the collective expanded to include Butler's brother Will Butler on keyboards and percussion, Tim Kingsbury on bass, Richard Parry on organ, Sarah Neufeld on violin, Howard Bilerman on drums, and multi-instrumentalist Jeremy Gara. In time, Bilerman left the group to pursue other projects, and horn player Pietro Amato and violinist Owen Pallett—who has released solo albums under his own moniker, Final Fantasy—signed on. This unusually large array of musicians brought with them skills on instruments rarely featured on rock records; in addition to the standard electric bass, guitar, and drums combination, Arcade Fire's songs include parts for violin, accordion, hurdy-gurdy, harpsichord, xylophone, stand-up double bass, and steel drums, among others. Win Butler and Chassagne's musical partnership soon turned personal, and the couple married in 2003.

Soon after forming, the group began playing shows, winning over Canadian audiences with its somewhat theatrical presence—Chassagne typically appears on stage in retro party dresses, while male members may sport suspenders—and unquestionably layered sounds. Arcade Fire quickly recorded an eponymous EP across the border in Maine, and on the strength of this self-released album and its live shows garnered a contract with independent label Merge Records. The group's resulting debut album, *Funeral*, reflected a series of personal tragedies that struck the musicians over the latter half of 2003 and early 2004. Chassagne's grandmother died, followed shortly by the Butlers' grandfather and Parry's aunt. Seeking to channel their grief, the group's members translated their feelings into sweeping songs organized around themes of death, grief, emotional connection, and loss.

Recorded on a slim $10,000 budget, *Funeral* became a breakout indie rock sensation. Blogs and music forums buzzed about it, and word-of-mouth spread quickly. Taste-making indie rock Web site Pitchfork Media gave the release an overwhelmingly positive review, with the site's David Moore proclaiming, "that it's so easy to embrace this album's operatic proclamation of love and redemption speaks to the scope of Arcade Fire's vision. It's taken perhaps too long for us to reach this point where an album is at last capable of completely and successfully restoring the tainted phrase 'emotional' to its true origin." Soon after, Kelefa Sanneh of the *New York Times* noted of the group's performance at the city's annual CMJ music showcase that "the seven members of Arcade Fire managed to exceed all expectations." Practically overnight, the group became an independent music sensation—albeit one that made barely a dent on the mainstream U.S. *Billboard* charts, despite performing well on organization's Heatseekers and Top Independent Albums rankings. In time, *Funeral* went on to sell some 750,000 copies worldwide. Late-night television performances and high-profile appearances at music festivals both in North America and abroad filled the group's schedule for the next several months.

Despite this apparent hype, *Funeral* has remained widely recognized as one of the most important and influential indie rock releases of the early 2000s. A number of similar-sounding groups followed in Arcade Fire's footsteps, and many ears turned anew to Canadian acts. At the close of 2010, Pitchfork Media named *Funeral* the second-best of the first decade of the twenty-first century, behind only long-standing alternative rock powerhouse Radiohead's *Kid A*, in a testament to its enduring legacy. Looking back on Arcade Fire's debut, Ian Cohen observed of its importance that "besides being a turning point for indie rock, *Funeral* was one for the indie community as well. Whether it's due to increasingly fractious listening habits or the increased ability for dissenters to be heard, *Funeral* keeps on feeling like the last of its kind, an indie record that sounded capable of conquering the universe and then going on to do just that."

During 2005, the group's star continued to rise. Rocker David Bowie joined Arcade Fire on stage to perform the Arcade Fire track "Wake Up" as part of VH1's *Fashion Rocks* event, and Irish megastars U2 invited the group to open for them on a few dates on their 2005 Vertigo tour, also joining them onstage to play a cover of 1970s Joy Division song "Love Will Tear Us Apart." Both *Funeral* and one-off track "Cold Wind," recorded for the HBO program *Six Feet Under,* received Grammy nominations, and the group picked up its first Juno Award for Songwriter of the Year in 2005.

In 2006, Arcade Fire began work on its second album in an unlikely recording venue: an old church located outside of Montreal. The group bought the building and refitted it as a recording studio and living space, spending the better part of the next several months residing in the church's basement and recording on its existing stage. These environs helped inspire the sounds—and title—of the resulting LP, *Neon Bible*. Centering on themes of the role of religion, bureaucracy, media, and other vast institutions to create a somewhat empty society, the album expanded Arcade Fire's lyrical focus while retaining its signature theatricality. Some of this distinctive sound can be attributed to the group's insistence upon maintaining artistic independence in an industry often dominated by the dictates of large corporations. Despite being courted by several major labels in the wake of *Funeral*'s success, Arcade Fire chose to stay with Merge. The group paid for the recording of *Neon Bible* itself, and retained ownership of all rights to its master recordings. "The idea of someone else owning what we do is insane when we did all the work," Win Butler told Darcy Frey of the *New York Times.*

Arcade Fire released *Neon Bible* to strong critical and commercial reception in March of 2007. The album debuted at number two on the *Billboard 200,* and critics such as Jody Rosen of *Entertainment Weekly* hailed it for its "immensity of the sound" and "majestic moments." Writing for *Allmusic,* James Christopher Monger assessed that "*Neon Bible* takes a few spins to digest properly … but there's no denying Arcade Fire's singular vision, even when it blurs a little." A frenetic round of touring followed that had the group play five consecutive sold-out shows in London, stage three consecutive sold-out dates in New York City, and make several highly billed appearances at worldwide music festivals such Great Britain's Glastonbury Festival and California's Coachella Arts and Music Festival. The recording of *Neon Bible* and subsequent tour also became the basis for the 2009 music documentary *Miroir Noir,* French for "black mirror"—a nod to one of *Neon Bible*'s best-known tracks. Awards committees again took notice of the group, with *Neon Bible* picking up a Grammy nomination for Best Alternative Album of the Year and the Juno award for Alternative Album of the Year.

In August of 2010, Arcade Fire released its highly anticipated third album, *The Suburbs.* Drawing on Butler's upbringing in suburban Houston, the album touched on themes ranging from the overt disaffection of middle-class suburban youth to feelings of entrapment. "*The Suburbs* is definitely a concept album: we know this because the word 'suburbs' appears in almost every song," assessed Michael Barclay in a review printed in the Kitchener, Ontario *Record.* "It's a rich theme, encompassing ennui of youth, wasted time, wasted potential, technological transformation, urban planning, and dreams of escape," he concluded. Bolstered by positive critical notices, the album debuted at number one in Canada, the United Kingdom, and the United States, where it beat out previous chart-topping albums by rapper Eminem and hard rockers Avenged Sevenfold. Nevertheless, the band remained modest about their success. "We have the #1 record, but we're still not that famous in the scheme of things," Will Butler told Ryan Dombal of Pitchfork Media. "America's a big country. There're still way more people who've never heard of us," added Win Butler. Indeed, despite this first-week success, the album's sales figures still hovered below the gold-selling 500,000 mark nearly a year after its release.

The critical success of *The Suburbs* included numerous nods from awards committees and best-of lists on both sides of the Atlantic. Listeners of the NPR program *All Songs, Considered* tapped the album as the best of 2010, while Pitchfork Media named it as the eleventh-best album of the year, with Mark Pytlik applauding it as "a full-bodied account of all the sweetness and strangeness of that life in all its multitudes." The Grammy committee nominated *The Suburbs*' track "Ready to Start" in the group Best Rock Performance category, along with the album itself for Best Alternative Album of the Year and Album of the Year. Although Arcade Fire failed to pick up the former trophy, it carried away the latter prize, shocking many commentators. Todd Martens of the *Los Angeles Times* Pop & Hiss music blog wondered in amazement, "the act with the most complex, thoughtful, and adventurous album actually won the Grammy for album of the year. When was the last time that happened?" In addition to this unanticipated accolade, *The Suburbs* earned the group four Juno Awards, a Shockwaves *NME* Award from the British music magazine *NME*, and two Brit Awards for Best International Album and Best International Group.

Arcade Fire continued to tour extensively to support their much-decorated album, performing at the U.S. music festivals Coachella and Bonnaroo before making the rounds of the European festival circuit in the summer of 2011. An expanded version of *The Suburbs* including new songs and a short film directed by Spize Jonze was also slated for release in August of that year. Despite this re-release and a busy touring schedule, the group did not plan to take a lengthy hiatus before beginning work on its fourth album. "Normally we'd take a pretty big break after touring … but … we paced ourselves a little better on this tour," commented Will Butler to Nick Patch of the *Canadian Press* in June of 2011. "So I don't think we're going to be quite so burned out. I mean, there's still months left to go on the road, but I think we'll be more fit to hop back into work quicker."

Selected discography

Funeral, Merge Records, 2004.
Neon Bible, Merge Records, 2007.
The Suburbs, Merge Records, 2010.

Sources

Books

Contemporary Canadian Biographies, Gale, 2005.
Contemporary Musicians, vol. 68, Gale, 2010, pp. 16-18.
Encyclopedia of Indie Rock, Greenwood Press, 2008, pp. 22-25.

Periodicals

Canadian Press (Toronto, Ontario, Canada), June 2, 2011.
Entertainment Weekly, March 9, 2007.
New York Times, October 18, 2004; March 4, 2007.
Record (Kitchener, Ontario, Canada), July 29, 2010, p. N6.

Online

"'All Songs' Listeners Pick the Best Albums of 2010," NPR, http://www.npr.org/2010/12/14/13205024.tif1/-all-songs-listeners-pick-the-best-music-of-2010 (June 2, 2011).
"Arcade Fire: *Funeral*," Pitchfork Media, http://pitchfork.com/reviews/albums/452-funeral/ (June 2, 2011).
"Grammy Awards: Arcade Fire shocks Streisand, the universe, with Grammy win," Pop & Hiss blog, *Los Angeles Times*, http://latimesblogs.latimes.com/music_blog/2011/02/grammy-awards-arcade-fire-shock-streisand-the-universe-with-grammy-win.html (June 2, 2011).
"Interviews: Arcade Fire," Pitchfork Media, http://www.pitchfork.com/features/interviews/7860-arcade-fire/ (June 2, 2011).
"Neon Bible," *Allmusic*, http://allmusic.com/album/neon-bible-r953023/review (June 2, 2011).
"The Top 50 Albums of 2010," Pitchfork Media, http://pitchfork.com/features/staff-lists/7893-the-top-50-albums-of-2010/4/ (June 2, 2011).
"The Top 200 Albums of the 2000s: 20-1," Pitchfork Media, http://pitchfork.com/features/staff-lists/7710-the-top-200-albums-of-the-2000s-20-1/2/ (June 2, 2011).

—*Vanessa E. Vaughn*

Heather Armstrong

Founder of Dooce.com

Born Heather B. Hamilton, July 19, 1975; married Jon Armstrong, 2002; children: Leta, Marlo. *Education:* Brigham Young University, B.A., 1997.

Addresses: *Office*—Blurbodoocery, 1338 Foothill Drive #230, Salt Lake City, UT 84108.

Career

Worked as a web designer, 1997-2002; founded Dooce.com, 2001.

Sidelights

Since 2001, Heather Armstrong has been blogging on her Web site, Dooce.com, dishing dirt about her life as an employee, a mother, and an ex-Mormon. The blog averages 1.5 million visitors a month and is known for Armstrong's funny, irreverent, and honest style.

Armstrong grew up in Memphis, Tennessee, in a very religious Mormon family. She studied English at Brigham Young University in Utah, and graduated in 1997. After college, she decided to make a break with her Mormon origins and moved to Los Angeles to find work.

In 2001, Armstrong was working for a web-design company in Los Angeles. At the time, she was single and enjoying her freedom, but she hated her job and the people she worked with, so she began blogging about how much they annoyed her. She also wrote about her family and her break with her Mormon upbringing, never thinking her family would find out what she was writing. She called her blog "Dooce," a personal joke based on the fact that when she sent instant messages to colleagues, she often started the message, "Dude," spelled "Doode," to be funny, but she consistently hit the wrong key, making it "Dooce," and this became her nickname.

Eventually her employer found out what she was writing about him and his company, and he was not amused. In 2002, Armstrong was fired for posting information about her employer and other people at her job. This situation led to a new slang word, "dooced," which meant getting fired for things one wrote on a Web site. Armstrong told a reporter for the States News Service that when she got fired, she "felt like I had ended my life. I was valedictorian at my school, I graduated with honors from college, and here I was getting fired for doing something really really dumb."

Armstrong temporarily stopped blogging. She eloped to marry Jon Armstrong after proposing to him in the comments section of his blog. Shortly after, he also lost his job, although not because of his blog. As Armstrong told a reporter for America's

Intelligence Wire, this was a time of transition: "We went from living in Los Angeles to both being unemployed to living in my mom's basement in Utah." Jon found a job fairly quickly. Their goal was to save money while they lived with her mother, and meanwhile look for work in Utah, because they couldn't afford to live in Los Angeles any more. Armstrong, who did not find a job, spent much of her time in the depressing, windowless basement, and as a form of self-therapy, she started blogging again.

Armstrong became pregnant in 2003, and her blogging naturally turned to that topic. When their daughter, Leta, was born, she suffered severe postpartum depression, taking medication and checking herself into a psychiatric hospital in order to prevent herself from committing suicide. She continued to blog, and the number of visitors skyrocketed. When she regained her equilibrium, she continued to write about the trials and tribulations of being a mother, one of many "mommy bloggers" whose popularity was growing not only among readers but also among advertisers, who realized the high volume of traffic on these sites was a potential goldmine of customers.

By 2005, Armstrong had turned her blog into a profitable business. Its monthly income was now more than her husband was making at work, so he quit his job and began working full-time managing the site and its advertisers. Although rumors abounded regarding how much money the site made, Armstrong would never confirm them. She told Lisa Belkin in the *New York Times*, "We're a privately held company and don't reveal our financials." She remarked to Molly Millett in America's Intelligence Wire, "The reason I also don't like to talk about money is I don't want people reading my site with the filter of a number in their head."

In 2009, Armstrong published a book, *It Sucked and Then I Cried: How I Had a Baby, a Breakdown, and a Much-Needed Margarita*. The book tells the story of Armstrong's pregnancy and the birth of her daughter, placed against the backdrop of her Mormon upbringing, her move to Los Angeles, and her return to Utah after her daughter was born. Armstrong was very open about the postpartum depression she suffered after her pregnancy, including the time she spent in a mental hospital as a result of that depression, as well as her struggles with chronic depression. She was also very open about the difficulties her depression caused in her marriage, and the fact that her psychological problems sometimes made it difficult for her to take care of her daughter. A *Kirkus Reviews* writer described the book as "a

truthful picture of what it takes to bring a life into the world, exposing Achilles heels large and small." Armstrong told Carol Memmott in *USA Today*, "I wanted it to be the funniest story about depression you've ever read."

In that same year, Armstrong was named No. 26 on *Forbes* list of the 30 "Most Influential Women in Media," coming in ahead of media journalists such as Soledad O'Brien and Andrea Mitchell. Armstrong and her husband also had another daughter, Marlo, in 2009.

In 2010, Armstrong signed a deal with the HGTV television network to blog on the network's site, as well as spots for video blogging, Twitter posting, and making appearances. Jim Samples, president of the network, told a reporter for America's Intelligence Wire that her popularity was not the only factor in the decision, but also her talent for design and photography. "She's clearly a great fit for us and our audience," he said.

Although it might seem as though no topic is off-limits for Armstrong, she told Memmott that if she and her husband get into a real fight, she won't mention it on her blog. "And I won't talk about our sex life," she added. She acknowledged that her honesty was a big part of her appeal for her audience, because "I will say what they're afraid to say."

Although many parents look at her life and wish they, too, could sit at home and make money through blogging, Armstrong's life does have a down side, mainly due to the lack of privacy. Sometimes her sheer lack of boundaries backfires on her. After she wrote a scathing report on Mormonism, her parents were devastated; her father didn't speak to her for months. Realizing that she had gone a little bit too far, she took down the posts, and decided not to write anything about her family that she wouldn't dare say to their faces, in front of other people.

She does get hate mail, often attacking her parenting style, and in one instance, she told Sue Shellenbarger of the *Wall Street Journal*, a woman she thought was a friend posted a comment on her site saying she wanted "to punch me in the face because she hated me so much." She added that because of the volume and intensity of the hate mail, she could understand why some famous people use drugs or commit suicide; however, she told Shellenbarger, most days she prints out the messages, lays them down in her driveway, and then drives over them with her car. She remarked to Shellenbarger, "That's the attitude I have, and it's made my life a thousand percent better."

Selected writings

It Sucked and Then I Cried, Simon Spotlight Entertainment (New York, NY), 2009.

Sources

Periodicals

America's Intelligence Wire, March 24, 2009; February 1, 2010.
Daily Record (St. Louis, MO), April 4, 2006.
Kirkus Reviews, February 15, 2009.
States News Service, August 8, 2010.
Sunday Times (London, England), April 27, 2008, p. 23.
USA Today, March 26, 2009, p. 5D
Wall Street Journal, April 10, 2008, p. D1.

Online

Dooce, http://www.dooce.com/ (February 11, 2011).
"Queen of the Mommy Bloggers," *New York Times,* http://nytimes.com/2011/02/27/magazine/27armstrong-t.html?_r=1 (February 25, 2011).

—*Kelly Winters*

Julian Assange

Activist, Web site owner, and software developer

Born July 3, 1971, in Townsville, Australia; son of John Shipton and Christine Assange (an artist); married, c. 1988 (divorced); children: Daniel. *Education:* Attended the University of Melbourne, 2003-06.

Addresses: *Contact*—c/o Box 4080, Australia Post Office, University of Melbourne Branch, Victoria 3052 Australia.

Career

Given Commodore 64, c. mid-1980s; became computer hacker, c. late 1980s; arrested for hacking into Nortel, 1991; started a free speech Internet service provider in Australia, 1993; served as a researcher on the book *Underground: Tales of Hacking, Madness and Obsession,* written by Suelette Dreyfus, 1997; co-invented a type of encryption to protect sensitive data collected by human rights workers, 1997; worked in computer security and software programs writing, c. late 1990s-early 2000s; founded WikiLeaks, 2006; faced criminal charges in Sweden, 2010.

Awards: Sydney Peace Foundation Gold Medal, 2011; Martha Gelhorn Prize for Journalism, 2011.

Sidelights

The founder and force behind the now-defunct controversial Web site WikiLeaks.org, Australian Julian Assange released numerous classified, sensitive, or otherwise contentious government documents, reports, and news stories. Calling himself the editor-in-chief of WikiLeaks, he was both criticized and lauded for publishing secret or confidential information as a means of challenging the establishment. Often called a whistleblower and watchdog, he maintained his Web site was a media organization that published essential journalism. The self-described renegade began as a teenage hacker and computer security expert. Notoriously, Assange faced serious rape charges in Sweden in 2010.

Born on July 3, 1971, in Townsville, Australia, he was the son of John Shipton and Christine Assange. He said his parents met at an anti-war rally protesting Vietnam, though his biological father left the family before he was two years old. When Julian was still a toddler, his artist mother married Brett Assange, an artist, who helped raise him. Assange's mother was skeptical of authority and institutions, and taught her son to distrust and not believe authorities and governments.

The Assange family moved often as they became involved in a left wing anti-establishment bohemian subculture. Assange's parents put on plays directed by his stepfather and for which his mother designed sets. His mother's marriage to Brett Assange ended when Julian was nine years old. His mother soon became involved with a musician who was a psychopath and manipulative. This boyfriend, who was accused of abusing children and being part of a cult, had a child with Assange's mother, who soon ended the relationship. From the age of 11 to 16, Assange, his mother, and his half-sibling had to live on the run to hide from him, sometimes taking assumed names.

Thus, by the time Assange was 14 years old, he had lived in 50 communities in Australia, including Perth, Adelaide Hills, Brisbane, Sydney, Magnetic Island, and Lismore. He received his education partially from homeschooling as his mother wanted him not to be affected by teachers and the lure of authority, though he did attend at least 37 schools for various amounts of time over the years. With this difficult life, Assange found solace in a Commodore 64 he was given as a teenager. He soon figured out how to hack into programs, skills which found use after he received a modem for his sixteenth birthday.

At 17, Assange married his 16-year-old girlfriend and became a father at 18, when she gave birth to their son Daniel. Assange worked as a freelance software developer and computer hacker for his own anti-establishment group known as the International Subversives. He and his friends hacked into computer systems in Europe and North America, such as the Canadian telecommunications group Nortel. Nortel sold high-tech equipment used by telephone companies in Australia and other countries, and he easily hacked into the system because Nortel lacked internal security. Assange and his friends gained access to many passwords and explored Nortel computers around the world, gathering information about new product development and raiding various sites.

The authorities caught on to the hacking, however, and Assange soon faced legal consequences. In October of 1991, he was arrested with a warrant by the Australian police for hacking into the Melbourne computers of Nortel, among other activities. When the police raided his home, he had a list of 1,500 accounts and their passwords, including the U.S. Air Force 7th Command Group. Around the time of his arrest, Assange's marriage fell apart and a nine-year custody battle over his son began, whom Assange and his mother believed was in danger from Assange's ex-wife's new boyfriend. Assange struggled with depression during this time, leading to periods of hospitalization.

Assange continued to work in computers and computer-related industry. By 1993, he started a free speech Internet service provider in Australia. De-spite the evidence of his hacking activities and 31 charges, Assange was not sent to prison. In December of 1996, he pled guilty to 24 of the charges and paid a $2,300 fine. He was also under a good behavior bond for three years. During this time, Assange spent years doing research for academic Suelette Dreyfus, the author of the 1997 book *Underground: Tales of Hacking, Madness and Obsession.* The book discussed the hacking actions of Assange (under the name of Mendax) and his friends in the International Subversives. Also in 1997, he co-invented a type of encryption to protect sensitive data collected by human rights workers.

In 1999, Assange's custody case was settled, with a custody agreement in place that left his son primarily in his care. Though he later became estranged from his son, the experience of fighting for Daniel through Australian bureaucracy left Assange with post-traumatic stress disorder. Assange traveled regularly during this period, riding a motorcycle across Vietnam while continuing to hold numerous computer jobs, focusing primarily on computer security and writing related software programs. Assange later founded a computer consultant firm. He tried to stay away from hacking by studying math and physics at the University of Melbourne and other universities in Australia off and on through 2007.

By this time, Assange had founded WikiLeaks. He created WikiLeaks with an international group of dissidents, academics, and mathematicians in 2006. He originally conceived of WikiLeaks as a place to reveal the truth about government and other conspiracies, and by leaking this truth, undermining authorities. Explaining his motivation in 2010, Assange told *Radio Free Europe*, "The vision behind it is really quite ancient: in order to make any sensible decision you need to know what's really going on, and in order to make any just decision you need to know and understand what abuses or plans for abuses are occurring. As technologists, we can see that big reforms come when the public and decision makers can see what's really going on." By being an activist, Assange hoped to create justice. WikiLeaks originally focused on Asia, the former Soviet Union and its satellites, sub-Saharan Africa, and the Middle East. Among its first postings was a rebel leader in Somalia's call to use criminals to assassinate government officials.

Because of the nature of WikiLeaks, Assange found it difficult to find an Internet service to host the Web site. He found a home in Sweden on PRQ, which hosted the legally questionable Pirate Bay Web site as well as other companies and people who participated in shadowy, if not illegal, activities. The demands of WikiLeaks were somewhat unique. To maintain anonymity, sources could upload documents anonymously to WikiLeaks using a form of encryption that both hid the content and the source. Assange stated that WikiLeaks was a media organization and he was editor-in-chief, even though it published primarily nonoriginal content. As Jason Pontin of the *Technology Review* wrote, "Perhaps the best way to conceive of WikiLeaks is this: it is a stateless, distributed intelligence network, a reverse image of the U.S. National Security Agency, dedicated to publicizing secrets rather than acquiring them, unconstrained and answerable to a single man."

It took time for WikiLeaks to grab attention. In 2007, WikiLeaks published many U.S. military records about the force structure in Afghanistan and Iraq but there was little notice. Over the next few years, WikiLeaks published information like data from the manuals of Guantanamo Bay, the emails of Sarah Palin, secret censorship briefs from China, a report about an accident at an Iranian nuclear facility, instructions from the British Ministry of Defense describing how to secure military computer systems from WikiLeaks and spies, bank documents related to the Icelandic financial meltdown, and official assassinations in Kenya and East Timor. Some of these stories became noteworthy, while others did not.

In April of 2010, Assange and WikiLeaks came to greater fame with the publication of an edited, highly classified military video *Collateral Murder* that used footage, shot from a U.S. helicopter, of the killing of alleged insurgents and two Iraqi employees of Reuters in New Baghdad. While this video led to more notice, WikiLeaks would become known worldwide because of its next leaks.

In July of 2010, WikiLeaks became a source of controversy with the release of what was dubbed the "Afghan War Diary," that included at least 91,000 reports. These documents included information from embassies in relation to Afghanistan, units in the field, informers, and intelligence officers. As Assange did with other massive releases in this time period, he shared this leak information with traditional news sources like the *New York Times,* the London *Guardian,* and the German *Der Spiegel.*

With the release of these unedited U.S. military reports from Afghanistan, the CIA and others accused Assange and his Web site of contributing to the deaths of civilians in the conflict because the reports contained the names of civilians who had helped British and American forces. Much of the data came from a disgruntled American soldier who was later arrested and faced charges in the United States. Bradley Manning was caught not because WikiLeaks released his identity, but because he bragged about what he had done to a former hacker who informed on him.

Maintaining Assange's continued stance that he was an editor and WikiLeaks was a media organization, WikiLeaks continued to release challenging material in August of 2010, publishing a CIA report on U.S. terror recruits known as the "Red Cell" report and dated February 2, 2010. The unedited report warned about how the world would view the United States as a supporter of terrorism for attacks by American-based or financed terrorists in support of Jewish, Muslim, and Irish nationalist causes. WikiLeaks also released hundreds of thousands of reports from soldiers in Iraq in October 2010, and more than a quarter million secret, confidential, sensitive diplomatic cables from the United States in November 2010.

As WikiLeaks became more notorious, many financial institutions refused to process any transactions intended for the Web site, including Bank of America in December 2010. In early 2011, WikiLeaks released documents from a Swiss bank. At the same time, Assange announced its next target would be a major American bank, suspected to be Bank of America.

While WikiLeaks was finally garnering worldwide attention, Assange himself soon faced legal issues and media scrutiny. In Sweden in August 2010, a warrant was issued for his arrest for sexually molesting two women who volunteered with WikiLeaks over a two-day period. Swedish prosecutors initially withdrew the warrant after 24 hours because of the lack of evidence, and Assange denied the accusations. Assange's supporters believed that the warrant was part of a smear campaign against him because of the nature of the information released by WikiLeaks; however, the charges did not go away.

By December 2010, multiple charges of rape were finally brought to court in Sweden. Assange turned himself into British police and was put in Wandsworth Prison. He was initially denied bail so that he could be extradited to Sweden, but eventually people, including filmmaker Michael Moore, paid his bail. To be released on bail, Assange had to surrender his passport, wear an electronic monitor, and submit to a curfew while living under house arrest in England until a scheduled July 2011 hearing about his extradition. Assange still planned on fighting extradition to Sweden and feared threats made on his life. The Swedish charges were not the only ones dogging Assange. He also potentially faced charges in the United States under the Espionage Act for releasing the diplomatic cables, war reports, and other documents through WikiLeaks.

As Assange dealt with his legal battles, he continued to run WikiLeaks until it was forced to shut down in December 2010. Still, the concept spawned new leak platforms like GreenLeaks, which focused on environmental issues, and Brussels Leaks, which focused on the European Union. Despite the controversy over what Assange had done and the outstanding charges, he received at least two prestigious awards in 2011.

In addition to the Martha Gelhourn Prize for Journalism, the Sydney Peace Foundation honored Assange with its Gold Medal for courage while pursuing human rights. In giving Assange the award, the foundation's director, Stuart Rees, told the *The Information Company*, "By championing people's right to know, WikiLeaks and Julian Assange have created the potential for a new order in journalism and in the free flow of information." Rees added, "We think the struggle for peace with justice inevitably involves conflict, inevitably involves controversy. We think that you and WikiLeaks have brought about what we think is a watershed in journalism and in freedom of information and potentially in politics."

Sources

Advertiser (Australia), December 11, 2010, p. 30.
Australian Womens Weekly, February 1, 2011.
Calgary Herald (Alberta, Canada), August 29, 2010, p. C2.
Christian Science Monitor, February 24, 2011.
Europe Intelligence Wire, June 2, 2011.
Guardian Unlimited, December 16, 2010; December 18, 2010; January 14, 2011.
The Information Company, May 11, 2011.
Maclean's, December 27, 2010, p. 28.
National Journal, December 14, 2010; December 16, 2010.
New York Magazine, December 13, 2010.
Radio Free Europe, July 27, 2010.
Technology Review, March-April 2011, p. 70.
Times (London, England), December 21, 2010, pp.12-13.

—A. Petruso

Kate Atkinson

Author

Born Kate Atkinson, December 20, 1951, in York, U.K.; married twice; children: two. *Education:* University of Dundee, M.A., 1974.

Addresses: *Publisher*—Transworld Publishers, 61-63 Uxbridge Road, London, W5 5SA, England. *E-mail*— info@transworld-publishers.co.uk

Career

Worked as a home help aid, legal secretary, and a teacher, mid- to late 1970s; began writing short stories, 1981; began writing for women's magazines after winning *Woman's Own* short story competition, 1986; published first novel, *Behind the Scenes at the Museum,* 1995; wrote *Nice* for the Traverse Theater in Edinburgh, 1996; wrote the play *Abandonment,* 2000.

Awards: Best short story, *Woman's Own,* short story competition, 1986; best short story, Ian St. James Award, for "Karmic Mothers," 1993; Book of the Year Award, Whitbread Book Awards, for *Behind the Scenes at the Museum,* 1995; Lire Book of the Year, for *Behind the Scenes at the Museum,* 1996; Best First Work, *Yorkshire Post* Book Award, for *Behind the Scenes at the Museum,* 1996; E. M. Forster Award, American Academy of Arts and Letters, 1997; Prix Westminster Award, for *Case Histories,* 2004; Scottish Book of the Year Award, Saltire Society, for *Case Histories,* 2005; Richard and Judy Best Read of the Year Award, British Book Awards, for *When Will There Be Good News?,* 2009.

Sidelights

Kate Atkinson is not easily categorized. She is an author with a way for words who earned her masters degree in English Literature at the University of Dundee, but after studying for her doctoral degree in American Literature failed at the viva stage which means that she did not pass her oral exam. While she has won such prestigious literary awards as the Whitbread Award, the British Book Award, and the E. M. Forster Award, she writes crime fiction that is typically thought of as being genre fiction. When Georgie Lewis, interviewing her for independent bookseller Powells' Web site, asked Atkinson about attempts to categorize her fiction, Atkinson responded "They annoy me." Atkinson went on to say in the same interview that she had spoken with Nancy Pearl—who is a librarian, radio show host, and author—and Pearl suggested that the best way to categorize Atkinson's fiction was within the designation of "comedies of manners."

Atkinson is very much an odd collection of dissimilarities. Tim Teeman, writing for the London *Times,* described her as "unapologetically tricky" and went on to relate that Atkinson did not understand why the journalist would want to write about her. A well-known, best-selling author whose income is based on how popular her books are and how much exposure she and her books can garner, Atkinson is nonetheless reticent about her past. When the *Times* article was written, Atkinson already had multiple best-selling books in the United Kingdom including *Behind the Scenes at the Museum, Human Croquet, Emotionally Weird,* and *Case Histories.* Atkinson has disclosed that in the past she was struck by a year long bout of agoraphobia that came out of nowhere. Rather than succumbing to it, she fought her way out of it. While socially Atkinson can appear quite jovial, displaying what Teeman described as "warm laughter and conversational scattiness" during an interview over tea and cake at a hotel, Teeman also quoted Atkinson as saying, in regards to several tabloids trying to dig up information about her two ex-husbands, "It made me want to kill. In fact several people are now dead. I have a huge amount of hatred, which is a very healthy thing to feel." However Atkinson revealed to Teeman that this was not her deep, dark secret. Her deep, dark secret was "not getting outside what was inside."

Atkinson's books are littered with dead bodies, including dead women dropped into canals or left in boats, and dead bodies decaying in their homes. When she was asked if she had ever had anything violent happen to her, Atkinson replied that she had not been the victim of any crime. She did confess that a friend of hers had a sister who had been murdered. Atkinson explores in her fiction the randomness of the intrusion of violence in people's lives. The main character of three of her novels is Yorkshireman Jackson Brodie, who is motivated to solve crimes because of the murder of his older teenage sister. He is a man of few words, capable of violence in the right situation, and confused by women. In *Started Early, Took My Dog* he compulsively visits every Betty's tea room, travels to ruined abbeys in the North of England, acquires a dog, and discovers a passion for poetry. When asked how she had created the character of Brodie, Atkinson stated that he just occurred to her and told Teeman that "a friend's daughter is called Brodie." She gave the character an interest in the poetry of Emily Dickinson because she always wanted to title a book after the poem "I started early, took my dog." Despite the seeming randomness of her creation of the character of Brodie, Dr. Jules Smith, writing for the British Council's Web site on Contemporary Writers, claimed "she is the most games-playing of writers, playing with literary genre conventions, eroding their boundaries and entertainingly subverting them." The numerous literary awards that Atkinson

has been given for her fiction will attest to the solid craftsmanship of her work and her intentionality in what she creates.

Stephen King, writing for *Entertainment Weekly,* declared that *Case Histories* was "Not just the best novel I read this year ... but the best mystery of the decade.... I defy any reader not to feel a combination of delight and amazement.... This is the kind of book you shove in people's faces, saying 'You gotta read this!'" Atkinson's books appear on the same shelves in a bookstore as Jane Austen who she asserts was just writing romantic fiction, Charles Dickens who was writing crime fiction, and Fyodor Dostoyevsky. They are all considered to be literary fiction, but the designation is not of importance to her. On her Web site it states that the theme that runs through her work is "the irrecoverable loss of love and how best to continue living once you have glumly recognised that" (taken from a *Sunday Times* review by Penny Perrick).

Atkinson has been married twice and is a mother. She gave birth to one of her daughters while she was completing her masters degree program. She has worked at a variety of different jobs over the course of her life, including being a home help aid, a legal secretary, and a teacher. She has written short stories, plays, and several novels. She dislikes explaining what her works mean to people and wrote in an article published in the *Guardian* that asking an author what a book is about is "the most loathsome question you could ask—why bother to write the thing if you then have to explain it?" She is a literary author who considers the designation elitist. She is also a writer of magical fiction that conjures a vision of the worst of this world. Finally, she is a woman whose words failed her and yet have given her tremendous success. Atkinson is categorically indefinable by choice and by design.

Selected writings

Behind the Scenes at the Museum, Doubleday UK (London), 1995.

Human Croquet, Doubleday UK, 1997.

Abandonment (a play), Nick Hern Books (London), 2000.

Emotionally Weird, Doubleday UK, 2000.

Not the End of the World (a collection of short stories), Doubleday UK, 2002.

Case Histories, Doubleday UK, 2004.

One Good Turn, Doubleday UK, 2006.

When Will There Be Good News?, Doubleday UK, 2008.

Started Early, Took My Dog, Doubleday UK, 2010.

Sources

Periodicals

Entertainment Weekly, December 23, 2005; February 1, 2007.

Guardian, November 1, 2008.

Publishers Weekly, January 10, 2011.

Sunday Times, August 6, 2006, p. 50.

Telegraph, August 18, 2010.

Times, August 8, 2008.

Online

"Kate Atkinson," British Council on Contemporary Writers, http://www.contemporarywriters.com/authors/?p=auth4 (February 20, 2011).

"Kate Atkinson," Good Reads, http://www.goodreads.com/author/show/10015.Kate_Atkinson (February 26, 2011).

Kate Atkinson's Official Web site, http://www.kateatkinson.co.uk (February 20, 2011).

"Kate Atkinson's Rescue Operatipon," Powells, http://www.powells.com/interviews/atkinson.html (February 20, 2011).

"*Not the End of the World* by Kate Atkinson," Bookslut, http://www.bookslut.com/fiction/2004_02_001530.php (February 20, 2011).

—*Annette Bowman*

Elizabeth Banks

Actress

Born Elizabeth Maresal Mitchell, February 10, 1974, in Pittsfield, MA; daughter of Mark (a factory worker) and Ann Mitchell; married Max Handelman (a sportswriter and executive), 2003; children: Felix. *Education:* University of Pennsylvania, B.A., 1996; American Conservatory Theater, M.F.A., 1998.

Addresses: *Web site*—http://www.elizabethbanks. com.

Career

Actress in films, including: *Surrender Dorothy,* 1998; *Shaft,* 2000; *Ordinary Sinner,* 2001; *Wet Hot American Summer,* 2001; *Catch Me If You Can,* 2002; *Spider-Man,* 2002; *Stella Shorts 1998-2002,* 2002; *Swept Away,* 2002; *Seabiscuit,* 2003; *The Trade,* 2003; *Spider-Man 2,* 2004; *The 40-Year-Old Virgin,* 2005; *The Baxter,* 2005; *Daltry Calhoun,* 2005; *Heights,* 2005; *Sexual Life,* 2005; *The Sisters,* 2005; *Invincible,* 2006; *Slither,* 2006; *Fred Claus,* 2007; *Meet Bill,* 2007; *Spider-Man 3,* 2007; *Definitely, Maybe,* 2008; *Lovely, Still,* 2008; *Meet Dave,* 2008; *Role Models,* 2008; *W.,* 2008; *Zack and Miri Make a Porno,* 2008; *Big Breaks,* 2009; *The Surrogates,* 2009; *The Uninvited,* 2009; *The Details,* 2010; *The Next Three Days,* 2010; *Our Idiot Brother,* 2011. Television appearances include: *Third Watch,* 1999; *Sex and the City,* 2000; *Law & Order: Special Victims Unit,* 2001; *Without a Trace,* 2002; *Stella,* 2005; *Scrubs,* 2006-09; *American Dad!,* 2007-08; *Wainy Days,* 2007-08; *Commanche Moon* (miniseries), 2008; *Modern Family,* 2009; *30 Rock,* 2010—.

Jason Merritt/Getty Images

Sidelights

Striding onscreen with a whiter-than-white smile, Elizabeth Banks' style and savvy might not be the first thing that one notices. But the actress whose premiere role was as Vicki in the movie *Surrender Dorothy* about sexual dominance and submission has humor, verve, intelligence, and a sense of style that has caused comparisons to be made between her and a *Breakfast at Tiffany's*-era Audrey Hepburn. Banks was not just another could-be pinup; she has played a wide range of characters and explored the feminine through such roles as a stepmother who makes the lives of her stepdaughters miserable, a doctor who is the love interest of another doctor, a nightclub singer, and First Lady Laura Bush. Banks has been a representative of the female condition across the spectrum—everything from being the face of L'Oréal cosmetics to doing speaking engagements in support of "A Woman is Not a Pre-existing Condition," a National Women's Law Center initiative to pass healthcare reform legislation that includes affordable coverage and benefits for reproductive health.

Banks, who changed her name from Elizabeth Maresal Mitchell so as not to be confused with another actress named Elizabeth Mitchell, was born in Pittsfield, Massachusetts in 1974. She was the eldest daughter of four children born to Mark and Ann Mitchell. Her father was a factory worker for General Electric. Growing up, Banks was a tomboy who enjoyed riding horses and going to baseball games. She dreamed of becoming an athlete until a disastrous slide into third base at a softball game resulted in a broken leg. Looking for other activities to do after school, Banks became involved with the school play. She played the role of Pontius Pilot in *Jesus Christ Superstar*, where the robe hid her cast. While playing the role of Aldonza/Dulcinea in *Man of La Mancha*, the unfortunate combination of a thunderstorm and open air vents in the auditorium meant that puddles of water collected onstage. Banks stuck to a longtime theater tradition, did not miss a beat, and the show went on.

Banks' good looks and winning smile won her her first taste of celebrity when she was named Harvest Queen in her hometown's annual autumn celebration. After graduating from Pittsfield High School in 1992, she attended the University of Pennsylvania where she demonstrated that she had more than just beauty by graduating magna cum laude in 1996. When her undergraduate days were coming to an end, Banks began interviewing for corporate positions that would help her to pay off her student loan debts. With her outstanding grades she had no difficulty getting interviews, but her heart was not in pursuing these jobs and interviewers were inclined to ask her if she really wanted the positions that they were willing to offer her. At the same time many of her friends who were in theater were applying to go on to drama school. Banks was torn. An uncle gave her the advice to go ahead and apply to drama school because the corporate jobs would still be available in two years after she completed a master's degree. Two years later, Banks earned her master of fine arts degree at the American Conservatory Theater in San Francisco where she appeared in a variety of stage productions, including *Hurly Burly, Bethlehem, A Midsummer Night's Dream, A Woman of No Importance, Uncle Vanya,* and *Summer & Smoke.*

Despite her titillating onscreen performances and the sizzling kiss in *Invincible* that earned her and Mark Wahlberg a nomination for "Best Kiss" at the MTV Movie Awards, Banks was happily married to Max Handelman. Banks met Handelman, who is a sportswriter and producer, on her very first day of college. When they married in 2003, she converted to Judaism and Banks' mother made the chuppah for the wedding ceremony from the groom's baby blanket, Banks' great-grandmother's hankie, and T-shirts from the couple's alma maters. Handelman and Banks co-founded Brownstone Productions.

Banks tried unsuccessfully for many years to conceive a child with her husband. She was quoted by Sarah Michaud of *People* as saying, "After years of trying to get pregnant, exploring the range of fertility treatments, all unsuccessful, our journey led us to gestational surrogacy." Banks stated that two miracles came into her life in her quest to have a child. The first miracle was in meeting the woman who carried and gave birth to Banks' child. The second was Banks' son Felix, born in 2011.

Immediately after graduating with her masters degree, Banks began taking whatever acting gigs she could get in order to pay off her student loans. She appeared in commercials for products like Dove soap, Crest toothpaste, and Zima beverages. When Handelman's job transferred him to the West Coast, the two moved and began their lives in California together. Fearlessly Banks accepted a role in the independent film *Surrender Dorothy* in which she played the character of Vicky. The movie was about a man who is frightened of women, psychologically manipulates a male heroin addict, and turns the addict into his sexual slave. It was an unconventional choice for a first movie for a budding actress. After this movie, Banks had a small role in the 2000 remake of *Shaft* starring Samuel L. Jackson. In 2001 Banks played the character of camp counselor Lindsay in the cult-classic film titled *Wet Hot American Summer*. The film launched the careers of a number of comedic actors including Paul Rudd, Michael Showalter, and Amy Poehler. Banks herself has credited the film with starting her on the comedic path.

Banks' role in *Wet Hot American Summer* helped her land a small but memorable role in *The 40-Year-Old Virgin*. Banks played a sex-crazed bookstore clerk whose bathtub scene scares away lead Steve Carell. Banks' homecoming queen good looks and down-to-earth nature made her a favorite among the band of writer/directors whose movies feature man-children and the women who fall for them. First David Wain cast her in *Wet Hot American Summer,* then Judd Apatow cast her in *The 40-Year-Old Virgin,* and in 2008 Kevin Smith cast her in the lead role opposite Seth Rogen in *Zack and Miri Make a Porno.* The film was about two longtime friends and roommates who decide to solve their financial woes by making a pornographic movie, and in the process figure out how to be romantically involved with one another. In each of these films Banks demonstrated her ability to deliver raunchy dialogue and realistically portray potentially embarrassing scenes with grace and good humor. Banks also showed a marked degree of comedic talent and was able to hold her own in scenes with such comedic heavy hitters as *30 Rock*'s Tina Fey and Alec Baldwin.

When *Zack and Miri Make a Porno* was released, Banks told Robert Abele of the *Los Angeles Times* that "Sex is ridiculous on all levels. As a woman, I don't see it as a big romantic thing. We have needs as human beings. I'm not a self-serious person in general, and I'm not somebody who believes that women have to uphold the code of morality for men." While Banks excelled in comedies that shaved close to the immoral, she described herself to the *Pennsylvania Gazette*'s Caroline Tiger as a "goody two-shoes," elaborating by saying, "I've been in the same relationship with the same person for 17 years, so, you know, you don't really get a reputation as being a wild woman." Banks' interest in portraying the characters that she took on in these films was purely a career decision. She explained to the *Los Angeles Times*' Abele that she would like to give up working on such films, but they pay her bills. In addition to the man-children comedies, she has played a number of second-tier female roles in such action and comedy movies as *Spider-Man, Spider-Man 2, Spider-Man 3, Fred Claus,* and *Slither.* Banks told Abele that she could "be in a female-driven indie and make two cents and maybe get an Independent Spirit Award, but then you can't pay your car lease." The practical-minded Banks, who almost went corporate after her undergraduate years, added that if Vince Vaughn makes a movie and needs a woman to be in it with him then it very well might be her.

Banks was as comfortable in dramatic roles as comedic roles. While filming *The Next Three Days* about a prisoner who had been falsely accused and wrongly imprisoned for murder, Banks appeared on *The Tonight Show with Jay Leno.* At the time her hair was dyed, making her a brunette rather than her usual blonde. She joked with Leno that it was her "serious" hair. Before this Banks earned critical acclaim in such dramatic roles as the bank teller who inadvertently teaches Leonardo DiCaprio's con man character in *Catch Me If You Can* how to create forgeries, Jeff Bridges' young wife in *Seabiscuit,* and a New York photographer in the indie film *The Heights.* In 2008 after meeting Banks, Oliver Stone was determined to have her play First Lady Laura Bush in his biopic about George W. Bush titled *W.* He was so convinced that she embodied First Lady Laura Bush that he called Banks "Laura" on the set. Other dramatic roles for Banks included portraying Janet Cantrell in *Invincible* with Mark Wahlberg, the character of Emily Jones in *Definitely, Maybe,* the character of Nancy Pecket in *The Sisters,* Rachel Summers in *The Uninvited*—in which Banks tried to make each of her lines have dual meaning—and Effie Trinket in *The Hunger Games.* While many fans wanted to see Kristin Chenoweth cast as Effie, Banks' landing of the role was lauded by critics as a good decision in order to bring forth the complexi-

ties of the character of Effie. Critics cited Banks' past work in bringing to life such characters as Rachel Summers.

As a working, talented, and versatile actress, Banks also appeared in a variety of television series such as *Third Watch, Sex and the City, Law & Order: Special Victims Unit, Without a Trace, Stella, American Dad!,* and *Modern Family.* Because of her work on *Wet Hot American Summer* David Wain called on her talents for his series *Wainy Days.* Banks starred in the television miniseries *Comanche Moon.* After the well-received initial appearance of the character of Dr. Kim Briggs on *Scrubs,* the role became recurring. Banks also played Avery Jessup on the hit comedy *30 Rock,* beginning in the fourth season.

Intelligent, funny, and beautiful, Banks brings a variety of charms and liveliness to any role that she takes on. The hardworking, girl-next-door actress illuminated a diverse cross section of female characters and brings thoughtfulness, depth, and commitment to each of the women she portrays, whether that woman is the love interest of the moment or the wife of a president.

Sources

Periodicals

Los Angeles Times, October 31, 2008.
Daily News (NY), March 31, 2011.

Online

"Elizabeth Banks: Address," Fanmail, http://www.fanmail.biz/90426.html (May 7, 2011).

"Elizabeth Banks: Biography," Moviefone, http://www.moviefone.com/celebrity/elizabeth-banks/2029482/biography (May 7, 2011).

"Elizabeth Banks: Biography," Rotten Tomatoes, http://www.rottentomatoes.com/celebrity/elizabeth_banks/biography.php (May 7, 2011).

"Elizabeth Banks: Biography," Yahoo! Movies, http://movies.yahoo.com/movie/contributor/18078163.tif51/bio (May 7, 2011).

"Elizabeth Banks," IMDB, http://www.imdb.com/name/nm0006969/maindetails (May 7, 2011).

"Elizabeth Banks Names 'Miracle' Baby Felix," *People,* http://www.people.com/people/article/0,,20477493.tif,00.html (May 7, 2011).

Elizabeth Banks' Official Web site, http://www.elizabethbanks.com/welcome.html (May 7, 2011).

"How To Succeed In Show Business By Really, Really Trying," *Pennsylvania Gazette*, http://www.upenn.edu/gazette/0110/feature3_1.html (May 7, 2011).

"*Hunger Games*: Why Elizabeth Banks Would Make the Perfect Effie," *Entertainment Weekly*, http://popwatch.ew.com/2011/04/19/hunger-games-elizabeth-banks-effie/ (May 7, 2011).

"Interfaith Celebrities: Meet Dave, Elizabeth Banks, and Jean Sarkozky," Interfaith Family, http://www.interfaithfamily.com/arts_and_entertainment/popular_culture/New_Movies_Interfaith_Connections.shtml?rd=2 (May 7, 2011).

—Annette Bowman

Simon Baron-Cohen

© *Brian Harris/eyevine/Redux*

Psychologist

Born August 15, 1958, in London, England; son of Vivian and Judith (Greenblatt) Baron-Cohen; married Bridget Lindley; children: Sam, Kate, Robin. *Education:* New College, Oxford, UK, M.A., 1981; University College, London, Ph.D., 1985; London Institute of Pschiatry, M.Phil., 1987.

Addresses: *Office*—Autism Research Centre, University of Cambridge, Douglas House, 18b Trumpington Rd., Cambridge, England CB2 2AH. *E-mail*—sb205@cam.ac.uk.

Career

Staff psychologist, Institute of Psychiatry, London, 1985-87; lecturer in psychology, University College, London, and St. Mary's Hospital Medical School, 1987-88; lecturer in developmental psychology, Institute of Psychiatry, 1988-94; lecturer in psychopathology, University of Cambridge, 1994-97, then reader in developmental psychopathology, 1998-2001, then professor of developmental psychopathology, 2001—; writer, 1993—. Director of the Autism Research Centre and the Cambridge Lifespan Asperger Syndrome Service.

Member: Association of Child Psychology and Psychiatry; National Autistic Society; British Psychology Society.

Awards: Research award, Association of Child Psychology and Psychiatry, 1986-87; research award, British Psychological Society, 1990; Spearman Medal for Trust Fellow, Wellcome Trust, 1990; research award, American Psychological Association, 1991.

Sidelights

Are there masculine and feminine ways of thinking? Does everyone have the capability of being able to empathize equally? Does environment or genetics play a greater role in the development of autism? These weighty questions are among those upon which the sometimes controversial and prominent British psychologist Simon Baron-Cohen has focused his career. His first employed position was at the Family Tree, a learning institute for individuals with autism, and this inspired him to go on to examine how autism comes about and how people with autism think. Baron-Cohen is a professor of developmental psychopathology at the University of Cambridge. He is also the director of the Autism Research Centre and the Cambridge Lifespan Asperger Syndrome Service. He has written many books about autism and is frequently asked to comment in the media about autism and psychology. Baron-Cohen lives in the United Kingdom with his wife and three children.

In 1997, Baron-Cohen wrote a book titled *Mindblindness: An Essay on Autism and Theory of Mind.* In this book he proposed that autistic individuals do not develop what he called a "theory of mind." He explained that a theory of mind was the ability to understand that other individuals have their own perspectives, thoughts, and feelings. He went further to explain that not only could individuals with autism not conceive that others had thoughts and feelings but they could not imagine what the thoughts and feelings might be and have an appropriate response to the feelings of others.

Since this first theoretical explanation for what skills individuals with autism might lack, Baron-Cohen has gone farther to find evidence to back up his "theory of mind." In 2003, Baron-Cohen wrote *Essential Difference: Men, Women and the Extreme Male Brain.* In this book he explained that women tend to be better at reading the emotions of other people and empathizing, while men tend to better at creating systems. He proposed that an extreme version of this male tendency was responsible for the malady of autism. In 2005 in an interview with the Web site Medscape Baron-Cohen explained that "In the general population you find that, on average, males have a stronger drive to systemize and females have a stronger drive to empathize. Those are the two cognitive processes we've been focusing on to try to understand autism and why it should be more common among boys than girls. We've found that people on the autistic spectrum show an exaggeration of the male profile." In the same interview he went on to explain that, when he first began researching his theory of mind, he set up his experiments to test for empathy and the ability to systemize as separate abilities. As he continued his research it become evident that the two abilities were correlated and seemed to compete for space in the brain. In other words, if a person proved to be good at empathizing they would not be as good at systemizing. As a further extreme of this model, he offered in the Medscape.com interview that autistic individuals who in the past had been labeled as cognitively impaired might not be but rather their ability to systemize was so exaggerated that it narrowed their focus in a dramatic way.

In looking for reasons for why this potentially overly male form of cognition would come about, Baron-Cohen considered genetics and the impact of the environment on individuals. In 2006, he cowrote a book titled *Prenatal Testosterone in Mind: Amniotic Fluid Studies* in which he published the results of research examining the testosterone levels of the amniotic fluid of women to get a picture if high levels of testosterone would impact the child's later development. He found that high levels of in utero testosterone were associated with the children making less eye contact at 12 months of age and developing language slower at 18 months of age. In other studies he also examined associative mating.

Associative mating is an idea from the field of genetics that purports that people with similar characteristics tend to mate. It has been proven to be true in regards to individuals with similar heights tend to have children. He did MRI scans on the parents of children with autism and found that both the mothers and fathers tended to think in similar ways and follow the pattern of being systematic thinkers. Further, in conducting this research he also found that the fathers of both the mothers and fathers of the autistic children tended to be engineers. Engineering is an occupation that requires systematic thinking.

As a child growing up in a Jewish household, Baron-Cohen's father told him about the Nazis and the atrocities that had been committed during World War II. In 2011 Baron-Cohen wrote *Science of Evil: On Empathy and the Origins of Human Cruelty.* The book has been very controversial among the communities of parents whose children have autism and of those who have been the victims of violent crimes. Baron-Cohen told Liz Else, writing for *New Scientist,* that this puzzle of how the Holocaust happened has been very influential on his thinking. In the book Baron-Cohen puts forth that the term evil is very subjective and that the concept of evil should be put in terms of empathy. He suggests that evil is a zero rating of empathy. Individuals who have such psychiatric disorders as psychopathic personality disorder, borderline personality disorder, and narcissism would all be considered to have a zero empathy rating. Individuals with autism would also be considered to have a zero empathy rating. A person with well-developed empathic abilities would have an empathy rating of six. Baron-Cohen also reiterates that the above mentioned psychiatric conditions might be caused by genetics, environment, or a combination of both and empathic education programs such as anti-bullying programs are necessary. He also states that individuals with autism can become super-moral if given empathic training. His theories have raised discussions about the nature of crime and what the judicial or rehabilitative response should be to crimes.

Selected writings

(Edited with H. Tager-Flusberg and D. J. Cohen) *Understanding Other Minds: Perspectives From Autism,* Oxford University Press (Oxford, U.K.), 1993.

(With P. Bolton) *Autism: The Facts,* Oxford University Press, 1993.

Mindblindness: An Essay on Autism and Theory of Mind, MIT Press/Bradford Books (Cambridge, MA), 1995.

The Maladapted Mind: Classic Readings in Evolutionary Psychopathology, Psychology Press (Hove, East Sussex, U.K.), 1997.

(Edited with J. Harrison) *Synaesthesia: Classic and Contemporary Readings,* Blackwell (Cambridge, MA), 1997.

(With M. M. Robinson) *Tourette Syndrome: The Facts,* Oxford University Press, 1998.

(With P. Howlin and J. Hadwin) *Teaching Children With Autism to Mind-Read: A Practical Guide for Teachers and Parents,* Wiley (New York, NY), 1998.

(With P. Howlin and J. Hadwin) *All About Emotions,* Wiley, 2000.

The Essential Difference: Men, Women and the Extreme Male Brain, Basic Books (New York, NY), 2004.

(With S. Wheelwright and P. Meyers) *An Exact Mind: An Artist with Asperger Syndrome,* Jessica Kingsley Publishers (New York, NY), 2004.

(With R. Knickmeyer and S. Lutchmaya) *Prenatal Testosterone in Mind: Amniotic Fluid Studies,* MIT Press (Cambridge, MA), 2006.

Autism and Asperger Syndrome, Oxford University Press, 2008.

Zero Degrees of Empathy: A New Theory of Human Cruelty, Allen Lane (New York, NY), 2011.

The Science of Evil: On Empathy and the Origins of Cruelty, Basic Books, 2011.

Sources

Books

Complete Marquis Who's Who, Gale Group, 2010.
Writers Directory, St. James Press, 2011.

Periodicals

New Scientist, April 13, 2011.
New York Times, June 13, 2011.
Telegraph, April 20, 2011.

Online

"An Interview With Simon Baron-Cohen on Zero-Empathy, Autism, and Accountability," Science20, http://www.science20.com/countering_tackling_woo/interview_simon_baroncohen_zeroempa thy_autism_and_accountability-79669 (November 20, 2011).

Contemporary Authors Online, Gale, 2011.

Gale Biography in Context, Gale, 2011.

"Neuropsychology of Autism and Pervasive Developmental Disorders—The Extreme Male Brain Theory: An Expert Interview With Simon Baron-Cohen, PhD, MPhil," Medscape, http://www.medscape.com/viewarticle/518449 (November 20, 2011).

—Annette Bowman

Rick Bass

Author

Born March 7, 1958, in Fort Worth, TX; son of C. R. (a geologist) and Lucy (an English teacher and homemaker) Bass; married Elizabeth Hughes (an artist); children: Mary Katherine, Lowry. *Education:* Utah State University, B.A., 1979.

Addresses: *Agent*—Bob Dattila, 216 South Yellowstone, Livingston, MT 59047.

Career

Worked as a petroleum geologist in Jackson, Mississippi, 1979-87; published first collection of essays, *The Deer Pasture,* 1985; moved to Montana, 1987; published nonfiction book, *Oil Notes,* 1988; published first collection of stories, *The Watch,* 1988; published first novel, *Where the Sea Used to Be,* 1998; published historical novel, *The Diezmo,* 2005; published country music novel, *Nashville Chrome,* 2010. Contributed essays and stories to periodicals, including *Sports Afield, Audubon, National Geographic Traveler, Atlantic Monthly, Sierra,* and *Texas Monthly.*

Member: Outdoor Writers of America, Sierra Club.

Awards: Younger Writers Award, General Electric, 1987; PEN/Nelson Algren Award for fiction, PEN American Center, for *The Watch,* 1988; James Jones Fellowship Award, James Jones Literary Society, for *Where the Sea Used to Be,* 1995; won multiple O. Henry Awards and Pushcart Prizes.

Sidelights

American author Rick Bass is best known for writing fiction and nonfiction about environmental topics like wilderness, the landscape, nature, wildlife, and wildness in well-known books like *The Book of Yaak* and *Where the Sea Used to Be.* He often includes personal reflections, observations about the natural world, and elements of story in both his fiction and nonfiction, and has a distinctive storytelling voice. Bass has passionately worked to conserve the Yaak, the valley in Montana where he lives, and he has spent much time and energy on this effort. Later in his career, Bass wrote on different topics, including Texas history and the country music pioneers the Browns in novels like *The Diezmo* and *Nashville Chrome,* respectively.

Discussing Bass as an author, Utah naturalist and author Terry Tempest Williams told Brandon Griggs of the *Salt Lake Tribune,* "Rick eats the landscape. It is his nourishment. It is his intensity. Rick Bass' emotions are on the page, and as a result, his readers feel very close to him." Bryan Woooley of the *Dallas Morning News* lauded, "Probably no American writer since Hemingway has written about man-in-nature more beautifully or powerfully than Rick Bass."

Born March 7, 1958, in Fort Worth, Texas, he was the son of C. R. and Lucy Bass. His father was a geologist and his mother was an English teacher. Raised in the suburbs of Houston, he often went deer hunting in the Texas hill country with his father and grandfather. From the latter, he heard stories and family myths, and Bass grew to love the outdoors.

A football player, Bass attended Utah State for whom he played flanker and tailback. (He chose Utah State over other schools because of the landscape depicted in the film *Jeremiah Johnson*.) He studied wildlife science before changing to geology. He spent much time camping in nearby mountains and twice took a writing course with Tom Lyon, who had an influence on the young writer.

After earning his degree in geology in 1979, Bass moved to Mississippi where he worked as a petroleum geologist from 1979 to 1987. As a geologist, he prospected for new oil wells. Essentially, Bass was a wildcatter who grew to love the land while searching for new wells. While living in Mississippi, Bass was given Jim Harrison's novella *Legends of the Fall* by a bookstore owner. The way that Harrison wrote about the Montana wilderness with straightforward eloquence inspired Bass to try writing fiction. He wrote on the side for several years, then went to the Writers at Work conference in Park City, Utah, where one of his stories got the attention of an editor at W.W. Norton, Carol Houck Smith. Smith asked to see more, and Bass sent her a number of them, leading to his first fiction publication, the short story collection *The Watch*.

His lauded Norton book—*The Watch*—was not Bass' first book. While still working as a geologist, Bass published his first book, the nonfiction *The Deer Pasture* in 1985. It was based on the experiences he had hunting with his grandfather in the Texas hill country. In 1988, Bass published *Oil Notes* which became one of his better-known nonfiction books. Written in the form of a journal, the book touches on the art and science of finding oil as well as words on the author's personal life and outdoor activities. Reviewing the book for the *St. Petersburg Times*, Andy Solomon wrote, "As in his stories, Bass speaks with the muscular voice of the youthful (31 this past March) naturalist outdoorsman in clipped, unadorned prose. And as with much best-selling fiction—*Jaws*, *Coma*, and *Shogun* come immediately to mind—he combines an absorbing blend of spirited writing with an area of technical expertise."

As Bass began focusing on writing, he left Mississippi with his girlfriend (later wife) Elizabeth Hughes, and they moved between New Mexico, Arizona, Colorado, Utah, and Idaho before settling in an isolated area of Montana. The Yaak was located in the far northwestern corner of the state where only 150 people lived without television or radio reception and many even lacked connection to an electric grid. He initially resided in a cabin without electricity in this essentially inaccessible piece of land before moving into a home with a generator. He regularly hiked over 10 miles a day on nearby acres owned by the federal government (the Yaak is part of the Kootenai National Forest) while taking notes and thinking about his work. He spent much of his time writing, and published prolifically for more than a decade. (Bass later lived near Troy, Montana, with a population of 900, before living part time in Missoula, Montana, as well as Yaak Valley in the early 2000s.)

Bass felt extremely protective of the Yaak, and was passionate about caring for the land and its purity. He worried that it would be developed and become infiltrated by developers, tourists, loggers, and miners. In turn, the area where he lived inspired much of his fiction and nonfiction directly or indirectly. Chris Solomon of the *Seattle Times* explained that Bass had written "a flurry of award-winning short stories and nonfiction that capture the gut essence of this place, its peculiar autumn softness and blue-cold winters, its characters and wild creatures, and the mysterious humming rhythms of nature still intact. He knows where he lives is special."

Nonfiction books like 1991's *Winter: Notes from Montana* and 1996's *The Book of Yaak* summarized the appeal of the area and offer his argument of what it was special about it. The Yaak, Bass explained in the latter book, contained the biodiversity of all the ecosystems of the West but was not protected from logging and thousands of miles of logging road scarred through the Purcell Mountains and into the forest. Bass worked hard to safeguard the last unroaded areas of the Yaak as wilderness so that logging was barred forever. In this capacity, he often wrote about the valley for magazines, visited elected officials in Washington, and composed many advocacy letters and editorials.

The effort to protect the Yaak sometimes took a toll on Bass. He told Solomon of the *Seattle Times*, "It's not the emotional turmoil. You know, great fiction, great art can come out of—does come out of—emotional turmoil. That's the least of it. It is the physical licking of stamps, the physical typing of the letters, the physical loading in of the data into the mind. That's probably where some of my, at times, bitterness comes from, from feeling like I have to work so much on political inanities, instead of just getting out and hiking and daydreaming and unmooring, and just cutting loose and going as deep into art as I want to go, day after day, night after night."

The Yaak was not Bass' only nonfiction topic. He also wrote nonfiction books filtered through other environmental concerns like animals. For example, 1992's *The Ninemile Wolves*, and 1998's *The New Wolves* focused on wolves and their plight. In 1995, he published *The Lost Grizzlies: A Search for Survivors in the Wilderness of Colorado*, which focused on grizzly bears. In it, he argued that such large predators should be allowed to thrive.

In the mid-1990s, Bass began focusing more on fiction. He primarily wrote short stories and often featured hunting, fishing, and drinking as themes. In 1994, he published the collection *Platte River*, and *In the Loyal Mountains* in 1995. In 1997, he published three novellas together, titled *The Sky, The Stars, The Wilderness*. In 1998, Bass published his first novel, *Where the Sea Used to Be*. This saga focused on Wallis, a petroleum geologist who goes to Montana at behest of a Texas oilman named Old Dudley. Living in an isolated part of Montana and searching for oil, Wallis lives with Mel, Old Dudley's daughter, and falls in love with her and the landscape. But Wallis also finds oil, bringing Dudley north to drill which affects the wilderness, his relationship with Mel, and his soul.

In 2000, Bass published another of his best known books *Colter: The True Story of the Best Dog I Ever Had*. He had mentioned his dog, a German shorthaired pointer, in previous essays and books. The book focuses on Bass' life and relationship with and loss of his beloved Colter who disappeared one winter evening and did not come home. Bass found his remains a year later and buried him. Also present in the book are bigger themes like the transformation of the American West, environmentalism, the beauty of hunting, and man's fate woven among the stories of man and dog. Writing in the *Austin American-Statesman*, Robert Braile called it a "simple, elegant book."

Bass continued to publish both nonfiction and fiction in the early 21st century. In 2002, he put out the story collection *The Hermit's Story*, which contains ten stories about the Montana countryside in the winter, offering studies of character and place. In 2005, Bass published his first historical novel, *The Diezmo*, which was based on the Mier Expedition of 1842 when 300 armed Texans crossed into Mexico to retaliate for a Mexican attack on San Antonio and take plunder. The raiding party was captured, forced to march for hundreds of miles, and suffer starvation, recapture after escaping, and assassination. Only one third of the original group made it back to Texas. Events and characters were true, but Bass invented the novel's narrator, James Alexander.

Bass' 2006 short story collection *The Lives of Rocks: Stories* was a Story Award finalist in 2007. In 2008, he published a memoir *Why I Came West*, which reflected on the 17 years he spent in Montana, and the hows and whys of where he ended up. The book was a National Book Critics Circle Award finalist in autobiography in 2008. He followed this with the 2009 nonfiction tome, *The Wild Marsh: Four Seasons at Home in Montana*, which took readers through a year in the life in the Yaak Valley, and the 2010 novel *Nashville Chrome*. Like *The Diezmo*, *Nashville Chrome* was not about Montana or the landscape, but about country music. It was a fictionalized account of the country music pioneers, the Browns. The Browns was a band that consisted of two sisters and a brother, sold millions of records, and became one of the first big crossover country music stars in the 1950s and 1960s.

Over the years, Bass also contributed essays and stories to such periodicals as *Sports Afield, Audubon, National Geographic Traveler, Atlantic Monthly, Sierra,* and *Texas Monthly*. He wrote about country music for various magazines as well. But it was nature that was the focus of Bass' most passionate, best known work. Bass told Bill Mintutaglio of the *Dallas Morning News*, "When we lose diversity and tolerance for places that are different, then we are sunk. We are going down like the Titanic. Creativity is lost, imagination is lost. We need that diversity in our movement, in our thinking, working and living. The wilderness is anything but abstract. When we lose wilderness, it is like we have lost a mirror in which to see ourselves."

Selected writings

Essay collections

The Deer Pasture, Texas A&M University Press (College Station, TX), 1985.
Wild to the Heart, Stackpole (Harrisburg, PA), 1987.
Oil Notes, Seymour Lawrence (New York, NY), 1988.
Brown Dog of the Yak: Essays on Art and Activism, Milkweed (Minneapolis, MN), 1999.

Nonfiction

Winter: Notes from Montana, Houghton Mifflin (Boston, MA), 1991.

The Ninemile Wolves, Clark City (Livingston, MT), 1992.

The Lost Grizzlies: A Search for Survivors in the Wilderness of Colorado, Houghton Mifflin, 1995.

The Book of Yaak, Houghton Mifflin, 1996.

The New Wolves, Lyons (New York, NY), 1998.

Colter: The True Story of the Best Dog I Ever Had, Houghton Mifflin, 2000.

Caribout Rising: Defending the Porcupine, Gwich-'in Culture, and the Arctic National Wildlife Refuge, Sierra Club Books (San Francisco, CA), 2004.

Why I Came West, Houghton Mifflin, 2008.

The Wild Marsh: Four Seasons at Home in Montana, Houghton Mifflin Harcourt (Boston, MA), 2009.

Story collections

The Watch, W.W. Norton (New York City), 1988.

Platte River, Houghton Mifflin, 1994.

In the Loyal Mountains, Houghton Mifflin, 1995.

The Hermit's Story, Houghton Mifflin, 2002.

The Lives of Rocks: Stories, Houghton Miffline, 2006.

Novella collections

The Sky, The Stars, The Wilderness, Houghton Mifflin, 1987.

Novels

Where the Sea Used to Be, Houghton Mifflin, 1998.

Fiber, University of Georgia (Athens, GA), 1998.

The Diezmo, Houghton Mifflin, 2005.

Nashville Chrome, Houghton Mifflin Harcourt, 2010.

Sources

Books

Environmental Encyclopedia, Gale, 2009.

Periodicals

Associated Press State & Local Wire, September 24, 2010.

Austin American Statesman, September 24, 2000, p. L9.

Booklist, May 1, 2009, p. 53.

Dallas Morning News, November 15, 1992, p. 23; November 3, 2002, p. 11C; May 30, 2005, p. 10E.

Houston Chronicle, June 29, 2008, p. 13.

Newsweek, January 9, 1989, p. 57.

Philadelphia Inquirer, November 17, 2010.

Salt Lake Tribune, August 16, 1998, p. J1.

Seattle Times, January 12, 1998.

St. Petersburg Times, August 20, 1989, p. 6D.

Texas Monthly, July 2010, p. 70.

Online

Contemporary Authors Online, Gale, 2011.

—*A. Petruso*

Jose Bautista

© AP Images

Professional baseball player

Born José Antonio Bautista, October 19, 1980, in Santo Domingo, Dominican Republic; son of Americo (a poultry farm operator) and Sandra (a certified public accountant) Bautista; companion of Neisha Croyle; children: one (with Croyle). *Education:* Attended Chipola Community College.

Addresses: *Office*—Toronto Blue Jays, Rogers Centre, 1 Blue Jays Way, Ste. 3200, Toronto, Ontario M5V 1J1 Canada.

Career

Played college baseball at Chipola Community College, c. 1998-2000; drafted by the Pittsburgh Pirates in the twentieth round, 2000; played for Pittsburgh's Class A team, Hickory, 2002; played in Lynchburg in the Carolina League, 2003; claimed by the Baltimore Orioles in the Rule 5 Draft, 2004; played for the Baltimore Orioles, Tampa Bay Devil Rays, Kansas City Royals, New York Mets, and Pittsburgh Pirates, 2004; spent most of season in Pirates' minor league system, 2005; traded to Toronto Blue Jays, 2008; made significant changes to approach to hitting, 2009; had career year, 2010; set record in All-Star balloting, 2011.

Awards: Silver Slugger Award, 2010, 2011; Hank Aaron Award, 2010, 2011; four Player of the Month Awards, 2010, 2011; four Player of the Week Awards, 2010, 2011; named to the Major League Baseball All-Star team, 2010, 2011.

Sidelights

At the end of the 2011 season, highly regarded Toronto Blue Jays player Jose Bautista was a prime candidate for the Most Valuable Player Award though he ultimately finished third. After changing his swing and mentality as a batter in 2009, the player saw his prowess at the plate increase greatly in 2010 and 2011, including setting league-leading statistics in a number of offensive categories. Primarily a third baseman, Bautista was able to play all outfield positions and second base. In 885 games played over the course of his career through the end of 2011, he had a career batting average of .254 with 455 hits, 156 homers, and an on-base percentage of .362. Bautista was also highly regarded as a leader in the clubhouse, with an outstanding work ethic and willingness to help others.

Born October 19, 1980, in Santo Domingo, Dominican Republic, he was the son of Americo and Sandra Bautista. His father operated a large poultry farm, while his mother was a certified public accountant. As a child, Bautista was raised in a middle class household and helped on the farm by giving vaccinations and setting up equipment. His parents wanted him to have a good education, so they enrolled him in private school when they were not happy with the education he was receiving at public schools. As a student, he was good at math, biology, and chemistry, and began studying English at the age of eight. He eventually focused his studies on business.

Bautista was also an active child, playing soccer, basketball, and baseball, often with small group of friends. He became particularly focused on baseball by the age of eight, and memorized the statistics of every Major League player. He told Mark Zwolinski of the *Waterloo Region Record*, "I played Little League. But I was always one of the smallest guys; that changed later on. But definitely I wasn't a power-hitting guy. I was a leadoff hitter and speedy." He was also disciplined and would round up teammates for games on Saturday mornings, not waiting for the set meeting time to see who would show up. With his academic success and baseball skills, he won a scholarship to Florida's Chipola Community College and played baseball while displaying what would become a career-defining sense of work ethic and focus. He soon caught the attention of Major League Baseball.

In 2000, Bautista was drafted by the Pittsburgh Pirates in the twentieth round. He signed and began playing Single A baseball in their system in 2002. Playing for Class A Hickory, Bautista hit .301 with 14 home runs and 57 runs batted over 129 games. In 2003, he played in Lynchburg in the Carolina League for 51 games, posting a .242 batting average, four home runs, and 20 runs batted in. He missed two months during the season because of a broken hand, but returned for the playoffs when he hit .375 and had a home run.

After the season ended, Bautista was left exposed in the Rule 5 draft. The Baltimore Orioles picked him up for spring training, and had to keep him on their major league roster all season or he would be offered to the Pirates for $25,000. Baltimore manager Lee Mazzilli spoke highly of him, telling the Associated Press State & Local Wire, "the kid can swing the bat a little bit. Hopefully, he's a diamond in the rough." Bautista played 16 games with the Orioles as an infielder and posted a .273 batting average before being moved to the Tampa Bay Devil Rays. He played 12 games with the Devil Rays, then was designated for assignment in June of 2004. The Kansas City Royals picked up Bautista from the Rays in exchange for cash. The Royals eventually sent him to the New York Mets, who traded him back to Pittsburgh at the end of July of 2004 as part of a trade involving Kris Benson.

During the 2005 season, Bautista struggled in the Major Leagues, so he spent much of the year in the Pittsburgh minor league system where he could play every day and build up his confidence. He then played 117 games for the Pirates in 2006. He had 58 runs and 94 hits with 16 home runs, the most he would hit in a season with Pittsburgh. In 2007, he played nearly a full season with Pittsburgh, 142 games. He had 75 runs, 135 hits, 36 doubles, and 15 home runs. Bautista had 63 runs batted in as well. In the off-season, Bautista and the Pirates were set to go to arbitration over his contract, but came to an agreement for a $1.8 million one-year contract.

In 2008, Bautista began the year with Pittsburgh. In early August 2008, the Pirates sent him down to their Triple A team. By late August 2008, the Pirates had traded him to the Toronto Blue Jays for catcher Robinzon Diaz. The Blue Jays were happy to acquire Bautista who had already hit more home runs than any player on the Toronto roster and was especially effective against left-handed pitchers. The Blue Jays were also stirred by his ability to play multiple positions, including third base, second base, and all three outfield positions. Bautista was on Toronto's radar after he made an impression on Blue Jay manager Cito Gaston when he hit a two-run home run to help the Pirates best Toronto in a mid-June game.

Bautista's move to Toronto was important to him as well. He told the *Toronto Star*, "I knew it was probably going to be my last chance to be a starter on a team. I was reaching the age of 30. My time was running out to prove that I was a capable starter. If I didn't prove that, then I was going to fall into a backup, utility role. And that was something I definitely did not want to happen." He finished 2008 having played 128 total games for both teams with 88 hits, 45 runs, 17 doubles, and 15 home runs. He also had 54 runs batted in.

In 2009, Bautista played 113 games for Toronto, with some improvements in his numbers. He had 54 runs, 79 hits, and 13 home runs. Though he had a powerful swing, it was also erratic. In late September, he began making significant changes to how he prepared at the plate including altering his setup, swing mechanics, timing, and mental approach to hitting, with the help of Blue Jays manager Gaston and hitting coach Dwayne Murphy. Bautista moved from being a hitter who guessed to one who looked for pitches in certain spots to hit with his uppercut, dead-pull swing. Between September 1, 2009, and August of 2010, he hit 46 home runs, more than anyone else in Major League Baseball. In roughly the same time period, his runs batted in, slugging percentage, and on base plus slugging percentage also vastly improved. As Craig Slater put in for Canwest News Service, "Without question, Bautista is a dangerous hitter and an intimidating presence in the batter's box."

Appearing in 161 games in total in 2010, Bautista had a career year with 109 runs, a Major League-leading 54 home runs, and 148 hits while playing both third base and in the outfield. Before joining the Blue Jays in 2008, Bautista had never hit more than 16 home runs in a year. By hitting 54 home runs, he broke George Bell's single season American League home run record of 47. Some skeptics wondered if Bautista's improvement came from the use of steroids or other drugs or chemicals. But as David McDonald wrote in the *Ottawa Citizen*, "There is ... not visible evidence Bautista is on the juice. A lean 6-1, 195 pounds, he looks pretty much the same as he did before the ball started flying out of the park. His hat size is unchanged. There are no suspicious urine samples that we know of."

Yet Bautista only earned $2.4 million in 2010. In the off-season, Bautista signed a new contract with Toronto. He was given a five-year deal worth $65 million. In 2011, Bautista was set to earn $8 million, then $14 million each of the following four seasons. The contact also included a $14 million option for 2016 with a one-million-dollar buyout.

While moving from third base to right field, Bautista continued on the torrid pace set in 2010 through the first third of the 2011 leading the Major Leagues with 20 home runs and the highest batting average at .348. He also led or was near the lead in other batting categories in the American League. Yet, Bautista sensed that pitchers were making adjustments to his changes and often walked him, so he had to modify his approach to the game. He told the *National*, "Everyone pitches me the same, it seems: hard, up and in. I need to be patient and I have been more patient this year than I was last year. I need to get the pitcher in a better hitting count, so I can get a pitch to hit."

In 2011 All-Star Game balloting, Bautista received a record number of fan votes to make the squad. He received 7.45 million votes, besting Ken Griffey Jr.'s 1994 record of 6.04 million. Shortly before the July 2011 game, Bautista was leading the Major Leagues with 29 homers. He participated in the Home Run Derby as well as the All-Star Game itself. However, after the All-Star break Bautista's productivity declined and he slumped badly in late July and early August; the slugger admitted he was not as disci-

plined at the plate. Bautista finished the year with .302 batting average, 43 home runs, 105 runs, 103 runs batted in, and an on-base percentage of .447. His success brought an excitement to the Blue Jays though post-season success remained elusive. By season's end, Bautista was considered a favorite for the American League Most Valuable Player Award in some circles, while others believed that because Toronto was not in contention for the playoffs, he would not win. He ultimately finished third with five first-place votes, losing the trophy to Detroit Tigers pitcher Justin Verlander.

Outside of baseball, Bautista was into fashion and clothes, seeking out interesting men's fashions to wear. His fashion sense emphasized smooth and stylish over loud or attention seeking as he favored pieces from Gucci, Prada, and Gieves. He told Zwolinski of the *Waterloo Region Record*, "I'm not an extravagant guy.... I don't like going over the top on anything. I have what I need and I try to keep it that way."

Bautista was also known for being a leader in the clubhouse. He went out of his way to learn perfect classic and American English, and helped other Spanish-speaking players adjust. Blue Jays first base coach Omar Malave told Zwolinski of the *Waterloo Region Record*, "One thing that Jose has is a big heart.... With [Yuni] Escobar, he tried to take him under his wing, he tried to show him things when the kid arrived in Toronto.... I am very happy to see that he is doing well now, he's worked hard for it."

Sources

Periodicals

Associated Press, June 25, 2004; January 17, 2008.
Associated Press State & Local Wire, March 1, 2004; August 22, 2008.
Associated Press Worldstream, February 17, 2011.
Canwest News Service, March 29, 2011; May 18, 2011; July 4, 2011; July 14, 2011; August 11, 2011.
Edmonton Journal (Alberta, Canada), September 19, 2011, p. C6.
Gazette (Montreal, Canada), September 26, 2011, p. A20.
Globe and Mail (Canada), July 9, 2011, p. S6.
National (United Arab Emirates), May 22, 2011.
Ottawa Citizen, September 5, 2010, p. C1.
Pittsburgh Post-Gazette, March 5, 2005, p. B1.
Sports Network, June 28, 2004.
Toronto Star, June 18, 2011, p. S1; September 6, 2011, p. S1.
Waterloo Region Record, August 17, 2010, p. D3.

Online

"Bautista Belts Way to Third in AL MVP Vote," Major League Baseball, http://mlb.mlb.com/news/article.jsp?ymd=20111121.tif&content_id=26017324.tif&vkey=news_mlb&c_id=mlb (November 21, 2011).

"Jose Bautista," BlueJays.com, http://toronto.bluejays.mlb.com/team/player.jsp?player_id=430832 (November 19, 2011).

"Jose Bautista," ESPN.com, http://espn.go.com/mlb/player/_/id/5890/jose-bautista (November 19, 2011).

—A. Petruso

Trevor Bayne

Professional race car driver

Born February 19, 1991, in Knoxville, TN; son of Rocky (a business owner) and Stephanie Bayne.

Addresses: *Office*—c/o Trevor Bayne, Inc., 124 Floyd Smith Dr., Ste. 325, Charlotte, NC 28262. *Web site*—http://www.trevorbayne.com/.

Career

Began racing at the age of five, c. 1996; competed on the go-kart circuit, c. 1996-2004; raced on Allison Legacy Race Series circuit, c. 2004-06; won Allison Legacy Race Series championship, 2005; raced on USAR Hooters Pro Cup Series circuit, c. 2006-08; entered driver development program with Dale Earnhardt, Inc., 2008; competed in NASCAR Camping World East series, 2008; had NASCAR series win at the Thompson International Speedway in Thompson, CT, 2008; raced for Michael Waltrip Racing on NASCAR Nationwide series, 2009-10; signed with Roush-Fenway Racing, racing on the NASCAR Nationwide series, 2010—; loaned to Wood Brothers Racing to compete part time on the NASCAR Sprint Cup Series, 2010—; won Daytona 500, 2011.

Awards: Rookie of the Year, Allison Legacy Race Series, c. 2004; rookie of the year, USAR Hooters Pro Cup Series, c. 2006; Sunoco Rookie of the Race, Irwindale Speedway's Toyota All-Star Showdown, 2009.

Sidelights

In 2011, race car driver Trevor Bayne became the youngest person to ever win the Daytona 500. The holder of 22 championships on the racetrack by the age of 20, Bayne won on every level he competed in, setting such records as youngest to win rookie honors on the USAR Hooters Pro Cup Series. Bayne was a natural behind the wheel. Eddie Wood of the Wood Brothers Racing family told Peter Kerasotis of the Gannett News Service, "He reminds me of the great ones. He will be a great one. I told somebody the other day that I felt like he just might be the next big deal, and I think he is."

Born on February 19, 1991, in Knoxville, Tennessee, he was the son of Rocky and Stephanie Bayne, the eldest of three. His father owned a business that provided service and maintenance for restaurant facilities. Bayne's grandfather, William, competed on dirt tracks in the Carolinas and Tennessee, inspiring his grandson's career. Though he began riding a mini-motorcycle at the age of three, Bayne's racing career began shortly after he turned five years old. Competing on the go-kart circuit for the next eight years, he was racing 43 weekends per year by the age of eight.

Go-kart racing proved costly but Rocky Bayne believed it was worth it. He told Mark Whicker of the *Orange County Register*, "People ask about those sacrifices, but a lot of people would spend that much to get their kids out of jail, or off drugs. I just looked at it as part of his life. I loved it as much as he did." Along the way, Bayne posted more than 300 victories, winning 18 track and state championships, and eight World Championships. Bayne told Gary Peterson of the *Contra Costa Times*, "My friends thought it was cool, so that sort of justified it for me. When I was in seventh grade I took a magazine to school to show my teacher. I was on the cover. She couldn't believe it."

When Bayne was 13 years old, he moved up to the Allison Legacy Race Series. He became the youngest to win top rookie honors in the series. Bayne spent two years racing in the series, winning 14 times in 41 starts. He also won 19 pole positions and finished in the top five 30 times. In 2005, he won the series' national championship.

At 15, Bayne moved to the USAR Hooters Pro Cup Series, competing in the Southern Division and being coached in the nuances of racing. He won top rookie honors here as well while competing in races at venues like Lonesome Pine Raceway in Coeburn, Virginia, and winning for the pole for Pro Cup race at Bristol Motor Speedway. Until the age of 15, Bayne was still attending school, but then stopped going to high school and completed his GED online to focus on racing. At that time, he moved from Knoxville to Mooresville, North Carolina.

In 2008, when Bayne was 17, he was signed to the Dale Earnhardt, Inc.'s (DEI) driver development program. Later that year, Bayne began competing in the NASCAR Camping World East series. On July 21, 2008, he landed his first NASCAR series win at the Thompson International Speedway in Thompson, Connecticut. While Bayne did not post another win in that series that year, he managed six top-five places and seven top-ten finishes. For this effort, he finished fourth in the standings for the year.

Bayne continued to race in the series in 2009, starting off the season with a second-place finish at the Irwindale Speedway's Toyota All-Star Showdown on January 24. With this finish, he won the Sunoco Rookie of the Race honors. However, the driver development program became a low priority by early 2009 when DEI—who was still dealing with money problems even after a merger with Ganassi Racing in late 2008—laid off 150 employees.

Bayne managed to compete on the NASCAR Nationwide Series through a hodge podge of a deal. While DEI continued to give Bayne some equipment and support, he drove Jimmy Mean Racing's number 52 car with some team support as well. Front Row Motorsports landed him a sponsor, a chain of local Taco Bell restaurants. Bayne himself spent hours working on the car with the crew as a shop hand. He told David Hooker of the *Knoxville News-Sentinel*, "I'm doing everything I can. I love being a part of it. I was in the shop a lot last year. But for this deal I've seen every piece that's been on the racecar." With this arrangement in place, Bayne competed in the March 21 Scotts Turf Builder 300 in the Bristol Motor Speedway, in Tennessee.

Bayne returned to the Nationwide Series on a more regular basis in 2009 when he began racing part-time for Michael Waltrip Racing in the number 99 Toyota Camry. In 15 races he finished in the top ten twice and the top 15 seven times. In 2010, Bayne began the year continuing to race on the Nationwide series for Michael Waltrip Racing. He started 28 races, and did well in the last 14. In those 14 races, he won three poles, posted five top-five finishes, and finished in the top ten nine times. Those three pole wins were consecutive and he became the youngest Nationwide driver to win three straight poles. The feat was last done 18 years previous. But Bayne had to leave Waltrip Racing because of the lack of a sponsor. In October of 2010, Bayne moved to Roush-Fenway Racing to finish off the Nationwide series for the year. He raced in a Roush-Fenway Ford, though he still could not attract a sponsor.

In 2011, Bayne continued to race in the Nationwide series for Roush-Fenway, with the goal of winning a series championship. Bayne also competed in some of NASCAR's top series, including the Sprint Cup series, for Wood Brothers Racing in the number 21 Ford on loan for 17 races from Roush-Fenway to get the young racecar driver experience. Unexpectedly, he impressed the NASCAR world when he won the first race of the year, the Daytona 500, and only his second Sprint Cup start. (He finished 17th at a 2010 Sprint Cup race in Texas.) At 20 years old (it was the day after his birthday), he was the youngest to win by five years. He won in spectacular fashion, never leading until the final laps but pushing others, blocking Carl Edwards, and keeping off every challenge until reaching the checkered flag. After the race was completed, Bayne did not know where Victory Lane was. He passed the turn, and had to go in reverse to get there to celebrate.

Though enthusiastic about the victory and its nearly $1.5 million purse, he told Kerasotis of the Gannett News Service, "I'm here to win just like they are." Yet Bayne also noted to Jenna Fryer of the Associated Press State & Local Wire, "I'm a little bit worried that one of them is going to come after me tonight. I'm going to have to sleep with one eye open. That's why I said I felt a little undeserving. I'm leading, and I'm saying, 'Who can I push?'"

It was also the first Daytona 500 win for Wood Brothers since 1976 and their first Sprint Cup series win in a decade. Donnie Wingo, the Wood Brothers' crew chief, told Kerasotis of the Gannett News Service, "At the end, he did what he needed to do. He adapts well to certain situations. Just the racing part of it; he catches onto the racing part and [doesn't] put [himself] in a bad position. That's the sign of a good racer." Even Jeff Gordon, who had previously been the youngest winner of the Daytona 500, was enthusiastic about the victory for Bayne and Wood Brothers. Gordon told Jenny Fryer of the Associated Press, "I think it's very cool. Trevor's a good kid, and I love the Wood Brothers. I'm really happy for him. And I think it's great for the sport. To have a young talent like that he's got that spark, you know?"

After the victory, Bayne could not celebrate with champagne because he was underage; however, he did play basketball with friends and skateboard on the infield of the Daytona track. With the win, Bayne faced hard choices. Because of new NASCAR rules, he could only compete for points in one series and had chosen Nationwide at the beginning of the season. While Bayne could change his mind and compete for points in Sprint Cup, the points from the Daytona 500 could not be applied retroactively.

Though the Chase committee ruled that the victory would count in seeding for the Chase for the Sprint Cup championship, Bayne was inclined to compete for points and a championship in the Nationwide series. One reason for this was Wood Brothers did not have funding or sponsorship for a full season, though they added the race at Martinsville to Bayne's Sprint Cup schedule. Bayne told Jenna Fryer of the Associated Press, "One thing I haven't really talked about is keeping our expectations realistic here. We won this race and that sets the bar high, but if we would have finished 15th, we would have been happy. We've got to remember that for the rest of the season. There are going to be a lot of times when we do struggle because I'm new at this. A lot of new pieces have come together, so I think we've got to keep that realistic and just race right now."

Despite the victories, Bayne still could not immediately find sponsors for his Nationwide series nor his Sprint Cup series cars. If he had a sponsor, he would have been able do a full season on the Sprint Cup series with the Wood Brothers. He also crashed during qualifying and during the race at Phoenix International Raceway the following week, finishing fortieth. His next few Nationwide and Sprint Cup races also had disappointing results. Despite these setbacks, Bayne did land a sponsor so that he could enter the Sprint All-Star Race in May 2011. Good Sam Club also sponsored Bayne for an April Sprint Cup race at the Talladega Superspeedway.

Bayne faced a bigger problem that limited his racing in April and May 2011. He was bitten by an insect in mid-April and developed a rash and numbness in his arm that seemed to be a result of the bite. While briefly hospitalized in mid-April, symptoms returned and grew worse forcing him to drop out of a late April Nationwide race at Richmond International Raceway. He missed multiple races, including the Sprint All-Star Race, with an inflammatory condition and symptoms like blurred vision, nausea, and fatigue. Treated at the Mayo Clinic for the condition over this time period, Bayne finally returned to the racetrack for an early June race. The STP 300 at the Chicago Speedway was part of the Nationwide series.

As Bayne achieved success, his parents continue to support their son, believing in his abilities and level-headedness. Faith was also important to him; for example, he organized a Bible study for the drivers before the 2011 Daytona 500. His mother, Stephanie Bayne, told Jenna Fryer of the Associated Press, "He's always been a mature kid, he's an incredible boy. He makes really smart choices, and I've never worried about him. He's a real likable boy." Bayne himself told Rick Minter of the *Atlanta Journal-Constitution*, "I just have to be true to who Trevor Bayne is. I don't ever want to have anything to hide. I want to be as public and truthful as possible and be the same person in the media and away from it. I have tried to do that, and I try to stay humble through it all."

Sources

Periodicals

Associated Press, July 31, 2010; February 21, 2011; February 28, 2011; April 16, 2011; April 28, 2011; May 15, 2011.

Associated Press Online, February 21, 2011; February 25, 2011.

Associated Press State & Local Wire, February 21, 2011; April 12, 2011.

Atlanta Journal-Constitution, February 26, 2011, p. 7C.

Bristol Herald Courier (VA), February 22, 2011.

Buffalo News, February 21, 2011, p. D1.

Contra Cost Times (CA), February 22, 2011.

Gannett News Service, February 20, 2011.

Knoxville News-Sentinel, March 19, 2009.

Orange County Register (CA), March 26, 2011, p. B.

Sports Network, May 19, 2011.

Tampa Tribune (FL), February 21, 2011, sec. Sports, p. 1.

Online

"Danica Patrick, Trevor Bayne Return to the Track," *Chicago Sun Times,* http://www.suntimes.com/sports/5763548-419/danica-patrick-trevor-bayne-return-to-the-track.html (June 4, 2011).

"Trevor Bayne Biography," Trevor Bayne Official Web Site, http://www.trevorbayne.com/?cid=biography (June 2, 2011).

—*A. Petruso*

Stacey Bendet

AP Images/Matt Sayles

Fashion designer

Born Stacey Wiener, c. 1978; daughter of Joseph D. (a fabric manufacturer) and Olivia Bendet Wiener; married Eric Eisner (a producer), 2008; children: Eloise Breckenridge, Scarlet Haven. *Education:* Earned degree in international relations from the University of Pennsylvania, c. 2000.

Addresses: *Home*—New York, NY. *Office*—Alice + Olivia, 80 West 40th St., New York, NY 10018. *Web site*—http://www.aliceandolivia.com.

Career

Flash Web designer, c. 2000-02; launched Alice + Olivia, 2002; opened first freestanding store, 2005; introduced Alice + Olivia for Payless, 2008.

Sidelights

Fashion designer Stacey Bendet is the creative talent behind the label Alice + Olivia. Though not formally trained, Bendet had been making clothes to fit her petite frame since her teens, and the line of women's trousers she launched with a friend in 2002 quickly grew into an entire contemporary women's apparel company. "From Day 1, she made money for me," said Andrew Rosen, founder of Theory, who invested $300,000 in the brand in 2003; four years later, Alice + Olivia was selling an estimated 100 times that annually, according to *Philadelphia Inquirer* journalist Elizabeth Wellington, who interviewed Rosen. "I knew she would be successful because she started with a singular idea. She made a name for herself by making pants better than anyone."

Bendet was in her mid-twenties when her company became practically an overnight sensation in the fashion world. Raised in Greenwich Village and then Chappaqua, New York, she attended Horace Greeley High School and then the University of Pennsylvania. Her degree in international relations included a stint in Paris, where she took a job with the Style Network. After earning her degree, she became a Web site designer while dallying over her next move; her parents hoped she would choose a law school. Instead her Web-design business grew to include a client base with some impressive names, including designer Shoshanna Lonstein Gruss and Paul Wilmot Communications, a major fashion public relations firm.

Bendet's father was a textile importer, and she had learned to sew at a young age. One day in 2001, she saw a retro, 1970s fabric in a store window, and impulsively bought a few yards to sew a pair of pants for herself. She was wearing them in Los Angeles when boutique owner Lisa Kline stopped her on the street and asked her about them, then ordered 20 pairs for the store. Bendet teamed up with a friend from college, Rebecca Winn Matchett, and launched Alice + Olivia in 2002, borrowing the first names of their mothers for their fledgling label.

They showed their first collection of women's slim-fitted trousers at the Russian Tea Room in New York City, and a buyer for Barneys New York ordered 100 pairs.

In 2003, Bendet inked a new deal with Andrew Rosen, the founder of contemporary women's apparel line Theory. The former Calvin Klein executive helped her grow the business, but the core remained her slim-fitted trouser, which she originally dubbed "Staceypants." "The concept was a pant that elongates, lengthens the look of the leg, and raises the butt," Bendet explained to Colleen Nika in *Interview* magazine online. "The pants are all cut slim at the hip to suck you in and make your body look leaner and straighter."

After two years of superb sales and revenues, Bendet began opening Alice + Olivia stores in 2005. The first was in the tony resort area of the Hamptons on Long Island, followed by one on Robertson Boulevard in Los Angeles in May of 2006. Later that year Bendet set up shop at 80 West 40th Street in Manhattan, followed by a second store in the trendy NoLita neighborhood, at 219 Mott Street in New York, in the spring of 2007. That same year Bendet's name was announced as the newest collaborator with Payless ShoeSource, the mass-market footwear retailer. Her Alice + Olivia line debuted at Payless in the spring of 2008.

Alice + Olivia expanded to new stores in Malibu, Beverly Hills, Miami, and the high-class enclave of Greenwich, Connecticut. Even through the sharp economic downturn that began in 2008—and hit high-end retailers and the apparel business particularly hard—Bendet was able to grow her business. "It's been a wake up call," she told Cayte Grieve on the Web site BlackBookMag. "We were a little bit more lax about things, and now we are very much about being lean and efficient. We re-staffed and re-structured in a way that is a little bit more reserved." She also noted that Alice + Olivia "made an effort to have products that are at a low price point. I won't compromise the quality of my fabrics or the garment for anything. I've tried to take a lower margin on some things so we can have a better price."

Bendet is married to Eric Eisner, an entertainment producer who is the son of onetime Disney CEO Michael Eisner. Their first child, a daughter they named Eloise, was born in 2008. Bendet gave birth to their second daughter, Scarlet Haven, on April 8, 2011, in New York City. The couple lives in Tribeca but spends one week of the month in the Los Angeles area for their respective work projects. In 2010,

Bendet bought a vintage Airstream trailer and toured several Southern states to promote Alice + Olivia, even stopping at the Bonnaroo Music & Arts Festival in Tennessee in June. She once appeared on *America's Next Top Model* as part of a job challenge for contestants, but Bendet told *New York* magazine online there was no reality series about her glamorous life in her future. "I really like to be alone," she told Mike Vilensky for the magazine. "And I also really like designing clothes. Being a celebrity is a job."

Rosen remains chief financial partner of Alice + Olivia; Matchett is a silent partner. Bendet is active on several philanthropic fronts in the New York social scene, including the prestigious American School of Ballet gala. A daily yoga practitioner, Bendet always tries to promote her favorite pet projects when giving media interviews about her company, such as Bent on Learning, which funds yoga classes in the New York City public schools. She was eager to avoid the socialite/designer designation, she told Wellington in the *Philadelphia Inquirer* interview. "There is not a person near me that won't tell you that I'm the hardest worker that you've ever met. I get up at 5 in the morning. I go to yoga at 5:45 a.m. I'm here [at the studio] by 7:30 and I'm here until 9:30 p.m. That's me. You can call me a socialite, but I'm a hard worker."

Sources

Periodicals

New York Times January 7, 2007, p. ST4.
Philadelphia Inquirer, July 29, 2007.
Vanity Fair, February 2004, p. 64; October 2008, p. 176.
WWD, October 6, 2005, p. 13; May 24, 2007, p. 8; January 31, 2008, p. 16.

Online

"Alice + Olivia Designer Stacey Bendet Doesn't Eat Animals, But Feels Glamorous Wearing Them," *New York* magazine, http://nymag.com/daily/fashion/2010/07/alice_olivia_designer_stacey_b.html (February 15, 2011).
"Industry Insiders: Stacey 'StaceyPants' Bendet," BlackBookMag, http://www.blackbookmag.com/article/industry-insiders-stacey-staceypants-bendet/7592 (February 17, 2011).
"Introducing: Stacey Bendet of Alice + Olivia," *Interview* magazine, http://www.interviewmagazine.com/blogs/fashion/2010-06-09/introducing-stacey-bendet-alice-and-olivia/ (February 17, 2011).

—*Carol Brennan*

Elizabeth Berg

Author

Born Elizabeth Hoff, December 2, 1948, in St. Paul, MN; daughter of Arthur and Jeanne Hoff; married Howard Berg (a marketing director), March 30, 1974 (divorced); partner of Bill; children: Julie, Jennifer (from marriage). *Education:* Attended University of Minnesota, 1966-69; St. Mary's College, A.A.S, 1974.

Addresses: *Agent*—Lisa Bankoff, International Creative Management, 40 W 57th St., New York, NY 10019. *Contact*—Elizabeth Berg, P.O. Box 707, Oak Park, IL 60202-0707.

Career

Worked as a registered nurse for ten years, and as a waitress, chicken washer, singer, and information clerk. Author, 1993—.

Awards: Best Book of the Year, American Library Association, for *Durable Goods,* 1993; Best Book for Young Adults, American Library Association, for *Joy School,* 1997; New England Booksellers Award for fiction, for body of work, 1997; Illuminator Award, AMC Cancer Research Center, 1998; honors from Boston Public Library and Chicago Public Library.

Sidelights

Elizabeth Berg is an American author best known for her warm, insightful novels about women undergoing life transitions and making choices. Her

Tom Williams/Roll Call/newscom

writing is honest and true-to-life, and resonates with readers who can identify with her characters and the dilemmas they face. Typically, her books are not heavily plot-based, but rely more on interest generated by the growth and depth of the characters.

Berg was born in St. Paul, Minnesota, the daughter of Arthur and Jeanne Hoff. Her father was a military man, and Berg's family moved often throughout her childhood; on her Web site, she commented that twice, she went to three schools in a single school year. Thus, to this day, when people ask her where she is from, she has a hard time answering, and often says, "Um ... nowhere?"

As a child, Berg loved books and reading, and she began writing as soon as she was able to hold a pencil. She submitted her first poem to *American Girl* magazine when she was nine years old. It was rejected, and the rejection stung so much that Berg did not submit her writing to any other market until 25 years later.

In the intervening time, Berg grew up and went to college, studying nursing and becoming a registered nurse; she worked in nursing for ten years. On her Web site, she commented that nursing was her version of writing school: "Taking care of patients taught me a lot about human nature, about hope and fear and love and loss and triumph and especially about relationships—all things that I tend to focus on in my work."

When she was 34 Berg entered a writing contest in a magazine and won. The win seemed to cancel out the rejection she had suffered so long ago, and it opened the door for her to write. She spent the next ten years writing for magazines, mainly articles about raising children and running a home, topics she knew well because she was living them at the time.

After ten years of writing nonfiction magazine articles, Berg began writing novels, averaging a book per year. Her first novel was *Durable Goods*, published in 1993. The book tells the story of Katie, a 12-year-old girl whose father is in the Army and who consequently has to move frequently. Her mother has died from cancer, and her father is abusive to her and her sister. She dreams of escaping from her father, and Berg shows her situation clearly, honestly, and with sensitivity. In the *New York Times*, Regina Weinreich called the book "luminous" and described it as "spare but rich." A *Kirkus Reviews* writer commented, "Hope and sorrow mingle at the close of this finely observed, compassionate book."

Berg's next novel, *Talk Before Sleep*, draws on Berg's experiences as a nurse to tell the story of Ann, a nurse who is caring for her dying friend Ruth. A *Publishers Weekly* reviewer remarked that readers might forget that the book is fiction because it is so emotionally accurate and includes many true-to-life details; the reviewer noted, "This book is a weeper, all right, but its effect is cathartic." In the *New York Times*, Lauren Belfer praised the book's unsentimental portrayal of the dying woman, calling it "haunting and sensitive."

Four years after the publication of *Durable Goods*, Berg released a sequel, *Joy School*. The book features Katie, now 13, as her family moves to Missouri. Her father has married his housekeeper, Ginger, and Katie's sister Diane has married and moved far away. Katie has trouble fitting in at her new school, and she is trying to unravel the meaning of romance and relationships. In a review for the *Virginian Pilot*, Diana Lynn Diehl wrote that Berg "captures the essence of adolescence with all of its highs and lows." In the Piedmont Triad *News and Record*, Ruth Moore wrote, "Berg's books are not for everybody, but once you develop a taste for what she does with language and deeply rooted emotions, you devour them."

Berg's 1998 novel, *What We Keep*, tells the story of Marion, a woman who has not seen her daughters for 35 years, and her reunion with them. Much of the story is told through flashback as Ginny, her daughter, remembers the summer her mother abandoned the family, and its aftermath. Through the book, and through Ginny's eyes, readers see Marion's growing sense of suffocation and alienation as she tries to be the perfect 1950s housewife, losing her own identity in the process. In the *Austin American-Statesman,* a reviewer wrote, "Grounded in domestic detail and told from the viewpoint of an unbiased 12 year old, the truths revealed in *What We Keep* are all too real."

Open House, released in 2000, became a *New York Times* best-seller, was an Oprah's Book Club selection, and was made into a CBS movie. The book tells the story of woman whose husband leaves her. In response to the financial difficulty this presents for her, she rents out rooms instead of selling her house. As a result, she meets a wide variety of people, and finds strengths in herself that she never knew she had, as well as a new view of what a truly loving relationship is. Joanna Burkhardt noted in *Library Journal*, "Berg writes with clarity.... Her characters are true to life."

Like *What We Keep,* 2004's *The Art of Mending* examined relationships between parents and children, as well as among siblings. In the novel, three siblings disagree about their childhoods: Laura and Steve believe they grew up in a happy family, whereas Caroline says their mother abused her. Initially, her siblings refuse to believe her, but eventually they learn that their mother was abusive to her, and that their grandmother also abused their mother. In *Booklist,* Joyce Saricks called the novel "emotionally satisfying" and "totally believable."

Berg's 2005 novel *The Year of Pleasures*, tells the story of a widow who tries to fulfill her husband's dying wish for her. She moves from Boston to a small town outside Chicago. Lonely, she looks up three college friends from the late 1960s, all of whom reenter her life and provide the support she needs to open her own store, called What a Woman Wants. She also begins to find romance returning to her life. In *Publishers Weekly*, a reviewer noted, like other commentators on Berg's fiction, that the novel is not heavy on plot, but follows a more serendipitous path, following the characters through their emotional changes. In *Library Journal,* Caroline M. Hallsworth praised the novel, noting, "Berg's talents grow richer with each book." *Library Journal* audiobook reviewer Denise A. Garofalo wrote, "Berg's prose brings a gentle beauty to the ordinary and domestic aspects of life."

Berg's 2007 novel, *Dream When You're Feeling Blue,* unlike her other books, is a historical novel set during World War II. The novel tells the story of the Heaneys, a Chicago family, particularly the three Heaney sisters, as they navigate through the years from 1943 to 1946, and adjust to the impact the war has on their lives. Calling it a "sentimental celebration of a bygone era," a *Publishers Weekly* reviewer also remarked that the book revealed changing attitudes toward working women and single mothers during the war years.

Berg departed from novels with 2008's *The Day I Ate Whatever I Wanted: And Other Small Acts of Liberation.* The book, a collection of 13 stories, tells the stories of women ranging from teenagers to octogenarians, who struggle with issues including aging, love, body image, loss, and moving into new lives. Some stories are sad, others humorous. On her Web site, Berg explained that the inspiration for the book came one day when she reflected on the fact that many women, when they go out to eat, order salad even though they may really want to eat something else—usually something more fattening. Berg told a friend, "One of these days I'm going to write a book called 'The Day I Ate Whatever I #%^*$ Wanted!'" And she did. "Only," she added on her Web site, "we edited the title just a wee bit—took out the expletive, even though I thought it added a lot of character."

The Last Time I Saw You, released in 2010, was inspired by computer ads that offer, "Find Your Classmates!" Berg wondered what impulse drove people go back and find classmates they hadn't seen or spoken to for decades, and why people's memories of high school remain so fresh and often so hurtful even after many years. Through the book, she vicariously had her own reunion. Berg wrote on her Web site, "I wanted to have FUN writing something, and I did have a really good time writing this book."

Despite her success, Berg has never forgotten what it feels like to be an aspiring writer, and she has always been encouraging to new writers. In 2000 she wrote *Escaping Into the Open,* a book that describes her own slow but sure route to successfully writing novels, and which contains, she wrote on her Web site, "everything I know and believe about writing," with advice and exercises for aspiring writers. In a 2010 interview published in *Writer's Digest* and reprinted on the magazine's blog, *Promptly,* she gave advice to those who want to write: "You need to write what's in your heart and soul, and let the chips fall where they may." She cautioned writers against thinking too much about their potential readers and twisting their work to appeal to them: "Let's say you try to accommodate this imaginary reader, and you produce a work that you're not particularly happy with. That will always stay with you, that you didn't write what was true for you." She also advised writers not to think about the business of publishing or listen too much to others' advice during the process of writing. Instead, she counseled, there is "something inside of a person that makes them be a writer in the first place. That's a strong and true thing." And, she said, writers should center their writing on that truth, rather than on what they think might sell.

Berg was married for 20 years, and then divorced. She had two daughters, Julie and Jennifer, and three grandchildren. As of 2011, she lived in Oak Park, Illinois, but also spent time in Boston and Wisconsin. On her Web site, Berg wrote that although she loves writing, "The prospect of retiring is beginning to sound better and better. I really want to live on a hobby farm with lots of animals, including a chicken. I'm dying for a chicken."

Selected writings

Novels

Durable Goods, Random House (New York City), 1993.
Talk Before Sleep, Random House, 1994.
Range of Motion, Random House, 1995.
The Pull of the Moon, Random House, 1996.
Joy School, Random House, 1997.
What We Keep, Random House, 1998.
Until the Real Thing Comes Along, Random House, 1999.
Open House, Random House, 2000.
Never Change, Pocket Books (New York City), 2001.
True to Form, Atria (New York City), 2002.
Say When, Atria, 2003.
The Art of Mending, Random House, 2004.
The Year of Pleasures, Random House, 2005.
We Are All Welcome Here, Random House, 2006.
The Handmaid and the Carpenter, Random House, 2006.
Dream When You're Feeling Blue, Random House, 2007.
Home Safe, Random House, 2009.
The Last Time I Saw You, Random House, 2010.
Once Upon a Time, There Was You, Random House, 2011.

Other

Family Traditions: Celebrations for Holidays and Everyday (nonfiction), Reader's Digest (Pleasantville, NY), 1992.

Escaping into the Open: The Art of Writing True (nonfiction), HarperCollins (New York City), 2000.

Ordinary Life (short stories), Random House, 2002.

The Day I Ate Whatever I Wanted: And Other Small Acts of Liberation (short stories), Random House, 2008.

Sources

Books

Complete Marquis Who's Who, Marquis Who's Who, 2010.

Contemporary Authors, New Revision Series, Gale (Detroit, MI), vol. 179, pp. 36-41.

Writers Directory 2010, Gale (Detroit, MI), vol. 1, p. 170.

Periodicals

Austin American-Statesman, June 7, 1998, p. D8.

Booklist, September 1, 2004, p. 142.

Kirkus Reviews, February 15, 1993.

Library Journal, June 15, 2000, p. 111; March 1, 2005, p. 74: October 5, 2005, p. 91.

News and Record (Piedmont Triad, NC), May 11, 1997, p. F5.

New York Times Book Review, October 24, 1993; May 22, 1994.

Publishers Weekly, February 21, 1994, p. 232; February 21, 2005, p. 154; March 19, 2007, p. 38.

Virginian Pilot, June 1, 1997, p. J2; July 21, 2002, p. E4.

Online

"Elizabeth Berg: 'If I Could Say Anything to Aspiring Writers, It's To Keep Your Own Counsel, First and Foremost,'" *Promptly* blog, *Writer's Digest,* http://blog.writersdigest.com/promptly/Elizabeth+Berg+If+I+Could+Say+Anything+To+Aspiring+Writers+Its+To+Keep+Your+Own+Counsel+First+And+Foremost.aspx (March 5, 2011).

Elizabeth Berg's Official Web site, http://www.elizabeth-berg.net/ (February 11, 2011).

—Kelly Winters

Ingrid Betancourt

© vario images GmbH & Co.KG/Alamy

Politician, activist, and author

Born December 25, 1961, in Bogota, Columbia; daughter of Gabriel Betancourt (a diplomat and ambassador) and Yolanda Pulecio (a diplomat and human rights activist); married Fabrice Delloye (a French diplomat), 1983 (divorced, 1990); married Juan Carlos LeCompte (an advertising executive), 1997; children: Melanie, Lorenzo (from first marriage). *Education:* Institute of Political Studies, diploma.

Addresses: *Office*—c/o Penguin Press, 375 Hudson St., New York, NY 10014.

Career

Worked as an advisor to her mother's senate campaign, 1990; worked in Colombia's finance and commerce ministries, c. 1990-94; served in Colombian chamber of representatives, 1994-98; founded Oxygen (a green party), Colombia, 1997; served in Colombia senate, 1998-c. 2001; served as Oxygen's presidential candidate, 2001-02; kidnapped by FARC, 2002; rescued by Colombian military, 2008; published *Even Silence Has an End: My Six Years of Captivity in the Colombian Jungle,* 2010.

Awards: Concord Award, Prince of Asturias Awards, 2008; Legion of Honor, 2008; Woman of the Year, World Awards Association, 2008.

Sidelights

While Ingrid Betancourt was a one-time presidential candidate in Colombia, she is perhaps best known as one of the most high-profile captives of FARC (Marxist Revolutionary Armed Forces of Colombia). Held from 2002 to 2008, she suffered unspeakable horrors during her time as a hostage. Betancourt was a target of FARC in part because she doggedly fought corruption in and the influence of drug traffickers on the Colombian government during her time as a representative and senator in the Colombian legislature. Betancourt also founded her own political party, the Oxygen party, and published three books about her life and experiences.

Betancourt was born on December 25, 1961, in Bogota, Colombia, the daughter of Gabriel Betancourt and Yolanda Pulecio. Her father was a diplomat and ambassador who served as the education minister in Colombia, as Colombia's ambassador to France, and as assistant director to UNESCO (United Nations Educational, Scientific, and Cultural Organization). Her mother was once a beauty queen who later became an activist and founder of the organization L'Albergue. It addressed the needs of street children living in Bogota. Pulecio also became involved in politics herself, serving as a diplomat and legislator.

Betancourt's childhood was spent in both France and Colombia. Though she primarily grew up in Paris, her parents instilled a deep love of Colombia in Betancourt, and she was often exposed to political debates among creative people who cared about its future. She grew up feeling a sense of responsibility because of the opportunities she was given as a child and her life of privilege. A good student, she was also a rebel. As Betancourt explained to Jeremy Lennard of the London *Guardian,* "I was born on December 25, but I'm not sure my father thought me much of a Christmas present. I was always doing everything I shouldn't."

Betancourt completed her education in Paris, earning a diploma in political science at the Institute of Political Studies. With her education complete, she married her first husband, a French diplomat. The couple had two children and lived well in France, Ecuador, the Seychelles, and the United States. Betancourt remained loyal to her homeland, however, and a visit with one of her children in 1986 increased her desire to help the Colombian people during a time of crisis. She was acutely aware of how her circumstances were much better than those of friends, relatives, and others living in Colombia, and felt she could help.

An incident involving her mother proved to be the catalyst. In 1989, her mother was an active participant in the campaign of Carlos Luis Galan for Colombia president. Galan was seen as someone who could turn Colombia around and greatly improve conditions for many people; however, Galan was assassinated in August of 1989 while on the campaign trail with Pulecio, Betancourt's mother, standing right behind him. Only the fact that Betancourt's mother had tripped because she was wearing high heels saved her from harm. The incident shook up Betancourt and compelled her to make some major life choices.

Wanting to both comfort her mother and move Colombia forward, Betancourt divorced her husband and moved with her two children back to her native country in January of 1990. She immediately began serving as an advisor to her mother's senate campaign. When the campaign was complete, she took positions on Colombia's finance and commerce ministries, but realized that corruption and ineptitude were the rule in the Colombian government. Frustrated, Betancourt resigned in 1994 and entered politics.

Betancourt ran for a seat in the Colombia chamber of representatives, promising to weed out corruption. Though an unknown before the campaign began, Betancourt received much attention by handing out condoms during her campaign to highlight how corruption was a disease. Her grassroots campaign was direct but effective with certain segments. She won the election as a liberal on her anti-corruption stance, garnering the most votes of anyone running for the chamber of representatives in Bogata. Betancourt began serving as a representative in 1994.

During her tenure in the chamber of representatives, Betancourt made fighting corruption the focus of her tenure. She tried to root out corruption in every aspect of government. For example, she worked to prevent a government arms contract to buy weapons that were outdated. Because of her high profile and controversial stances, Betancourt became the target of death threats.

In 1996, these threats compelled Betancourt to send her children to live with their father, who was then residing in New Zealand. They remained in his custody for the rest of their childhood as she continued to fight for the betterment of her country. Of this choice, Betancourt told Fabiola Santiago of the *Miami Herald* in 2002, "It's the most painful decision I've ever had to make. It's very difficult for me to talk about this because it hurts every day. I have been without my children for six years now, and there is not one day when I don't feel the pain."

In 1995, Betancourt had an enlightening experience meeting the heads of the Cali drug cartel, the Rodriguez brothers, that informed another crusade. She met them while serving on a national security commission investigating Cali's role in the 1993 killing of a prominent drug trafficker, Pablo Escobar. Through this meeting, she learned that almost a majority of those serving in the Colombia legislature were receiving funding from the cartel. The Cali drug cartel was also providing funds for the presidential campaign of Ernesto Samper, who later won the office. This experience made Betancourt take drastic action. One was to go on a hunger strike to force an independent inquiry into Samper's finances and actions. She also wrote *Si Sabia: Viaje a traves del expediente de Ernesto Samper,* published in 1996. This book was an investigation into the Samper's presidential campaign, specifically describing the Cali Cartel financing of Samper's campaign.

In 1997, Betancourt founded a new political party, the Oxygen Party. It was a green party which sought to empower those traditionally outside of political power in Colombia and continue her anti-corruption activities. Running under the Oxygen party, she ran for a seat in the Colombian senate and used attention-grabbing tactics during her campaign. Winning the seat in 1998, Betancourt found that her ideas were controversial at best. She tried to get legislation about housing, media ownership, and envi ronmental issues passed to no avail. Betancourt also tried to get legislation passed that would replace Colombia's congress with a new type of legislature, but this bill failed as well.

Finding her work in the senate frustrating, Betancourt resigned and began a campaign for the presidency on the Oxygen ticket in 2001 ahead of May 2002 elections. Competing against a handful of other candidates and initially facing low poll numbers, she campaigned endlessly using her trademark attention-grabbing methods, including passing out Viagra pills as a means of symbolizing the need to increase Colombia's vigor. Because her campaign focused on combating corruption, introducing reforms, fighting male domination, and encouraging democracy for Colombia, many of the drug cartels made threats against her.

While she was campaigning, Betancourt published the Spanish and English translation of her biography, *Until Death Do Us Part: My Struggle to Reclaim Colombia*, in early 2002. Originally published in French in 2001 because Colombia publishers were afraid to put it out, the biography spent weeks as the best-selling book there. It was eventually translated into 20 languages. The book covered the whole of her life, including her descriptions of the drugs and corruption in Colombia. Though considered a campaign tool, it also indicted the corruption in politics in Colombia.

The threats against Betancourt came to fruition in 2002. While campaigning for the presidency, Betancourt often took risks and travelled in rural areas. While traveling to the isolated community of San Vicente del Caguan in an overcrowded pickup truck, she was kidnapped by Marxist Revolutionary Armed Forces of Colombia (FARC) on February 23, 2002, along with her chief of staff, Clara Rojas. (FARC is a semi-Marxist organization, part of the Armed Forces of Colombia. It regularly takes hostages and is often allied with drug traffickers.) The kidnapping soon became an international incident with such leaders as United Nations Secretary General Kofi Anan and French President Jacques Chirac launching an international movement to press for her release. When elections were held a few months later, she did not win, but the campaign to free her from FARC continued.

Betancourt remained in FARC's control for six and a half more years. During her time in captivity, she suffered greatly. FARC marched her and other captives around for days on end, moving them between makeshift camps located deep in the Colombian jungle. She was often caged with no privacy and bored beyond belief. Betancourt was traumatized and subjected to cruelty daily, regularly ill from the conditions. She was exposed to swarms of mosquitoes, red ants, wasps, midges, ticks, scorpions, anacondas, and rivers full of piranhas. Betancourt felt the harsh sun as well as torrential rains. Bathroom facilities consisted of latrines dug by hands, while she was fed with meager rations.

Despite the hostile conditions, Betancourt continued to fight. She had at least three risky escapes, but was always caught and returned. Upon her recapture, she was subject to intense punishments, both mental and physical, such as being chained by her neck and sexually assaulted. Despite these often unspeakable acts of torture, Betancourt remained resolved to survive and retain her dignity; however, she and her fellow hostages were often put at odds with each other, and Betancourt was the object of scorn for her sophisticated background and attitude. Betancourt also experienced moments of kindness and affection. Throughout their captivity, Betancourt had a particularly complex, if not mercurial, relationship with Rojas as well as with her fellow hostages and even her captors.

While various entities, especially the French government, tried to negotiate with FARC for her release or rescue over the years, it was not until 2008 that FARC weakened. Betancourt was rescued by the Colombia military on July 2, 2008, in a heroic, dangerous, tricky rescue, with 14 other hostages. Shortly thereafter, the French government bestowed upon her the French Legion of Honor. She also published a book, *Letters to My Mother: A Message of Love, A Plea for Freedom*. After her release, Betancourt left Colombia and lived in Paris and New York City, rejecting any notion of returning to politics. Her visits of Colombia were brief at best and she rejected any request to run for its presidency in 2010.

In 2010, Betancourt published a book, *Even Silence Has an End*, which focused on what happened during her time as a hostage of FARC. It was published in six languages in 14 countries simultaneously. The book was reflective and full of self-criticism, but received with animosity by some, including a few fellow hostages, and embraced for its richness by others. Reviewing the book in the *Christian Science Monitor*, Sibylla Brodzinsky praised its "literary style, gripping account of her life in jungle prisons, and profound reflections on the human condition."

Shortly before the book was published, Betancourt sued the Colombian government for $6.8 million in damages for stress and time lost in captivity. When many Colombians reacted negatively to her demand because military personnel risked their lives trying to save her and the others, she withdrew her suit a short time later though many initially boycotted the publication of her book because of it. A reviewer of *Even Silence Has an End* understood Betancourt's point of view. Writing in the *New York Times*, Caroline Elkins wrote, "Regardless of her liberation and journey toward forgiveness, the time lost with loved ones cannot be recovered, nor can the humiliations be undone."

Discussing her future, Betancourt told Oscar Avila of the *Chicago Tribune*, "Captivity is like a hurricane that passes over one's life and destroys everything. So I need to rebuild my life. It is a process that takes time, and I need to give myself that time." She did not rule out a later return to politics, stating "I want to pursue the politics that I want, a politics based on emotion, on love, on tolerance, on compassion. I am conscious that because all of you [reporters] are here, there are people behind you who want to hear what I say. I owe them."

Selected writings

Si Sabia: Viaje a traves del expediente de Ernesto Samper, Ediciones Temas de Hoy (Santa Fe de Bogota, Colombia), 1996.
(With Lionel Duroy) *Until Death Do Us Part: My Struggle to Reclaim Colombia,* Ecco Press (New York City), 2002.
Letters to My Mother: A Message of Love, A Plea for Freedom, Abrams Image (New York City), 2008.

Even Silence Has an End: My Six Years of Captivity in the Colombian Jungle Penguin Press (New York City), 2010.

Sources

Books

Contemporary Hispanic Biography, vol. 2, Gale, 2002.

Periodicals

Atlanta Journal-Constitution, May 22, 2002, p. 5E.
Chicago Tribune, January 4, 2009.
Christian Science Monitor, September 21, 2010.
Economist, March 20, 2004.
Globe and Mail (Canada), April 10, 2008, p. A3.
Guardian (London, England), November 10, 2001, p. 97.
Harper's Bazaar, October 1, 2010, p. 291.
Miami Herald, January 12, 2002, p. 1E.
National Post (Canada), October 23, 2010, p. WP18.
New York Times, July 3, 2008, p. A1.
New York Times Book Review, October 3, 2010, p. 26.
Observer (England), November 30, 2008, p. 4.
Publishers Weekly, January 28, 2002, p. 143.

Online

Contemporary Authors Online, Gale, 2002.

—*A. Petruso*

Justin Bieber

© n8n photo/Alamy

Singer

Born Justin Drew Bieber, March 1, 1994, in London, Ontario, Canada; son of Jeremy Jack Bieber and Patricia Lynn Mallette.

Addresses: *Agent*—Creative Artists Agency, LLC, 162 Fifth Ave., 6th Fl., New York, NY, 10010. *Record company*—Island Records, 825 Eighth Ave., 28th Fl., New York, NY 10019. *Web site*—http://www.justinbiebermusic.com.

Career

Won a local singing competition in Stratford, Ontario, Canada, 2007; appeared singing in YouTube videos, 2007; signed to Island Records; released his first single *One Time*, 2009; recorded and released *My World*, 2009; recorded and released *My World 2.0*, 2010.

Awards: Artist of the year, American Music Awards, 2010; favorite pop/rock male artist, American Music Awards, 2010; T-Mobile breakthrough artist, American Music Awards, 2010; favorite pop/rock album, American Music Awards, for *My World 2.0*, 2010; favorite international artist, Meus Premios Nick Awards, 2010; best male award, MTV Europe Music Awards, 2010; best push act award, MTV Europe Music Awards, 2010; best new artist, MTV Video Music Awards, 2010; Choice Music: male artist award, Teen Choice Awards, 2010; Choice Music: breakout artist male award, Teen Choice Awards, 2010; Choice Summer Music Star: male award, Teen Choice Awards, 2010; Choice Music: pop album award, Teen Choice Awards, for *My World 2.0*, 2010; best international act, TRL Awards, 2010; newcomer of the year, Young Hollywood Awards, 2010; international breakthrough artist, Brit Awards, 2011; fan choice award, Juno Awards, 2011; pop album of the year, Juno Awards, for *My World 2.0*, 2011; favorite male singer, Nickelodeon Kids' Choice Awards, 2011; favorite song, Nickelodeon Kids' Choice Awards, for "Baby," 2011; top new artist, Billboard Music Awards, 2011; top social artist, Billboard Music Awards, 2011; top streaming artist, Billboard Music Awards, 2011; top digital media artist, Billboard Music Awards, 2011; top pop album, Billboard Music Awards, for *My World 2.0*, 2011; top streaming song, Billboard Music Awards, for "Baby," 2011.

Sidelights

In the song "Born to Be Somebody" Justin Bieber sang "I was born to be somebody / I was born to be / and this world will belong to me." Truer words were never sung. Bieber was discovered by agent Scooter Braun after his mother posted videos of him singing on YouTube and quickly rose to international fame. His haircut became a cultural phenomenon that inspired multitudes of young men and boys to emulate the style of the pop singer who required crowd control and protection from thousands of squealing pre-teen and teenage girls.

Bieber was born in London, Ontario, Canada, the son of single mother Patricia Mallette. Mallette was only 18 years old when she gave birth to him. She moved to Stratford, Ontario, where she lived with him in low-income housing and worked a series of low-paying office jobs in order to support herself and her son. Bieber's father, Jeremy Bieber, maintained contact with his son but married another woman with whom he had two children.

Both of Bieber's parents were instrumental in developing his talent. Bieber was interested in music from a young age and his mother gave him a drum set for his second birthday because he was banging on anything that would make noise. With this drum set Bieber taught himself to play the drums by the age of three. When Bieber was only 12 years old he entered a small talent contest in his hometown of Stratford and placed second. Bieber, who also taught himself how to play the guitar and piano, was shy about his musical abilities but, because of this win, was encouraged to continue singing. His mother wanted to show friends and family video clips of him singing and so began posting homemade videos on YouTube of him performing Stevie Wonder, Michael Jackson, and Ne-Yo covers. Ever supportive, Mallette traveled with Bieber and moved to Atlanta, Georgia, to assist him in pursuing his singing career. She also kept him grounded by insisting on a curfew and chores. Bieber's father expanded his musical knowledge. Bieber told Joey Bartolomeo of *People* magazine, "He's the one who got me into classic rock and then turned me on to stuff like Guns N' Roses and Metallica. He taught me how to drive too. He's cool."

In 2008 when Mallette began posting videos of Bieber, Scooter Braun, a talent agent and former So So Def marketing executive, stumbled across them. Braun had recently left So So Def Recordings and was reputedly looking for new acts to "discover." While at a basketball game he told his close friend Chaka Zulu that he wanted to find three breakout acts: the next white rapper, an all-female singing group, and a kid who, as Braun told *Billboard*, "could do it like Michael Jackson—sing songs that adults would appreciate and be reminded of the innocence they once felt about love." In Bieber he hoped he had found the latter. Braun was impressed with Bieber's talent in the YouTube videos and tracked down Mallette by calling the town of Stratford's school board. Mallette was initially nervous about her son leaving Stratford to go to Atlanta, Georgia, to meet Braun. Braun was able to convince her to fly with her son to Atlanta. Braun told *Billboard*, "That was the first time either of them had been on a plane. They weren't a wealthy family ... his mother worked different jobs and their grand-

parents kind of helped out, so they got by." That first meeting was historic in the chronology of Bieber. They all liked one another and Mallette and Bieber agreed to have Braun represent the budding star.

After Braun signed Bieber, the next thing they needed to do was find a major recording label that would partner with Braun and Bieber. This proved to be a difficult task because Bieber had not risen to attention through either Nickelodeon or Disney, which is how most young performers gain prominence. Braun approached Justin Timberlake, whom he knew through a past career as a party organizer, and Timberlake indicated that he was very interested in the young performer. Braun also received a call from Usher's road manager asking if he had signed any new young talent. Braun showed Usher Bieber's YouTube videos and within a day Braun arranged for the young singer to have an audition with the legendary entertainer. Usher and Timberlake engaged in a brief bidding war to sign the promising Bieber, but Usher's enthusiasm for Bieber and the proposed deal won out. Usher contracted Bieber along with Island/Def Jam chairman L. A. Reid.

After signing with Usher and Island Records, Mallette moved herself and her son to Atlanta and Bieber began recording music. To build his YouTube following, Braun had Bieber continue to create homemade-looking videos and post them online, but for the first time Bieber also recorded in a studio. After recording eight songs, Braun got the go ahead and a budget from Reid to create the "One Time" video. In May of 2009, Bieber released his first single, "One Time." To bolster the single, a popular video featuring Usher was simultaneously released. The song and video were not that popular until they became available on YouTube. At that time Bieber's subscription base included roughly 40 million people. "One Time" debuted at 95 on the *Billboard* Hot 100 in July of 2009. After that not only did the single peak in the top ten in Canada and chart in the top 30 in several international markets, "One Time" went platinum in both Canada and the United States.

The huge success of the single "One Time" was followed up by the seven-track EP *My World* in November of 2009. *My World* also went platinum in the United States. All seven songs landed on the *Billboard* Hot 100, a first for a debut album. In March of 2010 Bieber experienced similar success when he released his first full-length studio album, *My World 2.0*. It debuted at number one on the *Billboard* charts, within the top ten of the charts of several international countries, and the album went double platinum in the United States six months after it was released. The music video of "Baby" rose quickly to become the most viewed and discussed video on YouTube. Bieber followed up the release of *My World 2.0* with a headlining world tour titled the "My World Tour." In addition, two re-mix albums were also released, titled *My Worlds Acoustic* and *Never Say Never—The Remixes*. A top-grossing 3D biopic concert film titled *Justin Bieber: Never Say Never* was also released.

As if these efforts in the span of a mere two years were not enough, Bieber also chased up his successes and promoted his endeavors with guest appearances on a variety of television shows. He appeared on the *Today Show, Good Morning America, Chelsea Lately,* the *Wendy Williams Show,* and the *Ellen DeGeneres Show.* He performed at the White House on the televised Christmas special *Christmas in Washington.* He was also one of the entertainers who performed December 31, 2009, on *Dick Clark's New Year's Rockin' Eve.* Bieber also played at the White House Easter Egg Roll. He made appearances morning, noon, and late into the night, interviewing at radio stations for promotional events and taping television shows such the *Tonight Show With Jay Leno.* In April of 2010, Bieber was the musical guest on *Saturday Night Live*—a gig that only the most popular performers land.

In addition to double platinum record sales and chart-topping singles, Bieber's hard work paid off in other ways. He won numerous awards for his music. At the 2010 American Music Awards, Bieber won Artist of the Year, Favorite Pop/Rock Male Artist, T-Mobile Breakthrough Artist, and Favorite Pop/Rock Album for *My World 2.0.* He won international awards for best new artist, favorite international artist, and best pop act.

While Bieber had millions of fans, he also had a large number of detractors and was the subject of "malicious campaigns and pranks," wrote Nick Collins for the *Telegraph.* Bieber's Web site was hacked and an online poll was hijacked. The result was that half a million people voted to send Bieber to North Korea on his next tour. The group 4Chan promoted a campaign amongst its readers to put the words "Justin Bieber Syphilis" into Google to make it the number-one set of keywords on the search engine. A Facebook page called "I Hate Justin Bieber" acquired more than 180,000 fans and included such topics for discussion as "ways to kill Justin." In January of 2011 a Facebook virus appeared that promised video footage of Bieber hitting a girl. When an unsuspecting user clicked on the link, an application would post updates to the person's wall and send messages from his or her account.

Reasons cited for why Bieber is so hated by some are his meteoric rise to fame and also his carefully crafted image. Bieber, who grew up in a middle class neighborhood, often wore hoodies, oversized baseball caps, dog chains, and flashy sneakers. The look was not in keeping with his background and was criticized for being artificially streetwise. Similarly his manner of speech was seen as emulating that of some of the rappers he admires and not in keeping with his true self. His stylist has been derogatorily referred to as Bieber's "swagger coach." While these elements lend ammunition to his detractors, the adults who work hard to maintain his image, tutor him, and protect him find that they have a difficult job not only keeping him on the tracks to success but saving him from his success. While Bieber received criticism for his look, his voice and talent, famous hairstyle, boyish good looks, and morality caused young girls' hearts to race and consequently created even more of a commotion and possible threat to the young star.

Girls and women who have been seen with Bieber have received threatening messages from Bieber's fans. Both Taylor Swift and Selena Gomez, who reputedly dated Bieber at various times, received death threats. One of Bieber's tutors for his home-schooling program declined to have her last name published in an interview for fear of his fans. In 2009 Bieber was scheduled to appear at Long Island's Roosevelt Field Mall, but an out of control crowd led to the cancellation of the event. In April 2010 Australian police canceled another scheduled promotional performance after several girls were injured in a crowd crush. In Liverpool, police were brought in to do crowd control for one of his performances and there were reports that the local police threatened to arrest him for "inciting a riot" if he left his hotel.

Regardless of whether individuals hate or adore Bieber, it is appropriate that he named his debut albums *My World* and *My World 2.0* because he has the attention of the world. Island Records president Steve Bartels told *Billboard* that Bieber "is a phenom, but it's really backed up. He's got that viral cachet right now, but what he stands for at the end of the day is music. We're keeping our fingers crossed, obviously, but we think we have something here that has incredible longevity."

Selected discography

My World, Island Records, 2009.
My World 2.0, Island Records, 2010.
My Worlds Acoustic, Island Records, 2010.

My Worlds: The Collection, Island Records, 2010.
Never Say Never—The Remixes, Island Records, 2011.

Sources

Periodicals

Guardian, November 13, 2010; January 2, 2011.
Los Angeles Times, April 13, 2010.
New York Times, December 31, 2009.
Daily News (New York, NY), March 23, 2010.
PR Newswire, November 21, 2010.
Rolling Stone, February 18, 2011.
Telegraph, July 6, 2010.

Online

"Justin Bieber: Address," Fanmail, http://www.fanmail.biz/111653.html (May 26, 2011).

"Justin Bieber: A phenom on the verge of superstardom," *Billboard,* http://www.azcentral.com/thingstodo/music/articles/2010/03/19/20100031.tif9justin-bieber-billboard.html (May 26, 2011).

"Justin Bieber Biography," AOL Music, http://music.aol.com/artist/justin-bieber/biography (May 26, 2011).

"Justin Bieber Biography," *Billboard,* http://www.billboard.com/artist/justin-/bio/1099520#/artist/justin-bieber/bio/1099520 (May 26, 2011).

"Justin Bieber Biography," Biography, http://www.biography.com/articles/justin-bieber-522504 (May 26, 2011).

"Justin Bieber Biography," Internet Movie Database, http://www.imdb.com/name/nm3595501/bio (May 26, 2011).

"Justin Bieber Joins the Ranks of Youngest *SNL* Performers," MTV, http://newsroom.mtv.com/2010/02/22/justin-bieber-saturday-night-live/ (May 26, 2011).

"Justin Bieber: Phone Number," ChaCha, http://www.chacha.com/topic/justin-bieber-phone-number (May 26, 2011).

"Justin Bieber—The *Billboard* Cover Story," *Billboard,* http://www.billboard.com/news/justin-bieber-the-billboard-cover-story-10040746.tif92.story (May 26, 2011).

"Did Justin Bieber hit a girl? No, you got scammed," MSNBC, http://today.msnbc.msn.com/id/41122407.tif/ns/today-today_tech/t/did-justin-bieber-hit-girl-np-you-got-scammed/ (May 30, 2011).

"Meet Justin Bieber's Rockin' Dad," AOL Music, http://www.people.com/people/article/0,,20395400.tif,00.html (May 26, 2011).

"Neon Limelight Interviews: Usher Protege Justin Bieber: Accidental Star," Neon Limelight, http://neonlimelight.com/2009/08/11neon-limelight-interviews-usher-protege-justin-bieber-accidental-star/ (May 26, 2011).

"Police 'threaten to arrest' Justin Bieber 'for inciting a riot' in Liverpool," *Now* magazine, http://www.nowmagazine.co.uk/celebrity-news/teen-now/518861/police-threaten-to-arrest-justin-bieber-for-inciting-a-riot-in-liverpool/1/ (May 30, 2011).

"Temperature's rising as Justin brings Bieber fever to Birmingham," *Birmingham News* blog, http://blog.al.com/mcolurso/2010/12/temperatures_rising_as_justin.html (May 26, 2011).

"'Time' is right for teen singer Justin Bieber," Reuters, http://www.reuters.com/article/2009/07/19/us-bieber-idUSTRE5612BM20090719.tif (May 26, 2011).

"Top 10 YouTube Videos of All Time," ReadWriteWeb, http://www.readwriteweb.com/archives/top_10_youtube_videos_of_all_time.php (May 26, 2011).

"Usher and Justin Timberlake Battled It Out For Justin Bieber," MTV News, http://www.mtv.com/news/articles/1621324/usher-justin-timberlake-battled-it-out-justin-bieber.jhtml (May 26, 2011).

—Annette Bowman

The Black Keys

Rock group

Group formed in 2001 in Akron, OH; members include Dan Auerbach (born May 14, 1979, in Akron, OH; married), vocals, guitar; Patrick Carney (born April 15, 1980, in Akron, OH), drums.

Addresses: *Record company*—Nonesuch Records, 1290 Avenue of the Americas, New York, NY, 10104. *Web site*—http://www.theblackkeys.com.

Career

Formed in Akron, Ohio, 2001; signed to Alive, released debut album, *The Big Come Up*, 2002; signed to Fat Possum, released *Thickfreakness*, 2003; released *Rubber Factory*, 2004; signed to Nonesuch, released *Magic Potion*, 2006; released *Attack & Release*, 2008; released *Blakroc*, 2009; released *Brothers*, 2010; released *El Camino*, 2011.

Awards: Grammy Award for best alternative music album, National Academy of Recording Arts and Sciences, for *Brothers*, 2011; Grammy Award for best rock performance for a duo or group with vocal, National Academy of Recording Arts and Sciences, for "Tighten Up," 2011.

Sidelights

Grammy-award-winning rock duo the Black Keys steadily won increasing popular and critical recognition for their classic bluesy sounds and driving rhythms in the years following the limited release of their 2002 debut, *The Big Come Up*. Origi-

© *Ethan Miller/Getty Images*

nally hailing from the northeastern Ohio city of Akron, the group initially drew comparisons to fellow Midwestern guitar-and-drums outfit the White Stripes but evolved to develop their own distinctive sound. With the release of their Danger Mouse-helmed 2008 album *Attack & Release*, the Black Keys broke out from college radio popularity to mainstream success, and follow-up sixth studio album *Brothers* became a bona fide rock hit that debuted at number three on the *Billboard* charts and garnered the duo two Grammy Awards, for best alternative music album and best rock performance. High-profile appearances at music festivals, including Coachella and Bonnaroo, paved the way for the hotly anticipated 2011 release *El Camino*.

The Black Keys are comprised of Dan Auerbach on vocals and guitar and Patrick Carney on drums. This spare lineup first came together when the two were in high school, although they had known each other "since I started having memories," Auerbach told Austin Scaggs in *Rolling Stone*. "Our brothers were buddies. They told us to get together when I was 17 and Pat was 16," he continued. "We'd never hung out, but I walked to his house with a guitar and amp and went down to his basement and started [playing]. We hit it off immediately," he concluded. The two played together, drawing on influences ranging from Led Zeppelin to Nirvana, but did not formally form the Black Keys until about 2001. The duo took their name from a term used by local schizophrenic artist Alfred McMoore, who frequently left answering machine messages for Carney's journalist father that contained the phrase.

Before long, the duo began developing a regional fan base on the strength of live performances both in Akron and nearby Cleveland. California-based independent label Alive signed the Black Keys and their debut, *The Big Come Up*, appeared in the spring of 2002. "As minimal two-man blues-rock bands go, this has to be near the top of the heap," proclaimed Allmusic reviewer Richie Unterberger of the release. Early positive reviews and growing buzz helped raise the group's profile, and by 2003, the Black Keys had signed with Mississippi-based blues and rock label Fat Possum, which released the duo's sophomore effort *Thickfreakness*. A continuation of the duo's blues-influenced, spare-yet-raucous style, the album attracted national attention and pushed the duo for the first time into the lower reaches of the *Billboard* Independent Albums charts. Also writing for Allmusic, Mark Deming proclaimed that "the Black Keys' wail is hot, primal, and heartfelt.... If you want to hear a rock band confront the blues with soul, muscle, and respect, then *Thickfreakness* is right up your alley." Opening stints with performers such as Beck and Sleater Kinney brought the Black Keys to new audiences both in the United States and abroad.

The following year, the group released *Rubber Factory,* titled to reference the former Akron tire plant where they had recorded the album. "The title conjures a dank, mildewy, claustrophobic place," commented *Entertainment Weekly* reviewer David Browne, "and the music takes you there as well." Dense and gritty, the album saw the duo translate their classic rock and blues influences for 21st century alternative music fans through what was generally considered a more focused songwriting approach. *Rubber Factory* helped the Black Keys grow their audience, as did continued rounds of intensive touring, and the album hit number five on the *Billboard* Top Heatseekers Chart and nearly cracked the top ten of the organization's Independent Albums rankings, a considerable rise over their sophomore effort. A live DVD and a short album of covers of the music of bluesman Junior Kimbrough soon followed.

The Black Keys traded in record label Fat Possum for major label-distributed Nonesuch Records to release their fourth studio album, *Magic Potion.* Like its predecessors, the album saw the duo distill their blues-rock roots into sharply controlled modern rock packages to what was generally considered audible success. Although the label change prevented the group from continuing its slow but steady ascent up the independent charts, the album performed well and helped the group land higher-profile slots at music festivals such as Lollapalooza. Yet it failed to excite the same kind of overall enthusiasm as its predecessors. "On *Magic Potion,* the pleasures are coyer and the variations much more subtle from riff to riff, song to song. In other words, it's not the record I want to hear from the Black Keys," sighed Pitchfork Music reviewer Jason Crock.

A new creative force soon emerged in the group's sound, however. For their fifth studio album, the duo recorded for the first time with an outside producer, Danger Mouse, also known as Brian Burton. "I think Dan and I were intrigued to work with somebody as a producer because we both realized we couldn't teach ourselves anything more, and it was best to start learning from other people," Carney told National Public Radio. Despite this external creative vision, the album built primarily on the musical foundations that had long defined the group. As heard on tracks such as "Strange Times" and "I Got Mine," *Attack & Release* placed Auerbach's raw vocals against the duo's stripped down rock sound, but nevertheless incorporated some new sonic ideas from other contributors, including guitarist Marc Ribot and female backing singers. Several songs from the album were picked up for commercials and television programs, further helping to make the band's music familiar to many new listeners.

After *Attack & Release,* Auerbach and Carney seemed ready to explore other creative ventures. They recorded a rap-rock project under the direction of hip-hopper Damon Dash, *Blakroc,* that saw them partner with some of hip-hop's leading names, including Q-Tip, Ludacris, and RZA. Although the album failed to launch a true explosion of the hybrid musical form, it did manage to hit the number-five spot on the *Billboard* Rap Albums chart and generate generally positive reviews. "The rappers make it great, stepping up their game to flow with Auerbach and Carney's bluesy swing," commented Scott Frampton of *Esquire* about the 2009 release.

Along with their joint work, both Auerbach and Carney have pursued independent projects. In February of 2009, Auerbach released a solo album, *Keep It Hid,* with Nonesuch Records. Recorded at Auerbach's own Akron Analog studio, the album saw the musician channel his blues-inflected tunes into an a sound related to that of the duo but still individualistic. "*Keep It Hid* is at once completely similar and totally different than the Black Keys," argued Stephen Thomas Erlewine of Allmusic, who continued, "it really is something that he couldn't have made with Carney, and its existence winds up confirming the immense talents of both musicians." David Bevan agreed, applauding the "textures and layers [Auerbach's] voice hasn't reached before" in an *A.V. Club* review. Carney formed his own side project, Drummer, which featured—as the name suggests—several Ohio-based drummers, mostly filling other roles in the band's musical lineup. Carney served as the group's bassist, and Drummer released an album, *Feel Good Together,* in late 2009 on Carney's own Audio Eagle Records imprint. Although critics such as Pitchfork Music's Stephen M. Deusner hailed the release as "remarkably fleshed out, full of smart, focused, propulsive indie art-rock sounds that sound both purposeful and adventuresome," the album failed to attract much notice among listeners at large.

Luckily for the Black Keys, the same was not true of their next studio album together, 2010's *Brothers.* Released by Nonesuch Records in May of 2010, the album saw the duo return to their blues-rock roots with driving, gritty tracks such as "Tighten Up" and "Next Girl." Critics enthusiastically welcomed the open rock sound of *Brothers,* with Leah Greenblatt of *Entertainment Weekly* applauding its "real songwriting, and real hooks," even as Michael Connor of *Billboard* hailed its "spooky throwback sound, preternatural grooves, and dark bluesy jams." Fans flocked to support the record, sending it to the number-three spot of the *Billboard* 200 in its first week of release.

The album went on to achieve gold-selling status and racked up several critical nods, including the number-two position on *Rolling Stone*'s top albums of 2010 list and four Grammy nominations for best alternative music album, best rock song, best rock performance by a duo or group, and best rock instrumental performance. The nominations surprised no one more, perhaps, than the Black Keys themselves. "I think it's kind of weird," Auerbach told D. Patrick Rodgers of the *Nashville Scene.* "I never thought we would get nominated for a Grammy. I have been having kind of anxiety dreams about it.... We'll see what happens. I think maybe the only way we will win something is if we ... witness the head of the Grammys murder somebody. He'd owe us." Although this dramatic confrontation did not come to pass, the Black Keys did walk away with two trophies from the ceremony in early 2011, with *Brothers* earning a nod as best alternative music album and "Tighten Up" garnering the prize for best rock performance.

Brothers also attracted packaging for its simplistic album art. Comprising just two sentences against a black background—"This is an album by the Black Keys. The name of this album is Brothers."—the bare-bones styling was seen as a reflection of the changing nature of music consumption. "We thought, 'Are we allowed to do this?'" album designer Michael Carney, brother of the group's drummer, told David Browne of the *New York Times.* "The marketing people said, 'This is our dream!'" he concluded, going on to explain that he had taken into account the size constraints of music-buying services such as iTunes. Observers largely hailed the plain statement as both daring and modern, and the Grammy committee agreed, giving Carney a nod for best packaging.

Soon after the Grammys, the duo went back into the studio in their newly adopted hometown of Nashville, Tennessee. "I wasn't even in Akron that much because we were always on tour," Auerbach told Scaggs of *Rolling Stone* about the move. In December of 2011, the Black Keys released their seventh album, *El Camino,* written entirely in the studio during those Nashville sessions. Again teaming up with producer Danger Mouse, Auerbach and Carney took a conscious step away from the sounds of *Brothers,* combining speed and energy to produce a driving rock sound. "Almost every song on the record has a foundation of live drums and guitar together in the room," Auerbach explained to William Goodman of *SPIN.* "It's guitar bleeding into the drum mics. It's pretty raw," he concluded.

The album—led by the single "Lonely Boy"—quickly became a critical darling upon its release in December of 2011. Writing in *Entertainment Weekly,* Melissa Maerz hailed the record as "awesomely down-and-dirty," while Will Hermes of *Rolling Stone* proclaimed it "the Key's grandest pop gesture yet, augmenting dark-hearted fuzz blasts with sleekly sexy choruses and Seventies-glam flair." Backed by these strong notices and several appearances by the group on late-night television programs, including *Saturday Night Live, Colbert Report,* and *Late Night with David Letterman,* the album debuted in the number-two slot on the *Billboard* 200—the group's highest chart position to-date—with estimated sales of more than 150,000 units, double that of *Brothers* in its own debut week. The group's decision to curtail the album's online availability by blocking its distribution through popular streaming services such as Spotify and Rhapsody, was another possible contributing factor to these increased sales figures. With the release of the album came another spate of touring that took the Black Keys throughout Europe and North America into 2012.

Selected discography

The Big Come Up, Alive, 2001.
Thickfreakness, Fat Possum, 2003.
Rubber Factory, Fat Possum, 2004.
Magic Potion, Nonesuch, 2006.
Attack & Release, Nonesuch, 2008.
(With others) *Blakroc*, V2, 2009.
Brothers, Nonesuch, 2010.
El Camino, Nonesuch, 2011.

Dan Auerbach solo release

Keep It Hid, Nonesuch, 2009.

Patrick Carney solo release

(With Drummer) *Feel Good Together*, Audio Eagle, 2009.

Sources

Books

Contemporary Musicians vol. 64, Gale, 2008.

Periodicals

Billboard, June 19, 2010, p. 36.
Entertainment Weekly, September 3, 2004; May 21, 2010; December 9, 2011.
Esquire, January 2010, p. 22.
Nashville Scene, March 31, 2011.
New York Times, August 12, 2011.
Rolling Stone, November 24, 2011, p. 28; December 22, 2011-January 5, 2012, p. 85.

Online

"*The Big Come Up*," Allmusic, http://allmusic.com/album/the-big-come-up-r585141/review (December 13, 2011).
"Biography," Allmusic, http://allmusic.com/artist/the-black-keys-p527822/biography (December 13, 2011).
"The Black Keys, In Concert," National Public Radio, http://www.npr.org/templates/story/story.php?storyId=90270955.tif&refresh=true (December 13, 2011).
"The Black Keys: *Magic Potion*," Pitchfork Music, http://pitchfork.com/reviews/albums/9398-magic-potion/ (December 13, 2011).
"Dan Auerbach: *Keep It Hid*," A.V. Club, http://www.avclub.com/articles/dan-auerbach-keep-it-hid,23614/ (December 13, 2011).
"Drummer: *Feel Good Together*," Pitchfork Music, http://pitchfork.com/reviews/albums/13599-feel-good-together/ (December 13, 2011)
"In the Studio: The Black Keys," *SPIN*, http://www.spin.com/articles/studio-black-keys (December 13, 2011).
"*Keep It Hid*," Allmusic, http://allmusic.com/album/keep-it-hid-r1466387/review (December 13, 2011).
"*Thickfreakness*," Allmusic, http://www.allmusic.com/album/thickfreakness-r633586 (December 13, 2011).

—*Vanessa E. Vaughn*

David Boreanaz

Actor

Far Field Productions/Josephson Entertainment/Album/newscom

Born May 16, 1969, in Buffalo, NY; son of David Thomas (known professionally as Dave Roberts, a weatherman, television personality, and actor) and Patti (a singer and travel agent) Boreanaz; married Ingrid Quinn (a social worker and screenwriter), June 7, 1997 (divorced, 1999); married Jaime Bergman (an actress and model), November 24, 2001; children: Jaden Rayne, Bella Vita (second marriage). *Education:* Graduated from Ithaca College, 1991.

Addresses: *Office*—c/o *Bones*, 20th Century Fox Studios, 10201 West Pico Blvd., Bldg. 1, Ste. 100, Los Angeles, CA 90035.

Career

Actor on television, including: *Married with Children*, FOX, 1993; *Buffy the Vampire Slayer*, The WB then UPN, 1997-2003; *Baby Blues* (animated), 2002; *Angel*, The WB, 1999-2004; *Bones*, FOX, 2005—. Film appearances include: *Aspen Extreme*, 1993; *Best of the Best 2*, 1993; *Macabre Pair of Shorts*, 1996; *Valentine*, 2001; *I'm With Lucy*, 2002; *The Crow: Wicked Prayer*, 2005; *These Girls*, 2005; *The Hard Easy*, 2006; *Mr. Fix It*, 2006; *Suffering Man's Charity*, 2007; *Justice League: The New Frontier* (animated), 2008; *The Mighty Macs*, 2009. Stage appearances include: *Hatful of Rain*, Ensemble Theatre, Orange County, CA, 1993-94. Co-producer of *Bones*, 2007-09; producer of *Bones*, 2009—; director of television episodes including *Angel*, 2004; *Bones*, 2010, 2011.

Awards: Saturn Award for best genre TV actor, Academy of Science Fiction, Fantasy & Horror Films, for *Angel*, 2000; Young Alumni Award, Ithaca College, 2001; Saturn Award for best actor in a television series, Academy of Science Fiction, Fantasy & Horror Films, for *Angel*, 2003, 2004; Gold Medal (with Dave Roberts), Pennsylvania Association of Broadcasters, 2011.

Sidelights

Perhaps best known for playing brooding vampire Angel on the series *Buffy the Vampire Slayer* and *Angel*, actor David Boreanaz also gained fame for his portrayal as a reliable FBI agent on the hit FOX drama *Bones*. The actor received his first role of note in a guest spot on *Married with Children*, and appeared in a number of films over the years. Despite his success, Boreanaz kept his career in perspective, telling Mike McDaniel of the *Houston Chronicle*, "I work on a television show; that's what I do for a living. And I'm being recognized for that. There are a lot of people who don't work in television or film and work just as hard. To me, they're famous in my eyes. Fame—you take it for what it's worth. And always remind yourself where you come from."

Born on May 16, 1969, in Buffalo, New York, he was the son of David Thomas Boreanaz and his wife Patti. His father was known professionally as Dave

Roberts and worked in local television. In addition to being a weatherman, Roberts hosted a children's program called *Rocketship 7* and a local program called *Dialing for Dollars*. In 1978 the family, which included two older sisters, moved to Villanova, Pennsylvania, when Roberts landed a job at WPVI.

Boreanaz decided to be an actor when he was seven years old after seeing Yul Brynner in *The King and I*. He received his education at Rosemont School of the Holy Cross and Malvern Preparatory School for Boys in Malven, Pennsylvania. Also a football fan, he was a ball boy for the Pittsburgh Steelers as a child and played offense and defensive back for Malvern. He told Sean Mitchell of the *New York Times*, "I wasn't the best of players, but I could go across the middle and catch a ball." Boreanaz then studied cinema and photography at Ithaca College in New York. Upon earning his degree in 1991, Boreanaz moved to Los Angeles to pursue his life's goal, though he thought about working behind the camera at first.

Before landing his acting break, Boreanaz worked as a parking attendant, house painter, toilet cleaner, door-to-door gourmet food salesman, towel boy, and props department assistant. He was discovered by a talent manager walking his dog, which led to acting jobs like an appearance in a commercial for Foster's beer. His first noteworthy role came when he landed the role of Kelly Bundy's biker boyfriend on the hit FOX situation comedy *Married with Children*; Boreanaz played Frank on one episode in 1993. He was also an uncredited extra in two films in 1993, *Aspen Extreme* and *Best of the Best 2*. In addition, he appeared in smaller stage roles, such as *Hatful of Rain* at Orange County's Ensemble Theatre in 1993-94.

In 1997, Boreanaz landed a career-defining role when he was cast as the vampire Angel in the supernatural drama *Buffy the Vampire Slayer*. Angel was a brooding character, full of pain and torture in part because of a curse that ensured he could not experience true happiness. While the 240-year-old Angel had once been a bad boy, he came to the United States 80 years earlier, vowed to be good and not to do blood feedings or kill again.

Describing Angel to the *Chicago Daily Herald*'s Ted Cox, Boreanaz said, "He's trying so desperately hard to be good, and at the same time he's a [monster]. I really liked his evil side, and at the same time I really liked his good side. I kind of look at him as a recovering alcoholic, and he could easily slip off the deep end."

This vampire-with-a-conscience role was sometimes hard for the more free-spirited Boreanaz, who had limited training as an actor. He told Cox of the *Chi-* *cago Daily Herald*, "I didn't really know how to play this character. To this day, I just sort of let him evolve." But playing Angel made Boreanaz a star in part because of the tension and complex relationship he shared with the titular Buffy, played by Sarah Michelle Geller.

During this time period, Boreanaz married his first wife Ingrid Quinn. Their union faced challenges because of his growing fame and the couple divorced within two years. The year of his divorce, 1999, Boreanaz's career reached new heights when he was given his own spin-off show, *Angel*, which was also successful. He continued to make guest appearances on *Buffy* until that show ended its run in 2003.

In *Angel*, Boreanaz's vampire alter ego moves from Sunnydale, California, where *Buffy* is set, to Los Angeles. He makes the move because he cannot bear to be around Buffy, and finds his own path fighting other creatures of the night. As Boreanaz explained to Kinney Littlefield of the *Orange County Register*, "Angel is atoning for his own sins, but he'll also deal with demons and the human condition—which he's never been particularly good at—in the big city." Angel was also more adult in tone and content than the teen-oriented *Buffy*.

While starring on *Angel*, Boreanaz landed his first major film role. In 2001, Boreanaz played a sports journalist whose writer girlfriend is being stalked by a madman in the thriller *Valentine*. Telling Stephen Schaefer of the *Boston Herald* how he landed the role, the actor said, "*Valentine* came out of nowhere, and that's where I think life should be lived. I hear, 'You've got to meet this director' or 'You've got to do this role.'" He added, "If it's meant to be, it's meant to be." He also appeared in the film *I'm With Lucy* in 2002.

Angel was cancelled in the spring of 2004. By this time, Angel was operating an evil law firm, Wolfram and Hart. By show's end, he went back to being a vampire with a conscience and facing down long-running villains. Boreanaz also was able to fulfill his desire to work behind the camera when he directed an episode of the show, which aired in 2004. He told the *Daily Star*, "It was beautiful. I know what our talented cast can do, so I wasn't going to tell them how to do this or that. I learned the edited version is a lot different from the director's cut but I was pleased with the outcome."

After *Angel* ended its run, Boreanaz planned on traveling and spending time with his family, which included his second wife and a toddler son. He considered film offers and perhaps doing more stage work. But he returned to series television in 2005 with what proved to be another hit show, *Bones.* He played one of the leads, upright, hard-charging FBI Agent Seeley Booth. Boreanaz's Booth was assisted in his investigations by Emily Deschanel's Temperance Brennan, a talented but quirky forensic anthropologist. The series was inspired by Kathy Reichs, a best-selling novelist who also worked as a forensic anthropologist herself.

While the cases the pair worked on were key to *Bones,* the show focused more on the relationship between Booth and Brennan. Boreanaz compared their chemistry to the popular 1980s romantic comedy series *Moonlighting. Bones* was a hit from the first for FOX. Critics praised the show, with John Leonard of *New York Magazine* stating, "*Bones* is a sexed-up variation of all the CSIs." Leonard also lauded, "*Bones,* the best drama of the new network season, has established the terms of its screwball romantic comedy inside a procedural cop show: The FBI cares about people, both vic and perp."

Bones also proved his range as an actor as Boreanaz was able to avoid being typecast as an Angel-type of character. His Booth was—as Sean Mitchell of the *New York Times* described—"emotional and caring, an unmarried father who is seeking redemption for his past as an Army sniper." During the run of *Bones,* Boreanaz also began working with an acting coach, Ivana Chubbuck. She taught him to draw on his own experiences in his acting, making the process much more enjoyable. Boreanaz expanded his range in other ways as well. Beginning in 2007, Boreanaz was a co-producer on *Bones,* then became a full producer in 2009. He also directed at least three episodes in 2010 and 2011.

While starring on *Bones,* Boreanaz continued to take on a few film roles. He appeared in 2005's *The Crow: Wicked Prayer* and *These Girls.* The latter film was a Canadian-set independent comedy in which he played a hunky small-town husband and father who cheats on his wife with three teenage girls then tries to get out of the situation. Boreanaz took roles in other films, including two low-budget features released in 2006, *The Hard Easy* and *Mr. Fix It,* as well as 2007's *Suffering Man's Charity,* 2008's *Justice League: The New Frontier,* and 2009's *The Mighty Macs.*

While *Bones* was a hit that took chances by having the main characters grow even closer beginning in its third season, Boreanaz faced some difficulties in his personal life that earned him notoriety. Like his character in *These Girls,* he admitted in the spring of 2010 to being unfaithful to his wife with Rachel Uchitel (who had been involved with superstar golfer Tiger Woods) as well as at least one other woman. Boreanaz was also hit with a sexual harassment lawsuit by an extra named Kristina Hagan. The suit was later dismissed in early 2011.

Away from acting, Boreanaz loved dogs and sports. He was a football and hockey fan, especially the Philadelphia Flyers. He played golf, even taking trips to Ireland to play the game. Emphasizing a love of family, Boreanaz considered his father key to his life. He told Louis B. Hobson in the *Toronto Sun,* "My dad is also my best friend. We have a very special relationship. He's always been there for me. I talk to him every day." The actor also noted his dislike of living in Los Angeles, telling Hobson, "Hollywood is not my kind of town. I'm a small-town boy from the east, but this is where movies are made, so I make the best of my time here."

While *Bones* was scheduled to continue airing at least through the 2011-12 season, Boreanaz shot a film scheduled for release in 2012, *Officer Down.* Explaining his professional philosophy, he told Littlefield of the *Orange County Register,* "I'm just letting my life take its course. I mean, this could all be over very quickly. I don't think way ahead. I think definitely for the day and what it brings me for learning, and walking away with something from the scene."

Sources

Periodicals

Associated Press, July 23, 2010; March 30, 2011.
Boston Herald, February 1, 2001, p. 43.
Chicago Daily Herald, August 17, 1998, p. 6.
Contra Costa Times, May 4, 2010.
Daily Star, March 28, 2004, p. 13.
Edmonton Journal (Alberta, Canada), February 22, 2000, p. C1.
Houston Chronicle, January 22, 1998, p. YO4.
London Free Press (Ontario, Canada), April 6, 2010, p. C2.
New York Magazine, December 12, 2005.
New York Times, December 27, 2006, p. E1.
Orange County Register (CA), September 30, 1999, p. F4.
Ottawa Citizen, April 19, 2008, p. J3.
Peterborough Examiner (Ontario, Canada), March 23, 2006, p. C2.
Sun, March 27, 2004.
Toronto Sun, February 5, 2001, p. 41; May 19, 2004, p. 65; October 30, 2005, p. TV2.
UPI NewsTrack, May 3, 2011.
Vancouver Sun (British Columbia, Canada), September 2, 2009, p. D8.

Online

"David Boreanaz," Internet Movie Database, http://www.imdb.com/name/nm0004770/filmotype (May 26, 2011).

—A. Petruso

Alan Bradley

Author

Born October 10, 1938, in Toronto, Ontario, Canada; married Shirley (second marriage).

Addresses: *Contact*—c/o Delacorte Press, 1745 Broadway, New York, NY 10019. *E-mail*—info @flaviadeluce.com. *Web site*—http://www.flavia deluce.com/.

Career

Worked as an engineer at radio and television stations in Ontario, Canada, and the Ryerson Polytechnical Institute, Toronto, Ontario, Canada, through 1969; director of television engineering in media center and screenwriting and television production teacher, University of Saskatchewan, Saskatoon, Saskatchewan, Canada, 1969-94; wrote short stories for literary journals and CBC Radio while living in Saskatoon; published first book, *Ms. Holmes of Baker Street: The Truth About Sherlock*, 1988; published first Flavia de Luce mystery novel, *The Sweetness at the Bottom of the Pie*, 2009.

Member: Saskatoon Writers (first president), Saskatchewan Writers Guild (founding member), Casebook of Saskatoon (founding member).

Awards: Debut Dagger Award, British Crimewriter's Association, for *The Sweetness at the Bottom of the Pie*, 2007; Award for Children's Literature, Saskatchewan Writers Guild, for "Meet Miss Mullen" (a short story).

Sidelights

Canadian author Alan Bradley found success in his late sixties with his wildly popular series of mystery novels featuring the bright eleven-year-old detective Flavia de Luce, known as the Buckshaw Chronicles. With a winning submission to the Debut Dagger Award competition in 2007, Bradley unexpectedly landed a six-book deal to write the novels. He began his professional career as a radio and television engineer who was involved in the construction of several television stations. After retiring early from his position at the University of Saskatchewan, Bradley devoted himself to writing, creating unproduced screenplays and a published memoir. His best-known character, Flavia, unexpectedly popped to life while he was writing a different novel, and became a star in his 2009 debut novel, *The Sweetness at the Bottom of the Pie*. As H. J. Kirchhoff wrote of her in the *Globe and Mail*, "She's Harriet the Spy by way of Agatha Christie, with a dash of Lemony Snicket and the Addams Family. Who could resist?"

Bradley was born on October 10, 1938, in Toronto, Ontario, Canada. His father, a veteran of World War II, abandoned the family when Bradley was a toddler, and he and his two elder sisters were raised by his single mother in Cobourg, Ontario, Canada. Bradley's maternal grandparents came from England and helped raise him. Though he learned to read before entering kindergarten, Bradley was a poor student and defiant, though he loved to read. He wanted to be himself no matter what the cost.

As Bradley explained to Fiona Morrow of the *Globe and Mail* in reference to his best-known literary creation, "I really like the eleven-year-old idealism of Flavia. I remember that feeling of being absolutely unstoppable—that you could do anything. And, I remember how quickly that becomes repressed at school—when you run into a brick wall of people who don't think you can do anything at all. They just want you to conform, to sit down and listen and keep your mouth shut. I consciously sat down one day and asked myself if I was going to cave in and become one of them. And I decided that, despite how hard it would be, I would much rather just stay me."

In adulthood, Bradley studied electronic engineering, remained in Cobourg, and worked as an engineer for television and radio stations in Ontario. He focused on constructing and designing various electronic systems. For example, Bradley spent a year and a half working in Cornwall, Ontario, Canada, during the construction of the CJSS Channel 8 TV. He was later employed by the Ryerson Polytechnical Institute (now known as Ryerson University), for a brief period of time until a new position came his way. In 1969, Bradley moved to Saskatoon, Saskatchewan, Canada, to build a state-of-the-art broadcasting studio at the University of Saskatchewan. In addition to serving as the director of television engineering in media center, he also taught screenwriting and television production there through 1994, when he retired.

While living in Saskatoon, Bradley's life-long interest in writing came to fruition. He became active in the local literary scene and was a part of many local writing groups. He learned much from his fellow writers and aspiring writers. During this time period, he published a few short stories in literary magazines (including a number of stories for children published in *The Canadian Children's Annual*) and had some read on the air on CBC radio programs.

In 1988, Bradley published his first book, *Ms. Holmes of Baker Street: The Truth About Sherlock*. Written with William A. S. Sarjeant, it was a work of literary criticism that took ten years to write. The pair read every story and book about Sherlock Holmes, the detective created by Sir Arthur Conan Doyle, and devised a theory that Holmes was really female. They based their controversial theory on facts from Doyle's life, including his many close female relationships and that Holmes was created from characteristics of his friends. A second edition was published in 2004.

In 1994, Bradley took an early retirement from the University of Saskatchewan. He and his second wife, Shirley, moved to Kelowna, British Columbia,

Canada, when her employer transferred her there. In Kelowna, the couple lived in a faux Victorian villa and Bradley focused on writing. He concentrated on screenplays for many years. He wrote on the eighteenth-century Scotsman John Hunter who taught himself surgery and later operated his own medial school. Other topics included kids in a runaway plane and a western. In nine years, he wrote about seven or eight screenplays. While a few were optioned by Hollywood, no project made it to fruition.

Bradley's focus as a writer changed in 2003. That summer, the Okanagan Mountain Park fires nearly consumed his neighborhood. While Bradley and his wife managed to escape and their home was relatively unscathed, many of his neighbors were not so lucky. The haunting experience compelled him to focus on different projects. As he explained to Richard Helm of the *Edmonton Journal*, "That was just a horrible time, and I decided to turn to something a little quieter in my writing." He began working on nonfiction and literary fiction instead of screenplays. Bradley's second book was nonfiction. The 2006 memoir *The Shoebox Bible* focused on the author and his family. As a child, he found a shoebox full of unusual objects in his mother's closet, but did not learn the meaning of its contents until his mother was dying many years later.

Bradley became a literary sensation in 2009 with his first novel, a mystery with an eleven-year-old detective at its center. He was inspired to create Flavia de Luce while working on a different project, a work of fiction that focused on a female CBC broadcaster living in England in the 1950s as part of a BBC and CBC work exchange. Bradley became distracted by a new, unrelated character who emerged fully formed from his creative mind. Flavia took over what he was writing, and he abandoned his female broadcaster project after a few chapters to focus on his young detective.

With his wife's encouragement and love of this character, Bradley molded the idea for a fiction contest: the Debut Dagger operated by the U.K. Crime Writer's Association. It was sponsored by Orion, a British publisher, and required 3,000 words or fewer of a mystery novel and synopsis. The winner had a chance to be published by Orion. Bradley wrote 15 pages of what became *The Sweetness at the Bottom of the Pie*, and submitted it to the competition in early 2007. By June, he learned he was the winner and Orion began negotiating with his agent. A bidding war ensued and before picking up the award on July 5, 2007, Bradley had a three-book deal with Orion for British rights, with Bantam in the United

States, and with Doubleday in Canada. *The Sweetness at the Bottom of the Pie* was translated and published in a number of other countries as well, including Norway, Taiwan, and Slovakia. Bradley completed the novel in seven months.

In the first Flavia de Luce mystery novel, readers are introduced to the precocious detective. She lives in England in the 1950s with her two older sisters and their stamp collecting-obsessed father. Flavia and her sisters are allowed to follow their own interests with little guidance; Flavia's is chemistry, specifically the study of poisons. After a dead bird is left at the once-wealthy family's door at their manor home named Buckshaw and a murder is committed in her village of Bishop's Lacey, Flavia investigates, riding around the village on her BSA bicycle. Flavia finds the dead man's body in a cucumber patch on her family's ancestral estate. She also learns that her father might have a connection to the murder as he was involved in the suicide of a teacher years earlier. Though he is arrested, Flavia is able to prove his innocence.

Discussing his literary creation, Bradley told Mark Medley of the *Calgary Herald*, "Flavia's such a concoction of contradictions. It's one of the things that I very much love about her. She's eleven but she has the wisdom of an adult. She knows everything about chemistry, but nothing about family relationships."

Before the publication of *The Sweetness at the Bottom of the Pie*, Bradley had never been to England. He read many books about the subject and also drew on the memories and descriptions of his grandparents, especially his grandmother, a literary enthusiast. The story is filled with touches like old maiden aunts and afternoon teas. Bradley specifically chose the socially stratified yet innocent 1950s. He told Morrow of the *Globe and Mail*, "The response to living in disturbing times is to go to the polar opposite. And it seems to me that 1950s England is the polar opposite of where we are now."

The Sweetness at the Bottom of the Pie was popular worldwide with good reviews and appearances on various best-seller lists in a number of countries. Critics praised numerous aspects of the novel. In the *Vancouver Sun*, for example, Joe Wiebe lauded, "*The Sweetness at the Bottom of the Pie* is an entertaining, original page-turner with a fresh, unconventional heroine who will undoubtedly charm legions of readers."

In March of 2009, Bradley sold his home and began traveling around the world with his wife as he worked on the next Flavia de Luce novels. They eventually relocated to Malta where Bradley continued his writing routine that allowed him to produce 1,000 words per day. Bradley's second Flavia de Luce novel, *The Weed That Strings the Hangman's Bag*, was also popular and completed before he left on his travels. In the 2010 novel, Flavia uses her skills with chemistry and questioning adults to figure out who killed a television puppeteer putting on a show in her village while his van was being repaired. Like his first book in the series, Bradley's *The Weed That Strings the Hangman's Bag* was well received. Reviewing the second novel, a *Publishers Weekly* reviewer lauded, "The author deftly evokes the period, but Flavia's sparkling narration is the mystery's chief delight. Comic and irreverent, this entry is sure to build further momentum for the series."

Bradley's third Flavia de Luce novel was published in 2011. Titled *A Red Herring Without Mustard*, it features Bradley's young sleuth helping a gypsy who nearly dies at the hands of an unknown attacker. She also figures out the disappearance of a baby and reveals a ring that deals in forged antiquities. In addition, Flavia's family faces bankruptcy, and her father must sell his stamp collection and the silver. Reviewing the novel in the *Hamilton Spectator*, Gary Curtis lauds, "The author's prose remains quaint, effervescent, and playful, *A Red Herring Without Mustard* being among the very few sleuthing books suitable for both adults and children, as are its predecessors." Writing in *USA Today*, Carol Memmott praises the novel as well as its title, writing "if awards were given for great titles, Alan Bradley would nail it every time."

Six total Flavia de Luce novels were to comprise the series, with its trajectory already planned out by the author; however, Flavia will not age much and Bradley does not plan, at least at this stage of his career, on working with producers to turn the novels into television movies or films. Discussing the issue of aging, Nicholas Pashley wrote in Canada's *National Post*, "Bradley has said he does not want Flavia to grow older. Quite right: She is perfect as she is." Bradley also had other novels in the works, including *Upstairs at the Roxy*, which might see the light of day sometime in the future. Set in Cornwall, Ontario, Canada, the novel focuses on a movie house built in the early 1940s. The novel looks at the history of film through the filter of a projectionist, a job that Bradley always coveted and eventually performed when he worked briefly at a drive-in theater in Pembroke, Ontario, Canada. Of his success as a novelist, Bradley told Vit Wagner of the *Toronto Star*, "At my age, it's comforting to know what you're going to be doing in 2013."

Selected writings

Nonfiction

(With William A. S. Sarjeant) *Ms. Holmes of Baker Street: The Truth About Sherlock,* 2nd ed., University of Alberta Press (Edmonton, Alberta, Canada), 2004.
The Shoebox Bible, McClelland & Stewart (Toronto, Ontario, Canada), 2006.

Novels

The Sweetness at the Bottom of the Pie, Delacorte Press (New York City), 2009.
The Weed That Strings the Hangman's Bag, Delacorte Press, 2010.
A Red Herring Without Mustard, Delacorte Press, 2011.

Sources

Periodicals

Booklist, February 1, 2001, p. 38.

Calgary Herald (Calgary, Alberta, Canada), March 22, 2009, p. D1.
Canwest News Service, March 21, 2010.
Cornwall Standard Freeholder (Ontario, Canada), February 28, 2009, p. 2.
Edmonton Journal (Alberta, Canada), February 10, 2009, p. D1.
Globe and Mail (Canada), February 14, 2009, p. R1; March 27, 2010, p. F12.
Hamilton Spectator (Hamilton, Ontario, Canada), February 26, 2011, p. GO2.
National Post, March 13, 2010, p. WP17.
North Shore News (British Columbia, Canada), February 20, 2009, p. 21.
Publishers Weekly, January 25, 2010, p. 101.
Sherbrooke Record (Quebec, Canada), August 7, 2009, p. B4.
Toronto Star, February 15, 2009, p. E6.
USA Today, February 24, 2011, p. 5D.
Vancouver Sun (Vancouver, British Columbia, Canada), February 28, 2009, p. C6; March 13, 2010, p. C7.

Online

Contemporary Authors Online, Gale, 2010.

—*A. Petruso*

Keegan Bradley

Professional golfer

© *Stan Badz/US PGA Tour/Getty Images*

Born June 7, 1986, in Woodstock, VT; son of Mark (a golf professional) and Kaye Bradley. *Education:* St. John's University, New York City, sports management degree, 2008.

Addresses: *Agent*—Ben Harrison, Gaylord Sports Management, 13845 N. Northsight Blvd., Ste. 200, Scottsdale, AZ 85260. *Home*—Jupiter, FL. *Web site*—http://www.keeganbradley.com.

Career

Won several amateur golf tournaments, including Vermont High School Division 2 state individual championship, 2003, Wyoming State Amateur Championship, 2005, and Princeton Invitational, 2008. Turned professional, 2008. Professional golfer on the NGA Hooters Tour, 2008-09, Nationwide Tour, 2009-10, and PGA Tour, 2011—. Won HP Byron Nelson Championship, 2011, PGA Championship, 2011, and PGA Grand Slam of Golf, 2011.

Member: Professional Golfers' Association of America.

Awards: Massachusetts Golfer of the Year, Massachusetts Golf Association, 2004; PING Mid-Atlantic All-Region Team, Golf Coaches Association of America, 2008; Rookie of the Year, PGA Tour, 2011.

Sidelights

In the summer of 2011, American golfer Keegan Bradley was already on his way to a stellar rookie season on the Professional Golfers' Association (PGA) Tour with a victory in the Byron Nelson Championship and five other top-20 finishes. At the PGA Championship in August he overcame a five-shot deficit with three holes left to force a tie for the lead. His victory in a three-hole playoff made him only the third golfer in a century to win his first appearance in one of professional golf's four major tournaments. Noting that other golfers have failed to capitalize on spectacular debuts, Bradley told Alan Shipnuck of *Sports Illustrated* that "I don't want to be one of those guys that kind of disappears. I don't plan to."

Bradley was born on June 7, 1986, in Woodstock, Vermont, the eldest child of Mark and Kaye Bradley. Golf was an important part of his childhood; his father was an accredited PGA instructor and his aunt, Pat Bradley, won multiple major tournaments on the Ladies PGA circuit and made the World Golf Hall of Fame. Nevertheless, skiing was young Keegan's first sport. He began competing at age six, won state tournaments, and was talented enough to consider an Olympic career. Summers he put his skis away and spent time at his father's "office," playing golf and practicing putting. "Skiing and golf have a lot of similarities in terms of they're very mental," he told Shipnuck. "You're in that starting gate all by yourself with that scary course in front of you." By the time he entered high school, however, Bradley had decided to focus on golf.

Bradley attended a private golf school in Florida for a semester before deciding to return home to New England. The tuition was a stretch for his newly divorced parents, and the former skier did not fit in. "I didn't grow up like the kids in the South," Bradley told Jim McCabe of *Golf Week*. "I had long [periods] of time off where I didn't even hit balls." He attended Hopkinson High School in Massachusetts his senior year, helping his golf team win the state title by taking the individual championship. He also competed in American Junior Golf Association tournaments, but not as often as other aspiring golfers. "Obviously, I wish we could have let Keegan play more top junior tournaments and amateur tournaments," his father told McCabe. "But he knew we couldn't afford it, and he is such a great kid, he didn't complain. He appreciated what we could give him."

Despite his high school golfing success, Bradley was not heavily recruited by the major golf colleges in the South. Instead he chose St John's University in New York City, attracted by the courses in the metropolitan area. During his collegiate career, Bradley won nine tournaments but never received more than regional recognition for his performances. He was the team's Most Valuable Player his senior year and graduated in 2008 with a degree in sports management. Bradley turned professional that year and began competing on the National Golf Association's Hooters Tour, a developmental league funded mainly by entry fees. Over his 15 months on the tour, Bradley had seven top-ten finishes, including two wins. He attributed his persistence in following a challenging and sometimes discouraging career to his famous aunt: "Pat and I have a lot of similarities in our game, in our approach to the game, our work ethic," the golfer told Larry Dorman of the *New York Times*. "I look up to her in a lot of different ways, and one of the ways I try to emulate her is her toughness and work ethic."

In 2009, Bradley also played in two tournaments on the Nationwide Tour, the PGA's own developmental league. He made the cut (qualified to play the third and fourth round) in both events and decided to try the tour full-time. In 2010, his five top-ten Nationwide finishes—four of them coming during the last six weeks of the season—were enough to place him 14th on the tour money list, qualifying him for the PGA Tour in 2011. He made the cut in his first four PGA tournaments, earning top 20 finishes in two of them, and attracted major sponsors, including Putnam Investments, Oakley (golf clothing), and Cleveland Golf (clubs and accessories).

Bradley's first PGA Tour victory came less than five months into the season, at the HP Byron Nelson Championship in Irving, Texas. During the final round, playing in wind gusts up to 35 miles per hour, Bradley bogeyed (shot under par) only once and finished in a tie for first. He won the sudden-death playoff on the first hole to clinch the victory. While his quick rise to professional success surprised some observers, "Going under the radar is kind of my thing," the golfer told Ron Sirak of *Golf World*. "I hope someday not to go under the radar, but I'm fine with it."

A week after failing to capitalize on a second-round lead at the Bridgestone Invitational and finishing 15th, Bradley was in the mix at the PGA Championships. Trailing by two holes in the final round, he triple-bogeyed the 15th hole to fall five back of leader Jason Dufner. "I just kept telling myself, 'Don't let that hole define the whole tournament,'" Bradley told Barry Svrluga of the *Washington Post*. "I just didn't want to be remembered as the guy who tripled that hole and went on to bogey in or something." He made two birdies (one shot under par) and a par on his last three holes and ended up in a tie with Dufner for the lead. In the three-hole playoff, Bradley birdied the first hole, then held on to the lead to clinch the victory. The win made him only the third rookie in golf history to capture a major on his first try.

With two wins and 12 top-25 finishes, Bradley finished the 2011 PGA season with more than $3.75 million in earnings, making him 13th on the money list. As the winner of the PGA Championship, he also qualified for the PGA Grand Slam, a two-round competition held at the end of the season between the winners of pro golf's four majors. The rookie won the PGA Grand Slam by one shot, earning another $600,000 in unofficial earnings. He was also invited to the World Golf Championship-HSBC Championships in Shanghai, China. Bradley led after the first round but finished the tournament in a tie for 16th place. Just competing was exciting for the young golfer, who played alongside 2010 world number one Lee Westwood in the first round. "There are times," he told Lewine Mair on hsbcgolf. com, "when I feel like I have to pinch myself out here because of what's going on and just how much fun I'm having."

At the beginning of 2011, Bradley did not even appear on the list of the top 300 golfers as rated by the Official World Golf Ranking; however, by the end of 2011, the rookie was ranked 26th in the world and hoped to continue improving his standing. In December of 2011, he was named Rookie of the Year for the PGA Tour, while Player of the Year honors went to Luke Donald. Bradley's success—the money, the endorsements, the celebrity that allowed him to throw out the first pitch at a game of his beloved Boston Red Sox—was secondary to playing the game he loves. "Everything for me is a bonus out here. I didn't grow up with a lot so anything that happens out here is a huge bonus," Bradley told Tim Maitland on the PGA Web site. "I try to look at it that way. I got nothing to lose, pretty much. Dad was a club pro and I'd just travel around with him. I'd get up early and go to work with him and hang out at the course all day. Golf was what I always loved and I still love it. I'm lucky to be out here."

Sources

Periodicals

Golf World, June 6, 2011, p. 35.
New York Times, February 13, 2011, p. SP9.
Sports Illustrated, August 22, 2011.
Time, August 29, 2011.
Washington Post, August 15, 2011, p. D6.

Online

"Bradley Promises to Be a Threat to Win in First Attempt at WGC-HSBC," PGA Tour, http://www.pgatour.com/2011/tournaments/r489/10/24/bradley/index.html (November 7, 2011).
"Bradley, Roommate Take Divergent Career Paths," *Golf Week,* http://www.golfweek.com/news/2011/oct/18/bradley-roommate-take-divergent-career-paths/ (November 7, 2011).
"Keegan Bradley: Just Living the Dream," ESPN Boston, http://espn.go.com/boston/golf/story/_/id/6916568/keegan-bradley-just-living-dream (November 7, 2011).
"Keegan Bradley, Luke Donald Get Top PGA Tour Honors," *Boston Herald,* http://www.bostonherald.com/sports/golf/view/20111214.tifkeegan_bradley_luke_donald_get_top_pga_tour_honors/srvc=sports&position=also (December 15, 2011).
"Keegan Bradley Out in Front," HSBC Golf, http://www.hsbcgolf.com/news/98.html (November 7, 2011).
"Keegan Bradley," PGA Tour, http://www.pgatour.com/golfers/033141/keegan-bradley/ (November 7, 2011).
"The Unlikely Road to Bradley's PGA Title," *Golf Week,* http://www.golfweek.com/news/2011/aug/19/mccabe-unlikely-road-bradleys-pga-title/ (November 7, 2011).

—*Diane Telgen*

David Bromstad

Interior designer and television personality

Born David Reed Bromstad, August 17, 1973, in Cokato, MN; son of Richard and Diane (Krueger) Bromstad. *Education:* Ringling College of Art and Design, Sarasota, FL, B.F.A., 1996.

Addresses: *Agent*—Kenneth Slotnick, William Morris Endeavor Entertainment, 1325 Avenue of the Americas, New York, NY 10019. *Home*—Bal Harbour, FL. *Office*—c/o HGTV, 9721 Sherrill Blvd., Knoxville, TN 37932.

Career

Illustrator and set builder with the Walt Disney Company in Orlando, FL, after 1996; founder and principal, Bromstad Studio; won *HGTV Design Star* reality show series, 2006; host of *Color Splash with David Bromstad,* HGTV, 2007—; host of *Bang for Your Buck,* HGTV, 2009—; spokesperson, Mythic Paint, 2009—.

Sidelights

David Bromstad was a former Disney illustrator and struggling interior designer who specialized in extravagant children's rooms when he won HGTV's inaugural *Design Star* reality-competition series in 2006. The plum prize for the first-place winner was their own show on HGTV, and in March of 2007 Bromstad debuted with *Color Splash.* "I loved my life before," he told *Sacramento Bee* writer Debbie Arrington about his career coup. "I'm an artist. I paint. But I've really loved what's happened, too. I get to work with such wonderful people. It's so fabulous. I still pinch myself."

Bromstad was born in 1973 as the last of four children in his family. His earliest years were spent in Cokato, Minnesota, and then his family moved to the wealthy Minneapolis suburb of Wayzata when he was in middle school. A shy teen who dreamed of becoming an animator for the Walt Disney Company, Bromstad would later say that his years at Wayzata High School in the late 1980s and early '90s were "not a good time for me," he told *South Florida Sun-Sentinel* writer Charlyne Varkonyi Schaub. "Those hard times made me the person I am today."

Leaving Minnesota after his high school graduation, Bromstad enrolled in the Ringling College of Art and Design in Sarasota, Florida, which has a strong track record of placing graduates with jobs inside the Disney entertainment empire. One of his teachers, Joe Thiel, later spoke to Minneapolis *Star Tribune* staff writer Bill Ward about his former student, recalling that Bromstad's senior thesis project "was one of the most unusual we've had. The theme was Denny's at 3 a.m. He went and scouted it out and then basically set up a Denny's in our gallery."

After graduating from the Ringling College in 1996, Bromstad was able to land his dream job at Disney's Orlando studio, and spent the next several years building installations for theme-park attractions at Disney World, Universal Studios, and the Islands of Adventure. When the company suffered a downturn, Bromstad was laid off but decided to use the opportunity to start his own design firm, Bromstad Studio. Drawing on his Disney experience, he specialized in children's fantasy bedrooms and play spaces, but the business struggled to stay afloat in a tough economic climate.

It was the suggestion of a friend that prompted Bromstad to turn up at the Miami tryouts for a new reality series on HGTV, *HGTV Design Star*. He was one of ten young designers chosen to appear in its first season, which began airing in July of 2006. The eight episodes were taped in New York City and showed Bromstad and his competitors as they faced various challenges designed to test their mettle. For example, one challenge was to design a room entirely with items from a pet store, and on a budget of just $500. At the close of each episode, host Clive Pearse of HGTV's *Designed to Sell* and celebrity judges chose one contestant to eliminate. It was a grueling process, Bromstad later admitted, both professionally and personally. "I was really lucky," he told Schaub in the *South Florida Sun-Sentinel* interview. "My talent and personality got me through. I decided I was going to be me. I was not going to hold back because cameras are on me. I think America picked up on that, too."

Bromstad bested contestants that included a former Miss Utah and a pair of twins who both held architecture degrees from Harvard University. He found a way to differentiate himself from the other contestants by habitually taking his shirt off in the middle of the design-build-paint frenzy, showing off a chiseled physique and a few Asian-inspired tattoos. "They're like, 'You're doing a design show—you shouldn't have your shirt off,'" he was told at times, he confessed to Ward in the *Star Tribune* article. "And I'm like…. 'We're from Miami; we don't keep our clothes on.'"

The tight turnaround for the projects suited him, however, as he told Schaub in the *South Florida Sun-Sentinel* interview. "I'm a kind of procrastinator. I would always wait until the last minute to get things done. Doing a task in such little time was pretty much like I work." At the show's final episode, Bromstad beat out Alice Fakier to become HGTV's first *Design Star* winner. The finale on September 10, 2006, was a watershed moment for the network, posting the highest ratings in HGTV history for an original series.

Bromstad won a car, and a significant career boost for his Bromstad Studio business, but more importantly landed his own HGTV series. *Color Splash with David Bromstad* debuted on the network on March of 2007. Later that year he was a guest on the second season of *Design Star*, which filmed in Las Vegas. "I know all the tricks the production team will use to make [the finalists] tired and crying," he joked about his appearance in an interview with *Denver Post* writer Sheba R. Wheeler. "You only get to have two or three hours of sleep at night. You add that to a lack of food and intense emotions, and you do end up [bawling] and fighting. You are stressed out, and you feel like you are in a dream state. You really have to rely on your instincts, and that causes people's good and bad sides to come out."

Bromstad's fifth season as host of *Design Star* in 2009 coincided with a second series for HGTV, *Bang for Your Buck*. That same year, he became a spokesperson for the environmentally conscious Mythic Paint brand, whose products have a zero-V.O.C. (volatile organic compound) formulation. *Design Star* was taped in San Francisco, but Bromstad had settled in Miami Beach by then and acquired a larger living space in the form of a loft in Bal Harbour. In the interview with Arrington for the *Sacramento Bee*, he described the renovation as "probably my biggest design challenge yet because of the configuration and because it's my space. I'm really pushing myself to make it unique and make an impression on the world. I'm getting there slowly. But right now, it looks like a crayon box threw up in my house."

Sources

Periodicals

Denver Post, July 27, 2007.
Multichannel News, September 18, 2006, p. 30.
New York Times, July 22, 2006.
Sacramento Bee, April 20, 2009.
South Florida Sun-Sentinel (Fort Lauderdale, FL), September 21, 2006.
Star Tribune (Minneapolis, MN), March 12, 2007, p. 1E.
USA Today, March 16, 2007, p. 7E.

Online

"David Bromstad," HGTV.com, http://www.hgtv.com/david-bromstad/bio/index.html (April 11, 2011).

—*Carol Brennan*

Norbert Leo Butz

© *Andrew H. Walker/Getty Images*

Actor

Born January 30, 1967, in St. Louis, MO; son of Norbert and Teresa Ann Butz; married Sydney (divorced); married Michele Federer, 2007; children: Clara, Maggie (from first marriage), Georgia (from second marriage). *Education:* Webster University, BFA (acting); Professional Actor Training program, Alabama Shakespeare Festival, MFA, 1993.

Addresses: *Agent*—c/o Elin Flack Management, 435 West 57th St., Ste. 3M, New York, NY 10019.

Career

Actor on stage, including: *Rent,* 1996-98; *Cabaret,* 2000; *Juno and the Paycock,* 2000; *Saved,* 2001; *Thou Shalt Not,* 2001-02; *The Last Five Years,* 2002; *Buicks,* 2003; *Wicked,* 2003; *Dirty Rotten Scoundrels,* 2005-06; *Is He Dead,* 2007-08; *Speed-the-Plow,* 2008-09; *ENRON,* 2010; *Catch Me If You Can,* 2011. Film appearances include: *Went to Coney Island on a Mission from God, Be Back By Five,* 1998; *Looking for an Echo,* 2000; *New World Order,* 2002; *Noon Blue Apples,* 2002; *West of Here,* 2002; *Dan in Real Life,* 2007; *Higher Ground,* 2011.

Awards: Drama Desk Award for outstanding actor in a musical, Drama Desk, for *Dirty Rotten Scoundrels,* 2005; Drama League Award for distinguished performance, Drama League, for *Dirty Rotten Scoundrels,* 2005; Fred & Adele Astaire Award for best male dancer on Broadway, for *Dirty Rotten Scoundrels,* 2005; Outer Critics Circle Award for outstanding actor in a musical, for *Dirty Rotten Scoundrels,* 2005; Tony Award for best performance by a lead-ing actor in a musical, for *Dirty Rotten Scoundrels,* 2005; Drama Desk Award for outstanding actor in a musical, Drama Desk, for *Catch Me If You Can,* 2011; Fred & Adele Astaire Award for best male dancer on Broadway, for *Catch Me If You Can,* 2011; Tony Award for best performance by a leading actor in a musical, for *Catch Me If You Can,* 2011.

Sidelights

Norbert Leo Butz is an actor best known for his Broadway performances, who has also dabbled in film and television work. He is most well known for his appearances in the Broadway plays *Wicked, Dirty Rotten Scoundrels,* and *Catch Me If You Can.* He has won two Tony Awards.

Butz was born in St. Louis, Missouri, in 1967. He was the seventh of eleven children. He humorously told Nancy Rosati in *Talkin Broadway* that he has "the worst name in show business," and explained how he came to be named Norbert. Although he had six older brothers at the time he was born, he was the first one his father helped to deliver. His father Norbert, was so emotionally moved by the experience that he asked Butz's mother if he could name the child after himself. She said no, but while she was in the recovery room, he changed the name on the birth certificate to Norbert; originally, the name was Timothy James Butz. He never took a stage name, because his brothers would have teased him about it unmercifully. He told Joanne Kaufman in the *Wall Street Journal* that some people suggested he use the name Bert. "I don't do Bert," he told her.

Butz told Rosati that perhaps as a result of his unromantic name, he "always had low expectations of myself." He was shy and rather quiet; however, when he was in high school and college, he began acting in school plays, and was recognized for his talent. He told Rosati that acting was "the thing that always made sense to me."

He planned to major in journalism at the University of Missouri in Columbia, and won a scholarship to go there. At the same time, though, he secretly auditioned for an acting program at Webster University in St. Louis. A week before he was scheduled to begin his studies at the University of Missouri, he found out that he was accepted into the acting program. His parents were furious when he turned down the University of Missouri and entered the acting program. They felt that he should get a good, steady job, and do acting as a hobby; however, later in his life they became his biggest fans.

After graduating from Webster University, Butz worked in regional theater for five years, then earned a master of fine arts degree at the Alabama Shakespeare Festival as part of its Professional Actor Training program, and continued to work with the acting company at Alabama. He married Sydney, his first wife, and planned to settle down and stay in regional, repertory theater.

Before he got too settled, he decided to move to New York City and pursue a larger acting career. At 28, he went to New York and, a month after arriving, got a part in the hit Broadway musical *Rent*. Eventually he did six parts, including the two leads; often he would do both lead parts on the same day. Following *Rent*, he toured with *Cabaret*. His wife and two-year-old daughter toured with him; while in *Cabaret* he and his wife had another daughter, Maggie.

He followed this with parts in *The Last Five Years* and *Thou Shalt Not*, then made it really big when, in 2003, he played Prince Fiyero in *Wicked*. While he was working on *Wicked*, he and Sydney divorced, and he met Michelle Federer, whom he would marry in 2007. In 2004 he left *Wicked* to star in *Dirty Rotten Scoundrels* until 2006. His work in the show won him many awards, including the 2005 Drama Desk Award for Outstanding Actor in a Musical and a Tony Award for Best Performance by a Leading Actor in a Musical.

In 2009, Butz began appearing in the musical *Catch Me If You Can*, initially in a test run of the show in Seattle. The night before the show opened, Butz's family sustained a tragedy. His sister Teresa was fatally stabbed and her partner wounded by an intruder who entered their Seattle home. The attacker was later caught and tried, and in July of 2011 he was found guilty and sentenced to life in prison without the possibility of parole. Butz was deeply affected by the traumatic loss, and he later praised members of the cast and crew of the show for helping him get through such a dark and difficult time.

In 2010, Butz appeared in the Broadway show *EN-RON*, about the scandal-plagued financial collapse of the company by the same name. Butz played company president Jeffrey Skilling. In *Talkin Broadway*, Matthew Murray praised Butz's performance, calling him "legitimately impressive" and noting that his "coolly likeable manner and charming enthusiasm" perfectly portrayed the devious Skilling. Despite these comments and other critical praises, the show did not do well at the box office.

Butz appeared in the film *Higher Ground* in 2011. The film was widely praised by critics for its portrayal of a woman torn between skepticism and religious faith. More notably in 2011, Butz appeared in the Broadway performance of the acclaimed musical *Catch Me If You Can* as Carl Hanratty, an FBI agent who tracks down con artist Frank Abagnale Jr. Over time the two men come to a new understanding of themselves and of life. Jack O'Brien, director of the show, told Kaufman, "Norbert's performance as Carl is revelatory. He sings the blues. He sings his butt off. He's funny as hell and he's deeply moving." Butz won his second Tony Award for his work in the show. In his acceptance speech, Butz thanked his father and gave a tribute to his sister, saying "I love you Teresa. We remember you every night."

Sources

"Enron," *Talkin Broadway*, http://www.talkinbroadway.com/world/Enron.html (July 12, 2011).

"Kalebu Guilty of 2009 Rapes, Slaying in South Park Home," *Seattle Post-Intelligencer*, http://seattletimes.nwsource.com/html/localnews/20154862.tif42_kalebu02m.html (July 15, 2011).

"Norbert Leo Butz," Internet Movie Database http://www.imdb.com/name/nm0125475/ (July 11, 2011).

"Sister of Norbert Leo Butz Slain; Preview of *Catch Me If You Can* Is Postponed," *Backstage,* http://www.backstage.com/bso/news-and-features-news/sister-of-norbert-leo-butz-slain-10039960.tif94.story (July 12, 2011).

"Slain Seattle Woman Remembered in Tony Speech," *Seattle Post Intelligencer,* http://blog.seattlepi.com/thebigblog/2011/06/13/seattle-murder-victim-remembered-in-tony-speech/ (July 12, 2011).

"Spotlight On Norbert Leo Butz," *Talkin Broadway,* http://www.talkinbroadway.com/spot/nlb1.html (July 12, 2011).

"This Time He's Not the Con Man," *Wall Street Journal,* http://online.wsj.com/article/SB10001424.tif05274870.tif37125045.tif76240752.tif18598000.tif0.html (July 12, 2011).

"Tony Award Winner Norbert Leo Butz Gives Second Acceptance Speech at the *Catch Me* Curtain Call," *Playbill,* http://www.playbill.com/playblog/2011/06/tony-award-winner-norbert-leo-butz-gives-second-acceptance-speech-at-the-catch-me-curtain-call-video/ (July 12, 2011).

"*Wicked* Sweethearts Norbert Leo Butz and Michelle Federer Welcome Baby Girl Georgia," Broadway.com, http://www.broadway.com/shows/catch-me-if-you-can/buzz/154809/wicked-sweethearts-norbert-leo-butz-and-michelle-federer-welcome-baby-girl-georgia/ (July 12, 2011).

—Kelly Winters

Felipe Calderón

Saul Loeb/AFP/Getty Images

President of Mexico

Born Felipe de Jesús Calderón Hinojosa, August 18, 1962, in Morelia, Michoacán, Mexico; son of Luis Calderón Vega (an activist and historian) and Cameron Hinojosa Calderón; married Margarita Zavala; children: Maria, Luis Felipe, Juan Pablo. *Education:* Escuela Libre de Derecho, Mexico City, Mexico, bachelor's degree; Insituto Tecnológico Autónomo de México, Mexico City, Mexico, graduate degree; Harvard University, MPA, 1999.

Addresses: *Office*—Residencia Oficial de Los Pinos, Casa Miguel Alemán, Col. San Miguel Chapultepec, C.P. 11850, Mexico.

Career

Worked as youth organizer for the National Action Party, 1980s; elected to Mexico City assembly, 1988; elected to Mexican Congress, 1991; secretary-general, National Action Party, 1993-95, then president, 1996-99; director, National Bank of Public Works and Services, early 2000s; energy secretary of Mexico, 2002-04; president of Mexico, 2006—.

Sidelights

Felipe Calderón was elected to a six-year term as president of Mexico in a hotly contested race in the summer of 2006. A conservative politician and strong supporter of free trade initiatives, Calderón is the second consecutive Mexican chief executive from the nation's center-right National Action Party. Before winning the presidency, he spent several

years working to support his political party as secretary-general and later as party president. He also served in the government of President Vincente Fox as the nation's energy secretary. The 2006 presidential election in which Calderón ran against the left-wing mayor of Mexico City ended unclearly, leaving the actual winner undetermined for several weeks after polls closed. Although Calderón was eventually certified as the victor, accusations of voting irregularities and efforts to block his inauguration followed. After taking office, Calderón worked strenuously but largely ineffectively to end the drug-related violence that has caused tens of thousands of deaths in Mexico. While drug violence dominated Calderón's terms, other issues such as food prices, illegal immigration, and energy reform also required attention. Under Mexican law, Calderón was barred from running for reelection at the close of his term in 2012.

The president was born Felipe de Jesús Calderón Hinojosa in Morelia, Michoacán, Mexico, on August 18, 1962. Calderón was the youngest of the five sons of Carmen Hinojosa Calderón and Luis Calderón Vega, a co-founder of the Mexican political party Partido Acción Nacional, or National Action Party (PAN); Vega later became the party's official historian. The family's close ties to the party influenced the future president's political views from his early childhood, despite the PAN's often futile efforts to mount successful candidates at time when Mexico was essentially dominated by the Partido Revolucionario Institucional, or Institutional Revolution Party (PRI), which had formed out of the movement that ousted Mexican dictator Porfirio Díaz and installed a democratic government in the early twentieth century. Additionally, the PAN's close ties to the Catholic Church and its conservative social beliefs helped shape Calderón's views. In time, he came to embrace conservative economic policies favoring a flat tax and free trade, along with traditional social views including opposition to abortion and gay marriage.

From an early age, Calderón wished to enter politics. Even as a child, he campaigned for the PAN, and in time he came to head its youth organization. After completing secondary school in Morelia, Calderón pursued legal studies at Mexico City's Escuela Libre de Derecho (Free Law School) and continued on to earn a master's degree in economics from the Insituto Tecnológico Autónomo de México (Autonomous Technology Institute of Mexico). Some years later, he received a second master's degree in public administration from Harvard University's John F. Kennedy School of Government.

Calderón launched his formal political career in his mid-20s when he won election to Mexico City's municipal assembly in 1988. Three years later, he campaigned successfully as a PAN candidate for the Mexican Congress. While serving in the national assembly, Calderón met fellow party member Congresswomen Margarita Zavala. The two became engaged while working on a 1994 political campaign and, after marrying, settled in Mexico City. They had three children together: Maria, Luis Felipe, and Juan Pablo.

In 1993, the PAN tapped Calderón as its secretary-general. Two years later, he decided to return to his home state of Michoacán to run as the PAN candidate for governor. Although Calderón lost the election, he became the president of the PAN the following year. Under his watch, both the PAN and the leftist opposition party Partido de Revolución Demócratia, or Party of Democratic Revolution (PRD), succeeded in chipping away at the decades-long dominance of the PRI in Mexican elections. Their combined efforts helped PAN candidate Vincente Fox win the nation's presidency in 2000, becoming the first non-PRI politician to hold that position since the formal establishment of the PRI in the late 1920s.

With a PAN president in place, Calderón's ascent into the upper echelons of government continued. He served for a time as director of the state-run Banco Nacional de Obras y Servicios Públicos, or National Bank of Public Works and Services. In 2002, Fox named Calderón as energy secretary. He held this post for two years before stepping down in order to begin a run of his own for the presidency. However, his path to the nomination was far from a clear one; Fox supported Santiago Creel, a PAN politician who was then serving as secretary of the interior. Although Creel was considered the favorite, Calderón's long-standing connections to the party helped him garner the votes necessary to win its nomination in a closed primary the following year. He thus stood as the PAN candidate against PRD candidate Andrés Manuel López Obrador—the populist mayor of Mexico City—and PRI candidate and party leader Roberto Madrazo in the 2006 election to replace Fox.

The election proved highly contentious. Calderón and López Obrador quickly pulled ahead of Madrazo, making the race essentially a contest between the PAN and PRD candidates. López Obrador characterized his opponent as a representative of Mexico's minute economic elite who was likely to cater to the interests of the wealthy and powerful at the expense of ordinary Mexicans, of whom roughly half lived below the poverty line at the time of the campaign. Calderón, in response, attacked López Obrador as a dangerous leftist whose reckless spending would force the nation into immense debt while failing to solve its social problems. "The underlying message in most of Mr. Calderón's attack advertisements," noted James McKinley of the *New York Times*, "is that Mr. López Obrador is a leftist dictator in the making."

During much of the campaign, López Obrador led the polls, but as the election date neared the race became extremely tight, and analysts declined to predict a sure winner. The election itself failed to immediately resolve the question; in what was Mexico's closest-ever election results, unofficial counts placed Calderón ahead by just one percentage point out of some 43 million votes cast as both candidates declared victory. López Obrador demanded a strict recount and street protests broke out over a suspected three million uncounted votes. A final tally days later confirmed Calderón as the narrow winner, but protests continued well into the fall.

As a result of the closeness of the vote and the continuing claims of irregularities by the PRD, dramatic circumstances surrounded Calderón's inauguration before the Mexican Congress in December of 2006. Fights erupted between members of the PAN and the PRD when PAN politicians took the stage where the inauguration was to be held in order to prevent PRD members from blocking the inaugural ceremony. In order to ensure the transition of power in the event of a blacked inauguration, an unusual private investiture ceremony had been held the night before the planned public ceremony. Amidst the chaos in the assembly, however, a group of PAN members cleared the way for Calderón to enter and receive the presidential sash—the official symbol of office—from Fox. Sometimes violent protests over the inauguration also erupted around Mexico.

Once firmly—if somewhat controversially—inducted into office, Calderón began work on his signature law and order campaign initiative. He first sent thousands of Mexico military forces to Michoacán to crack down on drug cartel violence, and in time spread some 50,000 troops around the country's most violent areas. Calderón also worked to reorganize the regular police force to make it more effective. While these initiatives did allow authorities to capture or kill several top Mexican drug lords, they failed to reverse the trend of violence. Between the time of Calderón's inauguration and the spring of 2011, as many as 34,000 Mexicans had died as a result of cartel-related incidents, with 2010 the bloodiest year yet. The violence, largely concentrated near the U.S.-Mexico border, deterred tourists from visiting safer, more southern areas of the country, removing vital foreign dollars from the Mexican hospitality industry; however, by 2010, tourism seemed to be rebounding.

Despite these setbacks, Calderón reiterated his commitment to the crackdown, citing the United States as the ultimate source of much of the violence. The Mexican president pointed to the approximately 8,000 gun stores along the U.S-Mexico border as the origin of many of the weapons used in Mexican crimes, even as former president Fox suggested that the United States legalize drugs to curtail the demand for cross-border drug trafficking. "My government has seized more than 100,000 weapons in the past four years, 85 percent bought in the U.S.," Calderón was quoted as stating in a *Wall Street Journal* article by Peter Sanders. "It was exactly the moment the assault-weapon ban ended in the U.S. that criminals in Mexico started to get more powerful weapons," the leader concluded. These issues, along with concerns over illegal immigration from Mexico to the United States, further heightened already tense relations between Mexico and its northern neighbor.

Cross-border relations took another blow in late 2010, when the Web site WikiLeaks posted cables between U.S. diplomats in Mexico City and leaders in Washington, D.C., that criticized Mexico's handling of the drug cartel violence. The cables further expressed doubts in the nation's ability to end the violence, and reported on corruption and abuse within the Mexican military and police. Internationally embarrassed by the publication of the confidential cables, U.S. officials worked to restore diplomatic relations with Mexico, although leaders stopped short of making a formal apology to Calderón's government.

In March of 2011, Calderón paid an official visit to U.S. President Barack Obama to discuss the nations' concerns. The visit came short weeks after a U.S. immigration and customs agent was killed in Mexico by a drug cartel gunman, becoming the first U.S. official to die in the line of duty across the border in some 25 years. At the same time, U.S. officials made suggestions that Mexican drug cartel members could be affiliated with Muslim extremists or even have the potential to mount a coup against the Mexican government that would require U.S. military intervention to end. These statements greatly angered Mexican leaders, creating a tense atmosphere for the meeting. The talks seemed productive, however, and the two leaders presented a united front on the issues facing their shared border. "We are very mindful that the battle President Calderón is fighting in Mexico is not just his," Obama was quoted as stating at a press conference by Ginger Thompson of the *New York Times*. "It's also ours. We have to take responsibility, just as he's taking responsibility." Calderón agreed that the issues required fresh cooperation. "I think that here, not just in terms of weapons, guns, we have to think in a much more open manner and seek much more creative solutions. It seems to me that we are experiencing extraordinary circumstances that call for extraordinary actions by our governments," Thompson quoted the Mexican leader as saying.

A quick end to the violence was unlikely, however, and Mexican citizens seemed increasingly frustrated with Calderón and the PAN over the nation's problems. Although Calderón was constitutionally barred from seeking a second term, many political analysts believed that the 2012 presidential election would serve as a referendum on his often failed efforts to curtail violence. A year prior to the election, polls indicated strong voter support for Enrique Peña Nieto, the expected PRI candidate.

Sources

Books

Encyclopedia of Latin America: Amerindians through The Age of Globalization (Prehistory to the Present), vol. 4, Facts on File, 2010, p. 52.

Encyclopedia of World Biography, vol. 27, 2nd ed., Gale, 2007, pp. 68-70.

Periodicals

New York Times, June 17, 2006; July 4, 2006; July 5, 2006; December 11, 2010; March 3, 2011.

Times (London, England), December 1, 2006.

Wall Street Journal, March 3, 2011; April 13, 2011; May 19, 2011.

Online

"Presidente Felipe Calderón Hinojosa," Presidencia de la República, http://www.presidencia.gob.mx/oficina-de-la-presidencia/presidente/ (June 3, 2011).

"Profile: Felipe Calderón," BBC News, http://www.bbc.co.uk/news/world-latin-america-12242685.tif (June 3, 2011).

—*Vanessa E. Vaughn*

David Cameron

AP Images/Lefteris Pitarakis

Prime minister of the United Kingdom

Born David William Donald Cameron, October 9, 1966, in London, England; son of Ian Donald (a stockbroker) and Mary Fleur Mount (a justice of the peace) Cameron; married Samantha Sheffield (a luxury-goods executive), June 1, 1996; children: Ivan, Nancy, Arthur, Florence. *Education:* Oxford University, B.A., 1988.

Addresses: *Office*—10 Downing St., London SW1A 2AA, United Kingdom. *Web site*—http://www.number10.gov.uk/.

Career

Research assistant to a Conservative (Tory) Member of Parliament, early 1985; ship jumper, Jardine Matheson, 1985; began as associate researcher, Conservative Research Department, 1988, became head of its political section, early 1990s; special advisor to the Chancellor of the Exchequer, 1992-93; special advisor to the Home Secretary, 1993-94; director of corporate affairs, Carlton Communications, 1994-2001; elected to the House of Commons from the constituency of Witney, Oxfordshire, 2001, 2005, 2010; parliamentary posts include shadow deputy leader of the Commons, 2003, Conservative Party deputy chair, 2003-04; shadow minister for local government finance, 2004-05, and shadow education secretary, 2005; elected Tory leader, 2005, and became Leader of the Opposition in the House of Commons, 2005; became prime minister with the general election, 2010.

Sidelights

As head of Britain's Conservative (Tory) Party, David Cameron became one of the youngest prime ministers in British history in 2010. His party's victory in that spring's elections ended 13 years of Labour Party rule, which in part was credited to Cameron's dramatic efforts to overhaul the party's image as stuffy, elitist, and unfashionably conservative. "If there is such a thing as Cameronism," wrote Catherine Mayer in *Time*, "it's a melding of old-style Toryism—typified by its skepticism of European integration, plus bracing instincts toward individual effort and the size of the state—with modern, green-tinged, compassionate conservatism."

Cameron was born in 1966 in London into a wealthy family with deep roots in the British establishment. His mother was the daughter of Sir William Mount, a British Army officer and holder of a baronetcy, while his father's family were the descendants of Alexander Geddes, a Scot who made a fortune in the grain business in the United States in the mid-nineteenth century. Another ancestor on Cameron's paternal family tree is King William IV, who sired a number of children outside of his marriage. Cameron's father, Ian, was a stockbroker with Panmure Gordon & Co., a top investment banking firm in London.

One of four children, Cameron grew up in the Berkshire-area village of Peasemore, but was sent off to boarding school at a very young age—standard practice for affluent English families, including the royal offspring of the House of Windsor. He entered Heatherdown Preparatory School, just behind Queen Elizabeth II's third son, Prince Edward, where he proved a gifted student. After that he entered tony Eton College, England's best-known single-gender private academy. Also at Eton during Cameron's years were Charles Spencer, the future earl and brother to Diana, the late Princess of Wales, and the actor Dominic West, best known for his role on television's acclaimed HBO series *The Wire*.

Cameron began his career in politics during his "gap year," the customary time off for British students before they begin their university studies. He worked as a researcher for his godfather, who was a Member of Parliament (MP). Later in 1985 he spent some time working for a shipping company in Hong Kong before entering Brasenose College of Oxford University. He graduated with a first-class honors degree in PPE (Philosophy, Politics, and Economics) in 1988. While at Oxford Cameron was a member of one of the school's more notorious dining clubs, the Bullingdon, which had a long record of infamous pranks.

In September of 1988 Cameron began a five-year stint with the Conservative Research Department, eventually rising to the head of its political section. One of his job duties was to brief Prime Minister John Major, the Tory leader, before the weekly Questions to the Prime Minister period when parliament is in session. He also prepared Major during the run-up to the 1992 general election, when the Tories squeaked by with a surprising margin of victory over Labour. Later that year Cameron was serving as special advisor to the Chancellor of the Exchequer, Norman Lamont, when Major's government made a sudden withdrawal from the European Exchange Rate Mechanism (ERM) after a day of perilously erratic trading on the London financial markets. Known as Black Wednesday, the removal of the pound sterling from the ERM on September 16, 1992, proved a major setback for Major's government, but years later footage would surface of Lamont's nighttime press conference, where a 25-year-old Cameron can be seen behind the Chancellor of the Exchequer.

Lamont was forced out of office several months later, and in 1994 Cameron went to work for media firm Carlton Communications, a publicly traded company in the midst of a period of steady acquisition of television properties in Britain. Cameron held the title director of corporate affairs until 2001. He first ran for office in the 1997 general election from a constituency in Stafford, but the Labour Party won in a landslide that year, gaining or keeping several seats in the House of Commons, including the one Cameron sought. The Labour Party had been out of power since 1979, but was revitalized in the mid-1990s under new leader Tony Blair, a youngish former attorney and onetime rock musician. Blair's retooling of the party's political agenda to a more centrist approach brought back voters and prompted the 1997 landslide. Labour went on to win a stupendous victory in the 2001 general election, holding on to most of its seats in the House of Commons, but Cameron entered and won a race for the constituency of Witney in Oxfordshire. His opponent was the incumbent, Shaun Woodward, with whom Cameron had once worked at the Tory headquarters in early 1990s. Woodward had held the seat since the 1997 election, but made a shocking defection to the Labour Party in 1999; in the 2001 campaign Woodward was derided as the only Labour MP to employ a butler.

In the House of Commons, Cameron began to attract notice as one of the Tories' new younger wing of backbenchers, or junior MPs. After 2003 he was appointed to "shadow" or opposition posts, which are used to publicly assail the ruling government's policies and decisions, and then became head of Tory policy coordination. When Labour won again in the May 2005 general election, Tory leader Michael Howard was forced to step down. Four months later, Cameron announced he would run for the party leadership post at the next Tory conference. He was criticized for stepping up, for these party-chief roles generally go to those with a much more extensive resume than Cameron, who had only been an MP for a few years.

The Tories, however, were a divided party. Its base remained in the south of England, among the landed gentry and middle classes, and the average age of the typical Tory voter was climbing steeply. Labour, by contrast, held firm in the northern industrial cities, and was popular with younger voters, women, and Britons of color. The Tories were viewed as somewhat of an anachronism: In recent years they had engaged in bitter battles over immigration policy, even favoring a cap on immigration, and opposed same-sex unions and pro-environment policies. They even mounted an intense campaign against the ban on the use of dogs in blood sports like fox hunting.

Like Labour a decade earlier, the Tory Party was in dire need of new leadership. "Cameron represents the holy grail," wrote the *Guardian*'s Oliver Burkeman not long after the MP announced he would run for party leadership. "He's telegenic, approachable, sanely eurosceptic, socially liberal, unburdened by baggage.... Above all, he stands a chance of addressing the party's central image problem, which is that for years now, in many circles, admitting to being a Tory has meant admitting not just to certain socioeconomic beliefs, but to being, somehow, a bit weird."

Cameron cruised to a surprising victory at the Conservative Party conference on December 6, 2005, winning the party leadership. That also gave him the title of Leader of the Opposition in Parliament. He became one of the most visible faces during the Prime Minister's Questions period, famously harrying Blair and then Blair's successor as prime minister, Gordon Brown. It was the jousts with Brown, in particular, which helped the Tories gain a lead in polls. The Labour leader was burdened with a poor public image, and reports also surfaced that Brown was an ineffective leader, unable to quell the dissension within his party.

As Tory leader, Cameron set out to revitalize the party, shifting it to a new agenda he liked to frame around the phrase "compassionate conservatism." Labour and Liberal Democrats derided his speeches as lacking in any solid political strategy or policy goals. He was also slotted into what the media dubbed the "Notting Hill set," after the central London neighborhood where Cameron and scores of others from his background—moneyed, Eton- and Oxford-educated, often with high-profile careers— lived and socialized. The Tory old guard was also said to roundly disapprove of Cameron, but he was able to marshal enough support from within party ranks to curb its reputation as an aging, elitist lot of vituperative xenophobes. Cameron spoke of a need to create a greater sense of community in Britain, which included respect for the environment and the rights of others, and urged citizens to become more involved as volunteers. Typical of a Tory, he criticized what his party viewed as Labour's profligate spending on social-welfare programs.

As prime minister, Brown was able to avoid scheduling elections until the spring of 2010. To the surprise of many, both he and Cameron agreed to a three-way televised debate with Liberal Democrat leader Nick Clegg, a first in the history of British general elections. On the May 6 Polling Day, the Tories gained a stunning 97 seats in the House of Commons, but they needed 20 over the 306 constituencies won to give them a majority. The final tallies resulted in a hung parliament—the first time in Britain since 1974—which meant that a coalition government had to be cobbled together. After days of tension, Brown resigned as prime minister and Cameron announced that he had formed a coalition government with Clegg's Liberal Democrats. Just 43 years old, Cameron became the youngest prime minister of Britain since 42-year-old Lord Liverpool was appointed to the office in 1812.

Cameron named Clegg as deputy prime minister, but reserved key cabinet posts for fellow Tories, including former Bullingdon mate George Osborne, who became Chancellor of the Exchequer. With Britain still roiling from the global economic crisis that began in 2008, Cameron faced his toughest challenge in hammering out a budget that would pass in parliament. The 2011 plan featured heavy cuts in government spending, as expected. His most dramatic overhaul was the new Welfare Reform Bill, introduced in parliament in early 2011. It proposed to overhaul Britain's generous unemployment benefit and housing allowance, eradicating them altogether in favor of a so-called universal benefit, which would be capped at $42,000 per household per year.

Cameron's wife, Samantha Sheffield, was pregnant with their fourth child during the brief 2010 campaign season. Sheffield hails from a distinguished and titled family that includes the first Duke of Buckingham, who built Buckingham Palace, and Lord Astor, who became her mother's second husband in 1976. Sheffield wed Cameron in 1996, and for a number of years ran the luxury-goods firm of Smythson of Bond Street. The couple's first child, Ivan, was born in 2002 with cerebral palsy and a severe form of epilepsy. He required round-the-clock care and the prognosis was grim from birth, with doctors cautioning he would likely never walk or talk. "You are depressed for a while, yes, because you're grieving the difference between your hopes and the reality," Cameron said of his son in the 2005 *Guardian* interview with Burkeman. "But you do get over that, because he's wonderful ... you learn to adjust." Ivan died in February of 2009 at the age of six. The tragedy gave Cameron an unusual commonality with his main political enemy, Gordon Brown, whose ten-day-old daughter, born prematurely, died in 2002. Both Brown and Cameron have spoken highly of the professionals and caregivers of the National Health Service, Britain's government-run health-care system, which provides universal coverage to all.

Cameron and "Sam Cam," as the British tabloids call his wife, are parents to a daughter born in 2004, a son in 2006, and a second daughter born three months after they moved into 10 Downing Street, the British prime minister's official residence and office. In Cameron's first speech in front of his new home, he proclaimed that his goal as leader of the ruling party was to "help build a more responsible society here in Britain," he asserted, according to a BBC News report. "Those who can should and those who can't, we will always help. I want to make sure that my government always looks after the elderly, the frail, the poorest in our country."

Sources

Periodicals

Financial Times, March 4, 2006, p. 16; October 2, 2010, p. 1.

Guardian (London, England), September 29, 2005, p. 8.
New York Times, October 4, 2006.
Observer (London, England), December 18, 2005.
Time, April 26, 2010.

Online

"Cameron Is New UK Prime Minister," BBC News, http://newsvote.bbc.co.uk/mpapps/pagetools/print/news.bbc.co.uk/2/hi/uk_news/politics/election_2010/8675265.stm?ad=1 (February 6, 2011).

—Carol Brennan

Catherine, Duchess of Cambridge

Royal/Alamy

British Duchess

Born Catherine Elizabeth Middleton, January 9, 1982, in Reading, Berkshire, England; daughter of Michael (a company owner) and Carole (a company owner; maiden name, Goldsmith) Middleton; married William, Prince of Wales, April 29, 2011. *Education:* University of St. Andrews, M.A. (honors), 2005.

Addresses: *Office*—Clarence House, St. James' Palace, London, SW1A 1BA, England. *Web site*—http://www.princeofwales.gov.uk/personalprofiles/thedukeandduchessofcambridge/theduchessofcambridge/index.html.

Career

Assistant accessories buyer, Jigsaw, 2006-07; associate, Party Pieces, 2007-09.

Awards: By marriage created Her Royal Highness Princess William Arthur Philip Louis, Duchess of Cambridge, Countess of Strathearn, Baroness Carrickfergus, April 29, 2011.

Sidelights

Kate Middleton married William, Prince of Wales and heir to the British throne, on April 29, 2011, in a much-anticipated royal wedding viewed by an estimated global television audience of 300 million. The 29-year-old, who met the grandson of Queen Elizabeth II at the University of St. Andrews in Scotland, became the first "commoner"—that is, a per-

son with no title or blood ties to England's aristocracy—to marry a future King of England in more than 350 years. The Queen bestowed on the newlyweds the title to the Dukedom of Cambridge, making the former Miss Middleton officially "Her Royal Highness The Duchess of Cambridge."

In the months leading up to the Royal Wedding, an extraordinary amount of media attention was focused on the bride-to-be's middle-class roots. She was born Catherine Elizabeth Middleton on January 9, 1982, the first child of Carole Goldsmith Middleton, the daughter of a builder who had spent part of her infancy in a council estate, as public-housing apartment complexes are called in Britain. Carole's mother's family had been coal miners in the northeast of England as recently as the 1930s.

Middleton's parents met while working as cabin attendants for BOAC, the forerunner of British Airways. Michael Middleton, Kate's father, came from a more prosperous family than his wife's; in the nineteenth century his ancestors included wool merchants and attorneys in Leeds. Michael's great-grandfather died in 1921 and left a trust specifically for the purpose of providing his descendants with access to educational funds. Middleton's parents drew upon this to send Kate and her two siblings to some of Britain's most prestigious schools. Middleton's younger sister, Philippa Charlotte or "Pippa," was born in 1983, and a year later the family moved to Amman, Jordan, when Mike Middleton was transferred there by British Airways. They returned to Britain in September of 1986, several months before the birth of the Middletons' third child and only son, James William.

Middleton's early years were spent in Bradfield Southend, a town in the scenic Berkshire county in southern England. She began her elementary school education at St. Andrews School in Pangbourne around the time her mother started a mail-order business out of their home called Party Pieces, which furnished supplies and decorations for themed birthday parties for children. The business grew so successful over the next decade, expanding into the e-commerce realm, that the Middletons became millionaires; Mike Middleton even resigned from British Airways to help run the company. In 1995 the family of five moved into a much grander home in the parish of Bucklebury, in West Berkshire.

That same year, Middleton began school at nearby Downe House as a day student. In the spring of 1996 Middleton enrolled at Marlborough College in Wiltshire, a co-educational boarding school. She spent these high school years preparing diligently for the Advanced Level General Certificate of Education, better known as A-levels, which are required for university entrance. A top athlete at the school, she set records in the high jump and was captain of the girls' field hockey team.

Middleton was born the same year as Prince William, though she is five months his senior. The first son of Prince Charles and his 21-year-old wife, the former Lady Diana Spencer, William had endured a life in the media spotlight from the moment his parents first brought him out of the London hospital where he was born. Charles and Diana had been married in spectacular fashion in July of 1981 in a royal wedding that helped rekindle interest in the monarchy after years of disinterest, disapproval, and even calls to abolish it entirely. The obviously unhappy marriage of William's parents became fodder for England's tabloid newspapers, and finally Charles and Diana formally separated in 1992, with their divorce finalized in August of 1996. William and his younger brother Harry (Prince Henry, born in 1984), divided their time between their mother's house, Kensington Palace, and Highgrove House, Prince Charles' estate in Gloucestershire. Diana was killed in a car crash in Paris a year after her divorce, and her funeral became one of the most-watched television spectacles of the royal family saga, bookended by the elaborate 1981 wedding and the 2011 vows of Diana's son and Kate Middleton.

William and Harry were close to their grandmother, the Queen, and it was she who encouraged William to consider a university in Scotland, at a time when England was becoming more formally separated from Scotland, Northern Ireland, and Wales, each of which were granted devolution and the right to form their own parliaments, though they still remained part of the United Kingdom and under the British crown. He chose the University of St. Andrews in Fife, on Scotland's North Sea coast after graduating from one of England's top private single-gender schools, Eton.

University-bound British students commonly take a "gap year" after graduating from secondary school. Middleton spent part of hers in Florence, Italy, brushing up on her Italian in preparation for the art-history degree she planned to earn. She entered the University of St. Andrews at the same time as Prince William, in September of 2001, though with considerably less fanfare. Both lived in St. Salvator's, one of the residence halls, and reportedly met at the dining hall, though both were enrolled in the same art-history program and shared some lecture courses. William eventually switched majors to geography, and in their second year he and Middleton became flatmates in an off-campus apartment they shared with two other students. For a time, both were enmeshed in monogamous relationships with other students, with Kate dating a handsome, affluent older student named Rupert Finch. As England's most eligible single man, William dated a string of beauties, including several high-born members of what British tabloids dubbed the "Glossy Posse," the moneyed set who spent country weekends in Gloucestershire.

Tabloid lore fixes the date of March 27, 2002, as the turning point in the ostensibly platonic relationship between Middleton and the prince. That night, she modeled in a charity fashion event at St. Andrews Bay Hotel, and the press sensationalized the prince's reaction to the transparent dress Middleton wore, and the fact that William had paid a few hundred dollars for a front-row seat. In the fall of 2003, as they started their third year at St. Andrew's, they moved with friends to a private estate outside of town, Balgove House, which had to be specially outfitted with bulletproof windows and bombproof doors to ensure the safety of the heir. William was always accompanied by a phalanx of security men, even in his classes.

Middleton and the prince were often photographed socializing together, but always in a group. The first published pictures of them alone surfaced on April 1, 2004, when they shared a ski lift at the posh Swiss resort of Klosters. Both earned their university degrees in June of 2005 in a ceremony attended—in a first—by both Mike and Carole Middleton and the Queen and her husband, Prince Philip. Also present was Prince Charles and his new wife, the former Camilla Parker-Bowles, the woman whom Diana had blamed repeatedly in the press for the breakup of her marriage.

While William began his military career—obligatory for an heir to the British throne—at the Royal Military Academy Sandhurst, Middleton lived in a flat in London's ritzy Chelsea neighborhood that her parents had bought for their children to share. For a time, she worked as an accessories buyer for Jigsaw, a clothing chain, but was hounded relentlessly by paparazzi. When she was with William—either at London nightclubs, during his weekend breaks from Sandhurst, or on longer vacations at various luxury resorts—they were cosseted by his bodyguards. On her own, however, Middleton was followed everywhere, because as a mere girlfriend of a royal family member she was not entitled to her own security detail.

The next milestone in Middleton's public relationship to the prince came on December 15, 2006, when she was an official guest at his Passing Out Parade at Sandhurst. Tellingly, her parents were invited, too. William had spent many weekends with the Middletons at their home in Bucklebury, and reportedly loved the casual, close-knit normalcy of a family life he and his brother had never enjoyed because of their parents' high-profile, unhappy marriage. Middleton and William split briefly in the spring of 2007, in a break confirmed in dramatic fashion by the royal press office, but the pair reconciled within a matter of weeks. Middleton continued to be photographed at high-profile events and vacation spots with William, and was invited to stay at the royal family estates that were favorite retreats of the Queen, Sandringham and Balmoral. When his military service prevented him from attending his cousin Peter Phillips' wedding in May of 2008, Middleton attended in his stead. A few months later, William's press office at Clarence House—the palace that served as his and Harry's official residence in London with their father—announced that the heir to the throne would begin Royal Air Force training to become a search-and-rescue helicopter pilot.

With no formal engagement announcement forthcoming, the press dubbed Middleton "Waity Katie." The couple spent much of 2009 apart, with Middleton in Berkshire, where she worked for her parents'

company, while the prince completed his Royal Air Force training. They resumed living together in early 2010 after William was assigned to an air base on Anglesey Island in Wales. In October of 2010, the couple vacationed in Kenya, where William formally proposed to Middleton with his late mother's legendary diamond-and-sapphire engagement ring. The engagement was announced to the world on November 16, 2010, and the couple stood for a photo call at St. James' Palace, followed by a television interview to British broadcaster ITV. These were the first remarks ever voiced by Middleton to a media source. "Over the years William has looked after me, he's treated me very well, as the loving boyfriend he is," were among the first words she spoke, according to the *Times* of London. "He is very supportive of me through the good times and also through the bad times."

A few days later the date of the Royal Wedding was fixed for Friday, April 29, 2011. Media frenzy in the interim eclipsed that of Charles and Diana's wedding nearly 30 years earlier. On her wedding day, Middleton was ferried to Westminster Abbey with her father in a Rolls Royce Phantom VI limousine that was given to Queen Elizabeth II on the occasion of her Silver Jubilee in 1977. She emerged from the car in a long-sleeved dress made by Sarah Burton, creative director of the fashion house Alexander McQueen, one of the event's most closely guarded secrets. An estimated one million spectators lined the streets of London to hail the wedding procession both before and after the Westminster Abbey ceremony.

After the obligatory kiss she and William shared on the balcony of Buckingham Palace before a cheering throng, and a lunch reception hosted by the Queen, the new Princess of Wales donned a second wedding dress for the evening's festivities, which had been arranged in part by Pippa, who works as an event planner. The couple spent the weekend in seclusion, then returned to Anglesey on the following Monday. Now styled Her Royal Highness, The Duchess of Cambridge, the former Miss Middleton continued to be the focus of intense media fascination, as she would for the rest of her life. "One thing the wedding of William and Kate demonstrated is that the power of the British royals to rivet at a least a good portion of mankind persists, despite everything," commented *Guardian* journalist Tim Adams the next day. "The monarchy, of course, can never be democratic, but it can be more alive, and maybe more in love. That is what Diana apparently craved, it is also what her sons seem to place their faith in."

Sources

Periodicals

Daily Mail (London, England), April 19, 2011, p. 18.
Guardian (London, England), April 30, 2011.
New York, March 28, 2011.
Times (London, England), November 17, 2010, p. 1; April 30, 2011, p. 27.
Vanity Fair, November 2008, p. 198; December 2010.

Online

"Katie Nicholl: The Secrets of Kate and William's Lovers' Pact," *Vanity Fair*, http://www.vanityfair.com/online/daily/2011/03/-caption-here-weinstein-books.html (March 31, 2011).
"Royal Wedding: The Kate Middleton Story," BBC News, http://www.bbc.co.uk/news/uk-11767308.tif (March 31, 2011).

—Carol Brennan

Michael Cera

Actor

Born Michael Austin Cera, June 7, 1988, in Brampton, Ontario, Canada; son of Luigi (a Xerox technician) and Linda (a day care worker) Cera.

Addresses: *Management*—Thruline Entertainment, 9250 Wilshire Blvd. #100, Beverly Hills, CA 90212.

Career

Actor in films, including: *Frequency*, 2000; *Steal This Movie*, 2000; *Ultimate G's: Zac's Flying Dream*, 2000; *Confessions of a Dangerous Mind*, 2002; *Rolie Polie Olie: The Great Defender of Fun* (voice), 2002; *Darling Darling*, 2005; *Clark and Michael*, 2006; *Juno*, 2007; *Superbad*, 2007; *Extreme Movie*, 2008; *Nick and Norah's Infinite Playlist*, 2008; *Paper Heart*, 2009; *Scott Pilgrim vs. the World*, 2009; *Year One*, 2009; *Youth in Revolt*, 2009; *Bad Dads*, 2011. Television appearances include: *I Was a Sixth Grade Alien*, YTV, 1999; *Noddy*, 1999; *Switching Goals* (movie), 1999; *Twice in a Lifetime*, 1999; *La Femme Nikita*, 2000; *Real Kids, Real Adventures*, 2000; *Braceface*, 2001; *Doc*, PAX, 2001; *The Familiar Stranger* (movie), 2001; *The Grubbs*, 2001; *I Was a Rat* (movie), 2001; *My Louisiana Sky* (movie), 2001; *Stolen Miracle* (movie), 2001; *Walter and Henry* (movie), 2001; *The Berenstain Bears* (animated), 2003; *Custody of the Heart* (movie), 2003; *Exit 9* (movie), 2003; *Rolie Polie Olie* (animated), 2003; *Arrested Development*, FOX, 2003-06; *What Katie Did* (movie), 2004; *Wayside School* (animated special), Teletoon, 2005; *Tom Goes to the Mayor*, Cartoon Network, 2006; *Veronica Mars*, 2006; *Derek and Simon: The Show*, 2007; *Children's Hospital*, 2008-10; *Drunk History*, 2010. Film work includes: director, producer, writer and editor, *Clark and Michael*, 2006; composer, *Paper Heart*, 2009.

Awards: Future Classic Award (with others), TV Land Awards, for *Arrested Development*, 2004; Breakthrough Artist Award, Austin Film Critics Association, for *Juno* and *Superbad*, 2007; award for most promising performer, Chicago Film Critics Association, for *Juno* and *Superbad*, 2007; award for best performance by a male—film, Canadian Comedy Awards, for *Superbad*, 2008; best actor in a motion picture, comedy, or musical, Satellite Awards, for *Scott Pilgrim vs. the World*, 2010.

Sidelights

Canadian actor Michael Cera has built his career playing nerdy, often naive characters in popular teen films like *Superbad*, *Juno*, and *Nick and Norah's Infinite Playlist*. He began acting as a child growing up in Canada, first appearing in television commercials before moving on to television and films. Cera's breakout role came on American television, playing George Michael Bluth on the FOX comedy *Arrested Development*. While critics regularly lauded his ability to be a subtle, relatable actor, Cera did not take acting particularly seriously. He told Cass Bird of *GQ*, "I don't really think about my career. I could stop acting tomorrow."

Born on June 7, 1988, in Brampton, Ontario, Canada, he is the son of Luigi and Linda Cera. His father was a native of Sicily who worked as a Xerox technician while his mother was raised in Montreal and was employed as a day care worker. The middle child, Cera has an older sister, Jordan, and a younger sister, Molly. Cera was interested in acting from an early age. He told Maryam Siddiqi of Canada's *Financial Post*, "I'd been wanting to act since I was four. I've just always been into it." Two of his inspirations were Bill Murray and Mel Brooks.

Cera's first acting experience came at nine when he had an unpaid role in a Tim Horton's commercial for summer camps in Canada. He went on to appear in other television commercials, including Pillsbury, but once, at age ten, auditioned for 200 commercials in a row without being cast. Cera told Benjamin Leszcz of the *National Post*, "It's discouraging. Commercial producers want you to be really hammy. Finally, I said, 'Can we not go for commercials anymore?'"

By 1999, Cera was working professionally on television, with guest spots on shows like *Twice in a Lifetime* and *Noddy*. In 1999, he also spent a year on the YTV series *I Was a Sixth Grade Alien*. The following year, he made his first three films: *Ultimate G's: Zac's Flying Dream*, *Steal This Movie*, and *Frequency*. Over the next few years, Cera regularly took parts on television movies and small roles in Hollywood films like 2002's *Confessions of a Dangerous Mind*.

As he reached adolescence, Cera developed an enduring gawkiness that furthered his career. To really pursue acting, the young Cera began moving between his home in Brampton, a Toronto suburb, and Los Angeles. To facilitate his career, his mother quit her job so they could live in Los Angeles part time. He remained enrolled in a school in Brampton and completed work online when he worked in California.

This move was especially key when Cera was cast in a regular role on a series for a major American television network in 2003. On the cult hit situation comedy *Arrested Development*, he played George Michael Bluth, the son of Michael Bluth (played by Jason Bateman) and grandson of George Bluth (played by Jeffrey Tambor), who are the patriarchs of their odd, if not dysfunctional, family. Convicted of a white collar crime, George Bluth is serving time and Michael Bluth, the sanest member of his family, is trying to keep his family intact.

Describing his role, Cera told Leszcz of the *National Post*, "I'm glad I get to play a more humble, passive character. It's fun playing a part that's not a smart-

ass kid. I like how George Michael doesn't know how to react to his family, but doesn't want to show that he's weirded out." Critics responded positively to the sincerity of his character and he became a breakout star from the show.

Discussing the importance of the series to his career, Cera explained to Siddiqi of the *Financial Post*, "Being part of *Arrested Development* has meant a huge deal to me both professionally and personally. It's definitely the funniest thing I've ever worked on, and everyone involved in it is equally excited about getting to do it, which makes for an extremely pleasant work environment." Though *Arrested Development* won six Emmy Awards and was beloved by critics, it failed to find a large audience and was cancelled in late 2005. The last shows aired in 2006.

While appearing on *Arrested Development*, Cera worked on other projects, including more television movies and a web series made with friend Clark Duke. As he had throughout his career, he did voice work for animated series and specials. In 2001, he lent his voice to *Braceface*, while in 2003 he appeared on *The Berenstain Bears*. In 2005, Cera provided the voice of Todd in the animated special *Wayside School*, which made its debut on the Canadian network Teletoon. Based on the popular series of books for children, *Wayside School* is set at an elementary school that was built on its side 30 stories high. Cera greatly enjoyed doing animated work, telling Bill Brioux of the *Toronto Sun*, "Anyone can do it. You can feel awful. It's incredible. You're in and out in 15 minutes."

After the cancellation of *Arrested Development*, Cera took on a few guest spots on television series like *Veronica Mars*. In 2007, Cera's career took off again when he began appearing in a series of films about teenagers and young adults that were extremely popular at the box office and made Cera a star. The first was the raunchy teen comedy *Superbad*, written by Seth Rogen—a film and television star in his own right—and his writing partner, Evan Goldberg.

Superbad was a coming-of-age story with heart about two socially inept high school students and best friends—played by Cera and Jonah Hill—who are about to graduate and go to different colleges. The film focuses on one night where they have to purchase alcohol to get into a party at the house of a popular girl at school. As Cera explained it to Cindy Pearlman of the *Chicago Sun Times*, "This isn't the typical high school movie where it's the jocks vs. the loser. You can still be a loser, but you still get to say hi to the popular girls and you can be friends with them. You slip under the radar and these girls might even like you a little bit."

In conjunction with *Superbad*, Cera and Hill appeared on the cover of *Entertainment Weekly*, which gave both young stars the highest visibility of their young careers. Critics lauded the film, with Chris Hewitt of St. Paul, Minnesota's *Pioneer Press* calling it "the funniest movie of the year." Hewitt also commented, "Michael Cera is the funniest actor alive." A few months later, many more people agreed with the release of another big hit, *Juno*.

Written by Diablo Cody and directed by Jason Reitman, the low budget, independent *Juno* focused on the teenaged titular character (played by Ellen Page) who finds herself pregnant by Cera's character and must deal with the consequences. The poignant, smart comedy was a box office hit as film audiences and critics alike responded positively to the journey Juno goes on that leads to her giving up her child for adoption.

While Cera was not the co-star of the film as he was in *Superbad*, *Juno* established him as a box office attraction. His supporting turn as track nerd Paulie Bleeker attracted many positive reviews. As David Wiegand wrote in the *San Francisco Chronicle*, "Cera, of course, again proves himself a master of deadpan, a kind of modern-day Buster Keaton whose slightest gesture, the flicker of change in a facial expression, communicates every thought in his character's head and feeling in his heart."

Cera followed *Juno* with another intelligent independent comedy, 2008's *Nick and Norah's Infinite Playlist*. In the film, Cera starred as Nick, a music-obsessed recent high school graduate who has an adventure in Manhattan to find a secret concert by his favorite band. Along the way, he becomes involved with Norah (played by Kat Dennings), a similarly obsessed high school student who is interested in Nick because of the mix CDs his ex-girlfriend has thrown away. Elements of hipster and thriller also are found in the film, which was a minor hit.

Cera appeared in another film in 2008, *Extreme Movie*, then three more in 2009. Cera moved into a different kind of comedy with *Year One*. Directed and co-written by Harold Ramis and co-starring Jack Black, the film is set in primitive/Biblical times. A critical and box office failure, it saw Cera playing the shy and uncertain Oh, a Neanderthal living in exile in Sodom. Also released in 2009 were the romantic, extremely low budget independent faux documentary film *Paper Heart*—in which he played himself as the film documented him and his girlfriend's relationship—and the more widely seen *Youth in Revolt*, which gave Cera his first starring role.

In the smart teen comedy *Youth in Revolt*, Cera played two characters, Nick Twisp and his alter ego Francois Dillinger. Twisp is a teen obsessed with film who must deal with the bad life decisions of his mother and two of her boyfriends while winning the heart of the girl of his dreams. In the process, Cera also plays Twisp's alter ego, the smooth, womanizing lounge lizard Dillinger. While the film did not attract a wide audience, it did show Cera's ability to play a character other than his typical hesitant, shy guy. His Dillinger had swagger and an attitude not present in other performances, showing Cera's depth as an actor.

Youth in Revolt's director, Miguel Arteta, praised Cera's acting abilities. Arteta told Jay Stone of the Canwest News Service, "He's one of my favourite actors. He reminds me of an early Peter Sellers in his ability to be very subtle, but universally people can relate to him. Even though he's not moving his face, you can read his thoughts. You know when a thought is being formed in his head. You can see the thought process in his face without him doing anything at all. Most actors aren't that subtle."

Cera's next film was a cult hit and saw him take another leading role that carried the film. Based on a series of graphic novels, *Scott Pilgrim vs. the World* features Cera playing a 23-year-old musician who is out to win the heart of a new, impossibly cool girlfriend, Ramona Flowers (played by Mary Elizabeth Winstead). To do so, he must defeat all of her seven evil exes, and does so with surreal videogame flourishes. While the film was given critical kudos for its wit, dream-like nature, and vivid special effects, its audience was enthusiastic but limited.

Cera had more films in the works for 2011 and 2012, but he also enjoyed down time. In his free time, he plays guitar. His father played guitar and Cera picked it up from him as a child. Cera once stated that his most prized possession was a Fender Stratocaster. One of his indulgences while on *Arrested Development* was buying a Martin acoustic guitar for $1,000. He is also an enthusiastic golfer. Cera would like to write and direct his own film projects in the future.

Explaining Cera's appeal as an actor, Sonny Bunch of the *Washington Times* said, "Mr. Cera is a[n] ... unlikely leading man. Although he has an undeniable boyish charm, one would never confuse him for Paul Newman or Tom Cruise. But like Dustin Hoffman before him, Michael Cera has tapped into a very real current within the American consciousness. By choosing his projects wisely, Mr. Cera has developed broad appeal with both hipster tastemakers and the general public alike."

Sources

Periodicals

Canwest News Service, January 2, 2010; January 7, 2010.

Chicago Sun Times, August 12, 2007, p. D1; June 19, 2009, p. B1.

Financial Post (Canada), August 21, 2004, p. IN2.

GQ, October 2008, p. 208.

Mail on Sunday (London, England), February 3, 2008, p. 8.

National Post (Canada), January 4, 2006, p. AL1.

New York Magazine, January 4, 2010.

New York Times, November 9, 2003, sec. 13, p. 4.

Pioneer Press (St. Paul, MN), August 16, 2007.

San Francisco Chronicle, December 14, 2007, p. E1.

San Jose Mercury News, September 24, 2008.

Time Out, August 26, 2010, p. 20.

Toronto Sun, November 17, 2005, p. 110.

Washington Times, October 3, 2008, p. B1.

Winnipeg Sun (Manitoba, Canada), August 16, 2007, p. 18.

Wired, July 2010, p. 124.

Online

"Michael Cera," Internet Movie Database, http://www.imdb.com/name/nm0148418/ (February 22, 2011).

—A. Petruso

Georgina Chapman and Keren Craig

© McMullan Co/SIPA/newscom

Fashion designers for Marchesa

Born Georgina Chapman, April 14, 1976, in London, England; daughter of Brian Chapman (an organic coffee distributor) and Caroline Wonfor (a journalist); married Harvey Weinstein (co-founder of Miramax Films); children: India. Born Keren Craig in 1976 in England; married Piers North (an art director); children: Delilah. *Education:* Chapman: Wimbledon School of Art, 2001. Craig: Brighton Art College, 2000.

Addresses: *Office*—Marchesa, 601 W. 26th St., Ste. 1425, New York, NY, 10001. *Web site*—http://www.marchesa.com.

Career

Chapman: Actress in commercials and films including: Head and Shoulders and Soothers commercials; *Desire*, 2001; *Jeffrey Archer: The Truth*, 2002; *Shanghai Knights*, 2003; *Sons and Lovers*, 2003; *Bride and Prejudice*, 2004; *Piccadilly Jim*, 2004; *A Soldier's Tunic*, 2004; *Zemanovaload*, 2005; *The Business*, 2005; *Danny the Dog*, 2005; *Derailed*, 2005; *Match Point*, 2005; *Factory Girl*, 2006; *Awake*, 2007; *Grindhouse*, 2007; *Nanny Diaries*, 2007. Craig: Did textile design, 2000-04. Co-founders and co-owners, Marchesa, 2004—.

Sidelights

Marchesa Luisa Casati was an eccentric and glamorous socialite who wore live snakes as jewelry. She would take evening walks in nothing but her fur coats. She dined surrounded by wax mannequin figures rumored to contain the ashes of former lovers and was served by a staff of naked servants gilded in gold leaf. She traveled wherever her whims took her and collected castles and wild animals. She often walked a pair of cheetahs who wore diamond-studded collars. She was the most scandalous woman of her era. Georgina Chapman and Keren Craig named their fashion design house, Marchesa, after Luisa Casati. The duo decided that this more accurately represented the spirit of fashion that they wished to evoke, rather than simply calling their business Chapman and Craig, which Chapman felt sounded like a dentist's office.

The lives of Chapman and Craig are far from mundane. Both were born in Britain in 1976 and met when they were teenagers at the Chelsea College of Art and Design. While Chapman was in college, she began modeling to pay for her studies and to enable her to travel. A tall, lanky woman with beautiful green eyes and high cheekbones, Chapman was in demand and was seen in commercials for such products as Head and Shoulders and Soothers. She studied costume design at the Wimbledon College of Art. Just as Marchesa traveled the world, so has Chapman. In an interview with Lisa Grainger of the London *Telegraph*, when asked what was the "roughest" place to which she had traveled, Chapman responded that she had backpacked from Australia through Thailand and Vietnam to Nepal and India and that "some of the places had no heating and hundreds of bedbugs." When she and Craig were 19 they traveled together to Nepal and stayed in rest houses. In their mid-thirties the duo have an active schedule that includes a great deal of jet-setting around the world to premiere their beautiful designer fashions on runways and red carpets. Chapman told Grainger that she travels "at least once every four weeks."

Marchesa gowns are a combined effort, also drawing upon Craig's textile and embroidery design experience. Craig graduated from Brighton Art College with a bachelor's degree in fashion textiles and did freelance work in printmaking. Her skills are utilized to create or select the beautiful and unusual fabrics from which the gowns are constructed. Chapman's design sensibilities, drawing from her travels and experience in costume design, go into the creation of the structure of the gown. A Marchesa gown is a true piece of art and requires hours of skilled work before it is complete. A Marchesa dress might be prepared on a mannequin for months before it goes down a runaway.

The fact that Marchesa designs have come to be the haute couture of the red carpet and the night-out-on-the-town label for the rich and famous is testament to the quality of design, attention to detail, and fine craftsmanship that goes into every gown. Founded in 2005, Marchesa employs 40 people. Among the luminaries who have worn Marchesa gowns to A-list events are Sandra Bullock, who wore a Marchesa gown when accepting her Academy Award for Best Actress in 2011. Sarah Jessica Parker, Demi Moore, Rihanna, Blake Lively, Anne Hathaway, and Kristin Stewart have all chosen Marchesa dresses for big events.

Even though Chapman is married to Harvey Weinstein, co-founder of Miramax films, and has appeared in such movies herself as *Awake, Nanny Diaries, Grindhouse, Factory Girl, Piccadilly Jim, Derailed,* and *Shanghai Knights,* her Hollywood connections did not help her and Craig make Marchesa a success. The pair first began designing clothing together while they were in college. At one point, via a chance encounter, legendary fashion editor and muse Isabelle Blow saw the women's dresses and encouraged them to pursue fashion design. Chapman began making one-of-a-kind dresses for a small customer base out of her apartment in west London. After moving the tiny operation to an office in Soho, she asked Tamara Mellon of Jimmy Choo for advice on how to expand the business. Chapman told the *Telegraph*'s Francesca Babb that Mellon advised them to take their dresses to the Peninsula Hotel in Los Angeles during the awards season. Mellon said doing this and meeting with all the stylists to the stars was how she had been able to get her shoes worn by famous actresses. Chapman and Craig followed her advice and met celebrity stylist Rachel Zoe and publicist Nanci Ryder. They asked Ryder to represent them. She happened to also represent Renee Zellweger, who needed a gown for an event. Zellweger was the first celebrity to wear a Marchesa dress. After this the design house's gowns became well-known without being advertised simply because of the media photographing actresses and other notable people wearing the beautiful designs.

Even though their lives are filled with travel, celebrities, and glamour, Chapman and Craig work very hard to make their business a success. In 2009, just two days after giving birth to her daughter, Delilah, Craig was busy at a runway show. In addition to their well-known primary line of designer dresses, Marchesa also has a less expensive line of dresses called Notte by Marchesa. Chapman told Jane Keltner on the *Teen Vogue* Web site that they had received "loads of photographs from girls who've bought the dresses and worn them out to a big event. That's really great."

Sources

Books

Complete Marquis Who's Who, Gale, 2010.
People of Today, Debrett's Ltd., 2011.

Periodicals

People, December 4, 2006.
Telegraph, January 16, 2011; November 22, 2011.

Online

"About Casati," MarchesaCasati.com, http://www.marchesacasati.com/bio.html (November 22, 2011).
"Backstage Video: Marchesa's Georgina Chapman and Keren Craig on Just How Long It Takes to Make Those Fairy Princess Dresses," *New York* magazine, http://nymag.com/daily/fashion/2011/09/backstage_video_marchesas_geor.html (November 22, 2011).
Gale Biography in Context, Gale, 2011.

"Georgina Chapman: Designer to the Stars," *Telegraph,* http://fashion.telegraph.co.uk/news-features/TMG8246746/Georgina-Chapman-designer-to-the-stars.html (November 22, 2011).

"Georgina Chapman," Internet Movie Database, http://www.imdb.com/name/nm1312338/ (November 22, 2011).

"Georgina Chapman's Travelling Life," *Telegraph,* http://www.telegraph.co.uk/travel/celebritytravel/8907236/Georgina-Chapmans-travelling-life.html (November 22, 2011).

"Keren Craig," My Fashion Database, http://www.myfdb.com/people/51166-keren-craig (November 22, 2011).

Marchesa Official Web Site, http://www.marchesa.com/index.php (November 22, 2011).

"Marchesa," *Teen Vogue,* http://www.teenvogue.com/industry/designer/Marchesa (November 22, 2011).

—Annette Bowman

Laura Chinchilla

President of Costa Rica

Born Laura Chinchilla Miranda, March 28, 1959, in San José, Costa Rica; daughter of Rafael Ángel Chinchilla Fallas (a government official) and Emilce Miranda Castillo; married Mario Alberto Madrigal Díaz, January 23, 1982 (divorced, 1985); married José María Rico Cueto (a lawyer), March 26, 2000; children: son José Maria Rico (from second marriage). *Education:* Earned political science degree from the University of Costa Rica; Georgetown University, M.P.P., 1989.

Addresses: *Home*—San José, Costa Rica. *Office*—Casa Presidencial, San José, Costa Rica.

Career

Consultant to nongovernmental organizations (NGOs); vice minister for public security in the cabinet of Costa Rican President José Figueres Olsen, 1994-96; minister of public security, 1996-98; elected deputy from San José province to the National Assembly on the Partido Liberación Nacional (PLN) ticket, 2002; elected vice president of Costa Rica, 2006; resigned as vice president, 2008; won PLN presidential primary race, 2009; elected president of Costa Rica, 2009.

Sidelights

In 2010 Laura Chinchilla was sworn in as the first female president of Costa Rica. The Georgetown-educated candidate on the National Liberation Party ticket, Chinchilla is the protégé of her predecessor in the office, veteran political figure Oscar Arias

Sánchez. "Wives and working women continue overcoming barriers to make a greater Costa Rica," Chinchilla said in her victory speech on February 7, according to a report in the *Guardian.* "All the women and also the men who have accompanied us have made it possible that a daughter of this country can today be president."

Laura Chinchilla Miranda was born on March 28, 1959, in San José, Costa Rica's capital city. Her father, Rafael Chinchilla, went on to serve as government comptroller in the 1970s and '80s. Chinchilla grew up with three brothers who, she told Michelle J. Wong for the country's English-language newspaper, the *Tico Times,* "say I was bossy, that's the word they used. But the fact that my mother never made a distinction between me and my brothers is what made the difference for me."

At the University of Costa Rica, Chinchilla majored in political science and, like other Latin American university students around the world, showed her solidarity for leftist political movements across Latin America by wearing traditional textiles and other items of clothing made by indigenous or mestizo populations of the region. Her nation was an oasis of calm on the troubled Central American isthmus in the 1970s and '80s, thanks to a fortuitous decision years earlier to abolish its standing army after a six-week long civil war. Back in 1948, a leading political figure named José Figueras Ferrer ousted the junta that had seized control, and dissolved the military altogether, which prevented power from accumulating in any one sector. Costa Rica's neighbors, meanwhile—with the exception of Belize, a British colony until 1981—were subsequently torn by deadly political strife for decades. In places like El Salvador, Guatemala, and Nicaragua, military juntas either ousted democratically elected governments in the 1970s and '80s or propped up authoritarian right-wing regimes with the help of U.S. foreign-aid dollars and arms. In the case of the strategically sited Panama, home to the vital shipping canal of the same name, a large contingent of U.S. military personnel safeguarded any disruption to global maritime commerce.

Costa Rica, by contrast, invested in education and health care, and emerged as a peaceful, prosperous refuge on the isthmus that was often referred to as "the Switzerland of Central America." Its elections were free and fair, and the nation boasted one of the highest standards of living in all of Latin America. For decades Figueras' National Liberation Party (known by its Spanish-language acronym, PLN, for the *Partido Liberación Nacional*) held power, only occasionally losing elections to right-wing or center-right parties like the National Union Party or Christian Socialists. In 1986, Costa Ricans elected PLN candidate Óscar Arias Sánchez to the office of president. A year later, Arias was awarded the Nobel Peace Prize for successfully brokering a peace deal to end the devastating conflicts across Central America.

During this period Chinchilla was studying toward a master's degree in public policy at Georgetown University in Washington, which she earned in 1989. One of her professors was the formidable former U.S. ambassador to the United Nations, Jeane Kirkpatrick, a committed anti-communist whose arguments helped shape U.S. foreign policy in Latin America under President Ronald Reagan in the 1980s. The Reagan administration was criticized for allying with and providing support to groups who also fit the classic definition of terrorist outfits. Chinchilla was known to engage in voluble classroom debates with Kirkpatrick over U.S. foreign policy.

In the early 1990s, Chinchilla worked as a consultant to nongovernmental organizations, or NGOs. In the 1994 presidential contest, José Figueres Olsen—son of the three-term president and PLN founder—won the election, and appointed Chinchilla to serve as vice minister for public security. Two years later,

in 1996, President Figueres promoted her to the post of minister of public security, making her the first woman to serve in this post in Costa Rican history. Though she had no standing army to oversee, the country's national police force was well trained and equipped to deal with a variety of crises. Chinchilla warned that the same problems plaguing Costa Rica's neighbors—a sharp rise in violent crime and urban gang activity resulting from the underground drug-trafficking economy—could easily migrate into Costa Rica. She was criticized for being an alarmist, but her predictions would later prove true a decade later as crime rates in San José and other parts of Costa Rica began to spike.

Chinchilla was elected to Costa Rica's National Assembly in 2002 for a four-year term on the PLN ticket. In the 2006 presidential election, Arias returned to the ballot as the PLN candidate, and Chinchilla was chosen as one of his two vice presidential running mates. It was a close contest between Arias and the next leading candidate, Ottón Solís of the Citizen Action Party (Partido Acción Ciudadana, or PAC), but Arias won more than 40 percent of the vote and was declared the winner.

Chinchilla resigned her post as vice president in November of 2008 in order to prepare for a run to become the PLN candidate in the 2010 presidential election. She won the PLN primary race on June 8, 2009, besting her closest competitor, Johnny Araya, the former mayor of San José. In the February 2010 election, she faced several challengers, but the most significant among them were the PAC's Solís and Otto Guevara, a relative newcomer to politics in Costa Rica and the candidate for the Partido Movimiento Libertario, or Libertarian Movement Party (PML).

Official campaigning for the February 7 election kicked off a week earlier, on January 31. Chinchilla crisscrossed the country, even visiting a prison to ask for votes from inmates—a telling indicator of Costa Rica's generous approach to an inclusive, representative democracy—and speaking to crowds under signature green and white PLN banners and the slogan "Laura: Firme y Honesta" ("Laura: Firm and Honest"). Solís and Guevara, meanwhile, focused their attention on her close ties to Arias, claiming that if elected she would do little more than fulfill the outgoing president's mandate now that he was barred from seeking a third term in office.

Chinchilla won all seven of Costa Rico's provinces, a feat that rarely occurs in presidential contests in her country. She polled 47 percent of the vote, a solid 22 points ahead of Solís, and 26 points ahead of Guevara, who took 21 percent of the vote. She was not the first woman to run for Costa Rica's highest office, but she was the first to win it. "Today we are making history," she said in her victory speech, according to the Associated Press and the *New York Daily News*. "The Costa Rican people have given me their confidence and I will not betray it." She was sworn into office as the country's first female president on May 8, 2010, with her teenage son at her side. She is married to José María Rico Cueto, an attorney; an earlier marriage in the 1980s ended in divorce.

Costa Rica is a demonstrably Roman Catholic nation. There is even a section of the constitution that declares Roman Catholicism as the official state religion, and Chinchilla has stated her opposition to attempts to remove that declaration. While the PLN is a left-of-center party, Chinchilla has gained support from more conservative elements of the Costa Rican electorate by opposing the legalization of abortion and emergency contraception. On environmental issues, however, Chinchilla pledged to maintain the country's status as one of the "greenest" nations in the developed world; its biodiversity and impressive number of federally protected national parks and wildlife refuge areas helped make it one of the planet's top new eco-tourism sites. In 2007, Arias' government announced a program to make Costa Rica the world's first carbon-neutral nation by 2021, and Chinchilla affirmed her administration's allegiance to meeting that goal.

One of Chinchilla's first acts in office was to reimpose a ban on the controversial practice of open-pit mining, a ban that Arias had lifted. Even months later, the slurs of the campaign season still riled her. "The principal attack from my opponents was to call me, 'the Marionette of Oscar Arias,'" she told Wong in the *Tico Times* interview. "They would have never said that if [the candidate] had been a man; but they said it to me."

Chinchilla gained some international attention during her first year in office when Costa Rica and its neighbor, Nicaragua, seemed to be headed for potential conflict over an uninhabited island in the San Juan River, the waterway that serves as Costa Rica's northern border. Costa Rica's Isla Calero, or Calero Island, was a wilderness area in the river that had been the subject of dispute between the two countries for decades. The incident began in November of 2010 when the Nicaraguan government sent a dredging operation to the island. A Costa Rican newspaper asked the Nicaraguan official who was supervising the dredging why there were 50 soldiers on the island, and he told the reporter that Google Maps showed it as part of Nicaragua, not Costa Rica. That statement made headlines across the globe, reported *New York Times* journalist Robert Mackey. "The idea that Nicaragua had relied on Google Maps for a military deployment, and stumbled across a frontier because of a mistake by the search giant, set off peals of laughter worldwide, sent Google scrambling to explain and fix the error, and led journalists to discover another mistaken Google Map that could provoke an international incident."

But as Mackey's article noted, the two countries had been at odds over Calero Island for centuries. Chinchilla's government objected to the dredging operation because it was depositing silt on the Costa Rican banks of the river, and there were also fears that if untended the island could become a stopping point for drug traffickers. The Organization of American States (OAS) ordered both sides to refrain from sending any more personnel to the island. "This is not a border dispute," Mackey's report quoted her as saying. "We've had a lack of respect for the sovereignty of Costa Rica, primarily by the dredging of the river, affecting the Costa Rican bank, and secondly, with the entry of troops that remain."

Chinchilla is the fifth woman to lead a Latin American nation. The first was Nicaragua's Violeta Chamorro back in 1990, followed by the 1999 election of Mireya Moscoso in Panama. Chilean voters elected Michelle Bachelet to their nation's highest office in 2006, and a year later Cristina Elisabet Fernández de Kirchner became president of Argentina. A sixth woman, Dilma Rousseff of Brazil's Workers' Party, became the first woman to lead South America's largest economy when she was elected in October of 2010. Chinchilla faced some criticism for failing to attend Rousseff's inauguration on January 1, 2011, but her office said she had chosen to stay in San José and solve a potentially critical budget deficit of $997 million.

Chinchilla, her husband, and their son José Maria live in the Casa Presidencial in San José. In Latin American politics, her nation remains one of the few not marked by political instability in the modern era—Chamorro was the wife of a slain leftist leader, and even Rousseff had spent time as an underground operative for a Marxist guerrilla group in the 1960s. In Central America, only sleepy, posh Belize, which also lured valuable tourism revenue from abroad, boasts a similarly stable political history. Chinchilla's nation, wrote *Time*'s Tim Padgett, "has long given the isthmus a model to emulate—something it still urgently needs. Central

America may no longer be fighting the civil wars that ravaged it in the 1980s, but its problems are nonetheless mountainous and pose policy headaches for Washington in areas like the drug war, free trade, and illegal immigration."

Sources

Periodicals

Christian Science Monitor, February 8, 2010.
Guardian (London, England), February 8, 2010.

Online

"Chinchilla Forges Own Political Path," *Tico Times*, http://www.ticotimes.net/News/Top-Story/News/Chinchilla-forges-own-political-path_Friday-January-28-2011 (April 11, 2011).

"Costa Rica: A Woman in Charge?," *Global Post*, http://www.globalpost.com/dispatch/costa-rica/100204/laura-chinchilla-elections (April 11, 2011).

"Costa Rica Elects First Female President, Georgetown Grad Laura Chinchilla," Vox Populi Blog, *Georgetown Voice*, http://blog.georgetownvoice.com/2010/02/08/costa-rica-elects-first-female-president-georgetown-grad-laura-chinchilla/ (April 11, 2011).

"Costa Rica Elects Laura Chinchilla, Country's First Woman President," *New York Daily News*, http://articles.nydailynews.com/2010-02-08/news/27055682.tif_1_woman-president-costa-ricans-otton-solis (April 12, 2011).

"Costa Rica's Generational and Gender Changes," *Time*, http://www.time.com/time/world/article/0,8599,1963355,00.html (April 11, 2011).

"The Google Maps War That Wasn't, " The Lede blog, *New York Times*, http://thelede.blogs.nytimes.com/2010/11/19/the-google-maps-war-that-wasnt/?pagemode=print (April 12, 2011).

"Laura Chinchilla Wins Ruling Party's Primary Vote," *Tico Times*, http://www.ticotimes.net/dailyarchive/2009_06/060809.htm (April 12, 2011).

—*Carol Brennan*

Chris Colfer

Actor and singer

Born Christopher Paul Colfer, May 27, 1990, in Clovis, CA; son of Tim and Karyn Colfer.

Addresses: *Management*—Inphenate, 9701 Wilshire Blvd., 10th Fl., Beverly Hills, CA 90212.

Career

Joined Good Company Players, Fresno, CA, c. 2000; appeared in *Glee*, 2009—.

Awards: Teen Choice Awards for male scene stealer, Fox, 2010; SAG Award (with others) for outstanding performance by an ensemble in a comedy series, Screen Actors Guild, for *Glee*, 2010; Golden Globe for best performance by an actor in a supporting role, Hollywood Foreign Press Association, for *Glee*, 2011; Dorian Award for television comedy performance of the year, Gay & Lesbian Entertainment Critics Association, for *Glee*, 2011.

Sidelights

Singer-actor Chris Colfer quickly established himself as a breakout star of the musical hit comedy *Glee* shortly after it debuted in 2009. Among the cast, Colfer has been a steady scene-stealer with his portrayal of the sharp-witted, soprano-singing gay teen Kurt Hummel. In 2011, Colfer won a Golden Globe for best performance by an actor in a supporting role and found himself on the cover of *Entertainment Weekly* and among *Time* magazine's list of most influential people. With the help of Colfer's

acting ingenuity, *Glee* defied odds by surviving into its third season. Past music-based scripted shows never received the critical acclaim *Glee* has enjoyed. In explaining the *Glee* phenomenon to the *Telegraph*'s Craig McLean, Colfer summed up the show's popularity this way: "It's three things: there's something everyone can relate to, whether it's a character or a situation; it's the music—it just has this magical way of connecting everybody; and it promotes emotion. High school is such a trying, horrible time for everybody. Your hormones are crazy, your body's changing, all kinds of things are happening. It's the one hostage situation that everyone can relate to."

Christopher Paul Colfer was born on May 27, 1990, in Clovis, California, a conservative agricultural community in the San Joaquin Valley. Growing up, he struggled to fit in with his peers and his community. Colfer's Republican parents—Tim and Karyn Colfer—sent Colfer to Bible camp and dressed him in fancy Western gear before toting him off to the rodeo. In addition, the family had to deal with the medical issues surrounding Colfer's younger sister, Hannah, who suffers from severe epilepsy. Colfer found an outlet for his frustrations through acting. He began performing in elementary school, finding roles in local plays. Colfer portrayed

Snoopy in his first production. By the age of ten, he had joined the Good Company Players, a Fresno-based community theater company.

During his many years with the theater troupe, Colfer appeared in several shows, including *My Heart's in the Highlands, Second Space* and *Dad's Christmas Miracle.* Colfer also played the BB-gun wielding protagonist Ralphie in *A Christmas Story.* At the time, Colfer was homeschooled. This enabled him to stay out late for rehearsals and performances. Once Colfer reached his teens, he left the theater troupe so he could attend Clovis East High School. He also found a Hollywood agent to represent him and frequently made eight-hour round trips to Los Angeles for auditions but failed to land any roles.

Despite the setbacks, Colfer's parents remained hopeful and dedicated to his acting aspirations. In an interview with the *Los Angeles Times'* Maria Elena Fernandez, Karyn Colfer recalled her son's stage debut. "I saw a light go on in my son that has never turned off. We had this child, Christopher, who was extremely gifted in all areas. He was very smart academically. He was very mature for his age because of his sister's illness. And this was his outlet. It was a way for him to have something that was his very own, and his father and I committed to making sure that he went after this."

As for his adolescence, Colfer told *Entertainment Weekly's* Tim Stack that he never fit in. "The best way I can describe myself in high school was that I was kind of like a social llama. Like, where does the llama go? A llama's not a cow. It's not a horse. It might hang out with the duck once in a while, but it really has no place to belong. I was a social llama." During high school, Colfer was president of the writers' club and a member of the speech team. Colfer competed in several categories, including humorous interpretation, original prose and poetry, and dramatic interpretation. He earned awards at the local, regional, and state levels. During his senior year, Colfer qualified for the national competition but decided not to go because the event conflicted with an acting gig. During Colfer's senior year the school held a variety show. Most of his classmates performed gags and *Saturday Night Live*-type skits. Colfer, however, chose to write, star in, and direct a piece called *Shirley Todd*, a gender-switched musical spoof of *Sweeney Todd*.

Soon after his high school days came to a close, Colfer traveled to Los Angeles to audition for *Glee.* He tried out for the role of Artie, the show's wheelchair-driving, guitar-playing geek. Colfer sang "Mr. Cellophane" from the hit musical *Chicago*. Afterward, Colfer was not sure how well he did because he was nervous performing in front of the show's co-creator, Ryan Murphy, who had risen to fame as the mastermind behind the critically acclaimed drama *Nip/Tuck*. Murphy decided Colfer was not right for Artie but he wanted Colfer in the show, so he created a new character to explore Colfer's creative genius. "He's never been formally trained and I just thought he was so talented and gifted and unusual," Murphy told the *Los Angeles Times'* Fernandez. "I've never seen anyone who looks like him or acts like him or sounds like him. You'd think he'd been at Juilliard for six years but he hasn't."

Murphy chose to name Colfer's character Kurt Hummel because Colfer had played Kurt Von Trapp in a production of *The Sound of Music* and because Colfer reminded him of the cherub-faced porcelain Hummel figurines. Murphy called Colfer back to audition for the newly created character and ended up offering him the role before Colfer even returned home. In an interview with CNN's Piers Morgan, Colfer recalled the car ride home with his mother and that gleeful telephone call. "We were just passing Santa Monica Pier," Colfer said. "And the phone rang and she answered it. And then she just looked at me with that look, and I knew I had it." At the time, Colfer was working at a dry cleaner and had just begun classes at Fresno City College. Colfer happily dropped out to join the cast of *Glee.*

Glee kicked off its first season in September of 2009 and was nominated for 19 Emmy Awards and four Golden Globes. *Glee*—a mix of comedic wit, high drama, and choreographed musical numbers—centers around a high school glee club and follows storylines dealing with the characters' relationships, sexuality, and responses to societal influences. The school characters are fairly stereotypical of the average American teen. Characters include overachiever Rachel Berry (played by Lea Michele), the plus-size diva Mercedes Jones (played by Amber Riley), the juvenile jock Finn Hudson (played by Cory Monteith), the pregnant cheerleader Quinn Fabray (played by Dianna Agron), and Colfer's character, the effeminate glee guy. The glee club faculty sponsor is Will Schuester, played by Matthew Morrison, who starred in Broadway's *Hairspray*. Actress Jane Lynch also appears on the show, cast in the role of Sue Sylvester, the tracksuit-wearing, villainous coach of the school's cheerleading squad.

A typical show includes several converging storylines and three to five musical numbers. The *Glee* pilot aired in May of 2009 and included a rendition of Journey's "Don't Stop Believin'." The following day, the cast's choral remake of the song hit number one on the iTunes download chart. By the end of the first season, *Glee* had a regular following, with more than ten million viewers tuning in for the finale. The freshman show earned top honors at the 2010 Golden Globes, winning for best musical or comedy television series and besting veteran shows like *The Office* and *30 Rock*. In addition, Colfer turned his character into an award-winning role. In 2011, he won a Golden Globe for best performance by an actor in a supporting role. He used his acceptance speech to speak about bullying and reach out to kids who feel they do not fit in—much like he did in high school as a closeted gay teen.

From its inception, *Glee* generated a lot of interest—both positive and negative. Writing in *Slant Magazine*, television critic Julie Leung noted that *Glee* was similar to Disney's highly popular *High School Musical* franchise. Leung seemed to prefer *Glee*. "Unlike *High School*, though, Fox's musical comedy about a glee club full of misfits isn't as mind-numbingly white-bread or, for that matter, as annoying to watch. With classic Broadway and mainstream hits padding the pilot episode, and caricatures of high school faculty adding more generational depth, *Glee*'s charm is more akin to that of the *original* high school musical, *Grease*." On the flipside, the Parents Television Council spoke out against the show, specifically for a sexually-suggestive episode in which Gwyneth Paltrow, playing a substitute teacher, sang Joan Jett's "Do You Wanna Touch Me?"

One thing most television critics agree on is that Colfer is a touchstone for the show, often providing an emotional anchor for the storylines. Writing for the PhillyMag's *Philly Post*, Gail Shister praised *Glee* for supplying television with a "fully-realized adolescent homosexual"—a character Shister said had been missing from broadcast television since the mid-1990s when ABC aired *My So Called Life*. Shister praised Colfer for playing the role "to painful perfection."

Fellow cast member Mike O'Malley, who plays Colfer's father on the show, told *Entertainment Weekly*'s Stack that Colfer was easy to work beside. The episode where Colfer's character came out to O'Malley's character drew rave reviews. "He's able to inhabit this role in a way that is so easy to act opposite him if you have any sort of empathy," O'Malley said. "Anytime I'm in a scene with him, all I have to do is put my attention on him and what he is going through in the scene and then the words just come out."

Besides helping Colfer get his face out there, *Glee* has afforded Colfer the opportunity to get his voice out there as well. Each week, the songs featured on the show are available for download at iTunes. These remakes have been extremely popular. By the eighth episode of the first season, *Glee* had sold more than 2.5 million downloads. Downloads available from Colfer included "Defying Gravity" from the musical *Wicked*, a rendition of Beyoncé's "Single Ladies" and "Don't Cry for Me Argentina" from the famed 1970s musical *Evita*. In addition, the *Glee* cast released ten albums its first two seasons and in 2011 released *Glee: The Music, Presents the Warblers*, a disc of songs featuring Colfer and cast member Darren Criss. It debuted at number two on the *Billboard 200*.

After making a name for himself on *Glee*, Colfer branched out from acting and began writing scripts. He sold a pilot to Disney called *The Little Leftover Witch* about a little witch that gets lost on Halloween night and ends up in the care of a regular family. In addition, Colfer wrote *Struck by Lightning*, a coming-of-age movie about high school overachievers. Production began during the summer of 2011, with Colfer cast in the lead role. Colfer told *Entertainment Weekly*'s Stack that he enjoys screenwriting because he gets to create worlds and people. "I think I'm just addicted to storytelling whether I'm writing it or I'm acting it out. I'm just a born storyteller."

Selected discography

(With others) *Glee: The Music, Volume 1*, Columbia, 2009.

(With others) *Glee: The Music, Volume 2*, Columbia, 2009.

(With others) *Glee: The Music, The Power of Madonna*, Columbia, 2010.

(With others) *Glee: The Music, Volume 3 Showstoppers*, Columbia, 2010.

(With others) *Glee: The Music, Journey to Regionals*, Columbia, 2010.

(With others) *Glee: The Music, The Rocky Horror Glee Show*, Columbia, 2010.

(With others) *Glee: The Music, The Christmas Album*, Columbia, 2010.

(With others) *Glee: The Music, Volume 4*, Columbia, 2010.

(With others) *Glee: The Music, Volume 5*, Columbia, 2011.

(With others) *Glee: The Music, Presents the Warblers*, Columbia, 2011.

(With others) *Glee: The Music, Volume 6*, Columbia, 2011.

Sources

Periodicals

Back Stage, September 3, 2009, p. 8.
Entertainment Weekly, November 12, 2010, pp. 46-48.
Fresno Bee, May 18, 2009, p. D1; July 9, 2010, p. A1; January 16, 2011, sec. Spotlight, p. 8; January 20, 2011, p. B4.
Guardian (London, England), November 9, 2009, p. 2.
Rolling Stone, April 15, 2010; September 16, 2010, pp. 50-52.

Online

"Chris Colfer's Journey From Small Town to *Glee,*" *Los Angeles Times,* http://latimesblogs.latimes.com/showtracker/2009/09/glee-creator-and-executive-producer-ryan-murphy-discovered-chris-colfer-but-dont-tell-the-young-actor-that-it-makes-him-feel.html?cid=6a00d8341c630a53ef0120a78f0161970b (April 4, 2011).

"*Glee* Is Gay," *Philly Post,* http://blogs.phillymag.com/the_philly_post/2010/11/16/glee-is-gay (June 4, 2011).
"*Glee:* Season One," *Slant Magazine,* http://www.slantmagazine.com/tv/review/glee-season-one/100 (June 4, 2011).
"*Glee* Star Chris Colfer: Who Could've Predicted All of This?" CNN, http://www.cnn.com/2011/SHOWBIZ/05/20/piers.morgan.chris.colfer.glee/index.html (June 4, 2011).
"*Glee* Star Chris Colfer Discusses His New Pilot for Disney and Kurt's Return to McKinley," *Entertainment Weekly,* http://insidetv.ew.com/2011/04/22/glee-chris-colfer-disney-pilot/ (June 4, 2011).
"*Glee:* The Making of a Musical Phenomenon," *Telegraph,* http://www.telegraph.co.uk/culture/8271318/Glee-the-making-of-a-musical-phenomenon.html (June 6, 2011).
"*Glee* Warblers Album Flies High on Billboard 200," *Billboard,* http://www.billboard.com/news/glee-warblers-album-flies-high-on-billboard-10051558.tif42.story#/news/glee-warblers-album-flies-high-on-billboard-10051558.tif42.story (June 4, 2011).

—Lisa Frick

Suzanne Collins

Author

Born in 1962, in New Jersey; daughter of an Air Force officer; married Cap Pryor (an actor). *Education*: Indiana University, Bloomington, IN, B.A.; New York University, M.F.A.

Addresses: *Home*—Sandy Hook, CT. *Publisher*—c/o Scholastic Inc., 557 Broadway, New York, NY 10012-3999. *Web site*—http://www.suzannecollinsbooks.com/.

Career

Wrote scripts for children's television, 1990s—; published first novel, *Gregor the Overlander,* 2003; published *The Hunger Games,* 2008.

Awards: Children's book of the year, New Atlantic Independent Booksellers Association, for *Gregor the Overlander,* 2004; Cybils Award for young adult fantasy & science fiction, Children's and Young Adult Bloggers' Literary Awards, 2008; notable book, *New York Times,* for *The Hunger Games,* 2008; Fanfare award, *Horn Book Magazine,* for *The Hunger Games,* 2008; best book of the year, *Publishers Weekly,* for *The Hunger Games,* 2008; best book of the year, *School Library Journal,* for *The Hunger Games,* 2008; editors' choice book, *Booklist,* for *The Hunger Games,* 2008; best book of the year, *Kirkus Reviews,* for *The Hunger Games,* 2008; Georgia Peach Book Award for Teen Readers, Georgia Library Media Association, for *The Hunger Games,* 2010; TIME 100, *TIME* magazine, 2010; California Young Reader Medal, California Library Association, et al., for *The Hunger Games,* 2011.

Sidelights

Best-selling author Suzanne Collins is best known as the literary voice behind the popular young adult Hunger Games trilogy. Composed of 2008's *The Hunger Games,* 2009's *Catching Fire,* and 2010's *Mockingjay,* the series garnered numerous critical accolades for its gripping, unsparing depiction of a dystopian world in which a powerful government forces a small group of teenagers to compete in televised war games to the death. Readers quickly embraced the trilogy, keeping *The Hunger Games* on the *New York Times* best-seller list for more than 100 consecutive weeks, leading to the printing of more than six million copies of the trilogy's installments. In 2010, Collins' mass appeal earned her a spot on *TIME* magazine's list of the 100 most influential people of the year, with Lizzie Skurnick proclaiming that Collins was "a literary fusioneer, that rare writer who is all things to all readers." *Entertainment Weekly* also named her entertainer of the year for 2010. At the same time, pre-production had begun in earnest on a film adaptation of *The Hunger Games.* In addition to the Hunger Games trilogy, Collins is the author of the five-part children's series called the Underland Chronicles, the picture book *When Charlie McButton Lost Power,* and numerous scripts for television programs including *Clarissa Explains It All* and *The Mystery Files of Shelby Woo*.

The youngest of four children, Collins was born in 1962 in New Jersey and was raised mostly in Indiana and, later, Brussels, Belgium. Growing up, her father—a career Air Force officer and history enthusiast—introduced the future writer to the darker aspects of human civilization. Speaking in an interview published on the Scholastic Web site, Collins explained that "it wasn't enough to visit a battlefield, we needed to know why the battle occurred, how it played out, and the consequences.... He ... seemed to have a good sense of exactly how much a child could handle, which is quite a bit." Collins' father also influenced the content of the Hunger Games trilogy by actively hunting game and collecting edible plants as a way to supplement the family's food supplies, a remnant of his own experiences growing up during the Great Depression of the 1930s and a foreshadowing of the trilogy's characters' reliance on outdoor survival skills.

Collins attended Indiana University, where she met her husband Cap Pryor. After graduation, she moved to New York City and received a graduate degree in dramatic writing from the city's New York University. During the 1990s, she worked as a writer for children's television, contributing to such Nickelodeon programs as *Clarissa Explains It All, The Mystery Files of Shelby Woo, Little Bear, Oswald,* and *Wow! Wow! Wubbzy,* along with serving as head writer for the public television series *Clifford's Puppy Days,* and contributing scripts to the WB program *Generation O!* In 2001, she co-wrote the script for the Rankin and Bass holiday special *Santa Baby!* with Peter Bakalian that was nominated for a Writers' Guild of America award. Even after Collins transitioned to writing full-length children's books, she remained active as a television script writer, in part because of the opportunity to pursue a more uplifting storyline. "When I was working on *The Hunger Games*—there's not a lot of levity in it—I'd do a *Wubbzy* script," she told Rick Margolis of *School Library Journal.* "It's an enormous relief to spend some hours in Wuzzleburg ... where I know things are going to work out just fine and all the characters will be alive at the end of the program."

During the early 2000s, Collins shifted her focus from television to prose. The result was the *Underland Chronicles,* a series of five children's books following the story of eleven-year-old New York City resident Gregor in the fantastic world of the Underland. Hidden beneath the city, the Underland is home to a secret human society and a wide collection of talking creatures from cockroaches to massive spiders. Over the course of the series, Gregor takes part in the conflict brewing in the Underland and ultimately faces off against a giant evil rat called the Bane. In writing the series, Collins made a conscious decision to include dark topics and themes often left out of children's books. "Kids will accept any number of things," she told *Instructor* magazine. "The Underland Chronicles ... features death, loss, and violence. The third book has biological warfare, the fourth book has genocide, the fifth book has a very graphic war.... I think somehow if you went on that journey with me from the beginning, you kind of worked into the more violent places and were prepared by what had come before."

In 2008, Scholastic published *The Hunger Games,* the first novel in a planned trilogy of the same name. Like the Underland Chronicles, *The Hunger Games* combined elements of science fiction and adventure to create a distinctive world noticeably unlike those typically found in children's books. The novel takes place in a dystopian future in which climate change and war have greatly altered the face of North America to create the nation of Panem. A lengthy intercontinental war left the majority of the former United States under the iron rule of an authoritarian government. Based in an extremely wealthy capital city, the government and capital's citizens rely on the products made in Panem's remaining 12 administrative districts. To remind its subjects of its power over them and to punish them for their earlier rebellion, Panem's government requires each of the 12 districts to send one young man and young women between the ages of 12 and 18 to participate in a televised fight to the death known as the Hunger Games. The victor of this annual tournament reaps benefits for his or her home district and a lifetime of relative ease, but at the expense of the deaths of the remaining 23 contestants, known as "tributes." *The Hunger Games* follows the experience of Katniss Everdeen, a 16-year-old female tribute from District 12, Panem's poorest region, as she enters and competes in the Hunger Games.

Collins has often attributed the inspiration for the story to the Greek myth of Theseus and the Minotaur, in which the city of Athens was forced to send 14 young people to the island of Crete, where they were killed and eaten by a half-man, half-bull creature known as the Minotaur. The practice is eventually ended when the hero Theseus volunteers to enter the Minotaur's labyrinth and succeeds in killing the creature. "Katniss is a futuristic Theseus," Collins told Margolis in the same *School Library Journal* interview. "But I didn't want to do a labyrinth story. So I decided to write basically an updated version of the Roman gladiator games." The story also reflected the author's viewpoint on the popularity of modern reality television programs. Speaking to *Instructor* magazine, Collins commented, "while I think some of those shows can succeed on different levels, there's a voyeuristic thrill, watching people being humiliated or brought to tears or suffering physically. And that's what I find very disturbing. There's this potential for desensitizing the audience so that when they see real tragedy playing out on the news, it doesn't have the impact it should." Despite its grisly subject matter, young and adult readers alike embraced the novel, lavishing praise and sending the book to the top of the best-seller lists. Hailing the work as "brilliantly plotted and perfectly paced," John Green assessed in the *New York Times* that "the considerable strength of the novel comes in Collins' convincingly detailed world-building and her memorably complex and fascinating heroine. In fact, by not calling attention to itself, the text disappears in the way a good font does: nothing stands between Katniss and the reader, between Panem and America."

Anticipation was high for the second book in the series, 2009's *Catching Fire*. Picking up Katniss' story shortly after the conclusion of the first novel's Hunger Games, *Catching Fire* followed her travels throughout Panem as discontent began to turn into full-scale rebellion. The protagonist is forced to complete in a special 75-year anniversary Hunger Games that pits former victors against one another in the arena. Katniss' actions in the arena further encourage widespread unrest, and she and some of her fellow competitors eventually escape from the arena to the great anger of Panem's government. In doing so, Katniss discovers that District 13—an area long thought to have been completely destroyed in the wars that installed Panem's current government—had survived the conflict. The book debuted at the top of several best-seller lists and again garnered widespread critical accolades. Writing in *School Library Journal*, Megan Honig judged that "this sequel has enough action to please *Hunger Games* fans and leaves enough questions tantalizingly unanswered for readers to be desperate for the next installment," while *Booklist*'s Ian Chipman pointed out that "this book only needs to be good enough to satisfy its legions of fans. Fortunately, it's great."

Collins concluded Katniss' story in the third installment, 2010's *Mockingjay*. Another instant best seller, *Mockingjay* moved some 450,000 printed and electronic copies in its first week of publication. The events of this novel chronologically follow those of *Catching Fire* closely, and involve Katniss' role as the titular mockingjay—a genetically modified bird that the rebels adopt as their symbol. Despite her misgivings about being used as an engineered media focal point, Katniss helps the leaders of the rediscovered District 13 and others take on Panem's government in a full-scale invasion. Calling the series' final book "the grimmest yet," Sue Corbett of *People* judged it to be "a riveting meditation on the costs of war." Jane Henriksen Baird of *School Library Journal* agreed, noting, "Collins is absolutely ruthless in her depictions of war in all its cruelty, violence, and loss, leaving readers, in turn, repulsed, shocked, grieving and, finally, hopeful."

Although Collins has confirmed that Katniss' story ended with the close of *Mockingjay*, the Hunger Games series continued to have fresh life in a different medium. In 2009, production studio Lionsgate purchased the option to make *The Hunger Games* into a feature film. Drawing on her background as a television writer, Collins drafted her novel into a screenplay. "Adapting a book into a two-hour viewing experience is a challenge," she told Tina Jordan of *Entertainment Weekly*. "You want to preserve the essence while making the film stand on its own." Further refinements were made to the screenplay by *The Hunger Games* director Gary Ross. Fans closely watched the development of the film, particularly debating which actresses could best bring Katniss Everdeen to the big screen. In early 2011, Lionsgate and Collins announced their selection for this pivotal role: 20-year-old Academy Award-nominated actress Jennifer Lawrence. Although some fans questioned the actress' slightly more advanced age than the novel's lead, Ross and Collins firmly supported Lawrence's suitability. "I believed that this was a girl who could hold out that handful of berries and incite the beaten down districts of Panem to rebel.... Could [Lawrence] believably inspire a rebellion? Did she project the strength, defiance, and intellect you would need to follow her into certain war? For me, she did," Collins wrote in an open letter to fans quoted by Karen Valby of *Entertainment Weekly*. Additional cast announcements soon followed, including Josh Hutcherson as Peeta Mellark and Liam Hemsworth as Gale Hawthorne. This young cast was joined by seasoned film veterans such as Woody Harrelson in the role of Haymitch Abernathy, Elizabeth Banks in the role of Effie Trinket, and Donald Sutherland in the role of Panem's president. Filming began on location in North Carolina in the spring of 2011 for an anticipated release in March of 2012; Lionsgate also suggested that as many as three sequels could continue the series' story on the big screen.

Selected writings

Gregor the Overlander, Scholastic (New York City), 2003.
Gregor and the Prophecy of Bane, Scholastic, 2004.

Gregor and the Curse of the Warmbloods, Scholastic, 2005.

When Charlie McButton Lost Power, Putnam (New York City), 2005.

Gregor and the Marks of Secret, Scholastic, 2006.

Gregor and the Code of Claw, Scholastic, 2007.

The Hunger Games, Scholastic, 2008.

Catching Fire, Scholastic, 2009.

(Contributor) *12,* Feiwel and Friends (New York City), 2009.

Mockingjay, Scholastic, 2010.

Sources

Books

Contemporary Authors, New Revisions Series, Gale, 2011.

Periodicals

Booklist, July 1, 2009, p. 62.

Entertainment Weekly, December 10, 2010; April 1, 2011.

Instructor, September-October 2010, p. 51.

New York Times, November 7, 2008; April 8, 2011.

People, September 13, 2010.

School Library Journal, September 2008, p. 30; September 2009, p. 154; August 2010, p. 24; October 2010, p. 110.

Star (Cleveland Co., NC), June 4, 2011.

Online

"A Conservation with Suzanne Collins," Scholastic, http://www.scholastic.com/thehungergames/media/qanda.pdf (June 6, 2011).

"Suzanne Collins," *TIME,* http://www.time.com/time/specials/packages/article/0,28804,1984685_1984940_1985512,00.html (June 6, 2011).

—*Vanessa E. Vaughn*

Ally Condie

Author and teacher

Born c. 1978; married Scott (an economics professor); children: three sons. *Education:* Graduated from Brigham Young University.

Addresses: *E-mail*—ally@allycondie.com. *Publisher*—c/o Dutton Juvenile Publicity, 345 Hudson St., New York, NY 10014. *Web site*—http://www.allysoncondie.com/; http://www.matched-book.com/.

Career

Taught high school English in New York state and Utah, c. early 2000s; published first novel *Yearbook,* 2006; launched bidding war with *Matched* manuscript, 2009; published *Matched* with Dutton/Penguin, 2010.

Sidelights

Utah-based young adult author Ally Condie came to fame in 2010 for her dystopian teen novel *Matched,* the first in a planned trilogy. The former high school English teacher had previously published a number of young adult novels with Mormon publishers, including the high school-based Yearbook trilogy and the stand-alone 2008 release *Freshman for President.* Undoubtedly talented, Condie took her newfound fame in stride.

Born around 1978, Condie was raised in Cedar City, Utah. She loved poetry and writing stories from an early age. Condie earned an English teaching de-

gree from Brigham Young University, then taught high school English in upstate New York and Utah. A lifelong reader, she was particularly fond of Wallace Stegner and Agatha Christie. The former's style proved inspirational, while Condie looked to Christie for inspiration on dialogue, pacing, and revelations. Condie's favorite book by the prolific murder mystery author was *The Murder of Roger Ackroyd.*

Quitting teaching after a few years when the first of her three sons with husband Scott was born, Condie found she missed students and books. She began spending hours writing in the basement, making herself write every day. Obviously gifted, Condie began publishing books with Deseret Books Company, a Mormon publishing company. Targeted at young adult readers, they featured Mormon themes and concerns. Condie's first books were a trilogy known as the Yearbook series.

The first novel in the series, 2006's *Yearbook,* focuses on three students starting high school and dealing with the newness of the institution, the worries, and emotions that come with it. The next novel in the series, 2007's *First Day,* centers on a new set of Mormon students in their junior year of high school. They face challenges like final exams, romance, mission trips, family responsibilities, and church responsibilities. In the final installment, 2008's *Reunion,* Condie's characters are more mature and self-aware as they enter college and come into their own.

Condie's next two novels were stand-alone titles. The first was 2008's *Freshman for President,* put out by another Utah-based publisher, Shadow

Mountain. In this novel, 15-year-old Milo Wright runs for the presidency of the United States, funding his run with a lawn-mowing business. While the idea seems unusual and interesting at first, Milo's campaign is derailed by commitments to family, homework, and his soccer team. Critics praised the novel with *ForeWord* noting, "Its timeliness in an election year will make it a great choice for teachers looking for ways to excite students about the American electoral process." Condie returned to Deseret Books for 2010's *Being Sixteen,* another teen-focused novel.

After publishing these five books, Condie looked to broaden her audience. The resulting book drew on her experience teaching high school English as well as her husband's knowledge about game theory and probability. (Her husband worked as an assistant professor of economics at Brigham Young University.) *Matched* was primarily about marriage, inspired in part by a time when Condie and her husband chaperoned a prom. They also had interesting discussions about what would happen if the perfect algorithm for bringing couples together was discovered. The manuscript for *Matched* only took nine months to write and launched a bidding war among eight publishers, resulting in a seven-figure deal for the trilogy. Condie later sold foreign rights to 30 countries and landed a film rights contract with Disney.

Matched was published in December of 2010. The novel focuses on 17-year-old heroine Cassia Reyes and explores the dystopian civilization in which she lives. The Society is a well-planned social economy where each stage of life is decided upon in advance for best results. Marriage happens at 21, death happens by the age of 80, and the Society even determines how its people die. Occupations and homes are also determined for people by the Society. Truly satisfying food is only served on special occasions, while the nutritionally valuable but unappealing gray-brown oatmeal is eaten much more often. There is no personal choice because what is best and perfect has already been determined, even in terms of clothing, songs, poems, and paintings.

In *Matched*, Cassia learns through a microcard that her marriage match is a boy she has known for much of her life, Xander Carrow, but because of a glitch in the matching process, she is also matched to an unknown boy from the Outer Provinces named Ky Markham. Cassia becomes a rebel, inspired in part by Dylan Thomas' "Do Not Go Gentle Into That Good Night," a poem forbidden by the controlling Society. She questions the intentions of the Society and blossoms in her emotional develop-

ment as she moves from perfectionist to rebel after small events prove to her that the government does not have its citizens' best interests at heart. The novel also explores the tension between the assigned destiny of her first match as determined by the Society, and the potential for what could have been as well as what might be possible with Ky.

As Condie explained to Ben Fulton of the *Salt Lake City Tribune,* "What if you had a society that looked only at probability and didn't care about anything else? What if probability was their religion? That scenario interested me. So did the great dichotomy of being a teenager. It's a time when everything seems new, and is happening for the first time, but you feel like you don't have enough power to experience the way you like." In another interview with Fulton for the *Salt Lake City Tribune,* Condie focused on Cassie, telling him: "Especially as a teenager, choice is all you want, and it's taken away from you again and again. My book is the story of a girl who falls in love with someone she can't marry. She then tries to decide if she wants to turn the world on its head."

Reviewers compared *Matched* to Aldous Huxley's *Brave New World,* Stephanie Meyer's *Twilight* novels, and the dystopian trilogy The Hunger Games. Natasha Harding of England's *Sun* called *Matched* a "must-read," continuing, "The fictitious tale about a young girl living in a perfect world captures your imagination and plays on your mind, long after you've put it down." Susan Carpenter, in the Newark, New Jersey, *Star-Ledger,* lauds, "*Matched* is a wonderful debut with strong, rather than strident, feminist undertones—a primer for young minds encouraged to question."

Matched made the top ten of the *New York Times* best-seller list, and was named by *Publishers Weekly* as one of the best children's books of 2010. *Crossed* was the next book in the trilogy, scheduled for publication on November 1, 2011, with the third installment planned for 2012. Though Condie had not taught school in several years, she continued to take state exams to keep her teaching license. Amidst this whirlwind, Condie remained humble, telling the *Salt Lake City Tribune*'s Fulton about *Matched* that, "The book has gotten a lot of buzz, but a successful book is not like a successful movie. It's only been out a short time. I guess what I'm saying is, maybe it's too early to call myself a success."

Selected writings

(As Allyson B. Condie) *Yearbook,* Deseret Book Company (Salt Lake City, UT), 2006.

(As Allyson B. Condie) *First Day*, Deseret Book Company, 2007.

(As Allyson B. Condie) *Reunion*, Desert Book Company, 2008.

Freshman for President, Shadow Mountain (Salt Lake City, UT), 2008.

Being Sixteen, Deseret Book Company, 2010.

Matched, Dutton Juvenile (New York City), 2010.

Crossed, Dutton Juvenile, 2011.

Sources

Books

Contemporary Authors Online, Gale, 2011.

Periodicals

Associated Press, December 20, 2010.

Daily Variety, September 15, 2010, p. 1.

Deseret Morning News (Salt Lake City, UT), November 27, 2010.

ForeWord, August 19, 2009.

Salt Lake Tribune, April 15, 2010.

Star-Ledger (Newark, NJ), December 19, 2010, p. 8.

The Sun (England), December 3, 2010, p. 82.

Time Out, December 9, 2010, p. 60.

Online

"Author Bio," *Matched* Official Web site, http://www.matched-book.com/bio.html (June 4, 2011).

Contemporary Authors Online Gale, 2011.

"FAQ," Ally Condie Official Web site, http://www.allysoncondie.com/frequently-asked-questions-2/ (June 4, 2011).

"Romancing the Future: Ally Condie's *Matched*," *Salt Lake Tribune*, http://www.sltrib.com/sltrib/entertainment/50949533.tif-81/condie-book-books-matched.html.csp (June 4, 2011).

—*A. Petruso*

Bradley Cooper

© Anthony Jones/PA Photos/Landov

Actor

Born January 5, 1975, in Philadelphia, PA; son of George (a stockbroker) and Gloria (Campano) Cooper; married Jennifer Esposito, December 21, 2006 (divorced, November 10, 2007). *Education:* Georgetown University, B.A., 1997; Actors Studio Drama School, The New School, M.F.A., 2000.

Addresses: *Publicist*—WKT Public Relations, 9350 Wilshire Blvd., Ste. 450, Beverly Hills, CA 90212.

Career

Actor in films, including: *Wet Hot American Summer*, 2001; *Bending All the Rules*, 2002; *Changing Lanes*, 2002; *My Little Eye*, 2002; *Wedding Crashers*, 2005; *Failure to Launch*, 2006; *The Comebacks*, 2007; *The Midnight Meat Train*, 2008; *Older Than America*, 2008; *The Rocker*, 2008; *Yes Man*, 2008; *All About Steve*, 2009; *Case 39*, 2009; *The Hangover*, 2009; *He's Just Not That Into You*, 2009; *New York, I Love You*, 2009; *The A-Team*, 2010; *Valentine's Day*, 2010; *The Hangover Part II*, 2011; *Limitless*, 2011. Executive producer of films, including: *Limitless*, 2011. Television appearances include: *Sex and the City*, HBO, 1999; *Wall to Wall Records* (movie), 1999; *The $treet*, 2000-01; *Alias*, 2001-03, 2006; *The Last Cowboy* (movie), 2003; *Miss Match*, 2003; *I Want to Marry Ryan Banks* (movie), 2004; *Touching Evil*, 2004; *Jack & Bobby*, 2004-05; *Law & Order: Special Victims Unit*, 2005; *Law & Order: Trial by Jury*, 2005; *Kitchen Confidential*, FOX, 2005-06; *Nip/Tuck*, FX, 2007-09; *Saturday Night Live*, NBC, 2009. Stage appearances include: *Elephant Man*, Circle in the Square Theatre, New York City, c. late 1990s; *Three Days of Rain*, 2006.

Awards: Hollywood Comedy Award, Hollywood Film Festival, 2007; Special Award—Comedy Star of the Year, ShoWest Convention, 2009.

Sidelights

American actor Bradley Cooper became a star with his work in such films as *The Hangover, The Hangover Part II,* and *The Wedding Crashers*. The handsome actor is best known for his work in comedies, but also had memorable roles in dramas and action films. Cooper began his career on television, most notably on the series *Alias,* which had him temporarily typecast in good guy roles. His work as the villain in *The Wedding Crashers* changed his role choices to include bad boys and roguish men. Of his acting career in Hollywood, Cooper told Michael Cidoni of the Associated Press, "You know, you're one movie away from falling off or ascending. That's the beautiful thing about this business."

Born on January 5, 1975, in Philadelphia, Pennsylvania, he was the son of Charles and Gloria Cooper. His father was a college basketball star and stockbroker with Merrill Lynch. Cooper was educated at Germantown Academy in Fort Washington, Pennsylvania, and was academically focused in his youth. He graduated high school in 1993 and entered Georgetown University, where he was selected for the Honors English program. Cooper was also a member of the crew team, winning a medal for his participation on the men's heavyweight crew team.

After graduating college in 1997, Cooper moved to New York City and enrolled in the master of fine arts program at the Actors Studio Drama School, then part of the New School in New York City. Of this choice, he told Bob Thompson of the Canwest News Service, "I was a late bloomer, but I always secretly wanted to be an actor." During his student years, he spent weekends working with LEAP (Learning through the Expanded Arts Program). This non-profit organization educated inner-city school children in acting and movement. For his thesis performance, he played John Merrick in *The Elephant Man* at Circle in the Square Theatre.

While still a student in the acting program, Cooper began acting professionally. Much of his early work was in television, including a 1999 guest spot on the hit HBO show *Sex and the City*. Cooper also appeared in a film, the coming-of-age comedy *Wet Hot American Summer*, which was released in 2001. Its filming caused him to miss his college graduation. He also had a part in a second feature, 2002's *Bending All the Rules*.

Cooper was going to move to Los Angeles to further his career, but delayed the transfer when he was cast on another television series, *The $treet*, in 2000. He also landed a role in the feature *My Little Eye*, released in 2002. *The $treet* ended its run in 2001, and Cooper finally moved to Los Angeles when he was cast in the espionage series *Alias*.

Alias began airing in 2001, and Cooper played sensitive journalist Will Tippin on the show. His character was a nice guy and the best friend to Jennifer Garner's leading character; this led him to be typecast for a time in good-guy roles. Cooper played the role for two seasons before the show moved in a new direction and his character was essentially gone the following season. After leaving *Alias*, he appeared in television movies like 2003's *The Last Cowboy* and 2004's *I Want to Marry Ryan Banks*. Cooper landed roles in short-lived series like 2003's *Miss Match* and 2004's *Touching Evil*, He also appeared in *Jack & Bobby*, which lasted a full season, from 2004 to 2005.

Cooper's career took a new direction in 2005. That year, he had guest spots on *Law & Order: Special Victims Unit* and *Law & Order: Trial by Jury*. He also was the star of the FOX series *Kitchen Confidential*. On the program, Cooper played a chef named Jack Bourdain who was once famous but was seeking a second chance at his career and life. The show was canceled halfway through its first season.

Cooper was able to break out of the nice-guy roles with his work in the 2005 feature *Wedding Crashers*. The director, David Dobkin, had no idea who he was when he auditioned or that he had played the good guy on *Alias*. Cooper gained weight to do the film and played Sack Lodge, the sociopathic boyfriend of Rachel McAdams' character. Cooper then appeared in the 2006 romantic comedy *Failure to Launch*, which starred Matthew McConaughey as a slacker who lives with his parents until he falls in love with the girl of his dreams. Cooper's Demo was his best friend who encourages the relationship. Also in 2006, Cooper appeared on Broadway in *Three Days of Rain*.

In 2007, Cooper returned to television, taking a recurring role on the hit FX series *Nip/Tuck*. The show focused on plastic surgery, and Cooper's character, Aidan Stone, was an unstable dramatic actor. Of the role, Cooper told Ben Carrozza of the Canwest News Service, "He's crazy.... I got there the first day and was like, 'Ryan [Murphy, show creator], can I just go and try and come up with stuff? And if you hate it, just tell me and I won't do it anymore.' I think one of the first things we shot was one of the emergency room scenes, and, I don't know, I just sort of went nuts—and they left it in."

While working on *Nip/Tuck* for two seasons, Cooper's film career flourished and he appeared in numerous films, including 2007's *The Comebacks*, and 2008's *Older Than America, The Rocker, The Midnight Meat Train*, and *Yes Man*. In the comedy *Yes Man*, Cooper plays Peter, the best friend to the film's focal point, the morose Carl, played by Jim Carrey. While Peter tries to help Carl turn his life around, it is a self-help guru who makes a difference by advocating saying yes to everything that comes your way. Cooper related to the idea, telling Ben Carrozza of the Canwest News Service, "My better days have been the days where I've embraced life more than rejected it, that's for sure."

Cooper's career reached new heights in 2009. He appeared in five films, including *New York, I Love You*, the thriller *Case 39*, the comedy *All About Steve*, and the romantic comedy *He's Just Not That Into You*. In *All About Steve*, Cooper played the boy toy that Sandra Bullock's character wants, while in *He's Just Not That Into You*, he played a philandering husband.

The sixth film of Cooper's that was released in 2009 was *The Hangover*, which was the surprise hit of the summer of 2009, became the highest-grossing R-rated comedy of all time, and made the actor a star and leading-man material. Directed by Todd Phillips, the film focuses on a bachelor party in Las Vegas that goes horribly wrong. Discussing the film, Cooper told Bob Thompson of the Canwest News

Service, "What I liked about all the craziness is that it's embedded in a sense of reality. It's odd and funny, but not just a bunch of comedic set pieces."

In *The Hangover,* Cooper played Phil, a discontented teacher, father, and husband, who instigates shenanigans and leads the bachelor party group on a night they forgot but must reconstruct to find the missing groom. He is also the straight man to much of the comedy in the film. Of Phil, Cooper told Michael Ordoña of the *Houston Chronicle,* "I kind of fell in love with Phil. He reminded me a lot of fathers I've met; their bark is much bigger than their bite. They are great fathers, and they love their wives and their friends more than anything." After *The Hangover,* Cooper hosted an episode of *Saturday Night Live.*

Cooper only had two films released in 2010: the ensemble romantic comedy *Valentine's Day* and the film version of the hit 1980s series, *The A-Team.* In the latter film, he worked out and got himself in excellent physical shape to play Face, and only improved his fitness level as the shoot went on. Cooper's character was described by Jay Stone of the Canwest News Service as "the handsome lady-killer whose irresistibility is established with a few shirtless scenes and thereafter rests on Cooper's bad-boy smile." *The A-Team* focuses on how the unit of rogue soldiers came together and work outside of the system to correct wrongs. While the film was not critically acclaimed, it was a box-office success.

In 2011, Cooper starred in and served as executive producer on the thriller *Limitless.* In this film, he played Eddie Morra, a novelist who is struggling to write his overdue book to fulfill a contract. Morra's brother-in-law offers him a pill called NZT that allows a person to access all of his or her brain power, become fully engaged in the world, and meet his or her full potential. The genius Morra becomes involved with a shadowy financier, Carl Van Loon (played by Robert DeNiro). Cooper explained to Jamie Portman of the Victoria, B.C. *Times Colonist* that if he had this access to such a drug in real life, "I'd definitely try to learn as many languages as I could right away, I think. And then I would probably, after that, learn as many instruments as I could. It would be incredible to start jamming with all these great musicians, and communicating with people wherever you are in all the different dialects. I mean, it would be incredible. I don't know what I would do after that, but I would still be an actor."

Also in 2011, *The Hangover Part II* was released. While Cooper made $600,000 for *The Hangover,* he earned five million dollars for the sequel. He told Alison Jones of the *Birmingham Post,* "I never thought I would get paid that much money in my whole life. It is not unbelievable but for me it was just insane." It was greenlit shortly before the release of the original, and was nearly the box-office hit that *The Hangover* was.

In *The Hangover Part II,* the bachelor party is held in Thailand, where Stu, played by Ed Helms, is getting married. Like *The Hangover,* the bachelor party here goes awry, this time in Bangkok, and the men involved do not remember what happens and must trace their steps to find the bride's little brother, who is lost. Discussing the film with Patricia Sheridan of the *Pittsburgh Post-Gazette,* Cooper declared, "I'm really proud of this movie and I love playing Phil and I love Phil in this movie…. I thought it was better than the first one. It's a very strong movie. It's dark. It's comedy. It's this weird wonderful relationship these three guys have."

Firmly established as a box-office draw, Cooper had more films scheduled for release including *The Words* and *The Place Beyond the Pines.* Yet he still worked to land the parts that he wanted. He told Kat Angus of the Canwest News Service, "More doors have opened, for sure, but it's not like I sit back with a cigar on Monday morning and go through the scripts that have been offered. That's not the case. I still put myself on tape to audition for movies and try to get roles."

Sources

Periodicals

Associated Press, May 19, 2009.
August Chronicle (GA), December 5, 2003, p. D10.
Birmingham Post, March 17, 2011, p. 10.
Canwest News Service, December 17, 2008; June 1, 2009; June 10, 2010; March 27, 2011; May 25, 2011.
Daily News (New York, NY), February 26, 2006, p. 47.
Details, June-July 2009, p. 114.
GQ, December 2009, p. 240.
Houston Chronicle, July 11, 2009, p. 2; March 16, 2011, p. 1.
Metro (UK), March 17, 2011, pp. 34–35.
New York Sun, March 10, 2006, p. 15.
Pittsburgh Post-Gazette (PA), May 23, 2011, p. C1.
St. Paul Pioneer Press (MN), May 24, 2011.
Times Colonist (Victoria, BC, Canada), March 20, 2011, p. C9.

Online

"Bradley Cooper (I)," Internet Movie Database, http://www.imdb.com/name/nm0177896/filmtype (August 19, 2011).

—*A. Petruso*

Cat Cora

© Todd Williamson/WireImage/Getty Images

Chef and television personality

Born Catherine Cora, January 1, 1968, in Jackson, MS; daughter of Spiro Cora; partner of Jennifer Cora, 2001; children: Zoran, Caje, Thatcher Julius, Nash Lemuel (with partner). *Education:* University of Southern Mississippi, B.S.; Culinary Institute of America.

Addresses: *Agent*—William Morris Agency NY, 1325 Avenue of the Americas, New York, NY 10019. *Web site*—http://www.catcora.com/.

Career

Began working in restaurants, c. 1986; worked for Arcadia, Beekman Tavern, c. 1990s; apprenticed with George Blanc at Vonnas and Roger Verge, France, c. 1990s; worked as sous chef at Old Chatham Shepherding Company in New York City, and chef de cuisine at Bistro Don Giovanni, c. late 1990s-early 2000s; worked as executive chef at Postino in Lafayette, California, 2001, then partner; began appearing on television, c. early 2000s; published first cookbook, *Cat Cora's Kitchen: Favorite Meals for Family and Friends,* 2004; founded Chefs for Humanity, 2004; won *Iron Chef America,* Food Network, 2005; opened first restaurant, CCQ, Costa Mesa, CA, 2008; appeared in online series *The Muppets Kitchen with Cat Cora,* Disney.com, and *Hasty Tasty Cooking Tips with Cat Cora and the Muppets,* Family.com, 2010. Television appearances include: *Melting Pot,* Food Network, 2001; *My Country My Kitchen: Greece,* 2001; *Simply Your Life,* Fine Living, 2002; *Kitchen Accomplished,* 2004; *Iron Chef America,* Food Network, 2005—; *Celebrity Cooking Showdown* (miniseries), NBC, 2006; *What's Cooking with Cat Cora!,* 2008.

Member: Screen Actors Guild.

Awards: Teacher of the Year Award, *Bon Appétit,* 2006.

Sidelights

The first woman to be named an Iron Chef on *Iron Chef America,* Cat Cora was well-known for her creativity and emphasis on family friendly, fresh food informed by Greek and Southern influences. A graduate of the Culinary Institute of America, she worked in restaurants in New York and California before moving into television at the beginning of the twenty-first century. In addition to *Iron Chef,* she hosted *Kitchen Accomplished* and other Food Network programs. Cora also wrote three cookbooks that emphasized her cooking philosophy. Explaining her philosophy, she told John Griffin of the *San Antonio Express-News,* "I call it simple gourmet. I take things that are simple, quick, and easy, and refine it."

Cora was born on January 1, 1968, in Jackson, Mississippi, into a Greek-American family. Raised in a Greek community, her family was food-focused and her grandfather and father were restaurateurs. She was interested in becoming a chef herself from an early age. By the time she was 15 years old, she had written a business plan for her own restaurant. After high school, Cora attended the University of Southern Mississippi, studying exercise physiology and biology, and working in restaurants all the while. She was employed at an Italian bistro and a private dining club which focused on French cuisine during her undergraduate years.

After graduation, Cora worked as a server at Jackson's only four-star restaurant. During this time period, she met chef Julia Child at a book signing. Cora talked to the highly regarded chef, who encouraged Cora to apply to the Culinary Institute of America (CIA) in Hyde Park, New York. The next day, Cora sent in her application and she was accepted. While studying at the CIA, she was an apprentice at Arcadia for chef Anne Rozenweig, later transferring her apprenticeship into a job. Cora then found employment at the Beekman Tavern in California's Napa Valley, working under chef Larry Forgione. Cora continued her training in the culinary arts in Europe. She apprenticed with George Blanc at Vonnas and with Roger Verge, both three-star Michelin chefs, and learned much about French cuisine and culture. Of this experience, she told Aleta Capelle of the Rochester, Minnesota *Post-Bulletin*, "I apprenticed in France. I thought after I'd done that, I could do anything."

After returning to the United States, Cora found employment at the Old Chatham Shepherding Company in New York City, working as a sous chef. Cora then moved to Northern California, where she was chef de cuisine at Bistro Don Giovanni. By 2001, Cora was working as the executive chef at Postino in Lafayette, California. She eventually became a partner in the restaurant, which was located in an old post office. While the restaurant focused on country Italian cuisine, Cora was still fervent about her Greek and Southern background. She told Jackie Burrell of the *Contra Costa Sun*, "My real passion is Greek cuisine. I have to hold back the reins. But this is a beautiful, understated cuisine. Elegant, yet simple. The flavors are real, honest and pure. I like to take the tradition of country Italian cuisine and pair it with what is fresh from local farms."

In the early 2000s, Cora began sharing her love of cooking and cuisine with television audiences. After appearing on the local San Francisco-based morning show *Bay Cafe,* a tape of her work was sent to the Food Network, which contacted her a short time later. By 2001, she was co-hosting *Melting Pot* with Rocco DiSpirito on the Food Network. She went on to host *My Country My Kitchen: Greece* and *Simply Your Life* as well. In 2004, Cora appeared as host of *Kitchen Accomplished*, a surprise kitchen make-over show. Cora also made regular appearances on talk shows and morning programs, like *Today, The Wayne Brady Show,* and *Live with Regis and Kelly.*

Cora believed that the Food Network, among other networks, encouraged a greater interest in food and the food scene and allowed chefs like herself to share knowledge with a wide audience. She told Jan Norris of the *Palm Beach Post,* "I think the Food Network has been a huge part of a whole food explosion. It's made it possible for a lot of us to take our talents and share them with America—fantastic for all of us. PBS, too: They've allowed chefs to come on in a big way to share what we know. It's opened so many doors for so many, and been fun and rewarding."

As she became more widely known, Cora began teaching and writing cookbooks. In 2004, Cora published her first, *Cat Cora's Kitchen: Favorite Meals for Family and Friends*. The recipes were inspired by her family life, including both Greek and Southern influences. Philanthropy also became a major focus for Cora in this time period. She founded Chefs for Humanity in late 2004 in the wake of the devastating tsunamis in Asia. This non-profit organization raised money—sometimes through auctions of signed chef items—and used resources for emergency food relief and nutrition education among other concerns. Chefs for Humanity often partnered with groups like Second Harvest and the Red Cross. In 2005, her organization fed people in the Gulfport region after Hurricane Katrina. Chefs for Humanity later partnered with the United Nations World Food Programme, Action Against Hunger, and UNICEF. (Cora herself later became the nutritional spokesperson for UNICEF.)

Cora's career reached in new heights in 2005. That year, Cora was asked to appear on the Food Network's *Iron Chef America*. Of the selection, she told Heather McPherson of the *Orlando Sentinel,* "They came to me. They knew my work from other Food Network shows and my culinary background. It was time for a woman to be in the mix, and I was in the right place with the right skills." Cora won the competition over chefs like Alex Lee. She was the first woman to win, adding more victories in a number of subsequent competitions, and had one of the best records on the show. Cora eventually became one of the continuous Iron Chefs, and regularly appeared on the program. Talking about her appearances on *Iron Chef America*, she told Carrie Sturrock of the *San Francisco Chronicle,* "It will show that women can cook alongside men just as hard and just as well. You don't see that a lot on television. The shows are more how-to—'OK, we're going to crack an egg and make a meringue.'"

While continuing her appearances on Food Network, Cora took on a new challenge when she joined the five-night NBC miniseries *Celebrity Cooking Showdown* in 2006. On this show, which was compared to *Dancing with the Stars*, famous chefs and celebrities worked together in a timed cook-off competition. The show featured other celebrity chefs like Wolfgang Puck. That same year, she was named the executive chef of the magazine *Bon Appétit*, and began appearing in original content produced for MSN's online presence in conjunction with Kraft. In these video segments, Cora illustrated recipes targeted at busy moms.

In 2007, Cora published her second cookbook *Cooking from the Hip: Fast, Easy, Phenomenal Meals*. This tome emphasized simple, quality meals made with ingredients on hand at home. Describing the book to McPherson of the *Orlando Sentinel*, Cora stated, "I understand the stress of time and raising children. I'm a working mom. That's why the book is in four categories: fast—30 minutes or less; easy—interruption-proof; fun—food you can prepare with friends; and phenomenal—special dishes for special meals." *Publisher's Weekly* praised *Cooking from the Hip*, calling the results "pleasing and more accessible than many of the concoctions presented on TV by battling chefs." The review also notes "Cora's spontaneous, easygoing yet stylish way" and her "sunny, can-do attitutde."

In 2008, Cora began opening her own restaurants. Already affiliated with Macy's Culinary Council, a national culinary authority, she opened signature restaurants alongside Macy's department stores in the Los Angeles area. One was called CCQ (Cat Cora's Que), a barbecue restaurant located in Costa Mesa, California. Working under a fast casual concept, the restaurants were targeted at shoppers. She opened more restaurants over the next few years, including one at Macy's South Coast Plaza and Kouzzina at Walt Disney World in 2009. She also was a part of the Napa Farms Market in Terminal 2 of the San Francisco International Airport, where local chefs shared their dishes. The food was prepared with local ingredients. That year, Cora launched her own television series, *What's Cooking with Cat Cora!*, which was filmed in Orlando. She appeared in two online series in conjunction with Disney as well. Working with Muppets, she cooked and offered tips for moms and kids about activities to bring the family together in the series *The Muppets Kitchen with Cat Cora* on Disney.com and *Hasty Tasty Cooking Tips with Cat Cora and the Muppets* on Disney's Family.com in 2010.

Cora published her third book, *Classics with a Twist: Fresh Takes on Favorite Dishes*, in 2010. It focused on family friendly recipes taken from cultures around the world, but emphasized fast, healthy, and affordable meals. Reviewing the book, Greg Morago of the *Houston Chronicle* wrote that it "puts a new spin on family favorites by injecting everyday dishes with some pizzazz. The cookbook offers dishes with refreshing new takes, including Greek nachos, quick chicken curry, white bean and chicken chili, Middle Eastern turkey meatballs, and Asian salmon loaf." She told Morago how much she appreciated feedback, noting: "There's nothing worse than a recipe that doesn't turn out or something is left out. That's the aim: to make sure people are happy with them."

Part of Cora's philosophy, underscored in all her work, emphasized the importance of a sit-down dinner for family. Cora told Allen Pierleoni of the *Sacramento Bee*, "I'm a super-busy mom, but we try to sit down as a family as much as we can. What my mom did is what we do—shut the TV off during dinner so we can look each other and actually have a conversation.... I push that a lot."

In the future, Cora planned on opening more restaurants and developing new shows for various television networks, including potentially the Oprah Winfrey Network (OWN). She would also like to try acting. Cora told John Tanasychuk of the *South Florida Sun-Sentinel*, "In the next chapter of my life, I'd like to do some acting. I've always been a performer since I was really young doing school plays. I perform every day in front of thousands of people as a chef. I think it's something I would enjoy."

Selected writings

Cat Cora's Kitchen: Favorite Meals for Families and Friends, Chronicle Books (San Francisco), 2004.
(With Ann Krueger Spivack) *Cooking from the Hip: Fast, Easy, Phenomenal Meals*, Houghton Mifflin (New York City), 2007.
(With Ann Krueger Spivack) *Classics with a Twist: Fresh Takes on Favorite Dishes*, Houghton Mifflin, 2010.

Sources

Periodicals

Brandweek, September 25, 2006.
Business Wire, September 14, 2010.
Contra Costa Sun (CA), December 26, 2001, p. 2.
Curve, June 2008, p. 46.

Dallas Morning News, January 29, 2005, p. 3E.
Houston Chronicle, June 2, 2010, p. 1.
Orlando Sentinel (FL), April 18, 2007.
Palm Beach Post (FL), October 20, 2005, p. 1FN.
Pittsburgh Tribune Review, June 20, 2007.
Post-Bulletin (Rochester, MN), March 28, 2007.
Publishers Weekly, January 15, 2007, p. 45.
Sacramento Bee (CA), April 4, 2007, p. F1.
San Antonio Express-News (TX), March 2, 2005, p. 1F.
San Francisco Chronicle, April 1, 2005, F1.
San Jose Mercury News (CA), April 12, 2011.
South Florida Sun-Sentinel, June 28, 2010.
USA Today, March 31, 2006, p. 9D.

Online

"About Cat," The Official Cat Cora Web site, http://www.catcora.com/about (August 12, 2011).
"Cat Cora Bio," Food Network, http://www.foodnetwork.com/chefs/cat-cora/index.html (August 12, 2011).
"Cat Cora," Internet Movie Database, http://www.imdb.com/name/nm1752094/ (August 12, 2011).

—*A. Petruso*

Charlie Crist

© *PhotoStockFile/Alamy*

Attorney

Born July 24, 1956, in Altoona, PA; son of Charlie, Sr., (a family doctor) and Nancy Lee Crist; married first wife, c. mid-1980s (divorced, c. mid-1980s); married Carole Rome (a businessperson), December 12, 2008. *Education:* Attended Wake Forest University; Florida State University, B.A. 1978; Cumberland School of Law, J.D., 1981.

Addresses: *Office*—c/o 400 S. Monroe St., Tallahassee, FL 32399.

Career

Served as general counsel to the National Association of Professional Baseball Leagues, 1982-87; state director for U.S. Senator Connie Mack, 1987; attorney, Wood & Crist, Tampa, FL, 1987-89; member of the Florida State Senate, 1992-98; deputy secretary, Florida Department of Business & Professional Regulation, 1999-2000; education commissioner, State of Florida, 2000-02; attorney general, State of Florida, 2003-06; governor of Florida, 2007-11; joined law firm Morgan & Morgan, 2011.

Sidelights

Former Florida governor and U.S. Senate candidate Charlie Crist has been an extremely popular politician not only his home state but across the United States. A Republican, Crist was considered fiscally conservative but moderate, if not liberal, on social issues. He embraced environmental concerns, wanted Florida's government to be more open, and the best state for children to live in, but also en-

dorsed the dismantling of the Internal Revenue service, a nation-wide flat tax, and the return of chain gangs to Florida's prisons. Though there were some uncertainties about his leadership, he was popular with voters until he declared himself independent during the 2010 race for the U.S. Senate, which he lost to Republican Marco Rubio. After his political career ended in 2011, Crist returned to private legal practice.

Born on July 24, 1956, in Altoona, Pennsylvania, he was the son of Charlie Sr. and Nancy Lee Crist. His father was the son of a Greek Cypriot immigrant. After living in Atlanta while his father attended medical school, the family, including Crist's three sisters, moved to St. Petersburg, Florida, when he was a small child. His father had a family medical practice there and became politically active, running for a seat on the Pinellas County School Board; the ten-year-old Crist helped with the campaign. In his youth, Crist was enthusiastic about boating and fishing.

Educated in public schools, Crist was interested in politics and football by the time he was in high school. At St. Petersburg High School, Crist was both class president and starting quarterback for the football team. He then entered Wake Forest University, where he played football as a walk on, then transferred to Florida State University after an injury to improve his grades. His father encouraged him to pursue a medical career, but Crist struggled in science classes. After the transfer, he served as student body vice president at Florida State. In 1978, Crist earned his undergraduate degree from Florida State University.

Deciding on a legal career, Crist entered the Cumberland School of Law in Birmingham, Alabama. During his law school years, he served as an intern in the Florida state attorney's office. After completing his J.D. in 1981, he twice failed the Florida state bar before passing. Crist then served as general counsel to the National Association of Professional Baseball Leagues. Beginning in 1982, he worked in the association's minor league division. He left in 1987 and briefly worked as state director for U.S. Senator Connie Mack, then began working as an attorney in private practice with his brother-in-law. Their firm, Wood & Crist, was based in Tampa, Florida.

In the late 1980s, Crist's political ambitions emerged. He first ran for a Florida senate seat in 1986 representing parts of St. Petersburg, but lost. Undeterred, Crist sought the same office again 1992, and won. He was re-elected in 1994. During his tenure, served as the chairman of the Senate Ethics and Elections Committee as well as chairman of the Appropriations Criminal Justice Subcommittee. He was a dedicated advocate on such issues as public safety, sponsoring the Stop Turning Out Prisoners (STOP) bill that would require prisoners to serve 85 percent of their sentences. Crist also wanted the return of chain gangs for prison inmates, leading to his nickname "Chain Gang Charlie." In addition, Crist launched controversial investigations into calls made on behalf of Governor Lawton Chiles' campaign and Florida's $11 billion settlement with tobacco companies.

Instead of running for the state senate again, Crist pursued a U.S. Senate seat in 1998. He was the Republican candidate to incumbent Senator Bob Graham, a Democrat. During his campaign, Crist stated his support of the abolishment of the Internal Revenue Service and replacing it with a flat tax or national sales tax. Crist lost with only 38 percent of the vote.

Crist then took a position in Florida Governor Jeb Bush's government. Bush named Crist deputy secretary of the Florida Department of Business & Professional Regulation from 1999 to 2000. When the position of education commissioner became open and the subject of a special election, Crist ran for the office and won because of the name recognition he gained while running for U.S. Senate. He was the last person elected to the office, and served until 2002.

In 2002, Crist ran for a new office, attorney general for the State of Florida. Easily winning the election, he became the first Republican elected to the post. He served as attorney general until 2007. During his time in office, he emphasized civil rights issues. Among his accomplishments was reviving a 1951 case involving the murder of two civil rights activists. Crist also supported a bill that gave the attorney general's office the ability to take action against businesses that have discriminatory employment practices. Crist faced controversy as well because of the Terri Schiavo case. The brain-damaged Schiavo had been kept on life support for years, and her husband and parents were locked in a debate over the removal of her feeding tube. Crist ended official attempts to keep her alive and did not want the state to intervene in the family matter, a stance that was not supported by the right to life faction.

While still serving as attorney general, Crist decided to seek the Republican nomination for governor's office as Bush could not seek re-election because of term limits. Crist ran for governor of Florida in 2006, promising to lower costs for both people and businesses in Florida. He also wanted to make Florida's economy stronger and increase everyone's access to government. Children were also a key part of Crist's campaign. He wanted to make sure they lived safely and had access to a world-class education. In addition, Crist, supported civil unions for gay couples and stem cell research.

Because of some of his stances, Crist was labeled a liberal by his primary opponent in the Republican primary, Jay Gallagher, Florida's chief financial officer. Crist also took flack in the primary because of his unmarried state. He had briefly been married in the mid-1980s and engaged at one point years later, and his lack of wife or girlfriend compelled some to accuse him of being homosexual. Crist denied the rumor as well as an old claim that he fathered a child out of wedlock many years previous. Crist won the nomination easily with 64 percent of the vote. He then faced Democrat Jim Davis in the general election. Emphasizing fiscal conservatism and environmental issues, Crist spent $20 million on his campaign to Davis's $7 million. Crist won with 52 percent of the vote to Davis's 45 percent.

When Crist took the oath of office in January of 2007, he promised to be open and emphasize bipartisanship. According to J. Taylor Rushing of the *Florida Times-Union*, Crist said in his inauguration speech, "We face no obstacle greater than our abilities, no problem that cannot be solved. Our challenge [is] to recognize our common future, our common destiny. To understand that we are stronger in cooperation than in competition." After the inauguration, Crist opened the doors to the governor's mansion for three hours to everyone. Thousands showed up.

Crist then went to work. Within days of becoming governor, he founded the Office of Open Government by an executive order. This office was founded to make government more accessible to Floridians. Among his other early focuses were trying to rein in high property taxes and the high cost of property insurance. He was able to pass a number of homeowner's insurance measures such as a rate freeze. Another vow was taking a bipartisan approach to the legislature, and Crist tried to work with Democrats and Republicans on these issues.

Crist also tried to fulfill campaign promises related to Florida's children. Among his accomplishments in this area was his establishment of the Governor's Council on Physical Fitness, which encouraged exercise, activity, and healthy lives for Florida's school children. Another success was the founding of the Children and Youth Cabinet to advocate for child-related issues. Crist also worked to improve Florida's adoption process by appointing a Chief Child Advocate.

Environmental issues were also important to Crist who wanted to restore the Everglades and address climate change matters. Crist hosted the Florida Summit on Global Climate Change in July of 2007. This summit featured experts from around the world discussing greenhouse gas emissions. During the summit, Crist showed his support by signing three state executive orders related to the reduction of carbon emissions.

During his second year in office, Crist remained popular but was accused of not fulfilling enough campaign and inaugural promises. Despite this situation, he continued to work to improve life for Floridians by creating affordable health care for the working poor, increasing teacher's salaries, and giving tax breaks for certain businesses engaged in renewable energy. Crist also gained the national spotlight because of the 2008 Republican primary. Under a law signed by Crist in 2007, the Florida primary moved to January of 2008. Crist took a neutral stance until three days before the primary, when he announced his support for Senator John McCain.

McCain won the primary, and Crist was considered a potential running mate for McCain, who became the Republican nominee for president that year.

Yet Crist became estranged from his party as the national election neared. Crist was dismissive of the fraud allegations against ACORN, a voter registration group. He also made early voting hours longer, a position Republicans did not support. McCain ultimately lost the election to Democrat Barack Obama. Shortly after the election, Crist married Carole Rome on December 12, 2008.

Crist dealt with challenges, expected and unexpected, in 2009. Florida faced a multi-billion dollar budget shortfall in January of that year and was criticized by fellow Republicans for vetoing cuts to certain state programs. Politics also affected Crist. Instead of seeking a second term as governor, he announced his intention to seek the 2010 Republican nomination for U.S. Senate in May 2009. Crist faced an uphill battle in the Republican primary, however, as a tea party candidate (former Florida house of representatives speaker Marco Rubio) emerged as a significant challenger. Crist was accused of supporting establishment politics and roundly criticized for taking stimulus funds from and hugging President Obama in 2009. He also took flack for vetoing an education bill that called for linking teacher pay to the test scores of their students.

By January of 2010, Crist's campaign was suffering from unexpected setbacks including the ouster of his chosen Republican party chairman, his emergency management chief quitting, and his juvenile justice administrator being investigated for excessive travel. Despite the support of the national Republican party and a 30-point lead in the polls at one point in the election cycle, Crist believed that he could not win the August of 2010 primary as Rubio gained a 20-point lead of his own in the spring of 2010.

Crist took a risk in late April of 2010 by declaring himself an independent candidate, which meant the national Republicans no longer supported him or his campaign. Crist felt the change was for the better, telling Jane Musgrave of the *Palm Beach Post*, "I was glad to leave it, at least the right-wing part of it. I couldn't be comfortable with it anymore. Things do evolve and they change." In the November of 2010 elections, Crist faced both Rubio and the Democratic candidate Kendrick Meek. Despite a financial advantage, Crist ultimately lost the election to Rubio.

After losing the election and leaving the governor's office, Crist returned to private legal practice with the firm Morgan & Morgan. He continued to be interested in environmental issues. In February of 2011, he and former Florida Chief Financial Officer Alex Sink took part in the launch of a petition drive to get a constitutional amendment to ban oil drilling on the ballot in November of 2012. Always supportive of Florida's voters, Crist told Aaron Sharockman of the *St. Petersburg Times*, "This puts it in the hands of the people and that's exactly where it should be."

Sources

Books

Complete Marquis Who's Who, Marquis Who's Who, 2010.
State Directory, Carroll Publishing (Bethesda, MD), 2009.

Periodicals

Florida Times-Union (Jacksonville, FL), January 3, 2007, p. B1.
Miami Herald, August 20, 2006.
Palm Beach Post (FL), October 17, 2010, p. 1A.
South Florida Sun-Sentinel (Ft. Lauderdale, FL), January 2, 2008; February 20, 2008.
St. Petersburg Times (FL), January 9, 2010; May 5, 2010, p. 1A; May 13, 2010, p. 1B; February 10, 2011, p. 7B.
Tampa Tribune (FL), October 14, 1998, p. 3; August 10, 2002, p. 3.

Online

"Charlie Crist,"WhoRunsGov, http://www.whorunsgov.com/Profiles/Charlie_Crist (March 5, 2011).

—*A. Petruso*

Dennis Crowley

Co-founder of Foursquare.com

Born June 19, 1976, in the United States; son of Dennis and Mary Crowley. *Education:* Syracuse University, B.S., 1998; New York University, M.P.S., 2004.

Addresses: *E-mail*—dens@foursquare.com. *Web site*—http://www.teendrama.com.

Career

Worked as a snowboard instructor, after 1998; researcher, Jupiter Research, 1998-2000; product developer, Vindigo, 2000-01; wireless product developer, MTV Networks, 2003; game co-designer, PacManhattan, 2004; technical lead, ConQwest, 2004; co-founder and lead developer for Dodgeball, 2004-07; product manager, Google, 2005-07; adjunct professor, New York University, Interactive Telecommunications Program, 2005-06; worked for area/code, 2007-08; co-founder, Foursquare, 2009—.

Awards: One of the "Top 35 Innovators Under 35," MIT's *Technology Review* magazine, 2005; one of the "40 Under 40," *Fortune,* 2010.

Sidelights

Dennis Crowley, the upwardly mobile Internet innovator who helped to create social media location networking sites such as Dodgeball and Foursquare, has in the past been spotted at such diverse activities as dining at some of Silicon Valley's best restaurants, flying down mountain slopes

Andreas Rentz/Getty Images for Hubert Burda Media

where he taught snowboarding, winning the "Fast Money" bonus round on the set of *Family Feud,* speaking with investors in Boston, and taking in an NBA basketball game from courtside. He has even been seen in ads modeling chunky Gap cardigans near bus stops. Crowley has also admitted to working toward being the mayor of Scratchers—a bar not far from the headquarters of Foursquare. He worked as an adjunct professor at New York University's Interactive Telecommunications Program in addition to being a successful programmer and Internet entrepreneur.

In the early years of Internet social media there was a program called Friendster. Like Facebook, people could update their profiles and keep in contact with friends, but once the computer was turned off the experience was done. Adrianne Jeffries, writing for the *New York Observer,* quoted Crowley as saying, "In the past, I would spend all this time on my Friendster profile finding people and sharing the profile, and at the end of the day, it was close the lid on your laptop and that was it. It didn't do anything." Crowley and his friends wanted to change that. They wanted to make a social media application that was more interactive. While attending New York University's Interactive Technology Program, Crowley and fellow student Alex Rainert created a social networking site called Dodgeball for Crowley's graduate thesis project. In his online resume Crowley described Dodgeball as a product that combined "location-based services with social software on mobile devices." He went on to say that "the combination of the three leads to technology that facilitates serendipity." Before he and Rainert dove into developing Dodgeball, as described by Mathew Ingram for the Web site GigaOM, Crowley said he "went through three to four years thinking I was going to meet some magical engineer who would build all the stuff I was thinking about." Then Crowley decided that instead of listening to people who kept telling him that his ideas would not work, he would just find a way to improvise and make them work. He and Rainert would "roll out half-baked features a few times every week and were more worried about getting stuff in the hands of users than making sure it actually worked," Crowley told Ingram.

Dodgeball was founded as a company in 2004 by Crowley and Rainert. The way Dodgeball worked was that if someone was a registered user with the site, they could text a message to the site telling where they were. Dodgeball would then forward the message out to all the people that the user had listed as friends. Dodgeball's computer would check the user's location address against its list of geographical locations in 22 different cities. If someone who was not on the user's friend list had checked in within the last three hours and was within a ten block radius, Dodgeball's computer would notify both parties. If the user had identified someone as being a person that they had a "crush" on then that person would get a picture of the user and a message saying that the user was interested. The "crush" would then have the option to find the user or "dodge" them.

Google took note of Dodgeball and, in 2005, acquired the company and hired Crowley and Rainert. At the time Crowley's friends celebrated his accomplishment and everyone predicted that Dodgeball would become a huge success. In April of 2007, Crowley and Rainert left Google. Dodgeball was available for use at its most popular time period in the cities of Seattle, San Francisco, Portland, Los Angeles, Las Vegas, San Diego, Phoenix, Dallas-Fort Worth, Austin, Houston, New Orleans, Miami, Atlanta, Washington, D.C., Philadelphia, New York City, Boston, Detroit, Chicago, Madison, Minneapolis-St. Paul, and Denver. In January of 2009 Google announced that they were going to discontinue Dodgeball. That next month, Dodgeball was terminated and Google Latitude was introduced as a replacement although general consensus was that Twitter had largely replaced Dodgeball. The night that it was announced that Dodgeball

would be discontinued Crowley was at a party that became a wake of sorts for the now "dead" application. Despite little or no activity for two years on Dodgeball within Google, 17 people at the party were still registered users.

Dodgeball—and Crowley's interest in computer programming and developing location-based applications—may never have come about if he had not gone with a friend to what he described as a "weird art show at NYU," according to Kristine Jannuzzi, writing for *NYU Alumni Connect*. He had already graduated from Syracuse University and worked two separate jobs in New York City. One had been for an internet research firm and the other had been for a tech start-up. He was laid off in 2001 prior to the tragedy of 9/11 and was unemployed. He became a snowboard instructor for the winter season and began filling out an application to attend New York University's Stern Business School because he did not know what else to do. His heart was not really invested in attending business school to obtain a masters degree in business administration. He went to the art show at New York University's Interactive Technology Program and, he told Januzzi, "the first project I saw was someone who was making robots who follow robots who follow robots.... And as soon as I saw that, I was like, oh my God, I need to be here, I need to be doing this stuff. It was very clear to me."

After the frustrating experience with Dodgeball at Google, Crowley worked for a company called Area Code designing interactive games using real-world locations. It was like a giant game of Monopoly played by thousands of people using their locations as determined by GPS to make moves within the game. While he was at Area Code he met Naveen Selvadurai, who worked in the same building but for a different company. In the autumn of 2008, sitting at Crowley's kitchen table in his apartment in New York's East Village, the duo began working on the prototype of what would become Foursquare. Foursquare was introduced to a great deal of fanfare in 2009 at South By Southwest because, as John Fischer wrote for the New York Future Initiative Web site, it was predicted to change the way New Yorkers would get information about bars, stores, restaurants, lunch specials, landmarks, scenic views, weekend plans, and the like. It was described by ZDNet writer Jennifer Leggio as "one of the most deliciously addictive social applications on the planet."

Foursquare in many ways is the descendent of Dodgeball, which was adopted initially by tech and media types to coordinate social activities such as going out to a bar. Crowley explained that Dodgeball was really good for checking in with friends but not a great application if a person was on their own. He wanted Foursquare to have more features and be more widely usable by a greater range and number of people. Foursquare's official Web site description is as "a location-based mobile platform that makes cities easier to use and more interesting to explore."

Foursquare turns a user's social life into an interactive video game using the person's GPS chip in their phone. Registered users can earn points by checking in and giving their location. Crowley and Selvadurai programmed features into Foursquare where people can earn badges and become the mayor of a certain location if they are the person who has frequented that location the most within a two-month period. Becoming mayor of a location in some places has become a coveted and contested title that can be both easily won and easily lost. Different themed activities can earn badges. For instance, a user might obtain a "photogenic" badge for finding three different places with a photobooth in one week. Frequenting the same place three times in a week might earn the badge of being a "local." Users can also leave comments and tips about locations within the program and, similar to Dodgeball, users can notify their friends of their whereabouts. "Where we're trying to get to with it is that you can be walking down the street in a neighborhood you don't know around lunchtime, and your phone will suddenly buzz with the location of a sandwich shop near you that your friend has recommended," Crowley told New York Future Initiative's Fischer. Crowley hoped that Foursquare would help people by giving them "contextually relevant information" about the cities that they live in and that the information will come directly from friends, according to his interview with Fischer. His ambition was that Foursquare would encourage people to do more things and try different activities and venues. While Dodgeball was very much ahead of its time, Foursquare was not the only program available that used location-based social information. There was also Gowalla, Loopt, and Britekite, which were all startups doing similar things.

Crowley designed Foursquare to use behavior that he believes is ingrained in human beings. Rather than simply giving people the ability to broadcast their lives as Twitter does, Foursquare allows them to broadcast their lives with as much or as little openness as they desire, organizes the information from people's social lives, and lets them compete for social credibility and popularity. The biggest hindrance to Foursquare becoming a widely used application like Facebook or Twitter, as Crowley interprets it, is that people need to be made aware of the program, sign up, and get in the habit of using it because the content in the program comes from the users and there needs to be a critical mass of information to make the game as interesting as possible.

As of December 2010 Foursquare had "4.5 million users, a whopping 35 employees and $20 million in funding, and it recently opened a San Francisco office," reported Liz Gannes for the Web site NetworkEffect. On the Foursquare Web site the number of registered users jumped to 6.5 million users worldwide as of February 2011. The Web site also listed several investors, including Union Square Ventures, O'Reilly AlphaTech Ventures, and Andreessen Horowitz. Crowley continued to look for ways to expand the utility of Foursquare with such ideas as a cab sharing application, a couponing engine that gives rewards for statistics within the game, and ways for merchants to advertise new products or specials. Initially merchants would set up rewards within Foursquare where if someone visited the restaurant or bar they might get a free ticket to see a band or a free cup of coffee. The rewards merchants give based on Foursquare statistics have expanded to include such things as free drinks for the mayor of a particular yacht club, a free night at a hotel in Amsterdam, and free bottles of wine to frequent customers at a New York restaurant. As of December 2010, among the registered users for Foursquare only about 20 percent of the check-ins were considered out of the grid for the mapped areas that the program included. While the main demographic that used Foursquare seemed to be in the 24-35 age range and in urban areas, Foursquare was used in suburban areas for such things as parents connecting to other parents at playgrounds. It was also being used by high school students and college students to make social plans.

For his birthday in June of 2010, Crowley's mother made him a basket of cookies that represented the various badges within Foursquare. While Crowley is definitely an entrepreneur on the move, hopefully he will maintain the title of mayor of location-based social applications.

Sources

Periodicals

New York Observer, December 28, 2010.

Online

"40 under 40," CNN Money, http://money.cnn.com/galleries/2010/fortune/1010/gallery.40_under_40.fortune/29.html (February 20, 2011).

"100 Brains: Foursquare's Dennis Crowley and his geo-local revolution," ZDNet, http://www.zdnet.com/blog/feeds/100-brains-foursquares-dennis-crowley-and-his-geo-local-revolution/3034?tag=mantle_skin;content (February 23, 2011).

"Alumni Profile: Dennis Crowley (TSOA '04)," *NYU Alumni Connect*, http://alumni.nyu.edu/s/1068/index.aspx?sid=1068&gid=1&pgid=1614 (February 25, 2011).

"Breaking: Dennis Crowley Gets Foursquare Badge Cookies For His Birthday," *San Francisco Chronicle*, http://www.sfgate.com/cgi.bin/article.cgi?f=/g/a/2010/06/18/businessunsider-breaking-dennis-crowley-gets-foursquare-badge-cookies-for-his-birthday-2010-6.DTL (February 23, 2011).

"Dennis Crowley Biography," TechniFi, http://technifi.com/Businesspersons/Dennis-Crowley/bio (February 23, 2011).

"Dennis Crowley," Dennis Crowley's Web site, http://www.denniscrowley.com (February 20, 2011).

"Dennis Crowley," LinkedIn, http://www.linkedin.com/in/dpstyles (February 20, 2011).

"Dennis Crowley, 29," *Technology Review*, http://technologyreview.com/TR35/Profile.aspx?TRID=94 (February 20, 2011).

"Fabulous Life of Dennis Crowley, The Most Wanted Man In Silicon Valley," Business Insider SAI, http://www.businessinsider.com/foursquare-dennis-crowley-2010-04 (February 20, 2011).

"Foursquare," Foursquare Web site, http://foursquare.com (February 20, 2011).

"Foursquare's Dennis Crowley Live at Dive Into Mobile Conference," Network Effect, http://networkeffect.allthingsd.com/20101207.tif/dennis-crowley-live-at-dive-into-mobile/ (February 20, 2011).

"Foursquare wants to be the mayor of location apps," O'Reilly Radar, http://radar.oreilly.com/print/2010/03/foursquare-location-apps.html (February 23, 2011).

"Personal Branding Interview: Dennis Crowley," Personal Branding Blog, http://www.personalbrandingblog.com/personal-branding-interview-dennis-crowley/ (February 23, 2011).

"Resume," Dennis Crowley's Web site, http://www.denniscrowley.com/resume/index.html (March 29, 2011).

"Soliloquy for Dodgeball," Barbarian Blog, http://www.barbariangroup.com/posts/1562-soliloquy_for_dodgeballm (February 20, 2011).

"Startup Lessons From Foursquare's Dennis Crowley," GigaOM, http://gigaom.com/2010/11/29/startup-lessons-from-foursquares-dennis-crowley/ (February 20, 2011).

"With Foursquare, Dennis Crowley Aims Past the Nerds," New York Future Initiative, http://nyfi.observer.com/arts-culture/268/foursquare-dennis-crowley-aims-past-nerds (February 23, 2011).

—*Annette Bowman*

Mark Dayton

© Scott J. Ferrell/Congressional Quarterly/Getty Images

Governor of Minnesota

Born January 26, 1947, in Minneapolis, MN; son of Bruce (a businessman) and Gwendolen (Brandt) Dayton; married and divorced first wife; married Janice Haarstick (divorced); children: Eric, Andrew (first marriage). *Education:* Yale University, undergraduate degree (cum laude), 1969.

Addresses: *Office*—c/o Office of the Governor, 130 State Capitol, 75 Reverend Dr. Martin Luther King Jr. Blvd., St. Paul MN 55155. *Web site*—http://mn.gov/governor/. *Web site*—http://markdayton.org/.

Career

Worked as a teacher of general science, New York City, 1969-71; employed as a counselor and administrator, Social Services Agency, Boston, MA, 1972-76; employed as legislative aide to Senator Walter Mondale, U.S. Senate, c. 1976; staff member for Minnesota Governor Rudy Perpich, 1977; Commissioner of Economic Development, State of Minnesota, 1978, then Commissioner of Energy and Economic Development, 1983-86, then State Auditor, 1991-95; member of Senator Paul Wellstone's re-election campaign, 1995-96; U.S. Senator from Minnesota, 2001-07; elected governor of Minnesota, 2010.

Sidelights

The current governor of Minnesota and former U.S. Senator representing that state, Mark Dayton dismissed the life he could have led as a wealthy heir to a department store fortune to embrace one dedicated to public service. Known for his strong ideals and belief in radical ideas, Dayton had a reputation for being intense, competitive, idealistic, and committed, yet sometimes temperamental and flaky. Over the years, he ran for numerous political offices on the state and national level, serving for a time as Minnesota state auditor. While Dayton was not always effective in office, he had a sense of humor about himself and did his best to represent and meet the needs of his constituents.

Born on January 26, 1947, in Minneapolis, Minnesota, he was the son and eldest of four children of Bruce and Gwendolen Dayton. His father was the one-time chairman of the Dayton-Hudson Corporation, a department store chain founded by Dayton's great-grandfather, George D. Dayton, who also worked as a banker. He grew up in a Republican household that emphasized the value of hard work. Dayton told Bill Salisbury of the *Saint Paul Pioneer Press*, "My father often said, 'The only thing worse than a bum is a rich bum.' He made us understand that we were very fortunate, and with that came an opportunity and responsibility to give back." Yet his childhood had suffering as well. His mother was an alcoholic and often emotionally absent to her children. They felt shame at her behavior, but also developed empathy for those with troubled lives.

A shy child, Dayton attended public schools through second grade, then entered the private, exclusive Blake School. He played hockey in high school, winning a state championship. He was a goalie and loved the game his whole life. He also played golf, football, baseball, and basketball. Because he was not naturally gifted as an athlete, he had to work hard to achieve success. Dayton also achieved academically, participating in debate and dramatics. He ran for and won the position of lead boy, equivalent to student council president. In addition, Dayton had a strong faith, and for a time wanted to become a minister; however, at age 15 he began working as a hospital orderly, spending summers working in the emergency room and surgery units, which changed his career direction.

After graduating from Blake, Dayton entered Yale University, where he was pre-med. While earning a degree in psychology, he applied to medical school, but he withdrew his application during his senior year because he was unsure he wanted to commit to medicine as a career. Dayton was already developing an interest in politics and became involved in the anti-Vietnam War movement and other radical politics. Choosing Senator Robert Kennedy as a hero, Dayton became committed to living out his political consciousness the night that Kennedy was assassinated while on the campaign trail. Dayton graduated in 1969.

Despite being a multi-millionaire because of his inherited wealth, Dayton chose a career that would allow him to help others. After graduation, he moved to New York City and worked as a teacher at the rough P.S. 65 on the Lower East Side. Of the experience, Dayton told Doug Grow of the Minneapolis *Star Tribune*, "That taught me the difference between the haves and the have-nots. I realized, through circumstances of birth, that these kids were given so few opportunities, while I was given so many. I've believed in public service ever since." Burned out after a few years in the classroom, he then moved to Boston, where he worked at the Social Services Agency as a counselor to runaway teenagers. He eventually became the program's chief financial officer and began drumming up funding support in Washington, D.C. This experience led him to government and politics. Dayton told Salisbury in the *Saint Paul Pioneer Press* interview, "I saw government was the place where you could make a difference, for better or worse, in people's lives."

Moving into politics, Dayton's father helped his son get a job as a legislative aide to Minnesota Senator Walter Mondale. By 1977, Dayton was working on the staff of Minnesota governor Rudy Perpich. In 1978, he became the Commissioner of Economic Development for the state of Minnesota. In 1982, Dayton ran for a U.S. Senate seat, but lost. Returning to state politics, he served as the Commissioner of Energy and Economic Development for Minnesota from 1983 to 1986. He ran for and won the office of state auditor for Minnesota in 1990. He took office in 1991, and remained there for four years. During his tenure as auditor, he was known for being a watchdog over public funds. He was able to gain new limits on high-risk investments by state and local governments. Dayton was also a member of Senator Paul Wellstone's re-election campaign, from 1995 to 1996. Dayton also formed his own investment company and founded a nonprofit agency to encourage rural economic development at various points of his career.

In 1998, Dayton made a run for governor of Minnesota, but trailed far behind Hubert Humphrey III for the Democratic-Farmer-Labor (DFL) Party nomination. Dayton had little support, even from his own party and legislature, nor did he land any significant interest group endorsements. He also suffered from staffing problems, as he went through several campaign managers and significant exoduses of staff members. Dayton drew on his own personal fortune to run for the primary, but agreed to abide by spending limits, which amounted to spending only $1.9 million primarily on television advertising. During his campaign, Dayton advocated for rural issues, expanding health care coverage, making the tax structure increasingly progressive, and supporting an increase in the minimum wage. He also emphasized that he was a regular, anti-establishment guy, who was not controlled by labor unions or other interest groups. Dayton finished fourth, while Humphrey landed the nomination.

Despite the loss, Dayton did not give up on politics. He spent two years running his investment company and a beef farm he owned with his second wife. In April of 2000, Dayton announced that he was running for a U.S. Senate seat, challenging incumbent Republican Rod Grams. Again a DFL candidate, he was one of at least nine people seeking the nomination in the primary. Some criticized Dayton's candidacy as the actions of a bored rich man because he had no political base. Dayton answered such criticisms by telling Doug Grow of the Minneapolis *Star Tribune*, "There's this illusion if you have material wealth, your life must be happy and easy. I know that isn't true. On the other hand, Jesse Jackson says, there's learning by burning. I believe I have gained in experience; maybe I've even come to some wisdom."

Unexpectedly, Dayton won the DFL primary, defeating three major candidates. He spent five million dollars of his own money in his campaign, but emphasized his public service experience and his long-term financial support of his party. He entered the primary too late to gain any significant endorsements from DFL interest groups or other elected officials, and his reputation as quirky and temperamental did not help with his image. Dayton worked hard, and had a campaign staff that followed his lead yet ensured that he did not come off as off-kilter when being intense and passionate about discussing issues. Among his major issues during the primary was Social Security, health care, and the cost of prescription drugs. He instituted a campaign known as Healthcare Helpline, a phone service that provided callers with help with their insurers, especially those who were refused treatment coverage by their HMOs. Dayton also successfully defused his wealth as an issue in the campaign, and was able to defeat Grams in the general election.

As a U.S. Senator, Dayton continued to assist Minnesotans fighting their insurance companies and HMOs for needed treatments through his helpline, helping more than 800 people by 2003. While he promised to get Congress to pass a prescription drug plan under Medicare for the elderly, he failed to deliver on this promise in his first few years in office. By 2003, the liberal Dayton found it hard to advance any legislation or gain the public's attention. He also lost a mentor when friend Paul Wellstone died in October of 2002, days before Wellstone's possible re-election to the Senate. Yet Dayton continued to push for issues like more federal aid for disabled students, tax cuts for the lower and middle class, and promoting renewable energy sources. He also paid special attention to farm and military issues while serving on the agriculture and armed services committees. Dayton helped form the 2002 Farm Bill. Dayton also was critical of President George W. Bush, opposing his plan for tax cuts, the war in Iraq, and mandatory school testing program. Yet he supported the troops after the war was launched, and wanted a quick victory. As the war continued, he remained critical and demanded a timetable for troop withdrawal and that the Pentagon release more pictures of American soldiers abusing Iraqi prisoners. Dayton also garnered denigration for shutting his Senate office for 30 days during pre-election recess in 2004 because of concerns about terrorist attacks.

In early 2005, Dayton announced that he would not seek re-election to the Senate. Citing low poll numbers and a costly campaign battle, Dayton stated that he was not the best person to hold the seat for Democrats. He also loathed the fund-raising such a campaign would involve. He told Kevin Diaz of the Minneapolis *Star Tribune*, "I was into the fund-raising mode for the first time and it took a lot of my time.... [E]verybody said I was going to spend every waking moment of the next two years having to raise money, which I abhor. I didn't see how I could spend every waking moment raising money and running in a political campaign and then spend full-time also being a U.S. senator, which I love to do." Dayton left office when his term ended in 2007 and hinted that he might run for governor in the next election.

Despite his antipathy toward fund-raising, Dayton decided to seek public office again in 2009. That January, he filed paperwork to begin his campaign for the office of governor of Minnesota, hoping to defeat Governor Tim Pawlenty. Again facing a crowded field, Dayton decided not to self-finance his campaign but determine how much to raise by what his fellow candidates spent. During his campaign, Dayton emphasized the importance of job creation, education funding, aid to local governments, closing tax loops, and increasing taxes on the rich. He promised to boost education spending each year if he was elected governor. After winning the Democrat primary in 2010, Dayton faced a close race with Republican Tom Emmer, and received support in his campaign from many Democrats, including President Barack Obama. The election was close and it appeared on election day that Dayton won by only 9,000 votes. A recount was held and Emmer finally conceded to Dayton in early December.

When Dayton took office in January of 2011, he called on everyone to work together to improve Minnesota. Focusing on job creation, balancing a state budget in the face of a $6.2 billion deficit, and improving government services like education, Dayton wanted to raise taxes on high earners. Dayton's first few months in office were difficult, as he and the Republican-controlled legislature reached an impasse over the budget. In July of 2011, the government of Minnesota shut down for at least 19 days because the lack of agreement on the budget meant that the state ran out of appropriations and left 22,000 state employees temporarily out of work. In the end, Dayton had to give up his desire for new income taxes in favor of delaying payments to schools and selling tobacco payment bonds to bring $1.4 billion into the budget.

Despite this setback, Dayton believed Minnesota would improve during his tenure. As he stated in his inaugural address, as quoted by Paul Demko of the *Legal Ledger*, "Let us dedicate ourselves to rebuilding a successful state, one that again is the envy of the nation, a leader of the world. Let it be written that we were Minnesotans who led the way to something better than before, who created something greater than ourselves, who achieved together what none of us could have accomplished on our own."

Sources

Daily Globe (Worthington, MN), February 11, 2000.

Legal Ledger (St. Paul, MN), January 5, 2011.

Lewiston Morning Tribune (ID), July 15, 2011.

Saint Paul Pioneer Press (MN), October 16, 2000, p. 1A; November 30, 2002, p. 9B; April 2, 2003, p. A11; September 14, 2010; October 23, 2010; December 6, 2010; January 3, 2011; July 19, 2011.

Star Tribune (Minneapolis, MN), July 27, 1998, p. 1B; April 5, 2000, p. 2B; September 13, 2000, p. 1A; November 3, 2000, p. 20A; June 16, 2003, p. 1A; February 10, 2005, p. 18A; February 12, 2005, p. 1A; January 17, 2009; January 9, 2011, p. 1A.

—*A. Petruso*

Jim Denevan

Artist

Born in 1961 in San Jose, CA; son of Dorothy Denevan (a math teacher).

Addresses: *Office*—P.O. Box 2413, Santa Cruz, CA 95063-2413. *Web site*—http://jimdenevan.com/.

Career

Chef, Gabriella Café, Santa Cruz, CA, late 1990s; founder, Outstanding in the Field, 1999, and creative director, 1999—; began creating sand paint-

© *Brent Stirton/Getty Images*

ings in California, 1996; has exhibited works at the Yerba Buena Center for the Arts (San Francisco), 2005; PS1/MOMA (New York City), 2007; Parrish Art Museum (Southampton, NY), 2008; and Vancouver Biennale, 2010.

Sidelights

Jim Denevan's bifurcated career veers between building impermanent environmental artworks on the world's beaches and arranging novel pop-up outdoor dinners created entirely from locally sourced food products. Denevan's geometric-abstract sandscapes are made with the help of rakes and sticks and briefly adorn long stretches of beach before disappearing with the waves, though they live on in video documentary footage. Some of his dinner spectacles have been chronicled in a 2008 tome, *Outstanding in the Field: A Farm to Table Cookbook.* "There's a strange phenomenon in our culture that makes celebrities out of chefs while ignoring the people who actually produce our food," Denevan explained to a writer for *Sunset* magazine, Josh Sens, about his locavore dinners. "That's part of the idea, to focus our attention on the work they do."

Denevan was born in California in the early 1960s as one of nine children. His mother Dorothy was a math teacher who struggled to support her children after the death of their father; the Denevans' hardships were later compounded by diagnoses of schizophrenia that beset three of Denevan's older siblings. As a young adult he settled into a career as a self-trained chef, working at the Gabriella Café, a restaurant in Santa Cruz, California. The Outstanding in the Field events began as a way to introduce the Café's patrons to the local growers who supplied the restaurant. "People were becoming more interested in where their food comes from, but there wasn't much knowledge about the farmers or farms," he told *Miami New Times* journalist Lee Klein, "So I thought the moment was right for the farm-to-table idea—or I guess it's table-to-farm—and was thinking that I wanted to push in that direction."

Denevan and some fellow locavores launched Outstanding in the Field in 1999. The first dinners were held at the restaurant, but Denevan soon hit upon the idea of siting one at an apple orchard his brother owned in the Santa Cruz Mountains. That proved so popular that they soon found other farms willing to host outdoor dinners cooked by renowned local chefs, and the events migrated over to the San Francisco Bay area. The first Outstanding in the Field dinner on the East Coast was held in the Hudson

River Valley's Pocantico Hills, near the Rockefeller family estate, in advance of a new restaurant called Blue Hill at Stone Barns. Chef Dan Barber, who ran the Blue Hill restaurant in New York City, cooked the dinner.

A ticket to one of Denevan's Outstanding in the Field events can cost upward of $150, and sometimes guests are asked to bring their own plates. The outdoor locations have a fairy-tale quality, with an epic array of local delicacies cooked and served out of doors on white linen tablecloths and lit by candlelight. A core of dedicated volunteers helps Denevan arrange the events, which have been held on an isthmus in Seattle's Puget Sound and a sea cave in northern California. Any fishermen, farmers, vintners, dairy workers, or organic cattle ranchers involved in the process dine for free; the costs of the event are borne by ticket sales, which have attracted a semi-cultish national following. Denevan's idea proved so popular that in the summer of 2004 he bought an old bus, refitted it, and turned the Outstanding in the Field events into a literal movable feast, traveling across the United States and finding a farm or space in which to hold the next dinner.

In 2008 Denevan worked with coauthor Marah Stets to produce a 100-recipe cookbook, *Outstanding in the Field: A Farm to Table Cookbook,* published by Clarkson Potter, which brought in some much-needed revenue to Denevan's ongoing elite-picnic adventure project. In 2009 he set up events at the Queens County Farm Museum in New York City and another at a community garden in Lower Manhattan. In 2012 a Miami-area farm, Hani's Mediterranean Organics, hosted another highly anticipated Outstanding in the Field event.

For several years Denevan barely earned enough to keep the project in progress, taking out emergency loans from a line of credit backed by his mother's house in Santa Cruz, which she had left him after her death in 2000 from complications of Alzheimer's disease. "She always said I was a dreamer, that I should be more responsible," he mused in an interview with Kim Severson for the *New York Times Magazine.*

Denevan began creating his sand art projects just a few years before he started the Outstanding in the Field dinners, as a way to deal with his mother's illness and his siblings' plight. He began with a 12-foot-long fish drawing on a northern California beach in 1996, and the works evolved into epic, abstract land-art images that take hours to create but just minutes to erode once the tide comes in. Galleries in San Francisco and New York City have heralded his works, in photographic and video form, and he also participated in the 2010 Vancouver Biennale. "One part of drawing in the sand that's really great is that, no matter what I do, no matter how big it is, I have a completely clean sheet of paper," he explained to author Michael Welland in the book *Sand: The Never-ending Story*. "Meaning a completely clean strip of sand that I can return to every day, and there's an incredible freedom in that kind of artwork."

In 2010 Denevan traveled with a crew of volunteers and filmmakers to Lake Baikal, Siberia, where he created a massive installation of circle-art on ice spread across nine square miles. This was his largest project to date, and the process became the documentary movie *Art Hard*, which made the rounds of the 2011 film-festival circuit. The Lake Baikal effort can also be viewed at a Web site called TheAnthropologist.net, which is also the name of an arts foundation backed by the Anthropologie retail chain. "A chance to make geometry," Denevan wrote about the ordeal in verse form for the Web site. "Meaning: / A beginning and a completion of the motions, / A fulfillment between storms and days."

Selected writings

(With Marah Stets) *Outstanding in the Field: A Farm to Table Cookbook*, Clarkson Potter (New York City), 2008.

Sources

Books

Welland, Michael, *Sand: The Never-ending Story*, University of California Press, 2009, p. 214.

Periodicals

New York Times, September 2, 2009, p. A17.
New York Times Magazine August 21, 2005, p. 42.
Sunset, September 2008, p. 34.
Telegraph (London, England), July 3, 2008.
Toronto Star, July 27, 2009, p. E1.

Online

"Featured Contributor: Jim Denevan," TheAnthropologist.net, http://theanthropologist.net/#/JimDenevan(November 29, 2011).
"Outstanding in the Field Plans Big Eats at Hani Khouri's Farm," *Miami New Times*, http://blogs.miaminewtimes.com/shortorder/2011/11/outstanding_in_the_field_comin.ph (November 22, 2011).

—*Carol Brennan*

Al DiGuido

Chief Executive Officer of Zeta Interactive

Born in 1956, in New York, NY; son of a police officer and a homemaker; married Chris; children: Rosie, George, Diana. *Education:* St. Francis College, B.A., 1978.

Addresses: *Office*—Zeta Interactive, 99 Park Ave., 23rd Flr., New York, NY 10016.

Career

Began his advertising career with an outdoor billboard company; associate publisher, then executive vice-president, Ziff-Davis Publishing, 1987-2000; publisher, *Computer Shopper*, 1993-98; CEO, Expression Engines, c. 1999-2000; CEO, Bigfoot Interactive, 2000-03; founded charity, Al's Angels, 2004; president and CEO, Epsilon Interactive, 2006-07; founder, Zeta Interactive, 2007, and CEO, 2007—.

Awards: Tomorrow's Children's Fund Award, 1999; Rotary Sunrise Award/Paul Harris Fellowship, 2008; William A. Krause Jr. Humanitarian Award, 2009; Sons of the American Revolution Bronze Good Fellowship Award.

Sidelights

Al DiGuido is CEO and President of Zeta Interactive, a digital marketing services company. In the past, he has held senior management positions at Sports, Inc., Children's Television Network's magazine division, and *Parade* magazine. His passion for marketing, particularly online marketing, is well-known in his industry; in *Directmag*, Ken Magill called him "one of the most vocal evangelists in e-mail marketing."

DiGuido was born in the New York City borough of Brooklyn in 1956, one of seven children. His father was a New York City police officer and his mother was a homemaker. As a boy, he played baseball at his elementary school and softball at his high school, but he was best known for breaking the most windows when the neighborhood kids gathered on the street to play stickball. When he was 13 years old, his playtime was curtailed as he began working after school and on weekends to help support his family. He worked all through his years at St. Francis College in Brooklyn, earning a bachelor's degree in political science. While in college, he was the sports announcer at the school basketball team's games, and he also participated in the school's theater program, appearing in several productions—most notably in "Witness for the Prosecution."

While he was still in school, DiGuido began his life-long career in media and marketing through a chance event. Although he had applied to law school, he was not accepted into the schools he wanted, so he had to get a job. His mother went to a Brooklyn hair salon and while she was having her hair done, struck up a conversation with the woman next to her. She mentioned that her son, Al, was looking for a job. The woman replied that her husband had a recruiting firm. DiGuido went to see him, and was put in touch with a man who had an outdoor billboard advertising company and who wanted to hire someone who could learn that business. DiGuido took the job.

DiGuido eventually moved indoors, working in the publishing industry with Ziff-Davis from 1987 to 2000, including a stint as publisher of *Computer Shopper* from 1993 to 1998. He became chief executive officer of Bigfoot Interactive, an e-mail marketing company, from 2000 to 2003. In 2004, DiGuido founded a charity, Al's Angels. The organization helped needy families in Connecticut, New Jersey, and New York, providing food and toys during the holidays, and raised funds for families dealing with severe illness or financial hardship.

In 2005, the marketing company Epsilon Interactive acquired Bigfoot Interactive and then bought the e-mail marketing unit of advertiser DoubleClick. The changes led to friction between executives from Bigfoot and DoubleClick, and many DoubleClick staffers left. Those who remained were taken aback by DiGuido's passion for creating a full-service advertising agency, one that would provide not only advertising e-mail services, but also Web site design, social media services, and creative campaign development. Toward the end of his tumultuous tenure at Epsilon, an anonymous blogger, calling himself Pal Dodido, stirred up gossip about DiGuido in the relatively small e-mail marketing world by posting boasts about fooling venture capitalists and analysts into overvaluing his company. No one ever found out who the blogger was, and the posts eventually stopped. Nevertheless, in September of 2007, after repeated clashes, DiGuido was fired.

Within a year, DiGuido became chief executive officer of Zustek, an e-mail marketing company, and soon after that he acquired Adverb Media, an online marketing services agency. He renamed the combined company Zeta Interactive, and his focus was on online marketing and providing the comprehensive suite of services he was unable to provide at Epsilon. He realized that the old world of paper magazines and publishing was dying, and that advertisers would have to shift their efforts to the place where people spent the most time looking at media: the Internet. He chose the name Zeta because the letter Zeta comes after the letter Epsilon in the Greek alphabet; the name is a clever way of saying, "After Epsilon."

Zeta Interactive creates Web sites and email campaigns for its clients, and it also provides a "data mining" service that allows companies to determine whether people are reading their e-mails and Web sites. The company's tool, Zeta Buzz, can examine posts on Facebook and other social networks to tell marketers what people are interested in and most likely to buy. As DiGuido told Joan Verdon of the North Jersey *Record Online*, "There's 100 million people who blog [and post on social networking sites] every day. And this tool allows you to go in there and scrape content, real-time." Zeta Buzz included a tool that examined the sentence structure of what people posted in order to determine whether a comment was positive or negative.

DiGuido told Verdon that over the years, he had seen a huge shift in the ways people read and got their information. Magazines and newspapers all over the country were going out of business. He pointed out that this was not because people were no longer interested in the information that newspapers and magazines provided, but because people preferred to read online and that the old, paper-based business model was no longer sustainable. In response, his company created Zeta NextPage, which lets online readers electronically flip through pages of magazines and catalogs just as they would with a paper version.

As a result of these innovations, Zeta Interactive was named a Top 50 digital agency by the magazine *Advertising Age*. The company's clients include many Fortune 500 companies.

DiGuido currently lives in Westport, Connecticut, with his wife Chris and their three children. He is very active with Al's Angels as well as with his children's sports teams, the local chapter of Sons of Italy, and the local YMCA. DiGuido ran in the New York City Marathon in 2004. He has received awards for his charitable work, including the William A. Krause Jr. Humanitarian Award, the Bronze Good Citizenship Award from the Sons of the American Revolution, and the Rotary Sunrise/Paul Harris Fellowship.

Sources

Periodicals

Direct, December 12, 2006; October 3, 2007; November 16, 2007; November 20, 2007; February 12, 2008.
PR Newswire, February 24, 2011.

Online

"2009 Honorees: Al DiGuido," Sportsmen of Westport, http://www.sportsmenofwestport.org/2009_honorees.htm#AL0IGUIDO (February 11, 2011).

Al's Angels, http://www.alsangels.org/ (February 11, 2011).

"An Interview with Al DiGuido," *Promotion World*, http://www.promotionworld.com/interviews/080220AlDiGuido.html (February 15, 2011).

"Media Business CEO Started with Billboards," *Record Online*, http://www.northjersey.com/news/business/62785837.tif.html?page=all (February 11, 2011).

"Say It Ain't So, Al; What Will We Write About?" *Direct*, http://directmag.com/email/say_aint_so/ (February 11, 2011).

Zeta Interactive, http://www.zetainteractive.com/ (February 15, 2011).

—*Kelly Winters*

Rocco DiSpirito

Chef and television personality

Born November 19, 1966, in New York, NY; son of Raffaele and Nicolina DiSpirito; married Natalie David (divorced, 2000). *Education:* Graduated from Culinary Institute of America, Hyde Park, NY, 1986; studied at Jardin de Cygne, Paris, France; Boston University, B.A., 1990.

Addresses: *Web site*—http://www.roccodispirito. com

Career

Began working in a pizzaria, 1977; assistant chef, Adrienne, New York City, 1988; chef de partie, Aujourd'hui, Boston, c. late 1980s; worked at the French restaurant Lespinasse, New York City, c. early 1990s; founder and executive chef, Dava Restaurant, New York City, 1995-96; owner and executive chef, Union Pacific, 1997-04; host of television show *Melting Pot*, Food Network, 2000; published first cookbook, *Flavor*, 2003; consulting chef, Tuscan, New York City, 2003; founder and executive chef, Rocco's on 22nd, New York City, 2003-04; star of the reality television show *Restaurant*, NBC, 2003-04; radio host, WOR, New York City, 2004-05; participant, *Dancing with the Stars*, ABC, 2008; star of reality television show *Rocco Gets Real*, A&E, 2008—.

Awards: Best New Chef, *Food and Wine* magazine, 1999; Most Exciting Young Chef, *Gourmet* magazine, 2000; Sexiest Chef Alive, *People* magazine, 2002; Best Cookbook-cooking from a professional point of view, James Beard Award, for *Flavor*, 2004.

Sidelights

The focus of Rocco DiSpirito's life is family and food. Growing up in the borough of Queens in New York City, he was surrounded by his loving and large Italian-American family. As a child DiSpirito learned many traditional Italian recipes from his mother, grandmothers, and extended family. The dedication at the beginning of his cookbook *Flavor*, which won a James Beard Award in 2004, says "To my Grandma Anna-Maria, my mother Nicolina, my aunts, paisani and friends: Margarite, Maria, Elena, Isadore, Concettina, Guisseppina, Angelina, Emanuela, Raffielina, Camilla, Pasqualina, Vincenzina and all the other great women out there who give generously, cook, teach, nurture, inspire and bring the good life to the rest of us. It wouldn't be the same without you."

On Al Dente, an Amazon Food Blog, DiSpirito described how he and his siblings struggled with figuring out who they were. He wrote "My family exists at the center of the Italian way of life, the American way of life, and all the rich traditions that come with both cultures." Thanksgiving, a very American holiday, meant that there would be a turkey with all of the trimmings, but Christmas was a very different feast. On Al Dente, DiSpirito wrote "The Christmas we had was la Vigilia di Natale, the Feast of the Seven Fishes, on Christmas Eve, when we opened our gifts. Our Christmas Eve dinner was *off the charts*. It was the meal we looked forward to *all* year, my first cousins, second cousins, third cousins—everyone." With this emphasis on family and food, it is no surprise that DiSpirito became a celebrity chef who included his entire family in the reality television show *Restaurant* and who has a passion for helping home cooks to become better cooks.

Patty Adams, writing for *Page Six Magazine,* asked DiSpirito what it was like growing up in Jamaica, Queens. DiSpirito called his neighborhood a ghetto and told her that he was terrified everyday walking to school in his Catholic school uniform of brown corduroy trousers, a maroon jacket, and a tie that was printed with the words "Presentation of the Blessed Virgin Mary." He explained to Adams that he "was a walking target!" But Queens also had family, community, and pizza. When DiSpritio was eleven years old he went to work at a pizzeria. Answering questions by viewers of the *Rachel Ray Show* that were submitted on her official Web site, he wrote "There is no greater gift you can give than to cook for someone. It's what I fell in love with my first day on the job in that Queens pizzeria when I was eleven years old and to this day nothing makes me happier." Feeding people and creating great food became his passion.

When DiSpirito was only 16 years old he entered the world-famous Culinary Institute of America to further his cooking skills and his knowledge of food. After completing this program in 1986 and graduating with honors, he went to France and studied French regional cooking and wine at the Jardin de Cygne restaurant in Paris with Dominique Cecillon and Gray Kunz. Deciding that he would benefit from some business skills in addition to his culinary skills, DiSpirito attended Boston University where he earned a bachelor's degree in business and graduated cum laude in 1990. For hands on experience he worked as an assistant chef at Adrienne in Hotel Maxim's de Paris in New York in 1988, became Chef de Partie at Boston's Aujourd'hui, then returned to New York to study under great chefs Charlie Palm and Gray Kunz who later included DiSpirito in the opening team for the famous Lespinasse restaurant. In addition to learning French culinary techniques to add to his traditional Italian food knowledge, DiSpirito learned about Asian ingredients and techniques from Chef Mark Baker while he was at Aujourd'hui. All of these experiences led to DiSpirito developing his own theories about blending flavors and creating unique recipes.

After working to acquire his skills in the kitchen, DiSpirito wanted to strike out on his own and open his own restaurant. His first attempt was Dava Restaurant in midtown Manhattan which was open only for six months, but Ruth Reichl, the food critic at the *New York Times*, wrote in a review for Dava that "Rocco DiSpirito isn't a name you are likely to forget. But you are bound to be hearing a lot of it, because Mr. DiSpirito is turning out food so personal and intense you can't help asking, 'Who's the chef?'" After this he opened Union Pacific in 1997 in the Gramercy Park section of Manhattan. The first time Reichl reviewed Union Pacific she gave the restaurant only two stars. A second review in 1998 earned a third star and she wrote "The woman at the next table is moaning. I try to discover what has caused this reaction, but she has just finished the final forkful and all I can see is her eyes, wide with the wonder of whatever is in her mouth." She went on in the review to say "I have yet to taste anything on Mr. DiSpirito's menu that is not wonderful." After this review Union Pacific became a destination for people who were interested in exquisite dining and DiSpirito began his ascent into food superstardom.

While DiSpirito was becoming more famous, the producers for the television show *Restaurant* were looking for a chef willing to open a restaurant as part of a reality television series. Restaurateurs such as Drew Nierporent, Brian McNally, and Phil Suarez were approached. DiSpirito was signed on and Jeffrey Chodorow was the financier behind Rocco's, the restaurant that bore DiSpirito's name and was opened on 22nd Street in Manhattan. Chodorow had seen an episode of *Today* where DiSpirito made an Easter meal and this swayed him to work with the young chef. Chodorow was coming to the endeavor as a businessman with more than 20 other restaurants that collectively took in approximately $150 million annually. At first the show began as a somewhat comic romp with such dramas as a workplace romance, service troubles, and a kitchen fire. His mother, Nicolina, kept showing up and was a charming addition to the staff. DiSpirito did indeed involve his family. His mother was hired to make her special meatballs. His aunt was in the kitchen making pasta. His uncle worked in the restaurant as well. Rocco's was DiSpirito's dream and he had high ambitions of opening a series of Rocco's restaurants across the United States; then the troubles began.

At first Chodorow was barely present on the show, but as the restaurant grew more chaotic and less profitable, Chodorow became more and more in evidence. Tensions rose between Chodorow and DiSpirito and a theme began of the back-office financier battling with the passionate, brilliant, and idealistic front man. DiSpirito appeared to be a man under attack in his own kitchen when the second season was filmed in 2003-04. Chodorow then filed a lawsuit in the Supreme Court of the State of New York. He wanted to dissolve the business partnership with DiSpirito and he wanted DiSpirito to compensate him for side ventures that DiSpirito did that featured the restaurant. There were allegations that DiSpirito submitted bills to be paid for supplies for Rocco's that were sent over to DiSpirito's other restaurant, Union Pacific. Beth Landman, writing for *New York* magazine, quoted Chodorow as saying "My manager caught one of his people taking pasta out of the restaurant, which we know he was sending over to Union Pacific, and we were paying for the labor. Our flower bills were $1,400 a month—and we didn't have any flowers. I'm going to depose that flower woman and see if we were paying and she was really doing those flowers for Union Pacific."

The allegations stunned DiSpirito who had envisioned the restaurant as more of a tight, almost family like business. Chodorow had at first agreed to do *Restaurant* because he thought it would give the restaurant great advertising exposure and then more restaurants could be opened nationwide. He saw it as a winning proposition, but after the show aired Chodorow began to be concerned about his reputation as a businessman because he felt that the show portrayed the whole start-up of the restaurant in a negative light. Before the second season Chodorow approached the producers of the show with his complaints and they told him that if he could turn the restaurant around then they would broadcast it. Chodorow became the star of the second season and his conflict with DiSpirito took over the show. After Chodorow filed his lawsuit at the end of the filming of the second season, DiSpirito countersued. The divide between DiSpirito and Chodorow grew wider. In July of 2004, New York Supreme Court Judge Ira Gammerman issued an injunction against DiSpirito who could no longer go into Rocco's and also gave Chodorow the right to sell or reopen the restaurant. Rocco's on 22nd Street closed in September 2004 and was reopened in 2005 as a Brazilian steakhouse.

After the ordeal with *Restaurant*, which left many critics speculating about whether or not a celebrity chef could be called insulting names weekly on television and still be able to have a culinary career, DiSpirito left Union Pacific by mutual agreement with his partners. The restaurant where DiSpirito made his name announced it would be closing at the end of 2004 and that another chef would be the executive chef until then. DiSpirito was suddenly the most talented and celebrated chef in New York without a restaurant.

Following *Restaurant* and leaving Union Pacific, DiSpirito did not return to the restaurant business. He hosted a radio program in the New York City metro area from October 2004 through December 2005, was featured in a Lincoln MKX commercial, and made an appearance on the ABC sitcom *Knights of Prosperity.* He was a guest judge on Bravo's *Top Chef* reality chef competition show and returned for the third season finale to assist one of the contestants. He made another appearance on the show as a judge during the fourth season. He appeared on NBC's *Biggest Loser: Couples* to help contestants prepare healthy meals and on *Biggest Loser: Families* to teach contestants how to shop and cook healthy recipes. DiSpirito also competed on *Dancing With the Stars* during its seventh season, placing ninth overall.

When DiSpirito appeared on *Biggest Loser: Couples* and *Biggest Loser: Families,* it was after he had lost 30 pounds and begun doing triathlons. He told the participants how he had reached a hefty 216 pounds before deciding to lose the weight. In 2008 DiSpirito became the host of his own show on A&E titled *Rocco Gets Real.* The program was part cooking show and part lifestyle show in which DiSpirito went to people's homes and helped them to prepare meals for such events as the dinner for a marriage proposal, a feast for a family reunion, or a special family meal. He worked with the participants on the show to help them learn to cook and overcome any anxieties they had about preparing a menu and cooking a meal. DiSpirito has continued to write cookbooks and in 2009 published *Now Eat This.* He wanted a cookbook that was accessible, recreating recipes for traditional American fare but making them healthier, with less fat and fewer calories. DiSpirito may no longer be in the restaurant business, but he is reaching out to a greater audience and making his own family of food lovers.

Selected writings

Cookbooks

Flavor, Hyperion (New York City), 2003.
Rocco's Italian-American, Hyperion, 2004.
Rocco's 5 Minute Flavor: Fabulous Meals with 5 Ingredients in 5 Minutes, Scribner (New York City), 2005.
Rocco's Real Life Recipes; Fast Flavor for Everyday, Wiley (Hoboken, NJ), 2007.

Rocco Gets Real: Cook at Home, Every Day, Wiley, 2008.

Now Eat This! 150 of America's Favorite Comfort Foods, All Under 350 Calories, Ballantine Books (New York City), 2010.

Now Eat This! Diet: Lose Up to 10 Pounds in Just 2 Weeks Eating 6 Meals a Day!, Grand Central Life & Style (New York City), 2011.

Sources

Books

DiSpirito, Rocco, *Flavor*, Hyperion, 2003.

Periodicals

New York Times, October 13, 1995; August 5, 1998; September 29, 2004.

St. Petersburg Times (FL), November 9, 2009.

Online

"About Rocco DiSpirito," Al Dente: An Amazon.com Food Blog for Recipes, Cocktails, Food Buzz, and Kitchen Gadget Reviews, http://www.aldenteblog.com/rocco_dispirito.html (February 20, 2011).

"Food Networker," *New York* magazine, http://nymag.com/nymetro/food/industry/features/5155/ (March 2, 2011).

"On the Ranch with Rocco: Recipes and Tips from the *Biggest Loser* Chef," Delish, http://www.delish.com/cooking-shows/food-tv/rocco-dispirito-biggest-loser (Febrauary 20, 2011).

"Rocco DiSpirito," About.com, http://gourmetfood.about.com/od/chefbiographi2/p/roccodispirito.htm (February 14, 2011).

"Rocco DiSpirito Biography," Biography, http://www.biography.com/articles/Rocco-DiSpirito-368870 (February 20, 2011).

"Rocco DiSpirito," Cookstr.com, http://www.cookstr.com/users/rocco-dispirito/profile (February 20, 2011).

"Rocco DiSpirito," Internet Movie Database, http://www.imdb.com/name/nm1406387/ (March 2, 2011).

"Rocco DiSpirito," Rachel Ray's Official Web site, http://www.rachelray.com/food/rocco.php (February 20, 2011).

"Six Seconds With ... Rocco DiSpirito," *Page Six Magazine,* http://www.nypost.com/pagesixmag/issues/20081221.tif/Six+Seconds+Rocco+DiSpirito (February 20, 2011).

"Spaghetti Western," *New York* magazine, http://nymag.com/nymetro/food/features/n_10216/ (February 26, 2011).

—*Annette Bowman*

Jeffrey Donovan

AP Images/Peter Kramer

Actor

Born May 11, 1968, in Amesbury, MA; son of a factory worker. *Education:* Attended Bridgewater State College, c. 1986-87; University of Massachusetts—Amherst, B.A., 1991; New York University, M.F.A., 1994.

Addresses: *Office*—c/o USA Network, 30 Rockefeller Plaza, 21st Fl., New York, NY 10112.

Career

Actor in films, including: *Throwing Down*, 1995; *Sleepers*, 1996; *Catherine's Grove*, 1997; *Vegas Vacation*, 1997; *Bait*, 2000; *Book of Shadows: Blair Witch 2*, 2000; *Purpose*, 2002; *Final Draft*, 2003; *Sam & Joe*, 2003; *Hitch*, 2005; *Believe in Me*, 2006; *Come Early Morning*, 2006; *The Changeling*, 2008; *Hindsight*, 2008. Television guest appearances include: *Homicide: Life on the Street*, NBC, 1995; *Law & Order*, NBC, 1995, 2007; *Another World*, NBC, 1997; *Millennium*, FOX, 1997; *Spin City*, ABC, 1999; *The Beat*, UPN, 2000; *Witchblade*, TNT, 2002; *CSI: Miami*, CBS, 2005; *Monk*, USA Network, 2006; *Threshold*, CBS, 2006; *Yes, Dear*, CBS, 2006. Television movie appearances include: *Critical Choices*, Showtime, 1996; *When Trumpets Fade*, HBO, 1998; *Witness to the Mob*, NBC, 1998; *Touching Evil*, USA Network, 2004. Regular television appearances include: *The Pretender*, NBC, 1997-98; *Touching Evil*, USA Network, 2004; *Crossing Jordan*, NBC, 2007; *Burn Notice*, USA Network, 2007—. Stage appearances include: *Freedomland*, Wilder Theater, New York City, 1998; *A View from the Bridge*, Neil Simon Theater, New York City, 1998; *Things You Shouldn't Say Past Midnight*, Promenade Theatre, New York City, 1999. Made directing debut with a 2010 episode of *Burn Notice*, and directed *Burn Notice: The Fall of Sam Axe* (television movie), 2011.

Sidelights

Jeffrey Donovan starred in *Burn Notice*, one of the top-rated television series on basic cable in the early twenty-first century. The hour-long USA Network drama featured Donovan as Michael Westen, a former high-level foreign intelligence operative whose sudden dismissal—a "burn notice" in spy parlance—forces him back to Miami, where he takes private-investigation jobs while attempting to unravel the mystery surrounding his past life. "Michael Westen is no James Bond," asserted *Newsday* writer Joseph V. Amodio about Donovan's character. "He's Stephen Colbert armed with sunglasses, a hot babe sidekick, and perhaps some combustible homemade thermite powder, outwitting villains with levity as well as pyrotechnics."

Born in 1968, Donovan was a native of Amesbury, Massachusetts, a small town near the state's northern border with New Hampshire. He was the second of three sons in a single-parent household that was often in perilous financial straits. "My mother worked in a factory. We were off and on welfare, food stamps," he told Luaine Lee in the *South Florida Sun-Sentinel*. "We grew up in a very poor town, there wasn't a lot of money to be found." At Amesbury High School, Donovan was a solid athlete, but was drawn into the drama club, too.

Donovan attended Bridgewater State College near Boston before transferring to the University of Massachusetts at Amherst. He worked his way through the undergraduate theater program, driving a bus in the early-morning hours then bartending on weekends. When he graduated, he won a coveted slot in the graduate theater program at New York University's Tisch School of the Arts, but had $60,000 in student loan debt by the time he finished his master of fine arts degree in 1994. He made his film debut in an independently produced caper film, *Throwing Down,* that premiered at the 1995 Chicago International Film Festival but failed to find a distributor.

Fortunately, New York City provided Donovan with ample opportunity for work. He appeared in episodes of *Law & Order* and other television series, and had a small role in the 1996 drama *Sleepers,* which starred Robert De Niro and Dustin Hoffman. He also landed stage roles in a revival of Arthur Miller's *A View from the Bridge* and *Freedomland,* among other plays.

In 2000, Donovan returned to the big screen with a part in a Jamie Foxx action thriller called *Bait* and *Book of Shadows: Blair Witch 2.* It would take another four years of small parts and box-office duds before Donovan finally attained a starring role in a series. The show was *Touching Evil,* which ran for one season on the USA Network. Donovan played Detective David Creegan, who was shot in the line of duty, died for ten minutes, and was revived; though physically recovered, he struggles with a radically altered personality. Critics gave *Touching Evil* high marks, but the series was not renewed for a second season.

Donovan continued to land film roles, including a part in the 2005 Will Smith comedy *Hitch* and as the romantic lead opposite Ashley Judd in 2006's *Come Early Morning.* In 2007 he played a roguish attorney in the sixth and final season of the NBC crime drama *Crossing Jordan.* That was also the same year that *Burn Notice* premiered on the USA Network. One of new passel of original series on basic cable, the hour-long action drama took its title from a term used in intelligence operations when an agent is suddenly blacklisted. Donovan's Michael Westen is working for an unnamed agency in Nigeria when he is bundled into a car, which begins an arduous journey back to Miami. His termination means that not only is he blacklisted in the espionage community, but has also been expunged from all official records, including the pension rolls. Westen soon discovers he is also being blamed for unauthorized killings.

In Miami, Donovan's character picks up odd jobs as a private detective, using his superb Special-Operations military training to avenge wrongdoers. His mother, played by Sharon Gless, harasses him, and he remains on friendly terms with his ex-girlfriend, Fiona (Gabrielle Anwar), a weapons expert with ties to the Irish Republican Army. Westen has a tenuous relationship with the sole connection to his former career, an ex-spy named Sam Axe (Bruce Campbell). *Burn Notice* earned high marks from its debut season, with *Entertainment Weekly's* Gillian Flynn characterizing it as a fairly straightforward detective series "brightened by unusual characters and snazzy dialogue." Flynn also singled out "Donovan's knowing narration, which is a great blend of old-school, earnest noir and new-school, smart-ass sarcasm."

As the second season's episodes of *Burn Notice* rolled out in the summer of 2008, *New Yorker* television critic Nancy Franklin found the series a compelling watch. "Donovan has a hard, closed face, and he deploys a broad, deliberately insincere grin that conveys Westen's bitterness and cynicism," she wrote. Near the end of that sophomore season, *New York Times* journalist Ginia Bellafante theorized that "*Burn Notice* succeeds in some sense because it is a restitution drama without blatantly saying so. It lives by the voiceover, but its insouciance prevents us from hearing the deep thoughts that must be quaking in Michael's mind. He worked in the age of National Security Agency spying and unsound foreign policy."

The third season opener for *Burn Notice* pulled in six million viewers. The fourth season found Donovan's character further enmeshed in the clandestine world of counter-terrorism operations like overseas rendition. In one episode, Burt Reynolds starred as a bartender whose prior career shared eerie similarities to Westen's. USA Network executives, thrilled by the consistently strong ratings, ordered fifth and sixth seasons, plus a movie special that would fill in some of the back story on Axe and his run-ins with a Colombian drug cartel years before. Donovan was set to direct the 2011 telefilm.

Donovan has been linked romantically to Ellen Muth, who starred in the Showtime series *Dead Like Me,* and Kathryn Kovarik, a Los Angeles-area yoga instructor. His action-heavy role on *Burn Notice* required an extreme degree of physical fitness, and he worked out for several hours a day with a personal trainer to prepare for the shooting season. He admitted that he delved into spy memoirs when he first landed the lead in the series. "They all spoke about the same thing," he recounted in the interview with *Newsday*'s Amodio. "How boring and long the waiting is between actual missions. Kind of like sitting on a movie set."

Sources

Entertainment Weekly, June 29, 2007.
Newsday (Melville, NY), July 8, 2008.

New Yorker, August 11, 2008, p. 94.
New York Times, January 22, 2009, p. C3.
South Florida Sun-Sentinel, May 31, 2004, p. 3D.
Variety, April 15, 2010.

—*Carol Brennan*

Patrick Dougherty

Welsh Studios

Artist

Born in 1945, in Oklahoma; married first wife (divorced, 1985); married Linda Johnson (a museum curator), c. 1992: children: two from first marriage, son Sam (from second marriage). *Education:* University of North Carolina, B.A., 1967; University of Iowa, M.P.H., 1969; enrolled in graduate art program at the University of North Carolina—Chapel Hill, 1982.

Addresses: *Home*—Chapel Hill, NC. *Web site*—http://www.stickwork.net.

Career

Hospital administrator, U.S. Air Force, 1970s; artist, 1983—.

Awards: National Endowment for the Arts fellowship, 1990.

Sidelights

Artist Patrick Dougherty fashions immense, undulating works of environmental art entirely by hand from twigs, saplings, and other foliage elements. Every year, Dougherty creates nine or ten installations for museum, parks, and other community sites in the United States, Europe, and Asia, but the impermanent huts, towers, and tunnels degrade naturally back into the environment. "I try to use the craftiness that I see in animals as well as the human urges to use sticks," the artist explained in an interview with *Columbus Dispatch* writer Bill Mayr.

Dougherty was born in Oklahoma in 1945, but his family moved to North Carolina's secluded, scenic Moore County when he was ten. At the University of North Carolina's Chapel Hill campus, he majored in English, then went on to earn a master's degree in hospital administration from the University of Iowa in 1969. He spent time working for a U.S. Air Force medical center in West Germany before returning to North Carolina as a husband and father. Around 1973, he bought a ten-acre parcel in Chapel Hill, and set to work building his own home, a humble one-room cabin he erected with *Foxfire* guides, a series of books that originated as magazine articles on traditional Appalachian folk ways. "I didn't know much about building, and I was intimidated by people that did," he recalled in an interview with Penelope Green in the *New York Times*. "Also, I wanted to face the problems myself. It was a passage, finding my way through a house and into a life."

Dougherty's mastery of carpentry skills awakened his interest in art. One day, on a rural road, he pulled over to investigate an odd shape in the brush, marveling at the structures created by nature. In the early 1980s, he began taking graduate art courses at the University of North Carolina, but the professors were perplexed by his first works, which were life-sized figures created entirely from saplings, which are the young, more pliant new branches of a tree. He had his first solo show in 1983, and soon gained some regional recognition. In 1990, he was awarded a National Endowment for the Arts fellowship, and a year later was invited to participate in a group show at the Katonah Museum of Art in Westchester, New York. "Fully biodegradable and eminently uncollectable, the shapes recall not only tornadoes," wrote Vivien Raynor in the *New York Times* about Dougherty's swirled towers of twigs, "but also the leafy 'Bigfoot' who turns up in the pre-Christian mythology of northern Europe."

Over the next decade Dougherty traveled around the globe creating site-specific works for a shrine in Chiba, Japan, museums in Belgium, Kentucky, and New York City, and even a coil of branches that wrapped around the columns of the neoclassical Manchester City Art Gallery. Early in his career, Dougherty would use maple saplings from a North Carolina supplier, but eventually shifted to using native materials taken from a site near the planned commission. The process involves cutting the saplings, which he does himself, then creating an outline of the structure using the larger saplings. Then, the saplings are woven to create the form itself, sometimes using rope or twine to bend the shape to his liking, which is eventually removed.

Because Dougherty's works are almost always in public spaces, he fields incessant questions from passers-by, and began inviting some of the more serious ones to join him. He now works with teams of volunteers, some of whom have worked with him for years. But it is the pedestrian's reaction to his shapes and forms that remains paramount. "The public is absolutely unforgiving," he told Mayr, the *Columbus Dispatch* journalist. "They either like it or they don't."

In the twenty-first century, Dougherty has accepted commissions from the Smithsonian's National Museum of Natural History, the Honolulu Contemporary Museum, the Santa Barbara Botanic Garden, and one much-discussed, traffic-stopping façade for a new Max Azria store on Melrose Avenue in Los Angeles. There were also installations in Alabama, Minnesota, and Pennsylvania, and even a conference room for a cutting-edge advertising agency in Portland, Oregon. In France in 2008, he created "Sortie de Cave" ("Free at Last") for the Jardin des Arts in Chateaubourg, which resembled giant wine bottles with cutout windows, tilting against one another and hedges. Two years later, he built "Natural History" at the Brooklyn Botanic Garden, a quintet of pod-like huts created from willow saplings taken

from a protected wetland area on Staten Island. "In parks or gardens they look like primitive huts, witch's castles, enormous vases or nests for gigantic birds," wrote *Star Tribune* writer Mary Abbe about Dougherty's environmental installations. "For museums and galleries his designs are usually more abstract and conceptual—wild mats of greenery that drop from ceilings, swirl down stairways and flow outside to encircle trees or embrace the pillars of a porch."

Dougherty's works degrade naturally over an eight-season life cycle with the help of wind, rain, and sun, but sometimes he and his volunteers disassemble them. In 2010, Princeton Architectural Press published a monograph of his works to date, *Stickwork*, with the "Sortie de Cave" image on the cover. Photographs of past installations can also be found on his Web site, www.stickwork.net. "I make temporary work that challenges traditional concepts of sculpture," he once told a reporter, Stephen Henkin, for an article that ran in *Insight on the News*, asserting his mission was to create a body of work that "challenges permanent objects made to last for generations, which can be bought and sold and accrue value."

Art scholars categorize Dougherty's work as a new field of environmental art, linked to the large-scale installations of artists like Christo but also to the folk traditions of ancient and pre-modern cultures. Dougherty likes to remind visitors that the first structures humans ever built to shelter themselves were fashioned from wood. "Because the scale Dougherty works with is so large, it makes us think of the environments developers transform daily in real time and space on a similar scale in our cities, suburbs, rural areas that have no aesthetic of integration with site and space," wrote John K. Grande in a chapter devoted to Dougherty in the 2003 tome *Balance: Art and Nature*. "The physical scale and presence of Dougherty's art is a constant reminder that real world environments affect our senses more profoundly than any abstract conception of a place ever will."

Selected works

Selected temporary installations

Sticks and Stones (group exhibition), Katonah Museum of Art, Westchester, NY, 1991.
"Rip-Rap," Manchester City Art Gallery, Manchester, England, 1991.
"Holy Rope," Chiba, Japan, 1992.
American Craft Museum, New York City, NY, 1996.

Spalding University, Louisville, KY, 1996.

Cultural Arts Council, Houston/Harris County, TX, 1996.

"Watchamacallit," Smithsonian National Museum of Natural History, Washington, DC, 2000.

Atelier 340 Muzeum, Brussels, Belgium, 2003.

"Na Hale 'O Waiawi," Contemporary Museum, Honolulu, HI, 2003.

Twisted Logic (retrospective), Grounds for Sculpture, Hamilton, NJ, 2004.

Santa Barbara Botanic Garden, Santa Barbara, CA, 2005.

Franklin Park Conservatory, Columbus, OH, 2006.

"Just for Looks," Melrose Avenue, Los Angeles, CA, 2006.

"Stir Crazy," Frederik Meijer Gardens and Sculpture Park, Grand Rapids, MI, 2007.

"Sortie de Cave," Jardin des Arts, Chateaubourg, France, 2008.

"Catawumpus," Los Angeles County Arboretum & Botanic Garden, Arcadia, CA, 2008.

Florence Griswold Museum, Old Lyme, CT, 2009.

"Lookin' Good! Lookin' Good!," Montgomery Museum of Fine Arts, Montgomery, AL, 2009.

"Natural History," Brooklyn Botanic Garden, Brooklyn, NY, 2010.

Dumbarton Oaks, Washington, DC, 2010.

Palo Alto Art Center, Palo Alto, CA, 2011.

Guilford College, Greensboro, NC, 2011.

Purdue University, West Lafayette, IN, 2011.

Wegerzyn Gardens Metropark, Dayton, OH, 2011.

"Diamonds in the Rough," Lewis Ginter Botanical Garden, Richmond, VA, 2011.

Selected writings

Stickwork, Princeton Architectural Press (New York City), 2010.

Sources

Books

Grande, John K., "Patrick Dougherty: Wildness Fits," in *Balance: Art and Nature,* Black Rose Books Ltd., 2003, p. 234.

Periodicals

Arts & Activities, December 2009, p. 21.

Columbus Dispatch (OH), February 26, 2006.

Insight on the News, August 26, 1996, p. 38.

Interior Design, August 1, 2007, p. 182.

New York Times, July 14, 1991; October 31, 2004, p. 8; October 7, 2010, p. D1.

Star Tribune (Minneapolis, MN), May 21, 2010, p. 1E.

Online

Patrick Dougherty Official Web site, http://www.stickwork.net/ (May 16, 2011).

—*Carol Brennan*

Jonah Edelman

Activist

Born c. 1970, in Washington, D.C.; son of Peter (an attorney, government official, political aide, and law professor) and Marian Wright (an attorney and activist) Edelman; married Charese; children: Levi, Elijah (twins). *Education:* Yale University, B.A., 1992; Oxford University, M.A. and Ph.D, 1995.

Addresses: *Office*—Stand for Children Leadership Center, 516 SE Morrison St., Ste. 420, Portland, OR 97214.

Career

Helped organize the Stand for Children rally, Washington, D.C., 1996; co-founder and chief executive officer for Stand for Children, 1996—; helped get the Children's Investment Fund passed in Portland, OR, 2002, and renewed, 2008.

Awards: Prime Mover, Hunt Alternatives Fund, 2006; Innovator for the Public, Ashoka, 2008.

Sidelights

Activist Jonah Edelman is the co-founder of Stand for Children, and focuses on improving public education in the United States. His organization provides a political voice for students and making life better for children. Explaining the purpose of his organization, Edelman told Barbara Kessler of the *Dallas Morning News,* "The reality is that the United States, for all its resources, human and financial, does a terrible job of taking care of its children. We are at the bottom of industrialized nations in almost every category of child well-being, infant mortality, low-birth-weight babies.... But at the same time, I think that the average American wants to do well by children. So why have we allowed this to happen? I think it's because people have not translated their personal caring commitment to children into what they do as citizens." He added, "Because every child matters; there's nothing that matters more."

Born in Washington, D.C., he was the son of Peter and Marian Wright Edelman. His father was an attorney who was once an official in the U.S. Health and Human Services Department. He also worked as an aide to Robert F. Kennedy and was close to the presidential candidate. Peter Edelman later became a law professor. His mother was a civil rights leader who helped found and served as the head of the Children's Defense Fund. She was also a lawyer who became the first African-American woman to be admitted to the Mississippi Bar.

Edelman was educated at Yale University, where he majored in history and African-American studies. While a student there, he became interested in children's issues by tutoring. He told Kessler of the *Dallas Morning News,* "I was like many people who didn't know exactly how to get involved but wanted to make a difference in a child's life. So I started by tutoring a 7-year-old boy named Danny Zayas. He was a bilingual kid who didn't know how to read at that point.... And I taught him how to read. It was the most satisfying thing that I had ever done, and that really got me hooked."

While a student, Edelman eventually launched a mentoring program for students living in New Haven, Connecticut, called LEAP. It brought together children who lived in public housing with mentors from local high schools and colleges. Edelman also took part in partnership activities between Yale University and both the business and black communities, and organized a teenage pregnancy speaker's bureau where members of the community spoke to kids about being responsible and making good choices. He graduated from Yale University in 1992, then landed a Rhodes scholarship. Studying politics at Oxford University, he earned both a masters and Ph.D by 1995.

Edelman first gained noticed by helping to organize the Stand for Children founding rally in Washington, D.C., in 1996. Attended by 200,000 to 300,000 people, it was the largest rally for children in American history. Organizers, including Edelman, wanted to guarantee that Americans; legislators and government entities at the national, state, and local levels; nonprofits; and corporations all played an important role in assisting children in the United States and that children should be a priority to ensure a better future. Edelman told Desda Moss of *USA Today*, "We hope to raise awareness in the country that we need to act now for children. We are too locked in a framework where people say it's all about government or it's all about the individual."

By 1997, Edelman was serving as executive director of Stand for Children, which had been created by the Children's Defense Fund. Stand for Children was developing its agenda, which included addressing issue related to children such as lack of insurance, inadequate health care, insufficient child care, poverty, and the failings of the educational system. Edelman also addressed related topics like safe communities and legislation like federal welfare bills. To address these issues, Edelman and Stand for Children supported programs which supported children, including afterschool programs for at-risk youth, renovating playgrounds, and investing in prenatal care to ensure children are born healthy. To expand such support, Stand for Children held rallies all across the United States on June 1, 1997, with the goal of starting local "Children's Action Teams."

Moving to Portland, Oregon, in 1999, Edelman continued to expand the Stand for Children vision over the years, addressing issues like the rate structures for retailers supporting state lotteries to guarantee that rates would be beneficial for schools, and working toward policy changes that would benefit children and education. Stand for Children helped get Portland to pass the Children's Investment Fund levy in 2002, which invests millions of dollars every year into early education programs, after-school programs, and drop-out prevention programs. More than 16,000 children were helped each year in the program, which was renewed in 2008.

By 2010, the organization had affiliates in Oregon, Arizona, Illinois, Massachusetts, Tennessee, Washington, and Colorado, as well as members across the country. Grassroots advocacy was encouraged, with training provided on the state and local levels. Stand for Children advocates leveraged more than $2.3 billion in public funding for programs benefitting 2.5 million children in the United States. They also helped get legislation passed in six states in 2010, which would lead to more teachers in the classroom, increase the number of high-performing charter schools, turnaround poorly performing schools, and put rigorous high school graduation standards in place. By 2011, Stand for Children had an operating budget of $15 million, and was working on getting a comprehensive education improvement package passed in Illinois to allow local officials in Chicago to make the school day longer and implement new rules on tenure and performance that supported the best teachers instead of the longest-serving, and made it easier to fire bad teachers.

Known for his people and leadership skills, Edelman denied any interest in politics. Focusing all his attention on Stand for Children, he acknowledged that educational reform, like many of the issues his organization addressed, sometimes created difficult questions and debates. He told Amanda Paulson of the *Christian Science Monitor*, "We all want the best for kids, and we all want more students, regardless of their circumstances, to graduate high school ready for postsecondary education. There is a very legitimate debate about how best to get there." He added to Rebecca Napi of the *Spokesman Review*, "Whether you can see it or not in the moment, you are making a difference."

Sources

Periodicals

Business Wire, September 28, 2010.
Chicago Sun-Times, July 13, 2011, p. 12.

Christian Science Monitor, July 30, 2011.

Dallas Morning News, March 23, 1997, p. 1J.

New York Times, April 29, 2011, p. 23A.

Oregonian, April 8, 2005.

Spokesman Review (Spokane, WA), March 22, 2010, p. A5.

St. Louis Post-Dispatch (MO), April 27, 2011, p. A15.

USA Today, May 31, 1996, p. 3A.

US Fed News, April 12, 2009.

Washington Post, December 9, 1991, p. C7.

Online

"Activist Stands Up for Kids; And Group Takes Note," *Portland Tribune,* http://www.portlandtribune.com/news/story.php?story_id=11955115.tif91290566.tif00 (October 8, 2011).

"Jonah Edelman, Chief Executive Officer, Stand for Children," Stand for Children, http://www.stand.org/Page.aspx?pid=1271&chid=5 (October 8, 2011).

—*A. Petruso*

Carl Edwards

Race car driver

Born Carl Michael Edwards II, August 15, 1979, in Columbia, MO; son of Carl Edwards Sr. (a race car driver); married Katherine Downey, January 3, 2009; children: Anne, Michael. *Education:* Attended University of Missouri, Kansas City, MO.

Addresses: *Office*—Roush Fenway Racing, 4202 Roush Place, Concord, NC, 28027. *Web site*—http://www.carledwards.com.

Career

Began racing four-cylinder mini-sprints, 1993; won four feature races in the mini-sprints, 1994; switched to dirt racing, 1997; won NASCAR Truck Championship, 1999; became a full-time Truck Series competitor, 2003; made his Nextel Cup series debut, 2004; became a full-time driver in both the Nextel Cup and Busch Series circuits, 2005; placed second, NASCAR Nationwide Series, 2010; won Kobalt Tools 400 race, NASCAR Sprint Cup Series, 2011.

Awards: Rookie of the Year, IMCA modified division, 1998; Rookie of the Year award, NASCAR Craftsman Truck Series, 2003; Rookie of the Year, NASCAR Busch Series, 2005; Champion, NASCAR Busch Series, 2007.

Sidelights

Carl Edwards has been flipping for racing since he was a small child growing up in Columbia, Missouri. His father, Carl Edwards Sr., was a race

© *Michael Buckner/WireImage/Getty Images*

car driver who raced modified Volkswagens and midget cars in the United States Auto Club. Edwards' uncle, Bill Schrader, and his cousin, Ken Schrader, were also involved in auto racing. Ken Schrader even won a Nextel cup. Edwards was such an avid auto racing enthusiast that he reminisced in an interview to Matt Crossman of *Sporting News* that he could "remember going to school and playing at recess with the cars. People would be sliding the cars in the dirt, and they'd be doing it all wrong." Edwards would tell them that that was not how it was supposed to look.

When Edwards first began racing he was not even old enough to have a driver's license. His father told Kerri Reynolds, writing for the *Missourian* that "we would sneak him in the back of the truck. When it got dark we would put a helmet on him and put him in the race car." Race officials, other drivers, and the audience would assume that it was Carl Edwards Sr. who was driving the car. Once, after Edwards had won three or four races, he was stopped to be interviewed by a reporter who thought he was his father. Edwards was nervous, but calmed himself and gave his first interview. He was not yet 16 years old. After this Edwards' father came up with a solution. He told the *Missourian*'s

Reynolds, "We went and got my kid a fake drivers license. Not so he could drive, or drink, but so he could get in a doggone racetrack." The license said he was 16.

Edwards wanted to race so badly, that he and his father worked out a deal where Edwards would do all the maintenance on both of their cars in order to race. Edwards told Nikki Krone of the Web site Frontstretch that he "wanted to race so badly that it didn't really matter." Edwards' career began when he was 13 and started racing four-cylinder mini-sprints. A mini-sprint is an upright, open-wheeled racecar with a 600 cc to 1200 cc engine. His second year on the tracks, Edwards won four feature races in the mini-sprint series in Missouri and Illinois. He won an additional 14 times from 1995-96. In 1997, Edwards switched to dirt racing in the International Motor Contest Association modified division. During that year he slept on his mother's couch to save money, worked as a substitute teacher, and raced as much as he could. He quickly started racking up wins and showing that he had talent when it came to racing cars. He was named the Rookie of the Year in the modified division at Holt Summit, Missouri's Capital Speedway.

The *Sporting News*' Crossman asked Edwards about the experience of altered perception when he is driving a car and likened it to when an athlete gets into a zone and the action slows. Edwards responded "The first time that happened to me I was racing a guy for a win at a local dirt track. After the race, there were parts that I could tell you every little piece of dirt that was flying through the air. There were parts I couldn't remember. You get so focused in, weird things happen. It's like you're wearing the car." His ability to intuitively become one with his car benefited him. In 1999, just two years after joining the modified division, Edwards won 13 races and became the NASCAR Track Champion.

In 2002 Edwards competed in seven NASCAR Craftsman Truck Series events. Whether it was the business cards Edwards handed out or his driving (even though his best finish in all those races was eighth), he caught the attention of Jack Roush. Roush gave him his big break and Edwards began driving as a full-time Truck Series competitor in 2003. That year in addition to the three races that he won, he also won Rookie of the Year in the NASCAR Craftsman Truck series. In 2004 Edwards won three more races, including the Florida Dodge Dealers 250 at the Daytona International Speedway, finished fourth overall in the points ranking, and made his Nextel Cup Series debut.

The next year, Edwards achieved racing stardom when he won two separate races in one weekend in Atlanta, Georgia. On March 19, 2005, he won the Busch Series race and on March 20, 2005, he won the Nextel Cup race. He was the first driver to ever win both races in one weekend and these wins were his first in their respective series. He went on that year to win more races in both series including the Nextel Cup at the Pocono 500 and the Bass Pro Shops MBNA 500 at Atlanta Motor Speedway. He was named Rookie of the Year in the NASCAR Busch Series in 2005.

After a 52-race winless streak, Edwards won the Citizens Bank 400 in the Nextel Cup Series in 2007. After this he went on to win the Sharpie 500, which gave him a spot in the 2007 Chase for the Nextel Cup. He placed ninth in the overall standings in the Nextel Chase for the Championship. He was awarded the NASCAR Busch Series Championship that year as well.

Another two years of winless racing passed and then, in 2010, Edwards won the Nationwide Series race at Road America, the Nationwide Series race at Gateway, the Nationwide Series race at the Texas Motor Speedway, and the Kobalt Tools 500. In 2011 he won the Kobalt Tools 400 at Las Vegas and the NASCAR Sprint All-Star Race. He also signed a contract to continue racing with Roush-Fenway Racing.

When Edwards is not racing, he is at home with his wife, Katherine, and his two children. He is very athletic and enjoys working out at the gym and riding motorcycles. He is the owner of his own record label, Back40 Records. He also does volunteer work for organizations such as Victory Junction Gang Camp, Dream Factory, and various children's hospitals.

Sources

Books

Complete Marquis Who's Who, Marquis Who's Who, 2010.

Periodicals

New York Times, May 29, 2011, p. 6; August 7, 2011, p. 8.
Pittsburgh Tribune-Review, July 2, 2011.
PR Newswire, July 29, 2011.
Sporting News, July 14, 2006, p. 16.
USA Today, July 1, 2005; August 1, 2007; May 23, 2011; June 3, 2011; August 5, 2011.

Online

Biography in Context, Gale, 2009.

"Biography for Carl Edwards," Internet Movie Database, http://www.imdb.com/name/nm1907731/ (August 27, 2011).

"Carl Edwards Bio," Roush Racing, http://www.roushracing.com/?q=driver/edwards-bio (August 28, 2011).

"Carl Edwards Career Statistics," Racing Reference Info, http://www.racing-reference.info/driver/edwarca01 (August 28, 2011).

"Carl Edwards' father reminisces at races at Boone County Fair," *Columbia Missourian,* http://www.columbiamissourian.com/stories/2010/07/30/carl-edwards-father-racing-nascar-boone-county-fair-door-banger-nationals/ (August 27, 2011).

"Carl Edwards to compete for the ultimate Father's Day gift—back-to-back NEXTEL Cup victories," Frontstretch, http://www.frontstretch.com/nkrone/552/ (August 27, 2011).

"Carl's Bio," Aflac Racing, http://www.aflacracing.com/default.aspx#/team99/carls-bio (August 28, 2011).

NASCAR Driver Carl Edwards' Official Web site, http://carledwards.com/ (August 28, 2011).

—*Annette Bowman*

Liz Elting and Phil Shawe

Co-founders of TransPerfect

Elting: Born Elizabeth Louise Elting, c. 1967; daughter of Everett (an advertising executive) and Judy (a special education teacher) Elting; married Michael Burlant, 1999; children: Zachary, Jason. Shawe: Born Philip Shawe, c. 1970. *Education:* Elting: Trinity College, B.A., 1987; New York University Stern School of Business, M.B.A., 1992. Shawe: University of Florida, B.S.; New York University Stern School of Business, M.B.A., 1993.

Addresses: *Office*—TransPerfect, 3 Park Ave., 39th Fl., New York, NY 11016. *Web site*—http://www.transperfect.com.

Career

Elting: Your America (translation company), c. 1987-90; worked briefly in finance, early nineties; co-founder, TransPerfect, 1992. Shawe: Financial analyst, Chemical Bank; Global Custody Consultant, Merrill Lynch; co-founder, TransPerfect, 1992; founded Translations.com, 1999.

Awards: Together: Blue Chip Enterprise Initiative Award, U.S. Chamber of Commerce and *Nation's Business*, 1999; 5000 Award, *Inc.* magazine, 2000, 2009, 2010; Entrepreneur of the Year, Ernst & Young, 2001; "TransPerfect Day," New York City Mayor Michael Bloomberg, 2008; Stevie Award for Sales Meeting of the Year, Stevie Awards, Inc., 2009; Technology Fast 500, Deloitte, 2009, 2010. Elting: Entrepreneurial Excellence Award for Customer Service, *Working Woman* magazine, 1999; Woman of the Year, American Express/*Entrepreneur* magazine, 2004; Alumni Medal of Excellence, Trinity College, 2007; Distinguished Alumnae Award, New York University, 2011. Shawe: Entrepreneur of the Year, Ernst & Young, 2001; Technology Fast 50, Deloitte and Touche, for Translations.com, 2003, 2005, 2006, 2007; 40 Under 40, *Crain's New York Business* magazine, 2008.

Sidelights

TransPerfect is a New York-based company, founded by Liz Elting and Phil Shawe, that specializes in translations in a variety of fields, including law, life sciences, finance, and marketing. The company is known for its ability to deliver fast, accurate translations of complex and difficult documents. It is the largest privately held provider of language and business services in the world. TransPerfect provides services to companies that need to communicate verbally, in the form of documents, or electronically, around the globe.

Elting became interested in languages when she was eight years old and her family moved to Portugal. She studied Portuguese and French, and when the family moved to Toronto a year later, she continued to study French, adding Spanish and Latin. She attended Trinity University, where she majored in Spanish and French and spent a year in Spain. After graduating from Trinity, she pursued an internship in finance in Venezuela. After returning to the United States in 1987, she worked at the New York-based translation company Your America. While working there, she noted that when the company was unable to meet deadlines, it lost critical opportunities. She decided to pursue her own business goals, and enrolled in New York University's business school.

Shawe and Elting met in 1991, in an international finance class at New York University. Shawe had always thought he would become a banker, and had previously worked for both Chemical Bank and Merrill Lynch; however, while in graduate school he became interested in pursuing a different career. The two hit it off and began sharing their dreams, ultimately deciding to start their own translation company. Elting knew, from working in the translation industry, that the field was a patchwork of small companies that delivered variable levels of quality. She and Shawe decided that their company, TransPerfect, would be known for its fast service and its ability to deliver accurate translations of highly specialized documents. They also decided their company would eventually become a worldwide entity, with branches in every part of the world.

For their start-up, they opted not to pursue outside investment. They didn't want to waste time writing a lengthy business proposal and finding investors. They were used to living a frugal student lifestyle and decided they could start on their own, live cheaply, and put everything they had into the business. In 1992 they borrowed $5,000 on their credit cards and set up shop in a dorm room, using a rented computer, a fax machine, and a desk that was also their dining table. Subsisting on cheap ramen noodles, they worked seven days a week, from the moment they woke up until the time they went to bed. For the first three years, they allowed themselves a salary of $9,000 each, all of which they put back into the business. Shawe told Victoria Neal in *Entrepreneur*, "There was no difference between living expenses, food expenses and business expenses. We put as much as we could into the business, then we paid the utilities, then the rent—only then did we feed ourselves."

They began by calling both prospective clients and translators whom they hoped to hire. They made thousands of calls and sent out thousands of letters, hearing back from one in a thousand recipients if they were lucky. Slowly, they built up a network of subcontracted professional translators. Their first client was a law firm, who asked them to translate a short document from English to Slovak. They accepted the job, hiring a friend of a friend to do the translation.

Elting and Shawe's big break came when a U.S.-based company wanted them to translate a feasibility study regarding a potential gold mine in Russia. Other translation companies had refused the job, saying it was too technical and that the company wanted it done too quickly, but Elting and Shawe jumped on the opportunity. They hit the phones, calling their connections. There were only a handful of people in the world who had both the knowledge of geology and the linguistic ability to translate the document from Russian into English, but Elting and Shawe found them. They flew the translators to New York City, set them up in hotels, brought them to work in the dorm room, and handed the completed project in on time. The fee from that project allowed them to rent a one-room office and hire their first employee.

Their reputation for completing difficult projects with accuracy and speed led to contracts with other clients and long days and nights of work; one year, they spent Christmas Eve and Christmas Day on the market trading floor at the investment bank Goldman Sachs, working on a document about the privatization of a Latin American telecommunications company. Although being away from their families on the holiday made them wonder if all the work was worth it, the sacrifice paid off when Goldman Sachs become one of TransPerfect's regular clients.

In 1998, when Exxon and Mobil merged, TransPerfect translated a million words in just two weeks. The company has transcribed data from black boxes after airplane crashes, translated for mergers and acquisitions, and translated small but critical documents, such as the instructions for medical devices. It has also aided companies in developing culturally sensitive advertisements. In a notable case, the company translated tape recordings gathered by undercover agents who had infiltrated a drug cartel. The tapes included conversations in five languages, and the translations had to be impeccable because any errors might allow the criminals to go free. Company translators worked with prosecutors and undercover agents, helping to successfully convict the members of the drug cartel.

Shawe founded a sister company, Translations.com, in 1999. The company provided software and Web site localization for clients who want to do business in international markets. Like TransPerfect, it emphasized a high level of service and accuracy, and it has grown to include more than 50 offices around the world. Its customers fall into several areas: automotive, energy, financial services, industrial manufacturing, life sciences, retail, technology, travel and hospitality, telecommunications, and media/entertainment.

In 2004, Elting was awarded the Woman of the Year Award by American Express and *Entrepreneur* magazine. Rieva Lesonsky, senior vice-president and editorial director for *Entrepreneur,* remarked in PR Newswire, "As [Elting] described her goal-setting and employee-friendly corporate culture, as well as her charity and community service record, we at *Entrepreneur* realized we had found an unquestionably unique business owner whose company's reach is truly global." Shawe has also won awards. In 2008, Shawe was named to the *Crain's New York Business* "40 Under 40," an annual selection of people who have achieved outstanding success in business before the age of 40.

By 2010, TransPerfect had more than 1,500 employees who oversaw the work of 4,000 subcontracted linguists, and maintained offices in 57 cities in 18 countries. Shawe and Elting's 1992 dream of a worldwide company had become a reality, with revenues of $255 million and an annual growth rate of 30 percent. Its clients include more than three-quarters of U.S. Fortune 500 companies. In an article in *Forbes,* available on the company's Web site, Elting noted, "In today's world, information moves very quickly around the globe. One slip, one misunderstanding, and a critical business goal could be jeopardized.... Businesses need to select a translation provider with a proven track record in their industry. In the area of international business, the stakes are simply too high to do anything less."

Sources

Books

Dunung, Sanjyot P., *Straight Talk about Starting and Growing Your Business,* McGraw-Hill, 2005.

Greenberg, Herb, and Patrick Sweeney, *Succeed on Your Own Terms,* McGraw-Hill, 2006.

Yaverbaum, Eric, *Leadership Secrets of the World's Most Successful CEOs,* Kaplan Business, 2004.

Periodicals

Business Wire, February 23, 2005; March 3, 2008.

Crain's New York Business, February 14, 2000, p. 34.

Entrepreneur, November 1999; June 2004, pp. 38, 41.

Financial Times, April 9, 2007, p. 9.

Forbes, October 25, 2010.

O, the Oprah Magazine, September 2005, p. 238.

PR Newswire, May 24, 2004.

Reader's Digest, February 2010, p. 56.

Online

"An Entrepreneur Finds the Right Word in Record Time," *MOSAIC,* Trinity College, http://www.trincoll.edu/pub/Mosaic/5.00/Elting.htm (February 9, 2011).

TransPerfect Official Web site, http://www.transperfect.com/ (February 9, 2011).

—*Kelly Winters*

Recep Tayyip Erdogan

Prime minister of Turkey

Born on February 26, 1954, in Istanbul, Turkey; married Emine; children: Ahmet Burak (son), Mecmettin Bilal (son), Esra (daughter), Sumeyye (daughter). *Education:* Marmara University, Istanbul, Turkey, BS, 1981.

Addresses: *Office*—Vekaletler Caddesi Başbakanlik Merkez Bina, P.K. 06573 Kizilay / Ankara, Turkey.

Career

Became involved with Islamic political movement, 1970s; served as chair of the National Salvation Party youth branch, 1976; chair of the Welfare Party, Beyoglu district, 1984; chair of the Welfare Party for Istanbul, 1985; ran unsuccessful campaigns for various political offices, late 1980s-early 1990s; elected mayor of Istanbul, 1994; convicted of threatening the secular state, barred from politics, 1998; allowed to return to politics, elected prime minister, 2003.

Sidelights

As leader of the majority Justice and Development Party, Recep Tayyip Erdogan became the prime minister of the nation of Turkey in 2003. He assumed power after preceding officeholder Abdullah Gül helped pass legislation allowing Erdogan to return to politics following a ban of several years stemming from a conviction over a public reading of an Islamic poem in the late 1990s; Erdogan spent several months in jail as a result of the judgment. Before his enforced political hiatus, Erdogan served

as mayor of the Turkish city of Istanbul, and was active in a number of Islamic political parties from the 1970s onward. Although known for his staunch adherence to Islam in a nation governed by an intentionally secular constitution, Erdogan largely refrained from promoting religious views during his tenure as prime minister. His government presided over a period of extensive growth and modernization throughout Turkey, during which the economy grew dramatically, many aspects of the government underwent reforms, and the nation worked to both improve diplomatic relations with the Middle East and join the European Union. Western analysts have hailed Erdogan's government as a model of moderate Islamic rule, noting that his Justice and Development Party has successfully reached what the *Economist* called "people who mix Muslim piety with a taste for expensive cars."

The son of a Turkish Maritime Lines coastal captain father and a homemaker mother, Erdogan was born on February 26, 1954, in Istanbul, Turkey. His family returned to their native Black Sea coastal city of Rize when Erdogan was an infant, and remained there until the future prime minister was approaching his teen years. Hoping to give his children a better life, Erdogan's father then moved the family to Istanbul. Erodgan spent his teens in the city's Kacimpasha neighborhood, a lower middle class area in the bustling Beyoglu district, where he reportedly worked the streets selling lemonade and sesame buns. He remained a hero for the neighborhood throughout his political career and, many have noted the neighborhood's tough-talking, rough-and-tumble ways as a substantial influence on Erdogan's political style. The young Erdogan attended Piyale Pasa primary school and the Istanbul Imam Hatip secondary school, an institution dedicated to training young men to become imams, or Muslim religious leaders. This school instilled deep religious values in the young Erdogan, and helped him develop, in his own words, "patriotism, love for fellow human beings, service for the country, the worship of God, environmental sciences, the spirit of solidarity, and wishing for others what I want for myself," according an article from *Muslim World* by Metin Heper and Sule Toktas. After completing his basic education in 1973, Erdogan enrolled in Istanbul's Maramara University to pursue studies in economics and management. He finished his degree in 1981.

While he was still in high school, Erdogan became involved with two of the defining themes of his early life: soccer and politics. In 1969, he began playing soccer with an amateur club, and over the next dozen years played the sports at both the amateur and semi-professional levels. Politically, he was exposed to Islamic ideas through his secondary school. During his university years he became acquainted with Necmettin Erbakan, who eventually became the nation's first Islamic prime minister in the late 1990s, and this association encouraged Erdogan to further embrace Islamic ideals. He joined the National Turkish Students Association, then in the process of becoming a firmly Islamic organization, and in 1976 became the head of the youth division of the Islamist National Salvation Party's Beyoglu branch. Soon after, he was named the youth head for the Party at the citywide level. Although the party commanded a small portion of the Turkish electorate during the 1970s, it exercised influence within the era's national coalition governments until it was banned under the military government that came to power in 1980 as a potential threat to the secularity of the Turkish state. That year, Erdogan had his first clash with authorities over his beliefs when he lost his job with the city's transit authority by refusing to shave his mustache when ordered to by his supervisor, a retired colonel.

In 1983, the remains of the disbanded National Salvation Party helped form the Welfare Party, and Erdogan returned to politics as a member of this new group. The year after its formation, the party named Erdogan its head of the Beyoglu district, and in 1985 he rose to become the citywide party chair. A string of political failures followed over the next few years. In 1986, Erdogan mounted an unsuccessful campaign for the Turkish national legislature on the Welfare Party ticket, and three years later he failed to win election in a campaign to become Istanbul's mayor. He again stood for election to parliament in 1991, but failed to win a seat.

These setbacks ended in 1994 as both the national Welfare Party and Erdogan began to enjoy a rise in popularity. That year, Erdogan again ran for mayor of Istanbul, this time successfully with a plurality of roughly one-quarter of the total votes. In 1995, the Welfare Party made gains on a national scale, winning 158 of the national assembly's 500 seats, carrying the most popular vote of any one party in the election. Erdogan proved an effective and popular mayor, working to make the city cleaner and more pleasant for residents. His work as mayor helped make Erdogan a nationally known political figure, and the Welfare Party formed a coalition government in the national assembly with one of Turkey's center-right political parties, which led to the installation of Erdogan as prime minister. Supporters of Turkey's strict secularism resisted Erbakan's selection and the military led a movement to topple the coalition government in 1997. That government fell, and the Welfare Party lost support in the new coalition government that emerged in its wake; soon after, the party was disbanded. Amidst this turmoil, Erdogan was arrested and sent to prison for four months for publicly reciting a religious poem the year before that contained the lines, "the mosques are our barracks, the domes our helmets, the minarets our bayonets, and the faithful our soldiers," according to a BBC News profile. The conviction forced Erdogan to leave his mayoral office and barred him from running in future parliamentary elections. By 2001, Erdogan had organized the remnants of the Welfare Party into a new Justice and Development (AK) Party. This party focused less on strict Islamic ideals and more on conservative, democratic efforts, and thus soon won over a plurality of Turkish voters. In late 2002, the AK majority in the Turkish parliament overturned the ban, and Erdogan became prime minister the following year.

As prime minister, Erdogan showed his support for secular goals from the beginning. He stated his commitment to winning admission to the European Union for Turkey, a process long underway but often blocked by concerns over the political and cultural differences between Turkey and its western neighbors. He also initially continued a government ban on the wearing of traditional Islamic headscarves for women in official buildings for the first several years of his government; later efforts to ease that ban failed. Critics argued that Erdogan harbored a conservative Islamic agenda, pointing to social changes proposed under the Erdogan government by the ruling AK Party as potential threats to Turkey's secular nature. These included a proposal to make adultery illegal, and efforts to appoint Muslims to important government positions. Although Erdogan denied these allegations, tensions remained between conservative and secular groups. In 2007, some 300,000 protestors marched on the Turkish capital of Ankara to protest the possibility of an Erdogan presidency following the end of the administration of sitting president Ahmet Necdet Sezer; under Turkish law, the president is selected by parliament, not through a vote by the people. "I feel a little scared about the developments. I would not like to have an Islamic regime in Turkey," one protestor told BBC News. "I would like to protect the secular system. That's why I am here. Especially as a female, this is very important for me." Erdogan ultimately did not stand as a candidate for president, and Abdullah Gül was instead selected for the office. Despite such opposition, Erdogan and his AK Party have remained very popular among the majority of Turks, easily retaining control of parliament in elections in 2007 and 2011. Much of this popularity has been traced to the explosive economic growth that Turkey enjoyed from the beginning of Erdogan's government, with the size of the economy tripling and the value of exports growing by some $80 billion.

By 2010, Erdogan had begun to shift the country's diplomatic gaze east and south, seeking better relations with its Middle Eastern neighbors. He spoke out against an Israeli attack on a supply ship trying to reach the Gaza Strip—a reversal of Turkey's longtime support for Israel—and partnered with Brazilian president Lula da Silva to meet with Iranian leader Mahmoud Ahmadinejad. The group brokered an agreement known as the Tehran Declaration, which sought to allow Iran to receive nuclear fuel for research through a peaceful exchange. The following year, he sought to mediate the conflict in Libya, but ultimately called for that nation's longtime dictator Muammar al-Qadhafi to resign from office.

In August of 2011, Erdogan's control of power in Turkey was drawn into sharper focus following the resignations of four of the nation's top military officers in protest of the arrests of several high-ranking military generals accused of plotting a political coup some years previously. Erdogan accepted the resignations, replacing the heads of the Turkish army, navy, air force, and overall armed forces with his own choices. The change of command was hailed as the end of an era during which the Turkish military wielded a great deal of political power, as the new military leaders seemed more likely to accept the superiority of the civilian government's authority. While many Turks applauded this sea change as a sign of increased security from the military coups that had shaken the government in the past, others worried that the coalescence of power and support around Erdogan and his party could allow them to influence too much of Turkish society. "These people will never go away," commented Sevda Sunar in a story by Anthony Shadid of the *New York Times*. "They work hard, they're smart, they're well organized and they will bring their own system."

However, the actions and words of Erdogan's government seemed to contradict these worries of a new religious order in Turkey. In August of 2011, for example, the prime minister announced a plan to return property seized from members of religious minority groups since 1936 to their rightful owners or to provide compensation for those properties that had been sold. This policy stood in stark contrast to those of earlier, more avowedly secular governments that had permitted limitations on property ownership by non-Muslims. "Like everyone else, we also do know about the injustices that different religious groups have been subjected to because of their differences. Times that a citizen of ours would be oppressed due to his religion, ethnic origin, or different way of life are over," Erdogan was quoted as announcing in a *New York Times* article by Sebnem Arsu.

Sources

Books

Biographical Encyclopedia of the Modern Middle East and North Africa, Gale, 2008.
Encyclopedia of Political Communication, Sage, 2008.

Periodicals

Economist, June 10, 2010; August 6, 2011.
New York Times, August 1, 2011; August 4, 2011; August 28, 2011.

Online

"Gaza Flotilla: Prime Minister Recep Tayyip Erdogan Insists that Israel Apologize to Turkey," *Huffington Post*, http://www.huffingtonpost.com/2011/07/23/gaza-flotilla-recep-tayyip-erdogan-israel-apologize-turkey_n_907688.html (August 28, 2011).

"Recep Tayyip Erdogan," *New York Times*, http://topics.nytimes.com/topics/reference/timestopics/people/e/recep_tayyip_erdogan/index.html (August 28, 2011).

"Recep Tayyip Erdogan," *Time*, http://www.time.com/time/specials/packages/article/0,28804,2036683_2036767_2036779,00.html (August 28, 2011).

"Secular rally targets Turkish PM," BBC News, http://news.bbc.co.uk/2/hi/europe/6554851.stm (August 28, 2011).

"Turkey's charismatic pro-Islamic leader," BBC News, http://news.bbc.co.uk/2/hi/europe/2270642.stm (August 28, 2011).

—Vanessa E. Vaughn

Fantasia

Singer

Born Fantasia Monique Barrino, June 30, 1984, in High Point, NC; daughter of Joseph (a truck driver) and Diane (a pastor) Barrino; children: Zion.

Addresses: *Web site*—http://www.fantasiaofficial. com.

Career

Performed with family singing group the Barrino Family, 1990s; won third season of *American Idol*, 2004; released debut album, *Free Yourself*, 2004; published memoir *Life Is Not a Fairy Tale: The Fantasia Barrino Story*, 2005; appeared in Lifetime biopic based on her memoir, 2006; released second album, *Fantasia*, 2006; starred in Broadway production of *The Color Purple*, 2007; appeared in VH1 reality program *Fantasia for Real*, 2010; released third album, *Back to Me*, 2010. Television guest appearances include: *American Dreams*, 2004; *The Simpsons*, 2005.

Awards: Top Selling Single of the Year and Top Selling R&B/Hip-Hop Single of the Year *Billboard* Music Awards, both for "I Believe," 2004; Outstanding Female Artist, NAACP Image Awards, 2005; (with Jennifer Hudson) Outstanding Duo or Group, NAACP Image Award, 2009; Grammy Award for Best Female R&B Vocal Performance, National Academy of Recording Arts and Sciences, for "Bittersweet," 2011; Best Song, NAACP Image Awards, for "Bittersweet," 2011.

Sidelights

Grammy-award-winning R&B artist Fantasia Barrino—often known professionally simply as Fantasia—became famous around the world as the winner of the third season of the massively popular reality singing competition *American Idol* in 2004. Since that time, the performer has expanded on her *American Idol* success to build not only a music career, but also a stage and screen presence. In 2004, Barrino released her debut album, *Free Yourself*, which landed in the upper reaches of the charts and racked up platinum-level sales. Follow-up effort *Fantasia* appeared in 2006, not long after the release of the artist's memoir, *Life Is Not A Fairy Tale: The Fantasia Barrino Story*. Barrino then shifted to a new creative outlet with a long-running performance in the Broadway musical version of *The Color Purple* before returning to the studio to record her third album, *Back to Me*. Despite these achievements, Barrino suffered from personal turmoil that contributed to a suicide attempt in August of 2010. The singer soon bounced back, winning the starring role in a planned biopic of legendary gospel performer Mahalia Jackson and picking up her first Grammy award in early 2011.

The singer was born Fantasia Monique Barrino in High Point, North Carolina, on June 30, 1984, to truck driver Joseph Barrino and church pastor Diane Barrino. The Barrino family had a deep-rooted love of music; Barrino's father had performed in gospel quartets since his teen years, and her mother and brothers also enjoyed singing gospel music. "My father still wanted to be involved with singing and so did my mother.... My parents would sing at any opportunity that came to them," Barrino recalled in her memoir *Life Is Not a Fairy Tale.* This love of singing eventually led to the formation of a gospel group called the Barrino Family. Featuring a young "Tasia," as she was nicknamed, alongside several other family members, the group appeared at churches, revivals, and other local venues throughout the South. The Barrino Family received a recording contract with Universal, and in 2000 released an album, *Miracles,* on the First Lite imprint.

The young Barrino's involvement with gospel music also included performing with the choir at the church where her mother was co-pastor, High Point's Mercy Outreach Church of Deliverance. For a time, Barrino served as the church's choir director, a natural fusing of her passions for music and for Christianity. "When I was about nine, an elderly woman came up to me, crying, and said, 'I want you to know that you touched me,'" the singer told Oprah Winfrey in a 2007 *O* magazine interview. "My mother later told me that God had given me a gift," she continued, "but I had low self-esteem. I seemed so different from other kids; I grew up in church and felt a connection with God, and a lot of kids my age really didn't understand that." Despite winning a spot in the all-county chorus while attending Welborn Middle School in High Point, Barrino also faced difficulties in school, partially as a result of missing classes because of the Barrino Family's touring schedule and partially due to problems reading.

Barrino's personal challenges escalated after she entered Andrews High School. She became increasingly rebellious, and at the age of 14 was raped by a classmate in the school auditorium. Stunned, she returned home and retreated into herself, refusing to tell anyone what had happened for some time because of her shame over the event. "One point in time I was saying it was my fault—just because of the way I was dressed, I caused it on myself," Barrino was quoted as saying in an ABC News story. Later that school year, she dropped out of Andrews and moved out on her own into an apartment in a rough neighborhood of High Point. Boyfriend Brandel Schauss moved in, and the relationship became physically abusive.

In 2001, the 17-year-old Barrino gave birth to a daughter, Zion. Realizing that she was a role model for her newborn daughter, Barrino decided to leave her abusive boyfriend and start working to turn her life around. An opportunity to do that soon arrived in an unexpected form: auditions for singing competition program *American Idol.* Although Barrino was initially hesitant to sing for famously caustic judge Simon Cowell, her family convinced her to make the trip to Atlanta. Rather than criticizing her, Cowell became one Barrino's early supporters, and the judges selected her from a group of some 70,000 hopefuls to compete for the title and its accompanying recording contract. The young singer turned in a series of strong vocal performances, consistently winning over the judges but coming near elimination twice in the hard-fought competition. Despite facing criticism over her status as a single mother and high-school dropout, Barrino—who dedicated part of her time over the course of *Idol*'s run to studying for her high school equivalency degree—eventually made it to the final round along with young singer Diana DeGarmo. When the record-breaking 65 million votes were tallied, Barrino emerged the victor. "I've been through some things, but I've worked hard to get where I'm at. Thank you all so much," an emotional Barrino declared when her win was announced, according to a *People* magazine story.

Her win made Barrino an overnight global star. She made high-profile appearances, including stops on national talk shows and a performance at Washington, D.C.'s Kennedy Center Honors. Barrino's musical skills continued to be her strongest source of success. The young performer's debut single "I Believe," which Barrino sang on *American Idol*, became the first track to bow in the number-one position on the *Billboard* Hot 100. Less than six months after taking the title of American Idol, Barrino released her first album, *Free Yourself.* Recorded as part of her *Idol* prize with music industry veteran Clive Davis, the album showcased Barrino's powerful voice on a series of urban tracks produced by the likes of Missy Elliott, Jermaine Dupri, and Rodney "Darkchild" Jerkins. "If [the album] delivers no knockout punches, at least it maintains the mood and groove from beginning to end and is considerably more fashionable than anything *American Idol* has yet produced," assessed Stephen Thomas Erlewine of the Allmusic Guide. Although this measured opinion reflected general critical sentiment, music buyers flocked to the release, sending it to number two on the *Billboard* R&B chart and number eight on the *Billboard* 200. The Grammy committee also recognized *Free Yourself*, nominating the album and songs "Summertime" and "Free Yourself" for three awards. Despite these solid commercial and critical returns, Barrino's album failed to live up to the success of previous *Idol* releases, giving her a shadow of failure that may not have otherwise appeared.

In 2005, Barrino published a memoir, *Life Is Not a Fairy Tale*. Filled with revelations such as the circumstances of her rape as a teen and her own functional illiteracy, the memoir became a *New York Times* bestseller. The following year, television network Lifetime adapted the book as a biopic, with Barrino appearing as herself in the lead role. Although critics largely dismissed the film, the singer won some praise for her acting chops; Virginia Heffernan of the *New York Times* proclaimed that Barrino's performance was "like everything she touches … gold."

Indeed, Barrino's next creative endeavor literally turned to gold—certified sales of more than 500,000 copies. The singer released her sophomore album, simply titled *Fantasia*, in late 2006. Adhering more closely to a strictly R&B sound, the album saw the performer again displaying the strong voice that had helped her win *American Idol*. "The album's subtle appeal isn't evident on the first listen," noted Henry Goldblatt of *Entertainment Weekly*, yet he termed Barrino "an artist who has something original to contribute to the industry." However, with the buzz of *American Idol* no longer focused on Barrino, the album failed to rack up the same level of chart success as had its predecessor. Although "When I See U" topped the Hot R&B/Hip-Hop Singles & Tracks chart, *Fantasia* barely cracked the top 20 of the *Billboard* 200.

Again facing the perception of failure despite objective success, Barrino decided to take a hiatus from recording to star as Celie in the Broadway musical adaptation of *The Color Purple*. Bolstered by media attention from *Idol* and the *Oprah Winfrey Show*, Barrino's performance helped the show achieve record-breaking ticket sales, and she soon signed on to extend what was originally a six-month run. The artist spent much of the next several months appearing with the production, delaying plans for a third album.

In January of 2010, Barrino returned to television, this time as the star of a VH1 reality program *Fantasia for Real*. Criticized by some as just another in a string of celebrity focused programs for the network, the show followed Fantasia, her family, and others in their circle on various exploits to the backdrop of Barrino working on a comeback. Critic Brian Lowry of *Daily Variety* complained that the show "traffic[ed] in the kind of stereotypes—in 'Fantasia's' case, a shiftless black man mooching off his female relatives, test-driving Ferraris and aghast at the prospect of working—that would be rightfully pilloried in a scripted context." Not everyone agreed with this negative assessment; Amy Amatagnelo of the *Boston Herald* instead proclaimed that "Fantasia

shows off an infectious laugh and a tremendous work ethic. It's hard not to root for her. One can only hope that the show represents a turning point in her career and her life." The program returned for a second season in the fall of 2010.

Although plans for Barrino's third album moved forward, the performer herself continued to experience personal challenges throughout much of 2010. That summer, she became embroiled in scandal when it was revealed that the man she had been dating for several months, Antwaun Cook, had in fact been married during the course of their relationship. Barrino claimed repeatedly that she had believed him to be separated from his wife when they began dating. Amid the media hubbub that followed the accusations, Barrino was hospitalized in August after overdosing on a combination of aspirin and sleeping pills. She later confirmed that the overdose was a suicide attempt. "I wanted to be so away from all this noise in my world," she was quoted as explaining in the *Toronto Star*. Later, the singer testified in court during Cook's divorce proceedings that she had become pregnant by Cook, but had an abortion at about the time of the overdose attempt.

August also marked the release of Barrino's much-delayed third album, *Back to Me*. A slickly urban R&B effort, *Back to Me* saw the performer again summon up her famously raspy voice for what Erlewine of the Allmusic Guide termed "her most interesting album." The release soared to the upper reaches of the *Billboard* 200 and R&B albums charts, producing two popular singles, "Bittersweet" and "I'm Doing Me." *Back to Me* also garnered the artist another raft of Grammy nominations. At the ceremony in February of 2011, Barrino garnered her first Grammy award for "Bittersweet." The following month, Barrino picked up another win when "Bittersweet" garnered a trophy in the Outstanding Song category at the NAACP Image Awards.

Selected discography

Free Yourself, J Records, 2004.
Fantasia, J Records, 2006.
Back to Me, J Records, 2010.

Selected writings

Life Is Not a Fairy Tale; The Fantasia Barrino Story, Fireside (New York City), 2005.

Sources

Books

Barrino, Fantasia. *Life Is Not a Fairy Tale: The Fantasia Barrino Story*, Fireside, 2005.

Contemporary Black Biography, vol. 53, Gale, 2006, pp. 9-11.

Contemporary Musicians, vol. 61, Gale, 2008, pp. 55-57.

Periodicals

Boston Herald, January 11, 2010, p. 23.

Daily Variety, April 17, 2007, p. 1; January 11, 2010, p. 21.

Entertainment Close-Up, September 14, 2010.

Entertainment Weekly, December 22, 2006.

New York Post, August 11, 2010, p. 72; November 24, 2010, p. 89.

New York Times, August 18, 2006; July 13, 2007, p. E5.

O, The Oprah Magazine, September 2007, p. 318.

Toronto Star, September 11, 2010, p. E13.

Online

"Back to Me," *Allmusic Guide,* http://allmusic.com/album/back-to-me-r1830845/review (March 5, 2011).

"Fantasia's Memoirs Reveal Experiences with Illiteracy, Rape," ABC News, http://abcnews.go.com/2020/OnlyinAmerica/story?id=1170655&page=1 (March 5, 2011).

"Free Yourself," *Allmusic Guide,* http://allmusic.com/album/free-yourself-r719729/review (March 5, 2011).

"Public Picks Fantasia as American Idol," *People,* http://www.people.com/people/article/0,,642897,00.html (March 5, 2011).

—*Vanessa E. Vaughn*

Bruce Feiler

© Beowolf Sheehan/Zuma Press/Corbis

Author and journalist

Born October 25, 1964, in Savannah, GA; son of Edwin J. Jr. (a developer) and Jane (a small business owner) Feiler; married Linda Rottenberg (a nonprofit founder); children: Eden Elenor, Tybee Rose (twins). *Religion:* Jewish. *Education:* Yale University, B.A. (cum laude), 1987; Clare College, Cambridge University, M.Phil, 1991; attended Kansai Gaidai University, 1986, and the University of Oslo, 1989.

Addresses: *Contact*—c/o Author Mail, 11th Fl., HarperCollins Publishers, 10 E. 53rd St., New York, NY 10022. *Office*—120 Habersham St., Savannah, GA 31401.

Career

Taught at a junior high school in Sano, Japan, 1987-88; worked for Kyodo News Service, Tokyo, Japan, 1988-89; writer, 1991—; worked as a clown for the Clyde Beatty-Cole Bros. Circus, 1993; co-producer for *Abraham: A Journey to the Heart of Three Faiths* and *Walking the Bible: A Journey by Land Through the Five Books of Moses* (both miniseries), 2005; correspondent, *All Things Considered*, National Public Radio; contributed to periodicals including the *Washington Post, Gourmet, New York Times, New Republic,* and *USA Today.*

Awards: Deems Taylor Award, ASCAP (American Society of Composers, Authors, and Publishers), for *The New Republic*, 1997; Bert Green Award, International Association of Culinary Professionals, 2001; James Beard Award in journalism, James Beard Foundation, 2001, 2002, 2003.

Sidelights

Author and journalist Bruce Feiler has published a number of popular nonfiction works that chronicle his experiences with religions, culture, and life abroad. Some of his most popular books focus on Biblical figures, including the 2001 travel-inspired narrative *Walking the Bible: A Journey by Land Through the Five Books of Moses.* Another bestseller was more personal: *The Council of Dads: My Daughters, My Illness, and the Men Who Could Be Me,* published in 2010, describes his fight with bone cancer and making preparations for his daughters in the event of his death. Feiler's books greatly affected readers. Talking about *Walking the Bible* but perhaps applying to his other books as well, Feiler told John Keenan of the *Omaha World Herald*, "the number-one thing people have written to me or said to me is, 'Thank you for writing openly about your struggle.'"

Born on October 25, 1964, in Savannah, Georgia, he was the son of Edwin J. Feiler, Jr., a developer, and his wife, Jane, a small business owner. He spent his first 18 years in Savannah, where he was a fifth generation Savannah Jew. Explaining his attachment to Georgia, Feiler told William L. Hamilton of the *New*

York Times, "It's the heart of who I am. I love the South, the stickiness, the familyness, the storytelling. At the same time, as a Jew, you never feel like you are fully a part of that, that you fully belong."

Feiler received his education at Yale University, where he felt like a true outsider for the first time as a Southerner in the North. He began exploring regional experiences, a process which would become part of his perspective as a writer. While a student at Yale, he also spent time studying abroad at Kansai Gaidai University in 1986. After graduating from Yale cum laude with a degree in history in 1987, Feiler decided to continue exploring what it felt like to be an outsider.

To that end, Feiler returned to Japan to teach English and American culture at a junior high school in Sano, Japan, from 1987 to 1988. He was given this job as part of the Japan Exchange and Teaching program sponsored by the Japanese government's ministry of education. Sano was a rural community that had little contact with people from the west, and Feiler found the experience challenging. Remaining in Japan, he worked as a reporter for the Tokyo-based Kyodo News Service from 1988 to 1989.

Continuing his education, Feiler attended the University of Oslo in 1989, then moved to England to attend Cambridge University. In 1991, Feiler completed his M.Phil in international relations at Clare College, Cambridge. That year, Feiler became a full-time writer, focusing primarily on nonfiction. His first book was based on his experiences in Japan. First published in 1991, *Learning to Bow: Inside the Heart of Japan* was put in print again in 2004. In the book, Feiler chronicles the difficulties he faced in adjusting to life in Japan, including relationships with his fellow teachers, students, and other Japanese. He also describes what he learned about them and himself in the process.

In 1993, Feiler published his second book, *Looking for Class: Seeking Wisdom and Romance at Oxford and Cambridge*. This book was based on his experiences in England, where Feiler again faced difficulties adjusting to a new, unfamiliar culture. The traditions and code of conduct at Cambridge provided interesting yet sometimes challenging incidents and encounters. Because of his involvement with a Canadian student at Oxford, Feiler was able to have similar experiences at Oxford as well. By the end of *Looking for Class*, Feiler was comparing what he had done in Japan with what had happened in England.

By the time *Looking for Class* came out, Feiler was back living in the United States after years aboard. In 1993, Feiler was taking on new challenges as he

spent time working as a clown in the Clyde Beatty-Cole Bros. Circus, hoping to tour the United States and work with interesting people. While fulfilling his childhood dream, Feiler soon learned that the hours were long and life in the circus was not particularly exotic. The experience informed his third book, 1995's *Under the Big Top: A Season with the Circus*. In Feiler's tome, he looked at the subculture of the circus, detailing its high points and its low points with affection.

For Feiler's next project, he chose a topic close to his heart. A long-time fan of country music, he turned his attention to that genre and its home base of Nashville. In 1998's *Dreaming Out Loud: Garth Brooks, Wynonna Judd, Wade Hayes, and the Changing Face of Nashville*, he offers an examination of the country music business and industry in Nashville. Despite his love of country music, Feiler did not shy away from looking at the negatives as well as the positives. Feiler also places country music in the context of greater American culture. Critics praised the book for its comprehensive examination.

In the late 1990s, Feiler found a new focus that would lead to a handful of books. Visiting the Middle East, he began writing about Biblical and other ancient holy texts, using research and travels to the ancient lands to inform his words. Feiler's first project in this area focused on the Pentateuch, the first five books of the Bible. He went to the Middle East to find archaeological evidence for the stories included therein, interviewing both religious leaders and ordinary people while travelling 10,000 miles.

In 2001's *Walking the Bible: A Journey by Land Through the Five Books of Moses*, Feiler describes his journey with an archaeologist to related sites in places such Turkey, Israel, Syria, Egypt, and Jordan to find the locations associated with Biblical figures like Moses, Abraham, and Jacob. Critics noted that he made the Bible and its ancient figures seem real and vital.

For Feiler, it changed how he perceived the subject and himself. He told Cathy Lynn Grossman of *USA Today*, "This book changed how I knew myself. I gave up the question of proofs.... Proof is not the point. There will never be enough proof. The most powerful stories are not provable in archaeology.... The evidence is cultural and historical, not physical. And that is much more persuasive." *Walking the Bible* became a popular best-seller.

Feiler's next book looked specifically at Abraham, exploring questions related to the fact that three religions—Chrsitinaity, Judaism, and Islam—look to him as their founding father yet took different paths and have been in conflict. While Feiler conducted his research for 2002's *Abraham: A Journey to the Heart of Three Faiths* at a time when the region was torn apart by war, he took great personal risk to talk to people and leaders in all three religions to better understand Abraham and how each faith employs and interprets his teachings in their faith.

After *Abraham: A Journey to the Heart of Three Faiths*, Feiler returned to *Walking the Bible*-related projects. In 2004, he published a children's version titled *Walking the Bible: An Illustrated Journey for Kids Through the Greatest Stories Ever Told*, while in 2005, he put out the visually emphasized *Walking the Bible: A Photographic Journey*. Also in 2005, Feiler served as a co-producer on the miniseries version of two of his books, *Abraham: A Journey to the Heart of Three Faiths* and *Walking the Bible: A Journey by Land Through the Five Books of Moses*.

Feiler put out a book for adults as well in 2005, *When God Was Born: A Journey by Land to the Roots of Religion*. In this more personal tome, the honest Feiler looks at a question about religion serving as a source of conflict or the pathway to peace while describing his take on organized religion and new connection to his Jewish heritage. The author also states his support for moderates and belief that peace will someday come to the Middle East.

In 2009, Feiler published another Biblical-related book *Americas' Prophet: Moses and the American Story*. This book looks at the ways Moses has influenced Americans and American history, from the Founding Fathers to members of the Civil Rights Movement to contemporary times. By the time *Americas' Prophet: Moses and the American Story* came out, Feiler was facing a personal crisis of his own.

In 2008, he was diagnosed with rare type of bone cancer, osteogenic sarcoma, that was threatening to take his leg, if not his life. The father of young twin girls at the time, Feiler worried about who would help his wife raise their daughters. In the days after his diagnosis, he wrote letters to and visited six men to whom he was close and whom he wanted to help his daughters see the world, dubbing them the Council of Dads. Seriously ill for a year and a half, Feiler underwent chemotherapy to treat the disease and had to have his left leg reconstructed. By 2010, Feiler had finished treatment and was able to walk without aid.

Feiler wrote a book about his experiences, *The Council of Dads: My Daughters, My Illness, and the Men Who Could Be Me*. Written in three months, *The Coun-cil of Dads* was more than a memoir about his family and surviving cancer. As Feiler survived, the council evolved and became a support group for Feiler and his family—godparents for contemporary times. It also inspired others suffering from disease to create their own councils, including the creation of a related Web site and social networking site.

Still others took the book as a guide for fatherhood. Discussing this aspect of *The Council of Dads*, Feiler told Bo Emerson of the *Atlanta Journal-Constitution*, "People seem to be receiving it that way. I feel a couple of things about that: When I first had the idea it felt instantly old to me.... To me it's always been very, very intimate between me and my daughters. I wanted to get this story down so they would know. But from the very first time I showed the book, one thing everybody's said is the following; 'I think about you for three or four pages, then I think about me.' It seems to have a universal appeal."

While working on his books and other projects, Feiler also regularly contributed to numerous periodicals, including the *Washington Post, Gourmet, New York Times, New Republic*, and *USA Today*. He became a correspondent for the National Public Radio show *All Things Considered* as well; however, Feiler knows that his future is uncertain as the odds of his long-term survival because of the cancer are unclear.

Because of his Council of Dads, Feiler believes he has had one of the best experiences of his life and knows his family has support if he is taken from them. He told Steve Myall of the London *Mirror*, "The process made me focus on my friendships and the girls—it crystallised my wish not to leave them. It gave me something to fight for and created fight between the cancer and the girls. That fight was the reason I live today. In a way if it wasn't for the council I wouldn't be here."

Selected writings

Learning to Bow: Inside the Heart of Japan, Ticknor & Fields (New York City), 1991; reprinted, Harper-Perennial (New York City), 2004.

Looking for Class: Seeking Wisdom and Romance at Oxford and Cambridge, Random House (New York City), 1993; reprinted, HarperPerennial, 2003.

Under the Big Top: A Season with the Circus, Scribner (New York City), 1995.

Dreaming Out Loud: Garth Brooks, Wynonna Judd, Wade Hayes, and the Changing Face of Nashville, Avon Books (New York City), 1998.

Walking the Bible: A Journey by Land Through the Five Books of Moses, Morrow (New York City), 2001.

Abraham: A Journey to the Heart of Three Faiths, Morrow, 2002.

Walking the Bible: An Illustrated Journey for Kids Through the Greatest Stories Ever Told, HarperCollins (New York City), 2004.

Walking the Bible: A Photographic Journey, William Morrow (New York City), 2005.

When God Was Born: A Journey by Land to the Roots of Religion, William Morrow, 2005.

Americas' Prophet: Moses and the American Story, William Morrow, 2009.

The Council of Dads: My Daughters, My Illness, and the Men Who Could Be Me, William Morrow, 2010.

Sources

Periodicals

Atlanta Journal-Constitution, May 2, 2010, p. E5.
Mirror (London, England), May 21, 2010, p. 26.
New York Times, December 29, 2005, p. F1.
Omaha World Herald, December 4, 2001, p. 2E.
Philadelphia Inquirer, October 27, 2009, p. B2.
Times (London, England), May 4, 2010, p. 1.
USA Today, April 5, 2001, p. 10D.
Washington Post Book World, October 24, 1993, p. X8.

Online

Contemporary Authors Online, Gale, 2007.

—A. Petruso

Mark Feuerstein

Valerie Macon/Getty Images

Actor

Born June 8, 1971, in New York, NY; son of an attorney and a teacher; married Dana Klein (a writer), 2005; children: Lila Jane, Frisco Jones, Addie. *Education:* Princeton University, B.A., 1993; studied at London Academy of Music and Dramatic Art and L'Ecole Phillipe Gaulier as a Fulbright scholar.

Addresses: *Agent*—Framework Entertainment, 9057 Nemo St., Ste. C, West Hollywood, CA 90069.

Career

Actor in films, including: *Practical Magic*, 1998; *30 Days*, 1999; *Giving It Up*, 1999; *Muse*, 1999; *Rules of Engagement*, 2000; *What Women Want*, 2000; *Woman on Top*, 2000; *Abandon*, 2002; *Balkanization*, 2002; *Three Days of Rain*, 2002; *Two Weeks Notice*, 2002; *In Her Shoes*, 2005; *Lucid*, 2006; *Wedding Weekend*, 2006; *Defiance*, 2008; *Blessed Is the Match: The Life and Death of Hannah Senesh*, 2008; *Knucklehead*, 2010; *Love Shack*, 2010. Television appearances include: *Loving*, 1995-96; *Caroline in the City*, 1996-97; *Guiding Light*, 1997; *Fired Up*, 1997-98; *Conrad Bloom*, 1998; *Sex and the City*, 1999; *Ally McBeal*, 2000; *An American Daughter*, 2000; *Once and Again*, 2000-01; *Heart Department*, 2001; *West Wing*, 2001-05; *Good Morning, Miami*, 2002-04; *Last Comic Standing*, 2003; *Closer*, 2005; *Law & Order*, 2005; *3 lbs.*, 2006; *Masters of Horror*, 2006; *Dance Man* (movie), 2007; *Shark*, 2007; *Hustler*, 2009; *Royal Pains*, 2009-11; *Independent Lens*, 2010.

Sidelights

Mark Feuerstein is a nice guy who plays nice guy characters. When asked by Sheldon A. Wiebe of *Eclipse Magazine* what he shared with the character, Dr. Hank Lawson, he plays on *Royal Pains*, Feuerstein replied, "the aspiration of Hank, the hope that he is living the best life he can for who he is; I share that with Hank. Hank is trying to do the most good for the most people where he can ... and as an actor, you're always trying to find the best opportunities." While most of the members of Feuerstein's family were attornies, this was not Feuerstein's calling. He decided to become an actor and in this way find both the way to help other people and opportunity for himself.

Dr. Hank Lawson is a kind of knight in shining armor who makes house calls. Feuerstein described *Royal Pains* to Irene Lacher of the *Los Angeles Times* as "an answer to the failure of our healthcare system to make us feel we're taken care of, to make us feel safe.... And here's a guy who's willing to go out in the field and say, 'Knock knock, what's wrong with you?'" In other words, the show itself is a cure to help people feel better and Feuerstein is taking the opportunity to be part and to help people through his own particular gift as an actor.

Feuerstein was born in New York City to a Jewish family. His father was an attorney and his mother was a teacher. Feuerstein attended high school at the private, independent, co-ed Dalton School in New York City. While he did not participate in the performing arts curriculum in high school Feuerstein was on the wrestling team and won the state championship. He was also the captain of the football team and active in student government. The rigorous education that he received while in high school prepared him to go on to prestigious Princeton University where he intended to study international relations. Feuerstein told the *Daily Princetonian*, "In high school I was a total jock/extracurricular nerd/just plain nerd. When I got to college, I realized that building a resume to get into a good school was no longer necessary. I had already gotten into one. I might as well follow my bliss." Feuerstein remembered his eleventh grade modern drama class and how much fun it had been. On a whim he began auditioning for various student dramas and was cast in a play titled *Orphans*, written by Lyle Kessler. Where most young people might dream of becoming an actor and end up as an attorney, Feuerstein wanted to be an attorney when he was young and ended up an actor. After graduating from Princeton University in 1993, he was awarded a Fulbright scholarship and studied at the London Academy of Music and Dramatic Arts.

After studying at the London Academy of Music and Dramatic Arts he studied with the premiere clown teacher at Ecole Phillipe Gaulier in France. Feuerstein's natural sense of humor and uncanny knack for physical comedy earned him the nickname of "Chaplin" on the set of *Giving It Up*. He also had a physical impromptu slapstick exchange with Mel Gibson while the two were filming *What Women Want*, and on the set of *Royal Pains*, he and Paulo Constanzo have had a joking rapport. Feuerstein told *Eclipse Magazine*'s Wiebe, "If you came into the make-up trailer on any given day while we're getting ready for the day of work, you would see Paulo imitating 17 different characters from the crew or people who have been visiting our set and you would see me laughing hysterically and then jumping in and joining him." This sense of humor has served Feuerstein well in show business where auditions, rejections, and the cancellation of television programs are commonplace frustrations.

Feuerstein began his professional acting career on the daytime drama *Loving* on which he appeared for only one year. After this he had appearances in a number of television situation comedies. For one season he played the recurring role of Joe DeStefano in eight episodes of *Caroline in the City*. The character was a veterinarian wtih whom the main character had a relationship. They almost moved in together, but then he had an affair with an ex-girlfriend. Feuerstein received good reviews for the role and because of it he was later cast in other situation comedies. In 1997, Feuerstein played Dr. Steven Levine for one season on another daytime television drama, *Guiding Light*. Continuing his pattern of appearing for a short time in a television series, Feuerstein was next cast as Danny Reynolds, a philosophical bartender in the short-lived series, *Fired Up*. This was the first of several series that cast Feuerstein as a regular performer and were short lived, which earned him a reputation as being a sitcom killer. Other short-lived television series that Feuerstein was cast in included *Conrad Bloom, Once and Again, Good Morning, Miami,* and *3 lbs. Conrad Bloom* was something of a high-profile flop that lasted less than half a season and marred Feuerstein's ability to be cast in other television programs.

Despite these setbacks, Feuerstein continued his pursuit of being an actor. He took his skills to Broadway where he was cast as the lead in Alfred Uhry's Tony-winning play *Last Night of Ballyhoo*. His performance impressed critics and lead to Feuerstein being cast in *Practical Magic* as Sandra Bullock's character's cursed husband who dies young because he married into a family of witches. The role was a small one but it was his first role in a feature film. His performance in *Practical Magic* was so strong that it compelled Nancy Meyers, the director of *What Women Want*, to cast him in that film alongside heavy hitter Mel Gibson. In addition to these films, Feuerstein also performed in Albert Brooks' *Muse* and *Giving It Up*. In *Giving It Up*, Feuerstein's first leading role, he played a womanizing ad executive and the film won an award for Best Romantic Comedy at the New York International Independent Film and Video Festival.

Feuerstein was not a typical leading man. He was not smooth like George Clooney or Brad Pitt. He was not brooding like Colin Farrell. Feuerstein had boyish charm, humor, and an Upper East Side appeal. When he was cast as the lover who could not satisfy Miranda on *Sex in the City*, he took the shirtless role all in good humor even though he has stated that the role was not his favorite. When his scenes opposite Sandra Bullock were deleted from *Two Weeks Notice*, he took it in good stride and found work on *Last Comic Standing* and *Good Morning, Miami*. After these programs, he had a recurring part as Cliff Cailey on the successful political drama *West Wing*. In 2005, he was part of the cast of *In Her Shoes*, starring Cameron Diaz, Toni Collette, and Shirley MacLaine. He played the character of Simon Stein, who is engaged to be married to Collette's character.

Still looking for the role that was the perfect fit and would make him a star, Feuerstein had guest appearances on more television shows, including *Closer, Law and Order, Masters of Horror, Shark,* and *Hustler.* He also appeared in such films as *Wedding Weekend, Lucid, Defiance,* and *Knucklehead.* His big break finally came when he was cast as Dr. Hank Lawson on the USA Network's *Royal Pains.*

Eclipse Magazine's Wiebe asked Feuerstein if he had any advice to give those who wished to become actors. Feuerstein replied that while every actor has people helping them, such as agents and managers, it is still up to the actor to take responsibility, advocate, and pursue his goals for himself. Feuerstein went on to tell the story of how he was cast in the role of Dr. Hank Lawson. Out to lunch with a man who was both a producer and his friend, Feuerstein boldly took his friend's cell phone to call Andrew Lenchewski, a mutual acquaintance who would soon be shooting a new pilot for the USA Network. "Andrew," Feuerstein said, according to Wiebe, "first of all, I want to congratulate you on the fact you're making a pilot for USA and I heard it's about a doctor to the rich and the not-so-rich in the Hamptons, so second, I want to congratulate you on the fact that I'm going to be starring in it." A month later Feuerstein had the role.

Royal Pains was not just another medical drama. It was about a very successful Manhattan doctor who chose to save the life of a complete stranger rather than that of the elderly billionaire hospital trustee and experienced a plummet in his stature. The character, by way of looking for another chance in his career, took the position of concierge doctor to the wealthy who live in the Hamptons. The experience was transformative for Dr. Hank Lawson. Not only was the show about the quirky characters who reside in the Hamptons and their extravagant lifestyles, it was also about the relationships between the characters. Henry Winkler was brought into the cast as Lawson's estranged father. There was also a love interest named Jill. Further, there are the many patients that Dr. Lawson treats as a concierge doctor. To prepare for playing a doctor, Feuerstein followed doctors around. He met with concierge doctors and even sat in on a brain surgery. He also had an emergency room surgeon consulting on the set, who researched medical stories to be included in episodes of *Royal Pains.*

Feuerstein finally found his breakout role after weathering years of disappointments in show business. Other actors have not been so persistent. As the character of Dr. Hank Lawson, he had the opportunity to display his charm, wit, and intelligence. He had a growing base of fans as *Royal Pains* became a number-one show on the USA Network.

In 2005, Feuerstein married writer Dana Klein. The pair had three children named Lila Jane, Frisco Jones, and Addie. In 2010, Addie was diagnosed with a rare heart defect and spent 89 days in the hospital. It was a challenging and weird experience for Feuerstein, who went from using medical terminology on the set of *Royal Pains* to using the same words in an actual hospital in regards to his daughter. He told Nicki Gostin of PopEater that he had a greater appreciation for doctors and nurses than ever before. During the five months that *Royal Pains* was not in production, Feuerstein worked as a stay-at-home dad who enjoyed being with his children. Feuerstein was also a self-proclaimed outdoorsman with an unabashed love of mountain biking and marathons. He also wrestled and danced. His sitcom-killing days behind him, Feuerstein told Mandi Bierly of *Entertainment Weekly,* "It's such a relief to not have to talk to your uncle at Thanksgiving about 'I don't get your show, and I get why it's being canceled.' That conversation is now out the window."

Sources

Periodicals

Daily Princetonian, May 9, 2003.
Entertainment Weekly, July 24, 2009.
Los Angeles Times, June 13, 2010.

Online

"Mark Feuerstein," *AskMen,* http://www.askmen.com/celebs/men/entertainment/mark-feuerstein/ (May 7, 2011).

"Mark Feuerstein Bio," AOL TV, http://www.aoltv.com/celebs/mark-feuerstein/2001361/biography (June 4, 2011).

"Mark Feuerstein Biography," Star Pulse, http://www.starpulse.com/Actors/Feuerstein,_Mark/Biography/ (May 7, 2011).

"Mark Feuerstein," Internet Movie Database, http://imdb.com/name/nm0275417/maindetails (May 7, 2011).

"Mark Feuerstein Talks *Royal Pains,* Daughter's Illness," Popeater, http://www.popeater.com/2011/01/20/mark-feuerstein-royal-pains/ (May 7, 2011).

"*Pains* Star Mark Feuerstein Gets Pay Raise," Deadline Hollywood, http://www.deadline.com/2011/04/pains-star-mark-feuerstein-gets-pay-raise/ (May 7, 2011).

"*Royal Pains* Mark Feuerstein Talks all Things Hank-Med!," *Eclipse Magazine,* http://eclipsemagazine.com/hollywood-insider/22303/ (May 7, 2011).

—Annette Bowman

Katie Finneran

Actress

Born Kathleen Finneran, February 22, 1971, in Chicago, IL; daughter of Dennis (a financial-services executive) and Kitty (a school principal) Finneran; married Darren Goldstein (an actor), August 16, 2010; children: Ty Michael Goldstein. *Education:* Attended Carnegie-Mellon University, c. 1998-99.

Addresses: *Agent*—Innovative Artists, 235 Park Avenue South, 10th Fl., New York, NY 10003.

Career

Actress on the New York stage, including: *On Borrowed Time*, Circle in the Square Theater, 1991-92; *My Favorite Year*, Vivian Beaumont Theater, 1992; *Two Shakespearean Actors*, Cort Theater, 1992; *In the Summer House*, Vivian Beaumont Theater, 1993; *The Heiress*, Cort Theater, 1995; *Proposals*, Broadhurst Theater, 1997-98; *Bosoms and Neglect*, Signature Theater Company, 1998; *You Never Can Tell*, Roundabout Theater Company, 1998; *The Iceman Cometh*, Brooks Atkinson Theater, 1999; *Cabaret*, Studio 54, 2000-01; *Noises Off*, Brooks Atkinson Theater, 2001-02; *Pig Farm*, Roundabout Theater Company, 2006; *Mauritius*, Biltmore Theater, 2007; *Love, Loss, and What I Wore*, Westside Theater, 2009; *Promises, Promises*, Broadway Theater, 2010-11; has also appeared in *Present Laughter*, Hartford Stage, CT, 1994; *Beyond Therapy*, Williamstown Theater Festival, MA, and Bay Street Theater, Sag Harbor, NY, 2008. Television guest appearances include: *Sex and the City*, HBO, 1998; *Frasier*, NBC, 1999. Regular television roles include: *Bram and Alice*, CBS, 2002; *Wonderfalls*, FOX, 2004; *The Inside*, FOX, 2005. Film appearances include: *Night of the Living Dead*, 1990; *You've Got Mail*, 1998.

Awards: Tony Award for best featured actress in a play, American Theatre Wing/Broadway League, for *Noises Off*, 2002; Drama Desk Award for outstanding featured actress in a play, Drama Desk, for *Noises Off*, 2002; Tony Award for best featured actress in a musical, for *Promises, Promises*, 2010.

Sidelights

Katie Finneran is a veteran of several Broadway productions and is a two-time Tony winner. A triple threat who can dance and sing in musical comedies or convincingly emote in hard-hitting dramas, Finneran has won accolades for roles in productions as diverse as a bleak Eugene O'Neill classic to jazzy musicals like *Cabaret* and *Promises, Promises*.

Finneran was born in Chicago in 1971 and moved with her parents, Dennis and Kitty, to the Miami area as a child. Her father was a financial-services executive and her mother a teacher in a private school who was interviewed by *Miami Herald* journalist Christine Dolen years later. Kitty Finneran recalled that her daughter won "a lead role in sixth grade, and when she came offstage, she said, 'I think this is what I want to do.' She got an agent when she was 12, auditioned for commercials and got one."

Finneran spent her ninth-grade year at Southwood Middle School in Palmetto Bay, a performing-arts magnet school, and went on to the New World School of the Arts in Miami. She was part of its second graduating class, in 1989, and easily earned a spot in the prestigious drama program at Carnegie-Mellon University in Pittsburgh. One of her professors suggested she was already advanced enough to move to New York City, and Finneran left after a year. She also made her film debut around this time, winning one of the lead roles in the 1990 remake of *Night of the Living Dead,* which was filmed in the Pittsburgh area.

Finneran moved to New York City with her best friend from Florida, Andrea Burns, who would also go on to a Broadway career. At one point, they were living on such a limited budget that they shared a favorite dress for auditions. If each of them had an appointment, "we'd meet at various McDonald's around the city and hand off the dress," Finneran told Dolen in the *Miami Herald* article. "That dress could have auditioned by itself."

Finneran's breakthrough came when she landed understudy roles for a major Broadway revival of a period drama, *On Borrowed Time,* in the fall of 1991, in a production that starred George C. Scott and Nathan Lane. In early 1992, she won a small part in an original play that had a short run at Cort Theater, *Two Shakespearean Actors.* She went on to make her Broadway musical debut in a revival of *My Favorite Year* mounted at the Vivian Beaumont Theater at Lincoln Center in late 1992. This was a new musical adaptation of an acclaimed 1982 film that starred Peter O'Toole as a louche actor about to appear on a television variety show in the early 1950s, and reviewers panned it.

In the spring of 1994 Finneran won critical notice for her role in a revival of a Noel Coward play, *Present Laughter,* at the Hartford Stage in Connecticut. The farce, written decades earlier, featured David Birney as a monstrously egotistical movie star named Garry Essendine. "Katie Finneran is squealingly funny as the jumpy Daphne Stillington, an Essendine one-night conquest with long-range plans," declared *New York Times* critic Alvin Klein. "Otherwise, the performances are inexplicably weary or stale."

Finneran had a supporting role in *The Heiress* for much of 1995, the stage adaptation of Henry James' 1880 novel *Washington Square.* During this period she continued to take classes with famed drama coach Uta Hagen at HB Studio in Lower Manhattan.

"I remember the exhilaration the first time Uta Hagen said to me 'I have no criticism,'" Finneran said in a tribute to her teacher that ran in the *Village Voice* in 2004. "All of us in her class at HB Studio longed to hear those words. We all knew we were learning from a living legend, and these words meant that for a brief moment, our work had met her expectations. I heard them twice in 13 years."

Finneran spent some time searching for film and television roles. She had a comic part as a dinner-party hostess in the second episode of the hit HBO series *Sex and the City* in 1998 and appeared in two episodes of Season 7 of *Frasier* as Poppy Delafield, daughter of the radio station owner. In one of 1998's biggest box-office hits, the Tom Hanks-Meg Ryan romantic comedy *You've Got Mail,* she had a bit—but choice—role as the infamous nanny Maureen.

In between those jobs Finneran won a plum role in a new Neil Simon play, *Proposals,* that ran for just two months in late 1997-early 1998. She went on to earn excellent reviews in a revival of the George Bernard Shaw play *You Never Can Tell* at the Laura Pels Theater, the off-Broadway venue that is part of the Roundabout Theater Company. "Finneran is amusing in her haughty disdain for such old-fashioned sentiments as love and shattered with self-loathing once she succumbs to them," wrote Wilborn Hampton in a *New York Times* assessment.

Finneran earned even more ardent reviews later in 1998 for her appearance in *Bosoms and Neglect,* a revival of a two-decade-old John Guare play. She plays Deirdre, a rare-book dealer dreading the month her therapist will be on vacation, and who commiserates with another patient, Scooper. The story, written as a dark comedy, dealt with tough subject matter, and the two other leads were both stage veterans. As a relative newcomer, remarked *Village Voice* critic Michael Feingold, Finneran "holds her own, with a droll mix of regal bearing and abrupt starts that betray the woman whose life is, literally, fiction."

The accolades continued into the later half of the 1998-99 Broadway season, when Finneran appeared in a new production of the Eugene O'Neill classic *The Iceman Cometh* at the Brooks Atkinson Theater. The actor Kevin Spacey starred as Theodore "Hickey" Hickman, a longtime habitué of a Skid Row bar in New York City who returns to his old haunt on the eve of the first world war after a long sojourn. The sales rep proclaims himself a reformed alcoholic and attempts to convince his old drinking buddies to turn their lives around, too. Finneran was cast as Cora, an aging prostitute. Vincent Canby, writing in the *New York Times*, hailed the production as one of the most dazzling of the year. "You won't be able to avoid Ms. Finneran's expression as, near the end of the performance, Cora sits stoically, stage center, en route to oblivion once again. That image, unsentimental and brutally fixed, provides the evening with its haunting coda."

Finneran stayed in *The Iceman Cometh* until it closed in the summer of 1999. A little over a year later, she stepped into the juicy role of Sally Bowles in the hit musical *Cabaret,* a revival of the 1966 original whose film version made Liza Minnelli a star. In the fall of 2001, she was cast in a revival of Michael Frayn's 1982 hit *Noises Off.* She played the ditsy ingénue Brooke Ashton in the play-within-a-play comedy that pokes fun at "every smirky, double-entendre-clogged British sex farce there ever was," wrote *New York Times* theater critic Ben Brantley. His review commended "what will surely turn out to be the most fine-tuned ensemble of the season, featuring some very familiar presences … you'll now have trouble forgetting, especially a comic bombshell named Katie Finneran." That role won Finneran a Tony Award in 2002 for Best Featured Actress in a Play as well as a 2002 Drama Desk Award for Outstanding Featured Actress in a Play.

Finneran returned to television a few more times: in the fall of 2002 in a CBS sitcom called *Bram and Alice,* which was cancelled after just a few episodes, and in a 2004 FOX Television series, *Wonderfalls,* in which she played the lesbian sister of the lead character, Jaye Tyler, an Ivy League graduate who works in a gift shop in the tourist attraction on the U.S.-Canadian border, Niagara Falls. In 2005, she had a recurring role on a FOX crime drama, *The Inside,* that also failed to get picked up for a second season.

Finneran almost met her future husband through the 2006 play *Pig Farm,* an off-Broadway comedy from the duo who had the hit *Urinetown.* In *Pig Farm* she played Tina, the disconsolate wife of a financially troubled swine farmer. "It's like *Jaws,*" she told Robert Feldberg in the Bergen County *Record* about the premise, which did not include any actual pigs. "You very seldom see the shark. Here, all you see is one set, the kitchen." *Pig Farm* failed to replicate the success of *Urinetown,* which won two Tony Awards, but Finneran did invite her co-star Logan Marshall-Green to play matchmaker. He suggested a fellow actor named Darren Goldstein, but the two did not begin dating until they appeared together in *Beyond Therapy* at the Williamstown Theater Festival in Massachusetts in the spring of 2008.

Beyond Therapy was a revival of a 1981 play by Christopher Durang about a couple who allow their therapists an unusual degree of interference in their romance. Finneran was cast as Prudence, a magazine editor who answers the personal ad placed by Bruce, who is bisexual but seeks a traditional marriage and family. The two lead actors began dating as their careers jointly skyrocketed: Finneran replaced Kristin Chenoweth in *Love, Loss, and What I Wore,* a one-act play written by Nora Ephron and Delia Ephron that featured an all-star ensemble cast, while Goldstein originated two roles in the off-Broadway sensation *Bloody Bloody Andrew Jackson.*

Finneran won her second Tony Award for *Promises, Promises,* a mid-twentieth century period musical set at a Manhattan insurance agency. Based on the 1960 Jack Lemmon movie *The Apartment,* the plot centers on an ambitious young Chuck Baxter, who lets the senior-level executives use his apartment for romantic trysts. In the 2010 revival, that role was played by Sean Hayes of *Will & Grace* fame. Chuck has a crush on Fran Kubelik, played by Kristin Chenoweth, and is upset to learn his boss is romancing her. Finneran appears in the second act as Marge MacDougall, a blowsy redhead Chuck meets at a bar. They have one number together, "A Fact Can Be a Beautiful Thing," which features a raucous dance sequence.

Promises, Promises, opened in April of 2010 and was grossing $1 million a week for a time, though critics derided it as a lackluster attempt to horn in on the success of television's period-chic *Mad Men.* Brantley, writing in the *New York Times,* marked Finneran's performance as the high point of the show. "Nothing in the languorous first act prepares you for the jolt of energy that begins the second," he wrote, and described their duet as "a showstopper you wish would never end. Ms. Finneran is on view for only, say, a quarter of an hour. I can't be sure exactly, because it's true that time not only flies but also stretches deliciously when you're having fun. That means that once Ms. Finneran exits, it's all too easy to count the remaining minutes."

Finneran won her Tony Award in June of 2010, and announced in her acceptance speech that she and Goldstein had recently become engaged. They wed that August, and she bowed out of *Promises, Promises* in October, well into the second trimester of her pregnancy. Their son, Ty, was born in February of 2011. Their August wedding was featured in the *New York Times* "Vows" column, which runs in the Sunday "Styles" section. Before meeting Goldstein, she had not really considered dating any fellow actors, she told writer Paula Schwartz. "I'd always thought that I needed something opposite of that, so I would date bankers or people who did completely the opposite kind of thing." The couple wrote their own vows, which were repeated in the "Vows" column. "I love how you can perform in front of thousands of people every night and yet the post office intimidates you," Goldstein said, according to the *New York Times* article, and the declaration from an admittedly disorganized Finneran included the line, "I love that you don't seem to mind that the post office really does intimidate me."

Sources

Periodicals

Back Stage, November 16, 2001, p. 33.
Miami Herald, June 13, 2010.
New Yorker, October 15, 2007, p. 102.
New York Times, June 5, 1994; June 23, 1998; April 18, 1999; November 2, 2001; April 26, 2010; August 27, 2010; September 26, 2010.
Record (Bergen County, NJ), June 25, 2006, p. E7.
Village Voice, December 22, 1998; January 20, 2004.

Online

"Katie Finneran," Internet Broadway Database, http://www.ibdb.com/person.php?id=40531 (February 17, 2011).
"Katie Finneran's Baby Has Arrived," Broadway World.com, http://broadwayworld.com/article/ Katie_Finnerans_Baby_Has_Arrived_20110205.tif (February 17, 2011).

—Carol Brennan

Colin Firth

© Eamonn McCormack/WireImage/Getty Images

Actor

Born Colin Andrew Firth, September 10, 1960, in Grayshott, Hampshire, England; son of David (a university lecturer in history) and Shirley (a university lecturer in comparative religion) Firth; married Livia Giuggioli (a film producer), June 21, 1997; children: William Joseph Firth (with actress Meg Tilly), Luca, Matteo. *Education:* Attended Barton Peveril College and Drama Centre at Chalk Farm, London.

Addresses: *Agent*—Independent Talent Group Ltd., Oxford House, 76 Oxford St., London W1D 1BS, England. *Home*—London, England.

Career

Worked in the offices of London's Shaw Theatre and at the National Youth Theatre as a wardrobe assistant, c. late 1970s-early 1980s. Actor in films, including: *Another Country*, 1984; *A Month in the Country*, 1987; *Apartment Zero*, 1988; *Valmont*, 1990; *Wings of Fame*, 1990; *Femme Fatale*, 1991; *Out of the Blue*, 1991; *The Advocate*, 1994; *Playmaker*, 1994; *Circle of Friends*, 1995; *The English Patient*, 1996; *Fever Pitch*, 1997; *A Thousand Acres*, 1997; *Shakespeare in Love*, 1998; *The Secret Laughter of Women*, 1998; *My Life So Far*, 1999; *Relative Values*, 2000; *Londinium* (released as *Fourplay* in Britain), 2001; *Bridget Jones' Diary*, 2001; *The Importance of Being Earnest*, 2002; *Girl with a Pearl Earring*, 2003; *Hope Springs*, 2003; *Love Actually*, 2003; *What a Girl Wants*, 2003; *Bridget Jones: The Edge of Reason*, 2004; *Nanny McPhee*, 2005; *Where the Truth Lies*, 2005; *When Did You Last See Your Father?*, 2007; *St. Trinian's*, 2007; *Accidental Husband*, 2008; *Mamma Mia!*, 2008; *Easy Virtue*, 2008; *A*

Christmas Carol, 2009; *Dorian Gray*, 2009; *A Single Man*, 2009; *St. Trinian's II: The Legend of Fritton's Gold*, 2009; *The King's Speech*, 2010; *Main Street*, 2010; *Tinker Tailor Soldier Spy*, 2011. Television movie or miniseries appearances include: *Camille*, Hallmark Hall of Fame/CBS, 1984; *1919*, British Film Institute/Channel 4, 1984; *Lost Empires*, Granada, 1986; *The Secret Garden*, Hallmark Hall of Fame/CBS, 1987; *Tumbledown*, BBC, 1988; *Hostages*, HBO, 1993; *Master of the Moor*, ITV, 1994; *The Widowing of Mrs. Holroyd*, BBC, 1995; *Pride and Prejudice*, BBC, 1995; *Nostromo*, BBC, 1996; *Conspiracy*, HBO, 2001; *Born Equal*, BBC, 2006; *Celebration*, Channel 4 (UK), 2007. Stage plays include: *Another Country*, Queen's Theatre, London, UK, 1983; *The Caretaker*, Comedy Theatre, London, UK, 1991; *Chatsky; or, The Importance of Being Stupid*, Almeida Theater, London, UK, 1993.

Awards: Award for best male actor, Royal Television Society, for *Tumbledown*, 1989; best actor award, Broadcasting Press Guild, for *Pride and Prejudice*, 1996; SAG Award for outstanding performance by a cast (with others), Screen Actors Guild, for *Shakespeare in Love*, 1998; best actor award, Austin Film Critics Association, best actor award, San Diego Film Critics Society, best actor award, San Francisco Film Critics Circle, Coppa Volpi, Venice Film Festival, all for *A Single Man*, all 2009; BAFTA Film Award for best leading actor, British Academy of

Film and Television Arts, best actor award, Chlotrudis Awards, ALFS award for British actor of the year, London Critics Circle, outstanding performance award, Santa Barbara International Film Festival, best actor award, Vancouver Film Critics Circle, all for *A Single Man*, all 2010; best actor award, Austin Film Critics Association, best actor, British Independent Film Awards, best actor award, Chicago Film Critics Association; best actor award, Empire Awards, UK, best actor award, Florida Film Critics Circle, best actor award, Los Angeles Film Critics Association, best actor award, New York Film Critics Circle, award for best actor in a leading role, Phoenix Film Critics Society, best actor award, San Francisco Film Critics Circle, best actor in a motion picture—drama, Satellite Awards, best actor award, Washington DC Area Film Critics Association, all for *The King's Speech*, all 2010; Academy Award for best performance by an actor in a leading role, American Academy of Motion Picture Arts and Sciences, BAFTA Film Award for best leading actor, British Academy of Film and Television Arts, best actor award, Critics Choice award for best actor, Broadcast Film Critics Association, Empire Awards UK, Golden Globe award for best performance by an actor in a motion picture—drama, Hollywood Foreign Press Association, best actor award, Kansas City Film Critics Circle, ALFS award for actor of the year, London Critics Circle, best actor award, Online Film Critics Society, Jury Award for best ensemble cast (with others), Santa Barbara International Film Festival, SAG awards for outstanding performance by a cast in a motion picture and outstanding performance by a male actor in a leading role, Screen Actors Guild, best actor award, Vancouver Film Critics Circle, all for *The King's Speech*, all 2011; star on the Hollywood Walk of Fame, 2011.

Sidelights

British actor Colin Firth was earning rave reviews for his rare combination of talent and photogenic charm years before he won the Academy Award for Best Actor in 2011. His turn as England's King George VI—the father of reigning monarch Elizabeth II—in *The King's Speech* proved one of the season's most surprising box-office successes, with Firth enlivening a role other actors might have avoided: that of a stuffy, shy prince with a stammer who is unexpectedly thrust into the public spotlight after his brother abdicates the throne. Prior roles for the actor have included the heartthrob Mr. Darcy in the British Broadcasting Corporation (BBC)'s *Pride and Prejudice* adaptation back in the 1990s, which ignited interest in the novels of Jane Austen, and then as the handsome Mark Darcy in the Austen-inspired *Bridget Jones* movies.

Journalist William Leith has ventured the theory that part of Firth's appeal as the quintessentially British actor lay in his roots: both of his parents were raised in India in the waning days of British Empire rule on the subcontinent. Each set of grandparents were missionaries/aid workers, and his parents had known one another since childhood. By the time Firth was born in 1960 as the first of their three children the couple had settled in England, but Leith imagined that the Firth children grew up in a household that retained some of the archaic pronunciations and mannerisms of Britons who spent years in colonial isolation.

Firth's parents were university professors and the family lived in Hampshire, save for a stint in Nigeria, when his father took a job with that country's ministry of education, and another one in, improbably, St. Louis, Missouri, in the early 1970s. Firth has described himself as an indifferent student, excelling neither in academics nor sport, but said he had decided to become an actor by age 14. He finished his formal schooling at Barton Peveril College in Hampshire, then moved to London. He worked in entry-level backstage jobs at the Shaw Theatre and National Youth Theater before winning a spot at the Drama Centre London in its original location at Chalk Farm in north London. He first gained some notice in the Drama Centre's staging of *Hamlet*, in which Firth was cast in the title role.

Firth's star rose quite suddenly in British theater circles when he joined the cast of the sensational Julian Mitchell drama *Another Country*. Set during the 1930s at an elite boys' boarding school, the story was loosely based on several well-born political figures who were later accused of espionage and boldly defected to the Soviet Union. All had known one another at Eton, the school fictionalized in the play. The drama premiered at the Greenwich Theater in London in November of 1981 with novice Rupert Everett as the louche, possibly homosexual future spy Guy Bennett. A young Kenneth Branagh played another student, Tommy Judd, while the third element in their secretive, and later traitorous triangle, was played by Cary Elwes. Firth replaced Everett on stage as Bennett in 1983, then was cast opposite him in the 1984 screen version as Tommy Judd.

Firth began winning television and stage roles after the success of *Another Country*. One notable turn was in a 1986 miniseries called *Lost Empires* that marked one of the last appearances of one of England's greatest stage actors, Sir Laurence Olivier. Moving easily into leading roles, Firth then beat out several other actors for a highly coveted role as Scots Guard Robert Lawrence, who was paralyzed from a battle injury during the 1982 Falklands War.

The BBC drama *Tumbledown* was based on Lawrence's own memoir of the conflict and his difficult adjustment to life as a disabled vet. Firth won a won a Royal Television Society Award for best actor for *Tumbledown* and was also nominated for a British Academy of Film and Television Arts (BAFTA) Award for best actor.

Firth's first full-scale, big-budget film was *Valmont*, directed by the legendary Milos Forman. This was the second recent screen adaptation of the salacious eighteenth-century novel *Les Liaisons Dangereuses*; the first one, a standard Hollywood costume epic that was nominated for Best Picture, starred Glenn Close and John Malkovich as a scheming pair who set out to corrupt Uma Thurman and then Michelle Pfeiffer's characters; Keanu Reeves also makes an appearance. In Forman's *Valmont*, Firth was cast as the seductive nobleman of the title, with Annette Bening as his foil. "The film is rapturously beautiful, enticing us into a lush, aristocratic world," declared Peter Travers in *Rolling Stone*. "Firth's engaging portrayal of Valmont bears little resemblance to the viper that Malkovich played."

Canadian actress Meg Tilly played one of the targets of Valmont's advances in *Valmont*, and the pair became romantically involved off-screen, too. Tilly gave birth to a son, Will, in 1990, and for a few years the couple lived in a remote part of British Columbia. Dramatically distanced from the worlds of film and theater, Firth took almost no roles for a few years in the early 1990s. A low point came in 1994, when he played a killer in a television adaptation of a Ruth Rendell mystery, *Master of the Moor*.

Firth's comeback, and starmaking turn, came in 1995 with *Pride and Prejudice*. The six-part BBC miniseries, based on the 1813 novel by Jane Austen, pulled in ten million viewers in Britain and helped reignite interest in Austen's works, which serve as the literary forerunner of modern cinema's romantic-comedy tales. Jennifer Ehle was cast as female lead Elizabeth "Lizzie" Bennet, who is initially disdainful of the handsome, unattached aristocrat who comes into her social circle, Mr. Fitzwilliam Darcy. Firth admitted he had not actually read *Pride and Prejudice* before he saw the script. "Nineteenth-century literature didn't seem very sexy to me," he told Rachel Kelly in a *Times* of London interview. "I had this prejudice that it would probably be girls' stuff. I had never realised that Darcy was such a famous figure in literature."

Firth seemed a perfect match for the British period drama, managing to don full Regency England dress—waistcoats, breeches, billowing white shirts,

and even a magnificent pair of sideburns—with appealing panache. As Leith wrote in the *Observer* profile, his character "hung around in the background, not saying much. Firth did a lot of his acting with his eyes.... Late in the day, burning with passion and unfulfilled sexual desire, he jumped off his horse into a pond and emerged, his shirt dripping."

That was a shot that turned Firth into England's newest screen heartthrob overnight. He appeared in several more movies, including *The English Patient*, *Fever Pitch*, *Shakespeare in Love*, and *Londinium* before turning up as Mark Darcy in the much-anticipated screen adaptation of journalist Helen Fielding's novel *Bridget Jones' Diary*, a runaway bestseller in the U.K. Fielding had originally penned a tongue-in-cheek newspaper column about the perils of modern dating, then adapted them into a modern-day version of *Pride and Prejudice*, even naming the brooding attorney who is Bridget's foil "Mark Darcy." Fielding, it was said, was adamant about Firth in the role, and most critics pronounced him and his rival, played by Hugh Grant, the most polished performances in an otherwise clunky film.

Firth returned to period dramas with the 2002 film version of Oscar Wilde's *The Importance of Being Earnest*, which reunited him with Everett, and then portrayed seventeenth-century Dutch artist Johannes Vermeer in *Girl with a Pearl Earring* in 2003. He and Grant were part of a massive ensemble cast in *Love Actually*, a 2003 romantic comedy of epic proportions, then both reprised their roles in 2004's *Bridget Jones: The Edge of Reason*. The sequel kicked off with Darcy and Renee Zellweger's Bridget now firmly ensconced in a relationship. "With more time than in *Diary*, Firth balances Mark's emotional retentiveness, inner warmth and class hang-ups in a surprisingly edgy, unpredictable performance that gives the movie its few moments of real uncertainty," declared *Variety*'s Derek Elley.

Firth, who married Italian film producer Livia Giuggioli in 1997, became a father again in 2001 with the birth of his second son; a third was born in 2003. In his early 40s, he began taking on more mature roles, such as the hapless father in the popular *Nanny McPhee* kids' movie and the successful *St. Trinian's* franchise. There was also a 2008 appearance in *Mamma Mia!*, the film version of the hit stage musical, in which he was required to deliver a song from ABBA, the '70s Swedish pop sensation.

Firth reclaimed more serious ground in his career with *A Single Man*, fashion designer Tom Ford's directorial debut. Based on a Christopher Isherwood novel about a closeted gay man in the early 1960s, Firth starred as a lonely British expatriate teaching in sunny southern California and mourning the death of his lover. The film was released in late 2009 to a great flush of publicity, but reviews were mixed. "Firth's performance—which won the best actor award at the Venice Film Festival—is one of the finest of the year, a wondrous surprise at the heart of this otherwise preening, shallow movie," wrote Stephanie Zacharek in Salon. The Venice Film Festival award, called the Coppa Volpi, was followed by his first nomination for an Academy Award and a BAFTA Award for Best Actor in a Leading Role.

A drama about a World War II-era British monarch who suffered from a speech impediment well into his adult years seemed an unlikely formula for box-office gold, but that is exactly what Firth as King George VI and the team behind *The King's Speech* achieved. The screenplay was based on the true story of Lionel Logue, a self-taught Australian vocal coach who began working with England's Prince Albert, the Duke of York, in secret after the stuttering Duke's disastrous live radio broadcast at the British Empire Exhibition of 1925. Logue was played by Geoffrey Rush, while Helena Bonham Carter—who was once shortlisted for the *Bridget Jones* role—also gave a moving performance as Firth's spirited, devoted wife, the former Lady Elizabeth Bowes-Lyon, later to become Britain's venerated Queen Mum. Albert, called "Bertie," was the second son of his imperious, formidable father, King George V. Bertie's playboy brother David inherited the throne in 1936 as Edward VIII, but abdicated several tense months later in order to marry a twice-divorced American woman. At the time, the scandal was viewed as a grave threat to the future of the British monarchy, but in retrospect King George VI proved to be a much more solid leader during the devastating years of World War II.

The King's Speech garnered strong critical acclaim and was rolled out with major fanfare in the run-up to Oscar nominations. "In Firth's pale features—far more handsome than the real Bertie's, but pinched with trepidation at the thought of each public appearance—we sense a grownup boy who has spent his life tiptoeing through a minefield," wrote the *New Yorker* film critic, Anthony Lane. In *Entertainment Weekly*, Lisa Schwarzbaum commended Firth in the title role as "a performance of nuance and

soul that would be more astonishing only if we hadn't become almost spoiled by expecting such quality from him."

Firth took home the Oscar for Best Actor at the 83rd Annual Academy Awards in February of 2011. "I have a feeling my career's just peaked," he quipped on the podium, according to the *New York Times*. A more likely prospect would be a passel of first-rate leading roles, beginning with *Tinker Tailor Soldier Spy,* a big-budget adaptation of the acclaimed John le Carré spy thriller. In one interview to promote *The King's Speech,* Firth claimed that despite being a trained actor it was not overly difficult to portray a person with a nervous stammer. "Public speaking is terrifying," he told *Vogue*'s Gaby Wood. "Even people who have been nominated for awards will tell you that at the moment the nominations are read out, you are praying that it's not you."

Sources

Periodicals

Entertainment Weekly December 30, 2010.
New Yorker, November 29, 2010, p. 90.
New York Times, February 28, 2011.
Observer (London, England), April 9, 2000.
Sunday Times (London, England), December 4, 2005, p. 18.
Times (London, England), October 25, 1995, p. 15.
Variety, November 8, 2004, p. 38.
Vogue, December 2010, p. 292.

Online

"Colin Firth: By Anyone's Measure, A Leading Man," *Fresh Air,* National Public Radio, http://www.npr.org/templates/transcript/transcript.php?storyId=12328486.tif6 (June 22, 2011).
"*A Single Man*: Tom Ford's Shallow but Compelling Debut," *Salon,* http://www.salon.com/entertainment/movies/review/2009/12/09/a_single_man (June 28, 2011).
"*Valmont,*" *Rolling Stone,* http://www.rollingstone.com/movies/reviews/valmont-19891117.tif (June 28, 2011).

—*Carol Brennan*

James Franco

Helga Esteb/Shutterstock.com

Actor

Born James Edward Franco, April 19, 1978, in Palo Alto, CA; son of Doug and Betsy Franco. *Education:* University of California Los Angeles, B.A., 2008; Columbia University, M.F.A., 2010; graduate work at New York University, Yale University, Brooklyn College, Warren Wilson College, and the Rhode Island School of Design.

Addresses: *Management*—James/Levy/Jacobson Management, 3500 West Olive Ave., Ste. 1470, Burbank, CA 91505.

Career

Actor on television, including: *Pacific Blue*, USA Network, 1997; *1973* (movie), 1998; *Profiler*, NBC, 1999; *To Serve and Protect* (movie), 1999; *Freaks and Geeks*, 1999-2000; *At Any Cost* (movie), 2000; *James Dean* (movie), 2001; *The X Files*, FOX, 2001; *General Hospital*, ABC, 2009—; co-host of Academy Awards, 2011. Film appearances include: *Never Been Kissed*, 1999; *If Tomorrow Comes*, 2000; *Whatever It Takes*, 2000; *Mean People Suck*, 2001; *Blind Spot*, 2002; *The Car Kid*, 2002; *City by the Sea*, 2002; *Deuces Wild*, 2002; *Mother Ghost*, 2002; *Sonny*, 2002; *Spider-Man*, 2002; *You Always Stalk the Ones You Love*, 2002; *The Company*, 2003; *Spider-Man 2*, 2004; *The Ape*, 2005; *Fool's Gold*, 2005; *The Great Raid*, 2005; *Annapolis*, 2006; *The Dead Girl*, 2006; *Flyboys*, 2006; *Grasshopper*, 2006; *Tristan + Isolde*, 2006; *The Wicker Man*, 2006; *An American Crime*, 2007; *Finishing the Game: The Search for a New Bruce Lee*, 2007; *Good Time Max*, 2007; *In the Valley of Elah*, 2007; *Knocked Up*, 2007; *Spider-Man 3*, 2007; *Camille*, 2008; *Milk*, 2008; *Nights in Rodanthe*, 2008; *Pineapple Express*, 2008; *127 Hours*, 2010; *Date Night*, 2010; *Eat Pray Love*, 2010; *Howl*, 2010; *Masculinity Me*, 2010; *William Vincent*, 2010; *The Green Hornet*, 2011; *Your Highness*, 2011. Film work includes: executive producer, director, and writer, *The Ape*, 2005; writer and director, *Fool's Gold*, 2005; writer and director, *Good Time Max*, 2007; writer and director, *The Feast of Stephen*, 2009; writer and director, *Herbert White*, 2010; director, *Saturday Night*, 2010; writer and director, *The Clerk's Tale*, 2010; writer and director, *Masculinity & Me*, 2010.

Awards: Critics Choice Award for best actor in a motion picture made for television, Broadcast Film Critics Association, for *James Dean*, 2002; Golden Globe Award for best performance by an actor in a miniseries or a motion picture made for television, Hollywood Foreign Press Association, for *James Dean*, 2002; Hollywood Breakthrough Award for actor of the year, Hollywood Film Festival, 2008; Critics Choice Award (with others) for best acting ensemble, Broadcast Film Critics Association, for *Milk*, 2009; Independent Spirit Award for best supporting male, Film Independent, for *Milk*, 2009; Man of the Year, Hasty Pudding Theatricals, 2009; award for best actor, Dallas-Fort Worth Film Critics Association, for *127 Hours*, 2010; Sierra Award for best actor, Las Vegas Film Critics Society, for *127 Hours*, 2010; Teddy Award for best short film, Berlin International Film Festival, for *The Feast of Stephen*, 2010;

best actor, Central Ohio Film Critics Association, for *127 Hours*, 2011; actor of the year, Central Ohio Film Critics Association, 2011.

Sidelights

Actor James Franco may have established himself as a gifted star with award-winning turns in projects like *James Dean* and *127 Hours*, but he also was a dedicated student, artist, filmmaker, and author as well. As an actor, he could do both drama and comedy—two of his best known films are *City by the Sea* and *Pineapple Express*—and he often played troubled characters. A painter since his teen years, Franco made changes after finding a conventional career path for actors unsatisfying. As a result, the intelligent Franco worked on completing multiple graduate degrees in English, filmmaking, and fiction and poetry writing as well as creating related projects and his own artwork. Sam Anderson of *New York Magazine* wrote of Franco: "He's not a savant or an obvious genius—he's someone of mortal abilities who seems to be working immortally hard."

Born on April 19, 1978, in Palo Alto, California, he is the son of Doug and Betsy Franco. Raised with his two younger brothers, Tom and Dave, Franco was shy in his youth but always interested in acting. He was a math prodigy in his youth, but rebelled as a teenager and became interested in the arts. While attending Palo Alto High School, he joined the drama club senior year because he was jealous of his girlfriend who was appearing in a play that required kissing another guy. After graduating from high school in 1996, he entered the University of California Los Angeles (UCLA) where he studied English. Looking to overcome his shyness, he took an acting class and become hooked. Franco dropped out of UCLA after a year and spent the next year and a half intensely studying acting at Playhouse West.

In that time period, Franco landed some guest roles on series like *Pacific Blue* in 1997 and movies like 1998's *1973* and 1999's *To Serve and Protect*. The young actor had his first breakout role in the cult hit *Freaks and Geeks*. Though the show only aired from 1999 to 2000, it was a critical favorite and had a small, but loyal, audience. Set in the early 1980s, *Freaks and Geeks* focused on a group of high school students in Michigan generally marginalized in their social structure. Franco played Daniel Desario, a troubled but charismatic teen.

Franco was the first breakout star of *Freaks and Geeks*. During and shortly after the run of the show, he began appearing in films including 1999's *Never Been Kissed*, 2000's *If Tomorrow Comes* and *Whatever It Takes*, and 2001's *Mean People Suck*. In 2001, Franco had another career-defining role playing the title role in the television movie *James Dean*. Critics raved about his work playing the troubled actor, with Ann Hodges of the *Houston Chronicle* writing "He not only looks like Dean, but his mannerisms and his whole persona are startlingly real. This movie rests on his thin, hunched shoulders, and he carries it off." He won a Golden Globe for playing Dean.

The success of *James Dean* led to more roles in films for Franco. Within a few years, Franco was a true film star; however, his career did have its ups and downs. The actor auditioned for the role of Peter Parker/Spiderman, but lost to Tobey Maguire. Instead, Franco was cast as the villainous Harry Osborne in 2002's *Spider-Man*, a role he reprised in the sequels, 2004's *Spider-Man 2* and 2007's *Spider-Man 3*.

Franco did not only appear in Hollywood summer blockbusters like *Spider-Man*. He appeared in Hollywood films like *Deuces Wild* and the drama *City by the Sea*, both released in 2002. In *City by the Sea*, Franco played the troubled, drug-addicted son of a cop played by Robert De Niro. The legendary actor chose him for the role after seeing him in *James Dean*. Again praised for his authenticity, Franco took to the streets to research the role.

Over the next six years, Franco capitalized on his career momentum by appearing in a large number of films; however, the output was uneven and the quality was not always great. He appeared in five forgettable films in 2002, including *You Always Stalk the Ones You Love* and *Sonny*. Franco continued to take roles in a few films released in 2003 and 2005, including *The Great Raid*, to little acclaim.

In 2006, Franco had six films released, including *Flyboys*, in which he played a World War I fighter pilot. He played the lead in the studio film, which did not find much of an audience. He also had leading roles in films like *Tristan + Isolde* and *Annapolis*, two more studio films which were not particularly successful. Other films featuring Franco released in 2006 include *The Wicker Man* and *The Dead Girl*. One acclaimed film was 2007's *In the Valley of Elah*, a film about returning veterans starring Tommy Lee Jones. Franco also had a small role in the hit 2007 comedy, *Knocked Up*.

Unhappy with the direction of his career, Franco began taking different chances. As he told Glenn Whipp of the *Los Angeles Times*, "it's all connected to an attitude change. I just decided a career wasn't worth having unless I was doing things that interested me. For a while, I didn't think I should listen to my own taste. I didn't know that was something you could do. I thought you had to build a career … whatever that means." To that end, in 2008, he took roles in *Camille* and *Nights in Rodanthe*.

More importantly, Franco reunited with *Freaks and Geeks* co-star Seth Rogan in the popular buddy film comedy *Pineapple Express*. In the film, the actors switched from their typical roles. Franco played a stoner drug dealer to great comic effect, while Rogan played the straight man. Also in 2008, Franco appeared in the biopic *Milk*, about the life and assassination of San Francisco city councilman Harvey Milk. Franco played Milk's one-time lover, and won an Independent Spirit Award for his work in the role. With these new choices, things began to change. Franco also admitted that he stopped taking himself so seriously, which he believed helped his career.

Continuing that trend, Franco took on new challenges in 2009 when he joined the cast of the long-running soap opera *General Hospital* in the small, but recurring, role of a psychopathic killer/performance artist named Franco. He returned as Franco in 2010 for 20 episodes, and turned the role into a piece of performance art hosted by the Museum of Contemporary Art (MOCA) at the Pacific Design Center in Los Angeles called *Soap at MOCA*. In 2010, Franco also saw six films released, displaying the depth and breadth of his talent and interests.

Some were independent films like *Howl,* in which he played the poet Allen Ginsberg. The film focuses on the titular poem—arguably Ginsberg's best known work—the poet's love life, and the obscenity trial related to his work. Others were mainstream Hollywood films like the comedy *Date Night* and the Julia Roberts vehicle *Eat Pray Love,* based on the best-selling book by Elizabeth Gilbert. In the latter film, he played Roberts' character's boyfriend. Franco also appeared in the independent film, *William Vincent,* as well as *Masculinity Me.*

Franco's most acclaimed film of the year was *127 Hours.* Directed by Danny Boyle, the film tells the story of Aron Ralston who was forced to cut off his arm after it became lodged under a rock in an accident that occurred while he was hiking in Canyonlands National Park. The filming was challenging, as the director would let the camera role for 20 to 30 minutes, allowing the actor to struggle with the rock. As Franco explained to Devin Friedman of

GQ, "For Danny it was more having me go through the experience, so he'll have me at the beginning of the take and then 20 minutes later, where I'm physically exhausted. That's the only way to get that moment."

Critics and audiences responded positively to his depiction of Ralston in *127 Hours,* and Ralston himself approved. Ralston told the *Brentwood Gazette,* "James is so good that the first few times I watched it, it's so real I didn't even think he was acting. His response and his emotions are so realistic. I have to say that I think James does a phenomenal job with it and I'm really happy with what he does in the film." Franco won several awards for his work in the role, and he was nominated for a 2011 Academy Award for best actor.

In early 2011, Franco had a cameo in *The Green Hornet,* which was co-written by and starred Rogan. Franco also made headlines in 2011 for his continuing short-term appearances on *General Hospital* and for co-hosting the Academy Awards with actress Anne Hathaway. Franco's turn as co-host received mixed reviews, as it was unclear to viewers and critics if Franco was uncomfortable or merely playing the straight man to Hathaway's free spirited comedic stylings.

Away from acting, Franco spent his little spare time painting, a pursuit he had enjoyed since high school. He had his own production company, Rabbit Bandini Productions, and produced, directed, and wrote a number of films, some in conjunction with his academic programs, others outside of them. Franco also continued his education, finding the non-acting activity very satisfying. He went back to UCLA to finish his undergraduate degree in creative writing and English, graduating with a 3.5 grade point average. He later entered master's degree programs at New York University, where he studied film, and Columbia University, where he studied fiction writing. He also did graduate work in fiction writing at Brooklyn College and poetry at Warren Wilson College in North Carolina. He graduated with his master of fine arts degree from Columbia in 2010 and, that fall, enrolled at the Rhode Island School of Design to study art. As of 2011, Franco was also in an English literature Ph.D. program at Yale University.

Known for his high productivity level and ability to focus, Franco was a dedicated student and lover of learning. He also published short stories in *Esquire* and *McSweeney's.* Franco's student films created at New York University have made the rounds at film festivals. Franco dismissed criticism that he was spreading himself too thin, telling Sam Anderson of *New York Magazine*, "If the work is good, what does it matter? I'm doing it because I love it. Why not do as many things I love as I can? As long as the work is good."

Despite the academic and other demands, Franco continued to work regularly as an actor. He had a number of film projects lined up for release in 2011 and 2012, including a *Planet of the Apes* remake called *Rise of the Apes*. Other planned films included the comedy *Your Highness* and *Maladies*. Writers like Tom Chiarella of *Esquire* believed that Franco's acting career would continue to move to the next level. Chiarella claimed, "He's about to enter the realm of leading man simply because he does exactly what a movie star does: make you want a lot more of him."

Sources

Periodicals

Brentwood Gazette, January 12, 2011, pp. 8-9.
CosmoGIRL!, November 1, 2006, p. 39.

Daily News of Los Angeles, September 6, 2002, p. U4; August 3, 2008, p. L1.
Esquire, September 1, 2010, p. 122.
Evening Standard (London, England), March 1, 2011, p. 49.
GQ, December 2010, p. 286.
Houston Chronicle, August 5, 2001, p. 2.
Los Angeles Times, November 18, 2010, p. S20.
National Post, December 23, 2010, p. AL1.
New Yorker, July 12, 2010, p. 31.
New York Magazine, August 2, 2010.
St. Petersburg Times (FL), March 1, 2011, p. 2B.
Vancouver Sun (British Columbia, Canada), December 3, 2010, p. D7.

Online

"James Franco (I)," Internet Movie Database, http://www.imdb.com/name/nm0290556/ (February 22, 2011).

—*A. Petruso*

Brian Gallagher

Chief Executive Officer of United Way of America

Born c. 1959 in Chicago, IL; married; children: two. *Education:* Ball State University, Muncie, IN, bachelor's degree, 1981, honorary doctorate, 2003; Emory University, Atlanta, GA, M.B.A., 1992.

Addresses: *Office*—United Way of America, 701 North Fairfax St., Alexandria, VA 22314.

Career

Began career at United Way in management training program, 1981; assistant campaign director, United Way of Forsyth County, NC, 1982-84; associate executive director of resource development, United Way of Berks County, PA, 1984-87; senior vice president of donor services, United Way of Southeastern New England, 1987-90; group vice president, United Way of Metropolitan Atlanta, 1990-94; executive vice president and chief operating officer, United Way of Metropolitan Atlanta, 1994-96; president, United Way of Central Ohio, 1996-2002; president and chief executive officer of United Way of America, 2002—; head of United Way Worldwide, 2009—.

Member: Board of directors, United Way of America, 2002—.

Sidelights

Brian Gallagher became the fourth president and chief executive officer of the United Way of America in 2002 after more than 20 years of service with the non-profit organization, including a stint as president of the United Way of Central Ohio based in Columbus. In 2009, he was also named head of United Way Worldwide. As the CEO of these two organizations, Gallagher oversees a worldwide network of 1,800 community-based outreach and philanthropy groups spanning 45 countries and territories and raising more than $5 billion annually. From the beginning of his tenure, Gallagher strove to transform the United Way from an organization focused on local-level fund-raising to one working in concert to achieve specific, measureable goals such as those laid out by the organization in 2008 to create significant improvements in the areas of education, income stability, and health.

Gallagher was born around 1959 in Chicago, Illinois, but grew up in the northern Indiana community of Hobart. His youth was a difficult one. "Our family was really challenged," he recalled to Kathy Hoke of *Business First—Columbus*. "It wasn't always the most safe place in the world." Gallagher's family had only modest ambitions, and his parents did not encourage him to excel in school or attend college; however, from about the age of ten, Gallagher began forming relationships with authority figures at school or with the parents of friends, who gave him support and structure. He observed interactions among people and organizations in society, and began to notice differences in life goals and opportunities. This led Gallagher to apply to college on his own initiative. "Very early on, I understood the concept of personal accountability," he explained to Hoke. After high school, Gallagher won admission to Indiana's Ball University, becoming the first member of his family to attend college. There, he studied social work, and had his first exposure to the United Way through a senior internship at the organization's Muncie, Indiana outpost. The United Way's goals intrigued him, and Gallagher applied for and received a spot in the organization's management training program.

Gallagher began his career in earnest with the United Way in the management training program in 1981 after finishing his bachelor's degree, and advanced steadily within the organization over the next several years. The following year, he joined the staff of the United Way of Forsyth County in Winston-Salem, North Carolina, as an assistant campaign director. In 1984, he advanced to become the associate executive director for resource development at the United Way of Berks County in central Pennsylvania. He continued to move up the ladder in 1987, shifting to the United Way of Southeastern New England in Providence, Rhode Island, where he served as a senior vice president for donor services. His next stop was in Atlanta, where he became a group vice president. In 1992, Gallagher received his master's in business administration from Atlanta's Emory University. Two years later, he became the executive vice president and chief operating officer of the same Atlanta affiliate. From Atlanta, he went to Columbus, Ohio's United Way affiliate to serve as its president. There, he inaugurated the Family Housing Collaborative, a service organization aimed at reducing homelessness through community services to help people find affordable housing, child care, and job-skill training.

In 2002, Gallagher was named the president and CEO of the United Way of America, succeeding Betty Stanley Beene. He has quickly thrust into dealing with internal problems within the United Way system. At about the same time as Gallagher was named head of the national United Way, the organization began looking into suspicious spending at its affiliate in Washington, D.C. The investigation revealed fraud and other financial irregularities on the part of former affiliate president Oral Suer and then-current head Norman O. Taylor. In 2004, Suer pled guilty to embezzling nearly $500,000 of United Way funds, although the total amount stolen was estimated to be much larger; he was later sentenced to more than two years in prison. The scandal hurt United Way fund-raising efforts and tarnished the organization's image, already damaged from similar revelations of extortion at the national level a decade previously.

Gallagher's history of focusing on community initiatives rather than simply generating funds proved a good match for the organization's changing needs and mounting public relations issues. Among Gallagher's primary concerns at the time of his appointment was pressing for the United Way to measure its success by impact, not by dollars. "There were a number of local United Ways that were already making the transition on their own, defining the business of changing community conditions and outcomes in people's lives.... [W]e spent probably the first eight to ten months of my tenure just making the case for why local United Ways and the United Way movement should get back to ... trying to galvanize individual interests in communities around a common agenda focused on human need and potential," he told Matt Sinclair of *Philanthropy News Digest.*

This agenda was fully realized in 2008 when Gallagher and the United Way issued a ten-year plan titled "Goals for the Common Good." This initiative focused on enacting dramatic improvements in three broad areas: education, income, and health. In the field of education, the organization declared intentions to reduce the number of student dropouts by half; in income, to halve the number of financially unstable families; and in health, to raise the percentage of healthy Americans by one-third. Within these goals, the United Way set up measurable indicators by which to judge its own progress in a consistent way from community to community. This program emblemized the shift from fundraising to action that Gallagher had worked to enact since taking over the United Way's top job. "This is the next evolution of us, from a fund-raising mission to a community change mission, and this is really getting focused and declaring our commitment to national, long-term, very concrete goals that will then drive strategies that get created locally and nationally," he told Mark Hrywna in the *Non-profit Times.* "We believe that if real change is going to happen, we've got to commit ourselves to these goals." The following year, Gallagher was named the president and CEO of United Way Worldwide while retaining his post with United Way of America.

In order to support its ten-year plan to improve graduation rates, the United Way conducted a nationwide study during 2010 to learn how members of communities both large and small viewed the role of education. Finding a general trend toward community-based support for strong public school systems, the organization began a program the following year to recruit one million education volunteers to serve as readers, tutors, and mentors for young people around the country.

Sources

Periodicals

Business First—Columbus, December 14, 2001, p. A1.
Dallas Morning News, April 1, 2005.
New York Times, January 23, 2002, p. A16; March 5, 2004, p. A17.
Non-profit Times, March 1, 2002, p. 4; June 1, 2008, p. 34.

Online

"Brian Gallagher," United Way, http://liveunited. org/people/profile/brian-gallagher (August 26, 2011).

"Interview: United Way of America CEO Brian Gallagher," Philanthropy Action, http://www. philanthropyaction.com/articles/interview_ united_way_of_america_ceo_brian_gallagher/ (August 26, 2011).

"One Million Volunteers for America's Kids," United Way, http://liveunited.org/blog/entry/ one-million-volunteers-for-americas-kids/ (August 26, 2011).

"PND Newsmakers—Brian Gallagher," *Philanthropy News Digest,* http://foundationcenter.org/pnd/ newsmakers/nwsmkr.jhtml?id=18680000.tif2 (August 26, 2011).

—*Vanessa E. Vaughn*

Andrew Garfield

Actor

B orn Andrew Russell Garfield, August 20, 1983, in Los Angeles, CA. *Education:* Central School of Speech and Drama, London, England, 2004.

Addresses: *Management*—Creative Artists Agency, 2000 Avenue of the Stars, Los Angeles, CA 90067.

Career

A ctor on stage, including: *Kes*, Royal Exchange Theater, Manchester, England, 2004; *Mercy*, Soho Theater, London, 2004; *Hush*, Soho Theater, London, 2004; *Romeo and Juliet*, Royal Exchange Theater, Manchester, England, 2005; *The Laramie Project*, Sound Theater, London, 2005; *Beautiful Thing*, Sound Theater, London, 2006; *Burn/Chatroom/Citizenship*, Royal National Theater, London, 2006; *The Overwhelming*, United Kingdom tour, 2006; *Death of a Salesman*, Broadway Revival, 2012. Television appearances include: *Sugar Rush*, 2005; *Swinging*, 2005; *Simon Schama's Power of Art*, 2006; *Doctor Who*, 2007; *Freezing*, 2007; *Trial & Retribution*, 2007. Film appearances include: *Boy A*, 2007; *Lions for Lambs*, 2007; *The Imaginarium of Doctor Parnassus*, 2009; *Red Riding: In the Year of Our Lord 1974*, 2009; *Red Riding: In the Year of Our Lord 1980*, 2009; *Red Riding: In the Year of Our Lord 1983*, 2009; *Never Let Me Go*, 2010; *The Social Network*, 2010; *The Amazing Spider-Man*, 2012.

Awards: Most promising theater newcomer award, *Manchester Evening News*, 2004; named to *Variety* magazine's list of ten actors to watch, 2007; BAFTA award for best television actor, British Academy of

© *Michael Buckner/Getty Images*

Film and Television Arts, for *Boy A*, 2008; Hollywood Breakthrough Award for actor of the year, Hollywood Film Festival, 2010; Hollywood Film Award for ensemble of the year (with others), Hollywood Film Festival, for *The Social Network*, 2010; best ensemble acting (with others), Phoenix Film Critics Society Award, for *The Social Network*, 2010; Saturn Award for best supporting actor, Academy of Science Fiction, Fantasy & Horror Films, for *Never Let Me Go*, 2011; British Film Award for best actor, *Evening Standard*, for *Never Let Me Go* and *The Social Network*, 2011; British supporting actor of the year, London Critics' Circle, for *The Social Network*, 2011; ensemble cast award (with others), Palm Springs International Film Festival, for *The Social Network*, 2011; grooming icon, *Esquire* magazine, 2011.

Sidelights

S ony Pictures created a stir in 2010 when it tapped Brit-raised actor Andrew Garfield as the successor to the Spider-Man throne in a thoroughly scrutinized casting decision. Having arrived in the United States just four years earlier, Garfield remained relatively unknown among moviegoers when he was tagged to wear one of the most famous costumes in cinema, taking the mantle from Tobey Maguire, who had played Peter Parker—aka Spider-Man—in the first three installments of the film series.

Garfield beat out a long list of well-known Hollywood heartthrobs, including Jamie Bell (*Billy Elliot*), Frank Dillane (*Harry Potter and the Half-Blood Prince*), Josh Hutcherson (*The Kids Are All Right*), Aaron Johnson (*Kick-Ass*), and Anton Yelchin (*Star Trek*). According to the *Washington Post*'s Michael Cavna, Spider-Man director Marc Webb issued this announcement upon naming Garfield to the role: "Though his name may be new to many, those who know this young actor's work understand his extraordinary talents. He has a rare combination of intelligence, wit, and humanity. Mark my words, you will love Andrew Garfield as Peter Parker."

The film was slated for release in July of 2012. Meanwhile, eager Spidey fans were able to catch glimpses of Garfield in the 2010 releases *The Social Network* and *Never Let Me Go.* Garfield earned a Golden Globe nomination for best supporting actor for his role in *The Social Network*, a dramatization of the early days of Facebook.

A dual citizen of the United States and United Kingdom, Andrew Russell Garfield was born on August 20, 1983, in Los Angeles to a British mother and an American father. Garfield spent three years in the United States before the family of four—Garfield has an older brother—moved to Surrey, England, southwest of London. While Garfield was growing up, his parents ran an interior design business. Later, his father became head coach of the Guildford City Swimming Club and coached the British national team. His mother worked as a teacher.

As a child, Garfield tried swimming and gymnastics. He told the *Telegraph*'s Isabel Albiston that his parents encouraged him to start gymnastics at six. "I hated it to begin with but I got pretty good. I came third in the national championships when I was 12. I should have won it, but I bricked it in the set floor routine." Shortly thereafter, Garfield gave up the sport, feeling he had been pushed into it too hard and too young. In addition, he just did not see himself as a gymnast long-term. "There was nothing in a handstand that told me the meaning of life," he told the *Guardian*'s Chrissy Iley.

During another point in his childhood, Garfield envisioned himself becoming a singer-songwriter. His parents signed him up for classical guitar lessons, but he ended up hating it because the teacher never let him play anything he wanted and instead drilled him on a classic repertoire of music. After about two years of lessons, he gave up on guitar and never touched the instrument again.

By the time Garfield reached his teens, he felt unsettled. Because of his competitive nature, he had a hard time following in the footsteps of his older, over-achieving, and very intelligent brother. To give him an outlet for his emotions, Garfield's parents encouraged him to try something creative. He chose acting and began classes in the city of Guildford at the age of 15. One of his first roles was playing Fat Sam in the gangster musical *Bugsy Malone*.

Garfield attended the City of London Freeman's School. While there, he caught the attention of Phil Tong, the school's drama teacher, who encouraged Garfield to enroll in drama classes at the school. A defining moment came when Tong took Garfield's class on a field trip to the Royal Court Theater to see Kelly Reilly, who had become a mainstay of the British stage. Reilly had been a student of Tong's. Seeing Reilly on stage made an impression on Garfield and he began to believe he, too, could become a successful actor.

With Tong's encouragement, Garfield applied to London's Central School of Speech and Drama and was accepted. The school's graduates included such noteworthy stars as Judi Dench, Kathryn Turner, and James Nesbitt. By now, Garfield was sure he was on the right track. Speaking to director Terry Gilliam, for a piece in *Interview* magazine, Garfield noted that his temperament made him well-suited for acting. "I just think I've always been sensitive and had difficulty containing my feelings, and I've always searched for outlets for that, because otherwise those feelings come out in chaotic ways that aren't always great. So I think I was searching from the start of my conscious life for some kind of constructive way to work through my feelings, and I found acting."

To support himself in drama school, Garfield got a job at Starbucks. During his third year of school, Garfield landed his first major role, playing Billy in a 2004 stage production of Ken Loach's 1969 film *Kes* at the Royal Exchange Theater in Manchester, England. For his performance, Garfield was honored with the Most Promising Newcomer theater award from the *Manchester Evening News*.

Around that same time, Garfield landed a role in *Mercy* at the Soho Theater and appeared in *Hush* on the stage in London. The year 2005 found Garfield playing the title role in *Romeo and Juliet* for a production in Manchester and appearing in *The Laramie Project* during the show's UK premiere at the Sound Theater in London. As his stage career took off, Garfield found he was wanted for roles on British television as well. In 2005 he appeared in several episodes of the Emmy Award-winning teen comedy drama *Sugar Rush* and remained a TV staple, playing bit roles on *Swinging* in 2005, *Simon Schama's Power of Art* in 2006, and the police drama *Trial & Retribution* in 2007. He also appeared in two episodes of the famed long-running British science fiction series *Doctor Who.*

Garfield's most high-profile television turn came with the 2007 indie movie *Boy A*. The film, first released on British Channel 4, was featured at the 2007 Toronto Film Festival and later released in the United States. In *Boy A*, Garfield played a young man named Jack who had committed murder as a child and spent his youth institutionalized in a detention facility. The movie focused on Jack's release as a young adult as he tries to build a new life and escape his troubled past. Writing in the *Guardian*, Iley said Garfield nailed the role. "Andrew Garfield's performance as the 23-year-old, released from prison and struggling to adjust to a new life with a new identity, is rare and mesmerizing. The character's fragility, his inner turmoil and angst are on the surface: you feel everything." Garfield won a British Academy of Film and Television Arts (BAFTA) award for Best Television Actor for his work in *Boy A*.

The film's director, John Crowley, raved about Garfield's performance in an interview with Mark Olsen of the *Los Angeles Times*. "When we were editing, I'd often find him giving with glances or with looks what the text was also doing. We began cropping dialogue out because everything was already being communicated. The amount of emotional heat behind each take was always absolute."

Eventually, Garfield landed on the big screen in the United States, working with American director Robert Redford. Garfield caught the attention of Hollywood in 2006 when he appeared in a London production called *Chatroom*. An assistant to filmmaker Stephen Daldry saw the play and urged Daldry to screen-test Garfield for an upcoming film. Daldry's film fell through but Garfield's audition tape landed in the hands of New York-based casting director Avy Kaufman. At the time, Kaufman was seeking actors for an upcoming Redford-directed flick, *Lions for Lambs*. Garfield earned a part in the film and made his American film debut alongside Meryl Streep, Tom Cruise, and Redford, who also starred in the film. Released in 2007, the film was a box-office disappointment, but introduced Garfield to American moviegoers.

Garfield left the United Kingdom and moved to Hollywood in 2006, quickly adjusting to life in the United States. He wandered around Hollywood shooting baskets, riding his skateboard down concrete ramps, and surfing. "I knew no one," he told Jeff Gordinier of *Details*. "I got to know the city as a solitary individual." Garfield told Gordinier that he spent a lot of time on the streets—sometimes shooting hoops on the way to an audition—because his mind tends to get stuck in overdrive. "I think too much," he told Gordinier. "Being in my body is much more satisfying than being in my head."

In 2009, Garfield appeared in *The Imaginarium of Doctor Parnassus*, a dark yet stunning fantasy flick about a traveling theater troupe. Garfield played a sleight-of-hand magician. The director, Terry Gilliam, was only about one-third of the way finished with filming when one of the stars, Heath Ledger, died, though he managed to salvage the film with some rewrites and clever re-casting. Well-liked in Europe, the film received only lukewarm reception in the United States. In the end, it garnered two Academy Award nominations—for Best Costume Design and Best Art Direction.

In 2010 Garfield starred alongside Keira Knightley and Carey Mulligan in *Never Let Me Go*. In the film, Garfield played a young adult who had grown up at an English boarding school. He was a special kid, created by a laboratory as a future organ donor—meaning his life would be short-lived. Garfield earned best actor honors from the *Evening Standard British Film Awards* for his work in the film, beating out Oscar favorite Colin Firth who had won countless awards for his portrayal of King George VI in *The King's Speech*.

In 2010 Garfield also appeared in the highly acclaimed, surprise hit of the year *The Social Network*. The film, based on the book *The Accidental Billionaires*, focused on the early days of Facebook. Garfield played Eduardo Saverin, a close friend of Facebook co-founder Mark Zuckerberg. Saverin helped Zuckerberg launch the social networking site and initially served as Facebook's chief financial officer before he was ousted from the company.

Garfield read *The Accidental Billionaires* before filming began. The book largely centered on Saverin's perspective. "Saverin feels like he understands Mark better than anyone else, and I see their relationship as big brother-little brother," Garfield told *Daily Variety*'s Steve Heisler. "He's in awe of Mark's brilliance and really loves him, but he wants him all to himself. I also imagine this is the first time he's experienced real betrayal."

Meanwhile, as Garfield's face played on big screens around the world, he stayed busy filming his next project—*The Amazing Spider-Man*, the fourth film in the Columbia Pictures franchise. Filming began in December 2010 with the release scheduled for July 2012. The movie focuses on Parker's teen years during the time he developed his supernatural powers. Early rumors suggested the film would be a "reboot" of the franchise, similar to director Christopher Nolan's 2005 darker, more realistic image-shifting flick *Batman Begins*.

In early 2011, the studio released a picture of Garfield wearing the new Spider-Man suit, which led to more speculation that the film would be a re-imaging of the character. The *Guardian Unlimited* described the photo this way: "The shot depicts Garfield as a lean, bloody and brooding figure. Scratchmarks adorn his cheek and a strap sits on his shoulder, suggesting the webslinger may be heading straight from a night fighting crime on the street to high-school lessons."

Speaking to *Details'* Gordinier, Garfield acknowledged the struggle that lay in reinventing the character. "I see it as a massive challenge in many ways. To make it authentic. To make the character live and breathe in a new way. The audience already has a relationship with many different incarnations of the character. I do, as well. I'm probably going to be the guy in the movie theater shouting abuse at myself. But I have to let that go. No turning back. And I wouldn't want to."

Sources

Periodicals

Daily Variety, December 7, 2010, p. A4.
Details, February 2011, p. 62.
Guardian Unlimited (England), January 14, 2011.
Los Angeles Times, July 24, 2008, p. E3; January 6, 2011, p. S6.

Online

"Andrew Garfield: Biography," *TV Guide*, http://www.tvguide.com/celebrities/andrew-garfield/bio/293703 (November 8, 2011).
"Andrew Garfield," *Interview* magazine, http://www.interviewmagazine.com/film/andrew-garfield/ (November 8, 2011).
"Andrew Garfield: Playing Spider-Man is A Dream," *Sun*, http://www.thesun.co.uk/sol/homepage/features/3380075/Being-Spider-Man-is-a-dream-come-true.html (November 8, 2011).
"Andrew Garfield: Ready for Take-Off," *Telegraph*, http://www.telegraph.co.uk/culture/3668860/Andrew-Garfield-ready-for-take-off.html (November 8, 2011).
"Mad About the Boy," *Guardian*, http://www.guardian.co.uk/film/2008/apr/22/tvbaftas2008.television (November 8, 2011).
"This Just In: Hollywood's New Spider-Man Is ... Andrew Garfield," *Washington Post*, http://www.washingtonpost.com/blogs/comic-riffs/post/this-just-in-hollywoods-new-spider-man-isandrew-garfield/2010/12/20/ABSxNBG_blog.html November 8, 2011).

—Lisa Frick

Gabrielle Giffords

© Jim Harrison/AFP/Getty Images/newscom

U.S. congressional representative

Born Gabrielle Dee Giffords, June 8, 1970, in Tucson, AZ; daughter of Spencer J. and Gloria Kay Frazer Giffords; married Mark E. Kelly (an astronaut). *Education:* Scripps College, Claremont, CA, B.A., 1993; Cornell University, M.A., 1997.

Addresses: *Office*—1030 Longworth House Office Bldg., Washington, D.C., 20515; 3945 E. Fort Lowell Rd., Ste. 211, Tucson, AZ, 85712. *Web site*—http://giffords.house.gov/.

Career

Associate for regional economic development, Price Waterhouse, New York, NY, 1996; president and chief executive officer, El Campo Tire Warehouses, 1996-2000; congressional representative, Arizona House of Representatives, 2001-03; senator, Arizona State Senate, 2003-05; congressional representative, U.S. House of Representatives, 2007-12.

Member: Congressional Motorcycle Caucus; Tohono Chul Park; Beat Cancer Boot Camp; Metropolitan YMCA; 162nd Air National Guard Fighter Wing Minutemen Committee; Blue Dog Coalition; U.S. Holocaust Memorial Council; Anti-Defamation League Arizona Regional Board; chairwoman, Energy and Environment Subcommittee; Subcommittee on the Western Hemisphere; House Foreign Affairs Committee; chairwoman, Space and Aeronautics Subcommittee; U.S.-Mexico Interparliamentary Group; House Committee on Science and Technology; Armed Services Committee; Hadassah.

Awards: William J. Fulbright scholar, Fulbright Program, 1993-94; Rutgers University Fellow, Eagleton Institute, 2003; Fannie Mae Fellow, Harvard University School of Executive Management, 2003; Legislator of the Year award, Arizona Planning Association, 2003; Outstanding Legislator, Arizona Family Literacy, 2003; Legislator of the Year award, Coalition to Prevent Homelessness, 2003; Top 10 Tech award, Arizona Technology Council, 2003-04; Legislator of the Year award, Mental Health Association of Arizona, 2004; Young Leader Worth Watching award, Gannett News Service, 2004; Outstanding Alumna award, Scripps College, 2004; Award of Distinction, League Arizona Cities and Towns, 2005; Golden Eagle Award, Independent Insurance Agents and Brokers of Arizona, 2005; Eagle Enterprise award, Arizona Small Business Association, 2005; Women on the Move award, YWCA of Tucson, 2005; Most Valuable Player at Arizona Legislature award, Sierra Club, 2005; Woman of the Year award, Tucson Business Edge, 2005; Athena National award, Athena International, 2011; Tourism Champion of the Year award, Arizona Office of Tourism, 2011; Solar Champion award, Vote Solar, 2011.

Sidelights

It was eight months before Gabrielle Giffords learned of the fatal shooting in a Tucson Safeway parking lot. A victim of the shooting herself, the U.S. Representative from Arizona was shot in the head at the Congress on Your Corner event. Her husband, Mark E. Kelly, and other loved ones wanted to keep the news from her that her aide Gabe Zimmerman, close friend U.S. District Judge John Roll, and nine- year-old Christina-Taylor Green had been killed in the violent rampage, which claimed six lives in total with thirteen others wounded. Giffords' miraculous recovery took a great deal of her energy and on August 1, 2011, she appeared on Capitol Hill to vote in the important federal debt ceiling legislation.

Giffords' name may not have become so familiar outside of her congressional district if not for the tragic events that occurred on January 8, 2011, just three days after she was sworn in for her third term. Giffords is known for being friendly and kind, focusing on political issues that she believes passionately in, and making certain that the voices of those she represents are heard. She went that Saturday afternoon to the Safeway parking lot to personally meet her constituents, listen to their concerns, and to answer questions. As she met people at what was to be the first of several informal talks in various neighborhoods, Jared Lee Loughner shot Giffords in the head at close range. He then turned his gun on the crowd and shot many innocent bystanders and murdered six people. Loughner was eventually sent to a federal prison facility in Springfield, Missouri, after a federal judge deemed that he was mentally incompetent to stand trial on the 49 charges brought against him.

The incident quickly became politicized and polarized both conservatives and liberals despite Giffords' position as a moderate Democrat who has belonged to the Blue Dog coalition. The Blue Dogs are known for advocating fiscal responsibility, regulating immigration, and developing better relations with the Latin American countries. Giffords, being the only representative with an active serviceman as a spouse, has sat on the Armed Services committee. She has also sat on the Foreign Affairs and Science and Technology committees and is a proponent of an alternative energy policy. Even though she is the type of Democrat that the Republicans like to work with, she was targeted by the Tea Party to be voted out of office and they unsuccessfully ran a Tea Party activist against her in the previous election.

There was much controversy in the wake of the shooting because former vice presidential nominee Sarah Palin had posted a graphic on her Web site that showed Giffords' district in gunsight crosshairs, indicating that she was targeted to be elected out of office because of Giffords' vote on the federal Health Care Reform Bill. Giffords' office was also vandalized because of her voting for the Health Care Re-

form Bill. Liberals used these facts to point to a conservative conspiracy. Conservatives pointed fingers back, saying that the liberal media was distorting the facts. There was discussion about how far the rhetoric should go in campaigning and political discourse and whether or not it was appropriate to advocate for "targeting" an opponent or holding target shooting events as political fund-raisers. In the meantime, Giffords went through trauma surgery and then was transferred to the Memorial Hermann Hospital in Houston, Texas, where she began the long road to recovery. A memorial service was held for the victims of the shooting and, at that event, President Barack Obama himself announced the first good news about Gifford. He reported to the public that she had opened her eyes.

Giffords was born on June 8, 1970 to Spencer J. and Gloria Kay Frazer Giffords. Intelligent, passionate, and aware, she pursued first a bachelor's degree from Scripps College and then a master's degree in regional planning from Cornell University. Because of her outstanding academic abilities she was a William Fulbright scholarship recipient and studied in Chihuahua, Mexico. She also did research on the effects of Operation Gatekeeper II on the San Ysidro Port of Entry in San Diego. After her education was complete, Giffords worked as an associate for regional economic development at Price Waterhouse in New York City. From there she returned to her hometown of Tucson to take over the family business, which had been founded by her grandfather. She served as the president and chief executive officer of El Campo Tire Warehouse until it was sold to the Goodyear Tire Company in 2000. These experiences in the world of business helped prepare Giffords to understand the needs of business and to give her a unique understanding of factors that contribute to a successful climate for small business owners. This knowledge helped her in her bid for political office.

Giffords, who is a motorcycle-riding, gun-rights advocating woman of Jewish descent, was first elected to the Arizona House of Representatives in 2000. She then was elected in 2002 to the Arizona State Senate. She resigned before the end of her term in 2005 so that she could run for the U.S. Congress. Giffords was elected to the U.S. House of Representatives on November 7, 2006. After this she won successive terms in office in 2008 and again in 2010. She represents Arizona's Eighth Congressional District, which encompasses more than 9,000-square miles and shares a 114-mile border with Mexico. In addition to advocating for small businesses, Giffords worked on technology legislation and on furthering space exploration, is a proponent of the alternative energy policy that includes renewable sources of energy such as solar energy, and has consistently fought for border security.

It is no surprise that Giffords has advocated for legislation to benefit both service personnel and their families and to further technology and space exploration because Giffords' husband Mark E. Kelly is a U.S. navy captain, a naval aviator who flew during the Gulf War, and an astronaut. Kelly has been aboard four different space shuttle missions in differing capacities, including one in May 2011, only months after Giffords' gunshot injury. Giffords traveled to Florida for the launch; she had been at every shuttle launch to see him off into space since they met. C. J. Karamargin, Giffords' communication director, was quoted by USA Today's Donna Leinwand Leger as saying, "The congresswoman is one of the most ardent champions of the space program in Congress because of the power it has shown through its history to ignite the curiosity and imagination of America's school children." As the chairwoman of the House committee on Science and Technology, Giffords was glad that the National Aeronautics and Space Administration (NASA) received a proposal for increased funding to the space program for 2010, but she and the rest of the committee expressed concern that the direction Obama was proposing for NASA was a divergence from Project Constellation, an aim for NASA for a number of years. The concerns around having NASA shift its direction were based on already developed and developing technology and the highly educated and specialized personnel required to do the research and development. In 2009 States News Service quoted Giffords as saying, "NASA's technology development activities are critical not just to NASA's future, but to the quality of life of our citizens and our nation's competitiveness." She went on to give the example of the extensive number of NASA-developed technologies that have made the U.S. commercial aeronautics industry possible and pointed out that the widespread availability and safety of airplanes was only made possible because of NASA.

Giffords, who represents sunny Arizona, is an advocate for solar energy. One of the issues that Giffords is passionate about is creating a federal energy policy that focuses on sustainable energy. Giffords was quoted by States News Service as saying in regards to the Pentagon holding a forum on sustainable energy, "Our military leaders clearly understand that reducing our dependence on fossil fuels is essential for the safety of our troops. This is an issue of national security." Giffords also introduced a bill in 2010 titled "Department of Defense Energy Security Act." The purpose of the bill was to reduce the Pentagon's annual fuel costs through such measures as using biofuels for aviation and creating a number of large-scale renewable energy projects. Giffords has also promoted alternative energy projects in the private sector. She has spoken at the groundbreaking or initiation of several projects having to do with solar energy, including an event in 2010 when the National Bank of Arizona first turned on the power for their two million dollar solar energy system. In 2010 she welcomed to Tucson the participants in the Zero Emissions Race. The objective of the race was not to be the fastest vehicle, but rather it was a race to make smaller, greener, more efficient vehicles popular.

Giffords' congressional district is very large, encompassing such cities as Tucson and Tombstone and sharing a border with Mexico. After Cochise county rancher Rob Krentz was killed on isolated part of his ranch by what were believed to be members of a drug cartel, Giffords made an appeal to Obama to send in National Guard troops to help patrol the Mexican border. While Krentz's killers were never apprehended, they were tracked to within 20 miles of the Mexican border. Frequent skirmishes between the border patrol and drug cartel members in the early 21st century have found the border patrol seriously outmanned and outgunned. Giffords has made the case that patrolling the border is both an immigration issue and an issue of national security. After sending Obama two requests for deployment of the National Guard, she joined a group of lawmakers from five states to send a strongly worded letter requesting assistance. In regards to these requests, the States News Service reported Giffords as saying, "Border security is not a Republican issue or a Democratic issue, it's an American issue. Every American, no matter which party they belong to or where they live, is deeply concerned about restoring law and order in our border communities.... President Obama needs to immediately deploy the National Guard and send a clear message to the drug cartels: We will fight you, we will stop you, and we will never waiver in our commitment to securing our border."

When the state of Arizona passed a law mirroring federal immigration laws, making it a state offense to not be in compliance with such requirements as carrying identification and immigration status papers, and allowing state law enforcement personnel to enforce the state law, there was an uproar. State police officers could stop a person for a routine traffic violation and if the person could not produce a state driver's license, indicating that they may be in the state illegally, that individual could be arrested in violation of the state immigration law. There was a general boycott of the state of Arizona in response to the immigration law. Giffords, while stating that she personally did not agree with the law that had been passed by a large majority of state voters, appealed to the many agencies and organizations that cancelled conventions that were to be held in the state of Arizona. She also criticized two federal agencies that boycotted the state in regards to the immigration law and asked that they consider the many people within the state whose jobs might be lost in a recessive economy if all the conventions and events were cancelled.

On January 25, 2012, Giffords formerly resigned. "I will recover and will return," she said in a letter read aloud by her friend and colleague Rep. Debbie Wasserman Schultz. Giffords cast her final vote on a bill that she and U.S. Rep. Jeff Flake introduced to try and crack down on illegal drug smuggling across the U.S. border. The bill passed unanimously. Ever intelligent, aware, and a fighter, Giffords was engaged in many battles as Arizona's Representative to the U.S. Congress. She fought for the beleaguered NASA space program, petitioned for a sustainable energy policy, was a fierce advocate to maintain the borders of southern Arizona, and survived an assassination attempt.

Sources

Books

Complete Marquis Who's Who, Marquis Who's Who, 2010.

Periodicals

Economist, January 15, 2011, p. 30.
Globe & Mail (Toronto, Canada), February 4, 2011, p. L1.
New American, February 7, 2011, p. 10.
Newsweek, April 18, 2011, p. 26.
Phoenix Business Journal, July 16, 2011; August 16, 2011.

States News Service, October 22, 2009; February 25, 2010; April 28, 2010; June 22, 2010; July 8, 2010; August 18, 2010; October 15, 2010; October 22, 2010; October 27, 2010; November 22, 2010.
USA Today, April 29, 2011, p. 5A; August 3, 2011, p. 6A.

Online

"Bio: Arizona Rep. Gabrielle Giffords," Fox News, http://www.foxnews.com/us/2011/01/08/arizona-congresswoman-shot-married-astronaut/ (August 19, 2011).
"Biography for Gabrielle Giffords," Internet Movie Database, http://www.imdb.com/name/nm4259289/bio (August 27, 2011).
"Biography," Gabrielle Giffords Official Web Site, http://giffords.house.gov/about/ (August 19, 2011).
Biography in Context, Gale, 2011.
"Gabrielle Giffords Now Knows Who Died In Tucson Shooting, Aide Says," *Huffington Post*, http://www.huffingtonpost.com/2011/08/20/gabrielle-giffords-tucson-shooting_n_932062.html (August 20, 2011).
"Gabrielle Giffords resigns from Congress," CNN.com, http://www.cnn.com/2012/01/25/politics/gabrielle-giffords/index.html?hpt=hp_t1 (January 25, 2012).
"'Solar Champions' Honored at 5th Annual Equinox Celebration," Vote Solar, http://votesolar.org/press/vote-solar-honors-national-solar-champions-at-5th-annual-equinox-celebration/ (August 27, 2011).

—*Annette Bowman*

Julia Glass

Author

Born March 23, 1956, in Boston, MA; daughter of John and Kerry (a dog breeder) Glass; married first husband (divorced); life partner of Dennis Cowley (a photographer); children: Alec, Oliver (both with Cowley). *Education:* Yale University, B.A., 1978.

Addresses: *Office*—Author Mail, Pantheon Books, Random House, 1745 Broadway, New York, NY 10019.

Career

Employed at Fogg Art Museum, Harvard University, c. 1979-80; worked variously as a freelance copy editor, freelance writer, and hat maker, New York City, 1980-c. early 2000s; published first novel *Three Junes,* 2002; published fourth novel, *The Widower's Tale,* 2010. Contributor to periodicals including *Bellingham Review* and *Chicago Tribune.* Exhibited art at the Brooklyn Museum of Art and the National Academy of Design.

Awards: Richard Nelson Algren Award for a short story, *Chicago Tribune,* 1993; medal for best novella, Faulkner Society, for *Collies,* 1999; National Book Award for fiction, National Book Foundation, for *Three Junes,* 2002; two additional Nelson Algren Awards; Tobias Wolfe Award for fiction; Arnes Memorial Essay Award for nonfiction.

© *Nancy Kaszerman/ZUMA Press/newscom*

Sidelights

After beginning her career as a moderately successful artist, nonfiction writer, and editor, Julia Glass found success as novelist, winning the 2002 National Book Award with her debut novel *Three Junes.* As an author, she was often compared to nineteenth-century novelists like Charles Dickens, whose work featured large cast of characters and complexly woven stories. Critics praised her ability to juggle multiple storylines and create stories that resonate with emotional depth. Of her work style, Glass told Lindy Washburn of the *Record,* "Writing a story for me is like growing a tree. You plant a seed, and the seed is the first character you think of. It grows and it branches into other characters, and sometimes you step back and you prune it a little, but it continues to grow in this very organic way."

Glass was born on March 23, 1956, in Boston, Massachusetts, to John and Kerry Glass. Her mother worked as a dog breeder. Glass grew up loving to write and create art. She earned a bachelor's degree from Yale University in 1978, majoring in art and focusing on painting. Winning a fellowship, she then studied art in France after earning her degree. When she returned to the United States, she settled in Cambridge, Massachusetts, painted, and worked at the Fogg Art Museum at Harvard University, but soon sought new challenges. By 1980, Glass had moved to New York City. There, she painted and got her work exhibited in galleries and in a Brooklyn museum.

To make ends meet, Glass worked as a copy editor, taking on many types of projects including romance novels and corporate menus. She was employed by companies like J. P. MorganChase and *Cosmopolitan* magazine. She worked for the latter publication for two years. Of that experience, Glass told Joyce Prunick of the *New York Times*, "It was a hoot. You have never seen so many way-overqualified people doing something so utterly silly. It was the heyday of Helen Gurley Brown, who really is an extraordinary person. I think the only conversation I ever exchanged with her was when she complimented me on a pair of magenta pantyhose." Glass also worked as a writer, contributing book reviews to various publications, writing a pet column for *Glamour* magazine for a time, and even penning brochures.

Still trying to find her niche while living in New York City, Glass studied at the Fashion Institute of Technology and began making hats. While enjoyable, it proved not to be her life's calling. She found purpose when she tried to wrote a short story for *Cosmopolitan*. Something clicked and she began writing more stories, but because of their length they were never prominently printed. She won a number of literary awards for them, including a Nelson Algren Award for a short story featured in the *Chicago Tribune* in 1993. Yet she was still trying to do painting as well. Trying to do both, she told Claudia La Rocco of the Associated Press, "I'd feel guilty. But then I thought, this is ridiculous. If I want to write short stories, I'll write short stories."

One short story became a novella that was originally titled *Souvenirs*. *Souvenirs* was never published and was somewhat based on a visit she made to Greece in 1979. Glass later re-wrote it and re-named it *Collies*. This version of the novella won the Faulkner Society Medal for best novella. She then began working on a novel around 1992 when she was diagnosed with breast cancer and her younger sister, a veterinarian named Carolyn, committed suicide. She abandoned that novel for further work on *Collies*, which became part of her first published novel. Glass explained to La Rocco of the Associated Press, "As the novel grew out of these characters, I came to feel that what I wanted to write, in essence, was a book about living beyond incurable heartbreak and irreparable loss."

In 2002 Glass finally published *Three Junes* which won the National Book Award for fiction that year. It was a three-part novel that took place in June 1989, June 1995, and June 1999, and was tied together by the character of Fenno McLeod, a gay Scot who moves to New York City and runs a bookshop in Greenwich Village. Loss is one of the main themes of the book as Fenno loses a close friend to AIDS, while another is emotional isolation. In the section that consists of *Collies*, the novel focuses on Paul McLeod, a Scottish newspaper publisher who once wanted to be a novelist. He is grieving because his wife, Maureen, a breeder of collies, dies of lung cancer. Fenno is their eldest son. After her death, Paul goes on a group tour to Greece where he meets Fern, an artist, receives comfort from her, and makes a new life for himself on a Greek island. The second section "Upright," centers on Fenno and his younger twin brothers after Paul's death. The three men are arranging Paul's funeral. Much of the story describes Fenno and how he fits into gay society in the West Village. There, he becomes involved in the life of a music critic dying of AIDS who has a parrot, Felicity, that becomes a fixture at his bookstore. Fenno also is considering being a sperm donor to one of his brother's wives. The last section, "Boys," focuses on Fenno and David, one of his younger twin brothers, becoming closer. Fenno also meets Fern—now a book designer who gets a second chance at finding love—at the Fire Island home of his gay mentor Ralph Quayle. While Fenno never learns that Fern knew his father, the pair were involved with the same man, a photographer named Tony, at different times.

Critics praised *Three Junes*, with Katherine Wolff of the *New York Times Book Review* noting, "*Three Junes* affords many pleasures—sometimes witty, often solemn." Wolff concluded, "Masterfully, *Three Junes* shows how love follows a circuitous path, how its messengers come to wear disguises. Julia Glass has written a generous book about family expectations—but also about happiness, luck, and, as she puts it, the 'grandiosity of genes.'" In the *San Francisco Chronicle*, David Kipen called it "a warm, wise debut" and stated "life in *Three Junes* blindsides everybody, visiting joy and heartbreak on these exquisitely drawn characters with no warning whatsoever."

With the National Book Award and the acclaim that came with the novel, Glass finally felt she had found her path. She told Joyce Prunick of the *New York Times*, "I do finally feel I am doing what I am supposed to be doing." She added to La Rocco of the Associated Press, "The language part of my brain was meant to be used. Visual art is a foreign language I'm fluent at, but my native language is language." Yet she still worked as a freelance editor for a time. During an interview with Anita Creamer of the *Sacramento Bee*, Glass told her, "I just turned down an editing job today. But I've told all my regular clients not to take me out of their Rolodexes. You don't know as a writer where your career will take you. I'd love to have a life where I could devote all my time to my kids and to writing fiction, but I don't take that for granted."

Glass continued to write and her second novel, *The Whole World Over*, was published in 2006. At the heart of this novel is Greenie Duquette, an unhappy pastry chef living in New York City who becomes the personal chef to the governor of New Mexico. To take the job, she must leave her husband, Alan, behind; she takes their son with her. In New York, Alan is a depressed therapist who finds it hard to retain patients but has an interesting case in Saga, a patient with intermittent amnesia and other ailments who feels her life is without purpose. Also included in the novel are Fern and Fenno from the first novel, as well as a friend of Greenie's, a restaurant owner named Walter who is interested in a lawyer named Gordie, whose partner Stephen wants to become a father. The novel is tied up by the events of September 11, 2001.

Like *Three Junes*, critics gave *The Whole World Over* positive reviews. Lorraine Adams of the *New York Times Book Review* lauded, "Just when the reader feels sure of an outcome, other forces are set to work, shifting the momentum in unexpected directions. This is particularly admirable because Glass is so unobtrusive a writer, conveying meaning not through insightful asides, philosophical musings or verbal pyrotechnics but through storytelling." Dawn Baumgartner Vaughan of the Durham, North Carolina *Herald-Sun* wrote, "*The Whole World Over* forms the intricate kind of tapestry that is both treasured and worth closer examination of its complexities."

Glass' third novel, *I See You Everywhere*, was published in 2008. Focusing on a theme of competitiveness between women, the novel follows two sisters, Louisa and Clem Jardine, and examines their relationship. Louisa is very stable, a college graduate, and works as a potter and for an art magazine. Clem is more adventurous, working as a biologist who goes into the wilderness of Alaska, Wyoming, and Brazil to study animals. The novel covers 25 years of their lives beginning in 1980, and shows how the pair is often at odds but how they evolve into complex characters who are eventually forgiving. *I See You Everywhere* is considered the most autobiographical of Glass' novels, reflecting her own complicated relationship with her sister. Writing about the novel for the *New York Times Book Review*, Liesel Schillinger called it "Rich, intricate and alive with emotion." Schillinger concluded, "Glass has used the edges and color blocks of her own life to build an honest portrait of sister-love and sister-hate—interlocking, brave and forgiving—made whole through art, despite missing pieces in life."

In 2010, Glass published *The Widower's Tale*, her fourth novel. This multi-faceted book focuses on the changing life of Percival Darling, a widower and retired Harvard librarian living an isolated existence on his property in rural Matlock, Massachusetts. He lets his daughter begin a preschool, Elves and Fairies, on his land, and it changes his world as children, teachers, and parents all become regular parts of his life. Percival becomes less isolated in the process, forcing him to look at his life and choices, even as he becomes involved with single mom Sarah Straight. Also part of the novel is Percival's relationship to his oldest grandson, Robert, who considers abandoning his medical studies at Harvard to become an environmental activist. Other characters include Ira, a homosexual teacher at the school, and Celestino, a landscaper from Guatemala. In the *New York Times Book Review*, Maria Russo writes, "This energized, good-humored novel … smashes through … illusion, beginning as satire, becoming stealthily suspenseful and ending up with a satisfyingly clear-eyed and compassionate view of American entitlement and its fallout."

Despite finding greater success as an author than as a painter, Glass does not deny how much her painting played a role in her writing. Discussing *Three Junes*, she told Creamer of the *Sacramento Bee*, "At first I thought I'd wasted all those years painting. The truth is, from reading out loud from the book on tour, I've realized how very visual the way I write is. It's the way my eyes have been trained to look at the world. Painting absolutely has influenced my writing."

Selected writings

Novels

Three Junes, Pantheon (New York City), 2002.
The Whole World Over, Pantheon, 2006.
I See You Everywhere, Pantheon, 2008
The Widower's Tale, Pantheon, 2010.

Sources

Periodicals

Associated Press, December 31, 2002.

Chicago Daily Herald, June 3, 2006, p. 1.

Chicago Sun Times, June 25, 2006, p. B11.

Cookie, August 2008, p. 122.

Daily Telegraph (London, England), January 31, 2009, p. 24.

Herald-Sun (Durham, NC), June 18, 2006, p. E3.

Modesto Bee, September 28, 2003, p. E1.

New York Times, November 21, 2002, p. B11; January 13, 2003, p. B1.

New York Times Book Review, June 16, 2002, p. 16; June 11, 2006, p. 8; October 12, 2008, p. 16; September 12, 2010, p. 9.

Pittsburgh Post-Gazette, June 18, 2006, p. H6; September 6, 2010, p. B4.

Record (Bergen County, NJ), February 22, 2004, p. E1.

Sacramento Bee, October 22, 2003, p. E1.

San Francisco Chronicle, July 7, 2002, p. 1; July 6, 2006, p. H24.

Seattle Post-Intelligencer, July 7, 2006, p. 34.

Online

Contemporary Authors Online, Gale, 2011.

—*A. Petruso*

Jim Goodnight

© *Charly Kurz/laif/Redux*

Chief Executive Officer of SAS Institute

Born James H. Goodnight, January 6, 1943, in Wilmington, NC; son of Albert (a hardware store owner) and Dorothy (a hardware store owner; maiden name, Patterson) Goodnight; married Ann Baggett, 1966; children: Leah, Susan, James Arthur. *Education:* North Carolina State University, B.S., 1965, M.S., 1968, Ph.D, 1972.

Addresses: *Office*—SAS Institute, 100 SAS Campus Dr., Cary, NC 27513. *Web site*—http://www.sas.com.

Career

Computer programmer, National Aeronautics and Space Administration Apollo space program, 1966; member of the faculty, North Carolina State University, 1972-76, then adjunct professor, 1976; co-founder, president, chief executive officer, and computer programmer, SAS Institute, Cary, NC, 1976—.

Awards: Business leader of the decade, *Business Leader*, 1999; Influential Leaders Award, *CRM*, 2003.

Sidelights

Academic and entrepreneur Jim Goodnight co-founded SAS Institute, which became the largest private software company in the world. He became one of the richest men in the world with a multibillion-dollar fortune because of the success of his company. The business executive ran SAS in ways that were not often embraced by mainstream business culture such as selling its products on a subscription basis and providing many perks to employees, but such choices contributed to SAS being ranked year after year as one of the best companies in the world to work for. Explaining his business philosophy, Goodnight told Richard Fletcher of the London *Sunday Telegraph*, "People are our most important asset. Ninety-five percent of my assets drive out of the front gate at the end of every day. My job is to ensure they return. You look after your employees. They look after your customers. Customers look after you."

The son of Albert and Dorothy Goodnight, he was born on January 6, 1943, in Wilmington, North Carolina. Raised in Greensboro and Wilmington, his parents owned and operated a hardware store, where Goodnight began working as a teenager. Despite a love of basketball as a teen, Goodnight studied applied mathematics while an undergraduate student at North Carolina State University (NC State). As a sophomore, he took the only class available in computing and became interested in software and computer programming. During the summer after his sophomore year, he found a job in programming and decided that it would be his career.

After completing his undergraduate degree, Goodnight began graduate studies at NC State in statistics. He left school briefly in 1966 to work for NASA (National Aeronautics and Space Administration) and its Apollo space program. Goodnight's job was to work on engineering programs for GE (General Electric), which helped develop and run Apollo. Goodnight found the work itself thrilling, but the working conditions uninspiring as employees were not respected and much emphasis was placed on discipline. The experience helped mold the choices he made when he founded his own company a decade later.

Returning to NC State and his studies, Goodnight completed his master's degree in statistics in 1968, then his Ph.D in the same subject in 1972. By the time he graduated, Goodnight was already on the faculty at NC State. As part of his doctoral research, Goodnight worked with another NC State graduate, Anthony Barr, to develop a program that could be used to analyze all the agricultural data being sent to the school from other universities in the Southeast. It was called Statistical Analysis Software (SAS) and was developed with federal funding. Though this money dried up by 1972, Goodnight and Barr were able to get paid by the schools using SAS so that development could continue. Soon insurance and pharmaceutical companies began using SAS as well.

Goodnight and Barr had 120 clients by 1976, and SAS had become too big for a university-based research project. Partnering with John Sall and Jane Helwig, the SAS Institute was founded by these four people that year. Profitability was never an issue as the SAS Institute retained clients from its university days, and the company grew each year from 1976 onward. Within a few years, Barr and Helwig sold their shares, leaving Goodnight with two-thirds of SAS Institute. Though Sall retained one-third of the company, Goodnight was in charge of running SAS, serving as president and chief executive officer.

In 1980, Goodnight moved the SAS Institute headquarters to Cary, North Carolina, where he had bought large amounts of real estate. The company eventually had a 200-acre campus that was inspired by a university campus. The way SAS was organized was also different. Instead of following the industry standard of perpetual license billing, SAS software was sold on a subscription basis with yearly renewals. Thus, emphasis was placed on customer needs and satisfaction, and customers contributed to the direction of the company. Also, Goodnight and SAS spent more on research and development of software projects than sales and marketing.

Goodnight valued his employees as much as his customers. In addition to creating a work environment that was stimulating and pleasant, he also ensured that there was a balance between work and family, providing many generous benefits like onsite health care and day care, a massive fitness center, laundry services, classes, and flexible working hours. His staff turnover rate was only about four to five percent, 15 percent less than the industry norm, in part because of his emphasis on the importance of creative capital. Goodnight was not just an executive, but also did software programming for the company. He wrote code for SAS products until the late 1990s and tried to stay in touch with his employees and their needs. SAS also had a relatively flat hierarchy, with only four layers between Goodnight and the lowest level employee, and Goodnight cultivated a low-key, approachable style.

Former employee Philip Busby told Steven Eisenstadt and Elizabeth Wellington of the Raleigh News and Observer that Goodnight nevertheless expected much from his employees. Busby said, "He has an amazing ability to synthesize information quickly and get to the essence of a problem. And he'll zap you if you're not on the same wavelength. For people who are slow, he doesn't have a lot of patience. If you can't run with him, get out of the race."

While many in the business world were critical of Goodnight and SAS, sales reached one billion dollars in 1999. Still, Goodnight recognized the environment around business was changing in this time period as the business computer software market became more competitive. Though SAS previously had a very low profile, that situation started to change as Goodnight recognized that the company had to sell itself to executives instead of ride the wave of its reputation. Goodnight even considered taking SAS public in the early 2000s, in part to increase its chances of using stock options to recruit and retain the best employees.

Though internal moves were made in preparation to go public between 2000 and 2002, Goodnight decided to keep SAS private after the stock market crash in that time period and did not change his mind in subsequent years. Despite the turmoil, SAS retained its customers and staff and saw its revenue from software sales increase by 14 percent between 2002 and 2003. Goodnight continued to expand the company as well, developing new products like anti-money laundering software and acquiring new companies on occasion. By 2004, SAS programs were being used by 98 percent of Fortune 500 companies for analysis, data mining, and warehousing.

SAS also had a 98 percent customer retention rate, serving such businesses as insurance companies, retailers, professional sports teams, and financial institutions, among others.

As part of his more high-profile status, Goodnight became a leader and active speaker at the annual World Economic Forum. Outside of SAS, Goodnight emphasizes the importance of educational reform and believes that education is important for people to become successful as well as organizations and whole countries. He has used his financial success—worth an estimated $7.1 billion dollars in 2011—to endow several professorships at NC State, and he and his wife, Ann, cofounded an independent, private college prep day school, the Cary Academy, in 1996. To that end, SAS also launched SAS inSchool, which develops educational software that works to increase the use of technology in teaching. Goodnight is an active philanthropist in other areas as well, benefitting institutions such as the North Carolina Museum of Art.

Goodnight did not plan on stepping down from running SAS soon, or changing his philosophy toward business. He told Scott S. Smith of *Investor's Business Daily*, "I don't believe a business should be run by a bunch of analysts on Wall Street who take a cursory look at a company, then make sweeping judgments that are not always rooted in deep understanding of what it is trying to accomplish. There's also huge pressure to sacrifice long-term strength and stability for short-term gains. I plan to be around for a long time."

Sources

Books

International Directory of Business Biographies, St. James Press, 2005.

Periodicals

Business Wire, June 22, 2005.
ENP Newswire, April 17, 2009; January 24, 2011.
Fast Company, January 1999, p. 84.
Investor's Business Daily, August 3, 2009, p. A3.
National Post's Financial Post & FP Investing (Canada), July 17, 2010, p. FP3.
News and Observer (Raleigh, NC), July 21, 1996, p. A1; July 28, 2005; December 31, 2006, p. A1; November 13, 2007, p. D1; September 22, 2011.
Sunday Telegraph (London, England), November 24, 2002, p. 09.

Online

"Jim Goodnight," SAS, http://www.sas.com/company/about/bios/jgoodnight.html (October 8, 2011).

—*A. Petruso*

Nancy Grace

© *Jordan Strauss/Getty Images*

Television personality and attorney

Born Nancy Ann Grace, October 23, 1959, in Macon, GA; daughter of Mac and Elizabeth Grace; married David Linch (an investment banker), 2007; children: Lucy Elizabeth, John David (twins). *Education:* Mercer University, B.A., 1981; Walter F. George School of Law, J.D., 1984; New York University, master of law, c. 1985; also attended Valdosta State College.

Addresses: *Office*—CNN, New York bureau, One Time Warner Center, New York, NY 10019.

Career

Passed the Georgia State Bar Exam, 1984; served as a law clerk for a federal judge, c. 1984-85; practiced antitrust and consumer protection law with the Federal Trade Commission, c. 1985-87; served as an assistant prosecutor with the Georgia District Attorney's Office, Atlanta-Fulton County, 1987-96; anchor and host of *Cochran and Grace, Trial Heat,* and *Closing Arguments,* Court TV, 1996-2007; host of *Nancy Grace Investigates,* Court TV, 2004-07; a substitute host on *Larry King Live,* CNN, 2003-05; published *Objection!: How High-Priced Defense Attorneys, Celebrity Defendants, and a 24/7 Media Have Hijacked Our Criminal Justice System,* 2005; radio show host, *Rapid Fire with Nancy A. Grace,* KNEW-AM, 2005; host, *Nancy Grace,* CNN Headline News (later HLN), 2005—; published first novel, *The Eleventh Victim,* 2009; host, *Swift Justice with Nancy Grace,* syndicated, 2010-11; competed on *Dancing with the Stars,* ABC, 2011.

Awards: Gracie Award for individual achievement as best programming host, American Women in Radio and Television.

Sidelights

Though television legal commentator and host Nancy Grace considers herself an advocate for crime victims through her work on shows like *Closing Arguments* and *Nancy Grace,* many see her as controversial and unrelenting, unwilling to admit that some accused criminals are not guilty. Grace originally became a attorney after the murder of her fiancé, and went on to be a successful prosecutor in Atlanta. In the mid-1990s, Grace moved into television when she was hired as a legal commentator for Court TV. There, Grace found a forum in which she could express her opinions on the most prominent criminal cases of the day. She became a star after moving to CNN's Headline News in 2005 to host *Nancy Grace,* which was a hit from its first days on the network. As Kenneth Jautz, the executive vice president of CNN News Group told Steve Murray of the *Atlanta Journal-Constitution,* "There is nobody as compelling, as passionate or as knowledgeable on legal news as Nancy Grace. She brings an ex-practitioner's point of view. That, coupled with her passion and her interest in victims' rights, makes her unique and compelling to watch."

Born October 23, 1959, in Macon, Georgia, she was the daughter of Mac and Elizabeth Grace. She was raised in that small town and was encouraged to believe in herself from an early age. She told Craig Wilson of *USA Today*, "I grew up on a red dirt road with a tree growing right in the middle of it. We didn't have much, but it never occurred to me that if you wanted to do something you couldn't do it. You can do anything if you try." After completing high school, she entered Valdosta State College and intended to become an English teacher because of her love of Shakespeare. She had a boyfriend, Keith Griffin, who became her fiancé. In 1979, Griffin was murdered in a robbery gone wrong a few weeks before their wedding by a man who was out on parole. The event changed the course of her life. Grace lived with her sister in Wharton, Pennsylvania, for a year after his death while deciding on her future. She chose to become a victim's advocate and settled on a new career in law.

Grace returned to Georgia and earned her bachelor's degree from Mercer University in Macon in 1981. She then went on to complete her law degree at the Walter F. George School of Law in Macon in 1984. She also earned a master of law degree from New York University at a later date. In addition to passing the bar exam in the state of Georgia in 1984, she also clerked for a federal court judge. She then practiced anti-trust and consumer protection law with the Federal Trade Commission. In 1987, Grace joined the Atlanta-Fulton County District Attorney's Office as an assistant prosecutor, focusing on cases involving women and children. She had nearly 100 felony convictions and was known for her aggressiveness, especially in the courtroom. For her success, she was given the nickname "Amazin' Grace." Yet she was also reprimanded for stepping over the line in court more than once.

Because of her behavior and reputation, Grace caught the attention of the creator of Court TV, Steve Brill. Leaving the prosecutor's office in 1996, she took his offer to join the network. Just before she made the switch, she told Jay Croft of the *Atlanta Journal and Constitution*, "Every case took a piece of me; every one. For ten straight years, dealing with the most brutal people in our society just took its toll on me." Doing a television program was not a problem after years in the courtroom. She told Croft, "Nothing is scarier or more exciting than looking at 12 jurors. So looking at one camera is not intimidating. It's just a conversation. It's where it takes you, and you better be ready."

Grace became the anchor and host of Court TV's *Closing Arguments*. On the show, she shared her legal expertise and personal opinion on high-profile court cases. She continued to focus on advocating victims' rights on the show. Her original co-host on the show was O.J. Simpson defense attorney Johnnie Cochran, and it was originally titled *Cochran and Grace*. The pair took calls from listeners and hosted guests. The show was later re-titled *Trial Heat* before being re-named *Closing Arguments*. In 2005, Grace and Court TV gained ratings and national attention by hosting a series of primetime specials under the moniker *Nancy Grace Live* on the high-profile cases and related personalities such as convicted murderer Scott Peterson and his mistress Amber Frey. Grace also hosted another Court TV show, *Nancy Grace Investigates,* from 2004 to 2007.

While appearing on *Closing Arguments,* Grace also served as substitute host for *Larry King Live!* from 2003 to 2005. She had long been a regular guest on the show. In addition, Grace moved into radio in 2004 when she became the host of *Rapid Fire with Nancy A. Grace* for KNEW-AM. In 2005, Grace's television career reached new heights when she began working for CNN (which owned 50 percent of Court TV by this time). She joined CNN Headline News (later known as HLN) as the host of the show *Nancy Grace*. This program was also a legal affairs show similar in format to *Closing Arguments* with guests and calls from viewers, but *Nancy Grace* made her a breakout personality on cable television and gave Headline News its highest-rated show ever within a few months of its debut. Grace said she did not care about the ratings, telling Gail Shister of the *Philadelphia Inquirer*, "This is not a popularity contest. My purpose is to shine light on the justice system. I don't concern myself with ratings. I know you can be up one day, down the next."

One reason for Grace's success was her contentious, often divisive, personality. Describing Grace, Michael Learmonth of *Variety* wrote "Volatile, opinionated, and prone to tearing up, Grace is an unabashed crime-victim's advocate, equally comfortable arguing for Terri Schiavo's right to a feeding tube as for Scott Peterson's death sentence." Other cases covered and highlighted on Grace's show included the Michael Jackson molestation case, the Robert Blake murder trial, the Kobe Bryant rape case, Natalee Holloway's disappearance and presumed murder, the kidnapping of Elizabeth Smart, murder victims like Chandra Levy, the Casey Anthony murder trial, and runaway brides like Jennifer Wilbanks.

When discussing such cases, Grace often saw the world in black and white terms, good versus evil, victims and villains. She encouraged the use of tip lines and self-solving of crimes, and highlighted injustice in addition to legal commentary of the day. Observers saw Grace as an example of the trend of on-air news hosts with outspoken, sometimes outrageous, personalities which attracted viewers and encouraged conversations. Grace herself explained to the *Atlanta Journal-Constitution*'s Murray, "I've never pretended to be objective.... I'm a trial lawyer and a victims' rights advocate. I don't always fall on the side of the state. I like to think I fall on the side of the truth." An early definer of what came to be known as the "legal shout fest" format, Grace often gave disparaging labels to the accused and other alleged criminals.

The same year Grace joined CNN, she published her first nonfiction book, *Objection!: How High-Priced Defense Attorneys, Celebrity Defendants, and a 24/7 Media Have Hijacked Our Criminal Justice System*. Co-authored with writer Diane Clehane, the book took the tone of Grace's television show. She believed that the American justice system put plaintiffs and victims on the losing end, and defense attorneys often trumped common sense and the rule of law. In the book, Grace argues that defense attorneys are dangerous, unethical, and only care about winning, while prosecutors want to do what is right. She also analyzes high-profile cases and describes cases from her time as prosecutor. While *Objection!* debuted at number seven on the *New York Times* best-seller list, critics gave the book mixed reviews, with some noting the irony of her criticism as a member of the media who made much money from talking about difficult, horrible, notorious cases. Writing in the *Vancouver Sun*, Shelley Fralic called it "a 326-page diatribe against the U.S. justice system" and "a chatty, if cranky, account of all that is wrong with crime and punishment in Nancy Grace's world."

In 2006, Grace's bulldog style created controversy after the suicide of Melinda Duckett, a guest on the show. Duckett was a suspect in the disappearance of her two-year-old son Trenton, and Grace asked numerous difficult, if not badgering, questions of the woman. A day after Duckett taped the interview with Grace, she committed suicide, but Headline News continued to air parts of the interview after her death. MSNBC host Joe Scarborough told David Bauder of the Associated Press, "I don't fault Nancy Grace for asking the questions. That's her job. That's her shtick. She's an entertainer. The problem is what happened afterward. She's gone on a personal jihad against this woman. At what point does CNN step in and say 'enough's enough?'" The family of Duckett sued Grace and CNN, and the case was settled out of court in 2010.

Because of the success of *Nancy Grace*, Grace left *Closing Arguments* in 2007. Two years later, Grace published her first novel, *The Eleventh Victim: A Thriller*, which became a *New York Times* best seller. Grace admits that the novel drew on her own life. Main character Hailey Dean is an assistant district attorney in Atlanta whose fiancé is murdered. A success in court, she sends many to jail before suffering burn out. After she wins a case involving the murder of eleven prostitutes, Dean moves to New York City and becomes a therapist. When Dean's client turns up murdered in a similar way, she becomes a suspect, has to clear her name, and gets the real criminal prosecuted. She published a second novel, *Death on the D-List*, the following year.

While continuing to appear on *Nancy Grace* and provide commentary to HLN programming and other shows, Grace became the focus of a new syndicated program, *Swift Justice with Nancy Grace*, in 2010. *Swift Justice* was a courtroom show in which Grace acted as judge in minor civil cases. Grace left the show in 2011 and was replaced by Clark County District Judge Jackie Glass. In 2011, Grace took on new challenges when she agreed to compete on *Dancing on the Stars*. She had the support of viewer votes—gained from her daily television visibility from her show and her appearances as a commentator on other shows. She also regularly reminded viewers of *Nancy Grace* to vote for her. Grace nearly made it to the semifinals before being voted off.

While ratings for *Nancy Grace* were down significantly between 2009 and 2011 overall, the 2011 trial of Casey Anthony brought new attention to the television personality as she firmly believed Anthony—whom she dubbed "tot mom"—was guilty of murdering her two-year-old daughter Caylee. When the verdict was announced, HLN had its best ratings ever in its history with Grace at the center of the coverage.

Six years after joining HLN, Grace remained a focus of controversy in part because of the attitude she expressed about trials like Anthony's. Grace had supporters like Ernie Allen, the director of the National Center for Missing and Exploited Children, who told David Carr of the *New York Times*, "What Nancy Grace does so well is tell the story from the perspective of the victims. Her show is a way for the broad dissemination of information about the victims of crimes." Yet others saw her as a bully who never admitted she was wrong. Grace told Murray of the *Atlanta Journal Constitution*, "Want to know the truth? I learned it the hard way right there in Atlanta at the Fulton County Courthouse: Not everyone's gonna like what you have to say, but the minute you back down you lose not only your supporters, but your self-respect."

Selected writings

Nonfiction

(With Diane Clehane) *Objection!: How High-Priced Defense Attorneys, Celebrity Defendants, and a 24/7 Media Have Hijacked Our Criminal Justice System,* Hyperion (New York City) 2005.

Novels

The Eleventh Victim: A Thriller, Hyperion, 2009.
Death on the D-List, Hyperion, 2010.

Sources

Books

Complete Marquis Who's Who, Marquis Who's Who, 2010.

Periodicals

Associated Press, September 24, 2006; November 21, 2006; November 5, 2007; November 8, 2010; July 9, 2011.

Associated Press State & Local Wire, May 25, 2011.
Atlanta Journal and Constitution, December 21, 1996, p. 4D; April 25, 2005, p. 1C.
Broadcasting and Cable, November 15, 2010, p. 43.
Business Wire, January 6, 2005.
Christian Science Monitor, November 8, 2011.
Creators Syndicate, September 8, 2010.
Electronic Media, March 11, 2002, p. 6.
New York Times, May 23, 2011, p. B1.
Philadelphia Inquirer, April 11, 2005, p. D6.
Pittsburgh Post-Gazette September 10, 2010, p. C6.
Television Week, February 21, 2005, p. 6.
USA Today, August 10, 2009, p. 1D; November 14, 2011, p. 4D.
Vancouver Sun (British Columbia, Canada), July 30, 2005, p. F1.
Variety, March 28-April 3, 2005, p. 18.
Washington Post, June 27, 2005, p. C1; July 7, 2011, p. C1.

Online

Contemporary Authors Online, Gale, 2011.

—A. Petruso

Cee Lo Green

© Scott Gries/PictureGroup

Singer and television personality

Born Thomas DeCarlo Callaway, May 30, 1975, in Atlanta, GA; married Christina Johnson (divorced, 2005); children: Kingston, two adopted daughters.

Addresses: *Agent*—William Morris Endeavor Entertainment, 9601 Wilshire Blvd., 3rd Fl., Beverly Hills, CA 90210. *Web site*—http://www.ceelogreen.com/.

Career

Member of the Goodie Mob, c. mid-1990s-c. 2000; signed solo recording deal with Arista, c. 2000; released first solo album, *Cee-Lo Green and His Perfect Imperfections*, 2002; formed band Gnarls Barkley, c. 2004; found worldwide success with Gnarls Barkley single "Crazy," 2006; launched record label, Radiculture, 2007; signed with Elektra, 2009; re-united with the Goodie Mob for tour dates, 2010; released third solo album *The Lady Killer*, 2010; vocal coach for reality competition show *The Voice*, NBC, 2011—.

Awards: Grammy Award (with Gnarls Barkley) for best alternative music album, National Academy of Recording Arts and Sciences, for *St. Elsewhere*, 2007; Grammy Award (with Gnarls Barkley) for best urban/alternative performance, National Academy of Recording Arts and Sciences, for "Crazy," 2007; Grammy Award for best urban/alternative performance, National Academy of Recording Arts and Sciences, for "F*** You!," 2011.

Sidelights

A solo artist sometimes known just by his first name, Cee Lo Green came to fame in the early 2000s not only for his own work but also as a member of the duo Gnarls Barkley. Beginning his career as a member of the rap group the Goodie Mob, Green was perhaps best known for the major Gnarls Barkley hit "Crazy" and his own solo smash "F*** You!" A singer with a crooning style, he was influenced by soul singers like Jackie Wilson, Al Green, and Curtis Mayfield, as well as Motown, rap, Culture Club, ABC, and the Cure. In 2011, Green took on new challenges when he became one of the celebrity coaches on the reality competition show *The Voice*. It was Green's own voice that captured attention. Tom Horan of the London *Daily Telegraph* described his "extraordinary voice" as "pristine and soaring, the phrasing razor-sharp, evoking soul singers of the past … while radiating immediacy and modern attitude."

Born Thomas DeCarlo Callaway on May 30, 1975, in Atlanta, Georgia, Green was the son of two ordained ministers. His father died when he was two years old. His mother, who also was a volunteer firefighter, was paralyzed in a car accident when he was 16 years old. The young Green described himself as an angry young teen. He told Tom Horan of the London *Daily Telegraph*, "I was the polar opposite to how I am now. I was enraged. I was disgruntled, without an outlet. I took what I wanted, figuratively, literally. I was aggressive and I was pretty efficient with it—I took pride in that ability. I got up to be aggressive every day." Green was friends at school with André Benjamin who eventually formed OutKast, and the relationship was a positive one at a time when Green needed it.

By the mid-1990s, Green came to fame as a member of the Goodie Mob, one of the first Southern rap acts to become successful nationwide. This group helped define and create the Dirty South style of rap, along with OutKast, and emphasized social consciousness. Green was a crooner with the group, which included Khujo, T-Mo, and Big Gipp. The Goodie Mob debuted on OutKast's first album, *Southernplayalisticadillacmuzik*, in 1994, then recorded its debut with the same production team, Organized Noize. Green sang the hooks to some of their best known songs like "Cell Therapy," "Soul Food," and "Black Ice." The Goodie Mob's debut, 1995's *Soul Food*, was lauded by critics, produced three hit singles in the urban radio market, and landed on the *Billboard* album chart.

Green also appeared on 1998's *Still Standing* and 1999's *World Party*. Both Goodie Mob albums were also produced by Organized Noize. *Still Standing* was a hit that reached number six on the *Billboard* album charts. While *World Party* was less concerned with social commentary than previous efforts and more commercially focused, it failed to deliver a hit single and was not as highly regarded by critics or audiences. After this failure, Green left the Goodie Mob and focused on his own career, with an offer for a solo deal from producer/executive L. A. Reid in hand. The Goodie Mob continued after Green's departure, releasing an album in 2004 titled *One Monkey Doesn't Stop No Show*.

Reid believed that Green had a chance to be part of the burgeoning neo-soul movement led by singers like Alicia Keys and Macy Gray, and saw that OutKast's *Stankonia* was extremely successful. What Green created was unexpected, unique, and original, recorded and produced by himself at a small Atlanta-based studio to ensure minimal outside influence. Dropped in 2002, *Cee Lo Green and His Perfect Imperfections* was a critical success and debuted at number two on the *Billboard* R&B/Hip-Hop Album charts, but was a commercial failure, selling less than 300,000 copies by early 2004, despite Green's best efforts to promote it.

Reviews of *Cee Lo Green and His Perfect Imperfections* tried to explain the album in all its complexity. In the *Boston Herald*, Sarah Rodman wrote "Cee-Lo mixes gospel, funk, rap, and soul into a heady brew that careens from silly to spiritual to wordy provocation within the space of the same song." Malcolm X Abram of the *Akron Beacon Journal* explained "it was the insular sound of a frustrated artist indulging all the ideas he had had swirling around his head for years. Sometimes that kind of creative purge can result in a disjointed mess, but Green's self-produced debut was an eclectic, heady, fun, funky, and spiritual trip through his mind...." Green himself admitted to the *New York Post*, "This is not a safe album. It doesn't speak to the formula of the standard."

Green then produced a second album, *Cee Lo Green ... Is the Soul Machine*. More focused than his first album and less under his control, his sophomore effort featured tracks produced by names like Timbaland and the Neptunes. Released in 2004, Green wrote or co-wrote all the 18 tracks, and included guest appearances by artists like Pharrell, Ludacris, and Big Rube & G-Rock. The track "The One" was co-written, produced, and featured Jazze Pha, while DJ Premier produced "Evening News." The *Akron Beacon Journal*'s Abram noted "though Green has reined his muse in some, it's still different from 97.2 percent of the stuff that makes it to R&B/hip hop radio." Danny Hooley, in Raleigh, North Carolina's *News & Observer*, commented, "Green has an easygoing way with making something funky-fresh out of something old, and something new—a knack that eludes many of the kitchen-sink-rummagers of so-called neo-soul." Daniel Durchholz of the *St. Louis Post-Dispatch* concluded, "He lives up to his own hype, which is something too few hip-hop artists do these days."

In 2006, Green had the greatest success of his career to date as a member of Gnarls Barkley. The duo that included DJ/producer Danger Mouse (Brian Burton) had originally met in Atlanta in the late 1990s. They began recording together in the early 2000s, and the results were shared with many who knew them. Before their first album, *St. Elsewhere*, was released in late 2006, the pair had their first smash hit single, "Crazy" in the summer of 2006. In the United Kingdom, "Crazy" was the first song to reach number one on the British singles chart by download alone. The song was also a hit in the United States and was named the song of the year by *Rolling Stone* magazine. Green explained to Fred Shuster of the *Daily News of Los Angeles*, "I expected 'Crazy' to resonate. What's weird is when something that comes from a dimly lit private space touches so many people. We don't make music merely to entertain."

Gnarls Barkley's first album, *St. Elsewhere,* was also a success both critically and commercially in the United States and Europe. It was certified platinum in the United States for selling more than one million copies. (By October of 2010, it had sold 1.4 million.) While still working the R&B/hip-hop/neo-soul realm, Gnarls Barkley was also embraced as indie pop and landed five Grammy Award nominations. Yet this kind of honor meant little to Green, who told Shuster of the *Daily News of Los Angeles,* "We don't think about that kind of stuff. We don't aim for that. That's not why we make music. We don't want to be consumed by all that extraneous stuff. Music feeds us, not awards shows." Live, the band challenged and entertained audiences with odd costumes and unexpected covers.

In the wake of the success of Gnarls Barkley, Arista released a best of album for Green's solo albums and work with the Goodie Mob. Titled *Closet Freak: The Best of Cee Lo,* it was embraced by critics as a way of introducing the depth of Green's talent. Writing about the album in the Little Rock *Arkansas Democrat-Gazette,* Shon McPeace lauded, "It really doesn't matter whether Cee Lo is rhyming or singing, he does both in a very different and very wondrous way." Green also launched his own record label, Radiculture, in conjunction with Atlantic Records in 2007.

Gnarls Barkley recorded a second album, *The Odd Couple,* in 2008, and while it received three Grammy Award nominations, it could not match the dominant success of their first. Green told Jason Lipshutz of VNU Entertainment News Wire, "There were quite a few people who argued that *Odd Couple* came too soon after *St. Elsewhere,* and maybe they had a point. At the time, 'Crazy' was such a big thing that it was kind of hard to live down."

Still, the sound of *The Odd Couple* was embraced by critics and Green's honesty shone through. Writing in *Time Out,* Sharon O'Connell explained, "Helter-skelter lead single, 'Run' indicates that it's basically eccentric beats-driven, neo-vintage soul business as usual, an uplifting and genuinely emotion-filled affair with dashes of dark humour and plenty of rug-cutting opps, that sounds both warmly familiar and bracingly innovative." O'Connell noted the "profoundly deep partnership," and Danger Mouse told her, "We don't live or die by Gnarls Barkley, we do it because we want to. We're very lucky to have each other and I'm glad to be able to make something that Cee Lo wants to sing, stuff that he feels passionate about."

In 2010, Green joined the Goodie Mob on some tour dates in the United States. Later that year, he released his third solo album, *The Lady Killer,* this time on a new label, Elektra, that was dedicated to promoting him. It was recorded in Miami, London, and Atlanta, and influenced by soul rhythms, Serge Gainsbourg, and James Bond movies. The album featured the single "F*** You!," which was a hit before the album was even released. The single was co-written and produced by The Smeezingtons and went multiplatinum not only in the United States but in other countries as well. (In the fall of 2010, a clean version of the single called "Forget You" was released and found an audience as well.) Siobhan Murphy of *Metro* described the song as "a joyously potty-mouthed slice of Motown-infused pop-soul." Discussing the single's popularity, Green himself told Lipshutz of VNU Entertainment News Wire, "It's pleasantly surprising. But I'm poised for it, and I'm dressed for the occasion." The success of the single and the album proved that Green could be viable on his own. Other tracks on *The Lady Killer* were produced by such stars as Salaam Remi, Jack Splash, and Fraser T. Smith.

At the height of solo success, Green reached a new audience when he was part of the inaugural season of the NBC reality competition *The Voice* in 2011. Green was one of four well-known musical acts who picked teams from the various contestants to help mentor and develop them, leading to a winner. *The Voice* was an unexpected success, and Green and his fellow coaches—Adam Levine from the band Maroon 5, Christina Aguilera, and Blake Shelton—were expected to return for another season in 2012.

Green's future includes more solo albums, a new Gnarls Barkley album, and perhaps another with the Goodie Mob. He also planned to continue to collaborate, write, and produce tracks for and with other artists like Brandy, Solange, Jennifer Hudson, and the Pussycat Dolls, as he had for years. Of his success, Green told Murphy of *Metro,* "I was a success at being an outsider but I was in control of that. Now I've been invited inside but there's still a part of me that does not have to be 'the man.' I don't want it the way I've seen a lot of people want it; I only want what belongs to me."

Selected discography

(With Goodie Mob) *Soul Food,* LaFace Records, 1995.
(With Goodie Mob) *Still Standing,* LaFace Records, 1998.
(With Goodie Mob) *World Party,* LaFace Records, 1999.
Cee Lo Green and His Perfect Imperfections, Arista, 2002.
Cee Lo Green ... Is the Soul Machine, Arista, 2004.

(With Gnarls Barkley) *St. Elsewhere,* Downtown Music/Atlantic, 2006.
Closet Freak: The Best of Cee Lo, Arista, 2006.
(With Gnarls Barkley) *A Trip to St. Elsewhere,* CMP Entertainment, 2007.
(With Gnarls Barkley) *The Odd Couple,* Warner Bros., 2008.
The Lady Killer, Elektra/Warner Bros., 2010.

Sources

Periodicals

Akron Beacon Journal, March 7, 2004, p. E3.
Arkansas Democrat-Gazette, November 19, 2006.
Boston Herald, May 3, 2002, p. 22.
BPI Entertainment News Wire, January 12, 2004.
Daily News of Los Angeles, December 29, 2006, p. U22.
Daily Telegraph (London, England), October 30, 2010, pp. 10-11.
Los Angeles Times, May 10, 2011, p. D1.
Marketwire, August 26, 2010.
Metro (UK), October 4, 2010, pp. 34-35.
New Musical Express, May 8, 2007.
News & Observer (Raleigh, NC), March 14, 2004, p. G2.
New York Post, May 3, 2002, p. 57.
New York Times, July 1, 2011, p. C1.
PR Newswire, May 6, 2011.
St. Louis Post-Dispatch (MO), March 18, 2004, p. F3.
Time Out, March 27, 2008, p. 112; October 21, 2010, p. 110.
VNU Entertainment News Wire, October 18, 2010; May 19, 2011.

Online

"Cee Lo Green: Biography," AllMusic, http://www.allmusic.com/artist/cee-lo-green-p279684/biography (August 21, 2011).
"Cee Lo," Internet Movie Database, http://www.imdb.com/name/nm0123741/ (August 21, 2011).
"Gnarls Barkley: Biography," AllMusic, http://www.allmusic.com/artist/gnarls-barkley-p772553/biography (August 21, 2011).
"Goodie Mob: Biography," AllMusic, http://www.allmusic.com/artist/goodie-mob-p168624/biography (August 21, 2011).

—*A. Petruso*

Neil Patrick Harris

Actor

Born June 15, 1973, in Albuquerque, NM; son of Ron (an attorney) and Sheila (a writer and attorney) Harris; partner of David Burtka, 2004—; children: Gideon Scott, Harper Grace (twins).

Addresses: *Contact*—c/o Booh Schut Company, 11365 Sunshine Terrace, Studio City, CA 91604. *Office*—c/o *How I Met Your Mother*, 20th Century Fox Studios, 10201 W. Pico Blvd., Trailer 795, Los Angeles, CA 90035.

Career

Actor in films, including: *Clara's Heart*, 1988; *Purple People Eater*, 1988; *Animal Room*, 1995; *Starship Troopers*, 1997; *The Proposition*, 1998; *The Next Best Thing*, 2000; *The Mesmerist*, 2002; *Undercover Brother*, 2002; *Harold & Kumar Go to White Castle*, 2004; *Harold & Kumar Escape from Guantanamo Bay*, 2008; *Justice League: The New Frontier* (animated), 2008; *Cloudy with a Chance of Meatballs* (animated), 2009; *Batman: Under the Red Hood* (animated), 2010; *The Best and the Brightest*, 2010; *Beastly*, 2011; *Company*, 2011; *The Smurfs*, 2011; *A Very Harold & Kumar 3D Christmas*, 2011; *The Muppets*, 2011. Television appearances include: *Too Good to Be True* (movie), 1988; *B. L. Stryker*, 1989; *Home Fires Burning* (movie), 1989; *Doogie Howser, M.D.*, 1989-93; *Blossom*, 1991; *Stranger in the Family* (movie), 1991; *Captain Planet and the Planeteers* (animated), 1992; *Roseanne*, 1992; *Capitol Critters* (animated), 1992-95; *A Family Torn Apart* (movie), 1993; *Murder, She Wrote*, 1993; *Quantum Leap*, 1993; *Snowbound: The Jim and Jennifer Stolpa Story* (movie), 1994; *Legacy of Sin: The William Coit Story* (movie), 1995; *The Man in the Attic* (movie),

1995; *My Antonia* (movie), 1995; *Not Our Son* (movie), 1995; *The Outer Limits*, 1996; *Homicide: Life on the Street*, 1997; *The Christmas Wish* (movie), 1998; *Joan of Arc* (movie), 1999; *Stark Raving Mad*, 1999-2000; *Will & Grace*, NBC, 2000; *Ed*, 2001; *Son of the Beach*, 2001; *Static Shock* (animated), 2001; *Sweeney Todd: The Demon Barber of Fleet Street in Concert* (movie), 2001; *The Wedding Dress* (movie), 2001; *Touched by an Angel*, CBS, 2002; *Boomtown*, NBC, 2003; *Spider-Man* (animated), 2003; *Law & Order: Criminal Intent*, 2004; *The Christmas Blessing* (movie), 2005; *Jack & Bobby*, 2005; *Numb3rs*, CBS, 2005; *How I Met Your Mother*, CBS, 2005—; *Family Guy* (voice), 2007-09; *The 2008 World Magic Awards* (host), 2008; *Sesame Street*, PBS, 2008; *The 7th Annual TV Land Awards*, 2009; *The 63rd Annual Tony Awards* (host), CBS, 2009; *The 61st Primetime Emmy Awards* (host), 2009; *Batman: The Brave and the Bold* (animated), 2009; *Robot Chicken*, Cartoon Network, 2009; *Yes, Virginia* (movie), 2009; *The 64th Annual Tony Awards* (host), 2010; *The 65th Annual Tony Awards*, 2011; *Glee*, FOX, 2010; *The Penguins of Madagascar* (animated), Nickelodeon, 2010. Television work includes: Producer, *The 61st Primetime Emmy Awards*, 2009; producer, *The 65th Annual Tony Awards*, 2011. Stage appearances include: *Luck, Pluck and Virtue*, New York City, c. 1994; *Rent*, La Jolla, CA, and Los Angeles, CA, 1997-98; *Romeo and Juliet*, Old Globe Theatre, San Diego, CA, 1998; *Sweeney Todd, the Demon Bar-*

ber of Fleet Street, New York Philharmonic, New York City, 2000; *Proof*, Walter Kerr Theatre, New York City, 2001; *Cabaret*, Studio 54, New York City, 2003; *Assassins*, Studio 54, New York City, 2004; *Paris Letter*, Kirk Douglas Theater, Culver City, CA, 2005; *Tick, Tick...Boom!*, Menier Chocolate Factory, London, 2005; *All My Sons*, Geffen Playhouse, Los Angeles, CA, 2006. Also starred in the Web-only miniseries, *Dr. Horrible's Sing-Along Blog*, 2008.

Awards: Award for favorite male performer in a new TV series, People's Choice, 1990; Young Artist Awards for best young actor starring in a television series, Young Artist Foundation, for *Doogie Howser, M.D.*, 1990, 1991, 1992; The Trevor Life Award, The Trevor Project, 2009; Emmy Award for outstanding guest actor in a comedy series, Academy of Television Arts and Sciences, for *Glee*, 2010; Emmy Award (with others), outstanding special class programs, Academy of Television Arts and Sciences, for *The 63rd Annual Tony Awards*, 2010; award for favorite TV comedy actor, People's Choice, for *How I Met Your Mother*, 2011.

Sidelights

While actor Neil Patrick Harris is perhaps best known for his work on such television series as *Doogie Howser, M.D.* and *How I Met Your Mother*, his career also included memorable film and stage roles, a popular Web-only miniseries, and hosting duties for high-profile award shows like the Emmys and the Tonys. Harris began acting professionally as a teenager, and worked steadily into adulthood. Known for his sense of humor as well as his ability to sing, dance, juggle, and do magic, Harris is a rare complete package as a performer. Though his many appearances on stage, screen, television, and the Web could make audiences feel the fatigue of over-exposure, Harris has been deft in the career choices he makes. As Jon Hurwitz, the creator of the *Harold & Kumar* franchise, told T. L. Stanley of the *Los Angeles Times*, "It's impossible to get tired of him. When you see him, you smile."

Harris was born on June 15, 1973, in Albuquerque, New Mexico, to Ron and Sheila Harris. His father worked as an attorney while his mother was a writer and attorney. Harris became interested in acting at an early age, around the first grade. Accompanying his elder brother to auditions, he was cast as Toto in a school production of *The Wizard of Oz*. He told Howard Kissel of the New York *Daily News*, "Where I grew up, there wasn't much culture to be had—it was mostly football and soccer. At nine or ten, I was a high soprano in the church choir. Around the same time, I played John Darling in the Albuquerque Civic Light Opera's production of *Peter Pan*."

Harris also appeared in productions in Ruidosa, New Mexico, and attended drama camps. By 1988, Harris was acting professionally after being discovered at one such camp operated by screenwriter Mark Medoff. His first films included *Purple People Eater* and *Clara's Heart*. In the latter film, he played a young boy, David Hart, who becomes friend of a character played by Whoopi Goldberg. Harris was nominated for a Golden Globe for his work in the role. While finding employment as an actor, Harris was educated in New Mexico, at La Cueva High School in Albuquerque.

When Harris was 16 years old, he was cast in the leading role in the dramatic comedy series *Doogie Howser, M.D.*, created by Steven Bochco. Harris played a child prodigy who becomes a doctor at 14 and was a second-year resident in a hospital at 16. While the 16-year-old learned to cope with a world not always comfortable with such a young doctor, Howser also had to deal with his own maturation process, including the discovery of the opposite sex, and family life with his parents, like being a teen trying to borrow his father's car. Reviewing the pilot for the *Orange County Register*, Ray Richmond was somewhat skeptical of the premise but commented "Harris is so good, so convincing as Doogie that he actually makes us believe he's a doctor. That's no small feat. He rattles off the medical terminology without missing a beat and proves a charismatic presence in the premiere. Harris' performance is enough to carry the pilot episode and makes us care."

As *Doogie Howser* became a hit, Harris emerged as a teen heartthrob and cultural sensation in the process. For better or for worse, playing Howser defined and followed Harris through the whole of his career. He later acknowledged its importance in his life, telling Bob Thomas of the Associated Press State & Local Wire, "The series has granted me opportunities that I would never have had otherwise in my adulthood, freedoms that would have been unimaginable, financially, professionally, education-wise."

During the 1989 to 1993 run of *Doogie Howser*, Harris appeared in television movies like 1989's *Home Fires Burning*. He played Lonnie in the movie about three generations of the Tibbetts family living in a small Southern town during World War II. Michael E. Hill of the *Washington Post* praised Harris' work, writing "His acting is strong and steady, mature beyond his years, and even though he is not the narrator of the story, the film seems to take on his point of view." Harris' co-star, Barnard Hughes, told Hill of the *Post*, "I don't think anyone thought of him in any way but as an actor—not a child actor."

After *Doogie Howser* went off the air in 1993, Harris wanted to focused on stage work for a time as he longed to do since he began acting professionally. He had appeared in his senior play at La Cueva High School, playing Lazar Wolf the butcher in *Fiddler on the Roof* in 1991; however, it took several years for this desire to come to fruition. In the meantime, Harris appeared in a number of guest spots and television movies. He took on guest roles in series like *Quantum Leap* and *Murder, She Wrote* in 1993. Harris' television movies included 1993's *A Family Torn Apart*, 1994's *Snowbound: The Jim and Jennifer Stolpa Story*, and 1995's *The Man in the Attic* and *Not Our Son*. The dramatic *A Family Torn Apart* focused on the murder of seemingly perfect parents by one of their adopted sons, and gave Harris a chance to show his dramatic chops.

In the mid-1990s, Harris' stage ambitions were realized when he appeared in a New York production of *Luck, Pluck and Virtue*, then was cast as Mark Cohen in the West Coast production of *Rent*. The musical opened in La Jolla, California, before moving to Los Angeles. Harris dyed his hair blond. He also began appearing in films again, with roles in 1997's *Starship Troopers* and 1998's *The Proposition*. In addition, Harris continued to work in television, appearing in movies like 1998's *The Christmas Wish* and *Joan of Arc*. In 1999, Harris had another featured role in the television comedy *Stark Raving Mad*, in which he played a germaphobe book editor forced to help an eccentric horror author with writer's block. It was the first time that Harris had worked on a live-audience situation comedy, an experience that he found interesting. He told Bob Thomas of the Associated Press State & Local Wire, "It's a very odd and fairly surreal process, much different than I had anticipated. But good, challenging. When you watch these shows, you think it's a fairly simple formula. But it is really very complex, as far as the writing, your inflection, when to wait for the joke, when to pause." Despite winning a People's Choice award for Favorite New Television Comedy Series in January of 2000, *Stark Raving Mad* was canceled after one season.

Harris landed more stage roles in the early 2000s. His first part of note came in the concert version of *Sweeney Todd, the Demon Barber of Fleet Street*, singing the role of Tobias in the New York Philharmonic production. Harris' stage work reached new heights in 2001, when he made his Broadway debut in the dramatic Pulitzer Prize-winning play *Proof*. In 2003, Harris began working regularly in musical theater and took over the role of the emcee in the Broadway production of *Cabaret* for several months to much acclaim. In 2004, he appeared in the Broadway musical *Assassins*, playing Lee Harvey Oswald in the Stephen Sondheim musical.

Next, in 2005, he appeared in the London production of *Tick, Tick...Boom!*, with critics lauding his performance. Reviewing the production in *Variety*, Matt Wolf wrote "Harris is simply remarkable in his London debut, striking up an easy rapport with the audience.... On the same sure-footed vocal ground heard last year on Broadway in *Assassins*, the performer makes something both charming and eloquent out of self-doubt and indecision." In 2006, he played Chris Keller in a Los Angeles production of *All My Sons*, by Arthur Miller.

As Harris was finding success and fulfillment on stage, he continued to work in film and television. He had roles in films, including 2000's *The Next Best Thing* and the 2002 comedy *Undercover Brother*. In 2004, Harris played a fictionalized, exaggerated version of himself in the stoner comedy *Harold & Kumar Go to White Castle*, a role he reprised in *Harold & Kumar Escape from Guantanamo Bay*, released in 2008. For television, Harris provided the voice of Peter Parker/Spider-Man for the 2003 MTV animated series *Spider-Man*. In 2005, he had a guest spot on the long-running CBS series *Numb3rs*.

In 2005, Harris landed another career-defining role. He was cast as the ladies' man Barney Stinson in the hit situation comedy, *How I Met Your Mother*. Producers selected him for the role because of his work in *Harold & Kumar Go to White Castle*. Harris' Barney was a character known for his suits, love advice, and many catchphrases. The Emmy-nominated Harris loved playing the Lothario in the ensemble show, telling Virginia Rohan of the Bergen County *Record*, "Barney's sort of the Lenny and Squiggy of this comedy. He thinks he's incredibly cool, incredibly sexy.... Commitment—I don't think he's every heard that word before." During the run of the show, in 2006, Harris publicly announced he was gay because of on-going rumors and the chance he could be outed without his permission. He had been in a committed relationship with David Burtka since 2004, and in 2010, the couple had twins, Gideon and Harper, via a surrogate.

While *How I Met Your Mother* continued to be a hit, Harris found success in a new medium: the Internet. In 2008, he was the star of the extremely popular Web-only series *Dr. Horrible's Sing-Along Blog*. Harris also had roles in animated films like 2008's *Justice League: The New Frontier*, 2009's *Cloudy with a Chance of Meatballs* and 2010's *Batman: Under the Red Hood*. In 2011, Harris had a live-action role in a film version of the cartoon *The Smurfs*, which featured animated versions of the titular characters. Future films include a third Harold and Kumar film, and a role in the revival of *The Muppets*.

In addition to acting, Harris enjoyed singing—which came through in his stage work—and performing magic. He did tricks on the Jerry Lewis MDA telethon and various talk shows. Harris also gained acclaim for his award-show hosting ability. Among his well-received hosting gigs were the 2009 Emmy Awards and TV Land Awards as well as the Tony Awards in 2009 and 2011. When Harris hosted the 2009 Tonys, the audience increased 19 percent from the previous year's telecast. Discussing his hosting of the 2011 Tony Awards, Robert Lloyd of the *Los Angeles Times* noted, "Harris ... brings irony to a celebratory moment with no loss of edge or of joy: He never let the show get away from him, even when it might have." Harris was also a producer for the 2009 Emmys and 2011 Tonys.

Harris acknowledged his career had taken interesting turns. He told Rohan of the Bergen County *Record*, "It's a strange feeling having a modicum of success early on. You wonder if it will ever come again. You wonder if you can match it. It's great. I'm a big fan of working, so when I can do as many things as I can and try to parlay that into other work, I'm thrilled." On this topic, he also told T. L. Stanley of the *Los Angeles Times*, "I like to make decisions based on things I'm interested in doing, not what seems like the next move in my quote-unquote career. I'm not trying to climb a ladder—I'm casting a bit of a net."

Sources

Periodicals

Associated Press, November 17, 2003; October 16, 2010; May 10, 2011.

Associated Press Online, August 10, 1997; November 4, 2006.
Associated Press State & Local Wire, November 26, 1999.
Associated Press Worldstream, February 27, 2003.
Daily News (NY), April 30, 2000, p. 21.
Daily News of Los Angeles, April 20, 2008, p. L2.
Daily Variety, November 19, 1993; September 21, 1999, p. 14.
Deseret News (Salt Lake City, UT), November 7, 1997, p. W9.
Houston Chronicle, September 21, 2009, p. 1.
Los Angeles Times, June 13, 2011, p. D8; July 15, 2011, p. D1.
National Post, April 24, 2008, p. AL1.
New York Times, April 16, 2006, sec. 2, p. 17.
Orange County Register, October 5, 1988, p. L1; September 19, 1989, p. F1.
Record (Bergen County, NJ), December 18, 2005, p. E1.
Television Week, June 2, 2008, p. 26.
USA Today, January 27, 1989, p. 3D; February 22, 1990, p. 3D.
Variety, June 27, 2005-July 10, 2005, p. 71.
Washington Post, January 29, 1989, p. Y8.
Women's Wear Daily, July 29, 2011, p. 10.

Online

"Neil Patrick Harris," Internet Broadway Database, http://www.ibdb.com/person.php?id=87740 (August 20, 2011).
"Neil Patrick Harris," Internet Movie Database, http://www.imdb.com/name/nm0000439/ (August 20, 2011).

—*A. Petruso*

Thomas Heatherwick

© *Keith Morris/Alamy*

Designer

Born Thomas Alexander Heatherwick, February 17, 1970, in London, England; son of Hugh (a musician) and Stefany (a bead-store owner; maiden name, Tomalin) Heatherwick; married; children: two. *Education:* Attended Manchester Metropolitan University; Royal College of Art, M.A., 1994.

Addresses: *Office*—Heatherwick Studio, 364 Gray's Inn Rd., London WC1X 8BH, United Kingdom. *Web site*—http://www.heatherwick.com.

Career

Founder, Heatherwick Studio, 1994, and principal, 1994—; visiting lecturer: Chelsea School of Art and Design, 1999, Manchester Metropolitan University, 2000, Royal College of Art, 2000, 2002, Bartlett School of Architecture, 2001, Kingston University, 2001; consulting artist, St. Helier Waterfront, Jersey, 2000; consultant, Milton Keynes Council, 2001; senior fellow, Royal College of Art, 2004—; honorary fellow, Royal Institute of British Architects, 2008—.

Awards: Edward Marshall Prize, Edward Marshall Trust, 1994; Setting Up Grant, Crafts Council, 1995; Black Pencil (Gold Award), British Design & Art Direction, for *Autumn Intrusion*, 1997; Sustainable Furniture Competition, Earth Centre, Doncaster, 2000; Design Week Awards, 2001; Bombay Sapphire Prize, Bombay Sapphire Foundation, for "Glass Bridge," 2002; Yellow Pencil (Silver Award) for Environmental Design & Architecture—Design for Leisure, British Design & Art Direction, for *Blue Carpet*, 2003;

Structural Steel Design Awards, Corus, for *Rolling Bridge*, 2005; Walpole Award for Design, Walpole, 2005; Lovells Art and Work Award, for *Bleigiessen*, 2006; Prince Philip Designers Prize, Design Council, 2006; Black Pencil in Environmental Design—Retail & Services, British Design & Art Direction, for La Maison Unique, 2007; London Design Medal, London Design Festival, 2010; designer of the year, *Wallpaper Magazine*, 2011.

Sidelights

British designer Thomas Heatherwick creates dazzling large-scale sculptures and installations from unusual materials or tricks of mechanical virtuosity. In London, he devised a roll-up pedestrian footbridge over a canal, and for a Manhattan luxury-goods retailer he fashioned a staircase that appears to be made from waves of rubber and wood. But Heatherwick's most noteworthy work is the enormous, six-story "flower" made from 60,000 acrylic rods that swayed in the wind at the 2010 Shanghai World Expo in China. "I don't feel I'm trying to make art," Heatherwick told Steve Rose, a writer for the *Guardian*. "I'm trying to make interesting things. People can relate to that."

Heatherwick was born in London in 1970 into a creative family. His father was a musician, his mother owned a bead shop on the famed Portobello Road for two decades, and his grandmother had once run the textile design studio for Marks & Spencer, a major British retailer. Fascinated by anything tactile, movable, or mechanical at an early age, Heatherwick earned the nickname "How-Why" from classmates for his habit of persistently asking questions. He attended the tony Sevenoaks school in Kent before entering Manchester Metropolitan University's art program. Before earning his master's degree in three-dimensional design from London's Royal College of Art, he had already attracted the patronage of Sir Terence Conran, the visionary designer and founder of a high-end chain of furniture and housewares stores. Conran bought the work Heatherwick created for his 1994 degree exhibition, a curvilinear X-shaped plywood gazebo, and installed it on his Berkshire estate.

Heatherwick opened his London-based Heatherwick Studio in 1994. One of his first major commissions was a temporary installation at the upscale clothing retailer Harvey Nichols in Knightsbridge. Heatherwick's design was a massive laminated wood ribbon that wound through the windows of the flagship store during London Fashion Week in the fall of 1997. The extruded polystyrene and birch veneer ribbon, which he dubbed *Autumn Intrusion,* made it appear as if the building was encased in a giant, glowing pretzel, and won him the prestigious Black Pencil Award from the British Design & Art Direction foundation.

Another buzzed-about project from Heatherwick's studio was *Blue Carpet,* a public square in front of the Laing Art Gallery in the city of Newcastle-upon-Tyne. Made from a combination of resin, concrete, and reinforced glass, the surface rises up into seats, or gives a peekaboo look at what is underneath, including remnants of the city's past, which dates back to the Roman invasion of Britain. Its popularity was equaled by the *Rolling Bridge* over the Paddington Basin canal in London. Erected in 2004, the wooden footbridge rolls up by itself via hydraulic rams when a boat nears. Another popular London attraction is *Bleigiessen,* installed in the atrium of a new home for the biomedical research charity, Wellcome Trust. Unveiled in March of 2005, *Bleigiessen*'s 150,000 glass beads stretch into a multistory sculpture "shimmering ethereally in what seemed to be a permanent white mist, like a grounded UFO in some epic science-fiction movie," wrote *Times* of London journalist Richard Morrison, who also hailed Heatherwick as "perhaps the most daring creative brain that Britain has nurtured for a generation."

Heatherwick first worked with French luxury-goods retailer Longchamp back in 2003, which produced his dramatically ingenious Zip Bag. He had visited

a zipper factory and was stunned to learn that the closures can be manufactured in huge lengths; his Zip Bag for Longchamp doubles in size when unzipped. The company then commissioned him to design a staircase for its New York City store in SoHo, which opened in the spring of May of 2006. His studio worked with the store's architect and a Boston company to assemble a stunning, 55-ton steel and rubber staircase that waves upward and across the Longchamp store.

As it entered its second decade as a company, Heatherwick Studio began working on freestanding buildings. The first was the East Beach Café, on the West Sussex coastline. Heatherwick also won a commission at Aberystwyth University in Wales. "What could have been just another university building is instead an enchanted woodland community, albeit one that looks like something from a sci-fi movie, with crinkly walls that seem to have been made of tinfoil, although they are in fact stainless steel," reported Rose in the *Guardian* article. Heatherwick explained that stainless steel was a fantastically durable material, and noncorrosive, but was too costly to use as a primary building material. "We found a mill in Finland where they rolled it 0.1mm thick—the thickness of a coke can. The problem is, it crinkles. So we thought, 'What if we let it crinkle and enjoy that?'"

The most controversial project of Heatherwick's career has been the public sculpture *B of the Bang,* installed in front of the City of Manchester Stadium in 2005. It was an enormous, 184-foot-tall, pitched grouping of 180 steel spikes. The stadium was relatively new, and Heatherwick's work—which borrowed its title from an Olympic sprinter's explanation of needing to make a fast start when one hears the starting pistol of a footrace—was erected in commemoration of Manchester hosting the 2002 Commonwealth Games. When imagining what they might submit for the project, Heatherwick told Morrison in the *Times,* he and the other design and engineering professionals "wanted to avoid the usual cliché—depicting peace and harmony between nations. Top-class sport isn't peaceful at all. It's incredibly aggressive. So the challenge we set ourselves was: what is the most unpassive, aggressive, dynamic object we could build?"

For a time, Heatherwick's *B of the Bang* was the largest sculpture in the Britain Isles, dwarfing Antony Gormley's 66-foot-high *Angel of the North* in Gateshead; however, Heatherwick's work had to be dismantled when some of the steel tips on the spikes began falling off, creating a safety hazard. He had better luck with the stunning *Seed Cathedral,* which served as the British Pavilion at the 2010 Shanghai World Expo. Keeping with the fair's theme of sustainable development, Heatherwick's studio worked with the Royal Botanic Gardens' Millennium Seed Bank project to place one seed from its conservation archive into each tip of 60,000 acrylic rods, which swayed in the wind. It was one of the most talked-about buildings at the Expo and helped Heatherwick land a commission to design the Olympic Cauldron for the 2012 London Summer Games. "We don't work on rich patrons' bathrooms," the designer told Morrison, the *Times* of London journalist. "I try to take the long view: what is the best thing I can do now for people in 100 years' time?"

Sources

Daily Telegraph (London, England), November 25, 2006, p. 7.
Guardian (London, England), March 16, 2005; May 27, 2009.
Independent (London, England), March 16, 1998, p. 4.
New York Times, June 4, 2006; May 30, 2010.
Observer (London, England), December 29, 2002.
Times (London, England), January 12, 2005, p. 4.

—*Carol Brennan*

Daniella Helayel

Fashion designer

Born c. 1972, in Rio de Janeiro, Brazil; daughter of a teacher. *Education:* Attended college in New York City; took courses at the Fashion Institute of Technology, early 1990s.

Addresses: *Home*—London, England. *Office*—Issa London, Unit 11-12, 90 Lots Rd., London SW10 0QD, United Kingdom.

Career

Worked in the garment-manufacturing industry around Seventh Avenue in New York city as a broker and manufacturer's representative; founded own label, Issa, 2001.

Sidelights

Brazilian-born fashion designer Daniella Helayel is the founder of Issa, a women's clothing label that received a massive boost in sales after Kate Middleton, who married Prince William of Wales in 2011, was photographed wearing Helayel's sleek, sophisticated designs during their highly publicized courtship. In fact, the blue Issa dress that Middleton wore at the press conference announcing the couple's engagement in November of 2010 sold out in high-end retailers like Harvey Nichols within a matter of hours. The royal wedding ties helped Helayel's business, but Issa already had a devoted core of customers. "We cut the dresses to enhance the chest, hide the hips and make the waist look small," the designer explained to *WWD* writer Samantha Conti in 2005. "The whole point is to make comfortable clothes that enhance what's beautiful and hide what's not."

Helayel was born in Rio de Janeiro, Brazil, and grew up in coastal Niterói. Her mother, an early-elementary teacher, eventually divorced Helayel's father and remarried. Growing up, Helayel loved to visit her grandmother in another beach town, Buzios, that gained a measure of international fame years before when French screen siren Brigitte Bardot stayed there for several months. Helayel first visited New York with her mother as a tween, and vowed to come back permanently, even dreaming of becoming a fashion designer. Her chance came in the early 1990s, when she enrolled in college-level law classes, but she also managed to take classes at the Fashion Institute of Technology. "I was only allowed to study design if I also studied law," she told the *Daily Telegraph*'s Celia Walden about the bargain she brokered with her parents. "That was the deal."

Helayel spent most of the decade in the city. She eventually found a job in the Garment District, working as a broker for Brazilian textile firms and clothing manufacturers. Her creative urges were sated by buying vintage clothes, then refitting them to better suit her proportions. After a particularly rough breakup, she pulled up roots and resettled in London at the start of the new millennium, in 2000. "I had all these girlfriends who never wore dresses, then I came back from New York with a suitcase of vintage dresses and they went crazy for them," she recalled in an interview with *Times* of London journalist Lisa Armstrong. "So I thought, maybe I had a business plan."

Helayel launched Issa in 2001, borrowing the name from a word that Brazilian surfers yell out when they catch a particularly choice wave. It roughly translates as "lucky," but Helayel's first few years in business were anything but that as she made several costly errors. Despite her expertise in the business, she once paid retail, not wholesale, prices for her batch of fabrics, and sold that season's wares at an enormous loss. There were production issues that delayed deliveries, which in turn made retailers wary. Finally, the mother of one of her friends came on board to sort things out. Laura Moltedo, who had run luxury Italian leather-goods manufacturer Bottega Veneta for a few years, invested in Issa and helped Helayel focus on what she did well: a jersey wrap dress, similar to those popularized by designer Diane von Furstenberg in the 1970s, but in bold, Brazilian-inspired prints. When Helayel's fashionista friends wore them to high-profile events, it sparked interest, and Helayel earned a mention in the U.S. edition of *Vogue* in June of 2005 as one of the more intriguing new designers to watch.

Issa's first foray into London Fashion Week came in early 2006, when Helayel previewed her 2006-07 Autumn/Winter collection. Her company's fortunes were boosted when Net-a-Porter, the leading online retailer for higher-end fashion, began carrying the dresses. In October of 2006, pop star Madonna was interviewed by Oprah Winfrey via satellite link wearing one of Issa's wrap dresses, a teal pheasant print. Issa gained tremendous exposure and traction over the next year, and soon Helayel was able to move her home and office into the same space, a townhouse in Chelsea on its fabled Cheyne Walk, the Thames riverside drive with a long list of famous residents, including Henry James and Mick Jagger.

Helayel's dresses found their way into the closets of Princesses Beatrice and Eugenie, the daughters of the former Duchess of York, Sarah Ferguson, and her ex-husband Prince Andrew. Their princesses' cousin, Prince William, was dating a young woman from Berkshire named Kate Middleton, whom he had met while a student at St. Andrew's University in Scotland. For the first few years of their romance,

Middleton kept a low profile, but began to be seen in public with William after their 2005 graduation. Dubbed "Waity Katie" by the British tabloids for sticking with the prince through several separations due to his military-service commitments, Middleton began to be photographed with "Wills" and other members of the royal family, and polished up her image by adding demure, yet sophisticated ensembles that helped her weather the scrum of paparazzi who followed her everywhere in London. The first notable Issa addition to Middleton's closet was an evening-gown-length coral pink dress she wore to a charity boxing ball in June of 2008 that made the front pages of every British tabloid the next day.

Middleton was wearing a blue Issa dress from the 2004 collection when she and the prince appeared at a news conference just after his palace office at Clarence House issued the official word of their engagement. The pair posed for photographers, and sat for an interview with ITV News. The blue of the dress Middleton had chosen matched the deep blue of the legendary diamond-and-sapphire engagement ring worn by William's mother, the late Diana, Princess of Wales.

Helayel's name was mentioned as one of the possible designers for Middleton's wedding dress, which remained a closely guarded secret until the April 29 extravaganza. It was assumed the future Queen would choose a more established British designer who had more significant bridal or haute couture experience. Helayel, meanwhile, was making plans to expand her company on the Issa wave of royal wedding fever: the first standalone stores opened in 2011, and she also launched Baby Issa. "The one person I would really like to dress is the Queen," the exuberant Brazilian told Walden in the *Daily Telegraph*, referring to Elizabeth II, Prince William's grandmother. "She ... would look really cool in a silk cape like mine. The Queen of England is the ultimate style icon."

Sources

Daily Mail (London, England), October 27, 2008.
Daily Telegraph (London, England), September 17, 2008, p. 28.
Evening Standard (London, England), February 24, 2009, p. 35.
New York Times, November 25, 2010.
Sunday Times (London, England), July 12, 2009, p. 30.
Times (London, England), March 23, 2005, p. 13.
WWD, June 14, 2005, p. 14; December 28, 2010, p. 3.

—Carol Brennan

John Benjamin Hickey

© *Charles Sykes/AP Images*

Actor

Born June 25, 1963, in Plano, TX; partner of Jeffrey Richmond.

Addresses: *Agent*—Paradigm Agency, 360 N. Crescent Dr., Beverly Hills, CA 90210.

Career

Actor on stage, including: *Love! Valour! Compassion*, Walter Kerr Theatre, February-September 1995; *Cabaret*, Kit Kat Klub/Studio 54, February 1998-99; *The Crucible*, Virginia Theatre, March 2002-June 2002; *Mary Stuart*, Broadhurst Theatre, April 2009-August 2009; *The Normal Heart*, John Golden Theatre, April 2011-July 2011. Film appearances include: *The Bet*, 1992; *The Ref*, 1994; *Only You*, 1994; *Comfortably Numb*, 1995; *Eddie*, 1996; *Sin #8*, 1996; *The Ice Storm*, 1997; *Love! Valour! Compassion!*, 1997; *Finding North*, 1998; *The Bone Collector*, 1999; *General's Daughter*, 1999; *The Anniversary Party*, 2001; *Changing Lanes*, 2002; *Flightplan*, 2005; *The Ex*, 2006; *Flags of Our Fathers*, 2006; *Fast Track*, 2006; *Infamous*, 2006; *The Seeker: The Dark Is Rising*, 2007; *Freedom Writers*, 2007; *The Seeker: The Dark Is Rising*, 2007; *Then She Found Me*, 2007; *The Taking of Pelham 1 2 3*, 2009; *Transformers: Revenge of the Fallen*, 2009; *Civil Unions: A Love Story*, 2010. Television appearances include: *Normandy: The Great Crusade* (movie), 1994; *NYPD Blue*, 1994, 2001; *New York News*, 1995; *Nothing Sacred*, 1997; *3rd Rock from the Sun*, 1998; *Law and Order*, 1998, 2002, 2004-06; *Sex and the City*, 1998; *Homicide: Life on the Street*, 1999; *The Lady in Question* (movie), 1999; *D.C.*, 2000; *Hamlet* (movie), 2000; *Law and Order: Special Victims Unit*, 2000; *Perfect Murder, Perfect Town* (miniseries), 2000; *C.S.I.: Crime Scene Investigation*, 2001; *The Guardian*, 2001; *Life with Judy Garland: Me and My Shadows* (miniseries) 2001; *A Glimpse of Hell* (movie), 2001; *Hack*, 2002; *Law and Order: Criminal Intent*, 2003; *It's All Relative*, 2004; *Alias*, 2005; *Silver Bells* (movie), 2005; *A House Divided* (movie), 2006; *Brothers and Sisters*, 2006; *Justice*, 2006; *Stacked*, 2006; *Undercover History*, 2006-07; *Heartland*, 2007; *Situation Critical* (narrator), 2007; *Secrets of the Moon Landing* (narrator), 2007; *In Plain Sight*, 2008; *Living Proof* (movie), 2008; *Lincoln: American Mastermind* (movie; voice), 2009; *The Big C*, 2010—; *Law and Order: LA*, 2010; *The Good Wife*, 2011.

Awards: Obie Award (with others) for performance, *Village Voice*, for *Love! Valour! Compassion!*, 1995; Tony Award for best performance by a featured actor in a play, American Theatre Wing and the Broadway League, for *The Normal Heart*, 2011.

Sidelights

Actor John Benjamin Hickey has appeared in several Broadway shows and a number of films. A major triumph was the result of his appearance in the play *The Normal Heart*; he won a Tony Award in 2011. He is also a star on the Showtime television show *The Big C*.

Hickey grew up in Plano, Texas, near Dallas. He was interested in being an actor from an early age, and he was also aware that he was gay, but he kept that a secret. In the deeply conservative culture he lived in, as he told T. Michelle Murphy for New York's *Metro*, "I grew up thinking gay was not good, that gay was not something you had a choice to be. So I sublimated that part of myself."

As a young person his heroes were people in the theater world, including Tony Kushner, Craig Lucas, John Robin Baiz, and Paul Vogel. Like Hickey, all of these role models were gay and, as Hickey told a reporter for *Out* magazine, "They were all out, and they were all working and doing the kinds of things I wanted to do. I felt like if I wanted their respect, I had to stand up and be who I was." Hickey decided that he would have to leave Texas if he wanted to do what he wanted to do and live a truthful life in terms of his sexual orientation; however, he confessed to Murphy, "I have deep, deep roots in Texas. I love my home state and I love my family…. My feelings are no longer mixed, there's a lot of love for both places."

When he was 21, Hickey moved to New York City and studied at the acclaimed Juilliard School. He made his Broadway debut in 1995 in the show *Love! Valour! Compassion!* The play is about eight gay men who spend summer weekends together at a country house. In the play, Hickey played Arthur Pape, an accountant, whose rather conventional exterior hides the anger and fear he really feels deep down. He won an Obie Award for his performance in the play. After *Love! Valour! Compassion!* Hickey appeared in other Broadway shows, including *Cabaret* (1998-99), *The Crucible* (2002), and *Mary Stuart* (2009). Hickey has also appeared in films, including *Flags of Our Fathers* (2006), *Freedom Writers*, (2007), and *Transformers* (2009).

Starting in 2010, Hickey appeared on the Showtime network's new program, *The Big C*, with Laura Linney. In the show, he played Sean, a homeless-by-choice environmentalist who suffers from manic depression; Sean's sister is a cancer patient whose experiences with her illness are the focal point of the show. Despite its serious subject matter, the show had a comedic thread running through it, which Hickey found interesting and challenging. He told Murphy of the *Metro* that he took the role "not because of the heaviness, but because of trying to find the lightness."

Linney was one of the producers of *The Big C*, and she was good friends with the producer of a Broadway play, *The Normal Heart*. She made the introductions and soon Hickey was slated to star in the play, despite the fact that at the same time, he was regularly appearing on *The Big C*. This took some finagling, but the producers of both shows were on his side and willing to work to make it possible for Hickey. He was delighted and grateful to be involved in two great shows, shuttling back and forth between filming and performing, and he made it a policy to never, ever complain about having too much work, since so many actors struggle to find any work at all.

The Normal Heart, was written by gay activist Larry Kramer, who founded the Gay Men's Health Crisis to assist people suffering from the AIDS epidemic. The play surges with Kramer's intensity and anger over the way gay men's health, lives, and deaths were being ignored as the medical system, government, and public at large failed to respond to the AIDS crisis. Hickey told Bill Keith of *Out* magazine, "It's a universal cry for justice and love, that unless you are heard you disappear." In the play, Hickey portrayed Felix Turner, a closeted *New York Times* reporter who is Kramer's lover. In an interview with the Web site Broadway.com, Hickey noted that when he was first approached about the show, he thought it would be a rather stale period piece, given that it was set in 1985; however, he noted, the issues in the play were still relevant and it was "as tremulous and as powerful as ever." He remarked to Murphy that, in contrast to *The Big C*, which is a comedy with serious elements, *The Normal Heart* "has great laughs in it, but it is a deeply heartbreaking play. So I have to work very hard to shake it all off at the end of the day and keep my sense of humor."

Hickey won a Tony Award in 2011 for his performance in the play. When he heard the news, he told a reporter from the Web site Broadway World, "I was beside myself with pride and so proud to be part of the company. It is humbling and the experience has been incredible." He added that the first person he called to tell about the award was his mother, because "she has been waiting and wishing for this longer than anyone." In his acceptance speech for the award, he thanked her and several other people for their help and support, including his partner Jeffrey Richmond. Hickey remains positive about life and the future and is appreciative of the opportunities he has been given to do what he loves. When asked by *Metro* reporter Murphy if he had any advice for young actors or gay young people, Hickey replied, "Love yourself, be safe, come to New York."

Sources

"Big C Break," *New York Post,* http://www.nypost.com/p/entertainment/tv/big_break_2gIP6W2kjGOvrJCowpPpwO (July 15, 2011).

"Catching Up with John Benjamin Hickey," *Out*, http://www.out.com/detail.asp?id=30030 (July 15, 2011).

"John Benjamin Hickey," Filmbug, http://www.filmbug.com/db/277940 (July 15, 2011).

"John Benjamin Hickey," Internet Movie Database, http://www.imdb.com/name/nm0382632/ (July 15, 2011).

"John Benjamin Hickey Mentions His Same Sex Partner in Tony Speech," The New Civil Rights Movement, http://thenewcivilrightsmovement.com/tonys-john-benjamin-hickey-mentions-his-same-sex-partner-in-tony-win-speech/news/2011/06/12/21986 (July 15, 2011).

"John Benjamin Hickey on Learning Tony News at *The Big C*," Broadway World, http://broadwayworld.com/article/John-Benjamin-Hickey-on-Learning-Tony-News-at-The-Big-C-20110503.tif (July 15, 2011).

"John Benjamin Hickey Shares Humor and 'Heart,'" *Metro*, http://www.metro.us/newyork/article/860981--john-benjamin-hickey-shares-humor-and-heart (July 15, 2011).

"*The Normal Heart*'s John Benjamin Hickey on Juggling The Big C and Acting with Joe Mantello," Broadway.com, http://www.broadway.com/shows/normal-heart/buzz/156227/the-normal-hearts-john-benjamin-hickey-on-juggling-the-big-c-and-acting-with-joe-mantello/ (July 15, 2011).

"Theater Review: *Love! Valour! Compassion*," *New York Times*, http://theater.nytimes.com/mem/theater/treview.html?html_title=&tols_title=LOVE!%20VALOUR!%20COMPASSION!%20(PLAY)&pdate=19950215.tif&byline=By%20VINCENT%20CANBY&id=10770114.tif30638 (July 15, 2011).

—*Kelly Winters*

Laura Hillenbrand

Author

Born May 15, 1967, in Fairfax, VA; married G. Borden Flanagan (a history professor), 2008. *Education:* Attended Kenyon College, Gambier, OH, 1985-87.

Addresses: *Agent*—Janklow/Nesbit Associates, 445 Park Ave., New York, NY 10022-2606. *Home*—Washington, DC.

Career

Contributing editor, *Equus* magazine, 1989—; also contributor to *The Blood-Horse, Thoroughbred Times, The Backstretch, Turf* and *Sport Digest*; first book, *Seabiscuit: An American Legend*, published by Random House, 2001, and adapted for film as *Seabiscuit*, 2003.

Awards: Eclipse Award for Magazine Writing, National Turf Writers Association, for "'Four Good Legs Between Us,'" 1998.

Sidelights

Laura Hillenbrand turned out a sensational debut for a first-time writer: her 2001 book *Seabiscuit: An American Legend* spent six weeks at the No. 1 spot on the *New York Times* nonfiction best-seller list and went on to sell more than six million copies. The movie adaptation, released in the summer of 2003, was nominated for seven Academy Awards. Hillenbrand followed up with another bestseller, *Unbroken: A World War II Story of Survival, Resilience and Redemption*, in 2010.

Hillenbrand was raised in the middle of North America's elite equestrian circuit. She was born in 1967 in Fairfax, Virginia, the last of four children, and spent summers at a family farm in Sharpsburg, Maryland, where her father ran the region's unofficial horse-rescue operation. Once, Hillenbrand sold her musical instruments and her older sister used all her savings to purchase a three-year-old horse destined for the slaughterhouse. They named her Allspice, and "she blossomed into an extraordinarily beautiful creature who bonded with us the way dogs sometimes bond to their owners," Hillenbrand told Amy Blumenthal in the *Kenyan College Alumni Bulletin*. Allspice learned how to open doors with her mouth, and was known to occasionally stroll into the Hillenbrand home during dinnertime.

Hillenbrand followed her sister to Kenyon College in Gambier, Ohio, where she had a dual major in English and history. She met her future husband there, G. Borden Flanagan, and planned to spend her junior year at the University of Edinburgh. During spring break of her sophomore year, she and Flanagan drove to Florida for spring break with another friend. On the way back, just a half hour from campus, Hillenbrand recalled seeing a deer near the road, just as its knee was about to lock for a leap across their path. But it stayed in place as their car whirred past. "The bumper missed the deer's chest by an inch, maybe two," Hillenbrand wrote of the moment in an article that appeared in the *New Yorker* in 2003. "The animal's muzzle passed so close that I could see the swirl of hair around his nostrils. Then he was gone behind us. I blinked at the road. My eyes caught something else. A brilliant light appeared through the top of the windshield and arced straight ahead of the car at terrific speed. It was a meteor. It burned through the rising light of the horizon and vanished in the black place above the road and below the sky.... I was about to speak when an intense wave of nausea surged through me."

Hillenbrand returned to Kenyon with what appeared to be a case of food poisoning picked up on their road trip. Racked by fever and vomiting for days, then a debilitating exhaustion that refused to abate, she was forced to drop out of classes three weeks later. She moved back in to her mother's house and began seeking treatment for a medical condition that puzzled nearly every doctor she saw. One diagnosed it as strep throat, another claimed it was Epstein-Barr syndrome, and a third suggested it was psychosomatic. Meanwhile, Hillenbrand's boyfriend graduated from Kenyon, took a job in nearby Washington, D.C., and moved in to help care for her. "People told me I was lazy and selfish," she wrote in the *New Yorker*. "Someone lamented how unfortunate Borden was to have a girlfriend who demanded coddling."

Hillenbrand would later recall that she spent much of 1987 and 1988 in a "brain fog," as she described it in an interview with *New York Times* columnist Tara Parker-Pope. Finally, the chief of infectious diseases at Johns Hopkins University School of Medicine diagnosed Hillenbrand with chronic fatigue syndrome, or CFS. Some of her symptoms were treatable, and Hillenbrand worked hard to regain her physical strength and battle the depression her condition caused. She began writing articles for equestrian journals while living in Chicago with Flanagan, who was pursuing his graduate degree at the University of Chicago. It sometimes took her weeks to write an article, but she found it was something she could manage on her own, if she planned her day properly. "Whenever I overextended myself my health disintegrated," she wrote in *New Yorker*. "One mistake could land me in bed for weeks, so the potential cost of even the most trivial activities, from showering to walking to the mailbox, had to be painstakingly considered. Sometimes I relapsed for no reason at all."

Long a fan of thoroughbred horseracing, Hillenbrand and Flanagan made plans to visit the famed race track at Saratoga Springs, New York, in the summer of 1991. The trip was a disaster, and Hillenbrand suffered a major setback to her health, including the onset of terrifying bouts of vertigo. "While I was lying there, I began to believe that we had struck the deer back in 1987, that he had come through the windshield and killed me, and that this was Hell," she recalled in the *New Yorker* article.

Hillenbrand eventually rallied and was able to begin writing again. She had long known the story of Seabiscuit, a horse that was a household name in the United States in the late 1930s. At a neighborhood fair, she told Parker-Pope in the *New York Times*, "for a quarter I bought a book called *Come On Seabiscuit*. I loved that book. It stayed with me all those years. I was sick and housebound and looking for something I could write about. I wrote an article. I was partway through it and realized there was a huge untold story."

The article Hillenbrand wrote was titled "Four Good Legs Between Us." and appeared in the July-August issue of *American Heritage* magazine in 1998. It won her the Eclipse Award for Magazine Writing from the National Turf Writers Association, and a book deal from Random House. There was major buzz about *Seabiscuit: An American Legend* even before Hillenbrand finished the manuscript in September of 2000. The book was published early the next year.

As Hillenbrand's book recounts, few thought that Seabiscuit was destined for greatness in American thoroughbred racing. Though descended from a famous winning horse named Man o' War, Seabiscuit was below average in size and build. His knees did not lock, and he even slept lying down, unlike most horses. Trainers considered him lazy, but a former rodeo rider named Tom Smith discovered the three-year-old stallion in 1936 at a racetrack sale at Suffolk Downs, Massachusetts, and persuaded his boss to buy the horse for Smith to train. Smith worked for Charles Howard, a wealthy car-dealership magnate in California who was one of the original investors in the Santa Anita racecourse.

Seabiscuit had run in 17 races, but had not won any of them. Smith, a skilled trainer, worked with the horse and put a devoted jockey named Johnny (Red) Pollard on him. Hillenbrand's book is the story of these three men and the thoroughbred that went on to become the most famous racehorse in the United States. Seabiscuit missed out on the 1937 Santa Anita Handicap, with its $100,000 prize purse, by an inch to a horse called Rosemont. By 1938 the rivalry between Seabiscuit and the East Coast's best horse, War Admiral, was one of the biggest news stories of the year.

Hillenbrand's work won rave reviews and held down the top spot on the *New York Times* best-seller list for six weeks. Writing in the *New York Times*, Michiko Kakutani called *Seabiscuit* "an absorbing book that stands as the model of sportswriting at its best.... Hillenbrand gives us a visceral appreciation of that sport as refracted through the tumultuous lives of Seabiscuit and his human companions, while at the same time creating a keenly observed portrait of a Depression-era United States bent on escapism and the burgeoning phenomenon of mass-media-marketed celebrity." *Salon*'s Charles Taylor remarked that Hillenbrand skillfully sketched out an enormously appealing title character, though the animal had died 20 years before she was even born. "If you're crazy about animals, part of the reason to love this wonderful book is obvious," Taylor wrote. "Without sentimentality or anthropomorphism, Hillenbrand writes of an animal's intelligence and character."

The Hollywood version of *Seabiscuit* starred Tobey Maguire, Jeff Bridges, and Chris Cooper—while ten different horses stood in for the title role— and was nominated for the Academy Award for Best Picture. It was a gratifying success for Hillenbrand, who had spent much of the past 14 years housebound and even bedridden. "Writing gives me a means by which to redefine myself. It enables me to accomplish something that has nothing whatsoever to do with sickness, so it gives me a sense of dignity," she told Blumenthal in the *Kenyan College Alumni Bulletin*. "The only time I approach being unaware of physical suffering is when I am absorbed in my writing. I have chosen to write about these people and this horse in part because of the vigor of their lives."

Hillenbrand contemplated writing a Civil War-era book for her next project, but instead chanced upon a long-forgotten tale that was one of the feel-good stories in the media at the end of World War II: a California man spent 47 days adrift in the Pacific Ocean after the B-24 bomber carrying him and ten other members of the U.S. Army Air Corps went down due to mechanical failure in May of 1943. But Louis Zamperini was also an Olympic-caliber runner who had competed in the 1936 Berlin Summer Games, and his courage and cunning helped him and another survivor of the crash, pilot Russell Allen Phillips, stay alive for nearly seven weeks at sea without food or water.

Hillenbrand's second book, *Unbroken: A World War II Story of Survival, Resilience and Redemption*, recounts this ordeal and then the much longer one that followed, when Zamperini and Phillips were held in a Japanese prisoner-of-war camp for 25 months, enduring horrific conditions and even torture. As Hillenbrand recalled in the interview with Parker-Pope in the *New York Times*, it was research on her first book that led her to Zamperini's story. "Seabiscuit was famous at the same time. All the newspapers that covered Seabiscuit also covered Louis. I kept reading about him. When I got done with Seabiscuit, I wrote him a letter and called him, and he told me his life story." Zamperini was 93 years old in 2010 when Hillenbrand's book became a bestseller, and he actually carried out the book-tour duties that Hillenbrand was unable to do because of her CFS. "Hillenbrand is particularly well suited to tell this inspiring tale," asserted David Margolick in his *New York Times* review. "She is intelligent and restrained, and wise enough to let the story unfold for itself. Her research is thorough, her writing (even on complicated, technical wartime topics) crystalline. *Unbroken* is gripping in an almost cinematic way."

Hillenbrand and Flanagan were married in 2008. They live in Washington, D.C., where he teaches government at American University. In the *New Yorker* article, which appeared in 2003, Hillenbrand recalled that the sudden fame that came with the publication of *Seabiscuit* surprised both her and Flanagan, and prompted them to reexamine their relationship. There was a period when they agreed to break up, but were still living together. One night Hillenbrand went out into the backyard alone, and saw another meteor. "In the depths of illness, I believed that the deer had crashed through the windshield and ushered me into an existence in which the only possibility was suffering," she wrote. "I was haunted by his form in front of the car, his bent knee, the seeming inevitability of catastrophe, and the ruin my life became. I had forgotten the critical moment. The deer's knee didn't straighten. He didn't step into our path, we didn't strike him, and I didn't die. As sure as I was that he had taken everything from me, I was wrong."

Selected writings

Seabiscuit: An American Legend, Random House (New York City), 2001.
Unbroken: A World War II Story of Survival, Resilience and Redemption, Random House, 2010.

Sources

Periodicals

American Heritage, July-August 1998, p. 38.
New Yorker, July 7, 2003, p. 56.

New York Times, March 6, 2001; November 21, 2010.
Wall Street Journal, November 12, 2010.

Online

"An Author Escapes From Chronic Fatigue Syndrome," Well blog, *New York Times,* http://well.blogs.nytimes.com/2011/02/04/an-author-escapes-from-chronic-fatigue-syndrome/?scp=3&sq=%22laura+hillenbrand%22&st=nyt (April 7, 2011).
"Leading on the Backstretch, " *Kenyan College Alumni Bulletin,* http://bulletin.kenyon.edu/x1228.xml (April 13, 2011).

"Seabiscuit: An American Legend by Laura Hillenbrand," *Salon,* http://www.salon.com/books/review/2001/03/14/hillenbrand/index.html (April 13, 2011).

Transcripts

Weekend Edition, National Public Radio, November 20, 2010.

—*Carol Brennan*

Douglas Hodge

© Henry S. Dziekan III/WireImage/Getty Images

Actor

Born Douglas W. Hodge, February 25, 1960, in Plymouth, Devon, England; son of a civil service dock worker and a nurse; married Tessa Peake-Jones (an actress); children: Mollie, Charlie. *Education:* Attended the Royal Academy of Dramatic Art.

Addresses: *Agent*—United Agents, Ltd., 12-26 Lexington St., London W1F 0LE United Kingdom.

Career

Actor on stage, including: *The Admirable Bashville, The Dark Lady of the Sonnets, A Midsummer Night's Dream, The Taming of the Shrew,* all Open Air Theatre, London, all 1982; *Coriolanus,* Almedia Theatre, London, c. 1984; *Once Upon a Mattress,* Watermill Theatre, Newbury, England, 1985; *King Lear,* Olivier Theatre, London, 1987; *Antony and Cleopatra, Countrymania, Down Cemetery Road, Entertaining Strangers, Fathers and Sons, Hamlet, King Lear, Macbeth, The Magistrate, Mean Tears, Medea, Miss Julie, The Pied Piper, Rosmersholm, School for Wives, Six Characters in Search of an Author, A Small Family Business, Three Men on a Horse, Ting Tang Mine, Tomorrow Was War, Tons of Money, A View from the Bridge, Waiting for Godot, The Wandering Jew, Yerma,* all British National Repertoire Season at the Cottesloe Theatre, Lyttelton Theatre, and Olivier Theatre, London, all 1987; *No Man's Land,* 1992; *Moonlight,* Almeida and Comedy Theatres, London, 1993; *The Collection, A Kind of Alaska, The Lover,* all Donmar Warehouse Theatre, London, all 1998; *The Caretaker,* Comedy Theatre, London, 2000; *Three Sisters,* Playhouse Theatre, London, 2003; *Dumb Show,* The Royal Court, London, 2004; *Guys and Dolls,* Piccadilly Theatre,

London, 2005; *Titus Andronicus,* Globe Theatre, England, 2006; *La Cage aux Folles,* Longacre Theatre, New York City, 2010-11. Television appearances include: *Alas Smith & Jones,* 1985; *Sorry!,* 1986; *King & Castle,* 1988; *London's Burning,* 1988; *Rumpole of the Bailey,* 1988; *Ten Great Writers of the Modern World,* 1988; *Behaving Badly,* 1989; *Capital City,* 1989-90; *Anglo Saxon Attitudes,* 1992; *A Fatal Inversion,* 1992; *Broken Lives* (movie), 1994; *Middlemarch* (miniseries), 1994; *Open Fire* (movie), 1994; *Bliss* (movie), 1995; *It Might Be You* (movie), 1995; *My Wonderful Life,* 1996; *Only Fools and Horses ...,* 1996; *True Love* (movie), 1996; *Rules of Engagement* (movie), 1997; *The Uninvited,* 1997; *The Scold's Bride* (movie), 1998; *Shockers: Dance* (movie), 1999; *The Canterbury Tales,* 2000; *The Law* (movie), 2000; *The Russian Bride* (movie), 2000; *The Way We Live Now,* 2001; *Red Cap* (movie), 2001; *Blue Heelers,* 2002; *Red Cap,* 2003-04; *MI-5,* 2005; *The Lift* (movie), 2007; *Mansfield Park* (movie), 2007; *The Whistleblowers,* 2007; *Unforgiven,* 2009; *Outnumbered,* 2010; *Skins,* 2010; *One Night,* 2012. Film appearances include: *Salome's Last Dance,* 1988; *Dark Obsession,* 1989; *Dealers,* 1989; *Buddy's Song,* 1991; *The Trial,* 1993; *Saigon Baby,* 1995; *Hollow Reed,* 1996; *The Magic of Vincent,* 2000; *Out of Time,* 2004; *Vanity Fair,* 2004; *Scenes of a Sexual Nature,* 2006; *The Descent: Part 2,* 2009; *Robin Hood,* 2010. Stage productions as director include: *Dumb Waiter,* Oxford Playhouse, 2003; *See How They Run,* U.K. cities then West End production, 2006; *Absurdia*, Donmar Warehouse, London, 2007; *Last Easter*, Birmingham Rep, 2007; *Dimetos*, Donmar Warehouse, London, 2009.

Awards: Laurence Olivier Award for best actor in a musical, Society of London Theatre, for *La Cage aux Folles*, 2009; Antoinette Perry Award for best actor in a musical, American Theatre Wing and the Broadway League, for *La Cage aux Folles*, 2010; Drama Desk Award for outstanding actor in a musical, Drama Desk, for *La Cage aux Folles*, 2010.

Sidelights

British actor Douglas Hodge is perhaps best-known for his Tony Award-winning work in a revival of *La Cage aux Folles* as well as his first role in musical theater as Nathan Detroit in an acclaimed London production of *Guys and Dolls*. In addition, Hodge was highly regarded in the United Kingdom for his multiple appearances in plays by Harold Pinter and Shakespeare, including a well-received turn in the title role of *Titus Andronicus*. Hodge also appeared in television and film, with his best-known roles coming in such British television programs as *Capital City* and *Middlemarch*. When asked what was the biggest myth about acting by Laura Barnett of the London *Guardian*, Hodge summarized his philosophy about his craft simply: "When people go on about 'having to make brave decisions', and all that nonsense. It's not that difficult, acting."

Hodge was born on February 25, 1960, in Plymouth, England. His father was a civil service worker on the docks, while his mother was a nurse. Acting was part of his life from an early age. He told the Web site WhatsOnStage.com, "When I was a child, I was good at impersonations—teachers, friends, people on telly—and I thought that was acting. I stumbled into it accidentally from there." By the age of 14, he was doing these imitations at local working man's clubs and, later, as part of a tour of NATO bases around Europe. After winning a talent competition when he was 16, Hodge received formal acting training at the National Youth Theatre (NYT). Until he auditioned when he was 16 years old, he had not really been exposed to the theater. (Hodge remain involved with NYT as an adult, conducting a workshop every summer, directing productions featuring NYT students, and serving on its council.) Building on what he learned at NYT and its charismatic leader Michael Croft, Hodge entered the Royal Academy of Dramatic Art (RADA), though he did not complete the latter program. During his time at RADA, Hodge made the choice to become a director rather than an actor, but his plans got waylaid when he kept getting acting jobs and found it hard to tell people what to do.

Hodge's professional acting career began in the early 1980s with roles in plays in Nottingham, Birmingham, and York. In 1982, he landed roles in such Open Air Theatre productions as *The Dark Lady of the Sonnets, A Midsummer Night's Dream,* and *The Admirable Bashville*. His first big break came in the mid-1980s when he played the title role in *Coriolanus*, which eventually led to a even bigger breakout role in *King Lear*. In the 1987 production at the Olivier Theatre, Hodge played Edmund to Anthony Hopkins' Lear. In 1987, Hodge also appeared in numerous productions of Shakespeare and other plays as part of the British National Repertory Season at London's Cottesloe Theatre, Lyttelton Theatre, and Olivier Theatre.

While Hodge was establishing himself as a stage actor of note, he also worked in television and film. He made his television debut in 1985 in an episode of *Alas Smith & Jones*. Within a few years, Hodge had significant roles playing a yuppie named Declan in the 1989-90 series *Capital City*, and playing Dr. Tertius Lydgate in the 1994 adaptation of the classic nineteenth-century George Eliot novel *Middlemarch*. His idealistic Dr. Lydgate has forsaken his place in his titled family to focus on charity work and medical research in the titular town in Britain in the 1830s-set drama. Discussing the role, Hodge told Heather Neill of the *Times*, "I'd far rather play goodies than moustache-twirling villains. It's much more difficult to play people who are morally centered because they can be bland, but there is more room to invest them with mistakes, foibles, arrogances." Other noteworthy television roles for Hodge including playing Adam in the 1992 series *A Fatal Inversion* and a younger Gerald in the 1992 series *Anglo Saxon Attitudes*. Hodge's first film role came in the adaptation of Oscar Wilde's *Salome's Last Dance*, released in 1988.

Hodge continued to move between television and stage with a few film parts over the next few years. On television, he took roles in a series of movies in the mid- to late 1990s, including 1994's *Broken Lives*, the 1995 comedy *Bliss*, 1996's *True Love* and *My Wonderful Life*, 1997's *Rules of Engagement*, and 1998's *The Scold's Bride*. Throughout his career, Hodge was able to move between comedy and drama with ease, learning new skills along the way. For the 1999 dramatic movie *Shockers: Dance*, he had to learn the tango, applying the skills to playing widower Mike Swift who becomes involved with a woman who rekindles his interest in the dance but also wreaks havoc in his personal and family life.

In the 1990s, Hodge's name as an actor became linked with playwright Harold Pinter after first appearing in a 1992 production of Pinter's play *No*

Man's Land. In 1993, Hodge appeared in Pinter's *Moonlight* at the Almeida and Comedy Theatres in London, and the playwright was closely involved in the production. Pinter gave Hodge his seal of approval and Hodge was known for his respected interpretation of Pinter's characters. In 1998, Hodge appeared in three Pinter plays put on at the Donmar Warehouse Theatre: *The Collection, The Lover,* and *A Kind of Alaska.* Pinter himself was a co-star in *The Collection,* and he was present for rehearsals as well. Explaining Pinter's sometimes difficult texts, Hodge told Neill of the *Times,* "It's like playing a great piece of music, stylised and structured, but it is important not to be seduced by the enigma of it all. You have to find out what it is about and then work back to the music."

In 2000, Hodge starred in a new production of Pinter's first successful play, *The Caretaker,* at the Comedy Theatre in London. He played Aston, the brain-damaged brother of the sinister Mick. The production drew much acclaim, and Hodge himself was lauded for his pitch-perfect portrayal of Aston. Hodge's work in the role landed him a best supporting actor Laurence Olivier Theatre Award nomination in 2001. While Hodge appreciated the acclaim that playing Aston gave him, he also admitted that he thought about wanting to do television again. He told Jane Warren of the *Sunday Express,* "I tend to spend the whole time in the theatre longing to be in television, and the whole time I'm doing TV longing to be on stage. I love them both. It's the difference between a marathon runner and a sprinter. They're both running but they require totally different attitudes." Later in 2000, he returned to television with his first role as a policeman, in the movie *The Law.*

Hodge began focusing more on television in the early 2000s, with plum roles in a 2000 adaptation of *The Canterbury Tales,* and the dramatic movie *The Russian Bride* the same year. In 2001, he had a featured part in the costume drama *The Way We Live Now,* an adaptation of the satire by Anthony Trollope. Hodge played Roger Carbury, a decent, upstanding school landowner. Reviewing the series, Rob Driscoll of the *Stage* wrote, "Hodge puts in a tellingly subtle and sometimes heartbreaking performance." Other television roles of note in the early 2000s include the 2001 movie *Red Cap,* the 2003-04 series *Red Cap,* the 2007 movie *The Lift,* and the controversial 2010 series *Skins.* He also had roles in films such as the 2004 costume drama *Vanity Fair* and the 2010 version of *Robin Hood.*

But it was on the stage that Hodge began receiving the most acclaim as the first decade of the 21st century wore on. In addition to appearing in a 2003 production of Anton Chekhov's *Three Sisters,* he was nominated for *Evening Standard* Award for best actor for his work as the unfaithful drug-addicted comic Barry in *Dumbshow.* Being on a different kind of stage also added to Hodge's career. Though he had written songs since the age of 12, it was not until 2003 that he began playing gigs in his hometown of Oxford at open mic nights of folk clubs and pubs. In 2005, he released a five-song album of originals about life and love, *Cowley Road Songs,* and received much attention for it. He told the London *Telegraph's* Paul Morley, "At the clubs, I'm just known as Doug, and no one really knows that I'm an actor. That suits me fine. I don't want to be asked all the time what Ewan McGregor's like." He added, "My aim was to create something from scratch that people would get to hear without any fuss and like because they were good songs written from the heart."

Because of his singing side project, Hodge landed a role in his first musical. Director Michael Grandage had no idea the actor could sing and, after hearing his album, he cast him as Nathan Detroit in a new London production of *Guys and Dolls* in 2005. The role was made famous by Frank Sinatra and earned Hodge another Olivier Award nomination. Hodge enjoyed the fun, escapist tone of the musical, telling Morley of the *Telegraph,* "I never thought I'd end up doing show tunes, but it's the job of a life time. It's a bombshell musical, and such a pleasure to do."

After *Guys and Dolls,* Hodge returned to drama in a respected turn in the title role of Shakespeare's *Titus Andronicus* at the Globe Theatre in the summer of 2006. In 2008, Hodge had what was arguably his biggest success to date and a career-defining moment when he played Albin (and his drag queen alter ego Zaza) in a London revival of the farcical musical comedy *La Cage aux Folles.* It began its run at London's Menier Chocolate Factory before moving to the Playhouse Theatre in the West End. He won the 2009 Olivier Theatre Award for best actor for his work in the role. A revival of *La Cage aux Folles* on Broadway followed that wanted Hodge in the role, allowing him to make his Broadway debut in 2010. He won a Tony Award and Drama Desk Award and was nominated for a Drama League Award and an Outer Critics Award before the production closed. Reviews were great for Hodge's role on both sides of the Atlantic, though the actor told Kathy Henderson of the Web site Broadway.com that seeing himself in drag for the first time was "a terrible shock and disappointment," adding "In my head, I thought I looked like Audrey Hepburn, then I looked in the mirror and it was like seeing some terrible truck driver."

In addition to acting, Hodge was also a respected stage director. He directed his first play in 2003, the Oxford Playhouse production of *Dumb Waiter.* In addition to directing a triple bill of British Absurd-ist comedies at Donmar Warehouse, *Absurdia,* and *Last Easter* at Birmingham Rep, Hodge also directed a hit West End production of *See How They Run,* which toured cities in the U.K. Talking about direct-ing with WhatsOnStage.com, Hodge said "Being a director is, I think, a mixture of being able to be a showman—making sure the audience are given a wonderful evening's entertainment—and preparing the actors and the whole company to do their best work in every department."

Directing was not Hodge's only non-acting activity. He was also a passionate environmentalist and once ran for Parliament as a member of the Green Party. Hodge admitted he sometimes wanted to walk away from acting, and considered taking on other careers. He told Frances Hardy of the London *Daily Mail,* "Many times I've decided to do something else. Once I applied to be a fireman, but I didn't pass the physical tests—I think I was too old. I'm full of romantic notions; forever deciding I'll give it up. After I'd played Dr Lydgate, I decided I'd like to be a doctor, but I didn't have the right A-levels. It would have taken years to qualify. But I still wouldn't close the door on the notion of doing something else entirely."

Selected discography

Cowley Road Songs, Rightback Records, 2005.

Sources

Periodicals

Associated Press, April 18, 2010.
Birmingham Post, November 1, 1999, p. 13; October 17, 2007, p. 13.
Daily Mail (London, England), June 11, 2005, p. 20.
Daily Telegraph, June 14, 2006, p. 29.
Express, September 8, 2004, p. 30.
Houston Chronicle, April 10, 1994, p. 3.
Independent (London, England), November 12, 2000, p. 7.
New York Times, April 18, 2010, p. AR6.
Stage, November 15, 2001, p. 28.
Sunday Express, December 17, 2000, p. 67.
Sydney Morning Herald, May 18, 1998, p. 23.
This Is Oxfordshire, March 23, 2005.
Time Out, August 8, 2007, p. 117.
Times (London, England), May 30, 1992; May 11, 1998; October 30, 2000.

Online

"20 Questions With … Douglas Hodge," What'sOnStage.com, http://www.whatsonstage.com/interviews/theatre/london/E88211513.tif08275/20+Questions+With%85+Douglas+Hodge.html (November 16, 2011).
"Douglas Hodge: Actor/Voiceover," United Agents: The Literary & Talent Agency, http://unitedagents.co.uk/douglas-hodge#profile-1 (November 16, 2011).
"Douglas Hodge," Internet Movie Database, http://www.imdb.com/name/nm0388061/filmotype (November 16, 2011).
"Douglas Hodge: The Musical?," *The Telegraph,* http://www.telegraph.co.uk/culture/theatre/drama/3642935/Douglas-Hodge-the-Musical.html (November 16, 2011).
"Meet Douglas Hodge, the Breakout Star of *La Cage aux Folles,*" Broadway.com, http://www.broadway.com/shows/la-cage-aux-folles/buzz/151011/meet-douglas-hodge-the-breakout-star-of-la-cage-aux-folles/ (November 16, 2011).
"Portrait of the Artist: Douglas Hodge, Actor," *The Guardian,* http://www.guardian.co.uk/culture/2011/nov/14/portrait-of-the-artist-douglas-hodge?newsfeed=true (November 16, 2011).

—*A. Petruso*

Alice Hoffman

Author

Born March 16, 1952, in New York, NY; daughter of a teacher and social worker; married Tom Martin (a teacher and writer); children: Jake, Zack. *Education:* Adelphi University, B.A., 1973; Stanford University, M.A., 1975; additional graduate studies at State University of New York at Stony Brook.

Addresses: *Agent*—Elaine Markson Agency, 44 Greenwich Ave., New York, NY 10011. *Web site*—http://www.alicehoffman.com/.

Career

Became professional writer, 1975; published first novel, *Property Of*, 1977; wrote screenplay for *Independence Day*, 1983; co-founder of the Hoffman Breast Center, Mount Auburn Hospital in Cambridge, Massachusetts, c. 2001; published first young adult novel, *Aquamarine*, 2001; visiting research associate, Brandeis University's Women's Studies Research Center, c. 2011. Also contributed short fiction and nonfiction to the *New York Times, Redbook, Architectural Digest,* and *Gourmet*.

Sidelights

Best-selling American author Alice Hoffman was known for writing fiction which brought together fantasy and realism, and featured myths woven into everyday life. Her books sold millions of copies worldwide, included more than 100 foreign editions, and were translated into at least 20 languages. In such popular novels as *At Risk, Practical Magic, The Story Sisters,* and *The Dovekeepers,*

Hoffman often focused on domestic issues in tightly knit, well-crafted, fast-moving plots, well-blended structure, and intense imagery. Her characters survive the worst that life can throw at them and move on with only a sense of hope as a guide.

Magic and fairy tales were also important to Hoffman, and her books often incorporated magical events into every day life. She explained to Bob Hoover of the *Pittsburgh Post-Gazette,* "When I grew up, my favorite books were about magic. What you read as a child hugely influences you as a reader, as a writer, as a person. For me, magic is part of the whole literary tradition, whether it's fairy tales or folk tales or *Wuthering Heights,* which is really kind of a ghost story. Magic's all a part of the fabric of literature, and that's how I really see it."

Born on March 16, 1952, in New York City, Hoffman was raised in the suburbs on Long Island. Her mother was a teacher and social worker while her father was absent, especially after her parents divorced when she was eight. Hoffman's family life on the whole was generally unhappy, though she found solace in the film *It's a Wonderful Life* and venerated the house in which George Bailey lived. Hoffman wanted to be a veterinarian or a writer as a child, but she believed that as a girl she could not do either.

Books were thrilling to the young Hoffman. She told Hillel Italie of the Associated Press, "From the minute I could read and escape from reality, to me it was complete magic. To walk to the library, that was the biggest thrill. How cool it was picking those books, being able to escape into time." Still, she thought she would be a hairdresser or a secretary. As she told Ruth Reichl of the *New York Times*, "I didn't expect to go to college. I worked at horrible jobs. Then I decided that going to school would be easier."

While working on her undergraduate degree at Adelphi University, Hoffman found that she could write and she became interested in writing. She both read and wrote avidly. Receiving a scholarship to Stanford University to study creative writing as a graduate student, she studied with Albert Guerard, who proved to be a great influence on her. Hoffman also discovered the works of Grace Paley, who deeply affected many female writers of Hoffman's generation. Hoffman told the *New York Times'* Reichl, "Before I read her, I thought I didn't have anything to write about. I was a young woman; I had never been to war. Reading Grace Paley changed things a lot. I began to write." She was also a fan of William Faulkner and Gabriel García Márquez.

After Hoffman was granted her M.A. in 1975, she began working on a Ph.D. program at the State University of New York at Stony Brook, but dropped out because she did not like the experience. She also briefly lived in Manhattan before marrying her husband, Tom Martin, and the couple moved to Boston where he was a graduate student. Hoffman worked selling women's blouses for a time while completing her first novel. Hoffman's stint in retail was short-lived, however.

Hoffman published her first novel, *Property Of*, in 1977; it focused on a teenage girl pursuing a gang leader. Hoffman was successful from the first, with many of her novels, including *The Drowning Season* and *White Horses*, impressing critics and readers alike. As would be common throughout the course of her career, much of her fiction focused on children, death, and magical thinking. Many of her novels were set in provincial towns or suburbs in New York and Massachusetts where nearly everyone is the same but for one odd household.

As a writer, Hoffman drew on a sense of optimism which was buried under her wary pessimism. She told Italie of the Associated Press, "I feel like when I'm writing, I'm writing to make myself more optimistic. I'm also pessimistic, but I guess there

must be a kernel of complete optimism because that's what surfaces. It feels like being in a trance." Explaining herself further, Hoffman told Allen Pierleoni of the *Sacramento Bee*, "I write from such a subconscious place, it's almost like the elements of a dream. I don't understand what it means until I'm done. Sometimes I still don't understand it. That's where the readers put things together more quickly than the writer does."

Describing Hoffman's power as an author, Bill Copeland wrote in the *Sarasota Herald-Tribune*, "Alice Hoffman puts the reality of the soul into sharp perspective, each soul a memorable and individual entity, each with its own claim to the granted gift of life. You can't just read Alice Hoffman—you join her in a verbal vortex of enlightenment and extension."

Early in her career, Hoffman also wrote screenplays, though only one was made. She wrote the screenplay for 1983's *Independence Day*, which starred Kathleen Quinlan, David Keith, and Dianne Weist, and focused on spousal abuse. She later wrote screenplays with her teacher husband, though none were made.

After Hoffman began having children in the late 1980s, she felt her books changed as she had and her early novels had been written by someone else. The first book she wrote after her first son was born was *Illumination Night*. The novel focused on a character named Vonny who had agoraphobia, drawing on details that perhaps came from the author's own struggles with panic attacks.

Hoffman's sixth novel received much attention because it was controversial. Published in 1988, *At Risk* focused on an eleven-year-old girl with AIDS and how her family and the town she lives in reacts to her. The medical aspects of the disease were not highlighted, nor was there any type of death scene though the girl was slowly dying of AIDS-related illnesses. Hoffman wrote it just after the birth of her second son and she pondered how she would react to her boys being in school with a child with AIDS.

While *At Risk* was a Book of the Month Club selection, it was given mixed, if not hostile reviews. While the AIDS crisis was new, the author still expressed surprise by the reaction. She told Jill Lai of the United Press International, "It's interesting to me that not from my readers, not from any kind of political organizations, or gay organizations, but from some reviewers there has been a strange response, as if AIDS was not fit literary material for some reason. I don't understand it because I think that's the whole job of a fiction writer, to bring issues [to the reader's attention]."

Hoffman continued to write and publish best sellers in the 1990s and early 2000s. Each was challenging and unique. In 1994, she published *Second Nature,* about a woman who takes a man raised by wolves into her home on a lark and hides him from authorities. She teaches the man about civilization and falls in love with him. Hoffman sold the movie rights to Twentieth-Century Fox for one million dollars. A number of her novels were optioned for film.

Also optioned for film was 1995's *Practical Magic,* which focused on a pair of spinster witches. In the first section, all that goes wrong in a small Massachusetts town is blamed on these spinster witch sisters, yet some women seek them out for their special love potion. The witches have two nieces, Sally and Gillian, who vow as children not to let passion ruin their lives, but cannot live that way as adults, leading to tragedy. *Practical Magic* was adapted into a film starring Sandra Bullock and released in 1998.

Another acclaimed novel was 1997's *Here on Earth.* It took five years to write, and was a contemporary twist on the classic novel *Wuthering Heights,* set in Massachusetts. Hoffman consciously based the book on the Emily Bronte novel, and Hoffman thought it was more deep, disturbing, intense, and complicated than her previous books. Also in 1997, Hoffman published her first children's novel, *Fireflies,* which focused on a young boy lost on a snowy mountain. She asked her young son Zack for help in writing and editing the book. She told Erica Noonan of the Associated Press Online, "A lot of kids' books written by adults don't seem like kids' books. There's not child's point of view, not a kid's pacing. I wanted it to feel like a kid's book."

In 1998, Hoffman was diagnosed with breast cancer. As she underwent treatment and therapy, she wrote the novel *The River King* which was published in 2000. Writing the best-selling book provided her a sense of healing. Hoffman also founded the Hoffman Breast Center at Mount Auburn Hospital in Cambridge, Massachusetts, after her recovery. She told Pierleoni of the *Sacramento Bee,* "Whenever you have a life-threatening illness, there's a sense of a life before and a life after. I've certainly lost many people who I loved. I try my best to learn from other people who have managed to go forward, despite incredible loss in their lives. It's astounding what people are able to do."

In addition to writing children's books and novels for adults, Hoffman also ventured into young adult novels. Her first was *Aquamarine.* It was published in 2001 and focused on friendships among teenage girls. It was adapted into a film that was released in 2006. Other important adult books published in the early 2000s included 2003's *The Probable Future* and 2005's *The Ice Queen.* In 2007, she published *Skylight Confessions* which centered on a family after a young mother dies of cancer leaving her husband to cope with their two small children.

Hoffman put out another significant novel in 2009, *The Story Sisters.* Centering on three siblings, one of the sisters, Elv, invents a magical land to which she often escapes as a way of coping with family traumas. She shares stories of the demons and faeries that live there, and their language, with her sisters. The sisters speak in the secret language, which bonds and yet isolates them from the outside world. The novel follows the sisters from childhood to teen years and into young adulthood, marriage, and parenthood. It features themes like survival, betrayal, revenge, and loyalty. Subsequent works of fiction were set in the past, including 2010's *The Red Garden* and 2011's *The Dovekeepers.* The latter novel was concerned with the mass suicide at Masada in Israel during a first-century Roman siege.

Over the years, Hoffman's books were influenced by the various places she has lived and visited (including Masada), the books she read, films she saw, and the women she knew, especially her mother and grandmother. Their support was key to her success. Hoffman told Michele Dorgan of the Cox News Service, "My grandmother was extremely important in my writing life. She believed in me. She supported me, and I'm convinced all you really need is one person to believe in you."

Selected writings

Novels

Property Of, Straus (New York City), 1977.
The Drowning Season, Dutton (New York City), 1979.
Angel Landing, Putnam (New York City), 1980.
White Horses, Putnam, 1982.
Fortune's Daughter, Putnam, 1985.
Illumination Night, Putnam, 1987.
At Risk, Putnam, 1988.
Seventh Heaven, Putnam, 1990.
Turtle Moon, Berkley (New York City), 1993.
Second Nature, Putnam, 1995.
Practical Magic, Putnam, 1995.
Here on Earth, Putnam, 1997.

The River King, Putnam, 2000.
Blue Diary, Putnam, 2001.
The Probable Future, Doubleday (New York City), 2003.
The Ice Queen, Little, Brown (New York City), 2005.
Skylight Confessions, Little, Brown, 2007.
The Third Angel, Shaye Areheart (New York City), 2008.
The Story Sisters, Shaye Areheart, 2009.
The Dovekeepers, Scribner (New York City), 2011.

Short-story collections

Local Girls, Putnam, 1999.

Novels

Blackbird House, Doubleday, 2004.
The Red Garden, Shaye Areheart, 2010.

Young adult novels

Aquamarine, Scholastic (New York City), 2001.
Indigo, Scholastic, 2002.
The Foretelling, Little, Brown, 2005.
Incantation, Little, Brown, 2006.
Green Witch, Scholastic, 2010.

Children's books

Fireflies, Hyperion (New York City), 1997.
Horsefly, Hyperion, 2000.
(With Wolfe Martin) *Moondog*, Scholastic, 2004.

Sources

Associated Press, July 21, 1995.
Associated Press Online, November 6, 1997.
Cox News Service, November 6, 2002.
Hollywood Reporter, March 9, 2004.
Newsweek, August 1, 1988, p. 52.
New York Times, February 10, 1994, p. C1.
Ottawa Citizen, July 12, 2009, p. B1.
Pittsburgh Post-Gazette, January 21, 2007, p. F1; January 23, 2011, p. E5.
Sacramento Bee, January 29, 2007, p. E1; June 8, 2009, p. D1.
Sarasota Herald-Tribune (FL), November 16, 1996, p. 14E.
Star Tribune, October 2, 2011, p. 12E.
United Press International, July 29, 1988.
Washington Post, October 5, 2011, p. C4.

—*A. Petruso*

Freeman Hrabowski

President of the University of Maryland, Baltimore County

Carrie Devorah/WENN/CD1/newscom

Born Freeman Alphonsa Hrabowski III, August 13, 1950, in Birmingham, AL; son of Freeman (a teacher) and Maggie (a teacher) Hrabowski; married Jacqueline Coleman, 1970; children: Eric. *Education:* Hampton Institute, Hampton, VA, B.S., 1970; University of Illinois, Urbana-Champaign, IL, M.S., 1971, Ph.D., 1975 .

Addresses: *Office*—President, University of Maryland-Baltimore County, 1000 Hilltop Circle, Baltimore, MD 21250.

Career

Math instructor, University of Illinois, 1972-73; assistant dean for student services, University of Illinois, Urbana-Champaign, 1974-76; associate dean, Alabama A & M University, 1976-77; as dean of arts and sciences, Coppin State College, 1977-81, then vice-president for academic affairs, 1981-87; vice provost, University of Maryland, Baltimore County, 1987-90, then executive vice president, 1990-92, named interim president, 1992, president, 1993—. Author of books and articles including: *Beating the Odds: Raising Academically Successful African American Males*, Oxford University Press, 1998; *Overcoming the Odds: Raising Academically Successful African American Females*, Oxford University Press, 2002.

Member: American Academy of Arts and Sciences; American Philosophical Society; advisory council, Florence Crittenton Services Inc.; board of trustees, Baltimore City Life Museums; board of directors, American Council on Education; board of directors, Constellation Energy; board of directors, Baltimore Community Foundation; board of directors, McCormick & Company; board of directors, Mercantile Safe Deposit & Trust Company; board of directors, Merrick & France Foundation; board of directors, Suburban Maryland High-Technology Council; board of directors, Carnegie Foundation for the Advancement of Teaching; board of directors, Corvis Corporation; board of directors, Center Stage; board of directors, Joint Center for Political and Economic Development; board of directors, the Baltimore Equitable Society; board of directors, Maryland Humanities Council; board of directors, Alfred P. Sloan Foundation; board of directors, the Urban Institute; board of directors, chair, Marguerite Casey Foundation.

Awards: Scholarship for Study Abroad, American University, Cairo, Egypt, 1968-1969; Phi Delta Kappa, University of Illinois, Urbana-Champaign, 1971; Presidential Award for Excellence in Science, Mathematics, and Engineering Mentoring, National Science Foundation, 1996; BETA Award, GBC Technology Council, 1998; Marylander of the Year, *Sun*, 1999; Harold W. McGraw Jr. Prize, McGraw-Hill, 2001; Edward Bouchet Leadership Award in Minority Graduate Education, Yale University, 2002; one of the "10 Best College Presidents," *Time*, 2009; Theodore M. Hesburgh Award, TIAA-CREF, 2011; Outstanding Alumni Award, Hampton Institute, Baltimore Chapter; Outstanding Community Service Award, Tuskegee University; Education Achievement Award, National Science Foundation; Teachers College Medal for Distinguished Service, Columbia University.

Sidelights

An academic prodigy who earned his doctorate degree at the age of just 24, Freeman A. Hrabowski has dedicated much of his career to transforming the Baltimore County campus of the University of Maryland into a place where "it's cool to be smart" even among minority students more traditionally thought to excel at sports rather than math and science. "When most people see young black men walking across a campus," he told Chuck Salter of *Fast Company,* "they think, 'There goes the basketball team.' We want them to think, 'There goes the chemistry honors society.'" Under Hrabowski's leadership, the school has become as one the nation's strongest sources of African-American doctorates in math, science, and engineering through its respected Meyerhoff Scholarship Program. Since he became the campus's head in 1993, Hrabowski has earned nods as one of the United States' best college presidents from such publications as *Time* and *U.S. News & World Report* thanks to his efforts to encourage low-income and minority students to achieve rigorous academic goals.

Born Freeman Alphonsa Hrabowski III on August 13, 1950, in Birmingham, Alabama, the college president is himself the son of two teachers, Freeman and Maggie Hrabowski. The Hrabowskis valued education and challenged their son to strive for academic excellence. He met that goal by skipping two grades to enter high school at just 12 years old. As a child, Hrabowski was also attracted to the civil rights movement, taking part in anti-segregation demonstrations led by Dr. Martin Luther King, Jr. Along with a group of other young demonstrators, Hrabowski was arrested and jailed for his involvement with this Children's Crusade. "The lesson I learned from that experience," Hrabowski recalled to Michael Wamble of the Arlington Heights, Illinois *Daily Herald,* "is that even children can make choices." Supported by King's encouraging words and the presence of their parents outside the jail, the group emerged from jail nearly a week later as civil rights heroes. Later, the educator was featured in filmmaker Spike Lee's 1997 documentary *Four Little Girls* about the 1963 bombing of a Birmingham church.

After graduating from high school at the age of 15, Hrabowski enrolled at the Hampton Institute (now Hampton University) in Hampton, Virginia, to study mathematics. Despite an initial struggle to overcome expectations that he would not excel due to his race and background, the young scholar graduated with honors in 1970. He then continued his education at the University of Illinois at Urbana-Champaign, where he completed a master's degree in 1971 and a doctorate in higher education administration and statistics in 1975. During his graduate studies, Hrabowski founded a tutoring program for minority students. Partially on the strength of this program, he served as an assistant dean of student services for the university from 1974 to 1976, overseeing the lower-income and minority-focused support programs Project Upward Bound and the Educational Opportunities Program. He then briefly returned to Alabama to teach statistics at Alabama A&M University, where he also served as associate dean for graduate studies, before accepting a position as mathematics professor and dean of arts and sciences at Baltimore's Coppin State College. There, he soon advanced to become the institution's vice president for academic affairs.

Hrabowski remained at Coppin State until 1987, when he became the vice provost of the University of Maryland Baltimore County (UMBC). The following year he co-founded his signature initiative, the Meyerhoff Scholarship Program, in affiliation with the Robert and Jane Meyerhoff Foundation. Intended at first to support African-American men in the study of engineering and the sciences, the program quickly expanded to reach high-achieving male and female students of all races. The intensive program begins with a summer session to reinforce or introduce the math and science skills that low-income public high schools have often not provided in order to prepare students for undergraduate work. Meyerhoff Scholars then strive to attain high grades over the next four years, helping propel many of them—including traditionally underrepresented African-American students—to graduate work in the hard sciences and technology. Twenty years after its creation, the Meyerhoff program had graduated more than 600 science and engineering majors, paving the way for nearly 70 of them to achieve doctoral degrees. "Freeman is one of the rare figures who has single-handedly turned around a major institution," commented Amherst College president Anthony Marx to Kim Clark of *U.S. News & World Report* in 2008. "Along the way, he has taught all of higher education that minority and low-income students can and should be held to the highest standards, and can meet those standards and excel."

The influence of the Meyerhoff Scholarship Program has resonated throughout the UMBC campus. After Hrabowski became the university's president in 1993, he worked to foster an environment conducive to the study of mathematics, science, and engineering through such unconventional actions as refusing to field a football team in favor of supporting a championship chess team. Those efforts are increasingly attracting diverse, academically driven students to Hrabowski's "honors university," which might otherwise be simply a small commuter campus within the University of Maryland system. More than 40 percent of UMBC graduates complete a degree in the sciences, helping the university establish a growing reputation as a powerhouse in the field; U.S. News & World Report, for example, gave the institution a nod as the top "Up and Coming" campus in the United States in both 2009 and 2010. Nonetheless, Hrabowski has stated his intentions of developing the university's academic programs as a whole rather than focusing rigidly on math and science. "I often say to people that yes, over half of our students are in science fields, but the other half are in arts," he told Gilbert Cruz of Time in 2009. "We're working to build a university that has first-rate research across all disciplines."

Along with his work at UMBC, Hrabowski is active in numerous educational, corporate, and non-profit organizations. He has been a consultant to the National Science Foundation, the National Institutes of Health, and the National Academies, among other educational institutions. Hrabowski has also sat on the board of directors of the Constellation Energy Group, McCormick & Company, the Baltimore Equitable Society, the Carnegie Foundation for the Advancement of Teaching, the Maryland Humanities Council, the France-Merrick Foundation, the Alfred P. Sloan Foundation, the Urban Institute, and the Marguerite Casey Foundation.

Selected writings

(With others) Beating the Odds: Raising Academically Successful African American Males, Oxford University Press, 1998.

Overcoming the Odds: Raising Academically Successful African American Women, Oxford University Press, 2002.

Sources

Books

American Men & Women of Science, vol. 3, 27th ed., Gale, 2010, pp. 936-37.
Contemporary Black Biography, vol. 22, Gale, 1999, pp. 94-97.
Who's Who Among African Americans, 19th ed., Gale, 2006, pp. 603-04.

Periodicals

Daily Herald (Arlington Heights, IL), January 18, 2005, p. 9.
Fast Company, April 2002, p. 34.

Online

"The 10 Best College Presidents: Freeman Hrabowski," Time, http://www.time.com/time/specials/packages/article/0,28804,1937938_1937933_1937920,00.html (March 1, 2011).
"America's Best Leaders: Freeman Hrabowski, University of Maryland-Baltimore County," U.S. News & World Report, http://www.usnews.com/news/best-leaders/articles/2008/11/19/americas-best-leaders-freeman-hrabowski-university-of-maryland-baltimore-county (March 1, 2011).
"Freeman A. Hrabowski, III," University of Maryland Baltimore County, http://www.umbc.edu/aboutumbc/president/index.php (March 1, 2011).

—Vanessa E. Vaughn

Ben Huh

© Charles Sykes/AP Images

Internet entrepreneur

Born c. 1978, in South Korea; married to Emily. *Education:* Graduated from Northwestern University, 1999.

Addresses: *Office*—Cheezburger Network, 190 Queen Anne Ave. N., Ste. 310, Seattle, WA 98109. *Web site*—http://www.benhuh.com/; http://cheezburger.com/sites.

Career

Interned at newspapers while attending Northwestern University, c. late 1990s; employed at a newspaper, c. 1999; joined a dotcom, c. 2000; founded analytics Web site, c. 2001; worked in tech industry, c. 2001-07; acquired I Has Cheezburger blog, 2007; attracted venture capital funding for his company, Pet Holdings, Inc., 2011.

Sidelights

Internet entrepreneur Ben Huh is responsible for the exponential growth of such humor Web sites as I Can Has Cheezburger?, FAIL Blog, and The Daily What, showing how profitable such Web sites can be. The chief executive officer of the parent company to these blogs, Huh originally bought I Can Has Cheezburger? from its founders and grew the already successful company into an online empire. Drawing on popular concepts from the Internet, Huh and his staff would start a Web site or buy a Web site that focused on humorous content. Profitability also came from books and merchandising. Of his success, Huh told Brian Raferty of *Wired*, "I think

we're looking at a whole new generation of entertainment. It's not mainstream in any way, shape, or form, but it's becoming so."

Huh was born around 1978 in South Korea, and was raised in Hong Kong, where he attended Hong Kong International School while his father worked on the Hong Kong-Zhuhai bridge. After three and a half years, he and his family moved to Sacramento, California, where he became interested in publishing from an early age. By the time he was in high school, he was in charge of the school's yearbook and newspaper. He also tried and failed to start a radio station.

Studying journalism at Northwestern University, Huh interned at several newspapers. After earning his degree in 1999, he worked at a paper for some time but decided he needed to take his career in a new direction. As he explained to Kavita Daswani of the *South China Morning Post*, "although I worked for a newspaper, unlike most people I would get my news from the internet, reading off the wires. I found a paradox in my own behavior and decided this internet thing would be a lot more interesting. I was doing great in my job but decided I would take a risk."

Despite his career change, Huh retained a love of the profession of journalism, telling James Temple of the *San Francisco Chronicle,* "journalism to me is very, very fascinating, and I am constantly reading up on the life of journalists and the industry. I can't help but have a distinct notion that journalism is more vibrant today than ever before. There are more voices."

Huh took a post at a dotcom, but quit after seven months. He then launched an analytics startup Web site which went under several months later. He told Brian Raferty of *Wired,* "It was an abysmal failure. I hired too many people. I didn't raise enough money. We didn't actually have a product." Huh then took jobs in the tech industry, working variously at an Internet-radio startup and at a company that installed software. He and his wife also had a popular pet news blog called Itchmo, which led him to his next venture.

The I Can Has Cheezburger? Web site was founded in January of 2007 by Eric Nakagawa, a Hawaiian-based software developer, and his girlfriend Kari Unebasami. The Web site and its name had their origins in a photo Unebasami found on the Internet of a smiling cat with the caption "I Can Has Cheezburger?" Inspired by the humor, the couple decided to start a blog under that name. They began first with that photo, and soon added more photos of animals with funny captions. Within seven months, Nakagawa was selling ads for $500 to $4,000 per week for the blog, and was earning $5,600 per month for himself.

Nakagawa was a reader of Huh's blog, and linked to an Itchmo post from his blog in May 2007. Because of the increased traffic, Huh's site crashed. Once he understood why and began corresponding to Nakagawa, Huh learned about the success and continual growth of I Can Has Cheezburger. Huh soon began to talk to Nakagawa about buying the blog. For his part, Nakagawa was exhausted and burned out by the rapid growth of the blog.

Huh had to find investors first, and he assured them they could make money. He told Farhad Manjoo of *Slate Magazine,* "The pitch was that this was about humor and not all about cats. It's a lot about cats—but there was more opportunity there. People were like, So, are you going to create a dog site and a chicken site and a giraffe site? I was like, It's entirely possible that we may go into hippos, but it's more likely that we'll branch into something else." Nakagawa sold the blog to Huh and his investors in September of 2008 for $2.5 million. (Huh himself contributed $10,000.)

By May of 2008, the Web site was one of the most popular in the world, with 15 million unique versions. It garnered two million page views and 8,000 submissions per day in April of 2008; by October, it was 5.5 million hits per day. Most of the content on I Can Has Cheezburger? was added by its visitors, who created, submitted, and voted on Lolcats. (Lolcats are captioned photos of cats with character in different settings.) Each user could add their own caption to every photograph. The site also generated its own type of language known as Lolspeak or Kitty Pidgin, in which certain words are spelled in their own unique fashion. For example, Sunday could be "bunday," while human could be "hooman." As the Web site grew, news and objects were also added to the mix, so not all the humor was cute-focused and there was room for satire and more sophisticated jokes.

Explaining the humor of the Lolcats, Tom Cox of the London *Times* wrote, "The best cheezburger photo-caption combinations manage to sum up a dumb deviousness that's quintessentially feline (a ginger kitten on its hind legs, captioned with 'I baked you a cookie ... but I eated it.') or convey the sense that, in their hearts, cats believe they can outperform human beings at their own tasks (a cat on a dashboard, accompanied by 'GPS cat sez you lost.')" Cox added, "The genius of the site is managing to be mainstream yet making its users feel as if they are part of an exclusive club. The childish language is often mistaken for the textspeak of Generation Y, but its appeal goes far beyond millennials."

By late 2008, Huh added several sister humor Web sites, which were receiving a total of 6.3 million users per month. His parent company for all the Web sites, Pet Holdings, Inc., looked at what topics and areas of interest seemed to have a universal, long-term appeal, and either bought sites or built sites that met this criteria. The sister sites included FAIL Blog, which focused on stunning flops, while Engrish Funny featured signs that were poorly translated. GraphJam had users who created PowerPoint-like slides about life. Once Upon a Win focused on nostalgia by cataloging trends and fads from the past.

In this time period, the original Web site released its first book, also named *I Can Has Cheezburger: A LOLcat Colleckshun.* It became a best-seller on specialized lists at both Amazon.com and the *New York Times.* The book sold more than 100,000 copies. Huh's company published more books on a regular basis, based on all the Web sites. He had also had a best-seller with the second I Can Has Cheezburger book. Other titles include *I Has a Hot Dog.*

While some believed the I Can Has Cheezburger phenomenon might fade over time, the Web site only continued to grow under Huh's guidance. Traffic increased, and by the spring of 2009, the Web site had one million unique users per month. He also added new sites, like Tofulater, which allowed users to add captions to YouTube videos; That Will Buff Out, which focused on cars with problems; and Pundit Kiching, which focused on politics. All of the sites had a total of at least 5.5 million users per day, and generated millions in revenues. Huh's company was profitable because of its combination of advertising; merchandising, including calendars and a line of greeting cards; licensing; and publications. Huh told Manjoo of *Slate Magazine*, "That's the most interesting thing about this job— when people find out how big we are. They're like, Cheezburger's yours, and Failblog, holy crap! And then they're like, It's more than just you? They don't understand the scale of this. It's a proper sweatshop."

By early 2010, Huh's company had 30 aggregate sites that had 200 million page views per month. I Can Has Cheezburger alone had 18,000 images from readers submitted each day. He continued to actively find more ideas for sites, and had 150 ideas in development and 1,000 registered domain names. He and his staff continued to look at many pictures and videos on the Internet to see if humor trends could be spotted that might have long-term profitability. But even after launching a Web site or blog, Huh and his staff were not afraid to pull the plug if it did not attract enough users. Focusing on primarily user-generated content was a key to success, according to Huh. He told Brian Raferty of *Wired*, "I used to want to create memes more. But what's more satisfying: playing on the playground or building a playground for a bunch of people to enjoy? I'm much more the person who'd rather build it. That brings me satisfaction."

In 2011, Huh and his company reached new heights when Pet Holdings, Inc., the parent company of I Has Cheezburger and its sister sites, received $30 million in venture capital funding from the Foundry Group, Madrona Venture Group, and Avalon Ventures. The influx of capital allowed the company to double its staff, expand its international audience, gave Huh the freedom to take more risks and be more experimental in finding the next big thing,

and introduce other improvements. The extra funds also allowed the company to provide more content to users. By this time, the Cheezburger network of 45 Web sites had 16.5 million visitors monthly who generated 375 million page views. More than 500,000 photos and videos were uploaded monthly by users.

Huh believed the market for his type of product would only continue to grow. He told Rob Walker of the *New York Times Magazine*, "What interested me the most was there's this entire community of people devoted to following the rules and the system behind the framework of Lolcats. No one ever said, 'These are the rules.' But everybody said, 'I know the rules.'"

Of his philosophy toward his business, Huh explained to Michael Learmonth of *Advertising Age*, "We're just going through the process of creating content that makes people happy for just a few minutes a day. We are not trying to be a TV network; we're not trying to be a big media company. We are growing small things that are gathering loyal audiences. When you show up and you want to laugh or take a break from your daily work, then we have this little blog for you. You go, load the page, you scroll, and you're done."

Sources

Advertising Age, October 12, 2009, p. 3.
Austin American-Statesman, December 17, 2009, p. D1.
ComputerWorld, May 24, 2010.
Denver Post, January 18, 2011, p. B5.
Guardian (London, England), January 22, 2011, p. 41.
Guardian Unlimited (London, England), May 19, 2008.
New York Times, July 21, 2007, p. C5; April 18, 2009, p. B1; June 14, 2010, p. B1.
New York Times Magazine, July 18, 2010, p. 38.
Observer (England), March 9, 2008, p. 16.
San Francisco Chronicle, October 28, 2009, p. C1.
Slate Magazine, March 20, 2009.
South China Morning Post, August 1, 2010, p. 11.
Times (London, England), October 21, 2008, p. 6.
USA Today, November 25, 2008, p. 6D.
Wired, July 2008, p. 98; February 2010, p. 52.
Wireless News, April 8, 2008.

—A. Petruso

Nikki M. James

Actress

Born Nikki Michelle James, June 3, 1981, in Summit, NJ. *Education:* New York University, bachelor's degree.

Addresses: *Agent*—Abrams Artists Agency, 275 Seventh Ave., 26th Flr., New York, NY 10001.

Career

Appeared in commercials and walk-on roles, 1990s. Actress on stage, including: *Adventures of Tom Sawyer*, 2001; *All Shook Up*, 2005; *Bernanda Alba*, 2006; *The Wiz*, 2006; *Walmartopia*, 2007; *Romeo and Juliet*, Stratford Shakespeare Festival, 2008; *Caesar and Cleopatra*, Stratford Shakespeare Festival, 2008; *The Book of Mormon*, 2011—. Film appearances include: *Pizza*, 2005; *Caesar and Cleopatra*, 2009. Television appearances include: *Third Watch*, 2001; *The Jury*, 2004; *Law & Order: Criminal Intent*, 2003, 2009; *The Lot*, 2007; *30 Rock*, 2010.

Awards: Tony Award for best featured actress in a musical, American Theatre Wing/Broadway League, for *Book of Mormon*, 2011.

Sidelights

Actress Nikki M. James built her career through assorted film, television, and stage parts before breaking out to major success as a cast member of the comedic Broadway musical *Book of Mormon*. James' portrayal of Nabulungi won critical raves for both her acting and singing talents as well as gar-

nering her a Tony award in June of 2011. By that time, James had been performing for nearly 20 years, advancing from walk-on parts in soap operas and commercials as a young teen to making her Broadway debut in the short-lived musical *Adventures of Tom Sawyer* in the spring of 2001. She has also appeared in the Broadway production of *All Shook Up*, a 2006 revival of *The Wiz*, and as a lead performer in two plays at the 2008 Stratford Shakespeare Festival.

The performer was born Nikki Michelle James on June 3, 1981, in Summit, New Jersey, to a Haitian immigrant mother and a St. Vincentian immigrant father. She grew up in Livingston, not far from New York City. From a young age, James was attracted to reading and theater, making her performance debut singing the Whitney Houston song "Greatest Love of All" at her kindergarten graduation. Inspired by the aunt of a close friend who had a professional stage career, James told her mother that she wanted to be an actress even before she reached her teens. The 12-year-old James used money earned from babysitting to have head shots taken and soon—much to the surprise of her parents—found an agent. Before long, James had landed small roles in commercials and soap operas, fitting in filming after school. By the time she was 14 years old, James had enough experience to qualify for membership in the Actors' Equity Association. "I never, ever believed that I couldn't accomplish it as a young kid," James recalled to Mark Kennedy in a story published on the ABC News Web site. "It didn't occur to me that I was going to audition for jobs that I wouldn't get. I didn't know that it was difficult. And thank goodness, because it is hard. But I keep that little girl around with me a lot because she's much more brave than I am."

After graduating from high school, James began studying musical theater at New York University's prestigious Tisch School of the Arts. During the summer of 2000, she auditioned for the Broadway musical *Adventures of Tom Sawyer,* based on the Mark Twain novel of the same name, and was cast in the supporting role of Sabina Temple. To accommodate her rehearsal schedule, James took a semester off school, convinced that the show would be a great success. Despite high expectations, the musical closed less than three weeks after opening in April of 2001, failing to find an audience and suffering from what reviewers such as *Back Stage*'s Victor Gluck called its "pleasant and inoffensive, bland and uninspired" presentation. "It was a really interesting experience because, for all intents and purposes, it was a flop, a big flop," James told Andrew Gans of *Playbill.* "And so, that was a hard lesson to learn. I was 19 years old, and I thought I was going to be in this big Broadway show, and we closed two-and-a-half weeks after we opened." Undeterred, James returned to NYU and continued her degree work.

Over the next decade, James appeared in roles on both the big and small screens. In 2001, she had a two-episode arc on the television crime drama *Third Watch.* Two years later, she appeared on an episode of *Law & Order: Criminal Intent.* In 2005, she made her silver-screen debut in a small role in the comedy *Pizza.* Another stint on *Law & Order* and a guest spot in the NBC comedy *30 Rock* followed in 2009 and 2010, respectively.

James' greatest successes came in live theatrical performance. In 2005, she returned to Broadway in the musical production *All Shook Up.* The following year, she appeared in the off-Broadway musical *Bernanda Alba.* Although the production received only mediocre reviews overall, *Variety*'s David Rooney noted that James' Adela was "spirited and passionate." Later in 2006, James crossed to the West Coast to take on the role of Dorothy in the La Jolla Playhouse revival of *The Wiz. Variety*'s Bob Verini applauded James, declaring, "Any 'Wizard of Oz'

stands or falls on its Dorothy, and this production has both a Dorothy and a Toto for the ages. With the voice of an angel and strong acting chops, Nikki M. James is no weepy Nellie, but a confident young lady with good sense." A co-starring turn in the 2007 off-Broadway production of *Walmartopia* followed next.

In 2008, James helped open the Canadian Stratford Shakespeare Festival as a co-star in the classic Shakespeare play *Romeo and Juliet.* Later that summer, she appeared opposite Christopher Plummer in a festival production of the George Bernard Shaw comedy *Caesar and Cleopatra.* Critics were unenthusiastic about her performance as Juliet, with *Variety*'s Richard Ouzounian bemoaning the lack of chemistry between Gareth Potter's Romeo and James' Juliet, and sighing that "there's nothing in the thesp's training or resume to suggest she should be playing a major Shakespearean lead on the mainstage of one of the primary classical theaters in North America." However, her portrayal of Cleopatra garnered stronger notices. In a *Variety* review of *Caesar and Cleopatra,* Ouzounian applauded James' performance, noting, "she's grown a lot as an actress since [*Romeo and Juliet*] and also seems far more comfortable as a Shavian minx than as a Shakespearean heroine." The following year, a filmed version of a live performance of *Caesar and Cleopatra* enjoyed a limited cinema and DVD release.

The performer next returned to Broadway in the musical *Book of Mormon.* Created by *South Park* writers Trey Parker and Matt Stone, the show follows the adventures of two Mormon missionaries who travel to Uganda. James, as Nabulungi, played the daughter of a local chief who becomes interested in the religion as a way to escape from her difficult surroundings—only to receive a much-revised retelling of the Mormon scripture from one of the less knowledgeable missionaries in one of the show's signature numbers, "Joseph Smith American Moses." From early in its development, *Book of Mormon* received attention both for the notoriety of its creators and its potentially controversial subject matter. "I didn't worry about being offensive to Mormons," James explained to Simi Horowitz of *Back Stage.* "I was more concerned with the picture of Africans.... I was concerned with taking cheap shots at serious issues: baby rape, female circumcision, the AIDS epidemic. But some of the most interesting ways to deal with difficult subjects is by laughing at them," she concluded. The show opened to strong critical notices in March of 2011 and quickly became one of the leading musicals on Broadway. The following June, James was recognized for her performance with a Tony Award for

Best Featured Actress in a Musical. The actress expressed surprise and delight at her win, but noted that performing remained the best reward. "If I hadn't won this award tonight, doing my show every night is gift enough," she commented to Barbara Chai of *Wall Street Journal* just after her win.

Sources

Periodicals

Back Stage, May 11, 2001, p. 45; March 17, 2011, p. 12.
New York Times, May 13, 2011.
Variety, March 7, 2006, p. 5; October 16, 2006, p. 71; September 10, 2007, p. 96; June 2, 2008, p. 45; August 25, 2008, p. 90.

Online

"Diva Talk: Chatting with *Book of Mormon*'s Nikki M. James," *Playbill,* http://www.playbill.com/celebritybuzz/article/148048-DIVA-TALK-Chatting-with-Book-of-Mormons-Nikki-M-James (August 24, 2011).
"Nikki M. James on Her Tony Win for *The Book of Mormon*," *Wall Street Journal,* http://blogs.wsj.com/speakeasy/2011/06/13/nikki-james-on-her-tony-win-for-the-book-of-mormon/ (August 24, 2011).
"Star Rising: Nikki James of *The Book of Mormon*," ABC News, http://abcnews.go.com/Entertainment/wireStory?id=13619703.tif (August 24, 2011).

—Vanessa E. Vaughn

Clinton Kelly and Stacy London

Courtesy of TLC

Television hosts

Kelly: Born February 22, 1969, in Panama City, Panama. London: Born May 25, 1969, in New York, NY; daughter of Herbert (a social critic) and Joy (a venture capitalist) London. *Education:* Kelly: Boston College, B.S., 1991; Northwestern University, M.A., 1993. London: Vassar College, B.A.

Addresses: *Web site*—http://tlc.howstuffworks. com/tv/what-not-to-wear. *Web site*—http:// clintonkelly.com/.

Career

Kelly: Freelance journalist, 1990s; television presenter, Q2, 1990s; editor, *Marie Claire*, 1990s; senior editor, *Mademoiselle*, 1990s; executive editor, *Daily News Record*, early 2000s. London: Editorial assistant, *Vogue*, early 1990s; fashion stylist, 1990s—; host, *Fashionably Late with Stacy London*, 2007. Both: co-host, *What Not to Wear*, TLC, 2003—.

Sidelights

Best known as the hosts of long-running TLC fashion makeover reality program *What Not to Wear*, Clinton Kelly and Stacy London are fashion stylists, authors, and brand spokespersons as well as television personalities. Armed with trained eyes and sharps wits, the pair has guided numerous women to abandon outdated, inappropriate, or simply bland clothing choices in favor of modern, flattering looks. Both former magazine editors, Kelly and London co-authored the 2005 style manual *Dress Your Best: The Complete Guide to Finding the Style*

That's Right for Your Body. Each host has also engaged in a collection of solo activities. Along with acting as a spokesman for Macy's and launching a clothing line through QVC, Kelly has penned two additional lifestyle books—2008's *Freakin' Fabulous: How to Dress, Speak, Behave, Eat, Drink, Entertain, Decorate, and Generally Be Better than Everyone Else* and 2010's *Oh No She Didn't: The Top 100 Style Mistakes Women Make and How to Avoid Them*—while London has signed on as a spokesperson for brands including Pantene and Woolite and hosted her own small-screen programs, including 2007's *Fashionably Late with Stacy London*.

Before becoming television hosts, both Kelly and London built independent careers in the fashion industry. London was born on May 25, 1969, in New York, New York, and grew up in Manhattan. At the age of four, London was diagnosed with the skin disease psoriasis. Her childhood battle with the disease helped prepare the personality for her role as a professional critic on *What Not To Wear*. Speaking to Jocelyn Vena of *OK!* in 2007, London explained that using humor to accept her disease "made me constructively critical of other people. I know what's cruel and what isn't.... [T]here were people who could laugh with me and make fun of having a disorder with me, that I loved because I got it. I got the fact that they were accepting of me even when they were joking with me, and that's different than somebody being cruel." London eventually learned to manage the condition, but has admitted that she was nevertheless not a fashion icon during her youth thanks to braces, glasses, and the sometimes unflattering styles popular in the 1980s.

Far from being a fashionista, the young London had interests in other areas. After completing high school, she attended Vassar College in Poughkeepsie, New York. There, London studied both twentieth-century philosophy and German literature, writing her senior thesis on German philosophers Martin Heidegger and Friedrich Nietzsche and winning election to the academically rigorous Phi Beta Kappa society. After graduation, London began her career in fashion as an editorial assistant with *Vogue* magazine in New York City. At *Vogue* in the early 1990s, London saw the beginnings of a trend that she would later combat on *What Not to Wear,* which she termed the "casualization of America" to Naomi Schaefer Riley in the *Wall Street Journal.* "Grunge became a revolutionary fashion statement: Everything was a little sloppy, a little homeless," London explained in the same interview, continuing, "it took too long for the pendulum to swing back to elegance." Over the remainder of the decade, London worked as a fashion stylist for celebrities and magazines, as well as serving as a senior fashion editor at *Mademoiselle.*

Born on February 22, 1969, in Panama City, Panama, Kelly grew up in Port Jefferson Station on Long Island, New York. The teenaged Kelly made many of the same fashion faux pas of others of his generation, later admitting freely to Victoria Aheam in a *Toronto Star* interview that, "I was living at the epicentre of '80s fashion ... and so of course I made some mistakes.... I would do things like a Ralph Lauren polo shirt with acid-wash jeans.... And, you know, I had a mullet at one point." After completing high school, Kelly enrolled at Boston College to study communications. While at Boston College, the future fashion expert pursued a number of creative outlets, becoming the president of the University Chorale and taking a fiction workshop with author Robert Chibka that Kelly has identified as a life-changing experience. After completing his bachelor's degree in 1991, Kelly moved to Chicago to pursue graduate studies in journalism at Northwestern University. He earned a master's degree from the university's Medill School of Journalism in 1993.

Education completed, Kelly spent several years working as a freelance journalist and, for a time, hosting a program on shopping network QVC affili-

ate Q2. He served as an editor at women's magazine *Marie Claire* and deputy editor at *Mademoiselle,* where he wrote an advice column under the pen name Joe L'Amour. These gigs prepared him to become the executive editor of *Daily News Record* (*DNR*), a weekly publication for the men's fashion and retail industry. Soon after joining *DNR*, Kelly was tapped as a co-host for *What Not to Wear.* "On my first day, a casting director asked if I'd be interested in auditioning.... I thought, 'Yeah, sure, what the heck.' I already had a great job, so it was OK either way," he told Gina Roberts-Grey in an interview with *Lifescript.* The audition proved successful, and Kelly joined *What Not to Wear* as a co-host in the show's second season, replacing original male co-host Wayne Scot Lukas.

In the early 2000s, London was chosen as a co-host of the TLC program *What Not to Wear.* Based on a British fashion program of the same name, the show debuted in January of 2003 and followed a standard format. London, along with original co-host Lukas—later Kelly—surprised an unsuspecting person nominated by friends or family as a particularly poor dresser. The duo offered the nominee the opportunity to travel to New York City for several days to receive personalized fashion advice, a new hairstyle and makeover, and money to shop for a new wardrobe that followed the hosts' fashion rules, which were based on the subject's age, size, lifestyle, and other individual factors. The hosts offered feedback to the makeover subject during the shopping process and, at the end of the program, discussed why the new chosen looks worked well. The show—which initially featured both male and female makeover nominees—quickly proved popular. It was soon added to TLC's continuing programming lineup and eventually produced more than 250 episodes.

Viewers were attracted not just by the show's makeovers, but also by the down-to-earth attitudes of its presenters. The hosts emphasized that people of all ages, shapes, and sizes could dress well and look polished, rather than featuring only youthful looks or those best worn by the model-thin. London has noted in interviews that she has struggled with weight issues throughout her life, sometimes wearing as small as a size zero and at other times ranging up to a size 16; Kelly, at a lanky six-foot-four, has faced his own set of style challenges. These personal experiences informed the duo's witty, but not mocking, criticism of their subjects' poor sartorial selections. Additionally, Kelly and London treated their efforts as truly important to their subjects' lives and self-esteems. Rather than simply arguing that fashion must be followed for its own sake, Kelly and London are firm believers in the transformative power of style. "Every morning, when you get dressed you decide if you're going to propel yourself to your goal or hold yourself back," Kelly told Barbara Schneider-Levy of *Footwear News* in 2007. London has often pointed out the self-confidence that being well-dressed can encourage. "Imagine if everyone felt just incrementally better about themselves," she told *Daily Variety*'s Kate Hahn in 2010. "It would change the world."

On *What Not to Wear*, Kelly and London have also repeatedly striven to encourage women to accept some essential guidelines in choosing their clothing: dressing for one's present size, rather than waiting to lose weight or otherwise changing one's body shape; having clothing purchased off the rack professionally tailored to fit properly; and choosing fewer, higher-quality articles of apparel over many inexpensive disposable pieces. These concepts underlay Kelly and London's collaborative fashion book, *Dress Your Best: The Complete Guide to Finding the Style That's Right for Your Body*. Published in 2005, the book presents a visual guide to practically apply the *What Not to Wear* team's rules for a variety of both female and male body types—including their own. Brad Hooper of *Booklist* judged *Dress Your Best* to be a "delightfully upbeat and decidedly informative primer," while Sarah Aarthun noted that "if you like Stacy and Clinton's witty banter on the show, that same humor is sprinkled throughout the book, making it a fun yet useful read" in an article printed in the *Charlotte Observer*.

Kelly reiterated his style suggestions in two more books, *Freakin' Fabulous: How to Dress, Speak, Behave, Eat, Drink, Entertain, Decorate, and Generally Be Better than Everyone Else* and *Oh No She Didn't: The Top 100 Style Mistakes Women Make and How to Avoid Them*. The former work, which hit shelves in 2008, built on the information about dressing for specific body types to discuss appropriateness for various ages and events before delving into diverse lifestyle topics ranging from grammar to throwing parties to selecting and arranging furniture. "I just wanted to do a book about the things I love," Kelly told Donna Doherty of the *New Haven Register*. "Let's all be fabulous," he continued, "but I think the message is you have to put some work into it. Being an active participant in life is wanting to learn to cook new things, create a style that reflects your personality, a decor in your home to make you happy." Kelly returned to the written medium in 2010 with *Oh No She Didn't*, a guide to fashion infractions, ranging from the "mom jean" to wearing all black to poorly maintained hair coloring. In addition to these published works, Kelly has partnered with national retailer Macy's, launched a line of clothing on QVC, and made the rounds of the United States as a speaker on fashion.

At the same time, London continued to grow her style presence through television, public speaking, and product endorsements. London has anchored a special series called *Fashion Fanatic with Stacy London,* and in 2007, she hosted a TLC late-night talk show program titled *Fashionably Late with Stacy London.* The show failed to generate much of an audience, however, and was canceled after only a few episodes. Despite this, London remained a regular feature on television screens by making frequent stops on national talk shows such as *The Wendy Williams Show* and *Oprah,* as well as by occasionally guest hosting an hour of the morning program the *Today Show.* The fashion personality has partnered with numerous brands including Wonderbra, Woolite, Pantene, and Calvin Klein; London has also acted as a style consultant and speaker for major corporations such as Starwood Hotels. Over the years, she has been active with numerous charities, including the American Cancer Society and Triple Negative Breast Cancer Foundation, through which she has provided makeover services to cancer survivors who have had double mastectomies. London has also served on the board of the cancer foundation 96 Magnolia and acted as the spokesperson for the National Psoriasis Foundation's Psoriatic Arthritis Total Approach to Health (PATH) program.

London lives in Brooklyn, New York, with a pet cat or two and a shoe collection estimated at some 300 pairs. Kelly splits his time between Manhattan and a country house in Connecticut. He, too, admits to owning dozens of pairs of shoes.

Selected writings

Together

Dress Your Best: The Complete Guide to Finding the Style That's Right for Your Body, Three Rivers Press (New York City), 2005.

Clinton Kelly

Freakin' Fabulous: How to Dress, Speak, Behave, Eat, Drink, Entertain, Decorate, and Generally Be Better than Everyone Else, Simon Spotlight (New York City), 2008.
Oh No She Didn't: The Top 100 Style Mistakes Women Make and How to Avoid Them, Gallery Books (New York City), 2010.

Sources

Books

Kelly, Clinton, *Oh No She Didn't: The Top 100 Style Mistakes Women Make and How to Avoid Them,* Gallery Books, 2010.

Kelly, Clinton, and Stacy London, *Dress Your Best: The Complete Guide to Finding the Style That's Right for Your Body*, Three Rivers Press, 2005.

Periodicals

Booklist, August 2005, p. 1973.

Charlotte Observer (Charlotte, NC), November 9, 2005.

Daily Variety, January 29, 2010, p. A9.

Footwear News, July 23, 2007, p. 156.

New Haven Register (CT), December 8, 2008.

Toronto Star, March 4, 2011, p. E9.

USA Today, November 22, 2007.

Wall Street Journal, July 6, 2007, p. W9.

Online

"Clinton Kelly '91," Boston College, http://www.bc.edu/alumni/news/BCM/fall2008/kellyQA.html (April 23, 2011).

"Clinton Kelly: How to Dress with Rheumatoid Arthritis," http://www.lifescript.com/Body/Style/Your-Look/Clinton_Kelly_How_to_Dress_with_Rheumatoid_Arthritis.aspx?p=1 (April 23, 2011).

"Fashion Expert: Clinton Kelly," TLC, http://tlc.howstuffworks.com/tv/what-not-to-wear/about-clinton-kelly.htm (April 23, 2011).

"Fashion Expert: Stacy London," TLC, http://tlc.howstuffworks.com/tv/what-not-to-wear/about-stacy-london.htm (April 23, 2011).

"Q&A: Stacy London," *OK!*, http://www.okmagazine.com/2007/09/qa-stacy-london-1455/ (April 23, 2011).

—*Vanessa E. Vaughn*

John Key

© *Indranil Mukherjee/AFP/Getty Images*

Prime minister of New Zealand

Born John Phillip Key, August 9, 1961, in Auckland, New Zealand; son of George (an entrepreneur) and Ruth (a cleaning woman, milliner, and entrepreneur; maiden name, Lazar) Key; married Bronagh Dougan (a human resources specialist), 1984; children: Stephanie, Max. *Education:* University of Canterbury, B.Com., 1981.

Addresses: *Home*—Auckland, NZ. *Office*—Chief Executive's Office, Level 8, Executive Wing, Parliament Bldgs., Wellington 6011, New Zealand. *Web site*—http://www.johnkey.co.nz.

Career

Auditor with the firm McCulloch Menzies, after 1982; project manager with apparel manufacturer Lane Walker Rudkin; currency trader, Elders Merchant Finance, then head of foreign exchange trading desk, c. 1985-88; currency-trading executive, Bankers Trust New Zealand, 1988-95; director of Asian foreign exchange division, Merrill Lynch, 1995, then global head of foreign exchange, c. 1995-2001; member of the Foreign Exchange Committee, New York Federal Reserve Bank, 1999-2001; elected representative of the Auckland-area district of Helensville on the National Party ticket, Parliament of New Zealand, 2002; reelected 2005, 2008; became National Party finance spokesman in Parliament, 2004; became leader of the New Zealand National Party, 2008; became prime minister of New Zealand, 2008.

Sidelights

John Key led the New Zealand National Party to victory in the 2008 general election. The former currency trader and Merrill Lynch executive made an astonishingly quick rise to the prime pinister's office, which came just six years after he was first elected to the Parliament of New Zealand. His National Party's win on November 8, 2008, marked its return to full power after a 12-year absence. "Though he may not score highly on charisma," remarked Daniel Williams in *Time International*, "Key has inspired many New Zealanders, who see in him a combination of decency, cleverness, and determination that they believe could make him one of the nation's best prime ministers."

Key is also one of the youngest leaders in New Zealand history. He was born in 1961 in Auckland, the son of George and Ruth Key, and grew up with two sisters. Ruth Key was originally from Vienna, but her family's Jewish background put them in grave danger once Nazi Germany annexed Austria in 1938. The Lazars were moderately prosperous leather merchants, and Key's maternal great-aunt was able to flee the Continent and arrange a marriage to a British soldier for cash, which gave her

British citizenship and the ability to bring Ruth and three other members of the Lazar family to safety in England.

As a young immigrant in wartime England, Key's mother found work as a cleaning woman and then became a milliner before marrying George Key in 1950, the son of merchants and a veteran of both the Spanish Civil War and World War II. The couple relocated to New Zealand with the elder of Key's two sisters and, for a time, ran a small restaurant in St. Helier's, a beach town that is also a suburb of Auckland, New Zealand's largest city. But they struggled financially; Key's father drank heavily and died of a heart attack in May of 1969, a few months before his only son's eighth birthday. At that point, Ruth Key moved with her three children to Christchurch, New Zealand's second-largest metropolis, where they lived in government-subsidized housing. "Mum knew a couple of things: that education was a liberator, that was the thing they couldn't take away from you," Key recalled in an interview with Jonathan Milne for the *New Zealand Herald*. "And that you can and will face some real challenges in your life, that you ultimately get out of life what you put into it, that you will sometimes have to rebuild."

Like many struggling newcomers to New Zealand, Key's mother was an ardent supporter of the New Zealand Labour Party, the traditional center-left stronghold in national politics. Its chief rival for power was the old-guard National Party, which generally counted on support from New Zealand's business elite, Anglophiles, the religious right, and those opposed to the country's generous social-welfare system. Key announced his adherence to "the Nats," as the NP is casually called, while still in his teens. "I had really strong aspirations and I wanted to do something with my life. I liked the fact National stood for freedom and self enterprise," he told Warren Gamble in the *New Zealand Herald*. "You could exist on social welfare, but you could never get rich on it. I never wanted to live my life existing on it."

Until the early 1980s New Zealand had a tightly regulated economy that mirrored that of the United Kingdom, its former colonial ruler. Discovered by a Dutch seafarer and later mapped by sea captain James Cook in 1769, New Zealand consists of two main North and South Islands lying southeast of Australia. Its indigenous Maori unsuccessfully fought against massive European encroachment as New Zealand became part of the colonial territory called New South Wales, now the name of one of Australia's states. New Zealanders broke away from the Australian colony in the 1840s and were granted the right to form their own colonial parliament. Over the next century New Zealand prospered as the bucolic, hilly islands became a center of the whaling industry and major agricultural exporter to the rest of the world. In 1926 New Zealand leaders signed the Balfour Declaration with Britain, which gave it—along with South Africa and Canada—much greater autonomy, though even into the twenty-first century it retained nominal ties to England, with Queen Elizabeth II represented by a resident Governor General.

Key graduated from Burnside High School and entered the University of Canterbury near Christchurch. He earned a Bachelor of Commerce degree in accounting in 1981 and went to work for a firm called McCulloch Menzies as an auditor. He later joined Lane Walker Rudkin, a large apparel manufacturer. A television documentary on the exciting workdays of foreign-currency traders spurred him to land an interview with Elders Merchant Finance at the age of 24. He proved so successful at the fast-paced job that he was promoted rapidly to head of the firm's foreign exchange trading desk.

In 1988 Key took an executive position with Bankers Trust New Zealand, then moved over to Merrill Lynch as director of its Asian foreign exchange division seven years later. This was a Singapore-based job, and Key moved there with his wife Bronagh, whom he had met at Burnside High and married in 1984. The couple became parents to a daughter in 1993 and a son born two years later, and moved their family to London when Key was named Merrill Lynch's global head of foreign exchange. In the latter half of that decade Key made a small fortune for himself and Merrill Lynch, with his division's sales figures skyrocketing from $100 million to $1 billion in annual trading volume.

As a teenager Key had often stated his intention to enter politics and perhaps even become prime minister some day. It was his sister, Liz Cave, who helped arrange a crucial meeting with the head of the National Party when Key was still living in London. She was the efficient, respected gatekeeper receptionist at the executive offices of Lane Walker Rudkin, his old employer, when John Slater, the National Party chief, turned up for a meeting with company executives. She said that she had a brother about to return from overseas who was interested in entering politics as a second career, and Slater told Cave to have her brother call him.

After retiring from Merrill Lynch the year he turned 40, Key settled in Auckland and ran for a seat in the newly created electoral district of Helensville in the

2002 general election. As a new junior member from the Nats—which was the opposition party at the time—he gained a reputation for putting in long hours at the Beehive, the nickname for the tiered, circular building that houses parliamentary offices in Wellington, New Zealand's capital. In 2004 party leaders named him the spokesperson for finance, which made him the Nats' point person for a new tax plan. He was reelected to his Helensville seat in 2005, but the Labour Party remained in power during that election under Helen Clark, prime minister since 1999.

Key's rise to the National Party leadership came during a crisis in late 2006: internal party emails were leaked to journalist Nicky Hager, who wrote a telling exposé, *The Hollow Men: A Study in the Politics of Deception* that leveled such incendiary revelations about the party leadership that its publication was temporarily blocked by injunction. The book caused a sensation in New Zealand, especially in the link Hager traced back to potential support from a conservative Christian group called Exclusive Brethren, which has been placed on some cult watch lists. National Party leader Don Brash was forced to resign in November of 2006 and Key was elected the new head of the party.

Key worked to restore faith in the Nats and distance the party from some of the more conservative ideology, which tended to alienate younger, affluent urban voters. A general election was scheduled for November 8, 2008, and Key embarked on a campaign to win a majority of necessary seats in Parliament for his party to return to power. New Zealand operates by a Mixed Member Proportional system, or MMP. This means that voter cast two votes: one for their parliamentary representative, and another for the party of choice. Directly elected MPs hold 65 seats, and another 55 seats are reserved for "list" candidates on the party ballot; there are also seats reserved for Maori representatives.

New Zealand is one of the world's most prosperous, literate, and developed nations, but suffered in the global economic slump that began in 2007. Its housing market—with single-family homes comparable in price to those in sunny Southern California in some areas—was particularly hard hit. Opponents mocked his slogan, "Choosing a Brighter Future," pointing out that he had little political-leadership experience and, more tellingly, was one of New Zealand's richest citizens. He also had the highest net worth of any member of Parliament.

Key and the Nats squeaked by in the general election, taking 45 percent of the vote and 59 of the 122 seats. He negotiated an early transfer of power with Clark's team so that he could travel to Lima, Peru, as New Zealand's delegate to the Asia Pacific Economic Cooperation (APEC) summit, slated to begin on November 22, three days after his swearing-in. He allied with three other parties to form a coalition government, and won praise for taking a moderate course of action on economic matters and social issues.

As the two-year anniversary of his term neared, Key faced intense criticism for a deal his government struck to keep filmmaker Peter Jackson's next installment in the J. R. R. Tolkien novels, *The Hobbit*, on location in New Zealand. Jackson's earlier *Lord of the Rings* movies had provided an enormous boost to New Zealand tourism, but a labor dispute erupted that threatened to put an end to "Wellywood," as the city of Wellington had dubbed itself. The prime minister and other senior officials met with Hollywood studio executives and worked out a deal that included some revisions to New Zealand's labor laws and an incentive financing deal for *The Hobbit*. It was a potentially disastrous dilemma—Hollywood studios could decide to locate anywhere, or even create the lush Middle Earth topography using computer-generated imagery (CGI), while supporters of New Zealand's union-allied film workers threatened a massive boycott of the *Hobbit* franchise should they lose some of their workplace protections. Once the terms of the arrangement were announced, Labour Party politicians chastised Key's government for capitulating to the whims of Hollywood, essentially permitting a foreign company to influence legislation.

Key's leadership skills were tested in earnest on February 22, 2011, when a massive earthquake hit Christchurch during lunchtime. The death toll climbed to 182 as his government quickly moved to commit enormous resources to search-and-rescue and rebuilding operations. Two more significant aftershocks hit the city in mid-June of 2011, and social-service agencies reported signs that residents of the city and surrounding region of Canterbury were still fearful, even to the point of keeping their children home from school. "I think the most significant damage at the moment is to the confidence of Cantabrians who really want all this to end and to feel there's some clear air to start rebuilding their city," the prime minister was quoted as saying by the *Sydney Morning Herald*. He asked residents to stay and take part in the rebuilding effort. "We don't think it's a situation where people should give up hope in Christchurch. I haven't given up hope on Christchurch and I certainly won't be."

One highlight of Key's prime ministership was attending the 2011 wedding of Britain's Prince William and Catherine Middleton. That same spring, a photograph of 16-year-old Max Key appeared on a Facebook page titled "Planking New Zealand," showing Max in the prone position on a sofa, with his famous father looking on. The prime minister's office declined to comment.

Sources

Periodicals

Independent (London, England), June 1, 2011.
New York Times, October 27, 2010.
New Zealand Herald, March 23, 2002; November 27, 2006; November 16, 2008.
New Zealand Management, February 2010, p. 30.
Sydney Morning Herald, June 18, 2011.
Time, November 13, 2008.

Online

"About John Key," John Key, Prime Minister, NZ, http://www.johnkey.co.nz/pages/bio.html (June 30, 2011).

—*Carol Brennan*

Elena Kiam

Founder of Lia Sophia

Born Elena Margaret Hahn, c. 1964; daughter of Herbert (a corporate executive) and Ethelee (a foreign-language teacher) Hahn; married Tory Kiam, October 1991; children: Alexander, Sophia, Lia. *Education:* Harvard University, BS, 1985.

Addresses: *Office*—c/o Lia Sophia, 1235 N. Mittel Blvd., Wood Dale, IL 60191.

Career

Worked in corporate and personal finance, JP Morgan, 1980s-90s; founded Lia Sophia, 2004; executive vice president and creative director, Lia Sophia, 2004—.

Member: Board of directors, Dress for Success.

Sidelights

Entrepreneur and corporate executive Elena Kiam is the founder of Lia Sophia, the world's largest direct-sales jewelry company. After a 15-year career on Wall Street, Kiam left the corporate world to focus on raising her family; however, she was soon transforming a flagging family business into Lia Sophia. Since retooling the brand in 2004, Kiam—now Lia Sophia's senior vice president—has successfully helped grow the company's independent, overwhelmingly female team of fashion advisors and sellers to some 30,000. She considers part of Lia Sophia's success to be its support for women's professional and personal goals by providing an encouraging work environment for its sales force and helping women achieve a high-style look for an affordable price. "I like to believe that we empower women to become entrepreneurs," Kiam commented in an interview with the Real Style Network Web site.

A native of New York City, Kiam is the youngest of the four daughters of a corporate executive father and foreign-language teacher mother. The future jewelry maven enjoyed a comfortable upbringing, attending the city's prestigious and highly competitive Nightingale-Bamford School. Kiam later recalled that attending this all-girls school helped shape her confidence in her abilities as she entered traditionally male-dominated activities. "There were no male counterinfluences," she commented in a profile on the Web site WomensBiz.US. "I never questioned the abilities of girls to compete against men since I operated during those early years in an almost exclusively female environment." After graduating from Nightingale-Bamford in 1981, Kiam attended Harvard University.

Despite earning a degree in architecture in 1985, the recent graduate instead took a job with financial powerhouse JP Morgan. Much to Kiam's own surprise, this position became a 15-year career in financial services. Over the course of her tenure with JP

Morgan, Kiam worked in corporate finance and private banking. In the latter role, she traveled the country to work with individuals and businesses on wealth growth and management. To overcome clients' potential distrust of a female financial advisor, Kiam worked to develop her knowledge of her products and rely on humor to create relationships. In time, she rose to become one of the rare senior female executives at JP Morgan. "Women were typically pitted against one another and because there were so few positions, as I moved up the career ladder, it was very much a zero sum game where one woman's advancement meant one less place for another woman," Kiam recalled to Denise Albert of the *New York Daily News.*

However, Kiam had not focused entirely on her career during her corporate tenure. In 1991 she married business executive Tory Kiam and in time gave birth to three children, a son and two daughters. Kiam eventually decided to leave finance to focus on her growing family. "It was a terribly difficult decision," she explained in the same WomensBiz.Us profile. "I loved serving as a role model and mentor to young female executives who were also trying to break through. I couldn't imagine giving that up." A perhaps unexpected opportunity arose to allow Kiam to again work supporting women. Her husband's late father, Victor Kiam, had built the Remington company into a household name for shaving products during the late twentieth century. However, its Lady Remington division for direct jewelry sales had waned since its introduction in the mid-1980s.

In 2004, Kiam rebranded the failing company Lia Sophia, named after her two daughters. Her childrens' diverse personalities helped inspire their mother as she began overseeing the redesign of the Lia Sophia jewelry offerings to make them more modern and fashion-forward. "Sophia is more classic and elegant," Kiam told *People,* "while Lia is more whimsical.... I'm not devoted to what they say, but if both of them like a piece, I figure it's a keeper since it resonates with two different audiences." Lia Sophia operates on a direct-sales model in which independent sales associates known as "advisors" sell door-to-door or at in-home parties featuring the company's jewelry pieces. Guests then have the option to purchase or order pieces, and advisors earn a commission of 30 percent of each show's total sales. Hostesses receive discounts on jewelry and other incentives. This low-key model quickly proved its appeal to women seeking a flexible part-time job that fit their family commitments or as a post-retirement source of income, and Lia Sophia's team of advisors exploded from Lady Remington's 1,250 to some 30,000 worldwide in just six years. Kiam has noted that she strives to allow women to make money to support themselves while being able to work the hours that she herself wants to keep as a mother; some Lia Sophia representatives are reported to earn more than $100,000 annually. By 2011, the company's mass appeal had allowed it to establish a presence in the United States, Canada, and Germany.

Lia Sophia has attracted a bevy of celebrity fans, including singer Beyoncé, model Kate Moss, socialite Paris Hilton, media magnate Oprah Winfrey, and actress Lindsay Lohan, who once expressed interest in designing some jewelry pieces for Lia Sophia's more elaborate "Red Carpet" collection. Lia Sophia items have also graced the pages of numerous fashion and lifestyle magazines, and been worn by characters in popular television shows such as *Gossip Girl.* Kiam considers this notoriety a boon both for the brand and for the women who wear it, noting that it gives ordinary women an affordable connection to celebrity tastes and their accompanying perceived level of luxury.

With Lia Sophia, Kiam has also worked to help women by supporting Dress for Success, an organization that provides disadvantaged women with professional clothing and accessories to wear on job interviews and in the workplace, as well as offering a network of professional support programs. Noting that both organizations aim to give women self-confidence through a more polished appearance, Kiam explained to Albert that "with that confidence and self-esteem, women can accomplish amazing things that will benefit themselves and ultimately society." In 2009 and 2010, Lia Sophia donated some 170,000 pieces of jewelry to Dress for Success for the organization to distribute to its clients. In addition, Lia Sophia has encouraged its widespread team of sales advisors to take part in Dress for Success' mentoring program to help other women achieve their goals. Kiam has also served as a member of Dress for Success' Board of Directors.

Sources

Periodicals

New York Times, August 11, 1991.
Tribute, October/November 2010, p. 19.
WWD, July 15, 2009, p. 8.

Online

"A-list looks for less," *Daily News,* http://www. nydailynews.com/blogs/momsandthecity/2011/ 03/a-list-looks-for-less (June 1, 2011).
"Lia Sophia: A Fashion Jewelry Line with a Difference," Real Style Network, http://www.realstyle network.com/index.php/fashion-and-style/ 2010/05/lia-sophia-a-fashion-jewelry-line-with-a-difference/ (June 1, 2011).

"Lia Sophia's Elena Kiam Is Inspired by Daughters," Celebrity Baby Blog, *People,* http://celebrity babies.people.com/2011/02/04/lia-sophias-elena-kiam-is-inspired-by-daughters/ (June 1, 2011).

"Profiles: Elena Kiam: From Wall Street to Main Street," WomensBiz.US, http://www.womensbiz.us/archives/profiles0205.asp (June 1, 2011).

—*Vanessa E. Vaughn*

Christine Lagarde

© Panoramic/ZUMA Press/newscom

Managing director of the International Monetary Fund

Born Christine Madeleine Odette Lallouette, January 1, 1956, in Paris, France; daughter of Robert (a professor) and Nicole (a teacher; maiden name, Carré) Lallouette; married Wilfrid Lagarde, June 17, 1982 (divorced, April 1992); married Eachran Gilmour (an entrepreneur; divorced); children: (first marriage) Pierre-Henri, Thomas. *Education:* Earned degrees from University Paris X—Nanterre Law School, and the Institut d'études Politiques d'Aix-en-Provence.

Addresses: *Office*—International Monetary Fund (IMF), 700 19th St. NW, Washington, DC 20431.

Career

Congressional intern for U.S. Representative William S. Cohen (D-ME); attorney, Baker & McKenzie, 1981-87, made partner in 1987, co-managing partner of Paris office, 1991, member of executive committee, after 1995, chair of firm's European regional council, 1997-98, board chair, 1999-2004, president of global strategic committee, 2004-05; Minister for External Trade, France, 2005-07; Minister of Agriculture, 2007; Minister for Economic Affairs, Industry, and Employment, France, 2007-11; managing director, International Monetary Fund (IMF), 2011—.

Awards: Chevalier, Légion d'honneur (France), 2000.

Sidelights

Christine Lagarde advanced to one of the world's most powerful jobs in 2011 when she became the newest managing director of the International Monetary Fund, or IMF. She is the first woman to head the multinational economic organization, which wields immense influence on global exchange rates and trade- or loan-related transactions between nations. Silver-haired, gamine, and perpetually serene, Lagarde is an attorney by training and had previously served as France's Minister of Finance.

Christine Madeleine Odette Lallouette was born in Paris on January 1, 1956. The first of four children and only daughter of Robert and Nicole Lallouette, she grew up in the port city of Le Havre in a multilingual household: her mother taught classical languages, thus Lagarde and her brothers had a grasp of the basics of Latin and Greek at an early age, while their father was a professor of English at the University of Rouen. He died when Lagarde was 17, after which Lagarde's mother struggled to provide for the family.

Lagarde was a Girl Guide—the foreign counterpart to the U.S. Girl Scouts organization—and avid athlete. In 1973, her synchronized swim team took the bronze medal in French national championships. A year later, she graduated from the Lycée François Ier in Le Havre, and traveled to the United States after winning a scholarship from a foreign-exchange program to the Holton-Arms School, a single-gender boarding school in suburban Washington, D.C. After returning to France she studied law at the University of Paris' Nanterre X campus and earned a master's degree in political science from the Institut d'études politiques d'Aix-en-Provence, also known as Sciences Po Aix. Determined to enter one of France's elite national schools, which have rigorous entrance requirements and serve as a sort of French Ivy League, she sat twice for the exam to enter the prestigious École Nationale d'Administration, from which nearly all senior government officials in France graduate, but failed it both times.

Lagarde returned to the United States after landing a Congressional internship in the office of William S. Cohen, a Maine Democrat in the U.S. House of Representatives who would go on to the Senate and then serve as Secretary of Defense in the late 1990s. When she graduated from law school, Lagarde had an impressive command of English and Spanish, which helped her land a job in 1981 in the Paris office of Baker & McKenzie, a U.S. law firm with a wide global reach. She worked on antitrust and labor cases and was made partner in 1987. Four years later she became co-managing partner of the Paris office, and in 1995 was given a seat on the Baker & McKenzie executive committee. In the late 1990s she oversaw all eleven offices of the firm in Western Europe, and in October of 1999 was elected board chairperson of the firm, becoming the first woman ever to hold that post.

At the time, Baker & McKenzie was the second-largest law firm in the world, and Lagarde had been chosen by the balloting of 548 partners, only nine percent of whom were female professionals like herself. Her achievement merited an article in *New York Times,* but she took care to point out that though Baker & McKenzie was based in the United States it had an uncharacteristically large count of offices around the globe. "Our firm has to be extremely tolerant and open," she told *New York Times* journalist Melody Petersen. "Diversity is part of us. I think a lot of law firms tend to be more traditional, more clubby. Women are not so included in those firms as they are in my environment."

Lagarde moved to Chicago for her new role as head of Baker & McKenzie, but returned often to France. By that point she had two sons from a first marriage that ended in the early 1990s; the boys were nearly teens when she took the job in Chicago. During her time there she met a British entrepreneur named Eachran Gilmour, and was married a second time but later divorced. Several years later, after returning to France, she ran into a former Paris X—Nanterre law school classmate named Xavier Giocanti. Originally from Corsica, Giocanti was by then living in Marseille and running a company there. They have been together since 2006, though theirs is a commuter relationship.

In late 2004 Lagarde stepped down as chair of Baker & McKenzie and was put in charge of its global strategic committee. She was a surprising choice in the spring of 2005 when French Prime Minister Dominique de Villepin appointed her to serve as France's Minister for External Trade, for she had no previous government experience. Both de Villepin and the next French president, Nicolas Sarkozy, belonged to the center-right party *Union pour un Mouvement Populaire* (Union for a Popular Movement, UMP). Sarkozy took office in the spring of 2007 and made Lagarde the new Minister of Agriculture and Fisheries. A few weeks later, Sarkozy put her in charge of one of France's most vital cabinet departments, the Ministry of Economic Affairs, Industry, and Employment. She was the first woman to hold the post that in other European nations is usually called Finance Minister.

The French economy was lagging behind that of other nations, and Sarkozy installed Lagarde to help carry out his mission to revitalize it. On the agenda was a repeal of an annual wealth tax levied on the income *and* assets of some of the country's top earners, which had prompted many high-profile French celebrities to move out of the country. A more divisive goal of Sarkozy's was to reform some of the country's legendarily generous labor laws, which include a set 35-hour work week and eligibility to retire at age 50 for certain public sector workers in energy and transportation. Lagarde was in accord with Sarkozy on these points, telling the *Times* of London journalist Carl Mortished, "I was absolutely flabbergasted when I came back" after her five-year stint in Chicago, "to see how much people were talking about their holiday and their weekend and how many hours they were going to save to add up to their special time credit to add to their seventh week of vacation." The more left-of-center French media outlets quickly dubbed the new Finance Minister "l'Américaine" ("the American") because of her free-market views and time in Chicago, a corporate-law tenure that is quite rare for a French senior government official.

Several key industries in France are state-owned, but there are also powerful labor unions in France that respond quickly to any attempt to reduce their workers' benefits. They can call for paralyzing strikes, as happened in the early months of 2006 and again in late 2007 in protest of new government austerity measures. Yet Sarkozy's budget trims were modestly effective, and French economic indicators began to rise in 2008. Later that year, during the global economic meltdown that began in September of 2008 with the looming failure of some major Wall Street banks, Lagarde secured bailout funds for French banks whose incautious investments in American financial instruments had put them and their shareholders at risk.

A year later, at the annual G20 meeting—the "Group of Twenty" who are either finance ministers or central bank governors of the world's biggest economies—Lagarde took the opportunity to criticize U.S. banking executives for rewarding themselves with fat end-of-year bonuses after accepting federal bailout funds from U.S. taxpayers. She also warned of the risk of future financial catastrophes with the ongoing unregulated speculative trading arena. In 2009 the *Financial Times* of London ranked her as No. 1 in its annual assessment of Europe's finance ministers.

Lagarde spent much of 2010 handling a looming banking crisis in Europe, which had links back to the 2008 mortgage-backed securities debacle. Several countries, including Ireland and Greece, were in danger of defaulting on debt repayments, and it was Lagarde's role to work with other finance ministers in the Eurozone—the common economic and monetary union with 17 European Union member nations—to restructure their debt. In January of 2011, she turned up at the invitation-only World Economic Forum in Davos, Switzerland, and took the stage just after the head of one major British bank, American-born Robert Diamond, commended the finance ministers present for rallying to prevent a genuine global meltdown. That chief executive officer would later receive a $10.6 million bonus after stepping down as the head of Barclays Bank. "The best way for the banking sector to say thank you would be to actually have good financing of the economy, sensible compensation systems in place, and reinforcement of their capital," Lagarde said at the Davos panel in response to Diamond's remark, reported the *Guardian*'s Kim Willsher. It was a stinging semi-public rebuke that was met first with an astonished pause, and then applause from some observers.

Lagarde's name regularly appeared in news reports chronicling the ongoing Eurozone debt crisis until May 14, 2011, when the powerful head of the International Monetary Fund (IMF), Dominique Strauss-Kahn—one of her predecessors as French Finance Minister—was taken into custody at New York's John F. Kennedy International Airport on sexual assault charges. He was charged with attacking a housekeeper who had come to clean what the woman believed was an empty suite at the luxury Sofitel Hotel in Manhattan. Strauss-Kahn's arrest and detention by New York authorities was the main news story in both France and the United States for days.

Under pressure, Strauss-Kahn resigned as head of the IMF on May 18. Lagarde's name appeared in those first days as one of several contenders in the running to permanently replace the disgraced IMF chief, who was later exonerated. She had the early support of Sarkozy, and formally declared her candidacy for the IMF job on May 25.

The IMF was created in the final months of World War II, along with the World Bank, as an international intergovernmental organization whose member nations work together to promote global economic stability and cooperation. The head of the IMF, called a managing director, serves a five-year term and is appointed by a board of governors. The job has always gone to a European executive; the World Bank, by contrast, is traditionally headed by an American. Both organizations are headquartered in Washington, D.C.

On June 28, 2011, the IMF board voted in favor of Lagarde as the next managing director for a new, five-year term. Her job began on July 5, 2011, six days after she tendered her resignation as Finance Minister. Her most pressing new problem at the IMF was the complicated stew that was collectively known as the European sovereign debt crisis, which was tied to both the mortgage-backed securities debacle and the fiscal health of the European Central Bank.

Lagarde owns a country house near Rouen, where she tends roses and makes fruit jams in the warm-weather months. She is a vegetarian who rarely drinks and practices yoga in addition to swimming laps for exercise. Behind the scenes at the IMF, Lagarde hopes to bring the staid institution into the 21st century and add more diversity to its ranks. "Imagine a room with 24 men and you're the only woman," she recalled in an interview with Diane Johnson, a writer for the U.S. edition of *Vogue*, about the closed-door sessions with IMF's board of governors as she campaigned to become managing director. "The first day, I had to meet with each of them separately, 20 minutes each and then five minutes in-between time.... Then the next day, all 24, the whole boys' club, for a grilling. At the age of 55, I never thought I'd have to go through that again, studying, preparing—I felt as if I were 20 years old, interviewing for my first job."

Sources

Periodicals

Forbes, September 12, 2011, p. 78.
Guardian (London, England), November 7, 2009, p. 39; January 14, 2011, p. 16; May 29, 2011.
Independent (London, England), February 7, 2011, p. 24.
New York Times, October 9, 1999, p. C1; May 18, 2011, p. B1; September 24, 2011, p. 1.
Times (London, England), September 26, 2007, p. 56.
Vogue, September 2011, p. 706.

Online

"Christine Lagarde," International Monetary Fund Web Site, http://www.imf.org/external/np/omd/bios/cl.htmhtml (November 16, 2011).
"Is Christine Lagarde Right for the IMF?," *Business Week*, http://www.businessweek.com/print/magazine/content/11_25/b42330648.tif22844.htm (November 14, 2011).
"A New Leader for the IMF," *Der Spiegel*, http://www.spiegel.de/international/europe/0,1518,771278,00.html (November 12, 2011).

—*Carol Brennan*

Miranda Lambert

Singer and songwriter

Born November 19, 1983, in Lindale, TX; daughter of Rick (a detective agency owner and musician) and Beverly (a detective agency owner) Lambert; married Blake Shelton (a country singer), May 14, 2011.

Addresses: *Fan club*—P.O. Box 1270, Lindale, TX 75771. *Web site*—http://www.mirandalambert.com.

Career

Began performing in Texas bars and talent competitions, c. 1999; formed Texas Pride Band, c. 2000; actress in film *Slap Her, She's French*, 2001; released independent album *Miranda Lambert*, 2001; appeared on TV show *Nashville Star*, 2003; released first major-label single, "Me and Charlie Talking," 2004; released album *Kerosene*, 2005; released album *Crazy Ex-Girlfriend*, 2007; released album *Revolution*, 2009.

Awards: ACM award for top new female vocalist, Academy of Country Music, 2006; ACM award for album of the year, Academy of Country Music, for *Crazy Ex-Girlfriend*, 2007; ACM award for top female vocalist, Academy of Country Music, 2009; ACM award for video of the year, Academy of Country Music, for "White Liar," 2009; ACM award for album of the year, Academy of Country Music, for *Revolution*, 2009; ACM award for female vocalist of the year, Academy of Country Music, 2010; ACM awards for single record of the year, song of the year, and video of the year, Academy of Country Music, all for "The House That Built Me," all 2010;

Grammy Award for best female country vocal performance, National Academy of Recording Arts and Sciences, for "The House That Built Me," 2010; CMT Music Award for female video of the year, Country Music Television, for "White Liar," 2010; CMA awards for song of the year and music video of the year, Country Music Association, both for "The House That Built Me," both 2010; CMA award for female vocalist of the year, Country Music Association, 2010; CMA award for album of the year, Country Music Association, for *Revolution*, 2010.

Sidelights

Country singer/songwriter Miranda Lambert rose to fame with gutsy songs about extracting vengeance on wrongdoing men. Her tough persona proved popular and became part of a movement in contemporary country music away from soft, slick pop and back to the music's rough roots. Lambert wrote most of her own songs but also covered the work of well-established country songwriters, deftly building a career on both mass popularity and authenticity. She reached new heights in 2010 and 2011, when she won several prominent honors, including the Country Music Association's female vocalist of the year award, and married longtime boyfriend and fellow country star Blake Shelton.

"I can picture, like, my dad, driving down the road in our old $200 crap car that had no air conditioner and hardly started," Lambert told John Spong of *Texas Monthly*. "We're from Lindale, Texas, and we're poor and sweaty in our car that won't start. I want to hear a song about that. Because that's what country music is to me."

Lambert's father, Rick, was a country guitarist who also owned a private detective agency with his wife in Lindale, a small Texas town. Her memories of childhood include "sitting on the porch listening to my dad play Merle Haggard," she told Joanna Powell and Darla Atlas of *People*. "I was kind of ingrained that way. And I think that has a lot to do with who I am now."

Her career began at age 16 when she competed in a talent show at the Reo Palm Isle, a bar in Longview, Texas. A year later, she asked the bar owner if she could become the house singer. Still a high school senior, she performed at the Reo Palm Isle three nights a week from 9 p.m. to closing time. She left high school early, getting her degree through a ten-day program usually meant for troubled girls.

Lambert became a regular performer on the country bar circuit in Texas. She entered various country music talent contests as a singer, began writing songs, learned to play guitar, and formed a country band called the Texas Pride Band. She released the self-produced album *Miranda Lambert* in 2001, and her songs "Somebody Else" and "Texas Pride" became minor hits in the state. She appeared in a TV commercial and acted in *Slap Her, She's French*, a teen comedy produced in 2001.

In 2003, Lambert became a contestant on *Nashville Star*, a reality TV show and singing competition on the USA Network. She came in third, but attracted the attention of the record company Sony, which signed her to a contract. Sony released Lambert's first major-label single, "Me and Charlie Talking," on its Epic label in 2004.

For her first album for Epic, *Kerosene*, Lambert rejected several pop songs suggested by the label, choosing songs she wrote or co-wrote for ten out of the album's eleven tracks. "I went into the big board meeting, and I was like, 'Look, if you're going to try to change me and make me dance around and sing songs I don't want to sing, I'd rather just go back home and play,'" she told Amy Spencer of *Redbook*. "I was 19 and trying to stand my ground. And the president of Sony said, 'Make your record. We'll leave you alone.'" *Kerosene* eventually sold a million copies, including 40,000 in its first week on the market.

Touring with country stars such as Keith Urban helped Lambert grow her audience. So did a grueling schedule of small shows, including fairs and festivals popular with country music fans. "Every chili cook-off, she's there; every rib festival, she's there," her manager, Simon Renshaw, told Brian Mansfield of *USA Today*.

Fans found her tough personality appealing and a provocative contrast with her blond-haired good looks. After years in which mainstream country music had become more slick and pop-oriented, Lambert's angry, vengeful songs were fresh and provocative. In "Kerosene," the album's title track, she sang about burning down a cheating boyfriend's house. In an interview, she bragged about having a concealed handgun license. A tattoo on her left forearm also became her logo: two guns with wings behind them. "I don't write about angels, Jesus, happy days, kids," she told Chris Willman of *Entertainment Weekly*. "I grew up on drinkin', cheatin', [and] love gone bad."

By 2006, Lambert had bought her own house in Lindale, just down the street from her parents' home. She also opened the Miranda Lambert Store and Fan Club Headquarters in Lindale, which sold cowboy hats hand-painted by Lambert as well as CDs, posters, concert merchandise, and jewelry. Picnic tables with patio umbrellas outside the store became a place for musicians to play. Lambert dropped by to meet friends and fans on the 40 days or so per year that she was not touring.

Lambert truly established her stardom and her stage persona with her second album, *Crazy Ex-Girlfriend*, released in 2007. The album's songs "spun tales of cheating boyfriends and domestic abuse, and they almost always ended with the singer extracting violent, spectacular revenge on her aggressors," wrote Steve Leggett for the Web site AllMusic. For instance, "Gunpowder and Lead," the top-ten single from the album, played with feminine stereotypes while promising retribution. "I'm gonna show him what a little girl's made of: gunpowder and lead," she sang (as quoted by Melissa Maerz of *Rolling Stone*).

The album cemented Lambert's reputation as one of country music's bad girls. "People have asked me, literally, in interviews, 'You're not really going to shoot someone, are you?' Well, no," Lambert told Spong of *Texas Monthly*. "I mean, I would if I had to defend myself, but I'm not just waiting around for someone to shoot."

Crazy Ex-Girlfriend also showed off another element of Lambert's artistic stance, her insistence on staying close to her roots rather than let the Nashville-based country music establishment water down her music. "I dreamed of going to Nashville / Put my money down and placed my bet," she sang on "Famous in a Small Town," the first single off the album (as quoted by Spong in *Texas Monthly*). "But I just got the first buck of the season / I made the front page of the Turner town *Gazette*." Spong also noted the ring tone on Lambert's cell phone: "Red Bandana" by Merle Haggard, one of country's toughest outlaw singers.

For all the tales she sang about terrible exes, Lambert actually dated the same guy for years while writing many of those songs: fellow country singer Blake Shelton. The two began dating around 2005, the year they performed a duet of the song "You're the Reason God Made Oklahoma" for CMT Network's "100 Greatest Duets" special. Lambert and Shelton fished together during the summer and hunted together in the fall. "Some guys trade guns and knives with their buddies," Shelton told Maerz of *Rolling Stone*. "I do that with my girlfriend." Shelton released an album on the same day Lambert released *Crazy Ex-Girlfriend*; she teased him by saying her record would outsell his. By 2008, she had bought a farm a few miles from his in southeast Oklahoma.

"We have way different music tastes, Blake and I," Lambert told Ray Waddell of *Billboard*. "We don't listen to the same kind of music, and we don't record the same kind of music. But that's also kind of good in a way, because we each do our own thing and neither one of us tries to change the other." The two have also helped each others' careers. Lambert encouraged Shelton to join the social network Twitter, where he acquired 140,000 followers. They co-wrote three songs on her third album, *Revolution*.

Shelton also introduced her to another song she recorded for *Revolution*, "The House That Built Me," a ballad about the value of home and hard work. He was thinking of recording it himself, until he played it for her one night as they drove from Dallas to Oklahoma. "I looked over, and I could see from the dash lights that she was seriously bawling," Shelton told Mansfield of *USA Today*. "I said, 'If that song means that much to you, you should record it.' The crying tripled after that."

The song reminded Lambert of a tough time in her family's life, when little work was coming into her parents' detective business. "They lost everything and had to start over," Lambert told Spencer of *Redbook*. "We moved to this old farmhouse, and I think that shaped me to be who I am. We fixed it

up as the money came little by little, one room at a time. I remember my mom tacked pictures on the walls of what it was going to look like, every little detail." The family lived off the land, planting a garden and raising pigs and rabbits. Lambert built her own farm in Oklahoma with her parents' farm in mind.

Both Lambert and Shelton won awards at the 44th annual Country Music Association awards show in November of 2010. Lambert, nominated for nine CMA awards (a record), won the top female vocalist award, album of the year for *Revolution*, and song of the year and video of the year for "The House That Built Me." Shelton won top male vocalist. Lambert performed the John Prine song "That's the Way the World Goes 'Round" on the awards ceremony, which took place on her 27th birthday. Waddell of *Billboard* dubbed Lambert and Shelton "country's newly crowned power couple."

By performing songs by Prine and Fred Eaglesmith, both long-respected singer-songwriters, Lambert bolstered her identity as part of a rougher, less polished country style. The magazine *No Depression*, which usually celebrates critically acclaimed but non-mainstream alt-country singers, put Lambert on its cover. Talking with *Billboard*'s Waddell about *Revolution*, Lambert said, "For the first time, I could say, in all truth, 'I want to hand this record to my heroes. I feel confident enough about it.' She also said she'd received an immense compliment from one of country's elder stateswomen. "Loretta Lynn told me to my face, 'You're countrier than I am,' and I thought, 'This is coming from a woman who rhymes 'hard' with 'tired.'"

In May of 2011, Lambert and Shelton married at a ranch in Boerne, Texas, near San Antonio. A few days before the wedding, she posted a link on Twitter to a photo of venison from a deer she shot. "Last thing loaded for the wedding!!! Harvested by … me!!!!!" she tweeted, according to E! Online. The meat was served at the reception. Guests at the wedding included country singers Reba McEntire and Martina McBride, actress Katherine Heigl, and indie rock singer Cee-Lo.

The bride wore the same wedding gown her mother was married in, with cowboy boots. "I'm married to my best friend!" Lambert told *Us Weekly*. "Looking forward to a lifetime of laughter."

Before the wedding, Lambert told Spencer of *Redbook* that she was counting on marriage to give her and Shelton stability after the "glitz and glam" of stardom fades. But she shrugged off Spencer's suggestion that her next album might be softer because she was settling down. "I doubt if it'll be softer, because no matter how in love and happy I am, I still have that fiery side," Lambert replied. "And I always will."

Selected discography

Miranda Lambert, self-released, 2001.
Kerosene, Epic, 2005.
Crazy Ex-Girlfriend, Columbia, 2007.
Revolution, Sony Music, 2009.

Sources

Periodicals

Billboard, December 4, 2010, pp. 12-15.
Entertainment Weekly, April 27, 2007, p. 26.
Field and Stream, March 2008.
People, November 8, 2006, pp. 55-58.
Redbook, April 2011.
Rolling Stone, October 15, 2009, pp. 48-49.
Texas Monthly, October 2007.
USA Today, June 27, 2005, p. 3D; November 9, 2010, p. 1D.

Online

"About: Miranda Lambert," Miranda Lambert's Official Web Site, http://www.mirandalambert.com/about (May 22, 2011).
"Exclusive: Miranda Lambert Weds Blake Shelton!" *Us Magazine*, http://www.usmagazine.com/stylebeauty/news/miranda-lambert-weds-blake-shelton-2011145 (May 22, 2011).
"Miranda Lambert," AllMusic, http://www.allmusic.com/artist/miranda-lambert-p684675/biography (May 22, 2011).
"Royal Wedding This Ain't: Miranda Lambert Shoots Her Own Matrimonial Deer," E! Online, http://www.eonline.com/uberblog/b241494_royal_wedding_this_aint_miranda_lambert.html (May 22, 2011).
"See Miranda Lambert's Wedding Dress!" *Us Magazine*, http://www.usmagazine.com/stylebeauty/news/see-miranda-lamberts-wedding-dress-2011175 (May 22, 2011).

—Erick Trickey

Sanaa Lathan

© *Rob Kim/FilmMagic/Getty Images*

Actress

Born Sanaa McCoy Lathan, September 19, 1971, in New York, NY; daughter of Stan Lathan (a producer) and Eleanor McCoy (a dancer). *Education:* University of California, Berkley, B.A.; Yale School of Drama, M.F.A.

Addresses: *Office*—William Morris Agency, 151 El Camino Dr., Beverly Hills, CA 90212.

Career

Actress in films, including: *Blade*, 1998; *Best Man*, 1999; *Catfish in Black Bean Sauce*, 1999; *Life*, 1999; *Wood*, 1999; *Love and Basketball*, 2000; *Smoker*, 2000; *Brown Sugar*, 2002; *Out of Time*, 2003; *AVP: Alien vs. Predator*, 2004; *Something New*, 2006; *Family That Preys*, 2008; *Middle of Nowhere*, 2009; *Powder Blue*, 2009; *Wonderful World*, 2009; *Contagion*, 2011. Television appearances include: *In the House*, 1996; *Moesha*, 1996; *Built to Last*, 1997; *Drive*, 1997; *Family Matters*, 1997; *Miracle in the Woods* (movie), 1997; *NYPD Blue*, 1998; *Lateline*, 1998-99; *Disappearing Acts* (movie), 2000; *Nip/Tuck*, 2006; *Raisin in the Sun* (movie), 2008; *Cleveland Show*, 2009-11; *Family Guy*, 2010; *American Dad*, 2011; *Tilda* (movie), 2011. Stage appearances include: *Por' Knockers*, 1995; *A Star Has to Star in Black and White*, 1995; *Alexander Plays ... Suzanne in Stages*, 1996; *Our Town*, 1998; *Vagina Monologues*, 1999; *Measure for Measure*, 2001; *Raisin in the Sun*, 2004; *24 Hour Plays 2008*, 2008; *To Take Arms*, 2008; *Cat on a Hot Tin Roof*, 2009. Film producer of *Middle of Nowhere*, 2009.

Awards: Best actress, Black Entertainment Television, for *Love and Basketball*, 2001; Image award for outstanding actress in a motion picture, NAACP, for *Love and Basketball*, 2001; best actress, Black Reel Awards, for *Love and Basketball*, 2001; best actress, Black Reel Awards, for *Out of Time*, 2004.

Sidelights

The acting roles that Hollywood has traditionally given black female actresses has been limited. Black female performers have run into racial prejudice and harsh obstacles in pursuit of their art. For example, Hattie McDaniel, the first black woman to sing on the radio in the United States, won an Academy Award for her performance as a maid in *Gone With the Wind*. She appeared in more than 300 films but was only given credit in 80. Lena Horne had some of her solo singing performances in films censored out of showings in certain markets. She was also blacklisted in the 1950s for being involved in an interracial relationship. When Sanaa Lathan portrayed the namesake character who is a maid and aspiring actress in Lynn Nottage's play titled *By the Way, Meet Vera Stark*, ripples of multiple meaning crossed decades of history. This was not lost on Ben Brantley, writing for the *New York Times*, who titled his review "A Black Actress Trying to Rise Above a Maid."

Lathan, whose first name means "brilliance" in Arabic and "work of art" in Swahili, is a brilliant and talented artist who was trained at the Yale School of Drama. Despite the fact that she has a long list of film, television, and stage credits, her fame has been limited in proportion to her accomplishments. Lathan was exposed to the world of the performing arts early in her life. Her father, Stan Lathan, was a producer who earned his first television director's credit the year after Lathan was born with an episode of *Sanford and Son*. After this he worked on such acclaimed programs as *Barney Miller, Eight is Enough, Hill Street Blues, Fame,* and *Moesha*. Her mother, Eleanor McCoy, was a dancer. Lathan told Patrick Huguenin, writing for the New York *Daily News*, that she "grew up in the theater" and her "mother was one of the original Alvin Ailey dancers and was in *The Wiz* and *Timbuktu* on Broadway—and Eartha Kitt was in *Timbuktu*." She went on to explain to Huguenin that "as a very young kid, I was around Eartha Kitt all the time. My mother says I was always imitating her and doing her little growl." Lathan grew up surrounded by stars and the realities of show business.

Lathan was given gymnastic and dance training starting at a young age. When her parents divorced, she split her time between the two largest entertainment centers of North America, New York and Los Angeles. After graduating with a bachelor's degree in English from the University of California at Berkley, Lathan briefly considered going to law school, but because of her work with the Black Theater Workshop a recruiter from the Yale School of Drama suggested she audition for a slot in their master's program. Her father tried to dissuade her from becoming a performer and suggested she consider a more "stable" career. Lathan bravely chose to become an actress, knowing the pitfalls and obstacles.

Following her training at Yale, where she performed in many of Shakespeare's plays, Lathan moved back to New York. She appeared in numerous off-Broadway productions, including the sole female performance in Nottage's *Por'knockers*. The play concerns a group of terrorists who inadvertently kill children in the act of destroying a building. While the play was not given good overall reviews, Lathan's performance was praised.

After her father saw her perform in a number of stage productions and realized her skill and professional ambitions, he persuaded her to move to Hollywood. Without the help of her famous father, she landed roles in several television series, including *In the House, Moesha, NYPD Blue,* and *Family Matters*. She played opposite Della Reese in the made-for-television movie, *Miracle in the Woods*. She landed roles in two short-lived series titled *Built to Last*, which never made it to national distribution, and *Lateline*. Lathan received praise for her role as talent broker Briana on *Lateline*. In 1996 she appeared in her first feature-length film, *Drive*. The film was a biotech thriller that also starred Kadeem Hardison.

Between 1998 and 1999, Lathan was very busy and starred with many prominent leading men. She had a brief but noted role as the mother of Wesley Snipes' vampire-hybrid character in the action thriller *Blade*. In the comedy *Life* she played a girlfriend named Daisy opposite Eddie Murphy and Martin Lawrence. In *Wood* she first starred with Omar Epps, which fostered a real life friendship and, later, romantic involvement. In *Best Man* Lathan played the character of Robin, who was engaged to the main character, commitment-shy novelist Harper, played by Taye Diggs. Harper is going to the wedding of a friend in order to be the best man and Lathan's character warns him to remain faithful. He strays and has an affair with an old flame. The film was lauded for portraying a diversity of different black characters with unique personalities and motivations.

The film *Love and Basketball* depicted the ongoing relationship and development of two young people into star athletes. Lathan and Epps portrayed a pair of childhood friends who, as eleven-year-olds, have a love-hate relationship that lasts into high school. When Epps' character has a falling out with his father, he turns to Lathan's character. The two become romantically involved and then separate. The finale comes when the characters meet as professional basketball players for a game of one-on-one and the question of what is more important, love or basketball, becomes clear. In order to portray the character of Monica in this film that earned her an award for best actress from Black Entertainment Television, an Image Award for outstanding actress in a motion picture, and a best actress award from the Black Reel Awards, Lathan trained daily for four months to be in good enough shape to convincingly play a star athlete. Lathan had never played basketball in school or with any degree of seriousness as a hobby. She was not immediately offered the role until she was willing to demonstrate the dedication and physical skill that was necessary for a successful and authentic portrayal of Monica. When she began training, she trained with her brother and his friends. When Lathan demonstrated proficient athleticism and basketball handling, a coach was hired to work with her. All of her hard work paid off and her portrayal of Monica in *Love and Basketball* was hailed by critics.

Gina Prince-Bythewood, director of *Love and Basketball*, recognized the enormous talent that Lathan possessed and cast her opposite Wesley Snipes in the HBO made-for-television movie, *Disappearing Acts*. The movie was based on the best-selling novel by Terry McMillan. Lathan told *Jet* magazine, "I read the book when it first came out, and I loved it. I always thought, 'God, I would love to play Zora.' Terry McMillan's characters are so real and so modern. I knew the story and it was a dream role." In order to better depict the character of Zora Banks, Lathan gained 20 pounds. The story was about an aspiring singer and songwriter who falls in love with a carpenter. In addition to the two roles she did with Prince-Bythewood, Lathan also starred in a 2000 movie titled *Catfish in Black Bean Sauce*. The multiethnic comedy was about an African-American family that adopts two Vietnamese children. That same year, Lathan was dubbed one of *Ebony* magazine's "55 Most Beautiful People."

In 2002 Lathan again appeared with her co-star from *Best Man*, Diggs, in the romantic comedy *Brown Sugar*. The movie featured an all-star cast that included Queen Latifah and Mos Def. Lathan's performance drew acclaim and earned her a nomination for another NAACP Image award for outstanding actress in a motion picture.

In 2003 Lathan continued to be cast opposite some of Hollywood's top leading men. In *Out of Time* Lathan played the one-time high school sweetheart to Denzel Washington's character, a police chief in a small Florida town having an affair with Lathan's character, who is now married to the local bully. When a drug bust yields a suitcase of money that Washington's character must hold as evidence, he gives Lathan's character the money for a cancer treatment. A short time later, she is found dead, he is implicated, and the federal authorities want the missing money.

In 2004 Lathan diversified the types of categories that she has played by taking on the role of Alexa Woods in *AVP: Alien vs. Predator*. In the action-thriller Lathan portrayed an environmental technician and explorer who leads a team of scientists to the Antarctic where they discover a buried ancient pyramid. While on this expedition, the characters find themselves in the midst of a race war between two extraterrestrial species. Once again Lathan trained every day in preparation for her role. In an interview with Marti Yarbrough of *Jet* magazine, Lathan said, "I worked out for the whole movie, but after this I really have respect for action hero actors because it's really physically hard. If I wasn't working out I think I could have hurt myself."

Lathan returned to the stage in 2004 to star in the Broadway production of *A Raisin in the Sun* with Sean Combs, Audra McDonald, and Phylicia Rashad. Lathan received a Tony Award nomination for best performance by a featured actress for her portrayal of Beneathea Younger. In 2008 the cast reprised their roles in a made-for-television movie of the play, which was the first network television movie to be screened at the prestigious Sundance Film Festival.

In 2006 Lathan portrayed half of a couple in an interracial relationship in the movie *Something New*. The story concerned a 30-something black professional woman who is looking for a relationship and becomes involved with a white man. Considering that only five percent of African-American women marry outside of their race, the movie was a risk. Lathan recognized the historic significance of the story. She told Allison Samuels of *Newsweek*, "To be in a film where a black woman is desired by all men is something I feel grateful to be a part of." Lathan also portrayed the much younger wife of a Texas businessman in an interracial marriage on the television show *Nip/Tuck*.

In 2011, refusing to be typecast, Lathan took a role in the action-thriller *Contagion*. That same year, her portrayal of Vera Stark in the satiric play *By the Way, Meet Vera Stark* is informed by Lathan's knowledge of the history of show business and her own experiences as a black female actress. Lathan has steered her way through Hollywood and chosen roles that expanded her capabilities. She has also determinedly done whatever was necessary to make her portrayals as genuine as possible, whether it was training for months to be able to play basketball or gaining twenty pounds to look more like a character from a novel. While her name recognition is not in accordance with the solid career she has built over the years, her broad talent has added force to open the way for black actresses to be considered for roles beyond that of a maid or a love interest.

Sources

Books

Contemporary Black Biography, vol. 27, Gale, 2001.
Contemporary Theatre, Film and Television, vol. 102, Gale, 2010.
Who's Who Among African Americans, Gale, 2010.

Periodicals

Christian Century, November 15, 2003, p. 41.
Hollywood Reporter, February 6, 2008, p. 10.
Jet, December 11, 2000, p. 58; August 30, 2004, p. 54.

Newsweek, January 30, 2006, p. 60.

New York Times, May 10, 2011, p. C1.

Online

"Biography for Sanaa Lathan, " Internet Movie Database, http://www.imdb.com/name/nm0005125/bio (November 20, 2011).

"Meet 2econd Stage's Vera Stark, Tony Nominee Sanaa Lathan," Hartman Group PR, http://www.thehartmangrouppr.com/blog/?p=1274 (November 26, 2011).

"Sanaa Lathan Biography," Fandango, http://www.fandango.com/sanaalathan/biography/p237516 (November 22, 2011).

"Sanaa Lathan Biography," Starpulse, http://www.starpulse.com/Actresses/Lathan,_Sanaa/Biography/ (November 20, 2011).

"Sanaa Lathan," Yahoo! Movies, http://movies.yahoo.com/movie/contributor/18003167.tif07/bio (November 20, 2011).

"Stage Actress Sanaa Lathan plays a maid with dreams of movie stardom in Lynn Nottage's *Vera Stark,*" *Daily News,* http://articles.nydailynews.com/2011-04-28/entertainment/29497321.tif_1_movie-star-eartha-kitt-dreams (November 20, 2011).

—Annette Bowman

Frederick M. Lawrence

President of Brandeis University

Born c. 1955; married Kathy; children: Miriam, Noah. *Education:* Williams College, Williamstown, MA, B.S., 1977; Yale University, New Haven, CT, J.D., 1980.

Addresses: *Office*—Office of the President, Irving Enclave 113, MS 100, 415 South St., Waltham, MA 02453.

Career

Served as legal clerk for Judge Amalya L. Kearse, 1980; assistant U.S. attorney, southern district of New York, 1980s; law professor, Boston University Law School, 1988-2005; associate dean for academic affairs, Boston University Law School, 1996-99; Robert Kramer Research Professor of Law and dean, George Washington University Law School, 2005-10; president, Brandeis University, 2011—. Author of books and articles including *Punishing Hate: Bias Crimes Under American Law,* Harvard University Press, 1999.

Member: Trustee, Williams College; member, Board of Directors, Anti-Defamation League.

Awards: Metcalf Award for excellence in teaching, Boston University, 1996.

Sidelights

Legal scholar and higher education administrator Frederick M. Lawrence became the eighth president of Brandeis University on January 1, 2011. Before joining the Waltham, Massachusetts institution, Lawrence served as dean of George Washington Law School in Washington, D.C., and as a law professor at Boston University School of Law. During his lengthy career, Lawrence has gained a reputation as a prominent civil rights legal expert and led the national legal affairs committee of the Jewish civil rights organization the Anti-Defamation League for a time; he has also served on that organization's board of trustees. As president of Brandeis—a relatively young research university—the administrator faced new challenges of overseeing the institution's continued growth amid financial difficulties. "Fred Lawrence is an acclaimed educator, an expert on civil rights, and a proven leader with the ability to inspire the entire Brandeis community," assessed Brandeis Board of Trustees chair Malcolm L. Sherman in a press release reprinted in the *Jewish Journal.* "He is committed to the core values of academic excellence and social justice so essential to all that is Brandeis. He understands financial issues, has strong fund-raising skills, and connects on a very personal level with the university's heritage and its mission," Sherman concluded.

Born around 1955, Lawrence was raised on Long Island, New York. After completing high school, he enrolled at Williams College in Williamstown, Massachusetts, where he studied political economy.

Lawrence received his bachelor's degree magna cum laude in 1977 and then continued his studies at Yale University's law school in New Haven, Connecticut. In 1980, he completed his law degree at that institution and began his professional career as a clerk for Judge Amalya L. Kearse of the U.S. Court of Appeals' Second Circuit. Lawrence's next position was as assistant U.S. attorney for the southern district of New York state. In that role, he rose to head the district's Civil Rights Unit.

In 1988, Lawrence transitioned to the world of higher education when he became a faculty member at Boston University's law school. By that time, he had married Kathy, an American literature scholar, and the couple had had two children, Miriam and Noah. Over the next several years, Lawrence balanced raising his family in the Boston suburb of Brookline with teaching courses in civil rights crime, civil rights enforcement, criminal law, and civil procedure. In 1996, he received Boston University's prestigious Metcalf Award for teaching. That same year, Lawrence was named the law school's associate dean for academic affairs, a position he retained until 1999. During this period, Lawrence also authored the scholarly work *Punishing Hate: Bias Crimes Under American Law,* which was published by Harvard University Press in 1999.

In 2005, Lawrence joined the faculty of Washington, D.C.'s George Washington Law School as the Robert Kramer Research Professor of Law and the school's dean. As dean, Lawrence worked to attract elite students to the law program and build a faculty with diverse legal specialties. He oversaw the creation of the role of Lerner Family Associate Dean for Public Interest and Public Service Law, and added two new academic programs in national security and foreign relations law and business and finance law. Lawrence also strove to increase the university's international presence through the India Project and new foreign exchange programs that took students to the Netherlands and Italy. His financial management skills helped lessen the law school's debt and increase its endowment and financial aid programs. During his tenure at George Washington University, Lawrence also provided expert testimony to the U.S. Congress on hate crimes as part of the deliberation process on the Hate Crime Prevention Act of 2007. Speaking on George Washington University's Web site, university president Steven Knapp praised Lawrence as a "truly transformational dean and an exemplary university citizen."

In July of 2010, Brandeis University's search committee announced that it had selected Lawrence to replace long-time university president Jehuda Reinharz. Reinharz had made significant achievements during his 16-year tenure, including adding new endowed faculty chairs, opening new research centers, and expanding financial aid opportunities for the school's students. However, financial challenges placed such great pressures on the school, which relies heavily on donations to operate, that university administrators made the controversial decision to close Brandeis' art museum and auction off its valuable artwork in an effort to raise money. Although leaders eventually decided not to sell the art, cuts in faculty and academic programs followed in February of 2010 even as Reinharz announced plans to leave his position to head a Jewish educational foundation. The ensuing search for a new president led Brandeis to Lawrence, with search committee leaders drawn to his strong financial track record and his compatible human rights philosophy. "Brandeis is in its adolescence in a way; it's got some choices to make as it becomes a real grown-up world-class university," commented vice chairman of the Board of Trustees and search committee member Jack Connors, Jr., to Tracy Jan of the *Boston Globe.* "I think Fred will help guide the university to some wise decisions. There's only so [many] resources to go around, and I think he's thoughtful enough not to see them as an ox to be gored, but as a cow to be milked."

Lawrence left his position at George Washington University that fall to work with Reinharz for a time before officially assuming the presidency at Brandeis in January of 2011. His formal inauguration followed that March. "There is certainly a lot for me to absorb in a fairly short period of time and much to be done," commented the new president in a press release published by the States News Service during the transitional period. "[B]ut this period of discovery has left me even more excited for the challenges ahead. I look forward to meeting more students, faculty, and staff in the weeks ahead," he concluded. Among Lawrence's first duties was helping develop a plan to replace two top Brandeis administrators stepping down—provost and senior vice president for students and enrollment—along with considering how administrative positions of this type could be best structured for the university.

Selected writings

Punishing Hate: Bias Crimes Under American Law, Harvard University Press (Cambridge, MA), 1999.

Sources

Periodicals

Boston Globe, July 8, 2010.
Jewish Journal, July 12, 2010.

National Law Journal, July 8, 2010.

States News Service, July 8, 2010; September 1, 2010; January 1, 2011.

Online

"Frederick M. Lawrence Biography," Office of the President, Brandeis University, http://www.brandeis.edu/president/bio.html (May 21, 2011).

"GW Law Dean Frederick M. Lawrence Named Next President of Brandeis University," George Washington University, http://www.gwu.edu/explore/mediaroom/newsreleases/gwlawdean frederickmlawrencenamednextpresidentofbran deisuniversity (May 21, 2011).

—*Vanessa E. Vaughn*

Jennifer Lawrence

Actress

Born August 15, 1990, in Louisville, KY; daughter of Gary (a construction company owner) and Karen (a day camp manager) Lawrence.

Addresses: *Agent*—Creative Artists Agency, 2000 Avenue Of The Stars, Los Angeles, CA 90067.

Career

Actress on television, including: *Company Town*, 2006; *Not Another High School Show*, 2007; *The Bill Engvall Show*, 2007-2009. Television guest appearances include: *Monk*, 2006; *Cold Case*, 2006; *Medium*, 2007, 2008. Film appearances include: *The Burning Plain*, 2008; *Garden Party*, 2008; *The Poker House*, 2008; *Devil You Know*, 2009; *Winter's Bone*, 2010; *The Beaver*, 2011; *Like Crazy*, 2011; *X-Men: First Class*, 2011; *House at the End of the Street*, 2012; *The Hunger Games*, 2012.

Awards: Outstanding Performance Award, Los Angeles Film Festival, for *The Poker House*, 2008; Marcello Mastrocianni Award, Venice Film Festival, for *The Burning Plain*, 2008; (with others) outstanding young performers in a TV series, Young Artist Awards, for *The Bill Engvall Show*, 2009; NBR Award for best breakthrough performance, National Board of Review, for *Winter's Bone*, 2010; Rising Star Award, Palm Springs International Film Festival, 2011.

Sidelights

Actress Jennifer Lawrence gained widespread attention for her Academy Award- and Golden Globe-nominated performance in the 2010 independent drama *Winter's Bone*. The Grand Jury winner of that year's Sundance Film Festival, the movie catapulted its teenaged lead actress to great critical renown for her raw, powerful portrayal of a girl seeking her missing father in the crime- and drug-infused underworld of the impoverished Ozarks. Several more roles followed, most notably a turn in the 2011 summer blockbuster *X-Men: First Class* and a starring performance in the much-anticipated film adaption of the *Hunger Games*.

Born on August 15, 1990, in Louisville, Kentucky, Lawrence is the youngest of the three children of Gary Lawrence, a construction company owner, and his wife Karen, a day camp manager. Growing up, Lawrence had no particular attraction to acting; she attended public schools in Louisville, where she played sports and occasionally appeared in small local theater productions. Her life took a sharp turn, however, on a family spring break trip to New York City when Lawrence was 14. Speaking to Joseph Lord on the *Metromix Louisville* Web site, the actress remembered watching street dancers in the city's Union Square. "This guy was watching me, and he asked if he could take my picture. We didn't know that that was creepy, at the time. So we're like, 'Sure,'" she explained. "So he took my mom's phone number, and all of a sudden all these [modeling] agencies are calling. And that's when it all started," she concluded.

Soon after, Lawrence and her mother traveled back to New York in order for the teenager to audition for talent agencies. One agency praised her cold read for a candy commercial as the best it had ever seen for a person of her age, although Lawrence's mother—certainly not a budding stage parent—suggested that the company was lying; however, Lawrence had been bitten by the entertainment bug. She agreed to graduate from high school before making a serious effort to act, and completed her diploma two years ahead of schedule with a 3.9 average.

Lawrence and her mother then left Louisville for New York, where the teenager began auditioning for parts in earnest. Soon, she landed roles in commercials and picked up guest spots on television programs, including *Medium, Cold Case,* and *Monk.* In 2007, she debuted in her first regular television role on the TBC comedy *The Bill Engvall Show,* leaving New York for Los Angeles in order to film the program. The following year, Lawrence also appeared in a number of films: the small budget *Garden Party; The Poker House,* directed by actress Lori Petty; and *The Burning Plain,* which also featured stars Kim Basinger and Charlize Theron. Although the melodramatic film did not fare well commercially or critically, Lawrence's performance garnered her the Marcello Mastroianni Award at the 2008 Venice Film Festival.

Lawrence's next role proved to be the one that propelled her to stardom. Cast as the leading character of Ree Dolly in the dark drama *Winter's Bone,* the actress portrayed a teenager seeking to find her father so that he can appear for a scheduled court date, thus preventing the seizure of the family's home as part of his bail bond. In addition to her search for her father, Ree also cares for her younger brother and manages the household due to the practical catatonia of her mother. The events of the story are set in an impoverished rural area of the southern Missouri Ozarks, and the movie's depiction of the horrors of meth and its effects on people's lives were unstinting. Through the course of the film, Ree interacts with a number of meth-addled criminals, undergoes physical beatings, and endures a great deal of personal hardship. To portray the role

more realistically, the filmmakers had Lawrence actually undertake some of the actions performed by her character, such as skinning a squirrel and engaging in hard labor. "I've never been through anything that my characters have been through," the actress explained to Johanna Schneller of the Toronto *Globe and Mail.* "And I can't go around looking for roles that are exactly like my life. So I just use my imagination." Her imagination became the basis for what was widely considered one of the most powerful on-screen turns of 2010. "There's no denying the intensity in her *Winter's Bone* performance. Lawrence captures the fragility of this hardscrabble girl, seemingly doing so with ease," commented Steve Heisler of *Daily Variety.*

Despite being made on an extremely low budget, *Winter's Bone* was selected for inclusion at the highly respected Sundance Film Festival. There, it received a great deal of praise, ultimately carrying away the festival's top prize for drama and instantly making its star a talked-about contender for an Academy Award nomination—much to her surprise. "I got recognized on the street, and someone said, 'I love *Winter's Bone,*'" she told Jay A. Fernandez of the *Hollywood Reporter.* "And I was like, 'You saw *Winter's Bone*?'" The film was lauded at festivals that followed, and ultimately picked up several major award nominations. Lawrence herself earned both Golden Globe and Academy Award nominations as best lead actress, making her the second-youngest person to achieve that honor for the latter prize.

This growing notoriety and work schedule greatly changed Lawrence's life, taking her out of normal teenage activities in favor of life in front of the camera. "I've had a career since I was 14, I pay my own rent, I live on my own, and I'm not going to have a lot in common with somebody who's my age," she commented to Stephen Heyman of the *New York Times T* magazine in 2010. "And I know I sound like a jerk, but what are we going to talk about? Prom? I didn't go to prom. Or your boyfriend? I'm working—all the time."

In early 2011, Lawrence made headlines when she was cast in the starring role of Katniss Everdeen in the big-screen adaptation of the wildly popular young adult *Hunger Games* trilogy. Because the 20-year-old Lawrence was four years older than and physically unlike the dark-haired, olive-skinned character she was set to portray, some fans and others questioned the casting choice; however, film director Gary Ross and series creator Suzanne Collins stood by the decision to give the role to Lawrence. "We can't have an insubstantial person play [Katniss], and we can't have someone who's too young to play this," Ross argued in an *Entertainment Weekly* interview with Karen Valby. "Far from being too old, [Collins] was very concerned that we would cast someone who was too young. In Suzanne's mind, and in mine, Katniss is not a young girl. It's important for her to be a young woman.... [And] I promise all the avid fans of *The Hunger Games* that we can easily deal with Jennifer's hair color," he added. "Jennifer's just an incredible actress," agreed Collins in a separate statement printed in *Entertainment Weekly*. "So powerful, vulnerable, beautiful, unforgiving and brave. I never thought we'd find somebody this amazing for the role. And I can't wait for everyone to see her play it," she concluded. Production was soon underway, and the film was scheduled for a spring 2012 release. Lawrence was also attached to appear in the film adaptations of the two following books of the trilogy, *Catching Fire* and *Mockingjay.*

Short months after this high-profile casting announcement, Lawrence lit up the big screen in the comic book blockbuster *X-Men: First Class.* Cast as the youthful incarnation of Raven Darkholme/Mystique, Lawrence donned full-body blue makeup to act as the shape-shifting mutant, a character played by actress Rebecca Romjin in the series' first three films. The big-budget action film was a sharp departure from her earlier, independent dramas in what Lawrence acknowledged was an intentional creative shift. "It's easy to get pigeonholed, so I think it's important that when one thing gets really big, it's a wise decision to do the opposite," the actress explained to Danielle Nussbaum of *Teen Vogue.* Although the movie received some negative reviews—Joshua Zyber of *Home Theater* complained that "the screenplay is largely repetitive of story line[s] that have already been covered in prior movies. Young Mystique's character arc is virtually the same as Rogue's, and a subplot about a cure for mutantism is recycled straight from *The Last Stand*"—Lawrence generally won positive notices for her supporting role. "While their brief physiological transformations limit their expressiveness, [Nicholas] Hoult [as Beast] and Lawrence register poignantly as two young individuals trying to figure out their unique place in a hostile world," commented Justin Chang in *Daily Variety.*

The actress also performed in lower-key films throughout the year. She co-starred alongside Mel Gibson and actress/director Jodie Foster in *The Beaver,* a dark comedy about a depressed man (Gibson) who begins communicating with the outside world through the mouth of a beaver puppet. In *The Beaver,* Lawrence played the teenaged love interest of Gibson's character's son, portrayed by Anton Yelchin. The film received mixed reviews, with critics alternately praising and complaining about its complex, layered storyline, but Lawrence was hailed as "luminous" by Ross Douthat of the *National Review.* Later in 2011, the actress again teamed up with Yelchin in the independent romantic drama *Like Crazy.* The story of a pair of lovers separated by immigration problems, the film cast Lawrence as the sometimes-love interest of the male lead as time and distance keep the primary pairing apart. A film festival favorite, the work received generally positive critical nods for its complex acting.

Also scheduled for release in the spring of 2012 was a dark horror film titled *House at the End of the Street.* Starring Lawrence as a teenager who moves to a new city with her mother, the film follows the development of Lawrence's character's friendship with a neighborhood boy whose family was brutally murdered not long before in a house nearby. "The project is looking to be to *Psycho* what *Disturbia* was to *Rear Window*," surmised Borys Kit in a review for *Hollywood Reporter.* Originally filmed before the release of *Winter's Bone,* the film waited for several months to find distribution before being picked up by Relativity in April of 2011. Lawrence was also set to co-star alongside Bradley Cooper in *The Silver Linings Playbook,* a light-hearted film about the development of an unusual friendship between Cooper's and Lawrence's characters as Cooper's character tries to come to terms with his life after spending four years in a mental hospital. Helmed by Academy Award-nominated director David O. Russell, the movie began filming in late 2011, and was slated for release in the fall of the following year.

Despite her increasingly high profile and many star turns, Lawrence remained adamant that acting and fame were not the defining features of her life. In late 2010, she told Glenn Whipp of *Daily Variety* about the only magazine clipping of herself she had saved. "Somebody had drawn a moustache on me," she explained. "(My friend) sent it, writing, 'I didn't even do this. Somebody else doesn't like you.' Nobody really cares," she continued. "Acting's my job, but it has absolutely nothing to do with who I am."

Sources

Periodicals

Daily Variety, October 15, 2010, p. A2; October 25, 2010, p. A5; December 6, 2010, p. A1; May 31, 2011, p. 2.
Globe and Mail (Toronto, Canada), June 12, 2010.

Hollywood Reporter, June 4, 2010, p. 4; January 26, 2011, p. 50.
Home Theater, December 2011, p. 70.
National Review, June 6, 2011, p. 50.
Teen Vogue, May 2011, p. 110.

Online

"About Jennifer," Jennifer Lawrence Official Web site, http://jenniferslawrence.com/about-jen/ (November 21, 2011).
"*Hunger Games* director Gary Ross talks about 'the easiest casting decision of my life'—EXCLUSIVE," *Entertainment Weekly,* http://insidemovies.ew.com/2011/03/17/hunger-games-gary-ross-jennifer-lawrence/ (November 21, 2011).

"*Hunger Games*: Suzanne Collins talks Jennifer Lawrence as Katniss—EXCLUSIVE," *Entertainment Weekly,* http://insidemovies.ew.com/2011/03/21/hunger-games-suzanne-collins-jennifer-lawrence/ (November 21, 2011).
"Jennifer Lawrence: Bigger Things," *Metromix Louisville,* http://louisville.metromix.com/movies/article/jennifer-lawrence-bigger-things/1535101/content (September 21, 2011).
"The Nifty 50: Jennifer Lawrence, Actress," *New York Times T Magazine,* http://tmagazine.blogs.nytimes.com/2010/02/02/the-nifty-50-jennifer-lawrence-actress/ (September 21, 2011).

—Vanessa E. Vaughn

Eric Lefkofsky

Venture capitalist

Born September 1, 1969, in Detroit, MI; son of William (a structural engineer) and Sandy (a teacher) Lefkofsky; married Elizabeth Kramer (a philanthropist). *Education:* Earned undergraduate degree from the University of Michigan, 1991; University of Michigan Law School, J.D., 1993.

Addresses: *Office*—c/o Lefkofsky Family Foundation, 346 Grove St., Glencoe, IL 60022-2056; LightBank, Inc., 600 W. Chicago Ave., Ste. 700, Chicago, IL 60654. *Web site*—http://www.lefkofsky.com/.

Career

Founder and salesperson, Apex Industries, late 1980s; co-owner, Brandon Apparel, after 1993; co-founder, Starbelly, 1999; chief operating officer, Ha-Lo Industries, 2000-01; co-founder and senior executive of companies, including: InnerWorkings (founded 2001), Echo Global Logistics (founded 2005), MediaBank (founded 2006), ThePoint.com (founded 2007), Groupon.com (founded 2008), and LightBank (founded 2010). Created the Lefkofsky Family Foundation, 2006.

Sidelights

Eric Lefkofsky provided the funds to launch Groupon.com, the phenomenally successful e-commerce site, back in 2008. Groupon—short for "group coupon"—signs up users to receive a daily email offer for a local restaurant or service provider, often at an enticing discount. If enough users buy in, the deal becomes valid. Since its launch, the company, for which Lefkofsky serves as chair, has grown exponentially and was predicted to hit the $1-billion sales mark by 2011, making it the "the Fastest Growing Company Ever" in U.S. business history, as *Forbes* magazine called it.

Lefkofsky was born in 1969 and raised in a Detroit suburb. When he and his friend Noah Siegel were about to enter the University of Michigan, Siegel's father suggested they set up a business selling carpet remnants from the Siegel family store to incoming freshman to spruce up their dormitory rooms. The business was phenomenally successful, and Lefkofsky and Siegel expanded it to other colleges over the next few years. Before earning his degree in 1991, Lefkofsky used some of his profits to start a college-logo apparel company aimed at the children's market.

Lefkofsky earned his law degree at the University of Michigan in 1993, but continued to be drawn to entrepreneurial opportunities. With a fellow U-M alum named Brad Keywell, he bought an established Wisconsin-based clothing company in 1993, but the venture dissolved into a quagmire of debt and lawsuits. He and Keywell, undaunted, came up with an idea to sell specialty-promotional products like T-shirts and mugs in 1999 via the rapidly expanding world of e-commerce. "If you had a business plan" for a Web-based business back then, Lefkofsky recalled in an interview with Melissa Harris in the *Chicago Tribune,* "you could like roll it down the street and people would just throw money at it."

In early 2000 Lefkofsky and Keywell sold their company, called Starbelly, to Ha-Lo Industries in a deal worth $240 million, most of it in Ha-Lo stock.

Lefkofsky was brought on chief operating officer of Ha-Lo, but the company went bankrupt a year later when the dot-com bubble burst. Lefkofsky had better luck with his next venture, InnerWorkings, which was a web-based broker of printing services, helping companies find the lowest bidder for the job. In 2005 he and Keywell founded another company that also prospered, Echo Global Logistics. This was a freight logistics company, and became a publicly traded firm in 2009. It followed InnerWorkings' initial public offering (IPO) of stock in 2006, and Lefkofsky profited handsomely in both deals.

Lefkofsky, by this point married and living in Chicago, was busy running MediaBank, another company he had founded with Keywell, when a former InnerWorkings employee came to him with a business proposal. Andrew Mason, a musician and Northwestern University graduate, envisioned a Web site that could harness grass-roots support for user-created causes. Lefkofsky agreed to fund it, and ThePoint.com went live in late 2007 with a $1 million investment. The Web site quickly devolved into a chaotic free-for-all, gaining publicity for tongue-in-cheek fund-raising goals set up by users. One petitioner, for example, raised money to combat AIDS/HIV in Africa, but the bargain specified that if the target amount was met, Irish-born rock singer Bono would have to retire from public life forever. There was also a $10 million offer to force the band Weezer to break up.

Lefkofsky still believed in the original idea of collective action on the Web, and sat down with Mason to refocus the company as it plunged toward financial disaster. Mason had written a blog attached to ThePoint.com and had had surprising success with a "daily deal" offer. He and Lefkofsky decided to turn that idea into Groupon, which was originally called Getyourgroupon.com. Its first offer to subscribers was a half-off deal from a pizzeria in their office building.

Groupon was officially launched in November of 2008, offering local restaurant deals, personal-care services, and even a discount for a visit to an isolation tank. The deals operated on a limited-time-only basis, and if enough subscribers agreed to the deal, their credit or debit card would be charged. The venture proved especially popular with small businesses with little budget for advertising or promotion, and quickly expanded out of Chicago into Boston, New York, Washington, and other several other cities. It also spawned a rash of copycats, including LivingSocial.com. Hiring staff to roll out their expansion markets required infusions of venture capital, and as Groupon caught on with users Wall Street analysts pegged it as one of the hot new companies whose eventual IPO would make early investors rich.

In December of 2010, Google reportedly tried to buy Groupon for a sum rumored to be between $5 and $6 billion. Lefkofsky, Mason, and other key executives rejected the offer, preferring to wait for the IPO. Papers were filed in advance of that with the U.S. Securities and Exchange Commission in June of 2011, with the company valued at an astonishing $15 and $20 billion. Should Groupon become a publicly traded company in late 2011, Lefkofsky would become Chicago's wealthiest citizen. Asked about the prospect of surpassing even the famous Wrigley and Pritzker fortunes by Harris in the *Chicago Tribune* interview, Lefkofsky replied that "there comes a point where you reach a level of success, financial or otherwise, when you just kind of stop counting because, counting, it just doesn't change things."

Lefkofsky and his wife are active in several Chicago-area philanthropies, and funnel some of their wealth into the Lefkofsky Family Foundation, which supports children's charities. He teaches courses in entrepreneurship and the creation of technology-based businesses at the Booth School of Business at the University of Chicago and still funds start-up ventures through LightBank, Inc., a venture-capital firm he and Keywell founded in 2010. Groupon had become Chicago's first superstar tech company, and Lefkofsky hoped that LightBank could help turn the city into the Silicon Valley of the Midwest. "It's just the law of numbers," he told *Fortune* writer Dan Primack. "When you have thousands of smart people working on something, some of them will eventually start working on something else."

Sources

Periodicals

Chicago Tribune, December 5, 2010.
Forbes, August 30, 2010.
New York Times, November 17, 2010; June 19, 2011.

Online

"The Checkered Past of Groupon's Chairman," *Fortune*, http://tech.fortune.cnn.com/2011/06/10/groupon-eric-lefkofsky/ (August 4, 2011).
"Chicago Needs More 'Ego,'" *Fortune*, http://finance.fortune.cnn.com/2010/10/04/groupon-co-founder-chicago-needs-more-ego/ (August 1, 2011).
"Early Years," Lefkofsky.com, http://www.lefkofsky.com/blog/when-you-dont-know-what-to-say (August 1, 2011).
"More Wall Street Banks Grab Groupon I.P.O.," Dealbook, http://dealbook.nytimes.com/2011/07/14/more-wall-street-banks-grab-groupon-i-p-o/?scp=1&sq=lefkofsky&st=nyt (August 1, 2011).

—*Carol Brennan*

Maggie Q

© Jon Kopaloff/FilmMagic/Getty Images

Actress

Born Maggie Denise Quigley, May 22, 1979, in Honolulu, HI.

Addresses: *Agent*—Echelon Talent Management, 3674 Oxford St., Vancouver, BC V5K 1P3 Canada; William Morris Endeavor Management, 9601 Wilshire Blvd., 3rd Fl., Beverly Hills, CA 90210.

Career

Actress in films, including: *Gen-X Cops 2: Metal Mayhem*, 2000; *Model from Hell*, 2000; *Manhattan Midnight*, 2001; *Rush Hour 2*, 2001; *Naked Weapon*, 2002; *Around the World in 80 Days*, 2004; *Magic Kitchen*, 2004; *Rice Rhapsody*, 2004; *Dragon Squad*, 2005; *Taped*, 2005; *Mission: Impossible III*, 2006; *The Trouble-Makers*, 2006; *Balls of Fury*, 2007; *The Counting House*, 2007; *Live Free or Die Hard*, 2007; *Deception*, 2008; *Three Kingdoms: Resurrection of the Dragon*, 2008; *New York, I Love You*, 2009; *The Warrior and the Wolf*, 2009; *The King of Fighters*, 2010; *Operation: Endgame*, 2010; *Priest*, 2011. Television appearances include: *House of Harmony* (movie), 2005; *Nikita*, The CW, 2010—. Video game appearances include: *Need for Speed*, 2008. Stage appearances include *All Hallow's Eve*, Hong Kong, 2002.

Awards: Best supporting actress, Asian Excellence Awards, 2006; Person of the Year Award, PETA Asia-Pacific, 2008.

Sidelights

While Asian-American actress Maggie Q first found major success in Hong Kong as a model and actress, American audiences know her for her appearance in such blockbuster films as *Mission: Impossible III* and *Live Free or Die Hard*. She is perhaps best known for her starring role in the CW series *Nikita*, playing the titular rogue assassin. In many of her parts, Maggie draws on martial arts training she received from action star Jackie Chan. Authenticity in her work as an actress was important to Maggie who told Mike Gordon of the *Honolulu Star-Advertiser*, "I owe my audience something authentic. I feel if they are tuning in and if they like my work, then they should see something and experience something very real because I want it to be real for them, because it's definitely real for me."

Born Maggie Denise Quigley on May 22, 1979, in Honolulu, Hawaii, her father was an American of Polish descent and her mother was a native of Vietnam. Her mother worked as a property investor. Her parents met when her father served in Vietnam during the Vietnam War. She, her two older sisters, and two half-siblings from a previous marriage of her mother's, were raised in Hawaii. As a child, she was a swimmer and a runner, and wanted to become a veterinarian, but began modeling in Japan when she was 17 years old. She graduated from Mililani High School and began attending college. She also tried modeling in Taiwan for two months but with no luck. After a semester of school, she went to Hong Kong on a one-way ticket and found great success, modeling for the likes of Chanel and Gucci. By the time she was in her early twenties, Maggie became a supermodel in Hong Kong, appearing on many magazine covers and in several television commercials.

In the early 2000s, Maggie eventually turned to acting and became a major star in Asia. She was guided by martial arts action star Jackie Chan, who sought out new young actors and actresses to appear in films he was producing. His team trained actors and actresses like Maggie in various disciplines of martial arts. She told Sharon Lougher of *Metro*, "I think the biggest thing I learned from him was work ethic. I don't know a harder-working person. When you work with someone like that, who has come from nothing, he doesn't take s*** from anyone. You have to work really hard, otherwise you're gone.... If we dropped something and didn't pick it up, or didn't put something away, or weren't respecting somebody, we would get yelled at. It was know your place, do your job, do it well."

It was because of Maggie's acting career that she adopted the moniker "Maggie Q"—Chinese audiences found it difficult to pronounce Quigley. Her first film was 2000's *Model from Hell* followed by *Manhattan Midnight* and *Gen-X Cops 2: Metal Mayhem*. Maggie had a starring role in *Gen-X Cops 2*, playing a cool FBI agent. Her work in this film became an early highlight of her career, as was her stage debut in a Hong Kong production of *All Hallow's Eve* by David Pinner. As she took on more acting roles, Maggie was still labeled a model-turned-actress, though a good one. She told Lionel Seah of the Singapore *Straits Times*, "Yes, I'm a cliche. But I don't care." She continued, "I don't blame these stereotypes. Look at Cindy Crawford and Elle MacPherson. Just because one can doesn't mean one should."

While Maggie primarily appeared in Asian films throughout much of the first decade of the 2000s, she also dabbled in American films. She had a memorable cameo in 2001's *Rush Hour 2*, which starred her mentor Chan. Other noteworthy films included 2002's *Naked Weapon*, directed by Alfred Chung and featuring both Asian and American actors. Maggie received much attention for her work in the film because she appeared topless, creating a media firestorm. By 2003, Maggie was writing her own low budget film about a supermodel who turns the tables on her fans and stalks them, though the project did not reach completion.

Maggie began moving back and forth between films intended for Asian audiences and Hollywood films. Her Asian films included 2004's *Magic Kitchen* and *Rice Rhapsody*, 2005's *Dragon Squad*, and 2006's *The Trouble-Makers*. Her American films included 2004's *Around the World in 80 Days* (which also starred Chan) and 2005's *Taped*. In 2006, she had a significant supporting role in the Tom Cruise vehicle *Mission: Impossible III*, which marked the directorial debut of *Lost* creator J. J. Abrams. In this big budget action film, Maggie played Zhen, a member of the Mission team headed by Cruise's character, Ethan Hunt. Though Maggie developed kung fu skills in her Asian action films, *Mission: Impossible III* taught her combat skills, which she learned from hostage negotiators and military experts. She told Agence France Presse, "It was no joke. What I did in the film is real. I actually know how to rescue a hostage now. It was unbelievable and pretty surreal."

Building on the success of *Mission: Impossible III*, Maggie was cast in another high-profile Hollywood action film, *Live Free or Die Hard*, without even auditioning. The fourth installment of a popular Bruce Willis films series in which he plays maverick cop John McClane, Maggie's Mai was the villain and she used her kickboxing skills in the role to fight McClane. Maggie told Georgina Dickinson of the *News of the World*, "I'm totally into being strong and love whacking people.... I hate it when girls fight and they look too pretty or too smooth." *Live Free or Die Hard* was released in 2007, as was *The Counting House* and *Balls of Fury*. The latter film was a comedy about competitive ping pong while also being a spoof of martial arts films. Directed by Ben Garant (a star of the Comedy Central series *Reno 911!*), Maggie played a rule breaker and girlfriend of Randy Daytona, a ping pong protégée who choked at the 1988 Olympics and retired in shame.

Maggie appeared in two films in 2008—*Three Kingdoms: Resurrection of the Dragon* and *Deception*—and also was the star of a video game released by Electronic Arts, *Need for Speed Undercover*. She played Federal Agent Chase Linh in the racing game which featured big budget live action sequences. Her Linh was a sexy handler who recruits and guides players as they go undercover. Players took on dangerous jobs and compete in races to infiltrate and take down an international crime syndicate. In 2009, Maggie appeared in the Woody Allen film, *New York, I Love You*, as well as *The Warrior and the Wolf*.

She played the lead in the latter film, which was directed by Chinese Fifth Generation director Tian Zhuangzhuang and based on a short novel by Japanese author Inoue Yasushi. Maggie played a tribal woman living in the Harran village who gives shelter to a warrior general, Odagiri, in ancient China near the Silk Road.

In 2010, Maggie saw two more films released, *The King of Fighters* and *Operation: Endgame,* and also broke into American television. While she had previously appeared in a television movie, playing the title role of Harmony Petersen in *House of Harmony* in 2005, she became a television star with her leading role in the hit series, *Nikita,* which aired on the CW. *Nikita* was based on a 1990 French film, *La Femme Nikita* and another television series that aired in the late 1990s, but was not a rehash; instead it was a revamped version of the concept. Maggie played the titular Nikita, an operative trained to kill by a shadowy government agency called Division. She goes rogue with the intent of bringing down the agency to stop it from ruining other people's lives by forcing them to undergo the training to become a Division agent.

Playing Nikita, Maggie was able to show off the skills she gained in martial arts films over the years. She told Alex Strachan of the Canwest News Service, "I've done action movies, but I've never done an action television show, which is a whole other deal. Really, your level never goes down. You have to be on your game all the time." Maggie added that people have stereotyped her skills because of her ethnic background. She stated to Strachan, "Because I'm half Asian, people immediately go, 'Oh, well, you do kung fu.' Like, that's what we do, all of us."

Critics responded positively to Maggie's work in the role and *Nikata* as a whole. In the *New York Times,* Alessandra Stanley called it "a surprisingly sophisticated and satisfying adapation." Stanley also noted "how suited Maggie Q is to the role of Nikita; she has a solemn, exotic beauty and hauteur that echo the heroine's self-possession and cool relentlessness." Writing about the show in *USA Today,* Robert Bianco also praised the series and Maggie. Bianco said, "Q combines stunt-fighting chops and lithe beauty with an unusual-for-the-genre air of somber intelligence. Her Nikita is not above cracking a joke, but it's clear from Q's eyes and bearing that she has suffered at the hands of evil men, and she's not going to take it anymore." *Nikita* was renewed for a second season, and continued to draw an audience for its network.

Building on the success and celebrity that *Nikita* brought her in the United States, Maggie became a more outspoken supporter of animal rights. A vegetarian, she owned three dogs and was active with animal protection groups. She told Lynn Elber of the Associated Press, "I've never felt better in my life, ever. In terms of consciousness, what benefits our body and benefits animal welfare also benefits the planet. It's all connected." Continuing to work in film as well, Maggie had a role in the 2011 science fiction/western/vampire film *Priest,* playing a priest in a troubled post-apocalyptic world.

While Maggie landed parts in Hollywood films, television, and video games, she believed that Asian actors and actresses still had a hard time landing prime roles. Noting that American directors and producers are confused by her biracial background, she told Min Lee of the Associated Press, "They think, 'Wow, what is this? There's this girl. She's Asian, but she's not…. They're really not sure where to put me." She added, "It's a struggle. You got to win roles. You really got to fight for them. When I left Asia and went to the U.S., essentially I was starting over. It's very hard. It's a lot of work."

Sources

Periodicals

Agence France Presse, April 7, 2006.
Associated Press, October 14, 2008; September 30, 2010.
Business Wire, August 15, 2008.
Canwest News Service, September 2, 2010.
Daily Variety, June 9, 2011, p. A1.
Edmonton Journal (Alberta, Canada), May 14, 2011, p. C5.
Honolulu Star-Advertiser, October 24, 2010.
Metro (UK), October 7, 2010, pp. 38-39.
News of the World (England), July 1, 2007.
New York Times, September 8, 2010, p. C1.
Screen International, September 26, 2008.
Straits Times, December 16, 2000, pp. 4-5; August 17, 2003.
USA Today, September 9, 2010, p. 6D.
Vancouver Sun (British Columbia, Canada), August 29, 2007, p. D3.
Variety, May 8-14, 2006, p. 72; September 2010, p. 40.

Online

"Maggie Q," Internet Movie Database, http://www.imdb.com/name/nm0702572/filmotype (October 30, 2011).

—*A. Petruso*

Henning Mankell

Author

Born February 3, 1948, in Stockholm, Sweden; son of Ivar Mankell (a judge); married Eva Bergman (a choreographer and theater director), 1998; children: four sons (from other relationships before his marriage to Bergman).

Addresses: *Office*—Colombine Teaterförlag, Gaffelgränd 1A, SE-111 30 Stockholm.

Career

Worked as a merchant seaman, loading and unloading ships, before working in the theater and becoming a full-time writer with the publication of his first book, *The Rockblaster*, 1973. Author of novels and nonfiction, including: *The Prison Colony that Disappeared*, 1979; *The Eye of the Leopard*, 1990; *A Bridge to the Stars*, 1990; *Faceless Killers*, 1991; *Shadows in the Twilight*, 1991; *The Cat Who Liked Rain*, 1992; *The White Lioness*, 1993; *The Dogs of Riga*, 1994; *The Man Who Smiled*, 1994; *Chronicler of the Winds*, 1995; *Secrets in the Fire*, 1995; *Sidetracked*, 1995; *The Fifth Woman*, 1996; *When the Snow Fell*, 1996; *One Step Behind*, 1997; *Firewall*, 1998; *A Journey to the End of the World*, 1998; *The Pyramid*, 1999; *Daniel*, 2000; *The Return of the Dancing Master*, 2000; *Playing With Fire*, 2001; *Before the Frost*, 2002; *I Die, But the Memory Lives On*, 2003; *Depths*, 2004; *Italian Shoes*, 2006; *Kennedy's Brain*, 2005; *The Man from Beijing*, 2007; *The Troubled Man*, 2009. Head of the Kronobergsteatern in Växjö, Sweden, 1984—; head of the Teatro Avenida in Maputo, Mozambique, 1986—; founded Leopard Förlag publishing company, 2001; has written more than 30 plays, many of which have been performed at the Teatro Avenida or the Kronobergsteatern; the Wallander books have been adapted for television in Sweden and in the United Kingdom.

Awards: Best children's book, Rabén and Sjögren Award, for *A Bridge to the Stars*, 1990; best Swedish crime novel, Swedish Crime Writers' Academy, for *Faceless Killers*, 1991; Nils Holgersson Prize, for *A Bridge to the Stars*, 1991; Glass Key Award for best Nordic crime novel, for *Faceless Killers*, 1992; Deutsche Jugendliteraturpreis, for *A Bridge to the Stars*, 1993; best Swedish crime novel, Swedish Crime Writers' Academy, for *Sidetracked*, 1995; Astrid Lindgren Prize, Sweden, 1996; Gold Dagger for best crime novel of the year, Crime Writers' Association, for *Sidetracked*, 2001; Corine Literature Prize, for *One Step Behind*, 2001; Gumshoe Award for best European crime novel, *Mystery Ink*, for *The Return of the Dancing Master*, 2005; Corine Literature Prize for the German audiobook, for *The Man from Beijing*, 2008; honorary doctorate, University of St. Andrews, 2008.

Sidelights

Best-selling author Henning Mankell has sold more than 40 million books, and his work has been translated into 41 different languages. He is best known for his series of crime novels featuring police officer Kurt Wallander, but he has also written many books inspired by his experiences living in Africa and his youth as a merchant seaman.

Mankell was born in Stockholm, Sweden, in February of 1948. Mankell's mother left the family when he was one year old. As he told Nicholas Wroe in the *Guardian*, "She couldn't stand having children, which is a terrible thing for a child to deal with, but really she just behaved as many men do." He did eventually meet her, when he was 15, but he could not get over disliking her because she had abandoned him. She eventually committed suicide.

He and his older sister Helena were raised by his father, Ivar Mankell, a judge. When he was two years old, his father was offered a job in the small town of Sveg in northern Sweden, and Mankell grew up there in a small apartment on the floor above the law courts. Throughout his childhood, the children had to be very quiet on Mondays, when court was in session, and once during a case involving a traffic accident, a court official came upstairs to borrow Mankell's toy cars for a demonstration of the incident.

Mankell's father encouraged him to read but let him decide for himself what to read, and he chose to read about Africa, the farthest place he could imagine from his snowy town in Sweden. On his Web site, Mankell noted, "Africa was the most exotic place I could imagine—the end of the world—and I knew I would go there one day." In his imagination, he became an explorer in Africa, and the little river in Sveg became a tropical river filled with crocodiles. In his mind, he also created a mother who loved him and who was there for him, to replace the mother who had left.

When he was six his grandmother taught him to write, and the experience had a profound effect on him. As he wrote on his Web site, "I can still remember the miraculous feeling of writing a sentence, then more sentences, telling a story." The first thing he wrote was a retelling of the story of desert-island castaway Robinson Crusoe. He remarked, "It was at that moment I became an author." He told Bob Cornwell in an interview for the Tangled Web Books Web site that he "decided very early. I can't remember having any other dream in my life as a child than being an author. That was what I wanted."

When Mankell was 13, his family moved to Borås, on the west coast of Sweden. Bored in school, Mankell dropped out when he was 16 and went to Paris, but soon left that city and signed on as a merchant seaman. He worked loading and unloading a Swedish ship that carried coal and iron ore between Europe and the United States. On his Web site, he wrote, "I loved the ship's decent hard-working community. It was my real university."

He returned to Paris in 1966, and, after a year and a half there, he moved back to Stockholm, where he worked as a stagehand. During this time he wrote his first play, *The Amusement Park,* about Swedish colonial interests in 19th-century South America. He told Cornwell that directing plays was similar to writing, but that when he directed a play he had the pleasure of working with other people rather than alone. "And I was quite successful immediately," he told Cornwell. "It made it possible to let the theatre pay for my work as an author. If I directed one play, it would give me five months to write."

In 1973 Mankell published his first novel, *Bergspraengaren* ("The Rockblaster"), which was set in the midst of a workers' union movement. Mankell's father died shortly before the book was published, but Mankell wrote on his Web site that he always knew his father believed he would be successful as a writer.

Mankell used the money from the book to travel to Guinea-Bissau in Africa. He remarked on his Web site, "I don't know why but when I got off the plane in Africa, I had a curious feeling of coming home." Since that time, Mankell has spent much of his life in Africa.

In 1979, Mankell published the novel *Fåvårdskolonin som fösvann,* ("The Prison Colony That Disappeared") with the Ordfront publishing company. He worked with editor Dan Israel, beginning a long partnership. Ordfront published a Mankell novel almost every year from then until 2001. Many of the books have since been translated into English and other languages, but not necessarily in the order in which Mankell wrote them.

In 1984, Mankell became the head of Kronobergsteatern, a theater in Växjö, Sweden. His mission was to produce only Swedish plays, an unusual venture at the time, but it was successful. In 1986 he was invited to Maputo, Mozambique, to run a local theater, the Teatro Avenida. He has spent at least half of every year there since then, writing his books and working with the theater. The theater's mission is to examine the political and social issues that affect people in Mozambique. Mankell writes or cowrites many of the plays performed there. He told Wroe that "Three-quarters of the audience can't read or write, so live theatre is important."

Between 1984 and 1990, Mankell spent so much time working with the two theaters that he did not have time to write any new books. He returned to fiction in 1990, publishing two novels, *Leopardens öga* ("The Eye of the Leopard") and *Hunden som sprang mot en stjäma* ("A Bridge to the Stars"), both of which were eventually translated into English. *The Eye of the Leopard* contrasts a man's experiences growing up in Sweden with his life in Africa. *A Bridge to the Stars,* a young-adult novel about the adventures of 12-year-old Joel, a motherless boy growing up in northern Sweden, won the Rabén and Sjögren award for best children's book of the year.

In 1991, Mankell took a new direction with his writing, moving into the field of crime fiction. He had been in Africa for some time, and when he returned to Sweden he became deeply aware of the prevalence of racism in Swedish society. He wrote on his Web site, "To me racism is a crime, and I thought: Ok, I'll use the crime story. Then I realised I needed a police officer, and I picked the name Wallander out of the telephone directory."

His hero, Inspector Kurt Wallander, is troubled by issues affecting Swedish society, including racism, and wants to understand why people are racist, why they hurt children, and why they perpetrate horrible crimes. Wallander's questioning, probing nature regarding the ills of society gives the books a depth sometimes not found in crime fiction.

Mankell told Cornwell that he tries "to use the mirror of crime to look at a whole society." In his mind, the best crime stories ever written are *Macbeth* by Shakespeare and *Heart of Darkness* by Joseph Conrad. He added, to Cornwell, "I would never ever think of writing a crime story for the sake of itself. I really wanted to talk about certain things in society." As crime writer Ruth Rendell told Ian Thomson in the *Guardian,* "Mankell is modern, and he makes you reflect on society." Mankell takes pains to create detailed, realistic portraits of Wallander and his colleagues as people. Thomson also quoted novelist Maggie Gee, who praised Mankell's "leisurely, layered craft with which Mankell establishes the humanity of his policemen," and who noted that the Wallander books have "the density and pleasurable authority of a 19th-century novel."

The first book in the series, *Faceless Killers,* was immediately successful in Sweden, but it was not until two books later, with *The White Lioness,* that Mankell's books about Wallander became international bestsellers. *The White Lioness* was set partly in South Africa and was published simultaneously in several countries; as Markell wrote on his Web site, it "blew out the gates" and garnered him a legion of readers; however, Mankell was slow to gain fans

in the United States. His American translator, Steven Murray, told Thomson that he believed this was because Mankell emphasized "procedure and deduction, rather than action."

Mankell wrote nine books about Wallander, then decided to retire his detective; he did not want to keep writing the books until he was bored with them, and, by extension, readers became bored with them too. In the final book, *The Troubled Man,* Wallander is aging, suffering from occasional memory loss, but trying to figure out the most complicated case of his career. In the *Courier-Mail,* Bron Sibree called the book "deeply melancholy yet profoundly moving," and wrote that although it is a blend of spy thriller and police procedural, it "manages to transcend both genres."

Despite the end of the Wallander series, Mankell continued to write crime novels featuring Wallander's daughter, Linda; the first, *Innan Frosten* (2002; "Before the Frost"), involved a religious doomsday cult. Thomson noted that the character of Linda Wallander is based on a real female police officer somewhere in Sweden, who had shared her journals with Mankell. Her identity is still unknown.

While writing the Wallander series, Markell continued to write other novels. In 1991 he wrote a sequel to *A Bridge to the Stars,* titled *Skuggoma växeri skymningen* ("Shadows in the Twilight"). In this novel, Joel is hit by a bus but is miraculously unhurt, and he has to figure out some way to understand how this could be possible, and whether it demands some sort of response from him: why has he been saved? In the next book in the series, *Pojken som sov med snö i sin säng* ("When the Snow Fell"), Joel is now 14 years old and on the cusp of maturity. He ardently wants to escape the small, sleepy Swedish town that is his home and visit the sea.

In 1995, Mankell published *Eldens hemlighet* ("Secrets in the Fire"). It was the first book in a trilogy about a real African girl, Sofia, who lost her legs when she stepped on a hidden landmine. On his Web site, Mankell explained, "Sofia is one of my closest and dearest friends. No one has taught me as much as she has about the conditions of being human. Nor has anyone taught me more about poor people's unprecedented power of resistance." The first book in the trilogy was followed by *Eldens gåta* ("Playing with Fire") in 2001, and *Eldens vrede* ("The Fury in the Fire") in 2005. The Swedish government gave a free copy of the book to every schoolchild in Sweden; Mankell gave the proceeds to Sofia and her village.

In addition to working in the theater in Mozambique, Mankell has been deeply involved in another African project, the creation of "memory books" by the huge number of people who are dying of the AIDS epidemic in Africa. Parents record their lives in words and pictures, "not just for the children they leave behind, but also as a human chronicle," Mankell wrote on his Web site. He added, "Maybe in 500 years these 'memory books' will be a great record of African times. My hope is to store them in the new Alexandrian library in Egypt." These books are often small and slim, containing not only words but also pictures, a pressed butterfly loved by a lost mother, or even sand from a home village.

Mankell hoped to increase awareness of the AIDS epidemic with his 2003 book *Jag dör, men minnat lever* ("I Die, But the Memory Lives On"), which contained excerpts from these memory books. He has long been horrified by the fact that in the West, medicines are available that allow people with AIDS to live relatively normal lives, but in Africa, people simply die because they cannot afford the medicines. "I can't imagine a more cynical image of injustice," he wrote on his Web site. He added, "The worst thing in the world is that there is so much suffering that is absolutely unnecessary. We could stop it tomorrow.... It would cost the same amount of money as we spend on pet food in the West to teach every child in the world to read and write."

In 2001, Mankell and Dan Israel left Ordfront Publishing and founded their own publishing company, Leopard Publishing House. He has continued to write and to be an activist for the causes he believes in. Mankell told Sibree, "I wake up every day happy that when I go to bed I will have created something that I hadn't created yesterday."

Selected writings

Wallander novels

Mördare utan ansikte, Ordfront (Stockholm), 1991; translated as *Faceless Killers* by Steven T. Murray, Vintage (New York City), 2003.

Hundarna i Riga, Ordfront, 1992; translated as *The Dogs of Riga* by Laurie Thompson, Vintage, 2004.

Den vita lejoninnan, Ordfront, 1993; translated as *The White Lioness* by Laurie Thompson, New Press (New York City), 1998.

Mannen som log, Ordfront, 1994; translated as *The Man Who Smiled* by Laurie Thompson, New Press, 2005.

Comedia infantil, Ordfront, 1995; translated *Chronicler of the Winds* by Tina Nunnally, New Press, 2006.

Villospår, Ordfront, 1995; translated as *Sidetracked* by Steven T. Murray, New Press, 1999.

Den femte kvinnan, Ordfront, 1996; translated as *The Fifth Woman* by Steven T. Murray, New Press, 2000.

Steget efter, Ordfront, 1997; translated as *One Step Behind* by Ebba Segerberg, Vintage, 2002.

Brandbägg, Ordfront, 1998; translated as *Firewall* by Ebba Segerberg, New Press, 2002.

Pyramiden (short stories), Ordfront, 1999; translated as *The Pyramid* by Ebba Segerberg with Laurie Thompson, New Press, 2008.

Innan Frosten, Leopard, 2002; translated as *Before the Frost* by Ebba Segerberg, New Press, 2005.

Den orolige mannen, Leopard (Stockholm), 2009; translated as *The Troubled Man* by Laurie Thompson, Knopf (New York City), 2011.

Sofia novels

Eldens hemlighet, Ordfront, 1995; translated as *Secrets in the Fire* by Anne Connie Stuksrud, Annick Press (Toronto, Ontario, Canada), 2000.

Eldens gåta, Ordfront, 2001; translated as *Playing with Fire*, 2002.

Eldens vrede, Leopard, 2005; translated as *The Fury in the Fire*, Allen & Unwin (Sydney, Australia), 2009.

Joel Gustafson novels

Hunden som sprang mot en stjäma, Ordfront, 1990; translated as *A Bridge to the Stars*, Delacorte (New York City), 2007.

Skuggoma växeri skymningen, Ordfront, 1991; translated as *Shadows in the Twilight* by Laurie Thompson, Delacorte, 2008.

Pojken som sov med snö i sin säng, Ordfront, 1996; translated as *When the Snow Fell* by Laurie Thompson, Delacorte, 2009.

Resan till världens ände, Ordfront, 1998; translated as *The Journey to the End of the World*, Andersen Press (London), 2008.

For children

Katten som aelskade regn, Ordfront, 1992; translated as *The Cat Who Liked Rain*, Andersen Press, 2008.

Other books

Bergspraengaren ("The Rockblaster"), Foerfattarfoerlaget (Stockholm), 1973.

Vettvillingen ("The Madman"), Foerfattarfoerlaget (Stockholm), 1977.

Fåvårdskolonin som fösvann ("The Prison Colony that Disappeared"), Ordfront, 1979.

Dödsbrickan ("Badge of Death"), Ordfront, 1980.

En seglares död ("A Sailor's Death"), Ordfront, 1981.

Daisy Sisters, Ordfront, 1982.

Sagan om Isidor ("The Tale of Isidor"), Ordfront, 1984.

Leopardens öga, Ordfront, 1990; translated as *The Eye of the Leopard* by Steven T. Murray, New Press, 2008.

Danslärarens återkomst Ordfront, 2000; translated as *The Return of the Dancing Master* by Laurie Thompson, New Press, 2004.

Vindens son, Norstedt (Stockholm, Sweden), 2000; translated as *Daniel* by Steven T. Murray, New Press, 2010.

Tea-bag, Leopard, 2001.

(Nonfiction) *Jag dör, men minnat lever*, Leopard, 2003; translated as *I Die, But the Memory Lives On*, New Press, 2003.

Djup, Leopard, 2004; translated as *Depths* by Laurie Thompson, New Press, 2006.

Kennedys hjärna Leopard, 2005; translated as *Kennedy's Brain* by Laurie Thompson, Vintage, 2008.

Italienska skor, Leopard, 2006; translated as *Italian Shoes* by Laurie Thompson, New Press, 2009.

Kinesen, Leopard, 2007; translated as *The Man from Beijing* by Laurie Thompson, Knopf, 2010.

Sources

Periodicals

Courier-Mail (Brisbane, Queensland, Australia), May 14, 2011, p. 23.

Globe and Mail (Toronto, Canada), December 27, 2007, p. R3.

Guardian (London, England), February 20, 2010.

Times (London, England), March 25, 2006, p. 4; July 2, 2011, p. 43.

Online

"Detective Meets His End, Sort Of," *New York Times*, http://www.nytimes.com/2011/03/28/books/troubled-man-by-henning-mankell-review.html (November 4, 2011).

Henning Mankell's Official Web Site, http://www.henningmankell.com/ (November 4, 2011).

"The Mirror of Crime," Tangled Web Books UK, http://www.twbooks.co.uk/crimescene/hmankellintvbc.html (November 4, 2011).

"True Crime," *Guardian*, http://www.guardian.co.uk/books/2003/nov/01/featuresreviews.guardianreview13 (November 4, 2011).

—*Kelly Winters*

Bruno Mars

© George Pimentel/WireImage/Getty Images

Singer, songwriter, and producer

Born Peter Gene Hernandez, October 8, 1985, in Honolulu, HI; son of Pete (a percussionist) and Bernadette (a singer and dancer) Hernandez.

Addresses: *Office*—Atlantic Records, 1290 Avenue of the Americas, New York, NY 10104. *Web site*—http://www.brunomars.com/.

Career

Began appearing with family band, c. 1989; appeared as Elvis impersonator in film *Honeymoon in Vegas*, 1992; signed with Motown Records, 2003; moved to Los Angeles, CA, 2003; formed writing/producing/collaborating duo (later trio) the Smeezingtons, c. early 2000s; created hit songs (with Smeezingtons), 2008-10; signed with Elektra, 2009; released debut album, *Doo-Wops & Hooligans*, 2010; toured in support of album, 2010—.

Awards: Grammy Award for best male pop vocal, National Academy of Recording Arts and Sciences, for "Just the Way You Are," 2011.

Sidelights

Singer Bruno Mars is perhaps best known as a solo artist with a worldwide hit album, 2010's *Doo-Wops & Hooligans*, but also was notable for his work as part of the Smeezingtons as a writer/producer/collaborator responsible for popular songs by Cee-Lo Green, Travie McCoy, and B.o.B. Many of Mars' songs have global appeal, mixing pop, hip-hop, and reggae sensibilities with such varied influences as Elvis Presley, Michael Jackson, and Coldplay. A born performer, Mars began playing with his family's musical act as a small child and was once an impersonator not only of Presley but of Jackson as well. Summarizing Mars' appeal, Gym Class Hero frontman McCoy told Simon Vozick-Levinson of *Entertainment Weekly*, "He's got a really refreshing and effortless voice. And this dude could write a hit record sitting on the toilet. He's just got it in him."

Born Peter Gene Hernandez in 1985 in Honolulu, Hawaii, Mars was the son of Pete and Bernadette Hernandez. His father was from Brooklyn, had a Puerto Rican background, and was a Latin percussionist, while his mother was a vocalist, hula dancer, and a native of the Philippines. Mars was exposed to much music growing up, especially songs from the 1950s that were especially favored by his father but also the variety of influences that could be found in Hawaii. Mars was put on stage at an early age, the only one of his many siblings who longed to perform.

By the age of four, he was singing in the family band, the Love Notes, which performed locally. Mars was an Elvis impersonator for the band, and he became the youngest in the area in the process. He also sang tunes by Frankie Lymon and other doo-wop and 1950s artists. He told Jon Caramanica of the *New York Times*, "I can't believe that's my past. I wish I could tell you me and my rock band were traveling around, strung out. No, we were a family band. Straight Partridge Family."

At the age of six, Mars had a small part in the 1992 film *Honeymoon in Vegas*, singing Elvis' "Can't Help Falling in Love" as a mini Elvis impersonator. By the age of 14, Mars was a Michael Jackson impersonator, performing in the *Legends in Concert* show. Along the way, he learned to play piano, guitar, bass, and congas, mostly by teaching himself. He was respected for his professionalism, with Waikiki entertainer Tommy D. telling John Berger of the *Honolulu Star-Advertiser*, "He was always on time, he always showed up, he knew his show, he knew what he had to do ... and he could sing, he could dance and he could play five instruments." Tommy D. added that Mars was "one of the most incredible talents I've ever seen."

With his uncle's encouragement, Mars moved to California to pursue a music career after graduating from Roosevelt High School in 2003. Success did not come easy for Mars, though he had signed a deal with Universal Motown before arriving in Los Angeles because of a connection of one of his sisters. He told Vozick-Levinson of *Entertainment Weekly*, "I was just so young when I moved up here. You think it's like the movies, like you get signed and Pharrell and Timbaland are working with you. But it wasn't like that." The Motown deal did little to further Mars' career, and he spent months frustrated by his lack of success while also feeling homesick and somewhat uninspired. After a year and a half, he was dropped from the label after a few studio sessions resulted in Mars not releasing anything. Mars told Monica Herrera of *Billboard*, "I figured, 'I have to do everything myself, so I'm going to just produce and write these songs on my own and hopefully get lucky.'" He had a breakthrough when he met songwriter/former 'N Sync backup singer Phillip Lawrence, who encouraged Mars to write songs for other artists as his way into the industry.

Entering into a partnership with Lawrence (later adding Ari Levine, who focused on sound engineering) the duo dubbed themselves the Smeezingtons, and both produced and wrote songs for other artists when they found it lucrative and a way into the industry. Explaining their tastes, Mars told *Billboard*'s Herrera, "We're big fans of the Beatles, the Police, and Michael Jackson, so whether we're doing an R&B or a pop record, we're always trying to chase those big choruses that our idols have given us." After first selling a song to Menudo for $20,000 that Mars wrote when he was 17 ("Lost"), one of their first big successes came with the song "Long Distance," which was recorded by R&B singer Brandy in 2008. In 2009, the Smeezingtons had their first number-one hit with "Right Round," recorded by Flo Rida. Their track, recorded by Canadian hip-hop artist K'Naan, "Wavering Flags," served as the theme song for the 2010 World Cup.

In 2010, Mars achieved milestones not only as a songwriter but also as a singer. He co-wrote McCoy's hit "Billionaire," which was written in London while working with another artist and realizing how broke he and Levine were as they walked the streets of the city. He was the co-writer and co-producer on Cee-Lo Green's smash, "F**k You!," which was nominated for a Grammy Award. Mars' vocals were featured on the chart-topping pop hit "Nothin' on You," by rapper B.o.B. Mars also co-wrote and produced the number-one song. Other work as a member of the Smeezingtons included producing and writing Matisyahu's "One Day."

By this time, Mars had landed a record deal of his own. In 2009, he signed with newly revived Elektra, based on hearing early versions of "Billionaire" and "Nothin' on You." Mars' experience as a producer/writer/collaborator helped him be a better solo artist. He told Kevin C. Johnson of the *San Jose Mercury News*, "It's easier when you understand more about what you're doing. It's like a football player knowing the rule book in and out and knowing the sizes of the pads you wear when you go into the field. You have to know every detail about your craft, and when I was younger I didn't know. And I'm still learning every day."

The following year, Mars began putting out his own material. In May of 2010, he released his first EP, *It's Better If you Don't Understand*, which had songs from and was a preview for his forthcoming album. It was co-written and co-produced by Lawrence. It included the meaningful track, "The Other Side," which also featured vocals by Cee-Lo and contributions from B.o.B. Other tracks included "Somewhere in Brooklyn," with an electro-pop sound, the ballad "Talking to the Moon," and the more folk-oriented "Count on Me."

In October of 2010, Mars released his first full-length album, *Doo-Wops & Hooligans*, also produced by the Smeezingtons. The album had a number-one hit, "Just the Way You Are," even before the album hit the stores. It sold more than 4.5 million copies. Another memorable track was "The Lazy Song," which is a reggae-tinged ode to sloth, and the album's third single. Other notable songs show a variety of influences, including a second number-one hit "Grenade," which combines inspirations as different as 1980s pop and Kanye West percussion, and sold 4.4 million copies, while "Runaway Baby" shows the influence of Little Richard. "Liquor Store Blues" also has a roots reggae feel, while "Our First Time" sounds like Sade. "Marry You" shows the influence of Coldplay.

Critics responded positively to Mars and the album, with Jim Farber of the New York *Daily News* writing "The 24 year old has the ideal sound for the easy seasons. Pop, R&B, and reggae melodies flow in a footloose fashion, while his voice boasts the smooth texture and highflying pitch of prime Michael Jackson." The *New York Times'* Caramanica called Mars "one of the most versatile and accessible singers in pop, with a light, soul-influenced voice that's an easy fit in a range of styles, a universal donor. There's nowhere he doesn't belong." Of the album, Caramanica wrote, it is "an effortless, fantastically polyglot record that shows him to be a careful study across a range of pop songcraft."

As Mars' singing and performing career took off, he toured often, but still spent most of his down time at Levcon Studios where the Smeezingtons had been based for years. He told Vozick-Levinson of *Entertainment Weekly*, "I'm here from when I wake up to when I go to sleep, about six days a week. I haven't had a day off in a long time. But I can't complain. I've been chasing this s*** forever." The Smeezingtons essentially went on hiatus as Mars became a star in his own right, at least temporarily diverting focus from producing, songwriting, and collaborating activities.

Mars also faced legal problems just as his star was rising. In September of 2010, as he was he was preparing for the release of his album, Mars was arrested for cocaine possession in Las Vegas. He was found with 2.6 grams in a bathroom stall in the Hard Rock Hotel & Casino shortly after a performance, though he told the arresting officer he had never had done drugs before. While the arrest ruined his image as a clean-cut golden boy, he was neither expected to face jail time nor was it expected to hinder his career. In early 2011, he agreed to take a plea deal that involved him paying a $2,000 fine, serving probation for one year, performing 200 hours of community service, and completing drug counseling. In return, the felony cocaine possession charge against him would be dismissed and he would have no conviction on his record as long as he met the conditions for his agreement.

By November of 2010, Mars hit the road in support of *Doo-Wops*, traveling the world through much of 2011 as *Doo-Wops and Hooligans* became a number-one hit in Canada, Germany, Ireland, and the United Kingdom. British critics were somewhat dismissive of Mars, generally labeling him as derivative. Simon Price in the *Independent on Sunday*, for example, wrote "His stock in trade is bristling funk-pop, smooth soul-rock, and light acoustic reggae. He's Mike Posner meets Orson meets Maroon 5 meets Jack Johnson meets Mark Ronson. It's all mainstream fare, tailor made to be heard at low volume on the nation's office radios." He was also honored with seven Grammy Award nominations in 2011, not only for his solo work, but also for his contributions to the Cee-Lo hit and B.o.B. Mars won one award, Best Male Pop Vocal for "Just the Way You Are."

Doo-Wops and Hooligans sold at least 1.2 million units in the United States alone and 14 million worldwide through 2011, and he gained a new audience when his contribution to the *Twilight Breaking Dawn* soundtrack, "It Will Rain," was released in late September 2011. Mars' achievements surprised even him. He told Richard Smirke of *Billboard*, "It's a rare thing that happens, especially in this day, where it's real hard to sell albums. I'm traveling to places that I've never even heard of and there are all these people singing the songs back—and English is not even their first language. It's like, what the hell happened?" What happened, according to Atlantic Records chairman and chief operating officer Julie Greenwald, is simple, as she told Smirke. "The great thing about Bruno is that you can't put him in a box. That's why I think people are attracted to him and his music. You can put him with any type of artist from any genre and it will be beautiful. He understands music."

Selected discography

It's Better If you Don't Understand (EP), Elektra, 2010.
Doo-Wops & Hooligans, Elektra, 2010.

Sources

Periodicals

Alberni Valley Times (British Columbia, Canada), September 28, 2011, p. A12.
Associated Press, February 16, 2011.
Associated Press State & Local Wire, January 29, 2011.
Billboard, May 8, 2010; October 9, 2010.
Daily News (New York City), October 3, 2010, p. 12.

Honolulu Star-Advertiser, February 13, 2011.

Independent on Sunday (London, England), January 30, 2011, p. 50.

Live Design, July 1, 2011.

New Yorker, February 14, 2011, p. 120.

New York Times, October 6, 2010, p. C1.

Philippine Daily Inquirer, October 9, 2010.

San Jose Mercury News, December 15, 2010.

Star Phoenix (Saskatoon, Saskatchewan, Canada), August 2, 2011, p. C2.

Online

"Bio," Bruno Mars Official Web Site, http://www. brunomars.com/about/ (October 9, 2011).

"Bruno Mars: The *Billboard* Cover Story," *Billboard,* http://www.billboard.com/features/bruno- mars-the-billboard-cover-story-10052774.tif32. story#/features/bruno-mars-the-billboard-cover- story-10052774.tif32.story (October 9, 2011).

"Bruno Mars: Biography," Allmusic, http://www. allmusic.com/artist/bruno-mars-p1107691/ biography (October 9, 2011).

"Bruno Mars: Triumph and Trouble," *Entertainment Weekly,* http://www.ew.com/ew/article/ 0,,20428526.tif,00.html (October 9, 2011).

—A. Petruso

George R. R. Martin

Author

Born George Raymond Richard Martin, September 20, 1948, in Bayonne, NJ; son of Raymond Collins (a longshoreman) and Margaret Brady (a homemaker and factory manager) Martin; married Gale Burnick, 1975 (divorced, 1979); married Parris McBride, 2010. *Education:* Northwestern University. B.S. (journalism), 1970; Northwestern University, M.S. (journalism), 1971.

Addresses: *Office*—103 San Salvador, Santa Fe, NM 87501.

Career

Journalism instructor, Clarke College, 1976-78; writer-in-residence, Clarke College, 1978-79; story editor, CBS Television, then executive story consultant, then executive producer, 1986-1996; published *A Game of Thrones*, 1996; published *A Clash of Kings*, 1999; published *A Storm of Swords*, 2000; published *A Feast for Crows*, 2005; published *Shadow Twin*, 2005; published *Hunter's Run*, 2008; published *Dance with Dragons*, 2011.

Awards: Hugo Award for novella, World Science Fiction Society, for "A Song for Lya," 1974; Hugo Award for short story, World Science Fiction Society, for "The Way of Cross and Dragon," 1979; Hugo Award for novelette, World Science Fiction Society, for "Sandkings," 1979; Hugo Award for novella, World Science Fiction Society, for "Blood of the Dragon," 1997; Nebula Award for novelette, Science Fiction and Fantasy Writers of America, for "Sandkings," 1979; Nebula Award for novelette, Science Fiction and Fantasy Writers of America, for "Portraits of His Children," 1985; Daikon Award for best short fiction in translation, for "Nightflyers," 1982; Balrog Award for fantasy novel, for *The Armageddon Rag*, 1983; Gilgamesh Award for best collection/anthology, for *Songs the Dead Men Sing*, 1987; Daedalus Award, for *Wild Cards*, 1987; Bram Stoker Award for novelette, Horror Writer's Association, for "The Pear-Shaped Man," 1987; World Fantasy Award for novella, World Fantasy Convention, for "The Skin Trade," 1988; Locus Poll for best fantasy novel, *Locus* magazine, for *A Clash of Kings*, 1999; Ignotius Award for best foreign novel, for *A Game of Thrones*, 2002; 1 of the 100 most influential people, *TIME*, 2011.

Sidelights

George R. R. Martin is the best-selling author of the fantasy series "A Song of Ice and Fire." By April of 2011, he had sold more than 15 million books worldwide. Called "The American Tolkien" by some, he is noted for his complex characters, intricate world-building, and richly evolving plotlines.

Martin was born and raised in Bayonne, New Jersey, the son of a longshoreman. His family lived in a federal housing project and did not have money for travel, so, as Martin told Christopher John Farley in the *Wall Street Journal,* "My world was five blocks long." He watched the ships traveling past Bayonne and dreamed of the exotic places they might be traveling to and the adventures their crews might have. These dreams of adventure would later be incorporated into stories.

From an early age he loved to write and, as a child, wrote monster stories for other kids in his housing project for a penny a page. He began reading science fiction at a young age, beginning with Robert A. Heinlein's *Have Space Suit, Will Travel.* He was immediately hooked on the genre.

He also loved comic books, and at the age of 13 he wrote a fan letter to the *Fantastic Four* comic magazine. It was published. Shortly after that, as a result of having his address published in the magazine, he received a chain letter, the kind that asks you to send a quarter to someone on a list and in a few weeks you'd receive $64 back. Martin sent his quarter to the person on the list, and he never got the $64, but someone did send him a comics fanzine in exchange for his quarter. It was a homemade magazine in which fans discussed the comic books they loved. Martin was thrilled, and he began writing for fanzines, creating his own superheroes and writing stories for superheroes other people created. He continued to write for fanzines all through high school, progressing through the ranks to win an award for Best Fan Fiction. Along the way he learned from criticism and improved his technique.

By the time he got to college at Northwestern University, he was already thinking of himself as a writer, and he chose to major in journalism. At the same time, he took every fiction class he could, and he tried to write fiction for every course, even when the course had nothing to do with fiction; for example, he persuaded a Scandinavian history professor to let him write a historical fiction piece instead of a term paper. The professor liked the story so much that he submitted it to a journal called *American Scandinavian Review,* earning Martin his first professional rejection slip. Martin continued to write, collecting rejections, until selling his first story to *Galaxy* for $94 in 1971. In that same year he went to his first science fiction convention, where he met editor Gardner Dozois, who had published that first story, titled "The Hero."

Martin was a conscientious objector during the Vietnam War, and when he was drafted, he did alternative service, working with VISTA in the Cook County Legal Assistance Foundation. While working as a VISTA volunteer, he continued to write in his spare time. From 1976 through 1979, he taught writing at Clarke College in Dubuque, Iowa.

Martin met his current wife, Parris McBride, at a science fiction convention in 1975. At the time, he was engaged to Gale Burnick, whom he had also met at a science fiction convention. Martin and McBride went on with their lives—he married Burnick, and McBride went off to work with a traveling circus. By 1979 he and Burnick were divorced and he had moved to Santa Fe, while McBride was in Portland, Oregon, waiting tables in a restaurant. They began a long-distance romance, meeting at conventions and writing letters back and forth. In 1981, McBride moved to Santa Fe, and the two joined households; they eventually married in 2010.

Meanwhile, Martin continued to write for a variety of science fiction magazines. In 1986 he became a story editor for the *Twilight Zone* television show at CBS. In the following year he became an Executive Story Consultant for *Beauty and the Beast* at CBS.

By the early 1990s, Martin was growing tired of working in television, fed up with its limitations. His grand visions of castles, sweeping tides of war, and special effects were too expensive for television's small screen and careful budget. On paper, though, he could write stories filled with huge casts of characters, immense battle scenes, castles, and generations of conflict.

One day, an image appeared in his mind: a man taking a boy to observe a beheading. On the way, they find a direwolf (an especially large species of wolf) that has died while giving birth to a litter of pups. They rescue the pups. This image became the opening scene of Martin's novel *A Game of Thrones,* published in 1996. This 700-page epic told the story of the struggle for power in the Seven Kingdoms, a medieval setting based on the Wars of the Roses in England. Unlike many other fantasy novels, Martin's did not hinge heavily on magic, but had a more gritty, realistic bite.

The book did not immediately attract a great deal of public attention, but it won a few fans, who told their friends, who then told their friends. Through word of mouth, Martin's readership grew in a sporadic fashion. With the second book in the series, *A Clash of Kings,* published in 1999, and with *A Storm of Swords,* which came out in 2000, word of mouth continued to grow.

It took Martin five years to complete the next book, *A Feast of Crows,* but when it came out, his fan base had grown so much that the novel reached the number-one spot on the *New York Times* fiction best-seller list. *Time* magazine reviewer Lev Grossman dubbed Martin "The American Tolkien," but noted that in contrast to Tolkien, whose work tends to be G-rated, featuring a struggle between clearly good and clearly evil beings, many of whom are magical, Martin's work includes little magic, and much more sex, betrayal, and complex emotion. Characters who seem likable do horrible things, and characters who seem like villains do good things. Martin also keeps readers on their toes by being perfectly willing to kill off any character, even main characters or readers' favorites, at any time.

A Feast of Crows was only half of a 1,200-page novel that, at the time of publication, was still incomplete. The book introduced several new characters, and also left popular characters from his previous book hanging, their fates uncertain. This incompletion and suspense, along with the long hiatus in publishing that followed *A Feast of Crows,* annoyed and disappointed many fans. Readers were aggravated by a postscript Martin included in the book, in which he said he would probably finish the work within a year; by early 2011, no end was yet in sight. In blogs and on discussion boards, restive fans posted complaints and rumors about the delay. When Martin finally announce in March of 2011 that *A Dance With Dragons* would be published on July 12, fans reacted with anger and skepticism, doubting that it would ever actually happen.

Publication did happen, and the book hit number one on the Amazon best-seller list even before it came out. In the *New York Times,* Dana Jennings praised the book, saying that Martin was *not* the American Tolkien after all: "He's much better than that." She described the book as "a sprawling and panoramic 19th-century novel turned out in fantasy motley, more Balzac and Dickens than Tolkien." She also described Martin as "a literary dervish, enthralled by complicated characters and vivid language, and bursting with the wild vision of the very best tale tellers."

The book, like its predecessors, ended with many questions about the fate of its characters still unresolved, paving the way for future installments; Martin had at least two more planned, tentatively titled *The Winds of Winter* and *A Dream of Spring.*

When Martin writes, he has a general idea of where his story is going, but creates, or discovers, much about it along the way. When he creates a world, he generally only invents as much as he needs for his story, in contrast to his hero, fantasy writer J. R. R. Tolkien, who created lengthy histories, mythologies, and entire languages for his novels long before writing them. Some of Martin's fans assume that his world-building is as meticulous as Tolkien's, and write him to ask for more details about his languages or other aspects of Westeros, the world of his novels. As Martin told Laura Miller in the *New Yorker,* he has to confess that he has not done such detailed work. To a fan who asked for "a glossary and a dictionary and the syntax" of High Valyrian, one of Martin's invented languages, Martin noted, "I have to write back and say, 'I've invented seven words of High Valyrian.'"

Martin believes that writers owe a great deal to their fans, and he goes out of his way to cater to his. He keeps a regular blog to inform fans of his activities, stays late after readings to sign autographs, pose for photos, and chat with fans, and attends fan club meetings around the world in the course of his travels. Martin's fan group, which began at a Philadelphia science fiction convention in 2001, is called the Brotherhood Without Banners and, in keeping with the fandom of his and McBride's youth, it does not charge a membership fee or have any official structure or leader. Local gatherings of the Brotherhood are called "moots," and take place whenever it's convenient for fans, typically at conventions or book-signings. One custom of the Brotherhood is the midnight "Quest," in which Martin sends members out for local fast food, after which the fans are "knighted." One group, who tried unsuccessfully to find a particular dish after all the local restaurants had closed, looked in a restaurant's garbage and then tried to cook the food themselves; Martin dubbed them the Knights of the Dumpster.

Fans spend a great deal of time discussing the details of Martin's invented world; one of them, Elio Garcia, knows so much about it that Martin told HBO researchers to ask Garcia when they had questions about it. Garcia and Martin are collaborating on a guide titled *The World of Ice and Fire,* and Martin will often rely on Garcia's encyclopedic memory of his world, emailing him to ask if he had mentioned a detail before. With so many characters and such complex storylines, Martin has made occasional goofs, such as inadvertently changing the sex of a horse between books, or forgetting that a character's eyes are green, not blue.

Martin and his wife live in Santa Fe, New Mexico. Martin's office is located in a house across the street; in addition to writing there, Martin uses the house to display dioramas he has created with his large collection of medieval miniatures. Visitor opening closet doors in this house might find scenes from a medieval banquet, a castle siege, or an all-out battle.

In an interview with Tom Ashbrook in *On Point*, Martin joked that ever since he was a boy, his father noted that his son liked to read "weird stuff. He liked Westerns, So his taste was more grounded, at least in his view. I was always fighting a dragon or going off to the stars or something like that."

Selected writings

Novels

Dying of the Light, Simon and Schuster (New York City), 1977.
(With Lisa Tuttle) *Windhaven*, Timescape (New York City), 1981.
Fevre Dream, Poseidon Press (New York City), 1992.
The Armageddon Rag, Poseidon Press, 1983.
(With John J. Miller) *Dead Man's Hand*, Bantam Books (New York City), 1990.
(With Gardner Dozois and Daniel Abraham) *Shadow Twin*, Subterranean Press (Burton, MI), 2005.
(With Gardner Dozois and Daniel Abraham) *Hunter's Run*, Eos (New York City), 2008.

A Song of Ice and Fire

A Game of Thrones, Bantam Books, 1996.
A Clash of Kings, Bantam Books, 1999.
A Storm of Swords, Bantam Books, 2000.
A Feast for Crows, Bantam Books, 2005.
A Dance with Dragons, Bantam Books, 2011.

Short-story collections

A Song for Lya and Other Stories, Avon (New York City), 1976.
Songs of Stars and Shadows, Pocket Books (New York City), 1977.
Sandkings, Timescape, 1981.
Songs the Dead Men Sing, Dark Harvest (Chicago, IL), 1983.
Nightflyers, Bluejay Books (New York City), 1985.

Tuf Voyaging, Baen Books (New York City), 1986.
Portraits of His Children, Dark Harvest, 1987.
Quartet, NESFA Press (Framingham, MA), 2001.
GRRM: A Retrospective, Subterranean Press, 2003; also published as *Dreamsongs*, Bantam Books, 2007.
Starlady/Fast-Friend, Subterranean Press, 2008.

For children

(Illustrated by Yvonne Gilbert) *The Ice Dragon*, Starscape (New York City), 2006.

Sources

Periodicals

New Yorker, April 11, 2011, p. 32.

Online

"Books: The American Tolkien," *Time*, http://www.time.com/time/magazine/article/0,9171,1129596,00.html (July 13, 2011).
"A Dance with Dragons: George R. R. Martin," *On Point*, http://onpoint.wbur.org/2011/07/12/grrm (July 15, 2011).
"A Fantasy Realm Too Vile for Hobbits," *New York Times*, http://www.nytimes.com/2005/12/12/books/12crow.html (July 12, 2011.
"George R. R. Martin and Parris McBride Married," *Locus*, http://www.locusmag.com/News/2011/02/george-r-r-martin-parris-mcbride-married (July 15, 2011).
George R. R. Martin's Official Web Site, http://georgerrmartin.com/ (July 12, 2011).
"In a Fantasyland of Liars, Trust No One, and Keep Your Dragon Close," *New York Times*, http://www.nytimes.com/2011/07/15/books/a-dance-with-dragons-by-george-r-r-martin-review.html (July 15, 2011).
"Martin Spills the Secrets of *A Dance with Dragons*," *Wall Street Journal*, http://blogs.wsj.com/speakeasy/2011/07/08/game-of-thrones-author-george-r-r-martin-spills-the-secrets-of-a-dance-with-dragons/ July 12, 2011).

—Kelly Winters

Melissa McCarthy

Actress

Born August 26, 1970, in Plainfield, IL; daughter of Michael and Sandy McCarthy (both farmers); married Ben Falcone (a writer and actor); children: two daughters. *Education:* Studied textiles and fashion at Southern Illinois University; studied at the Actors Studio in New York City.

Addresses: *Office*—c/o *Mike and Molly,* Chuck Lorre Productions, 4000 Warner Rd., Bldg. 136, Rm. 127, Burbank, CA 91522.

Career

Performed stand-up comedy and studied at the Actors Studio in New York City, 1990-96; joined Los Angeles comedy troupe The Groundlings, 1997-2010; appeared in short films *God,* 1998 and *Go,* 1999. Actress on television, including: *D.C.,* 2000; *The Gilmore Girls,* 2000-07; *The Lost World,* 2001; *Kim Possible* (voice), 2002-05; *Curb Your Enthusiasm,* 2004; *Samantha Who?,* 2007-09; *Rita Rocks,* 2009; *Mike and Molly,* 2010—; *Private Practice,* 2010. Film appearances include: *Charlie's Angels,* 2000; *Drowning Mona,* 2000; *The Kid,* 2000; *Pumpkin,* 2002; *The Third Wheel,* 2002; *White Oleander,* 2002; *The Life of David Gale,* 2003; *Cook Off!,* 2006; *The Nines,* 2007; *Just Add Water,* 2008; *Pretty Ugly People,* 2008; *The Back-Up Plan,* 2010; *Life as We Know It,* 2010; *Bridesmaids,* 2011.

Awards: Emmy Award for outstanding lead actress in a comedy series, Academy of Television Arts and Sciences, 2011.

© *Silverstar/Polaris/newscom*

Sidelights

Melissa McCarthy is best known for her television work as the quirky chef Sookie St. James on the show *Gilmore Girls* and for her starring role on *Mike and Molly,* for which she won an Emmy award. McCarthy is known for her down-to-earth, just-plain-funny style. In the *Hollywood Reporter,* Lacey Rose praised McCarthy's "depth, comedic timing, and sheer likability."

McCarthy was born in Plainfield, Illinois, and grew up on a corn and soybean farm. Even as a child, she loved performing and making people laugh. She and her sister made up characters and acted out their exploits, and she sang long, rambling songs to her mother while her mother did the family laundry. In high school, she played tennis and was the captain of the cheerleading team; however, she became fed up with cheerleading at a pep rally when she heard a coach from the boys' team make a negative comment about the cheerleaders. As she told Andrew Goldman in the *New York Times Magazine,* she thought, "Are you kidding me? I'm out there doing back handsprings and aerials on blacktop to cheer for your stupid team that, by the way, is not doing that well. And you're in here with the guys making fun of it? I was like, I'm done." And with that, she quit cheerleading.

Throughout high school, she was hungry for an outlet for her creative energy, and she wanted to find other creative people to hang out with. She and her friends dressed Goth, with white face makeup, black clothes, and partly-shaved heads, and hung out with young men in the gay community. With them, she went to Chicago and snuck into bars, where they felt safer to be themselves in the relatively oppressive mid-1980s. She told Novid Parsi in *Time Out Chicago*, "My [gay] friends had to really watch it. It was just a whole different time."

Regarding her Goth appearance, she enjoyed the pageantry of the daily costuming, and the attention she garnered by dressing that way. As she told Ulrica Wihlborg in *People*, "I wasn't mopey enough [to be a Goth]. I would pretend to be, but I'd end up making people laugh." She became involved in acting during her senior year in high school, when she performed in a school play. She went on to study fashion and textiles at Southern Illinois University for a brief time before dropping out.

With the support of her parents she moved to New York City when she was 20, and did standup comedy and studied at the Actors Studio. In 1996 she went to Los Angeles, where she joined the Groundlings, a comedy troupe. She met her husband, Ben Falcone, another member of the Groundlings, whom she married in 2005; they would eventually have two daughters. While in Los Angeles, McCarthy won roles in John August's short film *God* (1998) and in August's drama *Go* (1999).

McCarthy was happy with her success so far, but she knew she might not go any farther in figure-conscious Hollywood because she had always found it easy to gain weight and difficult to lose it. In fact, a manager in Hollywood once told her she would never work if she did not lose weight. McCarthy told Wihlborg, "It really hurt my feelings. I understand that the odds are not as high as if I was skinny, but I still have talent. I thought, 'I'll show you!'" And indeed, her size proved not to be a limitation when, in 2000, she won a role as bubbly chef Sookie St. James on the television show *Gilmore Girls*. As Sookie, she was best friends with main character Lorelei Gilmore, played by Lauren Graham. Although her character was excitable and occasionally scatterbrained, McCarthy also revealed a more solid and healthy side of Sookie as she advised Lorelei about life and love.

The attention McCarthy received for her role on *Gilmore Girls* led to other small parts in movies such as 2000's *Charlie's Angels*, *Pumpkin*, and *The Third*

Wheel, both in 2002. In *Pumpkin* she played a woman who is set up on a date with a mentally handicapped man, and in *The Third Wheel* she played a coworker of Ben Affleck, and the two of them kibitzed about a date between two other characters. Beginning in 2002, McCarthy also provided the voice for Disney animated character DNAmy on the series *Kim Possible*.

Gilmore Girls was on the air from 2000 through 2007. When the show ended, McCarthy signed with another series, *Samantha Who?*, an ABC comedy series starring Christina Applegate as a woman who has recovered from an accident-induced coma and realized that she wanted to make amends for the selfish things she did before her accident. McCarthy played her needy best friend, Dena. The show did well in its first season, but was then repeatedly rescheduled, losing viewers, and it was eventually canceled.

McCarthy moved on to work in John August's 2007 film *The Nines*. She played three different roles in this complicated film about God and the nature of reality. McCarthy performed the role of a funny, loyal, and quirky best friend in the 2010 films *The Back-Up Plan* and *Life as We Know It*.

In that same year, she won a starring role on the CBS sitcom *Mike and Molly*. The show was about two people who met and fell in love at a meeting of Overeaters Anonymous. When she initially heard about the show she was not interested because she thought it was simply a show about fat people, and she thought that would be boring to participate in and would be nothing but a stream of fat jokes; however, when she read the script, she found that the show was deeper than that, that in fact it was a love story about two people who truly wanted to improve their lives and their love for each other. She accepted the part.

On the show, McCarthy's character Molly is dating Mike (played by Billy Gardell), a police officer. At *Yahoo Movies*, a reviewer called the show "a fine showcase for her talents," and remarked that the role "signaled the launch of her career as leading lady." For this show, her weight proved to be an asset, but McCarthy told Paulette Cohn in *Lifescript*, that she did not feel that her size was the only reason she got the part. "I've gotten it, hopefully, because they needed a funny person, and I was right for the part." Some critics panned the show, saying it was nothing but a series of set-ups for fat jokes. The reviewer who roused the most ire was a blog writer for *Marie Claire*, who wrote that the idea of watching two fat people kiss was revolting to her.

McCarthy was initially angered by the remarks, but then realized, as she told Karen Valby in *Inside Movies*, the writer was "a sad, troubled person." The blogger retracted her statement, claiming she had issues, but McCarthy wished that the blogger had had the guts to either think twice before publishing such mean-spirited things, or to own what she said and apologize for it.

Despite these initial critical responses, the show was popular with viewers, perhaps because the characters were so familiar to most Americans. Ann Oldenburg commented in *USA Today*, "The complaints have died down as fans have come to know that the show is, yes, bigger than just fat jokes." Unlike television shows featuring impossibly thin, rich, and chic characters, *Mike and Molly* presented people many Americans could relate to. A large percentage of Americans struggle with being overweight, but find few role models or vicarious companions in the world of TV. Gardell told Rose, "I think we take great pride in representing down-to-earth people who are just trying to get better. I think you have to have a deep soul to do that, and Melissa definitely has one." McCarthy told Craig Tomashoff in *Hollywood Reporter* "I read the script and felt like I knew these people. It was both real and funny, which is the heart of the show."

McCarthy has never forgotten that she grew up on a farm in Plainfield, Illinois, and does not view herself as a show-business kind of person. Sometimes her success comes as a surprise to her. In August of 2010, McCarthy and her parents were driving through Los Angeles when she saw a billboard for *Mike and Molly*. She immediately stopped the car, overwhelmed. "In other sections of the world it was just a billboard," she told Wihlborg. "But it was a big deal to me. I've never been on a billboard before!"

In 2011, McCarthy appeared in the Judd Apatow film *Bridesmaids*. Nathaniel Penn wrote in *GQ* that her character, Megan, was "a self-made woman of great machismo, voracious sexual appetites, mysterious financial resources, and a truly atrocious wardrobe." Despite her tasteless clothes and her butch appearance and attitude, Megan was truly confident in her sexuality, propositioning an air marshal (played by McCarthy's real-life husband) in the middle of an airline flight. McCarthy based the character on women she had seen throughout her life: "I love those no-bullsh** women with close-cropped hair that you'll see together and think, 'Is that her partner?' Then they talk about their husbands and six kids. I just love anybody who's that comfortable in her own skin,' she told Penn. And, she remarked to Valby, "Frankly I know a lot of women that are married, have kids, and that is how they look."

In the film, according to a *Yahoo! Movies* reviewer, she "nearly stole the show" from lead actress Kristen Wiig in her hilarious scenes. Dan Mecca wrote in *Film Stage* that she "stole every scene she was in" in the movie, helping to make the film a "surprise hit." Another factor in the movie's success was the fact that it included six large, rich parts for female comedians, unlike most comedy movies, which typically feature men.

In that same year, McCarthy was delighted to learn that she had won the Emmy Award for Outstanding Lead Actress in a Comedy Series for her portrayal of Molly on *Mike and Molly*. The day after the awards ceremony, the cast and crew of the show waited for her in the parking lot with a photo of her winning, and they all cheered for her. Gardell told Oldenburg, "Melissa brought us home the gold. We couldn't be more proud of her. That's a hell of an accomplishment."

In the fall of 2011, it was announced that McCarthy would star in a comedy film with Jason Bateman, titled *The ID Theft*. In addition to acting, McCarthy has always been interested in textiles, costumes, and clothing. She often makes her own clothes, because she feels that stylish clothes for plus-sized women are hard to find. She is thinking about starting her own clothing line for larger women; as she remarked to Cohn, clothing manufacturers "are missing out on a lot of money."

McCarthy is aware that in movies and television, some writers create roles for which the only qualification is that the actor be fat; the part is not thought-out and the character is not realistically human. As she told Parsi, "There's always some dingbat that's like, 'I've got a part for you.' And I think, You haven't written a part." What the person has written turns out to be a sight gag or a fat joke, and "That stuff I don't do." She is equally irked at reviewers who write that she is "playing" an overweight character. She sarcastically told Parsi, "Oh, I'm playing it. I must be amazing! As if at the end of the day, I unzip it I'm, you know, size six. I wish."

She told Wihlborg, "Being older, I'm not as hard on myself. The important things in my life—my family, my kids, my job—are so wonderful. I feel really lucky." And, she told Cohn, "I just like my life. I have a great husband and two great kids. I get to do what I want for a living. I think you have to be happy with what you do."

Sources

Periodicals

GQ, August 2011, p. 88.

Hollywood Reporter, September 20, 2010, p. 8; June 24, 2011, p. SS15; October 7, 2011, p. 34.
New York Times Magazine, October 16, 2011, p. 18L.
USA Today, October 3, 2011, p. 3D.

Online

"All I Want for Mother's Day Is for *Bridesmaids'* Melissa McCarthy to Be a Movie Star," *Inside Movies,* http://insidemovies.ew.com/2011/05/07/bridesmaids-melissa-mccarthy/ (November 4, 2011).
"ID Theft Gets Jason Bateman and Melissa McCarthy," *Movieweb,* http://www.movieweb.com/news/id-theft-gets-jason-bateman-and-melissa-mccarthy (November 4, 2011).
"Jason Bateman and Melissa McCarthy to Execute *ID Theft,*" *Film Stage,* http://thefilmstage.com/news/jason-bateman-and-melissa-mccarthy-to-execute-id-theft/ (November 4, 2011).

"Melissa McCarthy: Biography," *TV Guide,* http://www.tvguide.com/celebrities/melissa-mccarthy/bio/190575 (November 4, 2011).
"Melissa McCarthy: Her Moment to Shine," *People,* http://www.people.com/people/archive/article/0,,20472991.tif,00.html (November 4, 2011).
"Melissa McCarthy: Interview," *Time Out Chicago,* http://timeoutchicago.com/arts-culture/film/14751137.tif/melissa-mccarthy-interview (November 4, 2011).
"Melissa McCarthy," Yahoo! Movies, http://movies.yahoo.com/movie/contributor/18045040.tif85/bio (November 4, 2011).
"*Mike and Molly'*s Melissa McCarthy Finds Super-Sized Success," *Lifescript,* http://www.lifescript.com/Life/Timeout/Entertainment/Mike_and_Mollys_Melissa_McCarthy_Finds_Super-Sized_Success.aspx (November 4, 2011).

—Kelly Winters

Catherine McCord

Amanda Edwards/Getty Images Entertainment/Getty Images

Blogger

Born May 10, 1974, in Louisville, KY; married Jon; children: Kenya (son), Chloe. *Education:* Institute for Culinary Education, Manhattan, NY, 2002.

Addresses: *Web site*—http://weelicious.com/.

Career

Discovered at age 15 by Elite Model Management, 1989; modeled for such companies as L'eggs Pantyhose, Victoria's Secret, Calvin Klein, and Donna Karan. Actress in films, including: *Purpose*, 2002; *Winter Break*, 2003; *Stuck on You*, 2003; *Last Run*, 2004; *Raising Helen*, 2004; *Down Dog*, 2005; *Derailed*, 2005; *Gridiron Gang*, 2006; *Live!*, 2007; *Hotel for Dogs*, 2009; *Red State*, 2011. Television appearances include: *Ned and Stacey*, 1997; *Loveline* (co-host), 1999; *Once and Again*, 2000; *Two and a Half Men*, 2005; *Joey*, 2006; *Pandemic* (movie), 2007. Owner and creator of Weelicious, 2007—.

Sidelights

Born and raised in Louisville, Kentucky, Catherine McCord has an adventurous spirit that has made it possible for her to try diverse things. As a model she traveled the world and sampled cuisines far different from the culinary delicacies of her hometown. This passion for new flavors and experiences fed her desire to go to culinary school and introduce her now famous Web site, Weelicious, to the world so that other people would expand the foods on their plate and try new flavors.

Growing up, Catherine's family impressed upon her some of the values surrounding food and nutrition that she expounded upon on Weelicious. Sunday nights were a time when the whole family ate together and the preparation of the meal was a part of enjoying the dinner. McCord continued this and advocated on her Web site for children to be included in the selection and preparation of meals. She wrote on her Web site: "My advice is to try and cook with your kids at least one meal a week. Get them to participate in cooking with you, knowing where the produce comes from and how important the vitamins and minerals are in their little bodies in order to play and be active." McCord, who believes in shopping for food whenever possible at farmer's markets, added, "Part of the reason I love farmer's markets so much is that the food comes from the farm and then right to the market, so there's less handling. You're getting the freshest ingredients and you meet the people that grow it." Weelicious has a farmer's market location application to help people find the nearest market. McCord learned from her grandparents about respecting where food comes from and, just as she learned about these things from them, she told the Brooks Group that she is "Gardening, composting, canning, shopping at farmer's markets; these are traditions I'm now passing along to my children." Unlike other Web sites that give advice to parents about how to feed their children and get the children to eat nutritious food, Weelicious talks about educating children and involving them in the process of growing and cooking food in a meaningful way rather than trying to sneak healthy foods into the children's diets. The Web site has recipes for such wonderful things as homemade peanut butter and jelly toaster pastries, roast carrot coins, mini sweet potato muffins, and breakfast quesadillas.

Tall, beautiful, blonde, and athletic, McCord excelled in high school as a runner and a basketball player. She was hoping to earn an athletic scholarship to go to college when she experienced a hip injury that ruined any plans of participating in collegiate sports. Soon after this, a friend signed her up for a modeling contest. McCord was "discovered" by Elite Model Management when she was 15 years old. After this she began modeling for such companies and top designers as L'eggs Pantyhose, Victoria's Secret, Donna Karan, and Calvin Klein. She began traveling the world and spending time in such exotic places as New York, Paris, Milan, Tokyo, Morocco, and Sydney. On the Sohgave! Web site, McCord said, "I started modeling and traveling the world at a very young age, tasting and being turned onto foods that were exciting and exotic.... I became obsessed with learning about local cuisine." As McCord continued to model she began to appear in films and made guest appearances on various television shows. She appeared in such films as *Raising Helen, Derailed, Gridiron Gang,* and *Hotel for Dogs*. She was in the made-for-television movie *Pandemic* and had guest appearances on *Once and Again, Two and a Half Men,* and *Joey*. McCord was a co-host on MTV's *Loveline* in 1999.

The tragedy of 9/11 had a profound impact on McCord, who soon thereafter decided to make a career transition. McCord had managed to avoid all the dangers of modeling such as eating disorders and drugs because of the support of her family. Further, her father had always advised her to set money aside so that one day she could pursue whatever she wanted to do. McCord followed this advice and decided to go to culinary school. She continued to model and attended the Institute for Culinary Education in Manhattan. "It was a juggle," McCord told the Brooks Group. She worked in various restaurants in order to learn about food, cooking techniques, and to gain experience.

After marrying her husband, Jon, and moving to Los Angeles, she gave birth to her son, Kenya. Even though she knew a great deal about food and nutrition, she was surprised at the lack of information about how to feed children and teach them to eat a healthy diet. She began writing her blog, Weelicious, to share what she was learning on the job. At first Weelicious was a blog of homemade baby food recipes, but as her family grew, so did the blog. At first only family members and friends followed Weelicious, but slowly its readership grew into the millions. McCord posted daily recipes on the Web site, which features cooking videos, pictures of kids' lunches, a weekly menu planner, information about vitamins and minerals, and a recipe box where found recipes can be collected by individual subscribers. The Web site also has a store that recommends cooking equipment, culinary gadgets, storage items, and lunch boxes. Weelicious has been featured by prominent magazines, including *Parents, People,* and *Everyday with Rachel Ray*. McCord is a regular contributor to such sites as BabyCenter, Fox News Junior Foodies, and Babble. She has made appearances to promote Weelicious on *Good Morning America Health,* the *Today Show,* and *Fox News*. McCord's online recipes have inspired hundreds of families to eat in a more healthy manner. A cookbook will be published by William Morrow publishing.

Sources

"Catherine McCord, Founder of Weelicious.com and Mom," Jen and Barb, Mom Life, http://www.jenandbarbmomlife.com/catherine-mccord/ (June 2, 2011).

"Catherine McCord," Good Bite, http://www.goodbite.com/panelists/catherine-mccord (June 2, 2011).

"Catherine McCord," Internet Movie Database, http://www.imdb.com/name/nm0005201/bio (June 2, 2011).

"Catherine McCord's Biography," Brooks Group Web Site, http://www.brookspr.com/clients/catherine-mccord/ (June 2, 2011).

"Catherine McCord," Sohgave!, http://sohgave.com/chefs/catherine-mccord/ (June 2, 2011).

"Guest Blogger: Catherine McCord of Weelicious," Ladies' Lounge blog, *Ladies' Home Journal,* http://www.lhj.com/blogs/ladieslounge/2011/01/26/guest-blogger-catherine-mccord-of-weelicious/ (June 2, 2011).

"Learn More About Food Blogger Catherine McCord," *Parents,* http://www.parents.com/recipes/chefs/catherine-mccord/who-is-catherine-mccord/ (June 2, 2011).

"Meet Catherine McCord: An Interview With the Food Blogger," *Parents,* http://www.parents.com/recipes/chefs/catherine-mccord/meet-catherine-mccord--an-interview-with-the-food-blogger/ (June 2, 2011).

Weelicious, http://www.weelicious.com (June 2, 2011).

—*Annette Bowman*

Mike McCue

© Gabriela Hasbun/Redux

Co-founder of Flipboard

Born Michael S. McCue in 1968; son of Lucy Allan.

Addresses: *Contact*—Flipboard, 818 Emerson St., Palo Alto, CA 94301. *Web site*—http://www.flipboard.com.

Career

Wrote computer games as a high school student, early 1980s; joined IBM, 1980s; founded Paper Software, Inc., 1989; sold Paper Software to Netscape Communications Corp., 1995; vice president for technology, Netscape, 1996-98; co-founded TellMe Networks, Inc., 1999; sold TellMe to Microsoft, 2007; co-founded Flipboard, 2009; released Flipboard app for iPad, 2010.

Awards: Kilby International Young Innovator Award, North Dallas Chamber of Commerce High Tech Committee, 1996; TechFellow Award for Disruptive Innovation, Founders Fund, 2009; (with Evan Doll) Interactive Award, Brit Insurance Design Awards, 2011.

Sidelights

A tech-savvy creative genius, Mike McCue has been at the forefront of tech developments since he began writing videogames as a high school student in the 1980s. Since then McCue has founded and sold one Internet startup to Netscape and another to Microsoft. In 2010 McCue rolled out his

biggest game-changer, an iPad app called Flipboard. The app was developed by McCue's company of the same name, which he co-founded with Apple iPhone engineer Evan Doll. A social magazine application, Flipboard gathers content from a user's social networking sites, as well as information from Web site feeds, then presents them in an attractive and graphical magazine-like format. Utilizing the iPad's large touchpad screen, users can quickly "flip" through their content.

Speaking to *Net* magazine's Tom May, McCue described his app this way: "Flipboard is about taking the up-to-date information and interactiveness provided by the real-time web and marrying it to the timeless principles of print, the traditions of design typography, the rhythm of storytelling." *Time* magazine named Flipboard to its list of top 50 inventions for 2010 and Apple called it the iPad app of the year.

Born in 1968, McCue attended elementary school in Hopewell Junction, New York, and once wrote a report about his intention to become an astronaut. An imaginative boy, McCue spent his childhood building cardboard robots and constructed a calculator for a science fair project. "Everyone thought I was a little crazy because I didn't spend a lot of time out of the house," McCue told *Businessweek*'s John A. Byrne. "But I was too busy building things and dreaming."

McCue first worked with computers at his Cornwall, New York, high school, which had TI-99/4A computers, an early home computer designed by Texas Instruments. In 1981, writing in a programming language known as TI BASIC, McCue developed his first software program, a space-flight simulator called "Shuttle Flight." During his sophomore year, McCue's parents bought him a TI-99/4A and he started churning out video games, which he licensed to gaming magazines. McCue became so obsessed with software-creation that he would sit in class with a programming book hidden inside his textbook. He went on to write a game based on former President Jimmy Carter's 1980 failed helicopter rescue of Iran hostages. McCue sold the game, called "Night Mission," to a distributor in return for royalties.

During his teen years, McCue pursued his dream of becoming an astronaut by applying to the U.S. Air Force Academy. But the more he worked with computers, the more obsessed he became. "I was hooked on software and admired entrepreneurs like Steve Jobs, Mitch Kapor, and Bill Gates," McCue told *Tech N' Marketing*'s Hillel Fuld. "So by my senior year I had pretty much decided that rather than go to NASA I'd become a technology entrepreneur." After high school, McCue worked at a software store. Both Jobs and Gates had dropped out of college, so McCue saw no need for further education. Eventually McCue landed a job with IBM and created computer graphics for presentations given by company executives. He also developed a graphics management system before leaving the company in 1989.

After his stint at IBM, McCue felt ready to step out on his own and launched his first tech startup, Paper Software, Inc., in 1989 in Woodstock, New York. He intended to develop software that made operating a computer as easy as using a piece of paper. Success did not come quickly. To finance his business, McCue worked construction jobs and did tech consulting because he could not attract investors. Hoping to improve his image, McCue attended Toastmasters International to develop his speaking skills and enrolled in kung fu classes to build his confidence.

In his free time, McCue programmed and eventually created Sidebar, which became his company's first product. Sidebar—a launch-pad style icon toolbar—sat at the side of the monitor as a simplified "Windows-type" interface. In 1991, with his program complete, McCue enticed eight investors to give him $100,000. He took Sidebar on tour and received positive reviews from trade papers, though sales remained slim. In 1993, he licensed the program to IBM. McCue's next product was WebFX, a 3-D graphics plug-in for Netscape's Web browser. Impressed with McCue's work, Netscape Communications Corp. bought Paper Software in 1995 for an estimated $20 million and brought McCue on board as vice president for technology. At Netscape, McCue worked on the development of Netscape Netcaster before leaving the company in 1998, around the time it was acquired by AOL.

In 1999 McCue joined Angus Davis and Hadi Partovi to found Tellme Networks Inc. with the idea of creating a "voice" browser that utilized the Internet to deliver Web data over the phone. Davis had worked at Netscape with McCue and Partovi had worked at Microsoft. The company worked with voice-recognition software to create an interface that allowed users to vocally ask a simple question—such as "what is the weather forecast for St. Louis today?"—and receive the answer by voice or e-mail. The trio sold TellMe to Microsoft in 2007 for about $800 million.

In 2009, McCue co-founded another startup, Flipboard. He and his co-founder, Doll, had begun talking about how they would remake the Web if it was wiped out and they got to design a new one from scratch. Speaking to *Tech N' Marketing*'s Fuld, McCue described how the company came to be. "As our thought experiment progressed and interesting product ideas began to materialize we decided to start a company focused on improving how people discover, browse, and share content across social networks." What they ultimately created was the Flipboard app.

McCue believed Flipboard might ultimately lead to a revolution in how everyone views content over the Internet. Magazine publishers have contacted McCue, wondering if such an interface could help beautify their online publications and help them look more like their printed magazines. McCue told *Business Insider*'s Nicholas Carlson that he believed there would be other Flipboard platforms—perhaps for the iPhone or the Web—in the future, but he was going to take it slow. "I want to make sure we continue to build something here that's going to help publishers and it's going to help advertisers, and it's going to be a completely new kind of browsing experience for people who are using a tablet and are using the Internet. So that's going to take a lot of focus, a lot of energy and that's what we'll be doing for the foreseeable future."

Sources

Periodicals

Fast Company, November 2006, p. 31.
New York Times, April 21, 1999, p. C2.

Online

"An Interview with Mike McCue, the Genius Behind Flipboard," *Tech N' Marketing,* http://technmarketing.com/2010/11/an-interview-with-mike-mccue-the-genius-behind-flipboard/ (October 16, 2011).

"Flipboard's Mike McCue," *Net* magazine, http://www.netmagazine.com/interviews/in-depth/flipboards-mike-mccue (October 16, 2011).

"The Inside story: Flipboard's Crazy Launch and Its Plan to Save Media, *Business Insider,* http://www.businessinsider.com/flipboard-ceo-mike-mccue-2010-7 (October 16, 2011).

"Mike McCue—Director, Advanced Technology, Netscape Communications," *Businessweek,* http://www.businessweek.com/1997/34/b354158.htm (October 16, 2011).

"To Be Young, Gifted, and Geeky, *Businessweek,* http://www.businessweek.com/1996/12/b346722.htm (October 16, 2011).

—Lisa Frick

Cynthia McFadden

Television journalist

Henry S. Dziekan III/Getty Images Entertainment/Getty Images

Born Cynthia Graham McFadden, May 27, 1956, in Lewiston, ME; daughter of Warren Graham (a business executive) and Arlene (Ridley) McFadden; married Michael Davies (an editor and publisher), September 9, 1989 (divorced, 1996); children: Spencer Graham (with James Hoge, a magazine editor). *Education:* Bowdoin College, B.A. (summa cum laude), 1978; Columbia University, J.D., 1984.

Addresses: *Agent*—Creative Artists Agency, 2000 Avenue of the Stars, Los Angeles, CA 90067. *Office*—ABC News, 147 Columbus Ave., New York, NY 10023-5999.

Career

Executive producer of the Columbia University Seminars on Media and Society, 1984-91; senior producer and anchor, Court Television Network, 1991-94; network legal affairs correspondent, ABC News, 1994-96, then senior legal correspondent, 1996—; co-host, *Nightline,* 2005—.

Awards: Emmy Award (with others) for outstanding news and documentary program, National Academy of Television Arts and Sciences, for *ABC 2000: The Millennium,* 2000; Alfred I. DuPont Award, Graduate School of Journalism, Columbia University, 2002.

Sidelights

Cynthia McFadden's career at ABC News was cemented in 2005 when she was selected as one of the three new co-hosts of the network's long-running late-night staple, *Nightline.* She was the only female journalist among the trio chosen to replace *Nightline*'s founding anchor, Ted Koppel. Most television critics gave the retooled version little chance of survival in the highly competitive late-night ratings game, but McFadden and co-hosts Terry Moran and Bill Weir—who replaced veteran British journalist Martin Bashir—have managed to keep *Nightline* fresh and relevant. In 2009, the show even moved into the number-one spot as the most-watched television program in the United States in the 11:35 p.m. time slot.

Born in 1956 in Lewiston, Maine, McFadden was adopted by Warren McFadden, a business executive, and his wife Arlene, both of whom were natives of Auburn, Maine, where McFadden was raised. It was a private adoption, and therefore no records exist relating to her birth mother and father, but early on McFadden's parents would tell her the story of how they discovered her in a bassinet at a hospital and chose her among the other foundlings in the ward. When she was in middle school, a teacher's careless remark about biological versus adopted children troubled her, and she discussed this with her parents. "I know it doesn't feel this way just now, but you are so lucky," McFadden said her father told her in a 2003 article she wrote for *Good Housekeeping*. "Most of us can only hope to be as good-looking or as smart as the people in our families. But you are not limited by your mother and me. The Queen of England could be your mother. You can be anyone." Fortuitously, McFadden had just seen the medieval costume epic *The Lion in Winter*, which had won Katharine Hepburn another Academy Award for her portrayal of Eleanor of Aquitaine; McFadden imagined that the worldly, sophisticated Hollywood star—who had high cheekbones like her own—might actually be her mother.

A gifted student, McFadden planned on becoming a doctor, and entered Bowdoin College. By chance, her freshman-year roommate's parents lived next door to Hepburn on Connecticut's Long Island Sound. During the summer, McFadden visited her roommate's family in Fenwick, and was readying for a sail with the family when Hepburn walked past on the beach. They struck up a conversation and soon became friends, despite a nearly 50-year age difference. "Why she fascinated me was easy to understand. What she possibly saw in this kid on the beach was a mystery to me," McFadden told *Philadelphia Inquirer* columnist Gail Shister. She suggested that the veteran stage and screen star, who never had children, "was at a point in her life where she wanted to tell somebody the way she thought a good life should be lived. I was in the right place at the right time."

The college student quickly became part of Hepburn's close circle of friends. She stayed at the Fenwick house, and Hepburn even spent Christmas holidays with McFadden's parents at their Cundy's Harbor home. McFadden graduated from Bowdoin in 1978, with both summa cum laude and Phi Beta Kappa distinction, and went on to Columbia Law School in New York City, earning her juris doctor in 1984. While there, she became intrigued with the thriving graduate program at Columbia School of Journalism, run by a legendary former network news producer, Fred Friendly. Upon graduating in 1984, McFadden went to work for Friendly and his Columbia University Seminars on Media and Society, which were a long-running staple of the Public Broadcasting Service (PBS). She spent seven years as an executive producer of generously budgeted, intellectually rigorous series like *The Presidency and the Constitution*, a seven-part special that aired on PBS in 1987.

In 1991, McFadden was lured by an offer from a fledgling cable channel, Court Television Network. She signed on as a senior producer and anchor, and

appeared on the air daily as a legal analyst for high-profile criminal trials, beginning with the sexual assault case in Florida against William Kennedy Smith, a scion of the political dynasty. In 1994, she was hired by ABC News to be their network legal affairs correspondent. In that role, McFadden covered one of the most infamous trials of the twentieth century, when former professional football player O.J. Simpson was acquitted on charges that he had murdered his estranged wife and her friend.

McFadden was promoted to senior legal correspondent at ABC News in 1996. Her longtime friendship with Hepburn had continued over the years, with Hepburn occasionally attempting to play matchmaker for her protégé. In 1989, McFadden wed Michael Davies, the editor and publisher of the *Hartford Courant*, and the reception was hosted by Hepburn at her Fenwick estate. The couple divorced in 1996. In the winter of 1997-98, while covering a story in war-torn Bosnia, McFadden realized she was pregnant. Her son with James Hoge, the editor of *Foreign Affairs*, was born in July of 1998. It was Hepburn who suggested the infant's name, Spencer, in homage to the great love of her life, the actor Spencer Tracy.

McFadden regularly went to such remote locales to cover stories or court cases for ABC News. Her reports aired on *World News Tonight, Nightline,* and *Good Morning America,* and she also successfully pitched story ideas for special reports, including *Judgment at Midnight,* a one-hour special that made history when it aired in 1996. It marked the first time a television news team had been allowed inside a prison to track the final hours of a death-row inmate.

In 1996, McFadden became a correspondent for ABC's evening newsmagazine *Primetime,* and eight years later became one of its co-anchors. She also delivered stories for *20/20,* ABC's long-running newsmagazine, as one of its regular correspondents. The rights of women and children, and the hardships faced by many families, were her special focus. One story she did, about a five-year-old girl in Maine's foster-care system who died after being wrapped with duct tape by her foster mother, was part of a maelstrom of coverage that prompted state lawmakers to overhaul the entire foster-care system in Maine. For *Primetime,* McFadden followed the stories of children being raised by grandparents over a period of several years. She continued to report on high-profile trials, including the one that sent domestic doyenne Martha Stewart to prison in 2004 and the case of a pregnant California woman who went missing on Christmas Eve of 2002; the late Laci Peterson's husband was found guilty and sentenced to death.

Death penalty cases have always intrigued McFadden. In 2004, network executives agreed to another special segment, "In the Jury Room," which was the first time television cameras captured jury deliberations. Occasionally, she filled in as guest host for Ted Koppel on *Nightline*, the half-hour ABC News program that aired weeknights just after the local news, at 11:35 p.m. The show began back in 1979 as the network's special coverage of the ongoing hostage crisis in Iran, when Islamic militants took over the U.S. Embassy in Tehran and held several Americans hostage for more than a year. The show officially morphed into *Nightline* under Koppel in early 1980, and he remained its anchor for the next 25 years, one of the longest runs of a television journalist on a single program. Koppel was so closely identified with the show, in fact, that television critics assumed it would falter without him and eventually be cancelled.

ABC News executives decided to reformat the show slightly, giving *Nightline* three co-hosts who each delivered their own segment, instead of Koppel's singular focus on the day's most pressing story. They chose McFadden along with Terry Moran, who had served as chief White House correspondent for the network, and British import Martin Bashir, who had gained fame on both sides of the Atlantic for exclusive interviews with Diana, the Princess of Wales, and pop star Michael Jackson. The new anchors debuted in late November of 2005. Critics gave it a few weeks to find its footing, but remained skeptical. "The new *Nightline* isn't terrible, and some of the more recent segments have been quite good," wrote Alessandra Stanley in the *New York Times* on December 13. "But over all, the revised show is surprisingly ordinary, a flimsy, fast-moving magazine show like *20/20* that omits the kind of sustained, intelligent inquiry that turned Mr. Koppel's *Nightline* into a landmark."

A television journalist with an affable, friendly style—a cross between her network's most popular celebrity-interviewer Barbara Walters and the more cerebral Diane Sawyer—McFadden scored some major names for her *Nightline* segments. She sat down with U.S. Secretary of State Condoleezza Rice in 2007 and with President George W. Bush just a month after his 2008 reelection. She also managed to only mildly irritate pop superstar Madonna, who is famously reticent with the media. When McFadden toured Jennifer Aniston's spectacular newly renovated home for a profile that appeared in March 2010 issue of *Architectural Digest*, she elicited from Aniston the oft-repeated quote about the home, telling McFadden "it's like a big hug."

Michael Jackson's sudden demise in June of 2009 helped *Nightline* gain a lead over its competitors. With Bashir at the helm, the show devoted several nights of coverage to the singer's death, which brought a spike in the ratings. *Nightline*, to the surprise of many, grabbed the number-one spot in its time slot in the Nielsen ratings that year, and stayed there. This was an especially significant victory for the news team at ABC, who had long battled with network brass over the viability of the show, which was still the sole late-night national network news program on the air, as it always had been throughout its history. For years, it competed with Johnny Carson and then Jay Leno on *The Tonight Show* on NBC, against David Letterman and his *Late Show* on CBS, and there were times when network executives openly made moves to suggest they might replace *Nightline* with an entertainment show, or move comedian Jimmy Kimmel's 12:05 a.m. show forward a half hour. "We know we have to earn it every day," McFadden told Bill Carter in the *New York Times* about *Nightline*'s viability at the network.

McFadden was with Katharine Hepburn when the iconic movie star died at the age of 96 in June of 2003. Hepburn made McFadden co-executor of her will, and the process of settling the estate took several years. McFadden's mother Arline was still "my biggest supporter and my best critic," the journalist told gossip columnist Liz Smith in a 2005 *Good Housekeeping* article. "She watches news religiously and usually knows more than I do about many things. And she is tough. She called me last weekend and told me that she didn't like a piece that I had done. And she explained to me why. I have to tell you, it is really annoying, especially because she's usually right!"

Sources

Periodicals

Architectural Digest, March 2010, p. 56.
Good Housekeeping, May 2003, p. 121; February 2005, p. 129.
New York Times, December 13, 2005; July 27, 2009.
O, The Oprah Magazine, October 2004, p. 209.
Philadelphia Inquirer, August 31, 2006.
Portland Press Herald, August 19, 1996, p. 5B.

Online

"Cynthia McFadden," ABC News, http://abcnews.go.com/Nightline/story?id=128458&page=1 (March 30, 2011).

—*Carol Brennan*

Rory McIlroy

Professional golfer

© Vern Verna/Ai Wire/Landov

Born May 4, 1989, in Holywood, Northern Ireland, United Kingdom; son of Gerry (a bartender) and Rosie (a factory worker) McIlroy.

Addresses: *Management*—International Sports Management, Cherry Tree Farm, Rostherne, Cheshire WA14 3RZ United Kingdom. *Web site*—http://www.rorymcilroy.com/.

Career

Won European Amateur Championship, 2006; turned pro, 2007; joined European Professional Golfers Association Tour, 2008; joined U.S. Professional Golfers Association Tour, 2010; member of Ryder Cup-winning team, 2010; won U.S. Open, 2011.

Sidelights

In 2011, Rory McIlroy emerged as a new force in professional golf by winning the U.S. Open after a devastating loss at the Masters. A native of Northern Ireland, he played well from an early age and won the European Amateur Championship at 17. Turning professional in 2007, McIlroy's profile continued to build over the next few years, first in Europe then in the United States. With his U.S. Open victory, he was dubbed golf's next big star and had a large following not only in his native country but around the world. *Golf Digest* columnist and author Tom Callahan told Larry Dorman of the *New York Times*, "He's the one who's been on the horizon, the guy everybody has been hoping would come along. I'm ready for a sports hero who doesn't treat the world like his spittoon."

McIlroy was born on May 4, 1989, in Holywood, Northern Ireland, the only child of Gerry and Rosie McIlroy. His father worked three jobs to support his son's golf ambitions, including bartending at Holywood Golf Club, while his mother worked in a factory. McIlroy's father started teaching him to play golf at the age of four after the boy showed interest in the game by the age of two. The young McIlory could hit a long drive of 40 yards. By the age of seven, he belonged to the club, and qualified for his first professional tournament at the age 15. Along the way, he developed his game on courses in his area including Hazel Wood, Cherry Tree, Old Oak, Abbot's Wood, and Holly Bush. Describing film of a nine-year-old McIlroy, Jim White of the London *Daily Telegraph* wrote "Even then, he was in possession of the perfect swing, a gorgeous amalgam of art and function, a thing of such simplicity and grace it is enough to make the average weekend hacker weep at their own hopelessness."

By his mid-teens, McIlroy was considered a golf sensation in Ireland. Educated at Sullivan Upper School, he left school when he was 16 to focus on golf. Just after his sixteenth birthday, McIlroy played in his first senior pro game at the Dunlop Masters at the Forest of Arden. Of the experience, he told the *Mirror*, "Well, it was my first time out and I didn't know what to expect but it was tough. But I learned that they are not all Tiger Woods—the others don't hit it any better than I do, it's just about getting it around the golf course." The following week, he was given an invitation to play in the Nissan Irish Open at Carton House. He had played the course before, but only expected to make the cut.

In 2006, the 17-year-old won the European Amateur Championship. Continuing to shine, McIlroy was the top amateur at the British Open in 2007, finishing forty-second at Carnoustie. He had been third entering the second round. Also in 2007, he was a member of Britain and Ireland's Walker Cup team, which lost to the United States 12-11. Later in 2007, McIlroy turned professional. His first pro event was the British Masters, a stop on the European PGA (Professional Golfers Association) Tour. Of this even, the young golfer told the Associated Press Worldstream, "I'm not putting too much pressure on myself, but I would love to go out this week and play well. I think people have expectations of me and I have expectations of myself, so I hopefully can play well and live up to the expectations."

Shortly after turning pro, McIlroy began European PGA Tour qualifying school so that he could earn a tour card for 2008. He won the card and joined the European PGA Tour that year. Fellow Northern Irishman Darren Clarke served as his mentor. In 2009, McIlroy played primarily on the European tour, but also appeared in his first events on the U.S. PGA Tour. The first was the Accenture Match Play Championship, where he reached the quarterfinals. The following week, McIlroy played in his first strokeplay event on the American tour, the Honda Classic. During the first round, McIlroy was near the leaderboard but had a third round score of 71, which brought him back to Earth. He also played in the Houston Open and at his first Masters.

Early in 2010, McIlroy suffered his first major setback. After competing in two tournaments in Abu Dhabi and Dubai—finishing sixth in the latter and reaching number seven in the world rankings—the golfer suffered a back injury cased by too much practicing. While the long-term prognosis was good, there were concerns that his swing might be putting too much strain on his back. He recovered and joined the U.S. Professional Golfers Association Tour (though he spent much of the season in Europe after becoming homesick) and was a member of the European Ryder Cup winning team later in the year.

In 2011, McIlroy's career reached new heights, after one major low. Returning to the Masters, he was dominant in the first three rounds and seemed poised to win and become the youngest Masters champion since Woods; however, in the final round, McIlroy's game collapsed in spectacular fashion and he shot an 80. He admitted that what could have been a devastating loss was relatively easy to overcome. He told the Canwest News Service, "I felt like I got over the Masters pretty quickly." He proved this point by not only winning, but dominating, the U.S. Open at the Congressional Country Club a few months later. Playing flawless golf wire to wire, he finished the tournament 16-under par, eight shots ahead of Jason Day, who finished second. McIlroy was the youngest U.S. Open winner since Bobby Jones in 1923. In addition to setting a number of U.S. Open records, the victory boosted McIlroy's world ranking to four.

McIlroy was the second straight winner of the U.S. Open from Northern Ireland. Countryman Graeme McDowell won in 2010, and told Canwest News Service, "Nothing this kid does ever surprises me. He's the best player I've ever seen. I didn't have a chance to play with Tiger when he was in his real pomp, and this guy is the best I've ever seen. Simple as that. He's great for golf. He's a breath of fresh air for the game, and perhaps we're ready for golf's next superstar. And maybe, Rory is it."

After the U.S. Open, McIlroy's next important tournament was the 2011 British Open held at Royal St. George's, where he was treated like the star of the show though he did not play well. Though he played tournaments on both the European PGA Tour and the American PGA Tour, he concluded that he did better in the latter because he believed his game was better suited to that environment. He was even considering moving to Florida. Among the tournaments he played in upon his return to the States were the WGC-Bridgestone Invitational and the PGA Tour Championship.

With the U.S. Open win, McIlroy faced a surge in popularity, enhanced by his reputation for being nice, generous, and open with the public, fellow golfers, and the media. He was also UNICEF ambassador to Haiti in June 2011. Fellow elite golfer Phil Mickelson told Doug Ferguson of Associated Press Online, referring to McIlroy's U.S. Open win, "The thing about Rory is that he plays golf with a real flair and a real charisma, and I think fans are drawn to that. He plays it with this youthful exuberance, and it's fun to watch and see somebody play golf like that and really enjoy it. He played beautifully, obviously, and ended up winning. But it's not just how he won with his great play, but also the way he interacts with people."

Sources

Periodicals

Agence France Presse—English, June 19, 2011.
Associated Press Online, July 12, 2011.
Associated Press Worldstream, September 18, 2007.
Canwest News Service, June 19, 2011.
Daily Post (Liverpool, England), August 4, 2011, p. 34.
Daily Telegraph (London, England), June 21, 2011, p. 17.
Guardian Unlimited, February 8, 2010.
Mirror, May 19, 2005, p. 63.
New York Times, June 20, 2011, p. A1.

San Jose Mercury News, June 19, 2011.
Sunday Life, October 29, 2006, p. 86.
Sunday Times (London, England), March 8, 2009, p. 12; July 24, 2011, p. 14.
Vancouver Sun (British Columbia, Canada), August 9, 2011, p. F4.

Online

"Rory's World," *Sports Illustrated*, http://sports illustrated.cnn.com/vault/article/magazine/MAG1187576/index.htm (August 19, 2011).

—A. Petruso

Kevin Mitnick

© Kai Foersterling/EPA/Landov

Security consultant

Born Kevin David Mitnick, August 6, 1965, in Van Nuys, CA; son of Alan (a record promoter and general contractor) and Shelly (a waitress; maiden name, Jaffe) Mitnick; married Bonnie Vitello (in telecommunications; divorced).

Addresses: *Office*—Mitnick Security Consulting, LLC, 2564 Wigwam Parkway, Ste. 116, Henderson, NV 89074. *Web site*—http://mitnicksecurity.com/index.php.

Career

Convicted of stealing long-distance codes from MCI, 1989; worked for Tel Tec Investigations, c. 1992; charged with 48 counts of computer, wire, and cellphone fraud, 1995; pled guilty to seven charges, 1999; released from prison, 2000; published first book, *The Art of Deception: Controlling the Human Element of Security*, 2002; probation completed, 2003; founded and served as chief executive officer of Defensive Thinking LLC, c. 2003; founded Mitnick Security, c. mid-2000s.

Sidelights

Convicted of computer hacking in the late 1980s and late 1990s, Kevin Mitnick was once labeled the world's most wanted computer hacker and later became a respected computer security consultant after his release from prison. First arrested in his teens, his exploits included hacking into computers at various companies such as Pacific Bell and Digital Equipment Company, and stealing phone codes from MCI. He also hacked into long distance switching networks, pirated the Internet, and pirated cellular telephone companies, allegedly causing millions dollars worth of damage on corporate computer networks, but never stealing any money for himself. As Jonathan Littman of *Computerworld* wrote of Mitnick, "Even the most heavily guarded networks and highly touted security experts have been no match for Mitnick's unique double-barreled shotgun of technical savvy and old-fashioned con artistry."

Born on August 6, 1965, in Van Nuys, California, he was the son of Alan and Shelly Mitnick. His father worked as a record promoter and general contractor, while his mother was a waitress. Mitnick's parents divorced by the time he was three, and was raised in Panorama City, a suburb of Los Angeles, by his mother. Many of his relatives had trouble with the law, and Mitnick himself was regularly in trouble at school. By the time he was a teenager, he was an overweight loner and dropped out of high school. However he found he had a knack for manipulating gadgets like telephones and ham radios for pranks and other means of destruction. One of his first discoveries was "phone phreaks," teens who used stolen phone codes to make free long-distance calls. He and his friends also programmed phones of people they disliked to ask for 20 cents when the owners of the phones' picked up the receiver.

From phones, Mitnick moved into computers and computer hacking. He used information found in dumpsters for hacking purposes, and was persistent in using computers to gain power and violate privacy like breaking into voice mails and computer systems. He read through private files and regularly taunted those who crossed him. In 1981, Mitnick was arrested for the first time when he was caught hacking into the computers of Pacific Bell. He walked into a Pacific Bell office and took some computer manuals and codes to digital door locks. As a teenager, he also broke into a top secret military defense system, the North American Air Defense Command, and was believed to have stolen thousands of data files.

Mitnick was arrested again in 1988 for hacking into Digital Equipment Company, a crime that allegedly caused four million dollars in damage and led to a year in jail for him. Yet the true cost was later estimated to be $160,000 at most. The reason for his success at these crimes was his skill in social engineering. This means he tricked, threatened, or deceived people into giving out information and sensitive materials by pretending to be someone like a supervisor or new employee. Yet his mother was confused by the reputation his son was developing as a computer hacking expert, telling Estes Thompson of the Associated Press, "He's being talked about like he's some whiz kid. He's just not that smart. The kid never finished high school."

Despite the arrest, Mitnick continued to hack, focusing on telephone-related computer crimes. In 1989, he was convicted of stealing long distance codes from MCI telephone computers. As part of his defense, he stated he had an addiction to computers and hacking, a point with which the judge concurred. Because it was his third conviction, Mitnick served a year in federal prison, went to therapy, lost weight, and did a residential 12-step program. But he continued to hack after his release.

Mitnick was sought after for further allegations involving Pacific Bell in November of 1992. He evaded federal officials by hiding for more than two years, and he became the world's most wanted computer hacker in the process. The FBI (Federal Bureau of Investigation) followed him around the world. His location was revealed when he was caught hacking into a San Francisco Bay area network of 11,000 us-

ers called the Well. He read users' emails, and used the network to hide other activities. The beginning of the end came when he broke into the home computer of Tsutomu Shimomura, a computer security expert at the San Diego Supercomputer Center in 1994. Shimomura eventually helped them find Mitnick, who was living in Raleigh, North Carolina. During this time period, Mitnick also had 20,000 credit cards on his computer, copied from Netcom (an Internet service provider), but he had not used any of the accounts.

Finally arrested in February of 1995, Mitnick was initially charged with computer fraud and illegal use of a telephone access device. He was also wanted in California for violating the terms of his probation. At the time of his arrest, his former therapist, Harriet Rosetto, dismissed depictions of him as the most notorious cyberthief in history, telling Thompson of the Associated Press, "That's what I see, a sad, lonely, angry, isolated boy. I don't think he's that important a person. I think he's become mythical. That he's become public enemy No. 1 is kind of laughable. I think that had he found a way to be accepted in the mainstream, he would have joined the mainstream. He already had this reputation as this Svengali character. Nobody wanted to go near him." Yet Mitnick told Littman, "I don't consider the acts I'm accused of being heinous. There's no money I've stolen. Nobody made a profit." Mitnick also believed, "People who use computers are very trusting, very easy to manipulate. I know the computer systems of the world are not as safe as they think. Information is not safe. Only military computers are secure."

He eventually faced 48 charges of computer fraud, wire fraud, and cell phone fraud. He was accused of copying source code for cellular phone service, wiretapping FBI agents, and attempting to social engineer Department of Motor Vehicle officials. After four years in custody without a trial and the hacking community demanding justice for him, Mitnick pled guilty to seven charges in 1999 and ended up serving a total of five years behind bars. Upon his release in January of 2000, Mitnick said, according to Michael White of the Associate Press State & Local Wire, that prosecutors and the media greatly exaggerated his crimes. Mitnick stated, "My crimes were simple crimes of trespass.... My case is a case of curiosity. I wanted to know as much as I could find out about how phone networks worked, and the ins and outs of computer security."

Mitnick was then on probation for three years. He was not allowed on the Internet, to use computers, cell phones, or any other devices which could be linked to the Internet, have a permanent phone line, or even to work as a consultant to any business which dealt with computers during his probation without special permission. He was also supposed to stay within a seven-county area in California unless he had permission. He spent much of his time writing non-technology related articles for periodicals and giving interviews. Within a few months of his release, Mitnick was speaking to a Senate committee and offering his advice on how to keep government networks safe from hackers. His recommendations included focusing on simple safeguards like ensuring employees do not reveal passwords to sensitive systems. Discussing the experience, Mitnick told Ted Bridis of the Associate Press State & Local Wire, "I figured the United States of America was obviously my adversary for many years in this litigation, but I figured despite all that if I can serve country, I'll do it."

Because the restrictions of his probation limited his ability to find employment, the federal Probation Office made changes in July of 2000 which allowed him to pursue certain types of jobs, including working as a security consultant, and speaking publicly and writing about technology-related issues under certain circumstances. During his probation, he appeared as a hacker on the television series *Alias*, and began co-hosting a talk show on KFI that aired on Sunday mornings.

He also published a book, written with William L. Simon, *The Art of Deception: Controlling the Human Element of Security*, in 2002. In the book, which was intended for those who worked in Internet security and other interested parties, he described the social engineering methods he used to get access to sensitive information. He described how easy it is to get passwords, phone lists, and money transfer codes from people. Mitnick focused on how telephone contact is the most effective tool of a hacker, better than electronic and physical security breaches. He included many stories, both fictional and nonfictional, about hacking.

When his probation ended in the early 2003, Mitnick moved into information protection and founded Defensive Thinking, LLC, a computer security firm, with Alex Kasper, before founding a similar company a few years later, Mitnick Security. He helped companies by breaking into their computer networks to reveal weaknesses in their security systems, and teaching them how to protect themselves. He told Bob Mims of the *Salt Lake City Tribune*, "I know that is ironic. All those same skills I used to put into unethical activities I can now use legitimately, and in an ethical way. It's still basically

just solving a puzzle. Years ago, with poor judgment, I was intrigued to break through security on computer systems. Now I do it with the client's permission, for socially acceptable reasons."

An in-demand public speaker, Mitnick also made numerous appearances at related trade shows and conferences, and launched a quarterly publication, the *Mitnicknewsletter*. In 2005, Mitnick published another book, *The Art of Intrusion: The Real Stories Behind the Exploits of Hackers, Intruders, and Deceivers.* Offering an analysis of corporate hacking and ways that businesses can avoid being victims to such security breaches, Mitnick also criticized the way that hackers are treated and offered praise to hackers who show weaknesses in a system to its owners. The psychology of hacking and technical information on how computer security is breached are included.

In 2011, Mitnick published a memoir, *Ghost in the Wires: My Adventures as the World's Most Wanted Hacker.* He was unable to publish the book before 2007 because of a restriction placed on him by the U.S. government that banned him from profiting from his own story until that time. In the book, Mitnick tells his life story, from his early year as a loner kid, to discovering his purpose by hacking, his years dealing with law enforcement and prison, and becoming a public speaker and security consultant. He also deflates myths about himself and dismisses some accusations made against him by authorities.

In retrospect, Mitnick had mixed emotions about being labeled a computer addict during his hacking days. He told Stephen Lynch of the *Orange County Register*, "I've spent an unreasonable amount of time in front of a computer engaged in an activity where I make it a priority above everything else. I just enjoyed the thrill. But then I thought, what if I was a pro baseball player, and every day I went out to practice, because I wanted to be the best player there is. Is that different?" He also told Lynch that he was no longer a hacking addict, explaining "It's kind of like you grow out of it. It was a favorite pastime of mine, but it's not enticing anymore."

Selected writings

(With William L. Simon) *The Art of Deception: Controlling the Human Element of Security*, Wiley (Indianapolis, IN), 2002.

(With Simon) *The Art of Intrusion: The Real Stories Behind the Exploits of Hackers, Intruders, and Deceivers*, Wiley (Indianapolis, IN), 2005.

(With Simon) *Ghost in the Wires: My Adventures as the World's Most Wanted Hacker*, Little, Brown & Company (New York City), 2011.

Sources

Periodicals

Associated Press, February 17, 1995; March 18, 1999.
Associated Press State & Local Wire, January 21, 2000; March 2, 2000; July 13, 2000; June 30, 2002.
Computer Weekly, January 27, 2000.
Computerworld, January 15, 1996, p. 87.
Gazette (Montreal, Quebec, Canada), March 23, 1996, p. H1.
Globe and Mail (Canada), September 30, 2011, p. 10.
Guardian (London, England), December 13, 2002, p. 2.
Ha'aretz, April 4, 2000.
Herald-Sun (Dunham, NC), January 26, 1996, p. A1.

InfoWorld Daily News, December 1, 2000.
Irish Independent, September 1, 2011.
Irish Times, December 21, 1998, p. 8.
Jerusalem Post, February 24, 2006, p. 6.
New York Times, February 4, 1996, sec. 7, p. 14.
New York Times Book Review, August 14, 2011, p. 9.
Orange County Register (CA), November 8, 2001.
Salt Lake City Tribune, September 18, 2005, p. E1.
San Francisco Chronicle, April 21, 2003, p. E1.
Successful Meetings, July 2005, p. 136.

Online

Contemporary Authors Online, Gale, 2006.

—*A. Petruso*

Piers Morgan

Television personality

Born Piers Stefan O'Meara, March 30, 1965, in Newick, East Sussex, England; son of Vincent and Gabrielle (an artist and publican) O'Meara; stepson of Glynne Pughe-Morgan (a meat wholesaler and publican); married Marion Shalloe (a nurse), July 1991 (divorced, 2008); married Celia Walden (a journalist), June 24, 2010; children: Spencer William, Stanley Christopher, Albert Douglas (from first marriage). *Education:* Studied journalism at Harlow College.

Addresses: *Office*—CNN, One Time Warner Center, 10 Columbus Circle, New York, NY 10023.

Career

Clerk with Lloyd's of London, c. 1984; reporter for the Surrey and South London Newspaper Group, 1985-89; "Bizarre" columnist for *The Sun*, 1989-94; editor, *News of the World*, 1994-95; editor, *Daily Mirror*, 1995-2004; judge, *America's Got Talent*, 2006-2010, and *Britain's Got Talent*, 2007-2010; winning contestant on the seventh season of *Celebrity Apprentice*, 2008; host of *The Dark Side of Fame with Piers Morgan*, BBC, 2008; presenter, *Piers Morgan On...*, ITV1, 2009; host, *Piers Morgan's Life Stories*, ITV, 2009-10, and *Piers Morgan Tonight*, CNN, 2011—.

Sidelights

Piers Morgan was a household name in Britain as one of the more ruthless editors on Fleet Street, the section of London that is home to the offices of scores of daily newspapers. As editor of *News of the World* and then the *Daily Mirror*, he sent his journalists to ferret out salacious, headline-making scoops, often involving high-ranking politicians, members of the House of Windsor, or other assorted public figures. After a highly public sacking from the *Mirror* in 2004, Morgan fashioned a new multiplatform career as a newspaper columnist, television interviewer, and reality-television personality. He was the surprise choice of executives at the Cable News Network (CNN) to replace veteran broadcaster Larry King, who retired in 2010. Morgan made his debut in the 9 p.m. weeknight slot on January 17, 2011, as the host of *Piers Morgan Tonight*.

Morgan was the last of four children born to Gabrielle O'Meara, an artist, and her Irish-born husband, Vincent, on March 30, 1965, in the East Sussex town of Newick. Vincent died when Morgan was still an infant, and a few years later Gabrielle later married Glynne Pughe-Morgan, who ran a meat wholesale business. His stepfather—from whom Morgan took his name—later opened a pub, and Morgan speaks highly of both his mother and stepfather. "He took on two young boys when he was in his twenties and did a great job for us," a *Sunday Times* profile quoted him as saying. "We didn't have much money, but we had a great time."

As a youngster, Morgan enrolled in a boarding school, Cumnor House, but completed his education at the Chailey School, the local comprehensive academy. He was an admittedly rowdy kid, he told Simon Hattenstone in an interview for the *Guardian*. "People would say, 'God, he's become obnoxious,'" once he became famous on Fleet Street, but as Morgan pointed out, "I was always obnoxious. I was often thrown out of my local club and banned on Saturday nights for being shouty, mouthy, and drunken."

Unable to pass the foreign-language requirement on his first try for a slot at a university, Morgan went to work for insurance giant Lloyd's of London as a clerk. "It was good money," he told Hunter Davies in the London *Independent* in a 1994 interview, "but after nine months I was in tears with boredom." He entered Harlow College in Essex, which had an acclaimed journalism program, and during his summers off worked as a tree cutter. His first job as a journalist was with the Surrey and South London Newspaper Group. In 1989, Kelvin MacKenzie hired him as an entertainment reporter for one of Britain's top-selling tabloids, *The Sun*. Owned by Rupert Murdoch and his News Corporation, the daily newspaper concentrated on sensational headlines and scurrilous tales designed to appeal to the conservative, xenophobic reader.

Now using a shortened version of his name as his byline, Morgan penned *The Sun*'s "Bizarre" column, which featured blurbs about pop stars and other entertainment news. Morgan quickly became known for his uncanny ability to insert himself next to a celebrity at an event for a photograph, which then appeared in his column. In early 1994, Murdoch promoted the then-28-year-old Morgan to edit the Sunday tabloid *News of the World*, making him the youngest editor of a national newspaper in Britain in more than 50 years. *News of the World* was the top-selling newspaper in Britain at the time and, with newsstand sales of 4.7 million every Sunday, the best-selling newspaper in the Western world.

Morgan was admittedly nervous about his first *News of the World* edition, which was set to appear on February 6, 1994. Late on Saturday, he reached Murdoch by phone and went over the planned front-page stories, which Murdoch okayed. Then, a man in a red jumpsuit paraglided onto the roof of Buckingham Palace and stripped off his flight suit to crowds below, revealing green body paint. As Morgan recalled in an interview with *Esquire*'s Cal Fussman, "The staff comes to me. Boss, what are you going to do? I froze. Froze. A young guy, who I've got to be grateful to, piped up and said, 'Boss, one

question. How many times in your life do you think a bloke … is going to fly onto the roof of Buckingham Palace? If the answer is never again, put it on the front page.'"

Britain's royal family was a consistent source of fodder for scandal and speculation in the British press, a focus that intensified in the 1980s with the troubled marriage of the heir to the throne, Prince Charles, and his wife Diana. By the time Morgan took over at the *News of the World*, the marriage was effectively over, and Morgan's tabloid took the lead in publishing some of the most disastrous stories about Charles and Diana and their respective infidelities, which eventually prompted the Queen to order the couple to divorce. Morgan's paper famously broke the story about a series of harassing telephone calls to a married art dealer in 1993 and 1994 that, the newspaper claimed through its secret source, had been traced by investigators back to Kensington Palace, Diana's London home. That August story would quickly be eclipsed by revelations of a former British Army captain who claimed to have had a four-year affair with the princess. In early 1995, the *News of the World* paid the former valet to Prince Charles a large sum of money to divulge details, including that the heir to the throne still slept with his childhood teddy bear.

Morgan was publicly rebuked by Murdoch and Britain's Press Complaints Commission (PCC), however, for a *News of the World* story in which reporters gained entrance, under false pretenses, to a substance-abuse and eating-disorder treatment facility in Surrey upon hearing word that Princess Diana's sister-in-law was being treated there. The paper ran a photograph covertly taken of Countess Victoria Spencer, which prompted Murdoch to order Morgan to publicly apologize. A few months later, in August of 1995, Morgan jumped ship and went over to the rival *Daily Mirror*, another tabloid.

As *Mirror* editor, Morgan became one of the most publicly reviled figures in British journalism. His tenure there lasted nearly nine years, coinciding with the death of Princess Diana in a Paris automobile crash and the election of the first Labour government in Britain in nearly two decades. Morgan also became close to Britain's new prime minister, Tony Blair, but gave his reporters free rein to criticize Blair's wife, Cherie.

Morgan's paper was reprimanded several more times by the PCC, and in some cases was forced by a court to pay damages for libel to a person named in a story. Morgan himself became the subject of newspaper headlines when, in 2000, the *Mirror's* business writers touted a company called Viglen; the day before that story, Morgan had acquired £67,000 worth of shares under his wife's name. He claimed not to have known about the story, and the official inquiry finally decided there was insufficient evidence to prosecute him.

The *Mirror* was not always a scandal sheet; earlier in its history it had been a more sober voice of the British Labour and Socialist movement. After 9/11, Morgan guided the paper back into a "black top" masthead, denoting a newly serious tone and distance from the tabloids, which carry attention-grabbing "red tops" across their front page. The *Mirror* was named Newspaper of the Year in 2002 for Morgan's efforts. He went on to oppose Blair and Blair's support for the war in Iraq, but the rivers of anti-war rhetoric in the paper brought a decline in readership.

Morgan's greatest debacle came on Saturday, May 1, 2004, when the *Mirror* ran black-and-white photographs that allegedly showed members of the Queen's Lancashire Regiment abusing Iraqi prisoners. The Ministry of Defence immediately condemned the images as staged, noting that the truck, equipment, and even guns carried by the soldiers were not regulation British Army issue for its soldiers serving in Iraq. Morgan defended the veracity of the pictures, then went to battle against the *Mirror's* owners, Lord Rothermere and the Trinity Mirror media group, which ordered him to issue a retraction. When he refused, he was escorted out of the *Mirror's* offices.

For years Morgan had been involved in numerous high-profile feuds with other journalists or public figures. *Top Gear* host Jeremy Clarkson was one, who once threw a punch at Morgan at the 2004 British Press Awards over articles the *Mirror* had published about his marriage. The royal family was no doubt pleased about Morgan's downfall, for it had been Morgan who sent a reporter to interview for a footman's job at Buckingham Palace; the journalist was hired and the stories he later wrote in the *Mirror*, especially about the Windsors' preference for Tupperware containers to hold their breakfast cereal, caused another round of grumbling that Britain's press was simply out of control. Morgan defended his tactics as editor in the *Guardian* profile by Hattenstone, characterizing the news business as a competitive sport like cricket, which he played on weekends. "It is vile and vicious and great. I want absolute war on our sporting fields. It's much more fun that way, and the same with newspapers. Newspapers are at their best when they are going for each other in the most monstrous way."

Before taking the CNN job, Morgan founded *First News,* a weekly newspaper for young readers, and wrote a column for the *Evening Standard.* He also began appearing on reality-television programs, including *Britain's Got Talent* and then the American version, whose publicists attempted to portray him as a man more feared than *American Idol* judge Simon Cowell, a friend of Morgan's. The former editor also wrote a tell-all, *The Insider: The Private Diaries of a Scandalous Decade,* in which he revealed the details about some of his headiest triumphs in the tabloid business. "His memoir is historically negligible, analytically null, morally rudderless, sloppily edited, hopelessly written, boastful, whining, sentimental, thuggish and with all the fascination of a horrible accident," wrote Sam Leith in the *Spectator.* "Just like a red-top newspaper on a good day." Leith also reflected that the gory name-dropping served up by Morgan in the book "is the stuff of which red-tops are made. We pretend to disapprove of them, and they pretend to disapprove of each other, and they make gross intrusions into people's lives, and we devour them. Piers Morgan was a brilliant tabloid editor."

In 2008 Morgan's exposure to American audiences was heightened with his win on the seventh season of *Celebrity Apprentice.* In September of 2010, CNN executives confirmed reports that Morgan would replace Larry King, who had hosted an hour-long weeknight interview program on the network since 1985. The coup made Morgan the first major British journalist to appear regularly on American television since David Frost back in the 1970s. After sorting out a work visa issue, Morgan made his debut with *Piers Morgan Tonight* and a jazzed-up new set on January 17, 2011. His first guest was talk-show titan Oprah Winfrey, there to promote her new Oprah Winfrey Network (OWN) in a rare media interview. That was followed by a week of stellar names, including Howard Stern, George Clooney, and former secretary of state Condoleezza Rice.

When major world news erupted in the first months of 2011, Morgan accordingly switched the focus of his show to coverage of events in Egypt and Japan—particularly after an interview with reality-television stars Kim and Kourtney Kardashian. "I would've put good money on the Kardashians rating well, and they didn't," he admitted in an interview with Ben Grossman for *Broadcasting & Cable.* "I think the CNN audience, particularly when there are big news stories going on like the Middle East, they don't like if you interview people they think are pointless."

Selected writings

The Insider: The Private Diaries of a Scandalous Decade, Ebury Press (London), 2005.

Sources

Periodicals

Broadcasting & Cable, February 28, 2011, p. 8.
Esquire, February 2011, p. 96.
Guardian (London, England), March 5, 2005, p. 15; January 17, 2011, p. 6.
Independent (London, England), December 13, 1994.
New York Times, January 16, 2011.

Spectator, March 12, 2005, p. 46.
Sunday Times (London, England), April 6, 2008, p. 19.

Online

"Q&A: Piers Morgan, the Man Stepping into Larry King's Seat," *Time*, http://www.time.com/time/printout/0,8816,2030273,00.html (April 5, 2011).

—*Carol Brennan*

Muse

Rock group

Group formed in 1994 in Teignmouth, Devon, United Kingdom; members include Matthew James Bellamy (born June 9, 1978, in Cambridge, England, United Kingdom; children: Bingham [son; with Kate Hudson, an actress]), vocals, guitars, keyboards; Christopher Tony Wolstenholme (born December 2, 1978, in Rotterham, South Yorkshire, England, United Kingdom; married Kelly; children:

Alfie, Ava-Jo, Frankie, Ernie, Buster), vocals, bass; Dominic James Howard (born December 7, 1977, in Stockport, England, United Kingdom), drums.

Addresses: *Management*—Q-Prime Management, 729 Seventh Ave., Ste. 16, New York, NY 10019-6831. *Office*—Addis & Co., Emery House, 192 Heaton Moor Rd., Stockport, SK4 4DU, United Kingdom. *Web site*—http://muse.mu.

Career

Bellamy and Howard played in the band Carnage Mayhem and formed Gothic Plague; Gothic Plague reformed as Rocket Baby Dolls; Wolstenholme joined Rocket Baby Dolls, 1994; Rocket Baby Dolls won a "Battle of the Bands" contest, 1994; the name of the band was changed to Muse, 1994; Muse released its first album, *Showbiz*, 1999; released compilation album *Hullabaloo*, 2002; released the live album *HAARP*, 2008.

Awards: Best new band, NME Awards, 2000; best British band, Kerrang! Awards, 2001, 2007, 2011; best British live act, Kerrang! Awards, 2002; best album, Kerrang! Awards, for *Absolution*, 2004; best alternative act, MTV Europe Music Awards, 2004; best UK and Irish act, MTV Europe Music Awards, 2004, 2007; best live act, BRIT Awards, 2005, 2007; best live band, NME Awards, 2005, 2008, 2009; best alternative act, MTV Europe Music Awards, 2006; best live act, Kerrang! Awards, 2006; Headliner, MTV Europe Music Awards, 2007; anthem of the year, European Festival Awards, for "Uprising," 2010; best headliner, European Festival Awards, 2010; best special effects, MTV Video Music Awards, for "Uprising," 2010; favorite alternative artist, American Music Awards, 2010; Grammy Award for best rock album, National Academy of Recording Arts and Sciences, for *The Resistance*, 2011; International Achievement Award, Ivor Novello Awards, 2011.

Sidelights

Roger Morton, writing for *NME,* described the music of Muse as a "reinvention of grunge as a neo-classical, high gothic, future rock, full of flambéd pianolas and white-knuckle electric camp," which Morton considered a "precarious venture." Ever evolving, the group started as Gothic Plague, metamorphosed into the Rocket Baby Dolls, and then became Muse. They started as a glam and goth rock group intended only to perform to make a statement and have become the band identified as the best live-performance band in the world. Brian May, the guitarist of Queen—a band that Muse has

been compared to—was quoted by Tim Masters of *BBC News* as saying about Muse, "They are extraordinary musicians. Real virtuosos—much more than I am. I like the way they let their madness show through, always a good thing in an artist."

Muse began in the small seaside town of Teignmouth, Devon, in the United Kingdom. Matthew Bellamy, the group's lead singer, keyboardist, and guitarist moved to Teignmouth when he was ten years old. He grew up with music in his household. His father was in a band called The Tornadoes, who were the first band from the United Kingdom to get a U.S. number-one record. When Bellamy was 14 his parents divorced and he moved in with his grandparents. At that time he began playing the guitar. Bellamy has very diverse interests. According to Morton, he has "a taste for mushrooms, seances, and Hector Berlioz's 'Grande Messe Des Morts.'" At other times Bellamy has indicated interests in conspiracy theories, politics, and science fiction. Cameron Adams, writing for the *Herald Sun* quoted Bellamy as saying "It's good to spread the word that we are living in a relatively corrupt system at the moment. The way information reaches us is questionable, and where the information comes from is quite debatable. All those mishaps in intelligence have led us into what could be a world war. It's just going to keep escalating. It's not a case of inciting riots, but inciting change and the strength to make that change."

Dominic Howard moved to Teignmouth from Manchester when he was eight years old. He never had any interest in music and did not come from a family of musicians. He began playing the drums after hearing a jazz band play when he was in high school. He is wildly creative and experimental, like Bellamy. For example, while recording the album titled *Absolution*, Howard, who was working with engineer and producer Rich Costey, played drums in a pool, smashed cymbals in the water, and ran microphones up and down hallways to capture unique qualities of sound to enhance the songs on the album.

Christopher Wolstenholme started life in Rotterham, Yorkshire, before moving to Teignmouth at the age of eleven. Originally he played guitar, but when Bellamy and Howard asked him to join Rocket Baby Dolls, they also requested that he learn to play the bass. Wolstenholme took up the challenge. Wolstenholme's bass line is the lead instrument that carries the songs of Muse and Bellamy's guitar and vocals weave in and around the anchoring bass notes. Wolstenholme's sensibilities caused the band to refuse the Nestle company permission to use the song "Feeling Good" from the *Origin of Symmetry* album. When Nestle used the song without permission in one of their commercials, he was the one who wanted the band to sue the company; Wolstenholme objected to Nestle in part because Nestle markets powdered formula to mothers in third-world countries. The money that Muse won in the settlement was donated to the charitable organization Oxfam. Wolstenholme himself has struggled with alcoholism, and told *Q* magazine, as reported by the World Entertainment News Network, "I was actually losing my mind. I had to drink to get out of bed in the morning." The band was ignorant of his problem because of his prodigious musical talent. Wolstenholme did not appear impaired and the other members of the band assumed he needed to be by himself when he was, in reality, off drinking. Wolstenholme came to terms with his problem and stopped abusing alcohol. He has been dry since before the release of 2011's *The Resistance*.

As teenagers, the members of Muse entered a battle of the bands contest. Covered in goth make-up, they went onstage, played their hearts out, and destroyed all of their equipment while performing. They did not consider themselves the most musically accomplished group in the contest and did not think that they had a chance of winning. They were there to make a statement that the music should be about attitude and meaning. The band, known at that time as the Rocket Baby Dolls, won the contest. This win made them stop and reconsider their chances at being a successful rock band. They changed the name of the band from Rocket Baby Dolls to Muse because Bellamy had heard one of his teachers talk about the muses. Rather than use the word "muses" they shortened it to Muse.

Dennis Smith, who owned The Sawmill, a recording studio in Cornwall, knew Bellamy, Howard, and Wolstenholme. He had watched them grow up and form their band. Safta Jaffrey, who knew producers and had various contacts within the music industry, formed a partnership with Smith. Smith and Jaffrey wanted to record and promote the kinds of music that they felt passionate about. Smith sent Jaffrey some of Muse's early demonstration tapes and, as Jaffrey told Denny Hilton of the Web site Hit Quarters, Muse "sounded very different, articulate, and intelligent." Smith arranged for Jaffrey to hear Muse at the Cavern Club. At first no other labels or venues were interested in the group and it appeared as though no one understood what the band was creatively attempting, which was demoralizing for Bellamy, Wolstenholme, Howard, Smith, and Jaffrey.

Muse finally had its breakthrough at the *College Music Journal* (*CMJ*) Music Marathon in New York City. The *CMJ* festival is an annual event that has fea-

tured bands such as Green Day, Modest Mouse, My Chemical Romance, Mars Volta, Red Hot Chili Peppers, REM, Nirvana, Foo Fighters, and The Black Eyed Peas. Scouts from Columbia Records heard Muse play at the festival and liked what they heard. The Columbia scouts invited Muse to Los Angeles to play for Rick Ruben, the co-president of Columbia Records. Madonna's record company, Maverick Records, stepped forward first and offered the band a contract. Jaffrey, Smith, and Muse decided to deal with Maverick Records in the United States, but after an album was cut, Maverick felt that the band had not produced a single song that was radio worthy. Maverick asked Muse to change some of their songs, but Muse did not want to have the integrity of what they were trying to do as musicians altered and they refused. The partnership with Maverick was dissolved.

This initial contract worked better in the long run for Muse. They negotiated territorial deals with various companies, which enabled them to maintain creative control over their own material. This was an extremely important thing for Muse, a band that was pushing the envelope in different directions, experimenting with a variety of sounds, and evolving with each album. Jaffrey told Hit Quarters' Hilton that, had he signed "Muse to one label for the whole world, they would never have made it as a band. They were never radio friendly in those days. The music was too challenging."

Jaffrey, Smith, and Muse decided early on that the way for the band to promote itself was through touring. Each record deal in each part of the world included a large touring budget. Jaffrey and Smith, who were unofficially managing Muse, would look for the most exciting tours that they could find and Muse would do as many tours as they could. The first year that they toured, Muse was fortunate join the Red Hot Chili Peppers and the Foo Fighters, both popular acts. They also played at 54 international festivals.

In 2002, after Muse had recorded their first two albums, the band was trying to break into the American market and become a recognizable name. Celine Dion wanted to use the title "Celine Dion Muse" for a Las Vegas show that she was creating. The band owned the rights to the name "Muse" and told her that she could use the name as long as it was not associated with any title, album, or video created. Dion's management tried to buy the usage of the name for $50,000. Muse still refused and Bellamy, as reported by the *BBC News*, said, "We don't want to turn up there with people thinking we're Celine Dion's backing band." Dion backed down and used a different name.

Muse continued to create music and tour. With their third album, *Absolution*, they began to gain more recognition and the album charted at number one in the United Kingdom. At that time Jaffrey and Smith bowed out and new management and a new producer, Rick Costey, came in to work with Muse. In 2006, Muse released *Black Holes and Revelations*, also produced by Costey. The album reached number one on the charts in the United Kingdom, Europe, and Australia and was in the top ten on the *Billboard* charts in the United States. The album's themes dealt with science fiction ideas, political theories, and expressions of outrage. The cover had an image of four men sitting at a table located on Mars. The men represent the four horsemen of the apocalypse who have outgrown their horses. There is speculation on fan sites that the band has been said to be influenced by such diverse books as *1984* by George Orwell, *The Grand Chessboard: American Primacy and Its Geostrategic Imperatives* by Zbigniew Brzezinski, *Brainwashing: The Science of Thought Control* by Kathleen Taylor, and *Hyperspace* by Michio Kaku. After this album, Bellamy, Wolstenholme, and Howard were granted Honorary Doctorate of Arts degrees from the University of Plymouth for their contributions to music. In 2009, Muse released their first self-produced album, titled *The Resistance*. It was an instant success and was Muse's third album to reach number one in the United Kingdom. In 2011, Muse won a Grammy Award for Best Rock Album for *The Resistance*.

While Bellamy's fiancée, actress Kate Hudson, was pregnant and for the first few months of his son's life, Muse toured less. For the summer of 2011, Muse performed at only four festivals. After Bingham, Bellamy's son, was born, it was announced that Bellamy chose to have a smaller role in the creation of Muse's music and would be writing fewer songs; Wolstenholme would be taking over songwriting duties from Bellamy. According to the World Entertainment News Network, Wolstenholme told the *Sun* he thought Bellamy had "raised the bar quite high" and he was worried about writing a song that would bring down the band.

The sound of Muse keeps changing, and Bellamy, Wolstenholme, and Howard keep trying new things and testing their creativity, whether it is for a new single—such as "Neutron Star Collision" from the *The Twilight Saga: Eclipse* film soundtrack—or an entire new album. A Muse song is included in the popular video game Guitar Hero. The band continues to tour and perform before live audiences around the world. Describing their unique sound to Talia Soghomonian of the Web site MusicOHM, Bellamy said, "I don't think we really fit. I think we don't need to fit. We make our own music and people notice."

Selected discography

Showbiz, Taste Media, 1999.
Origin of Symmetry, Taste Media, 2001.
Hullabaloo (compilation), Taste Media, 2002.
Absolution, Taste Media, 2003.
Black Holes and Revelations, Helium 3, 2006.
HAARP (a live album), Helium 3, 2008.
The Resistance, Helium 3, 2009.
(Contributor) *The Twilight Saga: Eclipse*, Chop Shop/ Atlantic, 2010.

Sources

Books

Complete Marquis Who's Who, Marquis Who's Who, 2010.

Periodicals

Belfast Telegraph, April 14, 2008.
Guitar Player, July 2010, p. 70.
Herald Sun (Sydney, Australia), July 13, 2006.
Radio & Music, November 23, 2010.
Seattle Times, April 1, 2010.
World Entertainment News Network, May 31, 2011; June 30, 2011; August 15, 2011.

Online

"Band muses on Dion name victory," BBC News, http://news.bbc.co.uk/2/hi/uk_news/england/ 2339585.stm (August 12, 2011).
"Interview: Muse," MusicOMH, http://www. musicomh.com/music/features/muse_0706.htm (August 12, 2011).
"Interview with Safta Jaffrey," Hit Quarters, http:// www.hitquarters.com/index.php3?page= intrview/opar/intrview_Safta_Jaffrey_Interview. html (August 12, 2011).
"Lady Gaga, Muse, 30 Seconds to Mars Triumph at 2010 VMA Awards," *Live4ever* ezine, http:// www.live4ever.uk.com/2010/09/lady-gaga-muse-30-seconds-to-mars-triumph-at-2010-vma-awards/ (August 12, 2011).
"Lily Allen, Muse Soar to No. 1 on U.K. Charts," *Billboard*, http://www.billboard.com/bbcom/ news/article_display.jsp?vnu_content_... 00280231.tif0#/bbcom/news/article_display. jsp?vnu_content_id=10028023.tif10 (August 12, 2011).

"Matthew Bellamy," Internet Movie Database, http://www.imdb.com/name/nm1492114/bio (August 20, 2011).

"Muse," AllMusic, http://www.allmusic.com/artist/p142116/biography (August 12, 2011).

"Muse Bask in First Grammy Win, Make Plans For Kid-Friendly Album," MTV, http://www.mtv.com/news/articles/1657891/muse-grammy-awards.jhtml (August 12, 2011).

"Muse Biography," Ticketmaster, http://www.ticketmaster.ie/artist/944747 (August 12, 2011).

"Muse: *Black Holes & Revelations*," PopMatters, http://www.popmatters.com/pm/review/muse-black-holes-revelations/ (August 12, 2011).

"Muse," Internet Movie Database, http://www.imdb.com/name/nm0615614/otherworks (August 12, 2011).

Muse Official Web site, http://muse.mu/ (August 12, 2011).

"Muse: *Origin of Symmetry*," *NME*, http://www.nme.com/reviews/muse/5220 (August 12, 2011).

"Muse Receive Honorary Degrees," StarPulse, http://www.starpulse.com/news/index.php/2008/09/28/muse_receive_honorary_degrees_ (August 12, 2011).

"Muse Score Third U.K. No. 1 Album," *Billboard*, http://www.billboard.com/news/muse-score-third-u-k-no-1-album-100...464.story#/news/muse-score-third-u-k-no-1-album-10040144.tif64.story (August 12, 2011).

"Muse's Matt Bellamy Talks," Ultimate-Guitar, http://www.ultimate-guitar.com/news/interviews/muses_matt_bellamy_talks.html (August 12, 2011).

"Muse wins Grammy for Best Rock Album," Hollywood News, http://www.hollywoodnes.com/2011/02/13/muse-wins-grammy-for-best-rock-album/ (August 12, 2011).

"NME Albums & Tracks of the Year," *NME*, http://www.nme.com/reviews/albums/oftheyear (August 12, 2011).

"Queen star May hails Muse album," BBC News, http://news.bbc.co.uk/2/hi/8304176.stm (August 12, 2011).

"Rich Costey: Recording Muse's *Absolution*," Sound On Sound, http://www.soundonsound.com/sos/dec03/articles/richcostey.htm (August 12, 2011).

—*Annette Bowman*

Blake Mycoskie

Chief Executive Officer of TOMS Shoes

Born August 28, 1976, in Arlington, TX; son of Mike (a physician) and Pam (a cookbook author) Mycoskie. *Education:* Southern Methodist University, B.B.A., 1999.

Addresses: *Home*—Marina del Rey, CA. *Office*—TOMS Shoes Headquarters, 3025 Olympic Ave., Ste. C, Santa Monica, CA 90404. *Web site*—http://www.toms.com/.

Career

Co-founder, EZ Laundry, 1997; founder, Mycoskie Media, c. 2000; co-founder, Drivers Ed Direct, 2005; co-founder, TOMS Shoes, 2006, and chief executive officer, 2006—. Has also launched One Day without Shoes campaign in 2008, TOMS Eyewear in 2011, and is the author of *Start Something That Matters*, published by Spiegel & Grau in 2011.

Sidelights

Blake Mycoskie is the founder of TOMS Shoes, one of the most boldest social-entrepreneurship schemes to emerge in the new millennium. Designed as a global footwear initiative, TOMS donates one pair of shoes to a person in need for every pair it sells on the retail market. Mycoskie's innovative company grew rapidly within just a few short years and, in September of 2010—before it had even reached its five-year anniversary in business—TOMS hit the one-million mark for its shoe donations.

Mycoskie is a native of Arlington, Texas, where he attended James Martin High School. His father, Mike, is a doctor who once served as team physician for the Texas Rangers, the Major League Baseball franchise in Dallas-Fort Worth. In the early 1990s Mycoskie's mother, Pam, self-published a cookbook of her own low-fat recipes that went on to become the best-selling *Butter Busters* title. By then Mycoskie was one of the state's top-ranked junior tennis players and won an athletic scholarship to Southern Methodist University (SMU). With a friend, he launched his first money-making venture in the fall of 1997 while a student at SMU's Cox School of Business. Their EZ Laundry offered a low-cost alternative to the college's coin-operated laundry facilities and quickly became a campus success; Mycoskie and that business partner, Eric House, expanded to other colleges and were soon running a company with 40 employees.

Mycoskie left SMU with an undergraduate business degree in 1999. He traveled for a time before settling in Nashville, Tennessee, to open an outdoor-advertising company that sold space on the sides of multi-story buildings. That venture, called Mycoskie Media, was bought out by Clear Channel Communications, the radio-station and live-concert giant, when Mycoskie was just 25 years old. His third business venture was an online driver-education school, Drivers Ed Direct, that also snowballed into steady profitability within months of its founding in 2005. In between those projects Mycoskie and his sister, Paige, applied for and were accepted as contestants on Season 2 of the CBS reality series *The Amazing Race.* They steadily advanced through the challenges and elimination events on this worldwide scavenger hunt-style competition, and came within minutes of winning the first prize of $1 million. The journey took them from Brazil to Namibia, then Thailand, Australia, and finally back to the United States during its filming in early 2002.

In 2003 Mycoskie was involved with plans for an all-reality television network for cable. Two of his partners were veteran executives with experience at E! Entertainment and USA Network, but their venture tanked after the mighty FOX broadcasting and media empire came up with its own version, the Fox Reality Channel, which barely survived five years on the air before it was folded into another channel.

Mycoskie's entrepreneurial lifestyle and access to technology gave him adequate time for adventurous vacations. In January of 2006 he traveled to Argentina in order to learn the game of polo, a field sport in which horse-mounted players wield mallets to hit balls and score points against the opposing team. He also wanted to do some volunteer work while he was there, and signed up with an organization that donated shoes to impoverished children in the shantytowns that ring the wealthy, cosmopolitan capital of Buenos Aires. The sight of shoeless youngsters from the *villa miserias,* as the slums are known in Argentina, moved Mycoskie immensely and he started thinking about solutions to remedy what he realized was a worldwide dearth of footwear.

Conferring with his polo trainer, Alejo Nitti, Mycoskie came up with the idea to make and sell the humble *alpargata.* This was a simple canvas shoe worn by farmers and polo players alike in Argentina, but it also reminded Mycoskie of his favorite Vans, the slip-on sneaker popularized by American skateboarders in the 1980s. The shoes would be made locally, but sold globally, and Mycoskie inserted a clever concept into his business plan: for every pair sold, the company would donate a pair to a child in need. "It would be providing shoes for tomorrow," he explained to Jennifer Irwin for a *New York Times* article that ran in January of 2007.

Working with Nitti, Mycoskie contracted with local alpargata-makers, set up a Web site, and began contacting potential retail venues in the United States.

The buyer for a Southern California-based apparel chain, American Rag, placed an order, and Mycoskie eventually returned to the United States to sell his driver-education school to help finance TOMS' expansion. He moved into office space in Santa Monica with a skeleton staff and began traveling extensively to promote his global footwear initiative, which adapted a simple promotional slogan, "One for One." A major break came when Whole Foods Market began selling TOMS shoes in a selected stores. The shoe-donation sites also expanded to communities in Central America, Africa, and Asia. He and Nitti came up with a novel way to generate buzz for the donation events, inviting volunteers to join employees in "Shoe Drops" in remote locales, where as many as 10,000 pairs of kid-sized TOMS Shoes—the same style as sold in Whole Foods and other retailers—were handed out to youngsters.

Mycoskie also created a One Day without Shoes campaign in 2008 to raise awareness for the cause. In interviews to promote his company, he points out that in some parts of the world children cannot attend school unless they own a pair of shoes, and in places like Ethiopia and Haiti, where there is heavy concentrations of volcanic soil, those who go barefoot are at risk of contracting podoconiosis, a condition in which silica from the soil enters the body and causes the lower limbs to swell and harden.

Nordstrom, Urban Outfitters, and several other retailers sell various TOMS styles, priced between $45 and $85. In September of 2010 the company reached the one-million mark in donated footwear, and was busy launching another venture, TOMS Eyewear. Mycoskie chronicled his company's rapid rise in a 2011 book, *Start Something That Matters,* published by Spiegel & Grau. He has said in interviews that his start-up was funded with his own personal assets, but "if I would've taken half a million dollars and just bought shoes to give to the kids, I would've been able to give the shoes once," he told Mike Zimmerman in *Success.* "It never would've been as far-reaching and sustainable as TOMS Shoes is now."

Sources

Periodicals

Best Life, March 2007, p. 66.
Footwear News, December 1, 2008, p. 50.
Inc., March 2008, p. 89; June 2010, p. 112.
Newsweek, October 11, 2010, p. 50
New York Times, January 17, 2007.
Success, November 2009, p. 34. .

Online

"Blake Mycoskie," SMU Cox School of Business, http://cox.smu.edu/web/guest/blake-mycoskie (November 25, 2011).

Start Something That Matters, http://www.start somethingthatmatters.com/ (November 25, 2011).

—*Carol Brennan*

Diane L. Neal

Retail executive

Born Diane Lynn Neal c. 1957. *Education:* Michigan State University, B.S., 1979.

Addresses: *Office*—Bath & Body Works, Inc., 7 Limited Pkwy E., Reynoldsburg, OH 43068.

Career

Began at the Dayton-Hudson Corporation as a management trainee in merchandising, 1980; rose through company ranks to become president of Mervyn's, 2001-04; senior vice president for merchandising, Gap Inc., 2004-05; president, Gap Outlets, 2005-06; president and chief operating officer, Bath & Body Works, Inc., 2006-07, and chief executive officer, 2007-11.

Sidelights

Retail executive Diane L. Neal spent four years at the helm of Bath & Body Works after a long career with the Target Corporation (formerly known as the Dayton-Hudson Corporation). Neal's stint as chief executive officer of the personal-care and home-fragrance chain required a move to Ohio, where Bath & Body Works' corporate offices are located. In 2011, the company announced she was easing herself out of the role in order to move back to the West Coast, where she had spent several years as an executive with Mervyn's, formerly a Target Corporation subsidiary.

Neal uses a middle initial, L. (for "Lynn"), to distinguish her from the television actor Diane Neal, who is best known for her role on the NBC drama *Law &*

© Jemal Countess/Getty Images

Order: Special Victims Unit. Neal graduated from Michigan State University in 1979 with a degree in retailing. Her first job was with Dayton's, a high-end department-store chain that was a longtime fixture in the Minneapolis-St. Paul area. Back in the late 1960s, Dayton's had merged with a similar retailer in the Detroit area, the J. L. Hudson Company, to become the Dayton-Hudson Corporation. In 1978, two years before Neal was hired as a management trainee in merchandising, the company bought Mervyn's, a California-based discount department store. Mervyn's remained a subsidiary of the Dayton-Hudson Corporation, which already had Target stores, their own discount-goods chain, with a handful of stores in the Upper Midwest.

Neal rose through the ranks of Mervyn's inside the Dayton-Hudson Corporation, which changed its name to the Target Corporation in 2000 to reflect the growth and success of that division. A year later, she succeeded Bart Butzer as president of the 266 Mervyn's stores, working out of its headquarters in Hayward, California, a Bay Area municipality. She was only the second woman to run one of the Target Corporation's divisions, after Linda Ahlers took over at Marshall Field's five years earlier.

Neal's three-year tenure as president of Mervyn's was a time of immense struggle and seismic shifts in the American retail sector. Inside the parent company, Mervyn's stores were considered a distant, poorly performing cousin compared to the ever-expanding Target brand. The no-frills, low-key style of Mervyn's, furthermore, had been bested by Kohl's, a competitor in several key markets. Adding to the challenges was a sharp decline in consumer spending after 9/11.

Neal's name appeared in some national newspapers in 2003 when a disability rights group filed suit in Alameda County Superior Court charging the chain with refusal to abide by the 1990 Americans with Disabilities Act in its 125 stores in California. The plaintiffs claimed that Mervyn's had opted against widening pathways in its stores, a change that would have better accommodated shoppers who used wheelchairs, motorized scooters, or walkers. Neal testified in court and admitted that Mervyn's suggested store-architecture guidelines called for 32-inch pathways, but that executives had decided against a major renovation of all stores. A judge ruled in Mervyn's stores' favor in November of 2003.

In mid-2004 Target sold the ailing Mervyn's to a group of private investors. The group included Cerberus Capital Management, a private-equity firm that would later acquire a majority stake in Detroit automaker Chrysler. The new owners had a reputation for making drastic changes upon taking over, and Neal resigned ahead of her replacement by a new executive. She went to work for San Francisco-based apparel retailer Gap, Inc., as senior vice president for merchandising in 2004, and within a year was promoted to president of its Gap Outlets division. In October of 2006, the publicly traded company announced she was leaving. Her departure followed that of another key Gap executive, Jenny Ming, who had run its tremendously successful Old Navy spinoff. Ming had also started her career in retailing at Mervyn's at almost the same time as Neal had, then gone over to the Gap in the mid-1980s.

Neal had been lured to the Columbus, Ohio, area by Leslie H. Wexner, the retailing whiz who had started The Limited stores back in the 1960s in the city. The women's apparel chain had expanded nationally at a dizzying rate in the next three decades since, and Wexner eventually created a holding company called Limited Brands. Its subsidiaries included the Express clothing store chain, Lane Bryant, Victoria's Secret, and even upscale women's clothier Henri Bendel. In 1990 Wexner launched a new venture modeled after the successful global specialty-beauty retailer The Body Shop. Called Bath & Body Works, Wexner's knockoff grew phenomenally over the few years and was operating 1,500 stores when Neal came on board as president and chief operating officer in late 2006. Eight months later, in June of 2007, she was named chief executive officer of Bath & Body Works, replacing Neil Fiske, who was departing for Eddie Bauer, Inc.

Bath & Body Works was opening larger stores and had tried introducing some third-party brands under Fiske, but there were several issues with inventory and logistics. In late 2007, the company announced it was pulling back on the plan to use third-party suppliers. Aside from this relatively minor dilemma, Neal enjoyed a productive and prosperous tenure in her four years as CEO of Bath & Body Works. *Forbes* reported the combined value of her salary, pension, incentive pay, and stock options gave her a compensation package of $4.2 million in 2010. Her salary, however, hovered just under the $1 million mark, at $985,962.

In May of 2011 Neal announced she was leaving Bath & Body Works to return to California. "Diane has done amazing things at Bath and Body Works," Wexner said in a press release that appeared in *Digital Journal*. "I truly appreciate her expertise as a leader and merchant." There were rumors that Neal was set to either join or take over for former Gap, Inc., colleague Jenny Ming at women's-clothing retailer Charlotte Russe. Ming had been running the privately held chain, which is based in San Diego but has design offices in San Francisco, since 2009.

Sources

Periodicals

San Francisco Chronicle, August 22, 2003.
Star Tribune (Minneapolis, MN), March 22, 2004, p. 1D.
WWD, June 18, 2007, p. 3; June 7, 2011, p. 7.

Online

"Bath and Body Works Announces Executive Changes," *Digital Journal*, http://www.digitaljournal.com/pr/311730 (November 14, 2011).
"Diane L. Neal," *Forbes*, http://people.forbes.com/profile/diane-l-neal/96763 (November 14, 2011).
"Gap Outlet President Departing," The Street, http://www.thestreet.com/_googlen/newsanalysis/retail/10318002.tif.html?cm_ven=GOOGLEN&cm_cat=FREE&cm_ite=NA (November 17, 2011).

—*Carol Brennan*

Gina and Pat Neely

Television hosts

Born Gina Ervin, c. 1965; married first husband (divorced); married Pat Neely, 1994; children: Spenser (daughter from first marriage), Shelbi (daughter). Born Patrick Neely, July 20, 1964, in Detroit, Michigan; married first wife (divorced); married Gina Ervin, 1994; children: Shelbi (daughter). *Education:* Pat Neely: Attended Austin Peay State University, Clarksville, TN.

Addresses: *Contact*—c/o Neely's Bar-B-Que (East), 5700 Mt. Moriah, Memphis, TN 38115. *Web site*—http://www.neelysbbq.com/

Career

Pat Neely: Co-founded Neely's Bar-B-Que in Memphis, TN, 1988. Gina Neely: Worked as a jewelry buyer, bank manager, and events coordinator before working for Neely's Bar-B-Que. Both: Hosts of television series, including: *Down Home with the Neelys,* 2008—; *Road Tasted with the Neelys,* 2008. Television guest appearances, including: *Road Tasted,* 2007; *Paula's Party,* 2007, 2008; *Ace of Cakes,* 2010; *Meet the Browns,* 2010; *The Best Thing I Ever Ate,* 2010; *The Next Food Network Star,* 2011. Author of cookbooks, including: *Down Home with the Neelys,* 2009; *The Neelys Celebration Cookbook: Down Home Meals for Every Occasion,* 2011.

Member: Gina: Memphis Restaurant Association, Women's Empowerment Summit for the Memphis Housing Authority, Cordova High School Parent-Teacher-Student Association. Pat: Board of directors, Memphis Regional Chamber of Commerce; board of directors, Memphis Convention and Visitors Bureau.

Sidelights

Television hosts and restaurant owners Pat and Gina Neely have achieved national notoriety for their cooking instructional program, *Down Home with the Neelys,* and food travel show, *Road Tasted with the Neelys,* both on the Food Network. Along with Pat Neely's brothers, the husband-and-wife team has owned and operated three barbecue restaurants and a catering division in Memphis and Nashville, Tennessee, for more than two decades; a New York City outpost was scheduled to open in 2011. In 2008, *Down Home with the Neelys* became Food Network's highest-rated weekend cooking instructional series debut. The success of the program quickly gained the duo a great deal of popular attention, and they published their *New York Times* best-selling first cookbook, also titled *Down Home with the Neelys,* the following year. A second cookbook, *The Neelys Celebration Cookbook: Down Home Meals for Every Occasion,* was scheduled for publication in late 2011. "I was taught at a very young age to take advantage of what is offered to you," Pat Neely told Mary Constantine of the *Knoxville News.* "We certainly did not anticipate the success that we have had, but it's been incredible."

Patrick—often known simply as Pat—and Gina first met while attending Memphis' Melrose High

School. Although the two dated for a time as teenagers, their lives took separate paths following their 1983 graduations. Gina relocated to California and pursued a career in jewelry buying, while Pat attended Austin Peay State University in Clarksville, Tennessee, to play football. A knee injury soon ended his budding football career, however, and Pat returned to Memphis, where he began working at his uncle Jim Neely's barbecue restaurant. In 1988, he opened his first barbecue restaurant, Neely's Bar-B-Que, along with brothers Mark, Tony, and Gaelin. At first a tiny outpost with one barbecue pit, a few burners, and limited customer seating, that restaurant has become the heart of a small but thriving multi-location barbecue chain. During this time both Pat and Gina married other people, with Gina's marriage leading to the birth of daughter Spenser.

By the time of the erstwhile couple's ten-year high school reunion in 1993, both Pat's and Gina's marriages had ended. "I told her when we were in high school that I was madly in love with her," Pat commented to Constantine in the same *Knoxville News* story. "When she came back for the reunion, I realized I still was." The two rekindled their romance and, after Gina returned to Memphis, married the following year; Gina soon gave birth to the couple's daughter, Shelbi. After stints working as a branch manager at a Memphis bank and an events coordinator for a local public relations firm, Gina joined her husband's family business. Soon, she was helming a catering division that grew to generate 25 percent of the business' revenue. Over the next several years, the Neelys expanded their business venture to include a second Memphis location and an outlet in Nashville.

The Nashville restaurant proved the site of a pivotal moment in the couple's careers. In August of 2006, Bobby and Jamie Deen—then hosts of the Food Network food travel program *Road Tasted* and sons of network cooking star Paula Deen—visited the Neely's Nashville location to feature its barbecue. Both Pat and Gina made the trip from Memphis for the program, and their on-screen energy captured the attention of the program's producers. Over the next several months, producers tapped the Neelys to appear on Paula Deen's programs *Paula's Home Cooking* and *Paula's Party*. Their performances led to the development of their own cooking show, *Down Home with the Neelys*.

Food Network selected the Neelys to anchor a weekend cooking program at a time of change for the channel. Long-time affiliated chefs such as Emeril Lagasse and Mario Batali were being eased out of the network's lineup in favor of television chefs more closely tied to the network professionally and financially. "They don't need me," commented Batali on the transition to Elizabeth Jensen of the *New York Times*. "They have decided they are mass market and they are going after the Wal-Mart crowd…. [T]hey don't need someone who uses polysyllabic words from other languages," he concluded. *Down Home with the Neelys* exemplified the success of this new, mainstream appeal when it became the network's highest-rated instructional series debut in February of 2008. Filmed at the Neely home in Memphis, Tennessee, *Down Home with the Neelys* features comfort-food recipes often reflective of the pair's background with barbecue and Southern cuisine. The program was quickly renewed for additional seasons, and began airing both on weekend mornings and weekday afternoons to strong ratings. That summer, the Neelys returned to the retitled *Road Tasted with the Neelys*, this time as the program's hosts. The show saw them travel the United States seeking out unique family-run restaurants and food stores. The couple have also become regular guest stars on Food Network programs including holiday-themed specials and *The Best Thing I Ever Ate*.

The year after the premiere of their Food Network show, the Neelys authored their first cookbook, *Down Home with the Neelys*. Published by Knopf, the work featured recipes for the Neelys' spin on Southern family fare such as macaroni and cheese, pork ribs, and artichoke and collard greens dip. "We're really proud of the book," Pat told Jennifer Biggs of the Memphis *Commercial Appeal*. "It's home recipes. Gina and I only know one way, and that's the down-home-with-the-Neelys way." The Neelys also expanded their brand by offering cooking gear and a line of barbecue sauces available at national retail giant Wal-Mart. In 2010, the couple announced plans to open a barbecue restaurant, Neely's Barbecue Parlor, in New York City.

Despite their successes, the Neelys have worked to remain focused on their family. "The best part about this time in my life is that I'm able to share this with my wife," Pat commented to Marti Parham of *Jet*. "We're doing this together and I think that's what I get the biggest joy out of." The couple also maintains a strong community presence, with Pat having served on the boards of the Memphis Regional Chamber of Commerce and the Memphis Convention and Visitors Bureau and Gina having been a part of the Memphis Restaurant Association, the Women's Empowerment Summit for the Memphis Housing Authority, and the Cordova High School Parent-Teacher-Student Association. The couple also sponsors young athletics participation in Memphis and, through an endorsement agreement with Kraft Foods, nationwide hunger relief through the charity Feeding America.

Selected writings

Cookbooks

Down Home with the Neelys, Knopf (New York City), 2009.
The Neelys Celebration Cookbook: Down Home Meals for Every Occasion, Knopf, 2011.

Sources

Periodicals

Commercial Appeal (Memphis, Tennessee), May 13, 2009.

Knoxville News, May 17, 2009.
Jet, March 3, 2008, p. 50.
New York Times, December 17, 2007.

Online

"About," GPN, http://www.ginaandpat.com/about.html (May 30, 2011).
"Pat and Gina Neely," Food Network, http://www.foodnetwork.com/patrick-and-gina-neely/bio/index.html (May 30, 2011).

—*Vanessa E. Vaughn*

Téa Obreht

Author

Born Téa Bajraktarevic, September 30, 1985, in Belgrade, Yugoslavia; daughter of Maja. *Education*: University of Southern California, B.A., 2006; Cornell University, M.F.A., 2009.

Addresses: *Agent*—Seth Fishman, The Gernert Company, 136 E. 57th St., New York, NY 10022. *Web site*—http://www.teaobreht.com/.

Career

Contributor of short stories, articles, and essays to *Zoetrope: All-Story, Harper's,* the *New York Times, New Yorker, Atlantic,* and the *Guardian.* Instructor in creative writing at Cornell University; first novel, *The Tiger's Wife,* published by Random House, 2011.

Awards: Orange Prize for Fiction, for *The Tiger's Wife,* 2011.

Sidelights

Twenty-five-year-old Téa Obreht became the youngest writer ever to win Britain's Orange Prize for Fiction in 2011 for her debut novel, *The Tiger's Wife.* Hailed as a "beautifully executed, haunting, and lyrical" story about life, fables, and family in the former Yugoslavia by the *Independent*'s Lucy Popescu, Obreht's novel was the surprise winner of the Orange honor, given annually to a novel by penned by a female writer in the English language in the past year. Reviewing it for the *New York Times,* Michiko Kakutani asserted that "Obreht

© *Beatrice de Gea/The New York Times/Redux Pictures*

creates an indelible sense of place, a world, like the Balkans, haunted by its past and struggling to sort out its future, its imagination shaped by stories handed down generation to generation; its people torn between ancient beliefs and the imperatives of what should be a more rational present."

Critics were astonished not just by Obreht's relative youth, but by the fact she had sketched out so vividly a landscape she left at the age of seven. She was born Téa Bajraktarevic in 1985 in Belgrade, the Yugoslav capital and the largest city of the Socialist Republic of Serbia, one of Yugoslavia's constituent republics. The Balkan nation was a union of "south Slavic" (*jugo*-Slav) states whose federation was cobbled together by the firm rule of its longtime authoritarian president, Josip Broz Tito, in the years following World War II. Tito's unified one-party socialist state disintegrated into economic uncertainty and ethnic tensions in the decade following his 1980 death.

Obreht spent the first seven years of her life in Belgrade, where she was raised by Maja, her mother, and Maja's parents, Stefan and Zahida Obreht. Her grandfather was an aerospace engineer, and his marriage represented the ostensibly eroding boundaries among Yugoslavia's various ethnic and religious groups in the modern age: Stefan was from the province of Slovenia and raised Roman Catholic, while Obreht's grandmother was a Muslim from another republic of Yugoslavia, Bosnia-Herzegovina.

As a child Obreht spent hours with her beloved grandfather, who told her tall but semi-true tales that sparked her imagination. When they visited the Belgrade Zoo's lion and tiger exhibit, he would recount the time in his career when he called on an Ethiopian official at home and discovered several lions lounging about the man's front porch. There was also a story about one of the Belgrade Zoo tigers that had escaped from its confines during World War II after a particularly bad stretch of German aerial bombardment.

In the early 1990s Yugoslavia erupted into war. The various republics—including Serbia, Bosnia-Herzegovina, and Croatia—fought to secede from the union, and then, more drastically, began to exploit longstanding ethnic and religious tensions against one another. Obreht, her mother, and grandparents fled the violence, settling first on the Mediterranean isle of Cyprus, then in Cairo, Egypt, in 1993. It was there that an eight-year-old Obreht wrote her first "story" on a lumbering computer her mother used for her job. It was about a goat, she told the *Guardian*'s Kira Cochrane, and was just a few lines. "The goat has some sort of misadventure. All I really remember is the way the word 'goat' looked on screen. It was very attractive."

Obreht learned English quickly, and attended English-language schools in Cairo. In 1996, the family relocated to the United States, settling first in Atlanta. In time, her mother moved on to Palo Alto, California, and Obreht's grandparents returned to Belgrade. A top student who still loved to visit zoos, Obreht considered becoming a zoologist, but pursued a degree in English and creative writing at the University of Southern California (USC), which she entered at the age of 16. Four years later, she was on the verge of graduating when her grandfather fell ill. The question of whether to fly over to see him turned into "a big family conflict," she told Tim Teeman in a *Times* of London interview a few years later. In the end, it was decided she should stay in Los Angeles and focus on her final exams. "It took me about a year to come to terms with the fact he would never pick up the phone when I called Belgrade," she reflected. "I was asking myself: 'Where had he gone? Is death the end?' It also brought up, 100 percent, my own mortality."

After studying under T. Coraghessan Boyle at USC, Obreht entered the writing program at Cornell University, earning her master of fine arts degree in 2009. To honor her grandfather, she changed her name from Bajraktarevic to Obreht, and began publishing her first short stories under that name. Two were accepted for publication by a pair of prestigious magazines that serve as significant coups for a novice writer: a short story titled "The Tiger's Wife" appeared in the June 8, 2009, issue of the *New Yorker*, and in August the *Atlantic* ran her short story "The Laugh." The following summer, a third piece, titled "Blue Water Djinn," was selected for inclusion in the *New Yorker*'s annual "20 Under 40" special fiction issue. At 24, Obreht was the youngest among that year's crop of emerging writers.

"Blue Water Djinn" was based in part on a month that Obreht and her mother spent at a Red Sea resort shortly before immigrating to the United States. The sea and its mysterious pull play a large role in the plot, which revolves around a young boy whose mother works at just such a seaside hotel somewhere in the Middle East and a French hotel guest who has gone missing. "I wasn't a brave child," Obreht recalled in a *New Yorker* interview, "but the underwater world was so incredible to me that I was somehow able to overcome my terror of it.... [I]ts magic stayed with me for years."

Obreht set about tackling a larger piece of fiction, having begun work on the novel that would become *The Tiger's Wife*. As she told Teeman in the London *Times* interview, she wanted to pay homage to her beloved grandfather in the months following his death in 2006. "Writing the book extended my time with him and helped put my gutwrenching and obsessions onto the page," she said. At the same time, she recognized the challenges of crafting an entire novel. "When you write a short story you can see the whole thing right away," she explained to Jeffrey Brown, who interviewed her for the Public Broadcasting Series *PBS NewsHour*. "You write it possibly in a space of two nights and you see it from beginning to end and then you can restructure.... And then, a novel you realize you're not going to see the end until like a year has passed."

Obreht sent out 60 pages of her manuscript to literary agents, and The Gernert Company's Seth Fishman signed her on as a client. Fishman, in turn, sent out her manuscript to publishing houses, and piqued the interest of an editorial assistant at Random House named Noah Eaker. *The Tiger's Wife* became the first book Fishman sold, and Eaker moved up to become an editor at Random House and worked with Obreht on finessing it into its final form. There was one delay, which came after Fishman arranged a deal to send Obreht to the Balkans in the summer of 2009 on behalf of *Harper's* magazine to write a story about modern-day vampire hunters. "I rediscovered Belgrade," she told *New York Times* writer Charles McGrath about her trip. "I noticed changes in the city itself, in people's attitudes, and I got myself emotionally reconnected to the place and the culture in a way I needed to reshape the present-day story." She asked Random House for an extension, and rewrote significant chunks of the story.

The *Harper's* piece appeared in the November 2010 issue under the title "Twilight of the Vampires: Hunting the Real-Life Undead." A month later, a short piece by Obreht appeared in the *New York Times* in the "Holiday Fiction" section. As 2010 wound to a close, Obreht's name turned up in the *Village Voice* annual roundup of cultural and political milestones of the year as "Best New York Writer Young Enough to Make You Slit Your Wrists." The *Village Voice* blurb noted that Obreht's debut novel was set to be published in March of 2011, when she was still months away from her 26th birthday.

Random House published *The Tiger's Wife* on March 8, 2011. The anticipatory buzz for it was strong enough to merit a highly coveted cover spot on the March 13, 2011, issue of the *New York Times Book Review*. Critic Liesl Schillinger commended the first-time author for spinning a tale of the disastrous recent history of the former Yugoslavia in her debut—though the dramatic events of the 1990s are not actually recited. "Yet in its pages she brings their historic and human context to luminous life," Schillinger wrote. "With fables and allegories, as well as events borrowed from the headlines, she illustrates the complexities of Balkan history, unearthing patterns of suspicion, superstition, and everyday violence that pervade the region even in times of peace."

The Tiger's Wife recounts the journey of Natalia Stefanovic, a physician, who ventures into an unnamed country with another female doctor, her best friend, toting a stock of vaccinations they are to deliver at an orphanage. They cross a border—one that did not exist during Natalia's childhood—and Natalia learns that her grandfather, who had been coming to meet her, has died en route under suspicious circumstances. Natalia sets out to find his missing body and determine how he died. Interwoven through this story are tales her grandfather told her, including one about a tiger that escaped from a local zoo during World War II and turned up in her grandfather's village. The residents are understandably fearful, and their unease turns to the newly widowed wife of the village butcher, a deaf-mute Muslim woman. The superstitious townsfolk believe that the woman has befriended the animal

and is secretly colluding with it. Another tale involves a mysterious figure, the Deathless Man, whom Natalia's grandfather met at several crucial junctures in his life. This is Gavo, who claims to be immortal and manages to trick the grandfather into handing over his beloved copy of Rudyard Kipling's *The Jungle Book*, which he has carried on his person for most of his life. Over the course of *The Tiger's Wife* Natalia manages to unlock these mysteries while reflecting back on her own coming of age in a war-torn nation. The novel is dedicated to Obreht's late grandfather.

Obreht's debut won effusive praise from critics, earning comparisons to the fiction of Gabriel García Márquez and Mikhail Bulgakov, both literary giants in the genre of magical realism. "Some of the richest folklore in Europe, including the vampire myth, comes from the Balkans," remarked Popescu in the *Independent* review. "Obreht capitalises on this and, like a magician, conjures up a host of larger-than-life characters that become the stuff of modern legend." *The Tiger's Wife* also received a glowing review from Kakutani, the *New York Times'* longtime book critic, who described it as "a hugely ambitious, audaciously written work" for such a young author. "Obreht … writes with remarkable authority and eloquence, and she demonstrates an uncommon ability to move seamlessly between the gritty realm of the real and the more primary-colored world of the fable," declared Kakutani.

The Tiger's Wife won Obreht the Orange Prize for Fiction in June of 2011, one of the world's leading literary honors. She beat out a strong shortlist of fellow writers for the prize, including Nicole Krauss and Emma Donoghue. The win immediately propelled *The Tiger's Wife* to the *New York Times* hardcover best-seller list. "I still get floored by the fact that there is an actual book," she told Brown in the *PBS NewsHour* visit. "You know, it has a face. It's like meeting a stranger…. I've wanted to write my whole life and now people are reading what I've written. It's wonderful."

Selected writings

The Tiger's Wife, Random House (New York City), 2011.

Sources

Periodicals

Atlantic, July 2009.
Guardian (London, England), June 10, 2011; June 11, 2011.
Harper's, November 2010.
Independent (London, England), March 25, 2011.

New Yorker, June 14, 2010.

New York Times, March 10, 2011; March 11, 2011; March 14, 2011.

Publishers Weekly, January 17, 2011, p. 27.

Times (London, England), April 2, 2011, p. 9.

Online

"Conversation: Tea Obreht," *PBS NewsHour*, http://www.pbs.org/newshour/art/blog/2011/04/conversation-tea-obreht.html (July 12, 2011).

Joshua Onysko

Joshua Onysko

Founder of Pangea Organics

B orn c. 1978; son of Carol Onysko.

Addresses: *Office*—Pangea Organics, 6880 Winchester Circle, South Bay, Boulder, CO 80301.

Career

F ounded Pangea Organics, 2002; served as CEO of Pangea Organics, 2002—.

Awards: Ernst & Young Entrepreneur of the Year, 2007; Entrepreneur of Distinction (Espirit) Award, 2008; Ernst & Young Entrepreneur of the Year, 2008.

Sidelights

E ntrepreneur and corporate executive Joshua Onysko is best known as the founder and CEO of Pangea Organics, the top-selling organic skin care line in the United States. After spending his late teens and early 20s traveling the world, in 2001 Onysko turned to making organic soaps as a way to support his wanderlust. This small-scale soap making soon became the genesis of Pangea Organics, a line of fully organic soaps, skin cleansers, scrubs, creams, masks, toners, and other products, all sold in eco-friendly plantable or fully recyclable packaging. With fast-growing sales in excess of $10 million in 2010, Pangea markets its products through major retailers including Macy's, Sephora, and Whole Food Markets, along with small, independent environmentally friendly shops. Five percent of the line's profits go to the non-profit Pangea Institute, an organization established by Onysko to encourage sustainable business practices. "The vision is to create a role model for the corporate world," Onysko told Eric Peterson of *ColoradoBiz* in 2007. "Businesses can be responsible and still be profitable."

Born around 1978, Onysko grew up in Warwick, Rhode Island. At the age of nine, he left formal schooling to pursue a career in acting. His career failed to take flight, however, and Onysko returned to school a few years later, only to drop out at the age of 16 to travel. He eventually earned his GED. After spending time in Vermont, Wyoming, and coastal Rhode Island, Onysko traveled south to Central America. His passion for environmental protection was by then already apparent. "I moved ... to collect green sea turtle eggs on the beach and raise them in incubators; otherwise poachers would steal them and sell them on the black market," he explained in an interview on the Web site Planet Green.

In 1999, Onysko decided that he wanted to spend some time in India. Before setting out on his voyage, he made a fateful visit to his parents in Rhode Island, where he noticed a book on soap making. He and his mother made the first batch of soap—a recipe now available as Pangea Organics' Oatmeal and Italian Bergamot bar. "At the time, we didn't think it was going to amount to anything," commented mother Carol Onysko to Christina Dugas of *USA Today*. "But it has been an unbelievable journey. I look back, and I still can't believe it." Some bars from this initial soap-making session traveled with Onysko to India, Nepal, and Tibet. Several months later, Onysko returned to the United States. In need of money, he made a second batch of soap in a cleaned-out beer keg in a Wyoming barn using herbs he had picked from the nearby mountains. He soon sold these 1,000 bars in the parking lot of the Oregon Country Fair, earning $5,000 in three days. "I was like, This is great because I can keep making soap and traveling," Onysko later recalled to Adam Spangler of *Vanity Fair*. Using the proceeds from his soap sales, the budding entrepreneur went north to Alaska before traveling to Hong Kong. From there, he went to Tokyo, where he briefly sold counterfeit wrist watches and handbags on the street for the Japanese mafia to earn enough money to move on to Thailand and Cambodia.

By this time, Onysko had spent seven years criss-crossing the globe. He was tiring of the stresses of travel and becoming frustrated by what he had observed over the preceding years. As his biography on Pangea Organics' Web site put it, "Onysko had an epiphany: He realized that corporations were inheriting the earth and that by leading by example there was potential to influence others to reconsider their ways." To achieve this goal, he devised a plan to create a non-profit organization that would encourage the use of sustainable business practices. While visiting the Cambodian historical site Angkor Wat in 2002, Onysko shared his idea with a friend. This friend commented that Onysko should found a soap company to fund his dream, and name it Pangea after the ancient supercontinent. In that moment, Pangea Organics was born.

Days later, Onysko again returned to the United States, settling in Boulder, Colorado. There, he worked as a baker at a local Whole Foods Market by day and developed a cottage industry making soap by night. Pangea Organics grew quickly by selling its products at farmers' markets and festivals along the West Coast. Just six months later, Onysko was forced to give up making soap in his garage in favor of manufacturing soap and a new line of shower gels in a small Boulder factory. Although no longer handmade, the products remained entirely natural and organic, with Onysko actively working to use entirely edible ingredients, a rarity in the world of skincare. "I wanted to prove through ancient alchemy we could use nothing but edible ingredients to produce skin care that surpassed the efficacy of harsh chemically based products," he

told Spangler in the *Vanity Fair* interview. By 2003, the company had grown to have more than $100,000 in sales.

Two years later, Onysko expanded his vision with the help of San Francisco-based company IDEO. Together, they crafted sustainable packaging that, if planted, grows into a plant such as basil or amaranth. By 2007, this approach to natural skincare had helped Pangea Organics grow into a thriving business with 26 employees and sales of $2.7 million that encompassed a greatly expanded skincare product line. The following year, the company's sales figures in five countries worldwide doubled. By 2009, Pangea had grown its workforce to 32 and expanded into a 10,000-square foot production facility powered by sustainable wind energy. Employees, who receive a living wage and full company-paid health benefits, are also paid to work the 3,000-square foot organic garden attached to the company's facility that provides food for staff lunches.

Onysko considers these attributes a necessity to Pangea's commitment to responsible business practices. "Pangea is just a tiny company," he told Olivia Khalili of the Web site Cause Capitalism, "and if $10-million companies can't provide basic necessities to ensure that their employees are being treated fairly and can afford what they need to also thrive, then really what are they doing? Why produce a product that is not supporting the future of the world?"

Sources

Periodicals

Beauty Biz, August 1, 2006, p. 4.
ColoradoBiz, September 2007, p. 67.
USA Today, March 16, 2009, p. 5B.

Online

"Bio: Joshua Onysko," Pangea Organics, http://www.pangeaorganics.com/biography/biography/joshua_onysko_founder_and_ceo (June 2, 2011).

"Meet Josh Onysko of Pangea Organics," Planet Green, http://planetgreen.discovery.com/work-connect/change-makers-joshua-onysko.html (June 2, 2011).

"The Pangea Organics Adventure," *Vanity Fair*, http://www.vanityfair.com/online/beauty/2009/06/the-pangea-organics-adventure.html (June 2, 2011).

"Why Pangea Organics Founder Joshua Onysko Thinks 'Sustainability' is for Slackers," Cause Capitalism, http://causecapitalism.com/pangea-organics/ (June 2, 2011).

—*Vanessa E. Vaughn*

Carter Oosterhouse

Carpenter and television personality

Born September 19, 1976, in Traverse City, MI; son of Roland Oosterhouse and Mary Lopez. *Education:* Central Michigan University, B.A., 2000.

Addresses: *Office*—c/o HGTV, 500 W. Summit Hill Dr., Knoxville, TN 37902. *Web site*—http://www.carteroosterhouse.com.

Career

Worked as a carpenter, c. 1990s; production assistant, *Project Greenlight*, after 2000; model for print and television campaigns, after 2000; carpenter, *Trading Spaces*, 2003; host, *Carter Can*, 2007—; co-host, *Red Hot & Green*, 2008—.

Sidelights

Carter Oosterhouse is a television host who has appeared on several shows on the HGTV network. Known for his good looks and easygoing personality, he is a real-life carpenter who never dreamed that his summer jobs would lead him to a career as a celebrity.

Oosterhouse was born and raised in Traverse City, Michigan, the youngest of four children of Roland Oosterhouse and Mary Lopez. His mother, who is of Mexican descent, contributed to his dark-haired good looks. Home improvement seemed to run in his family; his two brothers eventually owned their own carpentry businesses, and his sister became an interior designer. During the summers, Oosterhouse

worked as a carpenter to make money. Traverse City is a tourist town, where summer residents enjoy building or remodeling their vacation homes, and work was plentiful. He started working when he was 13, picking up trash on his brothers' job sites; this fit in with the family work ethic instilled by his father, Roland. Oosterhouse told Caren Baginski on the HGTV Web site that when he and his siblings were younger, his dad would say, "You shouldn't watch TV—go outside and do something."

Oosterhouse was athletic and energetic, so in addition to his carpentry work, he played a variety of sports and eventually went to Central Michigan University on a rugby scholarship. After earning his degree in nutrition and communication, Oosterhouse moved to Los Angeles, hoping to find a career in nutrition, since he thought there would be a lot of people there who were interested in staying fit. He had a job in nutrition lined up when he moved out there, but it fell through and he found himself doing carpentry again.

He got a job as a production assistant with Matt Damon and Ben Affleck's *Project Greenlight*. Initially, he moved boxes and did other heavy work, but he soon moved into reading scripts and appearing in commercials. He also worked behind the scenes on *Project Greenlight* while it aired on HBO.

In 2003, Oosterhouse got his big break when he was hired as a carpenter on TLC's *Trading Spaces*. The show was a hit at the time, and it generated a lot of interest in Oosterhouse, who was soon named one of the "sexiest men alive" by *People* magazine. Oosterhouse was shocked by the attention, but as he commented to Ellen Sung in the Raleigh *News and Observer*, "That was definitely a perk."

When Oosterhouse was approached with the proposal for the show *Carter Can*, he was initially skeptical because the show sounded like every other home improvement show out there: go into people's homes, find out what they wanted to do, and help them do it. He thought about his dad's work ethic, which was to learn whatever he needed to in order to get things done, and translated it to the show: whatever the homeowner wanted, Oosterhouse would work to figure it out and get it done. In addition, on the show, Oosterhouse tried to implement solutions that save energy and reduce waste.

Oosterhouse told Baginski, "We get those people to shake a leg and try to get them to broaden their horizons." He is also sensitive to the feelings of homeowners, knowing that it can be nerve-wracking to have a stranger come in and start knocking down walls and moving things around. Oosterhouse told Baginski that this awareness of the homeowners' feelings was "the best part about it." He also wanted the homeowners to like the changes he made, unlike other members of the program who may focus more on creating a dramatic show than on the fact that after the television crew leaves, the homeowners have to live with what the crew has done.

Oosterhouse tries to build in a way that is safe for the environment, using "green" principles. He remarked to Baginski that he learned these principles from his family when he was young—they were interested in nutrition and living a clean lifestyle, and this translated, for him, into building clean. He told Baginski, "I feel a lot better when I can be green about my building than when I'm not."

Oosterhouse owns two homes, one in Los Angeles and the other in Michigan. The California house is minimalist and its decor is suited to the beach. The Michigan house is more than 100 years old and has a completely different feel, more traditional and comfortable. Although Oosterhouse does not know how to cook, the kitchen is the center of that house, with a large central island, custom concrete countertops, huge refrigerator and freezer, and a six-burner stove. He told Baginski, "The thing is I'm not even married yet or have kids, but I set it up for down the road. It's a great place to one day retire to."

Oosterhouse told Baginski that he loves doing carpentry because of the satisfaction in seeing a project through from beginning to end, and the enjoyment of seeing "a dramatic change in something that's physical, and right in front of your face that you crafted and put together."

Oosterhouse has modeled in advertisements for a variety of products, most notably a television commercial for the men's fragrance Voyage by Nautica; he has also appeared in print ads for Nivea, Lincoln, Hewlett Packard, and Miller Light. He doesn't like to dwell on his looks; he told Jeanine Falcon in *Canadian Living* that when he became a model and actor, "One of my biggest fears … was of becoming a Hollywood jackass." He prefers to focus on concrete, positive things, and credits his family's strong values for keeping him grounded.

Oosterhouse donates his time to a variety of children's charities, including Books for Kids, COACH (Community Outreach Assistance for Children's Health), and the Los Angeles Fulfillment Fund. He has created his own foundation, Carter's Kids, which develops and builds community parks and playgrounds to encourage kids to stay active and healthy.

Sources

Periodicals

Daily News (Los Angeles, CA), November 18, 2007, p. A2.
Houston Chronicle, September 19, 2010, p. 4.
News and Observer (Raleigh, NC), April 24, 2006.
St. Louis Post-Dispatch, January 9, 2010, p. L4.

Online

"6 Things to Know About Carter Oosterhouse," *Canadian Living*, http://www.canadianliving.com/style/beauty/6_things_to_know_about_carter_oosterhouse.php (February 11, 2011).
"Carter Oosterhouse," HGTV, http://www.hgtv.com/carter-oosterhouse/bio/index.html (February 11, 2011).
"Q & A with Carter Oosterhouse," HGTV, http://hgtv.com/home-improvement/qa-with-carter-oosterhouse/index.html (February 11, 2011).

—Kelly Winters

Paul Otellini

Chief Executive Officer of Intel

Born Paul S. Otellini, October 12, 1950, in San Francisco, CA; son of David (a butcher); married; children: two. *Education:* University of San Francisco, B.S., 1972; University of California, Berkeley, M.B.A., 1974 .

Addresses: *Office*—Intel, 2200 Mission College Blvd., Santa Clara, CA, 95054-1549.

Career

Began career at Intel, held various finance and marketing positions, 1974-80; account manager, 1980-87; general manager of Folsom operations, 1988; operating group vice president and served as technical assistant to company president, 1989; general manager of microprocessor division, 1990; corporate executive officer, 1991-93; senior vice president, 1993-96; executive vice president of sales and marketing, 1998-2002; executive vice president of architecture business group, 2002-05; chief executive officer, 2005—.

Member: Board of directors, Intel, 2002—; board of directors, Google.

Sidelights

Corporate executive Paul Otellini became the fifth chief executive officer of technology giant Intel on May 18, 2005. From 2002 until becoming CEO, he was Intel's president and chief operating officer. A career employee of the firm, Otellini had previously served as the head of the company's PC server and microprocessor division and the global sales and marketing division. Otellini was also named a member of Intel's Board of Directors in 2002. "At this point, it's hard for me to tell in what ways I've shaped Intel and in what ways Intel has shaped me," Otellini was quoted as observing by Gary Rivlin of the *New York Times*, shortly after his promotion to Intel's top job.

Born on October 12, 1950, in San Francisco, California, Otellini grew up in a working-class household; his father was a butcher, and his mother returned to work after Otellini and his brother began school. His family had deep roots in the San Francisco area, with one grandfather having a pivotal role in the building of the Golden Gate Bridge. As a boy, Otellini delivered newspapers, but his true interest lay in math and science. "I always liked solving problems and tinkering with things, including cars and other things that didn't work too well," he recalled in an oral history interview with Daniel S. Morrow for the Computerworld Honors Program International Archives. Later, Otellini worked in a men's clothing store and at a slaughterhouse. His Italian-American family held staunch Catholic views, and Otellini's father, a butcher, strongly encouraged his sons to join the priesthood. Although the future executive's brother did become a priest,

Otellini decided to pursue a secular career. He studied economics at the University of San Francisco, earning his bachelor's degree from the institution in 1972. Otellini then proceeded to graduate studies at the University of California in Berkeley, completing a master's in business administration two years later.

Shortly after finishing his education, Otellini decided to find a job in the emerging computer technology industry centered in Silicon Valley. After turning down offers from Fairchild Semiconductor and Advanced Micro Devices (AMD), he decided to sign on with the then-relatively new Intel. His first positions dealt with the company's finances, and he became interested in the technology behind the differing products. "There was something intriguing to me about a part that sold for $250 versus a lot of ones that we sold for $5.... I spent a lot of energy trying to figure out what they did and how they worked," he commented to Morrow of the Computerworld Honors Program International Archives. In 1980, he successfully lobbied for a transfer to the business division, and spent the next several years focusing his energies on sales to IBM. Between 1985 and 1989, he acted as General Manager of the Intel chip business at Folsom, California. This position brought a unique and tragic challenge after two Folsom employees committed suicide in unrelated incidents just months apart. To help his staff cope with the matter, Otellini brought in grief counselors and set up psychological counseling well before such measures were common corporate practice.

Otellini's work in Folsom brought him to the attention of then-Intel president Andrew Grove. In 1988, Otellini was named vice president of the company's operating group, and the following year advanced to become the president's technical assistant. Soon after, Otellini shifted roles again, this time to lead the microprocessor division. In 1991, he became a corporate executive officer; two years later, he was named a senior vice president. That same year, his group released the Pentium chip, and the processor's high speeds coupled with lower-than-anticipated prices helped it quickly become an industry leader. Otellini then became Intel's head of sales and marketing, although he did not actually want the job because it required a great deal of overseas travel. Otellini again advanced in 1998 to assume control of Intel's Architecture Group, which accounted for roughly 80 percent of Intel's overall business.

In 2002, Otellini was named as Intel's president and chief operating officer, a clear sign of the company's intention to groom him for the top job when then-

CEO Barrett retired in 2005. "We're giving him added responsibilities in anticipation of him moving forward," Barrett confirmed to Chris Gaither of the *New York Times.* "There are no guarantees in this world, but this is a pretty clear message." At the same time, Otellini joined Intel's Board of Directors. Despite this support from top-level management, Otellini's appointment had not been a sure thing; unlike all of the CEOs in the company's history to date, he had no formal training in engineering. Otellini's personal management style was also more soft-spoken and cooperative than that of his predecessors, although many within the company considered this a benefit for an Otellini-run Intel.

Over the next two years, Intel struggled to position itself in the rapidly maturing world of personal technology. The company strove to make technological products for wireless devices, but failed to achieve profitability; it also began developing chips for television sets, but ended work in 2004. Otellini was formally named to the role of CEO in late 2004 and, after assuming the office in May of 2005, he quickly began efforts to refocus Intel's product line on versatile platforms and chips designed to support portable multimedia applications. To this end, the company partnered with Apple, then worked to establish itself as a leader in the emerging mp3 player market. Intel launched its Core microprocessor, which boosted the company's competitiveness against its primary rival, AMD.

Nevertheless, global economic conditions toward the end of the decade hampered Intel's growth, and the company failed to promptly enter the burgeoning tablet market. In 2011, Otellini oversaw plans to shift Intel's products toward mobile devices in a major way, with the company planning to produce several new tablets with a lower-energy Intel chip, along with mobile phones and other portable devices. "We're still going to build products that scale up that dynamic range, for other market needs, obviously. But the center point is going to be about ultramobility," Otellini explained, as reported by Mark Hachman of *PC Magazine Online.* That same year, analysts noted that Otellini—approaching his sixtieth birthday, just five years from Intel's mandatory retirement age of 65—may have begun grooming his own successor by sending Intel executive vice-president Sean Maloney to Asia to head a new Intel strategy for the growing Chinese market.

Sources

Books

International Directory of Business Biographies, St. James Press, 2005.

Periodicals

Business Daily Update, May 25, 2011.

Digit, May 18, 2011.

New York Times, December 16, 1993; January 17, 2002; November 12, 2004, p. C5; December 30, 2005, p. C1; October 15, 2008, p. B11.

PC Magazine Online, May 17, 2011.

Online

"Paul Otellini Oral History," Computerworld Honors Program International Archives, http://www.cwhonors.org/archives/histories/Otellini.pdf (August 24, 2011).

—*Vanessa E. Vaughn*

Archie Panjabi

Actress

Born Archana Panjabi, May 31, 1972, in London, England; daughter of Govind (a restaurant owner) and Padma (a teacher); married Rajesh Nihalani (a tailor). *Education:* Brunel University, London, England, bachelor's degree.

Addresses: *Publicist*—Angelique O'Neil, 200 Riverside Blvd., Ste. 401, New York, NY 10069.

Career

Actress on television, including: *Under the Moon,* 1995; *Thin Blue Line,* 1996; *In the Beginning,* 2000; *The Bill,* 2001; *A Mind to Kill,* 2001; *Murder in Mind,* 2001; *Single Voices,* 2001; *Ivor the Invisible,* 2001; *The Secret,* 2002; *Holby City,* 2002; *My Family,* 2002; *White Teeth,* 2002; *Tough Love,* 2002; *Final Demand,* 2003; *This Little Life,* 2003; *Canterbury Tales,* 2003; *Postman Pat,* 2003; *Grease Monkeys,* 2003-04; *Sea of Souls,* 2004; *A Very Social Secretary,* 2005; *Life on Mars,* 2006-07; *Silent Witness,* 2007; *Love Triangle,* 2007; *Personal Affairs,* 2009; *The Good Wife,* 2009—. Film appearances include: *East is East,* 1999; *Bend It Like Beckham,* 2002; *Code 46,* 2003; *Cross My Heart,* 2003; *Yasmin,* 2004; *Chromophobia,* 2005; *The Constant Gardener,* 2005; *A Good Year,* 2006; *Flying Lessons,* 2007; *I Could Never Be Your Woman,* 2007; *A Mighty Heart,* 2007; *Traitor,* 2007; *Espion(s),* 2009; *The Infidel,* 2010.

Awards: Prix Ciné Femme, Mons International Festival of Love Films, for *Yasmin,* 2005; Shooting Star Award, Berlin International Film Festival, 2005; best actress award, Reims International Television Days, for *Yasmin,* 2006; Chopard Trophy, Cannes Film Festival, 2007; Primetime Emmy Award for outstanding supporting actress in a drama, Academy of Television Arts and Sciences, for *The Good Wife,* 2010.

Sidelights

Award-winning British actress Archie Panjabi is best known to U.S. audiences for her portrayal of Kalinda Sharma on the CBS television drama *The Good Wife.* Panjabi's embodiment of the character of Kalinda—a bisexual private investigator with a cynical streak and a penchant for knee-high leather boots—garnered her not only popular notice but also an Emmy Award for Outstanding Supporting Actress in a Drama in 2010 and a second nomination in 2011. The British actress first graced the screen in 1999 when she landed a supporting slot in the British comedy *East is East.* Roles in films including *Bend It Like Beckham, The Constant Gardener, A Mighty Heart,* and film festival favorite *Yasmin* followed, as did television appearances on shows such as *Grease Monkeys* and *Life on Mars.* In 2009, Panjabi inaugurated the career-shaping role of Kalinda, attracting critical acclaim and increased notoriety in the United States.

Born Archana Panjabi on May 31, 1972, in the London suburb of Edgware, Middlesex, England, Panjabi is the daughter of Hindu parents who immigrated to the United Kingdom from India before she was born; even earlier, her family had emigrated from Pakistan to India following the partition of

British India into Muslim Pakistan and Hindu India in 1947. Her father, Govind, ran a restaurant, and her mother, Padma, became a schoolteacher. The young Panjabi grew up mostly in the northwest London neighborhood of Harrow, but spent two years in Mumbai (Bombay), India as a child. Despite this multi-continental background, Panjabi's parents encouraged her to grow up as a member of British culture. "My mother always encouraged me to go to Sunday school and learn about the religion of the country we lived in, to fit in, to have friends from all backgrounds," Panjabi explained in an interview with Tim Teeman of the London *Times*. Practically from birth, Panjabi wanted to pursue acting, becoming fascinated both by Bollywood films and by British children's television. Although friends of the elder Panjabis dismissed acting as a low-class career, Panjabi's mother encouraged her daughter's dreams of performing. "My mother was never not supportive," the actress commented in the same interview with Teeman, "but I think she thought—and she was right—that acting in the only profession where the parts get fewer as you get older, so it was important to have something to fall back on." To that end, the aspiring performer took drama classes and found an agent as a teenager, but agreed to also fulfill her parents' hopes for her to achieve a traditional education. She attended London's Brunel University, receiving an undergraduate degree in management studies; plans to continue her education by pursuing a doctorate in that subject were derailed by her budding acting career.

Panjabi's acting career thus got off to a relative late start; she did not land her first role until she was cast at the age of 26 as the teenaged Meenah Khan in the film *East is East.* A comedy about a multicultural family in the early 1970s, the film made a stir in England upon its release in 1999 and helped propel Panjabi's career into action. Panjabi also married Rajesh Nihalani, to whom her mother had introduced her in the hopes of arranging a marriage, when she was 26 years old. Early in her career, she helped her husband run his high-end bespoke tailoring business while appearing in small but growing roles in British television programs such as *A Mind to Kill* and *The Bill.* She also landed parts in televised movies, including *In the Beginning* and the animated *Ivor the Invisible.* Panjabi returned to the silver screen in 2002 as Pinky Bhamra, the elder sister of main character Jess Bhamra, in the teen soccer film *Bend It Like Beckham.* "I played the slutty sister," she explained of her part to Andrew Davies in the *Birmingham Post & Mail.* "It was nice to play a tart with a heart. It was a different character. I get sent so many scripts, but this was really fun to play." The following year, Panjabi presented another aspect of the British Asian experience, playing the handy daughter in a family of South Asian car dealers and mechanics in the British television program *Grease Monkeys.*

Two years later, Paniabi took on a different type of role entirely when she appeared in the paranormal television drama *Sea of Souls.* The six-episode arc cast the actress in the role of Megan Sharma, a postgraduate parapsychology student working as an assistant to a paranormal investigator. Panjabi considered her casting in that role to be a particular triumph because the part of Megan had not been specifically written for a South Asian actress. "It is so refreshing to be able to be seen for a part where there is no reference to ethnicity," she told Jane Hall in the Newcastle, England *Journal.* "I believe one of the most important ways of combating racism—and trying to get people to accept everyone for who they are—is just to cast from a group of people and see which one is right," she concluded. That same year, Panjabi also starred in the award-winning *Yasmin.* The dramatic film followed the life of a young Muslim woman of Pakistani descent in Britain around the time of the devastating September 11, 2001 attacks in the United States. Panjabi's character grapples with the detention of the husband she has married only so that he can acquire residency in the United Kingdom, the anti-Muslim feeling rising in her community, and the crisis of identity created by the traumatic events of the time. Panjabi garnered accolades for her starring turn, picking up Best Actress nods at the Mons International Festival of Love Films in 2005 and the Reims International Television Days fest in 2006; *Yasmin* was released on television in Britain after failing to find cinema distribution.

Panjabi was not long absent from both the large and small screens. In 2005, she had a supporting role in the thriller *The Constant Gardener,* about the murder of a woman in Kenya and her husband's ensuing quest to discover the truth about her death. The film went to garner numerous award nominations and win an Academy Award. The following year, she appeared as Gemma in the lighthearted Russell Crowe vehicle *A Good Year.* Although the film received tepid reviews, Panjabi's performance was noted as a high point; "very little subtlety creeps into the acting," sighed Kirk Honeycutt of the *Hollywood Reporter* in a review. "One exception is Archie Panjabi, who as Max's assistant lets slight reproaches seep into exchanges with her boss without him seeming to notice." Also in 2006, Panjabi played a small role as the girlfriend of a police officer who is involved in a car crash and awakens more than 30 years in the past in the British television series *Life on Mars;* she reprised her role in an episode in the program's second season in 2007.

That same year, Panjabi appeared alongside Angelina Jolie in *A Mighty Heart,* a film based on the memoirs of Mariane Pearl, wife of murdered journalist Daniel Pearl. In *A Mighty Heart,* Panjabi portrayed Indian-American journalist Asra Nomani, a friend of the murdered reporter who helps his wife—played by Jolie—on her quest to discover what happened to him. Panjabi's performance was heralded by critics, and she won the prestigious Chopard Trophy for Female Revelation of the Year at the Cannes Film Festival. Panjabi developed a friendship with Jolie, noting the famous actress' professionalism and lack of conceit. Next up was the 2008 film *Traitor,* which saw Panjabi appear alongside Don Cheadle and Guy Pearce in another Middle Eastern-infused thriller. She then returned to Great Britain for a turn in the 2009 BBC television comedy *Personal Affairs.*

Later in 2009, Panjabi made her U.S. television debut in the role of Kalinda Sharma on the CBS legal drama *The Good Wife.* Starring Julianna Margulies as Alicia Florrick, the program followed the wife of a disgraced state attorney as she attempted to rebuild her law career and manage her family. Panjabi's character was the in-house detective for the law firm where Margulies' character found a job. Known for her cynical opinions of human behavior, occasional disregard for legal and ethical considerations, distinctly fierce persona, and leather boots and jackets, Kalinda was "the perfect foil to the buttoned-up Alicia," according to the South African newspaper the *Sunday Tribune.* Over the course of the first season, Panjabi's character became highly popular with the show's fans, who were attracted by her tough street smarts and practical abilities. "I think what people like about her is that she is able to say things that everyone else would like to say but doesn't," Panjabi suggested to Lorena Blas of *USA Today.* Critics agreed, and Panjabi was nominated for a Primetime Emmy Award for her work on the first season of *The Good Wife.* Up against actresses Christina Hendricks and Elisabeth Moss from critical favorite *Mad Men,* Panjabi hoped but did not expect to win at the 2010 Emmy ceremony; however, much to her surprise and delight, her name was called as the winner for Best Supporting Actress in a Drama. "When I started in the business in England, just getting a job was a dream. And to receive an Emmy now is just beyond my wildest dreams," she was quoted as stating after her win by Heidi Blake of the *Telegraph.* Panjabi was the only British performer to win a trophy at the 2010 Emmys, and only the fifth non-white woman to win her category in the Emmys' more than 50-year history. She was again nominated for the award for her work on *The Good Wife*'s 2010-2011 season.

In August of 2011, the actress signed on as an ambassador for the non-profit education organization Pratham USA, dedicated to improving educational opportunities for children in India. "The best way to shine the light on education in India is to continue to bring this incredibly important conversation to the global stage. These children are our future and in turn, we are theirs," Panjabi was quoted as stating by Seema Hakhu Kachru in a *Press Trust of India* article. As Panjabi's second chance at an Emmy approached soon after, the actress was set to return as Kalinda in the third season of *The Good Wife,* scheduled to premiere on CBS that fall. Despite her growing notoriety, she had no plans to seek a return to the silver screen or a starring vehicle of her own. "I'm happy doing *The Good Wife* right now and am honestly not even thinking about what I'm going to do next," Panjabi told Dipti Nagpaul D'souza of the *Indian Express* in the fall of 2010. "I've learned a lot more over the last one year than I did in my entire career spanning 15 years. When you shoot 22 episodes back to back and get the script merely two days before the shoot, you learn to become more spontaneous and think on your feet. With television, I feel I've grown as an actor."

Sources

Periodicals

Birmingham Post (Birmingham, England), April 9, 2003, p. 12.
Daily Mail (London, England), August 31, 2010, p. 6.
Guardian (London, England), September 4, 2010, p. 27.
Hollywood Reporter, September 11, 2006, p. 7.
Indian Express (New Delhi, India), September 5, 2010.
Journal (Newcastle, England), February 2, 2004, p. 20.
PTI—The Press Trust of India, August 26, 2011.
Sunday Mail (Glasgow, Scotland), June 14, 2009, p. 20.
Sunday Tribune (South Africa), July 25, 2010, p. 4.
Telegraph (London, England), August 31, 2010.
Times (London, England), September 4, 2010, p. 38.
USA Today, April 6, 2010, p. 08D.

Online

"Biography," Archie Panjabi Official Web site, http://www.archiepanjabi.com/biography.html (August 29, 2011).

—*Vanessa E. Vaughn*

Jim Parsons

Actor

Born James Joseph Parsons, March 24, 1973, in Houston, TX; son of a company president and a teacher. *Education:* University of Houston, B.F.A., 1996; University of San Diego, M.F.A., 1999.

Addresses: *Agent*—Innovative Artists, 1505 10th St., Santa Monica, CA 90401.

Career

Actor on stage, including: *Endgame, Marat/Sade, Othello, Suicide in B-flat, Woyzeck, Guys and Dolls, Eddie Goes to Poetry City, Jack, The Future is in Eggs, The Cherry Orchard, Camino Real, The Threepenny Opera, In the Jungle of Cities, Marie and Bruce, Last Rites, King Ubu is King, Tamalalia 3: The Cocktail Party,* and *Tamalalia 4: The Camp-Out,* all with the Infernal Bridegroom/Catastrophic Theater, 1995-2000; *Pitchfork Disney, Below the Belt,* and *Chili Queen,* Stages Repertory Theatre, late 1990s; *The Castle,* 2002; *Tartuffe,* 2002; *The Love for Three Oranges,* 2004; *The Mineola Twins,* 2004; *The Normal Heart,* 2011. Television appearances include: *Ed,* 2002; *Judging Amy,* 2004-05; *Why Blitt?,* 2004; *Taste,* 2004; *The Big Bang Theory,* 2007—; *Family Guy,* 2009; *Glenn Martin DDS,* 2010; *iCarly,* 2011; *Super Hero Squad Show,* 2011. Film appearances include: *Happy End,* 2003; *Garden State,* 2004; *The Great New Wonderful,* 2005; *Heights,* 2005; *The King's Inn,* 2005; *10 Items of Less,* 2006; *School for Scoundrels,* 2006; *Gardener of Eden,* 2007; *On the Road with Judas,* 2007; *The Big Year,* 2011; *Cooler,* 2011.

Awards: Individual achievement in comedy award, Television Critics Association, for *The Big Bang Theory,* 2009; Emmy Award for outstanding lead ac-

© *Janette Pellegrini/WireImage/Getty Images*

tor in a comedy series, Academy of Television Arts and Sciences, for *The Big Bang Theory,* 2010, 2011; Golden Globe Award for best actor in a television series (musical or comedy), Hollywood Foreign Press Association, for *The Big Bang Theory,* 2011.

Sidelights

Award-winning actor Jim Parsons is best known for his portrayal of the geeky particle physicist Sheldon Cooper on the popular CBS sitcom *The Big Bang Theory.* After the show's debut in 2007, Parsons received numerous critical accolades for his comedic performances, including two Emmy Awards for Outstanding Lead Actor in a Comedy Series in 2010 and 2011, and a Golden Globe Award for Best Actor in a Television Series (Musical or Comedy) in 2011. Parsons has also appeared in several other stage and screen roles during his career, including a recurring role on television program *Judging Amy* and small spots in films such as *Garden State* and *School for Scoundrels.* In 2011, the actor made his Broadway debut in a revival production of *The Normal Heart,* a play about a the emergence of AIDS in the early 1980s. Although the serious subject matter stood apart from Parsons' well-known comedy turns, the actor has acknowledged that he likes the challenge and variety of pursuing different types of work in the long run. "I guess my future hinges much more for me on the job I have right now.... You just pour yourself into it, and it'll lead to something else. Whenever this road ends, or even during this trip as we're going down it, I will do other things," he told Noel Murray of the A.V. Club Web site in 2009.

Born James Joseph Parsons on March 24, 1973, in Houston, Texas, the actor is the son of a plumbing company executive father who died in a car accident in 2001 and a mother who taught first grade. From childhood, Parsons was interested in performing, making his stage debut as a bird during an elementary school play. "From a very early age, I said 'movie star,'" in response to the question of what he wanted to be when he grew up, he later recalled in an interview with Andrew Dansby of the *Houston Chronicle*. "I couldn't have known what that meant, as far as fame—that didn't make sense to me. But I knew I wanted to act.... Why? I have no idea. I was given plenty of attention as a child," he concluded. After completing his high school education at Klein Oak High School in Spring, Texas, in 1991, Parsons enrolled at the University of Houston. Although interested in science classes—he later admitted to taking and failing a class in meteorology—he was drawn to acting, and in 1996 completed a bachelor's degree in theater at the university's School of Theatre and Dance. By that time, Parsons had made his professional stage debut in Houston in a Catastrophic Theatre production of *Endgame*. During the remainder of the 1990s, Parsons appeared in numerous theater productions around Houston, performing in shows including *Othello, Guys and Dolls, The Threepenny Opera*, and *Below the Belt*. In 1999, he left Houston for San Diego, where he completed graduate studies at the Old Globe/University of San Diego's Professional Actor Training Program.

Next, Parsons left the West Coast for a stint performing in off-Broadway productions in New York City, including an adaptation of Franz Kafka's *The Castle*, but soon returned to California. There, he appeared in supporting roles in productions at the respected La Jolla Playhouse, including *Tartuffe* and *The Love for Three Oranges*. At the same time, Parsons began seeking roles in film and television. Back in New York in 2002, he made his small-screen debut as a state park guide on the NBC sitcom *Ed*. More roles followed, with Parsons appearing in commercials for such companies as Quizno's, FedEx, and Stride gum, as well as landing a multi-episode stint as eager law clerk Rob Holbrook on the courtroom drama *Judging Amy*. He had a small part as a professional medieval re-enactor in the 2004 film *Garden State*, and had minor roles in other movies including 2006's *School for Scoundrels* and *10 Items or Less*.

In 2007, Parsons found the role that would make him famous: physicist Sheldon Cooper, one of four nerdy scientists anchoring the cast of the CBS sitcom *The Big Bang Theory*. The program followed the comedic interactions of the scientists and their attractive female neighbor using a more traditional—and unfashionable— sitcom format than many of its contemporaries. Unlike popular sitcoms such as *The Office*, for example, *The Big Bang Theory* relies on multiple-camera filming in front of a live audience and even a laugh track. "It's a dorky show about dorky people, but almost inexplicably, it works," commented Emma Rosenblum in *New York* magazine. Yet this unabashed dorkiness was one of the main factors attracting Parsons to the role; the challenge of presenting a main character who lacked the type of social charisma and outgoing personality that characterize most network leads drew the actor in. Parsons' portrayal of Sheldon captivated show creator Chuck Lorre, who was stunned by the actor's immediate understanding of the tricky scientist character. "We knew we were witnessing something astonishing," Lorre said of Parsons' audition in Dansby's article. "He's a force of nature. He really is that good," the show creator concluded.

Parsons' character Sheldon has also attracted popular attention for his sharply awkward mannerisms and personality. Many viewers and critics have observed that Sheldon seems to have a form of autism or the more specific Asperger's syndrome; both of these disorders can cause individuals to exhibit high degrees of interest and ability in specific areas while facing challenges relating to other people or social situations. The actor has noted, however, that the character of Sheldon is not specifically written as a person diagnosed with one of these disorders in order to allow both himself and the writers more leniency in the interpretation of the character. "I think a lot of this really intellectual work that somebody like Sheldon does, this way his brain works, it's so focused on the intellectual topics at hand that thinking he's autistic is an easy leap for people watching the show to make," Parsons told Murray in the A.V. Club interview. "The way Sheldon goes 'Huh?' to a social and emotional situation because he's so focused on what he's doing. His brain is so wrapped up in it," he added.

With so many of its characters written as scientific geniuses, *The Big Bang Theory* has undertaken considerable efforts to incorporate true-life, accurate scientific information into its scripts. The show employed David Saltzberg, a particle physicist who served on the faculty of the University of California in Los Angeles, as a technical adviser to ensure that its depiction of science was up to snuff. Sometimes, Saltzberg's suggestions directly shaped actions performed by Parsons' character. "Once Sheldon was working on a problem, and [the writers] needed it to be something where he would be putting balls on the floor, so that someone would come in and trip on them," Saltzberg recalled to Pearl Tesler of *Current Science.* "So why would he be putting balls all over the floor?" The real-life scientist hit on the idea of having Sheldon make a model of grapheme, a substance made of carbon atoms arranged in a honeycomb pattern—and, in fact, this was the explanation provided for the character's actions on the show. "They want to get everything right, and they actually know a lot of science," Saltzberg commented of the show's creators in the same interview. Nevertheless, Parsons has admitted that he sometimes had difficulty grasping the scientific jokes on the show, noting in a *TIME* interview, "That's not because it's not funny. It's because I am probably a little too dumb to get it. Every once in a while they write a joke in plain English that I don't understand how to make work.... That's been blessedly rare."

In fact, Parsons' portrayal of Sheldon became noted as one of the show's strongest aspects, and in time his character took on a larger and larger portion of the program's storylines. Critics formally recognized Parsons' acting achievement beginning in 2009, when he won the Television Critics Association Award for Individual Achievement in Comedy and garnered an Emmy nomination. The following year, Parsons won his first Emmy for Outstanding Lead Actor in a Comedy Series.

Parsons' sexuality has also been a topic of much debate among some fans. Although the actor has generally kept details of his personal life to himself, a 2010 story in the *National Enquirer* reported that Parsons was gay and newly engaged to his boyfriend of several years. Parsons made no comment on this story, but it fueled discussion of his sexuality on numerous LGBT Web sites; the tabloid also reported on supposed wedding plans that were later reputedly canceled. Despite the speculative nature of these stories, Parsons has been generally accepted as an open member of the gay community, although not one who chooses to bring his sexuality into the public sphere.

Popular and media focus has largely remained on Parsons' professional, rather than personal, accomplishments. *The Big Bang Theory* closed out 2010 as the most popular scripted series with the coveted 18-49 age group, averaging nearly 14 million viewers per episode. In 2011, Parsons picked up his first Golden Globe for his work on *The Big Bang Theory,* beating out several more high-profile actors for what was a somewhat unexpected honor.

The *Washington Post* noted that "it wasn't totally out of the blue for him to win.... But it was natural to think the Foreign Press might go with Alec Baldwin or *Glee*'s Matthew Morrison." Later that year, the Academy of Television Arts and Sciences again honored the actor with an Emmy nomination for Outstanding Lead Actor in a Comedy Series, an award he took home in September of 2011.

Parsons made his return to the stage in the spring of 2011 with a role in the Broadway revival of *The Normal Heart.* A heart-rending drama set in New York City in the early 1980s, the play first captured audiences upon its opening in 1985 for its harsh treatment of those unwilling to confront the then-new AIDS epidemic. Appearing alongside such renowned acting talents as Ellen Barkin and Joe Mantello, Parsons played the role of Tommy Boatwright, a Southerner involved in a group of politicizing gay men central to the play's story. Writing for the *New York Times,* Ben Brantley proclaimed that Parsons and his co-stars Lee Pace and Patrick Breen were "all terrific as very different types of gay men who band together and chafe and clash and ultimately explode," furthering noting that "Each has at least one outburst that leaves you as shaken as they are."

After the play completed its run in July of that year, Parsons returned to work on *The Big Bang Theory,* which CBS had renewed earlier that year through 2014. He was also set to appear on the silver screen in two films, the low-budget flick *Cooler,* about a hunt through Los Angeles for a lost cooler filled with bone marrow, and the higher-profile comedy *The Big Year,* which paired Parsons with such talent as Steve Martin, Rashida Jones, Owen Wilson, and Jack Black in a film following three dedicated bird watchers striving to find the most number of unusual bird species in North America.

Sources

Periodicals

Current Science, October 29, 2010, p. 4.
Houston Chronicle, September 20, 2009, p. 8.
New York, September 28, 2009.
New York Times, April 27, 2011.
Washington Post, January 18, 2011.

Online

"10 Questions for Jim Parsons," *TIME,* http://www.time.com/time/magazine/article/0,9171,2048322,00.html (August 29, 2011).

The Big Bang Theory Renewed for 3 More Seasons," AOL TV, http://www.aoltv.com/2011/01/12/the-big-bang-theory-renewed-for-3-more-seasons/ (August 29, 2011).

"Interview: Jim Parsons," A.V. Club, http://www.avclub.com/articles/jim-parsons,27415/ (August 29, 2011).

"Jim Parsons and Lee Pace Join the Cast of *Normal Heart* on Broadway," *New York Times*, http://artsbeat.blogs.nytimes.com/2011/03/07/jim-parsons-and-lee-pace-join-cast-of-normal-heart-on-broadway/?scp=1&sq=jim 0arsons&st=cse (August 29, 2011).

"More About Jim," Catastrophic Theatre, http://catastrophictheatre.com/page/more-about-jim (August 29, 2011).

—*Vanessa E. Vaughn*

Ron Perlman

Actor

Born Ronald Francis Perlman, April 13, 1950, in New York, NY; son of Dorothy (a municipal employee) Perlman and a drummer/TV repairman; married Opal (a fashion designer), 1981; children: Blake Amanda, Brandon. *Education:* Attended Lehman College in New York City, 1971; University of Minnesota College of Liberal Arts, M.F.A., 1973.

Addresses: *Office*—c/o Sons of Anarchy, Pacific 2.1 Productions, Occidental Studios, 7333 Radford Ave., North Hollywood, CA 91605.

Career

Actor in films, including: *Quest for Fire,* 1981; *The Ice Pirates,* 1984; *The Name of the Rose,* 1986; *Sleepwalkers,* 1992; *The Adventures of Huck Finn,* 1993; *Cronos,* 1993; *Romeo Is Bleeding,* 1993; *When the Bough Breaks,* 1993; *Double Exposure,* 1994; *Police Academy: Mission to Moscow,* 1994; *Sensation,* 1994; *The City of Lost Children,* 1995; *Fluke,* 1995; *The Last Supper,* 1995; *The Island of Dr. Moreau,* 1996; *Alien: Resurrection,* 1997; *Betty,* 1997; *Prince Valiant,* 1997; *Tinseltown,* 1997; *An American Tail: The Treasure of Manhattan Island* (voice; video), 1998; *Frogs for Snakes,* 1998; *I Woke Up Early the Day I Died,* 1998; *The Protector,* 1998; *Happy, Texas,* 1999; *The King's Guard,* 2000; *Price of Glory,* 2000; *Stroke,* 2000; *Titan A.E.* (voice), 2000; *Down,* 2001; *Enemy at the Gates,* 2001; *Night Class,* 2001; *Blade II,* 2002; *Crime and Punishment,* 2002; *Star Trek: Nemesis,* 2002; *Absolon,* 2003; *Boys on the Run,* 2003; *Hoodlum & Son,* 2003; *Looney Tunes: Back in Action,* 2003; *Rats,* 2003; *Two Soldiers,* 2003; *Hellboy,* 2004; *Quiet Kill,* 2004; *Missing in America,* 2005; *Second Front,* 2005; *5ive Girls,* 2006; *The Last Winter,* 2006; *Local Color,* 2006; *How to Go Out on a Date in Queens,* 2006; *Scooby-Doo! Pirates Ahoy!* (video), 2006; *In the Name of the King: A Dungeon Siege Tale,* 2007; *Hellboy II: The Golden Army,* 2008; *Mutant Chronicles,* 2008; *Outlander,* 2008; *Spirit of the Forest* (voice), 2008; *Uncross the Stars,* 2008; *Dark Country,* 2009; *The Devil's Tomb,* 2009; *I Sell The Dead,* 2009; *The Job,* 2009; *Acts of Violence,* 2010; *Bunraku,* 2010; *Killer by Nature,* 2010; *The Legend of Secret Pass* (voice), 2010; *Tangled,* 2010; *Bad Ass,* 2011; *Conan the Barbarian,* 2011; *Drive,* 2011; *Dark Star Hollow,* 2011; *The Littlest Angel,* 2011; *Season of the Witch,* 2011; *Crave,* 2012; *Frankie Go Boom,* 2012. Television appearances include: *Ryan's Hope,* 1979; *The Fall Guy,* 1985; *MacGruder and Loud,* 1985; *Our Family Honor,* 1985; *Insiders,* 1986; *Miami Vice,* 1987; *Beauty and the Beast,* 1987-90; *A Stoning in Fulham County* (movie), 1988; *The Legend of Prince Valiant,* 1991-92; *Blind Man's Bluff* (movie), 1992; *Animaniacs,* 1993; *Batman,* 1992-93; *Arly Hanks* (movie), 1993; *Bonkers,* 1993; *Untouchables,* 1993; *Aladdin,* 1994; *The Cisco Kid* (movie), 1994; *The Little Mermaid,* 1994; *Mighty Max,* 1994; *The Adventures of Captain Zoom in Outer Space* (movie), 1995; *Fantastic Four,* 1995; *Mr. Stitch* (movie), 1995; *Original Sins* (movie), 1995; *Picture Windows,* 1995; *Tiny Toons' Night Ghoulery* (movie), 1995; *Duckman: Private Duck/Family Man,* 1996; *Highlander: The Series,* 1996; *Iron Man,* 1996; *Mortal Kombat: Defender of the Realm,* 1996; *Phantom 2040,* 1996; *Skwids,* 1996; *Wing Commander Academy,*

1996; *Hey Arnold!*, 1996-98; *Perversions of Science*, 1997; *The Second Civil War* (movie), 1997; *Tracey Takes On...*, 1997; *The New Batman Adventures*, 1997-98; *Superman*, 1997-99; *Houdini* (movie), 1998; *The Outer Limits*, 1998; *A Town Has Turned to Dust*, 1998; *The Magnificent Seven*, 1998-2000; *Family Law*, 1999; *Primal Force* (movie), 1999; *Supreme Sanction* (movie), 1999; *Operation Sandman* (movie), 2000; *Sonic Underground*, 1999; *Buzz Lightyear of Star Command*, 2000; *Jackie Chan Adventures*, 2000; *The Trial of Old Drum* (movie), 2000; *The Wild Thornberrys*, 2000; *Charmed*, 2001; *The Tick*, 2001; *Static Shock*, 2003; *Justice League*, 2003-06; *Teen Titans*, 2003-06; *Danny Phantom*, 2004-06; *What's New, Scooby-Doo?*, 2005; *The Batman*, 2005-08; *Desperation* (movie), 2006; *Hellboy Animated: Sword of Storms* (movie), 2006; *Masters of Horror: Pro-Life*, 2006; *Afro Samurai* (mini-series), 2007; *Avatar: The Last Airbender*, 2007; *Hellboy Animated: Blood and Iron* (movie), 2007; *Hellboy Animated: Iron Shoes* (short), 2007; *Kim Possible*, 2007; *Star Wars: The Clone Wars*, 2008; *Chowder*, 2008-10; *Sons of Anarchy*, 2008—; *Robot Chicken*, 2009; *1000 Ways to Die*, 2009—; *Archer*, 2010; *Batman: The Brave and the Bold*, 2010; *Adventure Time*, 2011; *American Dad!*, 2011; *NASCAR on ESPN*, 2011; *Regular Show*, 2011. Has also done voice-over work for many films, television shows, and video games.

Awards: Golden Apple Award for male discovery of the year, Golden Apple Foundation, 1988; Golden Globe for best performance by an actor in a television series, Hollywood Foreign Press Association, for *Beauty and the Beast*, 1989; best actor award, Viewers for Quality Television, for *Beauty and the Beast*, 1988, 1989.

Sidelights

Ron Perlman is an American actor best known for roles in which his craggy, rugged looks are modified or hidden by makeup. His most famous role was that of Vincent, the "beast" in the 1980s television series *Beauty and the Beast*, which won him a Golden Globe award. He has also notably played Slade in the animated *Teen Titans* series; Clay Morrow in *Sons of Anarchy*, and Hellboy in the film franchise of the same name. He has also narrated the television series *1000 Ways to Die*. For more than three decades, Perlman has played characters ranging from Neanderthals to demons to transsexuals, always with depth and skill honed by his training in classical acting.

Perlman was born and grew up in the Washington Heights section of New York City. As a child, he was large and overweight, and his self-esteem suffered as a result. Ever since, despite slimming down and becoming a successful actor, he has thought of himself as a fat guy and an outsider. This feeling of desperate alienation perhaps gave him insight he would later use to portray characters who were outsiders, often because of their physical deformities or unusual looks.

Perlman had no thought of becoming an actor while he was growing up, and indeed, came into acting almost by chance. He made it onto his high school swim team, and one day a teacher from the drama department came in to talk to the swim coach. The drama teacher was putting on a play and he had a multitude of girls interested in acting in it, but no boys. As Perlman reported to John Tesh in an interview on the television program, *One on One* (transcript available on Perlman's unofficial fan Web site, The Perlman Pages), "I was this marginal swimmer so the guy says, 'Hey, Perlman, get out of the pool.'" He auditioned and got the lead part, and found that he loved acting and the audience's response to him.

Perlman went to Lehman College in New York City, then moved on to the University of Minnesota, where he earned a master of fine arts degree in theatre. In addition to his classical training in acting, he was greatly influenced by his father's taste in movies. To this day, his ten favorite movies of all time are identical to his father's. At an early age, his father made him watch Charles Lawton's famed portrayal of the hunchback in *The Hunchback of Notre Dame*. Perlman never forgot how deeply Lawton became the character, how he completely transformed himself to so believably play a role that was very different from his real life and appearance. Other heroes of both Perlman and his father include classic horror actor Lon Chaney and Marlon Brando. Perlman told Ethan Aames in *Cinecon* that as a child, watching Brando, "I was just tickled by how he disappeared into character and totally transformed himself role to role. You never saw Marlon, you just saw the guy." Only later in Perlman's life did he realize that the actors and roles he admired were the blueprint for the path he chose in his own acting life.

Initially, despite his acting degree, Perlman found it difficult to find work. He auditioned for soap operas and commercials, but his unusual looks—low brows, a long chin, and a tendency to appear as if he were scowling—made it hard for him to find roles. During this time, he was married and he and his wife had their first daughter, so he stayed home to take care of her. He told Tesh that from her first diaper in the morning to the last bottle at night, he was there. "It was tough while it was happening, but in retrospect, I think I was given this incredible gift."

Perlman did finally find work and began his long career of playing roles that require makeup or facial prosthetics with his very first foray into film. In Jean-Jacques Annaud's 1981 prehistoric-themed film *Quest for Fire*, he played a Neanderthal. He was nominated for a Genie award for that role; Annaud hired him again in 1986 to play a hunchbacked monk named Salvatore in *The Name of the Rose.*

This role garnered him enough attention to be cast in his breakout role: Vincent, a half-man, half-lion creature, in the much-loved series *Beauty and the Beast,* which began in 1987. The series, a huge hit with fans, lasted for three seasons and won him a Golden Globe Award.

Perhaps because he was so identified with this role in the minds of Americans, Perlman found it impossible to get work with American directors for the next ten years. He told Aaron Hillis in an interview for the IFC Web site, "Americans wouldn't hire me in the entire decade of the '90s. I couldn't get any American to freakin' hire me." He went where he could find work, and that turned out to be in Spain, where he appeared in *Cronos* (1993), directed by Guillermo del Toro. He laughingly told Hillis, "To this day, I don't know what the hell I was doing in that movie." However, he and del Toro formed a lifelong friendship as a result of his work on the film.

He next appeared in French director Jean-Pierre Jeunet's independent film *The City of Lost Children* (1995) in his first lead role. Jeunet was looking for a rough-hewn, innocent-bumpkin sort of character, and when he saw Perlman in *Cronos* he decided Perlman was perfect for the job. Perlman did not speak French, which made him seem even more unsophisticated and perfect for the part. In the movie, he had to speak French with a Russian accent, and he rose to this challenge. He followed this performance with his first mainstream film lead as Johner in Jeunet's 1997 science fiction film *Alien: Resurrection.*

Perlman continued to work steadily in film and television after appearing in these films. His next major role was as the title character in *Hellboy* (2004), based on the Mike Mignola comic book series; the part was written with him in mind by his old friend Guillermo del Toro. In the movie, based on the comic book, he played a demon. Initially, the studio had wanted someone more famous and "bankable" than character-actor Perlman, but director Guillermo del Toro insisted on Perlman. As a result, the movie brought Perlman's name to the forefront of the film industry and established him as a major actor. Perlman reprised the role in the sequel to *Hellboy, Hellboy II: The Golden Army* (2008).

When IFC's Hillis asked Perlman if he ever minded the four hours he had to spend every day in the makeup chair, Perlman replied that he did not, because "Generally, I like the guys I'm hanging out with. All the guys who put makeup on me are salt-of-the-earth people where the conversation flies, the music is cool and we take a lot of … breaks." He added, "It's never been a problem. It's always been a joy."

In 2008 Perlman moved to a set in which he could act without makeup when he played outlaw biker Clarence "Clay" Morrow in the FX television series *Sons of Anarchy.* Kurt Sutter, the creator of the series, wanted to portray the story of Shakespeare's play *Hamlet* in the context of a motorcycle gang. The series was a big hit, particularly among motorcycle riders, who showed up wherever the show was being filmed to see Perlman and the other actors and to share their stories and experiences with them. Because Perlman did not wear makeup for the role, he became more recognizable to the general public, and everywhere he went, fans would see him and call out, "Hey, Clay Morrow!"

Perlman noted the odd fact that although Morrow was the most physically natural character he had ever played, Morrow was actually the most alien to him of them all. Morrow had a narrow, one-sided view of every event and issue, and had no sense of humor; he was a serious man who, if need be, would do things that would lead to his own destruction rather than back down or compromise. Perlman told *Men's Health* writer J. Rentilly, "I'm very uncomfortable with him sometimes, which is a nice challenge."

In 2011 Perlman appeared, again without any facial alteration, in *Season of the Witch,* an action-horror movie set in medieval times. In the film, he played a sidekick to Nicholas Cage's main character. The two are chosen to escort a young woman who is accused of being a witch to trial. Perlman truly loved playing the role of the loyal friend and helper; he had long admired this role as it was played in many movies he enjoyed as a child. He and Cage also enjoyed the location of the filming, high in the Alps, in settings so beautiful they looked painted.

Perlman told Edward Douglas in *Crave Online* that he was truly delighted with the path his career had taken in recent years. In the early years of his career, he noted, "the roles were so disparate that it never gave anybody the opportunity to understand my essence and what I would be good at doing." He added, "It was only after *Hellboy II* where I began to see things coming my way that I said, 'I love this role.... This is something that I feel like I will be very engaged in, very challenged by, but also something that I feel like maybe I can be successful at.'"

Regarding his move to roles in which he did not need makeup, he told Douglas that he believed he chose "mask work" in his earlier years because "I just don't think I was that comfortable in my own skin.... I was such a late bloomer, I really didn't learn how to be me until I was in my late 40s, which is when I started playing roles that were closer to me." He did not, however, toss out the makeup jobs. Perlman continued to appear in movies such as 2011's *Conan the Barbarian* and the science fiction crime film *Bunraku*.

Throughout his career, Perlman has valued work based on his own perceptions of what is important in life. He explained to Renn Brown in *Chud*, "I have to feel I'm capable of playing the role. Second of all I have to feel I'm working around people who are doing it for the love of it, rather than some other network of reasons—whether they think it's the right career choice or they think it's going to be a blockbuster or going to get award consideration. Those things are of no meaning to me." He prefers to work on projects that have intelligence and depth, that are new and challenging to him, where he has to reach a little farther to fulfill the role. However, he acknowledged to Wilson Morales in *Black Film* that earlier in his career, he could not afford to take only these types of roles; sometimes he had to settle and take whatever was offered. "So there's a lot of stuff out there that I'm not proud, but I don't apologize. I'm raising kids and putting them through school and you got to do what you got to do. You take the good with the bad."

Perlman told Rentilly that he was truly happy as an actor. "I've never been pigeonholed and I've experienced so many different kinds of skin—what man will do and won't do, what you should do and shouldn't do. That's what's exciting about being an actor; where philosophy majors sit in classrooms or write books about human behavior, we're actually acting them out in front of cameras."

Perlman keeps busy with acting work, but he has not ruled out directing a movie of his own someday. He told Hillis, "I have a number of scripts I want to direct, but every time I seem to have a hole in the schedule, another acting gig comes up and it's an offer I can't refuse, so the whole thing keeps getting moved into the shed. One of these days...."

Sources

"A Chat with Ron Perlman," *Bullz-Eye*, http://www.bullz-eye.com/movies/interviews/2011/ron_perlman.htm (November 4, 2011).

"Exclusive Interview with Ron Perlman," *Crave*, http://www.craveonline.com/film/interviews/130810-exclusive-interview-with-ron-perlman (November 4, 2011).

"*Hellboy*: An Interview with Ron Perlman," *Black-film*, http://www.blackfilm.com/20040326.tif/features/ronperlman.shtml (November 4, 2011).

"IAR Exclusive Interview: Ron Perlman Talks," *I Am Rogue*, http://www.iamrogue.com/news/interviews/item/4926-iar-exclusive-interview-ron-perlman-talks-bunraku-drive-pacific-rim-and-the-future-of-sons-of-anarchy.html (November 4, 2011).

"Interview: Ron Perlman (*Bunraku, Drive, Mountains of Madness, The Help?*)," *Chud*, http://www.chud.com/68752/interview-ron-perlman-bunraku-drive-mountains-of-madness-the-help/ (November 4, 2011).

"Interview: Ron Perlman of *Hellboy*," *Cinecon*, http://www.cinecon.com/news.php?id=0403293 (November 4, 2011).

"The Many Mutations of Ron Perlman," *IFC*, http://www.ifc.com/fix/2009/04/ron-perlman (November 4, 2011).

"MH Interview: Ron Perlman," *Men's Health*, http://news.menshealth.com/mh-interview-ron-perlman/2011/09/06/ (November 4, 2011).

Perlman Pages Unofficial Fan Web Site, http://www.perlmanpages.com/ (November 4, 2011).

"Ron Perlman," Internet Movie Database, http://www.imdb.com/name/nm0000579/ (November 4, 2011).

"*Season of the Witch*: The Ron Perlman Interview," *Television Without Pity*, http://www.televisionwithoutpity.com/mwop/moviefile/2011/01/season-of-the-witch-the-ron-pe.php (November 4, 2011).

—Kelly Winters

Katy Perry

Helga Esteb/Shutterstock.com

Singer and songwriter

Born Kathryn Elizabeth Hudson, October 25, 1984, in Santa Barbara, CA; daughter of Keith (a pastor) and Mary (a pastor; maiden name, Perry) Hudson; married Russell Brand (a comedian and actor), October 23, 2010 (separated, 2011).

Addresses: *Management*—Direct Management Group, Inc., 947 North La Cienega Blvd., Ste. G, Los Angeles, CA 90069. *Record company*—Capitol Records, 1750 N. Vine St., Los Angeles, CA 90028-5209. *Web site*—http://www.katyperry.com/.

Career

Began career singing at church, c. 1990s; signed with Red Hill Records, c. 2000; released *Katy Hudson,* 2001; signed with Columbia, 2004; signed with Capitol Music Group, 2007; released first album on Capitol, *One of the Boys,* 2008; participated in the Vans Warped Tour, 2008; released *Teenage Dream,* 2010; released perfume, Purr by Katy Perry, 2010; appeared in acting role on *How I Met Your Mother,* CBS, 2011; provided voice of Smurfette in the feature film *The Smurfs,* 2011.

Awards: Best new act, MTV Europe Music Awards, 2008; international album of the year, Eska Music Awards, for *One of the Boys,* 2009; BRIT Award for international female solo artist, British Phonographic Industry, 2009; favorite pop song, People's Choice Award, for "I Kissed a Girl," 2009.

Sidelights

American singer Katy Perry is perhaps best known for hit songs like "I Kissed a Girl," "Hot N Cold," and "California Gurls." In her music, she emphasized entertainment over substance, fun over depth. Perry was not looking for critical praise, but giving the audience a sense of enjoyment. Yet, Perry was strong-willed with firm ideas about what her songs should say and sound like, as well as the nature of her public persona. She was true to herself, but loved to play around with outlandish, unique looks. Of her goal as a musician, she told Ashante Infantry of the *Toronto Star,* "I want to change peoples lives. I want to tell people stories. I don't just want to cater to radio and not have anything to back it up at the end of the day."

She was born Kathryn Elizabeth Hudson on October 25, 1984, in Santa Barbara, California, the daughter of Keith and Mary Hudson. Both of her parents were Christian pastors. Living in the lower-income areas of Santa Barbara with her sister and brother, she only listened to gospel music and attended Christian schools and camps. Describing her relationship with her siblings, Perry told Rose Apodaca of *Harper's Bazaar,* "We are like the Three Musketeers—actually the Three Stooges. I feel really blessed because of where I come from."

Perry began singing in church in the 1990s as a child. She was discovered there and began working on her first album, a Christian record with a gospel rock sound, in Nashville when she was 15 years old. Of her musical taste at the time, she told John Soeder of the Cleveland *Plain Dealer*, "My first door open into music was definitely through gospel, 'cause that there was kind of my world I lived in at that moment. At 15 and 16, everything that related to my life was about my faith and church and church friends. I didn't really have any grasp that there was a whole other world outside of that."

Around 2000, she signed with Red Hill Records, a gospel label. She put out her Christian album under her real name, Katy Hudson, in 2001. *Katy Hudson* went nowhere because the label folded soon after its release. Perry made the decision to switch from Christian to mainstream pop, and she moved to Los Angeles in 2003 looking for a record deal. (She changed her name, taking on her mother's maiden name to distinguish herself from the actress Kate Hudson.) She spent much of the next few years finding her career ambitions frustrated. She was signed by Island Def Jam at 17 and worked with hit making producer Glen Ballard on an album that never saw the light of day.

Perry then signed with Columbia Records in 2004, but was dropped before any product was released on the market even though the album she was working on was nearly complete. There was conflict between Perry and Columbia. Perry's manager Bradford Cobb told Cortney Harding of *Billboard,* "Columbia was never really willing to embrace Katy's vision. They were not willing to let her drive. Here was this ambitious young woman with a clear picture of who she was and the willingness to work hard, and Columbia just wouldn't put her in the driver's seat."

Of this frustrating time in her career, Perry told *Billboard*'s Monica Herrera, "I used to just feel numb. It was like taking a kid to Disneyland and then making them wait outside. The people just wouldn't let me through the gates—what could I do?" While searching for a new record deal, Perry took a draining job at Taxi Music, an independent A&R company, critiquing music sent in by aspiring artists.

In 2007, Perry was signed by Capitol Music Group and her singing career finally took steps forward with the support and freedom to do what she wanted. Having obtained the masters from her Columbia sessions, she had already completed much of what became her first album on Capitol, *One of*

the Boys, by the time she was signed. She co-wrote many of the songs on the album, which came out in 2008 and sold at least 1.2 million copies. It made the top ten of the *Billboard* album charts and was certified platinum. *One of the Boys* was a smash with hit singles including "I Kissed a Girl" and "Hot N Cold."

"I Kissed a Girl" was a number-one hit on the *Billboard* charts and sold at least 3.8 million downloads. It was an unexpected hit as the label was unsure that it would play, let alone catch on, in conservative parts of the country. The work of one person, Dennis Reese, who was the head of top 40 radio at Capitol, got the rest of the label behind the song, which greatly contributed to its success.

Describing "I Kissed a Girl," Perry told Infantry of the *Toronto Star*, "It's a song about curiosity. The fact of the matter is that girls smell much better than boys; we all know this. We're beautiful creatures, we've started wars, we've ended wars. Girl hangouts are very touchy; we have slumber parties, we have sleepovers, we choreograph numbers in our pajamas. And there's nothing perverted about that. It's just really sweet and innocent, and if Scarlett Johansson wanted to kiss me, I'm not sure I'd say no."

As the song began airing on radio and becoming popular, Perry toured in support of *One of the Boys*, participating in the Vans Warped Tour in the summer of 2008. She made sure her visual persona on the tour matched her reputation. She told Harding of *Billboard*, "I didn't wear the same outfit twice. I know how much people follow the visual aspect and they want to see eye candy. I used Freddie Mercury as my model—he was a serious artist and musician who never lost sight of the fact that you also need a good look." Perry later toured on her own worldwide in 2008 and 2009.

"Hot N Cold" was another number-one hit and sold at least 4.4 million downloads. The first release from *One of the Boys*, it was a caustic tune aimed a boyfriend who dumped her. "Ur So Gay" also had another target. Perry told Nekesa Mumbi Moody of the Associated Press, "It also takes a shot at the whole indie scene: The guys who are using the eyeliner, the straight irons, and my ex-boyfriends who would borrow my jeans and never give them back!"

Perry admitted that many of her songs, like "I Kissed a Girl" and "Hot N Cold," came from her interest in human behavior and her constant need to observe and listen to others. She told Sean Piccoli of the *South Florida Sun-Sentinel*, "I listen to people's conversations and pick up a phrase they say, and I'll stick it in my pocket." She added, "The art of people-watching is a beautiful thing, and I'm a big people-watcher. I've got eyes in the front of my head, the side of my head and the back of my head." She also described the importance of humor, telling Marian Liu of the *Seattle Times*, "I think the biggest ingredient in everything I do is my sense of humor.... And how I don't take myself, I don't take anything too seriously. At the end of the day, the world is still going to turn, honey."

Perry released her second album, *Teenage Dream* in the summer of 2010. Intentionally including more upbeat pop with a feel-good vibe, the album also had depth and received some positive reviews from critics. While "Circle the Drain" was inspired by Pat Benatar, for example, it was Perry's candid way of dealing with the end of her relationship with Gym Class Heroes frontman Travie McCoy.

Perry played a big role in the production of the album, working with producers like Tricky and songwriters like Mr. Luke to ensure every lyric and melody met her exacting standards. As she explained to Herrera of *Billboard*, "I think we rewrote 'Teenage Dream' five times for ten days straight. On the last day, I was so happy to finally get somewhere that we all agreed on."

This album produced Perry's third number-one hit with the summer anthem "California Gurls." It spent six weeks atop the *Billboard* Hot 100. Though "California Gurls" was a commercial success, Perry fully admitted that the song was about fun, not artistic genius. She told Herrera of *Billboard*, "I'm not saying, 'Oh, my God! "California Gurls" is a [...] genius opus!' I just know what kind of card this summer needs, and that's the one I'm playing." The power of such singles made *Teenage Dream* one of the best-selling albums of the year.

While Perry made promotional appearances in support of *Teenage Dream* in 2010, she focused on her personal life instead of touring in the second half of 2010. She married Russell Brand, a British comedian and actor, on October 23, 2010, in India. The couple had been dating since 2009 when they met while filming *Get Him to the Greek*. (Her cameo was cut in the final version.) She was also in the news for an entirely different reason. She filmed a segment, a duet with Elmo, for the long-running children's program *Sesame Street* only to see it dropped because some online viewers, who saw the segment before it aired, found her outfit bared too much cleavage and complained.

Perry finally began touring in support of *Teenage Dream* in early 2011. She continued to stretch her acting wings, playing Honey on an episode of the CBS situation comedy *How I Met Your Mother*. Perry also provided the voice of Smurfette for the semi-animated film *The Smurfs*, set for release in the summer of 2011.

Outside of music and acting, Perry marketed herself in other ways, primarily through her fashion choices. She had a distinctive look and was not afraid to take chances. She told David Curcurito of *Esquire*, "It's Lucille Ball meets Bob Mackie. It's about innuendo. I want everybody to get the joke, but I want them to think about it for a minute." She added to Rose Apodaca of *Harper's Bazaar*, "I have multipersonality disorder—in a very good way, of course—when it comes to my fashion choices."

Fashion was part of her marketing plan as an artist. When "I Kissed a Girl" was released, Perry had a marketing campaign in conjunction with Steven Madden shoes. While she eventually wanted to have her own line of clothing, she wanted to do it right and with focus and energy. By November of 2010, Perry had her own perfume, Purr by Katy Perry.

Of her persona and her music, Perry told Apodaca from *Harper's Bazaar*, "I'm kind of a good girl—and I'm not. I'm a good girl because I really believe in love, integrity, and respect. I'm a bad girl because I like to tease. I know that I have sex appeal in my deck of cards. But I like to get people thinking. That's what the stories in my music do."

Selected discography

Katy Hudson, Red Hill Records, 2001.
One of the Boys, Capitol Records, 2008.
Teenage Dream, Capitol Records, 2010.

Sources

Books

Contemporary Musicians, vol. 67, Gale, 2010.

Periodicals

Associated Press, March 14, 2008; August 23, 2010; September 23, 2010.
Associated Press Online, November 17, 2009.

Billboard, June 14, 2008; January 31, 2009, p. 20; July 31, 2010, p. 16.

Curve, April 2009, p. 32.

Esquire, April 2009, p. 112.

Harper's Bazaar, December 2010, p. 286.

Plain Dealer (Cleveland, OH), March 27, 2009, p. T14.

Press Enterprise (Riverside, CA), June 19, 2008, p. D4.

Seattle Times (WA), January 23, 2009.

South Florida Sun-Sentinel (Ft. Lauderdale, FL), July 12, 2008.

Toronto Star, June 15, 2008, p. E06.

Washington Post, September 24, 2010, p. C04.

Women's Wear Daily, July 22, 2010, sec. 1, p. 1.

Online

"Katy Perry," Internet Movie Database, http://www.imdb.com/name/nm2953537/ (February 27, 2011).

—A. Petruso

Drew Pinsky

Mario Anzuoni/Reuters

Physician, television personality, and radio host

Born David Drew Pinsky, September 4, 1958, in Pasadena, CA; son of Morton (a doctor) and Helene (a homemaker) Pinsky; married Susan Sailer, July 20, 1991; children: Jordan Davidson, Douglas Drew, Paulina Marie (triplets). *Education:* Amherst, undergraduate degree, 1980; University of Southern California School of Medicine, M.D., 1984.

Addresses: *Management*—Lapides/Lear Entertainment, 14724 Ventura Blvd. Penthouse, Sherman Oaks, CA 91403. *Web site*—http://www.drdrew.com/.

Career

Began appearing on *Loveline* radio program, KROQ, Los Angeles, 1983; co-host, *Loveline*, KROQ, 1984—; served residency in internal medicine at the University of Southern California County Hospital, then as chief resident at Huntington Memorial Hospital in Pasadena, CA, c. 1984; launched private practice, c. late 1980s; joined Las Encinas Hospital, Pasadena, CA, as the program medical director of the chemical dependency unit, c. early 1990s; launched Web site DrDrew.com, 1999; named clinical assistant professor of pediatrics at Los Angeles Children's Hospital, 2000; became clinical professor of psychiatry at the Keck School of Medicine at the University of Southern California, 2004; formed Dr. Drew Productions, 2010. Television appearances include: *Loveline*, MTV, 1996-2000; *Hollywood Squares*, 1998-99; *Big Brother*, CBS, 2000; *Men Are from Mars, Women Are from Venus*, 2001; *Strictly Sex with Dr. Drew*, Discovery Health Channel, 2005;

The Young and the Restless, 2008; *Celebrity Rehab with Dr. Drew*, 2008-11; *Sex Rehab with Dr. Drew*, 2009; *Sober House with Dr. Drew*, 2009-10; *Sex ... with Mom and Dad*, MTV, 2010—; *Dr. Drew*, HLN, 2011—.

Member: American College of Physicians, American Medical Association, American Society of Addiction Medicine, California Medical Association, American Society of Internal Medicine.

Awards: SHINE Award (with Adam Carolla) for best talk show, The Media Project, 2000; Larry Stewart Leadership and Inspiration Award, PRISM Awards, 2008.

Sidelights

After first coming to fame in the 1980s and '90s as the host of the popular call-in radio program *Loveline*, Dr. Drew Pinsky became a recognized expert on sex, relationships, and addictions through various television shows he has hosted since the mid-1990s. Also a board-certified internist and addictionologist who practices medicine, Pinsky hosted such shows as the television version of *Loveline*, the rehab reality show *Celebrity Rehab with Dr.*

Drew, and the news-oriented *Dr. Drew.* Pinsky was highly regarded for his even-handed demeanor and ability to be open minded yet honest with the questions about sex and relationships put before him. Of the queries he received on *Loveline* and other shows of that genre that he worked on, he told Sylvia Rubin of the *San Francisco Chronicle,* "I'm never shocked, but I am amazed, baffled, bewildered. I feel like Alice in Wonderland."

Born on September 4, 1958, in Pasadena, California, he was the son of Dr. Morton Pinsky and his wife, Helene. His father was a physician, while his mother was a homemaker. As a child, Pinsky would go with his father on house calls and decided that he would like to be a doctor himself. By high school, he was the captain of the football team and student body president. After graduating from Polytechnic High School in Pasadena in 1976, he majored in biology at Amherst College. While a high school student, he was an admitted overachiever, a trend that continued while in college. With his undergraduate degree in hand, Pinsky entered the University of Southern California School of Medicine, completing his M.D. in 1984. He told Josh Fischman of *U.S. News & World Report,* "I went through medical school thinking I'd be the traditional doctor, having a practice. I'm not a maverick, and really the I'm the last guy you'd expect to be involved in all this media craziness."

Pinsky's media career was launched when he was a third-year medical student in 1983. He began doing *Loveline* that year on local station KROQ, when some of his friends convinced the station to host a talk show about relationships and health which aired from midnight to 3 am on Sunday nights. Pinsky was asked to join the program to provide informed content on a volunteer basis because callers were asking intense questions about issues like sex and drugs. Of the experience, he told L. Kent Wolgamott of the *Lincoln Journal Star* "I had an absolute epiphany when I walked into that studio, listening to a young person bring their most important health issues to the table for some DJs to digest. Nobody was talking to them." During the early days of the shows, he was the first person working in mainstream media to talk about what later became known as AIDS.

In 1984, after earning his medical degree, Pinsky began serving his residency in internal medicine at the University of Southern California County Hospital, then became chief resident at Huntington Memorial Hospital in Pasadena, California. He continued to do *Loveline* for KROQ during this time period, and in 1993, the show went from one to five nights a week. By this time, Pinsky had become board certified in internal medicine, set up a private practice, and served as a program medical director of the chemical dependency unit at Las Encinas Hospital in Pasadena. In the early 1990s, when *Loveline* was still solely on KROQ, his co-host was Jim "Poorman" Trenton and featured celebrity guests. It emphasized practical information on any question on sex and relationships. In 1993, Pinsky told Carrie Borzillo of *Billboard* that *Loveline* is "the perfect public-health vehicle. In my profession, it's hard to reach this audience and this show is a way to get to them. Look at the statistics, some [diseases] are going up. Somewhere the system is failing badly."

Loveline soon became nationally syndicated and continued to air as it neared its third decade. As *Loveline* became popular in the early 1990s, MTV aired a television version of the radio show six nights a week from 1996 to 2000. Pinsky's co-host by this time was the droll Adam Corolla, who was handpicked by Pinsky to join *Loveline* in 1995 after Riki Rachtman declined to work on the television show as well. Corolla was a broadcaster and comedian who had a sensitive, caring touch with callers but also used his sense of humor to make the show entertaining as well. For several seasons, a third cohost, Diane Farr, added a female perspective on the television version. Pinsky noted to Sylvia Rubin of the *San Francisco Chronicle,* "I have no absolutely no idea what questions are coming until I hear them during the show. My role is to show how the physician's mind works and call it like I see it." He added to Sarah Van Boven of *Newsweek,* "The point is to create a coast-to-coast peer-counseling session, where listeners can learn from the consequences of the callers' actions."

Yet Pinsky's medical peers were not completely supportive. The medical director at Las Encinas Hospital, Dr. Joseph Haraszti, told Evan Henerson of the Los Angeles *Daily News,* "There was a lot of controversy when he was first going on TV, and people didn't want him to do it. I gave him a strong endorsement. It's a tremendous community service, a responsible and sober approach to sex education and relationship education to teens. Kids listen to him."

For a time, *Loveline* was one of the most popular shows on MTV, and the radio version attracted an average of three million listeners. In 1998, Pinsky and Corolla took *Loveline* on the road and let audiences—primarily college students—ask questions that were not broadcast or taped. The success of the MTV show led to further television opportunities for Pinsky, who became recognized as an expert on sex, relationships, and addiction, appearing regularly on morning, daytime, late night, and news shows. In the early 2000s, he became a frequent guest host for *Larry King Live* on CNN and contributed to NBC's *Today Show* on a regular basis.

Continuing to practice medicine and becoming board certified in addiction medicine in part because of the problems his callers brought to him, Pinsky was named the clinical assistant professor of pediatrics at Los Angeles Children's Hospital in 2000. He also branched out into a number of other shows and media projects while still working on the radio version of *Loveline*, which aired on at least 60 stations in this time period. In 1999, he signed a deal with Columbia TriStar to host a syndicated talk show, the same year he launched his Web site, DrDrew.com. The teen and young adult lifestyle Web site was funded by a $7.5 million investment from venture capitalists, but struggled behind the scenes to find its audience. In 2000, Pinsky appeared as the health and human relations expert on the CBS reality competition *Big Brother*. Of this experience, he told Henerson of the Los Angeles *Daily News*, "(It's) another opportunity to make something useful. It's kind of like walking onto a battlefield: 'Well, OK, I'll just dig in and try to help wherever I can.' I don't want to sound maudlin. When the day is done, I hope what I do really is useful. I hope it's not misinterpreted. I hope it does no harm."

In 2001, Pinsky hosted the short-lived talk show *Men Are from Mars, Women Are from Venus*, while in 2005, he hosted the similarly brief *Strictly Sex with Dr. Drew* on the Discovery Health Channel. The latter show featured sex-related knowledge and advice for everyone from singles to couples and both sexes, but was oriented more toward adults with topics like menopause, hormone replacements, and the female testosterone patches, but failed to catch on. While Pinsky had difficulties finding the right television outlet for himself in the early 2000s, he did become a clinical professor of psychiatry at the Keck School of Medicine at the University of Southern California in 2004.

Within a few years, however, Pinsky gained television fame with shows somewhat different from *Loveline*. In early 2008 he used his medical skills and knowledge of addiction to help people on the high-profile VH1 show *Celebrity Rehab with Dr. Drew*. Also serving as executive producer and host, the program featured nine celebrities struggling with addictions to alcohol, drugs, and other substances. *Celebrity Rehab* followed its participants continuously for three weeks as they underwent intensive therapy and detoxification. Pinsky guided their programs and helped them with their problems, even after production ended. While some found the program exploitative, others believed it showed how the process works and the effort and commitment needed to achieve sobriety. Pinsky himself was skeptical that the process he followed, rooted in Alcoholics Anonymous' 12-step program, could work on television, but saw the need as high-profile celebrities like Lindsay Lohan and Britney Spears struggled with their own addiction treatment programs and to show the general public how difficult recovery from such issues can be.

Filming the first season of *Celebrity Rehab* was powerful for Pinsky, who had to modify his usual treatment programs because of the nature of the show. He told Samantha Dunn of *O, The Oprah Magazine*, "It was so intense and anxiety producing, by the end of the show my radar was just not working well. It was like a fuse was blown. Which was okay for the patients, because the lion's share was done and I was able to let [the other counselors] come in more, but it was disconcerting for me because I am used to knowing what's going on with everybody instinctively." Despite this situation, the show was a hit for VH1 and aired for at least four more seasons through the summer of 2011 with a new set of celebrities and addiction problems.

The success of *Celebrity Rehab* led to two more reality shows that aired on VH1, both of which Pinsky also served as executive producer on. In 2009, he was the host of *Sex Rehab with Dr. Drew*, and from 2009-10, he was the host of *Sober House with Dr. Drew*. Pinsky moved to MTV for another show, *Sex ... with Mom and Dad*. After forming Dr. Drew Productions in 2010, Pinsky added another show to his repertoire when he began hosting *Dr. Drew* on HLN. *Dr. Drew* was a talk show on which he shared his opinions about what motivates people who are in the news. It featured relevant guests, like another recovering drug addict when a celebrity facing the same situation is in the headlines or trauma survivors when a devastating event occurs.

Pinsky also worked in another medium over the years: print. In addition to contributing to numerous magazines, he published several books, including *The Mirror Effect: How Celebrity Narcissism Is Seducing America*, written with S. Mark Young, and *Cracked: Putting Broken Lives Together Again*. Pinsky also took credit for publishing the first academic study of celebrities and narcissism in the *Journal of Research in Personality*. Talking about his professional life as a practicing doctor, television personality, and radio personality, Pinsky told Diane Lederman of the Springfield, Massachusetts *Republican,* "I'm living in different universes. I like the three different worlds. It's more interesting." He added, "I hope to make a difference, helping people understand what's healthy and what's not."

Selected writings

(With Adam Carolla and Marshall Fine) *The Dr. Drew and Adam Book: A Survival Guide to Life and Love,* Dell (New York City), 1998.

(With Marvin D. Seppala, Robert J. Meyers, John Gardin, William White, and Stephanie Brown) *When Painkillers Become Dangerous: What Everyone Needs to Know About OxyContin and Other Prescription Drugs,* Hazelden Publishing (Center City, MN), 2004.

Cracked: Life on the Edge in a Rehab Clinic, Regan-Books (New York City), 2003.

(With Dr. S. Mark Young) *The Mirror Effect: How Celebrity Narcissism Is Seducing America,* HarperCollins (New York City), 2009.

Sources

Periodicals

Associated Press, April 1, 2011.
Associated Press State & Local Wire, September 13, 1998; September 30, 2000.

Billboard, April 3, 1993, p. 84.
Daily News (Los Angeles, CA), August 21, 2000, p. L3.
Globe and Mail (Canada), December 21, 2010, p. R3.
Houston Chronicle, June 8, 2005, sec. STAR, p. 6.
Lincoln Journal Star (NE), February 20, 1998, p. 12.
London Free Press (Ontario, Canada), May 2, 2008, p. C10.
Newsweek, June 15, 1998, p. 62.
O, The Oprah Magazine, February 1, 2008, p. 119.
Pittsburgh Post-Gazette, May 17, 2010, p. C1.
PR Newswire, September 20, 2000; December 20, 2004; October 9, 2008; April 28, 2010.
Republican (Springfield, MA), April 7, 2010, p. C1.
San Francisco Chronicle, May 27, 1998, p. E1.
Spokesman Review (Spokane, WA), May 2, 2000, p. D1.
St. Petersburg Times (FL), April 4, 2011, p. 2B.
U.S. News & World Report, September 27, 1999, p. 63.

Online

"Drew Pinsky," Internet Movie Database, http://www.imdb.com/name/nm0005314/filmotype (May 26, 2011).

—A. Petruso

Kendell J. Powell

Andy Manis/Bloomberg via Getty Images

Chief Executive Officer of General Mills

Born Kendall J. Powell, c. 1954, in Denver, CO. *Education:* Harvard University, B.A., 1976; Stanford University, M.B.A., 1979.

Addresses: *Contact*—1 General Mills Blvd., Minneapolis, MN 55426.

Career

Marketing assistant, General Mills, 1979; marketing director, Cereal Partners UK, 1990; vice president and marketing director, Cereal Partners Worldwide; president, Yoplait, 1996-97; president, Big G Cereals, 1997-98; senior vice president, General Mills, 1998; chief executive officer, Cereal Partners Worldwide, 1999-2004, executive vice president, 2004-06, chief operating officer of US Retail, 2005-06, president of General Mills, 2006—, chief operating officer, 2006-07; chief executive officer, 2007—.

Member: Board, General Mills, 2006—; board, Medtronic, 2007—; John McCain campaign, 2008; McCain-Palin Victory campaign, 2008; board of directors, Minnesota Historical Society; Twin Cities Board, United Way.

Sidelights

Chances are good that most people have eaten something that has been made, packaged, and distributed by General Mills Company. It is one of the largest food companies in the world. General Mills is based in Minneapolis, Minnesota, and began in 1880 by selling Gold Medal Flour, which is still the best-selling flour on the market. In the fiscal year 2010 General Mills' global net sales was approximately $16 billion. Every day around the world General Mills products are eaten for breakfast, lunch, and dinner. The product line of General Mills includes such items as Cheerios cereal, Pillsbury dough, Bisquick biscuit mix, Cascadian Farms frozen fruit, Yoplait yogurt, Nature Valley granola bars, Hamburger Helper, Green Giant vegetables, and Betty Crocker baking mixes. The chief executive officer of General Mills, Kendall J. Powell, is making sure that the company remains profitable and keeps food on tables around the world.

Powell was born in Denver, Colorado. As an undergraduate student he majored in biology and received a bachelor's degree from Harvard University. For his graduate studies he went to Stanford University and attained a master's degree in business administration. Fresh from his master's degree in 1979, Powell was hired as a marketing assistant for General Mills. In his early years with the company he worked in a variety of different assignments and had positions in several different divisions of the company including Yoplait, Betty Crocker, Big G Cereal, and Cereal Partners Worldwide. Cereal Partners Worldwide is a joint partnership between General Mills and the Nestle Corporation. It operates throughout Europe, the Middle East, Africa, Latin America, Asia, and Oceania. Cereal Partners Worldwide is headquartered in Lausanne, Switzerland, and has 14 factories employing almost 4,000 people all over the world. Powell began to learn and advance through successive positions within General Mills and its partners. With each new assignment he learned a different aspect of the company and its operations and took on more and more responsibility.

In 1990 Powell was named as marketing director for Cereal Partners UK which is based in the United Kingdom. After this he became the vice president and marketing director of Cereal Partners Worldwide. During his tenure in this post Cereal Partners Worldwide experienced strong sales growth and developed the markets where it distributes its more than 50 brands of ready-to-eat cereals around the world. He helped to position the company to continue to grow and be profitable.

In 1996 Powell returned to the United States and became the president of Yoplait USA. General Mills is the franchisee for the brand of yogurt that is produced by a company owned by two French holdings, SODIAAL and PAI Partners. The name Yoplait comes from merging the names of the two farmer co-operatives that originally made the yogurt. During the 1990s the slogan for Yoplait yogurt was "Why dip a spoon into anything else?"

After a year and eight months with Yoplait USA, Powell transferred to Big G cereal in October of 1997 to become that division's president. The "Big G" of Big G cereal refers to the cursive letter G that is the division's logo. Big G cereals include such brand names as Cheerios, Chex, Lucky Charms, Total, Trix, and Wheaties. Powell did not stay for long as the president of Big G cereals; he was promoted to senior vice president of General Mills in May of 1998.

The first time that Powell became a chief executive officer was in September of 1999 when he was appointed back to Cereal Partners Worldwide in this capacity. He worked with Cereal Partners Worldwide until August of 2004. That month he once again returned to the parent company and served as executive vice president of General Mills. In May of 2005 Powell was elected executive vice president and chief operating officer of U.S. Retail. In June of 2006, he returned to familiar territory and became the elected president and chief operating officer of General Mills before becoming the chief executive officer on September 24, 2007. He was elected chairman of the board of General Mills in May of 2008.

Maintaining profitability for a food company is not an easy endeavor. The world's food is reliant upon the environment, climate, politics, and world economics. In December of 2010 the Food Price Index (maintained by the Food and Agriculture Organization of the United Nations) soared above the previous high from June of 2009, indicating that the price for all food commodities had increased. The cereal price index for such staples as rice, wheat, and maize showed a 39 percent increase. The cost of producing packaged foods for food companies must go up when the price for the commodities to make the foods goes up, but no food company wants to raise prices on their products if they can find a different way to absorb the cost and remain profitable.

Powell uses what is called "Holistic Margin Management" to make decisions within General Mills in order to keep the company profitable and keep costs down. Powell explained to Christina Veiders of *Supermarket News* that Holistic Margin Management "crosses functions and disciplines. It involves virtually everything, from product development to packaging innovations, convenience to product placement, from manufacturing to logistics to marketing to sales—with the business units taking the lead coordinating role." Under Powell's management this means that everyone looks for opportunities to maximize sales and find ways to cut costs. General Mills is still introducing new products in addition to looking for ways to optimize sales on existing products. For instance, during the Christmas 2010 season the team consisting of people within the marketing, research and development, and sourcing departments at General Mills came together and identified that they wanted to promote Chex rice cereal as being gluten free and that it could be made into Chex Party Mix. They found a new, cheaper supplier for rice and used the savings to advertise Chex rice cereal. Powell told Julie Gallagher of *Supermarket News*, "That contributed to retail sales growth of seven percent on Chex through our first three quarters of [fiscal] 2010, and will deliver significant annual cost savings for the brand." This brand of business savvy under the leadership of Powell has positioned General Mills to potentially continue to grow and maintain profitability into the future.

Sources

"Cereal Partners Worldwide-Nestlé and General Mills," Nestle Cereals, http://www.nestle-cereals.com/cpw/company.html (March 5, 2011).
"Executive Profile: Kendall J. Powell," *Bloomberg BusinessWeek,* http://investing.businessweek.com/businessweek/research/stocks/people/person.asp?personId=27475&ticker=GIS:US (February 14, 2011).

"Food Companies and the Unspoken Price Elephant in the Room," The Source blog, *Wall Street Journal,* http://blogs.wsj.com/source/2011/02/02/food-companies-and-the-unspoken-price-elephant-in-the-room/ (February 22, 2011).

"General Mills: Overview," General Mills, http://www.generalmills.com/~/media/Files/CorporateBrochure_090110_LowRez.ashx (March 5, 2011).

"GENERAL MLS INC Profile," Daily Finance, http://www.dailyfinance.com/company/general-mills-inc/gis/nys (February 22, 2011).

"Kendall J. Powell," General Mills, http://www.generalmills.com/en/Company/Leadership/Kendall_Powell.aspx (February 14, 2011).

"Kendall J. Powell," NNDB, http://www.nndb.com/people/493/00016998.tif3/ (February 14, 2011).

"Profile: Kendall J. Powell, 2009," *Supermarket News,* http://supermarketnews.com/profiles/kendall-powell-2009/ (February 14, 2011).

"Profile: Kendall J. Powell, 2010," *Supermarket News,* http://supermarketnews.com/profiles/kendall-powell-2010/ (February 14, 2011).

—*Annette Bowman*

Navinchandra Ramgoolam

Kamal Kishore/Reuters

Prime minister of Mauritius

Born July 14, 1947, in Mauritius; son of Seewoos-agur (a politician) and Sushil Ramgoolam; married Veena Brizmohun, 1979. *Education:* Royal College of Surgeons—Dublin, diploma-licentiates in medicine and surgery, 1975; London School of Economics and Political Science of the University of London, LLB (honors), 1990; completed vocational course at the Inns of Court School of Law, 1993.

Addresses: *Home*—Clarisse House, 37 Riverwalk, Vacoas, Plaines Wilhems, Mauritius. *Office*—Mauritius Labour Party, 7 Guy Rozemont Sq., Port Louis, Mauritius; Prime Minister's Office, Treasury Bldg., Intendance St., Port Louis, Mauritius.

Career

Medical resident, St. Laurence's Hospital in Dublin, 1975-76; intern, Monaghan County Hospital, Northern Ireland, 1976; resident medical officer, Dr. A. G. Jeetoo Hospital, Port Louis, Mauritius, 1976-77; clinical assistant in cardiology, University College Hospital, London, 1977-81; physician, Amersham General Hospital, Hammersmith Hospital (London), and Nunnery Fields Hospital (Kent), 1981-82; resident medical officer, Yorkshire Clinic, 1982-85; general practitioner in Mauritius, 1985-87; elected leader of the Labour Party of Mauritius, 1991; elected to the National Assembly of Mauritius, 1991; Leader of the Opposition, National Assembly 1991-95 and 2000-05; prime minister of Mauritius, 1995-2000, 2005—.

Awards: Grand Officier de la Légion d'Honneur, France, 2006.

Sidelights

Navinchandra Ramgoolam is only the fourth politician ever to serve as prime minister of the Indian Ocean island nation of Mauritius. The first in that line was his celebrated father, who became prime minister after Mauritius gained independence from Britain in 1968. Trained as both a doctor and a lawyer, Ramgoolam entered politics in the early 1990s when he became leader of the Parti Travailliste, or Labour Party of Mauritius. He served his first term as prime minister from 1995 to 2000, and returned to power again in 2005.

The main international airport in Mauritius is named for Ramgoolam's father, Sir Seewoosagur Ramgoolam, and a secondary school is named in honor of his mother, Lady Sushil Ramgoolam. Ramgoolam's father, whose own father had come to Mauritius from Calcutta, was educated in London and active in post-World War I British Socialist circles. He returned to the island to practice medicine and became involved in the growing movement for increased self-rule and eventual independence from the British Empire. Ramgoolam was born on July 14, 1947, seven years after his father took a seat on the Legislative Council as a Labour

Party representative. In 1948, the nation held its first general election, and the Labour Party won a majority. Twenty years later, Mauritius was granted independence and became a Commonwealth nation.

Ramgoolam's father, often called the father of the nation and known familiarly by Mauritians as "Cha Cha," served as first prime minister from 1968 to 1982 thanks to continued electoral support for the Labour Party. He kept the island on a stable development course and sought increased economic opportunities through foreign investment. The island, which Britain had originally taken from the French back in the Napoleonic Wars of the early nineteenth century, became a favorite tropical stop for wealthy vacationers in the 1960s and '70s, and also promoted its skilled labor force to textile manufacturers.

Ramgoolam was 18 years old when his father was knighted in 1965 as part of Queen Elizabeth II's annual birthday honors. Like many Mauritians hoping to study medicine, he traveled to Ireland for his education, for it was easier to win a place at the Royal College of Surgeons in Dublin than at the Royal College's Edinburgh or London sites. He spent seven years in Dublin, earning diplomas of licentiate from the Royal College of Physicians and Royal College of Surgeons of Ireland, then completing his training at St. Laurence's Hospital in Dublin in Monaghan County, Northern Ireland. In 1976, he returned to Mauritius and was appointed the resident medical officer at Dr. A. G. Jeetoo Hospital in Port Louis, the main city of Mauritius.

Mauritius first appeared on a European map in 1502, though Arab, African, and Indian traders had long visited the volcanic islands on their journey from East Africa or Madagascar—Mauritius' enormous island neighbor—to ports in Asia. Along with several other small islands it is technically known as the Mascarene Islands, after Portuguese explorer Pedro Mascarenhas. The Dutch set up a colony on Mauritius in 1598, naming it in honor of the Prince Maurice of Nassau. They depleted its significant stock of ebony forests, and then established lucrative sugar plantations staffed by slave labor from Madagascar and East Africa. In 1715 the French seized Mauritius and used it as their base of operations for the French East India Company. They lost it in their ongoing sea battles with the British Navy in 1810. Over the next few decades, as slavery ended on the island, British colonial authorities recruited indentured laborers from India. Ramgoolam's family has origins in the Indian state of Bihar, as do many other Mauritians. Though geographically Mauritius is part of sub-Saharan Africa, it considers itself more culturally aligned with the Indian subcontinent.

In 1977, Ramgoolam moved to London to become a clinical assistant in cardiology at University College Hospital. In 1981 and 1982, he trained at three separate medical centers in England, then took a post as resident medical officer of a Yorkshire clinic from 1982 to 1985. His father died in December of 1985, and Ramgoolam returned to the island with his wife, Veena, to practice medicine for two years. Switching careers to law, he enrolled at the London School of Economics and Political Science and was called to the Inner Temple of the United Kingdom Bar in 1993.

By this point Ramgoolam had already launched his career within the ranks of the Mauritius Labour Party. He became head of the party in 1991 and was elected to a seat in the National Assembly (NA) in the general election of 1991. For the next four years, he served as the official Leader of the Opposition in the NA while the Mauritian Militant Movement (MMM) and its offshoot, the Militant Socialist Movement (MSM) held power under Sir Aneerood Jugnauth, who succeeded Ramgoolam's father as prime minister in 1982.

The MMM and MSM gained traction thanks in part to Mauritius' healthy economic growth. Jugnauth's government set up a special export zone to lure retail giants like The Limited, Inc., which shifted some sewing operations to Mauritius. The island was also a signee to the Lomé Agreement, which meant that it had safe worker and fair-wage protection laws for its workers and for that received preferential trade status from European Union governments.

Since 1968, Mauritius had been a nation of the British Commonwealth. It was a parliamentary democracy with the reigning British monarch as head of state but represented there by an appointed governor-general. In 1992, the constitution of Mauritius was amended, with a president to serve as head of state and commander-in-chief. The president was to be elected by the members of the NA, which holds 60 seats.

With its main foe sundered into the MMM and MSM parties, the Labour Party seized an opportunity to return to power: Ramgoolam teamed with the MMM for the 1995 general election, and the alliance won. Ramgoolam was sworn in as only the third prime minister of Mauritius on December 15, 1995. He appointed the head of the MMM, Paul Bérenger, as his deputy prime minister, but fired him in 1997.

Bérenger is a Creole, a term denoting mixed African-European ancestry on Mauritius. The African ancestors were seized as slaves from Madagascar, Mozambique, and other parts of East Africa. Ramgoolam is of Indo-Mauritian descent, which is the largest demographic on the island. There were longstanding tensions between the two main ethnic groups that occasionally erupted into violence. Back in 1968, on the eve of independence, Creole Mauritians carried out acts of arson and violence in predominantly Indian communities. When unrest threatened overseas investments in the early 1970s, Ramgoolam's father declared a state of emergency to maintain control, which stayed in place for much of the decade. In the 1980s, wealthy Europeans who came for the pristine, environmentally unsullied beaches and waters of Mauritius—in contrast to the overdeveloped Mediterranean resorts—were ensconced in luxury compounds whose perimeters were carefully monitored by local law-enforcement authorities to prevent crime. One of the strongest voices of the Creole rights movement was a singer by the name of Kaya—born Joseph Reginald Topize—whose music fused native elements with reggae from the Caribbean world. In February of 1999, Kaya died in police custody, and the news prompted widespread unrest.

Ramgoolam's government lost the next general election, in September of 2000, to a new alliance between Jugnauth and Bérenger's parties. He kept his seat in the Assembly, becoming Opposition Leader once again. In 2005, his Labour Party, after combining forces with several smaller parties into the Alliance Sociale, took a majority of seats. Five years later, another coalition ticket—Alliance de L'Avenir, or Alliance of the Future—helped keep the Labour Party and Ramgoolam in control.

Ramgoolam holds the cabinet posts for Defense, Home Affairs, and External Communications. His administration is still dealing with a controversial decision made by his father on the eve of independence back in 1965, when British government officials pressured the leaders of the Mauritian national movement to accept a deal: hand over the tiny Chagos Archipelago, more than a thousand miles to the east, to the British, in return for a generous foreign-aid package once Mauritius gained independence. The British promised that the 2,000 inhabitants of the atoll would be resettled either on Mauritius or in Britain. The United Nations General Assembly registered its protest over the plan, but Britain gained control of the islands and over the next few years pressured the remaining Chagos Islanders to leave, first by halting ferry service to Mauritius, then imposing further economic hardships on the residents, known as *Ilois* or Chagossians. Britain then leased the archipelago to the U.S. government.

U.S. Navy vessels dropped off the last holdouts from Chagos at Port St. Louis in October of 1971. U.S. military personnel then began constructing an enormous military base on the island of Diego Garcia in the 1970s and '80s. Of strategic importance to the West because of its proximity to both the Arabian Gulf and Southeast Asia, the base at Diego Garcia was used as a staging point for the botched 1980 attempt to rescue American hostages at the U.S. Embassy in Tehran, Iran, and has also been used in the 1991 Gulf War and ongoing military operations against Iraq and Afghanistan. The Ilois, meanwhile, faced discrimination in Mauritius and in Britain, and fought for the return of their homeland. Many Mauritians have also objected to presence of a U.S. military base on what was historically part of their sovereign lands. There have also been allegations that Diego Garcia has been used as a secret site by the Central Intelligence Agency for questioning suspected terrorists.

Over the years, British officials have made various claims that the islands were unpopulated, or populated only by contract laborers, and finally that the Ilois had left willingly, which the deportees had been vehemently denying for decades. In 2010, Diego Garcia was still an American military base, and descendants of the Ilois maintained an ongoing battle in the British legal system for compensation. That same year, Britain moved to have Diego Garcia set aside as a protected marine reserve, but Ramgoolam's government claimed this was in violation of the 1982 United Nations Convention on the Law of the Sea.

Ramgoolam has supported the Ilois' bid to return to the Chagos archipelago permanently. "It is unacceptable that the British claim to protect marine fauna and flora when they insist on denying Chagos-born Mauritians the right to return to their islands all the while," he told *Times* of London correspondent Catherine Philp in March of 2010. "How can you say you will protect coral and fish when you continue to violate the rights of Chagos' former inhabitants?" Later in 2010, Ramgoolam moved decisively after secret diplomatic cables appeared on the Web site WikiLeaks in late 2010, showing that U.S. and British officials discussed the marine-reserve plan as a method of permanently evading any question of resettlement, even if the base was closed after its lease expired in 2014. "I feel strongly about a policy of deceit," a report in the *Guardian* quoted him as saying, and the prime minister added he had long believed the British to be harboring a "hidden agenda."

Sources

Books

Walker, Wendy, "Ramgoolam, Navinchandra (1947-)," in *Worldmark Encyclopedia of the Nations: World Leaders,* 10th ed., vol. 6, Gale Group, 2001.

Periodicals

Guardian (London, England), December 21, 2010; March 7, 2011.

Times (London, England), October 24, 1983, p. 18; December 16, 1985, p. 14; March 6, 2010.

Online

"75 Years of History," Mauritius Labour Party, http://www.labourparty.mu/pages/history/list. php?language_id=2&&info_id=8 (April 1, 2011).

"Prime Minister of the Republic of Mauritius," Republic of Mauritius, http://www.gov.mu/portal/ site/pmsite/menuitem.482a84fe37e55503040. tifd013400b521ca/ (March 30, 2011).

—*Carol Brennan*

José Reyes

Professional baseball player

B orn José Barnabas Reyes, June 11, 1983, in Villa Gonzalez, Dominican Republic; son of José Manuel and Josefina "Rosa" Reyes; married Katherine Ramirez, July 25, 2008.

Addresses: *Office*—c/o New York Mets, Citi Field, 12601 Roosevelt Ave., Flushing, NY 11368.

Career

S igned with New York Mets and played in the minor league teams, 1999-2002; shortstop, New York Mets, 2003—.

Awards: Larry Doby Award, MLB All-Star Futures Game, 2002; Minor League Player of the Year, *USA Today*, 2002; Player of the Week Award, National League, 2006 (twice); Silver Slugger Award, National League; Player of the Month Award, National League, April 2007.

Sidelights

J osé Reyes is a baseball player who has played for the New York Mets since 2003. He is noted for his gregarious personality, his coordination, and his ability to steal bases. His career has been marked by several injuries and downturns, but by 2011 he was a top player in the National League. Reyes was born in Villa Gonzalez in the Dominican Republic in 1983, the son of José Manuel and Josefina "Rosa" Reyes. He grew up in the village of Palmar Arriba, outside of Santiago. His family, like most of their

© *Scott Cunningham/Getty Images*

neighbors, did not have much money; they lived on a dirt road and did not have indoor plumbing, but Reyes and his sister, Meosote, never went hungry, and when Reyes began showing his innate athletic talent as a boy, his parents made sure that he got enough food to grow up strong and healthy.

Reyes' father and most of his friends played informal baseball games on a rough, homemade diamond. He was not particularly interested in the sport until he was around ten years old, and when he was about 12, he began playing every chance he got. He could not afford a catcher's mitt, so he made one out of a milk carton or played barehanded. By the time he was 15, he was the best player in town, and already had a fan base of neighbors who traveled to cheer him on when his youth league played in away games.

Because his family did not own a television, Reyes never saw any big-league games and he was free to evolve his own playing style. Before he was 16, he was already learning to switch-hit. In that same year, 1999, he went to a Mets tryout camp in Santiago. Eddy Toledo and Juan Mercado, scouts for the Mets, were immediately impressed by his strong pitching, coordination, and personal charm; however, at six feet tall and 130 pounds, Reyes seemed too skinny to be a ballplayer, and the scouts had to convince Mets general manager Jim Duquette to sign him. Reyes signed with the Mets in August of that year; he gave his $22,000 signing bonus to his parents, who used it to open a small store.

Reyes worked his way through the team's minor league, and by 2003 was ready for the major league. On June 10, 2003, he played in his first major league game, against the Texas Rangers, showing impressive skill and form. That great first season ended early for Reyes when he sprained his ankle, but for a rookie he did remarkably well, batting .307 with 32 RBIs (runs batted in) and 13 stolen bases.

In 2004 the Mets put Kazuo Matsui in the shortstop position, so Reyes had to play second base. In addition, early in the season he strained a hamstring and was on the disabled list (DL) until June 19. This injury, coupled with back pain and injuries among other Mets players led to the team's hovering around last place in the division.

In the 2005 season Reyes had a solid performance, with 733 appearances at the plate and only 27 walks. He also had 48 extra base hits, 60 stolen bases, and 58 RBIs. In 2006 the Mets hired Rickey Henderson to teach Reyes the finer points of getting on base and stealing bases, for which Henderson was known. In mid-June Reyes was playing excellently, with 30 hits in 57 at-bats, giving him a .526 batting average for that period; he was voted Player of the Week in the National League for two weeks in a row. In 2006 he won a Silver Slugger Award. The Mets made the playoffs that year, a thrilling event for Reyes. The Mets lost the playoffs after an exciting series, but Reyes played very well and was chosen to play in that year's Major League Baseball All-Star Series.

During the 2006 season Reyes also became known for his complicated handshakes, used to celebrate runs with other Mets, and his Spanish-language lessons given to fans in between innings on the stadium's giant screen. His personality, as well as his skills, made him a favorite among fans.

In August of 2007 he hit three home runs against the Philadelphia Phillies, and later became only the second player in Mets history to have 50 or more stolen bases in two consecutive seasons. Reyes played well until the end of the season, when he fell into a slump, batting .205 and ending the season with a .280 batting average. His exuberant dances and handshakes, formerly endearing to fans, were viewed as a silly distraction, and in 2008 he

decided to spend more energy on baseball and less on grandstanding to fans. On September 10 he set a new Mets record for stolen bases, with 282 stolen bases. On September 23, 2008, he reached 200 hits for the season, only the second Met ever to do so. He finished out the season with a batting average of .297.

In early 2009, Reyes injured his calf and ended up on the DL. While training to return to play, he incurred another injury and remained out of the game all summer; he then injured himself again in August, ending any hopes of playing that year. In March of 2010, Reyes was diagnosed with thyroid disease and had to stop playing for a while, missing the start of the season, but he came back and on May 25 he made his 1,000th career hit. He was chosen for the All-Star Team that year, but because of an injury, had to forego playing.

The season of 2011 saw Reyes stealing his 260th base, making him one of the top 100 all-time major-league base stealers. By July of that year Reyes was leading the National League with a .347 batting average. Once again, he was chosen for the All-Star Game but could not play because of an injury.

By 2011, Reyes and the Mets as a team were at a crossroads. Reyes was in his prime, playing at his peak. He was leading the National League in batting, hits, triples, and runs. Whether the Mets would trade him or re-sign him, and even whether they could afford to re-sign him, were hot topics in the baseball world, but Reyes decided that he would not discuss any contract negotiations until the end of the season.

Sources

Peroidicals

Daily News (New York), July 26, 2008.

Online

"Jose Reyes," Jockbio, http://www.jockbio.com/Bios/Reyes/Reyes_bio.html (July 20, 2011).
"Jose Reyes," New York Mets Official Site, http://newyork.mets.mlb.com/team/player.jsp?player_id=408314 (July 20, 2011),
"Reyes: Just What Game, and Mets, Need but His Future is a Mystery," *Sports Illustrated*, http://sportsillustrated.cnn.com/2011/writers/tom_verducci/06/21/jose.reyes.mets/index.html?sct=mlb_t11_a1 (July 12, 2011).

—*Kelly Winters*

Ryan Reynolds

Actor

Born Ryan Rodney Reynolds, October 23, 1976, in Vancouver, British Columbia, Canada; son of Jim (a former Mountie and food wholesaler) and Tammy (a retail store salesperson) Reynolds; married Scarlett Johansson (an actress), September 27, 2008 (filed for divorce, December 23, 2010). *Education:* Attended Kwantlen College.

Addresses: *Agent*—William Morris Endeavor Entertainment, 9601 Wilshire Blvd., 3rd Fl., Beverly Hills, CA 90210. *Contact*—c/o Dark Trick Films, 421 North Beverly Dr. Ste. 300, Beverly Hills, CA 90210.

Career

Actor on television, including: *Fifteen,* 1991-93; *The Odyssey,* 1993-94; *My Name Is Kate* (movie), 1994; *Lonesome Dove: The Outlaw Years,* 1995; *The Marshal,* 1995; *Serving in Silence: The Margarethe Cammermeyer Story* (movie), 1995; *The Outer Limits,* 1995, 1997, 1998; *In Cold Blood* (movie), CBS, 1996; *Sabrina the Teenage Witch* (movie), 1996; *A Secret Between Friends: A Moment of Truth Movie* (movie), 1996; *The X-Files,* FOX, 1996; *Tourist Trap* (movie), 1998; *Two Guys, a Girl and a Pizza Place,* ABC, 1998-2001; *Scrubs,* NBC, 2003; *Zeroman,* 2004-05; *School of Life* (movie), 2005; *My Boys,* TBS, 2007. Film appearances include: *Ordinary Magic,* 1993; *The Alarmist,* 1997; *Coming Soon,* 1999; *Dick,* 1999; *Big Monster on Campus,* 2000; *We All Fall Down,* 2000; *Finder's Fee,* 2001; *Buying the Cow,* 2002; *Van Wilder,* 2002; *Foolproof,* 2003; *The In-Laws,* 2003; *Blade: Trinity,* 2004; *Harold & Kumar Go to White Castle,* 2004; *The Amityville Horror,* 2005; *Just Friends,* 2005; *Waiting ...,* 2005; *Smokin' Aces,* 2006; *The Nines,* 2007; *Adventureland,* 2008; *Chaos Theory,*

Christopher Halloran/Shutterstock.com

2008; *Definitely, Maybe,* 2008; *Fireflies in the Garden,* 2008; *Paper Man,* 2009; *The Proposal,* 2009; *X-Men Origins: Wolverine,* 2009; *Buried,* 2010; *Green Lantern,* 2011.

Awards: Young Artist Award for next generation—male, Young Artist Foundation, 2003; Teen Choice Award for choice movie scary scene, FOX Network, for *The Amityville Horror,* 2005.

Sidelights

While Canadian actor Ryan Reynolds first came to fame on the situation comedy *Two Guys, a Girl, and a Pizza Place* in the late 1990s and early 2000s, he became better known as a film star after the show's run ended. His first notable hit was *Van Wilder,* and though comedy was his forte, Reynolds proved to be an actor with range. He had notable roles in horror films like *The Amityville Horror,* action films like *Blade: Trinity,* thrillers like *Foolproof,* and dramas like *Buried.* Of his career, Reynolds told Barbara Vancheri of the *Pittsburgh Post-Gazette,* "I was very fortunate to have success be incredibly incremental for me, it was an inch as a time. Because of that, I think it afforded me an opportunity to be working in different genres a lot."

Born on October 23, 1976, in Vancouver, British Columbia, Canada, he was the son of Jim and Tammy Reynolds. His father was a former Mountie and food wholesaler in that city while his mother worked in retail sales. The youngest of four boys, Reynolds began acting professionally as a teenager. His first role was in the *Beverly Hills 90210* knockoff *Fifteen*, which aired on Nickelodeon and on which he appeared from 1991 and 1993. Though the series featured many Canadian actors, it was shot in Florida, where Reynolds primarily lived during that time period. His work as Billy garnered him a Youth in Film Award nomination. He made his first film when he was 14 years old, 1993's *Ordinary Magic*.

After *Fifteen* ended its run, Reynolds returned to Vancouver where he took improv comedy classes and completed high school. While living there, he continued to act, primarily on television. From 1993 to 1994, Reynolds appeared on the series *The Odyssey*, as well as television movies like 1994's *My Name Is Kate*, 1995's *Serving in Silence: The Margarethe Cammermeyer Story*, and 1996's *In Cold Blood*. He also appeared in guest spots on the series *The Marshal* and *Lonesome Dove: The Outlaw Years*, also in 1995.

After Reynolds graduated from high school, he became disillusioned with acting, especially the roles he had in television movies. He told Glen Schaefer of the *Vancouver Province*, "I got tired of doing all these movies of the week. It was so uncreative. It was the disease of the week, playing the angry son that has to carry the drunk Donna Mills up the stairs every scene." He quit acting and began working in a Safeway grocery store as a shelf stocker on the overnight shift. Reynolds enjoyed his year working there, telling Schaefer, "I still look back on it as one of my favorite jobs because I was laughing the whole time—some truly great comedic minds inhabit these grocery stores from midnight to 8 a.m. The majority of the time it was a big food fight."

One morning after Reynolds' shift at Safeway, he met another Vancouver actor and friend, Chris William Martin, who convinced him to move to Los Angeles and pursue acting. When they first made the move with fellow actor Jonathan Scarfe, they lived in a cheap motel in Los Angeles. The first night in the city, Reynolds' jeep was stolen and recovered without its doors. He was forced to drive it that way for the next four months. While Reynolds struggled for a time as an actor, he auditioned regularly and was confident in his abilities. He told Marke Andrews of the *Vancouver Sun*, "I knew I could do sitcoms, but I just needed to have someone see me. The auditions were frustrating, because they would look at you, but not really notice you. Then, at one audition, the woman cocked her head and I thought, 'I have a chance.'"

Reynolds had a break in 1997 when he was cast in a new situation comedy, *Two Guys, a Girl and a Pizza Place*, as the smart alecky Berg. The show began airing in 1998, and was panned by critics for being mediocre and a stereotypical sitcom. Despite the negative reviews and limited audience after season one, its network, ABC, decided to give it a second chance. The show was revamped by Kevin Abbott, who had worked on the long-running hit *Roseanne*. The new version, later known as *Two Guys and a Girl*, became a minor hit. It aired through 2001 before being cancelled.

Though *Two Guys and a Girl* garnered only a small but loyal audience, Reynolds was the breakout star of the show and began appearing in film roles during its run. The actor had small parts in films like 1999's *Coming Soon* and *Dick*. He also appeared in both *Big Monster on Campus* and *We All Fall Down*, as well as *Finder's Fee* in 2001.

In 2002, Reynolds appeared in *Van Wilder*, his first major starring role. The film was a low-budget, raunchy college sex comedy in which he played a party guy and big man on campus who stays in college for the social life. His seven years in college threaten to come to an end when his wealthy father cuts him off, and Wilder has to put his skills to use as a party liaison to complete his degree. Reynolds was involved with the project from early drafts of the script and helped mold the film and his character. Labeled an updated version of *Animal House*, *Van Wilder* was shot primarily on the UCLA campus for $6 million, but the final product so impressed the film's backer, Artisan Films, that they invested $21 million promoting it.

Describing *Van Wilder*, Reynolds told Barrett Hooper of the *National Post*, "We weren't making *Apocalypse Van* or *National Lampoon's Sense and Sensibility*. It's more like *National Lampoon's Ferris Bueller*." Of his character, Reynolds told Hooper, "He has an ego in a Sam Malone kind of way but still remains a grounded person." *Van Wilder* was a minor hit and gave Reynolds a fun-loving reputation that followed him everywhere for years. Despite this success, he was ready to break out of the comedy mold and try working in different genres.

While many of Reynolds' film roles over the next few years were in comedies like 2003's *The In-Laws*, 2004's *Harold & Kumar Go to White Castle*, and 2005's *Just Friends*, he also sought out roles in other genres. In 2003, he appeared in the plot-heavy crime thriller *Foolproof*, while in 2004 he played the witty, outspoken vampire slayer Hannibal King in *Blade: Trinity*, an action-horror film, to much acclaim.

Of the role in *Blade: Trinity*, Reynolds told Jay Stone of the *Windsor Star*, "For me, it was a dream come true in terms of a role. In comic books you can imbue all the traits I love so much about Indiana Jones: these guys who get to be irreverent and not take themselves so seriously, and yet they also get to be the hero. That's the childhood dream part of it. I certainly couldn't do a film in this particular genre if I was just intermittently clinching my jaw muscles."

In 2005, Reynolds pushed himself further in a remake of *The Amityville Horror.* He played George, a new husband who becomes nasty and terrifying every time he is in his family's new home and eventually gives in to the evil in the house. The bearded Reynolds was hardly recognizable to fans of *Two Guys and a Girl* or *Van Wilder.* Though the horror film was not a particular success, it showed Reynolds' range as an actor and also contributed to making a greater variety of roles available to him.

After playing an FBI agent in the 2006 crime drama *Smoking Aces,* Reynolds was deeply affected by his turn in the extremely low-budget 2007 film *The Nines.* Made for less than a million dollars, Reynolds greatly enjoyed the process and the characters he played: an actor, a videogame designer, and writer whose lives are linked. Because of the experience, he became more selective in his roles and looked for certain types of films and more dynamic parts.

By 2008, Reynolds was seen as a leading man and had three major films released, including the romantic comedy *Definitely, Maybe.* Playing a political consultant on the verge of divorce, he has to explain to his ten-year-old daughter how he met and married her mother. The role required him to be more vulnerable and open as the film looks back at the loves of his character's life in flashbacks as his daughter guesses which one became his soon-to-be ex-wife. Reynolds connected with the script, telling Rachel Leibrock of the *Sacramento Bee,* "I was so moved by the journey Will takes with his daughter—not just to heal himself but to prepare for what's going to be a pretty rough road ahead. It brought me to tears when I was reading the script."

In 2009, Reynolds had roles in four films that showed off his range. For example, he appeared as the smooth-talking lothario Brad in the independent coming-of-age comedy *Adventureland.* The film's director, Greg Mottola, told Emma Rosenblum of *New York Magazine,* "I was looking for someone who could play against type, and it struck me that Ryan would be interesting playing wounded male pride. He created a nice tension by pulling way back on his natural charm. He's a smart actor; he understands that even people who behave badly have their reasons."

Also in 2009, Reynolds played the put-out assistant in the satiric romantic comedy *The Proposal.* The latter was a major hit in which Reynolds co-starred with Sandra Bullock. In the film, Bullock plays a high-powered Canadian book editor living in New York and facing deportation unless she marries. She tells immigration authorities that Ryan's character, her long-suffering assistant, is her fiancé. He only agrees to go along with the marriage if she will make him an editor and visit Alaska to meet his odd family. The film became one of the biggest hits of his career, taking in more than $300 million worldwide. Reynolds appeared in the comic book-inspired *X-Men Origins: Wolverine* as Wade Wilson/Deadpool and had a supporting role in the gentle comedy *Paper Man* in 2009 as well.

In 2010, Reynolds took on one of the most challenging roles of his career when appeared in *Buried.* In the film, he plays a civilian truck driver in Iraq who wakes up buried alive after a suffering a head injury and must get his ransom paid using a cell phone left in the box with him before he dies. Because of the challenges of playing the role, including more than two weeks spent inside a coffin, Reynolds became more appreciative of other film experiences. He also had to deal with emotional stress created by the role. It took him to unexpected places and made him deal with raw and frightening emotions. The film was a hit on the festival circuit.

Reynolds took on new, physical challenges when he played the superhero Green Lantern in a film set for release in the summer of 2011. He had previously expressed interest in playing the Flash, if DC Comics ever made a film adaptation, but no such project reached fruition. The hard-working Reynolds had a number of other films scheduled for 2011 and 2012 including *The Change-Up, The Croods,* and *Safe House.*

Reynolds was often in the news for other reasons as well. At the end of 2010, he received an unexpected honor when he was named the "Sexiest Man Alive" by *People* magazine. Reynolds was regularly the subject of celebrity news items, first for his long relationship with singer/actress Alanis Morrisette, to whom he was engaged from June 2004 to June 2006. In 2008, Reynolds married actress Scarlett Johansson. The couple separated late in 2010, and he filed for divorce on December 23, 2010.

Of his acting career, the amiable Reynolds told George M. Thomas of the *Akron Beacon Journal*, "I don't have a big trajectory in mind. I think I attribute most of my success to just the complete absence of expectation. So I'm always surprised, and I'm always happy with the new challenges that I take on. I don't place upon myself a tremendous amount of expectation, because that's a recipe for letdown. I want to continue growing and stretching as an actor."

Sources

Periodicals

Akron Beacon Journal (OH), December 10, 2004, p. E2.
Birmingham Post, April 14, 2005, p. 12.
Canwest News Service, October 1, 2010; December 23, 2010.
Daily News (NY), December 16, 2010, p. 5.
Globe and Mail (Canada), December 3, 2004, p. R39; October 1, 2010, p. R4.
Los Angeles Times, September 23, 2010, p. D1.
National Post (Canada), April 3, 2002, p. B1; February 11, 2008, p. AL4.
New York Magazine, May 4, 2009.
Pittsburgh Post-Gazette, October 8, 2010, p. E1.
Sacramento Bee (CA), February 10, 2008, p. TK6.
San Francisco Chronicle, November 23, 2005, p. E1; June 12, 2009, p. E1.
Toronto Star, June 11, 2009, p. E1.
Toronto Sun, October 3, 2003, p. E5.
Vancouver Province (British Columbia, Canada), April 1, 2002, p. B3.
Vancouver Sun (British Columbia, Canada), April 5, 2002, p. F1; November 18, 2010, p. C6.
Windsor Star (Ontario, Canada), April 3, 2002, p. B6; December 6, 2004, p. B3.

Online

"Ryan Reynolds (I)," Internet Movie Database, http://www.imdb.com/name/nm0005351/ (February 22, 2011).

—A. Petruso

Michelle Rhee

© ms4/ZUMA Press/newscom

Public school chancellor and teacher

Born December 25, 1969, in Ann Arbor, MI; daughter of Shang (a doctor) and Inza (a retailer) Rhee; married Kevin Huffman (divorced); married Kevin Johnson (a mayor and former professional basketball player), September 2011; children: Starr, Olivia (first marriage). *Education:* Cornell University, B.A., 1992; John F. Kennedy School of Government, Harvard University, M.P.P., 1997.

Addresses: *Office*—StudentsFirst, P.O. Box 5280, Sacramento, CA 95817.

Career

Joined Teach for America, 1992; teacher, Harlem Park Community School District, Baltimore, MD, 1993-96; founder, president, and chief executive officer, New Teacher Project, 1997-2007; chancellor, Washington, D.C. public schools, 2007-10; served on Florida Governor-elect Rick Scott's Education Transition Team, 2010-11; founded StudentsFirst (an advocacy group), 2010.

Awards: Women of Genius Award, Trinity Washington, 2007.

Sidelights

Unflappable and full of candor, Michelle Rhee became nationally known as an advocate of strong education reform in the United States. Gaining national attention for her contentious time as the head of the Washington, D.C. school district,

Rhee began her career as a Teach for America educator in Baltimore. Endlessly pushing for teacher accountability and doing what is best for students, Rhee was a lightning rod for controversy during her time in D.C. Rhee affected real change during her three years on the job, and went on to found a national education advocacy group, StudentsFirst. She had previously founded and helmed the teacher recruiting non-profit, the New Teacher Project. Her mentor, Joel Klein, who was the head the New York City public school system, told Evan Thomas, Eve Conant, and Pat Wingert of *Newsweek*, "She is without guile, so rare in public life."

Born on December 25, 1969, in Ann Arbor, Michigan, Rhee was the daughter of Shang and Inza Rhee. Her parents were Korean immigrants, and her father became a doctor while her mother owned a women's clothing store. She was raised primarily in Toledo, Ohio, and was an academic high achiever attending private schools for middle and high school. She had no clear career direction when she entered Cornell University, or when she earned her bachelor of arts degree in 1992. She then joined Teach for America. This program, founded by a Princeton University student, funneled bright college students into teaching positions at inner-city schools for at least a year. Of the program, Rhee told Lucia Graves of the *U.S. News & World Report*,

"I think what Teach for America has done quite brilliantly is to create something that's compelling and inspiring to people but also is going to be attractive to high-achieving people because it's very selective."

Rhee was assigned to work as a teacher the Harlem Park Community School District in Baltimore, Maryland. She taught second grade from 1993 to 1996 in one of the lowest-performing schools located in an underprivileged neighborhood. Rhee admitted to experiencing culture shock when she began teaching there. Most of her first year in the school, she suffered from extreme stress symptoms because she could not control her classroom. Her mother even encouraged her to apply to law school instead of return after Christmas break, but her father thought she should return. Rhee spent much of the next two years working hard with another teacher to improve as an educator and help her students have the educational experience she thought they deserved. Their standardized test scores greatly improved, becoming among the best in the district, in part because she gave them two hours of homework a night and had them come into school on Saturdays.

Rhee believed that it was her actions as a teacher that made the difference for the 70 kids in her charge in this time period. Instead of accepting that poor test results came from the often distressing environment in which the children were living, Rhee believed that teachers could be the catalyst to change. Referring to her 70 students, she told Thomas, Conant, and Wingert of *Newsweek*, "It drives me nuts when people say that two thirds of a kid's academic achievement is based on their environment. That is B.S. Those kids, where they lived didn't change. Their parents didn't change. Their diets didn't change. The violence in the community didn't change. The only thing that changed for those 70 kids was the adults who were in front of them every single day teaching them." She added to Lucia Graves of *U.S. News & World Report*, "People say that kids are disadvantaged because they come from poor homes or whatever. But the bottom line is that, if kids have teachers with extraordinarily high expectations of them, if they work hard and do the right things, they can absolutely achieve at the highest levels."

After leaving Baltimore in 1996, Rhee founded her own education organization, the New Teacher Project. She also served as president and chief executive officer of this national non-profit. It recruited gifted teachers to work in inner-city schools that found it hard to land quality educators willing to take jobs in their schools. She also started a family

with her first husband, Kevin Huffman, giving birth to two daughters, Starr and Olivia. In addition, Rhee earned a master of public policy degree from the John F. Kennedy School of Government at Harvard University.

In 2007, Rhee took on new, unexpected challenges when she agreed to become the chancellor of Washington, D.C. public schools, after initially turning it down and despite her lack of experience. Hired by the city's new mayor, Adrian Fenty, she was charged with reforming the notoriously poor school system. Though the Washington, D.C., school district spent more than every other big school district in the United States (except New York City), it had the lowest test scores and a poor reputation. Math and reading skills for many students were two or three years behind most other students in the United States. The D.C. school board fought reform efforts for years. Bureaucracy around the schools was known for its incompetence and distension, and its entrenched resistance to reform as well.

Rhee wanted to make radical changes to see results, and Fenty gave her backing, saying he would risk his own reputation to support her to make schools better. Rhee told Martha Brant of *Newsweek*, "If the rules don't make sense for kids, I'm not going to follow them. I don't care how much trouble we get in." Fenty backed Rhee, and her sometimes politically incorrect ways, from the first. To support her, he took away power held by the Washington D.C. school board, and gave her millions more in funding when she needed it.

Soon after taking the post, Rhee showed how she would challenge the status quo. She announced that she would fire more than 100 non-union administrative workers from their posts, fire 36 principals, and close 23 schools because they were not needed by the shrinking school system. This announcement riled both local unions and parents, as did her take-charge attitude. Also controversial was her meeting with school principals and telling them that they could lose their positions if test scores did not improve. Rhee became immersed in the job, involving herself even in seemingly mundane issues like repairing broken water fountains. Because of some of her actions, Rhee was screamed at and had things thrown at her by unhappy parents. She took it in stride, telling Thomas, Conant, and Wingert of *Newsweek*, "I don't take things personally."

Such an attitude helped Rhee as she worked to change the culture of the D.C. school system. She believed that the interests of teachers and administrators had been given more value than the interests of children and their classroom experience. Rhee did not believe that effectiveness in the classroom was more important than protecting the jobs of teachers, but had to fight the teachers' union to affect this change. While many affiliated with the school system disliked Rhee and her actions, she had supporters as well. PTA (Parent Teacher Association) co-chair Claire Taylor told Thomas, Conant, and Wingert of *Newsweek*, "Rhee's making decisions that should have been made years ago, and she's accountable for those decisions. And that is what is so disarming to parents who have been traumatized by this school system." Taylor added, "She clearly is a brave person. I have been in rooms where parents are hysterically upset and she walks in so quietly respectful, telegraphing accountability, and says 'I'm gonna do something you may not like, but it's for the good of the children, and I'm doing it, it's all me.'"

By 2008, Rhee had gotten rid of more central office employees, principals, and paraprofessionals. She offered buyouts to 700 teachers and put pressure on many more to leave, while bringing in ever greater numbers of Teach for America educators. A related major fight that Rhee took on was personally negotiating a new contract with the teachers' union. Her proposal involved teachers giving up tenure in exchange for becoming among the best paid in the country, but with the caveat that they could be fired if they prove themselves unable to perform well in the classroom during a one-year probationary period. Taking this deal would be optional for teachers already on staff, though all new teachers would be required to take it. Those who chose not to take the first deal would receive pay increases but lose the right to seniority, which meant that if their school closed or was overhauled, they could be out of a job. Also included in the contract was an increase in the amount of resources and professional development programs to which teachers had access. The union was very divided over whether or not to take the deal Rhee proposed, with many in the union resistant to the terms. After two years of negotiations, a version of Rhee's proposal passed.

Rhee was not done cleaning house. In July of 2010, Rhee fired more than 240 teachers and put another 731 on notice that they needed to improve within a year or leave; however, Rhee's controversial tenure as chancellor of Washington, D.C. public schools came to an end in October of 2010 when Fenty lost in his bid for re-election to Vince Gray. She stepped down, having made progress toward her and Fenty's goals of D.C. public schools becoming the highest-performing urban-school system in the country, closing the achievement gap between black and white students, and making the schools the first choice for families living in the district. On her last day in the post, Rhee took part in a ceremony that honored the 662 most effective teachers, held in the Kennedy Center for the Performing Arts. She later admitted she wished that her communication with the community and others had been more effective during her tenure.

By December of 2010, Rhee was serving as a member of Florida Governor-elect Rick Scott's Education Transition Team. In this position, she helped guide his education policy and the education-related choices he made as he took office. Also that month, Rhee announced the founding of a new education-related organization, StudentsFirst. A member-driven advocacy and lobbying group, it would support reform-focused political candidates and encourage policy changes around the country. Her goal was to affect positive change in public education through diversity, choice, efficiency, and community involvement. Its agenda focused on teaching as a profession, giving families empowering information, and encouraging accountability. Discussing the goals of StudentsFirst, Rhee told Christine Armario of the Associated Press, "These policies are a major disruption to the status quo. But at the same time, we believe it's really hard to argue against the things that we are pushing." Rhee hoped to raise one billion dollars in one year to support StudentsFirst, gain one million members, and work on the local, state, and national levels. Politics also seemed to be in her future as she hired a lobbyist in June of 2011 and looked to enter a race in her new home state of California.

As Rhee became a national spokeswoman for education reform and appeared in numerous magazines and on a variety of television shows, she received a lot of support but also was a source of controversy because of what happened during her tenure in D.C. and because of her outspoken beliefs about changes she believed needed to be made to improve education in the United States. Yet other states were adopting proposals similar to hers, including Indiana, Colorado, Ohio, and Idaho. Describing the problem of education in the United States to Harry Jaffe of the *Washingtonian*, Rhee said, "This country is in a significant crisis in education, and we don't know it. If you look at other countries, like Singapore—Singapore's knocking it out of the box. Why? Because the number-one strategy in their economic plan is education. We treat education as a social issue. And I'll tell you what happens with social issues: When the budget crunch comes, they get swept under the rug, they get pushed aside. We have to start treating education as an economic issue. We need America to become number one again, and the one thing that can drive us toward that is competition."

Sources

Associated Press, January 10, 2011.

Christian Science Monitor, December 6, 2010.

National Journal, December 6, 2010.

Newsweek, January 7, 2008, p. 64; September 1, 2008, p 54.

New York Times, November 13, 2008, p. A1.

Sacramento Bee, December 8, 2010, p. A1; June 11, 2011, p. A3.

South Florida Sun-Sentinel (Fort Lauderdale, FL), December 3, 2010.

U.S. News & World Report, October 27, 2008, p. 62; January 1, 2010, 38.

Washingtonian, December 2010, pp. 27-28, 30-32.

Washington Post, December 13, 2010, p. B4.

Washington Times, May 25, 2011, p. 1.

—*A. Petruso*

Ransom Riggs

Author

Born c. 1979 in Maryland; married. *Education:* Kenyon College, Gambier, OH, B.A.; University of Southern California, M.F.A.

Addresses: *Management*—Heroes and Villains Entertainment, 1041 N. Formosa Ave., Formosa Bldg., Ste. 202, Los Angeles, CA 90046. *Web site*—http://www.ransomriggs.com.

Career

Worked on several short films, including *Timing*, *Skinny Leg Blues*, and *Oblivion, Nebraska*, all 2006; wrote and directed short films, including *Spaceboy*, and *Portable Living Room*, both 2006; blogged for Mental Floss Web site, 2006-11; producer for short film *4?*, 2008; writer and voice director for video game *Infamous*, 2009; published *The Sherlock Holmes Handbook*, 2009; published *Miss Peregrine's Home for Peculiar Children*, 2011; published *Talking Pictures*, 2012.

Awards: Silver Award for best short film, WorldFest Houston International Film Festival, for *Portable Living Room*, 2007.

Sidelights

Author Ransom Riggs spent years working in the film industry and as a non-fiction writer before breaking out to widespread critical and commercial notice with his best-selling 2011 young adult debut, *Miss Peregrine's Home for Peculiar Children*. A dark tale weaving quirky characters and at times unsettling vintage photographs, the book was quickly optioned for production as a motion picture, with director Tim Burton attached to the project by the end of 2011. Riggs has himself worked as a screenwriter, producer, and director, helming short films, including *Spaceboy* and the award-winning *Portable Living Room*. As a longtime blogger for Web site Mental Floss, Riggs often featured found photographs with comic captions that led to the creation of a 2012 print collection, *Talking Pictures*.

Born around 1979 in rural Maryland, Riggs moved with his family to southern Florida when he was about five years old. Growing up in a place that the author later characterized on his Web site as having "lots and lots of old people and not very much for kids to do," Riggs became interested in storytelling as a way to entertain himself and his friends. He began writing and making home movies, delving into two fields that would later define his adult work. Riggs studied the former skill as a teen at the University of Virginia's Young Writer's Workshop and, later, as a student majoring in English at Ohio's Kenyon College before returning to the latter interest as a graduate student in the University of Southern California's Film School. There, he earned an master of fine arts degree in film production.

During and after his graduate studies, Riggs honed his skills as a short filmmaker. He worked on the crew of several 2006 shorts, including *Timing*, *Skinny Leg Blues*, and *Oblivion, Nebraska*, as well as writing and directing the short *Portable Living Room*. This piece, which depicted the imaginative world of a boy on a dull visit to his grandmother's house, garnered Riggs a Silver Award for best short film at the 2007 WorldFest Houston International Film Festival. Another Riggs-penned and -helmed graduate school short, *Spaceboy*, about a teenage boy who believes that he is actually an alien, was screened to positive reception at the Boston Science Fiction Film Festival that same year. In 2008, Riggs served as a producer on the short film *4?*, which told the story of a innocent man accused of a crime. Riggs also contributed as a writer and voice director to the 2009 video game *Infamous*.

During this period, Riggs also pursued work as a print and online writer. He was a regular blogger on the Web site *Mental Floss* from 2006 until 2011, posting on topics ranging from unusual stories spotted on the Internet to striking geographic landscapes that he photographed while traveling. In 2009, independent publisher Quirk published Riggs' printed debut, *The Sherlock Holmes Handbook: The Method and Mysteries of the World's Greatest Detective*. A mock-earnest instructional manual seeking to inform readers on to employ some of the legendary sleuth's skills for themselves, the *Sherlock Holmes Handbook* covered such topics as "How to Analyze Footprints" and "How to Survive a Plunge Over a Waterfall."

Riggs published his first fictional book, *Miss Peregrine's Home for Peculiar Children*, in June of 2011. A dark young adult story, the work follows the journey of a teenage boy named Jacob as he searches for—and visits—an unusual orphanage that his grandfather has told him stories about. There, Jacob meets a group of children called the Peculiars that Ruel S. De Vera of the *Philippine Daily Inquirer* noted were "each ... a startlingly original creation." Riggs supplemented the written descriptions of his tale with dozens of strikingly odd photographs that he had collected over the years. "They inspired the story," he explained to Mark Medley of the *National Post*. "I quickly discovered that photos of children from 80 or 100 years ago are almost universally creepy in some sort of undefinable way." This innovative storytelling technique led Laurel Bliss of *Library Journal* to dub the story "an original work that defies categorization," while *Publishers Weekly* hailed it as "an enjoyable, eccentric read." Audiences agreed, sending the book up the *New York Times* children's best-seller list shortly after its appearance on shelves.

The unusual characters and dark setting of *Miss Peregrine's Home for Peculiar Children* caught the attention of Hollywood even before its release, with film studio Twentieth Century Fox acquiring production rights in May of 2011. That fall, media outlets began reporting that director Tim Burton—known for such untradional takes on children's entertainment as *The Nightmare Before Christmas* and *Charlie and the Chocolate Factory*—had began negotiations to bring Riggs' story to the silver screen.

A few months after the publication of *Miss Peregrine's Home for Peculiar Children*, Riggs signed on with publisher Little, Brown to release two more books for young readers. The first of these, *Arcanum*, describes the effects of a discovery of a collection of unusual items in a small town museum attic by a group of local teens in what Rachel Deahl of *Publishers Weekly* dubbed, a "dark, creepy, and frightening story." Slated for release in 2014, the book presumably reflects Riggs' fascination with the name of the town of Arcanum, located in Darke County, Ohio; writing on his *Mental Floss* blog earlier in 2011, the author had enthusiastically declared that he believed Arcanum—a name meaning "deep, secret knowledge" in Latin—to be "a place where ... conspiracy theories must breed like crazy. Where Knights Templar and high-order Freemasons undoubtedly clink glasses in secret chambers."

The author also remained active in non-fiction, putting together a collection of found photographs, acquired over the years from flea markets, garage sales, and thrift stores, as the 2012 book *Talking Pictures*. A showcase of quirky vintage photographs featuring sometimes unintentionally comical handwritten captions from their original owners, *Talking Pictures* features several pictures originally published as part of Riggs' *Mental Floss* blog of the same name. The images range from the purposefully lighthearted—two apparently nude young women pose behind a large sign inscribed "Censored"—to the darkly droll—a caption declares one well-dressed man standing near an antique automobile to be "a good imitation of an idiot." Writing about the online series for the Web site Boing Boing, Maggie Koerth-Baker declared the captioned photographs to be the "multimedia equivalent of those ... ultra-short fiction stories.... [They] leave you wanting to know more."

Selected writings

The Sherlock Holmes Handbook: The Methods and Mysteries of the World's Greatest Detective, Quirk (Philadelphia, PA), 2009.

Miss Peregrine's Home for Peculiar Children, Quirk, 2011.

Talking Pictures, HarperCollins (New York City), 2012.

Sources

Periodicals

Library Journal, May 15, 2011, p. 77.
Philippine Daily Inquirer, August 13, 2011.
Publishers Weekly, April 25, 2011, p. 139; October 17, 2011, p. 7.

Online

"Anonymous Stories, Written on Found Photographs," Boing Boing, http://boingboing.net/2010/11/10/anonymous-stories-wr.html (September 21, 2011).

"Freak Chic: The 'universal creepiness' of Ransom Riggs' new novel," *National Post*, http://arts.nationalpost.com/2011/06/21/freak-chic-ransom-riggs-new-novel-uses-vintage-photography-for-universal-creepiness/ (September 21, 2011).

"The Most Mysterious-Sounding Village in Ohio," *Mental Floss*, http://www.mentalfloss.com/blogs/archives/80259 (September 21, 2011).

Ransom Riggs Official Web site, http://www.ransomriggs.com/ (September 21, 2011).

"Tim Burton Circles *Miss Peregrine's Home for Peculiar Children*," *Deadline*, http://www.deadline.com/2011/11/tim-burton-circles-miss-peregrines-home-for-peculiar-children/ (November 16, 2011).

—*Vanessa E. Vaughn*

Mary Roach

Author

Born March 20, 1959, in Etna, NH; daughter of Walter (a professor) and Clare (a secretary) Roach; married Ed Rachles (a graphic designer and illustrator); children: two stepchildren. *Education:* Weslyan College, Middleton, CT, B.A., 1981.

Addresses: *Agent*—Jay Mandel, William Morris Endeavor Entertainment, 1325 Avenue of the Americas, New York, NY 10019. *E-mail*—maryroach1gmail. com. *Publisher*—ATTN: Mary Roach, W. W. Norton & Co., 500 Fifth Ave., New York, NY 10110.

Career

Began as a freelance copy editor, 1981-84; worked in public relations, San Francisco Zoo; wrote freelance articles for local newspapers; wrote magazine articles for various publications including: *Outside, National Geographic, New Scientist, Wired,* and *New York Times Magazine.* Author of books, including: *Stiff: The Curious Lives of Human Cadavers,* 2003; *Spook: Science Tackles the Afterlife,* 2005; *Bonk: The Curious Coupling of Science and Sex,* 2008; *Packing for Mars: The Curious Science of Life in the Void,* 2010.

Awards: Engineering Journalism Award, American Association of Engineering Studies, for an article on earthquake-proof bamboo houses, 1996; *Elle* Reader's Prize, *Elle* magazine, for *Stiff: The Curious Lives of Human Cadavers; Elle*Reader's Prize, *Elle* magazine, for *Spook: Science Tackles the Afterlife,* 2005.

Sidelights

What happens to a human cadaver in an automobile crash test? Does the human soul weigh 21 grams? What is the best way to ensure that a sow will have a larger litter of piglets? What happens to a person living in a gravity-less environment where they cannot walk for more than a year? Could fleas really suck a cheetah dry? How many would it take to do so? These are all questions that the curious mind of Mary Roach has pondered.

While working in public relations for the San Francisco Zoo in an office next to Gorilla World, Roach discovered that she was far more interested in the science behind the removal of warts from an elephant's foot than in writing press releases. When a rumor about the cheetahs in the zoo being devoured by fleas prompted dozens of calls from concerned citizens, Roach found herself contemplating just how many of the small parasites it would take. This imaginative inquisitiveness lead Roach to write articles for a variety of science, technology, and travel magazines while she was still employed at the zoo. Roach wrote such articles as "How to Win at Germ Warfare," which was a National Magazine Award finalist, and an article on bamboo earthquake-resistant houses in Japan, which won the Engineering Journalism Award.

Prior to her employment at the zoo, Roach grew up in Etna, New Hampshire, where, as a child, she learned to drive a Skidoo and shoot a rifle—skills that she claims on her Web site to have never made much use of. She obtained a bachelors of arts degree from Weslyan College in 1981. After graduation she drove with some friends to San Francisco, where she worked as a freelance writer and copy editor before landing the job with the San Francisco Zoo public relations department.

Roach, who does not have a science degree, admits on her Web site that she sometimes must fake her way through interviews with experts who she cannot understand. While she used to write travel articles and has traveled to Antarctica three times, Roach told Matt Borony of the Web site Identity Theory, "I still enjoy travel, but prefer to be researching something that happens to be set overseas—rather than doing straight travel writing." For Roach the subjects that science writing provides are more fascinating and "much meatier," as she told Borondy. Roach's curiosity has sent her off to many exotic and unusual places, like India and the interior of an MRI machine in London, as she tackled such compelling subjects as death, the afterlife, the research of sex, and the quest to travel to Mars.

While writing a column for the online magazine *Salon*, Roach began doing research that would eventually lead her to write her first book, *Stiff: The Curious Lives of Human Cadavers*. She wrote three pieces that were about dead bodies rather than the living and these articles received some of the highest hit rates on *Salon*. The online magazine was considering starting a new column to be titled *Dead Beat* when budget cuts killed the idea before it had begun, but Roach had started her research. In the process of interviewing a man who designed crash test dummies, she learned that automative safety researchers used both the living and the dead in their studies. Obviously safety researchers could not use live volunteers for anything beyond mild crashes that would not hurt living people, but they still needed to know what kind of damage an impact would cause to a human body. Roach learned that cadavers were used in test crashes. She began researching the myriad places that bodies donated to science end up and discovered that there was "this whole work force of donated cadavers out there, being put through their paces in labs and universities," she said in an interview with the Web site Book Browse.

Many people would shy away from the subject of death and researching what happens to bodies after they are donated to science, but for an author who admits on her Web site that she has written columns about such unusual topics as "vaginal weight-lifting and amputee bowling leagues," dead bodies seemed a fitting subject. Identity Theory's Borondy told Roach that, with *Stiff*, she had "done quite a skillful job of balancing informative, often shocking content with a healthy dose of humor." *Stiff* became a best-seller after it was mentioned on the television program *Six Feet Under*.

While researching *Stiff*, Roach visited a lab where would-be plastic surgeons were learning the craft of the profession and practicing new techniques. In the laboratory there were 40 decapitated heads sitting in roasting pans lined up on tabletops. Roach told Book Browse, "Your brain doesn't really know what to do with this. Mine chose to pretend we were in a rubber mask factory, and these were just very realistic Halloween items being worked on." When she was asked if spending so much time around dead bodies had changed her view of death, Roach told Book Browse that the dead "are fairly easy to be around. They're the same sort of company as people across from you on subways or in airport lounges, there but not there. Your eyes keep going back to them, because they're the most interesting thing in the room, and then you feel bad for staring." In writing *Stiff* Roach was concerned about revealing all the various things that happen to cadavers who are donated to science for fear that she "might scare off potential body donors by giving out more information than they could handle," as she told Borondy in the Identity Theory interview. However, Roach has expressed that she herself likes the idea of donating her body to science although she had yet to fill out the paperwork to make her donation official. Roach, in various interviews, has said that she would like to be the skeleton in a human anatomy lab, have her organs plasticized and used in classrooms, or have her remains organically composted to provide nutrients to a tree.

Just as a person could be transformed into compost and reincarnated as a tree, there are many different beliefs about where humans go after life. This was the general topic of Roach's second book, *Spook: Science Tackles the Afterlife*. While she was gathering information for *Stiff* Roach met Duncan MacDougall, whose research involved determining the precise weight of the human soul by weighing bodies both before death and immediately after death. The discrepant amount of weight was approximately .75 ounces or 21 grams. Roach found this strange fact compelling and it prompted her to write *Spook*. While investigating and composing *Spook*, Roach knew she was choosing to enter a realm of science that was placed at the awkward intersection of science and belief and was rife with potential quackery.

At the onset of the book Roach described the parameters she used to pull together material for *Spook*. She decided to interview "people doing research using scientific methods, preferably at respected universities or institutions," and stated that "this is not a debunking book. I'm trying hard not to make assumptions, not to have an agenda."

In writing *Spook* Roach tracked down a sample of ectoplasm stored in the rare reading room of the library at Cambridge University. She noted that the ectoplasm looks somewhat like a woven material as opposed to the transparent, viscose green goo of *Ghostbusters*. She also learned that she was not the first person who thought that the sample of ectoplasm looked woven and that a researcher from 1921 attempted to ask disembodied spirits the cosmically significant question "Have you a loom in your world?" (according to a *New York Times* review).

As part of her *Spook* research, Roach traveled to India to interview a researcher investigating reincarnation. There she learned of another American reincarnation researcher who had published a scientific paper in the prestigious, peer-reviewed *Journal of the American Medical Association*. She went to the University of Virginia to an operating room where cardiologists had installed sensitive equipment in an effort to study out-of-body, near-death experiences. She tracked down electro-voice phenomena, which is considered to be a way of talking with the dead by using technology to pick up barely audible sounds supposedly uttered by those who have died. She enrolled in a school for mediums and experienced being "haunted" by being subjected to certain frequencies and levels of electromagnetism. The result of all of this tireless research was a book that Rick Kleffel, writing for the online Agony Column, described as "utterly engaging, charming, occasionally mind-boggling, and always informative."

For her third book Roach decided to write about yet another potentially awkward topic that would make people squirm. She chose scientific research about sex. Roach described *Bonk: The Curious Coupling of Science and Sex* to Joel Murphy of the pop culture Web site HoboTrashcan, giving her reason for picking this unusual topic: "There are tons of books about sex, but nobody's really written about sex research, partly because a lot of sex research isn't that interesting to read about. So I ferreted out the greatest hits."

Roach studied the scientific research of sex for two and a half years while writing *Bonk*. She told Murphy that "people were surprisingly supportive in light of the fact that when you do sex research, you're constantly exposing yourself to criticisms from family values groups and people who could interfere with your funding." Roach herself was supportive of the sex researchers and volunteered as a subject. She and her husband, Ed, flew to London to participate in a study at the University College London Medical School. Using ultrasound equipment, Dr. Jing Deng was working to capture a real-time image of human intercourse.

In addition to participating as a volunteer in Dr. Deng's study, Roach visited Danish pig farmers to learn about the Danish government's recommendations to increase the number of piglets born in a litter. She also traveled to Taiwan to witness an operation on a man to restore blood flow to his penis to correct his erectile dysfunction. She interviewed a woman who could think herself into an orgasmic state, and she delved into the history of Kinsey's notorious attic sex experiments. One of the recurring and serious themes that emerges in *Bonk* is the difficulty of funding sex research. The funding either comes from a grant and must be morally and politically correct or the funding comes from a corporation and must lead to a salable pharmaceutical product.

Roach's fourth book, *Packing for Mars: The Curious Science of Life in the Void*, was published in 2010. Paul Di Filippo, writing for the online *Barnes and Noble Review*, called the book "hilarious, yet journalistically and scientifically sound." In *Packing for Mars*, Roach once again goes for the uncomfortable topics in her writing. Rather than focusing on the gee-whiz, cutting-edge technology of space travel or the glorious vision of the conquest of space, she places the focus of her research and writing on the human aspects and things that need to be considered for a human being to travel into space. She ponders what happens to a person's emotional stability as well as to their body when they are no longer within the nurturing habitat of the earth and how sometimes an intoxicating ecstasy overcomes astronauts when they venture outside their spaceship. She writes about how bodily wastes would need to be dealt with in space on a long mission, such as traveling to Mars. She describes how the Japanese determine who will be their national space voyagers and NASA's simulation of capsule crashes using corpses and a giant gun. Her conclusion at the end of *Packing for Mars* is that, despite the many considerations that would have to be resolved, humankind should travel to Mars.

Roach's curiosity has led to four books that pull into the light four very different and problematic topics. Her humorous writing style makes these topics accessible to a wide audience who otherwise might not have thought about these subjects. Roach's curiosity has allowed everyone the opportunity to learn a few things they might not have known.

Selected writings

Stiff: The Curious Lives of Human Cadavers, Penguin (New York City), 2003.
Spook: Science Tackles the Afterlife, W.W. Norton (New York City), 2005.
Bonk: The Curious Coupling of Science and Sex, W.W. Norton, 2008.
Packing for Mars: The Curious Science of Life in the Void, W.W. Norton, 2010.

Sources

Periodicals

New York Times, October 6, 2005; March 30, 2008.

Online

"Getting to Know … Mary Roach," HoboTrashcan, http://www.hobotrashcan.com/2008/04/24/getting-to-know-mary-roach/ (May 7, 2011).

"Mary Roach: An interview," Book Browse, http://www.bookbrowse.com/author_interviews/full/index.cfm/author_number/898/mary-roach (May 7, 2011).

"Mary Roach," Identity Theory, http://www.identitytheory.com/interviews/roach_interview.html (May 7, 2011).

Mary Roach Official Web Site, http://www.maryroach.net/ (May 7, 2011).

"Mary Roach's Biography," Red Room, http://www.redroom.com/author/mary-roach/bio (May 7, 2011).

"Mary Roach," Squidoo, http://www.squidoo.com/mary-roach (May 7, 2011).

"Review of *Spook: Science Tackles the Afterlife,*" The Agony Column, Bookotron, http://www.trashotron.com/agony/reviews/2005/roach-spook.htm (May 7, 2011).

"Rocket Men Redux," *Barnes and Noble Review,* http://bnreview.barnesandnoble.com/t5/The-Speculator/Rocket-Men-Redux/ba-p/3089 (May 7, 2011).

"The Shorty Q&A with Mary Roach," The Rumpus, http://therumpus.net/2009/02/rumpus-original-the-shorty-qa-with-mary-roach/ (May 7, 2011).

—*Annette Bowman*

Aaron Rodgers

Jeff Haynes/Reuters

Professional football player

Born Aaron Charles Rodgers, December 2, 1983, in Chico, CA; son of Ed (a chiropractor) and Darla (a homemaker) Rodgers.

Addresses: *Contact*—Green Bay Packers, PO Box 10628, Green Bay, WI 54307-0628.

Career

Quarterback for Butte Community College, Oroville, CA, 2002; earned scholarship to the University of California, 2003; drafted by the Green Bay Packers, 2005; starting quarterback, Green Bay Packers, 2008—; won Super Bowl (with others), 2011.

Awards: All-USA Iron Man Team, JC Football Network, 2002; Holiday Bowl MVP, 2002; made list of top 100 junior college players, *SuperPrep* magazine, 2002; All-Pac 10 Honorable Mention, 2003; offensive MVP, Insight Bowl, 2003; First Team All-Pac 10, 2004; All-America honorable mention, *Sports Illustrated*, 2004; FedEx Air NFL Player of the Year, National Football League, 2010; Good Guy Award, Pro Football Writers of America, 2011; Super Bowl MVP, 2011.

Sidelights

During his first season as a starter for the Green Bay Packers, quarterback Aaron Rodgers faced a steady stream of put-downs from faithful Brett Favre fans who were angry to see Rodgers take the place of their legendary playmaker. Despite the unwelcoming atmosphere Rodgers jumped out to a good start, becoming the first National Football League (NFL) quarterback to pass for 4,000 yards in each of his first two seasons as a starter. During his third season (2010-11) at the helm of the Packers offense, Rodgers took his team to the Super Bowl and delivered a 31-25 victory over the much-favored Pittsburgh Steelers.

"When you step into a Hall of Famer's shoes like Aaron's had to in Green Bay and then perform as well as he's performed, it just goes to show what he's made of," two-time Super Bowl champ John Elway told *USA Today*'s Jim Corbett. "I've played golf with Aaron, a class kid with that demeanor that he's able to handle all the different things that have come at him. He's just moving into his prime."

Aaron Charles Rodgers was born on December 2, 1983, in the northern Sacramento Valley town of Chico, California. His father, Ed, played football at Chico State, where he earned all-conference honors. Ed Rodgers played three years of semi-professional football in Marysville, California, and later became a chiropractor. While Rodgers is said to have inherited his athletic abilities from his father, he acquired his nimble feet from his mother, Darla, who was a dancer.

Rodgers spent his childhood in Chico, growing up alongside an older brother, Luke, and younger brother, Jordan. Early on, Rodgers developed an obsession with football and, at the age of three, would sit through entire games, mesmerized by San Francisco 49ers quarterback Joe Montana. Rodgers collected football cards and learned addition by tracking player statistics. By the age of five, Rodgers could throw a football through a tire swing and identify the formations used by the 49ers.

As a youngster, Rodgers pushed himself athletically because he wanted to compete with his brothers—especially Luke, who was 19 months older. The Rodgers boys loved football, yet their father told them they could not play until high school because he feared they would burn out or get injured. Rodgers found a loophole, though, organizing football games at recess. He played Little League baseball and, though Rodgers was scrawny, his powerful arm helped him compete. Rodgers figured out how to use his small size to his advantage. During warm-ups as the opposing team watched, he gently lobbed the ball at the catcher, giving the impression he was easy to hit. Once the game started, Rodgers unleashed his fastball.

When Rodgers entered eighth grade, he persuaded his father to let him play football. He was still small a year later when he entered Chico's Pleasant Valley High, standing five-foot-two and weighing 130 pounds as a freshman. One friend nicknamed him "Hurley" in reference to Bobby Hurley, the lean but potent point guard who played basketball for the Sacramento Kings. His junior year, Rodgers earned the starting quarterback slot. During his two years quarterbacking, Rodgers set several records. He tossed six touchdowns in one game, a new school record. In addition, he set a record for most passing yards in one season at 2,176, and most total yards, at 2,466.

Despite his success, Rodgers failed to earn a scholarship to any big-name football programs. Of the more than 100 NCAA Division I schools, none came knocking. Many factors contributed to Rodgers' lack of recruitment. For starters, most colleges focused on California's larger metro areas when looking for talent, leaving Chico off the radar. In addition, Rodgers' coaches were not used to having talented prospects and did not know how to help him get a scholarship. Finally, Rodgers' lack of size turned schools away. As a senior, he had grown to six-foot-one and weighed 185 pounds, yet most colleges preferred larger quarterbacks.

Discouraged, Rodgers contemplated giving up football during the winter of 2001. About the time he hit bottom, Butte Community College football coach Craig Rigsbee stopped by the Rodgers home and asked Rodgers to join his team. Playing at the nearby junior college was not what Rodgers envisioned, but Rigsbee persuaded Rodgers that playing at Butte would give him the opportunity to polish his skills as he continued to grow into his late-blooming body. Rodgers told the *San Francisco Chronicle*'s Ron Kroichick that Rigsbee's optimism about his future proved to be a turning point. "I was kind of down and out about the whole thing, but he gave me my dreams back."

Rigsbee's hunch about the young quarterback's potential proved correct. Rodgers led the 2002 Roadrunners to a 10-1 record, tossing 28 touchdown passes his first and only season there. During the one game the Roadrunners lost, Rodgers set a school record for total offense, moving the ball 468 yards. The season's highlight included a trip to the Holiday Bowl, where Rodgers threw for 251 yards and two touchdowns for a 37-20 victory over San Joaquin Delta. Rodgers earned MVP honors for the bowl game and was named to *SuperPrep* magazine's list of top 100 junior college players.

Meanwhile, University of California (UC) coach Jeff Tedford was busy trying to recruit Rodgers' teammate Garrett Cross. While watching game films of the talented tight end, Tedford took notice of Rodgers. He traveled to Butte to watch the players and immediately offered Rodgers a scholarship to the Division I school. At the beginning of the 2003 season, Rodgers was listed second on the quarterback depth chart but earned the starting position a few weeks after play began. After Rodgers took over, he guided the team to a 7-3 record for the remainder of the season, though the Bears finished with an overall record of 8-6. The regular season ended with a win over Stanford in which Rodgers propelled the offense forward with 414 total yards. At the Insight Bowl, UC faced Virginia Tech, which jumped out to a 21-7 lead during the first quarter. Rodgers steadily cut into the lead, connecting on 27 of 35 pass attempts and setting a UC bowl record for passing with 394 yards. Under Rodgers' direction, the Bears scored 31 points the second half, winning 52-49 on a field goal kicked during the remaining seconds of play.

His junior year, Rodgers led the Bears to a 10-1 regular-season record. During the game the Bears lost, Rodgers set a school record for consecutive completed passes with 26 and tied an NCAA record of 23 consecutive completed passes in one game. Once again, the Bears earned a bowl game appearance, this time facing Texas Tech in the Holiday Bowl. Despite a 14-7 lead after the first quarter, the

Bears' defense could not contain the Red Raider quarterback, who passed for 520 yards, leading Texas to a 45-31 victory.

After Rodgers' junior year, mock draft predictions projected Rodgers as a top-five pick, prompting Rodgers to forgo his senior year and enter the 2005 NFL draft. Some football insiders thought Rodgers might be taken at number one, but once the draft began, Rodgers was left waiting, once again, just as he had his senior year of high school, wondering if he would be picked. Finally, he was chosen as the 24th draft pick by the Green Bay Packers and headed to Wisconsin to play backup behind Favre, the Packers' legendary pass-maker. During 2005, his first season with the Packers, Rodgers saw little playing time. He did not get much playing time the next season either, after breaking his left foot partway through. During the 2007 season, Rodgers made himself known during a November game against the Dallas Cowboys when he took over for Favre, who was injured. It was the second quarter and the Packers were down by 17. Completing 18 passes for 201 yards, Rodgers cut the deficit to three points but was unable to pull out a win.

During the off-season, in March 2008, Favre announced his retirement after 17 seasons. Rodgers spent the rest of the off-season preparing for his role as the Packers' starting quarterback, ready to take his turn in the spotlight. Then, in a bizarre twist, Favre "unretired" and hinted he wanted to return to the Packers. Favre showed up at the Packers' training camp but Packers management had already placed its trust in Rodgers and traded Favre to the New York Jets. Though Rodgers finally earned the chance to start for Green Bay, the whole ordeal left a sour taste in his mouth. Many Green Bay loyalists made it clear they would have preferred for Favre to stay.

When Rodgers took his place as quarterback during the first game of the 2008 season, it marked the first time since 1992 that Favre did not start a regular-season game for the Packers. Passing for 178 yards, Rodgers delivered a 24-19 win. The Packers won the next week, too, besting the Detroit Lions as Rodgers passed for 328 yards and three touchdowns. Though the Packers got off to a promising start, Rodgers had a tough time pulling out wins in close games. It proved to be a grueling season. The 6-foot-2, 220-pound Rodgers was booed on his home turf and was constantly grilled by members of the media who questioned his ability to fill Favre's shoes.

Rodgers grew a Tom Selleck mustache, hoping to deflect attention. "The questions got old," Rodgers told *Sports Illustrated*'s Damon Hack, "and I realized that if I could cut my facial hair into something crazy, maybe they'd ask me about that and every question wouldn't be about the guy who played before me." In the end, Rodgers led the team to a losing season, posting a record of 6-10. Favre had led the 2007 team to a 13-3 record and a playoff appearance, prompting Favre fans to continue questioning Rodgers' ability. Despite the Packers' record, Rodgers had put up great numbers. That season, he passed for 4,038 yards and 28 touchdowns.

Filled with hope for the 2009 season, Rodgers faced a tough first outing. In the first game of the season, Rodgers found his Packers trailing the Chicago Bears in the fourth quarter as the clock ticked away. But Rodgers pulled through, tossing a 50-yard touchdown pass on the way to a 21-15 victory. The Packers finished with an 11-5 record, a marked improvement over Rodgers' first season as the starter. In addition, he threw for 4,434 yards, making him the first starting quarterback to throw for 4,000 yards in each of his first two seasons.

In his spare time—often during the off-season—Rodgers raised money for the Midwest Athletes Against Childhood Cancer Fund. As for his personal life, Rodgers preferred to keep that private. As he told *USA Today*, "I don't think it's anybody's business, whether I am dating, not dating, who that person is, what they do; I really don't feel that's anybody's business."

In 2010, Rodgers helped deliver the Packers to a 10-6 regular-season record, though he missed playtime in two games after suffering concussions. He was healthy when the playoffs started and completed 71 percent of his passes to bring the Packers victories over the Philadelphia Eagles, Atlanta Falcons, and Chicago Bears on their way to the National Football Conference (NFC) Championship, earning Rodgers his first Super Bowl appearance. In the Super Bowl, the Packers faced the Pittsburgh Steelers, who were guided by quarterback Ben Roethlisberger. With two Super Bowl victories under his belt, Roethlisberger was heavily favored to bring his team to victory over the less-experienced Rodgers. In the end, Rodgers threw for 304 yards and three touchdowns to deliver his team a 31-25 victory and put to rest any lingering notions that Rodgers would be unable to follow in the footsteps of Favre. Rodgers' performance earned him Super Bowl MVP honors, a recognition that eluded Favre.

Sources

Periodicals

Chico Enterprise-Record (Chico, CA), January 4, 2005; February 6, 2011.
Dallas Morning News, February 1, 2011, p. CC1.

New York Times, January 31, 2011, p. D1.

Sports Illustrated, October 11, 2010, pp. 48-52.

USA Today, January 20, 2011, p. 1C; February 4, 2011, p. 14E; February 7, 2011, p. 5C.

Online

"Aaron Rodgers," California Golden Bears, http://www.calbears.com/sports/m-footbl/mtt/rodgers_aaron00.html (April 1, 2011).

"Chico Celebrates Its Native Son, Green Bay Packers Quarterback Aaron Rodgers," Santa Rosa *Press Democrat,* http://www.pressdemocrat.com/article/20110201.tif/WIRE/10202102.tif5 (April 4, 2011).

"Profile: Aaron Rodgers, Cal Quarterback," *San Francisco Chronicle,* http://articles.sfgate.com/2004-12-26/sports/17456978.tif_1_luke-t-shirt-aaron-rodgers (April 4, 2011).

—Lisa Frick

Andrew J. Rotherham

Policy analyst

Born c. 1971; son of James Rotherham and Barbara LaRock; married Julie Lynne Lusher, July 21, 2001; children: Elizabeth, Susan. *Education:* Virginia Tech, B.A., 1994; University of Virginia, M.Ed., 2000.

Addresses: *Home*—750 Montei Dr., Earlysville, VA, 22936.

Career

Served as legislative specialist and policy analyst for the American Association of School Administrators, mid-1990s; joined Progressive Policy Institute as director of the 21st Century Schools Project, 1998, named Special Assistant to the President for Domestic Policy, 1999; founded Eduwonk, 2004; co-founded Education Sector, 2005; co-founded Bellwether Education Partners, 2010. Editor of books and articles including: *Rethinking Special Education for a New Century*, 2001; *A Qualified Teacher in Every Classroom?: Appraising Old Answers and New Ideas*, 2004; *Collective Bargaining in Education: Negotiating Change in Today's Schools*, 2006.

Member: Board of Directors, Indianapolis Mind Trust; Virginia Board of Education, 2005-09; Board of Directors, University of Virginia Curry School, 2009—.

Sidelights

Educational policy expert and magazine journalist Andrew J. Rotherham is best known as the founder of the popular educational blog Eduwonk and a regular contributor to the educational sections of *TIME* and *U.S. News & World Report*. Rotherham began his career in education policy in the 1990s, serving as the director of the 21st Century Schools Project of the left-leaning Progressive Policy Institute and acting as a White House education adviser for the Clinton administration. The following decade, Rotherham co-founded the educational think tank Education Sector, served on the Virginia state school board, and co-founded a consulting firm aimed at improving educational efforts for low-income students, Bellwether Education Partners. A strong proponent of school choice and charter schools, Rotherham has also written extensively on topics including the role of teacher unions, school accountability, and federal educational policy reform.

A native of Virginia, Rotherham was born around 1971. Growing up in that state, he attended public schools. After completing high school, Rotherham continued his education at Virginia Tech, where he earned a bachelor's degree in history and political science, and later at the University of Virginia's Curry School of Education, where he completed a master's degree in education with a specialty in social foundations. He also completed coursework toward a doctorate in political science at the University of Virginia. Rotherham's involvement with that institution resumed in 2009 when joined the Curry School's Board of Directors; two years later, he became the board's vice-chairperson.

During the mid-1990s, Rotherham worked as a legislative specialist and policy analyst for the American Association of School Administrators. In 1998, he joined the Progressive Policy Institute (PPI), a center-left think tank that was a hub of policy for the New Democratic movement led by President Bill Clinton. There, he became the director of the institute's 21st Century Schools Project, which focused on educational reform. While with the PPI, Rotherham authored an influential position paper titled "Toward Performance-Based Federal Education Funding." Published in April of 1999, this paper argued for the creation of a system linking measurable school performance results with the receipt of federal funding dollars. "National benchmarks should be set and Washington should empower states and localities to make progress towards them. Most importantly, Washington should use its resources to drive and support ineffective practices and should not subsidize failure," Rotherham declared. "Ideally, state and school district performance should be measured against national benchmarks." The arguments set out in this paper formed the heart of a 2000 Democratic educational reform bill, the Public Education Reinvestment, Reinvention, and Responsibility Act—often called simply the Three Rs Bill. Although this bill failed to become law, some of Rotherham's ideas found a new home in the 2001 reauthorization of the Elementary and Secondary Education Act as the No Child Left Behind Act under the George W. Bush administration.

Less than a year after coming to the PPI, Rotherham took a leave of absence to join the Clinton White House as an adviser on educational policy. In doing so, he became the youngest person to date to serve in that role. "He's a rising star," commented Clinton domestic policy head Bruce Reed about Rotherham to Joetta L. Sack of Education Week. "What we need here at the White House is an aggressive team to help make sure the president can make the most of the bully pulpit on education." Rotherham was with the White House for several months. During this time, he worked with the administration on issues including school accountability, improved educational opportunities for low-income students, and the usage of charter schools and school of choice. Rotherham then returned to his position with the PPI, where he remained for the next several years. The PPI thus became the initial host of Rotherham's educational policy blog Eduwonk upon its launch in 2004.

The next year, Virginia Governor Mark Warner named Rotherham to a four-year term with the state board of education. "I'm excited to have the opportunity to give something back [to Virginia's public schools]," the new board member told Robert C. Johnston of Education Week. Later in 2005, Rotherham left the PPI to co-found an independent educational policy think tank, Education Sector, with educational policy expert and writer Thomas Toch. Education Sector's primary areas of focus include school accountability, public school choice and charter schools, staffing and human capital, and undergraduate education. To these ends, the organization investigated and critiqued such wide-ranging topics as teacher unions, charter school successes and failures, college student loan defaults, and the methods used to measure school performance under No Child Left Behind. Education Sector also became the new host of Eduwonk, and Rotherham used this platform to comment on a variety of educational issues outside of the official voice of his think tank. He also wrote a monthly education column for U.S. News and World Report, and contributed several opinion pieces to high-profile periodicals including the New York Times.

During the 2008 presidential election cycle, Rotherham served as an educational policy adviser to Democratic candidate Barack Obama's campaign. Rotherham's high profile, policy expertise, and previous White House experience later led to discussion in the media of the possibility that he would be named Secretary of Education for the incoming Obama administration later that year, but that position ultimately went to Chicago Public Schools superintendent Arne Duncan.

In 2010, Rotherham left Education Sector to co-found a new educational venture, Bellwether Education, with partners including Chicago-area education consultant Monisha G. Lozier, San Francisco-based education venture fund executive Kim Smith, and education consultant Mary K. Wells. Aiming to particularly support efforts for low-income students, Bellwether provides a host of educational consulting services, ranging from policy initiatives and publications to executive search and strategic planning; Rotherham heads the organization's thought leadership and policy analysis efforts. Explaining Bellwether's role in the educational landscape, cofounder Wells commented to Eliza Krigman of the National Journal that "we are trying to serve projects of strategic importance.... We are meeting a need that's very real. In a field where the organizations are quite small, many don't have the need or budget to engage with a large firm and do a big-scale project." With the establishment of Bellwether, Eduwonk again changed homes, moving with its writer to that organization.

Selected writings

(Co-editor) *Rethinking Special Education for a New Century*, Thomas B. Fordham Foundation (Washington, D.C.), 2001.

(Co-editor) *A Qualified Teacher in Every Classroom?: Appraising Old Answers and New Ideas*, Harvard Educational Publishing Group (Cambridge, MA), 2004.

(Co-editor) *Collective Bargaining in Education: Negotiating Change in Today's Schools*, Harvard Educational Publishing Group, 2006.

Sources

Books

Hunt, Thomas C., et al., eds., *Encyclopedia of Educational Reform and Dissent*, Sage, 2010.

Periodicals

Chronicle of Higher Education, November 14, 2008.
Education Week, August 4, 1999, p. 30; March 2, 2005, p. 17; January 27, 2010, p. 5.

Online

"About Andrew J. Rotherham," Eduwonk, http://www.eduwonk.com/2004/04/about-andrew-j-rotherham.html (November 17, 2011).

"New Group Targets Low-Income Education," *National Journal*, http://undertheinfluence.nationaljournal.com/2010/05/new-education-group-brings-tog.php (November 17, 2011).

"Toward Performance-Based Federal Education Funding," Democratic Leadership Council, http://www.dlc.org/documents/ESEA.pdf (November 17, 2011).

—*Vanessa E. Vaughn*

Dilma Rousseff

President of Brazil

Born Dilma Vana Rousseff, December 14, 1947, in Belo Horizonte, Minas Gerais, Brazil; daughter of Pedro (an attorney and entrepreneur) and Dilma Jane da Silva (a teacher) Rousseff; married Cláudio Galeno de Magalhães Linhares (a journalist), c. 1967 (separated, 1969; divorced, 1981); partner of Carlos Franklin Paixão de Araújo (an attorney and politician), 1969-2000; children: (with Araújo) Paula Rousseff de Araújo. *Education:* Attended the Minas Gerais Federal University School of Economics until 1969; graduated from Rio Grande do Sul Federal University, 1977; attended State University of Campinas.

Addresses: *Office*—Palácio do Planalto, Brasília, Brazilian Federal District, Brazil. *Web site*—http://www2.planalto.gov.br/presidenta.

Career

Active in the Comando de Libertação Nacional, or Command of National Liberation (COLINA) movement, late 1960s, and in the Vanguarda Armada Revolucionária Palmares, or Armed Revolutionary Vanguard of Palmares (VAR Palmares), after 1969; intern with the Fundação de Economia e Estatística (Foundation of Economics and Statistics, or FEE), after 1975; Municipal Secretary of Treasury for the city of Porto Alegre, after 1986; president of FEE, 1990-93; Secretary of Mines, Energy, and Communications for the state of Rio Grande do Sul, 1993-94, and again after 1998; appointed Brazilian Minister of Energy, 2002; served as President Lula's chief of staff, 2005-10; elected president of Brazil as the candidate of the Partido dos Trabalhadores or Workers' Party (PT), 2010.

© *Mauricio Lima/AFP/Getty Images*

Sidelights

Dilma Rousseff became president of Brazil, the world's fifth largest nation, on the first day of 2011. Impressively, Rousseff had won her first-ever bid for public office to lead the nation of 192 million, which boasts Latin America's most thriving economy. An economist by training, she was once jailed as a political prisoner in her twenties, and for many Brazilians of her generation represented a link to their own youthful resistance during a painful period of military dictatorship. "Even I think it is amazing," she told *Washington Post* senior editor Lally Weymouth when asked her thoughts on her historic first. "I believe that Brazil was prepared to elect a woman. Why? Because Brazilian women achieved that. I didn't come here by myself, by my own merits. We are a majority here in this country."

Rousseff was born in 1947 in the city of Belo Horizonte, the capital of the state of Minas Gerais. Her father was originally from Bulgaria, and changed the spelling of his name, Pétar Rúsev, to Pedro Rousseff once he settled in the South American nation. An attorney and supporter of leftist political groups, he had been forced to leave Bulgaria during a brutal political crackdown in the late 1920s. In

Brazil, Rousseff's father prospered and started a family that began with son Igor, born to Rousseff's mother, also named Dilma, who had been a teacher before her marriage to Pedro. Rousseff grew up the middle of three children, with younger sister Zana, in Belo Horizonte. Her father worked for German steel giant Mannesmann and also made profitable real estate investments, but he died in 1962, the year Rousseff turned 15.

Rousseff was educated at a French-language convent boarding school for young women, but finished her high school education at a co-educational public high school in Belo Horizonte. Two years after the death of her father, Brazil was rocked by coup that ended several years of democratically elected, predominantly left-of-center governments. In their place sat a widely reviled military dictatorship that would endure for the next 21 years.

Rousseff came of age in a growing, resource-rich nation that was home to several disparate elements. There were some descendants of original South American indigenous peoples, but most Brazilians traced their ancestry back to Portugal, which colonized it in the early sixteenth century, or to Africa, from whence large numbers of enslaved Africans had been transported in earlier centuries. Portuguese became the official language, and the European-heritage Brazilians controlled much of the nation's economic, cultural, and political capital after independence in 1822. There were many Brazilians, like Rousseff's late father, who were firmly in the middle class but fearful of right-wing repression, and they tended to vote into office candidates of the Brazilian Labor Party or Social Democratic Party. Those administrations worked to implement reforms that would help erase some of the country's widening gap between rich and poor, but were met with firm resistance by the country's more conservative elements, including top military officials fearful of a rising tide of Communist movements across Latin America in the twentieth century.

Once the military junta became firmly entrenched in the mid-1960s, young Brazilians rebelled in protest against the end of democracy. Rousseff was among those students who took to the streets, and then organized clandestinely to unseat the junta. In 1967 she joined a wing of the outlawed Brazilian Socialist Party, a faction that soon divided itself into two new groups. She followed the Marxist one that advocated armed struggle, the Comando de Libertação Nacional, or Command of National Liberation (known by its Portuguese-language acronym, COLINA). It looked askance on the efforts of the officially subdued center-left groups, which the junta

had organized into a single umbrella party called the Movimento Democrático Brasileiro, or Brazilian Democratic Movement (MDB). The only other party allowed to participate in elections during the military era was the right-wing Aliança Renovadora Nacional (National Renewal Alliance Party, or ARENA).

Rousseff was briefly married to a journalist and fellow activist named Cláudio Galeno de Magalhães Linhares in the late 1960s. He, too, was a COLINA member and was believed to have participated in one of the bank robberies for which the guerrilla group was gaining infamy in Belo Horizonte. During this period Rousseff was enrolled in the School of Economics at Minas Gerais Federal University. After a crackdown on COLINA operatives that resulted in an armed firefight between guerrillas and police officers, Rousseff and Galeno were forced to go underground. She eventually settled by herself in Rio de Janeiro, Brazil's largest city, and separated from Galeno after she became romantically involved with Carlos Franklin Paixão de Araújo, an attorney and fellow left-wing activist. Though the two never married, they had a daughter together in 1976 and remained involved with one another for nearly three decades.

The year 1969 was a tumultuous one for Rousseff, COLINA, and much of Brazil, riven by social unrest and anti-government violence. There were other left-wing groups working to destabilize the country, including the Movimento Revolucionário 8 de Outubro, (Revolutionary Movement of October 8), whose members kidnapped the U.S. ambassador to Brazil and held him for four days until their demands for the release of political prisoners were met. COLINA merged with another group to become the Armed Revolutionary Vanguard of Palmares, known in Portuguese as "Vanguarda Armada Revolucionária Palmares," or VAR Palmares. In June of 1969, the group masterminded the heist of a safe that was located in the house of a woman who was the former secretary to and suspected mistress of the onetime governor of the state of São Paulo, Adhemar de Barros, who had died in Paris three months earlier.

De Barros was famously corrupt and the *caixinha*, or safe, contained an estimated $2.5 million in U.S. dollars. VAR Palmares members dressed as federal police and swarmed the house of his former companion, while their comrades found the caixinha and spirited it out of a second-floor window. It was a spectacular heist and Rousseff would later be accused of having participated in it. Members of VAR Palmares who later admitted to the theft dispute this, as does she, along with charges that she managed the stolen funds and used some to purchase a Volkswagen Beetle for the group. She would later say that she indeed arranged the car purchase but disputed claims that the funds were from the safe heist.

The adage that both power and money corrupt seemed true for VAR Palmares, which disintegrated internally over the next few months. Furthermore, the military regime had adopted a draconian new tactic to fight domestic terrorism: mass-detentions known as Operação Bandeirantes. Rousseff was captured in one such raid in São Paulo in January of 1970, and was carrying a weapon. She was taken into custody and subject to torture, including electrical shocks and being hung upside down. She refused to give up names of her VAR Palmares associates, and a court handed down a sentence of six years in prison. Araújo was arrested in August of 1970 and for a time the two were in the same prison.

A court shortened Rousseff's sentence in 1972 and she was released, as was Araújo eventually. She settled in the city of Porto Alegre, where she finished her degree at the Rio Grande do Sul Federal University in 1977, a year after the birth of her daughter with Araújo, Paula. Her first legitimate career posts were with government-funded agencies, including the Fundação de Economia e Estatística (Foundation of Economics and Statistics, or FEE), and she and Araújo accepted government amnesty offers in the late 1970s designed to allow their generation to move forward in their professional careers.

In 1979 Rousseff and Araújo joined others to form the Partido Democrático Trabalhista, or Democratic Labor Party (PDT). By this point Brazil was slowly moving toward a restoration of democracy, with a loosening of authoritarianism and increasing support for MDB candidates, the only rivals to the ruling regime. There were massive pro-democracy rallies in 1984, followed by free elections a year later. Rousseff worked at the party level on a few campaigns that year and won an appointment as Municipal Secretary of Treasury for the city of Porto Alegre in 1986. In 1993 the newly elected governor of Rio Grande do Sul appointed her to serve as the state's Secretary of Mines, Energy, and Communications, a post she held again in the late 1990s. In between her government posts Rousseff served as president of FEE.

In 2000 Rousseff switched political allegiances, leaving the PDT to join the Workers' Party (*Partido dos Trabalhadores*, or PT). Since the restoration of democ-

racy in 1985 Brazil had limped along, beset by skyrocketing inflation, massive international debt, and political corruption. Successive administrations in Brasília, the federal capital, managed to bring some stability in the 1990s, but economic disparities remained painfully visible, most notably in the *favelas*, or shantytowns that ringed the main cities like Rio de Janeiro.

The Workers' Party pledged to enact reform measures to lift some of the country's poorest citizens out of dire poverty. In 2002 a former machinist named Luiz Inácio Lula da Silva ran for president, and Rousseff signed on to his campaign. Lula had left school after the fourth grade and had also been jailed back in the 1970s, though only for a few weeks for illegal strike activity. Lula won the election and named Rousseff as his cabinet's Minister of Mines and Energy. Though she was a virtual unknown in Brazilian national politics at the time, at the provincial level she was respected as a skilled administrator, astute political organizer, and government economist who put in long hours and had a solid, untarnished record of public service.

Rousseff wielded immense power as energy minister for the country, and her influence only increased when Lula made her chief of staff for his cabinet in 2005. She retained it after he was reelected to a second term in 2006. Enormously popular, Lula implemented sweeping social-welfare programs, including a generous family allowance that paid a stipend to parents whose children maintained solid school attendance records.

Brazil's constitution limited Lula to two terms, and few were surprised when Rousseff resigned as his chief of staff in March of 2010 to run in that year's coming presidential election as the PT candidate. Lula campaigned for her, which helped her win more than 46 percent of the vote on October 3. That tally, however, was still short of the 50 percent needed to avoid a runoff. On October 31 she faced off against José Serra, the candidate of the Partido da Social Democracia Brasileira, or Social Democratic Party of Brazil. She won the runoff with 56 percent of the vote to become the first woman to lead her nation.

Rousseff took the oath of office on January 1, 2011. She moved into the presidential palace in Brasília, the Palácio da Alvorada, with her mother and an aunt, and went to work in the grandly modernist Palácio do Planalto, or executive seat of government. During her first year in office she delivered the opening remarks to the General Debate session of the United Nations General Assembly and welcomed U.S. President Barack Obama. She was not expected to divert from Lula's extraordinarily successful domestic and foreign policies, and even at the U.N. visit took the opportunity to chide leaders of more powerful nations about growing global economic woes, including potential debt defaults in Europe, pernicious unemployment, and ongoing income disparities. "It is not for lack of resources that the leaders of the developed countries have not yet found a solution to the crisis," she said, according to the United Nations News Service. "It is the lack of political resources and of clarity of ideas that are to blame."

During her election campaign Rousseff was often forced to discuss her youthful days as a weapon-carrying Marxist. She admitted that she and others of her generation were misguided and used poor judgment at times, but asserted that she still believed in some of the core principles of the movement. Her time in prison had served her well, she told *Newsweek* writer Mac Margolis. "In jail you learn to survive, but also that you can't solve your problems overnight. In prison you do a lot of waiting. Waiting necessarily means hope, and if you lose hope, fear takes over. I learned how to wait."

Sources

Periodicals

Newsweek, September 26, 2011, p. 36.
New York Times, December 31, 2010, p. A8.
Washington Post, December 3, 2010.

Online

"Brazil Warns General Assembly of Global Rift unless Economic Crisis Is Resolved," United Nations, http://www.un.org/apps/news/story.asp?NewsID=39649 (November 14, 2011).
"President Dilma Rousseff," Brasil.gov, http://www.brasil.gov.br/para/press/files/profile-president-dilma-rousseff (November 17, 2011).

—*Carol Brennan*

Lisa Rudes-Sandel

Fashion designer

Born c. 1964 in Puerto Rico; daughter of George Rudes (a businessman); married Alex Sandel (an engineer); children: Max Isaac. *Education:* Graduated from the University of California Los Angeles.

Addresses: *Office*—NYDJ Apparel, LLC, 5401 South Soto St., Vernon, CA 90058. *Web site*—http://www.nydj.com/.

Career

Began working in various aspects of the garment industry worldwide, c. mid-1980s; eventually joined family business, St. Germain; founded Not Your Daughter's Jeans, 2003; released first product, Tummy Tuck Jeans, 2005; sold half of Not Your Daughter's Jeans to Falconhead Capital, 2008.

Sidelights

Entrepreneur and designer Lisa Rudes-Sandel is the creator of Tummy Tuck Jeans, targeted at women seeking to slim their midsections while wearing fashionable-looking jeans. She sold them through her Los Angeles-based company, Not Your Daughter's Jeans. Among the first Latinas to create a jeans company that achieved success, her family-run business reached $80 million in sales in 2008. The Tummy Tuck Jeans and other products were sold in at least 20 countries. In 2008, Rudes-Sandel and her family sold a stake in Not Your Daughter's Jeans to a private equity firm to help increase growth. Rudes-Sandel remained the company's spokeswoman and remained active in the design and marketing of its signature products. As she told Sarah Saffian of *Reader's Digest*, "The truth is I've never forgotten that woman I've been aiming for since day one."

Born around 1964 in Puerto Rico, she was the daughter of George Rudes, who worked in the apparel industry from his teen years. His father also worked in the industry in New York City, and George Rudes began his career by selling fabric for his father's company. After completing high school, Rudes-Sandel intended to be a plastic surgeon and entered University of California, Los Angeles. A biology class derailed her original goal, so she studied Italian and art history. She soon knew that she was going to work in the garment industry as well. When she graduated, she worked in many aspects of the garment business, primarily women's wear, in Europe and Asia. She held positions in design, production, marketing, and sales. Along the way, she became fluent in four languages. Rudes-Sandel eventually joined her father in the apparel business, working for the family company, St. Germain. This company made women's sportswear.

While shopping for jeans in the early 2000s, Rudes-Sandel realized that she could not find a fashionable pair that fit her body. Jeans were too small in key places because of the popular low-cut jeans look. It was not only because of the shape of her body and the effects of aging. She told Scott Malone of *WWD*, "I happen to be 40 years old, I am not in bad shape, I'm 5-foot-8-inches and I cannot put on a lot of these jeans. If I do get them on and they do fit, my butt shows. I have to take three or four sizes bigger" than her regular size 8. She saw an opportunity to create a new kind of jean for women who had been neglected by the mainstream market. Working with her father and with her siblings, Leslie and Kenneth, she founded a new company, Not Your Daughter's Jeans (NYDJ), in 2003 and put together an initial investment of $250,000. Rudes-Sandel served as president.

By April of 2005, Rudes-Sandel began marketing the Tummy Tuck Jean, which featured strategic reinforcements to ensure a flattering fit. This stretchy denim flattens the midriff, shapes hips, and lifts the backside of its wearer using patented crisscross stitching design panels that are built into the front pockets of the jeans. Talking to Maureen Jenkins of the *Chicago Sun-Times*, Rudes-Sandel explained that the jeans achieve this effect without "the feeling that you've got a girdle on. You feel like you're a wearing a normal pair of jeans, and you are." Rudes-Sandel added, "The fact the fabric stretches as it does allows you to go down one size. It does give the illusion of a narrower hip. They're so comfortable. It's like pulling on a legging." Made of 96 percent cotton and 4 percent spandex—a combination she found worked after much experimenation—the jeans were targeted at women older than 30 who sought both comfort and fashion.

Within a few months, Rudes-Sandel was selling her jeans in 500 specialty stores across the United States. A variety of styles and colors were available, initially retailing for $88 to $120. The first year, sales were $7 million. Because of the success of NYDJ, St. Germain was closed; its sales were only $2.2 million in 2004. Sales only increased in 2006, reaching $40 million as Tummy Tuck Jeans became available in department stores like Nordstrom, Dillard's, Macy's, Bloomingdales, and 1,000 specialty stores. By 2007, Tummy Tuck Jeans were available in Europe, South Africa, Canada, and Panama.

The jeans were made in the United States with denim imported from China. NYDJ, led by Rudes-Sandel, designed, finished, and shipped the jeans, and used factories in Los Angeles' extensive garment district to cut, sew, and launder them. Over the years, she added new washes, colors, and trendy details to her line. She also added plus and petite sizes by 2007. Rudes-Sandel's creation soon gar-

nered national media attention as well, appearing in *People* magazine's StyleWatch section. In 2007, Rudes-Sandel and her family were part of the NAS-DAQ opening bell ceremony on June 11, 2007, to celebrate the fiftieth anniversary of the Puerto Rican Day Parade in New York City.

In September of 2008, Not Your Daughter's Jeans sold a 50 percent stake in the company to private-equity firm Falconhead Capital. While Rudes-Sandel and her family remained an essential part of the company and served on the board, Edwin Lewis came aboard as chairman and chief executive officer, to execute a long-term, major growth plan. By 2008, Not Your Daughter's Jeans had $80 million in revenues, were sold in 3,000 specialty stores nationally and internationally, and he expanded the number of countries they were sold in, but to become bigger, the company needed an outside investor. Falconhead focused primarily on infrastructure while Rudes-Sandel and her family focused on product development, primarily expanding into using the Tummy Tuck technology on other types of pants, like dress pants, maternity jeans, and postpartum jeans, as well as shirts.

By 2009, Not Your Daughter's Jeans was the largest domestic manufacturer of women's jeans that cost less than $100. It was shipping 40,000 pairs per week to thousands of stores in 20 countries. Though Rudes-Sandel was no longer president (Kevin Mahoney took the post in 2011), she focused on design and marketing. She remained the company's spokeswoman as well, and sure of her vision for flattering jeans and other items for an often overlooked customer. As Rudes-Sandel explained to Helaine R. Williams of the *Arkansas Democrat-Gazette*, "There are a lot of people trying to … do what I'm doing. There are people that claim to have what I have and claim to do what I do…. They have one piece, they have one jean, they have one style…. My whole company is based on marketing all kinds of products for these women, not just one item."

Sources

Periodicals

Arkansas Democrat-Gazette, November 20, 2007.
Business Wire, September 26, 2008.
Chicago Sun-Times, July 21, 2005, p. 54.
Los Angeles Business Journal, June 6, 2011, p. 14.
Modesto Bee, January 12, 2007, p. G1.
New York Times, September 15, 2005, p. C7; September 21, 2006, p. C6.
PR Newswire, June 7, 2007; September 25, 2008.
Women's Wear Daily, September 2, 2004, p. 10; September 26, 2008, p. 22.

Online

"Dreamers: The Making of Not Your Daughter's Jeans," *Reader's Digest*, http://www.rd.com/money/dreamers-the-making-of-not-your-daughters-jeans/ (August 12, 2011).

"Good Jeans Bring Business Owner Success," Spell-Brand Brand Management, http://www.spellbrand.com/good-jeans-bring-business-owner-to-success (August 13, 2011).

—A. Petruso

Andra Rush

Founder of Rush Trucking

Born in 1961 in Michigan; children: three sons. *Education:* University of Michigan, B.S., 1982, M.B.A., 1983; Tuck School of Business at Dartmouth, 1998; Tuck Business School for Advanced Management at Dartmouth, 1999; Kellogg School of Management, 2003.

Addresses: *Office*—Rush Trucking, 35160 East Michigan Ave., Wayne, MI 48184-3698. *Web site*—http://www.rushtrucking.com/

Career

Worked as a nurse, 1980s; founded Rush Trucking, 1984.

Awards: Young Entrepreneurs Award for Business Founders, 1985; Entrepreneurial Spirit Award, Ford Motor Company, 2002.

Sidelights

Andra Rush is the founder of Rush Trucking, a Michigan-based trucking business that went from a one-woman company to a $400 million business. Rush, who is part Native American, makes sure that more than half of her employees are members of minorities, and that half are women. Rush Trucking is the largest Native-American-owned business in the United States.

Rush grew up in a middle-class family in Michigan. Her paternal grandparents were Native Americans from the Oshwegon Mohawk Reserve in Ontario, Canada. Rush grew up with an awareness of her Native American heritage, which she has carried through her life and work.

After high school, Rush went on to earn a nursing degree and began working at a local hospital; however, she chafed under the rigid hierarchy in the hospital, where she believed nurses were underpaid and treated unfairly. She looked at the organizational chart of the hospital's executives and decided that she would prefer to be a CEO.

Still working as a nurse on weekends, she enrolled in business school at the University of Michigan and, at the same time, worked an internship at an air freight company. While working there, she became interested in how products were shipped by truck, and thought she could do a better, faster job. The trucking industry was going through a period of deregulation, allowing entrepreneurs to enter the industry, and she liked the idea of being her own boss. So, after getting a feel for shipping and deciding that she could succeed in the business, in 1984 she started her own trucking business.

Rush spent all of her savings, and a $5,000 loan from her parents, to buy two used trucks and a van. She could not afford a cell phone, so she had potential customers leave messages for her at her grandmother's house. When she did talk to customers, she used several different voices and pretended to transfer callers to other departments, so they would think her company was large and well-established. She learned to repair trucks herself in order to save money. In the male-dominated world of trucking, she was often asked, "Who really runs this, your dad or your brother or are you the wife?" As she told Kimberlie R. Hall in an article from *News from Indian Country* that was reprinted on her Web site, she had to tell them, "No, it's really me."

Rush decided to specialize in fast, emergency shipping, and she never turned down a job, no matter how tight the deadline was. As she told Jacqueline Mitchell in the *Detroit News*, "I believed that if we could get the business, we would do a good job, and that would lead to repeat business and bigger contracts." At times she got up at 3 in the morning in order to deliver a shipment on time. Within six months, she had ten employees and clients like Ford and GM, who hired her to pick up small packages at the airport. Eventually they offered her bigger contracts to truck parts between their plants and their suppliers.

Rush's dedication to on-time service has at times led to creative solutions to difficult problems. After the terrorist attacks of September 11, 2001, the bridge across the Detroit River was closed. Rush needed to get auto parts shipments to the other side of the river, so she hired barges to take her trucks across. Rush told Michael Strong in *Crain's Detroit Business*, "I did this because I had a responsibility to customers to keep their goods flowing."

Rush also believes she has a responsibility to her drivers and other employees. As she told Margaret Heffernan in *Reader's Digest*, as a business, you have to serve customers, but you also "have to be focused on who's serving them. If we don't look after our drivers, they won't look after our customers."

In a tribute to her Native American heritage, Rush's company logo is a war staff with six feathers. The six feathers represent the Six Nations of the Iroquois people: Mohawk, Onondaga, Oneida, Cayuga, Tuscarora, and Seneca. Over time, Rush worked to do more for Native Americans. In 2002, as her business grew, she branched out from simply delivering parts to manufacturing them. She formed a joint venture with Intier Automotive, called Dakkota Integrated Systems. Dakkota develops and delivers all the interior components of a vehicle, excluding the seats. Rush chose to locate Dakkota's manufacturing facilities in Canada, near Native American reserves where people needed jobs.

Rush has also incorporated her Native American heritage in the decisions she makes regarding her business and her family. Traditionally, in Native American culture, people were taught to consider the impact of what they are doing on the people who will live seven generations from now; this has helped Rush make decisions with a long-term focus on people and the environment. As for her family, the entire extended family is involved in the upbringing of her three sons, from their dad and grandparents to their aunts and uncles. She also tries to make sure her employees are exposed to Native American culture and values as often as possible.

In addition to running her business, Rush sits of the boards of directors of the Michigan Minority Business Development Council, the Minority Enterprise Development/Minority Business Development Agency, the Minority Business Roundtable, and the Native American Business Alliance.

Diane Freeman, head of General Motors' supplier diversity program, told Nadine Heintz in *Inc.*, "She's made a lot of sacrifices to succeed. She's a risk taker." As for advice to others who want to start their own business, she told Hall, "Don't let people be your dreamstealers, just stay focused and committed.... When you decide to go for it, put your heart and soul in it and be committed."

Sources

Periodicals

Crain's Detroit Business, March 29, 2004, p. 20.
Inc., April 1, 2004.
News from Indian Country, July 2000, p. B4.
Reader's Digest, March 2010, pp. 55-56.

Online

"MBRT Board Officers: Andra Rush," Minority Business Round Table, http://www.mbrt.net/board/andra-rush.html (February 11, 2011.
"Native American Woman Drives Through Barriers," *Detroit News*, reprinted on Bad Eagle forum, http://www.badeagle.com/cgi-bin/il3/cgi-bin/ikonboard.cgi?act=ST;f=36;t=3639 (February 11, 2011).
"The Right Product to the Right Place at the Right Time," *News from Indian Country*, http://www.rushtrucking.com/rightproduct.shtml (April 2, 2011).
Rush Trucking Official Web site, http://www.rushtrucking.com/ (February 11, 2011).

—*Kelly Winters*

Juan Manuel Santos

President of Colombia

© *Joaquin Sarmiento/LatinContent/Getty Images*

Born Juan Manuel Santos Calderón, August 10, 1951, in Bogota, Colombia; married to María Clemencia Rodríguez; children: Martín, María Antonia, Esteban. *Education:* University of Kansas, B.S., 1972; London School of Economics, master's degree; Harvard University, master's degree; Fletcher School of Law and Diplomacy, Tufts University, Medford, M.A., master's degree.

Addresses: *Office*—Casa de Nariño, Carrera 8 No. 7-26, Edificio, Bogota, Colombia.

Career

Joined the National Federation of Coffee Growers, 1972; sub-director, *El Tiempo* newspaper, 1981; founded Good Government Foundation, 1990; Minister of Foreign Trade, Colombia, 1991; president, United Nations Conference on Trade and Development, 1992-96; vice president of Colombia, 1993-94; co-wrote *The Third Way* with British Prime Minister Tony Blair, 1999; Minister of Finance, Colombia, 2000-02; founded Partido de la U, 2005; Minister of Defense, Colombia, 2006-09; elected President of Colombia, 2010.

Awards: King of Spain's Prize for Journalism, 1985.

Sidelights

Juan Manuel Santos was elected President of the South American nation of Colombia in June of 2010, and assumed office in August. Before becoming president, Santos had served as Minister of Defense in the administration of his predecessor, President Alvaro Uribe; as Minister of Finance under President Andres Pastrana in the early 2000s; and as Minister of Foreign Trade under President César Gaviria in the early 1990s. Santos is also known for his leadership in Colombia's struggle against the leftist rebel group, the Revolutionary Armed Forces of Colombia (FARC). During his time as Minister of Defense, Santos oversaw efforts to dampen the power of the rebel group, but at the expense of conducting air raids over Ecuador without that nation's approval. After taking over Colombia's top job, Santos worked to improve relations with Venezuela and other world nations, helping position Colombia as a regional leader in foreign affairs. In the early months of his presidency, Santos enjoyed strong popularity, garnering a domestic approval rating of more than 70 percent roughly one year into his tenure in office for his center-right policies.

Born on August 10, 1951, in Bogota, Colombia, Santos comes from a family that has long wielded considerable influence in Colombia. His great-uncle, Eduardo Santos, was a newspaper publisher who operated the nation's largest newspaper, *El Tiempo*, and served as President of Colombia from 1938 to 1942. As a young man, Santos studied at the Naval Academy in Cartagena as a cadet before enrolling at the University of Kansas, which granted him a bachelor's degree in economics and business administration in 1972. Santos later pursued graduate studies at several prestigious world universities, eventually earning graduate degrees from the London School of Economics, Harvard University, and the Fletcher School of Law and Diplomacy at Tufts University near Boston. After completing his undergraduate studies, Santos began working with the London office of the National Federation of Coffee Growers. He remained with the organization from 1972 to 1981, serving for a time as the CEO. In 1981, Santos left London for Colombia, joining his family's publishing business as a newspaper executive. Four years later, Santos was named vice president of the Interamerican Society's Commission for Freedom of the Press. He remained in this position until he entered government service.

In 1990, Santos founded the Good Government Foundation, an organization that analyzes Colombia's governmental actions to ensure that they help the nation's people rather than devolving into ideological bickering. Santos' first government job came the following year, when he was named as Minister of Foreign Trade in the administration of then-Colombian President César Gaviria. The following year, Santos was appointed head of the United Nations Conference on Trade and Development; from 1993, he also led the Economic Commission on Latin America. Also in 1993, Santos became Colombia's vice president, a position he held for one year. During the 1990s, Santos held talks with members of the guerilla group FARC, eventually helping create a demilitarized zone that permitted peace negotiations to begin; however, these talks ended without any significant success. In 2000, Santos returned to government service as the Minister of Finance in the Pastrana administration; he held this position until 2002, when Uribe took office. Three years later, Santos founded Partido de la U, which had become the nation's largest political party by 2010. He joined the Uribe government in 2006 as Minister of Defense.

Santos' stint as defense minister experienced great successes, as he helped put down continuing attacks by leftist guerrillas and improve overall Colombian safety. In 2008, he oversaw an operation that freed several Colombian and American hostages held by FARC; however, several top-level government scandals also emerged during this time. In 2007, a former Colombian paramilitary death squad leader, Salvatore Mancuso, testified in court that Santos had conspired with paramilitary units in the mid-1990s to shake the government of then-President Ernesto Samper. At about the same time, information emerged revealing the existence of an illegal domestic spying program as well as evidence of connections between members of the Uribe administration and paramilitary leaders. The following year, Santos angered Ecuadorean leaders by authorizing an air raid over that nation's territory that resulted in the death of the number-two member of FARC along with some 25 others. Although the raid benefited Colombian security, it also violated foreign airspace and international law. Another military scandal called the "false positives" scandal came about in 2008 when information was revealed that Colombian military forces had been murdering innocent civilians and then making them look like dangerous insurgents by changing their clothing or planting weapons near them. As a result of the ensuing investigations, several high-ranking Colombian military officers resigned their posts.

In 2009, Santos resigned his post as Minister of Defense to be eligible to run for president in 2010; however, his candidacy remained in question until short weeks before the election as Uribe sought a constitutional amendment to allow him to run for a third term. When this proposal failed, Santos stepped in as a candidate and was immediately seen as the natural successor to Uribe's government and policies. The campaign thus became a referendum on the incumbent government, with Santos the candidate of continuation on the ticket of the Partido de la U, and his primary opponent, Green Party candidate and former mayor of Bogota Antanas Mockus, standing as the candidate of change. Although Santos was considered a favorite due to the popularity of Uribe, the outcome was not a foregone conclusion. "The Uribe government has been successful, nobody can deny that," commented think tank analyst Maria Victoria Llorente to Jeremy McDermott of the BBC News. "However it came at a cost, the dark side of the administration: paramilitarism, human rights abuses, and illegal wiretapping. Santos is associated with this." In the first polling on May 30, 2010, Santos won a plurality but not the majority needed to immediately claim office. During the runoff election between Santos and Mockus, the former Minister of Defense won a decided 69 percent of the vote to Mockus' 27.5 percent, a clear nod to support not just for Santos, but for his popular predecessor. "I went for Santos because we cannot lose what's been accomplished under Uribe," one Colombian voter told Simon Romero of the *New York Times* after the election. Two months later, Santos was inaugurated as President of Colombia.

Although many considered Santos' election an affirmation of the policies of his predecessor, the new president did not hesitate to strike his own course. During the first months of his presidency, Santos surprised analysts by reaching out to Venezuelan President Hugo Chavez, with whom Santos and the Uribe government had long had relations that could be termed shaky at best. Santos and the leftist Venezuelan leader repaired diplomatic relations to such an extent that the Colombian president was heard to refer to Chavez as his "best friend." Uribe spoke out against these efforts, commenting in an article reprinted by the BBC Monitoring International Reports service that "this is an excessively soft policy toward a dictatorship that has continued to grow stronger in Venezuela." The Santos administration also made efforts to repair diplomatic ties with Ecuador, which were still suffering from the FARC raid of 2008, and to build new ties with nations in Asia. In October of 2010, Colombia's international influence grew when the nation was unanimously elected to a non-permanent seat on the United Nations Security Council for the 2010-11 session.

These global efforts represented a shift in policy for Colombia, which had long looked to the United States as its most powerful ally and benefactor. Relations between the two nations had become somewhat strained over a lagging free-trade agreement and unflattering comments about Colombia in confidential documents published by renegade hacker group WikiLeaks. "I consider myself very pro-American; I want to continue and even strengthen our relationship, but it's common sense and common logic to diversify your international relations, especially in a world that is changing," Santos explained to Simon Romero of the *New York Times*. The Colombian leader met with U.S. President Barack Obama in April of 2011 to work toward the enactment of the stalled free-trade plan, with the two countries agreeing on an action plan to improve conditions for workers and labor activists in Colombia and thus remove the primary sticking point holding back the economic agreement.

Among Santos' primary stated goals was the reduction of the vast income gap between the nation's rich and poor, which was the second-largest in South America at the time of his inauguration. "If in four years they are going to call me the small Roosevelt of Colombia," he commented in the same interview with Romero, referencing the U.S. President Franklin Delano Roosevelt, "then I would be honored," Santos concluded. Along with foreign policy changes, Santos also began work to bring change to Colombia's domestic affairs. He proposed initiatives to beef up Colombia's infrastructure, ease tax collection procedures, and return or compensate individuals for land lost during the nation's lengthy civil war. This last proposal became law in June of 2011, with Santos estimating that total reparations paid would reach $20 billion over several years.

Two months later, Santos authorized some $65 million in funds to rebuild housing and services for residents of the city of Cartagena, who had been displaced by a geological fault resulting from an extended rainy period. But Santos did not just want to restore the residents' former homes; he wanted to ensure that "people who suffered the disaster are left better off than they were before," according to a story circulated on the UPI NewsTrack.

This combination of foreign and domestic initiatives proved a winning one for the new president. One year into his tenure, Santos enjoyed remarkable support from not only the people of Colombia, but also from its legislature. "Fortunately, I'm not in President Obama's position," commented Santos in an Associated Press article printed in the *Washington Times*, referencing the U.S. president's struggles with Republican opposition in Congress. "I'm fortunate to have 95 percent of the Congress with me," Santos concluded. The Colombian leader's legislative support was so broad, in fact, that even the Green Party—backers of his primary opponent in the previous year's presidential election—had joined with the ruling coalition government. With his nation's populace and media behind him, Santos, with his paired dedication to easing widespread poverty in Colombia and maintaining moderate political views, increasingly seemed poised to assume the role of a supranational leader. In August of 2011, he led a delegation to Mexico to discuss ways to prevent criminals from taking power within government-run institutions, drawing from efforts of Colombia's government to fight drug traffickers to inform the conversations. The talks also affirmed shared goals between the two governments in fighting against Latin American crime and violence. At about the same time, recently inaugurated Peruvian president Ollanta Humala reached out to Santos for advice on curbing Peru's own rising drug production and trafficking issues.

Despite this rising profile, Santos resisted being labeled a regional force. He did, however, express hopes that the 21st century would offer new opportunities for Central and South America as a whole. "This can and should be the decade for Latin America," proclaimed Santos at a meeting of the Economic Commission for Latin America and the Caribbean in Santiago, Chile, in August of 2011, according to the States News Service. "There are conceptual differences between the governments of the region, but we all seek the same objective: to improve our citizens' welfare. We must find our common denominators and in this way we will increase Latin America's prominence in the world," he added.

Selected writings

The Third Way, HarperCollins, 1999.

Sources

Periodicals

BBC Monitoring International Reports, August 11, 2011.

New York Times, May 16, 2007; October 29, 2008; May 30, 2010; June 20, 2010; March 5, 2011.

States News Service, August 17, 2011.

UPI NewsTrack, August 24, 2011.

Washington Times, August 29, 2011.

Online

"A look at Juan Manuel Santos, the enigmatic new president," France 24, http://www.france24.com/en/20100621.tif-new-president-colombia-juan-santos-uribe-successor-mockus-portrait-pragmatist (August 30, 2011).

"Alvaro Uribe casts long shadow over Colombia election," BBC News, http://www.bbc.co.uk/news/10131095.tif (August 30, 2011).

"Obama, Colombian Leader Agree on Changes to Trade Accord," Fox News Latino, http://latino.foxnews.com/latino/money/2011/04/08/obama-colombian-leader-agree-changes-trade-accord/ (August 30, 2011).

"President of the Republic," Republic of Colombia, http://wsp.presidencia.gov.co/En/Government/Paginas/President.aspx (August 30, 2011).

"Profile: Juan Manuel Santos," BBC News, http://www.bbc.co.uk/news/10317735.tif (August 30, 2011).

"Toxic fallout of Colombian scandal," BBC News, http://news.bbc.co.uk/2/hi/americas/8038399.stm (August 30, 2011).

—Vanessa E. Vaughn

Dan Savage

© Derek Storm/Splash News/newscom

Columnist, author, and gay rights activist

Born October 7, 1964, in Chicago, IL; son of William (a police officer) and Judy (a homemaker; maiden name, Sobieski) Savage; married Terry Miller; children: Darryl Jude (adopted). *Education:* University of Illinois, Champaign-Urbana, BA.

Addresses: *Office—Stranger,* 1535 11th Ave., 3rd Flr., Seattle, WA 98122.

Career

Worked for HIV activism organization ACT-UP, late 1980s; began writing sex-advice column "Savage Love," 1991; published *Savage Love: Straight Answers from America's Most Popular Sex Columnist,* 1998; published *The Kid: What Happened After My Boyfriend and I Decided to Go Get Pregnant: An Adoption Story,* 1999; published *Skipping Towards Gomorrah: The Seven Deadly Sins and the Pursuit of Happiness in America,* 2003; published *The Commitment: Love, Sex, Marriage, and My Family,* 2005; published *It Gets Better: Coming Out, Overcoming Bullying, and Creating a Life Worth Living,* 2011.

Awards: PEN West Award for Excellence in Creative Nonfiction, PEN Center USA, for *The Kid: What Happened After My Boyfriend and I Decided to Go Get Pregnant: An Adoption Story,* 2000; Lambda Literary Award for Humor, Lambda Literary Foundation, for *Skipping Towards Gomorrah: The Seven Deadly Sins and the Pursuit of Happiness in America,* 2003; September Sidney Award, Sidney Hillman Foundation, 2010; Family Equality Council Honoree, 2011; Webby Special Achievement Award, Webby Awards, for the It Gets Better Project, 2011.

Sidelights

Columnist, author, and gay rights activist Dan Savage is well known both for his syndicated sex-advice column "Savage Love" and for founding a gay-teen support organization, the It Gets Better Project. First published in 1991, Savage's advice column has grown to reach more than one million readers via more than 70 publications around the United States and several million more through the Internet. Known for his blunt, raunchy advice that is often at odds with traditional ideas about sex and relationships, Savage has attracted much attention for his sometimes controversial suggestions about modern sexuality. His frank style has garnered Savage both supporters and detractors, and the writer himself has made no secret of his disdain for those who disagree with him, particularly conservative Republican political leaders. In the fall of 2010, Savage made headlines for a new mission: providing moral support to gay teens in the wake of reports of school bullying and teen suicides due to sexual orientation. Beginning with one YouTube video posted by Savage and his partner Terry Miller, the It Gets Better Project grew to include thousands of offerings from people ranging from gossip columnist Perez Hilton to U.S. President Barack Obama.

Born on October 7, 1964, in Chicago, Illinois, Savage is the third of the four children of William, a police officer, and his wife, Judy, a homemaker. Savage's grandfather was a sportswriter for two local newspapers, and the family greatly valued reading. Even as a child, Savage was drawn to advice columns, developing an early affection for Ann Landers that later developed into a fascination with the sex columns printed in adult magazines such as *Penthouse* and *Playboy*. Growing up in Chicago's northern Rogers Park neighborhood, Savage attended Catholic schools, and the religion's ideals of a stable nuclear family and practices of instructing through analogy and personal fables have been noted as influences on the content and style of the columnist's advice well into his adult life. His late teen years involved a great deal of turmoil; Savage's parents divorced when he was 17, and the following year he informed his family that he was gay. At first, his mother was upset and told Savage not to bring home any boyfriends or other gay friends. When the family priest came to discuss the situation with Savage's mother, who wanted to put the teen into therapy, he proved an unexpected source of support. Speaking to Terry Gross of the NPR program *Fresh Air*, Savage recalled, "Father Tom put his hand on my mom's knee and said, 'Judy, I'm gay and it's better this way. It's better for Danny to be out than to live like I've lived.'"

After finishing high school, Savage enrolled at the University of Illinois at Champaign-Urbana, where he studied theater; however, he had decided by the end of his program that acting was not his calling. Following graduation, Savage moved to Madison, Wisconsin, to run the gay-rights group ACT-UP. While at ACT-UP, Savage undertook novel measures to raise awareness about the treatment of people suffering from the disease AIDS. When Wisconsin prison officials fulfilled a doctor's order to provide one afflicted inmate with nutritional supplements by giving him one additional peanut butter and jelly sandwich each day, for example, Savage and ACT-UP had one such sandwich sent to the governor's office daily for a year.

By 1991, Savage had begun working at a Madison video store. Through a friend there, he met Tim Keck, a co-founder of the satirical newspaper *The Onion*. When Keck told Savage that he was planning to start a new alternative newspaper in Seattle, Savage suggested he include an advice column. Keck in turn asked Savage to submit a sample, and—much to the surprise of Savage, who had no professional writing experience—offered him a job. "I'm often asked what professional qualifications I have, if any. Well, to be honest, none.... So besides reading advice columns all my life [and] listening to my mother give advice ... I can't claim to have

any 'real' qualifications," he admitted in the introduction to *Savage Love: Straight Answers from America's Most Popular Sex Columnist*. "But remember: Ann Landers ain't no shrink either, she's just a bright, brassy, opinionated midwestern gal," he pointed out. Savage's column debuted along with *Stranger*, and from the beginning exhibited a raunchy, insulting style quite unlike the more measured tones of Ann Landers or Dear Abby. Over time, Savage dropped some of the more blatantly offensive tones, and focused on providing direct, frank advice on both gay and straight sex and relationships. "Savage's sex advice puts me in mind of a smart, tough old grandmother, randy yet stern. It's Dr. Ruth if she were interested in bondage and threesomes," assessed Mark Oppenheimer in the *New York Times Magazine*. Through the 1990s, other newspapers picked up Savage's column, and by the end of the decade "Savage Love" reached an estimated 1.5 million people. A collection of highlights from the column was published in 1998 as *Savage Love*.

As Savage's column grew in readership, so did his work in other areas. During the mid-1990s, he hosted a late-night radio call-in program that offered listeners sex and relationship advice. Later in the decade, he began penning a toned-down version of his column for the ABC News Web site. In 1999, he wrote a book about the experiences that he and his partner, Terry Miller, had when deciding to adopt and raise a child, titled *The Kid: What Happened After My Boyfriend and I Decided to Go Get Pregnant: An Adoption Story*. The following year, the book won the PEN West Award for Excellence in Creative Nonfiction. Savage published a third book, *Skipping Towards Gomorrah: The Seven Deadly Sins and the Pursuit of Happiness in America*, in 2003. An exploration of how people in the United States sought happiness through indulgence in each of the Biblical seven deadly sins, the book received positive critical reception for its matter-of-fact look at how sin factored into modern life. "Common sense is Savage's strong suit, and he makes more of it than a preening moralist ever could," commented *Kirkus Reviews*. *Skipping Towards Gomorrah* earned Savage the Lambda Literary Award for Humor. A fourth book, *The Commitment: Sex, Marriage, and My Family*, followed in 2005.

In 2003, Savage made headlines for a creative—and somewhat outrageous—effort to fight comments made by then-Pennsylvania Republican Senator Rick Santorum that compared the right to have consensual homosexual sex to the right to bigamy, polygamy, adultery, incest, and even bestiality. Angered, Savage wrote an op-ed piece speaking out against Santorum's remarks in the *New York Times*, and later invited readers to write into his column to suggest new, highly sexual definitions for the word *santorum* after a reader complained that the story had fallen out of the news. More than 3,000 suggestions poured in, and Savage set up a Web site to ensure that the resulting intentionally crude definition became the top result when the senator's name was typed into a popular search engine. Three years later, Santorum lost his seat in the Senate; the issue flared again when the Republican considered a presidential run in 2011.

Savage's activism extends beyond blue political humor. In September of 2010, he began the It Get Better Project. "I was reading about teen suicides, speaking at colleges and thinking that what I should be doing is going to high schools," Savage explained in *TIME*. "But I would never get permission, as a gay adult, to speak to gay kids. Then it occurred to me that in the YouTube era, I was waiting for permission I no longer needed." Savage and his partner posted a video on YouTube urging gay teens to stay strong and have hope for the future even as they faced the difficulties of developing their identities and standing up to homophobia. The couple then asked others to contribute their own videos on the "it gets better" theme, but were stunned by the level of support the project received as gay adults shared their own stories of surviving bullying and opposition as teens because of their sexuality and straight supporters talked about their own experiences of enduring hurtful treatment or seeing others overcome challenges. Videos flooded in, and less than one year later users had contributed some 25,000 videos that had been viewed 40 million times. The project made headlines around the world, and soon began supporting other resources for gay, lesbian, bisexual, and transgender youth including the suicide prevention organization the Trevor Project; the Gay, Lesbian, and Straight Education Network; and the American Civil Liberties Union LGBT Project. In March of 2011, Savage and Miller also published *It Gets Better: Coming Out, Overcoming Bullying, and Creating a Life Worth Living*. A collection of essays, the book drew both on already available YouTube materials and new content contributed by public figures and celebrities from all walks of life: entertainment, politics, religion, literature, and even the military.

The outspoken Savage has sometimes generated attention for his unconventional ideas and pointed comments. In July of 2011, he was the subject of a profile by the *New York Times Magazine* in which he propounded the benefits of embracing unfaithfulness in marriage or long-term romantic partnering. "Given the rates of infidelity, people who get married should have to swear a blood oath that if it's violated, as traumatic as that would be, the greater good is the relationship," Savage told Oppenheimer. "The greater good is the home created for children.

If there are children present, they'll get past it. The cultural expectation should be if there's infidelity, the marriage is more important than fidelity," he concluded. Although this sentiment echoed the advice that Savage had long doled out in his column, the higher profile of the media outlet led to fresh discussion of Savage's ideas.

Soon after the *New York Times* magazine profile was printed, Savage appeared on the HBO talk program *Real Time with Bill Maher*. When Mahar made a comparison between congressional Republicans and the deceased Palestinian political leader Yasser Arafat, Savage shot back, "Unfortunately not exactly like him. I wish they were all ... dead," reported Jeremy Kinser in the *Advocate*. Soon thereafter Savage made a public apology for his statement. "It was a stupid, rude, thoughtless remark. I regret it and I retract it and I apologize to anyone watching at home," Savage posted on a blog on the *Stranger* Web site; *Newsweek* proclaimed the incident their "Apology of the Week." However, other comments made by Savage on the program angered a group on the other side of the political line: the National Organization for Women (NOW). A few days after the program aired, NOW released a statement condemning comments made both by Savage and fellow panelist, comedian Marc Maron, about having violent sexual intercourse with Republican politicians Michele Bachmann and Rick Santorum. "Political topics and satirical humor have always gone hand-in-hand, but joking about the sexual assault of anyone is in no way amusing.... It is deeply frightening that this needs to be said, but rape is not a joke, nor should it be used as a punch line for a political dig," the organization declared, according to the States News Service.

At the same time, Savage continued his public debate with Republican politicians over their lack of support for gay rights in general and the It Gets Better project specifically. After a representative of the National Republican Senatorial Committee argued that Savage was "lewd, violent, and anti-Christian," the columnist snapped back. In an e-mail posted by Ben Smith of the Web site Politico, Savage pointed out, "not a single GOP elected official can bring himself or herself to make a video, or participate in the creation of one.... No GOP elected can back the seemingly radical notion that LGBT kids shouldn't kill themselves, that they should have hope for their futures."

Selected writings

Savage Love: Straight Answers from America's Most Popular Sex Columnist, Plume (New York City), 1998.

The Kid: What Happened After My Boyfriend and I De-cided to Go Get Pregnant: An Adoption Story, Plume, 1999.

Skipping Towards Gomorrah: The Seven Deadly Sins and the Pursuit of Happiness in America, Dutton (New York City), 2002.

The Commitment: Love, Sex, Marriage, and My Family, Dutton, 2005.

It Gets Better: Coming Out, Overcoming Bullying, and Creating a Life Worth Living, Dutton, 2011.

Sources

Books

Contemporary Authors Online, Gale, 2011.

Savage, Dan, *Savage Love: Straight Answers from America's Most Popular Sex Columnist*, Plume, 1998.

Periodicals

Kirkus Reviews, September 1, 2002, p. 1288.

Newsweek, August 8, 2011, p. 18.

New York Times, April 25, 2003; June 30, 2011.

States News Service, July 20, 2011.

Time, March 28, 2011.

Washington Monthly, March-April 2011, p. 29.

Online

"An Apology," *The Stranger*, http://slog.thestranger.com/slog/archives/2011/07/15/an-apology (August 30, 2011).

"Dan Savage: For Gay Teens, Life Gets 'Better,'" NPR, http://www.npr.org/2011/03/23/13462875.tif0/dan-savage-for-gay-teens-life-gets-better (August 30, 2011).

"Dan Savage Wishes Death on Republicans, Apolo-gizes," *Advocate*, http://www.advocate.com/News/Daily_News/2011/07/18/Dan_Savage_Wishes_Death_On_Republicans,_Apologizes/ (August 30, 2011).

"Interview: Dan Savage," A.V. Club, http://www.avclub.com/articles/dan-savage,13972/ (August 30, 2011).

It Gets Better Project Official Web Site, http://www.itgetsbetter.org, (August 30, 2011).

"NRSC blasts 'lewd, violent, anti-Christian' Dan Savage," Politico, http://www.politico.com/blogs/bensmith/0711/NSRC_blasts_lewd_violent_antiChristian_Dan_Savage.html (August 30, 2011).

—*Vanessa E. Vaughn*

Mary Schapiro

Chief of the Securities & Exchange Commission

Born June 19, 1955, in Long Island, NY, daughter of an antiques dealer and a college librarian; married Charles A. Cadwell, December 13, 1980; children: three. *Education:* Franklin and Marshall College, Lancaster, PA, B.A., 1977; George Washington University, J.D., 1980.

Addresses: *Office*—U.S. Securities & Exchange Commission, 100 F. Street, NE, Washington, DC 20549.

Career

Trial attorney, 1980-81; counsel to the chairperson, Commodity Futures Trading Commission (CFTC), 1981-84; senior vice president, Futures Industry Association, 1984, then general counsel, 1984-88; commissioner, Securities & Exchange Commission (SEC), 1988-94 acting chairperson, then chairperson, CFTC, 1993-96; president, National Association of Securities Regulation, 1996-02; vice chairman and president over the regulatory policy oversight division, National Association of Securities Dealers (NASD), 2002-06, then chairperson and CEO, 2006-07; CEO, Financial Industry Regulatory Authority (FINRA), 2007-09; chairperson, U.S. Securities and Exchange Commission, 2009—.

Sidelights

In January of 2009, Mary L. Schapiro became the twenty-ninth chairperson and first female chair of the leading federal financial regulatory body, the Securities and Exchange Commission (SEC). A longtime public servant, Schapiro took the reins of the commission at a time when it was under a great deal of public fire for failing to prevent the financial meltdown that derailed the global economy in 2008. After winning confirmation as head of the SEC, Schapiro quickly began efforts to restore the organization's reputation by taking aggressive steps to crack down on financial sector abuses, including suing one of Wall Street's biggest firms, Goldman Sachs, on fraud charges stemming from the company's sales of toxic subprime mortgage investments. Before joining the SEC, Schapiro was the head of the Financial Industry Regulatory Authority (FINRA) and the chief regulator of the National Association of Securities Dealers (NASD). She also served in regulatory positions under the administrations of presidents Ronald Reagan, George H. W. Bush, and Bill Clinton."You don't survive in Washington for that many years by being colorful," commented financial counsel and former SEC officer David Martin to Alison Fitzgerald and Jesse Westbrook of Bloomberg News. "She is quite independent. She doesn't bring much of any agenda other than sensible regulation."

Born on June 19, 1955, in Long Island, New York, Schapiro is the second of the four children of an antiques dealer and a college librarian. Growing up in

Babylon, New York, the future regulator was exposed to Democratic politics from a young age; a maternal cousin, Terry Sanford, served as the Democratic governor of North Carolina between 1961 and 1965. Schapiro also showed an early competitive streak, participating in both high school and college sports. As an undergraduate at Lancaster, Pennsylvania's Franklin and Marshall College, Schapiro studied anthropology, focusing particularly on the culture of the Trobriand Islands near New Guinea. After completing her bachelor's degree in 1977, Schapiro enrolled in the law school at Washington, D.C.'s George Washington University. She completed her law degree in 1980.

Shortly after finishing law school, Schapiro embarked on a career in financial regulation when she accepted a position as a lawyer with the Commodity Futures Trading Commission (CFTC). She was thrust into a financial quagmire caused by the efforts of Texas speculators Nelson Bunker Hunt and William Herbert Hunt who tried to corner the silver market, driving up the price and causing a massive bubble that quickly collapsed. "I think it was the anthropologist in me that was fascinated by this idea that people thought they could control a world commodity," Schapiro later told Michael Scherer of *Time*. "Here they were, causing extraordinary pain to lots of people." She spent the next several years working as an attorney dealing with financial futures, which are short-term contracts linked to the purchase of financial products such as currencies, stock indices, or Treasury notes. In this capacity, Schapiro helped author new regulatory policies on the derivatives market—the market for futures or other types of forward-looking price-related financial instruments—after the 1987 stock market crash.

In 1988, President Ronald Reagan appointed Schapiro to what she told Scherer was known as the "woman's seat" on the Securities and Exchange Commission. She served for just six weeks before George H. W. Bush was inaugurated to the presidency, but retained her position after the new chief executive re-nominated her to the SEC. She remained with the agency for a total of six years, including a stint as Acting Chairman under the Clinton administration. Despite her status as a woman in what is largely acknowledged as the boys' club of high-stakes finance, Schapiro was unafraid to exercise her authority. Shortly after Clinton administration economic czar Robert Rubin named Schapiro the head of the Commodity Futures Trading Commission in 1994, she found herself at odds with then-Chicago Board of Trade head Thomas R. Donovan over her refusal to grant a requested exemption from certain financial regulations for Chicago traders. After Donovan publically stated that he

would not be intimidated by a five-foot-two-inch blonde woman, Schapiro famously snapped back that she was five-feet-five.

As its chair, Schapiro worked diligently to strengthen the CFTC, particularly in regards to its regulatory powers over the derivatives market, which had gone unregulated under the preceding Bush administration. "We did not give up the right to pursue anybody in that market for fraud," Schapiro stated in a *Washington Post* article quoted in her WhoRunsGov biographical profile. Although Schapiro helmed the CFTC for only a year, she increased regulatory enforcement investigations by half and more than doubled the amount of money collected in fines during her brief tenure. She also helped shore up the international economic base when a series of illegal trades caused a near-collapse of the massive British institution Barings Bank by making late-night phone calls to urge the Singaporean financial head to work to calm the nation's markets.

In 1996, Schapiro left her post with the CFTC to sign on with the National Association of Securities Dealers (NASD) as the head of its newly created regulatory arm. NASD is a self-regulating organization within the financial industry responsible for overseeing the NASDAQ stock exchange and more than 5,000 related brokerage firms. The experienced regulator stepped into an agency facing significant challenges. The SEC was in the midst of investigating the NASD for possible involvement in a price-fixing scandal, and the market additionally suffered from several problems related to listing standards and financial fraud. Schapiro quickly moved to beef up regulatory enforcement, pouring millions of dollars into the NASD. "The additional resources will insure we will have the ability to participate in sweeps and other focused regulatory or enforcement initiatives critical to the protection of investors and the maintenance of market integrity," she explained in a *New York Times* article by Floyd Norris.

Schapiro also put a swift halt to the trading of penny stock Comparator Systems, which rose swiftly in value for no apparent reason. "Clearly it's important for legitimate small companies to have an opportunity to come to market and for investors to have an opportunity to participate in their growth through buying their stock," Schapiro told Norris is a separate *New York Times* story. "On the other hand, there should be no market for companies who provide fraudulent information to the public and there need to be some listing standards." She also began work on effectively using a growing communication medium: the Internet. Under her direction, the

NASD worked to establish a system for consumers to report complaints to the organization and for regulators to monitor potentially misleading Internet chatter. Schapiro remained with the NASD for the next several years, advancing to become the organization's vice-chairman in 2002. The NASD spent much of the early twenty-first century battling financial scandal that followed the collapse of the tech bubble of the late 1990s, and Schapiro encouraged the adoption of new technology to help the regulatory body respond to increasingly rapid-changing financial markets. In 2005, she led a series of investigations into the use of gifts and entertainment expenses throughout Wall Street that uncovered a number of abuses.

In 2006, Schapiro again advanced with the NASD to assume the organization's top job. "I can't think of anyone better qualified to take this job," commented former SEC chair Arthur Levitt to Jenny Anderson of the *New York Times*. "The mark of a good regulator is balance. Mary didn't overplay her cards, and yet she took on the right issues and was tough when she needed to be," he concluded. Among Schapiro's most important achievements as CEO of the NASD was overseeing the organization's merger with the regulatory arm of the New York Stock Exchange in 2007. This merger created a new regulatory agency, the Financial Industry Regulatory Authority (FINRA). Schapiro became the first chief of FINRA, bringing her decades of regulatory experience to bear on a pool of some 5,000 banks and brokerage firms. In this role, she called for greater protections for individual consumers and for stricter regulation of the troubled mortgage market.

In December of 2008, President-elect Barack Obama nominated Schapiro as chair of the SEC. At the time, the federal regulator was embattled by scandals surrounding its inability to control the risky derivatives markets that had sparked a major economic downturn, its failure to recognize the actions of financier Bernie Madoff, and its continued employment of workers who were found to have viewed pornographic Web sites on the job. Although her qualifications were strong, Schapiro experienced some criticism for her long-standing connections to the family of rogue investor Madoff, who was arrested and imprisoned for a massive fraudulent Ponzi scheme—the use of one investor's money to pay off other investors without earning any real profits. Nevertheless, Schapiro won confirmation easily and assumed her new position shortly after Obama's inauguration in January of 2009.

She promptly set about restoring both the SEC's reputation and its effectiveness, hiring former federal prosecutor Robert Khuzami as the agency's chief enforcer. Under Khuzami's direction, the SEC more than doubled its number of investigations over 2008 numbers and greatly stepped up financial penalties for offending financial companies both large and small. "I wanted to do whatever I could do to strip out the inefficiencies and delays," Khuzami told Zachary A. Goldfarb of the *Washington Post*. "A large part of the deterrent impact of our actions has to do with the immediacy of our actions." In April of 2010, the SEC filed a lawsuit against financial giant Goldman Sachs that alleged that the company had fraudulently sold investors mortgage securities that were intended to lose, rather than gain, value.

Schapiro has also called for stricter financial regulation, particularly of the complex financial instruments known as swaps. A form of derivative, a swap is an agreement under which two parties trade the benefits of one party's financial instrument for those of the instrument owned by the party. Although swaps can help protect investors from certain risks, Schapiro believed that they carried enough financial risk to warrant greater scrutiny from regulators. Writing in the *Washington Post*, she explained, "such swap deals can be rife with conflicts of interest and ripe for abuse so long as they are invisible to regulators and others in the market. They can directly affect regulated markets and concentrate enormous risks in a handful of major financial institutions. And the failure of such institutions can impose costs on taxpayers and the broader economy."

Schapiro expressed support for the financial reform bill introduced by senators Chris Dodd and Barney Frank in the spring of 2010. As the result of that bill, the SEC undertook a major study of fiduciary standards that ended in January of 2011 with a recommendation that both financial brokers and advisers be held to the same standard: putting the interests of their clients ahead of their own financial interests. Yet the issue of a sole fiduciary standard was a controversial one, with two of the SEC's sitting commissioners arguing that the adoption of such a standard was not yet adequately supported by the data in the report. "We have a lot of work … ahead of us before we actually take a pen to paper and figure out what we might do in terms of writing any specific rule," Schapiro was quoted as stating in an *Investment News* article by Mark Schoeff, Jr. She further noted that the report "was really very much the first step in what will be a process."

Sources

Periodicals

Investment News, February 28, 2011, p. 10.

New York Times, May 16, 1996; June 2, 1996; January 13, 2006; April 13, 2008.

Time, May 13, 2010.

Washington Post, April 2, 2010, p. A17; April 6, 2010, p. A8; April 17, 2010, p. A1.

Online

"Mary L. Schapiro," WhoRunsGov, http://www.whorunsgov.com/Profiles/Mary_L._Schapiro (March 5, 2011).

"Schapiro Taking SEC's Reins Shows Regulator Dodged Cox Critics," Bloomberg News, http://www.bloomberg.com/apps/news?pid=newsarchive&sid=aZLII4ktuIAk&refer=home%29 (March 5, 2011).

"SEC's New Chairman: Who Is Mary Schapiro?" *Times,* http://business.timesonline.co.uk/tol/business/industry_sectors/banking_and_finance/article5364844.ece (March 5, 2011).

"Staying Ahead of the Scam Artists," *BusinessWeek,* http://www.businessweek.com/magazine/content/06_37/b4000074.htm (March 5, 2011).

—*Vanessa E. Vaughn*

Blake Shelton

© Kevin Winter/Getty Images for ACM

Singer and television personality

Born Blake Tollison Shelton, June 18, 1976, in Ada, OK; son of Dick (a used car dealer) and Dorothy (a beauty salon owner) Shelton; married Kaynette Williams, 2003 (divorced, 2006); married Miranda Lambert (a country music performer), 2011.

Addresses: *Record company*—Warner Music Nashville, 20 Music Square East, Nashville, TN 37203-4344. *Web site*—http://www.blakeshelton.com.

Career

Moved to Nashville, worked as songwriter, and signed record deal, late 1990s; released self-titled debut album, 2001; released *The Dreamer*, 2003; released *Blake Shelton's Barn and Grill*, 2004; released *Pure BS*, 2006; released *Startin' Fires*, 2008; released EPs *Hillbilly Bone*, and *All About Tonight*, 2010; became coach on *The Voice*, released *Red River Blue*, 2011.

Awards: Denbo Diamond Award for young performers, c. 1994; CMA Award for best male vocalist, Country Music Association, 2010; CMA award for musical event of the year (with Trace Adkins), Country Music Association, for "Hillbilly Bone," 2010; CMT Award for collaborative video of the year (with Trace Adkins), Country Music Television, for "Hillbilly Bone," 2010; CMT Award for male video of the year, Country Music Television, for "Who Are You When I'm Not Looking," 2011; CMT Award for web video of the year, Country Music Television, for "Kiss My Country Ass," 2011.

Sidelights

Singer, songwriter, and television personality Blake Shelton built a successful career as a country music performer before becoming a high-profile celebrity as a judge on the popular NBC singing competition *The Voice*. The nearly six-and-a-half-foot tall Shelton first became a sensation in 2001 with the release of his single "Austin," which topped the *Billboard* country charts for several weeks and helped his self-titled debut album go gold. Successive releases *The Dreamer*, *Blake Shelton's Barn and Grill*, *Pure BS*, and *Startin' Fires* also made waves with country audiences, helping establish Shelton as one of the most popular male country performers of the decade. In 2010, he released a pair of EPs, *Hillbilly Bone* and *All About Tonight*.

Several years into his career, Shelton expanded from music performance to television, signing on as a judge for *The Voice* in 2011. His sixth full-length studio album, *Red River Blue*, followed that summer, not long after Shelton married long-time girlfriend and fellow country performer Miranda Lambert. Despite his extremely busy schedule, the performer quickly made it clear that his new marriage was among his higher priorities. "The one thing we can't allow to happen is we get so busy that we lose each other. Do I want to be the biggest star on earth? Yeah. Am I willing to do what it takes to be that?" he told Jon Caramanica of the *New York Times* soon after his wedding. "Here came some cussing, before he concluded with a no," Caramanica added.

Born Blake Tollison Shelton on June 18, 1976, in Ada, Oklahoma, the performer was the youngest of the three children of used car dealer Dick Shelton and his wife, beauty salon owner Dorothy; Shelton's brother Richie died as the result of a car accident when the younger boy was still in his teens. From a young age, Shelton showed a flair for performance, making his stage debut singing the Bob Seger tune "Old Time Rock 'n' Roll" at a local talent show when he was just eight years old. By his mid-teens, the budding country artist had learned to play guitar and began touring local bars and music venues, winning Oklahoma's Denbo Diamond Award for young performers. He had also received career affirmation from respected songwriter Mae Boren Axton, who has contributed to songs performed by artists from Elvis Presley to Three Dog Night. Axton told Shelton that he had the potential to get a record deal after seeing one of the teen's performances in Ada. Encouraged by his early successes, Shelton moved to Nashville, Tennessee, just two weeks after graduating from high school to try to break into the country-music scene.

In Nashville, Shelton reconnected with Axton, who gave him a job painting houses and helped him network with local country-music figures. Soon, Shelton had sold songs to Nashville-area publishing houses including Naomi Martin Music, Warner/Chappell Music, and Jerry Crutchfield Music. He attracted the attention of country-music veteran Bobby Braddock, who propelled the young performer into his career. Before long, Shelton had signed a record deal with Giant Records and entered the studio to record his first album, with Braddock signing on to produce. The resulting first single, "Austin," recounted the story of a separated couple getting back together through a series of answering machine messages. The track, released in 2001, became a country-music hit, giving Shelton his first number one on the *Billboard* country songs charts and his first top-20 single on the mixed-genre *Billboard* Hot 100. When Giant went out of business later that year, Shelton was transferred to Giant's parent company, Warner Brothers, which released his self-titled debut in July of 2001. Hailed as "an earnest debut full of lots of promise and originality" by Maria Konicki Dinoia of Allmusic, the album sailed to the top of the *Billboard* country albums chart and was eventually certified gold.

Over the next decade, Shelton released several more albums for Warner Brothers. His sophomore effort,

The Dreamer, with featured popular single "The Baby" hit shelves in 2003. The album soared to the number-two spot on the *Billboard* country albums chart and peaked at number eight on the mainstream *Billboard* 200; like its predecessor, *The Dreamer* went gold in time. The year after the release of *The Dreamer,* Shelton returned with *Blake Shelton's Barn and Grill.* Termed "a happy balance between Nashville craft and pure country" by Stephen Thomas Erlewine of Allmusic, the album reflected Shelton's increasing maturity both as a person and as an artist. "As I'm getting a little older and really starting to settle into myself I realize I'm a pretty laid-back guy and that's alive in my music," Shelton commented to J. Adrian Stanley of the Colorado Springs *Gazette. Blake Shelton's Barn and Grill* produced the hit single "Some Beach," which topped the country charts, and itself cracked the top three of the *Billboard* country albums charts.

Shelton underwent changes in his personal life in 2006. He and his wife of three years, Kaynette Williams, divorced; soon after, Shelton began dating fellow country singer Miranda Lambert, who first rose to music success through the reality program *Nashville Star.* That same year, Shelton left Nashville to return to Oklahoma. He bought a 1,200-acre ranch in Tishomingo, Oklahoma, located in the southern tip of the state. Lambert purchased property just a few miles away, and the pair settled into true country life."[We'd] rather be at home cooking hamburgers or picking corn or something," Shelton told Chris Willard of *People* in 2008; however, with his divorce still fresh in his mind, Shelton was hesitant to jump straight into marriage with Lambert.

Returning to the recording studio, Shelton released *Pure BS* in 2007. Produced by Braddock along with Paul Worley and Brent Rowan, the album garnered positive critical notices. "Spanning love, heartache, drinking and just plain fun ... it's the best he has offered yet, judged Ken Tucker in *Billboard.* Thom Jurek of Allmusic agreed, proclaiming that "*Pure BS* is the album Shelton's been waiting to make his entire career and gives us an absolutely stunning new view of an established artist who is here to stay." Fans also signed on, sending *Pure BS* to the number-two spot of the *Billboard* country charts and to number eight on the *Billboard* 200. The following year, Shelton released *Startin' Fires,* his fifth full-length studio album and another solid success. Single "She Wouldn't Be Gone" took the performer back to the top of the *Billboard* country songs chart, and became Shelton's first gold-selling single.

In 2010, Shelton and Warner Brothers embarked on an unusual recording strategy. Instead of releasing a traditional full-length album backed by a series of radio singles, Shelton recorded two six-song EPs supporting just one single each. The first of these, *Hillbilly Bone,* hit shelves in March of 2010. The EP's hit track, which featured fellow country star Trace Adkins, topped the *Billboard* Hot Country Songs chart and helped make the overall EP a commercial success. As perhaps indicated by its backcountry title, the release saw Shelton nodding to traditionally rural working-class themes; writing for the *Washington Post,* reviewer Allison Stewart commented that much of *Hillbilly Bone* "labors aggressively to establish Shelton's country bona fides while being unnecessarily defensive at the same time." Jurek, however, argued in Allmusic that the EP was "a good-natured dig at city folks, and you can't help but like Shelton, no matter how many clichés he spews." Five months later, Warner Brothers released Shelton's second EP of the year, *All About Tonight.* By this time, Shelton had proposed to long-time girlfriend Lambert, and she appeared on two of the EP's tracks, including the duet "Draggin' the River." Both the title track and follow-up single "Who Are You When I'm Not Looking" topped the *Billboard* Hot Country Songs chart, and the EP itself took the top spot on the top country albums listing.

The country singer became a mainstream star with his participation on NBC singing competition *The Voice,* which premiered in April of 2011. Based on a Dutch singing program, *The Voice* brought together four successful music performers—Shelton, pop singer Christina Aguilera, rocker Adam Levine of Maroon 5, and hip-hop artist Cee-Lo Green—to serve as coaches for teams of aspiring singers. The four coaches chose their teams through a blind audition process, which featured an unusual twist in that the contestants were allowed to select their coach if more than one wanted to show him or her as a team member. Then, the celebrities helped guide the contestants through a series of head-to-head sing-offs that allowed both the coaches and the viewing audience to vote on the week's winners. A member of Shelton's team ultimately placed second in the overall competition. *The Voice* proved an instant hit, generating high ratings for NBC and introducing Shelton to new, non-country-listening audiences. Writing for *Entertainment Weekly,* Mandi Bierly noted that Shelton's "sense of humor, sensitivity (catch those smiles when contestants sang songs by his fiancée, Miranda Lambert?), and toughness (he still didn't pick either of 'em!)" gave him great appeal to new fans. The success of the program led to a quick renewal by NBC, and Shelton signed on to return for the show's planned second season in early 2012.

Shelton has also become known for his forthright nature and rustic charm, as well as his willingness to share information that celebrities often tried to keep quiet. He routinely posted personal comments about his drunken revelries or other matters on popular social Web site Twitter, using raw language that could be considered offensive. His record label urged him to stop making the posts, but Shelton resisted, telling Caramanica in the same *New York Times* interview, "If Hank Williams Sr. would have had a Twitter account, can you imagine [what he] would have said? Or George Jones?... It's O.K. to offend somebody.... If you don't stand for something, how can anyone respect what you do?" But even Shelton has, at times, apologized for his off-the-cuff comments. In May of 2011, he had a highly publicized Twitter conflict with gay and lesbian rights group GLAAD over a post in which Shelton seemed to be condoning and even encouraging violence against gay men in his rewrite of lyrics from a popular Shania Twain song. Shelton offered a public apology on Twitter, with *People*'s Dahvi Shira quoting him as explaining, "It honestly wasn't even meant that way.... But when it comes to gay/lesbian rights or just feelings … I love everybody."

Shelton's growing success continued into the summer as he won two trophies at the Country Music Awards in June, one for Male Video of the Year for "Who Are You When I'm Not Looking" and the other for Web Video of the Year for "Kiss My Country Ass," which had appeared on *Hillbilly Bone.* In July, Shelton released his sixth studio album, *Red River Blue.* Led by the chart-topping, platinum-selling single "Honey Bee," the album was recorded somewhat more quickly than anticipated in order to capitalize on the success of its first single. *Red River Blue* channeled a modern take of classic country sounds, combining honky-tonk rhythms with songs about standard country music themes like love, betrayal, and the blue-collar lifestyle. *Red River Blue* became Shelton's first *Billboard* 200 chart-topper as well as hitting number one on the *Billboard* country albums chart, selling 116,000 copies in its first week of release. To support *Red River Blue,* Shelton embarked on a tour, spending several weeks crisscrossing the United States and visiting a handful of Canadian cities.

Selected discography

Blake Shelton, Warner Brothers, 2001.
The Dreamer, Warner Brothers, 2003.
Blake Shelton's Barn and Grill, Warner Brothers, 2004.
Pure BS, Warner Brothers, 2006.
Startin' Fires, Warner Brothers, 2008.
Hillbilly Bone (EP), Warner Brothers, 2010.
All About Tonight (EP), Warner Brothers, 2010.
Red River Blue, Warner Brothers, 2011.

Sources

Books

Contemporary Musicians, vol. 45, Gale, 2004.

Periodicals

Billboard, May 5, 2007, p. 35.
Gazette (Colorado Springs, CO), August 6, 2004, p. GO19.
New York Times, July 10, 2011, p. 1.

Online

"Album Review: Blake Shelton, *Hillbilly Bone,*" *Washington Post,* http://blog.washingtonpost.com/clicktrack/2010/03/album_review_blake_shelton_hil.html (August 27, 2011).
"Biography," Allmusic, http://allmusic.com/artist/blake-shelton-p480679/biography (August 27, 2011).
"Blake Shelton," Allmusic, http://allmusic.com/album/blake-shelton-r541235 (August 27, 2011).
"Blake Shelton Apologizes for Offending Gays on Twitter," *People,* http://www.people.com/people/article/0,,20487562.tif,00.html (August 27, 2011).
"Blake Shelton is Single—For Now," *People,* http://www.people.com/people/article/0,,20208035.tif,00.html (August 27, 2011).
" *Blake Shelton's Barn and Grill,*" Allmusic, http://allmusic.com/album/blake-sheltons-barn-grill-r710843 (August 27, 2011).
"Hillbilly Bone," Allmusic, http://allmusic.com/album/hillbilly-bone-r1722820/review (August 27, 2011).
"Liking Blake Shelton on *The Voice*? Bet you'll like him even more after reading this!," *Entertainment Weekly,* http://popwatch.ew.com/2011/05/04/blake-shelton-the-voice-pop-culture-personality-test/ (August 27, 2011).
"Pure BS," Allmusic, http://allmusic.com/album/pure-bs-r1032581/review (August 27, 2011).

—*Vanessa E. Vaughn*

Yingluck Shinawatra

Prime minister of Thailand

Born on June 21, 1967, in Chiang Mai, Thailand; daughter of Lert Shinawatra (a politician) and Yindi Ramingwong; married to Anusorn Amornchat (a business executive); children: Supasek (son). *Education:* Chiang Mai University, bachelor's degree; Kentucky State University, M.P.A., 1991.

Addresses: *Office*—Office of the Prime Minister, Government House, Thanon Nakornpraton Dusit, Bangkok, 10300, Thailand.

Career

Worked for various corporations owned by the Shinawatra family, 1991-2011; began working for Shinawatra Directory, 1991; became managing director of Advanced Info Service, 2002; became executive president of SC Asset Corporation, 2006; elected prime minister of Thailand, 2011.

Sidelights

Yingluck Shinawatra was elected prime minister of Thailand in the summer of 2011 in one of the nation's most surprising and controversial political changeovers. The first woman to ever hold the top Thai political office, Shinawatra was the sister of former prime minister Thaksin Shinawatra, who was deposed in a 2006 coup. Prior to her election, Shinawatra had no political experience, making her win an apparent indication of popular support for her self-exiled brother rather than a sign of support for her own governmental qualifications. Many critics saw her election as a political front to return the deposed Thaksin Shinawatra to power, and the younger Shinawatra was criticized for what was seen as her government's first major attempt to secure his pardon and return to power short months after her election. Soon after taking office, Shinawatra also faced a significant challenge in the form of devastating flooding that greatly harmed the rural areas around Bangkok and in the country's north.

The youngest of the nine children of Lert Shinawatra and Yindi Ramingwong, Shinawatra was born on June 21, 1967. Her family was one of the wealthiest and most powerful in Chiang Mai, the leading city of northern Thailand, thanks to the family's diverse business holdings in telecommunications, transportation, cinemas, and textiles. Shinawatra's mother was the daughter of a princess, and her father was elected to the Thai parliament to represent the area in 1968 and later rose to become deputy leader of his political party. Although the family patriarch retired from political life in 1976, some of Shinawatra's older siblings carried on this tradition. One sister, Sujate Shinawatra, served as mayor of Chiang Mai, and another sister, Yaowapa Wongsawat, was the Thai first lady in 2008 during the tenure of her husband, Somchai Wongsawat, as prime minister. Other siblings served in the national legislature.

Politics thus played a major role in the young woman's life, and she decided to study the subject in college, earning first an undergraduate degree in political science from Chiang Mai University and, later, a master's degree in public administration from Kentucky State University in Frankfort, Kentucky. This family legacy of political involvement is not unusual in the region, explained Thai political science instructor Chalidaporn Songsamphan to Thomas Fuller of the *New York Times*. "Particularly in Southeast Asian countries, male and female politicians often enter politics because of their family connections. They enter politics because their fathers, mothers, brothers, sisters, cousins or even husband and wife are politicians," she explained. "Yingluck jumped into politics because of the needs of the family."

After completing graduate studies in 1991, Shinawatra returned to Thailand, where she worked in sales and marketing for a family-owned yellow pages company, Shinawatra Directory. In 1995, she married another businessperson, Anusorn Amornchat; the couple later had one son, Supasek. Over the next several years, Shinawatra rose through the corporate ranks of her family's holdings. She worked for a time for Advanced Info Service (AIS), the nation's largest mobile phone company, becoming that company's managing director in 2002. In 2006, Shinawatra shifted to another family corporation, the real estate firm SC Asset Corporation, when AIS was sold. She served as executive president of SC Asset Corporation.

Shinawatra's political career was inextricably linked with that of her brother, Thaksin Shinawatra, who became the Thai prime minister in 2001. His government was popular with the nation's poor rural residents, who believed that he worked to protect their interests through such programs as microloans and health insurance; however, Shinawatra also came under fire for human rights violations, corruption, and other political charges. In September of 2006, the military led a coup that ousted Shinawatra, temporarily suspended the constitution, and placed the nation under martial law. This action received a great deal of international criticism because the prime minister had been democratically reelected just months before. Opposition politicians within Thailand argued that the overthrow had been necessary. "I would say that nothing is worse than what Thaksin has done," commented former Thai senator Chirmsak Pinthong in a BBC News story. "Thaksin has already carried out what I would call a silent coup, because he called the country as a dictatorship by using money in a corrupt way." Two years later, the ousted leader fled Thailand for Dubai to avoid a prison sentence following conviction on charges of fraud.

In the spring of 2011, the Pheu Thai party—the latest in a series of parties created to support the political career of Thaksin Shinawatra—announced that Yingluck Shinawatra would be its standard bearer in that year's parliamentary elections. This nomination made her the first woman to stand for Thailand's top political job. The novice politician staffed her campaign with veterans of her brother's regime, allowing her to combine the attraction of being a new face in government with the experience of years of being in the system. As a reporter for the *Economist* observed during the campaign season, Shinawatra's "very appealing freshness, youth and easy-going nature are finely balanced against a hard-nosed, slick and pragmatic campaign that organizes every step she takes, every camera angle, and every handshake. Not a word or a smile is wasted." Hailed as being more natural with the average Thai citizen than her opponent, incumbent prime minister Abhisit Vejjajiva of the Democrat Party, Shinawatra proved a strong presence on the campaign trail. As the weeks went on, she gained increasing attention as a real contender for the prime minister's seat; when the election returns rolled in in July, the Pheu Thai party picked up a clear majority, giving the top job to Shinawatra. Although some political observers had questioned whether the military and other Thaksin opponents would allow his sister to form a government, the result went unchallenged.

Shortly after winning office, Shinawatra announced plans to create a coalition government, despite her Pheu Thai party picking up enough seats in the general election to dominate the national legislature on its own. The BBC News characterized this decision as a "a shrewd political move," noting that the coalition—which controlled nearly two-thirds of the parliamentary seats—"will make it easier ... to push through reforms promised during her election campaign and create a sense of stability." She soon announced the members of her 35-seat Cabinet, and observers noted the probable hand of her brother in the picks; most positions went to experienced members of the Pheu Thai party or to members of the coalition parties, with just a few people from outside the traditional government structure stepping in to fill roles, mostly in the economic and commerce ministries.

A major challenge for the prime minister followed soon after her assumption of office when a series of floods threatened Thailand in the fall of 2011. A combination of unusually heavy rainfall during the summer and early fall and rising runoffs from overtaxed dams formed massive floods that affected the nation's cities, agriculture, and industry. Media reports noted that rice fields had been completely destroyed and that the floodwaters had shut down more than 1,000 factories around the country even as hundreds of others faced lessened production, hobbling the nation's economy. Estimates suggested that some nine million Thai citizens were affected by the floods, with thousands forced to flee their homes and a death toll in the hundreds. Waters reached several feet in some areas as people abandoned houses filled waist-high with water.

Because of her lack of experience in the public sector, the situation was seen as a particularly sharp challenge for the new prime minister; Thaksin Shinawatra, widely speculated to be the real source of decision making behind the scenes of the ruling government, was simply too far removed from the problems on the ground to be able to guide his sister's actions. "Her mettle is being tested, and it certainly will define her leadership," commented Thitinan Pongsudhirak of Thailand's Chulalongkorn University to Seth Mydans of the *New York Times*. Shinawatra moved to protect the Thai capital city of Bangkok, home to more than 12 million residents, through a series of dams and other barriers that routed many of the floodwaters to the hinterlands surrounding the metropolitan areas. These actions worsened conditions in these already suffering regions, and ultimately failed to keep the city itself from being affected. "I have decided to ask Bangkok to open all gates, which could trigger an overflow, in order to drain water into the sea as soon as possible," she was quoted as stating by Mydans in the same article. "Floodwaters are coming from every direction, and we cannot control them because it's a huge amount of water. We will try to warn people," she concluded. Within days, residents of some areas began to speak out against the decision, with some taking measures to break open the dams and floodgates routing water to their neighborhoods; a new threat also emerged as crocodiles began to appear in flooded districts, prompting the government to offer bounties for animals caught alive. The situation remained unresolved as October 2011 drew to a close, with Thais throughout the nation dealing with high waters and Shinawatra facing criticism for her handling of a situation that offered no good options for action.

Even as political and human fallout from the flooding continued, Shinawatra's government faced fresh controversy when reports surfaced in November of 2011 that it was planning to provide a list of some 25,000 prisoners to the Thai king for him to pardon. Although the amnesty is an annual tradition in the nation's government, criticism immediately arose that the move was nothing more than an effort to clear the slate of the prime minister's exiled brother. "It's so obvious that this was done specifically for Thaksin," Abhisit Vejjajiva, the leader of the main Thai opposition party, told Fuller of the *New York Times* in a separate story. The press and protest leaders widely speculated that the disgraced former prime minister's name was included in the secret list, but—after initially refusing to confirm or deny the reports—the nation's Justice Ministry soon moved to refute these allegations. "Thaksin will not receive any benefit from the [royal] decree, and his name will not be included on the list of convicts eligible for a royal pardon," Justice Minister Pracha Promnok was quoted as stating in a story by Richard S. Ehrlich of the *Washington Times*. Reports continued to circulate that Thaksin Shinawatra had been included on an earlier draft of the amnesty list and was removed only after outcry forced the government to rescind its intentions; the former prime minister denied that any such effort had been made on his behalf.

Regardless of the controversy surrounding the still-young Shinawatra administration, the United States asserted its support for the sitting government. U.S. Secretary of State Hillary Rodham Clinton made an official visit to Bangkok while in Southeast Asia, during which she met with the prime minister and visited some families affected by the earlier floods. "We believe it is in the national security and political interest of the United States to have this government succeed," Ehrlich quoted a State Department representative as stating in the same *Washington Times* story, "and we will do what we can to support that going forward."

Sources

Periodicals

Bangkok Post, May 16, 2011.
New York Times, August 5, 2011; October 20, 2011; November 1, 2011; November 16, 2011.
Washington Times, November 23, 2011.

Online

"Election Q&A: What next for Thailand?," BBC News, http://www.bbc.co.uk/news/world-asia-pacific-14012310.tif (November 23, 2011).
"Flood Waters Free Crocodiles in Thailand," *New York Times*, http://thelede.blogs.nytimes.com/2011/10/25/flood-waters-free-crocodiles-in-thailand/ (November 23, 2011).
Gale Biography in Context, Gale, 2011.
"Profile: Yingluck Shinawatra," BBC News, http://www.bbc.co.uk/news/world-asia-pacific-13723451.tif (November 23, 2011).

"Thai PM deposed in military coup," BBC News, http://news.bbc.co.uk/2/hi/5361512.stm (November 23, 2011).

"Too Hot for the Generals," *Economist*, http://www.economist.com/node/21521969.tif (November 23, 2011).

"Yingluck Shinawatra, Thailand's 1st female prime minister," CBC News, http://www.cbc.ca/news/canada/story/2011/07/04/f-yingluck-shinawatra.html (November 23, 2011).

—*Vanessa E. Vaughn*

Alan Simpson

Co-chair of the National Commission on Fiscal Responsibility and Reform

Born Alan Kooi Simpson, September 2, 1931, in Denver, CO; son of Milward L. (an attorney and politician) and Lorna K. Simpson; married to Ann; children: three. *Education:* University of Wyoming, B.S., 1954, J.D., 1959.

Addresses: *Office*—1220 Sunshine Ave., Ste. B, Cody, WY 82414.

Career

Served in the U.S. Army, 1954-56; began practicing law in Cody, Wyoming, 1958; served as assistant attorney general of Wyoming, 1958-59; U.S. Commissioner, 1959-69; served in Wyoming House of Representatives, 1964-77; served in U.S. Senate, 1979-97; served as Republican whip, 1985-95; visiting lecturer, Harvard University, 1997-2000; began teaching at the University of Wyoming, late 1990s; named co-chair of a special deficit reduction committee, 2010. Author of books, including *Right in the Old Gazoo: A Lifetime of Scrapping with the Press*, 1997.

Member: Commissioner, American Battle Monuments Commission, 2001—; co-chairman, Continuity if Government Commission, 2002—; co-chairman, National Commission on Fiscal Responsibility and Reform, 2010—.

© *Roger L. Wollenberg/UPI/Landov*

Sidelights

Former U.S. Senator Alan K. Simpson served as a member of the Republican leadership of Congress' upper house during much of the 1980s and early 1990s despite disagreeing with the conservative wing over social issues such as abortion and homosexuality. Unafraid to stick to his own beliefs, the Wyoming politician used his sharp tongue and quick wit to develop a reputation as one of the most influential and outspoken members of the legislature. His Congressional legacy includes co-sponsorship of a controversial 1986 immigration reform law that granted amnesty to millions of undocumented immigrants and a tenure of nearly a decade as the Republican second-in-command in the Senate. Years after his retirement in 1996, Simpson returned to the capital to co-chair a presidential commission on deficit reduction. The committee's recommendations, issued in late 2010, came amid a major national discussion about the federal government's balance sheet. Although practically none of the recommendations came into practice, Simpson again became a sought-after expert on budgetary matters who was unafraid to challenge the anti-tax mantra of the contemporary Republican Party.

The future politician was born Alan Kooi Simpson on September 2, 1931, in Denver, Colorado, but grew up in Wyoming, where his family had long resided. Simpson's great-grandfather, Fincelius G. Burnett, had settled in the territory during the 1860s, selling supplies to soldiers at Fort Laramie and Fort Phil Kearney. His daughter, Margaret Burnett, was working on a Native American reservation as a teenager when she met Simpson's grandfather, a rough-and-tumble self-taught lawyer named William L. Simpson who went by the colorful nickname of "Broke-A** Bill." Their son, Milward L. Simpson became one of Wyoming's leading figures. A lawyer like his father, this Simpson served as Wyoming's governor during the late 1950s and later became one of the state's U.S. Senators. This familial dichotomy of Western independence and political astuteness helped shape the young Simpson's psyche, as did the Simpson clan's sharp sense of humor. "My mother's view was 'humor is the universal salve against the abrasive elements of life,'" the Senator told Chase Reynolds Ewald of *American Cowboy* in 1995. "And the old man's favorite phrase was 'I'm too busy loving to hate.'"

After graduating from high school in Cody, Wyoming, Simpson briefly attended the Cranbrook School near Detroit, Michigan, before returning to his home state to pursue law studies. While attending the University of Wyoming, Simpson was involved with student government and played both football and basketball. He completed a bachelor's degree in law in 1954. Soon after graduation, Simpson married fellow Wyoming native Ann Schroll; the couple later had three children. Simpson spent two years in the U.S. Army, serving mostly in the U.S.-occupied zone of West Germany. He left the military with an honorable discharge and resumed his education at the University of Wyoming, completing a post-graduate law degree at that institution in 1958.

Simpson spent the next decade working as an attorney in Cody, first entering politics in 1964 by winning election the state House of Representatives. He remained in state government until 1978, when he campaigned successfully for a seat in the U.S. Senate. As a new Senator, he was assigned to the Senate Judiciary Committee, and through this appointment was named a member of a presidential commission on immigration—despite representing a state with one of the lowest immigrant populations in the nation. Two years later, Republicans gained control of the Senate, and Simpson helped form a new subcommittee on the matter at the suggestion of Democratic Senator Ted Kennedy. Thus began Simpson's involvement with the issue that largely defined his first several years as a national legislator.

By 1982, Simpson had drafted the first version of a bill to reform U.S. immigration law with Democratic Representative Romano Mazzoli of Kentucky that was quickly dubbed the Simpson-Mazzoli Bill. This controversial legislation proposed a widespread amnesty for unauthorized aliens who had first entered and lived in the United States prior to 1982, placed greater responsibility on employers for affirming their workers' immigration status through the use of a national identification card system, and instituted quotas and restrictions on new immigration. Nationwide debate erupted over several provisions of the bill, particularly the identification card requirement, and the measure underwent revision multiple times before finally winning passage as the Immigration Reform and Control Act of 1986. Called "the most important immigration legislation in the last 20 years" by *New York Times* reporter Joel Brinkley in 1994, the finalized act instituted the originally proposed amnesty and allowed certain temporary workers to apply for documentation, thus allowing close to an estimated three million previously unauthorized immigrants to obtain legal residence in the United States. It also instituted legal penalties for employers who knowingly hired unauthorized workers among other efforts to curb illegal immigration. Despite its broad goals, the bill failed to truly solve immigration problems in the United States. Writing two decades after its passage, Rachel L. Swarns noted that "fraudulent applications tainted the process, many employers continued their illicit hiring practices, and illegal immigration surged"—the exact opposite result that Simpson and Mazzoli had hoped for. Immigration remained a hot-button issue in the United States well into the 21st century.

Along with immigration, the senator chaired a committee on veterans' affairs and participated in overall party leadership. In 1984, Simpson was elected whip—the second-highest leadership position within a political party in the Senate—at the same time that Senator Bob Dole was elected party leader. William E. Farrell and Warren Weaver Jr. of the *New York Times* noted that one Senate aide dubbed the polling results "the survival of the wittiest" in reference to the two leaders' famed droll styles. The Wyoming senator remained in this role until 1994, when he was unseated by the more conservative Mississippi Senator Trent Lott by just one vote. This shift reflected an overall rightward turn on social issues within the party, which set the pro-choice and pro-gay rights Simpson apart from his colleagues. In 1996, he chose not to run for re-election. The year following his retirement, Simpson, who had often clashed with reporters during his time in office, published a work on politics and the media titled *Right in the Old Gazoo: A Lifetime of Scrapping with the Press.*

After retirement, Simpson was a visiting lecturer at both Harvard University's John F. Kennedy School of Government and the University of Wyoming's political science program. Back in Wyoming, he also continued to practice law. In February of 2010, Simpson was thrust back into the political hot seat when President Barack Obama named him a co-chair to a bipartisan deficit reduction commission. Conservative political commentators attacked the former senator for working too closely with Democrats, but Simpson—channeling his signature independent streak—bluntly and colorfully dismissed their claims. As he told Weston Kosova of *Newsweek,* "it's all BS. I don't have to take that nonsense.... The people who distort the commission ... let's say they win the day, and we don't do anything to try to bring down this debt. Well, great. They've got grandchildren, too, and in 40 years they'll be sucking canal water and picking grit with the chickens."

The following November, the commission released its preliminary recommendations for how to reform the spiraling federal budget. Among their main recommendations were changing the structure of the Social Security system to index the retirement age to rising life spans, lower the annual cost-of-living increase amount, progressively reduce benefits for middle- and upper-earning retired individuals, and raise the cap on the dollar amount on salaries for which Americans pay Social Security taxes; decreasing Medicare and Medicaid costs by raising co-pays, requiring greater use of managed care, and creating a cap on program growth; cutting domestic spending in many ways, including freezing federal wages, eliminating several categories of government subsidies, and charging or raising admission fees at the Smithsonian museums and national parks; reducing defense spending by lowering troop and contract staff levels and canceling a number of military research programs; capping government expenditures and revenues at just over one-fifth of the nation's gross domestic product; and, finally, undertaking sweeping tax reform to lower the number of tax brackets and eliminate several tax deductions or credits.

The plan appealed to neither Democratic nor Republican orthodoxy. Democrats, who wished to protect social spending and domestic programs, opposed such measures as raising the retirement age for Social Security benefits. Yet even stronger opposition came from Republicans, who firmly opposed revenue increases through tax code reform, especially following sweeping Republican victories in the midterm elections of 2010 on promises of drastically cutting the size of government and slashing spending. Opposition within the deficit reduction panel prevented its recommendations from moving to Congress for a vote, and clashes over the nation's budget problems raged on. Simpson—known for his longtime support for reducing deficits even at the political cost of raising taxes—questioned the logic and motivations of the anti-revenue increase stance that derailed the committee's propositions. Speaking to Tim Dickinson of *Rolling Stone,* Simpson demanded, "whatever happened to common sense? People are going to look around in five or ten years and say, 'Whatever happened to the things that made me comfortable? That made our streets and schools good things?' And they'll look, hopefully, at Grover Norquist," referring to the head of anti-tax organization Americans for Tax Reform who has long asked GOP lawmakers to sign pledges agreeing to work to reduce all forms of federal taxes. "I can say to you with deepest sincerity: If this country and this legislature are in thrall to Grover Norquist, we haven't got a prayer."

Indeed, many analysts suggested that Republican lawmakers' pledge to Norquist's organization was a major sticking point in the deficit reduction talks that stalled compromise efforts to raise the U.S. debt ceiling during the summer of 2011. Because the overwhelming majority of Republican Congressional lawmakers had signed the pledge, they were forced to oppose any deal that included any form of revenue boosts through new taxes or even through allowing existing temporary tax cuts to expire. The influence and spending power of Norquist's organization could cost Republican lawmakers who broke their agreement their jobs. "Grover's got 'em terrified," Simpson told Dickinson in the same interview. "I always tell Republicans, 'Hell, Grover can't kill ya. He can't burn down your house. The only thing he can do to you is defeat you in re-election—and if re-election means more to you than your country, then you shouldn't be in the legislature," Simpson concluded bluntly. Members of the contemporary GOP leadership did not necessarily agree with the former senator's assessment, however. "Listen, our conference is opposed to tax hikes because we believe that tax hikes will hurt our economy and put Americans out of work," Speaker of the House John Boehner was quoted as saying in a *Washington Times* blog post by Sean Lengell.

Simpson remained a loud voice on budgetary issues into the fall of 2011 as the Congressional supercommittee charged with greatly trimming the federal budget failed to make its Thanksgiving deadline. Arguing that politicians were irresponsibly neglecting the nation's problem in favor of serving their political interests, Simpson chastised the committee members for not reaching an agreement and called for renewed political will to solve what he and co-chair Bowles dubbed "the most predictable economic crisis in history" in a press release reprinted on the Web site of the Moment of Truth Project.

Selected writings

Right in the Old Gazoo: A Lifetime of Scrapping with the Press, William Morrow (New York City), 1997.

Sources

Periodicals

American Cowboy, May/June 1995, pp. 51-55.
American Spectator, April 1993.
Newsweek, April 12, 2010, p. 35.
New York Times, December 7, 1984; October 24, 1990; September 15, 1994; May 23, 2006; December 1, 2010.
Rolling Stone, November 24, 2011, pp. 46-57.

Online

"Alan K. Simpson Bio," Made in Wyoming, http://www.madeinwyoming.net/profiles/extras/Alan-Simpson-bio.pdf (November 22, 2011).
"Alan Simpson: I'm Not Sticking With Republicans Who Are 'Homophobic,' 'Anti-Women,'" *Huffington Post,* http://www.huffingtonpost.com/2011/04/12/alan-simpson-abortion-gay-rights_n_848270.html (September 20, 2011).
"Boehner: Grover Norquist just a 'random' guy," *Washington Times,* http://www.washingtontimes.com/blog/inside-politics/2011/nov/3/boehner-grover-norquist-just-random-guy/ (November 22, 2011).
"Fiscal Commission Co-Chairs Simpson and Bowles Release Eye-Popping Recommendations," Talking Points Memo, http://tpmdc.talkingpointsmemo.com/2010/11/deficit-commission-co-chairs-simpson-and-bowles-release-eye-popping-recommendations.php (September 20, 2011).
"No-Tax 'Zealot' Norquist Emerges as Biggest Barrier to U.S. Deficit Deal," Bloomberg, http://www.bloomberg.com/news/2011-05-24/norquist-emerges-as-barrier-to-u-s-debt-deal.html (November 22, 2011).
"Simpson, Alan Kooi," Biographical Dictionary of the United States Congress, http://bioguide.congress.gov/scripts/biodisplay.pl?index=S000429 (September 20, 2011).
"Statement by Sen. Alan Simpson and Erksine Bowles on failure of select committee to reach agreement on deficit reduction plan," Moment of Truth Project, http://momentoftruthproject.org/publications/statement-sen-alan-simpson-and-erskine-bowles-failure-select-committee-reach-agreement- (November 22, 2011).

—Vanessa E. Vaughn

Ian Somerhalder

Actor

Born Ian Joseph Somerhalder, December 8, 1978, in Covington, LA; son of Robert (a building contractor) and Edna (a massage therapist) Somerhalder.

Addresses: *Office—Vampire Diaries* production company, 2364 Park Central Blvd., Decatur, GA 30035-3914. *Management*—1801 Century Park E., Ste. 700, Los Angeles, CA 90067.

Career

Began modeling at the age of ten, Ford Modeling Agency, 1989; began acting training at the age of 17, 1996; was signed for representation as an actor, 1998. Modeled for different designers including Ralph Lauren, Calvin Klein, Dolce and Gabbana, Gucci, and Guess. Actor in television, including: *Big Easy*, 1997; *Now and Again*, 1999; *Young Americans*, 2000; *Anatomy of a Hate Crime* (movie), 2001; *CSI: Crime Scene Investigation*, 2002; *CSI: Miami*, 2003; *Law and Order: Special Victims Unit*, 2003; *Fearless* (movie), 2004; *Smallville*, 2004; *Lost*, 2004-10; *Marco Polo* (movie), 2007; *Tell Me You Love Me*, 2007; *Lost City Raiders* (movie), 2008; *Fireball* (movie), 2009; *Vampire Diaries*, 2009—. Film appearances include: *Life as a House*, 2001; *Changing Hearts*, 2002; *Rules of Attraction*, 2002; *In Enemy Hands*, 2004; *Pulse*, 2006; *Sensation of Sight*, 2006; *TV: The Movie*, 2006; *Lost Samaritan*, 2008; *Tournament*, 2009; *Wake*, 2009; *How to Make Love to a Woman*, 2010.

Awards: Exciting New Face for a male actor, Young Hollywood Awards, 2002; (with others) SAG award for outstanding performance by an ensemble in a drama series, Screen Actors Guild, for *Lost*, 2006; Choice TV: Villain award, Teen Choice Awards, for *Vampire Diaries*, 2010.

Sidelights

Being a vampire who has trodden the earth for more than a 150 years is no delicate matter and Ian Somerhalder sinks his spectacularly white teeth into the role of Damon Salvatore on the hit television series *Vampire Diaries*. Somerhalder would also like to be known as someone who initiated the collective efforts of many people to make it possible for humans to not tread so heavily upon the earth and in the winter of 2011 started a foundation called the Ian Somerhalder Foundation to do just that. In an ironic turn of events a six-year-old fan of Somerhalder sent her tooth money from the tooth fairy to the foundation with a list of ideas to help. Somerhalder related the girl's words to Laura Prudon at TV Squad, "I'm sending you my tooth fairy money to the foundation to help save the planet, please let me know what I can do. I know I'm really young and I don't really have a voice yet, but, please let me help in my school."

Somerhalder stated that part of his reason for starting the foundation was to empower young people with a voice and a means to cooperatively create solutions to make the planet a healthier place. On the foundation Web site there is a page titled "Get Involved" and it asks people to email in their ideas, age, interests, passions, and skills. Somerhalder advocates for young people to become "youth catalysts." The stated mission of the Ian Somerhalder Foundation, according to the Web site, is "to empower, educate and collaborate with people and projects to positively impact the planet and its creatures." In addition to having young people collaborate and make change, the foundation desires to have existing organizations work in concert to make change in a similar fashion to the way that the earth and all of its living things are interconnected. The Web site states that "Nature does not behave independently. It works in unison with all its elements. Working independently to transform our planet is like trying to play a violin without strings. Communities of businesses, organizations, people and projects must begin to connect resources and skills to passions and projects."

Somerhalder, who used to drive a Land Rover, sold the gas guzzler and chose to buy a more fuel-efficient Audi. A native of Louisiana, Somerhalder's family was greatly affected by Hurricane Katrina in 2005. He described his mother Edna as being "very spiritual" and a huge Anne Rice fan. Environmental concerns and vampires seem natural interests for Somerhalder who auditioned for the role of Jason Stackhouse on the television series *True Blood* but did not get offered the role that Ryan Kwanten plays in the series. When the chance to audition for *Vampire Diaries* came up, Somerhalder seized the opportunity and enthralled the producers who cast him as Damon Salvatore. Damon is one of two brothers who were turned into vampires by a woman whom they both loved. The vampiric brothers have made their way to the small town of Mystic Falls where they find a young woman who reminds them both of the vampire who began their undead life. Somerhalder has stated that his favorite vampire film is *Shadow of the Vampire* starring Willem Dafoe and that he enjoys playing the same kind of creature on *Vampire Diaries.* MTV Movie News reporter Jocelyn Vena quoted Somerhalder as saying "Vampires are very hot. It's fun playing a vampire. You're 200 years old. You can fly around. You can eat beautiful girls—well, you can suck on their neck. I don't physically cut them up and eat them." About his character, Somerhalder said, "He's a lot of fun. He's charming and it's hard to hate him."

Somerhalder, who was best known for his breakout role as Boone Carlyle on J. J. Abrams' popular science fiction television series *Lost,* has a life that appears similar to that of a fictional character. His life is a story that began before he was even born. His last name came from his adoptive great grandfather who was an immigrant worker paid to marry the mistress of a wealthy English landowner. The mistress was pregnant and the baby needed a father to legitimize the birth.

Somerhalder was born north of New Orleans in Covington, Louisiana. Robert Somerhalder, his father, was a building contractor of French and English descent. His mother, Edna, who was a massage therapist, is of Choctaw and Irish descent and grew up on a pig farm in Mississippi. His parents divorced when Somerhalder was 13 years old. While his mother raised him on Eastern medicine and organic food, Somerhalder grew up doing typical boy activities such as boating, swimming, fishing, and training horses. When he was ten years old, he became a model, signing a three-year contract with the Ford Modeling Agency so that he could buy fishing equipment and a bicycle. While modeling for such designers as Ralph Lauren, Calvin Klein, Dolce and Gabbana, Gucci, and Guess kept him in New York for many summers and away from these activities, he chose to take time out from modeling in his young adolescence to go back to school where he acted in the school drama club and performed in a local theater group. He returned to modeling later when he had the opportunity to travel to Europe and model once more for the designers he had modeled for as a preteen. Somerhalder permanently left home a week after his 16th birthday. He does not like to speak about his years as a model for fear that people will get the impression that he is just another pretty face.

When he was only 17, Somerhalder decided to pursue acting and by the age of 19 he began studying with preeminent acting coach William Esper who is known for developing the talents of many luminaries of stage and screen, including Academy Award-winner Kathy Bates. Somerhalder was discovered like a Hollywood starlet of the glamourous past when he was working as an extra on the set of the feature film *Black and White* in the late 1990s. He was in the background in a club scene with 400 other people when the manager for another actor who was visiting the set saw him and immediately signed him for representation.

The actor made his small-screen debut in 1999-2000 in *Now and Again,* a science fiction television program about a man who has died and whose brain has been kept alive in a genetically engineered body. His next big role was as an angsty Rawley Academy student in the teen drama *Young Americans.* Somerhalder's character on the show falls for the daughter of the prep school's dean who is posing as a boy. Somerhalder's character questions his own sexuality in the confusion. Despite the fact that the television series was a spinoff from the wildly popular show *Dawson's Creek* only eight episodes ever aired.

Next came a small part in 2001 in *Life as a House,* which was a feature film starring Kevin Kline as a man who discovers that he has terminal cancer and wants to spend quality time with his teenage son who avoids him. In 2002 Somerhalder was cast in the role of Paul Denton in the feature film *Rules of Attraction,* which was about a love triangle between a drug dealer, a virgin, and a bisexual classmate amongst over-privileged college students. Returning once again to television, Somerhalder was cast as Adam Knight in the series *Smallville.* The character began as an unwilling pawn who was resurrected from the dead by Lionel Luthor and Dr. Lia Teng with the mission to befriend Lana Lang and spy on Clark Kent. Over the course of several episodes the character changed and ended as a murderer who killed Dr. Teng and her lab associates.

After *Smallville* Somerhalder was the first to be cast in *Lost,* Abrams' science fiction television series about the survivors of Oceanic Flight 815 who become stranded on a mysterious deserted island. Somerhalder played Boone Carlyle, a somewhat controlling and yet caring stepbrother to the character of Shannon Rutherford. The complex character cared for his spoiled and manipulative stepsister and was in love with her at the same time. The actress who played Shannon, Maggie Grace, became romantically linked to Somerhalder in real-life for a brief time. Even though Somerhalder's character was killed during the first season, the strange happenings on the island and flashbacks from other characters meant that Somerhalder continued to make guest appearances on the show during its run from 2004-10.

In 2006, Somerhalder starred with Kristen Bell in the teen horror movie titled *Pulse* which was about a computer hacker who hacks into a program that releases a mysterious wireless signal that unleashes an unimaginable evil. The movie was not well received by critics, with a mediocre box-office take. Also in 2006 Somerhalder played a drifter in the independent film *Sensation of Light.*

Somerhalder played the recurring character of Nick on HBO's highly acclaimed series *Tell Me You Love Me* in 2007. The television series depicted the lives of three couples going to a counselor who also has relationship difficulties. It generated a bit of controversy because of its extremely realistic depictions of sexual intercourse, oral sex, masturbation, and ejaculation which were repeatedly confirmed to be only simulated and not real. In 2007 the show was named number three on *Time* magazine's list of the top-ten new television series.

In 2008 Somerhalder played William Archer in *Lost Samaritan,* a feature film about a man who stops to help an injured motorist and becomes the target of two assassins. The movie was described in one review as being of inferior quality with a low budget and a poor storyline. It did not get critical acclaim or do very well at the box office.

In addition to landing a role on *Vampire Diaries,* 2009 was the year that Somerhalder starred in *Tournament,* a feature film about a contest between professional assassins who meet in an unsuspecting and designated town to duel until only one remains standing to collect the $10 million prize and the right to charge a million dollars per bullet for their services. Somerhalder was cast in the role of Miles Slade, a crazy Texan who shows up for the challenge to wreck havoc and create carnage. Somerhalder next appeared in the comedy feature film, *How To Make Love To A Woman,* released in 2010, but the movie was a flop.

Somerhalder, who is a more than 20-year veteran of the media and entertainment industry, continues to be someone recognized for his sultry, boyish good looks and easy manner. His face is memorable and he has been able to parlay a variety of roles into more leads and choice parts as he continues to expand his repertoire of credits. In addition to his acting abilities, the man who adopted a stray cat while on location in Hawaii for the filming of *Lost,* cares deeply for the planet and its creatures and hopes to make a difference and be seen for what lies beyond simply his surface attractiveness.

Sources

Periodicals

Time, December 9, 2007.

Online

"Ian Somerhalder," Internet Movie Database, http://www.imdb.com/name/nm0813812/maindetails (March 5, 2011).
"Ian Somerhalder Biography," Flixster, http://www.flixster.com/actor/ian-somerhalder/ian-somerhalder-biography (February 20, 2011).

"Ian Somerhalder Biography," TV.com, http://www.tv.com/ian-somerhalder/person/70561/summary.html (February 20, 2011).

"Ian Somerhalder Biography," Yahoo Movies, http://movies.yahoo.com/movie/contributor/18044639.tif86/bio (February 20, 2011).

Ian Somerhalder Foundation Web site, http://www.isfoundation.com/ (March 5, 2011).

"Ian Somerhalder Quotes," Flixster, http://www.flixster.com/actor/ian-somerhalder/ian-somerhalder-quotes (March 5, 2011).

"*Vampire Diaries* Star Ian Somerhalder on Playing the Bad Boy With a Conscience," TV Squad, http://www.tvsquad.com/2011/02/09/the-vampire-diaries-ian-somerhalder-interview/ (February 20, 2011).

"*Vampire Diaries* Star Ian Somerhalder Thanks *Twilight*," MTV Movie News, http://www.mtv.com/news/articles/1613202/vampire-diaries-star-thanks-twilight.jhtml (March 5, 2011).

—Annette Bowman

Esperanza Spalding

© Allstar Picture Library/Alamy

Musician

Born in 1984, in Portland, Oregon. *Education:* Berklee College of Music, Boston, MA, bachelor's degree, 2005.

Addresses: *Web site*—http://www.esperanzaspalding.com/

Career

Joined Noise for Pretend, 2000; released album *Happy You Near* with Noise for Pretend, 2002; toured with Patti Austin, toured with Joe Lovano, 2004-05; taught at Berklee College of Music, 2005-08; formed trio, released debut album *Junjo,* 2006; released *Esperanza,* 2008; released *Chamber Music Society,* 2010.

Awards: Scholarship for outstanding musicianship, Boston Jazz Society, 2004; Grammy Award for best new artist, National Academy of Recording Arts and Sciences, 2011.

Sidelights

Bass player, singer, and composer Esperanza Spalding made history and shocked industry observers and fans alike when she became the first jazz artist to take home the Best New Artist trophy at the Grammy Awards in February of 2011, beating out such heavy hitters as pop sensation Justin Bieber and urban music performer Drake. However, at the time of her win, Spalding was far from a newcomer to the music scene. After leaving high school as a teenager to pursue a music career, Spalding attracted such respect for her talents on the bass that she not only earned a bachelor's degree from Boston's respected Berklee College of Music, but also signed on as one of the school's youngest-ever instructors. Spalding has performed with artists including jazz singer Patti Austin and pop icon Prince, as well as playing at the 2009 Nobel Peace Prize ceremony at the request of U.S. President Barack Obama. In addition, she has released three solo albums, 2006's *Junjo,* 2008's *Esperanza,* and 2010's *Chamber Music Society;* a fourth solo album, *Radio Music Society,* was planned for late 2011. Despite her unexpected accolade, Spalding remained modest about her work, telling Philip Booth of *Bass Player,* "You never know why things happen the way they happen. I'm blessed. I think it's the hand of fate; I don't take full credit for it, because that would be arrogant."

Of mixed African American, Asian, Native American, and Hispanic heritage, Spalding was born the younger of two children in 1984 in Portland, Oregon. Raised by a single mother alongside a brother some seven years older than her, Spalding lived in some of the city's rougher neighborhoods as a child. After growing drug-related violence led to the death of a neighborhood child, her family left Portland's northeastern King neighborhood for what they hoped was a safer location, but to little success. Despite these difficult living environments and a constant struggle with poverty, Spalding did not develop the cynical attitude common of many of her peers. "You can grow up with literally nothing and you don't suffer if you know you're loved and valued," she told John Colapinto of the *New Yorker*. "A lot of people I grew up with, by the time they were eight they were completely disillusioned with the world. They already felt this system is wrecked and it's hopeless." In an effort to prevent that disillusionment from affecting her daughter, Spalding's mother withdrew her from Portland public schools and helped Esperanza educate herself through homeschooling.

Part of that somewhat informal education included music. From an early age, Spalding was attracted to diverse musical styles from Ludwig van Beethoven's symphonies to soul singer Smokey Robinson to the 1960s pop of the Monkees. She first began playing piano by ear at the age of four, and the following year became intrigued by string instruments after seeing cellist Yo-Yo Ma perform on the public television children's program *Mister Rogers' Neighborhood*. Through a community music program, Spalding began learning the violin; she eventually also took up the oboe, clarinet, and guitar. In time, the youthful musician won a seat in the Chamber Music Society of Oregon's advanced youth orchestra, serving for a period as its concertmaster. During this period, Spalding received a scholarship to attend the Northwest Academy, a private arts high school in Portland, where she first encountered and became enamored with the standup bass. "I could just tell: O.K., that's the instrument," one of Spalding's teachers recalled to Colapinto in the same *New Yorker* profile. "She just had that look in her eye. The connection was obvious." At about this time, Spalding also joined Portland indie trio Noise for Pretend, playing bass and singing background vocals.

Soon, Spalding left high school and received her GED. She then enrolled at Portland State University on a music scholarship. Despite being younger and less experienced than her peers, Spalding received support and encouragement from her instructors. "I was trying to play in these orchestras and do these Bach cello suites," she recalled in a biography published on her official Web site. "It wasn't really flying, but if nothing else, my teachers were saying, 'Okay, she does have talent.'" Spalding wrote a handful of songs that Noise for Pretend began playing, and the group attracted enough attention to land a record deal with indie imprint Hush. Label owner Chad Crouch suggested that Spalding take over lead vocal duties, which she did for the re-

cording of the group's album, *Happy You Near*. Shortly after the album's release in 2002, Noise for Pretend broke up and Spalding decided to pursue her studies outside of Oregon. She received a full scholarship to Boston's Berklee College of Music, and moved east that fall to attend the school.

Despite being still in college, Spalding continued on her professional career. She joined singer Patti Austin on tour for the performer's "For Ella" tour, which focused on the music of jazz legend Ella Fitzgerald. Back in Boston, she played around town as part of a jazz trio. That same year, she won the Boston Jazz Society scholarship for outstanding musicianship. While continuing her studies at Berklee, Spalding toured with jazz greats including saxophonist Joe Lovano. In 2005, she completed her bachelor's degree in music, with her professional achievements, including leading a band and recording an album, joining coursework as the basis of her accelerated studies. Explaining her formal studies to Booth in *Bass Player*, Spalding said, "I would take arranging, composition, vocal classes—all the things I wanted to have strong in my band—and courses in different musical styles, like world music, South American music, Brazilian music." After graduation, Berklee hired her as an instructor, making her one of the school's youngest-ever teachers.

In 2006, Spalding released her solo debut, *Junjo*, through an independent record label based in Barcelona, Spain. Despite limited distribution and promotion, the album, which featured Spalding playing alongside pianist Aruan Ortiz and drummer Francisco Mela, captured the attention of jazz fans for its blend of traditional jazz, South American, and Cuban influences. Writing for the Web site All-Music, Michael G. Nastos proclaimed the album "quite notable, considering the certainty of her concept and clarity of her vision.... *Junjo* is an auspicious beginning that should catch the ears of any lover of great music," he concluded. Paul Weideman agreed, writing in a review for the *Santa Fe New Mexican* that "Spalding's playing on *Junjo* is distinctive—fluid, energetic, subtle, wonderfully individual.... This is a pretty amazing debut album."

After the release of her debut, Spalding moved to New York City but continued to teach at Berklee even as she worked to get a record deal with a larger label. Major jazz imprint Blue Note passed on her demo—a decision that label head Bruce Lundvall later publicly admitted was a mistake—and Spalding instead signed with Cleveland-based independent imprint Heads Up. The resulting *Esperanza* appeared in 2008 to much wider notice than its predecessor. "Her album is a light, often delightful batch of effervescent, Latin-tinged jazz," commented reviewer Daniel Gewertz in the *Boston Herald*, while Ben Ratliff applauded its "accomplished jazz improvisation, funk, scat singing, Brazilian vernacular rhythm and vocals in English, Portuguese ,and Spanish" in the *New York Times*. These varied influences proved to resonate with jazz listeners, who pushed *Esperanza* to the number-one slot on *Billboard*'s Top Independent Albums charts and the number-two position of the *Billboard* Top Contemporary Jazz Albums; the album spent 70 consecutive weeks on the latter listing. Spalding also made a handful of television appearances supporting the album, including a stop at *Late Night with David Letterman* that inspired the host to call her "the coolest person we've ever had on the show" according to a *Billboard* article by Larry Blumenfeld.

Along with her televised performances, Spalding made a number of notable live appearances in 2008 and 2009. She played music festivals including Philadelphia's The Roots Picnic, Rhode Island's Newport Jazz Festival, Utah's Park City Jazz Festival, and New York City's JVC Jazz Festival and its Central Park SummerStage. Her most prestigious live appearances in 2009 included two performances for President Obama at the White House. The first came in February of 2009, when Spalding performed in honor of Stevie Wonder when he was presented with the Library of Congress Gershwin Prize for Popular Song; the second performance came just three months later at the White House poetry jam. In December of 2009, Obama requested that Spalding perform as part of the Nobel Prize awards ceremony in Oslo, Norway. "Isn't she terrific?" an online ABC News story quoted the president as commenting after a Spalding performance at a Democratic National Committee fund-raiser in Miami, Florida, in April of 2010. "I love listening to Esperanza, she is wonderful," he concluded. That spring, Spalding also toured as the opening act for the performer Prince.

With such appearances helping raise her public profile, Spalding released her third solo effort, *Chamber Music Society* in August of 2010. Backed by drummer Terri Lynne Carrington, pianist Leonardo Genovese, and percussionist Quintino Cinalli, along with a diverse collection of guest performers, Spalding continued her fusion of jazz and world sounds to what critics and listeners largely deemed great success. "*Chamber Music Society* is a more sophisticated offering than *Esperanza*," commented Thom Jurek of AllMusic. "That said, with its musical diversity, stylistic panache, humor, and soul, it's also a more enjoyable listen," he went on. In December of 2010, Spalding was nominated for the Grammy for Best New Artist along with Justin Bieber, Drake, indie group Florence and the Machine, and folk rockers Mumford & Sons. Speaking about her nomination with *Entertainment Weekly*, Spalding commented, "for jazz musicians, usually the recognition comes from your peers. If someone that you really respect artistically likes your record, that's all the award you need. But it is meaningful ... that someone outside of my little jazz circle knows about me and wanted to acknowledge me." As Spalding was widely acknowledged as the least well-known of the field of nominees—particularly in comparison to teen idol Bieber—viewers and critics alike were stunned when her name was announced as the award winner at the Grammy ceremony in February of 2011. Writing of the win in the *New York Times*, Jon Pareles commented that "Spalding astonished just about everyone, probably including herself." Her win was not Spalding's only appearance on stage that night; the Grammy committee also tapped her to co-host its pre-telecast ceremony with fellow jazz performer Bobby McFerrin. Following the Grammys, Spalding toured in support of *Chamber Music Society* through parts of Europe and the United States.

At the same time that Spalding recorded *Chamber Music Society* on her standup bass, she also recorded a series of tracks on the electric bass. Initially planned as the second disc of a double-disc release, these songs instead became the heart of Spalding's fourth album, *Radio Music Society*. "I wanted to find a way to incorporate jazz elements I find appealing into fun songs that could make it on the radio," she explained of her shift in style to Gail Mitchell of *Billboard*. "I don't want to be pigeonholed. My job is to do justice to the music that's speaking through me," she concluded. *Radio Music Society* was scheduled for release in late 2011.

Selected discography

(With Noise for Pretend) *Happy You Near*, Hush, 2002.
Junjo, Ayva Musica, 2006.
Esperanza, Heads Up, 2008.
Chamber Music Society, Telarc Jazz, 2010.

Sources

Periodicals

Bass Player, June 2008, p. 32.
Billboard, July 5, 2008, p. 52; August 7, 2010, p. 26.
Boston Herald, May 31, 2008, p. 26.
New Yorker, March 15, 2010, p. 32.

New York Times, May 26, 2008, p. E1; May 15, 2011, p. 4.
Santa Fe New Mexican, August 11, 2006, p. PA-84.

Online

"All About Me," Official Web site of Esperanza Spalding, http://www.esperanzaspalding.com/cms/?page_id=10 (June 6, 2011).
"Chamber Music Society," AllMusic, http://www.allmusic.com/album/chamber-music-society-r1830209/review (June 6, 2011).

"Esperanza Spalding: Who is the surprise Best New Artist?," *Entertainment Weekly*, http://music-mix.ew.com/2011/02/14/esperanza-spalding-best-new-artist/ (June 6, 2011).
"Junjo," AllMusic, http://www.allmusic.com/album/junjo-r840300 (June 6, 2011).
"Who Is Esperanza Spalding? President Obama Knows," ABC News, http://blogs.abcnews.com/politicalpunch/2011/02/who-is-esperanza-spalding-president-obama-knows.html (June 6, 2011).

—Vanessa E. Vaughn

Marla Spivak

Scientist

Born in 1955; daughter of a chemist and a teacher; children: one son. *Education:* Humboldt State University, B.A., 1978; University of Kansas, Ph.D., 1989.

Addresses: *Office*—Marla Spivak, 219 Hodson Hall, 1980 Folwell Ave., University of Minnesota, St. Paul, MN 55108. *Web site*— http://www.entomology. umn.edu/People/GradFaculty/Spivak/index.htm.

Career

Post-doctoral researcher, University of Arizona Center for Insect Science, 1989-92; assistant professor, University of Minnesota, 1993; McKnight Land-Grant Professorship, University of Minnesota, 1995-97; Distinguished McKnight Professor, University of Minnesota, 2009—.

Member: President, International Union for the Study of Social Insects—North American Section, 2008; Foundation for the Preservation of Honeybees; board of directors, Xerces Society for Invertebrate Conservation.

Awards: Distinguished Teaching Award (nontenured category), University of Minnesota College of Agricultural, Food and Environmental Science, 1996; Service Award for Outstanding Work in Apiary Research, Apiary Inspectors of America, 1999; Special Service Award, Wisconsin Honey Producers Association, 2002; J. I. Hambelton Award for Outstanding Research, Eastern Apicultural Society, 2003; Special Recognition/Merit Award, University of Minnesota College of Agricultural, Food and Environmental Science and College of Natural Resources, 2005, 2007; Faculty Award for Mentorship Entomology, University of Minnesota, 2007; University of Minnesota Distinguished McKnight Professor, 2009; McArthur Fellow, John D. and Catherine T. MacArthur Foundation, 2010.

Sidelights

A leading researcher in the field of honeybees, University of Minnesota entomologist Marla Spivak has spent her career helping protect honeybees from decimation. One of her biggest contributions to honeybee health included developing a line of honeybees—called the Minnesota Hygienic line—that can recognize diseased larvae and pupae and remove them from the hive. In 2010, Spivak was named a MacArthur Fellow in recognition of her work with honeybees. Nicknamed the "Genius Award," the $500,000 fellowships are doled out each year to about two dozen U.S. researchers, artists, and innovators to help support their work. "It's just a huge vote of confidence," Spivak told Ashley Mains of *Transitions* magazine. "I never in my wildest dreams imagined that I would have been considered or nominated. It means a lot to me to be able to increase awareness about the importance of bees."

Born in 1955, Marla Spivak grew up in Denver. Her mother was a teacher and her father, a chemist. Spivak graduated from Denver's George Washington High School, then headed to Arizona to attend Prescott College. One December night during her freshman year in 1973, Spivak found herself feeling lost and unsure of what direction to take in life. She went to the library looking for insight and picked up *Bees' Ways,* a book by beekeeper George DeClyver Curtis written from a naturalist's perspective. Spivak pulled an all-nighter reading the book. "I just couldn't put it down," she told Mains. "You know, I'm not sure I grabbed the book. I think the book grabbed me."

After reading the book, Spivak knew she had to work with bees. With the help of her college advisor and another faculty member, Spivak landed an internship with a commercial beekeeper in New Mexico who had more than 2,000 bee colonies living on an organic farm. Spivak spent a semester on the farm earning college credit while studying the bees and learning about their social behaviors. In 1974, Prescott College went bankrupt and Spivak transferred to Humboldt State University, located in Northern California. Spivak loved bees but chose to major in biology with an emphasis in invertebrate zoology. She did not see how her fascination with bees could lead to a career.

After graduating from Humboldt in 1978, Spivak traveled to South America and Central America with another keeper. Together, they sought out keepers to learn more about their beekeeping operations. Spivak became particularly interested in Africanized bees. The Africanized honeybee—popular in South America—is an aggressive bee hybrid known for swarming and defending its territory.

Initially, Spivak thought she would stay clear of research and the academic life it entailed, but the more she worked with bees, the more intrigued she became. Spivak discussed her change of heart with the Minneapolis *Star Tribune*'s Jenna Ross. She told Ross that she realized that in order to learn more about bees, she would have to go into research. "To pose a question, set up an experiment and have them answer you. Sometimes they start revealing secrets, telling you new stories." Taken with the idea of becoming a bee researcher, Spivak enrolled in a doctorate program at the University of Kansas and wrote her dissertation on the Africanized honeybee. After finishing her doctorate in entomology in 1989, Spivak completed post-doctoral work in Tucson, Arizona, at the Center for Insect Science.

Spivak joined the University of Minnesota in 1993 during a time when Midwestern beekeepers were struggling with mites. To fight the mite infestation, the keepers dumped pesticides on their hives but the mites were beginning to show resistance to the chemicals. Instead of dumping chemicals on the hives, Spivak took a different approach. She wondered if the problem could be solved by breeding bees that were mite-resistant. Spivak knew certain bees possessed a trait characteristic that prompted them to detect pupae infected with mites and remove them from the hive. Spivak decided to breed for that characteristic, hoping to lay off the pesticides.

"It was really a novel approach," her colleague, Bill Hutchison, told the *Star Tribune*. "As far as I know, she was the first person in the world to take that approach, and it worked. That catapulted her reputation, I think, worldwide." Once Spivak had bred her "Minnesota Hygienic" line, she made the bees available to U.S. beekeepers. In addition, Spivak traveled extensively, presenting programs to beekeepers to help them troubleshoot problems.

The plight of the honeybee hit critical mass in 2007 when the media reported on extensive colony collapses across the United States, which resulted in a widespread population decline. Speaking to LiveScience, Spivak discussed the role bees play in our ecosystems and why keeping them healthy is vital. "Research on bees has clear benefits to society: Bees are the most important insect pollinators of many fruits, vegetables, nuts and flowers. Promoting the health of bees involves promoting the health and stewardship of our urban, agricultural and natural ecosystems." It has been estimated that bees pollinate one-third of the U.S. food supply.

In 2010, Spivak won a MacArthur Fellowship in recognition for her work with honeybees. The award came with a $500,000, no-strings-attached grant to continue her research. Spivak had dreamed of establishing a bee center and might use some of the MacArthur funds to make that dream a reality. Spivak envisioned a bee center with a state-of-the-art research lab, museum, and honey-production facility. Such a center would be open to the public for education and perhaps include bee colonies complete with in-hive camcorders, allowing people to see and hear inside a hive.

Spivak also hoped to use the funds to continue her research on promoting bees' natural defenses. Her latest research—before winning the MacArthur—had focused on resins. Spivak noted that some bees collect a plant-derived resin to fix cracks in the hive. This resin, her researchers discovered, also helps the bees' immune systems and once back at the hive has an antimicrobial property. Spivak's research was looking at how to promote this resin-collecting trait among bees.

Speaking to LiveScience, Spivak expressed gratitude for her career. "I was lucky enough to find a passion early in life, which still drives me to learn more. I am very drawn to bees and beekeeping, and want to make sure my research is helpful to both. Personal success was never really on my radar, but in retrospect, extreme persistence and following my intuition have been key ingredients in all my endeavors."

Sources

Periodicals

Bee Culture, November 2010, p. 37.
Denver Post, October 10, 2010, p. B4.
Star Tribune (Minneapolis), September 29, 2010, p. 1A.

Online

"The Benefits of Studying Bees," LiveScience, http://www.livescience.com/14532-benefits-studying-bees-spivak-sl.html (October 11, 2011).
"Queen Bee," *Delta Sky Magazine*, http://www.xerces.org/wp-content/uploads/2011/01/rybak-2011-marla-spivak-delta-sky.pdf (October 12, 2011).
"The Ways of Bees," *Transitions*, http://agro.biodiver.se/wp-content/uploads/2011/03/transitions-spring11.pdf (October 12, 2011).

—*Lisa Frick*

Jason Statham

Actor

Born September 12, 1972, in London, England; son of Barry (a cabernet singer) and Eileen (a dancer) Statham.

Addresses: *Home*—Los Angeles, CA. *Management*—Steve Chasman, Ace Media, 9200 Sunset Blvd., Los Angeles, CA 90069.

Career

Actor in films, including: *Lock, Stock and Two Smoking Barrels*, 1998; *Snatch*, 2000; *Turn It Up*, 2000; *Mean Machine*, 2001; *The One*, 2001; *The Transporter*, 2002; *The Italian Job*, 2003; *Cellular*, 2004; *Collateral*, 2004; *Revolver*, 2005; *Transporter 2*, 2005; *Chaos*, 2006; *Crank*, 2006; *The Pink Panther*, 2006; *War*, 2007; *The Bank Job*, 2008; *Death Race*, 2008; *In the Name of the King: A Dungeon Siege Tale*, 2008; *Transporter 3*, 2008; *Crank: High Voltage*, 2009; *13*, 2010; *The Expendables*, 2010; *Blitz*, 2011; *Gnomeo & Juliet* (voice), 2011; *The Killer Elite*, 2011; *The Mechanic*, 2011.

Sidelights

Since hitting the big screen in 1998, British tough-guy actor Jason Statham has racked up a series of box office smashes to become Britain's most bankable action hero. Early in his career, the Olympic-trained platform diver and martial arts master established himself as the reigning king of the blue-collar action flick. A big draw at the box office, Statham became the star behind the high-grossing *Transporter* and *Crank* film franchises. Released in 2006, the initial installment of *Crank* grossed more than $40 million, providing the studio with an ample profit on a film that cost $12 million to make. Writing in the *Mail on Sunday*, Tiffany Rose attempted to explain Statham's unique appeal. "Described as a mean combo of Bruce Lee grace and Steve McQueen attitude, Statham's onscreen persona is that of a rough-edged tough guy with balletic charm. He may not possess quintessential matinee idol looks—his nose looks as if it's been broken a few times and the hairline is receding—but he's undoubtedly sexy. He's more loveable rogue than bad boy."

Statham was born on September 12, 1972, in the South London borough of Sydenham. His parents, Eileen and Barry Statham, had some experience with entertainment. Eileen Statham trained as a dancer and Barry Statham crooned Frank Sinatra hits as a cabernet singer. The family, however, made most of its money selling goods on the street. The Stathams ran a mock auction shop, selling hi-fi equipment, china, glassware, and cameras. Participating in the family business helped Statham sharpen his acting skills as he learned to channel his inner con artist in hopes of getting crowds to participate in the auctions at the family's shop. "It was a big, empty shop with a rostrum at the back," Statham told the *Sunday Times Magazine*'s Chrissy Iley. "It's a shop of what you would call 'liquidation goods.'" Statham went on to explain one ruse the family used to pique buyer interest. "You say, 'The boss has run away with my wife. What he's doing to her I'm going to do with his business!'"

As a youngster, Statham taught himself to box after a friend stole a punching bag. He later took kickboxing lessons at a local gym. At 15, Statham quit school to train as a high-board diver. He took an interest in the sport after watching a diver while on vacation. As a teen, Statham made the UK's national diving team and trained six days a week. He competed in the 1990 Commonwealth Games in Auckland, New Zealand. He also competed in Germany, France, Italy, and Russia. Statham placed twelfth in the 10-meter platform competition at the 1992 World Championships. Statham spent a dozen years diving for team England but never made the Olympic roster. After he quit diving, Statham went back to peddling cheap jewelry and perfume out of a suitcase. While he never succeeded at becoming a medal-winning elite diver, Statham's diving training and love for mixed martial arts left him with a toned body. Spotted at the local pool, he was offered a job modeling for a clothing line called French Connection and his picture ended up all over London.

Aspiring filmmaker Guy Ritchie saw the ad and began asking questions about Statham, eventually inviting him to read a script for *Lock, Stock and Two Smoking Barrels*. In an interview with Gabrielle Donnelly of the *Express*, Statham described how he hooked his first role. "What really happened was that Guy had come up with this script for *Lock, Stock* and he had a particular character in it who was a street corner conman. Rather than go to a drama school, pluck someone from there and try to teach them to pretend to have a street savvy, he decided to try to find someone who was authentic and knew the moves by intuition. And he found me."

Released in 1998, *Lock, Stock and Two Smoking Barrels* marked Ritchie's directorial debut, as well as Statham's acting debut. In the crime caper, Statham played a conman named Bacon. The movie opened with Statham's character conning a streetside crowd into buying stolen items. Just as sales pick up, the police arrive and a foot chase ensues. The scene marked the first of many chases Statham would perfect for the big screen. It was the ideal breakout role for Statham—playing a streetwise con artist was not much of a stretch. Ritchie enjoyed working with Statham and cast him in his next film, 2000's *Snatch*, another high-energy gangster flick. The cast included Brad Pitt and fellow Brit Vinnie Jones but failed to garner much attention.

In 2002, Statham appeared in *The Transporter*. The high-action, car chase and gunplay adventure showcased Statham's action-hero persona as he portrayed Frank Martin, a former Special Forces officer turned professional "transporter." Directed by action-flick choreographer Corey Yuen, the film was brutally physical, with Statham performing his own stunts. "It's not like a scene of dialogue where you can do 30 takes," Statham told the *Birmingham Post*'s Mike Davies, noting action sequences must be filmed in as few takes as possible "in order to retain that dynamic power. It is exhausting and you do get injuries. I pulled a hamstring and I had a shoulder injury ... so in this one scene where I have to smash through a door I could hardly lift my arm. But when you go into the deep end of a physical role, that's what you get."

The franchise was revived with *Transporter 2* in 2005, which opened atop the U.S. box office with ticket sales of $42 million. In this flick, Statham's character was asked to chauffeur a young boy. The child— the son of a wealthy, influential politician—gets kidnapped. Once again, Statham performed his own stunts, including a jet-ski jump. The final installment, *Transporter 3*, hit theaters in 2008 but failed to intrigue viewers like the first two flicks. During the mid-2000s, Statham also became the face of the well-received *Crank* franchise, playing contract killer Chev Chelios. *Crank* was released in 2006, followed by *Crank: High Voltage* in 2009.

Along the way, Statham snagged a role in 2003's *The Italian Job*, a remake of the 1969 cult classic. The ensemble cast included Seth Green, Mos Def, Ed Norton, Donald Sutherland, Charlize Theron, and Mark Wahlberg. Statham played Handsome Rob, an affable jewel thief whose specialty lies in his driving abilities, which help the gang elude capture. Statham and his cohorts pull off a heist, which leads to a Mini Cooper car chase through the streets of Los Angeles, with Statham driving one of the getaway cars. While insurance regulations prohibited Statham from driving all of the car-chase scenes, he was allowed to drive a boat for a chase sequence through Venice.

"I had never driven a boat in my life," Statham told the *Toronto Sun*'s Louis B. Hobson. Statham told Hobson he took a crash course in boat piloting "and then they stuffed me in the driver's seat and told me to drive." The stunt driving tested his nerves, Statham said, noting it was "scary because the tides would come in and then the boat would come so close to the pedestrian bridges that I was sure I'd give myself a haircut. They probably let me do so much of my own driving because the boat sequence was the last thing we shot. They probably felt I was expendable by that time." The film—which cost $60 million to make—was a lucrative success, grossing $97 million in the United States during its initial 13-week run.

In his interview with the *Express*, Statham told Donnelly his diving years helped prepare him for acting. "There is a parallel between acting and sports in that you have to be able to block everything else out and just focus on what you are doing in that moment. When you're on the edge of the diving platform waiting to go off it you're completely committed to what you're doing—you have to be. And in my acting I've been able to draw on these skills, which has given me a lot of confidence."

In 2008, Statham appeared in the sci-fi action flick *The Death Race*, which showcased his driving skills once again. In the film, Statham played Jensen Ames, a steelworker falsely imprisoned for murder. The warden offers Ames a chance at freedom by participating in "the death race," a competition that pits inmate against inmate, each equipped with high-powered weapons and armored cars. The winner gets freedom; the losers die. In the flick, Statham raced a Ford Shelby Mustang. Speaking to the *Mail Online*'s Simon Lewis, Statham bragged about the film's arsenal of vehicles. "We've got ejector seats and napalm that comes out and covers the car behind, and on the bonnet are two mini-guns that fire 4,000 rounds a minute. There's a Dodge Ram that fires missiles, a Buick Riviera, a Jaguar XJS, a classic Porsche. The cars will blow you away."

To prepare for the film, Statham trained with an ex-Navy Seal who pushed a grueling circuit-training regime. In a Statham profile that hit London's *Sunday Times Magazine* shortly after the release of *The Death Race*, Chrissy Iley wrote that Statham left her with "a tight chest" through the entire film. "You can't take your eyes off Statham. It's an intense and internal performance that works well with the hyper-speed action. And you can't take your eyes off his body either. His torso is a work of art. Every muscle group is defined in a way you never thought they could be on a human body." That same year, Statham hit the big screen in *The Bank Job*, a flick based on an actual 1971 London robbery of safe deposit boxes.

In 2010, movie director and action-flick heavyweight Sylvester Stallone tapped Statham to appear in *The Expendables*. The high-octane film included an all-star cast of veteran action heroes, including Jet Li, Mickey Rourke, Arnold Schwarzenegger, and Bruce Willis, with Stallone also starring. In the film, the characters attempt to rescue hostages taken by Somali pirates and overthrow a dictator. Filled with daunting stunts, never-ending explosions, and glistening muscles, *The Expendables* was a throwback to the popular men-on-a-mission action flicks of the 1980s. The film's bang-'em-up formula—and veteran cast—drew in viewers. With a production budget of $80 million, the film grossed more than $270 million worldwide. A sequel was planned for 2012.

As Statham's movies continued to find success, he was offered more and more roles. In 2011, Statham appeared as a detective in *The Blitz* and as an assassin in *The Mechanic*. He also voiced a bully gnome in the animated comedy *Gnomeo & Juliet*. That same year, Statham also completed filming for *The Killer Elite*, which afforded him the opportunity to play alongside Robert De Niro and Clive Owen.

With his career swimming full tilt ahead, Statham told the *Sunday Times'* Iley he was not sad about his failure to become an Olympic-winning diver, though he admitted he had not worked as hard as he could have. "That said, if I'd done better I might not be doing what I am now. So because I didn't fulfill my potential in that sport, I am able to direct all my concentration on something that is much more rewarding, and financially rewarding as well."

Sources

Periodicals

Birmingham Post, January 17, 2003, p. 16.
Express, September 17, 2003, p. 35.
Mail on Sunday (London, England), November 6, 2005.
Mirror (London, England), May 20, 2011, pp. 4-5.
National Post (Canada), April 23, 2009, p. AL3; January 29, 2011, p. TO8.
Sunday Times Magazine (London, England), October 5, 2008, p. 14.
Toronto Sun, August 31, 2003, p. 46.

Online

"Jason Statham: From Street Trader to Hollywood Star," *Mail Online*, http://www.dailymail.co.uk/home/moslive/article-511718/Jason-Statham-From-street-trader-Hollywood-star.html (June 5, 2011).

—Lisa Frick

Kristen Stewart

Actress

Born Kristen Jaymes Stewart, April 9, 1990, in Los Angeles, CA; daughter of John Stewart (a stage manager and television producer) and Jules Mann-Stewart (a script supervisor).

Addresses: *Agent*—The Gersh Agency, 9465 Wilshire Blvd., 6th Fl., Beverly Hills, CA 90212.

Career

Actress in films, including: *The Flintstones in Viva Rock Vegas*, 2000; *The Safety of Objects*, 2001; *Panic Room*, 2002; *Cold Creek Manor*, 2003; *Catch That Kid*, 2004; *Speak*, 2004; *Undertow*, 2004; *Fierce People*, 2005; *Zathura: A Space Adventure*, 2005; *The Cake Eaters*, 2007; *Cutlass*, 2007; *In the Land of Women*, 2007; *Into the Wild*, 2007; *The Messengers*, 2007; *Jumper*, 2008; *Twilight*, 2008; *What Just Happened*, 2008; *The Yellow Handkerchief*, 2008; *Adventureland*, 2009; *New Moon*, 2009; *Eclipse*, 2010; *The Runaways*, 2010; *Welcome to the Rileys*, 2010; *On the Road*, 2011.

Awards: MTV Movie Award for best female performance, MTV, for *Twilight*, 2009; MTV Movie Award (with Robert Pattinson) for best kiss, MTV, for *Twilight*, 2009; Teen Choice Award for choice movie actress: drama, FOX, for *Twilight*, 2009; Teen Choice Award (with Robert Pattinson) for choice movie liplock, FOX, for *Twilight*, 2009; People's Choice Award (with Taylor Lautner and Robert Pattinson) for favorite on-screen team, for *Twilight*, 2010; MTV Movie Award for best female performance, MTV, for *New Moon*, 2010; MTV Movie Award (with Robert Pattinson) for best kiss, MTV, for *New Moon*, 2010; Teen Choice Award for choice movie actress fantasy, FOX, for *New Moon*, 2010; Teen Choice Award for choice summer movie star: female, FOX, for *Eclipse*, 2010; Teen Choice Award (with Robert Pattinson) for choice movie: liplock, FOX, for *New Moon*, 2010; Teen Choice Award (with Robert Pattinson) for choice movie: chemistry, FOX, for *New Moon*, 2010; Orange Rising Star Award, British Academy of Television and Radio Arts, 2010; People's Choice Award for favorite actress, for *Eclipse*, 2011; People's Choice Award (with Taylor Lautner and Robert Pattinson) for favorite on-screen team, for *Eclipse*, 2011.

Sidelights

American actress Kristen Stewart is perhaps best known for playing Bella Swan in the popular series of *Twilight* films based on the best-selling series of novels. Stewart also had major roles in a number of independent films, both big and small, including *Adventureland* and *The Runaways*. Stewart often plays troubled teenagers or young adults, with a certain depth and confidence. Her roles have become increasingly confident over the years. Of acting, Stewart told Rick Bentley of the *Fresno Bee*,

"That is something I have to do." Yet she added to the *Daily News of Los Angeles*, "I don't know what the hell I'm doing; I'm just playing parts that speak to me."

Born on April 9, 1990, in Los Angeles, California, she is the daughter of John Stewart and his wife Jules Mann-Stewart. Her father is a stage manager and television producer who spent many years working at FOX and produced such shows as *On-Air with Ryan Seacrest* and *Lopez Tonight*. Her mother, a native of Australia, is a script supervisor on films. Stewart has an elder brother, Cameron, and two adopted younger brothers, Dana and Taylor. Raised primarily in the Los Angeles area, Stewart and her family also spent some of her childhood in Colorado and Pennsylvania.

Stewart's acting career began when she was in elementary school in Woodland Hills, California. She was in a school Christmas play when she was eight years old when a talent scout saw her performance and helped launch her career. Her parents were unsure about letting her go on auditions, well aware of how Hollywood could affect children, but she soon began landing parts. Her first roles were on television in small, nonspeaking roles, and in television commercials. She also had an uncredited role in the live-action movie *The Flintstones in Viva Rock Vegas* in 2000. Of her early career, Stewart told the *Daily News of Los Angeles*, "It's just something I fell into when I was a little kid. But I never got any of the Disney parts. I was told that I was uncharismatic and not cute and defiant."

The young actress' first role of note came in 2001 with *The Safety of Objects*. The following year, Stewart had her first role of substance in *Panic Room*, directed by David Fincher. She played Jodie Foster's diabetic daughter, Sarah Altman, in the dramatic thriller. The film focuses on a woman who is forced to hide in a panic room with her daughter on their first night in their new home when intruders invade looking for millions hidden by the home's previous owners. For her work in the role, Stewart was nominated for a Young Artist Award. Foster praised her young co-star, telling Brook Barnes of the *Edmonton Journal*, "Kristen isn't interested in blurting out her emotions all in front of her, and that results in really intelligent and interesting performances."

With this success, Stewart's career continued its forward momentum. Though her next film was not the box-office hit that *Panic Room* was, *Cold Creek Manor* saw Stewart earning more critical kudos. She was given a second Young Artist Award nomination.

Stewart continued to work regularly in her high school years. In 2004 alone, she appeared in three films: *Speak, Catch That Kid,* and the southern drama *Undertow.*

In *Speak,* she played a teenage girl who becomes selectively mute after being sexually assaulted. *Catch That Kid* was a children's film about three kids, including Stewart's character, who pull off a bank heist to raise money for an operation that her father needs. While Stephen Whitty of the *Times-Picayune* was generally dismissive of *Catch That Kid*, he said of her performance "Kristen Stewart is particularly good as Maddy, a rock-climbing girl whose dad's vague medical condition sets all this in motion."

In 2005, Stewart appeared in two films: one drama, *Fierce People,* and one science fiction film targeted at children, *Zathura: A Space Adventure.* The latter film, directed by Jon Favreau, focused on a trio of squabbling siblings who find an old game in the basement that, when played, sends them and their house to outerspace where they fight aliens and learn to get along before being sent home. Stewart plays the eldest of the three, a petulant teenager who must take care of her two younger brothers.

Stewart's film choices continued to mature as she aged. In 2007, she appeared in five films. They included *Into the Wild,* a biopic about Christopher McCandless (played by Emile Hirsch). Stewart played a teenage folksinger living in a commune who encounters McCandless on his journey. She was honored with another Young Artist Award nomination for her work in the small role. The other films that came out that year were smaller releases, including *In the Land of Women,* the thriller *The Messengers, The Cake Eaters,* and *Cutlass.* In *The Cake Eaters,* Stewart played a teenager facing terminal illness.

Stewart's career soon reached new heights when it was announced that she was selected to play Bella Swan in the film adaptation of a popular series novels by Stephanie Meyer. The *Twilight* novels focus on the love affair between Swan and a vampire named Edward Cullen, played by Robert Pattinson. The first film, titled *Twilight,* was released in 2008. Stewart won an MTV Movie Award for her performance in the role.

While playing Bella brought Stewart much fame, it also was accompanied by a greater sense of scrutiny, even animosity. As soon as it was announced that she was cast in the role, there were many negative, if not malicious, posts about her online. The negative nature of the comments left the young actress befuddled, though she did have a sense of humor about the situation. She told Bentley of the *Fresno Bee*, "One person said I walk funny. I think that is hilarious."

But Stewart also added to Bentley, "It's so weird to think that people put so much energy into, like, despising you so wholeheartedly, and they literally take time to go on message boards and talk about you. It's funny. I don't presume to know anything about anything.... I don't put too much stock into my own opinions so I don't put too much stock in other opinions." While there was a significant amount of negative reaction, Stewart had a legion of dedicated fans as well.

Before its release, Stewart had already decided that she was not going to let the success or failure of *Twilight* affect her career. She told Kevin Williamson of the *Toronto Sun*, "If this movie flops or if does fantastically, I'm still going to be able to do (what I want). This movie is either going to make easier for me to keep doing the things that I've been doing for almost ten years, or it's going to drop me right on my ass and I'm going to keep doing the same things that I've been doing—which are tiny little independent projects that no one sees."

Though many critics panned *Twilight*, it was a massive box-office success. Stewart reprised her role as Swan in sequels, including 2009's *New Moon* and 2010's *Eclipse*. Like *Twilight*, both were also box-office smashes worldwide but generally poorly received by critics. Roger Ebert of the *Chicago Sun Times* wrote in his review of *New Moon* that this sequel "takes the tepid achievement of *Twilight* ..., guts it, and leaves it for undead." Ebert also notes that, "The characters in this movie should be arrested for loitering with intent to moan. Never have teenagers been in greater need of a jump start."

Still, Stewart grew as an actress and public personality as she filmed these projects. She appeared increasingly more confident both on screen and in public with the release of *New Moon* and *Eclipse*. Yet media and fan scrutiny continued to follow her and intensify, especially as speculation ensued about her relationship with her co-star Pattinson.

Stewart continued to take on projects outside of the *Twilight* saga. Before Stewart began working on *Twilight*, she filmed an independent movie titled *Adventureland*. Set an amusement park in Pittsburgh in 1987, *Adventureland* is a coming-of-age comedy in which she played Em, a young worker there who is having an affair with the park's married electrician (played by Ryan Reynolds) and becomes the love interest of James (played by Jesse Eisenberg), a virginal college graduate who is forced to work in the park instead of travel to Europe before attending Columbia University for graduate school. Describing her interest in the film, she told Kevin Williamson of the *Toronto Sun*, "This was something I wanted to do because the characters were easy to invest in." Reviewing the film in the *New York Post*, Kyle Smith noted that her acting was "heartbreakingly good." It was released in 2009, after *Twilight*.

Stewart also appeared in the indie family drama *Welcome to the Rileys* in which she played an underage stripper and prostitute who helps fill a hole in the lives of a couple who are torn apart by the death of their daughter. It was released in 2010, as was *The Runaways*. In that film, Stewart played singer/guitarist Joan Jett in the biopic about her years as a teen rock sensation. Of Stewart's performance, Jett told Gary Graff in the *Vancouver Sun*, "Kristen was so into it, into the whole vibe of doing this. I think she felt a weight and a responsibility to interpret it correctly. She was really serious about it and was watching me and asking me all sorts of questions, from speech aspects to watching my body language, watching where I stood, watching my guitar playing. She really worked hard to get it right." While critics also praised Stewart's work in the role, *The Runaways* was not particularly successful.

Stewart was scheduled to appear in *On the Road*, an adaptation of the 1957 novel by Jack Kerouac, and the conclusion to the *Twilight* series, *Breaking Dawn* which will be released in two parts in 2011 and 2012. Discussing playing Bella, Stewart told Bob Thompson of *Calgary Herald*, "I'm very protective of her. I feel a shared ownership. It's weird: If you were to talk about the character in a way that was not thought out or flippant, I would be right there to say that you didn't know what you were talking about." Though the *Twilight* franchise was not always respected, there was little doubt about Stewart's future. As Brooks Barnes wrote in the *Edmonton Journal*, "Stewart is considered one of the most promising actresses of her generation, with Oscar winners like Sean Penn and Jodie Foster lining up to offer praise."

Sources

Periodicals

Atlanta Journal-Constitution, November 11, 2005, p. 4E.
Calgary Herald (Alberta, Canada), November 18, 2009, p. E1.

Chicago Sun Times, November 20, 2009, p. 26; July 2, 2010, p. B4.

Daily News of Los Angeles, November 21, 2008, p. L1; February 26, 2010, p. L1.

Edmonton Journal (Alberta, Canada), November 21, 2009, p. D1.

ENP Newswire, February 22, 2010.

Fresno Bee, November 19, 2008, p. E1.

Globe and Mail (Canada), November 21, 2008, p. R5.

Los Angeles Times, October 28, 2010, p. D1.

Metro (UK), July 6, 2010, pp. 26-27.

New York Post, April 3, 2009, p. 35.

Ottawa Citizen, June 26, 2010, p. H1.

San Francisco Chronicle, March 19, 2010, p. E1.

Times-Picayune (New Orleans, LA), February 6, 2004, p. 10.

Toronto Sun, November 21, 2008, p. E3; April 5, 2009, p. E4; June 27, 2010, p. 60.

USA Today, March 29, 2002, p. 4E.

Vancouver Sun (British Columbia, Canada), April 29, 2009, p. F3.

Online

"Kristen Stewart (I)," Internet Movie Database, http://www.imdb.com/name/nm0829576/ (February 22, 2011).

—A. Petruso

Kathryn Stockett

Author

Born in 1969 in Jackson, MS; daughter of Robert (a businessman) and Ruth Elliot Stockett; married Keith (divorced, 2011); children: Lila. *Education:* University of Alabama, Tuscaloosa, B.A.

Addresses: *Home*—Atlanta, GA. *Publisher*—Amy Einhorn Books, Penguin Group, 375 Hudson St., New York, NY 10014. *Web site*—http://www. kathrynstockett.com.

Career

Worked for nine years in magazine publishing and marketing, New York City; published first novel, *The Help,* 2009.

Awards: Readers award, BookBrowse, for *The Help,* 2009.

Sidelights

In 1962 black student James H. Meredith became the first black student enrolled at the University of Mississippi. This momentous event occurred despite segregationist Governor Ross Barnett opposing a federal ruling declaring that Meredith should be allowed to enroll at "Ole Miss." Riots broke out and Meredith had to be escorted by federal marshals. Two people were killed in the riots and President John F. Kennedy was concerned that a small-scale civil war would occur on campus. Bob Dylan's song "Oxford Town" is loosely based on these events. The Ole Miss riot is considered by many historians to be a pivotal event of the U.S. civil rights movement. Kathryn Stockett, author of *The Help* set her story in Mississippi in 1962.

While much of the civil rights movement involved shouting, violence, courage, and publicly standing up for one's beliefs in order to cause change or fight change, the tagline for *The Help* is "Change begins with a whisper." The whispers referred to are the hushed conversations between the gentile, prejudiced, white ladies of Jackson, Mississippi, who may only discuss "ladylike" subjects; the angry and frightened discussions of the maids amongst themselves; and the hushed tones of the maids telling Skeeter about the families that they work for. Skeeter is a 22-year-old woman who has graduated from Ole Miss and has come back to Jackson unmarried. She writes a domestic tips column, using the ideas of Aibileen who is a maid for one of her former college roommates. Skeeter, who aspires to be an author, decides to write a book of transcribed conversations with 12 of the maids in the Jackson area.

The Help was a controversial novel for several reasons: the racial subject matter, because Stockett wrote from the perspective of black maids, because she used a heavy dialect to portray the maids, and because she was a white woman from a wealthy background who drew on her childhood experience of being raised by a black maid to write her novel. In the London *Daily Mail,* online, Stockett pointed out, "Although Jackson's population was half white and half black, I didn't have a single black friend or a black neighbor or even a black person in my school. Even in the 1970s we were staunchly separated." In *The Help* the character of Skeeter is appalled when she hears that the Junior League wants to implement the Home Help Sanitation Initiative, which will decree that all domestic help should have separate lavatories outside the house in order to not spread disease. While she was growing up, Stockett never even realized that her beloved maid Demetrie had to go to the bathroom in facilities outside of the house. She told Jessamy Calkin of the London *Telegraph* in regards to Demetrie, "We would tell anybody, 'Oh, she's just like a part of our family,' and that we loved the domestics that worked for us so dearly—and yet they had to use a bathroom on the outside of the house."

When Stockett was six years old, her mother and father divorced. At the time her mother, Ruth Elliot Stockett, was a young and good-looking woman whom Stockett has described as wild. Stockett told Calkin that her mother "wore high heels and low-cut sweaters and she dated a journalist who travelled all over the world." Stockett's mother would hand the children over to her father and leave for periods of time. Stockett's father, Robert Junior Stockett, owned Ramada Motels in Mississippi. Sometimes the children would stay in one of the motels and sometimes they would stay at their grandfather's house. Either way Demetrie, a black maid who worked for her grandfather, would care for them.

Stockett's wealthy grandfather ran a stable with retired horses given to him by the Southern Calvary. The stables were well known and a number of prominent people would gather there informally. Stockett told Calkin that "there were more laws made on the porch of Stockett Stables than in the state capital." Eudora Welty, one of Stockett's literary heroes, used to come and enjoy the fresh air at the stables to help with her tuberculosis. Stockett liked being at her grandfather's house because people would catch horses for her and she could ride anywhere that she liked. She liked that things did not change at her grandparents' house. If a visitor came once for lunch, it was expected that they would stay and be there for the next meal. Things were idyllic, but Stockett always felt a bit unsettled because, as she told Calkin "I didn't always know where my mother was, I didn't know where my father was, but I always knew where Demetrie was. I would go to my grandparents' [house] six days a week. Demetrie was always there."

Stockett attended the University of Alabama and graduated with an bachelor's degree in English literature and creative writing. With dreams of working in the publishing industry, she headed to New York, where she worked in magazine publishing and marketing for nine years. When the planes crashed into the World Trade Center towers on September 11, 2001, Stockett had taken time off to work on some of her own projects. She was at home when the tragedy occurred. Power and Internet services were down for days and she felt isolated and frightened. She had written a novel that had been deemed not very good by a writing instructor, but in that moment of fear generated by the circumstances of the terrorist attack in New York, Stockett began to write for comfort. She wrote in Demetrie's voice. She had only ever seen Demetrie in her white maid's uniform and the clothing that Demetrie had worn when she was lying in her coffin. She had only ever gone to Demetrie's house once when she was seven years old. Stockett was quoted by Calkin as saying about the experience "It was a strange feeling to realise that Demetrie had another life; it was my first awakening that she was a person with an identity outside the Stockett family." In the afterward to *The Help,* Stockett quotes Howell Raines from his Pulitzer Prize winning essay, "Grady's Gift": "There is no trickier subject for a writer from the South than that of affection between a black person and a white one in the unequal world of segregation. For the dishonesty upon which a society is founded makes every emotion suspect, makes it impossible to know whether what flowed between two people was honest feeling or pity or pragmatism."

Stockett worked on *The Help* for five years. When she began writing, she felt no anxiety about writing in the voice of a black maid because she thought no one would ever read the book and it would never be published. She sent it to her mother to read and her mother told her that it was quite good and encouraged her. After her initial manuscript was complete, she sent it to a variety of literary agents. but it was rejected by each of them in turn, so she revised. As she wrote, Aibileen, Minny, Skeeter, and Hilly grew. She honed the story and the characters came more fully to life with each revision. After doggedly sending it to 60 agents, Susan Ramer at Don Congdon Associates took on the book with enthusiasm. Within a week Ramer found a publisher; Amy Einhorn of G.P. Putnam and Sons Publishing Company used *The Help* to launch her own imprint. According to Tirdad Derakhshani of the *Philadelphia Inquirer,* the book that had been rejected by 60 literary agents had spent as of the spring of 2011 "103 weeks on the New York Times best-seller list, six at No. 1. There are three million copies of the hardback in print." The film rights to *The Help* were sold early on to one of Stockett's longtime friends with whom she grew up, Tate Taylor. Taylor read one of the original manuscripts and felt homesick for the South. It reminded him of the maid, Carol Lee, who had cared for him when he was growing up. He told Sandy Cohen in the New York *Daily News* online, "It was just so nostalgic for me, and I was like, 'Oh my God, people need to see this.' I just wanted to tell this story." The movie version of *The Help* was released on August 12, 2011, and starred Viola Davis, Emma Stone, Octavia Spencer, and Bryce Dallas Howard. The movie grossed more than $26 million in its opening weekend.

For Stockett, success has continued to roll her way, past the moment when she pulled into a truck stop on a drive between Mississippi and Alabama to avoid a tornado and received a call from her publisher telling her that she was on the *New York Times* best-seller list, past the multi-city book tours, and past seeing her characters come to life on the big screen, but she has also received criticism. Literary agent Faith Childs told Motoko Rich of the *New York Times*, "Very often, when there is something that captures a particular voice or a particular time period where African Americans are subservient, it finds a large and willing audience—and one wonders why." Janet Maslin, in a review for the *New York Times*, explains how "It's a story that purports to value the maids' lives while subordinating them to Skeeter and her writing ambitions. And it celebrates noblesse oblige so readily that Skeeter's act of daring earns her a gift from a local black church congregation." Lynn Crosbie, writing for Toronto's *Globe & Mail*, criticized *The Help*, arguing that, "Stockett, a white Mississippi native, seems, incredibly, unaware of her competition—her novel is not only devoid of any deep insight into black women's lives, it exists in a cultural vacuum, seemingly oblivious to the impact of black artists and activists of the era she writes about." Crosbie goes on to question the appropriation of the black maids' voices and stories, and speculates why they could not publish their own stories in their own voices without the need for Skeeter. She gives the example of Harriet Wilson, who published an autobiographical slave narrative in 1859. Crosbie goes on to write that "white folks are always plunging back into times of monstrous oppression against blacks, out of an interest that feels only self-serving."

The idea of the appropriation of voice has taken Stockett and *The Help* beyond the realm of literary criticism and discussion regarding racism. Ablene Cooper, the longtime nanny for Stockett's brother filed a lawsuit against Stockett, accusing her—according to *Salon*'s Laura Miller—of causing Ablene to "'experience severe emotional distress, embarrassment, humiliation, and outrage' by appropriating 'her identity for an unpermitted use and holding her to the public eye in a false light.'" This accusation is based on similarities between Cooper's name and the character's name, and other characteristics that they hold in common such as a gold tooth. Skeptics of the lawsuit have pointed out that the white characters in Stockett's novel are portrayed in a much worse light than the black characters; Aibileen is portrayed as noble and virtuous. Stockett's brother, Robert, took Cooper's side and told her to pursue the lawsuit.

In the United Kingdom, the cover of *The Help* has a photograph that was pulled from the National Congress archives. It is a photograph from the period of the novel and portrays a little white girl in a stroller with two black maids in starched white uniforms on either side of her. This cover was considered to be too controversial to be used in the United States in 2009, a year after a black president was elected. While the Civil Rights Act was passed in 1964, two years after James H. Meredith registered for classes at Ole Miss amidst riots and during the events of *The Help,* controversy and heated discussion still arise as people seek to make sense of the past and what it means for the future. Stockett, who is not afraid of controversy and is working on a novel about a Christian family during the Depression, may not be shouting to incite change but perhaps she is whispering in people's ears.

Selected writings

The Help, Amy Einhorn Books (New York City), 2009.

Sources

Books

Stockett, Kathryn, *The Help,* Amy Einhorn Books, 2009.

Periodicals

Globe & Mail, August 6, 2011.
New York Times, February 19, 2009; November 3, 2009.
Philadelphia Inquirer, May 12, 2011.
Telegraph, July 16, 2009.
Time, November 11, 2009.

Online

"Black Maid Sues, Says *The Help* Is Humiliating," ABC News, http://abcnews.go.com/Health/lawsuit-black-maid-ablene-cooper-sues-author-kathryn/story?id=12968562.tif (August 12, 2011).

Contemporary Authors Online, Gale, 2010.

Kathryn Stockett Official Web Site, http://www.kathrynstockett.com (August 12, 2011).

"The dirty secrets of *The Help*," *Salon*, http://entertainment.salon.com/2011/02/22/the_help_lawsuit/ (August 12, 2011).

"*The Help*," BookBrowse, http://www.bookbrowse.com/reviews/index.cfm/book_number/2232/the-help (August 20, 2011).

The Help, Internet Movie Database, http://www.imdb.com/title/tt1454029/ (August 21, 2011).

"The Power of Friendship," *Daily News*, http://thedailynewsonline.com/lifestyles/article_81435af9-94ea-52da-94d3-f54e1033ee3e.html (August 12, 2011).

"This Life: Kathryn Stockett on her childhood in the Deep South," *Daily Mail* Online, http://www.dailymail.co.uk/home/you/article-1199603/This-Life-Kathryn-Stockett-childhood-Deep-South.html (August 12, 2011).

—*Annette Bowman*

Julia Stuart

Author

Born c. 1968 in the West Midlands, England; married. *Education:* Bachelor's degree in journalism.

Addresses: *Publisher*—HarperCollins, 10 East 53rd St., New York, NY 10022.

Career

Wrote for various British newspapers, including the *Independent*, 1990s-mid-2000s; published *The Matchmaker of Périgord*, 2008; published *The Tower, the Zoo, and the Tortoise*, 2010.

Sidelights

British author Julia Stuart captured audiences on both side of the Atlantic with the publication of her whimsical second novel, *The Tower, the Zoo, and the Tortoise.* The book won over U.S. readers—including President Barack Obama—with its quirky tale of a London Beefeater overseeing the British queen's menagerie while dealing with the effects on his family of the death of his only child. *The Tower, the Zoo, and the Tortoise* became a *New York Times* bestseller shortly after its publication in August of 2010. Before writing this novel, Stuart had published *The Matchmaker of Périgord* in her native England in 2007, and also worked for several years as a journalist with British newspapers, including the *Independent.*

A native of the West Midlands region of England, Stuart studied Spanish and French growing up, later attending college to complete an undergraduate degree in journalism. After finishing her education, Stuart taught English for a time in both Spain and France. Returning to the United Kingdom, she worked for a number of regional newspapers for about six years before landing a position with the high-circulation national British newspaper the *Independent.* At the *Independent,* Stuart served as a features writer both for the standard daily edition and for the special *Independent on Sundays.* Stuart was also attracted to fiction writing. "The beauty about non-fiction is that once the interview and research is done you already have the story. All you have to do is assemble it in a comprehensive and interesting fashion.... I think it's that thrill of not knowing precisely what's going to happen by the end of a sentence, the freedom to choose what to write about, and the liberty to express it in the precise words of your choosing that eventually draws journalists to writing fiction," she explained in an interview posted on the Web site of publisher HarperCollins.

Published in England in mid-2007 and by HarperCollins in the United States the following year, Stuart's first foray into fiction was *The Matchmaker of Périgord.* Partially inspired by a series of visits to the southwestern French region of Périgord, the novel told the fictional story of French barber Guillaume Ladoucette. Finding his business in decline as the residents of his community age and lose their hair, Ladoucette decides to embark on a new career: matchmaker. His attempts do not always end in success despite his enthusiastic efforts to bring together lovelorn villagers. Critics greeted *The Matchmaker of Périgord* warmly, hailing the novel for its depiction of the fictional French village of Amour-sur-Belle, its collection of unusual but engaging characters, and its light-hearted, witty style. "Debut novelist Stuart infects Amour-sur-Belle's byzantine lore with whimsy ... the usual beefs ... and sensual detail," assessed a review in *Publishers Weekly*, while *Library Journal's* Leigh Wright praised the novel as "an enjoyable trip through the sweetness, sadness, and hilarity that love—and life—often brings." By mid-2010, Stuart had sold the rights for a film production of *The Matchmaker of Périgord* to British screenwriter Andrew Birkin; however, no firm plans to bring the book to the screen had been set.

Pleased with the success of *The Matchmaker of Périgord*, HarperCollins picked up the rights for Stuart's planned second novel, then tentatively titled *The Raincatcher*, during the summer of 2009. The completed novel was first published the following spring in England as *Balthazar Jones and the Tower of London Zoo*, a reference to the main character and his unusual new line of work. In the novel, Jones, a Beefeater—one of the traditional guards of the Tower of London—is charged with looking after the exotic animals of the royal menagerie following that collection's move to the Tower; at the same time, he and his wife are dealing with their grief following the death of their only son. The novel also featured a cast of unusual dwellers of the Tower, where Beefeaters and their families are required to live.

Although the book received moderate praise for what critics generally agreed was a both absurd and touching story, the novel truly found its audience following its arrival on U.S. shelves in August of 2010. American audiences and booksellers lined up to shower enthusiastic praise on *The Tower, the Zoo, and the Tortoise*, as the book was retitled for the American market. Muriel Dobbin of the *Washington Times* proclaimed the novel to be "a marvelous confection of a book," and Karen Valby of *Entertainment Weekly* applauded the story's ability to combine lighthearted sweetness with a "sense of heartbreak and longing that holds it all together." Stuart and her book made worldwide news when *The Tower, the Zoo, and the Tortoise* was the only work by a non-American author to accompany U.S. President Barack Obama on his summer vacation that year. "I'm not quite sure why America has taken to it with such affection. Perhaps it's the history, or the love stories. Maybe it's the monkeys that flash their private parts when feeling threatened. Whatever the reason, I'm stunned and eternally grateful," Stuart wrote in a blog for the Web site *Huffington Post*.

In October of 2007, Stuart moved to the Middle Eastern nation of Bahrain for her journalist husband's work. The couple remained in the town of Janabiya for about two and a half years. Speaking to Alicia de Haldevang of the *Gulf Daily News*, Stuart explained that Bahrain had given her some creative ideas and she might someday feature the location in a book. "I do have an idea for a novel that was inspired by my stay in Bahrain, but it will remain just a vague notion at present," she qualified. Her surroundings had a direct effect on the writing of *The Tower, the Zoo, and the Tortoise*, however. One of Stuart's neighbors was a Greek woman, Maria Stanley, who often used Greek sayings that intrigued the writer. Stuart decided to make the wife of the novel's main character of Greek origin, and allow the character to voice many sayings like those used by Stanley in real life. "While the character in the novel isn't Maria, it was certainly inspired by her," the writer explained in a separate article in the *Gulf Daily News*.

By mid-2010, Stuart and her husband had left Bahrain for Cairo, Egypt, where Stuart was continuing to write. Speaking to Craig Wilson of *USA Today* in the late summer of 2010, she speculated on possible topics for her follow-up to *The Tower, the Zoo, and the Tortoise*. "I'm researching my third novel and wondering whether introducing a little monkey wearing red velvet trousers is too ridiculous. Probably not by my standards," she concluded.

Selected writings

The Matchmaker of Périgord, HarperCollins (New York City), 2008.
The Tower, the Zoo, and the Tortoise, HarperCollins, 2010.

Sources

Books

Contemporary Authors, vol. 237, Gale, 2010.

Periodicals

Entertainment Weekly, August 13, 2010.
Gulf Daily News (Manama, Bahrain), March 14, 2010; September 19, 2010.
Independent (London, England), August 15, 2007.
Library Journal, July 1, 2008, p. 68.
Publishers Weekly, April 14, 2008, p. 33.
USA Today, August 10, 2010, p. 1D.
Washington Times (Washington, D.C.), October 21, 2010, p. B6.

Online

"Author Interview: Julia Stuart," HarperCollins, http://www.harpercollins.com/author/author Extra.aspx?authorID=33124&displayType= interview (August 28, 2011).

"How a Beefeater and a Tortoise Captured America's Attention," *Huffington Post*, http://www.huffing tonpost.com/julia-stuart/how-a-beefeater-and-a-tor_1_b_691533.html (August 28, 2011).

—*Vanessa E. Vaughn*

Lisa Switkin

© *Dimitrios Kambouris/WireImage/Getty Images*

Landscape architect

Born Lisa Tziona Switkin, June 25, 1974, in St. Louis, MO; daughter of Sheldon and Linda Switkin; married Elijah Saintonge, November 6, 2011. *Education:* University of Illinois, B.F.A.; University of Pennsylvania, M.L.A; studied at Hebrew University, Jerusalem, Israel.

Addresses: *Office*—James Corner Field Operations, 475 Tenth Ave., 10th Flr.,New York, NY 10018.

Career

Design project manager of High Line project, James Corner Field Operations, New York, NY, 2004-07, associate partner and managing director by 2011. Previously worked as a landscape designer for W Architecture and Landscape Architecture, New York, NY; Marpillero Pollak Architects, New York, NY; Abel Bainnson Butz, New York, NY; and Bell Slater Partnership, London, England. Has also worked on the Champaign Revitalization Project, Champaign, IL, and East St. Louis Action Project, East St. Louis, IL. Teacher of graduate-level landscape architecture classes at University of Pennsylvania, Philadelphia; lecturer at universities, symposiums, foundations and institutions around the world.

Awards: ASLA Design Award, American Society of Landscape Architects, and AIA Staten Island Award, American Institute of Architects, both with Marpillero Pollak Architects for "Thresholds of Eibs Pond Park," both 2003; Honorable Mention and New York Heritage Award, Designing the High Line Competition, New York, 2003; Rome Prize, Fellow in Landscape Architecture at the American Academy in Rome, 2007-08; Shine On Award, *Good Housekeeping*, 2011.

Sidelights

Lisa Switkin had already been recognized as an innovator in landscape design before she became design project manager for New York City's High Line in 2004. Her work in converting the former elevated train line into a public park, however, brought her to the attention of an appreciative public. The High Line received more than two million visitors in 2010 alone, and in 2011 the designer was recognized by *Good Housekeeping* magazine with a Shine On Award as a woman who is "making a difference."

Switkin was born in 1974 in St. Louis, Missouri, but grew up in Columbus, Ohio. As a child she spent much of her time reading, preferring stories that engaged her imagination, such as Madeleine L'Engle's award-winning fantasy *A Wrinkle in Time.* Another childhood favorite was Frances Hodgson Burnett's classic *The Secret Garden*; its tale of how caring for a neglected garden heals a family foreshadowed her own interest in landscape architecture. After high school, Switkin attended the University of Illinois, where she studied urban and regional planning and received a bachelor in fine arts. She also spent time studying abroad at Hebrew University in Jerusalem, Israel.

After graduating, Switkin remained in Illinois and applied her skills to creating community stabilization plans for the East St. Louis Action Project. She also worked on economic development plans for the Champaign Revitalization Project, also in Illinois. Deciding to further her education, Switkin attended the University of Pennsylvania to study landscape architecture. While there she received a Faculty Medal for Excellence and an Honor Award from the American Society of Landscape Architects. After receiving her master's in landscape architecture, Switkin moved to New York City, where she could focus on blending natural elements into the urban landscape.

Switkin worked for a time with Marpillero Pollak Architects (MPA) in New York City. She contributed to an upgrade of Harlem RBI's Youth Baseball Park that brought social elements like a picnic area and memorial garden to help integrate the ballpark into the neighborhood. With MPA she also worked on the award-winning design for the Threshold to Eibs Pond Park in Staten Island, a project to help revitalize a neglected 17-acre wetland by making the edges accessible and inviting to the public. Switkin also collaborated on Abel Bainnson Butz's initial development of the Hudson River Park in New York City. The project repurposed a disused industrial waterfront into a recreational area, transforming piers into parks with fountains, gardens, and play areas. A similar conversion came out of her work with W Architecture and Landscape Architecture on the West Harlem Waterfront Project. The project took a formerly industrialized waterfront and built park areas that included river access for fishing and kayaking.

Switkin joined the firm of James Corner Field Operations to work on the High Line project and began serving as the design project manager in 2004. An elevated railway, the High Line was built in the 1930s to carry freight to New York's West Side, an area with meatpacking plants, factories, and warehouses. The railway fell into disuse in the 1980s and by 1999 it was overgrown with native flora and the city planned to tear it down. The nonprofit Friends of the High Line formed to save the structure and eventually got support from the City of New York to transform the line into a public park. After a six-month design competition, landscape architects James Corner Field Operations and architects Diller Scofidio + Renfro were selected to design the site. Construction started in 2006, with Switkin managing the landscape design.

The renovation began by removing the surfaces of the existing structure and repairing the underlying steel and concrete. New drainage and irrigation systems were installed to help make the new High Line a green structure, a "living roof" that absorbs heat and keeps most rain water in the plant beds, drastically reducing the amount ending up in sewers. The majority of the 210 plant species used in the park's gardens were native to New York—including the grasses, plants, and even trees that grew on the abandoned structure—and many were drought resistant. Interspersed among the gardens were water features, seating areas, viewing platforms, and even gathering spots for public events. Many of the High Line's original steel rails were reused and interwoven into the landscape, and a concrete path, handicap-accessible through one of the park's elevators, wound the entire length of the park.

Switkin wrote of her goals for the project in the High Line Blog: "I hope the magical sense of surprise and bewilderment that the site produces itself, along with the legible and deliberate elongated transitions embedded into the design—from streetside to topside, hard to soft, woodland to grassland, river to city—give people the opportunity to see the City in new and unexpected ways." She achieved this when the first section of the High Line opened to the public in 2009; as *New York Times* writer Nicolai Ouroussoff noted, "what's really unexpected about the park is the degree to which it alters your perspective on the city." The critic called the High Line "one of the most thoughtful, sensitively designed public spaces built in New York in years," adding that the park's founders and designers "have given New Yorkers an invaluable and transformative gift." Visitors were charmed as well by the park's combination of natural beauty, man-made elements, and unique views of the city. The High Line quickly became a popular destination, with up to 20,000 daily visitors; in 2011 a second section of the park opened and the development of the final section was approved.

After completing the High Line design, Switkin spent time in Italy on an American Academy in Rome fellowship, studying how monuments affect city planning and development. When she returned to Field Operations, it was to manage other projects that aimed to transform urban, industrial environments into beautiful public spaces. These included redesigning Seattle's Central Waterfront into a public space with access to the water; transforming Philadelphia's Race Street Pier from an industrial site to a public park; and developing seven acres of a former corporation headquarters into a park with a garden walk in the center of Santa Monica, California. About the Santa Monica Civic Center Parks, Switkin told the *Architect's Newspaper* that Field Operations' emphasis on a site's history, local environment, and place within a community won the job. "We are good listeners. We try to understand the site, not come in with a design and retrofit it to what people like." Rather than start designing from scratch, she noted, "we like to amplify the site's existing characteristics." It is this imaginative aspect of landscape design that keeps her fascinated, Switkin told Farai Chideya in *Good Housekeeping:* "Part of the skill and fun of the job is being able to see the potential of places that might otherwise be overlooked."

Sources

Periodicals

Good Housekeeping, May 2011, p. 99.
New York Times, June 10, 2009, p. C1.

Online

"About the High Line," High Line Web site, http://www.thehighline.org/about/ (November 8, 2011).
"Guest Blog: Lisa Switkin, Landscape Architect," High Line Blog, http://thehighline.org/blog/2009/06/23/guest-blog-lisa-switkin-landscape-architect (November 9, 2011).
"Santa Monica Cornered: Field Operations Tapped to Design Major Civic Park," *The Architect's Newspaper*, http://archpaper.com/news/articles.asp?id=4284 (November 9, 2011).

—*Diane Telgen*

Sam Taylor

Chief Executive Officer of Oriental Trading Company

Born c. 1961. *Education:* Brigham Young University, bachelor's degree, 1985; Harvard University, M.B.A., 1992.

Addresses: *Office*—Oriental Trading Company, 4206 S. 108th St., Omaha, NE 68137.

Career

Worked for Exxon as project engineer, 1985; case team leader, Bain & Company, 1986-95; director of strategic planning and European regional manager, Disney Catalog and Disney Store Online, 1995-2000; vice president of eCommerce and international operations, Lands' End, 2000-04; senior vice president of online stores and marketing, Best Buy, 2004-06; senior vice president of direct to consumer sales and HP.com, Hewlett Packard, 2006-08; president and CEO, Oriental Trading Company, 2008—.

Sidelights

Sam Taylor became the president and CEO of Oriental Trading Company—a large direct retailer of party supplies, toys, novelties, and other goods—in May of 2008, following the resignation of CEO Stephen Frary, who had headed the firm since 2000. Before signing on with Oriental Trading Company, Taylor had run technology corporation Hewlett Packard's Web site and global direct-to-consumer business, and, earlier, managed e-commerce and international operations for clothing retailer Lands' End and entertainment giant Disney. Taylor guided Oriental Trading Company through a challenging time, including a difficult recession and a bankruptcy filing in 2010. In February of 2011, the Oriental Trading Company emerged from bankruptcy, thanks in part to strong sales, and also to what Taylor described to Steve Jordon in the *Omaha World-Herald* as "employees who believe in the company, and [are] passionate about taking care of our customers."

Born around 1961, Taylor attended American Fork High School in American Fork, Utah, a small town in north-central Utah. After graduating from high school, he attended Provo's Brigham Young University, graduating as valedictorian of his class in 1985 with a degree in chemical engineering. He worked briefly as a project engineer with energy company Exxon, leaving in 1986 to take a job with global management consulting firm Bain & Company. At Bain & Company, Taylor worked in customer retention, retail, and consumer products practice to enhance business performance and help generate revenues for clients throughout North America. Taylor remained with that company for about a decade, taking time in the early 1990s to also study for a master's degree in business administration from the prestigious Harvard Business School.

Taylor left Bain & Company in 1995 to join global powerhouse Disney. He worked with the company's European affairs, first helping launch a European Disney catalog and overseeing its operations and, later, acting as the European e-commerce director and general manager of the subsidiary Disney Store Web site, run from the company's French offices. After five years with Disney, Taylor decided to return to the United States to take a position with clothing catalog Lands' End, based in Wisconsin. He rose from director of e-commerce to the position of vice president in mere months, assuming responsibility for several Lands' End's international Web sites and print catalog subsidiaries, and beginning work on European expansion. "Sam's extensive experience in international business gives him the knowledge and skills necessary to lead our worldwide growth," commented Lands' End senior vice president Bill Bass in a statement released through PR Newswire. Taylor applied new models of customer acquisition for the digital era to help Lands' End grow their worldwide business for less money than was possible using print products; instead of renting lists of customer names and mailing out numerous paper catalogs that incurred postage and printing costs, the company first launched a Web presence and built a customer base through the Internet. "At some point in the future, once the business is big enough, we will launch a paper catalog [in a foreign market], but not before the business is ready," Taylor told Carol Sliwa in a *Computerworld* interview. Under Taylor, Lands' End also launched a line of customized clothing options that proved more popular than originally anticipated.

Taylor's next leap was to senior vice president of online stores and marketing for big box giant Best Buy's online arm in May of 2004. He remained with the company for two years before moving to HP, where he served as senior vice president consumer direct sales and HP.com. In April of 2008, Oriental Trading Company announced its selection of Taylor as the new president and CEO, effective the following month. "I am pleased and honored to have the opportunity to lead Oriental Trading Company," commented Taylor in a press release published on the Carlyle Group's Web site, citing factors such as the firm's strong customer service ethic and Midwestern location as influential in his decision in an interview with Jim Tierney of *Multichannel Merchant*. He joined a company in need of new leadership amid lagging sales and crushing debt. Two years previously, equity investment firm the Carlyle Group had purchased Oriental Trading Company for $1 billion, instantly saddling the company with a massive debt burden. At the same time, the company had failed to fully embrace the digital era, and Taylor faced the challenge of transforming it into a strong online retailer. Sales began to decline as the recession pummeled the economy in 2008 even as costs rose and the debt burden remained at over $700 million. Taylor cut the Oriental Trading Company's staff by one-third and worked to lower expenses in other areas of the company to help stabilize its finances.

Oriental Trading Company was in the news in 2009, not for Taylor's efforts, but for a scandal surrounding Terry Watanabe, son of company founder Harry Watanabe. The younger Watanaba—who led the firm from the late 1970s through 2000—had accrued millions of dollars in gambling debt at casinos owed by Harrah's Entertainment. Watanabe claimed that the casino empire had supported his gambling problems by giving him prescription drugs and alcohol, and the two parties entered into a lawsuit. Although the case went to arbitration the following summer, Oriental Trading Company's problems were not over.

By May of 2010, Oriental Trading Company still had some $640 million in debt and was no longer able to make interest payments on part of that obligation. Although the firm had renegotiated some of its loans earlier in 2010, it continued to suffer rapidly dwindling cash balances and struggled against rising postage and dismal economic conditions. In August that year, Oriental Trading Company voluntarily filed for Chapter 11 bankruptcy protection in order to continue operating while restructuring its finances in conjunction with its creditors. "We are pleased with the ongoing support we have received from our lenders and believe this process will lead to a sustainable, long-term financial foundation for the company," Taylor commented in a separate story by Jordon of the *Omaha World-Herald*. Over the next several months, Taylor worked to restructure the company's debt load, and Oriental Trading Company announced it was emerging from bankruptcy just six months later, in February of 2011. The firm's debt was reduced by more than $400 million, and ownership of the company was shifted from the Carlyle Group and Brentwood Associates to a collection of the business' creditors. "Today marks the beginning of a new era of growth for Oriental Trading Co," Taylor told Jordon.

Sources

Periodicals

Chain Store Age, September 2002, p. 78.
Computerworld, April 30, 2001, p. 40.
Multichannel Merchant, June 1, 2008.
New York Times, July 21, 2010.
Omaha World-Herald, August 26, 2010; February 15, 2011.
PR Newswire, May 22, 2000.

Online

"Oriental Trading Company Names Sam Taylor as Chief Executive Officer; e-Commerce Executive Will Accelerate OTC's Growth Strategy," Carlyle Group, http://www.carlyle.com/media%20room/news%20archive/2008/item10358.html (August 26, 2011).

—Vanessa E. Vaughn

Steven Tyler

© Jeff Kravitz/KCA2011/FilmMagic/Getty Images

Singer and television personality

Born Steven Victor Tallarico, March 26, 1948, in Yonkers, NY; married Cyrinda Foxe, September 1, 1978 (divorced, 1987); married Teresa Barrick, May 28, 1988 (divorced, January 2006); children: Liv Tyler (with Bebe Buell), Mia Tyler (first marriage), Chelsea Tallarico, Taj Tallarico (second marriage).

Addresses: *Agent*—Paradigm, 509 Hartnell St., Monterey, CA 93940. *Management*—Tenth Street Entertainment, 700 San Vicente Blvd., Ste. G410, West Hollywood, CA 90069. *Web site*—http://www.aerosmith.com/; http://www.steventyler.com/.

Career

Formed band Aerosmith, 1970; Aerosmith signed with Columbia, 1972; released debut album, *Aerosmith*, 1973; Aerosmith's revival begins with *Permanent Vacation*, 1987; Aerosmith re-signs with Columbia, 1991; published autobiography, *Steven Tyler: Does the Noise in My Head Bother You?*, 2011; judge on *American Idol*, 2011—.

Awards: Soul Train Music Award (with Aerosmith and Run-D.M.C.) for best rap—single, for "Walk This Way," 1987; Grammy Award (with Aerosmith) for best rock performance by a duo or group with vocal, for "Janie's Got a Gun," 1990; MTV Video Music Award (with Aerosmith) for best metal/hard rock video, for "Janie's Got a Gun," 1990; Viewer's Choice Award (with Aerosmith), MTV Video Music Awards, for "Janie's Got a Gun," 1990; MTV Video Music Award (with Aerosmith) for best metal/hard rock video, for "The Other Side," 1991; Grammy Award (with Aerosmith) for best rock performance by a duo or group with vocal, for "Livin' on the Edge," 1993; Viewer's Choice Award (with Aerosmith), MTV Video Music Awards, for "Livin' on the Edge," 1993; Grammy Award (with Aerosmith) for best rock performance by a duo or group with vocal, for "Crazy," 1994; MTV Video Music Awards (with Aerosmith) for video of the year and best group video, both for "Cryin'," 1994; Viewer's Choice Award (with Aerosmith), MTV Video Music Awards, for "Cryin'," 1994; MTV Video Music Award (with Aerosmith) for best rock video, for "Falling in Love (Is Hard on the Knees)," 1997; Grammy Award (with Aerosmith), for best rock performance by a duo or group with vocal, for "Pink," 1998; MTV Video Music Award (with Aerosmith) for best rock video, for "Pink," 1998; MTV Video Music Award (with Aerosmith), for best video from a film, for "I Don't Want to Miss a Thing," 1998; Rock and Roll Hall of Fame inductee (with Aerosmith), 2001; Berklee College of Music, honorary degree, 2003.

Sidelights

The hyperactive, charismatic frontman of rock band Aerosmith, Steven Tyler is known for his showmanship, vocal abilities, and survival instincts.

Branded as one of the Toxic Twins with Aerosmith guitarist Joe Perry, Tyler and his band have sold more than 100 million albums over more than four decades. Tyler also has struggled with addiction issues and the band's many ups and downs, events chronicled in his 2011 autobiography, *Steven Tyler: Does the Noise In My Head Bother You?* Also in 2011, Tyler took on a new challenge when he became a judge on *American Idol.* As Rob Sheffield wrote in the *New York Times,* "Tyler has devoted his improbably long musical career to testing the limits of incoherence, loudness, and his mouth."

Tyler was born Steven Victor Tallarico on March 26, 1948, in the borough of Yonkers in New York City, the son of a music teacher. Music was a part of Tyler's life from an early age. He began as a drummer. Influenced by British invasion bands like the Beatles, the Rolling Stones, and the Yardbirds, he eventually became a singer as well. As a teenager, music was not his only pursuit; he also made money by working in a bakery. As a teen, Tyler began using drugs while hanging out in the Village and watching beatniks.

In the late 1960s, Tyler met guitarist Joe Perry who was working at an ice cream parlor in New Hampshire. Perry and bassist Tom Hamilton were the members of a somewhat successful band, the Jam Band. Tyler, Perry, and Hamilton formed a power trio, then added a second guitarist, Ray Tabano (replaced shortly by Brad Whitford). Tyler was both drummer and singer until the addition of drummer Joey Kramer, when Tyler focused exclusively on singing. The band took on a new name, Aerosmith, and moved to Boston by the end of 1970. As the band found success in New York and Boston with a sound that melded a blues and hard rock, influenced by the Rolling Stones and Led Zeppelin, the singer took on the name Steven Tyler. Tyler already had a flair for the theatrical with his gypsy-like stage getups and scarves tied to his microphone stand.

In 1972, the band signed to Columbia Records and released its first album, *Aerosmith,* the following year. Tyler and Perry were compared to Mick Jagger and Keith Richards of the Rolling Stones incessantly. Tyler told Edna Gundersen of *USA Today,* "The critics always slam-dunked us. They were too busy shining up the stars that were already shiny. Most journalists look at me, they look at (Mick) Jagger, they see big lips and they make a comparison. They never talked about the music or the lyrics."

Still, the band built up a following by touring in support of groups like the Kinks and Mott the Hoople and creating word of mouth. During the mid-1970s, Aerosmith became stars with the hard rock sounds found on some of their best known albums, including 1974's *Get Your Wings,* 1975's *Toys in the Attic,* and 1976's *Rocks. Toys in the Attic* was a breakthrough album, which showed the band at its hard rock best. Hit singles included the prototypical power ballad "Dream On," the bluesy rock song "Walk This Way," and the anthemic "Sweet Emotion." Tyler took charge of writing the lyrics, including many witty jokes and double entendres. Aerosmith sold out arenas all over the world.

Fame proved difficult for the band. Tyler and his bandmates all developed hardcore alcohol and drug problems, and Tyler and Perry were often at odds. The band's next albums, including *Draw the Line, Live Bootleg,* and *Night in the Ruts,* were not as coherent as previous efforts, but still were major hits on the charts. Because of ongoing tensions, Perry quit Aerosmith in 1979 to form the Joe Perry Project and Whitford followed in 1980. Describing the situation a few years later, Perry told Karen Knutson of the *Arkansas Democrat-Gazette,* "If we'd had leveler heads, we would have taken a vacation in 1979. If we'd had better and wise management, if we had known ourselves better, we'd have stopped right then…. It's not really that we hated each other, it's just that the drugs, insanity, pressure were all at work trying to destroy the magic we had as a band."

While living with a significant drug addiction to heroin, Tyler kept Aerosmith going with replacement members and a relatively unsuccessful album in 1982's *Rock in a Hard Place.* Also recovering from a serious 1981 motorcycle accident, Tyler could not keep the success going on his own, and the band faced bankruptcy and playing in smaller venues. In 1983, Perry returned to Aerosmith, with Whitford shortly thereafter. Though drug and alcohol issues were still present, the band toured again in 1984 and Tyler collapsed on stage at one point during the tour. The band signed with Geffen, and released an album, *Done with Mirrors,* that showed it had a future. After the album was released, Tyler and the rest of the band entered and completed rehabilitation programs. Tyler conquered his addictions to heroin, cocaine, and alcohol. In 1986, Tyler and Perry appeared on Run-D.M.C.'s cover of "Walk This Way," a major hit. The duo also appeared in the video, bringing them MTV stardom and paving the way for Aerosmith's true comeback.

Tyler and Aerosmith underwent a renaissance, and became a dominant force in music again, bigger in this time period than in the 1970s. The band released more multi-million selling albums including 1987's *Permanent Vacation,* and 1989's *Pump.* Hit singles from these releases included "Love in an Elevator," "Janie's Got a Gun," "Livin' on the Edge," and "Cryin'." As Aerosmith became dominant again, Tyler became one of the most respected frontmen in the history of rock and roll, with the lead singers of many hard rock bands mimicking him, his look, and the way he delivered his vocals. He credited his band with making it so. Tyler told Gundersen of *USA Today*, "We make beautiful music together. The kind that no one else on this planet can make. We finally came to realize that. We built and destroyed this band, and rebuilt it."

During the 1990s, Tyler and Aerosmith continued to stay in the spotlight. In 1991, they signed a $50 million deal with Columbia, even though they still owed two albums to Geffen. The Geffen contract was fulfilled with 1993's *Get a Grip* and 1998's *A Little South of Sanity*. *Get a Grip* was the first Aerosmith album to debut at number one. Talking about the band's chemistry during the recording of *Get a Grip*, Tyler told *USA Today*'s Gundersen, "There's tension, but we have a common vision. The internal friction is part and parcel of the process. While it's going down, you're ripping your guts apart. I cried a lot during this album." Tyler was also happy with the way that *Get a Grip* turned out, telling Craig Rosen of *Billboard*, "It makes me feel really good that when we put an album out that we love so much, that everybody else loves it. It's like, wow, there it is, the circle is completed."

The first album released under the Columbia deal was *Nine Lives*, which came out in 1997. This recording process was also difficult as the band found it hard to settle on a producer or songwriter. The band's long-time manager, Tim Collins, was also fired, and he implied that Tyler was using drugs again. Though Tyler denied the allegations, such implications would follow him for years. *Nine Lives* had some positive reviews and debuted at number one, but fell off the charts. While Aerosmith was still a live draw, its subsequent original albums were far apart and not particularly commercially successful. They included *Just Push Play*, released in 2001, and 2004's *Honkin' on Bobo*. Despite the lack of album success, Tyler and Aerosmith were inducted in the Rock and Roll of Fame in 2001.

While still active in Aerosmith in this time period, Tyler had major health problems. In 2006, he had throat surgery that could have been career-ending. During his recovery, the band had to stay off the road for months. That same year, Tyler was treated for Hepatitis C. Two years later, Tyler had surgeries to repair damage to his feet, and he checked into a rehabilitation clinic to recover. In 2009, Tyler fell off the stage in South Dakota and broke his shoulder. The band had to cancel dates during his recovery, and it was rumored that Tyler was either quitting the band or being forced out. While Perry even announced that Tyler was leaving the band to become a solo artist, Tyler countered that he was not leaving. Drug issues also resurfaced, and Tyler sought treatment for an addiction to prescription painkillers in 2010.

The in-fighting was somehow resolved and the band toured in 18 countries in 2010. Among the stops was an August 2010 sold-out show at Fenway Park in Boston. Aerosmith began recording their next album in 2011, and planned on continuing to tour indefinitely. Also in 2011, Tyler published his autobiography. In the book *Steven Tyler: Does the Noise in My Head Bother You?*, he chronicles the whole of his life, including extensive information and details about his drug use. Reviewing the book, Sheffield of the *New York Times* noted, "It ends up doing for Keith Richards's memoir *Life*, what Aerosmith originally did for the Rolling Stones: it's faster, sleazier, and pulpier, and somehow (as if just to prove it's possible) makes even less sense."

In 2011, Tyler reached a new audience when he agreed to become a judge on the long-running reality series *American Idol*, along with pop singer Jennifer Lopez; they both joined Randy Jackson. Longtime judge Simon Cowell left at the end of 2010, as did Ellen DeGeneres, who appeared on the show for only one season. Discussing Tyler agreeing to join the show, Crush Management founder Jonathan Daniel told Ann Donahue of *Billboard*, "Steven Tyler is not an obvious choice—but he's an awesome personality and maybe this, in his mind, is something where he can be real outspoken and interesting." Tyler told Alex Strachan of the *Vancouver Sun* that his ideal winner has certain qualities: "You need the whole deal. The voice, the personality, the attitude."

While talking about joining *American Idol*, Tyler revealed how being a survivor helped him as a judge and a musician. He told Ben Kaplan of the *National Post*, "Everything that came my way has cut me into what I am today—a grateful, recovering drug addict-alcoholic. I'm not without my marks and scars, but I show people them, and I think that's why they love my music—because I'm honest."

Selected discography (With Aerosmith)

Aerosmith, Columbia, 1973.
Get Your Wings, Columbia, 1974.
Toys in the Attic, Columbia, 1975.

Rocks, Columbia, 1976.
Draw the Line, Columbia, 1977.
Live Bootleg, Columbia, 1978.
Night in the Ruts, Columbia, 1979.
Rock in a Hard Place, Columbia, 1982.
Done with Mirrors, Geffen, 1985.
Permanent Vacation, Geffen, 1987.
Pump, Geffen, 1989.
Get a Grip, Geffen, 1993.
Nine Lives, Columbia, 1997.
A Little South of Sanity, Geffen, 1998.
Just Push Play, Columbia, 2001.
Honkin' on Bobo, Columbia, 2004.
Rockin' the Joint, Columbia, 2005.

Sources

Periodicals

Arkansas Democrat-Gazette (Little Rock, AR), April 1, 1988.
Atlanta Journal and Constitution, October 2, 1998, p. 4P.
Billboard, May 8, 1993, p. 9; August 14, 2010.
Boston Magazine, October 2005.
Canwest News Service, May 14, 2011.
National Post, January 19, 2011, p. B3.
New York Times, June 26, 2011, p. 27.
St. Louis Post-Dispatch, April 10, 1997, p. 8.
USA Today, October 6, 1989, p. 1D; April 20, 1993, p. 10D; August 15, 1991, p. 2D.
Vancouver Province (British Columbia, Canada), April 23, 2002, p. B11.
Vancouver Sun (British Columbia, Canada), January 12, 2011, p. D8.

Online

"About Steven Tyler," Steven Tyler Official Web Site, http://www.steventyler.com/bio (August 22, 2011).
"Aerosmith: Biography," AllMusic, http://www.allmusic.com/artist/aerosmith-p3508/biography (August 22, 2011).
"Steven Tyler: Biography," AllMusic, http://www.allmusic.com/artist/steven-tyler-p133400/biography (August 22, 2011).
"Steven Tyler Biography," Biography.com, http://www.biography.com/articles/Steven-Tyler-16472561.tif?print (August 22, 2011).
"Steven Tyler," Internet Movie Database, http://www.imdb.com/name/nm0878911/ (August 22, 2011).

—*A. Petruso*

Justin Verlander

Professional baseball player

Born February 20, 1983, in Manakin-Sabot, VA; son of Richard (a union official) and Kathy Verlander. *Education:* Attended Old Dominion University, 2001-04.

Addresses: *Agent*—SFX Baseball, 400 Skokie Blvd., Ste. 280, Northbrook, IL 60062. *Home*—Lakeland, FL and Goochland, VA. *Office*—c/o Detroit Tigers, Comerica Park, 2100 Woodward Ave., Detroit, MI 48201.

Career

Pitcher, Old Dominion University, 2002-04; pitcher for Team USA (U.S. national team), Pan-American Games, 2003; signed by Detroit Tigers, 2004; professional pitcher for minor-league teams Lakeland Tigers (Florida State League, A-Advanced), 2005, and Erie Seawolves (Eastern League, AA), 2005; starting pitcher for Detroit Tigers, 2006—.

Member: Major League Baseball Players Association.

Awards: Rookie of the year, Colonial Athletic Association, 2002; First-Team Freshman All-American, *Collegiate Baseball* and *Baseball America*, 2002; silver medal in baseball (with Team USA), Pan-American Games, 2003; Minor League Starting Pitcher of the Year and Class A Starting Pitcher of the Year, Minor League Baseball, 2005; Minor League All-Star and High Class A All-Star, *Baseball America*, 2005; Rookie of the Year, American League (AL), 2006; Tigers Rookie of the Year, Baseball Writers Association of America (BBWAA), 2006; All-Star, Major League Baseball (MLB), 2007, 2009-11; Player of the Year, *Sporting News*, 2011; MLB Players Choice Awards for Player of the Year and AL Outstanding Pitcher, MLB Players Association, 2011; AL Cy Young Award and AL Most Valuable Player Award, BBWAA, 2011. Also winner of player of the week and pitcher of the month awards in college and the minor and major leagues.

Sidelights

In 2011, starting pitcher Justin Verlander of the Detroit Tigers had one of the most dominating seasons in recent memory. He led all of Major League Baseball (MLB) in wins—24, the most for any pitcher since 2002—strikeouts (250), and the number of walks and hits per innings pitched (0.92 WHIP). He also led the American League (AL) with an earned run average (ERA) of 2.40 and was a unanimous selection for the AL Cy Young Award, given annually to the league's best pitcher. His performance, especially during a 12-game winning streak at the end of the season, helped the Tigers run away with their first division crown since 1987, earning him the AL Most Valuable Player (MVP)

Award. Verlander knew he had the potential for excellence. "I worked extremely hard for this, and I told you [reporters] a few times, if you expect greatness it shouldn't surprise you," the ace told Jason Beck of the MLB Web site. "I've always expected myself to be able to pitch this way. It still doesn't surprise me that I did."

Verlander was born in 1983 and was raised in Goochland, Virginia, outside the state capital of Richmond. When he began playing organized baseball at seven or eight, he demonstrated a strong arm, if not the best aim. "A couple of kids quit because I hit them a few times," the pitcher told John Lowe of the *Detroit Free Press.* "A few kids were crying on deck before they faced me. They knew I might hit them in the head or something." Richard Verlander knew his son had unusual potential when, at the age of nine, young Justin threw a rock into a pond twice as far as his father had. By 13, Verlander was throwing so fast his father could not catch his pitches; he got further training at a baseball academy.

By his junior year at Goochland High School—where the high-energy Verlander earned good grades but was sometimes scolded for talking—the young pitcher's fastballs were attracting major league scouts. After strep throat sapped his strength early in his senior season, his fastballs slowed below the 90-plus miles per hour that major-league pitchers regularly reach. His stock dropped, and despite finishing high school averaging two strikeouts per inning, Verlander went undrafted in 2002. He decided to attend Old Dominion University in Richmond instead.

At Old Dominion, as Verlander worked on his mechanics and lifted weights to increase his strength, his fastball speed began reaching the high 90s. "I grew into myself [at ODU]," Verlander recalled to Joan Tupponce in *Richmond Magazine.* "In high school, I was tall, lean, and lanky. I couldn't run. I could just throw. In college I worked out and became an athlete." After the 2002 season, Verlander's 1.90 ERA earned him Colonial Athletic Association rookie of year honors. Throughout college Verlander developed other pitches, adding a curveball (a pitch that dives as it approaches the plate) and a change-up (a slower pitch that is delivered like a fastball) to his killer fastball. "I kind of realized I couldn't blow the ball by everybody," Verlander told Will Kimmey of *Baseball America.* "In high school I could do that, but now it's not going to work. I need to pitch." Verlander set school and conference records with 427 career strikeouts; he also earned Old Dominion's single-season record for strikeouts, with 151 his junior year.

In 2003 Verlander competed in the Pan-American Games with the U.S. baseball team. His 5-1 record, 1.29 ERA, and team-leading 41 strikeouts helped the team earn a silver medal. The pitcher skipped his senior year of college after the Detroit Tigers drafted him in 2004 with the second pick overall. He spent most of the 2005 season in the minors, at Class A Lakeland (Florida) and then Class AA Erie (Pennsylvania). After 16 games in the minors with a combined 1.29 ERA and 136 strikeouts in 119 innings, Verlander was called up for his major league debut on July 4, 2005. He made two spot starts that month before returning to Erie, and although both were losses, his pitches and calm demeanor impressed both opponents and teammates.

Verlander made the Tigers roster in 2006 as a starting pitcher. His first game was a seven-inning, two-hit shutout of the Texas Rangers, the first of 17 wins that year. Batters all over the league were stunned by his fastball, which often approached 100 miles per hour, even in late innings. Verlander's final win of the season clinched the playoffs for the Tigers, and he won Game 2 of the AL Championship Series. In the World Series, he started two games against the St. Louis Cardinals, but lost both as the Cardinals took the series four games to one. With his 17-9 regular-season record and 3.63 ERA, Verlander became the overwhelming choice for the AL Rookie of the Year. Nevertheless, he knew he had room to improve. "If you asked me what I'm working on 15 years from now," the pitcher told Steve DiMeglio of *USA Today,* "I'd tell you the same thing I'll tell you now—everything."

Verlander did improve in the 2007 season, leading the Tigers with 18 wins and receiving his first All-Star bid. On June 12, he pitched his first no-hitter, beating the Milwaukee Brewers with 12 strikeouts and only four walks. In the final inning Verlander had one pitch register 101 miles per hour. "I like to challenge hitters with a 'Here it is, hit it,' attitude," Verlander explained to Jeff Berlinicke in *Baseball Digest.* "It is my biggest part of the game, especially when I get in situations where I need it. I always try to save a little bit so it's there for me at the end, but I like to keep hitters off balance." Verlander finished the season with an 18-6 record, 183 strikeouts, and a 3.66 ERA.

In 2008, Verlander was named Detroit's opening-day pitcher for the first time. Nevertheless, it was a down year for the hurler; although he occasionally pitched a gem, he finished the year 11-17, with a 4.84 ERA. Verlander told Paul Woody of the *Richmond Times-Dispatch,* "I was expecting more from myself, and the team was expecting more out of me. But it's nothing to hang my head about when know I did everything I could." He spent the off-season determined to work on his strength and endurance so that his arm would be as strong in September as in April.

Some observers might have worried in 2009 when Verlander started the season 0-2 after his first four starts; however, Verlander knew that the problem was not with his mechanics. "I sat down and asked myself what was different," he told Woody. "The answer I came up with was my mentality. So the last few weeks, I've just had an aggressive mentality, from the time I wake up in the morning until the end of the game." After this adjustment he won seven straight on the way to his second All-Star citation. He led the American League in wins (19), innings pitched (240), and strikeouts (269), and showed no signs of slowing at the end of the season. Hall-of-Fame pitcher Nolan Ryan—Verlander's childhood idol—saw the young pitcher strike out 13 with no walks against the Texas Rangers in July. That September, Ryan told Ben Shpigel of the *New York Times*, "This still holds true today—it was the best stuff I've seen all year. Just overpowering."

Tigers' management agreed with this assessment and in 2010 signed Verlander to a five-year contract extension worth $80 million. He expected another good year, having proven his stamina to last the whole season. "Last year, I felt like everything came together great for me," Verlander told Steve Greenberg of the *Sporting News*. "I pitched well and felt good all year. I can't remember one time when my arm was really sore." He had a 4-1 record in September on the way to another All-Star season for the Tigers, finishing in the top five of the American League in wins (18), innings pitched (224), and strikeouts (219). The pitcher was not satisfied with his performance, however. "I know I've had success," Verlander told Steve Kornacki of MLive.com during the off-season, "but I need to become more consistent with my fastball location. And I need to find a quick way to easier outs, eliminating most of those eight- and nine-pitch at-bats. That's what [Cy Young winners] Cliff Lee and Roy Halladay do."

Consistency helped Verlander achieve a remarkable performance in 2011. On May 7, against Toronto, he earned his second career no-hitter; in June he came close with a two-hit shutout of Cleveland. The ace told Paul White of *USA Today* that his one goal when pitching is to throw a no-hitter: "I'm not afraid to say it. That's my job. Why would I say I want to give up a hit? You know everybody thinks it. Nobody will say it." Verlander went on to have a stand-out season, with seven-game and 12-game

winning streaks to lead the Tigers to a division championship. Verlander won the AL triple crown with the most wins and strikeouts and the best ERA; he also led the majors in wins, strikeouts, innings pitched (251), and batting average against (.192). His dominance—including a 16-3 record pitching after a Tigers' loss—led to talk of a potential MVP Award, rarely given to pitchers. Trying to explain his outstanding year, Verlander told Ben Reiter of *Sports Illustrated*, "It's hard for me to put a finger on what I know, but it's there. Time. Experience of pitching at this level for a while now. You log it all away, and it opens up a new game to you, almost."

With Verlander leading the rotation, Detroit fans had high hopes for the 2011 postseason. Bad weather hampered the pitcher, raining out his first playoff game after one inning. Although in his next game he struck out eleven Yankees in a Detroit victory, several rain delays led to an early exit and a loss for Verlander in his first League Championship game against the Texas Rangers. In Game 5, with the Tigers facing elimination, manager Jim Leyland declared his two top relievers would not be available. Verlander pitched into the eighth inning, helping the Tigers to a 7-5 victory, but the Tigers lost the series, and Verlander finished the postseason with a 5.31 ERA, albeit against two of the best lineups in the game. MLB awards do not consider postseason performance, and here Verlander dominated once again. In awards voted on by players, he received the *Sporting News* MLB Player of the Year and the MLB Players Choice Player of the Year, becoming only the second pitcher to win the latter. He was also a unanimous selection for the AL Cy Young Award, given to the league's best pitcher by the Baseball Writers Association of America. The writers also gave Verlander the AL MVP Award, making him the first starting pitcher in 25 years to be so honored.

After his amazing season, Verlander took a month off to recharge and then returned to training full-time. "I've had some good years in the past, but nothing like this," the pitcher told Jon Robinson of ESPN. "That's why I continue to work hard, because you never know what the ceiling is. I'm not saying that this year is the ceiling. Who knows? Just continue to work hard and it's amazing to see what can happen." In his free time, the pitcher planned to enjoy golf, video games—he was excited to be on the cover of the popular *MLB 2K12* game—poker, movies, and spending time with his longtime girlfriend Emily Yuen and their dog Riley. The star also participated in several Tigers' charities and founded Verlander's Victory for Veterans, which brought veterans and their families to Verlander's suite in Comerica Park to watch games. The pitcher also donated his MLB Players Choice Award prize money, adding $30,000 of his own, to two veterans' hospitals in the Detroit area. Although more awards may be in his future, Verlander told Greenberg he has only one specific career goal: "I want to be in the Hall of Fame. I figure if I'm in the Hall of Fame, everything else will take care of itself."

Sources

Periodicals

Baseball Digest, May 2007, p. 56.
Detroit Free Press, February 21, 2006; June 12, 2007; June 12, 2008.
New York Times, September 18, 2009, p. B10; June 16, 2011, p. B12; October 14, 2011, p. B11.
Richmond Times-Dispatch, May 30, 2009.
Sporting News, March 15, 2010, pp. 52-57.
Sports Illustrated, May 28, 2007, p. 14; September 19, 2011.
USA Today, June 26, 2006, p. 1C; July 8, 2011, p. 1C; October 5, 2011, p. 4C.

Online

"Ferrari Parked in Garage, Tigers' Justin Verlander Has Eyes on Fast Track to Cooperstown," MLive. com, http://www.mlive.com/tigers/index.ssf/2011/03/ferrari_parked_in_garage_tiger.html (November 28, 2011).

"Justin Verlander Talks 'MLB 2K12,'" ESPN.com, http://espn.go.com/espn/thelife/videogames/blog/_/name/thegamer/id/7187804/justin-verlander-talks-mlb-2k12-nolan-ryan (November 28, 2011).

"Live from Detroit, It's Justin Verlander," *Richmond Magazine,* http://www.richmondmagazine.com/?articleID=b41eafc4f3d37f8b09a1c86c81378d79 (November 28, 2011).

"Tigers' Justin Verlander Adds AL MVP to His Award Haul," *Detroit Free Press,* http://www.freep.com/article/20111121.tif/SPORTS02/11112104.tif7 (November 28, 2011).

"Verlander: Dominant Stuff, Inconsistent Command," Baseball America, http://www.baseballamerica.com/today/2004draft/040324verlander.html (November 28, 2011).

"Verlander Takes Home Player of the Year Honors," Major League Baseball, http://mlb.mlb.com/news/article.jsp?ymd=20111103.tif&content_id=25895840.tif&vkey=news_det&c_id=det (November 28, 2011).

—*Diane Telgen*

Scott Walker

Darren Hauck/Reuters

Governor of Wisconsin

Born Scott Kevin Walker, November 2, 1967, in Colorado Springs, CO; son of Llewellyn (a pastor) and Patricia Walker; married Tonette; children: Matt, Alex. *Education:* Attended Marquette University, Milwaukee, WI, 1986-90.

Addresses: *Office*—115 East Capitol, Madison, WI 53702. *Web site*—http://walker.wi.gov; http://www.scottwalker.org.

Career

Worked for IBM, c. late 1980s; financial development staffer, American Red Cross, c. early 1990s; elected to Wisconsin State Assembly, 1993; elected Milwaukee County executive, 2002; elected governor of Wisconsin, 2010.

Sidelights

Wisconsin Governor Scott Walker, a Baptist minister's son, became a controversial national figure in 2011 when he championed an effort to severely limit the rights of public employee unions in his state to bargain with the government. Liberal activists swamped Wisconsin's capital, Madison, in massive protests to try to stop the law. The drama highlighted Walker's sudden status as the most prominent of several new Republican governors attempting to remake state public policies along more conservative lines.

Walker was born on November 2, 1967, in Colorado Springs, Colorado. He grew up in Plainfield, Iowa, and moved with his family to Delavan, Wisconsin,

in 1977. His father, Llewellyn, was a Baptist minister. "Friends of mine, when they would swear in front of me, would apologize," Walker told Bill Glauber of Milwaukee's *Journal Sentinel.* He became involved in scouting and rose to the rank of Eagle Scout.

Walker became interested in government while in high school, when he participated in the Boys Nation program in Washington, D.C. He attended college at Marquette University in Milwaukee and worked for IBM while in school. He left college in his final semester to take a full-time job in financial development with the American Red Cross.

In 1993, Walker was elected to the Wisconsin State Assembly as a Republican. He wrote several bills that became law, including truth in sentencing rules and the elimination of a statute of limitations for sexual assault. He ran for Milwaukee County executive in 2002, though he was a Republican in a Democratic county. "I remember, universally, people said I had lost my mind," Walker told Glauber of the *Journal Sentinel.* "One, you can't win. Two, if you do win, it's a political dead end."

But voters were ready for a change. Walker campaigned on a promise to clean up the county government after a scandal that had stuck taxpayers with millions of dollars in pension obligations. The government, he later told Monica Davey of the *New York Times,* was "addicted to other people's money."

While Walker was county executive, his proposals to privatize the county's food service and cleaning service, and change employee contributions to health and pension plans were often opposed by the Milwaukee County Board of Supervisors. Walker even questioned whether the county government was necessary and briefly proposed that it abolish itself. He and his wife, Tonette, regularly gave back a portion of his salary to the county. Walker spent eight years as county executive and boasted afterward that he had cut the county's workforce and debt, balanced the budget without raising property taxes, and recorded a budget surplus in 2009.

In 2010, Walker ran for governor of Wisconsin, emphasizing his frugality. He often told campaign audiences that he packed the same brown-bag lunch every day for two years: two ham and cheese sandwiches, with mayonnaise, on wheat bread. He outlined a three-point economic philosophy on his campaign Web site, ScottWalker.org: "1. Don't spend more than you have. 2. Smaller government is better government. 3. People create jobs, not government." He set a goal of creating an economic climate that would allow Wisconsin businesses to create 250,000 new jobs by 2015.

Walker beat his Democratic opponent, Milwaukee Mayor Tom Barrett, 52 to 46 percent. His victory was part of a Republican wave that swept through Wisconsin in the 2010 election. His party also won one of Wisconsin's U.S. Senate seats and majorities in the State Assembly and State Senate.

Once he became governor, Walker hung a sign on his office's doorknob that read, "Wisconsin is open for business" (according to the *New York Times*). He rejected an $810 million federal grant to build a train line connecting Milwaukee with Madison, arguing that the train would cost the state too much to operate. He announced that the state's commerce department would become a partially private organization and that the department's workers would have to reapply for their jobs. Walker and the Republican-controlled state legislature also implemented $117 million in tax cuts, many of them for businesses, set to take effect in 2012.

Most controversially, Walker declared that Wisconsin needed to cut the benefits of Wisconsin's public employees and sharply reduce their rights to collec-

tively bargain with the government. Doing so, he said, would address a $137 million state deficit anticipated in 2011 and a projected $3.6 billion shortfall in the two years after. "We can't have a society anymore where public employees are the haves and the taxpayers who pay the bills are the have-nots," Walker had told the *Journal Sentinel* editorial board during his campaign. He complained that most state employees' benefits, such as health care, were paid for completely by the state, while outside of government, employees and employers both contributed to benefit plans. To address that, his bill took away unions' right to bargain over pensions and health care. It also limited public employees' raises to the inflation rate and restricted unions' ability to collect membership dues.

Walker's move sparked rage and protests from Wisconsin's teachers, police, firefighters and other public employees in the winter of 2011. Their dramatic protests at Wisconsin's capitol building in Madison became national news and made Wisconsin the center of attention in a larger debate over public employee unions in other states, from New Jersey to Ohio. President Barack Obama called Walker's proposal an attack on unions, while John Boehner, speaker of the U.S. House of Representatives, said Walker's plan confronted long-avoided problems.

Walker shrugged off the protests. "This doesn't faze me one bit," he told Davey of the *New York Times* as thousands of demonstrators loudly occupied most of the capitol building. "I'm not going to be intimidated." He predicted that the "vast majority" of Wisconsin residents would eventually "realize this was not nearly as bad as they thought it was going to be."

The Wisconsin Senate's Democrats left the state in an attempt to prevent the Senate from voting on Walker's bill about bargaining rights, taking advantage of a rule that required a certain number of senators to be present to vote on bills that spent money. In late February 2011, Walker was embarrassed by a prank call from an editor of a Buffalo, New York-based Web site who posed as David Koch, a billionaire active in conservative causes and a major contributor to Walker's 2010 campaign. In the phone call, Walker repeatedly complained about the Senate Democrats and mentioned a plan to trick them into coming back to Madison by inviting them to a meeting, then holding the vote. In the end, Republicans passed Walker's proposal through the Senate in March, without any Democratic senators present, after removing the funding provisions in the bill. Walker signed the bill into law. As of early summer 2011, it had not gone into effect because of court challenges.

Another dramatic standoff took place inside the capitol's Assembly chamber that March. Walker presented his budget plan, which called for $1.5 billion in cuts to public schools, local governments, and other programs, and no increases in taxes or fees. Hundreds of protesters outside the capitol building pounded drums and chanted for Walker's recall.

Walker defended his actions in an opinion article in the *Wall Street Journal*. He argued that public employees would retain better benefits under his plan than those his brother received as a hotel banquet manager and bartender. "When Gov. Mitch Daniels repealed collective bargaining in Indiana six years ago, it helped government become more efficient and responsive," Walker argued. "The average pay for Indiana state employees has actually increased, and high-performing employees are rewarded with pay increases or bonuses when they do something exceptional."

By early summer 2011, the political battles over Walker's agenda had spread and deepened. Walker had signed a bill requiring that citizens show a photo ID to vote. Opponents argued that the bill discriminated against poor voters who do not own cars or have driver's licenses. A poll in late May found that 54 percent of Wisconsin residents disapproved of Walker's performance as governor and that 50 percent wanted to recall him, while 47 percent were opposed to a recall. Democratic activists had gathered enough signatures to force six Republican state senators who had voted for Walker's union law into recall elections in July. At their state convention in June, Democrats announced plans to try to recall Walker in 2012, two years before his term is scheduled to end.

Sources

Periodicals

Journal Sentinel (Milwaukee, WI), October 17, 2010; May 25, 2011; June 3, 2011.
New York Times, February 19, 2011.
Time, March 12, 2011.
Wall Street Journal, March 10, 2011.

Online

"About Governor Walker," Office of the Governor: Scott Walker, http://walker.wi.gov/category.asp?linkcatid=3599&linkid=1709&locid=177 (May 22, 2011).
"'I'll declare an economic emergency in the state,'" *Journal Sentinel*, http://www.jsonline.com/news/opinion/10507166.tif9.html (May 22, 2011).
"Meet Scott Walker" Scott Walker for Wisconsin Governor, http://www.scottwalker.org/about/biography (May 22, 2011).
"Times Topics: Scott K. Walker" New York Times, http://topics.nytimes.com/top/reference/timestopics/people/w/scott_k_walker/index.html (May 22, 2011).

—*Erick Trickey*

Jessica Watson

Sailor

Born Jessica Watson, May 18, 1993, in Gold Coast, Queensland, Australia; daughter of Roger and Julie Watson.

Addresses: *E-mail*—frase@5oceansmanagement. com. *Web site*—http://www.jessicawatson.com.au/.

Career

Sailed non-stop and unassisted around the world using a Southern hemisphere route, 2010.

Awards: Spirit of Sport Award, Sport Australia Hall of Fame, 2010; Young Performer of the Year, Sports Performer Awards, 2010; Adventurers of the Year, National Geographic Society, 2010; Young Australian of the Year, Australian Government, 2011.

Sidelights

Many people dream of heading off to the high seas and sailing around the world. It is a very fanciful and romantic dream and most people do not realize the difficulties and dangers of such an adventure. They think only of tall ships and tropical sunsets. Jessica Watson did more than just fantasize about circumnavigating the globe; she singlehandedly completed the arduous voyage despite high winds, enormous swells, days of drizzle, and critics who felt that a 16-year-old girl lacked the maturity and expertise for such an undertaking. But Watson was no ordinary teenager.

Watson, daughter of Roger and Julie Watson, was born in 1993 in Gold Coast, Queensland, Australia. She is one of four children. When she, her brother, and her sisters were children, they took sailing lessons. At first Watson was reluctant to try sailing. Jessica's mother Julie told Mike Colman of Queensland's *Courier Mail*, "Jessica didn't take to it straightaway. She was so tiny and thin, but in the end I think she got sick of sitting on the shore while the others were out having fun." After Watson's parents sold their home and successful real estate business, they decided to have a special double decker bus built to live in so that the family could travel. While they were waiting for the bus to be built, someone at the yacht club they frequented suggested that they buy a boat. They bought a 16-meter cabin cruiser and the entire family lived on the boat for more than five years. In addition to living on the sailboat, which they traveled with when the weather was good and stayed docked in port when the weather was inclement, the family also lived in the double decker bus and traveled around Australia. The children were home-schooled via a distance education program.

When Watson was still a preschooler she was diagnosed as having severe dyslexia. Her mother has described Watson's learning disability as being so severe that she could not count to ten or say the alphabet. Watson was still being read to at the age of eleven so that the world of books could be made more accessible to her. The desire to reach for the grand adventure of sailing around the world came from one of the books that Watson's mother read to her. That book was *Lionheart: A Journey of the Human Spirit* by Jesse Martin. Jesse Martin is another Australian who has sailed non-stop and unassisted around the world. Watson was inspired by his story and decided that she wanted to join the very exclusive numbers of people who had accomplished this extraordinary feat.

When Watson first approached her parents just after her 12th birthday with the idea that "maybe" she would like to sail around the world it was not really a maybe. She had already made up her mind. Colman described Watson's decision as a "a call to arms" and went on to say that it was an "almost personal challenge to become the youngest person to sail around the world alone." Watson had many obstacles to overcome to make this self-imposed challenge a reality. Not only did she have to become proficient as a sailor in order to be able to operate her sailboat and obtain a skipper's license, she had to find sponsors, get a sailboat, and learn how to repair engines. She had to work out for herself how to make the whole thing happen. Watson told Colman, "I was always the girl who had no confidence but you just stand up and you try. When we first started sailing I was always the one tagging along, but as I started doing things I started to get more confidence ... you set yourself a challenge so you have to deal with things, and you can." Watson responded to the media, confronted critics, and took classes in a variety of skills to prepare herself. Whenever someone was fixing a car engine or any other type of engine at the marina she volunteered to help so that she could learn. She also needed to have time on various boats and practice sailing. She washed dishes at a local restaurant to earn the money for return airplane fares when she sailed abroad to learn seamanship. Watson prepared for her solo journey for three years prior to sailing out of the harbor in Sydney, Australia.

All of Watson's determination and hard work paid off. Watson convinced people to assist her in her quest. She e-mailed Don McIntyre and he and his wife took a special interest in Watson; they not only gave her sailing tips and advice, they also bought and loaned her a yacht to use for her journey. Bruce Arms, another solo yachtsman, a boat builder, and a painter from Mooloolaba, Australia, was so won over by Watson's determination that he had her co-skipper his boat from Plymouth, New Zealand, to Mooloolaba and he donated two months of his time to fitting out Watson's boat, the *Ella's Pink Lady*. She was also able to get more than 36 sponsors for her endeavor, including such companies as Panasonic, Iridium, Ella Bache of Paris, Bainbridge International, and SatCom Global.

Watson's critics derided her parents for allowing her to undertake the journey and expressed concerns that she was too young and inexperienced to safely complete the route that she was proposing. Watson and her goal to sail around the world made her the girl who launched a thousand heated discussions around kitchen tables and in bars in Australia and around the world. People wondered what her parents were thinking. During a test run on September 9, 2009, to prepare for her longer journey, Watson was sailing in the busy shipping lane off of Queensland's coast. It was night and according to Yachtpals.com she had just written on her blog, "Ok, I better go and fire the radar up, turn the navigation lights on and have one last check of everything on deck before it gets dark. Then I might think about some dinner before grabbing some cat naps of sleep." Shortly after this entry Watson's boat, which is a 10.23 meter Sparkman and Stephens S&S 34, collided with the *Silver Yang*, a 63,000-ton bulk carrier. This collision lent validity to the concerns of Watson's critics. The *Ella's Pink Lady* was dismasted and Watson could have been badly injured. The final report by the Australian Transport Safety Bureau which was released in June 2010 stated that both Watson and the watchkeepers for the *Silver Yang* had failed to maintain an adequate lookout and that both had failed to properly employ navigational aids. The then acting premier of Queensland, Paul Lucas, expressed concern and advised that Watson should abandon her quest to sail around the world. Despite the fact that the collision gave Watson's critics ammunition, Watson took heart from the collision. She felt that it gave her confidence that she could respond to any severe emergency and she was even more determined to follow through with her plans to sail out of Sydney harbor on October 18, 2009, in her pink-hulled boat.

Watson's planned route was to take eight months, start and end in Sydney, Australia, and to pass near New Zealand, Fiji, Kiribati, Cape Horn, Cape of Good Hope, Cape Leeuwin, and South East Cape. She planned on sailing through some of the most difficult waters on the planet. Her course first took her past Tonga and she sailed clear of New Zealand and Fiji early in November 2009. As required by the World Sailing Speed Record Council's criteria for full circumnavigation of the globe she crossed the equator near Jarvis Island on November 19, 2009 before rounding Kiritimati on November 22, 2009 and recrossing the equator going in a southeasterly direction toward Cape Horn. At Christmas time of that year she was at the place located farthest from land, called Point Nemo. On January 13, 2010, she passed Cape Horn and had completed 9,800 nautical miles in 87 days. She was ahead of her schedule of trying to maintain a pace of 100 nautical miles per day. At this point in her voyage everything seemed to be going smoothly.

However, her journey was not to be all smooth sailing. On January 23, 2010, she encountered a storm and experienced four knock downs in which her boat was rocked and the mast hit the water. She rode out the storm with its ten-meter-high waves and winds that were measured at more than 70 knots. Her boat had minor damage as a result of the storm and her emergency beacon was accidentally activated, but she made it through.

She passed the halfway point of her voyage on the 100th day, January 25, 2010. On February 15, 2010, she crossed the Prime Meridian, passing from the Western Hemisphere to the Eastern Hemisphere. On February 24, 2010, she reached Cape Agulhas at the southernmost tip of Africa and then sailed the more than 5,000 nautical miles to reach Western Australia. Just prior to coming in to Sydney to round out her journey, she wrote of the mix of weather on her blog, "My perfect conditions came to an end late on Tuesday with thunderstorms then this freezing cold southerly wind (brrrr!). Yesterday the wind was gale force but today it's eased off to 30 knots, giving us great surfing conditions with the sea standing up as it meets the east coast current." On May 15, 2010, after battling mountainous waves, intense loneliness that caused her at more than one point to re-examine her decision to undertake her journey, and critics who disbelieved she could make it, Watson was escorted into Sydney Harbor by an enthusiastic, ad hoc flotilla of small craft and larger vessels who welcomed her home.

After climbing off of her boat, waving off an offer of a ride on a golf cart, she walked on unsteady legs and told the waiting crowd, as reported by Sydney correspondent Bonnie Malkin of the London *Daily Telegraph*, "As a little girl people don't think you're capable of these things, they don't realize what young people, 16 year olds and girls are capable of. But it's amazing what you can do."

After Watson completed her journey she was not given credit for circumnavigating the world. Not only did the World Speed Sailing Record Council decide to end its under-18 category, but they determined that Watson had not sailed far enough by not going far enough north of the equator to log the requisite number of nautical miles. Her logs indicate that she had sailed approximately 23,000 nautical miles, which is well over the necessary 21,600 nautical miles, but her route was not a straight route. Some of the zigzagging that Watson did to complete her journey added miles that cannot be included in the total. While the World Speed Sailing Record Council will not even consider her journey because of her age, in addition, they estimate that she is 2,000 nautical miles short of meeting their requirements. The BBC News quoted Watson as saying "If I haven't been sailing around, then it beats me what I've been doing out here all this time!" Watson's drive and determination are evident by any standards and she received the Young Australian of the Year Award in 2011 from the Australian government and has since written a book about her voyage titled *True Spirit,* available on her Web site.

Sources

Periodicals

Courier Mail (Queensland, Australia), June 13, 2009; January 31, 2010.
Guardian (England), May 15, 2010.
Herald Sun (Victoria, Australia), April 29, 2010.
Los Angeles Times, May 5, 2010.

Online

"Australia hails Jessica Watson, 16, for sailing record," BBC News, http://news.bbc.co.uk/2/hi/asia-pacific/8684120.stm (February 19, 2011).
Jessica Watson Official Web site and Blog, http://www.jessicawatson.com.au/ (February 19, 2011).
"Jessica Watson—Youngest Round Hopeful Collides at Sea," Yacht Pals, http://yachtpals.com/jessica-watson-7021 (February 19, 2011).
"Round the World Sailor Jessica Watson Arrives Back in Sydney," *Daily Telegraph,* http://www.telegraph.co.uk/news/worldnews/australiaandthepacific/australia/7727819/Round-the-world-sailor-Jessica-Watson-arrives-back-in-Sydney.html (February 19, 2011).

—*Annette Bowman*

Tim Westergren

Founder of Pandora Radio

Born Timothy Brooks Westergren, December 21, 1965, in Minneapolis, MN. *Education:* Stanford University, B.A., 1988.

Addresses: *Home*—San Francisco, CA. *Office*—Pandora Media, Inc., 2101 Webster St., Ste. 1650, Oakland, CA 94612.

Career

Musician, late 1980s-c. 1995; played in the bands Late Coffee and Oranges, Barefoot, and Yellowwood Junction; also worked as a hotel-bar pianist; founded Savage Beast Technologies, 2000, and served as chief executive officer until 2004; launched Pandora Radio, 2005, and served as chief strategy officer, 2005—.

Sidelights

Tim Westergren is the founder and chief strategy officer of Pandora, the Internet radio station that features a novel, and addictive, music recommendation engine. The site was launched in 2005 when the company was already five years old and had struggled financially for nearly all of that time. Westergren, a former musician, was forced to revise his business strategy several times to avoid a total shutdown and bankruptcy. "I've never, ever given up, even when we were in the most depressive bleak times," he told *Inc.* writer Stephanie Clifford. "I always thought it was a good idea."

Born in Minneapolis in 1965, Westergren emerged as a talented musician in his teens. He played several instruments, including piano, various wood-

winds, and the drums, and studied music theory and music-computer applications at Stanford University, where jazz great Stan Getz was one of his teachers. After earning his degree in 1988, Westergren spent several years playing in various San Francisco bands, including Barefoot and Yellowwood Junction; however, by the mid-1990s, he tired of eking out a living on the road and turned his focus to composing scores for independent films. One aspect of this line of work surprised him: when directors would try to tell him what they wanted the music to express for a scene, Westergren noted that they struggled to explain themselves, though these were people not inexperienced in expressing their creative ideas verbally.

Westergren came up with the idea of breaking down a song through several traits, much like the way in which DNA carries the uniquely individual characteristics of a organism on a gene. Calling it the Music Genome Project, he teamed with two friends— one with business experience and the other with a software development background—and launched Savage Beast Technologies in January of 2000. He hired musician-friends to help him build a database, coming up with a method of analyzing each song by about 400 attributes, such as tempo, harmony, and lyrics. The database was then plugged into an algorithm that could predict similar songs that a listener might like.

Initially, Westergren had no intention of starting an Internet radio station. His original plan was to build the business by licensing its proprietary methods to other, much larger companies. For a time, electronics retailer Best Buy was a client and installed music-listening kiosks designed to boost sales of CDs, but Westergren's company struggled to meet overhead and payroll costs. He asked employees to defer their salaries, and some agreed to stay on while he sought venture-capital funding to keep the company afloat. In 2003, he learned this was a violation of California labor laws, and the state regulatory agency agreed with a few disgruntled employees who had filed a lawsuit for back pay. At that point, Westergren was forced to lay off everyone, but some stayed and agreed to work for free. Finally, in early 2004 Westergren convinced a venture-capital firm to provide some seed money for his idea. It had been his 348th pitch to potential investors.

The $9 million infusion allowed Westergren to hire a more experienced chief executive officer named Joe Kennedy, whose resume included stints at Saturn and e-Loan. Kennedy convinced Westergren to sell his idea directly to consumers, forgoing third-party licensing deals with Best Buy and Borders, the bookstore chain which had also tentatively signed on, then retreated. Pandora Internet Radio went live in September of 2005, and proved so successful in its first week that the company had to double their server capacity three times. Users created their own "station" by selecting a single song or artist they liked, and then fine-tuned their preferences via a thumbs-up or thumbs-down vote on each song the Music Genome recommended.

Pandora offered new users a ten-hour free trial, after which the service was a mere $36 per year. Users found ways around that annual charge by simply signing up with a different email address. Once again, Westergren opted to try another strategy: selling ad space on the site. To advertisers, the captive audience of Pandora users was a veritable goldmine of readily accessible marketing data. With demographic information already on file, ads could be targeted at their most optimum audience.

Westergren regularly held town-hall style meetings across the United States to meet with Pandora users face-to-face and listen to their suggestions on how to improve the service. A little over two years in operation, Pandora had six million subscribers and was adding thousands more every day. The next challenge came from the recording industry itself: in the spring of 2007, the Copyright Royalty Board of the Library of Congress announced plans to revise fees that Internet radio stations would pay. "It would be the end of Pandora," Westergren said to *Newsweek*'s Steven Levy about the proposed change. "It's wildly counterproductive for everybody. It triples our cost, and that's in a business that already does not have a big margin to it."

Westergren led a grass-roots campaign to call attention to the new rates, and emails from Pandora urged subscribers to contact their Congressional representatives to protest the hikes. Other Internet radio sites joined in, and the offensive worked, though Pandora eventually had to pay a lump sum of $30 million in 2009 for past-due royalties.

Pandora's next phase was to generate new users via multiple devices. It launched an iPhone application that brought in a stunning 35,000 new listeners a day in 2008, and two years later inked a deal with Ford to feature the service in the automaker's new Sync dashboard-electronics system. Comedy Central's Stephen Colbert invited Westergren on his show, *The Colbert Report*, to discuss Pandora in the summer of 2010, when the service was nearing the 50-million user mark. Colbert asked Westergren why he named his company after the storied female from Greek mythology—Pandora was told never to open a certain box, but her curiosity prevailed and when she opened the chest, the miseries of the world were unleashed. "Is that what the Internet is? You click open the box and evil comes out your speakers?," Colbert joked, according to *Billboard*. "Surprises come out," Westergren answered, adding, "and at the bottom of that box was hope."

Sources

Periodicals

Billboard, July 17, 2010, p. 14.
Inc., October 2007, p. 101.
Newsweek, April 16, 2007.
New York Times, March 7, 2010; March 5, 2011.

Online

"Pandora Founder Rocks the Music Biz," CNN Money, http://money.cnn.com/2010/06/29/technology/westergren_pandora.fortune/ (April 7, 2011).

—*Carol Brennan*

Betty White

Actress

Born Elizabeth Marion White, January 17, 1922, in Oak Park, IL; daughter of Horace (an electrical engineer and traveling salesperson) and Tess (a homemaker); married Dick Barker (a chicken farmer and military pilot), 1945 (divorced, c. 1945); married Lane Allen (an agent), 1947 (divorced, 1949); married Allen Ludden (a television host), 1963 (died June 9, 1981).

Addresses: *Agent*—William Morris Endeavor Entertainment, One William Morris Place, Beverly Hills, CA 90212.

Career

Actress in films, including: *Time to Kill*, 1945; *Advise and Consent*, 1962; *A Different Approach*, 1978; *Rockin Road Trip*, 1986; *Big City Comedy*, 1986; *Holy Man*, 1998; *Hard Rain*, 1998; *Dennis the Menace Strikes Again!*, 1998; *The Story of Us*, 1999; *Gaia Symphony II*, 1999; *Lake Placid*, 1999; *Tom Sawyer*, 2000; *Whispers: An Elephant's Tale*, 2000; *She Turned the World on With Her Smile: The Making of "The Mary Tyler Moore Show,"* 2002; *Bringing Down the House*, 2003; *The Third Wish*, 2005; *Where's Marty?*, 2006; *Your Mommy Kills Animals*, 2007; *In Search of Puppy Love*, 2007; *Sea Tales*, 2007; *Love N' Dancing*, 2008; *The Proposal*, 2009; *You Again*, 2010. Television appearances include: *Hollywood on Television*, 1949; *Life with Elizabeth*, 1953-54; *The Betty White Show*, 1954-55; *Make the Connection*, 1955; *What's My Line?*, 1955, 1960, 1961, 1963, 1965, 1966; *The Millionaire*, 1956; *A Date with the Angels*, 1956-58; *The Betty White Show*, 1958; *Modern Romances*, 1958; *The Jack Paar Tonight Show*, 1958; *To Tell the Truth*, 1961; *The United States Steel Hour*, 1962; *Password*, 1963, 1972, 1973, 1975; *You Don't Say*, 1963, 1975; *Girl Talk*,1964; *Match Game*, 1964, 1967, 1969, 1973, 1974, 1975, 1982; *The 78th Annual Tournament of Roses Parade*, 1967; *Snap Judgment*, 1967, 1968; *That's Life*, 1968; *Petticoat Junction*, 1969; *Liars Club*,1969; *The Tournament of Roses Parade*, 1970-90; *The Pet Set*, 1971; *Vanished*, 1971; *The Odd Couple*, 1972; *O'Hara: U.S. Treasury*, 1972; *The Mary Tyler Moore Show*, 1973-77; *Password*, 1975; *Ellery Queen*, 1975; *Lucas Tanner*, 1975; *Showoffs*, 1975; *The Magnificent Marble Machine*, 1975; *The Carol Burnett Show*, 1975, 1976, 1978; *Dinah!*, 1975, 1976; *The Paul Lynde Halloween Special*, 1976; *Liars Club*, 1976-77; *The Peter Marshall Variety Show*, 1976; *Celebrity Sweepstakes*, 1976; *The Sonny and Cher Show*, 1976, 1977; *The Cross-Wits*, 1976, 1977; *Circus of the Stars #2*, 1977; *The John Davidson Christmas Show*, 1977; *The Betty White Show*, 1977-78; *With This Ring* (movie), 1978; *The Best Place to Be*, 1979; *Before and After* (movie), 1979; *Circus of the Stars #3*, 1979; *Paul Lynde at the Movies*, 1979; *Password Plus*, 1979, 1980, 1981, 1982; *The Big Show*, 1980; *The Love Boat*, 1980, 1981, 1982, 1984, 1985; *The Gossip Columnist* (movie), 1980; *Macy's Thanksgiving Day Parade*, 1980-90; *Bob Hope: Stand Up and Cheer for the National Football League's 50th Year*, 1981; *Eunice* (movie), 1982; *The Shape of Things*, 1982; *Love, Sidney*, 1982; *Best of the West*, 1982; *Madame's Place*, 1982; *Just Men!*, 1983; *Mama's Family*, 1983-86; *Fame*, 1983; *Hotel*, 1984; *Super Password*, 1984, 1986, 1988;

Helga Esteb/Shutterstock.com

The Love Report, 1984; *Those Wonderful TV Game Shows,* 1984; *Joan Rivers and Friends Salute Heidi Abromowitz,* 1985; *Who's the Boss?,* 1985; *St. Elsewhere,* 1985; *The New Hollywood Squares,* 1986, 1988; *The Golden Girls,* 1985-92; *Celebrity Double Talk,* 1986; *Walt Disney World's 15th Birthday Celebration,* 1986; *America Talks Back,* 1986; *NBC 60th Anniversary Celebration,* 1986; *The Television Academy Hall of Fame,* 1986; *Barbara Walters Special,* 1986; *This Is Your Life,* 1987; *Happy Birthday, Hollywood!,* 1987; *ALF Loves a Mystery,* 1987; *D.C. Follies,* 1987; *Matlock,* 1987; *Santa Barbara,* 1988; *Days of Our Lives,* 1988; *Win, Lose, or Draw,* 1988; *The $10,000 Pyramid,* 1988; *Animal Crack-Ups,* 1988; *Liars Club,* 1988; *Sweethearts,* 1988; *Another World,* 1988; *Happy Birthday, Bob—50 Stars Salute Your 50 Years with NBC,* 1988; *The Hollywood Christmas Parade,* 1988; *The Magical World of Disney,* 1988; *Super Bloopers & New Practical Jokes,* 1988; *Empty Nest,* 1989, 1992; *Bob Hope's Love Affair with Lucy,* 1989; *Friday Night Surprise!,* 1989; *Hanna-Barbera's 50th: A Yabba Dabba Doo Celebration,* 1989; *The Valvoline National Driving Test,* 1989; *The American Red Cross Emergency Test,* 1990; *Night of 100 Stars III,* 1990; *Time Warner Presents the Earth Day Special,* 1990; *The Tube Test,* 1990; *Carol & Company,* 1990; *Nurses,* 1991; *Doris Day: A Sentimental Journey,* 1991; *Funny Women of Television: A Museum of Television and Radio Tribute,* 1991; *Mary Tyler Moore: The 20th Anniversary Show,* 1991; *The Meaning of Life,* 1991; *The Walt Disney World Happy Easter Parade,* 1991; *Chance of a Lifetime* (movie), 1991; *The Golden Palace,* 1992-93; *Bob Hope and Other Young Comedians: The World Laughs, Young and Old,* 1992; *Hats Off to Minnie Pearl: America Honors Minnie Pearl,* 1992; *Starathon 2: A Weekend With the Stars,* 1992; *Walt Disney World Very Merry Christmas Parade,* 1992; *Bob Hope: The First Ninety Years,* 1993; *The Ninth Annual Television Academy Hall of Fame,* 1993; *Throwaway Pets,* 1993; *Bob,* 1993; *Bob Hope's Birthday Memories,* 1994; *Diagnosis Murder,* 1994; *Great Love Songs,* 1995; *Maybe This Time,* 1995-96; *The Story of Santa Claus,* 1996; *A Weekend in the Country* (movie), 1996; *Suddenly Susan,* 1996; *The John Larroquette Show,* 1996; *50 Years of Television: A Celebration of the Academy of Television Arts & Sciences,* 1997; *Intimate Portrait: Mary Tyler Moore,* 1997; *L.A. Doctors,* 1998; *Noddy Holiday Special: Anything Can Happen at Christmas,* 1998; *Behind the Laughs: The Untold Stories of Television's Favorite Comedy,* 1998; *The Lionhearts,* 1998; *Hercules,* 1998-99; *Me & George,* 1998; *Ladies Man,* 1999-2001; *Ally McBeal,* 1999; *Hollywood Squares,* 1999, 2003; *King of the Hill* (voice), 1999, 2002; *The Television Academy Hall of Fame,* 1999; *The '70s: The Decade That Changed Television,* 2000; *Intimate Portrait: Rue McClanahan,* 2000; *Intimate Portrait: Sharon Lawrence,* 2000; *Intimate Portrait: Betty White,* 2000; *Tom Sawyer* (movie), 2000; *The Simpsons* (voice), 2000, 2007; *The Retrievers* (movie), 2001; *Intimate Portrait: Estelle Getty,* 2001; *Lifetime Presents: Disney's American Teacher Awards,* 2001; *The Wild Thornberries: The Origin of Donnie* (movie), 2001; *That '70s Show,* 2002; *NBC 75th Anniversary Special,* 2002; *The Mary Tyler Moore Reunion,* 2002; *Yes, Dear,* 2002; *Providence,* 2002; *Pyramid,* 2002; *I'm With Her,* 2003; *Grim & Evil,* 2003; *Gary the Rat,* 2003; *Everwood,* 2003; *Great Women of Television Comedy,* 2003; *Intimate Portrait: Bea Arthur,* 2003; *Reel Comedy: "Bringing Down the House,"* 2003; *The Golden Girls: Their Greatest Moments,* 2003; *Lifetime's Achievement Awards: Women Changing the World,* 2003; *CBS at 75,* 2003; *Intimate Portrait: Vicki Lawrence,* 2003; *Return to the Batcave: The Misadventures of Adam and Burt* (movie), 2003; *Stealing Christmas* (movie), 2003; *TV Land Moguls,* 2004; *TV's Greatest Sidekicks,* 2004; *Higglytown Heroes,* 2004-05; *My Wife and Kids,* 2004; *Malcolm in the Middle,* 2004; *Father of the Pride,* 2004; *Complete Savages,* 2004, 2005; *Joey,* 2005; *Annie's Point* (movie), 2005; *Boston Legal,* 2005-06; *Family Guy* (voice), 2006; *Gameshow Marathon,* 2006; *CMT: The Greatest—Sexiest Southern Man,* 2006; *CMT: The Greatest—20 Greatest Country Comedy Shows,* 2006; *Comedy Central Roast of William Shatner,* 2006; *The Real Match Game Story: Behind the Blanks,* 2006; *The Bold and the Beautiful,* 2006-07; *Back to the Grind,* 2007; *Ugly Betty,* 2007; *Pioneers of Television,* 2008; *Million Dollar Password,* 2008; *My Name is Earl,* 2009; *30 Rock,* 2009; *Glenn Martin DDS,* 2009-10; *Saturday Night Live,* 2010; *Storyline Online,* 2010; *The Middle,* 2010; *You Again,* 2010; *Community,* 2010; *Pound Puppies,* 2010; *Hot in Cleveland,* 2010—; *Barbara Walters Presents the 10 Most Fascinating People of 2010,* 2010; *Night of Too Many Stars: An Overbooked Concert for Autism Research,* 2010; *Inside the Actors' Studio,* 2010; *The Lost Valentine* (movie), 2011. Author of books, including: *Betty White's Pet-Love: How Pets Take Care of Us,* Morrow, 1981; *Betty White In Person,* Doubleday, 1987; *The Leading Lady: Dinah's Story,* Bantam, 1991; *Here We Go Again: My Life in Television,* Scribner, 1995.

Awards: Emmy Award for outstanding continuing performance by a supporting actress in a comedy series, Academy of Television Arts & Sciences, for the *Mary Tyler Moore Show,* 1975, 1976; Golden Mike Award for outstanding achievements in television, Pacific Pioneers in Broadcasting, 1976; Patsy Award for Special Service, American Humane Association, 1978; Daytime Emmy Award for outstanding daytime game show host, National Academy of Television Arts & Sciences, for *Just Men!,* 1982; Daytime Emmy Award for outstanding game show host, National Academy of Television Arts & Sciences, for *Just Men!,* 1983; Emmy Award for outstanding actress in a comedy series, Academy of Television Arts & Sciences, for *Golden Girls,* 1986; Golden Apple Award for star of the year, Hollywood Women's Press Club, 1986; funniest female performer in a leading role in a television series, American Comedy Awards, 1987; best actress in a quality comedy series, Viewers for Quality Television, for *Golden Girls*, 1987, 1988; Lifetime Achievement Award, American Comedy Awards, 1990; inducted into the Television Hall of Fame, 1995; received a star on the Hollywood Walk of Fame, 1995; Emmy Award for outstanding guest actress for a comedy series, Academy of Television Arts & Sciences, for the *John Larroquette Show*, 1996; funniest female guest appearance in a television series, American Comedy Awards, for "Seeing Green," *Ally McBeal*, 2000; (with others) quintessential non-traditional family, TV Land Awards, for *Golden Girls*, 2003; (with others) groundbreaking show award, TV Land Awards, for the *Mary Tyler Moore Show*, 2004; Pop Culture Award, TV Land Awards, 2008; Lifetime Achievement Award, Screen Actors Guild, 2010; Emmy Award for outstanding guest actress in a comedy series, Academy of Television Arts & Sciences, for *Saturday Night Live*, 2010; (with Sandra Bullock) choice movie: dance, Teen Choice Awards, for *The Proposal*, 2010; outstanding performance by a female actor in a comedy series, Screen Actors Guild, for *Hot in Cleveland*, 2011.

Sidelights

In 2010, television icon Betty White enjoyed a career renaissance that rekindled the public's affinity for the actress' decades-spanning television career. One of the medium's female pioneers, she was among the first women to form her own production company and to be inducted into the Television Hall of Fame, as well as being the first woman to win an Emmy Award for hosting a game show. The actress has won five additional Emmys for her work, along with numerous other trophies including a Lifetime Achievement Award from the Screen Actors Guild; she also has a star on the Hollywood Walk of Fame. White's involvement with television began in the late 1930s and, after a stint in radio, she became a fixture of the small screen when the medium exploded in popularity during the 1950s. Over the next 60 years, the comedienne graced a variety programs, sketch shows, game shows, sitcoms, and even a handful of dramas. Among her best-known roles were Sue Ann Nivens, the "Happy Homemaker" of the popular 1970s program *The Mary Tyler Moore Show*, and the sweetly innocent Rose Nylund of the following decade's hit sitcom *The Golden Girls*. After a continuing string of guest appearances and recurring roles, White returned as a series regular with the 2010 premiere of TV Land sitcom *Hot in Cleveland*. In addition to her acting work, White is well-known for her advocacy of animal welfare issues.

Born Elizabeth Marion White on January 17, 1922, in the Chicago suburb of Oak Park, Illinois, White was the only child of electrical engineer and travel-

ing salesman Horace White and his homemaker wife, Tess, both first-generation Americans. When White was two years old, she moved with her family to Los Angeles, California. There, the Whites seem to have enjoyed a relatively comfortable lifestyle despite the looming Great Depression; by 1930, the family had purchased a house and a radio. The young White was initially attracted to writing rather than acting, and discovered performance only when she appeared in the lead role of a production of a play that she had written while attending Horace Mann Grammar School. "It was then that I contracted showbiz fever," recalled White in her memoir, *Here We Go Again: My Life in Television*, "for which there is no known cure." At Beverly Hills High School, White continued to hone her budding craft by writing and acting in school productions.

Shortly after graduating from high school in January of 1939, White made her professional acting debut at Beverly Hills' Bliss Hayden Little Theater. She appeared in several major roles on the Bliss Hayden stage as she also began building a career in radio, with appearances on programs including *Blondie* and *The Great Gildersleeve*. By the end of the decade, White began dabbling in the new but growing medium of television. She became a regular performer on Los Angeles-area programs such as *Tom, Dick, and Harry* and *Hollywood on Television*. The latter program saw White appear with Los Angeles personality Al Jarvis as he played records, performed comedy sketches, and held interviews. In 1952, Jarvis left the show, leaving White to assume duties as the program's host.

Also in 1952, White co-founded a production company, Bandy Productions, in order to create a sitcom featuring her acting. Over the next several years, White's involvement with Bandy Productions made her one of only two women in early television to have creative input on a program from both sides of the camera. Soon she became the star of her first television series, *Life with Elizabeth*. A situational comedy focusing on the events in the lives of a young married couple played by White and actor Del Moore, *Life with Elizabeth* was typical of its era in that it focused on light-hearted humor rather than character depth. Sometimes compared to the contemporary *I Love Lucy*, *Life with Elizabeth* initially played on KLAC in Los Angeles but was soon syndicated to nationwide broadcast markets. White's performance as the slightly daffy young wife garnered her her first Emmy nomination and helped set her on the path to television stardom. During the last year of *Life with Elizabeth*'s run, White also served as the host of her own NBC daytime program, *The Betty White Show*. Both programs ended in 1955, although *Life with Elizabeth* continued to air in syndication for some time.

One year later, White returned with a new sitcom that she co-created, *A Date with the Angels*. In this series, the actress portrayed newlywed Vicki Angel opposite Bill Williams as screen husband Gus. A fairly typical sitcom exploring the trials of a couple in its first year of marriage, *A Date with the Angels* failed to attract a substantial audience and aired for only a brief time before being replaced with a second incarnation of the *Betty White Show*. However, that program did not gain momentum, and was cancelled in the spring of 1958. During the 1960s, White remained a popular television personality who appeared often on variety programs and game shows. She was a frequent guest on the *Jack Paar Show*, and a regular panelist on *To Tell the Truth, What's My Line, The Match Game,* and *Password*. Over time, *Password* became a part of White's personal as well as professional life; the actress met and married the game show's host, Allen Ludden. The couple remained together until Ludden's death in 1981.

After more than two decades in television, White finally emerged as a true popular sensation when she was cast as Sue Ann Nivens, the hostess of the "Happy Homemaker" on the *Mary Tyler Moore Show* in 1973. The script writers had called for an "icky sweet Betty White" when developing the character, and the show's producers decided to attempt to cast the actress in what proved to be a happy marriage of inspiration and reality. Over the next four years, White's character became a series favorite despite appearing in fewer than half of the show's episodes in any given season. The actress' portrayal of the catty, man-crazed Sue Ann—whose true personality was at extreme odds with that of the "Happy Homemaker" she played on the show-within-the-show—earned White two Emmy Awards for Best Supporting Actress and helped make her a household name.

The 1980s proved a fruitful decade for the actress. In 1983, she served as the host of the game show *Just Men!*, in which White and a rotating cast of male guests helped two female contestants win prizes. Although the game show lasted just six months, White's performance made such an impact that she garnered two Emmy Award nominations for Best Game Show Host, becoming the first woman to take home the trophy in that category. Two years later, the actress began a run as one of the four leading ladies in the popular sitcom *Golden Girls*. As the naïve but charming Rose Nylund, White consistently won over audiences during the show's seven-year NBC run and garnered seven Emmy nominations along with one win in the category of Outstanding Lead Actress in a Comedy Series. After NBC cancelled the show, White appeared along with two of her co-stars in the short-

lived sequel *Golden Palace*, which saw the characters acting as proprietors of a Florida hotel. When that program ended its brief run, White moved on to a recurring slot on the Bob Newhart sitcom *Bob*, for part of 1994. The following year, she published a memoir of her lengthy television career, *Here We Go Again: My Life in Television*.

Despite lacking a steady performance vehicle for the next several years, White remained a common sight on the big and small screens alike. She had recurring roles on television programs including *Maybe This Time, The Lionhearts, Ladies Man, The Practice,* and *Boston Legal*, as well as a run on daytime soap opera *The Bold and the Beautiful*. White also made notable one-off guest appearances, including Emmy-nominated performances in *The John Larroquette Show, Suddenly Susan, Yes, Dear,* and *My Name is Earl*. A handful of small but memorable film appearances also added to the veteran actress' résumé. In 2003, she appeared in the comedy *Bringing Down the House*, which starred Steve Martin and Queen Latifah. Six years later, White played the role of Grandma Annie in the Sandra Bullock-Ryan Reynolds romantic comedy *The Proposal*. This appearance garnered White award nominations from some perhaps unexpected sources; the MTV Movie Awards named the actress as a contender in its Best WTF Moment category, and the Teen Choice Awards gave White and Bullock a shared trophy in the Choice Movie: Dance category.

In 2010, White embarked on what Lauren Zima of *Variety* declared "will surely be known as the Year of the Betty, when … White became a household name to a whole new generation." In January of 2010, a grassroots Facebook campaign promoting the selection of White as guest host of the long-running comedy skit program *Saturday Night Live* began; after attracting hundreds of thousands of supporters, the campaign resulted in NBC's naming of White as the host of a May episode alongside musical guest Jay-Z. Her appearance also drew several of the show's former female cast members, including Tina Fey and Amy Poehler, to make rare cameo performances. "It took on a groundswell," show creator Lorne Michaels told Gary Levin of *USA Today*. "It isn't something we would have said no to…. It was the outpouring of affection from fans, and we feel the same way." In fact, the program had previously approached White to host, but to no avail. "I had turned down *SNL* three times before because I thought I might feel like a fish out of water," she told Marc Berman of *MEDIAWEEK*. "But when the whole Facebook brouhaha started, which just baffles me, my agent told me I just had to do it. So I did, but boy was I terrified." At 88 years old, White became the oldest person to host the program; however, her age did not impede her comedic chops, and the actress picked up her an Emmy Award for her performance.

Short weeks after her *Saturday Night Live* hosting gig, White returned to television full-time with a starring role in the TV Land network's first scripted program, *Hot in Cleveland.* A sitcom following the exploits of a group of aging Hollywood performers who adopt the Rust Belt city of Cleveland as their hometown, *Hot in Cleveland* cast White as a wise-cracking Polish house caretaker who looks after the house rented by the displaced Californians. The show's premiere won TV Land its highest-ever audience and the program was soon renewed for a second season. Critics also saw the program's appeal. Writing in the *Hollywood Reporter*, Barry Garron declared that *Hot in Cleveland* "has charm, wit, and actresses who could coax laughs reading the fine print of a credit card agreement." White's work in the series earned a SAG Award for Outstanding Performance by a Female Actor in a Comedy Series at the ceremony in January of 2011. In March of 2011, NBC announced that White was slated to be the new host of a hidden camera prank show featuring senior citizens pulling pranks on younger people.

White embraced her unexpected octogenarian career revival with a mixture of surprise and cheerfulness. Writing in the introduction to the 2010 edition of her memoir, she observed that, back in 1995, "I figured I would soon be forced to pack in my career—not by choice but because I had been around so long. Who could have dreamed at the time that, 15 years later, I would still be hanging in there, busier than ever before. How lucky can an old broad be?"

Sources

Books

Riggs, Thomas, ed. *Contemporary Theatre, Film, and Television,* vol. 86, Gale, 2008, pp. 327-33.
White, Betty. *Here We Go Again: My Life in Television,* Scribner, 1995.

Periodicals

Hollywood Reporter, June 15, 2010, p. 23; June 18, 2010, p. 2.
MEDIAWEEK, July 12, 2010, p. 34.
USA Today, March 12, 2010.
Variety, November 15, 2010.

Online

"Betty White (I)," Internet Movie Database, http://www.imdb.com/name/nm0924508/ (March 7, 2011).
"Betty White," Paley Center for Media, http://www.shemadeit.org/meet/biography.aspx?m=117 (March 7, 2011).
"Betty White to Host a Hidden-Camera Prank Show on NBC," http://artsbeat.blogs.nytimes.com/2011/03/31/betty-white-to-host-a-hidden-camera-prank-show-on-nbc/?hp *New York Times,* (April 2, 2011).
"Betty White: White—Hot in Cleveland or Not," *Huffington Post,* http://www.huffingtonpost.com/megan-smolenyak-smolenyak/betty-white-white-hot-in_b_614937.html (March 7, 2011).

—*Vanessa E. Vaughn*

Kristen Wiig

Actress and screenwriter

Born Kristen Carroll Wiig, August 22, 1973, in Canandaigua, NY; married Hayes Hargrove (an actor and comedian), 2005 (divorced, 2009). *Education:* Attended the University of Arizona.

Addresses: *Web site*—http://kristenwiig.com/.

Career

Held jobs such as sales, retail, floral design, waitress, and commercial actress, c. mid-1990s-2000; began working with the Groundlings, c. 2000; member of the Groundlings Sunday Company, then Groundlings Main Company, both Los Angeles, CA, c. 2000-05; cast on *Saturday Night Live*, 2005; starred, co-wrote, and co-produced *Bridesmaids*, 2011. Television appearances include: *The Joe Schmo Show*, 2003; *The Drew Carey Show*, ABC, 2004; *I'm With Her*, 2004; *June* (movie), 2004; *My Life, Inc.* (pilot), 2004; *Saturday Night Live*, NBC, 2005—; *Home Purchasing Club*, 2006; *30 Rock*, NBC, 2007; *Global Warming*, 2008; *Saturday Night Live: Weekend Update Thursday*, NBC, 2008-09; *The Flight of the Conchords*, HBO, 2009; *SNL Presents: A Very Gilly Christmas* (movie), 2009; *Bored to Death*, 2009-10; *The Cleveland Show* (voice), FOX, 2010; *Legend of the Boneknapper Dragon* (movie), 2010; *Ugly Americans* (voice), Comedy Central, 2010; *The Women of SNL* (special), 2010; *The Looney Tunes Show* (voice), 2010-11; *The Simpsons* (voice), 2011. Film appearances include: *Carnata*, 2000; *Melvin Goes to Dinner*, 2003; *Life, Death and Mini-Golf*, 2004; *The Enigma with a Stigma*, 2006; *The Brothers Solomon*, 2007; *Knocked Up*, 2007; *Meet Bill*, 2007; *Walk Hard: The Dewey Cox Story*, 2007; *Forgetting Sarah Marshall*, 2008; *Ghost Town*, 2008; *Pretty Bird*, 2008; *Semi-Pro*, 2008; *Adventureland*, 2009; *Extract*, 2009; *Ice Age:*

Dawn of the Dinosaurs (voice), 2009; *One Night Only*, 2009; *Whip It*, 2009; *All Good Things*, 2010; *Date Night*, 2010; *Despicable Me* (voice), 2010; *How to Train Your Dragon* (voice), 2010; *MacGruber*, 2010; *Sticky Minds*, 2010; *Bridesmaids*, 2011; *Friends with Kids*, 2011; *Paul*, 2011. Film work includes: associate producer, *Boobie*, 2011; co-producer and screenwriter, *Bridesmaids* 2011.

Sidelights

A star on *Saturday Night Live* (*SNL*), Kristen Wiig has been nominated for at least three Emmy Awards for her work on the show. While Wiig was the most prominent female performer on *SNL* by 2010, she also had developed a strong secondary career in film and other television projects. Her film roles were usually supporting ones, including memorable turns in *Knocked Up* and *Adventureland*. Wiig was also the creative force and star of the 2011 hit film *Bridesmaids*. On *SNL*, Wiig's characters were often neurotic, self-absorbed, talkative, and even deformed. Wiig told Olivia Barker of Gannett News Service, "Sometimes when you're writing, it's more fun to describe someone who looks a little off, who acts a little strange. To me, it's more fun to play the weird lady at the party."

Wiig was born on August 22, 1973, in Canandaigua, New York, and raised in Rochester, New York. Wiig liked to watch female comic actors from the time she was a child and wanted to be on *Saturday Night Live* as a teen, but did not try performing. Instead, she majored in art at the University of Arizona, then moved to Los Angeles where she worked in retail and other odd jobs while trying to decide on her future. She told David Germain of the Associated Press, "You get this idea that you've figured out your life, and you go for it, so I moved to L.A. and immediately got scared and partially changed my mind. Thought, what the hell am I doing?... I was like, 'I took Acting 101. Hi, L.A.! I'm ready to be discovered!' Which really didn't happen."

After several years of working a floral designer, acting in commercials, and waiting tables at the Universal Pictures commissary, Wiig discovered the Groundlings, a legendary Los Angeles-based improv company that produced many *Saturday Night Live* performers. She began working with the group by 2000, and was soon a member of the Groundlings Sunday Company. After a year, she joined the Groundlings Main Company in Los Angeles. She was a part of the company through 2005, and appeared in numerous stage shows, including the 2005 revue *Groundlings May Be Closer Than They Appear.* While appearing with the Groundlings, she began working in film and television. Her films included 2000's *Carnata*, 2003's *Melvin Goes to Dinner*, and 2004's *Life, Death and Mini-Golf.* Wiig had a regular role in *The Joe Schmo Show* in 2003, guest spots on shows like *I'm With Her* and *The Drew Carey Show*, and failed pilots like *My Life, Inc.* and *McGrubbers.*

Wiig joined *Saturday Night Live* in the middle of the 2005-06 season. She landed a role on the show with tapes of her performances with the Groundlings. She was hired on a Wednesday and debuted on an episode that aired on Saturday in November of 2005. Soon after joining the show, Wiig gained notice for her characters. She told Sara Stewart of the *New York Post*, "The first recurring character I had on the show was the Target Lady—that was huge for me because I did that character at the Groundlings.... So to have a character that came back, that they wanted me to write, was a great feeling." Other memorable recurring characters included Penelope, who one-upped everyone and exaggerated everything, Aunt Linda, a film reviewer who hates everything, and the female half of the A-holes, an obnoxious high maintenance couple. Wiig was not afraid to retire recurring characters and develop new ones.

Wiig's impressions include actress Megan Mullally, actress/singer Judy Garland, Speaker of the House Nancy Pelosi, actress/producer Drew Barrymore, talk show host Kathie Lee Gifford, actress Jamie Lee Curtis, and CNBC financial advisor Suze Orman. Orman believed the impression was spot on. She told Jacob Bernstein of *Women's Wear Daily* that it was "the greatest honor of my career. I love it. I was in the audience for it recently. The real problem is that now, I do my own show every Saturday night and I start doing all these things that make me go, 'Ugh. I'm playing Kristen Wiig.' I mean, it's just very good. She has got me down."

More television roles came Wiig's way during her *SNL* tenure. She had guest starring roles on comedies like *30 Rock, The Cleveland Show, Ugly Americans*, and *The Flight of the Conchords.* Like her *SNL* cast mates, Wiig appeared on *Saturday Night Live: Weekend Update Thursday* from 2008 to 2009. This show took the news segment from the main show and expanded it to a half-hour format. Wiig played Gilly, one of her recurring characters, as host on the Christmas special, *SNL Presents: A Very Gilly Christmas*, in 2009. Beginning in 2010, Wiig voiced the recurring character of Lola Bunny on *The Looney Tunes Show.*

Wiig's film career took off as well, though she mostly appeared in memorable small or supporting roles. She told Katherine Monk of the Canwest News Service, "(Movie acting) is just like *SNL*—except that there are no cue cards. But it's still the same exercise. You're looking for the funny pieces, and what's going to make something funny ... so even if the acting style is completely different, it's still about funny." Of her film career, she told Monk, "I don't have ambitions of being a big movie star. I'm a private person. I'd rather have a small part in a big movie than a big part in a small one. I'm not a classically trained actor. I go on instinct."

In addition to 2006's *The Enigma with a Stigma*, Wiig had roles in four films in 2007: *Knocked Up, The Brothers Solomon, Meet Bill*, and *Walk Hard: The Dewey Cox Story.* In the Judd Apatow-directed *Knocked Up*, Wiig played a passive-aggressive television executive. Apatow told Germain of the Associated Press, "when we screened the movie, the first sentence out of her mouth would tear down the house. They loved her instantly." While *The Brothers Solomon* was critically panned, Wiig's work as Janine, the character hired by the titular dimwitted brothers to undergo artificial insemination because they believe that giving their domineering father a grandchild will wake him from his coma, received some positive notices. Better received was *Walk Hard: The Dewey Cox Story*, a parody of the Johnny Cash biopic *Walk the Line* and other music-related biographical films. Wiig played Edith, the first wife of Cox, a woman who is constantly pregnant.

Wiig appeared in four films in 2008 as well: *Pretty Bird, Semi-Pro, Forgetting Sarah Marshall*, and *Ghost Town.* In *Ghost Town*, Wiig had a small role as a colorectal surgeon in the Ricky Gervais vehicle. In 2009, Wiig had roles in five films, including *Adventureland, Extract, Whip It, One Night Only,* and the animated *Ice Age: Dawn of the Dinosaurs.* In *Adventureland,* a coming-of-age independent comedy set in an amusement park, Wiig had a supporting role as one of the co-managers with Bill Hader, a cast mate at *SNL.* The characters played by Wiig and Hader were a couple, odd and co-dependent. *Extract* was directed by Beavis and Butt-head creator Mike Judge, and focused on the life of the owner of a bottling plant, played by Jason Bateman. Wiig played Suzie, the wife of Bateman's character, and the pair had an unhappy marriage. *Whip It* focused on roller derby and the freedom to be one's self that the main character, Bliss (played by Ellen Page) finds in the sport. As in many of her films, Wiig has a memorable supporting role as Maggie Mayhem, a veteran member of the roller derby team Bliss joins.

By 2010, Wiig was becoming a dominant force on *SNL,* arguably its leading lady after the departure of female mainstays like Tina Fey and Amy Poehler, and the lack of other major, memorable female performers on the show. She appeared in many sketches each week, and a backlash was developing against her because of what many perceived as overexposure. As Jaime J. Weinman wrote in *Maclean's,* "Have you seen the *SNL* sketch where Kristen Wiig plays a horrible person that gets on our nerves? Oh, wait, that's all of them…. [S]he hasn't created many characters who are likeably funny like Will Forte's MacGruber and Bill Hader's Italian talk-show host. Instead, Wiig specializes in playing people who are absurdly unpleasant to be around."

Despite such criticism, Wiig remained a key player on *SNL* and continued to nurture her film career. In 2010, she had roles in at least six films, including a featured role as Vicki St. Elmo in the poorly received *MacGruber,* based on the *SNL* sketch. Two of her films released in 2010 were animated features: *How to Train Your Dragon* and *Despicable Me.* In the latter film, she provided the voice for Miss Hattie, the warden of an orphanage from which the main character, a villain looking to be more evil (voiced by Steve Carrell), adopts three little girls as part of his plan. Also in 2010, Wiig had roles in *Sticky Minds, Date Night,* and *All Good Things.*

In 2011, Wiig's career reached new heights as she co-wrote, co-produced, and starred in a hit film, *Bridesmaids.* In her first lead in a feature, Wiig plays Annie, a sweet but depressed woman whose life has gone downhill after the failure of her bakery and unsatisfying relationship. Annie's best friend, Lillian, asks her to be maid of honor in her wedding, but Annie finds it hard to pull off the perfect wedding as her life becomes more difficult. The meddling of one of the other bridesmaids, the wife of the boss of the groom, does not help matters. Critics generally responded positively and *Bridesmaids* was a hit. For the Canwest News Service, Jay Stone wrote "The result is a very funny movie, part indie comedy and part frat-girl raunch … that manages to get at some of the sly truths of female friendship. There's love and support here, but also jealousy and poop jokes. There's even a wedding."

Wiig has said that she was not a typical comedian because she did not have a depressive personality, but instead was upbeat. She was also quite reserved, if not shy, personally. She expressed a desire to be known not only for comedy but also for acting abilities, and wanted to try dramatic roles in the future; however, comedy is what she is best known for and what she has spent most of her time perfecting. Wiig told Emma Rosenblum of *New York Magazine,* "I guess I have a weird sense of humor. Weird to me is a compliment…. Comedy is so subjective. You could have an Ace Ventura movie, where someone like Jim Carrey is really big. An then you can have an Annie Hall comedy that's more subtle. I think comedians are the same way." Wiig also noted to Germain of the Associated Press, "Comedy is tough, and sometimes the more you try, the more it doesn't work."

Sources

Periodicals

Associated Press, May 9, 2011.
Canwest News Service, September 19, 2008; May 12, 2011.
Chicago Sun Times, September 4, 2009 p. B1; October 2, 2009, p. B1.
Daily Variety, July 12, 2005, p. 26; December 17, 2007, p. 6; June 10, 2010, p. 8.
Gannett News Service, May 20, 2010.
Los Angeles Times, May 8, 2011, p. D1.
Maclean's, April 12, 2010, p. 61.
New York Magazine, April 6, 2009.
New York Post, December 16, 2007, p. 65.
Times Colonist (Victoria, British Columbia, Canada), January 10, 2009, p. C14.
USA Today, December 2, 2005, p. 2E.
Variety, September 10-16, 2007, p. 84; March 21, 2011, p. 22.
Women's Wear Daily, March 20, 2009, p. 12.

Online

"Kristen Wiig," Internet Movie Database, http:// www.imdb.com/name/nm1325419/ (August 20, 2011).

—*A. Petruso*

Isabel Wilkerson

Journalist

Born in 1961 in Washington, D.C.; married. *Education:* Howard University, B.A., 1983.

Addresses: *Office*—Boston University College of Communication, 640 Commonwealth Avenue, Boston, MA 02215.

Career

Feature writer, *Detroit Free Press*, 1983-84; metropolitan reporter, *New York Times*, 1984-86, then national correspondant, 1986-91, then Chicago bureau chief, 1991-95, then senior writer, 1995—; Ferris Professor of Journalism, Princeton University, 1996-97; James M. Cox Professor of Journalism, Emory University, 2006—; Kreeger-Wolf endowed lecturer, Northwestern University, professor of journalism, Boston University, 2009—.

Member: Board, National Arts in Journalism Program, Columbia University.

Awards: George S. Polk Award, 1993; Pulitzer Prize in journalism, 1994; Journalist of the Year, National Association of Black Journalists, 1994; National Book Critics Circle Award for Nonfiction, National Book Critics Circle, for *The Warmth of Other Suns*, 2010; NAACP Nonfiction Award for a Debut Writer, 2010.

© *Erik Lesser/The New York Times/Redux Pictures*

Sidelights

Isabel Wilkerson is a journalist who won the Pulitzer Prize in journalism for her work as the Chicago bureau chief of the *New York Times*. She has also received the George S. Polk Award, a Guggenheim fellowship, and the Journalist of the Year Award from the National Association of Black Journalists. Her 2010 book *The Warmth of Other Suns*, explores the huge wave of African-American migration out of the South during most of the twentieth century.

Wilkerson grew up in Washington, D.C., but her parents were originally from the South. Her mother was from Georgia, and her father was from southern Virginia. Both had left the South and moved north in search of a better life. Like her parents, most of her friends' parents were also originally Southerners from South Carolina, North Carolina, and Georgia. They were part of an underreported mass migration that took place during the twentieth century, during which six million African Americans left the South and moved to the North. This "Great Migration" resulted in vast changes for both the South and the North. The African-American population of cities such as New York, Chicago, and Detroit grew by 40 percent, and the number of African Americans working in northern industries almost doubled. The migrants influenced contemporary music and culture, and the patterns of settlement that they were forced into later shaped both suburbanization and the existence of racially segregated ghettos in northern cities.

Wilkerson was always interested in writing as a child, and excelled in her English classes. Perhaps she inherited her gift from her grandfather, Charles Richardson, who dreamed of becoming a writer, but as an African American, was not even allowed to walk through the door of his local newspaper office. Wilkerson told Erik S. Lesser in the *New York Times*, "He wrote reams and reams of what was probably a memoir that no one took seriously. I wish we had paid more attention." To this day, she still has his old typewriter.

Wilkerson's parents sent her to an integrated school on the other side of Washington, D.C. At this school, many of the students came from other countries or were descended from immigrants. Wilkerson felt left out because unlike them, she did not have any stories she could tell about her ancestors' immigration. It would be many years later when she realized that she, and many other African Americans, did have a story of people making a long journey in search of a new and better life.

Wilkerson wrote stories for her high school newspaper, and eventually became its editor. She chose to go to college at Howard University in Washington, D.C. because, of all the colleges she was considering, it had the best newspaper. From the very beginning of her college experience, she wanted to be the editor of the *Hilltop*, Howard's newspaper. She began working for the paper as a freshman, and eventually did become the paper's editor-in-chief. During the summer, she took internships at various newspapers, including the *St. Petersburg Times*, the *Atlanta Journal-Constitution*, the *Los Angeles Times*, and the *Washington Post*. One of the stories she wrote as an intern, about a Washington, D.C. office cleaner, earned her the Mark of Excellence award, one of the highest honors for a college writer.

New York Times editor Anna Quindlen read the story and was impressed by it. According to Kim Urquhart in the *Emory Report*, Quindlen told Wilkerson, "If you could do this as a college student, I know you can do even greater things." Quindlen gave Wilkerson a reporting job at the *New York Times*, beginning a long and successful career. She eventually became the Chicago bureau chief for the paper.

When Wilkerson was growing up, she was only dimly aware that her family and and others were part of a large migration of African Americans, but when she began working as a journalist for the *New York Times*, she met many African Americans and spent time in various cities, such as Chicago, Detroit, and Los Angeles. Wherever she reported from, whenever she wrote about African Americans, she found they had a connection to the South. In each city, different parts of the South were represented, showing patterns of this migration. As she told Charlie Rose on the *Charlie Rose Show*, "I began to put that all together and realize that there were multiple migration streams. This is much bigger than just my experience growing up around people from North or South Carolina and Georgia and Washington, D.C."

She became curious about how and why so many African-American people from the South had moved to the North, and she also wondered why this story had not been told before. Initially, she tried to determine what the patterns of migration had been. As she found out, African Americans had started to leave the South about the time of World War I. At that time, 90 percent of all African Americans in the United States were living in the South. Waves of migrants left the South and kept coming through 1970, so the migration included several generations of people. Many of them wanted to escape the repressive "Jim Crow" laws of the South, which entailed daily humiliations as well as the regular and horrific violence against African Americans. Beatings, lynchings, and hangings were common.

As Wilkerson told Rose, "I really believe that in some ways it was a seeking of political asylum.... There was a rigid caste system in the south ... that continued on until the Civil Rights Act of 1964 and 1968." She noted that when the Civil Rights Acts were passed, the migration ended. By that time, half of all African Americans were living outside the South.

Wilkerson received a Guggenheim grant to further her work, and she spent two years traveling throughout the United States, visiting senior centers, quilting groups, churches, and other places where African-American people gathered. She found that in many cases, people had retained their Southern roots, often forming clubs representing their original hometowns and socializing with other people who had also migrated from there. She talked to more than 1,200 people and found that, despite the existence of these hometown clubs, many migrants had never told their stories. Many had changed their names and tried to blend into their new home in the North, putting their Southern experience behind them and not talking about it with their children. Most of them had no idea that they were part of a much larger wave of migrants.

As part of her research, Wilkerson moved from Chicago to Atlanta in hopes of finding glimpses of what the migrants had left behind. Settling into a house in the Virginia Highland area of Atlanta, she planted a large garden and began collecting art from the 1940s, mainly portraits of unknown African Americans. She wanted to connect with the spirit of the people she was writing about, and find out what they had left behind when they moved north. She told Charles McGrath in the *New York Times*, "I needed to look through the exile's heart and feel that distant, rejecting, hurtful feeling. I needed to come here to see what they left."

Of the many people Wilkerson interviewed, she decided to choose three that she viewed as representative of the migration: three people who would allow the reader to see what their lives were like, why they left their homes in search of something better, and what that journey felt like for them. She looked for people who had made the decision to move and who had actually made the move themselves: not the children or grandchildren of migrants, but the migrants themselves. Mainly, she wanted first-hand accounts of the decision to leave: what was the last straw that forced people into a decision, what was the journey like, and how did they settle into their new life?

She chose George Starling, a citrus picker from central Florida who moved to Harlem after finding out that the owners of the citrus grove were going to lynch him for trying to organize the pickers; Ida Mae Gladney, a sharecropper's wife from Chickasaw County, Mississippi, who moved to Chicago after her husband's cousin was brutally beaten by white people for a crime he didn't commit; and Dr. Robert Foster, who worked as a surgeon in the Army during World War II, but moved to California because he was not allowed to practice medicine in his hometown of Monroe, Louisiana. He eventually became the personal physician of Ray Charles.

Wilkerson immersed herself in research, talking to her subjects in great detail for months and, as best she could, reliving their lives. For example, when Foster drove from Louisiana to California, he could not find a single place on the route where an African American could safely stop and rest. Wilkerson, while writing about his journey, rented a Buick, the same model as his car, and drove the same route, nonstop like he did, so that she too could feel his exhaustion and anxiety.

She told these stories in her book *The Warmth of Other Suns*, published in 2010. The book weaves their stories together with more general sections that discuss what was going on in the country at that time. Each person migrated at a different time and to a different place; each had his or her own reasons for making the journey.

Because of these intimate portraits, the book sometimes has the immediacy and interest of a novel. In the *Wall Street Journal*, John Stauffer compared it to John Steinbeck's novel *The Grapes of Wrath*, about migrants from Oklahoma to California during the Dust Bowl. Stauffer noted that Wilkerson "humanizes history, giving it emotional and psychological depth.... She gets inside the heads of the people she's writing about and gives readers a penetrating sense of what it felt like." In the *New York Times*, Janet Maslin called the book "mesmerizing" and noted that it "creates a wide swath of human drama."

Beginning in 2009, Wilkerson taught writing at Boston University. As a nonfiction writer, Wilkerson values storytelling, and she believes that if narrative, storytelling elements are incorporated into nonfiction, this method can "lift anything from the mundane to something special," according to Urquhart. Wilkerson also told Urquhart, "In the end, nothing really matters until I can see from the perspective of the human heart."

Selected writings

The Warmth of Other Suns: The Epic Story of America's Great Migration, Random House (New York City), 2010.

Sources

Periodicals

America, November 1, 2010, p. 19.

Online

"Great Migration: The African-American Exodus North," National Public Radio, http://www.npr.org/templates/story/story.php?storyId=12982744.tif4 (July 12, 2011).
"The Great Northern Migration," *Wall Street Journal*, http://online.wsj.com/article/SB10001424.tif05274870.tif34670045.tif75463852.tif82397849.tif6.html (July 15, 2011).

"Interview with Isabel Wilkerson," *Atlanta Magazine*, http://www.atlantamagazine.com/onlineextra/wilkersonQandA.aspx (July 12, 2011).

Isabel Wilkerson's Official Web Site, http://www.isabelwilkerson.com/ (July 12, 2011).

"The Lives Gained by Fleeing Jim Crow," *New York Times*, http://www.nytimes.com/2010/08/31/books/31book.html (July 12, 2011).

"Write from the Heart," *Emory Report*, http://www.journalism.emory.edu/program/wilkerson.cfm (July 12, 2011).

"A Writer's Long Journey to Trace the Great Migration," *New York Times*, http://www.nytimes.com/2010/09/09/books/09wilkerson.html (July 12, 2011).

Transcripts

Charlie Rose Show, PBS, October 14, 2010.

—Kelly Winters

Sam Worthington

Actor

Born Samuel Henry J. Worthington, August 2, 1976, in Godalming, Surrey, United Kingdom; son of Ronald (a power plant worker) and Jeanne (a homemaker) Worthington; emigrated to Australia, c. 1982. *Education:* National Institute of Dramatic Art, Sydney, Australia, degree, 1998.

Addresses: *Agent*—Creative Artists Agency, 2000 Avenue of the Stars, Los Angeles, CA 90067.

Career

Actor in films, including: *Bootmen*, 2000; *Dirty Deeds*, 2002; *Hart's War*, 2002; *Getting' Square*, 2003; *Somersault*, 2004; *Thunderstruck*, 2004; *The Great Raid*, 2005; *Pros and Ex-Cons*, 2005; *Fink!*, 2006; *Macbeth*, 2006; *Rogue*, 2008; *Terminator: Salvation*, 2009; *Avatar*, 2009; *Clash of the Titans*, 2010; *Last Night*, 2011; *The Fields*, 2011; *The Debt*, 2011. Television appearances include: *JAG*, 2000; *Water Rats*, 2000; *Blue Heelers*, 2000; *Love My Way*, 2004-05; *The Surgeon*, 2005; *Two Twisted*, 2006.

Awards: Best actor in a lead role for *Somersault*, Australian Film Institute, 2005; Saturn Award for best actor, Academy of Science Fiction, Fantasy, & Horror Films, for *Avatar*, 2010; male star of the year, ShoWest Convention, 2010.

Sidelights

Actor Sam Worthington spent several years building a career in Australian theater, film, and television before breaking out to mainstream Hollywood success with appearances in a series of high-profile films including *Terminator: Salvation, Avatar,* and *Clash of the Titans* in 2009 and 2010. During his years in Australia, the actor won a great deal of critical acclaim for his screen performances, garnering an AFI—the Australian equivalent of an Academy Award—for his role in the 2004 film *Somersault*. Often hailed as one of Hollywood's fastest-rising male action stars, Worthington has expanded his repertoire beyond the science-fiction genre to play characters in dramas and thrillers. Speaking to Bryan Alexander of *Time* in 2010, Worthington explained that he drew inspiration from actors who blended toughness with sensitivity. "I look at people like Harrison Ford and Mel Gibson," he explained. "They had humor and romance and vulnerability in their action movies. That's what I have striven to do."

Born Samuel Henry J. Worthington on August 2, 1976, in Godalming, Surrey, United Kingdom, Worthington is the son of a power plant worker and a homemaker. When the future actor was very young, the Worthington family left Britain to relocate to the western Australian city of Perth. Growing up in Australia, Worthington displayed an early charm and affinity for performance. "He was Mel Gibson from the time he was young and he was focused from day one," former schoolmate Shelley Kot Parsons recalled in a 2009 *Daily Telegraph* article. Despite this perceived talent, Worthington entered into a distinctly unglamorous profession after completing school: bricklaying. It was while working in this field that he accidentally embarked on a career in acting when he accompanied a girlfriend to an audition at an Australian drama school to provide moral support. He was persuaded to perform a reading, and although his girlfriend did not receive a slot, Worthington did.

Having earned a scholarship, Worthington enrolled at the National Institute of Dramatic Art near Sydney, Australia. There, he studied acting, and quickly found that his ignorance upon entering study was an advantage. "I didn't know what wings on the stage were. I thought Chekov was on the Starship Enterprise on *Star Trek*. I didn't realize he wrote plays. So I was a sponge that took everything in.... I'm still an infant in this, but it's been ten years," Worthington commented to Kevin Williamson in the *Toronto Sun* in 2009. Shortly after graduating from the drama program in 1998, Worthington got a break, winning a role in a stage production of *Judas Kiss*. Soon, he began landing roles on both the large and small screen. In 2000, he appeared in an episode of the American television program *JAG*, the Australian programs *Water Rats* and *Blue Heelers*, as well as in the Australian film *Bootmen*. After appearing in a couple of short films and in a small role in *Hart's War*, Worthington won a prominent role in the coming-of-age film *Somersault*. Released in 2004, *Somersault* garnered numerous critical accolades and carried away several trophies at the Australian Film Institute awards, including one for Worthington.

The actor continued to build his career in Australia, appearing in recurring roles on television programs *Love My Way* and *The Surgeon*, along with spots in films including *The Great Raid, Fink!*, and a modern reinterpretation of Shakespeare's *Macbeth*. His rising notoriety earned him an audition to assume the character of James Bond in 2006. "You come back, exhausted, laughing that you went and did Bond," he told Steve Dow of the *Sydney Morning Herald*. "It's like any big movie; you go and meet big directors. It's not a disappointment because it puts heat on you. You become well known for going in and doing your job," he explained of his reaction to losing the role to British actor Daniel Craig. However, Worthington may not have lost all chance of becoming Bond; in 2010, his name was a source of frequent speculation as a successor to Craig in future installments of the series.

By 2007, Worthington had sold all of his belongings and begun living in his car; however, his luck soon turned around. A successful audition for acclaimed director James Cameron landed the actor a role in the 2009 science-fiction film *Avatar*. Cameron, who originated the *Terminator* series, also recommended Worthington for a role in the 2009 action flick *Terminator: Salvation*. Released several months before *Avatar*, the film paired the Australian actor as Marcus Wright, a mysterious character who has been turned into a cyborg, with Christian Bale's John Connor. Writing in *Variety*, John Anderson observed that "Worthington ... heists *Terminator Salvation* from Bale, for the most ironical of reasons: In a movie that poses man against machine, Worthington's cyborg is the far more human character." Although the movie failed to excite critics, it helped establish Worthington as an up-and-coming Hollywood action star.

The Christmas 2009 release of *Avatar* served to confirm Worthington's rising star. Set in the future on the fictional world of Pandora, the film followed the story of Worthington's Jake Sully, a paraplegic ex-Marine who must choose between fighting on behalf of the planet's native people or to support the human race in its goal of exploiting Pandora's resources. Critics hailed the film's groundbreaking special effects and epic storytelling, but noted that those same special effects dampened the impact of the acting. Speaking of the characters' signature blue faces, Owen Gleiberman of *Entertainment Weekly* noted that "the faces lack idiosyncrasy, and after a while it's hard not to notice that that's what the characters are lacking too. Worthington, both as the 'real' Jake and his avatar, is eager, bright-eyed, and wholesomely defiant," he concluded. Bolstered by its groundbreaking techniques, *Avatar* became a film juggernaut, grossing some $750 million in the United States and more than $2 billion internationally during its theatrical run—and sparking a 3D revival that included films ranging from a reinterpretation of *Alice in Wonderland* to horror flick *The Final Destination*. Although Worthington did not receive an individual nomination among the film's many Academy Award nods, he did win a Saturn Award from the Academy of Science Fiction, Fantasy, and Horror Films, and picked up nominations at the MTV Movie Awards and the Teen Choice Awards.

Worthington's notoriety continued to grow in 2010 with his appearance as the mythological hero Perseus in the 3D action-fantasy film *Clash of the Titans*. Appearing alongside acting heavyweights such as Liam Neeson and Ralph Fiennes, Worthington performed the lead role inaugurated by Harry Hamlin in the original 1981 *Clash of the Titans*. Although not the record-breaking commercial success that *Avatar* had been, *Clash of the Titans* proved a more than respectable blockbuster, easily winning its opening weekend with ticket sales of more than $60 million and ultimately grossing nearly some $493 million worldwide; however, this commercial success was not matched by critical accolades. Notices were mixed, with reviewers generally dismissing the film as what Manohla Dargis of the *New York Times* characterized as a "self-consciously kitsch retread." Worthington's performance struck many as overly serious for the somewhat overdone tone of the film. "Worthington ... comes equipped with the same buzz cut and sexy scowl that served him well during the live-action sequences in *Avatar*. That glower suggests that Mr. Worthington either believes he's in a significant movie or worries he's made a huge career mistake," Dargis concluded, while Colin Covert of the Minneapolis *Star-Tribune* observed that "Worthington has a hearty masculinity, and he's remarkably resourceful at hacking and slashing. He's sort of a stiff, though, even when the movie gives him comedic opportunities."

That same year, the actor also made a high-profile appearance in another medium: video games. He lent his voice to the character of central protagonist Alex Mason in the multi-platform action game *Call of Duty: Black Ops*, released in November of 2010. Also featuring voice acting by Hollywood actors Ed Harris and Gary Oldman, the game proved a massive seller, moving a record-breaking 5.6 million units in the United States alone within 24 hours of its release.

As 2011 began, Worthington remained in demand for Hollywood film projects. He appeared in the lead role in the crime thriller *The Fields*, scheduled for release in the summer of 2011. Directed by Ami Canaan Mann, the film was based on the true story of murders in the oil fields of Gulf Coast Texas. Worthington's character, police detective Jake Souder, teams up with a New York homicide detective played by Jeffrey Dean Morgan of *Watchmen* and *Grey's Anatomy* to investigate three decades' worth of unsolved crimes. "It's a brilliant screenplay, filled with ... things you would have had to find the dead bodies in a heroin operation to understand. That's why it's such a haunting piece," commented co-producer Michael Mann to Mike Fleming of *Deadline Hollywood*. "This is such a spooky zone in Texas where cell phones don't work, where the homes sit on trailer stilts, and where there's a hand-painted sign on the bridge that reads, 'You Are Now Entering the Cruel World'."

Scheduled for release through Focus Features in the fall of 2011 was the Miramax film *The Debt*. Starring Worthington and respected British actress Helen Mirren, the movie tells the story of three Israeli secret agents who have pursued a Nazi war criminal for decades; the Australian actor portrayed the young version of the secret agent played by Irish actor Ciarán Hinds. "The picture is taut with nail-biting tension and spotlights powerful performances," declared Focus CEO James Schamus in a *Daily Variety* story by Rachel Abrams. The film *Last Night*, a relationship drama starring Worthington and British actress Keira Knightley, was also picked up for planned U.S. distribution in mid-2011.

Worthington was also slated to star opposite actress Elizabeth Banks in the thriller *Man On a Ledge*. As the titular character, Worthington portrayed Nick Cassidy, a former police officer who is on the run and has positioned himself on the ledge of a New York City high-rise; Banks played the police negotiator who attempts to talk him off the ledge. "The longer they are on the ledge, the more she realizes he might have an ulterior objective," explained Borys Kit in a *Hollywood Reporter* preview of the film. The film was scheduled for release in late 2011 or early 2012.

The actor's schedule also included recurring roles in the follow-ups to some of his earlier breakthrough performances. He signed on to reprise the role of Perseus in the sequel to *Clash of the Titans*, the 2012 release *Wrath of the Titans*. Worthington was also expected to again appear as Jake Sully in two sequels to *Avatar*, tentatively scheduled for release in late 2014 and late 2015. "In the second and third films, which will be self-contained stories that also fulfill a greater story arc, we will not back off the throttle of *Avatar*'s visual and emotional horsepower, and will continue to explore its themes and characters, which touched the hearts of audiences in all cultures around the world," returning director James Cameron told Pamela McClintock of *Daily Variety*.

Sources

Periodicals

Daily Variety, October 28, 2010, p. 1; February 10, 2011, p. 5.
Entertainment Weekly, December 25, 2009.
Hollywood Reporter, October 7, 2010, p. 3.
New York Times, April 2, 2010.
Star-Tribune (Minneapolis, MN), April 2, 2010.
Sydney Morning Herald, September 15, 2006.
Time, April 12, 2010, p. 75.
Variety, May 17, 2009.
Washington Post, November 13, 2010, p. C1.

Online

"Avatar first reviews, Sam Worthington next Hollywood star in the making," *Daily Telegraph,* http://www.dailytelegraph.com.au/entertainment/movies/avatar-first-reviews/story-e6frexli-12258094.tif45878 (March 6, 2011).

"From living in a car to *Avatar* star," *Toronto Sun,* http://www.torontosun.com/entertainment/columnists/kevin_williamson/2009/12/15/12167126.tif.html (March 6, 2011).

"Michael Mann on Daughter's Directing Gig; Dad Producing & Sam Worthington Starring; QED Selling Foreign In Berlin This Week," *Deadline Hollywood,* http://www.deadline.com/2010/02/michael-manns-daughter-to-direct-hot-title-dad-producing-foreign-rights-selling-at-berlin-film-festival/ (March 6, 2011).

"Sam Worthington," Internet Movie Database, http://www.imdb.com/name/nm0941777/ (March 6, 2011).

—Vanessa E. Vaughn

Caroline Wozniacki

Professional tennis player

B orn July 11, 1990, in Odense, Denmark; daughter of Piotr (a tennis coach) and Anna (a volleyball player) Wozniacki.

Addresses: *Management*—SFX Tennis, 846 Lincoln Rd., 5th Fl., Miami Beach, FL 33139. *Web site*—http://www.carolinewozniacki.dk.

Career

B ecame a professional tennis player, 2005; made her first top 100 finish by reaching the second round of Wimbledon, 2007; winner, doubles tournament at the China Open in Beijing, 2008; winner, singles tournament at the Nordic Light Open in Stockholm, Sweden, 2008; winner, singles tournament at Pilot Pen in New Haven, CT, USA, 2008; champion, Women's Tennis Association (WTA) Ponte Vedra Beach tournament, 2009, 2010; champion, WTA Eastbourne tournament, 2009; champion, WTA New Haven tournament, 2009, 2010; champion, WTA Copenhagen tournament, 2010; champion, WTA Montreal tournament, 2010; winner, U.S. Open Summer Series, 2010; champion, WTA Tokyo tournament, 2010; champion, WTA Beijing tournament, 2010; ranked number one, Sony Ericsson WTA Tour, 2010; champion, WTA Dubai tournament, 2011; champion, WTA Indian Wells tournament, 2011; champion, WTA Charleston tournament, 2011; winner, Brussels Open tournament, 2011; winner, Copenhagen Open, 2011.

Awards: Newcomer of the Year award, Women's Tennis Association, 2008; Player of the Year award, International Tennis Federation, 2010.

Toru Yamanaka/AFP/Getty Images

Sidelights

C aroline Wozniacki is the sizzling young tennis star who has been heating up the courts in more than one way. While much attention has been paid to the young Danish athlete's blonde tresses, curvy figure, and short dresses, her mastery of the game of tennis is the real eye catcher. Wozniacki became a professional tennis player at the tender age of 15 just eight days after her birthday. In 2010 she finished the year ranked the number-one player on the Sony Ericsson Women's Tennis Association (WTA) Tour.

Wozniacki was born in Denmark in 1990 to a family of athletes. Her parents had immigrated to Denmark from Poland when her father, Piotr, signed on to play for the Danish soccer team, Boldklubben. Her mother, Anna, played volleyball and represented her native country of Poland on the national volleyball team. Wozniacki's brother, Patrik, is a professional soccer player in Denmark who plays for Hvidovre IF. Wozniacki told Runa Bhattacharya of *Teen Vogue* that tennis was her first love and she "really loved playing tennis from the first time I held a racquet in my hand." Wozniacki also said that she likes handball, swimming, boxing, soccer, and other non-sports related activities such as playing the piano. She does not like to run but ran anyway because it was a good way to stay in shape. She recommended that all young girls move their bodies and stay healthy because it gives confidence and helps one to feel better about oneself. Wozniacki told Bhattacharya that her family has contributed to her success as an athlete, because "my parents knew what is was all about and they have been very supportive. They know it's hard work that pays off and it helps that they have been there before."

Wozniacki's preferred type of tennis racket was a Babolat and she used an Aeropro Drive until 2011. She switched to a Yonex racquet in 2011 to smash the ball across the net with her powerful right-handed serves that can reach speeds of up to 199 kilometers per hour. Bhattacharya reported that Wozniacki looked up to such tennis greats as Switzerland's Martina Hingis and Germany's Steffi Graf when she was younger. Since debuting on the WTA circuit in 2005, Wozniacki has consistently improved her year-end rankings. She won three WTA single titles in 2008, three in 2009, six in 2010, and four in 2011. In 2006 she won the Wimbledon Girls' Singles and she holds two WTA titles in doubles.

Wozniacki, who said that she felt no pressure to perform as a young athlete and can go out there and just play, began playing tennis at the age of seven. She has been nicknamed "Sunshine" by the press because of her height, blonde hair, and sunny disposition. When she comes out to play tennis, her smiles match the results of her matches. Wozniacki's game, as described by the Web site FootFault, has been "built around the defensive aspects of tennis." Her game has been typified by her natural athletic ability and seen as being centered around her ability to anticipate where the ball will land, move with agility to that spot, and lob it back onto her opponent's side of the net. She is known for covering the court and being in the correct place to return the ball. FootFault wrote that "her determination and resilience are a well-documented aspect of her game and a rare quality among the 20-year-old's generation."

From an analysis of her playing, her backhand has been identified as the shot most frequently used and is her favored shot. It allows her to turn her defensive playing style offensive because of the control and accuracy with which she wields it. She is good at retrieving and returning as many balls as possible and FootFault claimed "her consistency and unwillingness to miss is a prominent part of Wozniacki's game." Her trademark "moonballs" are returned far into her opponent's side of the net. To win her matches, she is seen as relying on errors on the part of her opponent and her game has been described as lacking and one dimensional.

Wozniacki has also suffered from injuries over the course of her career. In 2008 Wozniacki twisted her ankle in the Amelia Island Tennis Tournament and was unable to play for three weeks. In 2009 Wozniacki retired at the Luxembourg Open when she suffered a hamstring injury. At the time she was one win away from defeating Anne Kremer. Because her father—also her coach—was overheard telling Wozniaki to quit before winning there was a surge in online betting that Kremer would win, resulting in a minor scandal that the game had been rigged. Wozniacki and her father were later seen as totally oblivious to the situation and no punishment was even considered. In 2010, while playing against Vera Zvonareva in the Family Circle Cup in Charleston, South Carolina, Wozniacki was forced to retire after she rolled her ankle chasing a ball close to the net. She recovered quickly and was back playing tennis within a few weeks. She played after this injury in Stuttgart, Rome, Madrid, and at the French Open.

Wozniacki is predicted to continue to be a force to reckon within professional tennis for many years to come. In 2008 she was awarded the WTA Tour's Most Impressive Newcomer of the Year award. In 2010 she was awarded the International Tennis Federation's Player of the Year award. As of 2011, she was sponsored by a variety of companies including Oriflame, Compeed, Sony Ericsson, Danske, Adidas, and Yonex. She was also a spokesperson for Turkish Airlines.

Sources

Periodicals

Copenhagen Post, March 27, 2009.
Independent, October 26, 2009.

Online

"20 Questions with Tennis Phenom Caroline Wozniacki," *Teen Vogue*, http://www.teenvogue.com/beauty/blogs/beauty/2008/11/20-questions-with-tennis-pheno.html (June 3, 2011).
"Caroline Wozniacki: An Analysis," Foot Fault, http://www.footfault.net/2010/08/06/caroline-wozniacki-an-analysis/ (June 3, 2011).
"Caroline Wozniacki—Denmark," Tennis Now, http://www.tennisnow.com/2010_news/shoes_racquet/caroline_wozniacki_tennis.aspx (June 3, 2011).
"Caroline Wozniacki (Den)," Tennis.com, http://www.tennis.com/players/player_bio.aspx?player_name=Caroline+Wozniacki (June 3, 2011).

"Caroline Wozniacki," Fanmail, http://www.fanmail.biz/98993.html (June 3, 2011).

Caroline Wozniacki's Official Web Site, http://www.carolinewozniacki.dk/ (June 3, 2011).

"Caroline Wozniacki," WTA Tennis, http://www.wtatennis.com/player/caroline-wozniacki_2257889_12631 (June 3, 2011).

Other

Additional information was obtained from a post-match press conference and interview released on April 17, 2010, through the Family Circle Cup.

—Annette Bowman

Jacob Zuma

AP Images/Yves Logghe

President of South Africa

Born Jacob Gedleyihlekisa Zuma, April 12, 1942, in Nkandla, KwaZulu-Natal, South Africa; son of a police sergeant and a domestic; married Sizakele Khumalo, 1973; married Nkosazana Dlamini (a physician and politician) (divorced, 1998); married Kate Mantsho (died, 2000); married Nompumelelo Ntuli, 2008; married Thobeka Madiba, January 2010; children: 20.

Addresses: *Office*—Tuynhuys Bldg., Private Bag X1000, Parliament St., Cape Town 8000, South Africa. *Office*—Union Bldgs., Private Bag X1000, Government Ave., Pretoria 0001, South Africa. *Web site*—http://www.thepresidency.gov.za/.

Career

Joined African National Congress (ANC), 1958, and enlisted in its armed resistance militia Umkhonto we Sizwe, 1962; spent ten years as a political prisoner on Robben Island, 1963-73; underground ANC organizer in KwaZulu-Natal, 1974-75, and then from exile in Swaziland; member of ANC's National Executive Committee after 1977; ANC deputy chief representative, then chief representative in Mozambique, early 1980s; member of ANC Military Committee and Political Committee, mid-1980s; director of ANC underground operations and chief of intelligence from Zambia after 1987; elected ANC chair in Southern Natal, 1990; elected ANC deputy secretary-general, 1991; elected ANC chair, 1994; held government posts in KwaZulu-Natal after 1994; appointed deputy president of the Republic of South Africa, 1999 (resigned, 2005); elected ANC president, 2007; became president of South Africa, 2009.

Sidelights

Jacob Zuma advanced to the office of president of South Africa in 2009. The first person of Zulu descent to lead South Africa and the sole representative among the world's G20, or Group of 20, with no formal education whatsoever, Zuma is known for his formidable political skills. South African journalist Jeremy Gordin called him "our first African president" in an interview with the British newspaper the *Guardian*. "Nelson Mandela transcended everything and was a world figure. Thabo Mbeki spent a lot of time in England wearing pinstripe suits and smoking a pipe. Zuma is a real African."

Zuma comes from exceedingly humble circumstances. He was born in 1942 in Nkandla, a town in what was then Natal Province. This was the historic homeland of the Zulu, a well-organized group that rose to dominate a large swath of southern Africa in the early nineteenth century. The Zulu Kingdom battled with British colonial forces well into the 1870s, and the threat they posed was finally checked after the Bambatha Rebellion of 1906.

In the Union of South Africa, as it was known when Zuma was born, Natal was one of several provinces, but blacks who lived there were primarily confined to the rural, undeveloped northern regions like Nkandla. His father was a police sergeant who died when he was a toddler, and his mother worked as a domestic. As a youngster Zuma looked after goats and cattle, but was eager to learn. He would ask other children if he could look at their prized school textbooks, and a local woman who had some education taught him to read and write. He also learned traditional Zulu arts, like stick fighting. In his village were two aging survivors of the notorious Bambatha uprising, who told stories about this final armed conflict between Zulus and white settlers in the region. "I then understood that the white man had actually taken the rights, and the land, of the black man," he told Douglas Foster in the *Atlantic.*

Zuma was six years old when the new ruling party in South Africa began implementing a drastic policy of racial segregation known as apartheid. What little political rights black or mixed-race South Africans held vanished under the new laws, and blacks were subject to increasing restrictions on basic freedoms, like the right to assemble or even relocate to another part of the country. Zuma's mother was able to find a job in Durban, the coastal city of Natal, and brought her sons to live in the shantytown settlement where blacks were permitted to live. There, Zuma began attending meetings of the African National Congress (ANC), which was founded in 1912 as the South African Native National Congress. Zuma had an older half-brother who was involved in the ANC, and formally joined the organization in 1958.

Zuma was still in his teens when he joined the ANC, which was outlawed by the South African government in 1960. Across Africa, groups similar to the ANC had successfully agitated for self-rule, and colonial powers like Britain and France were divesting themselves of these overseas territories and granting sovereignty in the 1950s and early '60s. The ruling National Party of South Africa, however, maintained a tight control over the country's media, and it was at ANC meetings that Zuma and others learned of successful black-nationalist movements in places like Kenya and Senegal. In fact, the South African government kept such a tight hold on freedom of the press that the country did not even launch a national television network until 1976.

The ANC had long adhered to policy of nonviolence, but a younger cadre of members disagreed with this. A young lawyer named Nelson Mandela was among the leaders of this faction, which formed a guerrilla group, Umkhonto we Sizwe (Spear of the Nation), in 1961. Zuma was 20 years old when he joined the MK, as it became known, in 1962. The MK carried out scores of attacks and acts of sabotage, but the group was routed in a 1963 raid, and Zuma was among several figures arrested that year. Mandela and top MK leaders were tried for treason and sentenced to life imprisonment at the notorious Robben Island detention facility, a former leper colony off the coast of Cape Town.

Zuma, too, was sentenced to Robben Island, but the court mandated a ten-year prison term. It was a devastating period for the ANC, with its main leadership permanently jailed, but the prisoners were allowed contact with one another and Zuma was remembered as a jovial cellmate who told long Zulu stories, organized a choral society, and captained a soccer team to maintain morale among his fellow detainees. Govan Mbeki, a Marxist scholar, taught him to read and write in English.

Released in 1973, Zuma looked up his former girlfriend, Sizakele Khumalo, and pledged that his political career was over when they wed. It was not. He went underground, organizing ANC cells in Natal province, and in 1975 was forced to flee to neighboring Swaziland. He spent the next 14 years in exile, living in the black-ruled nation and then in Mozambique, where he recruited new MK soldiers for the cause. He received advanced military training in the Soviet Union in the mid-1970s.

Mozambique was embroiled in a deadly civil war, and after a plane carrying its first black president was shot down inside South Africa there was a regime change and Zuma was expelled. He went to Zambia, where he served as head of intelligence services for the ANC, and was by then also a member of the ANC's national executive committee. This was a period when the MK used a secret security unit with broad powers known as Mbokodo, or "the stone that crushes," to root out infiltrators and informants. Zuma was a part of the Mbokodo unit but has refused to discuss its operations or this period of his career with the ANC.

Finally, after years of international pressure on South Africa, Nelson Mandela was released from prison in early 1990. Zuma was able to return to South Africa that same year, along with other exiled ANC leaders, and was part of the negotiating team that hammered out a deal for a transitional period toward majority self-rule with the National Party and South African government. South Africa held its first free elections in April of 1994, with ANC candidates winning by a landslide. Mandela became the first black president of the Republic of South Africa.

Mandela and his deputy president, Thabo Mbeki—whose father had been jailed with Zuma—were of Xhosa ethnicity. In Zuma's Zulu-dominated homeland of KwaZulu-Natal, as it was now known, opposition to the ANC remained strong, and Zuma was dispatched there to quell tensions before the April election date. He worked with the Zulu chief Mangosuthu Buthelezi, who was head of the Inkatha Freedom Party, to stabilize the area. Later in 1994 Zuma was elected as chair of the ANC, succeeding Thabo Mbeki. For the next five years he held various posts in the provincial government of KwaZulu-Natal. When Mbeki, as the new ANC candidate for president, won the election in 1999, Zuma was named his deputy president.

Not long after this point, relations between Zuma and Mbeki deteriorated. In the five years since majority rule, South Africa had prospered and failed to dissolve into a bloody civil war with racial overtones, as many had predicted. Mandela was revered by South Africans and feted around the globe for his role in bringing the nation peace and justice. Mbeki did not possess the same level of charisma—or political resume—as Mandela. Mbeki had spent many years in England, where he earned advanced degrees, and later worked for the ANC in exile in Zambia. He won a second term as president in 2004, but the Mbeki government was forced to implement harsh economic policies that further alienated him from South African's poorest citizens, some of whom had never held a job in their lives.

Zuma was targeted in an anti-corruption investigation. One of his longtime friends, a Durban businessperson named Schabir Shaik, was arrested on a charge of attempting to solicit a bribe from a French armaments manufacturer. At Shaik's trial, prosecutors produced documents showing that Shaik had made numerous gifts to Zuma over the years. But non-whites like Shaik, who was of South Asian descent, had also participated in the struggle against apartheid and had funded the ANC/MK pipeline during its underground era; actual ANC leaders like Zuma had no assets nor work experience when they returned to South Africa in the early 1990s, and they received gifts from entrepreneurs and other business elite. Even Mandela accepted such largesse.

Mbeki used the trial as a pretense to force Zuma to resign as deputy president in June of 2005. Zuma countered that he was the victim of a political witch-hunt, and vowed to fight the corruption charges. Later in 2005, he was charged with criminal sexual conduct when an AIDS activist claimed Zuma had raped her at his Johannesburg house. Zuma asserted the encounter was consensual, but his trial was a media sensation for its revelations. The victim was HIV-positive, but Zuma said during testimony that he had showered afterward, which he believed was protection from contracting a sexually transmitted disease. He also made some incautious remarks about women and sexual behavior.

The controversy surrounding Zuma dragged on for the next few years. He was acquitted on the rape charge, and battled the corruption charge. The scandals split the ANC, too, and Zuma rallied support from a faction who were unhappy with Mbeki's policies. At the ANC party conference in December of 2007, Zuma challenged Mbeki for the party leadership post, and won a clear majority of the 4,000 votes cast. Mbeki was forced to resign as president of South Africa. An interim president, Kgalema Motlanthe, was appointed to fill the remainder of Mbeki's term.

Weeks before the April 2009 election day, the corruption charges against Zuma were dismissed; the court found evidence that there had indeed been political interference. Zuma was the ANC candidate and the party won heavily in balloting, taking 279 seats in the National Assembly. Zuma was sworn into office on May 9, 2009, becoming president of a nation of 49 million and overseer of Africa's largest economy.

The biggest event of Zuma's presidency was the month-long World Cup, the quadrennial soccer championship of FIFA (Fédération Internationale de Football Association), held from June 11 to July 11 of 2010. It was the first time the tournament was ever held on the African continent, and though the South African national team did not advance very far, it marked a milestone for the nation. "We knew from that moment that South Africa would never be the same," Zuma said in remarks to journalists a few days before the kickoff, according to ESPN. "It is clear that millions of our people have waited for years and look upon this tournament with hope, pride, and a sense of belonging."

In its modern, post-apartheid era, South Africa has a media that is indisputably free. In the daily tabloid newspapers, news of Zuma and his personal life are regularly front-page stories. Polygamy is a Zulu custom and is permitted by South African law. Zuma is still wed to Sizakele Khumalo, but later took second and even third wives. One was Nkosazana Dlamini-Zuma, a physician who served as a cabinet minister in Mbeki's government after their divorce in 1998. Another was a woman from

Mozambique, who committed suicide in 2000. His fourth marriage was to a much younger woman, Nompumelelo Ntuli, in 2008, and two years later he married a fifth time, to Thobeka Madiba, not long after allegations surfaced that he had fathered what is believed to be his 20th child with another woman. "The question is: How do you carry yourself? Many people have got one wife, but they've got many mistresses," Zuma said in his defense in an interview with Charlayne Hunter-Gault for the *New Yorker* in 2010. "The only thing is that the mistresses are not talked about."

Sources

Periodicals

Atlantic, June 2009, p. 72.
Guardian (London, England), April 20, 2009, p. 16.
New York Times, June 7, 2010.
New Yorker, July 5, 2010, p. 24.

Online

"The Contender," *Time,* http://www.time.com/time/printout/0,8816,1682289,00.html (February 6, 2011).
"Jacob Gedleyihlekisa Zuma, Mr.," South African Government Information, http://www.info.gov.za/leaders/president/index.htm (February 24, 2011).
"Profile: South Africa's President Jacob Zuma," BBC News, http://news.bbc.co.uk/go/pr/fr/-/2/hi/africa/4615019.stm (February 6, 2011).
"Zuma: South Africa Poised for Spotlight," ESPN, http://espn.go.com/espn/print?id=5257401&type=story (February 24, 2011).

—Carol Brennan

Obituaries

Dede Allen

Born Dorothea Carothers Allen, December 3, 1923, in Cleveland, OH; died of complications from a stroke, April 17, 2010, in Los Angeles, CA. Film editor. Dede Allen, a film editor, helped assemble some of the masterpieces of twentieth-century American cinema. Her best-known works include *The Hustler, Bonnie and Clyde,* and *Reds,* and she was one of the first among her profession to earn a screen mention in the opening credits of a film. Before that, such post-production professionals were "largely anonymous," noted her *Times* of London obituary, "rarely afforded a mention in reviews. But Dede Allen was a rare exception. She was widely credited with revolutionising editing in Hollywood movies in the 1960s, with dramatic jump-cuts, sound that overlapped more than one scene and other techniques from European cinema."

Allen was a native of Cleveland, Ohio, where she was born in 1923. Her interest in the entertainment business came partly from her mother, who had done some acting. Allen's father, an executive with the chemical giant Union Carbide, and the family's modest affluence afforded Allen the chance to major in architecture at Scripps College in Claremont, California. Her career plans changed when she landed a job at Columbia Pictures as a messenger, and she eventually found her way into the sound effects department at the studio. A more experienced colleague, Carl Lerner, taught her how to edit film. The first feature film she completed was 1948's *Because of Eve,* a rather salacious work that skirted local censorship laws by posing as an instructional movie about human sexuality.

It would be nearly a decade before Allen worked on another film. The end of World War II brought an influx of men back into the civilian workforce, and she had trouble finding work in Hollywood. In the late 1940s she had married television news producer Stephen Fleischman, and the couple lived New York City and Europe with their two small children for a few years. After working on industrial films and television commercials, she was finally hired by director Robert Wise on Lerner's recommendation. Prior to his career as a director Wise had been a top film editor, and had even been nominated for the Academy Award for Film Editing for Orson Welles' 1941 classic, *Citizen Kane.*

Allen worked on Wise's 1959 *noir* thriller *Odds Against Tomorrow.* Her next project was *The Hustler,* a 1961 film by Robert Rossen that helped vault Paul Newman into stardom. In collaboration with Rossen, she devised novel ways to frame and pace the billiards game sequences by which Newman's titular character earns his living. "The players circling, the cue sticks, the balls, the watching faces—that implies the trance-like rhythm of the players," wrote film critic Roger Ebert of Allen's work, according to the *Los Angeles Times.* "Her editing 'tells' the games so completely that if we don't understand pool, we forget that we don't."

Director Arthur Penn hired Allen for his seminal 1967 gangster flick, *Bonnie and Clyde.* Based on the tale of the real-life bank robbers who eluded authorities across several states in the 1930s, the film starred Faye Dunaway and Warren Beatty and was nominated for a slew of Academy Awards. Allen worked with Penn to assemble the final shootout scene, which is considered one of the most dramatically edited sequences in the history of American cinema: the lawless duo, ambushed on a country road, are riddled with bullets in a montage that lasted a little more than one minute but contained 50 edits. The scene was controversial for its graphic nature—showing just how violent death by gunshot actually is—and was the topic of much debate at the time. Pauline Kael, the longtime film critic for the *New Yorker,* asserted (according to the London

Times) that "the rag-doll dance of death as the gun blasts keep the bodies of Bonnie and Clyde in motion, is brilliant. It is a horror that seems to go on for eternity, and yet it doesn't last a second beyond what it should."

Allen worked with Penn on several other films, including *Alice's Restaurant.* Another leading name in contemporary filmmaking, Sidney Lumet, hired her to edit his 1973 New York City police corruption drama *Serpico.* Two years later, she joined Lumet again for the bank robbery standoff tale *Dog Day Afternoon,* which resulted in her first nomination for an Academy Award for Film Editing. By this point Allen had perfected one of the hallmarks of her editing style, staccato cutting, sometimes called shock cutting. She was also one of the first to overlap sound between scenes. Her talents were so prized she eventually began asking for a cut of a movie's profits, and was the first film editor to receive solo credit on screen at the beginning of a film. Her second nomination for an Academy Award came in 1981 with Warren Beatty's Russian Revolution saga *Reds.*

The twilight years of Allen's career turn up a few surprise credits: she edited John Hughes' angsty teen drama from 1985, *The Breakfast Club,* and the 1991 screen adaptation of the popular 1960s television sitcom featuring the proto-Goth *Addams Family.* She spent much of the 1990s as a post-production executive at Warner Brothers. Her third and final nomination for an Academy Award came for the 2000 film *Wonder Boys.* Her last screen credit for film editing was *Fireflies in the Garden,* a 2008 drama that starred Willem Dafoe, Julia Roberts, and Ryan Reynolds.

Allen was felled by a stroke at the age of 86. She died at her Los Angeles home on April 17, 2010. Survivors include her husband; her daughter, Ramey; and her son, Tom, a sound engineer who has worked on scores of major Hollywood films. **Sources:** *Los Angeles Times,* April 18, 2010; *New York Times,* April 19, 2010; *Times* (London), May 2, 2010.

—*Carol Brennan*

Avigdor Arikha

Born Avigdor Dlugacz, April 28, 1929, in Radautz, Bukovina, Romania; died from complications of cancer, April 29, 2010, in Paris, France. Painter. Avigdor Arikha was one of the few figurative and objective painters of his era. Also a draftsman and printmaker, Arikha became one of the most notable modern Israeli artists, and was best known for his images of daily life. "He had an exceptional gift for capturing something deep in people and expressing their mystery," Frederic Mitterrand, Culture Minister of France, was quoted as saying in the *Los Angeles Times.*

Arikha learned the importance of expression through art during his childhood, when he sketched scenes from the concentration camp in which he was a prisoner during the Holocaust. Though he began his career in art as an abstract artist, he grew disillusioned with the form during the 1960s, and he instead created realistic, objectivist paintings, including portraits of Queen Elizabeth, the Queen Mother, and playwright Samuel Beckett, who was a close friend. Though he was Israeli, he spent most of his life in France.

Born in 1929 in Romania, Arikha was the son of Haim-Karl and Perla Kom Dlugacz, a German-speaking Jewish couple. He spent his early childhood in Bucharest, where he attended Hebrew school and developed a fondness and talent for art. The family moved to the Romanian town of Czernowitz (now part of the Ukraine) in 1940; they were sent to Lucinetz, a concentration camp in the Western Ukraine, in July of 1941. Arikha's father was beaten to death; the rest of the family was transferred to Mogilev, where Arikha was used for forced labor, but his mother and sister were safer.

While at Mogilev, Arikha, only 12 years old, began drawing images of the life around him as a way to cope. Of the 17 sketches of Arikha's that survived the war, one was of a wagon loaded with corpses while a naked body was tossed into a grave. The sketches were discovered by the International Red Cross, who intervened for Arikha's and his sister's freedom. His mother also survived the war; she, like her children, moved to Palestine, but she did not see Arikha again until 1958 when they met in Vienna, Austria.

In Palestine, Arikha and his sister lived in a kibbutz near Jerusalem, where Arikha was given his new surname, as well as military training. He enlisted in the Jewish Defense Force, the precursor to what would become the Israeli army, and he fought in the battles that led to the creation of Israel as a sovereign nation. He was wounded in battle in 1948, but joined the Israeli army after his recovery.

Alongside his military involvement, Arikha attended Jerusalem's Bezalel School of Arts and Crafts. He first enrolled in 1946; his attendance was interrupted by the Arab-Israeli conflict and then the Arab-Israeli War. After the latter concluded in 1949, Arikha attended the school full time; he won a scholarship to study in Paris at the Ecole de Beaux Arts. He traveled there and spent most of the rest of his life in Paris.

During his 30s, Arikha had much success as an abstract artist, but in the 1960s he grew disillusioned with the form. According to the *New York Times,* Arikha once explained, "People who think there is anything new in the arts are idiots." In trying to create new work, he said, he ended up repeating his own forms. He decided to make a return to a more traditional style and created representational paintings. Despite turning away from abstractionism, his realistic work retains some of the geometric basis that formed his earlier abstract work; Arikha referred to his style, which combined elements of both forms, as post-abstract naturalism. This naturalistic style also required another element from Arikha: he did not want his work shown under artificial light. He worked during daylight hours and used only natural lighting while painting. He also worked quickly; he felt that the basis of the work should be done in a day, and this led Arikha to trust his artistic intuition rather than agonizing over details. His works are notable for their asymmetry, often through use of color and tone, which can lead viewers to experience sensations of freedom and oppression in the same glance. His portraits were known for their odd angles, which sometimes cut off part of the subject's body.

Arikha was as interested in art history as he was in art. This led him to write and lecture extensively throughout his career. Along with his writings, he curated exhibits of the works of other artists at museums, including the "J. A. D. Ingres: Fifty Life Drawings from the Musée Ingres at Montauban" exhibition, which was shown at both the Frick Collection in New York and Houston's Museum of Fine Arts. Arikha was awarded with an honorary doctorate degree from the Hebrew University of Jerusalem.

Critics did not always agree with Arikha's art criticism or his own chosen style. Many felt that his return to representational art was a backwards step from his earlier, abstract work; however, others found value in his contrasting imagery and inventive use of color.

In 2008, Arikha was made a Chevalier in France's Legion of Honor. He died on April 29, 2010, at his home in Paris, the day after his 81st birthday. His works are on display in such museums as the National Portrait Gallery and the Tate Gallery in Lon-

don, the Louvre in Paris, and the Metropolitan Museum of Art in New York. **Sources:** *Los Angeles Times,* May 3, 2010; *New York Times,* May 1, 2010; *Times* (London), May 4, 2010; *Washington Post,* May 5, 2010, p. B7.

—*Alana Joli Abbott*

James Black

Born June 14, 1924, in Uddington, Scotland; died March 22, 2010. Scientist. Dr. James Black, also titled Sir James Black, was a pharmacologist who pioneered drugs known as beta blockers. His discoveries not only shaped the pharmaceutical industry, with developments for treating heart disease and acid reflux, but they earned him a Nobel Prize and an appointment to the Order of Merit. The drugs that Black developed—propanolol, sold under the brand name Inderal, and cimetidine, sold under the brand name Tagamet—are among the world's most widely prescribed drugs. Through their development, Black helped bring relief to a vast number of patients. In addition, he was noted for his approach to drug development through rational process, using known facts about biochemical and physiological processes, rather than through chance, which had previously been the strategy for many pharmacologists.

Black's research was based on previous studies by American scientist Raymond Ahlquist. In 1948, Ahlquist recorded two receptors, which he named alpha and beta, that regulated the contraction and relaxation of muscles. Black wanted to improve heart medications, which at the time were designed to bring more oxygen to the heart. Black focused instead on reducing the heart's need for oxygen by slowing down stress hormones like adrenaline and nonadrenaline that made the heart work harder. Black used studies of chemicals that were known to block or bind the beta receptor, and his team developed propanolol in 1962. Cimetidine, which uses the same science to block the beta receptors involved in heartburn and acid reflux, was developed in 1975. Black shared the 1988 Nobel Prize in Physiology or Medicine with Gertrude Elion and George Hitchings, a pair of Americans working with a similar philosophy in their cancer research. The three scientists were rare in that all of them made their discoveries while working in industry, rather than in academia.

Black's work eventually changed the field of cardiology. At the time, drugs used to treat angia pectoris, an extremely painful condition, were nitrate drugs, such as nitroglycerine. Though this helped with the pain, it did not affect heart rhythm abnormalities or blood pressure the way that propanolol did. In addition, Black's theory of using beta blockers has been applied in a number of different conditions, including migraine headaches and anxiety.

Black was born and grew up in Uddingston, a suburb of Glasgow, Scotland. His father was an engineer and colliery manager at the local mine. The education available to Black in Uddingston was not spectacular; he was a bright child and breezed through his classes at a rundown school near a mine. He had not intended to continue his scholarship, but after a teacher convinced him to take the entrance exam for the prestigious St. Andrews University when Black was only 15, Black won a scholarship and attended the university. He went into medicine after becoming interested in the textbooks of an older brother, who had previously gone to St. Andrews.

While at St. Andrews, Black met his future wife, Hilary Vaughan; after Black graduated in 1946, they were married. After Hilary's graduation in 1947, Black's job search took him to Singapore, where he worked at the King Edward VII College of Medicine. The pair returned to the United Kingdom two years later with no prospects. Eventually, Black found a position at the University of Glasgow Veterinary School, where he founded the school's physiology department. He worked there for eight years, where he began researching Ahlquist's ideas and taught himself experimental science, in which he had never been formally trained.

Having begun to think about beta receptors, Black was confident that he could make progress doing his own research. He sought funding through the Imperial Chemical Industries; they countered by offering him a job in their own research facilities. He took the opportunity, despite the opinion of the academia that no good scientists moved into industry. Black and his team began work on a drug to block the beta receptors in the heart. In 1962, they developed pronethalol, which worked as a heart relaxant and confirmed Ahlquist's theories; however, the drug had severe side effects and the team continued working on an alternative. Two years later, they ran clinical trials on propanolol, which succeeded with Black's goals. The drug could be used in treatment for heart murmurs and arrhythmic heartbeats, as well as high blood pressure. Use of the drug reduced the chance of death from a heart attack.

Though propanolol, under the brand name Inderal, brought huge success to Imperial Chemical Industries, Black was wary of staying with the company.

He wanted to pursue his own research applying the same beta-blocking technique to histamines. Believing that if he stayed at Imperial Chemical Industries he would have to continue to focus on Inderal, Black took a job at Smith, Kline & French Laboratories. There he worked with a team, searching for drugs that would block histamine receptor H2. Current drugs only blocked histamine receptor H1. He particularly applied this idea to the histamine that stimulated acid production in the stomach, which is a contributing factor in ulcers. The group produced metiamide, but the side effects of the drug made it unusable. In 1975, they developed cimetidine, which they found could be used on peptic ulcers with only minor side effects. The drug, marketed as Tagamet, was extremely successful. It became the first drug to bring in sales of more than a billion dollars per year.

Black spent much of the rest of his life in academia, joining the University College London in 1973. He held a position at the Wellcome Foundation from 1978 through 1984, when he returned to University College London. He was appointed chancellor of the University of Dundee in 1992.

Black's first wife Hilary died in 1986; Black remarried in 1994. In 2010, Black died at the age of 85. He is survived by his second wife, Rona Mackie, and his daughter, Stephanie. **Sources:** *Los Angeles Times*, March 25, 2010; *New York Times*, March 22, 2010; *Times* (London), March 24, 2010.

—Alana Joli Abbott

Manute Bol

Born October 16, 1962, in Turalei, Warrap State, South Sudan; died of complications from Stevens-Johnson syndrome, June 19, 2010, in Charlottesville, VA. Professional basketball player. Manute Bol towered above teammates and opponents alike as one of the tallest athletes ever to play in the National Basketball Association (NBA). The star shot-blocker from Sudan stood a stunning seven feet, seven inches, and was a fearsome presence on the court during his ten seasons with the Washington Wizards, Philadelphia 76ers, and other NBA teams in the 1980s and '90s. But Bol was also respected and admired for his genial personality and generosity in aiding his troubled African homeland. "You know, a lot of people feel sorry for him, because he's so tall and awkward," his Philadelphia 76ers teammate Charles Barkley once said about him, according to the *Washington Post*. "But I'll tell you this—if everyone in the world was a Manute Bol, it's a world I'd want to live in."

Bol did not possess an actual certificate of birth, but cited October 16, 1962, as his birthdate. He came from a settlement of Turalei in Warrap State, a corner of southern Sudan that was one of several counties to successfully secede from greater Sudan in 2011 after years of ethnic and religious warfare. Bol's family was of Dinka ethnicity and he was descended from a line of local chieftains. The Dinka were primarily cattle herders and Bol spent his childhood years tending to his family's cows; in an oft-repeated tale, he once felled a predatory lion with a well-aimed throw of his spear. His height was not unusual in his family, which included several relatives well over six feet.

Bol was in his late teens when he started playing basketball, eventually making his way to the Sudanese capital, Khartoum. In 1982 Don Feeley, a basketball coach from Fairleigh Dickinson University in New Jersey, traveled to Sudan to participate in a coaching camp. Feeley was stunned by Bol's height and helped arrange a move to the United States, but Bol faced several setbacks on his journey to NBA stardom. There was an offer from the San Diego Clippers (later the Los Angeles Clippers) in 1983 that officials later decided was invalid because Bol had not filed the necessary forms to enter that year's NBA draft. He spent some time in Cleveland, Ohio, where officials at Cleveland State University arranged English-language tutoring and other assistance. That was followed by a year at the University of Bridgeport in Connecticut, then a season with the U.S. Basketball League and its Rhode Island Gulls team.

Bol made his NBA debut with the Washington Bullets on October 25, 1985, in a game against the Atlanta Hawks, which the Bullets won by a score of 100 to 91. The rookie center emerged as one of the most popular new NBA stars the season, in part for his exotic backstory and full height of seven feet, six-and-three-quarter inches—usually rounded up to seven inches—and phenomenal shot-blocking ability. He could touch a basketball rim without lifting his heels, and opponents trying to score or move past him faced Bol's impressive wingspan of eight feet, six inches. Bol's rookie season with the Bullets ended with a total of 397 shots blocked, which remained the second-highest number for an NBA rookie a quarter-century later.

Bol played three seasons with the Bullets—whose owner would eventually change the team name to the Washington Wizards—then played two seasons with California's Golden State Warriors. In the early 1990s he went to the Philadelphia 76ers, and between 1993 and 1995 moved several more times, from Miami to Washington and Philadelphia again before playing his final five games with the Golden State Warriors in Oakland. Bol was the tallest athlete ever to play in the league until 1993, when Romanian Gheorghe Mureşan joined the league, but Mureşan's height of seven feet, seven inches was due to a pituitary gland disorder.

When Bol retired from the NBA in November of 1994, he had played in 624 games and averaged 2.6 points-per-game and 3.3 shots blocked. Over the years he had maintained close ties with his homeland, which became enmeshed in a devastating civil war for much of the 1990s. Bol donated to humanitarian causes and invested in risky projects, eventually settling there and taking another wife, as Sudan's plural-marriage laws permitted him to do. But the increasing instability in Sudan drained his financial wealth, as did a growing family. In 2004, after moving back to the United States, Bol was a passenger in a taxicab in Hartford, Connecticut, that was involved in a serious accident; the driver died and Bol suffered a broken neck and other injuries, but recovered. In his final years he lived in Olathe, Kansas, and worked on behalf of a Kansas City foundation that built schools in Sudan.

In the spring of 2010 Bol returned to his homeland to campaign for a presidential candidate, and apparently contracted a rare skin disorder known as Stevens-Johnson syndrome that can be a side effect of various medications. He was treated in a hospital in Nairobi, Kenya, before flying back to the United States. His flight back to Kansas had a layover, and his health was failing so rapidly that he was taken to the University of Virginia Medical Center in Charlottesville, where he died of kidney failure and complications from the syndrome four weeks later, on June 19, 2010.

The 47-year-old Bol was survived by his current wife and several children, including a newborn daughter. His cordial, open-hearted personality made him one of the most respected NBA players of his era, and his post-career efforts to help Sudan cemented his reputation as a genuine role model. "I am never bothered by the fact that I am tall," he told *Sports Illustrated* writer Leigh Montville. "When I was younger, I was bothered, but not now. My height is a gift from God.... You have to live with what you are given. Who knows what God is dreaming for us? There is a reason. Look at what he has dreamed for me." **Sources:** *Los Angeles Times,* June 20, 2010; *New York Times,* June 19, 2010; *Sports Illustrated,* June 28, 2010; *Washington Post,* June 20, 2010.

—Carol Brennan

Robert C. Byrd

Born Cornelius Calvin Sale, Jr., November 20, 1917, in North Wilkesboro, NC; died June 28, 2010, in Fairfax, VA. U.S. Senator. For five decades—more than a third of the 144 years that West Virginia has been a state and nearly a quarter of the history of the United States—Robert C. Byrd served as West Virginia's representative to the U.S. Senate. A Democrat, he served as Democratic whip, and as the majority leader twice during his tenure as a senator. At the time of his death in 2010, Byrd held the records for the most congressional votes cast and for being the longest-serving member of Congress in the history of the United States.

Over the course of his nine terms in the Senate, Byrd served as the chair of the Appropriations Committee, which handles the nation's budget, and changed his mind on policies such as segregation, which he initially supported in 1964, but later in his life denounced. Byrd instead fought for equality, including the right for gays to serve in the military. A supporter of education, Byrd is the only senator to have successfully put himself through law school while serving as a member of Congress.

Byrd was born in 1917 as Cornelius Calvin Sale, Jr. After the death of his mother during the 1918-19 influenza pandemic, Byrd was sent to live with his aunt and uncle in West Virginia. His father was alive, but was never part of his son's life; Byrd grew up not knowing his birth name or an accurate birth day; in 1971, Byrd discovered he was actually two months older than he had thought.

The Byrd family was poor, and Byrd grew up expected to contribute; his first job was collecting garbage from the property of the local coal company to feed the family pigs. He excelled at school and was the valedictorian of his high school, but was unable to attend college due to the Depression, instead finding menial work to support himself and, in 1937, his wife, Erma Ora James. The pair had two daughters, and Byrd worked to find a better-paying job; he studied to become a meat cutter and became

the head butcher at a grocery store, a position he held into the 1940s. As a young man, Byrd was an active and enthusiastic member of the Ku Klux Klan.

During World War II, Byrd worked in Baltimore as a shipyard welder. After returning home to West Virginia, he opened a grocery store, started a Bible study, and began broadcasting a Christian fundamentalist radio program, becoming a local celebrity. In 1946, made his first run for office, seeking a position in the West Virginia House of Delegates. At the age of 28, Byrd had charmed his district and won a seat in the state House by overwhelming majority. Four years later, he ran for state Senate, a campaign that was equally successful. But during his 1952 run for U.S. House of Representatives, his opponent revealed Byrd's former association with the Ku Klux Klan. Byrd broadcast his apology for his earlier position via radio, and he spent many years apologizing for belonging to the organization. He won the election and was sworn in as a congressman in 1953, during the last days of President Harry S Truman's administration.

After spending three terms in the House, Byrd was elected to the Senate, where he worked for nine full terms. His early years were marked by his support of segregation; in 1964, he filibustered for 14 hours to try to defeat the Civil Rights Act, which ultimately passed. He was a supporter of the Vietnam War, but he was not afraid to criticize when he felt the war was being handled badly; he stated that the 1968 Tet offensive, which helped to turn the opinion of American citizens against the war, should not have been a surprise, and that U.S. intelligence had failed. Though he was initially pro-segregation and supported war, in his later terms these positions changed: he fought for equality, including supporting the Equal Rights Amendment and standing against changing wording in the Constitution to support heterosexual-only marriage, and he was a strong critic of America's Iraq War. He also changed his position on District home rule for Washington D.C., at first firmly against it, but later convinced that local government needed to take more responsibility for the city.

Byrd was consistent in his belief in the American system of check and balances, always supporting the power of the legislative branch and mourning the accumulation of power by the White House. He fought against the balanced-budget amendment of the mid-1990s, which he felt would strip Congress of its control over national spending; he lamented the passing of the presidential line-item veto in 1996, which was later deemed unconstitutional; and he spoke against the number of White House staff members assigned to policy areas during the Obama administration.

Despite being well known for upholding the rights of Congress to control the budget, Byrd was notorious for sending federal money to West Virginia. He helped to expand the highway system through West Virginia, and through his work, the state houses Treasury and IRS offices, a NASA research center, a Fish and Wildlife Service training center, an FBI fingerprint center, a Bureau of Alcohol, Tobacco, Firearms and Explosives office, and Navy and Coast Guard offices. His request to move 3,000 employees of the CIA into West Virginia was, however, denied.

In addition to his political career, Byrd penned a two-volume history of the Senate, a 2005 memoir titled *Robert C. Byrd: Child of the Appalachian Coalfields*, and 2004's *Losing America: Confronting a Reckless and Arrogant Presidency*, which was his criticism of the Iraq War. Byrd was committed to American history, and he carried a copy of the U.S. Constitution with him in his shirt pocket.

Still actively serving at the age of 92, in June of 2010 Byrd was hospitalized for heat exhaustion and dehydration. He became critically ill and died on June 28. He is survived by two daughters, five grandchildren, and seven great-grandchildren. **Sources:** *Los Angeles Times*, June 29, 2010; *New York Times*, June 28, 2010; *Time*, June 28, 2010; *Washington Post*, June 28, 2010.

—*Alana Joli Abbott*

Dixie Carter

Born Dixie Virginia Carter, May 25, 1939, in McLemoresville, TN; died of complications from endometrial cancer, April 10, 2010, in Houston, TX. Actress. Dixie Carter was a stage and small-screen veteran best known for her role on the CBS sitcom *Designing Women*. "[She was] an actress who gave strong, opinionated Southern women a good name," wrote *New York Times* journalist Anita Gates. Carter spent seven seasons as the feisty Julia Sugarbaker, a principal in an Atlanta interior design firm.

Julia Sugarbaker was a role not too removed from Carter's own roots: she was born in 1939 in McLemoresville, Tennessee, where she grew up the daughter of a local merchant. At the age of four she heard her first radio opera broadcast and decided that would become her career, but her vocal prowess was hampered by an improperly done tonsillectomy during her youth. In her teens she played both piano and trumpet before entering the University of Tennessee. She graduated from Memphis State University with an English degree and made her professional debut in a 1960 Memphis production of the musical *Carousel*.

Three years later, Carter moved to New York City, where theater director Joseph Papp cast her in a New York Shakespeare Festival staging of *A Winter's Tale*. Papp once told her, according to her *Los Angeles Times* obituary, "that some of the biggest successes in New York were country bumpkins because they were so unsophisticated they'd try anything." She soon joined the Music Theater of Lincoln Center, and also honed her improvisational skills at a popular revue called Upstairs at the Downstairs. In 1967 she married a man who shared her Carter surname, investment banker Arthur Carter, and left show business for a time to devote herself to raising their two daughters. "Eventually I lost the idea that I could have a career," Carter once said, according to Gates' *New York Times* tribute. "I thought I was too old."

Carter had been away from the public for eight years when she landed a role in a new Broadway musical, *Sextet*, that ran for just one week in March of 1974. That same year she won a replacement part on the daytime drama *One Life to Live*, which led to a two-year-long gig as a public prosecutor named Brandy Henderson on *The Edge of Night* on CBS. She and Arthur Carter were divorced in 1977, and her second marriage to Broadway musical veteran George Hearn ended in 1979. Her first ex-husband went on to found the successful *New York Observer* newspaper in the late 1980s.

Carter relocated to Los Angeles in order to land more television roles. Her break came in 1981, when an Emmy-nominated freelance writer for *M*A*S*H** named Linda Bloodworth-Thomason cast her in a new sitcom about a dysfunctional Southern clan. *Filthy Rich* lasted just two seasons on CBS before the network cancelled it, and Carter went on to appear in the sixth and seventh seasons of the popular NBC series *Diff'rent Strokes* following that. But Bloodworth-Thomason had been pleased with Carter's performance on *Filthy Rich* as well as the work of Delta Burke, who had played a young widow that schemed with Carter's character on the series. "From the day I met Dixie, I wanted to cast her in everything I had," Bloodworth-Thomason was quoted as saying by *Entertainment Weekly* online. "She wasn't like anybody else. She had such charisma."

Bloodworth-Thomason pitched a show built around Carter and Burke to CBS, and *Designing Women* debuted in September of 1986. Carter played Julia Sugarbaker; her sassier, more indolent younger sister, Suzanne, was played by Burke. The cast included Jean Smart, Annie Potts, and Meshach Taylor, and vaulted into the top ten in ratings in its sixth season, though it always had a strong following among female viewers. "In an age of shifting values and changing identities, she evinced an independence and assurance that seemed appealing," wrote Martin Weil in the *Washington Post* about Carter's liberal-minded Julia Sugarbaker. "The show caught on, and made her well known and well off."

Carter later said that she was still a stiff Southern conservative on many political issues, and sometimes battled with the show's producers when she was given lines she felt were far too liberal for her own personal views; she cut a deal with Bloodworth-Thomason that any time that happened, they would write in a bit where she could sing, which she still dreamed of doing on stage. In 1990, Carter landed a highly coveted spot at Manhattan's vaunted Café Carlyle as a cabaret act, for which she earned terrific reviews.

Designing Women ended its seven-season run in May of 1993. Carter returned to Broadway in *Master Class* playing opera icon Maria Callas, and worked on her 1996 memoir, *Trying to Get to Heaven: Opinions of a Tennessee Talker*. From 1999 to 2002 she appeared on the CBS legal drama *Family Law* as divorce attorney Randi King. In 2007 she was nominated for the first primetime Emmy Award of her career for her turn as Gloria Hodge on *Desperate Housewives*.

Carter married actor Hal Holbrook in 1984, who shared screen credit with her in her final movie, 2009's *That Evening Sun*. She died from complications of endometrial cancer on April 10, 2010, in Houston, Texas, at the age of 70. Holbrook survives her, as do her two daughters by Arthur Carter, Ginna and Mary Dixie. **Sources:** CNN.com, http://www.cnn.com/2010/SHOWBIZ/TV/04/10/dixie.carter.obit/index.html (July 11, 2011); *Entertainment Weekly*, http://www.ew.com/ew/article/0,,20361292.tif,00.html (July 11, 2011); *Los Angeles Times*, April 12, 2010; *New York Times*, April 12, 2010; *Washington Post*, April 11, 2010.

—*Carol Brennan*

Alex Chilton

Born William Alexander Chilton, December 28, 1950, in Memphis, TN; died of a heart attack, March 17, 2010, in New Orleans, LA. Singer and songwriter.

Though Alex Chilton never became a huge commercial success, his work with the band Big Star had a significant impact on the pop music industry. A reporter for *Rolling Stone* once wrote, as quoted in the *Los Angeles Times*, "It's safe to say there would have been no modern pop movement without Big Star."

Using influences that included the Beach Boys and the Beatles, Big Star did not follow the trends of popular music in the 1970s. Instead of producing songs full of idealism and calls to activism that were successful at the time, Big Star echoed earlier decades, singing about dreams, but confessed that those dreams had not been fulfilled. Their work was occasionally somber, but it experienced a resurgence long after the band had split up, with a cover of one of their tunes, "In the Street," being used as the theme song for FOX television's *That '70s Show*. Chilton, who made several solo albums, was referenced in a song by Minnesota band the Replacements, who titled a song "Alex Chilton" after his influence on popular music. Among the bands Chilton and Big Star influenced are R.E.M., the Bangles, Teenage Fanclub, and Counting Crows.

Chilton was born in 1950, the son of two musicians. His father, Sidney, was a jazz trumpeter; his mother, Mary, was classically trained, and she made sure that her children were exposed to music by hosting jam sessions at the family home in Memphis.

During high school, Chilton formed a band with Gary Talley, a guitarist, called the Devilles. After gaining notice at a talent-show competition, producer Dan Penn took Chilton and the group under his wing. They were rechristened the Box Tops, and with Penn's help, they were a huge success. As a white group that sang soul music, they were considered a rarity, with Chilton particularly being noted for his gravely, soulful voice.

But Chilton and other members of the Box Tops were frustrated at how often they were removed from the recording studio to make room for more notable groups. They were also discouraged from recording their own works, and Chilton, who was a songwriter, grew increasingly frustrated with the lack of freedom he had with the Box Tops. The group split up in 1970, and Chilton approached his friend, singer-guitarist Chris Bell, to see if Bell would be willing to work with him. Instead, Bell invited Chilton to join his band, Icewater, which already included Jody Stephens on drums and Andy Hummel on bass. With Chilton added to the group, they renamed themselves Big Star and were signed to Ardent Records.

Although *Rolling Stone* later declared Big Star's first album, *No. 1 Record,* to be a near-perfect project, it was not a great commercial success. Ten of the 12 songs were written as Bell-Chilton collaborations, and all of the tunes had the potential to be released as singles, according to *Rolling Stone.* Full of pop music in an era when concept albums were what was selling, *No. 1 Record* suffered from poor marketing and promotion. The album's commercial failure drove a wedge between Chilton and Bell, who were already experiencing tension in their relationship. Big Star broke up, only to reform shortly afterward without Bell. Unfortunately, they experienced the same problems with their second album, *Radio City,* which featured a harder edge as Chilton's work lost the light-hearted influence of Bell. Despite being well received by critics, the album was another flop. Chilton and Big Star made one final effort, but because Chilton's work was so different from what was selling at the time, the album, *Third/Sister Lovers,* was released in 1978, four years after Big Star had split up.

Chilton went on to have a solo career that did little better than Big Star's efforts. Lost and depressed, Chilton turned to drugs and alcohol, and for a time stopped making music all together. But during this struggle, Big Star's reputation began to grow and take on a cult status. Bands like R.E.M. and the Replacements promoted Big Star to their fans, and the band took on the appeal of a rediscovery. Their songs were covered by the Posies and the Bangles; Cheap Trick covered "In the Street" as the theme song for the sitcom *That '70s Show.* Given the new, belated acclaim, and Chilton's dedication to getting and staying clean, he launched a reformed Big Star with fellow original member Stephens and former Posies members Jon Auer and Ken Stringfellow. The group went on tour and completed a live album. In 1998, Chilton reformed the Box Tops as well.

Big Star's studio album, and Chilton's last album, *In Space,* was released in 2005. The date came shortly after Chilton had been evacuated from his New Orleans home during the destruction of Hurricane Katrina. He died on March 17, 2010, in New Orleans.

Chilton's death took place just before he was to have had a reunion performance with Big Star at the South By Southwest Music Conference. The other members of Big Star held their reunion as a tribute in Chilton's honor. John Fry, the studio owner who produced many of Chilton's records, said in the *Los Angeles Times,* "You can't throw a rock at South By Southwest without hitting someone who was influenced by Big Star." Chilton was 59 years old.

Sources: *Entertainment Weekly,* April 2, 2010; *Los Angeles Times,* March 18, 2010; *New York Times,* March 19, 2010; *Times* (London), March 18, 2010; *Washington Post,* March 19, 2010, p. B7.

—*Alana Joli Abbott*

Lucille Clifton

Born June 27, 1936, in Depew, NY; died of a bacterial infection, February 13, 2010, in Baltimore, MD. Poet. Award-winning poet Lucille Clifton shared the truths of her experiences as an African-American woman of the twentieth century. She revealed the hardships she faced without ever showing herself as a victim. Her short poems contained intensity within a simplistic style, often ignoring punctuation and capitalization in favor of clarity of meaning. With rhythms that echoed the oral tradition of African Americans, an earthy humor, and a strong emotional core, Clifton's poems reached a wide audience and earned her high critical praise.

The author of eleven poetry collections and 20 books for young readers, Clifton served as the poet laureate of Maryland from 1979 to 1985, the second woman and first African American to hold the position. A 1988 collection was a finalist for the Pulitzer Prize, and a collection of her poetry published in 2000 won her the National Book Award. In 2007, Clifton received the Ruth Lilly Poetry Prize, a $100,000 award that gave her a mark of distinction, not only as a poet, but as the first African-American woman to receive the award.

The daughter of a worker and a laundry woman, Clifton was born in Depew, New York, in 1936, and grew up in nearby Buffalo. Her mother was an accomplished poet despite not having attended school beyond the elementary grades; however, when offered the chance to publish her work, Clifton's mother was denied by her husband, who proclaimed that he would not have a wife who was a poet. One of Clifton's poems, "fury," recalls her mother burning her poems in the furnace after being denied her dream. In the same piece, Clifton reveals that her dedication to the art of poetry is in part dedication to her mother.

In 1953 Clifton left New York to study at Howard University in Washington, D.C., but left after two years to pursue her career in poetry. She moved back to Buffalo to join a group of African-American intellectuals and artists, among whom was poet and philosopher Fred Clifton. The two were married in 1958, and they later settled in Baltimore, Maryland, where they raised their six children.

Clifton's first book of poetry was published in 1969, and due to its success, she was appointed as the writer-in-residence at Baltimore's Coppin State University during the 1970s. Some of Clifton's work written during this period was featured in an anthology, edited by Langston Hughes and Arna Bontemps, *The Poetry of the Negro, 1746-1970*. She continued to publish and her poetry was frequently anthologized. In 1979, she became the poet laureate of Maryland, and her collection *Two-Headed Woman* was released the next year.

After the death of her husband in 1984, Clifton was offered a teaching position at the University of California, Santa Cruz, where she taught until 1989. She returned to Maryland, where she taught at St. Mary's College and continued to write. *Good Woman: Poems and a Memoir, 1969-1980*, published in 1987, was a finalist for the Pulitzer Prize in Poetry. Two other collections were published before her *Blessing the Boats: New and Selected Poems, 1988-2000* received the National Book Award. Also in 2000, Clifton was featured on a program with Bill Moyers on PBS. In addition to her poetry, Clifton wrote picture books and novels for children, including a popular series about Everett Anderson, a young boy living in the inner city. Despite her critical acclaim, Clifton lived a fairly simple and grounded life, alternating such hobbies as listening to Bach with watching *The Price Is Right* or traveling to Atlantic City to gamble. In a 1988 interview with the *Christian Science Monitor*, quoted in the *Washington Post*, she explained, "Poetry is not my life. My life is my life."

Despite that distinction, Clifton's poetry clearly reflects her life, from her experiences with motherhood to her feelings about her body to the exploration of childhood abuse at the hands of her father. "Her poems are at once outraged and tender, small and explosive, sassy and devout," Christian Wiman, editor of *Poetry* magazine, said when presenting Clifton with the Ruth Lilly Poetry Prize in 2007 (as quoted by the *Washington Post*). "She sounds like no one else, and her achievement looks larger with each passing year." Wiman also described Clifton's style in an interview in the *Baltimore Sun*, quoted in Clifton's *Los Angeles Times* obituary, "I like the short, distinctive music that the poems make.... It's admirable how simple and clear the surfaces are. But when you study her best poems, they keep opening into depths of complexity."

Clifton suffered from breast and stomach cancer; in 1998 she received a kidney transplant from one of her daughters. She entered the hospital after being ill with an infection, and she died on February 13, 2010. Clifton was predeceased by a son and a daughter, but is survived by her four remaining children, her sister, and three grandchildren. She also leaves behind more than 30 published books, and the legacy of her life experience through the words of her poems and memoir. She was 73 years old. **Sources:** *Los Angeles Times*, February 17, 2010; *New York Times*, February 17, 2010; *Washington Post*, February 21, 2010, p. C6.

—*Alana Joli Abbott*

Art Clokey

Born Arthur Charles Farrington, October 21, 1921, in Detroit, MI; died January 8, 2010, in Los Osos, CA. Animator. Few people knew Art Clokey's name, but he is easily recognized through his creation, the character Gumby. A ubiquitous part of pop culture, the green clay figure with impossibly bendable limbs was originally introduced in the 1950s. He experienced a resurgence of popularity in the 1960s with a cartoon show, in the 1980s through Eddie Murphy's *Saturday Night Live* parody, and in the 1990s with a full-length animated feature, directed by Clokey.

Millions of Gumby dolls have been sold since the character's creation. The clay figure appears in video games and is referenced in movies. Versions of Gumby have been made to dangle from rearview mirrors. Another mark of Gumby's ubiquitous status is that the character has thousands of fans on Facebook.

Born Arthur Charles Farrington, Clokey grew up on his grandparents' farm in Michigan. At an early age, he started forming figures out of mud, paving the way for his clay sculptures later in life. When Clokey was eight, his parents divorced. He lived with his father until a tragic car accident ended Farrington's life. Sent to California to live with his mother, Clokey was rejected by his step-father and sent to live in a children's home.

At the age of eleven, Clokey was adopted by Joseph Waddell Clokey, a music teacher and a composer of secular and sacred music at Pomona College. Clokey considered his adoptive father to be a loving parent, and the composer taught Clokey to draw, shoot film, and paint, as well as exposing him to books and culture. The pair traveled to Mexico and Canada together. Clokey was enrolled at the Webb School, which sponsored annual fossil hunting expeditions that gave Clokey a taste for adventure and inspired Gumby's adventures later on.

During World War II, Clokey served in the military by doing photo reconnaissance over France and North Africa. He graduated from Miami University in Ohio and went to Hartford Seminary in Connecticut, with the intention of becoming an Episcopal minister. In Hartford, he met Ruth Parkander, who was the daughter of a minister, and the pair discovered a shared passion for filmmaking. They married and moved to California, where they intended to create films with a spiritual focus. Both Clokey and his wife got positions teaching at the Harvard School for Boys (now Harvard-Westlake) in Los Angeles. At night, Clokey studied filmmaking at the University of Southern California under the modernist filmmaker Slavko Vorkapich.

Clokey's career began to take shape with his student film, *Gumbasia*, a stop-motion animated film that featured characters dancing to jazz music. The film was a reference to the Disney animated feature *Fantasia*, which also featured music accompanied by animation. The president of 20th Century Fox, Sam Engel, who was also the father of one of Clokey's students, saw *Gumbasia* and was impressed; he invited Clokey to develop a children's program based on that film's concept. Gumby was brought to life soon after: a green character—because Clokey was an environmentalist—with an angular head. The shape was a reference to Clokey's biological father, who had a cowlick that made his hair appear to tilt off to one side of his head. The character debuted on the *Howdy Doody Show* in 1956 and was popular enough to earn his own television program.

The Gumby Show launched in 1957 and featured Gumby and his horse, Pokey. The pair went on many adventures, and the program was one of the first lengthy stop-motion animation programs on television. The cartoon offered a simple spiritual message: "If you've got a heart, then Gumby's a part of you." The program initially had a short run, but it was brought back in the 1960s with a new series, and the bendable toy featuring the character was released. During that time period, Clokey and his wife also created a more overtly spiritual series, Davey and Goliath, about a boy and his dog. This cartoon also featured stop-motion animation, but rather than clay figures, the characters were made from foam and other puppet materials.

In the 1970s, cartoons became more violent, and Gumby fell out of popularity. Clokey was hit with financial struggles, and his marriage to Ruth ended in divorce. He pursued spiritual studies, traveling to India and learning about Zen Buddhism. He once tried LSD under medical supervision, but the experience was long after Gumby's creation. In the 1980s, Eddie Murphy revitalized Gumby's popularity through a parody on *Saturday Night Live*. The comedian depicted Gumby smoking a cigar and using crass language, much to the delight of his adult audience. Clokey also enjoyed Murphy's performances, according to his son, Joe Clokey, though he was glad that the show was late at night, when children would not be awake to watch it. The resurgence in popularity brought enough attention for Gumby to merit his own full-length animated feature in 1995: *Gumby: The Movie*.

In 1976, Clokey remarried, and his second wife, Gloria, was the art director for the Gumby projects in the 1980s and 1990s. She died in 1998. Clokey was the subject of a documentary film, *Gumby Dharma*, in 2006.

In later years, Clokey's health declined. After a series of bladder infections, Clokey died in his sleep on January 8, 2010. He is survived by his son Joe, from his first marriage, and his stepdaughter Holly Harman. Clokey was 88 years old. **Sources:** *Los Angeles Times*, January 9, 2010; *New York Times*, January 11, 2010; *Washington Post*, January 10, 2010, p. C7.

—*Alana Joli Abbott*

Gary Coleman

Born February 8, 1968, in Zion, IL; died of a brain hemorrhage, May 28, 2010, in Provo, UT. Actor. From being a national icon for his child-star role in television program *Diff'rent Strokes* to his downward spiral into tabloid fodder, Gary Coleman never succeeded in moving his career beyond the role that made him famous. At ten years of age, he starred as eight-year-old Arnold Jackson, whose classic line "Wat'chu talkin' 'bout, Willis?" became a household phrase.

Despite the rave reviews for his comedic timing, his career after the show was plagued by heartache and misunderstanding. Diagnosed at a young age with a kidney disease, treatments stunted his growth so that, as an adult, Coleman only ever reached a height of 4-feet 8-inches. Coleman became embroiled in a lawsuit against his parents, whom he felt mismanaged or stole money from him while he was a minor; he later became a tabloid feature due to his hot temper. Though he made a run for California governor during the recall election of 2003 and placed eighth out of the 135 candidates who ran, he was never able to overcome the legacy of childhood stardom.

Coleman was born in Zion, Illinois, in 1968. At four days old, he was adopted into a blue-collar family: W.G. "Willie" and Edmonia Sue Coleman. When Coleman was 18 months old, it was discovered that he had been born with an atrophied kidney. Doctors diagnosed that the other kidney was likely to fail. He had his first kidney transplant when he was five years old, and had a second before he was 14. The dialysis medications used to treat his condition permanently stunted his growth.

But that side-effect made him a more appealing child actor, as he looked younger than his real age. He got into modeling and commercials; an advertisement for a Chicago bank brought him to the attention of television producer Norman Lear. Lear brought Coleman on as a guest in episodes of *Good Times* and *The Jeffersons*. The producer quickly realized Coleman's appeal and began designing a show around the young actor.

Diff'ent Strokes was the story of two young boys from Harlem whose mother, a housekeeper, dies. Her employer, a wealthy white New Yorker played by Conrad Bain, promises the woman he will take in her sons, and as the show begins, the world of Arnold (Coleman) and Willis (played by Todd Bridges) changes as they start to make their home in a very different world. Bain's character, a widower with a teenage daughter, eventually adopts the two boys, consistently introducing them as his sons throughout the series. Howard Rosenberg of the *Los Angeles Times* wrote of the show's 1978-79 debut season, "Its appeal rests chiefly on Gary, a black Pillsbury Doughboy, tiny and cuddly with a face like a pincushion.... But from his mouth come words ... well, you just have to be there."

Coleman was hailed for his comedic timing by such comic greats as Lucille Ball and Bob Hope; magazine articles at the time compared him to Jack Benny, Groucho Marx, and Richard Pryor. He had an undeniable presence that kept audiences turning their sets to *Diff'rent Strokes* for eight seasons. At the series' height, Coleman earned $64,000 per episode, and his net worth was $18 million. He was cast in films and television movies, and at one point had his own animated Saturday morning program, *The Gary Coleman Show.*

When *Diff'rent Strokes* concluded in 1986, Coleman was 18 years old. He became convinced that his parents and his former business manager, Anita De-Thomas, had stolen more than a million dollars from his trust. He brought suit against them in 1989; the three countersued for defamation and breach of contract. Santa Monica Superior Court ruled in favor of Coleman, awarding him $1.28 million. His parents continued to state their belief that they had done nothing wrong, and maintained to the press that they would welcome Coleman back into their lives; however, Coleman remained estranged from his parents for the rest of his life.

In the 1990s, Coleman made occasional guest appearances and did some voice acting in video games and for commercials. He also found work as a commercial pitchman and, more famously, as a mall security guard. It was in that latter role that Coleman made headlines; a female fan who outweighed him by more than a hundred pounds began harassing him for an autograph. Coleman lost his temper and engaged in a fist-fight with the woman. He was fined and required to take anger-management classes. He also was involved in domestic violence charges with his wife, the much younger Shannon Price. The pair had many heated squabbles, and both were accused of acts of violence against the other. Shortly after their 2007 marriage, they appeared on the reality television program *Divorce Court* to work out their differences. Some sources state that Coleman and Price divorced in 2008, though they were still living together in 2010.

In May of 2010, Coleman suffered an accidental fall. Due to his many health issues, the fall was serious, and he had a brain hemorrhage. Price accompanied Coleman to the hospital, and after Coleman fell into a coma, Price made the final decision to take him off of life support on May 28, 2010. He was 42 years old. **Sources:** *Chicago Tribune,* May 29, 2010; *Los Angeles Times,* May 29, 2010; *New York Times,* May 29, 2010; *People,* June 14, 2010, pp. 66-71; *Washington Post,* May 29, 2010, p. B4.

—*Alana Joli Abbott*

Mary Daly

Born October 19, 1928, in Schenectady, NY; died January 3, 2010, in Gardner, MA. Philosopher and theologian. Mary Daly, a theologian who criticized the Roman Catholic church for its treatment of women, became known as a pioneer in feminist philosophy. Her radical positions, such as her refusal to allow men into her upper-level courses on feminism, often irked her Boston College employers. But her writings led her to influence a generation of feminists. Activist and writer Robin Morgan, whose 1970 book *Sisterhood Is Powerful* included a profile of Daly as a major figure in feminism, told the *Los Angeles Times*, "She was the first feminist philosopher, really.... She opened the door for women to question everything."

Daly began her career as a radical Catholic, hoping that she could help to reform the church to draw it away from its patriarchal history. But later in her career she lost hope for being able to change the institution and considered herself a "post-Christian." She also identified herself as a pagan, eco-feminist, radical feminist, and "positively revolting hag." She was forced into retirement to end a lawsuit brought against Boston College due to her barring men from her classes.

Daly was the only child of Irish immigrants. Her father was an ice cream freezer salesman and her mother was a telephone operator. She became outraged at the inequality between sexes at a very young age when a male classmate, who was an altar boy, taunted her that she would never be able to serve Mass. Though she once stated that she hated the Bible, and she described her own spiritual awakenings as an adolescent through her connection with the natural world, she pursued studies in theology and religion.

Daly graduated from the College of Saint Rose in Albany, New York in 1950, holding a degree in English and Latin, and she earned a master's degree in English from Catholic University of America. Though she hoped to teach theology, as a Catholic woman she was not permitted to either teach or study theology. Instead, she pursued a doctorate in religion from St. Mary's College in Notre Dame, Indiana. She applied to the doctorate program in philosophy at the University of Notre Dame, but was denied entrance because she was a woman, or so she stated. Refusing to give up, she applied to the University of Fribourg in Switzerland, which was government-supported and, thus, required to admit women. There she earned doctorates in both philosophy and theology.

In 1966, Daly was hired at Boston College, where she became the first woman to teach theology among their faculty. In 1968, her book *The Church and the Second Sex*, which was highly critical of the Roman Catholic church's attitude toward women, was released. Her position maintained that the church was engaged in the systematic oppression of women. The administration at Boston College was not pleased with her stance, and in response denied her tenure and offered her only a one-year contract, effectively firing her. Her situation was brought to the attention of the media, particularly after 1,500 students, most of them men, signed a petition in support of her. In 1969, the college revised its position and offered her tenure.

In 1971, Daly became the first woman to preach the Sunday sermon at Harvard's Memorial Church. She encouraged the congregation to walk out of the church in rejection of patriarchy. That same year, she stated that the trinity in Christianity was a rip-off of the ancient triple-goddess religions. In 1973, her book *Beyond God the Father: Toward a Philosophy of Women's Liberation* was published. The title criticized the many misogynistic religions in which women are oppressed.

Despite her continued clashes with the administration at Boston College, where she was denied raises and promotions, Daly published widely. Her books include *Gyn/Ecology: The Metaethics of Radical Feminism, Pure Lust: Elemental Feminist Philosophy, Outercourse: The Be-Dazzling Voyage, Containing Recollections From My Logbook of a Radical Feminist Philosopher (Be-ing an Account of My Time/Space Travels and Ideas—Then, Again, Now, and How)* and *Websters' First New Intergalactic Wickedary of the English Language*, the last, written with Jane Caputi, being a book of plays on words that engage in social critique.

Daly was again the center of highly charged controversy in 1998, when Boston College faced a lawsuit from male student Duane Naquin, who Daly had barred from her advanced feminism classes. Daly felt that the presence of men in these advanced courses would stifle conversation and keep female students from freely speaking their minds. She offered instead to tutor any men who wished to take the courses, and she did allow male students to take her introductory courses in feminism. With the threat of the lawsuit, the administration of Boston College encouraged—or, as Daly claimed, forced—her to retire. Her courses were stripped from the course catalog in 1999, and she sued the college for breach of contract. A private settlement ended the debate in 2001, when the college announced Daly's official retirement.

Daly had a neurological disorder and her health had been failing for several years before her death in January of 2010. Though she has no immediate survivors, she leaves behind her a library of works, and a legacy of radical feminist thought that shaped her academic field. **Sources:** *Los Angeles Times,* January 10, 2010; *New York Times,* January 7, 2010; *Washington Post,* January 10, 2010, p. C7.

—*Alana Joli Abbott*

John Dankworth

Born September 20, 1927, in Woodford, Essex, England; died February 6, 2010, in London, England. Jazz saxophonist, composer, and band leader. For more than 60 years, saxophonist, band leader, and composer Sir John Dankworth made his mark on British jazz. Considered one of the most renowned British jazz musicians of his time, Dankworth was known for his movie and television themes of the 1960s, including the theme song for *The Avengers,* and for his work as the musical director for jazz singer Cleo Laine, his wife, whose career he launched in the early 1950s.

Inspired by Charlie Parker, Dankworth performed with such big names in jazz as Ella Fitzgerald and Nat "King" Cole. His orchestra was the first British band ever to perform at the elite Newport Jazz Festival in Newport, Rhode Island. Trained in classical music from a young age, Dankworth attempted to mix jazz and classical elements in some of his compositions, and he was a conductor of the "Pops" performances of the London Symphony Orchestra and the San Francisco Symphony Orchestra. He was knighted by Queen Elizabeth II in 2006, nine years after Laine was made a dame.

Born John Philip William Dankworth in 1927, Dankworth studied violin as a child. He penned his first musical arrangement, a setting of "The Daring Young Man on the Flying Trapeze," at the age of eight. As a teen, he loved the swing style of artists like Benny Goodman, and he decided to study the clarinet. In 1944, he won a soloist's prize on that instrument in a national competition. Dankworth continued to pursue his clarinet studies at the Royal Academy of Music, but the faculty did not support jazz music, and he stayed for only two years. During this time, he first encountered the music of Charlie Parker, whose musical influence led Dankworth to take up the alto saxophone.

After leaving the Royal Academy of Music to perform jazz with a dance band aboard the ocean liner the *Queen Mary,* Dankworth founded, with other

musicians, Club Eleven in London's Soho. The club became renowned as a home for England's jazz scene, particularly the jazz musicians partial to bebop. In 1950, Dankworth formed the Johnny Dankworth Seven, which debuted in the London Palladium. In 1951, after having performed with a number of guest singers, the band added a permanent singer to their number: Clem Campbell, who was renamed Cleo Laine by her band mates, and whom Dankworth married in 1958.

The Johnny Dankworth Seven was disbanded in 1953, and Dankworth put together a 20-piece orchestra to perform big band music. Dankworth's arrangements for this larger group came under some criticism for their unconventional style, but Dankworth was undiscouraged. He explained in a 1969 interview with Les Tomkins, quoted in the London *Times,* "The hardest thing to do is to swing quietly, with control and restraint. Lots of bands swing loudly. I refuse to let my band play loudly in order to try to swing when it isn't swinging softly…. I think that the best jazz in the long run is jazz that is controlled and will swing on its own terms."

Dankworth could clearly arrange in more traditional styles, as well. A 1956 recording, "Experiments with Mice," featured the band performing arrangements of "Three Blind Mice" in the styles of a number of well-known jazz composers, from Glenn Miller to Stan Kenton, and finally, in Dankworth's own signature style. During this part of his career, Dankworth focused more on his compositions than on his performances, feeling he was never the same level of virtuoso that critics often compared him to. His focus on his compositions allowed him the chance to listen to his work and revise in a way that performance had not.

Through the 1960s, Dankworth's music was commonly heard in the movies and on television. His scores were featured in British movies such as *We Are the Lambeth Boys, The Criminal,* and *Modesty Blaise.* He also wrote the themes for *Tomorrow's World* and *The Avengers.* With the pay coming in from the film industry, Dankworth could focus on "concept" albums that did not have the same earning potential. His most famous of these was the 1965 *Shakespeare and All That Jazz,* in which Laine performed Shakespeare's verse in jazz settings. Dankworth became a teacher at the Royal Academy of Music, and in 1971, he became Laine's musical director, stepping out of the spotlight for a time to promote her career. Dankworth also composed musicals in which Laine performed.

In addition to his compositions and performances, which he continued throughout his life, Dankworth founded and built a venue on the grounds of his home with Laine, called The Stables. The auditorium featured performances, not only of jazz, but of classical, folk, cabaret, and pop music as well. The couple also founded Wavendon Allmusic Plan, a charity for musical education.

After a long struggle with illness, Dankworth died on February 6, 2010. He was hospitalized at the time of an anniversary concert at the Stables, and Laine announced his death officially at the concert. She told the artists in advance, "I'll go on and I'll have a lump in my throat, and I might crack," Monica Ferguson reported to the *Los Angeles Times*. Laine made it through the announcement, however, and the concert featured performances by Dankworth and Laine's children: Alec, a bass player, and Jacqui, a singer and actress. Dankworth was 82 years old. **Sources:** *Los Angeles Times*, February 8, 2010; *New York Times*, February 11, 2010; *Times* (London), February 8, 2010; *Washington Post*, February 10, 2010, p. B6.

—*Alana Joli Abbott*

Victoria Manolo Draves

Born December 31, 1924, in San Francisco, CA; died of complications of pancreatic cancer, April 11, 2010, in Palm Springs, CA. Diver. Victoria Manalo Draves made history when she became the first woman to win two gold medals in diving events at the same Olympics. During London's 1948 Olympics, she won both the three-meter springboard and the ten-meter platform events. She was also one of the two first Asian Americans to win Olympic gold medals; the other was Sammy Lee, the men's platform winner.

Despite her long career as a swimmer, Draves did not begin diving until she was 16. As a child, she was afraid of the water, and she did not learn to swim until she was nine or ten years old. Born in 1924, Draves was the child of a father who immigrated from the Philippines and a mother who was an English immigrant. She was one of three sisters, and as a child, had dreams of being a ballet dancer. When Draves was 16, she went with her sisters to a pool for a swim, where Draves met Phil Patterson, who became her first coach.

Though Patterson started her career, Draves faced prejudice from him early on. Rather than allowing Draves to join the Fairmont Hotel Swimming and Diving Club, Patterson created the Patterson School of Swimming and Diving for her specifically. Draves believed that this was not a favor to her, but instead, it was to keep her separated from the other swimmers. In addition, Patterson would not allow her to compete under her last name, Manalo, forcing her to change to her mother's maiden name, Taylor, so that she did not sound Asian American.

While Draves was working with Patterson, coach Lyle Draves of the Athens Athletic Club in Oakland, California, noticed her competing and knew she would be a champion. Lyle Draves began training Draves in 1944, when she was 19, and under his tutelage she began to improve. The pair were married in 1946, and from 1946 to 1948, Lyle Draves coached his wife to five championships in the United States. Those three years, she was the national platform diving champion and the national indoor springboard champion. In 1948, Draves qualified for the Olympics, and she traveled to London to compete in the diving events. Her gold medal performances in the three-meter springboard and the ten-meter platform made her a household name. She was named by *Life* magazine, along Olympic decathalon gold medalist Bob Mathias, as the top U. S. athlete at the London games.

After returning from the Olympics, Draves was offered several movie opportunities in Hollywood and the Philippines. An attractive woman at only five foot one inch tall, her contagious smile made her seem a natural for stardom. But due to the types of roles she was offered—the studios wanted to cast her as a South Seas beauty—she turned down a career in movies. Instead, she became a professional swimmer. She joined Larry Crosby's aquatic show "Rhapsody in Swimtime," which played at Chicago's Soldier Field in 1948. Subsequently, she joined "Aqua Parade," directed and organized by Buster Crabbe. She toured with that performance throughout the United States and Europe.

In the early 1950s, Draves and her husband decided to start a family, so Draves ended her touring career and, with her former coach, started a training program for swimmers and divers. They first operated out of Indian Springs at Montrose, California, and later moved to Encino. Among the trainees in the program were future Olympic champions Patricia McCormick and Sue Gossick. In addition to her career swimming and coaching swimmers, Draves spent some time working as a secretary. She also raised four boys.

In 1969, Draves was honored for her Olympic achievements when she was elected to Fort Lauderdale, Florida's International Swimming Hall of

Fame. Among the other honors given to Draves was the building of a two-acre park in Draves' old neighborhood in San Francisco in 2005, which was named in her honor.

Draves suffered from pancreatic cancer, and on April 11, 2010, she died due to complications from the disease. The death was not widely publicized and was announced after the fact. Draves was 85 years old. In an obituary in the *Los Angeles Times*, fellow Olympic medalist Sammy Lee, who gave Draves away to her husband at her wedding, praised her work. "She was such a beautiful, graceful diver," Lee said. "She worked very hard on both the springboard and on the platform. I'd say her workouts were harder than the average top woman diver in those days." Patricia McCormick, for whom Draves was a role model, also praised Draves' legacy in the *Los Angeles Times*, saying, "She had a winning spirit, she had the skills, she had the consistency, and she was one heck of a competitor."

Draves is survived by her husband, their four sons, eight grandchildren, and her twin sister. Many of her memories of her career were published in an oral history by the Amateur Athletic Foundation of Los Angeles in 1991. **Sources:** *Los Angeles Times*, April 29, 2010; *New York Times*, April 29, 2010; *Washington Post*, April 30, 2010, p. B6.

—Alana Joli Abbott

Jaime Escalante

Born Jaime Alfonso Escalante Guitérrez, December 31, 1930, in La Paz, Bolivia; died of pulmonary arrest brought on by pneumonia, March 30, 2010, in Roseville, CA. Teacher. In 1982, a scandal rocked the education community: Of the 18 students from Garfield High School in East Los Angeles who took the Advanced Placement (AP) calculus exam, 14 were accused of cheating. The students, and their teacher, Jaime Escalante, believed they were victims of a racial profile. They were Hispanic, and attended a school that had nearly lost its accreditation a few years before. Escalante encouraged the students to retake the test, and 12 of them did, again passing, five of them with the highest marks. This proved that the students had earned their passing marks, and that Escalante's teaching methods had led his underprivileged students to their success.

Escalante's work might have been a footnote in educational news if the story had not sparked the interest of Hollywood. In 1988, Escalante and his suc-

cessful AP calculus program became the subject of the feel-good film, *Stand and Deliver*. Edward James Olmos, who played Escalante, received an Oscar nomination for his performance, propelling Olmos and Escalante into fame. Escalante continued to teach, but also became a motivational speaker and education advisor for politicians including California Governor Arnold Schwarzenegger. His dedication to students who had previously been dismissed by the public school system as unlikely to achieve proved that with the proper work ethic and encouragement, disadvantage students could out-perform their more privileged peers.

Born in La Paz, Bolivia, in 1930, Escalante was the son of two schoolteachers. His parents divorced when he was only nine; Escalante lived with his mother and attended San Calixto Jesuit school, a well-regarded school in La Paz. He often got into trouble due to his quick wit and mischievous demeanor. He served briefly in the army and considered going into engineering. Instead, he went to the state teacher's college, Normal Superior, in Bolivia. There he met his future wife, Fabiola Tapia. Escalante's first job was teaching physics at the American Institute when he was 21 years old. He taught at three highly rated Bolivian schools before earning his degree.

To earn extra money, and to handle his growing popularity as a teacher, Escalante worked at one school in the morning, another in the afternoon, and often tutored in the evening. But while Escalante's career was a success, his wife wanted to make sure that their son would have greater opportunities in his life than he could receive in Bolivia. She convinced Escalante that they should move to California, which they did in 1963. Escalante was frustrated to discover that none of his teaching credentials would carry over from Bolivia to the United States.

Escalante began his American life with a job in a coffee shop in Pasadena, California; he was quickly promoted to cook. While working, he also devoted himself to earning an American education: he took English classes at Pasadena City College and earned an associate's degree. With these new academic qualifications, he was offered better jobs; he was hired by a Pasadena electronics company as a technician, where he made a much better salary than he had before. Despite his second successful career, Escalante missed teaching. He pursued his teaching credentials, earning a scholarship to California State University at Los Angeles.

In 1974, at the age of 43, Escalante took a teaching position at Garfield High School, taking a large pay cut from his former job. Worse, Escalante discovered that he would be teaching the lowest level math courses, using textbooks he considered appropriately leveled for fifth grade math students in Bolivia. Nevertheless, Escalante brought his untraditional teaching style—which included using sports allusions, driving remote-controlled vehicles, and playing rock music—to students that other teachers—and the school system—had given up on. The administration noticed his success in turning around hard-to-reach students, and when Escalante wanted to start an AP calculus program, he had the school's support. In 1978, his first AP class had 14 students; five completed the course, and only two passed the AP test. In 1980, however, seven of his nine students passed; the next year, 14 of 15 passed. In 1982, all 18 of his students succeeded with either 4s or 5s (the highest score).

Success was followed by controversy when his students were accused of cheating. Escalante supported them, and when they were exonerated, Escalante's program became even more popular. By 1987, Garfield High, the low-income, dominantly Hispanic high school that had nearly lost its accreditation, held fifth place among schools taking and passing the AP calculus exam. In 1988, *Stand and Deliver* won Escalante national acclaim, but also created difficulties for him among his fellow teachers. Escalante was known for being blunt, and was not shy about criticizing teachers he felt were underperforming. The teacher's union undercut his classes by saying they exceeded the union's rules about how many students could attend classes by one teacher. Sick of the politics, Escalante left Garfield in 1991; the AP calculus program lost strength without its mentor and guide, and Garfield went back to underperforming in calculus.

Escalante taught for seven years at Hiram Johnson High School in Sacramento, near where his son lived. He never felt he had the same support at Hiram Johnson that he had received at Garfield, and despite his best efforts, his students never had more than a 75 percent rate of passing. He had achieved a 90 percent pass rate for his Garfield students. Frustrated, Escalante decided to return to Bolivia, where he taught calculus until 2008, but he spent a lot of time in the United States as well, doing motivational speaking and advising Schwarzenegger on educational policies.

Escalante suffered from bladder cancer, and was in poor health during the last months of his life. He traveled frequently to the United States for cancer treatments, but in 2010, he succumbed to pulmonary arrest due to pneumonia; he was 79. He died at his son's home in Roseville, near Sacramento, on March 30, 2010, leaving behind his wife, two sons, and a legacy of students who succeeded because Escalante believed in them. **Sources:** *Los Angeles Times*, March 31, 2010; *New York Times*, March 31, 2010; *Washington Post*, March 31, 2010, p. B5.

—*Alana Joli Abbott*

Doug Fieger

Born Douglas Lars Fieger, August 20, 1952, in Detroit, MI; died of lung cancer, February 14, 2010, in Woodland Hills, CA. Musician. Doug Fieger was frontman for The Knack, the Los Angeles-based power-pop band whose debut was one of the top-selling albums of 1979. Their first single, "My Sharona," spent six weeks at the No. 1 spot on the U.S. singles chart and turned Fieger and his bandmates into overnight stars. None of the band's follow-up singles ever matched the sales of "My Sharona," but their signature tune had a long afterlife as a cover song and periodically turned up in movies and commercials. "I've had ten great lives," Fieger said in an interview a few weeks before his passing, according to the *Los Angeles Times*. "And I expect to have some more. I don't feel cheated in any way, shape, or form."

Fieger was born in 1952 in Detroit, and grew up in suburban Oak Park. His mother was a teacher and his father a local civil rights attorney. In high school, Fieger started a band called Sky that played at noted Detroit venues and managed to get signed to RCA Records. They went to England to record with Jimmy Miller, a producer for the Rolling Stones and other major rock acts, but the two records that Sky made failed to achieve any success in an already glutted market. The band broke up, and Fieger played in a German progressive-rock outfit called Triumvirat before moving to Los Angeles.

In 1978 Fieger put together a new band, The Knack, with three other L.A. musicians—guitarist Berton Averre, bassist Prescott Niles, and drummer Bruce Gary. They played their first show at the Whisky a Go-Go, a celebrated West Hollywood rock club, on June 1, 1978. Their energetic, stripped-down tracks, which owed as much to the recent New Wave trends coming out of England as they did to the snappiest power-pop tunes from rock pioneers like Buddy Holly, quickly incited a bidding war among record labels, and they were signed to Capitol Records. The group endured some critical backlash for their decision to pose on their debut album's cover in what looked to be a homage to the Beatles' first record, replete with white shirts and black ties.

That album, *Get the Knack,* was released in the spring of 1979 and was an instant success. Fieger had penned the lyrics to its first single, "My Sharona," about his girlfriend at the time, Sharona Alperin, who was a 17-year-old Fairfax High School student when she met the 25-year-old Fieger a few years before. Alperin even appeared on the picture sleeve for the single, which soared to No. 1 and stayed there for much of the summer. The Knack's stunningly successful hit, wrote Ben Sisario in the *New York Times* "celebrated teenage lust in unabashed terms.... [A]nd came to symbolize the commercial arrival of new wave, the poppier, snazzier-dressed cousin of punk rock." At the time, however, critics were scathing in their reviews of the band, deriding their success as little more than a fluke.

Fieger's band had a second hit, "Good Girls Don't," also from *Get the Knack,* but their second album, *...But the Little Girls Understand,* failed to replicate the commercial success of their debut. There was even a "Nuke the Knack" campaign that originated in the Los Angeles New Wave scene. The staffers of influential *Rolling Stone* magazine promoted the anti-Knack sentiment, and one of the magazine's star critics delivered a brutal assessment of the Knack's second LP—though, to be fair, *Rolling Stone* journalists also derided another fairly popular new act, Devo, as little more than a bag of gimmicks. Fieger and his bandmates put out a third record, 1981's *Round Trip,* then broke up.

"My Sharona" was resurrected on the charts in 1994 when it was used in the film *Reality Bites.* Around this same period, Fieger's older brother, Geoffrey, gained a measure of national fame as the attorney for a Michigan physician, Dr. Jack Kevorkian, when prosecutors brought murder charges against Kevorkian for assisted suicide. In 1998, Fieger reunited with Averre, Niles, and a new drummer, Terry Bozzio of Missing Persons fame, for a tour and new Knack album, *Zoom.*

Fieger was diagnosed with lung cancer in 2005 and underwent surgery for a brain tumor a year later. He died of cancer at his home in Woodland Hills, California, on February 14, 2010, at the age of 57. He and Alperin dated for four years, but never married; she went on to become a successful real estate agent whose clients included some of Hollywood's biggest names. Fieger is survived by his brother, sister Beth, and ex-wife Mia, who cared for him in his final months. *Globe & Mail* rock critic Jonathan

Gross interviewed Fieger at the peak of the band's success, then caught up with him in 1998, when a reunited Knack was on tour. "He talked of plans to make more records, to kick-start the career. His confidence was palpable," Gross wrote. "And now he's gone as are many of the places and people mentioned here. *Rolling Stone* is still around though resigned to featuring no talent lip-synching on its cover in the absence of anything of substance. By comparison, Doug Fieger was John Lennon." **Sources:** *Globe & Mail* (Toronto, Canada), February 20, 2010, p. M12; *Los Angeles Times,* February 15, 2010; *New York Times,* February 16, 2010; *Times* (London), February 18, 2010, p. B8.

—Carol Brennan

Sid Fleischman

Born March 16, 1920, in New York, NY; died of cancer, March 17, 2010, in Santa Monica, CA. Author. Sid Fleischman was a successful adult novelist and screenwriter before he contemplated writing for children. Wanting to give his children an idea of what he did working from home, he wrote a children's book and sent it to his agent, expecting little to come of it. That book launched Fleischman on a long career in children's literature, and set him on the path that would win him a Newbery Award.

Fleischman's 1987 novel, *The Whipping Boy,* earned him the Newbery Medal and established him as an important children's writer. By the end of his career in 2010, Fleischman had published more than 50 books for young readers, including novels, picture books, tall tales, and biographies.

Fleischman was born in the borough of Brooklyn in New York City in 1920, but he grew up in San Diego, California. He was interested in magic, and as a teen, he taught himself magic tricks. He became accomplished enough at sleight of hand that he found work at nightclubs and vaudeville shows, including Mr. Arthur Bull's Francisco Spook Show. He wrote a book about performing magic tricks, which was published when he was 19. Though he changed his career focus to writing, he retained an interest in magic throughout his life. In 1993, he published a book of magic tricks for professional magicians: *The Charlatan's Handbook.*

During World War II, Fleischman served in the Navy Reserve, after which he attended and graduated from San Diego State University. While an undergraduate, he began to place short stories in magazines; after graduation, he got a job working as a journalist for San Diego's *Daily Journal.* Later, he found work as an editor at a small magazine; but he wrote in the meantime, and in 1951, he was ready to leave his job to focus exclusively on his writing. He had begun writing suspense novels in the late 1940s, and these books—including *The Straw Donkey Case* (1948), *Shanghai Flame* (1955), and *Blood Alley* (1955)—made it possible for him to begin his career as a writer.

The adult novels led to work on a screenplay. He was asked to write the adaptation of his own novel, *Blood Alley*, for the film of the same title. The film was released the same year as the book, and the movie starred John Wayne and Lauren Bacall. Fleischman wrote additional screenplays, including *Lay-fayette Escadrille,* based on one of his own short stories, and *The Deadly Companions.*

A visit by children's author and illustrator Leo Politi to Fleischman's daughter's school spurred him to write books for children. When his daughter Jane raved about meeting Politi, Fleischman reminded her that he was also a writer. As Fleischman recounted in his Newbery acceptance speech, Jane countered her father' reminder with, "Yes, but no one reads [Daddy's] books." Feeling that his children should form part of his audience, Fleischman began writing the book of an Old West traveling magician. Published in 1962, *Mr. Mysterious and Company* was an immediate sale, accepted by the first publisher who read it. This marked a turning point in Fleischman's career, and he focused his work on writing for children.

Well known before his Newbery win, Fleischman reached new critical acclaim with his novella for middle grade readers, *The Whipping Boy*, in 1987. Fleischman used a historical occurrence—the use of a whipping boy who would take the beatings for a rich or spoiled child whenever the child deserved punishment—and created the tale of a relationship between a young prince and the independently minded street boy who becomes the prince's whipping boy.

Along with Fleischman's Newbery winner, he has written titles such as *Humbug Mountain* and the "Josh McBroom" series, about a one-acre farm that produces an abundance of crops. Fleischman has also written several books of nonfiction for young readers, particularly focusing on biographies. The people about whom he has written include magician Harry Houdini, author Mark Twain, and actor Charlie Chaplin.

Fleischman died at his home in Santa Monica, California, the day after his 90th birthday. At the news of his death, Lin Oliver, who is the executive director of the Society of Children's Book Writers and Illustrators, told the *Los Angeles Times,* "Sid was a national treasure in the field of children's books.... He was a true master of the craft and a writer's writer." Oliver continued, "He was somebody, more than anyone I know, who loved his work; he *loved* to write." She also described Fleischman's commitment to the practice of magic, saying, "I think he regarded writing as magic." Fleischman is survived by his son Paul, his daughters, Jane and Ann, and his sister. He and his son are the only father-son pair of Newbery Award winners. **Sources:** *Los Angeles Times,* March 21, 2010; *New York Times,* March 25, 2010; *Washington Post,* March 29, 2010, p. B5.

—Alana Joli Abbott

Dick Francis

Born Richard Stanley Francis, October 31, 1920, in Lawrenny, Wales; died of natural causes, February 14, 2010, in the Cayman Islands. Author. Over the course of 40 years, former jockey Dick Francis published 42 successful mystery novels set in the world of horse racing, selling more than 60 million copies of his books. The recipient of three Edgar Allan Poe Awards from the Mystery Writers of America, Francis was named a grand master in 1996. He was made a Commander of the Order of the British Empire and won the prestigious Diamond Dagger Award from the Crime Writers Association of Great Britain. Several of Francis' novels have been adapted as films and television shows.

"I never really decided to be a writer," Francis explained in *The Spot of Queens,* his autobiography, quoted in the *New York Times.* "I just sort of drifted into it." In fact, he described writing fiction as a challenging and difficult profession. "Writing a novel proved to be the hardest, most self-analyzing task I had ever attempted, far worse than an autobiography," Francis was reported as having said in the *New York Times.*

The son of a steeplechase jockey and stable manager, Francis was introduced to riding at an early age. He served in the Royal Air Force during World War II, first in Egypt and later as a pilot of Spitfires, Wellingtons, and Lancasters. After the war, he became a steeplechase trainer's assistant at his father's stables. In 1948 he became a professional jockey, beginning a nine-year career in which he won nearly 350 out of more than 2,300 races. He reportedly had falls in about ten percent of his races, which was very hard on his body, and his various injuries included six broken collar bones, a fractured skull, five broken noses, a broken back, dislocated shoulders, and several broken ribs. Over the course of his career, he competed in 12 races with a broken arm, two of which he won.

The most memorable moment of his career was not a success, however: in 1956, he rode Devon Loch, the horse of the Queen Mother, in the Grand National. Ahead by lengths, Francis was posed to win, until suddenly the horse went sprawling. The mystery of what happened may have inspired Francis' choice of genre. But the novels did not start immediately; after Francis' retirement the following year, an agent recommended that he write an autobiography, which was met with critical success. Francis became a racing correspondent for London's *Sunday Express,* but finding that the column did not pay his bills, he began writing a mystery about a jockey killed during a race. The novel, *Dead Cert,* was released in 1962, and became the first of a long stream of novels set in the horse-racing world.

Though Francis' novels are often considered formulaic, and do not stray from the themes of racing, the formula was certainly a successful one. Francis tended to introduce readers to the racing subculture, add an element of danger and mystery, then put the hero, usually a jockey or a retired jockey, in the center of it all. After setting the high moral ground and taking on the villain himself, usually after torture, the hero would bring the mystery to a close and the evil-doer to justice. Typically as likely to chase women as another fictional British hero, James Bond, Francis' heroes would often get the girl at the end—but would know that he was the type likely to make a good husband.

The books are filled with details about racing, as well as details about the physical trauma the hero suffers, leading one of Francis' fans, the Queen Mother, to write him, "How do you think these stories up? You're getting more bloodthirsty than ever," according to the *Washington Post.* While some critics disparaged the formula, others praised his authenticity and pacing. The *New York Times* quoted critic John Leonard as having written, "Not to read Dick Francis because you don't like horses is like not reading Dostoyevsky because you don't like God." Author Carol Flake was quoted in the *Washington Post* as having once commented on the speed of the plot in one of Francis' novels, writing "one is tempted to handicap his books rather than review them, assigning each a speed rating and a weight allowance."

Francis suffered a tremendous set back to his career when his wife, Mary, who had been instrumental in his research and editing process, died in 2000. Their son Felix Francis, quoted by the *Los Angeles Times,* described his mother and father as "Siamese twins conjoined at the pencil." Francis would write out a draft in long hand, which Mary would edit, and then Francis would transpose into the computer. After losing his inspiration and partner, Francis did not release another novel for six years. Following that, he teamed up with his son Felix to write four subsequent books.

Diagnosed with prostate cancer in the 1990s, Francis died in 2010 of natural causes at the age of 89. Once afraid of being remembered as "the man who didn't win the National," according to the *Washington Post,* Francis is instead likely to be remembered as a Grand Master of mystery whose novels brought readers so vividly into the world of horse racing.

Francis' final novel, *Crossfire,* written with Felix, was published after his death. He is survived by both Felix and another son, Merrick, as well as five grandchildren and a great-grandchild. **Sources:** *Los Angeles Times,* February 15, 2010; *New York Times,* February 15, 2010; *Times* (London), February 21, 2010; *Washington Post,* February 16, 2010, p. B4.

—*Alana Joli Abbott*

Frank Frazetta

Born Frank Frazzetta, February 9, 1928, in New York, NY; died of a stroke, May 10, 2010, in Fort Myers, FL. Fantasy artist. Though the most famous paintings of Frank Frazetta were done in oil on canvas, his works were not typically seen by museumgoers. Instead, they were prominent and iconic works on the covers of fantasy novels, including the paperback reissues of the "Conan the Barbarian" series by Robert E. Howard and the "Tarzan" series by Edgar Rice Burroughs. Throughout the 1960s, Frazetta's art, featuring muscled warriors, scantily-clad women, and gruesome monsters, had a huge impact on the fantasy genre.

Oscar-nominated writer and director Guillermo del Toro, who, according to the *Los Angeles Times* called Frazetta "an Olympian artist that defined fantasy art for the 20th century," found it hard to state Frazetta's impact on the world of fantasy to anyone unfamiliar with the genre. "He gave the world a new pantheon of heroes.... [He] added blood, sweat and sexual power" to the legacy of earlier fantasy artists.

Born in the New York City borough of Brooklyn in 1928, Frazetta (who dropped the second z in his original surname) had an early talent for art. At the age of eight, he was enrolled at the Brooklyn Academy of Fine Art. One of his early influences was Hal Foster, the artist for the "Tarzan" comic strip. He began working professionally as an illustrator at the age of 16.

Much of Frazetta's early career was in comics. He did work on DC Comics' *Shining Knight*, provided art for the western series *Ghost Rider*, and illustrated a number of science fiction tales for EC Comics. In the early 1950s, he wrote his own, short-lived comic called *Johnny Comet*, and he worked, uncredited, under Al Capp on *Li'l Abner*, a job he held until he left the comics industry in the 1960s.

In a 1964 issue of *Mad* magazine, Frazetta's parody of a shampoo advertisement, featuring a member of the Beatles, drew the attention of Hollywood studio United Artists. They saw the work, thought it was in the right tone for an upcoming Woody Allen comedy, and hired Frazetta to paint the movie poster for 1965 film *What's New Pussycat?* Frazetta worked on other film posters, including *The Fearless Vampire Killers* in 1967 and the Clint Eastwood film *The Gauntlet* ten years later.

But Frazetta was finding larger successes beyond comics in the 1960s. In 1966, he painted the cover for a short story collection, *Conan the Adventurer*, by Conan-creator Robert E. Howard and L. Sprague de Camp. The image depicted the a well-muscled, shirtless warrior with long hair staring out at the reader, standing atop a hill of what appears to be slain enemies, his sword thrust downward into them; an apparently naked, buxom young woman rests at his feet, clinging to one of his ankles. The image was at once gruesome and sexual, and it almost immediately challenged the idea of what a fantasy paperback cover should look like. Frazetta became known for lush, almost erotic covers, which brought an aspect of sexuality to fantasy novel covers.

Frazetta illustrated the paperback reissues of a number of other Conan titles, including *Conan the Conqueror*, also released in 1966. The original painting for that cover later sold for a million dollars. According to the *New York Times*, by the 1970s, paperback publishers had "been known to buy one of his paintings for use as a cover, then commission a writer to turn out a novel to go with it." That must have suited Frazetta well, as he declared that he never read the novels he created covers for. "I didn't read any of it," he is quoted as having said in the *Washington Post*. "It was too opposite of what I do.... I drew [Conan] my way. It was really rugged. And it caught on. I didn't care about what people thought. People who bought the books never complained about it." In 1977, *The Fantastic Art of Frank Frazetta*, a collection of Frazetta's drawings, sold more than 300,000 copies.

The popularity of Frazetta's artwork hit its peak during the 1970s, just as heavy metal began to surge into prominence on the music scene. Frazetta did a number of album covers, such as *Expect No Mercy* by Nazareth and *Flirtin' with Disaster* by Molly Hatchet. Yngwie Malmsteen and Wolfmother also featured album covers by Frazetta. The artist also worked in animation and commercial art.

It was largely due to Frazetta's art that Conan, as a character, experienced a resurgence in popularity. Marvel comics picked up Conan as a comic franchise during the 1970s. In 1982, the film *Conan the Barbarian*, featuring Arnold Schwarzenegger, was released, its imagery drawing heavily upon the art created by Frazetta.

In 1995, Frazetta suffered a stroke, which forced him to retrain himself as an artist, changing from his formerly right-handed style to a left-handed brush technique. In 2009, his wife of 53 years, Eleanor Kelly, died; she had also served as Frazetta's business partner. After Kelly's death, Frazetta's children quarreled over the rights to Frazetta's works, culminating in Frazetta's oldest son attempting to remove the collection from Frazetta's small family museum. Charges were brought against the son, Frank Jr., but were later dropped after the family resolved the dispute. On May 10, 2010, Frazetta died in Fort Myers, Florida, after suffering a stroke. He is survived by his four children. **Sources:** *Los Angeles Times*, May 11, 2010; *New York Times*, May 10, 2010; *Washington Post*, May 13, 2010, p. B7.

—*Alana Joli Abbott*

Miep Gies

Born Hermine Santrouschitz, February 15, 1909, in Vienna, Austria (then the Austro-Hungarian Empire); died January 12, 2010, in Hoorn, the

Netherlands. Rescuer. During World War II, a brave young Jewish girl named Anne Frank hid with her family in an annex in one of her father's office buildings in Nazi-occupied Amsterdam. She recorded the experience in a diary that survived the war largely thanks to Miep Gies, one of the caretakers who helped keep the Franks hidden for 25 months. Gies was at the canal-side office building where the Franks were hidden when the Gestapo came to arrest them, less than a year before the end of the war.

Though Gies became a noted figure after the publication of *The Diary of Anne Frank,* she wrote in her own autobiography, *Anne Frank Remembered,* "I am not a hero. I stand at the end of the long, long line of good Dutch people who did what I did and more—much more—during those dark and terrible times years ago, but always like yesterday in the heart of those of us who bear witness." Despite her own beliefs that she was not a hero, she was presented with the highest honor given to civilians by the West German government in 1989, and she was knighted in 1996 by Queen Beatrix of the Netherlands.

Gies was born Hermine Santrouschitz, the daughter of a very poor couple in Vienna, which was the capital of the Austro-Hungarian empire. World War I took a tremendous toll on the poor in Austria, and many children, like Gies, were malnourished. At the age of 11, Gies was one of the children selected by the Dutch workers' association to be sent to the Netherlands and placed in the care of an adoptive family until she could regain her health. Rather than stay for only a few months, as the program anticipated, Gies was taken in by her new Dutch family and effectively adopted. They gave her the nickname Miep, and she lived with them until she was 18. Gies fell in love with Amsterdam when the family moved there, and she remained in the city after finishing school.

Beginning her career as an office assistant, Gies had trouble finding work when the recession hit Amsterdam in 1933. When there was a vacancy at a company called Opekta, which made pectin, an ingredient in jam, she applied. Otto Frank, a Jewish businessman who had moved from Germany (and was later followed by his family, including his youngest daughter, Anne) ran the company. Because Frank's Dutch was still rudimentary, Gies' ability to speak German fluently and her willingness to teach Frank Dutch was an asset. She became the head of information and complaints, which typically meant that she fielded calls from housewives who had made mistakes using the company's product. Opekta was a small company, and Gies became close friends with the Frank family.

In 1941, Gies was nearly extradited to Austria because she had never become an official citizen of the Netherlands. She had been seeing Jan Gies, but the pair elected not to marry due to financial insecurity. When her Austrian passport was questioned, the Gieses changed their plans and were married. Their wedding ceremony was the last public celebration that Anne Frank is known to have attended, as only a few months later, Otto Frank decided that the family should go into hiding, rather than be taken to a concentration camp by the German occupiers of the Netherlands. Frank confided to Gies what they were planning and asked if she would be willing to be one of their caretakers. Gies responded, immediately, "Of course." According to the *Los Angeles Times,* asked later about her quick response, she replied that if she had not helped, she "could foresee many sleepless nights," because "remorse and regret can be worse than losing your life." The *Washington Post* reported her as having said, "We did our duty as human beings. Helping people in need."

For 25 months, the Franks, the van Pels family, and a Jewish dentist named Fritz Pfeffer lived in a small annex in a canal-side office of the Opekta company. Gies continued to work for Opekta, keeping business normal, and she bought food and supplies for the hidden families. Jan Gies was already a part of the Dutch resistance, and, using forged ration cards and visiting several stores across the city to keep from buying too much in any location, they were able to get the food needed without raising suspicions. Gies also took out library books and baked a holiday cake to try to keep up the spirits of her friends.

As the war neared its end, the Franks believed they would survive without being caught, but it was not to be. An anonymous source told the Gestapo where the Franks were hiding, and on August 4, 1944, the police came to arrest them and transport them to concentration camps. Gies was at the office when the police arrived, and was not arrested, most likely because the leading officer was from Vienna and he wanted to spare his countryman. After the arrest, Gies hurried to the annex, where she saw loose papers containing Anne's writing, as well as her diary. Gies grabbed the papers and hid them in an unlocked desk drawer, where she intended to keep them until Anne's return. She also made the attempt, with help from the other caretakers, to bribe the Gestapo into releasing their friends, but she was unsuccessful. Anne and her sister were taken to Bergen-Belsen, where Anne died of typhoid only a few weeks before the camp was liberated by the Allies.

After the war, Otto Frank, the only one who had hidden in the annex who survived, returned to Amsterdam and lived for a time with the Gieses. Gies gave him Anne's papers when her death was reported, but refused to read or listen to any excerpts. She did not look at them until the second printing of their publication because she was afraid they would hold too much grief for her. The publication of Anne's diary made Gies a desired speaker, and after writing her own memoir, she visited classrooms to talk about her experiences during the war.

Gies died in 2010 at the age of 100. She was the last remaining caretaker of the Frank family. Gies is survived by a son and three grandchildren. **Sources:** *Los Angeles Times,* January 12, 2010; *New York Times,* January 12, 2010; *Times* (London), January 13, 2010; *Washington Post,* January 12, 2010, p. B5.

—*Alana Joli Abbott*

William E. Gordon

Born January 8, 1918, in Paterson, NJ; died of natural causes, February 16, 2010, in Ithaca, NY. Engineer and scientist. While William Edwin Gordon may not be a household name, his famous radio telescope, featured in such films as Robert Zemekis' *Contact* (starring Jodie Foster) and the 1995 James Bond movie *Golden Eye,* is a familiar science icon. Built in 1963 and expected to last only ten years, the Arecibo radio telescope in Arecibo, Puerto Rico, has enabled scientists to create three dimensional images of the universe, glimpse planets beyond the solar system, and map Mars, Venus, and the Moon in detail.

The telescope was used by Dr. Joseph Taylor and his student Russell Hulse at Princeton University to discover a binary pulsar. Their data led them to prove the existence of Einstein's hypothesized gravity waves, an achievement that earned the pair the 1993 Nobel Prize in physics. Because of the instrument's sensitivity, it is also involved with the search for extraterrestrial life, which the movie *Contact* (based on Carl Sagan's novel of the same name) popularized. Despite these uses for research in astronomy, Gordon initially conceived the telescope as primarily useful for meteorology research, which was his area of study.

Born in New Jersey in 1918, Gordon earned both his bachelor's and master's degrees from Montclair State Teacher's College, which is now Montclair State University. He enlisted in the U.S. Army Air Corps as a meteorologist in 1942, where he was as-

signed to study the effects weather had on radar. The military wanted answers about why radar could be effective beyond a 100-mile radius, but did not work close by. Gordon's work on these projects led him to continue his studies at Cornell University, where he earned his doctorate in engineering. There, he researched how radar functions in the ionosphere, an upper layer of atmosphere off of which radio waves are reflected.

In order to further his research, Gordon determined he needed a powerful transmitter with a large antenna beyond the scope of anything previously designed. He hoped to measure the ionosphere, and study the way electrons behaved in that part of the atmosphere, to improve radio transmissions. In order to secure funding for his research, he pitched the project to the military, assuring them that it would provide them with a chance of picking up Soviet radio signals. The research arm of the Defense Department granted him funding.

In order for Gordon's telescope to work, it would have to be far larger in scale than any previous project. The military had already run into trouble building receiving dishes. In order for them to be large enough to collect the data they needed, the dishes were too heavy to be supported off the ground. Gordon countered this problem by finding a location where a grounded receiving dish would work. The site needed to be located near the equator to lend the best view of the planets. Gordon found a limestone pit in Arecibo that was then being used as a tobacco farm. The sinkhole was perfect to support the dish.

The largest radio telescope before the Arecibo radio telescope was built measured 150 feet across the receiving dish. The Navy had attempted to build a 600-foot radio telescope in the 1950s, but it collapsed due to its weight. Gordon's plans required a dish with a 1,000-foot diameter. Rather than requiring the dish to move the way earlier models had, Gordon's curved dish reflected radio waves back at a moveable, suspended focal point.

The entire process from concept to completion took only five years, with Gordon spearheading every aspect of the project. Many experts said that what Gordon envisioned could not be done. According to the *Los Angeles Times,* at the fortieth anniversary celebration of the telescope's dedication, Gordon said, "We were young enough that we didn't know we couldn't do it…. [W]e were in the right place at the right time and had the right idea and the right preparation. We had no rules or precedents." That lack of doubt in their own abilities led to a tool of tremendous usefulness to astronomy. And despite its planned obsolescence, the Arecibo radio telescope remained in use for decades past its ten-year life expectancy. It has gone through two upgrades, and has gained ten times its sensitivity every ten years of its operation.

Gordon taught at Cornell from 1953 through 1965, and he served as the director of the National Astronomy and Ionosphere Center for the National Science Foundation during the first two years of that organization's existence. The telescope continued to be operated by that organization as of 2011, in cooperation with Cornell. In 1965, Gordon took a position at Rice University in Houston, Texas. He served as dean of natural sciences, vice president, and provost. He was one of two faculty members at Rice to have earned the title of distinguished professor emeritus.

Gordon's wife of 61 years died in 2002. Gordon died of natural causes on February 16, 2010, shortly following hip surgery; he was 92. He is survived by his second wife, two children, four grandchildren, and three great-grandchildren. **Sources:** *Los Angeles Times*, February 18, 2010; *New York Times*, February 27, 2010; *Washington Post*, February 21, 2010, p. C6.

—*Alana Joli Abbott*

Bruce J. Graham

Born Bruce John Graham, December 1, 1925, in La Cumbre, Colombia; died of complications from Alzheimer's disease, March 6, 2010, in Hobe Sound, FL. Architect. Bruce Graham was the architect behind two Chicago landmarks: the John Hancock Center off Michigan Avenue, and the Sears Tower, which for 25 years stood as the world's tallest building. A partner for decades at the leading architectural firm of Skidmore, Owings and Merrill, Graham devised the novel X-braced tube shape of both iconic buildings, which were completed in 1970 and 1973, respectively. "With those two skyscrapers he singlehandedly put Chicago back on the map," Joseph Rosa, head of the Art Institute of Chicago's department of architecture and design, told William Grimes in the *New York Times* about Graham's legacy. "Without them, Chicago architecture would have been frozen in time. They expressed the optimism in Chicago and pointed toward what the future could be."

Graham was the son of an international banker of Canadian extraction, and was born in 1925 in La Cumbre, Colombia, where his father and mother, a native of Peru, were living at the time. They later settled in San Juan, Puerto Rico, and Graham grew up speaking Spanish as his first language and displayed an early interest in urban planning by mapping out San Juan's slums as a hobby. A gifted student, he won a scholarship to the University of Dayton at the age of 15 to study engineering.

During World War II, Graham served in the U.S. Navy, then went on to earn his architecture degree from the University of Pennsylvania in 1948. After moving to Chicago, he wrangled a meeting with the famed Mies van der Rohe, one of the pioneering names in twentieth century Modernist architecture. Van der Rohe helped Graham secure an apprenticeship at a top firm called Holabird, Root and Burgeeat. In 1951 Graham joined Skidmore, Owings and Merrill (SOM), a highly regarded Chicago firm that built some of the most iconic American skyscrapers of the century.

One of Graham's first major projects to see completion was the Inland Steel Building, which in 1957 became the first new office building in Chicago's Loop, or downtown business district, since the 1920s. In 1960 he became a design partner at SOM, and spent the next few years working on two more landmarks in the city: the Equitable Building and Chicago Civic Center, both of which went up in 1965.

Graham's mixed-use building that eventually became the John Hancock Center was erected over a forgotten and shabby part of the city called Streeterville, between Michigan Avenue and Lake Michigan. The project was plagued by problems during construction, and initially critics were dismissive of Graham's idea to build a skyscraper whose supports—X-braces and vertical columns—would be visible on the exterior, a plan he devised with SOM's chief structural engineer, Fazlur Khan. But the office space, condominiums, and observation deck and restaurant proved popular with businesses, residents, and tourists, and instantly became one of the city's most eye-catching landmarks.

Graham pursued a more daring goal with the Sears Tower, which was situated at 233 S. Wacker Drive. This was planned to serve as the headquarters of the Sears, Roebuck and Company retail giant, and Graham convinced his client to add 50 more floors onto the original 60, so that the Sears Tower would surpass the recently completed Twin Towers of the World Trade Center in New York City as the world's tallest building. "As Mr. Graham, a smoker, related the story of Sears Tower's origins, he was lunching with Khan and grabbed a handful of cigarettes, cupped some in his hands and placed a smaller group on top, demonstrating what came to be called the 'bundled tube' concept," wrote Blair Kamin in the *Chicago Tribune.*

The Sears Tower proved to be less a destination site than the Hancock Center, and Sears executives later relocated to suburban Chicago. Many years later, a British insurance firm acquired the property, and it was renamed the Willis Tower. It remained the world's tallest building until 1998, when the Petronas Twin Towers in Kuala Lumpur, Malaysia, were completed, but the Willis Tower remains the tallest skyscraper in the United States.

Graham designed smaller, yet equally prestigious Chicago landmarks during his long career at SOM. These include the 57-story pink granite tower known as One Magnificent Mile, which houses an entire shopping mall on its first floors, and the Quaker Tower, home of the Quaker Oats Company, both of which were added to the skyline in the 1980s. Graham was also active in urban planning efforts in the city. He played a key role in shaping the controversial Chicago 21 plan in the 1970s, which proposed a solution to stem the tide of middle-class residents leaving the city. His suggestions included the resurrection of Navy Pier as a pedestrian-recreation zone and a more integrated layout for the campus that houses the Adler Planetarium, the Shedd Aquarium, and the Field Museum, both of which were realized.

Graham retired from SOM in 1989, and went on to start his own firm, Graham & Graham, with his second wife Jane Abend, who had been the chief interiors designer at SOM. She died in 2004. Graham spent his last years in a waterfront home on stilts in Hobe Sound, Florida, where he died of complications from Alzheimer's disease on March 6, 2010; he was 84. Survivors include his son George and daughters Lisa and Mara, plus six grandchildren. "Graham was deeply critical of the negative impact of mid-20th-century planning, which devastated urban communities with the construction of freeways, the expansion of the suburbs and the emptying of city centres," wrote Ricky Burdett in the London *Guardian* about his former colleague's achievements. "Today, Chicago is seen as a U.S. metropolitan success story, with more people moving back into the centre, as Graham had envisaged decades ago." **Sources:** *Chicago Tribune,* March 8, 2010; *Guardian* (London), March 26, 2010, p. 46; *New York Times,* March 10, 2010.

—*Carol Brennan*

Kathryn Grayson

Born Zelma Kathryn Elisabeth Hedrick, February 9, 1922, in Winston-Salem, NC; died February 17, 2010, in Los Angeles, CA. Operatic film star. Kathryn Grayson made her name as a coloratura soprano in Hollywood musicals alongside actors like Gene Kelly, Frank Sinatra, and Howard Keel. While her vocal style is no longer in vogue, at the time she was lauded as a great singer. Often cast in films as an opera star, Grayson followed her two decades in Hollywood with a career in opera. She performed through the 1990s, touring as a one-woman show or in the company of her former co-star Van Johnson.

Hired by MGM, Grayson produced 20 films for the company from 1941 through 1956. Best known for *Show Boat, Anchors Aweigh,* and *Kiss Me, Kate,* Grayson frequently starred alongside Keel or tenor Mario Lanza. She was paired twice with Sinatra and Kelly, and she also worked with Gordon MacRae and Mickey Rooney. Grayson also performed on television and was nominated for an Emmy Award in 1956.

Grayson was born Zelma Kathryn Elisabeth Hedrick, the daughter of a building contractor and real estate agent. The family moved from North Carolina to St. Louis when Grayson was a child. She studied voice from an early age—she was discovered singing to an empty opera house when she was 12—and hoped to become a professional opera singer. When she was an early teen, her family moved to California, where she had more opportunities to pursue her career. By the time she was 15, she was signed to RCA Victor Records' classical imprint, Red Seal. MGM Studios was impressed with her sound and, hoping to bring back the operettas that had been popular in the 1930s, they recruited her into the studio.

Like other MGM recruits, including Lana Turner and Donna Reed, Grayson began her career with an audition to be Rooney's love interest in one of his Andy Hardy films. She made her debut as the titular secretary in *Andy Hardy's Private Secretary* in 1941. Grayson performed two classical pieces, including an aria, onscreen in the film.

Grayson soon became a regular player in MGM's musicals. Following a few minor parts, including an Abbott and Costello musical and a revue in which she played Kelly's girlfriend, Grayson was cast in *Anchors Aweigh.* The role, in which she played a Hollywood hopeful who becomes the love interest for two sailors, played by Kelly and Sinatra, marked her as a star. She played the daughter of a steam boat captain who falls in love with a gambler in *Show Boat* in 1951, and as an actress who resembles her Shakespearean counterpart in *Kiss Me, Kate,* which retells the story of *The Taming of the Shrew* as a modern musical. Grayson later performed in both *Show Boat* and *Kiss Me, Kate* on stage.

She starred opposite Lanza in *That Midnight Kiss* and *The Toast of New Orleans* in 1949 and 1950. Grayson praised Lanza as a performer, but complained of his vulgar language and his behavior on set. In fact, it was in part due to problems with Lanza that Grayson left her Hollywood career. The tenor did not show up to film Paramount's *The Vagabond King*; because his stand-in was not an English speaker, Grayson had to also speak Lanza's lines. The actor dubbed his voice over hers after the filming. "It never should have been made," Grayson was quoted as having said in the *Washington Post.* Her *Los Angeles Times* obituary quoted her from a *Toronto Star* interview as explaining, "I didn't like it. So I called it a day: no more movies."

After playing roles as opera stars, including her portrayal of Grace Moore in the biographical film *This Is Love* in 1953, moving on to stage performances suited Grayson well. She made her opera debut in 1960, performing in *Madame Butterfly.* In 1962, she took over Julie Andrews' role of Guenevere in *Camelot* on Broadway. She also performed in *Naughty Marietta, The Merry Widow,* and *Rosalinda,* as well as nightclubs and concerts.

Beginning in the 1950s, Grayson took on television roles. She performed in *Playhouse 90* and *General Electric Theater,* earning an Emmy nomination for a dramatic performance in the latter. Her last appearance on screen was in 1989 on the television program *Murder, She Wrote,* in which she played one of the residents of the show's small-town setting.

Grayson performed throughout the 1980s and 1990s, first touring in a one-woman show, and later touring with Johnson. As she looked back on her career, she criticized the Hollywood studios for trying to make cheaper movies, which led to the decline of Hollywood musicals.

Grayson died at her home in Los Angeles, California, on February 19, 2010; she was 88. Twice married and divorced, Grayson is survived by her daughter from her second marriage, Patricia Towers. **Sources:** *Los Angeles Times,* February 19, 2010; *New York Times,* February 19, 2010; *Sunday Times* (London, England), February 21, 2010; *Washington Post,* February 19, 2010, p. B06.

—*Alana Joli Abbott*

Moshe Greenberg

Born July 10, 1928, in Philadelphia, PA; died May 15, 2010, in Jerusalem, Israel. Biblical scholar. A highly influential Jewish biblical scholar, Moshe Greenberg was known for works that drew connections between the works of ancient Jewish sages and more modern religious scholarship. He is best known for his two-volume commentary on the Book of Ezekiel, and his scholarship drew a connection between the taboo against murder in Abrahamic religions and the belief that humans are closely connected to God. In 1994, with a colleague, Greenberg won the first Israel Prize for Bible research; the award is the highest civilian honor given out by the nation of Israel.

Greenberg taught Bible and Jewish studies both in the United States, at the University of Pennsylvania, and in Israel at the Hebrew University of Jerusalem. His impact on the field of religious studies in the United States broke through a tradition of having biblical study dominated by Christian scholars. Though American by birth, he immigrated to Israel, and his scholarship sometimes verged on political in the context of his new nation. Some scholars supported the idea that the Book of Joshua offered Israel justification in using some types of normally prohibited violence in defense of the nation; Greenberg countered those ideas.

Born in Philadelphia in 1928, Greenberg was the son of a rabbi, Simon Greenberg, who became the vice chancellor of the Jewish Theological Seminary of America in New York. The younger Greenberg attended the University of Pennsylvania, from which he earned his doctorate. He was ordained a Conservative rabbi in 1954, but he never led a congregation.

The University of Pennsylvania broke convention after Greenberg earned his doctorate by hiring him to teach biblical studies, as well as Hebrew and Semitic languages and literature. In the 1950s, it was rare for a Jew to be hired into a biblical studies department; Professor Jonathan D. Sarna of Brandeis University explained in the *New York Times,* "The concept was that Jews could not be objective about teaching the Bible." Instead, Jewish scholars focused on the Talmud, a collection of rabbinic writings on Jewish law and doctrine. "The appointment of Greenberg to teach Bible at a secular university was a milestone," Sarna said.

Unlike other Jewish scholars at the time, Greenberg was willing to look at the Bible with the historical-critical approach, which supports the idea that many of the books of the Bible, including the first five books, were written by multiple authors. This concept flies in the face of Jewish dogma, which states that the first five books—called the Torah—were given, whole, to Moses. Greenberg investigated not only at the idea of multiple authorship, but also how the stylistic components came together to form the whole. He taught his students to examine how the compilers put the books together, and looked at how multiple writers combined their ideas, creating a unified theme.

Greenberg taught in Philadelphia from 1954 through the late 1960s. In 1970, he immigrated with his family to Israel, where he taught Bible and Jewish studies at the Hebrew University of Jerusalem for 26 years. In part, the move was brought about because he was one of the few Jewish biblical scholars in the United States. Given the focus by other Jewish scholars on the Talmud, Greenberg sought to widen the scholarship of the Bible by other Jewish scholars, something he felt he could best accomplish in Israel.

Over the course of his career, Greenberg wrote ten books and more than 200 articles. In addition to his historical-critical scholarship, Greenberg was an expert in Assyriology, which is the study of the language, archaeology, and history of ancient Mesopotamia. Using that expertise in conjunction with Hebrew studies, Greenberg was able to show distinctions between the ancient Israelites and their contemporaries in the region.

Greenberg's 1983 work, *Biblical Prose Prayer*, is a deep look into the way that people pray in the Bible. Much of the prayer is done by common people, or people without priestly training. That spontaneous prayer is so frequently present in the Bible shows how those early people expressed not only their humility, but their dependence on God for strength. It also shows that no priests were necessary for them to direct their prayers, an egalitarian idea reflected in modern Jewish culture and synagogues, in that Jews do not need an intermediary—like a priest—to deliver their prayers to God, or to help them repent of wrongdoing.

Greenberg's *Ezekiel*, a two-volume commentary on the biblical book of the same name, is considered by many to be a definitive work. He also wrote commentary, drawing on medieval Hebrew scholarship, on the Torah, particularly on the Book of Exodus.

Greenberg died on May 15, 2010, at his home in Jerusalem. He is survived by his wife of 61 years, Evelyn Gelber; their sons Joel, Rafi, and Ethan; and nine grandchildren. **Sources:** *Los Angeles Times*, May 21, 2010; *New York Times*, May 20, 2010; *Washington Post*, May 18, 2010, p. B5.

—*Alana Joli Abbott*

Doris Haddock

Born Ethel Doris Rollins, January 24, 1910, in Laconia, NH; died of emphysema, March 9, 2010, in Dublin, NH. Activist. The saying that retirement is when your life really begins certainly describes the life of Doris "Granny D" Haddock. At the age of 88, she began a cross-country trek, skiing when snow made walking impossible, to bring attention to campaign finance reform. When she was 94 she became the oldest non-incumbent candidate supported by a major party to run for a contested seat in the U.S. Senate.

Haddock is also the author of two books about her politics and her life, the second of which was published after her death in 2010. The *Washington Post* quoted the introduction to her memoirs, *My Bohemian Century*, in which Haddock wrote, "You have to keep the young adventurer inside your heart alive long enough for it to someday re-emerge. It may take some coaxing and some courage, but that person is in you always—never growing old."

Born Ethel Doris Rollins, Haddock later dropped her first name and officially adopted the middle name "Granny D" after her long campaign walk. Haddock attended Emerson College, where she studied acting. Never one to blindly follow rules, Haddock secretly married Amherst student James Haddock while she was still at Emerson. The secret got out, however, and Haddock was expelled, as married women could not attend college.

After moving to Manchester, New Hampshire, Haddock worked at a shoe factory for 20 years while her husband worked as an electrical engineer. Haddock's first political activity took place in 1960 when, alongside her husband, she protested the proposed testing of hydrogen bombs in Alaska. The campaign was successful, and was later given credit for saving Point Hope's Inuit village.

In 1972, the Haddocks retired to Dublin, New Hampshire. Haddock ran for the local planning board and was elected. Her husband suffered from Alzheimer's disease; he died in 1992. It was after his death that Haddock became more politically active, taking part in an exercise and politics discussion group called the Tuesday Morning Academy. She became interested in campaign finance reform when, in 1995, a bill sponsored by Senators John McCain and Russ Feingold that would have regulated unlimited financial contributions failed. Wanting to do something to bring public attention to the issue, in 1998 Haddock came up with the idea, along with the Academy members, of walking across the country. She trained by walking around Dublin for the rest of the year and, on New Year's Day 1999, she began her famous walk.

Haddock set out from Pasadena, California, less than a month before her 89th birthday. Awareness of her walk built slowly, but soon the media was following her. Her route, which took her through the desert, through the Appalachian mountains, and through a snow-covered Maryland, covered 3,200 miles. Haddock's pace was set at ten miles per day. Due to weather and conditions, Haddock suffered from dehydration and pneumonia over the course of her walk, and was hospitalized in Arizona. Later, she was nearly delayed from reaching her end goal by the snow in Maryland, so she skied 100 miles. She carried a banner that read "Granny D for Campaign Finance Reform," met with reporters, and posed in photos with politicians who also supported the issue. "It just infuriates me!" she explained to a *New York Times* reporter. "I feel we are losing our democracy. The corporations are taking over and deciding who gets elected."

Haddock's walk ended 14 months after it began, and she was welcomed in Washington, D.C., by dozens of members of Congress who walked alongside her from Arlington Cemetery to the Capitol. Politicians mentioned her as an inspiration: Al Gore invoked her name when he talked about campaign finance reform during his presidential bid. The McCain-Feingold Act was finally passed in 2002. But Haddock's walk was only the beginning of her activism. In fact, weeks after the walk was completed, she returned to Washington, D.C., to participate in a protest inside the Capitol Rotunda. She was arrested for illegal demonstration, but the crowds of bystanders applauded her efforts by cheering "Go, Granny, go," according to the *New York Times.*

In October of 2003, Haddock traveled around the country again—this time by vehicle rather than on foot—to promote voter-registration among American working women. The trip ended just in time for Haddock to make a bid for a Senate race. The Democratic candidate running against Senator Judd

Gregg, the incumbent Republican, had bowed out when his campaign manager was accused of financial fraud. Haddock took over the Democratic spot on the ticket and, without accepting private campaign contributions, she won 34 percent of the vote.

Though her run for office was unsuccessful, Haddock continued to press for finance reform, issuing statements about decisions, such as the Supreme Court ruling that the government could not ban corporations from spending money politically, right up into her hundredth year. Haddock died of emphysema on March 10, 2010, at her home in Dublin, New Hampshire. **Sources:** *Los Angeles Times,* March 11, 2010; *New York Times,* March 11, 2010; *Times* (London), March 15, 2010; *Washington Post,* March 13, 2010, p. B6.

—*Alana Joli Abbott*

Alexander Haig

Born December 2, 1924, in Bala Cynwyd, PA; died of a staphylococcal infection, February 20, 2010, in Baltimore, MD. General and politician. Retired Army General Alexander Haig was best known by the public for his involvement in convincing U.S. President Richard Nixon to resign from office rather than be impeached. Haig was also noted for his proclamation that he was in control of the White House on the day that President Ronald Reagan was shot, despite four others being in the line of succession ahead of him. Considered ambitious and highly competent, both as a leader and as a diplomat, Haig had a military and civilian career full of controversy.

Haig was one of the rare career military men who became a politician. Throughout his career, he moved back and forth between serving in the field and working in an administrative position. He was attached to a number of high-profile people, including Henry Kissinger, General Douglas MacArthur, and Robert McNamara. He was also surrounded by controversy throughout his career.

Born Alexander Meigs Haig, Jr., in Bala Cynwyd, Pennsylvania, in 1924, Haig was the second child of three. His father died when Haig was only ten years old, and Haig assumed a leadership responsibility for his family. Raised in the Roman Catholic Church, Haig first attended the University of Notre Dame for college. He was appointed to West Point Academy, graduating in 1947, and ranked 214 in his class of 310 students. Though Haig's grades were not the best, his abilities to think subtly and evade or out-maneuver bureaucracy were compared to Kissinger's.

Haig was stationed in Japan as a junior aide on MacArthur's staff. There he met Patricia Fox, whose father was a general on MacArthur's staff, and whom he married in 1950. Then a lieutenant, Haig served under Major General Edward M. Almond in the Korean War. Haig was present for the Battle of Inchon, for which he was awarded two Silver Stars and a Bronze Star. After the Korean War ended in 1953, Haig secured administrative posts domesti-cally, and he pursued a master's degree at George-town University.

As the Vietnam War loomed on the horizon, Haig was promoted to the military assistant to Army Sec-retary Cyrus Vance; later, he became the deputy to Joseph Califano, special assistant to McNamara, who was the Defense Secretary. During the war, Haig served overseas as the head of the 1st Infantry Division battalion. In 1967, when Haig was flying in a helicopter to join his battalion, who were pinned by the Viet Cong, his helicopter was shot down. Alongside his troops, he held back the enemy, often with odds that were three to one against the Ameri-can soldiers. In addition to receiving the Purple Heart medal due to injuries received from the shrap-nel of an exploding grenade, Haig was awarded the Distinguished Service Cross.

Haig became a military assistant for the National Security Council under Kissinger. He took on the role of a liaison between the Defense Department and the State Department in the White House, pre-paring daily reports for Nixon. Beginning in his po-sition as a colonel, Haig was elevated to brigadier general after only nine months of his work in the White House. From 1969 through 1971, Haig helped in wiretapping certain phones for reporters and gov-ernment officials. He also toured Southeast Asia sev-eral times between 1970 and 1973, convinced that the Vietnam War was not being fought correctly. In 1972 Haig helped pave the way for Nixon to appear in communist China. He attended the peace nego-tiations that took place in Paris in 1973. Already during this period, Haig's ambitions were showing: Haig reported Kissinger's plans to Nixon, using transcripts of Kissinger's own private calls as evidence.

Nixon wanted to keep Haig working closely with the White House, so he promoted Haig to four-star general. The president also gave Haig the position of the Army's vice chief of staff, skipping Haig over 240 other generals who had greater seniority. De-spite the promotion, Haig's tenure in the position didn't last. Months after the position was awarded, Nixon brought Haig into the civilian government as White House chief of staff. Accepting the position meant retiring from the military. But the position also meant a great deal of political power and influ-ence, which Haig utilized to help convince Nixon that he needed to resign rather than face the possi-bility of impeachment. As other staffers were being tried or asked to step down, Haig paved the way for a smooth transition in the White House. He con-tinued on for a few weeks under President Gerald Ford before asking to be recalled into the military. Ford sent Haig to Europe to become the Supreme Allied Commander Europe (SACEUR), a position in which he was considered extremely effective.

Although he toyed with the idea of running for president in 1980, he instead became the Secretary of State under Reagan. His appointment was con-tested, particularly given his close ties to Nixon, but he was appointed to the position. Unfortunately, it was never a good fit. Though he shared many stances on issues with Reagan, they often disagreed on how to handle problems. They also disagreed on how much power Haig should wield, and he tended to overstep his responsibilities. This was demon-strated to the general public after an assassination attempt on Reagan's life. With Vice President George H. W. Bush on his way back from Texas dur-ing the incident, Haig claimed the mantle of respon-sibility for the government. However, there were several others in the appropriate succession. Even-tually, his disagreements with Reagan led to the president requesting that Haig resign from his position.

In 1988, Haig made a run for the Republican nomi-nation for president, but his campaign never had enough support. He decided against campaigning in Iowa, where he finished poorly in the caucuses, and he dropped out of the running before the pri-mary in New Hampshire. He later endorsed candi-date Bob Dole. Leaving behind a career in politics, Haig ran a civilian company, Worldwide Associates, and occasionally appeared as an analyst on Fox News.

In 2010, Haig developed a staphylococcal infection and went to the hospital. He died on February 20, 2010; he was 85. He is survived by his wife, three children, and eight grandchildren. **Sources:** *Los An-geles Times*, February 21, 2010; *New York Times*, Feb-ruary 20, 2010; *Times* (London), February 22, 2010; *Washington Post*, February 21, 2010, p. A1.

—*Alana Joli Abbott*

Corey Haim

Born December 23, 1971, in Toronto, Ontario, Canada; died of pneumonia and related conditions, March 10, 2010, in Burbank, CA. Actor. Teen idol Corey Haim, who was most famous for his films in the late 1980s, struggled with drug problems through most of his career. The actor described himself as a "chronic relapse," according to sources including the London *Times,* and when the actor died at the age of 38 in March 2010, there was much speculation that he had once again fallen off the wagon.

Haim once described himself as idolizing James Dean, hoping that he would be remembered alongside that star who also died too early; however, Dean made only three movies and Haim made nearly 40. Haim was primarily associated not with the early films for which critics praised his acting ability, but for the downward spiral that enveloped his life. Several comeback attempts started off well later in his career, but friends, including frequent co-star Corey Feldman, recognized that Haim had an ongoing problem. As Feldman told *People* in 2008, distancing himself from Haim, "I am not going to watch him destroy himself." Despite this public statement, the two did remain friends until Haim's death.

Haim came to acting as a career differently from most child actors; his parents encouraged him to take acting classes to overcome his shyness. By the age of ten, the Canadian-born actor was starring in commercials. As a young teen, he had his first film role in the romantic comedy *Murphy's Romance,* starring Sally Field. Haim played the title character, an awkward teen, in *Lucas,* alongside Charlie Sheen and Kerri Green.

But it was with the 1987 film *The Lost Boys,* directed by Joel Schumacher, that Haim hit his highest level of fame. The vampire film also starred Corey Feldman, and the pair became idols together, featuring frequently in pin ups for teen lockers. Known as the Two Coreys, the pair worked together on other films, including *License to Drive* and *Dream a Little Dream.* Haim also appeared in films such as *Silver Bullet, Firstborn,* and *Watchers,* and was a regular on the television sitcom *Roomies.* Critics praised his acting ability, and his path toward success seemed set.

While his career was reaching its highest points of fame, however, Haim was becoming entrenched in the Los Angeles drug scene. "I lived in L.A. in the '80s, which was not the best place to be," he once told the *Los Angeles Times.* "I did cocaine for about a year and a half, then it led to crack." He and other young stars, too young to legally be allowed into bars, were often waved in and told not to drink—while being handed bottles of hard liquor. Haim made his first trip to rehab in 1989, but after he was released, he became addicted to prescription drugs, particularly Valium. At one point, he told the *Los Angeles Times,* he was taking 85 pills of Valium per day, and complementing that with other drugs besides.

By the 1990s, drugs had caused Haim's career and reputation to be so damaged that he was unable to find work. He appeared in straight-to-video movies, but did little that helped him have a come-back. It wasn't until 2006, when Haim collaborated with Feldman and his wife on an A&E reality show, that things began to look hopeful. The series, called *The Two Coreys,* featured Haim as a semi-permanent house guest of the Feldmans. Unscripted, the show offered several heartbreaking moments, including Haim's revelation that he had been raped by an older man when he was a teenager, and the relapsed Haim finding out that he was not being asked to star alongside Feldman in a sequel to their 1987 hit *The Lost Boys.* But while the show revealed Haim trying to pull his life back together, it also showed the strain Haim's relapsing had on Feldman, who himself had once been addicted to drugs, but got clean. Feldman declined to renew the show after its second season, unable to watch Haim suffer when Haim was unwilling to seek help.

Despite Feldman's frustrations and worries, Haim was serious about wanting to make a comeback. In 2008, he took out an ad in *Variety,* proclaiming himself clean and ready to get back to work. He worked on several independent films and was planning to direct two small films that were in pre-production at the time of his death. Due to Haim's continued relationship with prescription drugs, the officer at the scene told reporters it looked as though Haim had overdosed. His agent did not believe that Haim had been abusing again, however; several friends also told the press that they believed Haim had been pulling his life back together.

Though an investigation found that Haim was involved—possibly without his knowledge—in a prescription drug ring, and that false prescriptions for OxyContin had been filled out for him, the coroner eventually determined that drugs were not the cause of Haim's death. Haim, who had told his mother he had flu symptoms and was taking over-the-counter medication to combat the illness, died of a combination of pneumonia, damage to his lungs, and a genetic heart problem.

Haim, who had been living with his mother and supporting her in her struggle with breast cancer, collapsed in front of her in their apartment on March 10, 2010. He was 38 years old. **Sources:** *Chicago Tribune,* March 11, 2010; *Entertainment Weekly,* http://www.ew.com/ew/article/0,,20354564.tif,00. html (June 5, 2011); *Los Angeles Times,* March 10, 2010; *New York Times,* March 11, 2010; *People,* March 29, 2010, pp. 56-67; *People,* http://www.people. com/people/article/0,,20366327.tif,00.html (June 5, 2011); *Times* (London), March 10, 2010; *Washington Post,* March 11, 2010, p. B6.

—*Alana Joli Abbott*

Dorothy Height

Born March 24, 1912, in Richmond, VA; died April 20, 2010, in Washington, D.C. Activist. Though most American students are familiar with the name of civil rights activist Rosa Parks, who refused to give up her bus seat for a white passenger, fewer know the name of Dorothy Height. Considered something of an unsung hero of the civil rights movement, Height was one of the earliest and longest-lasting leaders in the fight for equality. Height had been an activist since the New Deal era; she served as the leader of the National Council of Negro Women for four decades and, at the time of her death in 2010, she was the president emerita of that group.

Height's career in activism lasted for nearly 80 years. She was active in protests against lynching in the 1930s, and she advised U.S. presidents from Dwight Eisenhower to Bill Clinton. President Barack Obama, the first African-American president of the United States, declared her the "godmother of the civil rights movement and a hero to so many Americans," according to the *New York Times.* According to the London *Times,* the president also said that Height had witnessed "every march and milestone along the way…. Even in the final weeks of her life … Dr. Height continued her fight to make our nation a more open and inclusive place for people of every race, gender, background, and faith." Height had witnessed Obama's oath of office, taken on January 20, 2009, from a place of honor on the dias.

Height was born in 1912, the daughter of a building contractor and a nurse. Both of her parents had been previously widowed, and Height was the youngest of several siblings and half-siblings. As a child, she had severe asthma, and she was not expected to live to adulthood. When Height was four, the fam-

ily moved from Richmond, Virginia, to Rankin, Pennsylvania, where Height's father was better able to grow his business. Despite the prosperity of Height's father's business in the North, her mother was unable to find work as a nurse because hospitals felt that white patients would not want to be cared for by a black nurse. Height also felt prejudice leveled against her by her peers; she went to an integrated school, but when she was eleven, her best friend, who was white, said they could no longer be friends. Height did not let this rejection stop her from making friends; when she attended her junior prom, she went with a white boy as her date.

The early personal rejection was followed by early academic rejection as well. During high school, Height entered a speech contest on the topic of the Constitution of the United States. Height was the only black student to advance to the national finals, and she was awarded first place, and a scholarship, by the all-white jury. But although she was accepted at Barnard, when she arrived, she was told she would not be admitted, as the college had already met their quota of African-American students— two—for the year. Heartbroken but unwilling to give up, Height took her Barnard acceptance letter to New York University, where she was quickly admitted; she earned both her bachelor's and master's degrees from that university.

Height began her career as a caseworker with the New York City Welfare Department. She worked for the Harlem YWCA as executive director in the late 1930s. In that position, she alerted the public to the way African-American women were hired as domestic day laborers, picked up from the street corners of Brooklyn and the Bronx that were referred to by locals as "slave markets," according to the *New York Times.* These women were paid 15 cents per hour by the suburban housewives who hired them. The media attention that Height gathered on the topic forced the market underground for a time. Height was promoted to a national leadership position at the Y in 1946, from which she oversaw the project of desegregating Y facilities. She also founded the Center for Racial Justice at the Y, and led that initiative from 1965 through 1977.

Height became a member of the National Council of Negro Women in the late 1930s and worked with Mary McLeod Bethune, who became Height's mentor. Despite the growing leadership she assumed in the National Council of Negro Women, Height often found herself pushed out of the spotlight as a women's rights activist due to her race, and as an activist for equality of African Americans due to her gender. She was often the only woman included in strategy meetings with Dr. Martin Luther King, Jr., and other members of the "Big Six," as they are called by historians. But while Height did not take the spotlight, she was there; she was instrumental in organizing the March on Washington in which King delivered his "I Have a Dream" speech. She helped to found the National Women's Political Caucus. She advised presidents on civil rights issues. Her memoir, *Open Wide the Freedom Gates,* serves as an overview not only of Height's own life, but of the civil rights movement in which she was constantly involved.

In 1994, Height was awarded the Presidential Medal of Freedom by President Bill Clinton. She was also a recipient of the Congressional Gold Medal, awarded by President George W. Bush in 2004. That same year, Height was belatedly named an honorary graduate of Barnard College, which had turned her away 75 years before. She also received more than 30 honorary doctorates. Height, who never married, died on April 20, 2010, at the age of 98. **Sources:** *Los Angeles Times,* April 20, 2010; *New York Times,* April 20, 2010; *Times* (London), April 22, 2010, p. 64;

—Alana Joli Abbott

Dennis Hopper

Born May 17, 1936, in Dodge City, KS; died of complications from metastasized prostate cancer, May 29, 2010, in Venice, CA. Actor. In the move that defined his early career, Hollywood rebel Dennis Hopper co-wrote, directed, and starred in the unexpected 1969 hit *Easy Rider,* a low-budget film based on the idea of replacing the horses in a Western with motorcycles and delving deeply into 1960s counterculture. Throughout the 1960s and 1970s, Hopper was almost as well known for his wild, drug-related antics as for his acting career; his work on *Easy Rider* and other films, however, helped change the way that Hollywood made films.

From the mid-1980s through 2010, after getting sober and going straight, Hopper experienced a resurgence in his career, filming 25 films between 2000 and 2010 alone. Reportedly, he would not turn down a role, and he played a number of characters in film and television whose roles were defined by prior drug use.

Hopper, the son of a railroad postal worker, was born in Kansas in 1936. His family moved to San Diego when he was a child, and Hopper apprenticed at the La Jolla Playhouse. Film actress Dorothy McGuire encouraged him to make his name in Hollywood, and after graduating high school in 1954, he made the move, acting in his first television role on the show *Medic* in 1955.

Hopper's first movie role was in the 1955 James Dean film *Rebel without a Cause,* and Hopper was enamored of Dean's style. He asked the other actor for advice, and Dean recommended that he be more intuitive in his acting, and that he never deliver a line the same way twice. While Hopper had additional early successes, including a second film with Dean in which Hopper played the son of Elizabeth Taylor and Rock Hudson in *Giant,* he ran into trouble in the late 1950s. A quarrel with Henry Hathaway, a well-known and well-established Hollywood director, over how to deliver a line in *From Hell to Texas,* led to Hathaway declaring Hopper would never work in Hollywood again. The blacklisting largely succeeded for years; Hopper moved to New York and found work on stage and in television, but until he married his first wife, Brooke Hayward, a member of the Hollywood elite, he was denied regular film roles, winning only small parts in films like *Cool Hand Luke* and *Hang 'Em High.*

Hayward had been childhood friends with actor Peter Fonda, and Hopper and Fonda developed a friendship also. Together, the pair and Fonda's writer friend Terry Southern, pitched the idea for a film about a pair of motorcycle-riding drug dealers seeking for truth as they journey from Mexico to New Orleans. A large studio would not take a risk on the venture, so the trio found independent financers, penned the script themselves, and Fonda and Hopper starred in the film, with Hopper directing. The result was *Easy Rider,* which became the touchstone of a generation, and proved to Hollywood that the same films they had been making were no longer in touch with a modern audience. *Easy Rider* won the 1969 Cannes Film Festival prize for best first film (though it had only one competitor) and proved to Hollywood that there was a market for showing counterculture in films. It also opened doors for young directors like Stephen Spielburg, George Lucas, and Francis Ford Coppola.

The film's success drove Hopper into a spiral of drug abuse and paranoia. Believing that eccentricity was simply a part of fame, Hopper let the fame go to his head, and he heavily indulged in alcohol and illegal drugs, at one point hiring security guards to keep watch on the roof of his New Mexico home. His substance abuse made him unreliable to work with, and he soon found himself again at odds with Hollywood, with fewer roles being offered. Notable exceptions during this time include *Apocalypse Now,* in which he played a drug-addled photojournalist during the Vietnam War.

In 1984, after a violent hallucination, Hopper spent time in the psychiatric ward of a Los Angeles hospital. It was this event that turned his life around; he abandoned drug culture and dove into his work. From the mid-1980s to 2010, Hopper performed in scores of movies and television programs, including *Hoosiers,* for which he earned an Academy Award nomination; *Blue Velvet,* in which he played a sadistic killer; *Colors,* which he also directed; and Keanu Reeves action film *Speed,* where Hopper once again played the villain. Because his characters were frequently off-beat, intense, and often off-putting, film critic Roger Ebert once called him the "most dependable and certainly the creepiest villain in the movies," according to the *Washington Post.* He earned an Emmy nomination for his performance in the television movie *Paris Trout,* worked in commercials, and performed in television series.

Hopper was diagnosed with prostate cancer in 2000, but his struggle with the disease was not revealed until October of 2009 while Hopper was starring in the Showtime television program *Crash.* His health was deteriorating, although he was able to attend the ceremony at which his star on the Hollywood Walk of Fame was unveiled in March of 2010. Hopper filed to divorce his wife of 14 years, Victoria Duffy, during his struggle with cancer; he died of complications from the disease on May 29, 2010. He is survived by daughters from his first, third, and fifth marriages and a son from his fourth marriage. He appeared in more than 115 films over the course of his career. **Sources:** *Los Angeles Times,* May 30, 2010; *New York Times,* May 30, 2010; *People,* June 14, 2010, pp. 76-78; *Washington Post,* May 30, 2010, p. C6.

—*Alana Joli Abbott*

Albert Montgomery Kligman

Born Albert Montgomery Kligman, March 17, 1916, in Philadelphia, PA; died of a heart attack, February 9, 2010, in Philadelphia. Dermatologist. Dr. Albert M. Kligman made several important discoveries in dermatological science during his long career with the University of Pennsylvania. His pioneering research led to a patent for Retin-A, an anti-acne treatment that was later found to reverse signs of the aging process. Kligman's achievements were, unfortunately, also usually mentioned along with a number of controlled scientific trials he conducted at a Philadelphia jail from 1951 to 1974. The resulting investigation led to tough new federal statutes that restricted medical studies using prison inmates.

Kligman was born in 1916 in Philadelphia into a Jewish immigrant family. He had little contact with nature until he began taking part in field trips and campground activities with his Boy Scout troop, and became fascinated by plants and botanical science. He earned his undergraduate degree in botany from Pennsylvania State University in 1939, and pursued a doctorate in the subject at the University of Pennsylvania. At one point, he was recruited for a secret mission to South America during World War II, when U.S. military officials sought to find plants with antimalarial properties to reduce casualties in the Pacific theater. But Kligman was removed from the project when it was discovered he had once joined the Communist Party.

At the time, Kligman was married to Beatrice Troyan, who was in medical school. Unsure of his future career direction, he decided to join her, and graduated with his M.D. from the University of Pennsylvania in 1947. An expert in fungi, he had already authored a book on mushrooms, and decided to make dermatology his specialty, because certain skin conditions like athlete's foot and ringworm were caused by fungus pathogens. After graduating he joined the dermatology faculty at the University of Pennsylvania, where his research led to an invitation by officials at Holmesburg Prison in Philadelphia to help solve recurring outbreaks of athlete's foot. The controlled, captive audience of a prison population was, to Kligman, an unparalleled scientific research opportunity. "All I saw before me were acres of skin," he told a journalist in 1966, according to the *Los Angeles Times.* "It was like a farmer seeing a fertile field for the first time."

Kligman soon set up a cottage industry at Holmesburg, conducting scores of product trials for federal agencies and pharmaceutical companies. Generously compensated inmates tested skin ointments, deodorants, and shampoos, but there were also experiments with psychoactive drugs and radioactive materials. In the most controversial trial, inmates were exposed to dioxin, an extremely toxic compound found in the defoliant Agent Orange, which was used by the U.S. military during the Vietnam War. The Vietnamese who came in contact with Agent Orange suffered horrific birth defects, and even soldiers who took part in aerial spraying flights reported that their wives suffered an unusually high number of miscarriages once they returned home. In the wake of these and other scandals at Holmesburg—the warden was slain in a particularly well-organized 1973 uprising—Kligman's experiments ended, and the resulting Congressional investigation led to strict new federal laws enacted 1978 that curtailed medical research in prison.

Kligman's remark to the journalist back in 1966 was later used by Allen M. Hornblum for the title of his 1998 exposé, *Acres of Skin: Human Experiments at Holmesburg Prison—A True Story of Abuse and Exploitation in the Name of Medical Science.* The book led to a spate of lawsuits against Kligman and prison officials by former inmates, but Kligman defended the trials, noting that both a breakthrough treatment for poison ivy and Retin-A had been developed there.

Retin-A remains Kligman's most enduring contribution to his field. This Vitamin A derivative, tretinoin, had been initially isolated by European scientists, but as a topical agent it proved a major skin irritant. Kligman tinkered with various formulations and developed a less irritating recipe that was also an effective anti-acne treatment. The U.S. Food & Drug Administration patent for Retin-A was granted in 1967 to Kligman and the University of Pennsylvania, and they licensed it to Johnson & Johnson, which sold it as a prescription treatment. Kligman initially dismissed reports that some older acne sufferers who used Retin-A claimed it gave them smoother, younger-looking skin, but he conducted his own study, as did other researchers, and Retin-A became the first known agent proven to reverse some of the effects of the aging process. Kligman and the University of Pennsylvania repatented it in 1986, and it went on to earn millions more as a prescription-only treatment sold under the brand name Renova.

Kligman was an expert in sun-related skin damage. He devised the term "photo-aging" to describe the how exposure to ultraviolet rays prematurely ages skin, and also came up with the word "cosmeceutical" to refer to drugs that could have dramatic, but purely cosmetic, effects. He donated many of his royalties to the University of Pennsylvania's medical school and its department of dermatology, which helped make the school a research leader in the field.

Kligman died on February 9, 2010, at Pennsylvania Hospital in Philadelphia, at the age of 93. His third wife, Lorraine, survives him, as do three children, Gail, Michael, and Douglas, along with two stepchildren and six grandchildren. He defended the Holmesburg experiments decades after they ended.

"I've always offered that, if anyone was ever injured in any way, come to us and we'll take care of you," he told one news outlet in 2003, according to the *Los Angeles Times*. "We're sorry if we did anything like that. And you know what? Not one person has ever come." **Sources:** *Los Angeles Times*, February 24, 2010; *New York Times*, February 22, 2010; *Times* (London), February 23, 2010; *Washington Post*, February 22, 2010, p. B4.

—*Carol Brennan*

Juanita M. Kreps

Born Blair Juanita Morris, January 11, 1921, in Lynch, KY; died of complications of Alzheimer's disease, July 5, 2010, in Durham, NC. Economist and former commerce secretary of the United States. Though she did not consider herself a women's liberationist, Juanita M. Kreps was the first woman in many of the positions she held as an economist throughout her career. She served under U.S. President Jimmy Carter as the first female commerce secretary of the United States. Only three other women had previously served in the cabinet. Despite her soft-spoken nature, she was noted for standing firm by her opinion, and for being willing to speak her mind.

In her position as commerce secretary, Kreps halted moves to dismantle the Commerce department and reorganized the department to strengthen its role in both foreign trade and the economic development of urban areas. Because of her previous roles as a business director for major corporations, and through her positions on policy in favor of business, she was well thought of by the business community. In turn, this allowed her to influence businesses to think from a more civic perspective.

Born in 1921 in the Appalachian Mountain region of Kentucky, Kreps was the daughter of Elmer M. Morris, a coal-mine operator, and Larcenia Blair Morris. Her parents divorced when she was very young, and her mother raised her as a single parent. Kreps attended a Presbyterian boarding school beginning at the age of 12, where she was an excellent student. In college, she decided to pursue a degree in economics, because, having grown up during the Great Depression, she felt understanding the economy would give her better insight into the way the world worked. She graduated from Berea College with high honors in 1942, and she received both a master's degree and a doctorate in economics from Duke University.

Kreps married her husband, economics professor Clifton H. Kreps, Jr., in 1944. The pair searched for universities or cities where they could both hold posts, which took them to New York City, where Kreps taught at Denison University, Hofstra College, and Queens College. They returned to Duke University in North Carolina, where Kreps became a member of the faculty in 1955; after several publications, in 1968 she became a full professor. Four years later, she was made the James B. Duke professor of economics, the first woman to hold that chair. She was also Woman's College dean, associate provost, and vice president of the university during her tenure there.

But her role in economics was not limited solely to academics. She was the first woman to be named a director on the New York Stock Exchange, and she was director for several large corporations, including Eastman Kodak, J.C. Penney, R.J. Reynolds, Citicorp, and AT&T.

Despite not thinking of herself as actively involved in the women's liberation movement, many of her articles focused on the labor demographics of women and older workers. Her books include *Sex in the Marketplace: American Women at Work, Lifetime Allocation of Work and Leisure: Essays in the Economy of Aging,* and *Women and the American Economy.* Like the subjects of her research, she faced conflicts between her career and her home life. In 1977, she was offered a position on President Jimmy Carter's cabinet as secretary of commerce. Her husband, however, was unwilling to give up his post as Wachovia professor of banking at the University of North Carolina at Chapel Hill. She commuted back to her family on the weekends in order to balance work and home, but her term was cut short when her husband suffered a self-inflicted gunshot wound to the head, which might have been a suicide attempt, and which he survived. In 1979, Kreps resigned from her position on the cabinet and returned to Duke; she eventually retired from that university as a vice president emerita.

Despite her shortened term, Kreps accomplished a great deal with the Commerce department during her time on the cabinet. As an economist, she hoped to change the position of the Commerce department, which was threatened with cuts and was frequently criticized, into a larger voice when it came to economic policy. She fought with the Treasury over which department was better suited to enforce trade regulation, and she came into conflict with the State Department over the commercial attachés who promoted American businesses in foreign economies. She butted heads with the national security adviser over what technology it was safe to export into Communist countries. She managed 38,000 employees, six billion dollars in public works projects, and oversaw the varied responsibilities of the department, including taking the census, standardizing weights and measures, charting seas, and collecting statistics on goods and services. Her efforts to promote international trade helped businesses see her as an ally, and she was able to help Carter and business leaders see eye-to-eye, restoring business confidence in the administration. Kreps negotiated trade missions in various nations, including a historic agreement with China, which had previously been closed to American business, in 1979.

Despite not being a member of Carter's inner circle, she made herself a voice on the cabinet, supporting privacy laws to protect consumers. She also helped to influence the business community into taking greater social responsibilities for the welfare of their employees, particularly in regards to affirmative action. She proposed an audit of social responsibility, done by the federal government, to measure how companies contributed to their civic environment, but the proposal was not adopted before Kreps' resignation in 1979.

In 1985, Duke University created the Juanita and Clifton Kreps chair in economics. Kreps remained active in academics and in governmental affairs throughout her career, received many awards, and was given fifteen honorary degrees. In her later life, she suffered from Alzheimer's disease, complications of which eventually lead to her death on July 5, 2010. She is survived by two of her children; she was 89 years old. **Sources:** *Los Angeles Times,* July 8, 2010; *New York Times,* July 7, 2010; *Washington Post,* July 8, 2010, p. B7.

—*Alana Joli Abbott*

Benjamin Lees

Born Benjamin George Lisniansky, January 8, 1924, in Harbin, China; died of heart failure, May 31, 2010, in Glen Cove, NY. Composer. Well known for his versatility and his disdain for modern musical trends, Benjamin Lees was an American composer who wrote for orchestra, solo instruments, voice, and chamber ensembles. His works were widely considered to be listenable and approachable to audiences, and he favored a lyrical, tonal style.

Frequently described as a Neo-Classical or conservative composer, Lees is best known for his 1985 Symphony No. 4, titled "Memorial Candles," which commemorated the 40-year anniversary to the end of the Holocaust; his 1985 Symphony No. 5, "Kalmar Nyckel," named after the ship that brought the first colonists from Sweden to Wilmington, Delaware, which earned him a Grammy nomination; and Concerto for String Quartet and Orchestra, one of his most frequently performed pieces, which was written in 1964.

The child of Jewish parents who had moved to China from the Ukraine, fleeing the pogroms there, Lees was born Benjamin George Lisniansky in January of 1924. When Lee was still a baby, the Lisniansky family moved to the United States, where they changed their name to Lees and settled in California. Lees received music lessons from an early age, playing piano at five and writing his first compositions as a teen.

During World War II, Lees served in the army. He married his wife, Leatrice Luba, in 1948, and the couple had a daughter, Janet. Lees studied music at the University of Southern California, but was offered the chance to apprentice American modernist composer George Antheil if he dropped out. Antheil told Lees that the university had taught him nothing, and so Lees privately studied for several years under Antheil, who also felt strongly about writing music an audience would connect to, rather than analyze.

Lees first came to public attention in 1954, when his "Profile for Orchestra" was performed on a national broadcast by the NBC Symphony Orchestra. The recipient of Guggenheim and Fulbright fellowships, Lees moved his family to Europe for seven years. In Paris, France, where they spent several years, Lees formed friendships with Surrealist artists, whose art influenced his compositions.

After returning to the United States, Lees taught composition at several universities and conservatories throughout the 1960s and 1970s. The schools where he lectured include the Peabody Conservatory in Baltimore, Maryland; Queens College of the City University of New York; the Manhattan School of Music; and the Juilliard School. Ultimately, he decided that he was not well suited to teaching and he returned his focus to composition.

In 1985 Lees penned the work that many consider to be his masterpiece. Symphony No. 4, "Memorial Candles," commemorated the fortieth anniversary of the end of the Holocaust. The piece includes poetry written by a Holocaust survivor. According to Lees' brother, Mark, quoted in the Los Angeles Times,

"It took a year of solid emotional work for him to complete it." The work was commissioned by the Dallas Symphony Orchestra. Other notable commissions by Lees include String Quartet No. 3, written for the Tokyo String Quartet; String Quartet No. 4, written for San Francisco's Aurora String Quartet; the Concerto for Brass Choir and Orchestra, which was also commissioned by the Dallas Symphony Orchetra; and a Horn Concerto, which he wrote for the Pittsburgh Symphony Orchestra.

Noting that Lees was well-liked rather than well known, Mark Swed, a critic for the Los Angeles Times, said that Lees' work "was appealing and ever-so-slightly quirky within a very conventional style." In a 1960 review of Symphony No. 2, performed by the Cleveland Orchestra in Carnegie Hall, Howard Taubman wrote in the New York Times that with the piece, Lees "proclaims himself as a composer of marked individuality." Unwilling to subscribe to a single particular style, Lees was difficult to pigeonhole as a composer. He disdained many of the styles embraced by other twentieth-century composers, such as atonalism, minimalism, and serialism. The most consistent quality in his pieces is the accessibility of the music to his audience. He was quoted by the New York Times as having once said, "I want a composer who communicates, not one who plays cerebral games."

By 1974, Lees was making his income entirely from music commissions. But he did not stop writing. He was nominated for a Grammy in 2004 for Symphony No. 5, and he was working on a piece of music for violin on May 31, 2010, when he died of heart failure; he was 86. He had once told the Los Angeles Times that composers did not retire: "We work until we cannot hold the pencil anymore."

Lees is survived by his wife of 62 years, his daughter, and two grandchildren. His work, which has been widely recorded and performed by such notable artists as pianist Gary Graffman, violinist Ruggiero Ricci, and the Tokyo and Budapest String Quartets, is the legacy he leaves behind. **Sources:** Los Angeles Times, June 11, 2010; New York Times, June 4, 2010; Washington Post, June 12, 2010, p. B5.

—Alana Joli Abbott

Art Linkletter

Born Gordon Arthur Kelly, July 17, 1912, in Moose Jaw, Saskatchewan, Canada; died May 26, 2010, in Los Angeles, CA. Radio and television personality, writer, and entrepreneur. Best known for his hilarious interviews with young children as a part of his radio and television shows *House Party* and *People Are Funny*, Art Linkletter was an innovative television personality who brought the funny side out of the people in his audiences and entertained millions at home. His programs were typically ad-libbed, with Linkletter strolling his studio audience to chat with them, or challenging normal people with ridiculous stunts. Due to the unscripted nature of his programs, some have considered him one of the pioneers of reality television.

In addition to his successful television and radio career, Linkletter used material he had developed for that media in several successful books. He wrote three autobiographies and produced a Grammy-winning spoken word record, *We Love You, Call Collect*, with his daughter Diane. The album, which had an anti-drug theme, came out months before Diane committed suicide in 1969, which the Linkletter family blamed on a previous bad LSD trip. The tragedy spurred Linkletter to become a spokesperson against drugs, serving on President Nixon's National Advisory Council for Drug Abuse Prevention. Linkletter was also a public speaker on the topic of enjoying the later years in life, as well as a highly successful entrepreneur.

Linkletter did not begin his life with financial success, however. Born in Moose Jaw, Saskatchewan, Canada in 1912, Linkletter was abandoned by his birth parents just months after his birth. He was adopted by Fulton John and Mary Metzler Linkletter, who were middle-aged, and whose own children had died. Linkletter's father was a cobbler and an evangelist, and the family was so poor that Linkletter later claimed not to have even noticed the impact of the Great Depression. The family settled in California when Linkletter was a child.

After graduating high school at age 16, Linkletter decided to see the world. With only ten dollars in his pocket, he hopped on a freight train and lived as an itinerant worker. Linkletter was a fast typist, and in New York, he found work as a typist, but was let go during the stock market crash of 1929. After serving as a merchant seaman, Linkletter returned to California.

Attending college with the intention of becoming an English teacher, Linkletter was hired to make radio announcements during his senior year in 1934. Though he graduated and was offered work as a teacher, Linkletter decided to continue to work in radio, as the pay was better.

His role expanded from spot announcer to radio personality. He was also asked to be the program director for the 1935 California International Exposition in San Diego, the radio director of the 1936 Texas Centennial Exposition, and the radio director for the San Francisco World's Fair in 1937. Though he quickly became well known and respected in the San Franscisco area, he initially had a hard time adjusting to the atmosphere of Hollywood, where he moved with his family in 1942. His first program was cancelled after Linkletter, covering a beach party, tripped over a piece of driftwood and lost his microphone.

One of his largest successes soon followed; Linkletter and John Guedel brought the program *People Are Funny* to the radio. The show featured audience members participating in crazy stunts: Linkletter would give an audience member a thousand dollar bill and ask him to buy a piece of gum, or would ask an audience member to cash a check for a large amount of money, but written on the skin of a watermelon. In one segment, he sent several balls adrift in the Pacific Ocean, saying that the first person to find one would receive a thousand dollars; the prize was claimed by a resident of the Marshall Islands two years later. The tremendously popular show ran from 1942 through 1960 on the radio, and was adapted for television, again with Linkletter as the host, from 1954 through 1961.

A second, similar program debuted in 1945 on the radio. Called *House Party*, the program was a looser version of the show, focusing more on Linkletter's ad-libbed conversations with audience members and less on stunts. The show also featured Linkletter's iconic conversations with children at the end of each program, in which the host invariably prompted hilarious remarks from the under-ten interviewees. Those conversations were compiled in the book, *Kids Say the Darndest Things*, and its sequel; in a reprint of the first book, Linkletter wrote, "Children under ten and women over 70 give the best interviews for the identical reason: they speak the plain unvarnished truth." In 1998 a television show named after Linkletter's book, hosted by Bill Cosby, was built around the same theme; Linkletter co-hosted the first program and was treated to a surprise by the producers: the entire studio audience was populated by adults who had once been children on *House Party*.

In his later years, Linkletter was a well-received public speaker who most often spoke on how to make the best of your senior years. He was so optimistic about his future, he was booked for a speaking engagement in Washington, D.C., for July 17, 2012, in honor of his 100th birthday. He died on May 26, 2010, two years short of that engagement in his home in Los Angeles, California, at the age of

97. **Sources:** *Entertainment Weekly,* http://news-briefs.ew.com/2010/05/26/art-linkletter-dead/ (May 26, 2010); *Los Angeles Times,* May 27, 2010; *New York Times,* May 26, 2010; *Washington Post,* May 27, 2010, p. B6.

—Alana Joli Abbott

Charles McCurdy Mathias

Born July 24, 1922, in Frederick, MD; died from complications of Parkinson's disease, January 25, 2010, in Chevy Chase, MD. Senator. Despite never considering himself a liberal, Republican Senator Charles McCurdy Mathias was best known throughout his long career in politics as a supporter of civil rights, an environmentalist, and a thorn in the side of his party. Mathias was a champion of the Chesapeake Bay, forming a federal and state initiative to clean up and protect the waterway. He was a major contributor to 1964's Civil Rights Act. His ideals often aligned more closely with the Democratic Party than with Republicans, and though he initially supported President Richard Nixon, he later became one of the president's most troublesome opponents. Due to his commitment to campaign finance reform, he was called "the conscience of the senate" by then-Democrat Majority Leader Mike Mansfield.

"I'm not all that liberal," Mathias said in 1974, according to the *Washington Post.* "In fact, in some respects, I'm conservative. A while ago, I introduced a bill preserving the guarantees of the Bill of Rights by prohibiting warrantless wiretaps. I suppose they'll say it's another liberal effort, but it's as conservative as you can get. It's conserving the Constitution." In a 1996 interview about the future of the Republican Party, Mathias said, "I'd like to think there would be a place for Abraham Lincoln, a place for Theodore Roosevelt, and a place for Dwight D. Eisenhower. If there's a place for them, I'd like to think I could find a small niche," the *Washington Post* reported.

Born in 1922 in Frederick, Maryland, Mathias came from a long line of Republican politicians. In the 1869s, his great-grandfather was a representative in the Maryland legislature. His grandfather served as a state senator who campaigned with Theodore Roosevelt. As a child, Mathias visited the White House with his father, meeting presidents Calvin Coolidge and Herbert Hoover.

After graduating from Frederick High School, Mathias spent a year at a prep school in New York. He attended Haverford College for two years before enlisting in the Navy in 1942. While in the Navy, he attended Yale and Columbia universities, and was able to apply credits from those courses to his Haverford degree, which he earned in 1944.

As an ensign in the Navy, and later as a captain in the Naval Reserve, Mathias served in the Pacific during World War II. He was stationed on a communications ship based out of the Philippines. After the war, he visited Hiroshima and Nagasaki to view the damage wrought by the atomic bomb. Viewing those sites made him wary of using nuclear arms unchecked. Mathias returned to the United States and studied law at the University of Maryland, from which he graduated with a law degree in 1949, and practiced law in his hometown of Frederick. He served as an assistant state attorney general and a city attorney for Frederick from 1954 to 1959. Even at that point in his career, his dedication to civil rights was clear: he participated in desegregating the Frederick Opera House. In 1958, he was elected to the Maryland House of Delegates. Two years later, he was elected to the U.S. House of Representatives.

Mathias was expected to serve in the House as a moderate Republican, but he soon felt that the party was moving further to the right. He considered himself a member of the "party of Lincoln," as was the tradition of Republicans in his family, which gave him a more liberal outlook on matters of race than others in his party. Over the course of four terms in the House, he sponsored civil rights legislation and opposed some of the U.S. actions in North Vietnam, giving him a reputation for going against the party line. His politics were based, he said, on principle rather than on political expediency.

In his first campaign for a Senate seat, Mathias ran against a friend and former University of Maryland classmate, Daniel Brewster, who was the Democratic incumbent. Mathias was the godfather of Brewster's son; Brewster had been an usher at Mathias' wedding. The campaign was difficult, and Mathias accused his friend of cowing to the Johnson administration and siding with labor lobbyists. It was a three-way race, with Mathias winning 48 percent of the vote. The day after the election, Mathias and his eldest son, Robert, went to visit Brewster to shake hands and make sure their friendship would recover. Mathias later served as a character witness for Brewster when the latter faced charges of bribery.

During his three terms in the Senate, Mathias continued to be active in supporting civil rights legislation. He voted for the District of Columbia to self-govern, supported gun legislation that would ban Saturday night specials (an inexpensive handgun), and voted against the Nixon administration's efforts to weaken the voting rights act of 1965. He called for investigation into the robbery at Watergate, at first supporting Nixon and believing the president had nothing to do with the scandal. He later changed his position when evidence gave a clearer idea that Nixon was indeed involved. Mathias also challenged two of Nixon's appointments to the Supreme Court; both candidates that Mathias challenged were not appointed. In 1973, Mathias laid the groundwork for a group effort, joining the governments of three states, the District of Columbia, and the federal government, to clean up and preserve the Chesapeake Bay. During his 1974 re-election campaign, he committed to a transparent financial campaign, pledging to reject cash donations and take no more than $100 from any single individual. Mathias advocated these same changes to be made law, and after his re-election, the measures were confirmed by the senate the following year.

Mathias' disagreements with his party led to his being blocked from positions of increasing power. Senator Strom Thurmond prevented Mathias from becoming the senior Republican on the Judiciary Committee; Mathias instead served as chairman of the less powerful Rules and Administration Committee. Despite these conflicts, and his support for initiatives that undermined Reagan administration efforts, he was known for earning respect from colleagues on both sides of the aisle. Mathias retired from the Senate in 1986, after which he practiced law with the Jones, Day, Reavis, & Pogue firm. He oversaw the dissolution of First American Bankshares following the banking scandal of the 1990s. He continued to take positions on issues in the press, stating his opposition to the Iraq War in 2002 and endorsing Barack Obama as presidential candidate in 2008.

Mathias suffered from Parkinson's disease, complications of which caused his death on January 25, 2010. He is survived by his wife and two sons. **Sources:** *Los Angeles Times,* January 27, 2010; *New York Times,* January 26, 2010; *Washington Post,* January 26, 2010, p. A1.

—*Alana Joli Abbott*

Malcolm McLaren

Born Malcolm Robert Andrew McLaren, January 22, 1946, in London, England; died of mesothelioma,

April 8, 2010, in Switzerland. Music promoter. Malcolm McLaren was a London tastemaker, music promoter, and retailer who is perhaps better known as the godfather of punk rock. The guiding force behind the Sex Pistols, an iconic band that gave increasingly disenfranchised British youth both a sound and a look, McLaren shaped the scene and made headlines himself in the late 1970s. "McLaren's provocative influence," asserted Dave Simpson in a tribute that appeared in Britain's *Guardian* newspaper, "can be detected in everything from Damien Hirst's art and contrary bands such as the Libertines and Oasis to the mainstream punk clothes on sale in Top Shop."

Born in 1946, McLaren grew up in Hackney, East London. He was a rebellious teen who dropped out of or was ejected from several schools. "Be childish. Be irresponsible. Be disrespectful. Be everything this society hates," he wrote around 1969 in a manifesto for his never-completed thesis film for Goldsmiths' College, according to the *Times* of London. His artistic philosophy was guided in part by the Dadaists of the 1920s and the Situationist International movement that grew in force during the social unrest of the late 1960s.

McLaren attended Harrow Art College, where he met budding fashion designer Vivienne Westwood. The pair began dating and had a son, Joseph, in 1967. In late 1971 McLaren and Westwood opened a clothing store at 430 Kings Road they named Let It Rock. For a time, McLaren worked with the New York Dolls, a notorious glam-rock band best known for wearing makeup and women's clothing, but the band soon broke up.

In the spring of 1973 McLaren and Westwood changed the name of their store to Too Fast to Live Too Young to Die, a slogan popularized by teens who were fans of the late actor James Dean. It would be renamed and remodeled several more times, usually with the aim of ridding the scene-y store of its more disruptive clientele. Its next incarnation was as "Sex" when the duo began selling their designs based on fetish wear, the bondage-and-discipline items known at the time to only an underground fraction of the public who were fans of kink. In 1976, the store became Seditionaries.

McLaren was still involved in the music scene and eventually met up with a struggling band formed in 1974 called the Strand, after the Roxy Music song. He retooled its line-up, selecting a local thug named John Lydon, who favored a Pink Floyd T-shirt with the words "I HATE" scrawled above the band name, as the new lead singer. Lydon became "Johnny Rotten" and his friend from a squat in Hampstead who eventually joined the band as a replacement bass player was known as Sid Vicious. McLaren and Westwood outfitted the band in gear drawn from an array of styles—the biker jackets worn by fans of James Dean, spiked accessories collected by fetishists, and Westwood's popular zippered and slashed T-shirts and pants. McLaren named the band the Sex Pistols and they played their first show at St. Martin's School of Art in London on November 6, 1975, where they were predictably booed off stage after two songs.

McLaren harnessed that scorn and strove to create a band that would be the most widely loathed, talentless musicians ever to sign a recording contract. The ploy worked: By the fall of 1976 the band was signed to EMI, which exited the deal a few months later when Lydon gave a profanity-laced television interview in the wake of their first single, "Anarchy in the U.K." McLaren negotiated an even better deal with A&M Records just in time to issue a second single, "God Save the Queen," as Queen Elizabeth II's Silver Jubilee approached. The song was banned by British Broadcasting Corporation Radio and McLaren was arrested for his part in staging a riverboat performance by the Sex Pistols in front of the Houses of Parliament. What may have been the stunning end result of McLaren's marketing strategy came in October of 1977, when the band's first and only album, *Never Mind the Bollocks, Here's the Sex Pistols* became number one in the U.K.

The Sex Pistols quickly disintegrated in a stew of drugs, infighting, and a felony murder rap. Lydon, in particular, would spend years criticizing McLaren publicly and battling him in court over copyright claims, even for the use of the name Johnny Rotten. Vicious died of a heroin overdose in 1979 while free on bail and awaiting trial for the fatal knifing of his girlfriend at New York's Chelsea Hotel.

McLaren had a long and productive post-Pistols career. He worked with Adam & the Ants, created the '80s band Bow Wow Wow, then produced his own solo records. These include 1983's *Duck Rock*, which introduced scratching, breakdancing, and other New York-centric hip-hop elements to a wider audience, and 1984's *Fans*, an attempt to blend hip-hop with classic opera that earned surprisingly strong reviews. In his later years he was a business partner with his longtime girlfriend, Young Kim, and his son Joe Corré in a luxury lingerie line called Agent Provocateur. In the fall of 2009 McLaren was diagnosed with mesothelioma, a cancer of the tissue linings, and died on April 8, 2010; he was 64. Mesothelioma is linked to the building material asbes-

tos, and McLaren may have been exposed while renovating the Kings Road store back in the 1970s. "The whole thing probably wouldn't have taken off the way it did without him, there's no doubt about that," former Sex pistols bassist Steve Jones told the *Los Angeles Times* about McLaren and the birth of punk rock. "But his downfall is that he spent the rest of his life trying to take credit for *all* of it." **Sources:** *Guardian* (London), April 9, 2010; *Los Angeles Times*, April 9, 2010; *New York Times*, April 9, 2010; *Times* (London), April 11, 2010.

—*Carol Brennan*

Alexander McQueen

Born Lee Alexander McQueen, March 17, 1969, in London, England; committed suicide, February 11, 2010, in London, England. Fashion designer. Lee Alexander McQueen—professionally known as Alexander McQueen—became recognized as one of fashion's most provocative designers for his challenging clothing and sensational runway shows during the 1990s. His meteoric rise to widespread acclaim saw the designer launch his own design house and join the prestigious luxury brand Givenchy as its head designer while still in his mid-20s. "He was talented beyond his years," commented actress and client Sarah Jessica Parker to Clarissa Cruz of *Entertainment Weekly*. "There has never been anyone like him. And there simply never will be." His clothes made headlines both as red carpet wear for A-list celebrities and as daring, even macabre works of fabric art; however, McQueen's personal life saw considerable turmoil and these challenges eventually contributed to his death at the age of 40.

The youngest of the six children of cabdriver father Ron McQueen and social science teacher and homemaker mother Joyce McQueen, the future fashion designer grew up in a working class area of London. At the age of eight, he realized that he was homosexual, and endured taunts from peers at the city's Rokeby Comprehensive School for Boys over his sexuality for the next several years. Although his father hoped that the young McQueen would pursue a career as a plumber or electrician, McQueen left school when he was 16 to take an apprenticeship with Anderson & Sheppard, a tailor on Savile Row, London's upscale menswear district. McQueen's next stop was Gieves & Hawkes, best known as the tailor to the British armed forces. During this period, the future designer worked on clothing for world dignitaries including Soviet leader Mikhail

Gorbachev and Britain's Prince Charles, in whose jacket lining McQueen legendarily claimed to have once written an offensive slur. The crisp lines and attention to detail that McQueen acquired during this period informed his later womenswear designs.

After stints working with theatrical costumier Angels & Bermans, Japanese designer Koji Tatsuno, and Italian designer Romeo Gigli, McQueen returned to London and applied for a job as a tutor in patternmaking with St. Martin's College of Art and Design. McQueen's application portfolio so impressed the school, however, that he was entered into its graduate program in fashion design. His graduate collection caught the attention of influential British stylist Isabella Blow, then on staff at British *Vogue*. She bought all of the young designer's pieces and steered him to launch his own fashion line. In 1996, French luxury brand Givenchy named McQueen its head designer. The partnership proved a rocky one—McQueen called the brand's founder "irrelevant" to his face shortly after signing on—but helped propel McQueen to greater notoriety, if more for his disputes with management than for his Givenchy designs. The young designer's strong fashion statements under his own name garnered him greater artistic notice. Among McQueen's most influential designs were his low-cut "bumster" trousers, later acknowledged as the forerunner of the low-rise jeans that dominated fashion during the first decade of the twenty-first century. His clothing typically featured impeccably tailored lines, skin-tight construction, and gothic imagery such as skulls.

McQueen remained with Givenchy until 2001, one year after he had signed a deal with Gucci Group giving that company a 51 percent stake in his own eponymous line. This agreement saw McQueen open single-branded stores in major world cities including London, Milan, Las Vegas, and Los Angeles. A menswear line; lower-priced diffusion women's line, McQ; a line of athletic shoes and luggage for sports brand Puma; and a series of McQueen-branded fragrances followed. The partnership also afforded McQueen, as the creative director of his own house, immense artistic control. He channeled his vision into, at times, shocking runway shows that saw models variously teeter on 12-inch heels, extend their middle fingers to the audience, appear as chess pieces and mental patients, and walk the runway apparently beaten and abused in what was known as the "Highland Rape" collection. "He was brilliant," commented model Karen Elson, a friend of McQueen's, to Suzanne Zuckerman of *People* after the designer's death. "Maybe from all of that passion comes something dark."

These daring collections and presentation won McQueen great acclaim and recognition from the fash-ion industry. He earned the title of British Designer of the Year four times between 1996 and 2003, and was named a Commander of the British Empire in 2003. McQueen also clothed numerous celebrities, including Madonna, Rihanna, Gwyneth Paltrow, Kate Winslet, and Lady Gaga. A McQueen design for Icelandic singer Björk appeared on the cover of the musician's 1997 album *Homogenic*.

The designer was found dead at his home the morning of February 11, 2010, short days after the death of his mother, who had declined from a long illness. He had reportedly hung himself. Although McQueen had experienced personal problems including drug abuse, his death shocked friends and peers alike. "Creativity is a very fragile thing, and Lee was very fragile," commented Philip Treacy, a milliner and acquaintance of McQueen, to Eric Wilson and Cathy Horyn of the *New York Times*. "It's not easy being Mr. McQueen.... We're all human. His mum had just died. And his mum was a great supporter of his talent." The 2007 suicide of longtime McQueen friend and advocate Blow was also noted as a contributing factor in the designer's own death. McQueen is survived by his father and five siblings. The fashion house that he founded also ensured McQueen's creative vision would live on. **Sources:** *Entertainment Weekly*, February 26, 2010; *Los Angeles Times*, February 12, 2010; *New York Times*, February 11, 2010; *People*, March 1, 2010; *Times* (London), February 12, 2010.

—*Vanessa E. Vaughn*

Carlos Monsiváis

Born May 4, 1938, in Mexico City, Mexico; died after a long struggle with lung disease, June 19, 2010, in Mexico City, Mexico. Writer. Though Carlos Monsiváis was never well known outside of his native Mexico, in his home country his prolific writings made his voice more recognizable than political officials and elected officials. Over five decades, he shared his observations on politics, liberalism, popular culture, and the Mexican identity in newspapers, magazines, and books. His writings helped to shape the contemporary political and cultural life of Mexico.

Part of the surge of Latin American writers whose works reached the wider world during the 1960s, Monsiváis was known for focusing less on the universal concerns embraced by his counterparts, such as Carlos Fuentes, and more on the ordinary problems that faced common people in Mexico. An activist supporting gay rights and liberal causes, Monsivá often wrote about events and issues as a participant.

Monsiváis, who was affectionately known as Monsi, was born in Mexico City on May 4, 1938. He attended the National Autonomous University of Mexico, where he studied in the schools of economics and arts and letters. Active in the student movement while attending university, Monsiváis began to write literary chronicles of his experiences after graduating. His early works have been compared to the New Journalism movement of the United States in the 1960s.

Throughout the 1960s, Monsiváis wrote articles, essays, and columns for newspapers and magazines, and he was often featured in the most prominent of these. In 1968, just before the start of the Mexico City Olympics, Monsiváis became involved in the student protests at Tlatelolco Plaza, which ended in tragedy. The army massacred scores of student protestors, and the event spurred on Mexico's pro-democracy movement. Originally covering the protests as a participant, Monsiváis revisited the event in a 1999 book titled *War Report*, in which he produced documents that showed the direct involvement of then-Mexican President Gustavo Díaz Ordaz in the massacre.

Monsiváis' articles also covered the tragic 1985 earthquake, which had a death toll in the thousands. His political concerns continued in articles about the Zapatista guerrilla uprising of 1994, which he supported, and the 2006 campaign of presidential candidate Andrés Manuel López Obrador, whom Monsiváis hoped would win, but who narrowly lost to current Mexican president, Felipe Calderón. Unsurprisingly, he was highly critical of Calderón's administration. Despite not seeing eye to eye, when Monsiváis died in 2010, Calderón expressed "profound sorrow" that the writer had died, according to the *Los Angeles Times*. The quote in the *Los Angeles Times* continued with Calderón calling Monsiváis "an exceptional pen, an exceptional intellect." According to the *New York Times*, the Mexican president also said that Monsiváis' "literary and journalistic work is a necessary reference for understanding the richness and cultural diversity of Mexico.... He was a chronicler and witness for his era."

While Monsiváis is perhaps best known for his writings on the serious topics of disasters and politics, he also enjoyed writing about lighter-hearted topics in popular culture, such as art, movies, literature, and soccer. He was the recipient of many awards, including Mexico's National Journalism Award. His tone when discussing both weighty and superficial material tended to include humor and irony. An article in the *New York Times* referenced his 1997 book *Mexican Postcards*, one of the few works he wrote that has been translated into English, as a prime example of his use of sarcasm. He wrote of Mexico: "A decent society with noble sentiments loves the home as if it were the nation, and venerates the nation as if it were a mother: there is no such thing as virtue outside of official engagements, no true love outside marriage, and no civic pride that is far removed from the respectful laying of bouquets and wreaths."

Putting forward a persona as both a curmudgeon and an everyman, Monsiváis was well loved by the Mexican public. He was a people's philosopher, an intellectual who would be recognized on the streets of Mexico City. Monsiváis had had a long struggle with lung disease and was hospitalized in April of 2010. He died on June 19, 2010, at the age of 72 in the city of his birth. Monsiváis left behind no immediate survivors, but gave Mexico a legacy of books.

After his death, a public viewing of his coffin was offered to the public of Mexico City. His coffin was draped in the national flag, the flag of his university, and the gay rights rainbow flag. Thousands of citizens came to honor him. Writer and friend of Monsiváis' Elena Poniatowska, in a public tribute, was quoted in the *Los Angeles Times* as having said, "This is an enormous loss for Mexico, an enormous loss for the Spanish-speaking world.... [Monsiváis] was always on the side of those who suffered most."

Monsiváis' early articles have been collected in books, including *Days to Remember, Scenes of Modesty and Frivolity,* and *The Rituals of Chaos,* all of which were popular in Mexico. Monsiváis' ashes have been added to the collection of the Estanquillo Museum, a popular culture museum in Mexico City that Monsiváis helped to create in 2006. **Sources:** *Los Angeles Times,* June 20, 2010; *New York Times,* June 22, 2010; *Washington Post,* June 21, 2010, p. B4.

—*Alana Joli Abbott*

Patricia Neal

Born Patsy Louise Neal, January 20, 1926, in Packard, KY; died of lung cancer, August 8, 2010, in

Edgartown, MA. Actress. Stage and screen veteran Patricia Neal earned accolades for her moving portrayals of women in turmoil, but the star's own personal setbacks brought her tremendous public sympathy. The Academy Award-winning actor had five children with the writer Roald Dahl, one of whom died at age seven. Three years later, Neal was pregnant with a fourth daughter when she suffered a series of debilitating strokes, but recovered and resumed her career, going on to earn an Academy Award nomination.

Neal was born in 1926 in Packard, a town in Kentucky's coal-mining region. Her father worked in mine management and the family eventually moved to Knoxville, Tennessee, where Neal showed an early talent for poetry recital. After two years at Northwestern University, she moved to New York City in 1945. Her breakout role came in a new Lillian Hellman play on Broadway, *Another Part of the Forest*, which opened in late 1946. For it, Neal won the first-ever Tony Award (Antoinette Perry Award for Excellence in Theater) for Best Featured Actress in a Play at the inaugural Tony ceremony.

Neal's triumph on Broadway led to studio offers from Hollywood, and she signed with Warner Brothers, who put her in a few substandard projects before handing her a much-coveted role in *The Fountainhead*, the screen adaptation of Ayn Rand's best-selling novel. The movie tanked at the box office, and its production also led Neal into an affair with her married co-star, Gary Cooper, who was 25 years her senior. This was a disastrous period of her personal life she detailed in her compelling 1988 memoir, *As I Am*.

Neal's professional career seemed to be derailing, too. Warner Brothers continued to assign her inferior projects, or lent her out to other studios. She was traumatized at having to appear in a 1951 science-fiction drama *The Day the Earth Stood Still,* but the film would later be considered one of the most cerebral and chilling sci-fi dramas of the era. Dejected, Neal returned to the New York stage, taking a role in a revival of another Lillian Hellman play, *The Children's Hour*. Through Hellman she met British author Roald Dahl, and the couple were married in New York City in 1953. Her husband would go on to pen several sophisticated and much-loved children's stories, including *Charlie and the Chocolate Factory* and *James and the Giant Peach*.

Neal's career shift into more nuanced roles came in the late 1950s. Director Elia Kazan cast her in a dark farce about fame and the media age, *A Face in the Crowd,* and she also turned up as the Manhattan so-cialite carrying on with George Peppard's character in *Breakfast at Tiffany's* in 1961. Neal's breakthrough role came with *Hud* in 1963. It starred Paul Newman as a callous cowboy from a wealthy Texas ranching family, and though Neal's role was not a lead, her performance earned her an Academy Award for Best Actress.

Neal was originally slated to play the part that went to Anne Bancroft in *The Graduate,* the 1967 comedy that made a star out of Dustin Hoffman. But Neal's home life had been beset by a series of tragedies: in December of 1960, her third child with Dahl, a son named Theo, was involved in a traffic accident in Manhattan while outside in a carriage with his nursemaid; he suffered brain damage and underwent multiple surgeries. Theo had followed Olivia, born in 1955, and Chantal, born in 1957; after Theo's accident Dahl decided to move the family to rural England, where Olivia died at the age of seven after contracting measles and then encephalitis. A fourth daughter, Ophelia, was born in 1964, and in early 1965 Neal was three months pregnant with her fifth child when she suffered a series of hemorrhagic strokes.

The family was in the Los Angeles area at the time, and Dahl rushed his wife to UCLA Medical Center. After hours in surgery, Neal remained in a coma for two weeks and finally awoke with her right side paralyzed, unable to walk or talk. Fortunately she delivered her daughter, Lucy, in August of 1965, and slowly recovered through a long and arduous rehabilitation period. "I loathed life," she said of this ordeal, according her *Los Angeles Times* obituary. "I had exercises to do every day. My husband had people coming in to teach me—three a day. I wanted to commit suicide, but I didn't know how."

Neal made a triumphant return to the public sphere in March of 1967, when a speech she delivered at a New York City benefit dinner for children with brain injuries brought the crowd to its feet and resulted in newspaper headlines across the country. She followed that a few weeks later by an appearance at the Academy Awards as a presenter. Hailed as a hero, Neal spoke candidly about her stroke and recovery efforts, and became a lifelong advocate for stroke awareness and rehabilitation services.

At the time, few thought Neal would be able to return to her career. But the director of an upcoming screen adaptation of an acclaimed Broadway play delayed production until she felt up to tackling the job. That movie was *The Subject Was Roses* and co-starred her with Jack Albertson and a young Martin Sheen. Her performance was nominated for an Academy Award.

Neal's name returned to newspaper headlines in 1983, when her 30-year marriage to Dahl ended after revelations that her husband had been having a years-long affair with one of her friends. Their oldest surviving daughter, Chantal, became a writer under the name Tessa Dahl; Tessa's daughter is British model/actress Sophie Dahl. Neal's children and several grandchildren were present at her home on Martha's Vineyard, Massachusetts, when she died on August 8, 2010. She was 84 and had been suffering from lung cancer. The epitome of graciousness to the end, she told her family the night before she passed, "I've had a lovely time," according to the *Los Angeles Times*. **Sources:** *Guardian* (London), August 9, 2010; *Los Angeles Times*, August 10, 2010; *New York Times*, August 9, 2010; *Washington Post*, August 10, 2010.

—Carol Brennan

Marshall Warren Nirenberg

Born April 10, 1927, in New York, NY; died of cancer, January 15, 2010, in New York, NY. Biologist. In the race to decipher the code that allows genetic information in DNA to be translated into proteins, Marshall Warren Nirenberg was an unexpected hero. Employed for his entire career by the National Institute of Health (NIH), Nirenberg was an outsider to molecular biology's academic circles. That he, with fewer resources and a smaller staff, was able to beat other labs to the solution to the genetic code earned him a Nobel Prize in 1968, making him the first NIH employee to receive the honor.

After receiving the Nobel, Nirenberg continued to perform research in molecular biology and, later, neurobiology. His additional significant discoveries include work in culturing neural cells, the discovery of a fruit fly gene that is essential for heart development, and innovations in screenings for addictions and disorders. He was known for his collegial nature, and in his Nobel speech, he offered credit to all of those he had worked with on the project, saying, "One individual alone creates only a note or so that blends with those produced by others. The advances that have been described here today are due to the efforts of investigators throughout the world." NIH Director Francis S. Collins called him "one of science's great titans," according to Nirenberg's *Washington Post* obituary.

Nirenberg was born in the New York City borough of Brooklyn in 1927. As a child, he developed rheumatic fever and, to help him recover, his family moved to the more hospitable climate of Orlando, Florida. There, Nirenberg developed an interest in the natural world, studying the swamps and becoming a bird-watcher and amateur entomologist. He studied zoology and chemistry at the University of Florida, graduating with his bachelor's degree in 1948. He earned his master's in biology in 1952, and went on to receive a doctorate in biochemistry from the University of Michigan five years later. Nirenberg accepted a postdoctoral fellowship at the NIH under the National Institute of Arthritis and Metabolic Diseases (later the National Institute of Arthritis and Musculoskeletal and Skin Diseases).

Focusing on the synthesis of proteins, Nirenberg began his studies in the contemporary way: looking at cell-free systems, which were used to synthesize proteins with enzymes from bacteria that had been crushed to break their cell walls. When James Watson and Francis Crick discovered the structure of DNA (a double helix composed of four repeating nucleotides) in 1953, the field began to change. Scientists posited theories about the quantity and organization of nucleotides needed to specify the 20 different amino acids in proteins. Crick suggested that three nucleotides would be necessary, and that there would be 64 combinations. The sequence of the nucleotides would be called a codon.

While other groups of scientists formed to tackle the problem, Nirenberg and his postdoctoral fellow, German biochemist J. Heinrich Matthaei, designed an experiment using the cell-free system: they would put known fragments of RNA, which they knew carried the genetic information from DNA, and see what proteins formed. The experiment should not have worked—as it was later discovered, RNA carries a "start" codon that needed to be disabled. Nirenberg and Matthaei happened to be using a protein synthesis solution that contained twice the amount of magnesium as found in natural protein production, which disabled the start codon. They selected an RNA fragment containing only uracil and found that it produced the amino acid phenylalanine. This meant that the codon of only uracil (U-U-U) would always create a protein of only phenylalanine.

Nirenberg presented his findings at a conference that summer in Moscow, but because he was an unknown, very few scientists attended his lecture. One of the biochemists who was in attendance realized the significance of what Nirenberg had decoded and persuaded Crick to have Nirenberg offer the presentation a second time. This session was packed, and Nirenberg's work was soon adapted by other scientists who hoped to decode the other 63 codons first.

Nirenberg's NIH lab had less funding and fewer staff members to work on the project, so it looked as though it would fall behind despite the fact that Matthaei had managed to uncover the second codon.

Nobel laureate Severo Ochoa seemed the most likely candidate to identify the other 62 codons first. He had a large laboratory at New York University's medical school and could apply plenty of resources to the project. While the NIH win seemed unlikely, Nirenberg continued his research—and soon other NIH staffers took time away from their projects to assist Nirenberg. "Faced with the possibility of helping the first NIH scientist win a Nobel Prize, many NIH scientists put aside their own work to help Nirenberg," the NIH said of the event on its Web site, according to the *Washington Post*. "All in all, more than 20 people came through Nirenberg's laboratory." With the additional assistance from fellow NIH scientists, Nirenberg pulled ahead, and soon Ochoa bowed out of the race, seeing that Nirenberg was closing in on the goal. By 1966, Nirenberg and his colleagues had identified 61 of 64 codons; the last three were identified the following year. In 1968, Nirenberg was one of three researchers to share the Nobel Prize in physiology or medicine, alongside Har Gobind Khorana, who was honored for work in synthesizing nucleic acids, and Robert W. Holley, who discovered transfer-RNA's chemical structure.

Though Nirenberg was offered many opportunities after winning the Nobel Prize, including positions at institutions worldwide, he decided to stay at NIH. As he explained in the *New York Times*, "I have been tempted to leave but I always ask myself, could I do better work someplace else, and I don't think I could. The salary here is relatively low, but the advantage to NIH is that you can use your time completely for research without the distraction of teaching or committee work." Though he never held a teaching position, he did serve as a mentor for researchers who worked under him, including two who later became Nobel laureates as well.

Nirenberg suffered from cancer and died on January 15, 2010 at his home in New York. He is survived by his second wife and four stepchildren. **Sources:** *Los Angeles Times*, January 29, 2010; *New York Times*, January 21, 2010; *Washington Post*, January 18, 2010, p. B4.

—*Alana Joli Abbott*

Kenneth Clifton Noland

Born April 10, 1924, in Asheville, NC; died of kidney cancer, January 5, 2010, in Port Clyde, ME. Painter. The paintings of Kenneth Noland marked him as one of the most influential abstract painters, particularly in post-Abstract Expressionism, during the 1950s through the 1980s. Though scholarly and critical conversation about Noland's pieces cooled as postmodernism became the dominant artistic movement, Noland is essential to the understanding of American abstract art in the twentieth century. *New York Times* critic Hilton Kramer once wrote, according to the *Washington Post*, "Noland is one of the artists who have decisively shaped American painting. The fate of abstract art in America in the 1960s and '70s can scarcely be understood without some knowledge of his work." Alongside Morris Louis, Noland became one of the best known representatives of the color-field school.

Noland and other artists working at around the same time began to reject some of the principles of Abstract Expressionism, choosing to abandon representations of spiritual meaning and evocative emotion in their works to focus on a more intellectual and technical style of art. In Noland's case, the artist focused primarily on color and its use with basic geometric forms, such as concentric circles, chevrons, diamonds, and stripes in oversized compositions. "I wanted to have color be the origin of the painting," Noland once told the *Washington Post*. "I was trying to neutralize the layout, the shape, the composition.... I wanted to make color the generating force."

Noland was born in 1924 in Asheville, North Carolina. His father, Harry Noland, was a pathologist and an amateur painter. As a teen, Noland visited the National Gallery in Washington, D.C., where the Monets particularly impressed him. His father loaned him art materials so that Noland could experiment with his own artistic impulses. At the age of 18, Noland was drafted into the Army Air Corps, and he served as a glider pilot and cryptographer from 1942 through 1946.

Returning from war and armed with the G.I. Bill, Noland entered Black Mountain College, with which musicians and artists such as John Cage, Willem de Kooning, and Josef Albers are associated. There, he studied with Russian artist Ilya Bolotowsky and Paul Klee, whose sense of surrealism impacted Noland's early work. From 1948 through 1949, Noland lived in Paris and worked with sculptor Ossip Zadkine and was introduced to the works of Matisse. He had his first exhibition in a Paris gallery in 1949.

Noland returned to the United States and took teaching positions at the Institute of Contemporary Arts and the Catholic University of America, both in Washington, D.C. He soon became friends with Louis, who taught alongside him at the evening school, Washington Workshop Center of the Arts. The pair studied with Helen Frankenthaler, who influenced them in staining their unprimed canvases with liquid pigment. The effect created translucent layers of color and eliminated effects like brush strokes, distancing the viewer from the artist's intentions and heightening the visual impact of the work. Critic Clement Greenberg became a supporter of both Noland's and Louis' works and included Noland in an *Emerging Talent* exhibition in 1954. Dorothy Miller also included a painting by Noland, *In the Mist,* in her traveling *Young American Painters* exhibition. Noland had his first one-man show at the Tibor de Nagy Gallery in 1957.

During the 1950s, Noland created a series of nearly 200 paintings of concentric circles that floated in the center of each canvas. A pulse of color around the far ring often framed these circles. He began experimenting with ovoid shapes in the 1960s, and then started working with horizontal stripes, plaids, and chevrons. In the early 1960s, he moved from Washington to New York City. He settled in South Shaftsbury, Vermont in 1963, living on a farm that had previously been owned by the poet Robert Frost. The move to Vermont introduced him to local artists Jules Olitski and sculptor Anthony Caro, with whom he developed close working relationships.

Starting in the 1970s, there was a move away from the style of expressionism that Noland embraced, as artists criticized the style, and Noland's work in particular, as unemotional and unconcerned with social issues. Nonetheless, Noland continued to work throughout the 1990s, returning to his early concentric circle work and using shaped canvases to further explore geometric patterns. Noland offered symposiums and lectures, speaking as a continued supporter of modernist art. "It's a fertile field that we barely have explored," he was quoted as having said in the *New York Times,* "and young artists will return to it. I'm certain."

Noland suffered from kidney cancer, and he died at his home in Port Clyde, Maine, on January 5, 2010. Noland is survived by his fourth wife and editor in chief of *Architectural Digest,* Paige Rense; his sons William and Samuel Jesse, and his daughters Cady and Lyn. **Sources:** *Los Angeles Times,* January 11, 2010; *New York Times,* January 6, 2010; *Times* (London), January 9, 2010; *Washington Post,* January 7, 2010, p. B6.

—*Alana Joli Abbott*

Merlin Olsen

Born Merlin Jay Olsen, September 14, 1940, in Logan, UT; died of mesothelioma, March 11, 2010, in Duarte, CA. Professional football player and actor. Few football players have captured the imaginations of audiences as much as the "Fearsome Foursome" of the Dodge Rams team in the 1960s. These men included David "Deacon" Jones, Roosevelt "Rosey" Grier, Lamar Lundy, and Merlin Olsen, a Hall of Fame player who was not only known for his size and strength on the defensive, but also as a highly intelligent and strategic player. He was named the most valuable player of the National Football League (NFL) in 1974, and he was elected to the Pro Football Hall of Fame in the very first year he was eligible, 1982. The Rams retired his jersey number, 74. Olsen's team record of 915 tackles went unbeaten throughout his life.

Olsen not only had a successful football career, but he made a name for himself as a broadcaster and actor after retiring from football. The size (he was six feet, five inches and 275 pounds) that made him stand out as a player continued to make him noticeable in roles on television, including an ongoing part on *Little house on the Prairie.* He held the starring role in the television show *Father Murphy,* and he was also recognizable as the face of FTD florists for many years.

Olsen was the second child in his family and was born in Utah in 1940. As a high school student, Olsen was awkward, and was actually discouraged from continuing in sports. Olsen stubbornly persisted and he went on to help revive the football program at Utah State. He led the team at the Sun Bowl and the Gotham Bowl, and he was a named All-American three times in his undergraduate career. In 1962, he won the Outland Trophy.

Olsen graduated summa cum laude, was elected to the Phi Beta Kappa honor society, and even while playing football professionally, he pursued his master's degree in economics from Utah State, showing his interest and ability in the academic world. He received his graduate degree in 1970. "I was amazed by his size just like everybody else, but more than that at his great intelligence," Irv Cross, a former teammate of Olsen's who later worked as a CBS analyst, was quoted as having said in the *Los Angeles Times.* "His ability to analyze the game was something everybody on the team recognized. It was just unbelievable that any one person would be gifted in so many ways."

In the 1962 NFL draft, Olsen was the third player selected, and he immediately became a starting player. The Rams were a dreadful team during

Olsen's rookie season, winning a single game. The team remained weak until the late 1960s, when Olsen and the other members of the "Fearsome Foursome" changed the way defense was viewed in the NFL. They made the defensive plays as exciting for fans to watch as the offense; they created "stunting" and "looping" techniques, crossing each other's paths and rushing the player passing the ball. Olsen's teammate Jones popularized the term "sack" to refer to tackling the quarterback behind the scrimmage line. In their 14-game season in 1968, the Rams' defense set an NFL record for yielding the fewest yards.

After a 15-season career, Olsen retired from football and became an analyst. He started off working for NBC with Dick Engberg, and the pair became well known for calling Rams' games. He also worked for CBS as an analyst later in his career, matching his 15 seasons in football with 15 seasons reporting on the game.

Because Olsen's contract with NBC gave him the option to act, Olsen asked how to get training so that he could become an actor. When he discovered there was no program at NBC to facilitate his career in that direction, he sought out his own training. He approached Michael Landon, an actor, producer, and director, who took Olsen under his wing. He later cast Olsen as Jonathan Garvey in *Little House on the Prairie,* a series based on the popular children's novels about pioneer days by Laura Ingalls Wilder. Olsen went on to star in *Father Murphy* from 1981 through 1983. In that series, Olsen played the role of a frontiersman who disguised himself as a priest in order to help a group of orphans. He also acted in *Fathers and Sons* and *Aaron's Way.*

In 2009, Olsen was diagnosed with mesothelioma, a type of cancer that affects the membrane covering internal organs of the body, including the lungs. Mesothelioma can be caused by long-term exposure to asbestos, a cause that led Olsen to sue NBC Studios and several other companies he had worked for, claiming that the companies had been responsible for his exposure, and thus, his condition. On March 11, 2010, Olsen died of the disease. He is survived by his wife of 48 years, Susan, two daughters, a son, and his brothers, who also played professional football. He was 69 years old. **Sources:** *Los Angeles Times,* March 12, 2010; *New York Times,* March 11, 2010; *Washington Post,* March 12, 2010, p. B7.

—*Alana Joli Abbott*

Harvey Pekar

Born October 8, 1939, in Cleveland, OH; died of an accidental overdose of prescription medication, July 12, 2010, in Cleveland, OH. Comic book writer. Harvey Pekar was among a small group of underground comic book writers who helped push the industry toward the creation of graphic novels, increasing the range of stories being told in the illustrated medium beyond adventure tales and into the realms of memoir and more serious topics. Pekar "recognized that there was no intrinsic reason comic books could not explore the same human terrain as prose literature," wrote one of his collaborators, Joe Sacco, in *Time.* Pekar's long-running *American Splendor,* largely based on his own life, opened the door for other comics writers and artists to tell their own stories in a comic medium.

Born in Cleveland, Ohio, in 1939, Pekar was the son of Jewish immigrants from Poland. The family lived above a neighborhood grocery store run by his father, who was a Talmudic scholar. Pekar went to college at what is now Case Western Reserve University before dropping out and serving in the Navy during the 1950s. A working-class artist throughout his life, he worked several low-paying jobs before finding work as a filing clerk at a VA hospital in Cleveland. Despite how popular his comic would become, Pekar worked at that same job for 30 years.

Though Pekar himself could never draw anything more than stick figures, he became close friends with cartoonist Robert Crumb, who published as R. Crumb, in the early 1960s. The pair bonded over a shared love of jazz—Pekar worked as a freelance jazz critic—and Crumb's success in the underground comics movement inspired Pekar. He brought Crumb storyboards, populated with stick figures, showing the story he wanted to tell. Crumb offered to collaborate with him, as well as put him in touch with other illustrators.

The work became *American Splendor,* which Pekar self-published, beginning in 1976 and continuing with one book per year, illustrated by a number of artists, including Crumb, Frank Stack, Gary Dumm, Spain Rodriguez, Bill Griffith, Gilbert Hernandez, Drew Friedman, Alison Bechdel, and Sacco. According to the *Washington Post,* Pekar once explained that when he began the project "I was single and I was spending thousands of dollars on rare records, so I thought I'd put out a comic. And so I lost money on that instead." He later featured his autobiographical character in *American Splendor* commenting that it did not matter if he lost a couple thousand dollars a year, so long as he was doing something creative.

Pekar was married three times; his third marriage was to one of his fans, a civic activist, teacher, and writer named Joyce Brabner. They corresponded, and when they first met in person, Brabner was violently ill over the home-cooked meal Pekar provided. That Pekar immediately took care of her during the situation convinced her, even on the first date, that he would be an excellent husband. Pekar proposed on their third date, and the two were married in 1983. In addition to their marriage, Babner and Pekar collaborated on a novel-length comic, *Our Cancer Year*, in 1994, after Pekar was diagnosed with lymphoma.

In all his works, Pekar was known for depicting mundane encounters without shying away from the idea that they happened to everyone. He drew heavily on his work at the hospital, and some peers suspected that he kept the job in order to continue gaining material for his comic, rather than due to a financial need. As a character, he depicted himself as cranky and odd, a bit of an outcast. He was critical of power and privilege and on the side of outsiders. Crumb once said of Pekar's work, as quoted in the *Los Angeles Times* that he featured topics "so staggeringly mundane it verges on the exotic." Bechdel wrote in the *Chicago Tribune*, "What his work told me was that you don't have to have grand themes to do great work, that you can just write honestly and grand themes would emerge." The result was also funny, and Pekar's works are noted for their use of mordant humor.

The first book-length compilation of *American Splendor* received the National Book Award in 1987. The comic also inspired the film adaptation, also called *American Splendor*, in 2003, which won the Grand Jury Prize for drama at the Sundance Film Festival.

In addition to the long-running comic *American Splendor*, Pekar wrote *The Quitter*, a book-length look at his early life, illustrated by Dean Haspiel, and books about the Beat Generation. In addition to his own autobiographical content, he wrapped the stories of others into *American Splendor*, including the Vietnam War experience of one of his coworkers at the hospital in the 2003 *American Splendor: Unsung Hero*.

Pekar also earned some fame—or notoriety—in his regular appearances on *Late Night with David Letterman*. From 1986 to 1988, he was a frequent guest, and his verbal sparring with the host, often about the lack of on-air time he received, was entertaining. An on-air argument kept him from being a guest on the show for several years, but he eventually reappeared in 1993.

Pekar retired from his job as a clerk in 2001, but continued to write. On July 12, 2010, he was found dead in his Cleveland home by Brabner. He had suffered from cancer and clinical depression for years, but at the time of his death, no cause was determined; a few months later it was released that he had accidentally overdosed on two anti-depressant medications. He was 70 years old. **Sources:** *Chicago Tribune*, July 13, 2010; *Los Angeles Times*, July 13, 2010; *New York Times*, July 12, 2010; *Time*, July 26, 2010; *Washington Post*, July 13, 2010, p. B5.

—*Alana Joli Abbott*

Teddy Pendergrass

Born Theodore DeReese Pendergrass, March 26, 1950, in Kingstree, SC; died of colon cancer, January 13, 2010, in Bryn Mawr, PA. Singer. A five-time Grammy Award nominee for best male R&B singer, Teddy Pendergrass was a super star in make-out music. His smooth baritone sound, first made popular with Harold Melvin and the Blue Notes and later just as popular in his own solo career, helped to make ten consecutive albums hit more than one million copies sold. Tunes such as "If You Don't Know Me By Now" and "Love TKO" became classic examples of a sound known as "Philly soul."

Along with his sensual voice, Pendergrass also had the looks of a sex icon. At the height of his career, he hosted midnight shows for "women only." A car crash in 1982 left him paralyzed from the waist down, but he returned to both stage and recording to produce more hits, appearing in the stage musical *Your Arms Too Short to Box with God*, and performing on television. Pendergrass wrote his autobiography, *Truly Blessed*, and he continued to serenade audiences from the stage for the duration of his career.

Born in 1950, Pendergrass grew up with his mother, Ida Pendergrass, in Philadelphia. His father left their family early on and was killed in a knife fight when Pendergrass was only seven. Ida Pendergrass, who was a nightclub performer, recognized her son's musical talent very early on and brought him up singing gospel at the Glad Tidings Holiness Church. Pendergrass was ordained as a minister at the age of ten. While he had a strong base in sacred music, he wanted to perform in the secular world. As a teen, he received a set of drums from his mother, and he left high school before graduating to become a musician.

In the mid-1960s, Pendergrass joined the Cadillacs as their drummer. The group merged with the better-known Harold Melvin and the Blue Notes in 1969, and the Cadillacs effectively became the back-up band for the vocal group. Melvin was the bandleader, but the lead singer was John Atkins, who left the group. When Melvin heard Pendergrass singing before a recording session, he realized the phenomenal talent Pendergrass had and invited him to take Atkins' place.

The Philadelphia International label picked up the Blue Notes, and the group produced some hit singles, including "I Miss You" in 1972, and "If You Don't Know Me By Now" later that year. More hits followed, and the sound of the group became known as "Philly soul." Pendergrass was called "the Black Elvis" by label producer Kenny Gamble, and it was clear that much of the group's success was due to Pendergrass's dynamite vocals. But despite their continued production of hits, not all was well with the band. Pendergrass and Melvin were in conflict, in part because of Melvin's greater billing with the group. For a short time, the group went by the awkward name Harold Melvin and the Blue Notes featuring Teddy Pendergrass. Pendergrass later said that he learned everything he knew about the music business from Melvin, good and bad, but that Melvin considered his band members expendable. Their professional differences could not be overcome, and Pendergrass left the group to go solo in 1976.

While the Blue Notes languished after Pendergrass left them, Pendergrass's solo career continued to produce hit after hit. Starting in 1978, he began producing platinum albums, and his reputation as a man's man, who performed exclusive concerts for women, was solidified. At his women-only concerts, the audience members would often throw lingerie and stuffed animals—usually teddy bears—at the stage.

Tragedy struck in 1982. While driving his Rolls-Royce to a Philadelphia night club, Pendergrass crashed into a metal guardrail and a tree. He was not wearing a seat belt, and the car was crushed, trapping him for 45 minutes before help arrived. His neck was broken, and his spinal cord was partially severed, paralyzing him from the waist down. Though he could still sing, the physical injuries for a star who had based so much of his career on machismo were devastating. Pendergrass first went into isolation, suffering from depression and refusing to work toward a physical recovery. Eventually, he began rehabilitation, and he worked for two years to recover enough to begin recording in the studio. But his confidence was shot, and he suffered from stage fright. In 1985, he made his first return to stage, performing as one of the few black soul artists at the Live Aid concert at Philadelphia's JFK Stadium. The fan response was overwhelming: 90,000 people in the audience celebrated Pendergrass's performance with a standing ovation. The experience encouraged Pendergrass to return to performing on stage.

In 1996, Pendergrass was cast in a revival of the musical *Your Arms to Short to Box with God*, in which a new song and role had been created specifically for him. In 2001, he made a concert tour, and sang from his wheelchair. Pendergrass retired in 2007, but returned to the stage in 2008 on a charity tour.

Along with his music career, Pendergrass founded the Pendergrass Institute for Music and Performing Arts and created a charity, the Teddy Pendergrass Alliance, to support others who suffered from spinal cord injuries. In August of 2009, he began being treated for colon cancer, the disease that led to his death at the age of 59. He is survived by his wife, Joan; his mother, Ida; three children, and two stepchildren. A musical based on Pendergrass' life story, *I Am Who I Am*, was performed in Chicago in 2008. **Sources:** *Los Angeles Times*, January 15, 2010; *New York Times*, January 15, 2010; *Times* (London) January 15, 2010; *Washington Post*, January 15, 2010, p. B6.

—*Alana Joli Abbott*

Frances Reid

Born December 9, 1914, in Wichita Falls, TX; died February 3, 2010, in Beverly Hills, CA. Actress. Frances Reid was a familiar face to generations of daytime drama viewers in her role as matriarch Alice Horton on NBC's *Days of Our Lives*. Since its debut in November of 1965 Reid had played the kindly grandmother, physician's wife, and community-service volunteer whose children and grandchildren tried her patience with their romantic contretemps, criminal acts, and general dysfunction. Her last appearance on the serial came in late 2007, but she remained under contract with the *Days* and was the last remaining original cast member before her death.

The daughter of a banker, Reid was born in 1914 in Wichita Falls, Texas. She grew up in Berkeley, California, and as a young woman took acting classes at the Pasadena Community Playhouse. Her first credited film role came in a 1938 Myrna Loy romantic comedy, *Man-Proof*, and a year later the ingénue appeared on Broadway in a revival of *Where There's a Will*. She spent much of the 1940s on the New York stage, appearing in new works like *The Patriots* and *Highland Fling* and some outstanding revivals of Shakespearean classics like *Hamlet* and *Twelfth Night*. She also won the part of Roxane in a revival of *Cyrano de Bergerac*, which co-starred José Ferrer. They later reprised those roles for a 1949 episode of the *The Philco Television Playhouse*.

Reid found steady work in the emerging medium. She was offered the role in her own daytime drama for CBS in 1954, *Portia Faces Life*, as the newly married title character, a crime-fighting attorney; the show had been a long-running radio serial and this was its first television incarnation. Reid found the demands of a new script and broadcast every day too demanding, however, and left after a year. Already in her forties by then, she discovered that film and television roles were scarcer, and returned to the genre in 1959 when she was cast as Grace Baker on another CBS soap, *As the World Turns*.

During this era, daytime dramas were generally a half-hour in length, and performed live, not taped. Reid found the process challenging, and she was wary when Ted and Betty Corday, the husband-and-wife producers of a new series planned for NBC, asked her to play the matriarch of the Horton family in the fictional town of Salem. She initially agreed to appear on *Days of Our Lives* just for a short time, and debuted with the show in its opening episode on November 8, 1965. Alice Horton was the wife of Dr. Tom Horton, a respected physician at Salem General Hospital, with five grown children. In the first episode, Alice learns that her headstrong granddaughter Julie has been arrested for shoplifting a fur coat. Though the show struggled to attract viewers in its first few years, it vied for the number-one spot in the daytime ratings race for much of the 1970s, and was one of the first American network soap operas to expand to a full hour format.

Alice Horton's perennial worries over the lives of her children and grandchildren—in a rapidly changing world where divorce, premarital sex, and unplanned pregnancies seemed to predominate—struck a chord with *Days of Our Lives* viewers. "Alice was known to *Days* aficionados for her spirited, loving nature, her sound counsel, her family values, her annual Christmas tree decorating party, and her homemade doughnuts," wrote Bruce Weber in the *New York Times*. "Over the years she was a homemaker, a hospital volunteer and board member, a cosmetics company investor and the co-founder of a shelter for teenage runaways and destitute families."

Alice Horton was widowed in 1994, the same year the actor playing her on-screen husband, Macdonald Carey, passed away. Several years later, *Days* fans were shocked when Alice was the victim of a serial killer stalking Salem residents; but her death by asphyxiation, after choking on a doughnut, turned out to be part of a clever scheme to entrap the real killer, and she was found alive and well on an island where Salem had been recreated in its entirety. The murder-mystery/science fiction angle had become standard fare in the storylines of daytime dramas as they struggled to hold on to a dwindling viewership.

Reid made her last appearance as Alice Horton on December 26, 2007, but characters still mentioned her and she remained under contract. She died on February 3, 2010, in Beverly Hills, California, at the age of 95. Her exit as Alice Horton was written into the storyline of *Days of Our Lives*, with family members coming to Salem to pay their respects. Reid's 42-year-long stint as Alice Horton was not the longest continuous role by a single performer in the history of daytime drama—that honor goes to Helen Wagner, who put in 54 years as Nancy Hughes on *As the World Turns*—but she was the sole surviving original *Days* cast member.

Reid was married to actor Philip Bourneuf, who had roles in *Perry Mason* and *Dr. Kildare*, for 39 years. He died in 1979. In her later years, she was an inveterate traveler, and once suffered a stroke that partially paralyzed her while on safari in Africa, but fully recovered. **Sources:** *Los Angeles Times*, February 5, 2010; *New York Times*, February 5, 2010; SoapCentral, http://www.soapcentral.com/days/news/2010/0203-reid_obit.php (April 14, 2011).

—*Carol Brennan*

Pernell Roberts

Born Pernell Elvin Roberts, May 18, 1928, in Waycross, GA; died of pancreatic cancer, January 24, 2010, in Malibu, CA. Actor. Television actor Pernell Roberts was best known for his role on the popular NBC series about the Wild West, *Bonanza*, and on *Trapper John, M.D.*, which ran on CBS from 1979 to 1986. During his stint as Adam Cartwright on *Bonanza* in the early 1960s, Roberts famously assailed television writing standards of the era. "They take a plot and write it six different ways for six different Sundays," he said, according to the *Times* of London. "One week it's lawyers night, next week it's ranchers night. You change protagonist, but it's the same old plot."

Born in 1928, Roberts grew up in a modest home in rural Waycross, Georgia. He demonstrated a musical talent at a young age, performing in church and school productions, and mastered the tuba and other horn instruments. He spent some time at the Georgia Institute of Technology, but left before earning a degree. Enlisting in the U.S. Marine Corps in 1948, he was given a plum assignment as part of the Marine Corps band, which played for White House events and other special occasions. He used his G.I. Bill benefits to return to school after his discharge, taking courses at the University of Maryland.

Roberts began working with a Washington, D.C. theater group in 1950, and showed enough promise that others encouraged him to try his luck in New York. Between 1952 and 1957 he landed a series of increasingly impressive stage roles, working with the North American Lyric Theater and winning a 1955 Drama Desk Award for an off-Broadway staging of the Shakespearean classic *Macbeth*. In the original *New York Times* review, theater critic Brooks Atkinson called the young actor "thoroughly masculine—a ruffian who bulls his way through the plot," according to Roberts' obituary in the same paper. Roberts went on to appear in another Shakespeare work, the comedic *Taming of the Shrew* on Broadway, before moving to Hollywood in 1957.

After signing with Columbia Pictures, Roberts made his screen debut in 1958's *Desire Under the Elms*, the film adaptation of a Eugene O'Neill play with a top-notch cast that included Sophia Loren and Anthony Perkins. In 1959, he landed a starring role in a new NBC series, *Bonanza*, as the educated Adam Cartwright, eldest of three sons who help their father manage a vast cattle ranch near Lake Tahoe in the mid-nineteenth century. His father Ben was played by Lorne Greene, and Adam's half-brothers were the bumbling Hoss (Dan Blocker) and impetuous Little Joe (Michael Landon). After a rocky start, the hourlong dramatic series became a huge hit, and was one of the first to be filmed in color. Spectacular Nevada scenery, horsemanship, gunfights, and the requisite fraternal rivalries were the elements that helped make the show a success, and *Bonanza* made Roberts a star. The show was such a ratings draw that he and his castmates negotiated a new record high for actors' wages in television, bagging $10,000 per episode.

Roberts was not averse to openly criticizing the show, however. He derided the formulaic plot lines the writers devised along with the patriarchal deference the Cartwright sons showed to Lorne Greene's character. "Isn't it just a bit silly for three adult males to get father's permission for everything they do?," Roberts said in a 1963 interview with the *Washington Post*. "I haven't grown at all since the series began four years ago." Roberts, who participated in the 1965 Selma March—the last major protest action of the civil rights movement—also chided NBC for failing to cast minorities on the show and in the network's other series.

Roberts quit *Bonanza* after its sixth season in 1965, but soon learned that his outspoken nature made film and television executives wary about hiring him. He returned to the stage, appearing in regional theater, and made guest appearances in scores of popular television dramas, including *Hawaii Five-O*. There was the occasional feature film, but certainly the low marks of Roberts's once-promising career were a stint in daytime drama and playing Captain von Trapp in the popular musical *The Sound of Music. Bonanza*, meanwhile, ran for another eight seasons, bowing out after the 1972-73 season as the second-longest running television western after *Gunsmoke*.

In 1979, Roberts was hired as the lead in a new medical drama, *Trapper John, M.D.*, on CBS, which resurrected his career. The title character was borrowed from a popular sitcom of the era, *M*A*S*H**, about army doctors in the Korean War. *M*A*S*H** was still running on CBS, but the series showed Dr. John McIntyre in the present, as chief of surgery at a San Francisco hospital, and its producers avoided copyright conflicts by basing the character on the original book that inspired Robert Altman's movie, both of which predated the sitcom. Roberts' character showed integrity and compassion, mentoring a young doctor, Dr. George Alonzo "Gonzo" Gates (Gregory Harrison) whose rebellious nature recalls the surgeon's own early-adult years. Toward the end of the show's seven-season run, Trapper John's fast-talking, ambitious son joins the hospital staff as a new resident. This character was played by Timothy Busfield, who would go on to appear in *Thirtysomething* and then have a long career as a television director.

Roberts had one son, Christopher, who died in a 1989 motorcycle accident. He was divorced three times: from a professor named Vera Mowry in the 1950s, from the actress Judith LeBreque in 1971, and from Kara Knack in 1996. At the time of his death from pancreatic cancer on January 24, 2010, at the age of 81 at his Malibu home, he was married to Eleanor Criswell, who survives him. His second wife went on to a bit of cult-film history with her appearance in David Lynch's first film, *Eraserhead,* in 1977. **Sources:** *Los Angeles Times,* January 25, 2010; *New York Times,* January 26, 2010; *Times* (London), January 27, 2010; *Washington Post,* January 27, 2010, p. B5.

—Carol Brennan

Robin Roberts

Born September 30, 1926, in Springfield, IL; died of natural causes, May 6, 2010, in Temple Terrace, FL. Professional baseball player. One of the greatest pitchers of the 1950s, Robin Roberts led the Philadelphia Phillies to the National League pennant. He was known as one of the "Whiz Kids," a group of upstart ball players whose fresh faces—and continued wins against older, better-known players—earned them a place in the hearts of Philadelphia fans.

From 1951 through 1955, Roberts led the National League twice in strikeouts and four times in victories. He pitched at 95 to 100 miles per hour. In 1952, his peak season, Roberts won 28 games, and his earned run average was 2.59. Working for nearly two decades as a pitcher, Roberts started 609 games, of which he completed 305. He pitched 45 shutouts, and he was included in seven All-Star teams. Over the course of his career, he won 286 games, and for six consecutive seasons, he had 20 wins per season.

Born in 1926 in Springfield, Illinois, Roberts grew up on a farm with his Welsh immigrant parents. His father, who was a coal miner, had brought a cricket bat with him from Wales to the United States, and Roberts grew up learning to swing. He was also talented in sports other than baseball, and he won himself a scholarship to Michigan State for basketball. After serving in the Army Air Force during World War II, Roberts went to Michigan State, where in addition to being the team captain on the basketball team, he tried out for the baseball team. Willing to take any position they would give him, Roberts founded out they needed a pitcher and declared that this was his preferred position.

To improve his pitching, Roberts joined the Vermont summer league, where he was spotted by the Phillies. After being hired on, he pitched a half season for the minors. His Philadelphia debut came in 1948, but it wasn't until two years later that he began to capture the imaginations of fans.

In the 1950 season, the Phillies, who had not performed well for decades, put together a team that included a number of young, promising players. Called the Whiz Kids, they proved their worth by taking first place in the season, defeating the Brooklyn Dodgers in their last game and giving the Phillies their first pennant win in 35 years. The game also marked a personal success for Roberts, as it was his 20th win of the season, making him the first Phillie to win 20 games since 1917. This was just the beginning of Roberts' stardom: for six consecutive seasons, he matched that record, continuing to have more than 20 wins under his belt per season.

Roberts' best season came two years after the pennant win; his season score of wins was 28, versus seven losses, and Roberts completed 30 games of 37 starts. He pitched 300 innings every season for six seasons.

Best known for that series of games with the Phillies, Roberts did play for other teams. He was sold to the Yankees when the 1961 season concluded, but never played for the team. Instead, he pitched for the Chicago Cubs, the Baltimore Orioles, and the Houston Astros. Over the course of his career, it was his ability to concentrate in the stress of a game that he found to be his strongest asset; however, players on opposing teams felt the speed of his pitch was what made Roberts a force to be reckoned with. "He had the best fastball I ever faced," Hall of Fame slugger Ralph Kiner was quoted as having said in the *New York Times.* Despite these strengths, Roberts was far from perfect; in his 1956 season, he yielded 46 home run hits. Over the course of his career, he yielded a record 505 home runs.

Roberts retired in 1966, but his jersey number for the Phillies, 36, retired four years earlier, making it the first number to be retired from the Phillies. He worked as an investment executive, working for a firm from 1977 through 1985. Roberts also became a baseball coach at the University of South Florida in Tampa. The Phillies brought him back on board to work as a minor league instructor, as well. Roberts was elected into the Hall of Fame in 1976.

Along with his work on the field, Roberts helped to form the players' union. He also worked closely with others in the hiring of Marvin Miller, who became the first president of the Major League Baseball Players Association. He was a member of the Baseball Hall of Fame's board of directors.

Roberts died of natural causes in March of 2010 at the age of 83. His wife, Mary, to whom he had been married for 55 years, predeceased him by five years.

Roberts is survived by four sons, a brother, seven grandchildren, and a great-grandchild. **Sources:** *Los Angeles Times Blog,* http://latimesblogs.latimes. com/sports_blog/2010/05/hall-of-fame-pitcher-robin-roberts-dies-at-83.html (May 6, 2010); *New York Times,* May 6, 2010; *Washington Post,* May 7, 2010, p. B6.

—*Alana Joli Abbott*

Carolyn M. Rodgers

Born December 14, 1940, in Chicago, IL; died of cancer, April 2, 2010, in Chicago, IL. Poet. Chicago poet Carolyn M. Rodgers was a voice of the Black Arts Movement in the late 1960s, and continued her career beyond her identity as a revolutionary poet. She explored her newly found spirituality in her 1976 National Book Award finalist *How I Got Ovah: New and Selected Poems,* in which she embraced her femininity in a new way through her acceptance of Christianity.

Rodgers' poetic voice was noted for her use of vernacular spellings and the slang and profanities of the Chicago street. Along with writing, Rodgers was a regular coffeehouse performer, particularly during the Black Arts Movement. She was widely considered a compelling reader and speaker, and she taught her literary theories of the black aesthetic in academic settings as well. Involved in founding Third World Press, through which two of her early works were published, Rodgers also created her own publishing company, Eden Press.

Born in 1940, Rodgers was the last of four children, and was the only one of her siblings to be born in Chicago. The family had moved from Little Rock, Arkansas, before Rodgers' birth. Rodgers and her siblings grew up in the Hyde Park area of Chicago's South Side. Both parents—a welder and a homemaker—were readers, and they encouraged their children to read. Rodgers began experimenting with writing her own poetry from an early age.

Rodgers graduated from Roosevelt University with her bachelor's degree in 1965 and later received her master's from the University of Chicago. She was also involved in writing workshops sponsored by the notable literary collective, the Organization of Black American Culture. She studied under Pulitzer Prize-winner Gwendolyn Brooks, one of the major voices on the literary side of the black power political movement.

Like the poems of her mentor Brooks, Rodgers' early poems were militant free-verse, full of the anger of the black power movement and free with the profanities and slang that filled the language of Rodgers' Chicago neighborhood. Her poetry focused particularly on the experience of being a black woman, and explored self-identity and relationships. Black women in Rodgers' poems are presented as strong survivors, rather than as victims. Despite the politics clear in her early works, the poems tend to be introspective rather than broad proclamations. Throughout her career, her poetry was full of her own, individual passions, and she identified herself as a woman who was unique even in her own community.

"Carolyn Rodgers was one of the finest poets to come out of the Black Arts Movement," Haki Madhubuti, professor, poet, and publisher at Third World, said of Rodgers in the *Chicago Tribune.* In the *New York Times,* he elaborated, "What made her important was her unique use of language and her descriptions of our community. When she read, people would sit up and take notice."

Rodgers published her poetry in a number of collections, including *Paper Soul, Songs of a Blackbird,* and *How I Got Ovah.* The last, which was a finalist for the National Book Award, explored her growth as a poet between the beginning of her career in the 1960s and the book's publication in 1976. Her earlier righteous fury faded into a more spiritual understanding of herself and her work. Despite the spiritual nature of the work, and the topic of Rodgers' Christianity, *How I Got Ovah* remains a sensual work, continuing her earlier theme of experiencing life as a black woman. Her poetry focused on hope and the ability of women to survive and overcome the challenges facing them.

In addition to her poetry, Rodgers penned short stories and essays about both poetry and black culture, many of which were published in academic journals. She was a teacher and lecturer at a number of universities, including the University of Washington, Indiana University, Fisk University, Emory University, and three schools in her native Chicago: Columbia College, Harold Washington College, and Malcolm X College. She was also a playwright. Her play *Love* was produced in the early 1980s in the Manhattan off-Broadway New Federal Theater. She also served as a mentor to the children of family friend, Dr. Linda Powell, particularly spending time with a boy who hoped to become a writer.

Along with her other honors, Rodgers was inducted into the International Literary Hall of Fame for Writers of African Descent, located in the Gwendolyn

Brooks Center for Black Literature and Creative Writing at Chicago State University in 2009. She was also honored with a gospel music tribute broadcast on *With Ossie and Ruby,* a public television program hosted by actors and activists Ossie Davis and Ruby Dee. At the age of 69, Rogers was put into hospice care at Mercy Hospital in Chicago, due to cancer. She died on April 2, 2010. Rogers is survived by her mother, Bazella, who was 99 at the time of her daughter's death, and her sisters Nina and Gloria. **Sources:** *Chicago Tribune,* April 13, 2010; *Los Angeles Times,* April 19, 2010; *New York Times,* April 19, 2010; *Washington Post,* April 23, 2010, p. B06.

—Alana Joli Abbott

Eric Rohmer

Born Jean-Marie Maurice Schérer (some sources say Maurice Henri Joseph Schérer), March 21, 1920, in Nancy (some sources say Tulle), France; died January 11, 2010, in Paris, France. Filmmaker. Over the course of five decades, French filmmaker Eric Rohmer created dozens of films in his own distinct style. Focusing on conversation between characters and stories of manners more than great actions, Rohmer brought to life characters who were tempted to stray from their own romantic commitments, but who eventually showed the strength to hold to their own morals. His characters discussed philosophy, romance, religion, and morality, often in a light, chatty fashion, leading the films to say more about what goes on in the minds of the characters, and their motives for the actions they take, or refrain from taking, over the course of the story.

Rohmer often compared his films to novels, finding their content similar to what would more often be found in a prose format. Early in his career, he penned a novel under the name Gilbert Cordier, and his successful films, particularly in his cycle of "moral tales," were based on prose sketches he created before becoming a filmmaker. His filmmaking style, conversational and typically low-budget, was iconic, and was praised and criticized in equal proportions. A famous line from the Hollywood film *Night Moves,* delivered by Gene Hackman, compared watching a Rohmer film to "watching paint dry." But Rohmer was also an Oscar nominee, and in 2001, he was awarded a Golden Lion at the Venice Film Festival to honor his body of work.

Rohmer, who was secretive about his personal life, was born either Jean-Marie Maurice Schérer or Maurice Henri Joseph Schérer in 1920. His birthplace was either Nancy or Tulle, France. He grew up in the Limousin area of France and studied art at the University of Nancy. His career began as a teacher and film critic. After starting his own, short-lived magazine, Rohmer joined the staff at *Cahiers du Cinéma,* where he worked until 1963.

Several of Rohmer's colleagues at *Cahiers* were also filmmakers. Rohmer had attempted to make his first feature film in 1952, but found himself short on funds; he had another chance when several of his colleagues began finding popularity with their "New Wave" films. Rohmer made *The Sign of Leo* in 1959, but it did not receive the type of critical attention that allowed him to leave his day job. In 1962, however, he found the success he needed with his 26-minute short, *The Bakery Girl of Monceau,* which allowed him to leave *Cahiers* and begin work on what would become his "Six Moral Tales" series. The second, *Suzanne's Career,* was also a short film, and was released in 1963.

My Night at Maud's, the third episode in the series, but the fourth to be filmed, brought Rohmer even greater critical attention when it was nominated for an Oscar. The story of a young engineer who spends a chaste night with a tempting femme fatale, the film was a prime example of Rohmer's themes: conversation, moral dilemma, and ultimate triumph of will over desire. Three more films followed in that series, after which Rohmer attempted two period films. *The Marquise of O...,* made in Germany and filmed in German, was based on a nineteenth century novel about the ethical dilemmas of an unmarried, pregnant girl. The film used many of the same stylistic choices as original Rohmer material, and was greeted with success. The following medieval film, *Percival le Gallois,* was too heavily stylized, however, and did not find an audience.

In 1981, Rohmer launched a new series of six films, "Comedies and Proverbs," based on sayings and quotations, that featured more fickle characters than had appeared in his earlier works. Some critics felt they had an air of misanthropy. His final series, "Tales of the Four Seasons," returned to his earlier, philosophical style, with love stories that were both earnest and genuine. Later in his career, Rohmer did work for television; he also created the digital film *The Lady and the Duke,* the true spy tale *Triple Agent,* and the seventeenth century love story *Astrée and Céladon,* which would be his last film.

Rohmer was a tall man with blue eyes and a quiet, intense demeanor, who inspired a hushed atmosphere on his sets. He was meticulous with his film schedule and with his plans for filming. For *Claire's*

Knee, he planted roses a year in advance of filming to be sure that the blossoms would appear as he wanted them in a particular scene. He planned to film a snow scene for *My Night at Maud's* months in advance, to be rewarded when the weather cooperated with snow on the day of filming. This level of preparation often meant fewer takes during the actual shooting of the film.

Highly protective of his personal life, Rohmer rarely appeared in photographs or interviews, and he once wore a disguise, including a fake moustache, to a New York premiere to avoid being recognized. He did not own a telephone or a car. According to rumor, his wife, Thérèse Barbet, thought he was a businessman rather than a filmmaker. In January of 2010, Rohmer was hospitalized, and he died in Paris on January 11, 2010. He is survived by Barbet, their two sons, and his brother, philosopher Rene Schérer. **Sources:** *Los Angeles Times,* January 12, 2010; *New York Times,* January 12, 2010; *Times* (London), January 12, 2010; *Washington Post,* January 12, 2010, p. B5.

—*Alana Joli Abbott*

Moishe Rosen

Born Martin Meyer Rosen, April 12, 1932, in Kansas City, MO; died of prostate cancer, May 19, 2010, in San Francisco, CA. Minister. Moishe Rosen founded the controversial Christian religious organization known as Jews for Jesus. A convert from Judaism to the Baptist faith, Rosen devoted his life to persuading other Jews to become "born again" evangelical Christians. Jews for Jesus provoked immense debate, and the group and its tactics were roundly condemned by mainstream Jewish leaders. "Rosen," opined Ruth Tucker on the *Christianity Today* Web site, "was the most colorful Jewish evangelist of the twentieth century—perhaps since the apostle Paul."

Rosen was born into an Orthodox Jewish family in Kansas City, Missouri, in 1932. His family later moved to Denver, Colorado, where he married his high-school girlfriend Ceil Starr in 1950. She, too, came from a Jewish family, but befriended a Christian woman and began leaning toward conversion. Rosen was aghast and read the books of the Bible's New Testament—the holy texts authored by followers of Jesus, who broke with Judaism formally around 70 CE—in order to rebut her arguments. Instead of bolstering his own faith, the New Testament scriptures caused Rosen to question it instead, and by 1953 both he and his wife had formally converted to Christianity. Rosen's family wholly disowned him for his decision.

Missionary efforts to recruit Jews to Christianity were controversial and, Jewish leaders asserted, played upon a sense of shame and discrimination that Jews felt as outsiders in a predominantly Christian society. Official Jewish teachings revered Christ as a prophet, but not as the son of God. Christianity, by contrast, was a faith whose central tenet posited that Christ was the Messiah, the human representative of God on earth. Jews who accepted this were called "Messianic" Jews, but they were judged by mainstream Jewish religious leaders as possessing heretical beliefs. Jewish theology maintained that the two religions were incompatible on this essential question, and that a believer could not worship Christ as their savior and remain part of the Jewish community of faith.

Following a stint at the University of Colorado, Rosen enrolled at the Northeastern Bible Institute in New Jersey to study theology and was ordained a Baptist minister in 1957. In the years following a mass-scale effort to exterminate Jews in the Holocaust during World War II, groups whose mission was to convert Jews to Christianity fell out of favor and were largely disdained by both Christian and Jewish theologians. One that was still nominally active was the American Board of Missions to the Jews, which later evolved into Chosen People Ministries. Rosen worked for the Board in New York and Los Angeles before arriving in San Francisco in the late 1960s.

At the time, the Bay Area was the locus of a massive cultural change, with student demonstrations on California college campuses for freedom of speech spiraling into several submovements, including black militantism and gay rights. Rosen adapted the mischievously defiant tactics of the countercultural scene for his own mission, initially aiming propaganda materials at young Jews who had rejected the rigid conformity of their parents' generation; "God likes beards too," read one of his early tracts. The rallies and pamphlets eventually crystallized in 1973 into the organization Rosen controversially called "Jews for Jesus."

Rosen's group was assailed by leaders of mainstream Jewish organizations, and it fought court battles on freedom-of-speech principles for passing out literature in public places. There were also charges that Jews for Jesus used cult-like recruiting and training methods. Prominent Jews such as Elie Wiesel, who wrote extensively on the Holocaust, along with the American Jewish Committee and the Jewish Community Relations Council of New York also criticized Rosen. "What they are attempting is spiritual genocide," asserted the latter group's director, Philip Abramowitz, according to the *Washington Post*. "They want to see Judaism destroyed as an entity."

Rosen remained executive director of Jews for Jesus until 1996. He was a born-again Christian, but still adhered to some traditional Jewish rites, including the Passover seder and fasting on Yom Kippur. He laid out his arguments in several books over the years, including *The Sayings of Chairman Moishe*, a nod to the popular Communist tract from China, *The Sayings of Chairman Mao*. One of his famous quips posed the question, "If the Jews didn't need Jesus, why didn't he come by way of Ireland?," according to Tucker's tribute to him in *Christianity Today*. Rosen died of prostate cancer on May 19, 2010, in San Francisco. Survivors include his wife; his daughter Lyn, who works for the Chicago branch of Jews for Jesus; and his daughter Ruth, who helps run the national office in San Francisco. "You can take from me everything but my Jewishness and my belief in God," Rosen once said, according to his *Washington Post* obituary. "You can say I'm a nuisance, a Christian, out of step with the Jewish community, but you can't say I'm not a Jew." **Sources:** *Christianity Today*, http://www. christianitytoday.com/ct/2010/mayweb-only/30-52.0.html (November 26, 2011); *Jewish Chronicle*, http://www.thejc.com/news/world-news/31908/jews-jesus-founder-moishe-rosen-dies (November 26, 2011); *Los Angeles Times*, May 23, 2010; *New York Times*, May 22, 2010; *Washington Post*, May 21, 2010.

—Carol Brennan

J. D. Salinger

Born January 1, 1919, in New York, NY; died January 27, 2010, in Cornish, NH. Author. During his college years, J. D. Salinger was said to have announced that he intended to write the Great American Novel. With the 1951 publication of *The Catcher in the Rye*, it became arguable that this is exactly what he had done. The author wrote from the voice of Holden Caulfield, a teenaged, misfit narrator who was disillusioned with adult life, which he considered "phony," and who came to embody the attitude of a generation. Despite mixed critical reviews, the novel was a best-seller, and it continues to be one of the most-taught and most-banned books in the United States.

The mythology that grew up around Salinger was in part due to his writing, but also in part due to his absolute rejection of fame. After he achieved such great success with the publication of *The Catcher in the Rye* and several other short stories and novellas, partially collected in *Nine Stories, Franny and Zooey*, and *Raise High the Roof Beam, Carpenters and Seymour: An Introduction*, Salinger ceased publishing his work. He left New York for Cornish, New Hampshire, where he lived in seclusion, with the exception of his wife and children, for more than 50 years. He refused interviews and did not allow his photograph to appear in the media. But rather than keeping him out of the public eye, this self-exile only heightened the mystique. A few rare interviews, and memoirs published by those who knew him, implied that he was still writing, and critics and fans alike eagerly awaited the possibility of new Salinger works; however, at the time of his death in 2010 no new works had been published, in part because, as Salinger explained in a rare interview with the *New York Times* in 1974, that he found "a marvelous peace in not publishing."

Salinger was born on New Year's Day in 1919 in the New York City borough of Manhattan. He and his elder sister, Doris, were the children of a Jewish importer of meats and cheese and his Scots-Irish wife. This mixed-heritage was later reflected in Salinger's Glass family of characters. The family lived on the East Side in Manhattan.

A poor student, much like his character Holden Caulfield, Salinger went to several public schools and the prestigious, progressive private McBurney School. He was noted by school officials to have plenty of ability and talent, but lacked any desire to complete his work. Failing out of McBurney, Salinger was sent to Valley Forge Military Academy in Wayne, Pennsylvania, which became the model for the prep school Holden ran away from in *The Catcher in the Rye*. Salinger managed the school fencing team and was the school yearbook literary editor. He graduated in 1936, earning his sole diploma.

Salinger attended New York University but dropped out after only a few weeks, instead traveling to Europe with his father, who hoped Salinger would take over his import business. The life of a businessman did not appeal, and Salinger attempted college again, this time at Ursinus College, where he was said to have bragged about his writing abilities and declared he would write the Great American Novel. He completed about a semester before dropping out. Living with his parents in Manhattan, Salinger took courses in writing at Columbia

University from Whit Burnett, who also edited *Story* magazine. Burnett was sufficiently impressed by Salinger's work that he published "The Young Folks" when Salinger was 21.

The early stories that Salinger published in *Story, Esquire,* and *Collier's* were fairly formulaic, and showed little of the style that would become associated with his writings. Salinger submitted works to the *New Yorker,* as well, and after a year of rejections, the magazine agreed in 1941 to publish "Slight Rebellion Off Madison," a story that later became part of *The Catcher in the Rye;* however, as the United States entered World War II, the magazine decided to postpone publication, not wanting to encourage children to run away from school.

Salinger was drafted into the Army in 1942, but he did not stop writing. His typewriter accompanied him on his tour in Europe, where he reportedly wrote even from foxholes. Several of his stories written during the war were published in the *Saturday Evening Post.* Salinger served in counterintelligence and fought in the bloody battles of Normandy and the Battle of the Bulge, events that impacted the rest of his life. He spent some time in the hospital for "battle fatigue," which was usually used to describe a mental breakdown, but he stayed in Europe after the end of the war to interview and chase Nazi agents.

After "Slight Rebellion Off Madison" was eventually published in 1946, Salinger developed an exclusive relationship writing for the *New Yorker.* In 1951, the publication of *The Catcher in the Rye* launched Salinger into stardom. The novel stayed on the bestseller list of the *New York Times* for 30 weeks and, by the 1960s, it had become not only well-loved and largely considered a classic, but also course reading in several high schools and universities. But fame did not sit well with Salinger, and for the second printing of the novel, he demanded his publishers remove his photograph from the jacket cover. In 1953, the year his *Nine Stories,* which showed his increased interest in Zen Buddhism, was published, he moved to New Hampshire to get away from the press and publicity.

Salinger's works from 1953 to 1965, when his last long piece was published in the *New Yorker,* focused on the Glass family. Like Holden, the Glass family members never quite fit in to the world around them. Salinger clearly loved the characters, which some critics embraced, while others scorned them as too well-loved by their author. After 1965, Salinger largely disappeared from the public view, surfacing in the 1970s in a lawsuit attempting to prevent the publication of an unauthorized collection of his short stories, in the late 1990s with the publication of a former lover's memoirs, and in the 2000s with his daughter's memoirs and another lawsuit, this one attempting to prevent the publication of an unauthorized sequel to *The Catcher in the Rye,* which also featured Salinger as a character.

In 2009, Salinger broke his hip, but he recovered well. A sudden decline in health in the first few weeks of 2010 was a surprise, and Salinger died of natural causes on January 27 of that year. Newspapers speculated on whether or not new Salinger works would be released now that the author no longer had to suffer the intrusions on his privacy that publishing had brought him. Regardless of future publications, his legacy was well established from the publication of *The Catcher in the Rye.* He is survived by his third wife, Colleen O'Neill; his children Matthew and Margaret; and three grandsons. **Sources:** *Entertainment Weekly,* February 5, 2010; *Los Angeles Times,* January 29, 2010; *New York Times,* January 29, 2010; *Times* (London), January 29, 2010; *Washington Post,* January 29, 2010, p. A1.

—*Alana Joli Abbott*

Erich Segal

Born Erich Wolf Segal, June 16, 1937, in New York, NY; died of a heart attack, January 17, 2010, in London, England. Author. Erich Segal's first novel, *Love Story,* was a publishing sensation in 1970 and timed to coincide with its equally blockbuster screen adaptation. The book spent a year on the *New York Times* best-seller list and was the top-grossing movie of 1971, though critics effusively disparaged both the schmaltzy novel and Hollywood version that starred Ryan O'Neal and Ali MacGraw. "Segal, who taught Greek and Roman literature at Yale University, might have been an unlikely author of a heart-tugging tale of doomed romance," wrote *Washington Post* reporter Matt Schudel, "but his story captured the spirit of the time, and its signature line became a catch phrase: 'Love means never having to say you're sorry.'"

The son of a rabbi, Segal was born in the New York City borough of Brooklyn in 1937 and was a preternaturally gifted student. In his teens, he attended both Midwood High School of Brooklyn College and a Jewish theological seminary. Fluent in three ancient languages—Hebrew, Greek, and Latin—he graduated from Harvard University in 1958 as the class poet and deliverer of the traditional Latin oration at commencement. He and a classmate took a musical based on Greek history's Helen of Troy to an off-Broadway production in the early 1960s, and his work on other projects led to an offer to retool the script for the 1968 Beatles movie *Yellow Submarine*. He began teaching at Yale in 1964, a year before he earned his Ph.D. in comparative literature from Harvard, and worked on original screenplays in his off-hours.

Segal knew a young model, Wellesley College grad Ali MacGraw, who became famous almost overnight in 1969 for her role in the screen version of *Goodbye Columbus*, the Philip Roth story about a romance between two American Jews from different backgrounds. MacGraw wed a rising studio executive, Robert Evans, and convinced him to acquire Segal's screenplay, which was simply titled *Love Story*. Few at Paramount Pictures wanted to make the movie, and Evans even had trouble finding a director. He convinced Segal to turn the screenplay into a novel first, and then stuck a deal with Harper & Row to share some of the promotional costs. The gambit worked: the novel became a bestseller overnight, and Paramount rushed out the movie in time for the 1970 holiday season.

Love Story recounted, in flashback form, the romance between Harvard student Oliver Barrett IV (O'Neal), scion of an old-money Boston family, and Jenny Cavilleri (MacGraw), a music student at Radcliffe College, the women's adjunct of Harvard before it became a co-ed institution. Jenny comes from a humble Italian-American background and is shocked when she visits the estate where Oliver grew up, where his elitist parents treat her frostily. When the couple marry, Oliver's parents disown him. He finishes law school and the couple moves to New York City, where Jenny learns she has a fatal disease. In the final scenes, Oliver reconciles with his now-contrite father, played by Ray Milland.

When *Love Story* was released in paperback form, it marked the largest-ever print run for a title at 4.3 million copies. The movie was the number-one box-office draw of 1971, and is considered one of the first genuine blockbuster films in cinema's modern era. It cost Paramount just $2 million to make, but grossed more than $200 million worldwide, and even rescued the studio itself: the board of directors had so little faith in Evans' judgment they were considering selling the studio, but Evans persuaded them to wait for *Love Story*'s release. Paramount was then able to start production on its next major effort, an adaptation of Mario Puzo's mob saga *The Godfather*.

Segal made a mint from *Love Story*, but was treated coolly by his classics-department colleagues at Yale and denied tenure in 1972. He went on to write several other novels, including a much-anticipated sequel, *Oliver's Story*, for which O'Neal reprised his screen role. Both the movie and the film, which follow the widower's career turmoil and romance with a department-store heiress played by Candice Bergen, failed to replicate the success of *Love Story*. His other books include the novels *The Class* and *Doctors*, along with a well-received survey of the art of stage comedy in Western civilization, *The Death of Comedy*, published by Harvard University Press in 2001.

Segal quit teaching in the 1980s, settling in London with his wife and two daughters. He was an avid runner and veteran Boston Marathon finisher, and even served as a commentator for ABC Sports for the 1972 and 1976 Olympic Games. His athletic and academic pursuits were curtailed in his final years by Parkinson's disease, and he died at age 72 at his London home on January 17, 2010, after suffering a heart attack. His wife Karen James survives him, as do daughters Miranda and Francesca.

Despite the critics' jibes and the passage of time, the popularity of *Love Story* endured. A few months after Segal's death, the story was turned into a musical that premiered at the Duchess Theatre in London's West End. Former U.S. vice president Al Gore knew Segal when Gore was an undergraduate at Harvard in the late 1960s and the roommate of future Hollywood star Tommy Lee Jones; Segal later said that the character of Oliver Barrett was a composite of Gore, Jones, and a few other student-athletes he knew. Even Harvard distanced itself from the success of the movie, rarely granting any other filmmakers permission to shoot on its storied campus. The success of his first novel "totally ruined me," Segal once said, according to the *Los Angeles Times*. "But I'm not going to say I'm sorry."

Sources: *Independent* (London, England), January 22, 2010, p. 46; *Los Angeles Times*, January 20, 2010; *New York Times*, January 20, 2010, p. A15; August 20, 2010; *Times* (London), January 20, 2010, p. 52; *Variety*, May 1, 2000, p. 1; *Washington Post*, January 20, 2010, p. B5.

—*Carol Brennan*

Cesare Siepi

Born February 10, 1923, in Milan, Italy; died of respiratory failure following a stroke, July 5, 2010, in

Atlanta, GA. Opera singer. For more than 40 years, bass opera singer Cesare Siepe entertained audiences the world over with his warm performance style. He was noted for not just singing the roles, but bringing the characters he acted to life for his audiences. "I think he was one of the greatest basses of his time, if not the greatest," wrote Martin Bernheimer in the *Los Angeles Times,* for which he served as a music critic from 1965 through 1996. "He was never content to just sing, he created a character."

Featured in nearly 500 performances with the Metropolitan Opera, for which he played 17 roles, Siepi was noted for the variety in his performances. He excelled at roles both serious and comic, though some critics, such as Peter G. Davis, found his performances "intelligent, consistently professional," instead of giving "arresting artistic" interpretations, according to the *New York Times.* Other critics embraced him eagerly, and he became a favorite to perform the title role in Mozart's *Don Giovanni,* due to his virtuoso vocal performance, coupled with his natural good looks and charismatic stage presence.

Born in Milan, Italy, in 1923, Siepi was the son of an accountant and a homemaker. The family enjoyed music but showed no particular talent for it. When Siepi was 16, his father died; his half-brother was killed on the Russian front during World War II, making Siepi the only source of support for his mother. Initially, he hoped to become a boxer, but it was in his voice where he found his real calling.

Siepi was largely self-taught as a musician, though he won a scholarship to a conservatory in Milan, where he studied. Having joined a madrigal group when he was 14, Siepi performed publicly as a teen, and made his first concert performance at 17. When he was 18, he was persuaded by friends to enter a vocal competition in Florence, for which he won first place.

A manager who had attended the competition offered Siepi the role of Sparafucile in Verdi's *Rigoletto.* The role—that of a hired assassin—is quite low in range, particularly for a man so young, but Siepi played it effectively enough that, despite fleeing to Switzerland during World War II, he immediately launched into a successful Italian career upon his return. He performed at La Scala in Milan, in a production of Verdi's *Nabucco,* for his first performance after the theatre was reconstructed following the war. That role began Siepi's relationship with La Scala, which endured for the rest of his vocal career.

Siepi's international breakthrough came almost by accident. Though he had already been featured in operas and concerts throughout Europe, it was a 1950 invitation to perform at the Metropolitan Opera in New York City that opened him up to the rest of the world. General manager Rudolf Bing had hoped to hire Bulgarian-born Boris Christoff for the 1950 performance of Verdi's *Don Carlo,* but when Christoff was mysteriously denied his visa, Bing hurriedly contacted Siepi to take on the role of King Philip II. With only a few weeks' notice, Siepi came to New York, missing several rehearsals, but ultimately stepping into the role and winning high critical praise. Virgil Thomson of the *New York Herald Tribune,* quoted in the *Washington Post,* wrote at the time that Siepi was "Clearly a fine musician and an artist.... His rich bass voice, moreover, is both vibrant and warm. It is a beautiful voice and seems to be thoroughly schooled. Mr. Siepi's dramatic performance was no less distinguished than his vocal work."

Thus began a relationship between Siepi and the Metropolitan Opera that lasted for 23 years. He was also a regular performer at London's Covent Garden, where he debuted in 1950. He became well-known for his performances of King Philip II in *Don Carlo,* Don Giovanni in the opera of the same name, the title character in Mussorgsky's *Boris Godunov,* Figaro in *The Marriage of Figaro,* and Gurnemanz in Wagner's *Parsifal,* among others. Of a 1970 performance of *Parsifal,* British critic Herbert Weinstock of *Opera* wrote, as quoted in the *New York Times,* Siepi "really sang the role rather than growling it and acted with touching conviction," performing the words in Wagner's script "as if born to them." Along with these serious roles, he was also known for his comedic performance of Don Basilio in the *Barber of Seville* by Rossini.

Along with his stage performances, Sipei recorded widely, particularly during the 1950s at the peak of his career. He earned high praise at the Salzburg Festival, at which he made live recordings, and performed with the Vienna Philharmonic on the recordings of two of Mozart's operas. He worked with record labels including Decca and Naxos, and he performed show tunes by Cole Porter on one album, showing his versatility. Siepi attempted a Broadway career, performing in *Bravo Giovanni* in 1962 and the 1979 show *Carmelina.* Niether was a critical success.

In concerts, Siepi showed his range, performing music by Schubert, Schumall, and Brahms at a 1986 recital at UCLA. Siepi retired from opera in 1989. In 2010, he suffered a stroke and was taken to the hospital in Atlanta, the city where he had lived for 25 years. A few days later, on July 5, 2010, Siepi died of respiratory failure; he was 87. He is survived by his wife Louellen Sibley—whom he had met through the Metropolitan Opera, where she worked as a dancer—and their two children. **Sources:** *Los Angeles Times*, July 6, 2010; *New York Times*, July 7, 2010; *Washington Post*, July 7, 2010, p. B7.

—Alana Joli Abbott

Jean Simmons

Born Jean Merilyn Simmons, January 31, 1929, in London, England; naturalized U.S. citizen, 1956; died of lung cancer, January 22, 2010, in Santa Monica, CA. Actress. British screen star Jean Simmons was one of the most lauded young talents to migrate from England to Hollywood in the years following World War II. Co-star to Laurence Olivier, Marlon Brando, Kirk Douglas, and scores of other leading names, Simmons first found fame because of "her beguiling beauty and demure British manners," asserted the *Sunday Times*. "But she disliked being required only to look dignified and pretty [and] also had an independent streak, fighting off the tentacles of the tycoon Howard Hughes as a young star."

Born in 1929, Simmons grew up in the suburbs of north London. Her father was a physical education teacher and former Olympic gymnast. In her early teens, Simmons began classes at the Aida Foster School of Dancing, where a talent scout found her and cast her in the 1944 comedy *Give Us the Moon*. A year later, Simmons made a brief but memorable appearance in *The Way to the Stars*, a patriotic drama about the England's Royal Air Force flyers, as the singer of a wartime ditty, "Let Him Go, Let Him Tarry."

Simmons, under contract to the British film studio owned by J. Arthur Rank, made dozens of films during these early years of her career, but a few are notable. There was David Lean's 1946 adaptation of the Charles Dickens novel *Great Expectations*, which made her a star, and the 1947 melodrama *Black Narcissus*, which starred Deborah Kerr as an Anglican nun in a remote Himalayan convent. Simmons played Kanchi, the temple dancer who seduces an Indian prince whom the nuns are tutoring. That choice role led to an offer from Laurence Olivier to star in his new screen version of *Hamlet*, in which he took the title role and also directed. It was a tremendous coup for any young star, and Simmons' famous beauty and relative inexperience made her Ophelia an unexpectedly successful one. She was

just 18 when they shot the movie, and 19 when she appeared on the June 28, 1948, cover of *Time* magazine, whose critic declared that Simmons "has an oblique, individual beauty and a trained dancer's continuous grace. As a result, she jerks genuine tears during scenes which ordinarily cause Shakespeare's greatest admirers to sneak out for a drink. Compared with most of the members of the cast, she is obviously just a talented beginner. But she is the only person in the picture who gives every one of her lines the bloom of poetry and the immediacy of ordinary life."

Simmons was nominated for an Academy Award as Best Supporting Actress for *Hamlet*. In 1950, she married British actor Stewart Granger, and the two moved to Hollywood. Rank had sold her contract to RKO Pictures, which came under ownership of aircraft mogul Howard Hughes. "The strange tycoon was obsessed with her personally, and he laid siege to her romantically and professionally so that she did not work for [more than] a year," wrote David Thomson in the London *Guardian*. Hughes did let her make one project, director Otto Preminger's 1952 noir thriller *Angel Face* in which she starred as a vindictive young woman who sets out to destroy her widowed father's second marriage, seducing tough-guy actor Robert Mitchum into her murderous scheme. Another director, William Wyler, wanted to cast her in the lead in *Roman Holiday*, but Hughes refused; the part went to Audrey Hepburn instead, who won an Academy Award for it.

Simmons finally took Hughes and RKO to court and won; for the rest of her career she avoided further contractual obligations. She starred in the MGM costume epic *Young Bess* as Elizabeth I, and with another fellow Brit, Richard Burton, in the 1953 biblical drama *The Robe*. She played the mistress *Désirée* to Marlon Brando's Napoleon Bonaparte, and appeared again with Brando in the sole screen musical of her career, *Guys and Dolls*. She won a Golden Globe for her portrayal of the Salvation Army worker Sarah Brown. The director, Joseph L. Mankiewicz, would later hail her as "an enormously underrated girl," according to Thomson's *Guardian* tribute. "In terms of talent, Jean Simmons is so many heads and shoulders above most of her contemporaries, one wonders why she didn't become the great star she could have been."

Simmons appeared in the 1958 western *The Big Country* and in that same year's *Home Before Dark*, about an unhappy housewife whose husband has her committed to a psychiatric hospital. She was the love interest to Kirk Douglas in *Spartacus*, Stanley Kubrick's Roman Empire epic. In 1960, her marriage to Granger ended and she married the director Richard Brooks, who helmed her in one of the last great roles of her career, the female evangelist who lures sinners in road-show revival meetings with the help of Burt Lancaster's *Elmer Gantry*.

The mother of two daughters by the early 1960s, Simmons worked only intermittently for the remainder of her career. She was nominated for a Best Actress Academy Award for *The Happy Ending*, a 1969 movie written and directed by her husband about a woman who drinks. Several years after her second marriage ended, Simmons admitted that she had undergone treatment for alcohol abuse at the Betty Ford Clinic in the mid-1980s. For much of that decade, Simmons appeared in television miniseries, including *The Thorn Birds*, for which she won an Emmy Award.

Simmons continued working well into her seventies. She delivered a voice for the English version of the Japanese animated sensation *Howl's Moving Castle*, and appeared in a 2009 British drama, *Shadows in the Sun*. She died of lung cancer at her home in Santa Monica, California, just a few days shy of what would have been her 81st birthday. Survivors include her daughter with Granger, Tracy, and Kate, from her second marriage. Both daughters were named after two of Simmons' close friends, the actors Spencer Tracy and Katherine Hepburn. **Sources:** *Guardian* (London), January 24, 2010; *New York Times*, January 24, 2010; *Sunday Times* (London), January 24, 2010, p. 12; *Time*, June 28, 1948; *Times* (London), January 25, 2010, p. 55.

—*Carol Brennan*

Ted Stevens

Born Theodore Fulton Stevens, November 18, 1923, in Indianapolis, IN; died of injuries sustained in a plane crash, August 9, 2010, in Alaska. U.S. Senator. Known fondly to his constituents as "Uncle Ted," former Alaska Senator Ted Stevens, a Republican, served in the U.S. Senate for 40 years. He was the longest-serving Republican in the history of the Senate. He was noted for his penchant for channeling federal funds to his home state, and often commented that his most important job was standing up for the rights of Alaska.

Historian Stephen Haycox said in the *Washington Post*, "The job of Alaska's congressional delegation has always been to pursue any project that has any promise of economic development," an idea that Stevens understood implicitly and consistently acted upon. Haycox continued by stating that Stevens is likely "the most important Alaskan in shaping modern Alaska."

Born in Indianapolis, Indiana, in 1923, Stevens lived with various relatives after his parents divorced when he was only six. He spent much of his later childhood in Manhattan Beach, California, with an aunt and uncle, where he practiced surfing; in later years, in his Senate office, he kept a surfboard he purchased during the 1940s as a reminder.

During World War II, Stevens served in the Army Air Forces, joining as a pilot at the age of 19. He flew transports over the Himalayas on a dangerous route, known as "the Hump," throughout the war, supplying Chinese nationals in their efforts against the Japanese occupying forces. In his service, he twice earned the Distinguished Flying Cross and additionally received two Air Medals.

Though none of his family had attended college, Stevens used money from the G.I. Bill to receive an education. He graduated from the University of California at Los Angeles in 1947; he pursued his law degree at Harvard, from which he graduated in 1950. In 1952, the year that Stevens married Ann Mary Cherrington, he took a job in the then-federal territory of Alaska, where he became a federal prosecutor. Within the next few years, he had a job as an Interior Department lawyer in Washington, D.C., where he lobbied for Alaska to become a state. The goal was achieved in 1959, when Alaska was made the 49th state. The following year, he returned to Alaska and opened a private law firm; he also entered politics, losing two races for U.S. Senate before winning a seat in the Alaska state legislature in 1964.

In 1968, Stevens' goal of becoming a representative in the U.S. Senate was realized. Senator Edward L. Bartlett, a Democrat, died while in office. Alaska Governor Walter Hickel, a Republican, appointed Stevens to take Bartlett's seat. Early on he showed an ability to help pass major legislation due to his willingness to form alliances with Democrats as well as members of his own party. In 1972, he was named to the Appropriations Committee and, in his position there, he traded favors with other senators, helping them to secure funds for their own home-state projects in return for their alliance on Alaska-related issues.

Stevens' willingness to work with members of both parties was one of the hallmarks of his career in office. He was known as a senator who could prepare, and bring to fruition, bipartisan bills. Typically on federal-level votes, he sided with his party, but he occasionally voted with the Democrats, as in his 1999 vote against tax cuts (he was in favor of spending surplus) and his vote against President Bill Clinton's impeachment.

Stevens was a favorite target of lobbyists advocating limits on government pork barrel spending. He funneled billions of dollars into Alaska on a variety of projects, such as the Trans-Alaska Pipeline, authorized by a bill in 1973; the pro-environment 2006 Magnuson-Stevens Act, which was put in place to protect against over-fishing; the infamous 2005 "bridge to nowhere"; and legislation to improve the quality of life in rural Alaska, including changes to the cost of groceries delivered by mail, and funding improvement in sewage systems and other public health concerns. In his farewell speech to the Senate, he stated that his philosophy throughout his career had been, according to the *Los Angeles Times,* "to hell with politics. Do what's right for Alaska."

Stevens' political career ended in 2008, when he narrowly lost his seat to Democrat Mark Begich, who had been the mayor of Anchorage. The race was impacted by charges against Stevens for concealing income in gifts; he faced seven felony counts of lying on Senate disclosure forms, and was believed to have concealed $250,000 in gifts. Stevens protested the allegations, particularly in the case of discounted home renovations, stating that he had paid his bill, assuming that the charges accurately reflected the work done by the contractor. Eight days before the 2008 election, Stevens was convicted. Within the next six months, the U.S. Attorney General had the indictment dismissed, explaining that evidence that would have supported the defense had been withheld by federal prosecutors.

In 1978, Stevens survived a plane crash that killed his wife and four other passengers. He remarried in 1980. On August 9, 2010, he was involved in another plane crash; the injuries from this second crash ended his life. He was 86 years old. He is survived by his second wife, Catherine Chandler, five children from his first marriage, a daughter from his second marriage, and eleven grandchildren. **Sources:** *Los Angeles Times,* August 11, 2010; *New York Times,* August 10, 2010; *Washington Post,* August 11, 2010, p. A1.

—Alana Joli Abbott

Stewart Udall

Born January 31, 1920, in St. Johns, AZ; died of natural causes, March 20, 2010, in Santa Fe, NM. Interior secretary and politician. Former Interior Secretary Stewart L. Udall served under presidents John F. Kennedy and Lyndon B. Johnson and led Congress initiatives to aid victims of radiation exposure. He is best known for his efforts to expand the national park lands of the United States. "Any wilderness area, any national park and national monument—wherever you live in the United States now, there is one relatively close to you," Carl Pope, chairman of the Sierra Club, was quoted as having said in the *Los Angeles Times.* "[Udall] created the spirit that made all those things possible."

During Udall's tenure, he helped to add large amounts of land to the national parks. Working with other lawmakers, environmentalists, conservationists, and writers, Udall paved the way toward the development of laws dedicated to conserving air, water, and land in the United States, including 1964's Wilderness Act, the Land and Water Conservation Fund Act of 1965, the Water Quality Act and the Solid Waste Disposal Act that same year, the Endangered Species Preservation Act in 1966, and 1968's Wild and Scenic Rivers Act.

Udall was born in St. Johns, Arizona, the town founded by his grandfather, David King Udall, in 1880. Udall's grandfather was a Mormon missionary; his father, Levi Udall, was a chief justice in Arizona's Supreme Court. Despite his father's political position, the family lived on a subsistence farm where Udall grew up with four siblings. The farm was not far from the Zuni and Navajo reservations in the northeast part of the state.

A Mormon, like his grandfather before him, Udall interrupted his studies at the University of Arizona to go on his mission service in New York and Pennsylvania. During World War II, Udall served as a B-24 tail gunner in the 15th Army Air Forces, and fought over Italy. He returned home to finish college and went on to law school, graduating in 1948. He founded a law firm in Tucson, and later, his brother Morris joined him as a partner.

Udall was elected to Congress in 1954. He held his seat in Congress up until Kennedy appointed him to the position of Secretary of the Interior in 1960. Despite Udall's move, his congressional seat remained in the family; his brother Morris was elected into the spot. Careers in politics continued to run in the family. Both Morris' son Mark and Udall's son Tom were elected to the Senate in 2008; the former a senator for Colorado, and the latter, for New Mexico.

As Secretary of the Interior, Udall was instrumental in increasing public holdings, acquiring 3.85 million acres of new territory. This included four new national parks: Utah's Canyonlands, Redwood National Park in California, Washington state's North Cascades, and the Guadalupe Mountains in Texas. The acreage also included six national monuments, eight national seashores, 20 historic sites, and 50 wildlife refuges. Udall's conservation efforts were not limited to the environment; he also helped preserve Carnegie Hall when the building was threatened with destruction. Udall's ideas about the environment were not only about conservation, however; he understood the economic value of having public land like parks. Roger G. Kennedy, a former director of the National Park Service, was quoted as having said of Udall in the *New York Times*, "[he] escaped the notion that all public land was essentially a cropping opportunity—the idea that if you cannot raise timber on it or take a deer off it, it wasn't valuable." The opposite ended up being true, as Udall suspected: his creation of national shoreline has driven the tourist industry in places like Cape Cod, Massachusetts, and Cape Hatteras, North Carolina.

Among the writers and artists Udall considered his friends were Robert Frost, whom Udall suggested recite a poem at the inauguration of Kennedy, poet Carl Sandburg, author Wallace Stegner, and actor Hal Holbrook. Udall supported environmentalist Rachel Carson's pivotal work *Silent Spring* and wrote his own treatise on environmentalism, *The Quiet Crisis*, in 1963.

Although Udall retired from government in 1969, he remained in Washington for another ten years, where he practiced law and wrote. In 1979, after spending some time teaching at Yale in New Haven, Connecticut, Udall returned to Arizona. There he continued his campaign to fight for victims of radiation, representing Navajo men who had developed cancer, possibly due to their being exposed to radioactive materials while mining uranium. Despite Udall's efforts, and an initial success in 1984, the suit failed in the appeals court. Dissatisfied with the result, Udall approached Congress with legislation ideas that would protect others from being harmed by radiation; in 1990 the Radiation Exposure Compensation Act, which provided up to $100,000 to people who became sick due to radiation exposure, was made law by President George H. W. Bush.

Udall continued to weigh in on national policies from retirement, and had much to say about America's relationship with atomic weapons in his 1994 book *The Myths of August: A Personal Exploration of Our Tragic Cold War Affair with the Atom*. Udall criticized the dropping of the atomic bombs on the Japanese cities of Hiroshima and Nagasaki during World War II and claimed that both politicians and scientists were too enamored with nuclear weapons to see the consequences clearly.

Udall's passion for the outdoors led him to accomplish several difficult physical feats, including climbing Mount Kilimanjaro in East Africa and Japan's Mount Fuji. In his later years, Udall continued to enjoy the wilderness that he had helped to protect. While he was in his eighties, he and a grandson hiked from the floor of the Grand Canyon to the South Rim—a distance of 7,000 feet. The National Park Service offered him a mule, which he refused; after finishing the ascent, he celebrated at the Tovar Lodge bar with a martini. At the age of 90, Udall suffered a fall that kept him bedridden. Shortly thereafter, on March 20, 2010, he died of natural causes. He had been the last surviving member of the original Kennedy cabinet. His wife of 55 years predeceased him; their six children and eight grandchildren survive him. **Sources:** *Los Angeles Times,* March 21, 2010; *New York Times,* March 20, 2010; *Washington Post,* March 21, 2010, p. A5.

—*Alana Joli Abbott*

Edgar Wayburn

Born September 17, 1906, in Macon, GA; died of natural causes, March 5, 2010, in San Francisco, CA. Conservationist and physician. Over the course of five decades, volunteer conservationist Edgar Wayburn was credited by U.S. President Bill Clinton for having "saved more of our wilderness than any other person alive," according to the *New York Times*. Despite his efforts, Wayburn was never as well known as other activists who gave the media a higher profile. Instead, Wayburn, who was a physician, maintained his full-time job while spending his off-duty hours working to prevent development, primarily in his home state of California and, later, Alaska. His work helped preserve more than 100 million acres of wild land.

Alongside his wife, fellow conservationist Peggy, Wayburn was involved in the projects to create the Golden Gate National Recreation Area, Point Reyes National Seashore, and Redwood National Park. He was a leader of the lobbying for the Alaska National Interest Lands Conservation Act, which passed in 1980. Wayburn served five terms as the president of the Sierra Club and was named their honorary president in 1993. In 1999, four years after receiving the Albert Schweitzer Prize for Humanitarianism, Wayburn received the Presidential Medal of Freedom, the highest honor that a civilian can be awarded by the U.S. government.

Born in Macon, Georgia, in 1906, Wayburn visited his mother's native San Francisco every summer, where his uncle ran a tuberculosis sanatorium. As a child he enthusiastically read nature books. After graduating from the University of Georgia at the age of 19, Wayburn went to Harvard Medical School. He moved to San Francisco to practice medicine, and was a physician who made house calls.

Wayburn initially joined the Sierra Club in 1939, not because he was planning to become an activist, but because he wanted to go on a burro trip in Yosemite that the group was sponsoring. After returning from his service as a doctor in the Air Force during World War II, Wayburn became more active in the Sierra Club, starting his chapter's first conservation committee. On his return to California, Wayburn noticed how the cities and suburbs had not yet spread out into the Marin Hills near San Francisco, and he wondered how long they would last.

In 1946, Wayburn met Peggy Elliott, a former editor at *Vogue* magazine. On their first date, they went hiking at Mount Tamalpais, and they were married six months later. The pair took trips, and later family vacations, to wilderness areas, returning with maps they would spread out at home, marking off areas they thought should become parks. In 1958, Wayburn won his first conservation victory by convincing politicians in California that the Mount Tamalpais State Park should be expanded. They voted to increase the boundaries of the park to seven times its original size.

Wayburn was a major force behind establishing the Point Reyes National Seashore in 1962. In 1968, Redwood National Park, which he and Peggy had dreamed up, spreading out maps on the floor of the secretary of the interior's office, became a reality. Wayburn's relationship with the secretary of the interior, Rogers Morton, was a surprising one, as Morton had previously been no friend to environmentalists. In fact, his appointment had been opposed by the Sierra Club. But, after a quiet persistence and a genteel attitude, complimented by his Georgia charm, Wayburn brought Morton around to his perspective on a number of issues, including the expansion of Golden Gate National Recreation Area. Rather than accepting the boundaries proposed by the National Park Service, Morton supported the much larger area proposed by the Sierra Club. (The national recreation area, one of the largest urban parks in the world, was established in 1972.) Morton was not the only politician to be won over by Wayburn. According to current Speaker of the House Nancy Pelosi, as quoted in the *New York Times*, "Legislators know that if Dr. Wayburn comes into your office, what might have been inconceivable at the beginning of the conversation is inevitable by the end of it."

Wayburn's first trip to Alaska was in 1967, and he and Peggy were immediately won over by the beauty of the untouched landscape. After several trips to the state, Wayburn convinced the Sierra Club to support the proposals of ten areas that would become national parks. The preservation of these areas was signed into law in 1980, securing more than 104 million acres of wilderness and doubling the size of the national parklands in the United States.

Along with his conservation efforts, Wayburn practiced medicine for more than 50 years and taught medical students for more than 40. He was the president of the San Francisco Medical Society and was a teacher at Stanford Medical School and the University of California at San Francisco. His thoughts about the combination of medicine and conservation were quoted in the *Washington Post*: "I have loved medicine and conservation. In one sense, my involvement with both might be summed up in a single word: survival. Medicine is concerned with the short-term survival of the human species, conservation with the long-term survival of the human and other species as well. We are all related."

Wayburn's wife Peggy died in 2002. Eight years later, at the age of 103, Wayburn died at his home in San Francisco. He is survived by three daughters, a son, and three grandchildren, and he leaves behind him a legacy of millions of wild acres preserved for the future. **Sources:** *Los Angeles Times*, March 8, 2010; *New York Times*, March 10, 2010; *Washington Post*, March 9, 2010, p. B7.

—Alana Joli Abbott

Earl Wild

Born November 26, 1915, in Pittsburgh, PA; died of congestive heart failure, January 23, 2010, in Palm Springs, CA. Pianist. Rather than taking the traditional path of a classical pianist, Earl Wild shunned popular expectations by embracing the Romantic performance style and taking positions with popular media, including radio and television. He performed and composed for Sid Caesar, and he accompanied Eleanor Roosevelt on a tour of the United States. While some criticized his lack of intellectual approach, Wild was typically lauded by musicians as a great pianist, a brilliant technician, and a refreshing performer. His style in performing the great virtuoso pieces was at odds with his contemporaries, who performed in a more sober, and less flamboyant, fashion.

A student in the lineage of Franz Liszt, Wild helped to rescue that composer from the doom of being considered unfashionable. Critics, including Harold C. Schonberg of the *New York Times,* have cited his championing the works of Liszt to be one of his most important contributions to modern pianism. Schonberg wrote, "By any standards, Mr. Wild has one of the great piano techniques of the 20th century, and with it a rich, sonorous tone." Wild was also known for his performance of four Rachmaninoff concertos, the recordings of which professor of keyboard studies Stewart Gordon told the *Los Angeles Time* were "the quintessential, definitive performance of those works."

Despite his chosen career and natural talent, Wild did not come from a particularly musical family. Wild was born in Pittsburgh in 1915; his father was a steelworker and his mother, a hatter. The family did own a piano, and Wild showed an affinity for the instrument at the age of three. His mother brought home a recording of an opera, and upon hearing the opening chord, Wild reached up to play the notes on the piano. He began studying at the age of four, and by age six, listeners were already commenting on his fluid technique. He attended the Pittsburgh Musical Institute from the age of six until he was 12, when he became a pupil of Selmar Jansen.

Under Jansen, Wild was first introduced to the music of Liszt, who had taught Jansen's teachers Eugen d'Albert and Xaver Schwarenka. He also began performing radio recitals for Pittsburgh stations. Wild progressed in his studies, also learning from notable pianists Paul Doguereau and Egon Petri, and when Wild was 14, he became a pianist and celesta player for the Pittsburgh Symphony Orchestra, then directed by Otto Klemperer. At 15, he performed Liszt's Piano Concerto No. 1 with the Minneapolis Symphony.

Wild attended Carnegie Tech, now Carnegie Mellon University, as a music student, learning to play cello, flute, and bass in addition to continuing his piano studies. In 1937, he began his career by joining the NBC Symphony Orchestra as the staff pianist, under the direction of Arturo Toscanini. Two years later, he gave the first-ever televised piano recital. His fame began in 1942, when Toscanini featured him in a radio broadcast of George Gershwin's "Rhapsody in Blue," which began his reputation as a performer of popular and Romantic music.

During World War II, Wild served in the Navy, playing the flute in the U.S. Navy Band. He performed piano solos with the Navy Orchestra as well, and he gave recitals at the White House. When First Lady Eleanor Roosevelt toured the United States, Wild traveled with her, playing "The Star Spangled Banner" before she spoke. Although he left the Navy in 1944, his relationship with the White House continued; he performed at John F. Kennedy's inauguration, and he was invited to the White House to perform for six consecutive presidents.

After leaving the Navy, Wild took a position with ABC as staff pianist, conductor, and composer, which he held until 1968. His large-scale oratorio, "Revelations," was written while at ABC, and was first broadcast by that network in 1962. In addition to his work for ABC, he also composed parodies of operas for NBC's Sid Caesar. By performing in the media, as well as through his concert performances as a soloist or with violinists and singers, Wild focused much of his career on entertaining, reaching a wide audience with his charismatic style.

Though best known for performing works from the Romantic school, Wild developed an extensive repertoire, from Buxtehude to Bach, from Gilbert and Sullivan to Gershwin. He debuted pieces by modern composers including Paul Creston, Martinu, and Morton Gould. He composed his own works, including the choral work "The Turquoise Hare" and the "Doo-Dah" variations for piano and orchestra, based on a theme by Stephen Foster. He performed on recordings throughout his career, beginning in 1939, and totaling more than 700 solo piano scores, 35 concertos, and 26 chamber works. In 1997, when he was 80 years old, he won a Grammy Award for his album *Earl Wild: The Romantic Master.*

In the 1970s and 1980s, Wild taught piano at Juilliard; he also taught at the Eastman School of Music, Penn State University, his alma mater Carnegie Mellon, Ohio State University, and the Manhattan School of Music. The Hungarian government honored Wild in 1986 by awarding him the Liszt Medal. Wild formed his own record label in the 1990s to produce his recordings. His final concert was given in 2008 at Walt Disney Concert Hall in Los Angeles, where he was awarded the President's Merit Award by the National Academy of Recording Arts and Sciences.

Wild spent his final years writing his autobiography. He died on January 23, 2010, at the age of 94. He is survived by Michael Rolland Davis, his companion of 38 years. His legacy remains in his multitude of recordings, and his autobiography, published by Carnegie Mellon the year after his death. **Sources:** *New York Times*, January 24, 2010; *Times* (London), February 9, 2010; *Washington Post*, January 28, 2010, p. B5.

—*Alana Joli Abbott*

John Wooden

Born October 14, 1910, in Hall, IN; died June 4, 2010, in Los Angeles, CA. Basketball coach. John Wooden was known as college basketball's most successful coach during his long tenure as the coach of the UCLA Bruins. He was called the "Wizard of Westwood," a moniker he never particularly cared for; he was known for focusing on team effort above the talent of individual players. His winning record of four consecutive undefeated seasons and 88 consecutive games has never been equaled in any major college sport. "He is the greatest coach in the history of sports, not just basketball but in any sport," Ben Howland, UCLA basketball coach, was quoted as having said in the *Washington Post*.

Wooden was born in 1910 in Hall, Indiana, one of the four sons of Dutch-Irish parents. His father was a farmer who introduced Wooden to the sport of basketball with a simple bushel basket nailed to the side of the barn and a black cotton sock stuffed with rags to be used for a ball. The farmhouse had few amenities, no electricity, and no indoor plumbing. When he was a teenager, his parents lost their farm, and the four boys moved to Martinsville, where Wooden excelled in high school basketball. He led his team to three consecutive state finals, one of which they won. Wooden fell in love with classmate Nellie Riley, who he married.

Though he won no scholarship, Wooden went to Purdue University, supporting himself through college with money from working construction during the summers. Again, he led the basketball team as a guard and the team captain. In 1932, he competed with Purdue at the Helms Foundation's unofficial national championship, at which he was named player of the year. But athletics was not his only focus; he majored in English and maintained the highest grade-point average among the Purdue athletes the year he graduated.

Wooden began his career as an English teacher and coach at Dayton High School in Dayton, Kentucky. Along with basketball, he coached tennis and baseball. After only two years, he found a job teaching English and coaching basketball in his native Indiana at South Bend Central High School. He worked there for nine years, and at the end of his high school coaching career, his record was 218-42.

During World War II, Wooden served as a physical education instructor for combat pilots in the Navy. When he returned to Indiana, he was hired by Indiana State Teachers College (now Indiana State University) to be the athletic director, basketball coach, and baseball coach. He had two winning seasons before he was offered the job that would define his career: basketball coach at UCLA.

No one expected much of the UCLA Bruins when Wooden took on the team. They were, at the time, the worst team in the Pacific Coast Conference. The first years had successes and failures, with a few teams making it into the NCAA tournament, but others having average records. Wooden did not focus on winning; he focused on creating players who would be quick, who would achieve their best possible physical condition, and who would work together. In 1963, that strategy for quickness paid off, when his team, featuring no players over the height of six-feet five-inches, made the NCAA tournament undefeated and won their championship game 98-83. The team continued to win the following season, losing only two games and taking home another championship. After a mediocre season in 1965-66, the team hit another winning streak, led by player Kareem Abdul-Jabbar; Bill Walton led the team starting in 1971, beginning the winning streak for which Wooden is known.

Wooden was a strict coach, requiring a conservative appearance and priorities that reflected his own. Walton was nearly removed from the team for not cutting his hair appropriately; Wooden famously told the player he respected him for standing by his beliefs, and that they would miss him on the team. Walton responded by immediately getting his hair cut and returning for the last half-hour of practice. In another case, Walton and others asked for permission to stage an anti-war protest during the Vietnam War; Wooden asked them if such an action aligned with their beliefs, and they said it did, but Wooden responded that his beliefs dictated that if they missed a practice they would be off the team. Walton wrote of his experience with Wooden, as quoted in the *Washington Post*, "When I left UCLA in 1974 and became the highest-paid player in the history of team sports at that time, the quality of my life went down. That's how special it was to have played for John Wooden and UCLA."

Along with his strict coaching, Wooden was also known for his moral code, including no swearing or drinking. Though some of his peers derisively nicknamed him "St. John," others pointed out his habit of heckling referees and players on other teams. He once said that talking to the opposing players was what he was most ashamed of in his career.

Wooden retired from coaching in 1975, after UCLA defeated Kentucky in the championship. But the former coach continued to attend basketball games at UCLA, signing autographs until the year he turned 97, at which point his family and the university requested privacy. After his retirement, he wrote several books on his coaching philosophy and gave speeches, speaking for up to an hour without notes during his later years. He offered the same life lessons to his audiences that he had given his players while coaching.

Though his teams were known for winning, he was proudest of the success his players achieved after leaving college. The majority of his players graduated, something uncommon in the modern era of basketball, in which players often leave college to start in the NBA after completing only two years of post-secondary studies. Of Wooden's players, 30 became attorneys, and others succeeded as teachers, doctors, and ministers. Wooden died on June 4, 2010, just months short of his 100th birthday. His wife predeceased him in 1985, after 53 years of marriage; he leaves behind two children, seven grandchildren, and eleven great-grandchildren. **Sources:** *Los Angeles Times*, June 4, 2010; *New York Times*, June 4, 2010; *Washington Post*, June 4, 2010.

—*Alana Joli Abbott*

Howard Zinn

Born August 24, 1922, in New York, NY; died of a heart attack, January 27, 2010, in Santa Monica, CA. Historian and activist. Best known for his popular history, *A People's History of the United States*, Howard Zinn was an activist and historian who believed and taught that change is generated, not by people in power, but by common workers. Over the course of his long career, he participated in many political protests, demonstrations, and sit-ins to advocate progressive changes. Though he served in World War II, his experiences there made him believe there could be no such thing as a just war, and he spoke out against wars and armed conflict from the Vietnam War to the Iraq War. Though his radi-

cal ideas were not always embraced by his colleagues, his book, *A People's History of the United States*, was one of the earliest revisionist histories, and its publication has helped to change the way that American history is taught.

His career in academia was occasionally troubled by his political stances. He once lost a job for insubordination, and he had an ongoing feud with the president of Boston University, where he taught for 24 years. But his popular image was bolstered by references in films like *Good Will Hunting*, written and directed by Ben Affleck and Matt Damon, who had grown up in Zinn's neighborhood. In 2009, the History Channel aired a documentary called *The People Speak*, based on Zinn's work. The film brought a renewed interest in Zinn's ideas.

The son of Jewish immigrants, Zinn was born in the New York City borough of Brooklyn in 1922. His parents had four boys, and the family was working class. Zinn once recalled that they had moved a lot when he was young, trying to stay "one step ahead of the landlord.... I lived in all of Brooklyn's best slums." Though neither parent was well-educated, they supported Zinn's education, and they gave him books by Charles Dickens, which helped to form his ideas about wealth, class, and poverty. After graduating from Thomas Jefferson High School, where he added the works of Karl Marx to his reading, he took work as a pipe fitter in a Brooklyn Navy Yard. There, he met Roslyn Shechter, who shared his political beliefs and whom he married. They remained married until her death in 2008.

When the United States became involved in World War II, Zinn, who was a dedicated anti-Fascist, joined the Army Air Corps. He served as a bombardier over Germany for two and a half years. Though he believed that Hitler needed to be opposed, his experiences at war changed his ideas about armed conflict. That the United States won seemed to make it too easy for the nation to always believe it was in the right, regardless of who the country opposed. According to the *New York Times*, Zinn said, "I would not deny that [World War II] had a certain moral code, but that made it easier for Americans to treat all subsequent wars with a kind of glow. Every enemy becomes Hitler." After he returned from war, he placed his medals in an envelope that he labeled "Never Again."

Zinn worked in manual labor to pay the bills until he and his wife moved to public housing, and Zinn used the G.I. Bill to attend college. He received his bachelor's degree from New York University, then went on to earn his master's and doctoral degrees from Columbia University. He began his teaching career at Spelman College in 1956, which was, at the time, an all-black women's college. There, he met former California state Senator Tom Hayden, with whom he later worked on social justice issues. He taught such notable students as novelist Alice Walker and Marian Wright Edelman, who founded the Children's Defense Fund. Oftentimes with his students, Zinn participated in protests and marched for civil rights, which eventually got him into trouble with the administration. He was fired for insubordination, but soon got a job at Boston University.

From 1964 to 1988, Zinn was a professor at Boston University, despite his ongoing conflicts with then-university president, John Silber, who was a political conservative. After traveling to North Vietnam to recover prisoners of war with the radical priest Daniel Berrigan, he wrote one of the first books that spoke out against the Vietnam War: *Vietnam: The Logic of Withdrawal*. The next year, he published *Disobedience and Democracy*, in which he discussed the idea of dissent as a patriotic duty.

In 1980, his most famous work, *A People's History of the United States* was published. Only 5,000 copies were initially printed; by the time of Zinn's death in 2010, nearly two million copies had been sold. The text, one of the first to look at history not from the perspective of its supposed heroes, but from the perspective of those who had been conquered or abused by the writers of the nation's history, became a staple of college and high school classrooms.

It was nominated for the National Book Award, and it won the Prix des Amis, a French honor sponsored by *Le Monde Diplomatique*.

Even after retiring from academics in 1988, Zinn continued to be active in the political world, participating in demonstrations, criticizing presidential policies, and opposing war. He was an active speaker and guest lecturer; he gave the commencement speech for the 2005 graduation at Spelman College. Zinn was due to speak at the Santa Monica Museum of Art for an event titled "A Collection of Ideas ... the People Speak" in 2010, when he died from a heart attack on January 27; he was 87. Zinn is survived by his son and daughter.

Zinn "had a profound influence on raising the significance of social movements as the real forces of social change in our country," Hayden told the *Los Angeles Times*. "He gave us our heritage and he gave us a pride in that heritage." Activist, MIT professor, and friend Noam Chomsky said in the *Washington Post*, that Zinn's "writings have changed the consciousness of a generation, and helped open new paths to understanding and its crucial meaning for our lives. When action has been called for, one could always be confident that he would be on the front lines, an example and trustworthy guide." **Sources:** *Los Angeles Times*, January 28, 2010; *New York Times*, January 28, 2010; *Times*, (London), February 2, 2010; *Washington Post*, January 28, 2010.

—*Alana Joli Abbott*

2012 Nationality Index

This index lists all newsmakers alphabetically under their respective nationalities. Indexes in softbound issues allow access to the current year's entries; indexes in annual hardbound volumes are cumulative, covering the entire *Newsmakers* series.

Listee names are followed by a year and issue number; thus **1996**:3 indicates that an entry on that individual appears in both 1996, Issue 3, and the 1996 cumulation. For access to newsmakers appearing earlier than the current softbound issue, see the previous year's cumulation.

AFGHAN
  Karzai, Hamid 1955(?)- **2002**:3

AFRICAN
  Brutus, Dennis 1924-2009
    Obituary **2011**:4

ALGERIAN
  Bouteflika, Abdelaziz 1937- **2010**:2
  Zeroual, Liamine 1951- **1996**:2

AMERICAN
  Aaliyah 1979-2001 **2001**:3
  Abbey, Edward 1927-1989
    Obituary **1989**:3
  Abbott, George 1887-1995
    Obituary **1995**:3
  Abbott, Jim 1967- **1988**:3
  Abdul, Paula 1962- **1990**:3
  Abercrombie, Josephine 1925- **1987**:2
  Abernathy, Ralph 1926-1990
    Obituary **1990**:3
  Abraham, S. Daniel 1924- **2003**:3
  Abraham, Spencer 1952- **1991**:4
  Abrams, Elliott 1948- **1987**:1
  Abrams, J. J. 1966- **2007**:3
  Abramson, Lyn 1950- **1986**:3
  Abzug, Bella 1920-1998 **1998**:2
  Achtenberg, Roberta **1993**:4
  Ackerman, Will 1949- **1987**:4
  Acuff, Roy 1903-1992
    Obituary **1993**:2
  Adair, Red 1915- **1987**:3
  Adams, Amy 1974- **2008**:4
  Adams, Don 1923-2005
    Obituary **2007**:1
  Adams, Patch 1945(?)- **1999**:2
  Adams, Scott 1957- **1996**:4
  Adams, Yolanda 1961- **2008**:2
  Adams-Geller, Paige 1969(?)- **2006**:4
  Addams, Charles 1912-1988
    Obituary **1989**:1
  Adelson, Jay 1970- **2011**:1
  Adkins, Trace 1962- **2012**:1
  Adler, Jonathan 1966- **2006**:3
  Adu, Freddy 1989- **2005**:3

  Affleck, Ben 1972- **1999**:1
  AFI **2007**:3
  Agassi, Andre 1970- **1990**:2
  Agatston, Arthur 1947- **2005**:1
  Agee, Tommie 1942-2001
    Obituary **2001**:4
  Agnew, Spiro Theodore 1918-1996
    Obituary **1997**:1
  Aguilera, Christina 1980- **2000**:4
  Aiello, Danny 1933- **1990**:4
  Aikman, Troy 1966- **1994**:2
  Ailes, Roger 1940- **1989**:3
  Ailey, Alvin 1931-1989 **1989**:2
    Obituary **1990**:2
  Ainge, Danny 1959- **1987**:1
  Akers, John F. 1934- **1988**:3
  Akers, Michelle 1966- **1996**:1
  Akin, Phil
    Brief entry **1987**:3
  Akon 1973- **2012**:1
  Alba, Jessica 1981- **2001**:2
  Albee, Edward 1928- **1997**:1
  Albert, Eddie 1906-2005
    Obituary **2006**:3
  Albert, Marv 1943- **1994**:3
  Albert, Stephen 1941- **1986**:1
  Albom, Mitch 1958- **1999**:3
  Albrecht, Chris 1952(?)- **2005**:4
  Albright, Madeleine 1937- **1994**:3
  Alda, Robert 1914-1986
    Obituary **1986**:3
  Alexander, Jane 1939- **1994**:2
  Alexander, Jason 1962(?)- **1993**:3
  Alexander, Lamar 1940- **1991**:2
  Alexie, Sherman 1966- **1998**:4
  Ali, Laila 1977- **2001**:2
  Ali, Muhammad 1942- **1997**:2
  Alioto, Joseph L. 1916-1998
    Obituary **1998**:3
  Alkalay, Yael 1969- **2012**:1
  Allaire, Jeremy 1971- **2006**:4
  Allaire, Paul 1938- **1995**:1
  Allard, Linda 1940- **2003**:2
  Allen, Bob 1935- **1992**:4
  Allen, Debbie 1950- **1998**:2
  Allen, Dede 1923-2010
    Obituary **2012**:3

  Allen, Joan 1956- **1998**:1
  Allen, John 1930- **1992**:1
  Allen, Mel 1913-1996
    Obituary **1996**:4
  Allen, Ray 1975- **2002**:1
  Allen, Steve 1921-2000
    Obituary **2001**:2
  Allen, Tim 1953- **1993**:1
  Allen, Woody 1935- **1994**:1
  Allen Jr., Ivan 1911-2003
    Obituary **2004**:3
  Alley, Kirstie 1955- **1990**:3
  Allgaier, Justin 1986- **2011**:3
  Allison, Jr., Herbert M. 1943- **2010**:2
  Allred, Gloria 1941- **1985**:2
  Allyson, June 1917-2006
    Obituary **2007**:3
  Alsop, Marin 1956- **2008**:3
  Alter, Hobie
    Brief entry **1985**:1
  Altman, Robert 1925- **1993**:2
  Altman, Sidney 1939- **1997**:2
  Alvarez, Aida **1999**:2
  Ambrose, Stephen 1936- **2002**:3
  Ameche, Don 1908-1993
    Obituary **1994**:2
  Amory, Cleveland 1917-1998
    Obituary **1999**:2
  Amos, Tori 1963- **1995**:1
  Amos, Wally 1936- **2000**:1
  Amsterdam, Morey 1912-1996
    Obituary **1997**:1
  Anastas, Robert
    Brief entry **1985**:2
  Ancier, Garth 1957- **1989**:1
  Andersen, Chris 1978- **2010**:2
  Anderson, Brad 1949- **2007**:3
  Anderson, Gillian 1968- **1997**:1
  Anderson, Harry 1951(?)- **1988**:2
  Anderson, Laurie 1947- **2000**:2
  Anderson, Marion 1897-1993
    Obituary **1993**:4
  Anderson, Poul 1926-2001
    Obituary **2002**:3
  Anderson, Sunny 1975- **2012**:4
  Anderson, Tom and Chris DeWolfe
    2007:2

Bell, Art 1945- **2000**:1
Bell, Ricky 1955-1984
    Obituary **1985**:1
Bellamy, Carol 1942- **2001**:2
Belle, Albert 1966- **1996**:4
Bellissimo, Wendy 1967(?)- **2007**:1
Bellow, Saul 1915-2005
    Obituary **2006**:2
Belluzzo, Rick 1953- **2001**:3
Belushi, Jim 1954- **1986**:2
Belzer, Richard 1944- **1985**:3
Ben & Jerry **1991**:3
Benatar, Pat 1953- **1986**:1
Benchley, Peter 1940-2006
    Obituary **2007**:1
Bendet, Stacey 1978- **2012**:1
Benes, Francine 1946- **2008**:2
Bening, Annette 1958(?)- **1992**:1
Benjamin, Regina 1956- **2011**:2
Bennett, Joan 1910-1990
    Obituary **1991**:2
Bennett, Michael 1943-1987
    Obituary **1988**:1
Bennett, Tony 1926- **1994**:4
Bennett, William 1943- **1990**:1
Benoit, Joan 1957- **1986**:3
Benson, Ezra Taft 1899-1994
    Obituary **1994**:4
Bentley, Dierks 1975- **2007**:3
Bentsen, Lloyd 1921- **1993**:3
Berg, Elizabeth 1948- **2012**:1
Bergalis, Kimberly 1968(?)-1991
    Obituary **1992**:3
Bergen, Candice 1946- **1990**:1
Berger, Sandy 1945- **2000**:1
Bergeron, Tom 1955- **2010**:1
Berkley, Seth 1956- **2002**:3
Berle, Milton 1908-2002
    Obituary **2003**:2
Berle, Peter A.A.
    Brief entry **1987**:3
Berlin, Irving 1888-1989
    Obituary **1990**:1
Berliner, Andy and Rachel **2008**:2
Berman, Gail 1957(?)- **2006**:1
Berman, Jennifer and Laura **2003**:2
Bern, Dorrit J. 1950(?)- **2006**:3
Bernanke, Ben 1953- **2008**:3
Bernardi, Herschel 1923-1986
    Obituary **1986**:4
Bernardin, Cardinal Joseph
    1928-1996 **1997**:2
Bernhard, Sandra 1955(?)- **1989**:4
Bernsen, Corbin 1955- **1990**:2
Bernstein, Elmer 1922-2004
    Obituary **2005**:4
Bernstein, Leonard 1918-1990
    Obituary **1991**:1
Berresford, Susan V. 1943- **1998**:4
Berry, Chuck 1926- **2001**:2
Berry, Halle 1968- **1996**:2
Besser, Richard 1959- **2010**:2
Bethe, Hans 1906-2005
    Obituary **2006**:2
Bettelheim, Bruno 1903-1990
    Obituary **1990**:3
Beyonce 1981- **2009**:3
Bezos, Jeff 1964- **1998**:4
Bialik, Mayim 1975- **1993**:3
Bias, Len 1964(?)-1986
    Obituary **1986**:3
Bibliowicz, Jessica 1959- **2009**:3

Biden, Joe 1942- **1986**:3
Bieber, Owen 1929- **1986**:1
Biehl, Amy 1967(?)-1993
    Obituary **1994**:1
Bigelow, Kathryn 1951- **2011**:1
Bigelow, Kathryn 1952(?)- **1990**:4
Bikoff, J. Darius 1962(?)- **2007**:3
Bikoff, James L.
    Brief entry **1986**:2
Billington, James 1929- **1990**:3
Birch, Thora 1982- **2002**:4
Bird, Brad 1956(?)- **2005**:4
Bird, Larry 1956- **1990**:3
Bishop, Andre 1948- **2000**:1
Bishop, Joey 1918-2007
    Obituary **2008**:4
Bissell, Patrick 1958-1987
    Obituary **1988**:2
Bixby, Bill 1934-1993
    Obituary **1994**:2
Black, Carole 1945- **2003**:1
Black, Cathleen 1944- **1998**:4
Black, Jack 1969- **2002**:3
Black Eyed Peas **2006**:2
The Black Keys **2012**:4
Blackmun, Harry A. 1908-1999
    Obituary **1999**:3
Blackstone, Harry Jr. 1934-1997
    Obituary **1997**:4
Blaine, David 1973- **2003**:3
Blair, Bonnie 1964- **1992**:3
Blakey, Art 1919-1990
    Obituary **1991**:1
Blanc, Mel 1908-1989
    Obituary **1989**:4
Blass, Bill 1922-2002
    Obituary **2003**:3
Bledsoe, Drew 1972- **1995**:1
Blige, Mary J. 1971- **1995**:3
Bloch, Erich 1925- **1987**:4
Bloch, Henry 1922- **1988**:4
Bloch, Ivan 1940- **1986**:3
Block, Herbert 1909-2001
    Obituary **2002**:4
Bloodworth-Thomason, Linda 1947-
    1994:1
Bloom, Amy 1953- **2011**:3
Bloomberg, Michael 1942- **1997**:1
Blume, Judy 1936- **1998**:4
Blumenthal, Susan J. 1951(?)- **2007**:3
Bly, Robert 1926- **1992**:4
Blyth, Myrna 1939- **2002**:4
Bochco, Steven 1943- **1989**:1
Boehner, John A. 1949- **2006**:4
Boggs, Wade 1958- **1989**:3
Bogle, Bob 1934-2009
    Obituary **2010**:3
Bogosian, Eric 1953- **1990**:4
Bohbot, Michele 1959(?)- **2004**:2
Boiardi, Hector 1897-1985
    Obituary **1985**:3
Boies, David 1941- **2002**:1
Boitano, Brian 1963- **1988**:3
Bolger, Ray 1904-1987
    Obituary **1987**:2
Bollinger, Lee C. 1946- **2003**:2
Bolton, Michael 1953(?)- **1993**:2
Bombeck, Erma 1927-1996
    Obituary **1996**:4
Bonds, Barry 1964- **1993**:3
Bonet, Lisa 1967- **1989**:2
Bonilla, Bobby 1963- **1992**:2

Bon Jovi, Jon 1962- **1987**:4
Bonner, Robert 1942(?)- **2003**:4
Bono, Sonny 1935-1998 **1992**:2
    Obituary **1998**:2
Bontecou, Lee 1931- **2004**:4
Boone, Mary 1951- **1985**:1
Booth, Shirley 1898-1992
    Obituary **1993**:2
Bopp, Thomas 1949- **1997**:3
Boreanaz, David 1969- **2012**:2
Borel, Calvin 1966- **2010**:1
Borlaug, Norman 1914-2009
    Obituary **2011**:1
Borofsky, Jonathan 1942- **2006**:4
Bose, Amar
    Brief entry **1986**:4
Bosworth, Brian 1965- **1989**:1
Bosworth, Kate 1983- **2006**:3
Botstein, Leon 1946- **1985**:3
Boudreau, Louis 1917-2001
    Obituary **2002**:3
Bourdain, Anthony 1956- **2008**:3
Bowe, Riddick 1967(?)- **1993**:2
Bowen, Julie 1970- **2007**:1
Bowles, Paul 1910-1999
    Obituary **2000**:3
Bowman, Scotty 1933- **1998**:4
Boxcar Willie 1931-1999
    Obituary **1999**:4
Boxer, Barbara 1940- **1995**:1
Boyer, Herbert Wayne 1936- **1985**:1
Boyington, Gregory Pappy
    1912-1988
    Obituary **1988**:2
Boyle, Gertrude 1924- **1995**:3
Boyle, Lara Flynn 1970- **2003**:4
Boyle, Peter 1935- **2002**:3
Boyle, T. C. 1948- **2007**:2
Boynton, Sandra 1953- **2004**:1
Bradford, Barbara Taylor 1933- **2002**
    :4
Bradley, Bill 1943- **2000**:2
Bradley, Ed 1941-2006
    Obituary **2008**:1
Bradley, Keegan 1986- **2012**:4
Bradley, Todd 1958- **2003**:3
Bradley, Tom 1917-1998
    Obituary **1999**:1
Bradshaw, John 1933- **1992**:1
Brady, Sarah and James S. **1991**:4
Brady, Tom 1977- **2002**:4
Brady, Wayne 1972- **2008**:3
Braff, Zach 1975- **2005**:2
Brando, Marlon 1924-2004
    Obituary **2005**:3
Brandy 1979- **1996**:4
Bratt, Benjamin 1963- **2009**:3
Braun, Carol Moseley 1947- **1993**:1
Bravo, Ellen 1944- **1998**:2
Bravo, Rose Marie 1951(?)- **2005**:3
Braxton, Toni 1967- **1994**:3
Bray, Libba 1964- **2011**:1
Brazile, Donna 1959- **2001**:1
Breathed, Berkeley 1957- **2005**:3
Brees, Drew 1979- **2011**:2
Bremen, Barry 1947- **1987**:3
Bremer, L. Paul 1941- **2004**:2
Brennan, Edward A. 1934- **1989**:1
Brennan, Robert E. 1943(?)- **1988**:1
Brennan, William 1906-1997
    Obituary **1997**:4
Brenneman, Amy 1964- **2002**:1

Carter, Chris 1956- **2000**:1
Carter, Dixie 1939-2010
  Obituary **2012**:3
Carter, Gary 1954- **1987**:1
Carter, Jimmy 1924- **1995**:1
Carter, Joe 1960- **1994**:2
Carter, Nell 1948-2003
  Obituary **2004**:2
Carter, Ron 1937- **1987**:3
Carter, Rubin 1937- **2000**:3
Carter, Stephen L. **2008**:2
Carter, Vince 1977- **2001**:4
Cartwright, Carol Ann 1941- **2009**:4
Caruso, David 1956(?)- **1994**:3
Carver, Raymond 1938-1988
  Obituary **1989**:1
Carvey, Dana 1955- **1994**:1
Case, Steve 1958- **1995**:4
Casey, William 1913-1987
  Obituary **1987**:3
Cash, Johnny 1932- **1995**:3
Cash, June Carter 1929-2003
  Obituary **2004**:2
Cassavetes, John 1929-1989
  Obituary **1989**:2
Cassidy, Mike 1963(?)- **2006**:1
Cassini, Oleg 1913-2006
  Obituary **2007**:2
Castelli, Leo 1907-1999
  Obituary **2000**:1
Castellucci, Cecil 1969- **2008**:3
Castillo, Ana 1953- **2000**:4
Catlett, Elizabeth 1915(?)- **1999**:3
Cattrall, Kim 1956- **2003**:3
Caulfield, Joan 1922(?)-1991
  Obituary **1992**:1
Cavazos, Lauro F. 1927- **1989**:2
Caviezel, Jim 1968- **2005**:3
Centrello, Gina 1959(?)- **2008**:3
Cerf, Vinton G. 1943- **1999**:2
Chabon, Michael 1963- **2002**:1
Chaing Kai-Shek, Madame
  1898-2003
  Obituary **2005**:1
Chamberlain, Joba 1985- **2008**:3
Chamberlain, Wilt 1936-1999
  Obituary **2000**:2
Chamberlin, Wendy 1948- **2002**:4
Chambers, John 1949- **2010**:2
Chancellor, John
  Obituary **1997**:1
Chandler, Kyle 1965- **2010**:4
Chaney, John 1932- **1989**:1
Channing, Stockard 1946- **1991**:3
Chao, Elaine L. 1953- **2007**:3
Chapman, Tracy 1964- **1989**:2
Chappell, Tom 1943- **2002**:3
Chappelle, Dave 1973- **2005**:3
Charisse, Cyd 1922-2008
  Obituary **2009**:3
Charles, Ray 1930-2004
  Obituary **2005**:3
Charlesworth, Sarah 1947- **2010**:3
Charron, Paul 1942- **2004**:1
Chase, Chevy 1943- **1990**:1
Chase, Debra Martin 1956- **2009**:1
Chase, Robin 1958- **2010**:4
Chast, Roz 1955- **1992**:4
Chastain, Brandi 1968- **2001**:3
Chatham, Russell 1939- **1990**:1
Chaudhari, Praveen 1937- **1989**:4
Chavez, Cesar 1927-1993

Obituary **1993**:4
Chavez, Linda 1947- **1999**:3
Chavez-Thompson, Linda 1944-
  1999:1
Chavis, Benjamin 1948- **1993**:4
Cheadle, Don 1964- **2002**:1
Cheatham, Adolphus Doc 1905-1997
  Obituary **1997**:4
Cheek, James Edward
  Brief entry **1987**:1
Chen, Steve and Chad Hurley **2007**
  :2
Chenault, Kenneth I. 1951- **1999**:3
Cheney, Dick 1941- **1991**:3
Cheney, Lynne V. 1941- **1990**:4
Chenoweth, Kristin 1968- **2010**:4
Cher 1946- **1993**:1
Chesney, Kenny 1968- **2008**:2
Chesnutt, Vic 1964-2009
  Obituary **2011**:4
Chia, Sandro 1946- **1987**:2
Chiasson, William 1953- **2011**:4
Chidsey, John 1962- **2010**:4
Chihuly, Dale 1941- **1995**:2
Chiklis, Michael 1963- **2003**:3
Child, Julia 1912- **1999**:4
Chilton, Alex 1950-2010
  Obituary **2012**:3
Chiquet, Maureen 1963- **2010**:1
Chisholm, Shirley 1924-2005
  Obituary **2006**:1
Chittister, Joan D. 1936- **2002**:2
Chizen, Bruce 1955(?)- **2004**:2
Cho, Margaret 1970- **1995**:2
Chouinard, Yvon 1938(?)- **2002**:2
Christensen, Kate 1962- **2009**:4
Christian Jacobs and Scott Schultz
  1972- **2011**:4
Christie, Chris 1962- **2011**:1
Christopher, Warren 1925- **1996**:3
Chu, Paul C.W. 1941- **1988**:2
Chu, Steven 1948- **2010**:3
Chung, Connie 1946- **1988**:4
Chung, Doo-Ri 1973- **2011**:3
Chyna 1970- **2001**:4
Cipriano, Salvatore 1941- **2011**:4
Cisneros, Henry 1947- **1987**:2
Claiborne, Liz 1929- **1986**:3
Clancy, Tom 1947- **1998**:4
Clark, J. E.
  Brief entry **1986**:1
Clark, Jim 1944- **1997**:1
Clark, Kenneth B. 1914-2005
  Obituary **2006**:3
Clark, Marcia 1954(?)- **1995**:1
Clark, Mary Higgins 1929- **2000**:4
Clark, Maxine 1949- **2009**:4
Clarke, Richard A. 1951(?)- **2002**:2
Clarke, Stanley 1951- **1985**:4
Clarkson, Kelly 1982- **2003**:3
Clarkson, Patricia 1959- **2005**:3
Clavell, James 1924(?)-1994
  Obituary **1995**:1
Clay, Andrew Dice 1958- **1991**:1
Cleaver, Eldridge 1935-1998
  Obituary **1998**:4
Clemens, Roger 1962- **1991**:4
Clements, George 1932- **1985**:1
Cleveland, James 1932(?)-1991
  Obituary **1991**:3
Cliburn, Van 1934- **1995**:1
Clifton, Lucille 1936-2010

Obituary **2012**:2
Clinton, Bill 1946- **1992**:1
Clinton, Hillary Rodham 1947- **1993**
  :2
Clinton Kelly and Stacy London
  1969- **2012**:2
Clokey, Art 1921-2010
  Obituary **2012**:1
Clooney, George 1961- **1996**:4
Clooney, Rosemary 1928-2002
  Obituary **2003**:4
Close, Glenn 1947- **1988**:3
Clowes, Daniel 1961- **2007**:1
Clyburn, James 1940- **1999**:4
Cobain, Kurt 1967-1944
  Obituary **1994**:3
Coburn, James 1928-2002
  Obituary **2004**:1
Coca, Imogene 1908-2001
  Obituary **2002**:2
Cochran, Johnnie 1937- **1996**:1
Coco, James 1929(?)-1987
  Obituary **1987**:2
Codrescu, Andreaa 1946- **1997**:3
Cody, Diablo 1978- **2009**:1
Coen, Joel and Ethan **1992**:1
Coffin, William Sloane, Jr. 1924- **1990**
  :3
Cohen, Arianne 1981- **2011**:2
Cohen, William S. 1940- **1998**:1
Colasanto, Nicholas 1923(?)-1985
  Obituary **1985**:2
Colbert, Stephen 1964- **2007**:4
Colby, William E. 1920-1996
  Obituary **1996**:4
Cole, Anne 1930(?)- **2007**:3
Cole, Johnetta B. 1936- **1994**:3
Cole, Kenneth 1954(?)- **2003**:1
Cole, Natalie 1950- **1992**:4
Coleman, Dabney 1932- **1988**:3
Coleman, Gary 1968-2010
  Obituary **2012**:4
Coleman, Mary Sue 1943- **2010**:1
Coleman, Sheldon, Jr. 1953- **1990**:2
Coles, Robert 1929(?)- **1995**:1
Colescott, Robert 1925-2009
  Obituary **2010**:3
Colfer, Chris 1990- **2012**:2
Collier, Sophia 1956(?)- **2001**:2
Collins, Albert 1932-1993
  Obituary **1994**:2
Collins, Billy 1941- **2002**:2
Collins, Cardiss 1931- **1995**:3
Collins, Eileen 1956- **1995**:3
Collins, Kerry 1972- **2002**:3
Collins, Suzanne 1962- **2012**:2
Colwell, Rita Rossi 1934- **1999**:3
Combs, Sean Puffy 1970- **1998**:4
Commager, Henry Steele 1902-1998
  Obituary **1998**:3
Como, Perry 1912-2001
  Obituary **2002**:2
Condie, Ally 1978- **2012**:2
Condit, Phil 1941- **2001**:3
Condon, Bill 1955- **2007**:3
Condon, Richard 1915-1996
  Obituary **1996**:4
Conigliaro, Tony 1945-1990
  Obituary **1990**:3
Connally, John 1917-1993
  Obituary **1994**:1
Connelly, Jennifer 1970- **2002**:4

Connelly, Michael 1956- **2007**:1
Conner, Bruce 1933-2008
  Obituary **2009**:3
Conner, Dennis 1943- **1987**:2
Connerly, Ward 1939- **2000**:2
Connick, Harry, Jr. 1967- **1991**:1
Conrad, Pete 1930-1999
  Obituary **2000**:1
Convy, Bert 1934(?)-1991
  Obituary **1992**:1
Conyers, John, Jr. 1929- **1999**:1
Cook, Robin 1940- **1996**:3
Cooke, Alistair 1908-2004
  Obituary **2005**:3
Coolio 1963- **1996**:4
Cooper, Alexander 1936- **1988**:4
Cooper, Anderson 1967- **2006**:1
Cooper, Bradley 1975- **2012**:3
Cooper, Chris 1951- **2004**:1
Cooper, Cynthia **1999**:1
Cooper, Stephen F. 1946- **2005**:4
Coors, William K.
  Brief entry **1985**:1
Copeland, Al 1944(?)- **1988**:3
Copland, Aaron 1900-1990
  Obituary **1991**:2
Copperfield, David 1957- **1986**:3
Coppola, Carmine 1910-1991
  Obituary **1991**:4
Coppola, Francis Ford 1939- **1989**:4
Coppola, Sofia 1971- **2004**:3
Cora, Cat 1968- **2012**:3
Corbett, John 1962- **2004**:1
Corea, Chick 1941- **1986**:3
Cornell, Brian C. 1959- **2009**:2
Cornum, Rhonda 1954- **2006**:3
Cornwell, Patricia 1956- **2003**:1
Corwin, Jeff 1967- **2005**:1
Cosby, Bill 1937- **1999**:2
Cosell, Howard 1918-1995
  Obituary **1995**:4
Cosgrove, Miranda 1993- **2011**:4
Costas, Bob 1952- **1986**:4
Costner, Kevin 1955- **1989**:4
Counter, Nick 1940-2009
  Obituary **2011**:3
Couples, Fred 1959- **1994**:4
Couric, Katherine 1957- **1991**:4
Courier, Jim 1970- **1993**:2
Courtney, Erica 1957- **2009**:3
Cousteau, Jean-Michel 1938- **1988**:2
Covey, Stephen R. 1932- **1994**:4
Cowen, Scott 1946- **2011**:2
Cowley, Malcolm 1898-1989
  Obituary **1989**:3
Cox, Courteney 1964- **1996**:2
Cox, Richard Joseph
  Brief entry **1985**:1
Cozza, Stephen 1985- **2001**:1
Craig, James 1956- **2001**:1
Crais, Robert 1954(?)- **2007**:4
Cram, Donald J. 1919-2001
  Obituary **2002**:2
Crandall, Robert L. 1935- **1992**:1
Cranston, Bryan 1956- **2010**:1
Craven, Wes 1939- **1997**:3
Crawford, Broderick 1911-1986
  Obituary **1986**:3
Crawford, Cheryl 1902-1986
  Obituary **1987**:1
Crawford, Cindy 1966- **1993**:3
Cray, Robert 1953- **1988**:2

Cray, Seymour R. 1925-1996
  Brief entry **1986**:3
  Obituary **1997**:2
Creamer, Paula 1986- **2006**:2
Crenna, Richard 1926-2003
  Obituary **2004**:1
Crewe, Albert 1927-2009
  Obituary **2011**:3
Crichton, Michael 1942- **1995**:3
Crist, Charlie 1956- **2012**:1
Cronkite, Walter Leland 1916- **1997**:3
Crosby, David 1941- **2000**:4
Crosley, Sloane 1978- **2011**:4
Crothers, Scatman 1910-1986
  Obituary **1987**:1
Crow, Michael 1956- **2011**:3
Crow, Sheryl 1964- **1995**:2
Crowe, Cameron 1957- **2001**:2
Crowley, Dennis 1976- **2012**:1
Cruise, Tom 1962(?)- **1985**:4
Crumb, R. 1943- **1995**:4
Crump, Scott 1954(?)- **2008**:1
Cruz, Nilo 1961(?)- **2004**:4
Cruzan, Nancy 1957(?)-1990
  Obituary **1991**:3
Cryer, Jon 1965- **2010**:4
Crystal, Billy 1947- **1985**:3
Cugat, Xavier 1900-1990
  Obituary **1991**:2
Culkin, Macaulay 1980(?)- **1991**:3
Cunningham, Merce 1919- **1998**:1
Cunningham, Michael 1952- **2003**:4
Cunningham, Randall 1963- **1990**:1
Cunningham, Reverend William
  1930-1997
  Obituary **1997**:4
Cuomo, Andrew 1957- **2011**:1
Cuomo, Mario 1932- **1992**:2
Curran, Charles E. 1934- **1989**:2
Curren, Tommy
  Brief entry **1987**:4
Curry, Ann 1956- **2001**:1
Curtis, Ben 1977- **2004**:2
Curtis, Jamie Lee 1958- **1995**:1
Cusack, John 1966- **1999**:3
Cyrus, Billy Ray 1961(?)- **1993**:1
Cyrus, Miley 1992- **2008**:3
Dafoe, Willem 1955- **1988**:1
Dahmer, Jeffrey 1959-1994
  Obituary **1995**:2
Daily, Bishop Thomas V. 1927- **1990**
  :4
D'Alessio, Kitty
  Brief entry **1987**:3
Daly, Carson 1973- **2002**:4
Daly, Chuck 1930-2009
  Obituary **2010**:3
Daly, Mary 1928-2010
  Obituary **2012**:1
D'Amato, Al 1937- **1996**:1
Damon, Johnny 1973- **2005**:4
Damon, Matt 1970- **1999**:1
Danes, Claire 1979- **1999**:4
Dangerfield, Rodney 1921-2004
  Obituary **2006**:1
Daniels, Faith 1958- **1993**:3
Daniels, Jeff 1955- **1989**:4
Danticat, Edwidge 1969- **2005**:4
Danza, Tony 1951- **1989**:1
D'Arby, Terence Trent 1962- **1988**:4
Darden, Christopher 1957(?)- **1996**:4
Darling, Erik 1933-2008

  Obituary **2009**:4
Daschle, Tom 1947- **2002**:3
Davenport, Lindsay 1976- **1999**:2
David, George 1942- **2005**:1
David, Larry 1948- **2003**:4
Davis, Angela 1944- **1998**:3
Davis, Bette 1908-1989
  Obituary **1990**:1
Davis, Eric 1962- **1987**:4
Davis, Geena 1957- **1992**:1
Davis, Miles 1926-1991
  Obituary **1992**:2
Davis, Noel **1990**:3
Davis, Ossie 1917-2005
  Obituary **2006**:1
Davis, Paige 1969- **2004**:2
Davis, Patti 1952- **1995**:1
Davis, Raymond, Jr. 1914-2006
  Obituary **2007**:3
Davis, Sammy, Jr. 1925-1990
  Obituary **1990**:4
Davis, Terrell 1972- **1998**:2
Davis, Todd 1967- **2010**:1
Davis, Viola 1965- **2011**:4
Dawson, Rosario 1979- **2007**:2
Day, Dennis 1917-1988
  Obituary **1988**:4
Day, Pat 1953- **1995**:2
Dayton, Mark 1947- **2012**:3
Dean, Howard 1948- **2005**:4
Dean, Laura 1945- **1989**:4
Dearden, John Cardinal 1907-1988
  Obituary **1988**:4
DeBakey, Michael 1908-2008
  Obituary **2009**:3
DeBartolo, Edward J., Jr. 1946- **1989**
  :3
DeCarava, Roy 1919- **1996**:3
De Cordova, Frederick 1910- **1985**:2
Dee, Sandra 1942-2005
  Obituary **2006**:2
Deen, Paula 1947- **2008**:3
Dees, Morris 1936- **1992**:1
DeGeneres, Ellen **1995**:3
de Kooning, Willem 1904-1997 **1994**
  :4
  Obituary **1997**:3
De La Hoya, Oscar 1973- **1998**:2
Delany, Dana 1956- **2008**:4
Delany, Sarah 1889-1999
  Obituary **1999**:3
de la Renta, Oscar 1932- **2005**:4
De Laurentiis, Giada 1970- **2011**:1
DeLay, Tom 1947- **2000**:1
Dell, Michael 1965- **1996**:2
DeLuca, Fred 1947- **2003**:3
DeLuise, Dom 1933-2009
  Obituary **2010**:2
De Matteo, Drea 1973- **2005**:2
DeMayo, Neda 1960(?)- **2006**:2
de Mille, Agnes 1905-1993
  Obituary **1994**:2
Deming, W. Edwards 1900-1993
  1992:2
  Obituary **1994**:2
Demme, Jonathan 1944- **1992**:4
Dempsey, Patrick 1966- **2006**:1
Denevan, Jim 1961- **2012**:4
De Niro, Robert 1943- **1999**:1
Dennehy, Brian 1938- **2002**:1
Dennis, Sandy 1937-1992
  Obituary **1992**:4

Denver, Bob 1935-2005
Obituary **2006**:4
Denver, John 1943-1997
Obituary **1998**:1
De Palma, Brian 1940- **2007**:3
de Passe, Suzanne 1946(?)- **1990**:4
Depp, Johnny 1963(?)- **1991**:3
Dern, Laura 1967- **1992**:3
Dershowitz, Alan 1938(?)- **1992**:1
Deschanel, Zooey 1980- **2010**:4
Desormeaux, Kent 1970- **1990**:2
Destiny's Child **2001**:3
Deutch, John 1938- **1996**:4
Devine, John M. 1944- **2003**:2
DeVita, Vincent T., Jr. 1935- **1987**:3
De Vito, Danny 1944- **1987**:1
Diamond, I.A.L. 1920-1988
Obituary **1988**:3
Diamond, Selma 1921(?)-1985
Obituary **1985**:2
Diaz, Cameron 1972- **1999**:1
DiBello, Paul
Brief entry **1986**:4
DiCaprio, Leonardo Wilhelm 1974-
1997:2
Dickerson, Nancy H. 1927-1997 **1998**
:2
Dickey, James 1923-1997 **1998**:2
Dickinson, Brian 1937- **1998**:2
Dickinson, Janice 1953- **2005**:2
Diddley, Bo 1928-2008
Obituary **2009**:3
Diebenkorn, Richard 1922-1993
Obituary **1993**:4
Diemer, Walter E. 1904(?)-1998 **1998**
:2
Diesel, Vin 1967- **2004**:1
DiFranco, Ani 1970(?)- **1997**:1
Diggs, Taye 1971- **2000**:1
DiGuido, Al 1956- **2012**:1
Diller, Barry 1942- **1991**:1
Diller, Elizabeth and Ricardo
Scofidio **2004**:3
Dillon, Matt 1964- **1992**:2
DiMaggio, Dom 1917-2009
Obituary **2010**:2
DiMaggio, Joe 1914-1999
Obituary **1999**:3
Di Meola, Al 1954- **1986**:4
Dimon, Jamie 1956- **2010**:3
Dinkins, David N. 1927- **1990**:2
Disney, Lillian 1899-1997
Obituary **1998**:3
Disney, Roy E. 1930- **1986**:3
DiSpirito, Rocco 1966- **2012**:1
Dith Pran 1942-2008
Obituary **2009**:2
Divine 1946-1988
Obituary **1988**:2
Dixie Chicks **2001**:2
Doctorow, E. L. 1931- **2007**:1
Doherty, Shannen 1971(?)- **1994**:2
Dolan, Terry 1950-1986 **1985**:2
Dolan, Tom 1975- **2001**:2
Dolby, Ray Milton
Brief entry **1986**:1
Dole, Bob 1923- **1994**:2
Dole, Elizabeth Hanford 1936- **1990**
:1
Dolenz, Micky 1945- **1986**:4
Domar, Alice 1958- **2007**:1
Donahue, Tim 1950(?)- **2004**:3

Donahue, Troy 1936-2001
Obituary **2002**:4
Donghia, Angelo R. 1935-1985
Obituary **1985**:2
Donnellan, Nanci **1995**:2
Donovan, Jeffrey 1968- **2012**:1
Donovan, Landon 1982- **2011**:4
Donovan, Shaun 1966- **2010**:4
Dorati, Antal 1906-1988
Obituary **1989**:2
Dorris, Michael 1945-1997
Obituary **1997**:3
Dorsey, Thomas A. 1899-1993
Obituary **1993**:3
Doubilet, Anne 1948- **2011**:1
Doubleday, Nelson, Jr. 1933- **1987**:1
Dougherty, Patrick 1945- **2012**:2
Douglas, Buster 1960(?)- **1990**:4
Douglas, Marjory Stoneman
1890-1998 **1993**:1
Obituary **1998**:4
Douglas, Michael 1944- **1986**:2
Douglas, Mike 1925-2006
Obituary **2007**:4
Dove, Rita 1952- **1994**:3
Dowd, Maureen Brigid 1952- **1997**:1
Downey, Bruce 1947- **2003**:1
Downey, Morton, Jr. 1932- **1988**:4
Downey, Robert, Jr. 1965- **2007**:1
Dr. Demento 1941- **1986**:1
Dr. Dre 1965(?)- **1994**:3
Dravecky, Dave 1956- **1992**:1
Draves, Victoria Manolo 1924-2010
Obituary **2012**:3
Drescher, Fran 1957(?)- **1995**:3
Drexler, Clyde 1962- **1992**:4
Drexler, Millard S. 1944- **1990**:3
Dreyfuss, Richard 1947- **1996**:3
Drysdale, Don 1936-1993
Obituary **1994**:1
Duarte, Henry 1963(?)- **2003**:3
Dubrof, Jessica 1989-1996
Obituary **1996**:4
Duchovny, David 1960- **1998**:3
Dudley, Jane 1912-2001
Obituary **2002**:4
Duff, Hilary 1987- **2004**:4
Duffy, Karen 1962- **1998**:1
Dukakis, Michael 1933- **1988**:3
Dukakis, Olympia 1931- **1996**:4
Duke, David 1951(?)- **1990**:2
Duke, Doris 1912-1993
Obituary **1994**:2
Duke, Red
Brief entry **1987**:1
Dunagan, Deanna 1940- **2009**:2
Duncan, Arne 1964- **2011**:3
Duncan, Tim 1976- **2000**:1
Duncan, Todd 1903-1998
Obituary **1998**:3
Dunham, Carroll 1949- **2003**:4
Dunham, Katherine 1909-2006
Obituary **2007**:2
Dunlap, Albert J. **1997**:2
Dunn, Jancee 1966- **2010**:1
Dunne, Dominick 1925- **1997**:1
Dunst, Kirsten 1982- **2001**:4
Dunwoody, Ann 1953- **2009**:2
Dupri, Jermaine 1972- **1999**:1
Durocher, Leo 1905-1991
Obituary **1992**:2
Durrell, Gerald 1925-1995

Obituary **1995**:3
Duval, David 1971- **2000**:3
Duvall, Camille
Brief entry **1988**:1
Duvall, Robert 1931- **1999**:3
Dworkin, Andrea 1946-2005
Obituary **2006**:2
Dyer, Wayne 1940- **2010**:4
Dykstra, Lenny 1963- **1993**:4
Dylan, Bob 1941- **1998**:1
Earle, Steve 1955- **2011**:2
Earle, Sylvia 1935- **2001**:1
Earnhardt, Dale 1951-2001
Obituary **2001**:4
Earnhardt, Dale, Jr. 1974- **2004**:4
Eastwood, Clint 1930- **1993**:3
Eaton, Robert J. 1940- **1994**:2
Eazy-E 1963(?)-1995
Obituary **1995**:3
Eberhart, Richard 1904-2005
Obituary **2006**:3
Ebersole, Christine 1953- **2007**:2
Ebert, Roger 1942- **1998**:3
Ebsen, Buddy 1908-2003
Obituary **2004**:3
Eckert, Robert A. 1955(?)- **2002**:3
Eckhart, Aaron 1968- **2009**:2
Ecko, Marc 1972- **2006**:3
Eckstine, Billy 1914-1993
Obituary **1993**:4
Edelman, Jonah 1970- **2012**:4
Edelman, Marian Wright 1939- **1990**
:4
Ederle, Gertrude 1905-2003
Obituary **2005**:1
Edmonds, Kenneth Babyface
1958(?)- **1995**:3
Edwards, Bob 1947- **1993**:2
Edwards, Carl 1979- **2012**:3
Edwards, Harry 1942- **1989**:4
Efron, Zac 1987- **2008**:2
Eggers, Dave 1970- **2001**:3
Ehrlichman, John 1925-1999
Obituary **1999**:3
Eilberg, Amy
Brief entry **1985**:3
Eisenman, Peter 1932- **1992**:4
Eisenstaedt, Alfred 1898-1995
Obituary **1996**:1
Eisner, Michael 1942- **1989**:2
Eisner, Will 1917-2005
Obituary **2006**:1
Elders, Joycelyn 1933- **1994**:1
Eldridge, Roy 1911-1989
Obituary **1989**:3
Elfman, Jenna 1971- **1999**:4
Ellerbee, Linda 1944- **1993**:3
Elliott, Missy 1971- **2003**:4
Ellis, David 1971- **2009**:4
Ellis, Perry 1940-1986
Obituary **1986**:3
Ellison, Larry 1944- **2004**:2
Ellison, Ralph 1914-1994
Obituary **1994**:4
Ellroy, James 1948- **2003**:4
Ells, Steve 1965- **2010**:1
Elway, John 1960- **1990**:3
Emanuel, Rahm 1959- **2011**:2
Eminem 1974- **2001**:2
Engelbreit, Mary 1952(?)- **1994**:3
Engibous, Thomas J. 1953- **2003**:3
Engler, John 1948- **1996**:3

Obituary **2003**:4
Frankenthaler, Helen 1928- **1990**:1
Frankfort, Lew 1946- **2008**:2
Franklin, Aretha 1942- **1998**:3
Franklin, Kirk 1970- **2010**:2
Franklin, Melvin 1942-1995
  Obituary **1995**:3
Franks, Tommy 1945- **2004**:1
Franz, Dennis 1944- **1995**:2
Franzen, Jonathan 1959- **2002**:3
Fraser, Brendan 1967- **2000**:1
Fraser, Claire M. 1955- **2005**:2
Frazetta, Frank 1928-2010
  Obituary **2012**:4
Frazier, Charles 1950- **2003**:2
Freeh, Louis J. 1950- **1994**:2
Freeman, Cliff 1941- **1996**:1
Freeman, Jr., Castle 1944- **2010**:2
Freeman, Morgan 1937- **1990**:4
Freiberg, Steven 1957- **2011**:4
Freleng, Friz 1906(?)-1995
  Obituary **1995**:4
French, Marilyn 1929-2009
  Obituary **2010**:2
French, Tana 1973- **2009**:3
Freston, Kathy 1965- **2009**:3
Friedan, Betty 1921- **1994**:2
Friedman, Milton 1912-2006
  Obituary **2008**:1
Friedman, Rose 1910-2009
  Obituary **2010**:4
Friend, Patricia A. 1946- **2003**:3
Frist, Bill 1952- **2003**:4
Fudge, Ann 1951- **2000**:3
Fulbright, J. William 1905-1995
  Obituary **1995**:3
Fulghum, Robert 1937- **1996**:1
Fuller, Millard 1935-2009
  Obituary **2010**:1
Funt, Allen 1914-1999
  Obituary **2000**:1
Furchgott, Robert 1916-2009
  Obituary **2010**:3
Furman, Rosemary
  Brief entry **1986**:4
Furyk, Jim 1970- **2004**:2
Futrell, Mary Hatwood 1940- **1986**:1
Futter, Ellen V. 1949- **1995**:1
Gabor, Eva 1921(?)-1995
  Obituary **1996**:1
Gacy, John Wayne 1942-1994
  Obituary **1994**:4
Gaines, William M. 1922-1992
  Obituary **1993**:1
Gale, Robert Peter 1945- **1986**:4
Galindo, Rudy 1969- **2001**:2
Gallagher, Brian 1959- **2012**:3
Gallagher, Peter 1955- **2004**:3
Gallo, Robert 1937- **1991**:1
Galvin, John R. 1929- **1990**:1
Galvin, Martin
  Brief entry **1985**:3
Gandolfini, James 1961- **2001**:3
Gandy, Kim 1954(?)- **2002**:2
Ganzi, Victor 1947- **2003**:3
Garbo, Greta 1905-1990
  Obituary **1990**:3
Garcia, Andy 1956- **1999**:3
Garcia, Cristina 1958- **1997**:4
Garcia, Jerry 1942-1995 **1988**:3
  Obituary **1996**:1
Garcia, Joe

Brief entry **1986**:4
Garcia, Juliet 1949- **2011**:1
Gardner, Ava Lavinia 1922-1990
  Obituary **1990**:2
Gardner, David and Tom **2001**:4
Gardner, Randy 1957- **1997**:2
Garner, Jennifer 1972- **2003**:1
Garnett, Kevin 1976- **2000**:3
Garofalo, Janeane 1964- **1996**:4
Garr, Teri 1949- **1988**:4
Garrison, Jim 1922-1992
  Obituary **1993**:2
Garson, Greer 1903-1996
  Obituary **1996**:4
Garzarelli, Elaine M. 1951- **1992**:3
Gates, Bill 1955- **1987**:4
Gates, Melinda 1964- **2010**:4
Gates, Robert M. 1943- **1992**:2
Gathers, Hank 1967(?)-1990
  Obituary **1990**:3
Gault, Willie 1960- **1991**:2
Gayle, Helene 1955- **2008**:2
Gebbie, Kristine 1944(?)- **1994**:2
Gee, E. 1944- **2011**:3
Geffen, David 1943- **1985**:3
Gehry, Frank O. 1929- **1987**:1
Geisel, Theodor 1904-1991
  Obituary **1992**:2
Geithner, Timothy F. 1961- **2009**:4
Gelbart, Larry 1928-2009
  Obituary **2011**:1
Gellar, Sarah Michelle 1977- **1999**:3
Geller, Margaret Joan 1947- **1998**:2
Gentine, Lou 1947- **2008**:2
George, Elizabeth 1949- **2003**:3
Gephardt, Richard 1941- **1987**:3
Gerba, Charles 1945- **1999**:4
Gerberding, Julie 1955- **2004**:1
Gere, Richard 1949- **1994**:3
Gergen, David 1942- **1994**:1
Gerrity, Sean 1958- **2011**:3
Gerstner, Lou 1942- **1993**:4
Gertz, Alison 1966(?)-1992
  Obituary **1993**:2
Gerulaitis, Vitas 1954-1994
  Obituary **1995**:1
Getty, Estelle 1923-2008
  Obituary **2009**:3
Getz, Stan 1927-1991
  Obituary **1991**:4
Gevinson, Tavi 1996- **2011**:1
Giamatti, A. Bartlett 1938-1989 **1988**:4
  Obituary **1990**:1
Giamatti, Paul 1967- **2009**:4
Giannulli, Mossimo 1963- **2002**:3
Gibson, Althea 1927-2003
  Obituary **2004**:4
Gibson, Kirk 1957- **1985**:2
Gibson, William Ford, III 1948- **1997**:2
Gifford, Kathie Lee 1953- **1992**:2
Giffords, Gabrielle 1970- **2012**:3
Gilbert, Elizabeth 1969- **2011**:1
Gilbert, Walter 1932- **1988**:3
Gilford, Jack 1907-1990
  Obituary **1990**:4
Gill, Vince 1957- **1995**:2
Gillespie, Dizzy 1917-1993
  Obituary **1993**:2
Gillespie, Marcia 1944- **1999**:4
Gillett, George 1938- **1988**:1

Gilruth, Robert 1913-2000
  Obituary **2001**:1
Gina and Pat Neely 1965- **2012**:2
Gingrich, Newt 1943- **1991**:1
Ginsberg, Allen 1926-1997
  Obituary **1997**:3
Ginsberg, Ian 1962(?)- **2006**:4
Ginsburg, Ruth Bader 1933- **1993**:4
Gioia, Dana 1950- **2008**:4
Gish, Lillian 1893-1993
  Obituary **1993**:4
Giuliani, Rudolph 1944- **1994**:2
Gladwell, Malcolm 1963- **2010**:3
Glaser, Elizabeth 1947-1994
  Obituary **1995**:2
Glass, David 1935- **1996**:1
Glass, Ira 1959- **2008**:2
Glass, Julia 1956- **2012**:3
Glass, Philip 1937- **1991**:4
Glasser, Ira 1938- **1989**:1
Glaus, Troy 1976- **2003**:3
Glazman, Lev and Alina Roytberg **2007**:4
Gleason, Jackie 1916-1987
  Obituary **1987**:4
Glenn, John 1921- **1998**:3
Gless, Sharon 1944- **1989**:3
Glover, Danny 1947- **1998**:4
Glover, Savion 1973- **1997**:1
Gobel, George 1920(?)-1991
  Obituary **1991**:4
Gober, Robert 1954- **1996**:3
Goetz, Bernhard Hugo 1947(?)- **1985**:3
Goizueta, Roberto 1931-1997 **1996**:1
  Obituary **1998**:1
Gold, Thomas 1920-2004
  Obituary **2005**:3
Goldberg, Gary David 1944- **1989**:4
Goldberg, Leonard 1934- **1988**:4
Goldberg, Whoopi 1955- **1993**:3
Goldblum, Jeff 1952- **1988**:1
Golden, Thelma 1965- **2003**:3
Goldhaber, Fred
  Brief entry **1986**:3
Goldman, Duff 1974- **2010**:1
Goldman, William 1931- **2001**:1
Goldman-Rakic, Patricia 1937- **2002**:4
Goldwater, Barry 1909-1998
  Obituary **1998**:4
Gomez, Lefty 1909-1989
  Obituary **1989**:3
Gomez, Selena 1992- **2011**:1
Gooden, Dwight 1964- **1985**:2
Gooding, Cuba, Jr. 1968- **1997**:3
Goodman, Benny 1909-1986
  Obituary **1986**:3
Goodman, Drew and Myra **2007**:4
Goodman, John 1952- **1990**:3
Goodnight, Jim 1943- **2012**:4
Goody, Joan 1935- **1990**:2
Goody, Sam 1904-1991
  Obituary **1992**:1
Gorder, Genevieve 1974- **2005**:4
Gordon, Dexter 1923-1990 **1987**:1
Gordon, Gale 1906-1995
  Obituary **1996**:1
Gordon, James 1941- **2009**:4
Gordon, Jeff 1971- **1996**:1
Gordon, Michael 1951(?)- **2005**:1
Gordon, William 1918-2010

Kallen, Jackie 1946(?)- **1994**:1
Kamali, Norma 1945- **1989**:1
Kamen, Dean 1951(?)- **2003**:1
Kanakaredes, Melina 1967- **2007**:1
Kandel, Eric 1929- **2005**:2
Kane, Patrick 1988- **2011**:4
Kanokogi, Rusty
  Brief entry **1987**:1
Kapor, Mitch 1950- **1990**:3
Karan, Donna 1948- **1988**:1
Karmazin, Mel 1943- **2006**:1
Karr, Mary 1955- **2011**:2
Kasem, Casey 1933(?)- **1987**:1
Kashuk, Sonia 1959(?)- **2002**:4
Kaskey, Ray
  Brief entry **1987**:2
Kassebaum, Nancy 1932- **1991**:1
Kathwari, M. Farooq 1944- **2005**:4
Katz, Alex 1927- **1990**:3
Katz, Lillian 1927- **1987**:4
Katzenberg, Jeffrey 1950- **1995**:3
Kaufman, Charlie 1958- **2005**:1
Kaufman, Elaine **1989**:4
Kavner, Julie 1951- **1992**:3
Kaye, Danny 1913-1987
  Obituary **1987**:2
Kaye, Nora 1920-1987
  Obituary **1987**:4
Kaye, Sammy 1910-1987
  Obituary **1987**:4
Kazan, Elia 1909-2003
  Obituary **2004**:4
Keating, Charles H., Jr. 1923- **1990**:4
Keaton, Diane 1946- **1997**:1
Keaton, Michael 1951- **1989**:4
Keeling, Charles 1928-2005
  Obituary **2006**:3
Keeshan, Bob 1927-2004
  Obituary **2005**:2
Keillor, Garrison 1942- **2011**:2
Keitel, Harvey 1939- **1994**:3
Keith, Brian 1921-1997
  Obituary **1997**:4
Keith, Louis 1935- **1988**:2
Kelleher, Herb 1931- **1995**:1
Kellerman, Jonathan 1949- **2009**:1
Kelley, DeForest 1929-1999
  Obituary **2000**:1
Kelley, Virginia 1923-1994
  Obituary **1994**:3
Kelly, Ellsworth 1923- **1992**:1
Kelly, Gene 1912-1996
  Obituary **1996**:3
Kelly, Jim 1960- **1991**:4
Kelly, Maureen 1972(?)- **2007**:3
Kelly, Patrick 1954(?)-1990
  Obituary **1990**:2
Kelly, R. 1968- **1997**:3
Kelly, William R. 1905-1998 **1998**:2
Kemp, Jack 1935- **1990**:4
Kemp, Jan 1949- **1987**:2
Kemp, Shawn 1969- **1995**:1
Kendrick, Anna 1985- **2011**:2
Kendricks, Eddie 1939-1992
  Obituary **1993**:2
Kennan, George 1904-2005
  Obituary **2006**:2
Kennedy, John F., Jr. 1960-1999 **1990**
  :1
  Obituary **1999**:4
Kennedy, Rose 1890-1995
  Obituary **1995**:3

Kennedy, Ted 1932-2009
  Obituary **2011**:1
Kennedy, Weldon 1938- **1997**:3
Kenny G 1957(?)- **1994**:4
Keno, Leigh and Leslie 1957(?)- **2001**
  :2
Kent, Corita 1918-1986
  Obituary **1987**:1
Keough, Donald Raymond 1926-
  1986:1
Keplinger, Dan 1973- **2001**:1
Kerger, Paula A. 1957- **2007**:2
Kerkorian, Kirk 1917- **1996**:2
Kerr, Clark 1911-2003
  Obituary **2005**:1
Kerr, Cristie 1977- **2008**:2
Kerr, Jean 1922-2003
  Obituary **2004**:1
Kerr, Walter 1913-1996
  Obituary **1997**:1
Kerrey, Bob 1943- **1986**:1
Kerrigan, Nancy 1969- **1994**:3
Kerry, John 1943- **2005**:2
Kesey, Ken 1935-2001
  Obituary **2003**:1
Kessler, David 1951- **1992**:1
Ketcham, Hank 1920-2001
  Obituary **2002**:2
Kevorkian, Jack 1928(?)- **1991**:3
Keyes, Alan 1950- **1996**:2
Keyes, James 1955- **2011**:3
Keys, Alicia 1981- **2006**:1
Kiam, Elena 1964- **2012**:2
Kidd, Jason 1973- **2003**:2
Kidd, Michael 1915-2007
  Obituary **2009**:1
Kid Rock 1972- **2001**:1
Kilar, Jason 1971- **2010**:1
Kilborn, Craig 1964- **2003**:2
Kilby, Jack 1923- **2002**:2
Kiley, Dan 1912-2004
  Obituary **2005**:2
Kilgore, Marcia 1968- **2006**:3
Kilmer, Val **1991**:4
Kilpatrick, Kwame 1970- **2009**:2
Kilts, James M. 1948- **2001**:3
Kim, Eugenia 1974(?)- **2006**:1
Kim Barnouin and Rory Freedman
  1971- **2009**:4
Kimmel, Jimmy 1967- **2009**:2
Kimsey, James V. 1940(?)- **2001**:1
King, Alan 1927-2004
  Obituary **2005**:3
King, Bernice 1963- **2000**:2
King, Coretta Scott 1927- **1999**:3
King, Don 1931- **1989**:1
King, Larry 1933- **1993**:1
King, Mary-Claire 1946- **1998**:3
King, Stephen 1947- **1998**:1
Kingsborough, Donald
  Brief entry **1986**:2
Kingsley, Patricia 1932- **1990**:2
Kings of Leon 1982- **2010**:3
Kingsolver, Barbara 1955- **2005**:1
Kinison, Sam 1954(?)-1992
  Obituary **1993**:1
Kinney, Jeff 1971- **2009**:3
Kiraly, Karch
  Brief entry **1987**:1
Kirchner, Leon 1919-2009
  Obituary **2011**:1
Kirk, David 1956(?)- **2004**:1

Kirkpatrick, Jeane 1926-2006
  Obituary **2008**:1
Kissinger, Henry 1923- **1999**:4
Kissling, Frances 1943- **1989**:2
Kistler, Darci 1964- **1993**:1
Kitaj, R. B. 1932-2007
  Obituary **2008**:4
Kite, Tom 1949- **1990**:3
Kitt, Eartha 1927-2008
  Obituary **2010**:1
Klass, Perri 1958- **1993**:2
Klein, Calvin 1942- **1996**:2
Kligman, Albert Montgomery
  1916-2010
  Obituary **2012**:2
Kline, Kevin 1947- **2000**:1
Kloss, Henry E.
  Brief entry **1985**:2
Kluge, John 1914- **1991**:1
Knievel, Evel 1938-2007
  Obituary **2009**:1
Knievel, Robbie 1963- **1990**:1
Knight, Bobby 1940- **1985**:3
Knight, Philip H. 1938- **1994**:1
Knight, Ted 1923-1986
  Obituary **1986**:4
Knight, Wayne 1956- **1997**:1
Knotts, Don 1924-2006
  Obituary **2007**:1
Knowles, John 1926-2001
  Obituary **2003**:1
Koch, Bill 1940- **1992**:3
Koch, Jim 1949- **2004**:3
Kohnstamm, Abby 1954- **2001**:1
Kolff, Willem 1911-2009
  Obituary **2010**:2
Koogle, Tim 1951- **2000**:4
Koons, Jeff 1955(?)- **1991**:4
Koontz, Dean 1945- **1999**:3
Koop, C. Everett 1916- **1989**:3
Kopits, Steven E.
  Brief entry **1987**:1
Koplovitz, Kay 1945- **1986**:3
Kopp, Wendy **1993**:3
Koppel, Ted 1940- **1989**:1
Kordich, Jay 1923- **1993**:2
Koresh, David 1960(?)-1993
  Obituary **1993**:4
Korman, Harvey 1927-2008
  Obituary **2009**:2
Kornberg, Arthur 1918(?)- **1992**:1
Kors, Michael 1959- **2000**:4
Kostabi, Mark 1960- **1989**:4
Kostova, Elizabeth 1964- **2006**:2
Kovacevich, Dick 1943- **2004**:3
Kozinski, Alex 1950- **2002**:2
Kozol, Jonathan 1936- **1992**:1
Kramer, Jack 1921-2009
  Obituary **2011**:1
Kramer, Larry 1935- **1991**:2
Kramer, Stanley 1913-2001
  Obituary **2002**:1
Krantz, Judith 1928- **2003**:1
Krause, Peter 1965- **2009**:2
Kravitz, Lenny 1964(?)- **1991**:1
Krebs, Edwin 1918-2009
  Obituary **2011**:4
Kreps, Juanita M. 1921-2010
  Obituary **2012**:4
Krim, Mathilde 1926- **1989**:2
Kroc, Ray 1902-1984
  Obituary **1985**:1

Obituary **2001**:3
Lindsay-Abaire, David 1970(?)- **2008**:2
Lines, Ray 1960(?)- **2004**:1
Ling, Bai 1970- **2000**:3
Ling, Lisa 1973- **2004**:2
Linklater, Richard 1960- **2007**:2
Linkletter, Art 1912-2010
    Obituary **2012**:4
Linney, Laura 1964- **2009**:4
Lipinski, Tara 1982- **1998**:3
Lipkis, Andy
    Brief entry **1985**:3
Lippman, Laura 1959- **2010**:2
Lipsig, Harry H. 1901- **1985**:1
Lipton, Martin 1931- **1987**:3
Lisick, Beth 1969(?)- **2006**:2
Lithgow, John 1945- **1985**:2
Little, Benilde 1959(?)- **2006**:2
Little, Cleavon 1939-1992
    Obituary **1993**:2
Litzenburger, Liesel 1967(?)- **2008**:1
Liu, Lucy 1968- **2000**:4
Lively, Blake 1987- **2009**:1
Livingston, Ron 1968- **2007**:2
Liz Elting and Phil Shawe 1967-
    2012:1
LL Cool J 1968- **1998**:2
Lobell, Jeanine 1964(?)- **2002**:3
Locklear, Heather 1961- **1994**:3
Lodge, Henry Cabot 1902-1985
    Obituary **1985**:1
Loewe, Frederick 1901-1988
    Obituary **1988**:2
Lofton, Kenny 1967- **1998**:1
Logan, Joshua 1908-1988
    Obituary **1988**:4
Lohan, Lindsay 1986- **2005**:3
Long, Nia 1970- **2001**:3
Long, Shelley 1950(?)- **1985**:1
Longo, Robert 1953(?)- **1990**:4
Lopes, Lisa 1971-2002
    Obituary **2003**:3
Lopez, George 1963- **2003**:4
Lopez, Jennifer 1970- **1998**:4
Lopez, Mario 1973- **2009**:3
Lopez, Nancy 1957- **1989**:3
Lord, Bette Bao 1938- **1994**:1
Lord, Jack 1920-1998 **1998**:2
Lord, Winston
    Brief entry **1987**:4
Lords, Traci 1968- **1995**:4
Lott, Trent 1941- **1998**:1
Louganis, Greg 1960- **1995**:3
Louis-Dreyfus, Julia 1961(?)- **1994**:1
Louv, Richard 1949- **2006**:2
Lovato, Demi 1992- **2011**:2
Love, Courtney 1964(?)- **1995**:1
Love, Susan 1948- **1995**:2
Loveless, Patty 1957- **1998**:2
Lovett, Lyle 1958(?)- **1994**:1
Lovley, Derek 1954(?)- **2005**:3
Lowe, Edward 1921- **1990**:2
Lowe, Mitch 1953- **2011**:2
Lowe, Rob 1964(?)- **1990**:4
Lowell, Mike 1974- **2003**:2
Lowry, Adam and Eric Ryan **2008**:1
Loy, Myrna 1905-1993
    Obituary **1994**:2
Lucas, George 1944- **1999**:4
Lucci, Susan 1946(?)- **1999**:4
Luce, Clare Boothe 1903-1987

Obituary **1988**:1
Lucid, Shannon 1943- **1997**:1
Lucke, Lewis 1951(?)- **2004**:4
Ludacris 1977- **2007**:4
Ludlum, Robert 1927-2001
    Obituary **2002**:1
Lukas, D. Wayne 1936(?)- **1986**:2
Lupino, Ida 1918(?)-1995
    Obituary **1996**:1
LuPone, Patti 1949- **2009**:2
Lutz, Robert A. 1932- **1990**:1
Lynch, David 1946- **1990**:4
Lynch, Jane 1960- **2011**:2
Lyne, Susan 1950- **2005**:4
Lynn, Loretta 1935(?)- **2001**:1
Lysacek, Evan 1985- **2011**:2
Mac, Bernie 1957- **2003**:1
MacCready, Paul 1925- **1986**:4
MacDonald, Laurie and Walter
    Parkes **2004**:1
MacDowell, Andie 1958(?)- **1993**:4
MacFarlane, Seth 1973- **2006**:1
Machover, Tod 1953- **2010**:3
Mack, John J. 1944- **2006**:3
Mackey, John 1953- **2008**:2
MacKinnon, Catharine 1946- **1993**:2
MacMurray, Fred 1908-1991
    Obituary **1992**:2
MacNelly, Jeff 1947-2000
    Obituary **2000**:4
MacRae, Gordon 1921-1986
    Obituary **1986**:2
Macy, William H. **1999**:3
Madden, Chris 1948- **2006**:1
Madden, John 1936- **1995**:1
Madden, Steve 1958- **2007**:2
Maddow, Rachel 1973- **2010**:2
Maddux, Greg 1966- **1996**:2
Madonna 1958- **1985**:2
Maggie Q 1979- **2012**:4
Maglich, Bogdan C. 1928- **1990**:1
Magliozzi, Tom and Ray **1991**:4
Maguire, Tobey 1975- **2002**:2
Maher, Bill 1956- **1996**:2
Mahony, Roger M. 1936- **1988**:2
Maida, Adam Cardinal 1930- **1998**:2
Mailer, Norman 1923- **1998**:1
Maiman, Theodore 1927-2007
    Obituary **2008**:3
Majerle, Dan 1965- **1993**:4
Malda, Rob 1976- **2007**:3
Malden, Karl 1912-2009
    Obituary **2010**:4
Malkovich, John 1953- **1988**:2
Malloy, Edward Monk 1941- **1989**:4
Malone, John C. 1941- **1988**:3
Malone, Karl 1963- **1990**:1
Maltby, Richard, Jr. 1937- **1996**:3
Mamet, David 1947- **1998**:4
Manchin, Joe 1947- **2006**:4
Mancini, Henry 1924-1994
    Obituary **1994**:4
Manheimer, Heidi 1963- **2009**:3
Maniscalco, Chuck 1953- **2010**:3
Mankiller, Wilma P.
    Brief entry **1986**:2
Mann, Sally 1951- **2001**:2
Manning, Eli 1981- **2008**:4
Manning, Peyton 1976- **2007**:4
Mansfield, Mike 1903-2001
    Obituary **2002**:4
Mansion, Gracie

Brief entry **1986**:3
Manson, JoAnn E. 1953- **2008**:3
Manson, Marilyn 1969- **1999**:4
Mantegna, Joe 1947- **1992**:1
Mantle, Mickey 1931-1995
    Obituary **1996**:1
Mapplethorpe, Robert 1946-1989
    Obituary **1989**:3
Maraldo, Pamela J. 1948(?)- **1993**:4
Maravich, Pete 1948-1988
    Obituary **1988**:2
Marchand, Nancy 1928-2000
    Obituary **2001**:1
Marchetto, Marisa Acocella 1962(?)-
    2007:3
Marcus, Stanley 1905-2002
    Obituary **2003**:1
Mardin, Brice 1938- **2007**:4
Margolis, Bobby 1948(?)- **2007**:2
Margulies, Julianna 1966- **2011**:1
Marier, Rebecca 1974- **1995**:4
Marin, Cheech 1946- **2000**:1
Marineau, Philip 1946- **2002**:4
Maris, Roger 1934-1985
    Obituary **1986**:1
Mark, Mary Ellen 1940- **2006**:2
Marky Mark 1971- **1993**:3
Maroon 5 **2008**:1
Marriott, J. Willard 1900-1985
    Obituary **1985**:4
Marriott, J. Willard, Jr. 1932- **1985**:4
Mars, Bruno 1985- **2012**:4
Marsalis, Branford 1960- **1988**:3
Marsalis, Wynton 1961- **1997**:4
Marshall, Penny 1942- **1991**:3
Marshall, Susan 1958- **2000**:4
Marshall, Thurgood 1908-1993
    Obituary **1993**:3
Martin, Agnes 1912-2004
    Obituary **2006**:1
Martin, Billy 1928-1989 **1988**:4
    Obituary **1990**:2
Martin, Casey 1972- **2002**:1
Martin, Dean 1917-1995
    Obituary **1996**:2
Martin, Dean Paul 1952(?)-1987
    Obituary **1987**:3
Martin, George R.R. 1948- **2012**:3
Martin, Judith 1938- **2000**:3
Martin, Lynn 1939- **1991**:4
Martin, Mary 1913-1990
    Obituary **1991**:2
Martin, Steve 1945- **1992**:2
Martinez, Bob 1934- **1992**:1
Marvin, Lee 1924-1987
    Obituary **1988**:1
Mary Mary 1972- **2009**:4
Mas Canosa, Jorge 1939-1997 **1998**:2
Mashouf, Manny 1938(?)- **2008**:1
Master P 1970- **1999**:4
Masters, William H. 1915-2001
    Obituary **2001**:4
Matalin, Mary 1953- **1995**:2
Mathews, Dan 1965- **1998**:3
Mathias, Bob 1930-2006
    Obituary **2007**:4
Mathias, Charles McCurdy
    1922-2010
    Obituary **2012**:1
Mathis, Clint 1976- **2003**:1
Matlin, Marlee 1965- **1992**:2
Matlovich, Leonard P. 1944(?)-1988

Onassis, Jacqueline Kennedy
1929-1994
  Obituary **1994**:4
O'Neal, Shaquille 1972- **1992**:1
O'Neil, Buck 1911-2006
  Obituary **2007**:4
O'Neill, Ed 1946- **2010**:4
O'Neill, Paul H. 1935- **2001**:4
O'Neill, Tip 1912-1994
  Obituary **1994**:3
Ono, Yoko 1933- **1989**:2
Onysko, Joshua 1978- **2012**:2
Oosterhouse, Carter 1976- **2012**:1
Orbach, Jerry 1935-2004
  Obituary **2006**:1
Orbison, Roy 1936-1988
  Obituary **1989**:2
O'Reilly, Bill 1949- **2001**:2
Orman, Suze 1951(?)- **2003**:1
Ormandy, Eugene 1899-1985
  Obituary **1985**:2
Ornish, Dean 1953- **2004**:2
Orr, Kay 1939- **1987**:4
Osborne, Joan 1962- **1996**:4
Osgood, Charles 1933- **1996**:2
Osteen, Joel 1963- **2006**:2
O'Steen, Van
  Brief entry **1986**:3
Ostin, Mo 1927- **1996**:2
Ostroff, Dawn 1960- **2006**:4
Otellini, Paul 1950- **2012**:3
Otte, Ruth 1949- **1992**:4
OutKast **2004**:4
Ovitz, Michael 1946- **1990**:1
Owens, Buck 1929-2006
  Obituary **2007**:2
Owens, Delia and Mark **1993**:3
Oz, Mehmet 1960- **2007**:2
Paar, Jack 1918-2004
  Obituary **2005**:2
Pacelle, Wayne 1965- **2009**:4
Pacino, Al 1940- **1993**:4
Pack, Ellen 1963(?)- **2001**:2
Packard, David 1912-1996
  Obituary **1996**:3
Padron, Eduardo 1946- **2011**:2
Page, Bettie 1923-2008
  Obituary **2010**:1
Page, Geraldine 1924-1987
  Obituary **1987**:4
Pagels, Elaine 1943- **1997**:1
Paglia, Camille 1947- **1992**:3
Paige, Emmett, Jr.
  Brief entry **1986**:4
Paige, Rod 1933- **2003**:2
Paisley, Brad 1972- **2008**:3
Pakula, Alan 1928-1998
  Obituary **1999**:2
Palahniuk, Chuck 1962- **2004**:1
Palance, Jack 1919-2006
  Obituary **2008**:1
Paley, William S. 1901-1990
  Obituary **1991**:2
Palin, Sarah 1964- **2009**:1
Palmeiro, Rafael 1964- **2005**:1
Palmer, Jim 1945- **1991**:2
Palmer, Keke 1993- **2011**:3
Palmer, Violet 1964(?)- **2005**:2
Palmisano, Samuel J. 1952(?)- **2003**:1
Paltrow, Gwyneth 1972- **1997**:1
Panetta, Leon 1938- **1995**:1
Panettiere, Hayden 1989- **2008**:4

Panichgul, Thakoon 1974- **2009**:4
Panofsky, Wolfgang 1919-2007
  Obituary **2008**:4
Pantoliano, Joe 1951- **2002**:3
Papp, Joseph 1921-1991
  Obituary **1992**:2
Paretsky, Sara 1947- **2002**:4
Parker, Brant 1920-2007
  Obituary **2008**:2
Parker, Colonel Tom 1929-1997
  Obituary **1997**:2
Parker, Mary-Louise 1964- **2002**:2
Parker, Sarah Jessica 1965- **1999**:2
Parker, Suzy 1932-2003
  Obituary **2004**:2
Parker, Trey and Matt Stone **1998**:2
Parker, Willie 1980- **2009**:3
Parks, Bert 1914-1992
  Obituary **1992**:3
Parks, Gordon 1912-2006
  Obituary **2006**:2
Parks, Rosa 1913-2005
  Obituary **2007**:1
Parks, Suzan-Lori 1964- **2003**:2
Parsons, David 1959- **1993**:4
Parsons, Gary 1950(?)- **2006**:2
Parsons, Jim 1973- **2012**:3
Parsons, Richard 1949- **2002**:4
Parton, Dolly 1946- **1999**:4
Pascal, Amy 1958- **2003**:3
Pass, Joe 1929-1994
  Obituary **1994**:4
Pastorius, Jaco 1951-1987
  Obituary **1988**:1
Pataki, George 1945- **1995**:2
Patchett, Ann 1963- **2003**:2
Paterno, Joe 1926- **1995**:4
Patrick, Danica 1982- **2003**:3
Patrick, Robert 1959- **2002**:1
Patterson, Richard North 1947- **2001**
:4
Patton, John 1947(?)- **2004**:4
Paul, Les 1915-2009
  Obituary **2010**:4
Pauley, Jane 1950- **1999**:1
Pauling, Linus 1901-1994
  Obituary **1995**:1
Paulsen, Pat 1927-1997
  Obituary **1997**:4
Paulucci, Jeno
  Brief entry **1986**:3
Pausch, Randy 1960-2008
  Obituary **2009**:3
Pavin, Corey 1959- **1996**:4
Paxton, Bill 1955- **1999**:3
Payne, Alexander 1961- **2005**:4
Payton, Lawrence 1938(?)-1997
  Obituary **1997**:4
Payton, Walter 1954-1999
  Obituary **2000**:2
Pearl, Minnie 1912-1996
  Obituary **1996**:3
Pearl Jam **1994**:2
Peck, Gregory 1916-2003
  Obituary **2004**:3
Pedersen, William 1938(?)- **1989**:4
Peebles, R. Donahue 1960- **2003**:2
Peete, Calvin 1943- **1985**:4
Peete, Holly Robinson 1964- **2005**:2
Pei, I.M. 1917- **1990**:4
Pekar, Harvey 1939-2010
  Obituary **2012**:4

Peller, Clara 1902(?)-1987
  Obituary **1988**:1
Pelosi, Nancy 1940- **2004**:2
Peltier, Leonard 1944- **1995**:1
Peluso, Michelle 1971(?)- **2007**:4
Pendergrass, Teddy 1950-2010
  Obituary **2012**:1
Pendleton, Clarence M. 1930-1988
  Obituary **1988**:4
Penn, Irving 1917-2009
  Obituary **2011**:2
Penn, Kal 1977- **2009**:1
Penn, Sean 1960- **1987**:2
Penn & Teller **1992**:1
Pennington, Ty 1965- **2005**:4
Penske, Roger 1937- **1988**:3
Pep, Willie 1922-2006
  Obituary **2008**:1
Pepper, Claude 1900-1989
  Obituary **1989**:4
Percy, Walker 1916-1990
  Obituary **1990**:4
Perdue, Frank 1920-2005
  Obituary **2006**:2
Perelman, Ronald 1943- **1989**:2
Perez, Rosie **1994**:2
Perkins, Anthony 1932-1992
  Obituary **1993**:2
Perkins, Carl 1932-1998 **1998**:2
Perlman, Ron 1950- **2012**:4
Perlman, Steve 1961(?)- **1998**:2
Perot, H. Ross 1930- **1992**:4
Perry, Carrie Saxon 1932(?)- **1989**:2
Perry, Harold A. 1917(?)-1991
  Obituary **1992**:1
Perry, Katy 1984- **2012**:1
Perry, Luke 1966(?)- **1992**:3
Perry, Matthew 1969- **1997**:2
Perry, Tyler 1969- **2006**:1
Perry, William 1927- **1994**:4
Pesci, Joe 1943- **1992**:4
Peter, Valentine J. 1934- **1988**:2
Peters, Bernadette 1948- **2000**:1
Peters, Mary E. 1948- **2008**:3
Peters, Tom 1942- **1998**:1
Petersen, Donald Eugene 1926- **1985**
:1
Peterson, Cassandra 1951- **1988**:1
Peterson, Roger Tory 1908-1996
  Obituary **1997**:1
Petty, Tom 1952- **1988**:1
Peyton, Elizabeth 1965- **2007**:1
Pfeiffer, Michelle 1957- **1990**:2
Phair, Liz 1967- **1995**:3
Phelan, John Joseph, Jr. 1931- **1985**:4
Phelps, Michael 1985- **2009**:2
Phifer, Mekhi 1975- **2004**:1
Philbin, Regis 1933- **2000**:2
Phillips, John 1935-2001
  Obituary **2002**:1
Phillips, Julia 1944- **1992**:1
Phillips, Sam 1923-2003
  Obituary **2004**:4
Phoenix, Joaquin 1974- **2000**:4
Phoenix, River 1970-1993 **1990**:2
  Obituary **1994**:2
Piazza, Mike 1968- **1998**:4
Pickett, Wilson 1941-2006
  Obituary **2007**:1
Picoult, Jodi 1966- **2008**:1
Pierce, David Hyde 1959- **1996**:3
Pierce, Frederick S. 1934(?)- **1985**:3

Reubens, Paul 1952- **1987**:2
Reverend Ike 1935-2009
  Obituary **2010**:4
Rey, Margret E. 1906-1996
  Obituary **1997**:2
Reynolds, Paula Rosput 1956- **2008**:4
Reznor, Trent 1965- **2000**:2
Rhee, Michelle 1969- **2012**:3
Rhodes, Dusty 1927-2009
  Obituary **2010**:3
Ribicoff, Abraham 1910-1998
  Obituary **1998**:3
Ricci, Christina 1980- **1999**:1
Rice, Anne 1941- **1995**:1
Rice, Condoleezza 1954- **2002**:1
Rice, Jerry 1962- **1990**:4
Rice, Susan E. 1964- **2010**:3
Rich, Buddy 1917-1987
  Obituary **1987**:3
Rich, Charlie 1932-1995
  Obituary **1996**:1
Richards, Ann 1933- **1991**:2
Richards, Michael 1949(?)- **1993**:4
Richardson, Steve 1939- **2010**:4
Richmond, Julius B. 1916-2008
  Obituary **2009**:4
Richter, Charles Francis 1900-1985
  Obituary **1985**:4
Rickover, Hyman 1900-1986
  Obituary **1986**:4
Riddle, Nelson 1921-1985
  Obituary **1985**:4
Ridge, Tom 1945- **2002**:2
Rifkin, Jeremy 1945- **1990**:3
Riggio, Leonard S. 1941- **1999**:4
Riggs, Bobby 1918-1995
  Obituary **1996**:2
Riggs, Ransom 1979- **2012**:4
Rigopulos, Alex 1970- **2009**:4
Riley, Pat 1945- **1994**:3
Riley, Richard W. 1933- **1996**:3
Rimes, LeeAnn 1982- **1997**:4
Riney, Hal 1932- **1989**:1
Ringgold, Faith 1930- **2000**:3
Ringwald, Molly 1968- **1985**:4
Riordan, Richard 1930- **1993**:4
Ripa, Kelly 1970- **2002**:2
Ripken, Cal, Jr. 1960- **1986**:2
Ripken, Cal, Sr. 1936(?)-1999
  Obituary **1999**:4
Ritchie, Dennis and Kenneth
  Thompson **2000**:1
Ritter, John 1948- **2003**:4
Ritts, Herb 1954(?)- **1992**:4
Rivera, Geraldo 1943- **1989**:1
Rivers, Joan 1933- **2005**:3
Rizzo, Frank 1920-1991
  Obituary **1992**:1
Roach, Mary 1959- **2012**:2
Robards, Jason 1922-2000
  Obituary **2001**:3
Robb, Charles S. 1939- **1987**:2
Robbins, Harold 1916-1997
  Obituary **1998**:1
Robbins, Jerome 1918-1998
  Obituary **1999**:1
Robbins, Tim 1959- **1993**:1
Roberts, Brian L. 1959- **2002**:4
Roberts, Cokie 1943- **1993**:4
Roberts, Doris 1930- **2003**:4
Roberts, Julia 1967- **1991**:3
Roberts, Nora 1950- **2010**:3

Roberts, Oral 1918-2009
  Obituary **2011**:4
Roberts, Pernell 1928-2010
  Obituary **2012**:1
Roberts, Robin 1926-2010
  Obituary **2012**:3
Roberts, Steven K. 1952(?)- **1992**:1
Roberts, Xavier 1955- **1985**:3
Robertson, Nan 1926-2009
  Obituary **2010**:4
Robertson, Pat 1930- **1988**:2
Robinson, David 1965- **1990**:4
Robinson, Earl 1910(?)-1991
  Obituary **1992**:1
Robinson, Eddie 1919-2007
  Obituary **2008**:2
Robinson, Frank 1935- **1990**:2
Robinson, Max 1939-1988
  Obituary **1989**:2
Robinson, Sugar Ray 1921-1989
  Obituary **1989**:3
Robinson, V. Gene 1947- **2004**:4
Roche, Kevin 1922- **1985**:1
Rock, Chris 1967(?)- **1998**:1
Rock, John
  Obituary **1985**:1
Rock, The 1972- **2001**:2
Rockwell, David 1956- **2003**:3
Roddenberry, Gene 1921-1991
  Obituary **1992**:2
Roddick, Andy 1982- **2004**:3
Rodgers, Aaron 1983- **2012**:2
Rodgers, Carolyn M. 1940-2010
  Obituary **2012**:3
Rodin, Judith 1945(?)- **1994**:4
Rodman, Dennis 1961- **1991**:3
Rodriguez, Alex 1975- **2001**:2
Rodriguez, Narciso 1961- **2005**:1
Rodriguez, Robert 1968- **2005**:1
Roedy, Bill 1949(?)- **2003**:2
Roemer, Buddy 1943- **1991**:4
Rogers, Adrian 1931- **1987**:4
Rogers, Fred 1928- **2000**:4
Rogers, Ginger 1911(?)-1995
  Obituary **1995**:4
Rogers, Roy 1911-1998
  Obituary **1998**:4
Rogers, William P. 1913-2001
  Obituary **2001**:4
Roizen, Michael 1946- **2007**:4
Roker, Al 1954- **2003**:1
Roker, Roxie 1929(?)-1995
  Obituary **1996**:2
Rolle, Esther 1922-1998
  Obituary **1999**:2
Rollins, Henry 1961- **2007**:3
Rollins, Howard E., Jr. 1950- **1986**:1
Romano, Ray 1957- **2001**:4
Romijn, Rebecca 1972- **2007**:1
Romo, Tony 1980- **2008**:3
Roncal, Mally 1972- **2009**:4
Rooney, Art 1901-1988
  Obituary **1989**:1
Roosevelt, Franklin D., Jr. 1914-1988
  Obituary **1989**:1
Rose, Axl 1962(?)- **1992**:1
Rose, Charlie 1943- **1994**:2
Rose, Lela 1969- **2011**:1
Rose, Pete 1941- **1991**:1
Rosedale, Philip 1968- **2011**:3
Rosen, Moishe 1932-2010
  Obituary **2012**:4

Rosenberg, Evelyn 1942- **1988**:2
Rosenberg, Steven 1940- **1989**:1
Rosendahl, Bruce R.
  Brief entry **1986**:4
Rosenfeld, Irene 1953- **2008**:3
Rosenthal, Joseph 1911-2006
  Obituary **2007**:4
Rosenzweig, Ilene 1965(?)- **2004**:1
Rosgen, Dave 1942(?)- **2005**:2
Ros-Lehtinen, Ileana 1952- **2000**:2
Ross, Herbert 1927-2001
  Obituary **2002**:4
Ross, Percy
  Brief entry **1986**:2
Ross, Steven J. 1927-1992
  Obituary **1993**:3
Rossellini, Isabella 1952- **2001**:4
Rossner, Judith 1935-2005
  Obituary **2006**:4
Rosten, Leo 1908-1997
  Obituary **1997**:3
Roth, Philip 1933- **1999**:1
Roth, William Victor, Jr. 1921-2003
  Obituary **2005**:1
Rothenberg, Susan 1945- **1995**:3
Rotherham, Andrew 1971- **2012**:4
Rothstein, Ruth **1988**:2
Rothwax, Harold 1930- **1996**:3
Rourke, Mickey 1956- **1988**:4
Rouse, James 1914-1996
  Obituary **1996**:4
Rove, Karl 1950- **2006**:2
Rowan, Carl 1925-2000
  Obituary **2001**:2
Rowan, Dan 1922-1987
  Obituary **1988**:1
Rowe, Jack 1944- **2005**:2
Rowe, Mike 1962- **2010**:2
Rowland, Pleasant **1992**:3
Rowley, Coleen 1955(?)- **2004**:2
Rowley, Cynthia 1958- **2002**:1
Roybal-Allard, Lucille 1941- **1999**:4
Royko, Mike 1932-1997
  Obituary **1997**:4
Rozelle, Pete 1926-1996
  Obituary **1997**:2
Rubin, Jerry 1938-1994
  Obituary **1995**:2
Rudd, Paul 1969- **2009**:4
Rudes-Sandel, Lisa 1964- **2012**:3
Rudner, Rita 1956- **1993**:2
Rudnick, Paul 1957(?)- **1994**:3
Rudolph, Wilma 1940-1994
  Obituary **1995**:2
Ruehl, Mercedes 1948(?)- **1992**:4
Ruffalo, Mark 1967- **2011**:4
Ruffin, David 1941-1991
  Obituary **1991**:4
Rumsfeld, Donald 1932- **2004**:1
Runyan, Marla 1969- **2001**:1
RuPaul 1961(?)- **1996**:1
Ruppe, Loret Miller 1936- **1986**:2
Rush, Andra 1961- **2012**:1
Rusk, Dean 1909-1994
  Obituary **1995**:2
Russell, Keri 1976- **2000**:1
Russell, Kurt 1951- **2007**:4
Russell, Mary 1950- **2009**:2
Russell, Nipsey 1924-2005
  Obituary **2007**:1
Russert, Tim 1950-2008
  Obituary **2009**:3

Russo, Patricia 1952- **2008**:4
Russo, Rene 1954- **2000**:2
Russo, Richard 1949- **2002**:3
Rutan, Burt 1943- **1987**:2
Ryan, Meg 1962(?)- **1994**:1
Ryan, Nolan 1947- **1989**:4
Ryder, Winona 1971- **1991**:2
Saberhagen, Bret 1964- **1986**:1
Sachs, Jeffrey D. 1954- **2004**:4
Safire, William 1929- **2000**:3
Sagal, Katey 1954- **2005**:2
Sagan, Carl 1934-1996
    Obituary **1997**:2
Sagansky, Jeff 1952- **1993**:2
Sajak, Pat
    Brief entry **1985**:4
Salazar, Ken 1955- **2011**:4
Salbi, Zainab 1969(?)- **2008**:3
Saldana, Zoe 1978- **2010**:1
Salerno-Sonnenberg, Nadja 1961(?)-
    1988:4
Sales, Soupy 1926-2009
    Obituary **2011**:2
Salinger, J. D. 1919-2010
    Obituary **2012**:1
Salk, Jonas 1914-1995 **1994**:4
    Obituary **1995**:4
Salzman, Mark 1959- **2002**:1
Sammons, Mary 1946- **2007**:4
Sample, Bill
    Brief entry **1986**:2
Sampras, Pete 1971- **1994**:1
Sams, Craig 1944- **2007**:3
Samuelson, Paul 1915-2009
    Obituary **2011**:4
Sanchez, Loretta 1960- **2000**:3
Sanders, Barry 1968- **1992**:1
Sanders, Bernie 1941(?)- **1991**:4
Sanders, Deion 1967- **1992**:4
Sandler, Adam 1966- **1999**:2
Sanger, Steve 1946- **2002**:3
Saporta, Vicki
    Brief entry **1987**:3
Sapphire 1951(?)- **1996**:4
Saralegui, Cristina 1948- **1999**:2
Sarandon, Susan 1946- **1995**:3
Sarazen, Gene 1902-1999
    Obituary **1999**:4
Satcher, David 1941- **2001**:4
Satriani, Joe 1957(?)- **1989**:3
Saul, Betsy 1968- **2009**:2
Savage, Dan 1964- **2012**:3
Savage, Fred 1976- **1990**:1
Savalas, Telly 1924-1994
    Obituary **1994**:3
Sawyer, Diane 1945- **1994**:4
Scalia, Antonin 1936- **1988**:2
Scardino, Marjorie 1947- **2002**:1
Scavullo, Francesco 1921-2004
    Obituary **2005**:1
Schaap, Dick 1934-2001
    Obituary **2003**:1
Schaefer, William Donald 1921- **1988**
    :1
Schank, Roger 1946- **1989**:2
Schapiro, Mary 1955- **2012**:1
Scheck, Barry 1949- **2000**:4
Scheider, Roy 1932-2008
    Obituary **2009**:2
Schembechler, Bo 1929(?)- **1990**:3
Schenk, Dale 1957(?)- **2002**:2
Schiavo, Mary 1955- **1998**:2

Schilling, Curt 1966- **2002**:3
Schirra, Wally 1923-2007
    Obituary **2008**:3
Schlessinger, David
    Brief entry **1985**:1
Schlessinger, Laura 1947(?)- **1996**:3
Schmelzer, Sheri 1965- **2009**:4
Schmidt, Eric 1955- **2002**:4
Schmidt, Mike 1949- **1988**:3
Schnabel, Julian 1951- **1997**:1
Schneider, Rob 1965- **1997**:4
Schoenfeld, Gerald 1924- **1986**:2
Scholz, Tom 1949- **1987**:2
Schott, Marge 1928- **1985**:4
Schreiber, Liev 1967- **2007**:2
Schroeder, Barbet 1941- **1996**:1
Schroeder, William J. 1932-1986
    Obituary **1986**:4
Schulberg, Budd 1914-2009
    Obituary **2010**:4
Schultes, Richard Evans 1915-2001
    Obituary **2002**:1
Schultz, Howard 1953- **1995**:3
Schulz, Charles 1922-2000
    Obituary **2000**:4
Schulz, Charles M. 1922- **1998**:1
Schumacher, Joel 1929- **2004**:3
Schuman, Patricia Glass 1943- **1993**
    :2
Schwab, Charles 1937(?)- **1989**:3
Schwartz, Allen 1945(?)- **2008**:2
Schwartz, David 1936(?)- **1988**:3
Schwarzenegger, Arnold 1947- **1991**
    :1
Schwarzkopf, Norman 1934- **1991**:3
Schwimmer, David 1966(?)- **1996**:2
Schwinn, Edward R., Jr.
    Brief entry **1985**:4
Scorsese, Martin 1942- **1989**:1
Scott, Gene
    Brief entry **1986**:1
Scott, George C. 1927-1999
    Obituary **2000**:2
Scott, H. Lee, Jr. 1949- **2008**:3
Scott, Jill 1972- **2010**:1
Scott, Pamella 1975- **2010**:4
Scott, Randolph 1898(?)-1987
    Obituary **1987**:2
Sculley, John 1939- **1989**:4
Seacrest, Ryan 1976- **2004**:4
Sears, Barry 1947- **2004**:2
Sebelius, Kathleen 1948- **2008**:4
Sebold, Alice 1963(?)- **2005**:4
Secretariat 1970-1989
    Obituary **1990**:1
Sedaris, Amy 1961- **2009**:3
Sedaris, David 1956- **2005**:3
Sedelmaier, Joe 1933- **1985**:3
Sedgwick, Kyra 1965- **2006**:2
See, Lisa 1955- **2010**:4
Segal, Erich 1937-2010
    Obituary **2012**:1
Segal, Shelden 1926-2009
    Obituary **2011**:2
Segal, Shelli 1955(?)- **2005**:3
Seger, Bob 1945- **1987**:1
Seidelman, Susan 1953(?)- **1985**:4
Seidenberg, Ivan 1946- **2004**:1
Seinfeld, Jerry 1954- **1992**:4
Selena 1971-1995
    Obituary **1995**:4
Selig, Bud 1934- **1995**:2

Semel, Terry 1943- **2002**:2
Senk, Glen 1956- **2009**:3
Seo, Danny 1977- **2008**:3
Serra, Richard 1939- **2009**:1
Serrano, Andres 1950- **2000**:4
Serros, Michele 1967(?)- **2008**:2
Sethi, Simran 1971(?)- **2008**:1
Sevareid, Eric 1912-1992
    Obituary **1993**:1
Sevigny, Chloe 1974- **2001**:4
Sexton, John 1942- **2011**:4
Seyfried, Amanda 1985- **2009**:3
Shabazz, Betty 1936-1997
    Obituary **1997**:4
Shaich, Ron 1953- **2004**:4
Shakur, Tupac 1971-1996
    Obituary **1997**:1
Shalala, Donna 1941- **1992**:3
Shalikashvili, John 1936- **1994**:2
Shandling, Garry 1949- **1995**:1
Shanley, John Patrick 1950- **2006**:1
Sharkey, Ray 1953-1993
    Obituary **1994**:1
Sharpe, Sterling 1965- **1994**:3
Sharpton, Al 1954- **1991**:2
Shaw, Artie 1910-2004
    Obituary **2006**:1
Shaw, Carol 1958(?)- **2002**:1
Shaw, William 1934(?)- **2000**:3
Shawn, Dick 1924(?)-1987
    Obituary **1987**:3
Shawn, William 1907-1992
    Obituary **1993**:3
Shea, Jim, Jr. 1968- **2002**:4
Sheedy, Ally 1962- **1989**:1
Sheehan, Daniel P. 1945(?)- **1989**:1
Sheen, Charlie 1965- **2001**:2
Sheen, Martin 1940- **2002**:1
Sheffield, Gary 1968- **1998**:1
Sheindlin, Judith 1942(?)- **1999**:1
Sheldon, Sidney 1917-2007
    Obituary **2008**:2
Shelton, Blake 1976- **2012**:3
Shepard, Alan 1923-1998
    Obituary **1999**:1
Shepard, Sam 1943- **1996**:4
Shepherd, Cybill 1950- **1996**:3
Sherman, Cindy 1954- **1992**:3
Sherman, Russell 1930- **1987**:4
Shields, Brooke 1965- **1996**:3
Shields, Carol 1935-2003
    Obituary **2004**:3
Shilts, Randy 1951-1994 **1993**:4
    Obituary **1994**:3
Shimomura, Tsutomu 1965- **1996**:1
Shirley, Donna 1941- **1999**:1
Shocked, Michelle 1963(?)- **1989**:4
Shoemaker, Bill 1931-2003
    Obituary **2004**:4
Shore, Dinah 1917-1994
    Obituary **1994**:3
Shreve, Anita 1946(?)- **2003**:4
Shriver, Eunice 1921-2009
    Obituary **2011**:1
Shriver, Lionel 1957- **2008**:4
Shriver, Maria
    Brief entry **1986**:2
Shue, Andrew 1964- **1994**:4
Shula, Don 1930- **1992**:2
Shulman, Julius 1910-2009
    Obituary **2010**:4
Shyamalan, M. Night 1970- **2003**:2

Duhalde, Eduardo 1941- **2003**:3
Fernández de Kirchner, Cristina
  1953- **2009**:1
Herrera, Paloma 1975- **1996**:2
Maradona, Diego 1961(?)- **1991**:3
Pelli, Cesar 1927(?)- **1991**:4
Sabatini, Gabriela
  Brief entry **1985**:4
Sosa, Mercedes 1935-2009
  Obituary **2011**:2
Timmerman, Jacobo 1923-1999
  Obituary **2000**:3

ARMENIAN
Sargsyan, Serzh 1954- **2009**:3

AUSTRALIAN
AC/DC Grammy Awards- **2011**:2
Allen, Peter 1944-1992
  Obituary **1993**:1
Allenby, Robert 1971- **2007**:1
Anderson, Judith 1899(?)-1992
  Obituary **1992**:3
Assange, Julian 1971- **2012**:2
Baker, Simon 1969- **2009**:4
Bee Gees, The **1997**:4
Blackburn, Elizabeth 1948- **2010**:1
Blanchett, Cate 1969- **1999**:3
Bloom, Natalie 1971- **2007**:1
Bond, Alan 1938- **1989**:2
Bradman, Sir Donald 1908-2001
  Obituary **2002**:1
Bright, Torah 1986- **2010**:2
Byrne, Rhonda 1955- **2008**:2
Clavell, James 1924(?)-1994
  Obituary **1995**:1
Collette, Toni 1972- **2009**:4
Freeman, Cathy 1973- **2001**:3
Gibb, Andy 1958-1988
  Obituary **1988**:3
Gibson, Mel 1956- **1990**:1
Gillard, Julia 1961- **2011**:4
Helfgott, David 1937(?)- **1997**:2
Hewitt, Lleyton 1981- **2002**:2
Hughes, Robert 1938- **1996**:4
Humphries, Barry 1934- **1993**:1
Hutchence, Michael 1960-1997
  Obituary **1998**:1
Irwin, Steve 1962- **2001**:2
Jackman, Hugh 1968- **2004**:4
Kidman, Nicole 1967- **1992**:4
Klensch, Elsa **2001**:4
Larbalestier, Justine 1968(?)- **2008**:4
Ledger, Heath 1979- **2006**:3
Luhrmann, Baz 1962- **2002**:3
McMahon, Julian 1968- **2006**:1
Minogue, Kylie 1968- **2003**:4
Mueck, Ron 1958- **2008**:3
Murdoch, Rupert 1931- **1988**:4
Norman, Greg 1955- **1988**:3
Powter, Susan 1957(?)- **1994**:3
Rafter, Patrick 1972- **2001**:1
Rudd, Kevin 1957- **2009**:1
Rush, Geoffrey 1951- **2002**:1
Stone, Curtis 1975- **2011**:3
Summers, Anne 1945- **1990**:2
Travers, P.L. 1899(?)-1996
  Obituary **1996**:4
Tyler, Richard 1948(?)- **1995**:3
Urban, Keith 1967- **2006**:3
Watson, Jessica 1993- **2012**:1
Webb, Karrie 1974- **2000**:4
Worthington, Sam 1976- **2012**:1

AUSTRIAN
Brabeck-Letmathe, Peter 1944- **2001**
  :4
Brandauer, Klaus Maria 1944- **1987**:3
Djerassi, Carl 1923- **2000**:4
Drucker, Peter F. 1909- **1992**:3
Falco
  Brief entry **1987**:2
Frankl, Viktor E. 1905-1997
  Obituary **1998**:1
Hrabal, Bohumil 1914-1997
  Obituary **1997**:3
Jelinek, Elfriede 1946- **2005**:3
Lamarr, Hedy 1913-2000
  Obituary **2000**:3
Lang, Helmut 1956- **1999**:2
Lorenz, Konrad 1903-1989
  Obituary **1989**:3
Mateschitz, Dietrich 1944- **2008**:1
Perutz, Max 1914-2002
  Obituary **2003**:2
Porsche, Ferdinand 1909-1998
  Obituary **1998**:4
Pouillon, Nora 1943- **2005**:1
Puck, Wolfgang 1949- **1990**:1
Strobl, Fritz 1972- **2003**:3
von Karajan, Herbert 1908-1989
  Obituary **1989**:4
von Trapp, Maria 1905-1987
  Obituary **1987**:3
Waltz, Christoph 1956- **2011**:1
Wiesenthal, Simon 1908-2005
  Obituary **2006**:4

AZERI
Aliyev, Ilham 1961- **2010**:2

BANGLADESHI
Nasrin, Taslima 1962- **1995**:1
Yunus, Muhammad 1940- **2007**:3

BARBADIAN
Rihanna 1988- **2008**:4

BELARUSSIAN
Lukashenko, Alexander 1954- **2006**:4

BELGIAN
Clijsters, Kim 1983- **2006**:3
Henin-Hardenne, Justine 1982- **2004**
  :4
Hepburn, Audrey 1929-1993
  Obituary **1993**:2
Verhofstadt, Guy 1953- **2006**:3
von Furstenberg, Diane 1946- **1994**:2

BENGALI
Khan, Ali 1922-2009
  Obituary **2010**:3

BOLIVIAN
Morales, Evo 1959- **2007**:2
Sanchez de Lozada, Gonzalo 1930-
  2004:3

BOSNIAN
Izetbegovic, Alija 1925- **1996**:4
Obreht, Tea 1985- **2012**:3

BRAZILIAN
Bundchen, Gisele 1980- **2009**:1

Cardoso, Fernando Henrique 1931-
  1996:4
Castaneda, Carlos 1931-1998
  Obituary **1998**:4
Castroneves, Helio 1975- **2010**:1
Collor de Mello, Fernando 1949-
  1992:4
Costa, Francisco 1961- **2010**:2
Fittipaldi, Emerson 1946- **1994**:2
Helayel, Daniella 1972- **2012**:2
Ronaldinho 1980- **2007**:3
Ronaldo 1976- **1999**:2
Rousseff, Dilma 1947- **2012**:4
Salgado, Sebastiao 1944- **1994**:2
Senna, Ayrton 1960(?)-1994 **1991**:4
  Obituary **1994**:4
Silva, Luiz Inacio Lula da 1945-
  2003:4
Szot, Paulo 1969- **2009**:3
Xuxa 1963(?)- **1994**:2

BRITISH
Adams, Douglas 1952-2001
  Obituary **2002**:2
Adamson, George 1906-1989
  Obituary **1990**:2
Adele 1988- **2009**:4
Ali, Monica 1967- **2007**:4
Altea, Rosemary 1946- **1996**:3
Amanpour, Christiane 1958- **1997**:2
Ambler, Eric 1909-1998
  Obituary **1999**:2
Ames, Roger 1950(?)- **2005**:2
Amis, Kingsley 1922-1995
  Obituary **1996**:2
Amis, Martin 1949- **2008**:3
Andrews, Julie 1935- **1996**:1
Ashcroft, Peggy 1907-1991
  Obituary **1992**:1
Ashwell, Rachel 1960(?)- **2004**:2
Atkinson, Kate 1951- **2012**:1
Atkinson, Rowan 1955- **2004**:3
Baddeley, Hermione 1906(?)-1986
  Obituary **1986**:4
Banksy 1975(?)- **2007**:2
Barker, Clive 1952- **2003**:3
Barker, Pat 1943- **2009**:1
Baron Cohen, Sacha 1971- **2007**:3
Baron-Cohen, Simon 1958- **2012**:4
Barrett, Syd 1946-2006
  Obituary **2007**:3
Bates, Alan 1934-2003
  Obituary **2005**:1
Beck, Jeff 1944- **2011**:4
Beckett, Wendy (Sister) 1930- **1998**:3
Beckham, David 1975- **2003**:1
Bee Gees, The **1997**:4
Bell, Gabrielle 1975(?)- **2007**:4
Berners-Lee, Tim 1955(?)- **1997**:4
Blair, Tony 1953- **1996**:3
Bloom, Orlando 1977- **2004**:2
Bonham Carter, Helena 1966- **1998**:4
Bowie, David 1947- **1998**:2
Boyle, Danny 1956- **2009**:4
Bradford, Chris 1937- **2011**:1
Brand, Russell 1975- **2010**:2
Branson, Richard 1951- **1987**:1
Broadbent, Jim 1949- **2008**:4
Brown, Gordon 1951- **2008**:3
Brown, Tina 1953- **1992**:1
Burgess, Anthony 1917-1993
  Obituary **1994**:2
Burnett, Mark 1960- **2003**:1
Bush, Kate 1958- **1994**:3

Obituary **1999**:1
McEwan, Ian 1948- **2004**:2
McIlroy, Rory 1989- **2012**:3
McKellen, Ian 1939- **1994**:1
McLaren, Malcolm 1946-2010
Obituary **2012**:3
McQueen, Alexander 1969-2010
Obituary **2012**:2
Mercury, Freddie 1946-1991
Obituary **1992**:2
Michael, George 1963- **1989**:2
Milligan, Spike 1918-2002
Obituary **2003**:2
Milne, Christopher Robin 1920-1996
Obituary **1996**:4
Minghella, Anthony 1954- **2004**:3
Mirren, Helen 1945- **2005**:1
Molina, Alfred 1953- **2005**:3
Montagu, Ashley 1905-1999
Obituary **2000**:2
Moore, Dudley 1935-2002
Obituary **2003**:2
Moore, Henry 1898-1986
Obituary **1986**:4
Morgan, Piers 1965- **2012**:2
Morrissey 1959- **2005**:2
Moss, Kate 1974- **1995**:3
Murdoch, Iris 1919-1999
Obituary **1999**:4
Muse 1978- **2012**:3
Newkirk, Ingrid 1949- **1992**:3
Newton-John, Olivia 1948- **1998**:4
Nolan, Christopher 1970(?)- **2006**:3
Norrington, Roger 1934- **1989**:4
Northam, Jeremy 1961- **2003**:2
Nunn, Trevor 1940- **2000**:2
Oasis **1996**:3
Ogilvy, David 1911-1999
Obituary **2000**:1
Oldman, Gary 1958- **1998**:1
Oliver, Jamie 1975- **2002**:3
Olivier, Laurence 1907-1989
Obituary **1989**:4
Osborne, John 1929-1994
Obituary **1995**:2
Osbournes, The **2003**:4
Owen, Clive 1964- **2006**:2
Owen-Jones, Lindsay 1946(?)- **2004**:2
Page, Dick 1955- **2010**:1
Palmer, Robert 1949-2003
Obituary **2004**:4
Panjabi, Archie 1972- **2012**:3
Park, Nick 1958- **1997**:3
Patten, Christopher 1944- **1993**:3
Pattinson, Robert 1986- **2010**:1
Pegg, Simon 1970- **2009**:1
Penrose, Roger 1931- **1991**:4
Philby, Kim 1912-1988
Obituary **1988**:3
Pleasence, Donald 1919-1995
Obituary **1995**:3
Pople, John 1925-2004
Obituary **2005**:2
Porter, George 1920-2002
Obituary **2003**:4
Potts, Paul 1970- **2009**:1
Princess Margaret, Countess of
Snowdon 1930-2002
Obituary **2003**:2
Pullman, Philip 1946- **2003**:2
Queen Elizabeth the Queen Mother
1900-2002

Obituary **2003**:2
Radcliffe, Daniel 1989- **2007**:4
Radiohead **2009**:3
Ramsay, Gordon 1966- **2008**:2
Rattle, Simon 1955- **1989**:4
Redgrave, Lynn 1943- **1999**:3
Redgrave, Vanessa 1937- **1989**:2
Reisz, Karel 1926-2002
Obituary **2004**:1
Rendell, Ruth 1930- **2007**:2
Rhodes, Zandra 1940- **1986**:2
Rice, Peter 1967(?)- **2007**:2
Richards, Keith 1943- **1993**:3
Richardson, Natasha 1963-2009
Obituary **2010**:2
Ritchie, Guy 1968- **2001**:3
Robinson, Peter 1950- **2007**:4
Roddick, Anita 1943(?)- **1989**:4
Ronson, Charlotte 1977(?)- **2007**:3
Roth, Tim 1961- **1998**:2
Runcie, Robert 1921-2000 **1989**:4
Obituary **2001**:1
Rylance, Mark 1960- **2009**:3
Saatchi, Charles 1943- **1987**:3
Saatchi, Maurice 1946- **1995**:4
Sacks, Oliver 1933- **1995**:4
Schlesinger, John 1926-2003
Obituary **2004**:3
Scott, Ridley 1937- **2001**:1
Scott Thomas, Kristin 1960- **2010**:2
Seal 1962(?)- **1994**:4
Sentamu, John 1949- **2006**:2
Seymour, Jane 1951- **1994**:4
Smith, Paul 1946- **2002**:4
Smith, Zadie 1975- **2003**:4
Spice Girls **2008**:3
Springer, Jerry 1944- **1998**:4
Springfield, Dusty 1939-1999
Obituary **1999**:3
Statham, Jason 1972- **2012**:2
Steptoe, Patrick 1913-1988
Obituary **1988**:3
Stevens, James
Brief entry **1988**:1
Stewart, Patrick 1940- **1996**:1
Stewart, Rod 1945- **2007**:1
Sting 1951- **1991**:4
Stone, Joss 1987- **2006**:2
Stoppard, Tom 1937- **1995**:4
Strummer, Joe 1952-2002
Obituary **2004**:1
Stuart, Julia 1968- **2012**:3
Styler, Trudie 1954- **2009**:1
Sullivan, Andrew 1964(?)- **1996**:1
Swinton, Tilda 1960- **2008**:4
Taylor, Elizabeth 1932- **1993**:3
Taylor, Graham 1958(?)- **2005**:3
Temperley, Alice 1975- **2008**:2
Thatcher, Margaret 1925- **1989**:2
Thompson, Emma 1959- **1993**:2
Tilberis, Elizabeth 1947(?)- **1994**:3
Trotman, Alex 1933- **1995**:4
Tudor, Antony 1908(?)-1987
Obituary **1987**:4
Uchida, Mitsuko 1949(?)- **1989**:3
Ullman, Tracey 1961- **1988**:3
Ustinov, Peter 1921-2004
Obituary **2005**:3
Ware, Lancelot 1915-2000
Obituary **2001**:1
Watson, Emily 1967- **2001**:1
Watts, Naomi 1968- **2006**:1

Weisz, Rachel 1971- **2006**:4
Westwood, Vivienne 1941- **1998**:3
Wiles, Andrew 1953(?)- **1994**:1
Wilkinson, Tom 1948- **2003**:2
Wilmut, Ian 1944- **1997**:3
Wilson, Peter C. 1913-1984
Obituary **1985**:2
Winehouse, Amy 1983- **2008**:1
Winslet, Kate 1975- **2002**:4
Wintour, Anna 1949- **1990**:4
Woodward, Edward 1930-2009
Obituary **2011**:3
Wright, Joe 1972- **2009**:1
Wright, Richard 1943-2008
Obituary **2009**:4

BRUNEI
Bolkiah, Sultan Muda Hassanal
1946- **1985**:4

BULGARIAN
Christo 1935- **1992**:3
Dimitrova, Ghena 1941- **1987**:1

BURMESE
Suu Kyi, Aung San 1945(?)- **1996**:2

CAMBODIAN
Lon Nol
Obituary **1986**:1
Pol Pot 1928-1998
Obituary **1998**:4

CAMEROONIAN
Biya, Paul 1933- **2006**:1

CANADIAN
Altman, Sidney 1939- **1997**:2
Arbour, Louise 1947- **2005**:1
Atwood, Margaret 1939- **2001**:2
Balsillie, Jim and Mike Lazaridis
2006:4
Barenaked Ladies **1997**:2
Bieber, Justin 1994- **2012**:2
Black, Conrad 1944- **1986**:2
Bouchard, Lucien 1938- **1999**:2
Bourassa, Robert 1933-1996
Obituary **1997**:1
Bourque, Raymond Jean 1960- **1997**
:3
Bradley, Alan 1938- **2012**:1
Buble, Michael 1975- **2010**:4
Burr, Raymond 1917-1993
Obituary **1994**:1
Campbell, Kim 1947- **1993**:4
Campbell, Neve 1973- **1998**:2
Campeau, Robert 1923- **1990**:1
Candy, John 1950-1994 **1988**:2
Obituary **1994**:3
Carrey, Jim 1962- **1995**:1
Cavanagh, Tom 1968- **2003**:1
Cera, Michael 1988- **2012**:1
Cerovsek, Corey
Brief entry **1987**:4
Charney, Dov 1969- **2008**:2
Cherry, Don 1934- **1993**:4
Chretien, Jean 1934- **1990**:4
Christensen, Hayden 1981- **2003**:3
Coffey, Paul 1961- **1985**:4
Copps, Sheila 1952- **1986**:4

Cronenberg, David 1943- **1992**:3
Cronyn, Hume 1911-2003
  Obituary **2004**:3
Crosby, Sidney 1987- **2006**:3
Dewhurst, Colleen 1924-1991
  Obituary **1992**:2
Dion, Celine 1970(?)- **1995**:3
Doherty, Denny 1940-2007
  Obituary **2008**:2
Eagleson, Alan 1933- **1987**:4
Ebbers, Bernie 1943- **1998**:1
Egoyan, Atom 1960- **2000**:2
Erickson, Arthur 1924- **1989**:3
Fillion, Nathan 1971- **2011**:3
Fonyo, Steve
  Brief entry **1985**:4
Foster, David 1950(?)- **1988**:2
Fox, Michael J. 1961- **1986**:1
Frank, Robert 1924- **1995**:2
Frye, Northrop 1912-1991
  Obituary **1991**:3
Fuhr, Grant 1962- **1997**:3
Furtado, Nelly 1978- **2007**:2
Garneau, Marc 1949- **1985**:1
Gatien, Peter
  Brief entry **1986**:1
Giguere, Jean-Sebastien 1977- **2004**:2
Gilmour, Doug 1963- **1994**:3
Gold, Christina A. 1947- **2008**:1
Gordon, Mary 1947- **2011**:4
Graham, Nicholas 1960(?)- **1991**:4
Granholm, Jennifer 1959- **2003**:3
Green, Tom 1972- **1999**:4
Greene, Graham 1952- **1997**:2
Greene, Lorne 1915-1987
  Obituary **1988**:1
Gretzky, Wayne 1961- **1989**:2
Haggis, Paul 1953- **2006**:4
Haim, Corey 1971-2010
  Obituary **2012**:2
Haney, Chris
  Brief entry **1985**:1
Harper, Stephen J. 1959- **2007**:3
Harris, Michael Deane 1945- **1997**:2
Hayakawa, Samuel Ichiye 1906-1992
  Obituary **1992**:3
Hennessy, Jill 1969- **2003**:2
Hextall, Ron 1964- **1988**:2
Hill, Graham 1971- **2010**:3
Hull, Brett 1964- **1991**:4
Jennings, Peter Charles 1938- **1997**:2
Johnson, Pierre Marc 1946- **1985**:4
Jones, Jenny 1946- **1998**:2
Juneau, Pierre 1922- **1988**:3
Jung, Andrea **2000**:2
Karsh, Yousuf 1908-2002
  Obituary **2003**:4
Keeler, Ruby 1910-1993
  Obituary **1993**:4
Kent, Arthur 1954- **1991**:4
Kielburger, Craig 1983- **1998**:1
Kilgore, Marcia 1968- **2006**:3
Korchinsky, Mike 1961- **2004**:2
Lalonde, Marc 1929- **1985**:1
Lang, K.D. 1961- **1988**:4
Lanois, Daniel 1951- **1991**:1
Lansens, Lori 1962- **2011**:3
Lavigne, Avril 1984- **2005**:2
Lemieux, Claude 1965- **1996**:1
Lemieux, Mario 1965- **1986**:4
Leaavesque, Reneaa
  Obituary **1988**:1

Levy, Eugene 1946- **2004**:3
Lewis, Stephen 1937- **1987**:2
Mandel, Howie 1955- **1989**:1
Marchionne, Sergio 1952- **2010**:4
Markle, C. Wilson 1938- **1988**:1
Martin, Paul 1938- **2004**:4
McKinnell, Henry 1943(?)- **2002**:3
McLachlan, Sarah 1968- **1998**:4
McLaren, Norman 1914-1987
  Obituary **1987**:2
McLaughlin, Audrey 1936- **1990**:3
McTaggart, David 1932(?)- **1989**:4
Messier, Mark 1961- **1993**:1
Morgentaler, Henry 1923- **1986**:3
Morissette, Alanis 1974- **1996**:2
Moss, Carrie-Anne 1967- **2004**:3
Mulroney, Brian 1939- **1989**:2
Munro, Alice 1931- **1997**:1
Musk, Elon 1971- **2011**:2
Myers, Mike 1964(?)- **1992**:3
Nickelback **2007**:2
O'Donnell, Bill
  Brief entry **1987**:4
O'Hara, Catherine 1954- **2007**:4
Ondaatje, Philip Michael 1943- **1997**
  :3
Osgood, Chris 1972- **2010**:1
Paquin, Anna 1982- **2009**:4
Parizeau, Jacques 1930- **1995**:1
Peckford, Brian 1942- **1989**:1
Penny, Louise 1958- **2011**:1
Peterson, David 1943- **1987**:1
Peterson, Oscar 1925-2007
  Obituary **2009**:1
Pocklington, Peter H. 1941- **1985**:2
Pratt, Christopher 1935- **1985**:3
Raffi 1948- **1988**:1
Randi, James 1928- **1990**:2
Reisman, Simon 1919- **1987**:4
Reitman, Ivan 1946- **1986**:3
Reitman, Jason 1977- **2011**:3
Reuben, Gloria 1964- **1999**:4
Reynolds, Ryan 1976- **2012**:1
Rhea, Caroline 1964- **2004**:1
Richard, Maurice 1921-2000
  Obituary **2000**:4
Richards, Lloyd 1919-2006
  Obituary **2007**:3
Rogen, Seth 1982- **2009**:3
Rovinescu, Calin 1955- **2010**:3
Roy, Patrick 1965- **1994**:2
Rypien, Mark 1962- **1993**:3
Sainte-Marie, Buffy 1941- **2000**:1
Sakic, Joe 1969- **2002**:1
Scott Moir and Tessa Virtue 1987-
  2011:2
Shaffer, Paul 1949- **1987**:1
Shields, Carol 1935-2003
  Obituary **2004**:3
Short, Martin 1950- **1986**:1
Stephens, Arran and Ratana **2008**:4
Strong, Maurice 1929- **1993**:1
Sutherland, Kiefer 1966- **2002**:4
Tilghman, Shirley M. 1946- **2002**:1
Trebek, Alex 1940- **2010**:4
Trudeau, Pierre 1919-2000
  Obituary **2001**:1
Twain, Shania 1965- **1996**:3
Vander Zalm, William 1934- **1987**:3
Vardalos, Nia 1962- **2003**:4
Vickrey, William S. 1914-1996
  Obituary **1997**:2

Villeneuve, Jacques 1971- **1997**:1
Weir, Mike 1970- **2004**:1
Whitehead, Robert 1916-2002
  Obituary **2003**:3
Williams, Lynn 1924- **1986**:4
Wilson, Bertha
  Brief entry **1986**:1
Wood, Sharon
  Brief entry **1988**:1
Young, Neil 1945- **1991**:2
Yzerman, Steve 1965- **1991**:2

CENTRAL AFRICAN
  Bozize, Francois 1946- **2006**:3

CHADIAN
  Deby, Idriss 1952- **2002**:2

CHILEAN
  Arrau, Claudio 1903-1991
    Obituary **1992**:1
  Bachelet, Michelle 1951- **2007**:3
  Lagos, Ricardo 1938- **2005**:3
  Pinera, Sebastian 1949- **2011**:2
  Pinochet, Augusto 1915- **1999**:2

CHINESE
  Chaing Kai-Shek, Madame
    1898-2003
    Obituary **2005**:1
  Chan, Jackie 1954- **1996**:1
  Chen, Joan 1961- **2000**:2
  Chen, T.C.
    Brief entry **1987**:3
  Deng Xiaoping 1904-1997 **1995**:1
    Obituary **1997**:3
  Fang Lizhi 1937- **1988**:1
  Gao Xingjian 1940- **2001**:2
  Gong Li 1965- **1998**:4
  Guo Jingjing 1981- **2009**:2
  Hatem, George 1910(?)-1988
    Obituary **1989**:1
  Hou Hsiao-hsien 1947- **2000**:2
  Hua Guofeng 1921-2008
    Obituary **2009**:4
  Hu Jintao 1942- **2004**:1
  Hu Yaobang 1915-1989
    Obituary **1989**:4
  Hwang, David Henry 1957- **1999**:1
  Jiang Quing 1914-1991
    Obituary **1992**:1
  Jiang Zemin 1926- **1996**:1
  Lee, Ang 1954- **1996**:3
  Lee, Henry C. 1938- **1997**:1
  Li, Jet 1963- **2005**:3
  Lord, Bette Bao 1938- **1994**:1
  Lucid, Shannon 1943- **1997**:1
  Ma, Jack 1964- **2007**:1
  Ma, Pony 1971(?)- **2006**:3
  Tan Dun 1957- **2002**:1
  Weihui, Zhou 1973- **2001**:1
  Wei Jingsheng 1950- **1998**:2
  Woo, John 1945(?)- **1994**:2
  Wu, Harry 1937- **1996**:1
  Wu Yi 1938- **2005**:2
  Yao Ming 1980- **2004**:1
  Ye Jianying 1897-1986
    Obituary **1987**:1
  Yen, Samuel 1927- **1996**:4
  Zhang, Ziyi 1979- **2006**:2
  Zhao Ziyang 1919- **1989**:1

COLOMBIAN

Betancourt, Ingrid 1961- **2012**:1
Botero, Fernando 1932- **1994**:3
Garcia Marquez, Gabriel 1928- **2005**
:2
Juanes 1972- **2004**:4
Leguizamo, John 1965- **1999**:1
Pastrana, Andres 1954- **2002**:1
Santos, Juan Manuel 1951- **2012**:3
Schroeder, Barbet 1941- **1996**:1
Shakira 1977- **2002**:3
Uribe, Alvaro 1952- **2003**:3

CONGOLESE

Kabila, Joseph 1971- **2003**:2
Kabila, Laurent 1939- **1998**:1
Obituary **2001**:3
Mobutu Sese Seko 1930-1998
Obituary **1998**:4

COSTA RICAN

Arias Sanchez, Oscar 1941- **1989**:3
Chinchilla, Laura 1959- **2012**:2

COTE D'IVOIRIAN

Gbagbo, Laurent 1945- **2003**:2

CROATIAN

Ivanisevic, Goran 1971- **2002**:1
Mesic, Stipe 1934- **2005**:4
Tudjman, Franjo 1922- **1996**:2
Tudjman, Franjo 1922-1999
Obituary **2000**:2

CUBAN

Acosta, Carlos 1973(?)- **1997**:4
Canseco, Jose 1964- **1990**:2
Castro, Fidel 1926- **1991**:4
Castro, Raúl 1931- **2010**:2
Cruz, Celia 1925-2003
Obituary **2004**:3
Cugat, Xavier 1900-1990
Obituary **1991**:2
Estefan, Gloria **1991**:4
Garcia, Andy 1956- **1999**:3
Garcia, Cristina 1958- **1997**:4
Goizueta, Roberto 1931-1997 **1996**:1
Obituary **1998**:1
Gutierrez, Carlos M. 1953- **2001**:4
Murano, Elsa 1959- **2009**:1
Palmeiro, Rafael 1964- **2005**:1
Saralegui, Cristina 1948- **1999**:2
Zamora, Pedro 1972-1994
Obituary **1995**:2

CYPRIAN

Chalayan, Hussein 1970- **2003**:2
Kyprianou, Spyros 1932-2002
Obituary **2003**:2

CZECH

Albright, Madeleine 1937- **1994**:3
Hammer, Jan 1948- **1987**:3
Hasek, Dominik 1965- **1998**:3
Havel, Vaclav 1936- **1990**:3
Hingis, Martina 1980- **1999**:1
Hrabal, Bohumil 1914-1997
Obituary **1997**:3
Jagr, Jaromir 1972- **1995**:4
Klima, Petr 1964- **1987**:1
Kukoc, Toni 1968- **1995**:4
Maxwell, Robert 1923-1991

Obituary **1992**:2
Porizkova, Paulina
Brief entry **1986**:4
Reisz, Karel 1926-2002
Obituary **2004**:1
Serkin, Rudolf 1903-1991
Obituary **1992**:1
Stoppard, Tom 1937- **1995**:4
Trump, Ivana 1949- **1995**:2
Zatopek, Emil 1922-2000
Obituary **2001**:3

DANISH

Bohr, Aage 1922-2009
Obituary **2011**:1
Borge, Victor 1909-2000
Obituary **2001**:3
Hau, Lene Vestergaard 1959- **2006**:4
Kristiansen, Kjeld Kirk 1948(?)- **1988**
:3
Lander, Toni 1931-1985
Obituary **1985**:4
Rasmussen, Anders Fogh 1953- **2006**
:1
Wozniacki, Caroline 1990- **2012**:2

DJIBOUTI

Guelleh, Ismail Omar 1947- **2006**:2

DOMINICAN

Balaguer, Joaquin 1907-2002
Obituary **2003**:4
Bautista, José 1980- **2012**:4
de la Renta, Oscar 1932- **2005**:4
Fernández, Leonel 1953- **2009**:2
Pujols, Albert 1980- **2005**:3
Ramirez, Manny 1972- **2005**:4
Reyes, Jose 1983- **2012**:3
Soriano, Alfonso 1976- **2008**:1
Sosa, Sammy 1968- **1999**:1

DUTCH

Appel, Karel 1921-2006
Obituary **2007**:2
de Hoop Scheffer, Jaap 1948- **2005**:1
de Kooning, Willem 1904-1997 **1994**
:4
Obituary **1997**:3
Duisenberg, Wim 1935-2005
Obituary **2006**:4
Gies, Miep 1909-2010
Obituary **2012**:1
Heineken, Alfred 1923-2002
Obituary **2003**:1
Juliana 1909-2004
Obituary **2005**:3
Koolhaas, Rem 1944- **2001**:1
Matadin, Vinoodh and Inez van
Lamsweerde **2007**:4
Parker, Colonel Tom 1929-1997
Obituary **1997**:2

ECUADORAN

Correa, Rafael 1963- **2008**:1

EGYPTIAN

Chahine, Youssef 1926-2008
Obituary **2009**:3
ElBaradei, Mohamed 1942- **2006**:3
Ghali, Boutros Boutros 1922- **1992**:3
Mahfouz, Naguib 1911-2006
Obituary **2007**:4

Mubarak, Hosni 1928- **1991**:4
Rahman, Sheik Omar Abdel- 1938-
1993:3

ERITREAN

Afwerki, Isaias 1946- **2010**:1

ESTONIAN

Ilves, Toomas Hendrik 1953- **2007**:4

FIJI ISLANDER

Mara, Ratu Sir Kamisese 1920-2004
Obituary **2005**:3
Singh, Vijay 1963- **2000**:4

FILIPINO

Aquino, Corazon 1933- **1986**:2
Aquino III, Benigno 1960- **2011**:4
Lewis, Loida Nicolas 1942- **1998**:3
Macapagal-Arroyo, Gloria 1947-
2001:4
Marcos, Ferdinand 1917-1989
Obituary **1990**:1
Natori, Josie 1947- **1994**:3
Pacquiao, Manny 1978- **2011**:1
Ramos, Fidel 1928- **1995**:2
Salonga, Lea 1971- **2003**:3
Sin, Jaime 1928-2005
Obituary **2006**:3

FINNISH

Halonen, Tarja 1943- **2006**:4
Kekkonen, Urho 1900-1986
Obituary **1986**:4
Ollila, Jorma 1950- **2003**:4
Torvalds, Linus 1970(?)- **1999**:3

FRENCH

Adjani, Isabelle 1955- **1991**:1
Agnes B 1941- **2002**:3
Albou, Sophie 1967- **2007**:2
Arnault, Bernard 1949- **2000**:4
Baulieu, Etienne-Emile 1926- **1990**:1
Becaud, Gilbert 1927-2001
Obituary **2003**:1
Bejart, Maurice 1927-2007
Obituary **2009**:1
Besse, Georges 1927-1986
Obituary **1987**:1
Binoche, Juliette 1965- **2001**:3
Blanc, Patrick 1953- **2011**:3
Bourgeois, Louise 1911- **1994**:1
Brando, Cheyenne 1970-1995
Obituary **1995**:4
Bruni, Carla 1967- **2009**:3
Calment, Jeanne 1875-1997
Obituary **1997**:4
Cardin, Pierre 1922- **2003**:3
Cartier-Bresson, Henri 1908-2004
Obituary **2005**:4
Chagall, Marc 1887-1985
Obituary **1985**:2
Chirac, Jacques 1932- **1995**:4
Colbert, Claudette 1903-1996
Obituary **1997**:1
Conseil, Dominique Nils 1962(?)-
2007:2
Cotillard, Marion 1975- **2009**:1
Cousteau, Jacques-Yves 1910-1997
1998:2
Cousteau, Jean-Michel 1938- **1988**:2
Cresson, Edith 1934- **1992**:1

Daft Punk 1975- **2009**:4
Delors, Jacques 1925- **1990**:2
Deneuve, Catherine 1943- **2003**:2
Depardieu, Gerard 1948- **1991**:2
Derrida, Jacques 1930-2005
   Obituary **2006**:1
Dubuffet, Jean 1901-1985
   Obituary **1985**:4
Duras, Marguerite 1914-1996
   Obituary **1996**:3
Fekkai, Frederic 1959(?)- **2003**:2
Gaultier, Jean-Paul 1952- **1998**:1
Ghosn, Carlos 1954- **2008**:3
Godard, Jean-Luc 1930- **1998**:1
Grappelli, Stephane 1908-1997
   Obituary **1998**:1
Guillem, Sylvie 1965(?)- **1988**:2
Indurain, Miguel 1964- **1994**:1
Jarre, Maurice 1924-2009
   Obituary **2010**:2
Klarsfeld, Beate 1939- **1989**:1
Kouchner, Bernard 1939- **2005**:3
Lacroix, Christian 1951- **2005**:2
Lagarde, Christine 1956- **2012**:4
Lefebvre, Marcel 1905- **1988**:4
Levi-Strauss, Claude 1908-2009
   Obituary **2011**:3
Louboutin, Christian 1963- **2006**:1
Malle, Louis 1932-1995
   Obituary **1996**:2
Marceau, Marcel 1923-2007
   Obituary **2008**:4
Mauresmo, Amelie 1979- **2007**:2
Mercier, Laura 1959(?)- **2002**:2
Millepied, Benjamin 1977(?)- **2006**:4
Mitterrand, Francois 1916-1996
   Obituary **1996**:2
Nars, Francois 1959- **2003**:1
Parker, Tony 1982- **2008**:1
Pépin, Jacques 1935- **2010**:2
Petrossian, Christian
   Brief entry **1985**:3
Phoenix **2011**:1
Picasso, Paloma 1949- **1991**:1
Ponty, Jean-Luc 1942- **1985**:4
Prost, Alain 1955- **1988**:1
Rampal, Jean-Pierre 1922- **1989**:2
Reza, Yasmina 1959(?)- **1999**:2
Rohmer, Eric 1920-2010
   Obituary **2012**:1
Ronis, Willy 1910-2009
   Obituary **2011**:1
Rothschild, Philippe de 1902-1988
   Obituary **1988**:2
Rykiel, Sonia 1930- **2000**:3
Saint Laurent, Yves 1936-2008
   Obituary **2009**:3
Sarkozy, Nicolas 1955- **2008**:4
Simone, Nina 1933-2003
   Obituary **2004**:2
Starck, Philippe 1949- **2004**:1
Tautou, Audrey 1978- **2004**:2
Thom, Rene 1923-2002
   Obituary **2004**:1
Thomas, Michel 1911(?)- **1987**:4
Tillion, Germaine 1907-2008
   Obituary **2009**:2
Touitou, Jean 1952(?)- **2008**:4
Ungaro, Emanuel 1933- **2001**:3
Villechaize, Herve 1943(?)-1993
   Obituary **1994**:1

Xenakis, Iannis 1922-2001
   Obituary **2001**:4

GABONESE
Bozize, Francois 1946- **2006**:3

GEORGIAN
Saakashvili, Mikhail 1967- **2008**:4

GERMAN
Barbie, Klaus 1913-1991
   Obituary **1992**:2
Bausch, Pina 1940-2009
   Obituary **2010**:4
Becker, Boris
   Brief entry **1985**:3
Bernhard, Wolfgang 1960- **2007**:1
Bethe, Hans 1906-2005
   Obituary **2006**:2
Beuys, Joseph 1921-1986
   Obituary **1986**:3
Blobel, Gunter 1936- **2000**:4
Boyle, Gertrude 1924- **1995**:3
Brandt, Willy 1913-1992
   Obituary **1993**:2
Breitschwerdt, Werner 1927- **1988**:4
Casper, Gerhard 1937- **1993**:1
Dietrich, Marlene 1901-1992
   Obituary **1992**:4
Etzioni, Amitai 1929- **1994**:3
Fischer, Joschka 1948- **2005**:2
Frank, Anthony M. 1931(?)- **1992**:1
Graf, Steffi 1969- **1987**:4
Grass, Gunter 1927- **2000**:2
Gursky, Andreas 1955- **2002**:2
Hahn, Carl H. 1926- **1986**:4
Hess, Rudolph 1894-1987
   Obituary **1988**:1
Honecker, Erich 1912-1994
   Obituary **1994**:4
Kiefer, Anselm 1945- **1990**:2
Kinski, Klaus 1926-1991 **1987**:2
   Obituary **1992**:2
Klarsfeld, Beate 1939- **1989**:1
Klemperer, Werner 1920-2000
   Obituary **2001**:3
Klum, Heidi 1973- **2006**:3
Kohl, Helmut 1930- **1994**:1
Krogner, Heinz 1941(?)- **2004**:2
Lagerfeld, Karl 1938- **1999**:4
Max, Peter 1937- **1993**:2
Mengele, Josef 1911-1979
   Obituary **1985**:2
Merkel, Angela 1954- **2010**:2
Mutter, Anne-Sophie 1963- **1990**:3
Newton, Helmut 1920- **2002**:1
Nowitzki, Dirk 1978- **2007**:2
Nuesslein-Volhard, Christiane 1942-
   1998:1
Pfeiffer, Eckhard 1941- **1998**:4
Pilatus, Robert 1966(?)-1998
   Obituary **1998**:3
Polke, Sigmar 1941- **1999**:4
Rey, Margret E. 1906-1996
   Obituary **1997**:2
Richter, Gerhard 1932- **1997**:2
Sander, Jil 1943- **1995**:2
Schily, Otto
   Brief entry **1987**:4
Schrempp, Juergen 1944- **2000**:2
Schroder, Gerhard 1944- **1999**:1

Schumacher, Michael 1969- **2005**:2
Schwarzkopf, Elisabeth 1915-2006
   Obituary **2007**:3
Sonnenfeldt, Richard 1923-2009
   Obituary **2011**:2
Tillmans, Wolfgang 1968- **2001**:4
Von Hellermann, Sophie 1975- **2006**
   :3
Werner, Ruth 1907-2000
   Obituary **2001**:1
Witt, Katarina 1966(?)- **1991**:3
Zetsche, Dieter 1953- **2002**:3

GHANAIAN
Annan, Kofi 1938- **1999**:1
Atta Mills, John 1944- **2010**:3
Chambas, Mohammed ibn 1950-
   2003:3
Kufuor, John Agyekum 1938- **2005**:4

GREEK
George and Lena Korres 1971- **2009**
   :1
Huffington, Arianna 1950- **1996**:2
Karamanlis, Costas 1956- **2009**:1
Papandreou, Andrea 1919-1996
   Obituary **1997**:1
Stefanidis, John 1937- **2007**:3

GUATEMALAN
Berger, Oscar 1946- **2004**:4
Menchu, Rigoberta 1960(?)- **1993**:2

GUINEA-BISSAUNI
Makeba, Miriam 1934- **1989**:2
Ture, Kwame 1941-1998
   Obituary **1999**:2

GUYANESE
Jagdeo, Bharrat 1964- **2008**:1

HAITIAN
Aristide, Jean-Bertrand 1953- **1991**:3
Cedras, Raoul 1950- **1994**:4
Danticat, Edwidge 1969- **2005**:4
Preaaval, Reneaa 1943- **1997**:2

HONDURAN
Lobo, Porfirio 1947- **2011**:3

HONG KONGER
Chow, Stephen 1962- **2006**:1
Chow Yun-fat 1955- **1999**:4
Lee, Martin 1938- **1998**:2

HUNGARIAN
Dorati, Antal 1906-1988
   Obituary **1989**:2
Fodor, Eugene 1906(?)-1991
   Obituary **1991**:3
Gabor, Eva 1921(?)-1995
   Obituary **1996**:1
Grove, Andrew S. 1936- **1995**:3
Ligeti, Gyorgy 1923-2006
   Obituary **2007**:3
Polgar, Judit 1976- **1993**:3
Solti, Georg 1912-1997
   Obituary **1998**:1

ICELANDIC

Bjork 1965- **1996**:1
Finnbogadoaattir, Vigdiaas
  Brief entry **1986**:2

INDIAN

Adiga, Aravind 1974- **2010**:3
Chopra, Deepak 1947- **1996**:3
Devi, Phoolan 1955(?)- **1986**:1
  Obituary **2002**:3
Durrell, Gerald 1925-1995
  Obituary **1995**:3
Gandhi, Indira 1917-1984
  Obituary **1985**:1
Gandhi, Rajiv 1944-1991
  Obituary **1991**:4
Gandhi, Sonia 1947- **2000**:2
Gowda, H. D. Deve 1933- **1997**:1
Iyengar, B.K.S. 1918- **2005**:1
Khosla, Vinod 1955- **2011**:2
Kundra, Vivek 1974- **2010**:3
Mahesh Yogi, Maharishi 1911(?)-
  1991:3
Mehta, Zubin 1938(?)- **1994**:3
Mittal, Lakshmi 1950- **2007**:2
Mother Teresa 1910-1997 **1993**:1
  Obituary **1998**:1
Musharraf, Pervez 1943- **2000**:2
Narayan, R.K. 1906-2001
  Obituary **2002**:2
Nooyi, Indra 1955- **2004**:3
Prowse, Juliet 1937-1996
  Obituary **1997**:1
Rajneesh, Bhagwan Shree 1931-1990
  Obituary **1990**:2
Ram, Jagjivan 1908-1986
  Obituary **1986**:4
Rao, P. V. Narasimha 1921- **1993**:2
Rushdie, Salman 1947- **1994**:1
Sharma, Nisha 1982(?)- **2004**:2
Vajpayee, Atal Behari 1926- **1998**:4
Wahid, Abdurrahman 1940- **2000**:3

INDONESIAN

Habibie, Bacharuddin Jusuf 1936-
  1999:3
Megawati Sukarnoputri 1947- **2000**:1
Suharto 1921-2008
  Obituary **2009**:2
Yudhoyono, Susilo 1949- **2009**:4

IRANIAN

Ahmadinejad, Mahmoud 1956- **2007**
  :1
Ebadi, Shirin 1947- **2004**:3
Khatami, Mohammed 1943- **1997**:4
Khomeini, Ayatollah Ruhollah
  1900(?)-1989
  Obituary **1989**:4
Rafsanjani, Ali Akbar Hashemi
  1934(?)- **1987**:3
Satrapi, Marjane 1969- **2006**:3
Schroeder, Barbet 1941- **1996**:1

IRAQI

al-Ani, Jananne 1966- **2008**:4
Hussein, Saddam 1937- **1991**:1
Kamel, Hussein 1954- **1996**:1
Saatchi, Maurice 1946- **1995**:4
Salbi, Zainab 1969(?)- **2008**:3

IRISH

Adams, Gerald 1948- **1994**:1
Ahern, Bertie 1951- **1999**:3
Ahern, Cecelia 1981- **2008**:4
Beckett, Samuel Barclay 1906-1989
  Obituary **1990**:2
Best, George 1946-2005
  Obituary **2007**:1
Binchy, Maeve 1940- **2010**:2
Bono 1960- **1988**:4
Branagh, Kenneth 1960- **1992**:2
Brosnan, Pierce 1952- **2000**:3
Byrne, Gabriel 1950- **1997**:4
de Valois, Dame Ninette 1898-2001
  Obituary **2002**:1
Doyle, Roddy 1958- **2008**:1
Enya 1962(?)- **1992**:3
Farrell, Colin 1976- **2004**:1
Geldof, Bob 1954(?)- **1985**:3
Heaney, Seamus 1939- **1996**:2
Herzog, Chaim 1918-1997
  Obituary **1997**:3
Hillery, Patrick 1923-2008
  Obituary **2009**:2
Hume, John 1938- **1987**:1
Huston, John 1906-1987
  Obituary **1988**:1
Jordan, Neil 1950(?)- **1993**:3
Keyes, Marian 1963- **2006**:2
Laird, Nick 1975- **2010**:4
McCourt, Frank 1930- **1997**:4
McGahern, John 1934-2006
  Obituary **2007**:2
McGuinness, Martin 1950(?)- **1985**:4
Neeson, Liam 1952- **1993**:4
O'Connor, Sinead 1967- **1990**:4
O'Sullivan, Maureen 1911-1998
  Obituary **1998**:4
Power, Samantha 1970- **2005**:4
Rhys Meyers, Jonathan 1977- **2007**:1
Robinson, Mary 1944- **1993**:1
Trimble, David 1944- **1999**:1
U2 **2002**:4

ISRAELI

Agassi, Shai 1968- **2010**:3
Arens, Moshe 1925- **1985**:1
Arikha, Avigdor 1929-2010
  Obituary **2012**:3
Arison, Ted 1924- **1990**:3
Barak, Ehud 1942- **1999**:4
Begin, Menachem 1913-1992
  Obituary **1992**:3
Elbaz, Alber 1961- **2008**:1
Elon, Amos 1926-2009
  Obituary **2010**:3
Greenberg, Moshe 1928-2010
  Obituary **2012**:4
Herzog, Chaim 1918-1997
  Obituary **1997**:3
Levinger, Moshe 1935- **1992**:1
Levy, David 1938- **1987**:2
Mintz, Shlomo 1957- **1986**:2
Netanyahu, Benjamin 1949- **1996**:4
Peres, Shimon 1923- **1996**:3
Rabin, Leah 1928-2000
  Obituary **2001**:2
Rabin, Yitzhak 1922-1995 **1993**:1
  Obituary **1996**:2
Shcharansky, Anatoly 1948- **1986**:2
Weizman, Ezer 1924-2005
  Obituary **2006**:3

ITALIAN

Agnelli, Giovanni 1921- **1989**:4
Andreotti, Lamberto 1952- **2012**:1
Armani, Giorgio 1934(?)- **1991**:2
Bartoli, Cecilia 1966- **1994**:1
Benetton, Luciano 1935- **1988**:1
Benigni, Roberto 1952- **1999**:2
Berio, Luciano 1925-2003
  Obituary **2004**:2
Berlusconi, Silvio 1936(?)- **1994**:4
Capra, Frank 1897-1991
  Obituary **1992**:2
Cavalli, Roberto 1940- **2004**:4
Ciampi, Carlo Azeglio 1920- **2004**:3
Clemente, Francesco 1952- **1992**:2
Coppola, Carmine 1910-1991
  Obituary **1991**:4
De Luca, Guerrino 1952- **2007**:1
Dolce, Domenico and Stefano
  Gabbana **2005**:4
Fabio 1961(?)- **1993**:4
Fabris, Enrico 1981- **2006**:4
Fano, Ugo 1912-2001
  Obituary **2001**:4
Fellini, Federico 1920-1993
  Obituary **1994**:2
Ferrari, Enzo 1898-1988 **1988**:4
Ferre, Gianfranco 1944-2007
  Obituary **2008**:3
Ferretti, Alberta 1950(?)- **2004**:1
Ferri, Alessandra 1963- **1987**:2
Fo, Dario 1926- **1998**:1
Gardenia, Vincent 1922-1992
  Obituary **1993**:2
Gassman, Vittorio 1922-2000
  Obituary **2001**:1
Gucci, Maurizio
  Brief entry **1985**:4
Lamborghini, Ferrucio 1916-1993
  Obituary **1993**:3
Leone, Sergio 1929-1989
  Obituary **1989**:4
Masina, Giulietta 1920-1994
  Obituary **1994**:3
Massimo and Lella Vignelli 1931-
  2010:1
Mastroianni, Marcello 1914-1996
  Obituary **1997**:2
Michelangeli, Arturo Benedetti 1920-
  1988:2
Montand, Yves 1921-1991
  Obituary **1992**:2
Pavarotti, Luciano 1935- **1997**:4
Piano, Renzo 1937- **2009**:2
Ponti, Carlo 1912-2007
  Obituary **2008**:2
Pozzi, Lucio 1935- **1990**:2
Prada, Miuccia 1950(?)- **1996**:1
Rizzoli, Paola 1943(?)- **2004**:3
Rosso, Renzo 1955- **2005**:2
Siepi, Cesare 1923-2010
  Obituary **2012**:4
Sinopoli, Giuseppe 1946- **1988**:1
Staller, Ilona 1951- **1988**:3
Tomba, Alberto 1966- **1992**:3
Valli, Giambattista 1966- **2008**:3
Versace, Donatella 1955- **1999**:1
Versace, Gianni 1946-1997
  Brief entry **1988**:1
  Obituary **1998**:2
Zanardi, Alex 1966- **1998**:2
Zeffirelli, Franco 1923- **1991**:3

NAMIBIAN

Nujoma, Sam 1929- **1990**:4

NEPALI

Shah, Gyanendra 1947- **2006**:1

NEW ZEALANDER

Campion, Jane **1991**:4
Castle-Hughes, Keisha 1990- **2004**:4
Crowe, Russell 1964- **2000**:4
Frame, Janet 1924-2004
  Obituary **2005**:2
Hillary, Edmund 1919-2008
  Obituary **2009**:1
Jackson, Peter 1961- **2004**:4
Key, John 1961- **2012**:3
Kleinpaste, Ruud 1952- **2006**:2
Shipley, Jenny 1952- **1998**:3

NICARAGUAN

Astorga, Nora 1949(?)-1988 **1988**:2
Cruz, Arturo 1923- **1985**:1
Obando, Miguel 1926- **1986**:4
Ortega, Daniel 1945- **2008**:2
Robelo, Alfonso 1940(?)- **1988**:1

NIGERIAN

Abacha, Sani 1943- **1996**:3
Babangida, Ibrahim Badamosi 1941-
  1992:4
Obasanjo, Olusegun 1937(?)- **2000**:2
Okoye, Christian 1961- **1990**:2
Olajuwon, Akeem 1963- **1985**:1
Olopade, Olufunmilayo 1957(?)-
  2006:3
Sade 1959- **1993**:2
Saro-Wiwa, Ken 1941-1995
  Obituary **1996**:2
Yar'Adua, Umaru 1951- **2008**:3

NORWEGIAN

Brundtland, Gro Harlem 1939- **2000**
  :1
Cammermeyer, Margarethe 1942-
  1995:2
Carlsen, Magnus 1990- **2011**:3
Olav, King of Norway 1903-1991
  Obituary **1991**:3
Stoltenberg, Jens 1959- **2006**:4
Svindal, Aksel 1982- **2011**:2

PAKISTANI

Bhutto, Benazir 1953- **1989**:4
Zia ul-Haq, Mohammad 1924-1988
  Obituary **1988**:4

PALESTINIAN

Abbas, Mahmoud 1935- **2008**:4
Arafat, Yasser 1929- **1989**:3
Darwish, Mahmud 1942-2008
  Obituary **2009**:4
Freij, Elias 1920- **1986**:4
Habash, George 1925(?)- **1986**:1
Husseini, Faisal 1940- **1998**:4
Nidal, Abu 1937- **1987**:1
Sharon, Ariel 1928- **2001**:4
Terzi, Zehdi Labib 1924- **1985**:3

PANAMANIAN

Blades, Ruben 1948- **1998**:2

PARAGUAYAN

Lugo, Fernando 1951- **2010**:1
Stroessner, Alfredo 1912-2006
  Obituary **2007**:4

PERUVIAN

Fujimori, Alberto 1938- **1992**:4
Garcia, Alan 1949- **2007**:4
Perez de Cuellar, Javier 1920- **1991**:3
Testino, Mario 1954- **2002**:1

POLISH

Begin, Menachem 1913-1992
  Obituary **1992**:3
Eisenstaedt, Alfred 1898-1995
  Obituary **1996**:1
John Paul II, Pope 1920- **1995**:3
Kaczynski, Lech 1949- **2007**:2
Kieslowski, Krzysztof 1941-1996
  Obituary **1996**:3
Kosinski, Jerzy 1933-1991
  Obituary **1991**:4
Masur, Kurt 1927- **1993**:4
Niezabitowska, Malgorzata 1949(?)-
  1991:3
Rosten, Leo 1908-1997
  Obituary **1997**:3
Sabin, Albert 1906-1993
  Obituary **1993**:4
Sendler, Irena 1910-2008
  Obituary **2009**:2
Singer, Isaac Bashevis 1904-1991
  Obituary **1992**:1
Walesa, Lech 1943- **1991**:2

PORTUGUESE

Cavaco Silva, Anibal 1939- **2011**:3
Saramago, Jose 1922- **1999**:1

PUERTO RICAN

Alvarez, Aida **1999**:2
Del Toro, Benicio 1967- **2001**:4
Ferrer, Jose 1912-1992
  Obituary **1992**:3
Julia, Raul 1940-1994
  Obituary **1995**:1
Martin, Ricky 1971- **1999**:4
Novello, Antonia 1944- **1991**:2
Trinidad, Felix 1973- **2000**:4

ROMANIAN

Basescu, Traian 1951- **2006**:2
Ceausescu, Nicolae 1918-1989
  Obituary **1990**:2
Codrescu, Andreaa 1946- **1997**:3

RUSSIAN

Brodsky, Joseph 1940-1996
  Obituary **1996**:3
Ginzburg, Vitaly 1916-2009
  Obituary **2011**:3
Gorbachev, Raisa 1932-1999
  Obituary **2000**:2
Gordeeva, Ekaterina 1972- **1996**:4
Grinkov, Sergei 1967-1995
  Obituary **1996**:2
Kasparov, Garry 1963- **1997**:4
Kasyanov, Mikhail 1957- **2001**:1
Konstantinov, Vladimir 1967- **1997**:4
Kournikova, Anna 1981- **2000**:3

Lapidus, Morris 1902-2001
  Obituary **2001**:4
Lebed, Alexander 1950- **1997**:1
Medvedev, Dmitry 1965- **2009**:4
Moiseyev, Igor 1906-2007
  Obituary **2009**:1
Ovechkin, Alexander 1985- **2009**:2
Primakov, Yevgeny 1929- **1999**:3
Putin, Vladimir 1952- **2000**:3
Rostropovich, Mstislav 1927-2007
  Obituary **2008**:3
Safin, Marat 1980- **2001**:3
Sarraute, Nathalie 1900-1999
  Obituary **2000**:2
Schneerson, Menachem Mendel
  1902-1994 **1992**:4
  Obituary **1994**:4
Sharapova, Maria 1987- **2005**:2
Solzhenitsyn, Aleksandr 1918-2008
  Obituary **2009**:4
Titov, Gherman 1935-2000
  Obituary **2001**:3

RWANDAN

Kagame, Paul 1957- **2001**:4

SALVADORAN

Duarte, Jose Napoleon 1925-1990
  Obituary **1990**:3

SAUDI

Fahd, King of Saudi Arabia
  1923(?)-2005
  Obituary **2006**:4

SCOTTISH

Black, James 1924-2010
  Obituary **2012**:3
Butler, Gerard 1969- **2011**:2
Coldplay **2004**:4
Connery, Sean 1930- **1990**:4
Ferguson, Craig 1962- **2005**:4
Ferguson, Niall 1964- **2006**:1
Franchitti, Dario 1973- **2008**:1
Macquarrie, John 1919-2007
  Obituary **2008**:3
McGregor, Ewan 1971(?)- **1998**:2
Mina, Denise 1966- **2006**:1
Paolozzi, Eduardo 1924-2005
  Obituary **2006**:3
Ramsay, Mike 1950(?)- **2002**:1
Rankin, Ian 1960- **2010**:3
Rowling, J.K. 1965- **2000**:1

SENEGALESE

Senghor, Leopold 1906-2001
  Obituary **2003**:1

SERBIAN

Djokovic, Novak 1987- **2008**:4
Patriarch Pavle 1914-2009
  Obituary **2011**:3
Tadic, Boris 1958- **2009**:3

SLOVENIAN

Obreht, Tea 1985- **2012**:3
Turk, Danilo 1952- **2009**:3

SOMALI

Ahmed, Sharif 1964- **2010**:3
Iman 1955- **2001**:3

SOUTH AFRICAN

Barnard, Christiaan 1922-2001
  Obituary **2002**:4
Blackburn, Molly 1931(?)-1985
  Obituary **1985**:4
Botha, P. W. 1916-2006
  Obituary **2008**:1
Buthelezi, Mangosuthu Gatsha
  1928- **1989**:3
Coetzee, J. M. 1940- **2004**:4
de Klerk, F.W. 1936- **1990**:1
Duncan, Sheena
  Brief entry **1987**:1
Fugard, Athol 1932- **1992**:3
Hani, Chris 1942-1993
  Obituary **1993**:4
Horn, Mike 1966- **2009**:3
Makeba, Miriam 1934- **1989**:2
Mandela, Nelson 1918- **1990**:3
Mandela, Winnie 1934- **1989**:3
Matthews, Dave 1967- **1999**:3
Mbeki, Thabo 1942- **1999**:4
Oppenheimer, Harry 1908-2000
  Obituary **2001**:3
Paton, Alan 1903-1988
  Obituary **1988**:3
Ramaphosa, Cyril 1953- **1988**:2
Sisulu, Walter 1912-2003
  Obituary **2004**:2
Slovo, Joe 1926- **1989**:2
Suzman, Helen 1917- **1989**:3
Tambo, Oliver 1917- **1991**:3
Theron, Charlize 1975- **2001**:4
Treurnicht, Andries 1921- **1992**:2
Woods, Donald 1933-2001
  Obituary **2002**:3
Zuma, Jacob 1942- **2012**:1

SOUTH KOREAN

Ban, Ki-moon 1944- **2011**:2
Kim, Yu-Na 1990- **2011**:2

SOVIET

Asimov, Isaac 1920-1992
  Obituary **1992**:3
Chernenko, Konstantin 1911-1985
  Obituary **1985**:1
Dalai Lama 1935- **1989**:1
Dubinin, Yuri 1930- **1987**:4
Dzhanibekov, Vladimir 1942- **1988**:1
Erte 1892-1990
  Obituary **1990**:4
Federov, Sergei 1969- **1995**:1
Godunov, Alexander 1949-1995
  Obituary **1995**:4
Gorbachev, Mikhail 1931- **1985**:2
Grebenshikov, Boris 1953- **1990**:1
Gromyko, Andrei 1909-1989
  Obituary **1990**:2
Karadzic, Radovan 1945- **1995**:3
Milosevic, Slobodan 1941- **1993**:2
Molotov, Vyacheslav Mikhailovich
  1890-1986
  Obituary **1987**:1
Nureyev, Rudolf 1938-1993
  Obituary **1993**:2
Sakharov, Andrei Dmitrievich
  1921-1989
  Obituary **1990**:2

Smirnoff, Yakov 1951- **1987**:2
Vidov, Oleg 194- **1987**:4
Yeltsin, Boris 1931- **1991**:1
Zhirinovsky, Vladimir 1946- **1994**:2

SPANISH

Almodovar, Pedro 1951- **2000**:3
Ayala, Francisco 1906-2009
  Obituary **2011**:3
Banderas, Antonio 1960- **1996**:2
Bardem, Javier 1969- **2008**:4
Blahnik, Manolo 1942- **2000**:2
Calatrava, Santiago 1951- **2005**:1
Carreras, Jose 1946- **1995**:2
Cela, Camilo Jose 1916-2001
  Obituary **2003**:1
Chillida, Eduardo 1924-2002
  Obituary **2003**:4
Cruz, Penelope 1974- **2001**:4
Dali, Salvador 1904-1989
  Obituary **1989**:2
de Larrocha, Alicia 1923-2009
  Obituary **2011**:1
de Pinies, Jamie
  Brief entry **1986**:3
Domingo, Placido 1941- **1993**:2
Juan Carlos I 1938- **1993**:1
Lopez de Arriortua, Jose Ignacio
  1941- **1993**:4
Miro, Joan 1893-1983
  Obituary **1985**:1
Moneo, Jose Rafael 1937- **1996**:4
Montoya, Carlos 1903-1993
  Obituary **1993**:4
Nadal, Rafael 1986- **2009**:1
Samaranch, Juan Antonio 1920- **1986**:2
Sanz, Alejandro 1968- **2011**:3
Segovia, Andreaas 1893-1987
  Obituary **1987**:3
Wences, Senor 1896-1999
  Obituary **1999**:4

SRI LANKAN

Bandaranaike, Sirimavo 1916-2000
  Obituary **2001**:2
Ondaatje, Philip Michael 1943- **1997**:3
Wickramasinghe, Ranil 1949- **2003**:2

SUDANESE

al-Bashir, Omar 1944- **2009**:1
Bol, Manute 1962-2010
  Obituary **2012**:4
Turabi, Hassan 1932(?)- **1995**:4

SWEDISH

Bergman, Ingmar 1918- **1999**:4
Cardigans, The **1997**:4
Carlsson, Arvid 1923- **2001**:2
Garbo, Greta 1905-1990
  Obituary **1990**:3
Hallstrom, Lasse 1946- **2002**:3
Lidstrom, Nicklas 1970- **2009**:1
Lindbergh, Pelle 1959-1985
  Obituary **1985**:4
Lindgren, Astrid 1907-2002
  Obituary **2003**:1
Mankell, Henning 1948- **2012**:4
Nilsson, Birgit 1918-2005
  Obituary **2007**:1
Olin, Lena 1956- **1991**:2
Palme, Olof 1927-1986

  Obituary **1986**:2
Persson, Stefan 1947- **2004**:1
Renvall, Johan
  Brief entry **1987**:4
Soderstrom, Elisabeth 1927-2009
  Obituary **2011**:3
Sorenstam, Annika 1970- **2001**:1

SWISS

del Ponte, Carla 1947- **2001**:1
Federer, Roger 1981- **2004**:2
Frank, Robert 1924- **1995**:2
Vasella, Daniel 1953- **2005**:3
Vollenweider, Andreas 1953- **1985**:2

SYRIAN

al-Assad, Bashar 1965- **2004**:2
Assad, Hafez 1930-2000
  Obituary **2000**:4
Assad, Hafez al- 1930(?)- **1992**:1
Assad, Rifaat 1937(?)- **1986**:3

TAHITIAN

Brando, Cheyenne 1970-1995
  Obituary **1995**:4

TAIWANESE

Chen Shui-bian 1950(?)- **2001**:2
Ho, David 1952- **1997**:2
Lee Teng-hui 1923- **2000**:1
Ma Ying-jeou 1950- **2009**:4

TANZANIAN

Nyerere, Julius 1922(?)-1999
  Obituary **2000**:2

THAI

Shinawatra, Yingluck 1967- **2012**:4
Thaksin Shinawatra 1949- **2005**:4

TRINIDADIAN

Headley, Heather 1974- **2011**:1
Ture, Kwame 1941-1998
  Obituary **1999**:2

TUNISIAN

Azria, Max 1949- **2001**:4

TURKISH

Ecevit, Bulent 1925-2006
  Obituary **2008**:1
Erdogan, Recep Tayyip 1954- **2012**:3
Gul, Abdullah 1950- **2009**:4
Ocalan, Abdullah 1948(?)- **1999**:4
Pamuk, Orhan 1952- **2007**:3

UGANDAN

Amin, Idi 1925(?)-2003
  Obituary **2004**:4
Museveni, Yoweri 1944- **2002**:1

UKRAINIAN

Baiul, Oksana 1977- **1995**:3
Gelfand, Israel 1913-2009
  Obituary **2011**:2
Tymoshenko, Yulia 1960- **2009**:1
Yanukovych, Viktor 1950- **2011**:4
Yushchenko, Viktor 1954- **2006**:1

URUGUAYAN
Vazquez, Tabare 1940- **2006**:2

UZBEKISTANI
Karimov, Islam 1938- **2006**:3

VENEZUELAN
Caldera, Rafael 1916-2009
Obituary **2011**:4
Chavez, Hugo 1954- **2010**:4
Hernandez, Felix 1986- **2008**:2
Herrera, Carolina 1939- **1997**:1
Perez, Carlos Andre 1922- **1990**:2
Santana, Johan 1979- **2008**:1

VIETNAMESE
Dong, Pham Van 1906-2000
Obituary **2000**:4
Le Duan 1908(?)-1986

Obituary **1986**:4
Le Duc Tho 1911-1990
Obituary **1991**:1

WELSH
Bale, Christian 1974- **2001**:3
Dahl, Roald 1916-1990
Obituary **1991**:2
Hopkins, Anthony 1937- **1992**:4
Jenkins, Roy Harris 1920-2003
Obituary **2004**:1
Jones, Tom 1940- **1993**:4
Macdonald, Julien 1973(?)- **2005**:3
William, Prince of Wales 1982- **2001**
:3
Zeta-Jones, Catherine 1969- **1999**:4

YEMENI
Saleh, Ali Abdullah 1942- **2001**:3

YUGOSLAVIAN
Filipovic, Zlata 1981(?)- **1994**:4
Kostunica, Vojislav 1944- **2001**:1
Pogorelich, Ivo 1958- **1986**:4
Seles, Monica 1974(?)- **1991**:3

ZAIRAN
Mobutu Sese Seko 1930-1997 **1993**:4
Obituary **1998**:1

ZAMBIAN
Chiluba, Frederick 1943- **1992**:3

ZIMBABWEAN
Mugabe, Robert 1924- **1988**:4
Smith, Ian 1919-2007
Obituary **2009**:1

2012 Occupation Index

This index lists all newsmakers alphabetically by their occupations or fields of primary activity. Indexes in softbound issues allow access to the current year's entries; indexes in annual hardbound volumes are cumulative, covering the entire *Newsmakers* series.

Listee names are followed by a year and issue number; thus **1996**:3 indicates that an entry on that individual appears in both 1996, Issue 3, and the 1996 cumulation. For access to newsmakers appearing earlier than the current softbound issue, see the previous year's cumulation.

ART AND DESIGN

Adams, Scott 1957- **1996**:4
Adams-Geller, Paige 1969(?)- **2006**:4
Addams, Charles 1912-1988
  Obituary **1989**:1
Adler, Jonathan 1966- **2006**:3
Agnes B 1941- **2002**:3
al-Ani, Jananne 1966- **2008**:4
Albou, Sophie 1967- **2007**:2
Allard, Linda 1940- **2003**:2
Alvarez Bravo, Manuel 1902-2002
  Obituary **2004**:1
Anderson, Laurie 1947- **2000**:2
Anderson, Sunny 1975- **2012**:4
Ando, Tadao 1941- **2005**:4
Appel, Karel 1921-2006
  Obituary **2007**:2
Arikha, Avigdor 1929-2010
  Obituary **2012**:3
Arman 1928- **1993**:1
Armani, Giorgio 1934(?)- **1991**:2
Ashwell, Rachel 1960(?)- **2004**:2
Aucoin, Kevyn 1962- **2001**:3
Avedon, Richard 1923- **1993**:4
Azria, Max 1949- **2001**:4
Badgley, Mark and James Mischka **2004**:3
Baldessari, John 1931(?)- **1991**:4
Ball, Michael 1964(?)- **2007**:3
Banks, Jeffrey 1953- **1998**:2
Banksy 1975(?)- **2007**:2
Barbera, Joseph 1911- **1988**:2
Barks, Carl 1901-2000
  Obituary **2001**:2
Barnes, Ernie 1938- **1997**:4
Barry, Lynda 1956(?)- **1992**:1
Batali, Mario 1960- **2010**:4
Bean, Alan L. 1932- **1986**:2
Beene, Geoffrey 1927-2004
  Obituary **2005**:4
Bell, Gabrielle 1975(?)- **2007**:4
Bellissimo, Wendy 1967(?)- **2007**:1
Bendet, Stacey 1978- **2012**:1
Beuys, Joseph 1921-1986
  Obituary **1986**:3
Bird, Brad 1956(?)- **2005**:4
Blahnik, Manolo 1942- **2000**:2

Blass, Bill 1922-2002
  Obituary **2003**:3
Bohbot, Michele 1959(?)- **2004**:2
Bontecou, Lee 1931- **2004**:4
Boone, Mary 1951- **1985**:1
Borofsky, Jonathan 1942- **2006**:4
Botero, Fernando 1932- **1994**:3
Bourgeois, Louise 1911- **1994**:1
Bowie, David 1947- **1998**:2
Boynton, Sandra 1953- **2004**:1
Breathed, Berkeley 1957- **2005**:3
Bromstad, David 1973- **2012**:2
Brown, Bobbi 1957- **2001**:4
Brown, Howard and Karen Stewart **2007**:3
Brown, J. Carter 1934-2002
  Obituary **2003**:3
Buchman, Dana 1951- **2010**:2
Bundchen, Gisele 1980- **2009**:1
Bunshaft, Gordon 1909-1990 **1989**:3
  Obituary **1991**:1
Burch, Tory 1966- **2009**:3
Calatrava, Santiago 1951- **2005**:1
Cameron, David
  Brief entry **1988**:1
Campbell, Ben Nighthorse 1933- **1998**:1
Campbell, Naomi 1970- **2000**:2
Cardin, Pierre 1922- **2003**:3
Cartier-Bresson, Henri 1908-2004
  Obituary **2005**:4
Cassini, Oleg 1913-2006
  Obituary **2007**:2
Castelli, Leo 1907-1999
  Obituary **2000**:1
Catlett, Elizabeth 1915(?)- **1999**:3
Cavalli, Roberto 1940- **2004**:4
Chagall, Marc 1887-1985
  Obituary **1985**:2
Chalayan, Hussein 1970- **2003**:2
Chapman, Georgina 1976-. See Georgina Chapman and Keren Craig
Charlesworth, Sarah 1947- **2010**:3
Chast, Roz 1955- **1992**:4
Chatham, Russell 1939- **1990**:1
Chia, Sandro 1946- **1987**:2

Chihuly, Dale 1941- **1995**:2
Chillida, Eduardo 1924-2002
  Obituary **2003**:4
Choo, Jimmy 1957(?)- **2006**:3
Christo 1935- **1992**:3
Chung, Doo-Ri 1973- **2011**:3
Claiborne, Liz 1929- **1986**:3
Clemente, Francesco 1952- **1992**:2
Clokey, Art 1921-2010
  Obituary **2012**:1
Cole, Anne 1930(?)- **2007**:3
Cole, Kenneth 1954(?)- **2003**:1
Colescott, Robert 1925-2009
  Obituary **2010**:3
Conner, Bruce 1933-2008
  Obituary **2009**:3
Cooper, Alexander 1936- **1988**:4
Costa, Francisco 1961- **2010**:2
Courtney, Erica 1957- **2009**:3
Craig, Keren 1976-. See Georgina Chapman and Keren Craig
Crumb, R. 1943- **1995**:4
Dali, Salvador 1904-1989
  Obituary **1989**:2
David Neville and Marcus Wainwright 1976- **2010**:3
Davis, Paige 1969- **2004**:2
DeCarava, Roy 1919- **1996**:3
de Kooning, Willem 1904-1997 **1994**:4
  Obituary **1997**:3
de la Renta, Oscar 1932- **2005**:4
Denevan, Jim 1961- **2012**:4
Diebenkorn, Richard 1922-1993
  Obituary **1993**:4
Diller, Elizabeth and Ricardo Scofidio **2004**:3
DiSpirito, Rocco 1966- **2012**:1
Dith Pran 1942-2008
  Obituary **2009**:2
Dolce, Domenico and Stefano Gabbana **2005**:4
Donghia, Angelo R. 1935-1985
  Obituary **1985**:2
Doubilet, Anne 1948- **2011**:1
Dougherty, Patrick 1945- **2012**:2
Duarte, Henry 1963(?)- **2003**:3

Miyake, Issey 1939- **1985**:2
Miyazaki, Hayao 1941- **2006**:2
Mizrahi, Isaac 1961- **1991**:1
Moneo, Jose Rafael 1937- **1996**:4
Moore, Henry 1898-1986
    Obituary **1986**:4
Morris, Robert 1947- **2010**:3
Motherwell, Robert 1915-1991
    Obituary **1992**:1
Mueck, Ron 1958- **2008**:3
Mumford, Lewis 1895-1990
    Obituary **1990**:2
Murakami, Takashi 1962- **2004**:2
Mydans, Carl 1907-2004
    Obituary **2005**:4
Nara, Yoshitomo 1959- **2006**:2
Nars, Francois 1959- **2003**:1
Natori, Josie 1947- **1994**:3
Nauman, Bruce 1941- **1995**:4
Nechita, Alexandra 1985- **1996**:4
Neiman, LeRoy 1927- **1993**:3
Nevelson, Louise 1900-1988
    Obituary **1988**:3
Newman, Arnold 1918- **1993**:1
Newton, Helmut 1920- **2002**:1
Nipon, Albert
    Brief entry **1986**:4
Noland, Kenneth Clifton 1924-2010
    Obituary **2012**:1
Ogilvy, David 1911-1999
    Obituary **2000**:1
Oldham, Todd 1961- **1995**:4
Olsen, Sigrid 1953- **2007**:1
Ono, Yoko 1933- **1989**:2
Oosterhouse, Carter 1976- **2012**:1
Page, Bettie 1923-2008
    Obituary **2010**:1
Page, Dick 1955- **2010**:1
Panichgul, Thakoon 1974- **2009**:4
Paolozzi, Eduardo 1924-2005
    Obituary **2006**:3
Parker, Brant 1920-2007
    Obituary **2008**:2
Parker, Suzy 1932-2003
    Obituary **2004**:2
Parks, Gordon 1912-2006
    Obituary **2006**:2
Pépin, Jacques 1935- **2010**:2
Pedersen, William 1938(?)- **1989**:4
Pei, I.M. 1917- **1990**:4
Pelli, Cesar 1927(?)- **1991**:4
Penn, Irving 1917-2009
    Obituary **2011**:2
Penn & Teller **1992**:1
Pennington, Ty 1965- **2005**:4
Peyton, Elizabeth 1965- **2007**:1
Piano, Renzo 1937- **2009**:2
Picasso, Paloma 1949- **1991**:1
Pinto, Maria 1957- **2011**:2
Plater-Zyberk, Elizabeth 1950- **2005**:2
Polke, Sigmar 1941- **1999**:4
Portman, John 1924- **1988**:2
Posen, Zac 1980- **2009**:3
Potok, Anna Maximilian
    Brief entry **1985**:2
Pozzi, Lucio 1935- **1990**:2
Prada, Miuccia 1950(?)- **1996**:1
Pratt, Christopher 1935- **1985**:3
Predock, Antoine 1936- **1993**:2
Puryear, Martin 1941- **2002**:4

Queer Eye for the Straight Guy cast
    2004:3
Radocy, Robert
    Brief entry **1986**:3
Raimondi, John
    Brief entry **1987**:4
Raskin, Jef 1943(?)- **1997**:4
Rauschenberg, Robert 1925- **1991**:2
Reese, Tracy 1964- **2010**:1
Rhodes, Zandra 1940- **1986**:2
Richardson, Steve 1939- **2010**:4
Richter, Gerhard 1932- **1997**:2
Ringgold, Faith 1930- **2000**:3
Ritts, Herb 1954(?)- **1992**:4
Roberts, Xavier 1955- **1985**:3
Roche, Kevin 1922- **1985**:1
Rockwell, David 1956- **2003**:3
Rodriguez, Narciso 1961- **2005**:1
Roncal, Mally 1972- **2009**:4
Ronis, Willy 1910-2009
    Obituary **2011**:1
Ronson, Charlotte 1977(?)- **2007**:3
Rose, Lela 1969- **2011**:1
Rosenberg, Evelyn 1942- **1988**:2
Rosenthal, Joseph 1911-2006
    Obituary **2007**:4
Rosenzweig, Ilene 1965(?)- **2004**:1
Rosso, Renzo 1955- **2005**:2
Rothenberg, Susan 1945- **1995**:3
Rouse, James 1914-1996
    Obituary **1996**:4
Rowley, Cynthia 1958- **2002**:1
Rudes-Sandel, Lisa 1964- **2012**:3
Rykiel, Sonia 1930- **2000**:3
Saatchi, Charles 1943- **1987**:3
Saint Laurent, Yves 1936-2008
    Obituary **2009**:3
Salgado, Sebastiao 1944- **1994**:2
Scavullo, Francesco 1921-2004
    Obituary **2005**:1
Schnabel, Julian 1951- **1997**:1
Schulz, Charles 1922-2000
    Obituary **2000**:3
Schulz, Charles M. 1922- **1998**:1
Schwartz, Allen 1945(?)- **2008**:2
Scott, Pamella 1975- **2010**:4
Segal, Shelli 1955(?)- **2005**:3
Serra, Richard 1939- **2009**:1
Serrano, Andres 1950- **2000**:4
Shaw, Carol 1958(?)- **2002**:1
Sherman, Cindy 1954- **1992**:3
Shulman, Julius 1910-2009
    Obituary **2010**:4
Simmons, Laurie 1949- **2010**:1
Simpson, Lorna 1960- **2008**:1
Skaist-Levy, Pam and Gela Taylor
    2005:1
Slick, Grace 1939- **2001**:2
Smith, Paul 1946- **2002**:4
Smith, Willi 1948-1987
    Obituary **1987**:3
Som, Peter 1971- **2009**:1
Spade, Kate 1962- **2003**:1
Spiegelman, Art 1948- **1998**:3
Sprouse, Stephen 1953-2004
    Obituary **2005**:2
Starck, Philippe 1949- **2004**:1
Stefani, Gwen 1969- **2005**:4
Stefanidis, John 1937- **2007**:3
Stella, Frank 1936- **1996**:2
Stockton, Shreve 1977- **2009**:4
Stone, Curtis 1975- **2011**:3

Sui, Anna 1955(?)- **1995**:1
Switkin, Lisa 1974- **2012**:4
Takada, Kenzo 1938- **2003**:2
Tamayo, Rufino 1899-1991
    Obituary **1992**:1
Tange, Kenzo 1913-2005
    Obituary **2006**:2
Taniguchi, Yoshio 1937- **2005**:4
Temperley, Alice 1975- **2008**:2
Testino, Mario 1954- **2002**:1
Thiebaud, Wayne 1920- **1991**:1
Tillmans, Wolfgang 1968- **2001**:4
Tompkins, Susie
    Brief entry **1987**:2
Touitou, Jean 1952(?)- **2008**:4
Trudeau, Garry 1948- **1991**:2
Truitt, Anne 1921- **1993**:1
Tunick, Spencer 1967- **2008**:1
Twombley, Cy 1928(?)- **1995**:1
Tyler, Richard 1948(?)- **1995**:3
Ungaro, Emanuel 1933- **2001**:3
Valastro, Buddy 1977- **2011**:4
Valli, Giambattista 1966- **2008**:3
Valvo, Carmen Marc 1954- **2003**:4
Varvatos, John 1956(?)- **2006**:2
Venturi, Robert 1925- **1994**:4
Versace, Donatella 1955- **1999**:1
Versace, Gianni 1946-1997
    Brief entry **1988**:1
    Obituary **1998**:2
Von D, Kat 1982- **2008**:3
von Furstenberg, Diane 1946- **1994**:2
Von Hellermann, Sophie 1975- **2006**:3
Vreeland, Diana 1903(?)-1989
    Obituary **1990**:1
Wagner, Catherine F. 1953- **2002**:3
Walker, Kara 1969- **1999**:2
Wang, Alexander 1984- **2011**:4
Wang, Vera 1949- **1998**:4
Warhol, Andy 1927(?)-1987
    Obituary **1987**:2
Washington, Alonzo 1967- **2000**:1
Waterman, Cathy 1950(?)- **2002**:2
Watterson, Bill 1958(?)- **1990**:3
Wegman, William 1942(?)- **1991**:1
Westwood, Vivienne 1941- **1998**:3
Whitney, Patrick 1952(?)- **2006**:1
Wilson, Peter C. 1913-1984
    Obituary **1985**:2
Winick, Judd 1970- **2005**:3
Wintour, Anna 1949- **1990**:4
Witkin, Joel-Peter 1939- **1996**:1
Wu, Jason 1983- **2010**:3
Wyeth, Andrew 1917-2009
    Obituary **2010**:1
Wyland, Robert 1956- **2009**:3
Yamasaki, Minoru 1912-1986
    Obituary **1986**:2
Yeang, Ken 1948- **2008**:3
Yosca, Gerard **2011**:2

BUSINESS
Abraham, S. Daniel 1924- **2003**:3
Ackerman, Will 1949- **1987**:4
Adams-Geller, Paige 1969(?)- **2006**:4
Adelson, Jay 1970- **2011**:1
Adler, Jonathan 1966- **2006**:3
Agnelli, Giovanni 1921- **1989**:4
Ailes, Roger 1940- **1989**:3
Akers, John F. 1934- **1988**:3
Akin, Phil

Dolce, Domenico and Stefano
 Gabbana **2005**:4
Donahue, Tim 1950(?)- **2004**:3
Doubleday, Nelson, Jr. 1933- **1987**:1
Downey, Bruce 1947- **2003**:1
Drexler, Millard S. 1944- **1990**:3
Drucker, Peter F. 1909- **1992**:3
Duisenberg, Wim 1935-2005
 Obituary **2006**:4
Dunlap, Albert J. **1997**:2
Dupri, Jermaine 1972- **1999**:1
Dyson, James 1947- **2005**:4
Eagleson, Alan 1933- **1987**:4
Eaton, Robert J. 1940- **1994**:2
Ebbers, Bernie 1943- **1998**:1
Eckert, Robert A. 1955(?)- **2002**:3
Ecko, Marc 1972- **2006**:3
Egan, John 1939- **1987**:2
Eisner, Michael 1942- **1989**:2
Elbaz, Alber 1961- **2008**:1
Eliasch, Johan 1962- **2011**:3
Ellis, Perry 1940-1986
 Obituary **1986**:3
Ellison, Larry 1944- **2004**:2
Ells, Steve 1965- **2010**:1
Engibous, Thomas J. 1953- **2003**:3
Engles, Gregg L. 1957- **2007**:3
Engstrom, Elmer W. 1901-1984
 Obituary **1985**:2
Epstein, Jason 1928- **1991**:1
Ertegun, Ahmet 1923- **1986**:3
Estes, Pete 1916-1988
 Obituary **1988**:3
Evans, Nancy 1950- **2000**:4
Eyler, John. H., Jr. 1948(?)- **2001**:3
Factor, Max 1904-1996
 Obituary **1996**:4
Fassa, Lynda 1963(?)- **2008**:4
Fekkai, Frederic 1959(?)- **2003**:2
Feld, Kenneth 1948- **1988**:2
Fender, Leo 1909-1991
 Obituary **1992**:1
Ferrari, Enzo 1898-1988 **1988**:4
Ferre, Gianfranco 1944-2007
 Obituary **2008**:3
Ferretti, Alberta 1950(?)- **2004**:1
Fertel, Ruth 1927- **2000**:2
Fields, Debbi 1956- **1987**:3
Fieri, Guy 1968- **2010**:3
Fiorina, Carleton S. 1954- **2000**:1
Fireman, Paul
 Brief entry **1987**:2
Fisher, Mel 1922(?)- **1985**:4
Fleming, Claudia 1959- **2004**:1
Flynt, Larry 1942- **1997**:3
Fodor, Eugene 1906(?)-1991
 Obituary **1991**:3
Fomon, Robert M. 1925- **1985**:3
Forbes, Malcolm S. 1919-1990
 Obituary **1990**:3
Ford, Henry II 1917-1987
 Obituary **1988**:1
Ford, William Clay, Jr. 1957- **1999**:1
Foreman, George 1949- **2004**:2
Francis, Philip L. 1946- **2007**:4
Frank, Anthony M. 1931(?)- **1992**:1
Frankfort, Lew 1946- **2008**:2
Freeman, Cliff 1941- **1996**:1
Freiberg, Steven 1957- **2011**:4
Frieda, John 1951- **2004**:1
Fudge, Ann 1951- **2000**:3
Fuller, Millard 1935-2009

Obituary **2010**:1
Furse, Clara 1957- **2008**:2
Gallagher, Brian 1959- **2012**:3
Galliano, John 1960- **2005**:2
Ganzi, Victor 1947- **2003**:3
Garcia, Joe
 Brief entry **1986**:4
Garzarelli, Elaine M. 1951- **1992**:3
Gates, Bill 1955- **1987**:4
Gatien, Peter
 Brief entry **1986**:1
Gaultier, Jean-Paul 1952- **1998**:1
Gentine, Lou 1947- **2008**:2
George and Lena Korres 1971- **2009**
 :1
Gerstner, Lou 1942- **1993**:4
Ghosn, Carlos 1954- **2008**:3
Gilbert, Walter 1932- **1988**:3
Gillett, George 1938- **1988**:1
Ginsberg, Ian 1962(?)- **2006**:4
Glass, David 1935- **1996**:1
Glazman, Lev and Alina Roytberg
 2007:4
Goizueta, Roberto 1931-1997 **1996**:1
 Obituary **1998**:1
Gold, Christina A. 1947- **2008**:1
Goldberg, Leonard 1934- **1988**:4
Goodman, Drew and Myra **2007**:4
Goodnight, Jim 1943- **2012**:4
Goody, Sam 1904-1991
 Obituary **1992**:1
Gordon, Michael 1951(?)- **2005**:1
Gorman, Leon
 Brief entry **1987**:1
Grace, J. Peter 1913- **1990**:2
Graden, Brian 1963- **2004**:2
Graham, Bill 1931-1991 **1986**:4
 Obituary **1992**:2
Graham, Donald 1945- **1985**:4
Graham, Katharine Meyer 1917-
 1997:3
 Obituary **2002**:3
Graham, Nicholas 1960(?)- **1991**:4
Graves, Ron 1967- **2009**:3
Green, Philip 1952- **2008**:2
Greenberg, Robert 1940(?)- **2003**:2
Greenwald, Julie 1970- **2008**:1
Gregory, Dick 1932- **1990**:3
Gregory, Rogan 1972- **2008**:2
Greiner, Helen 1967- **2010**:2
Griffin, Merv 1925-2008
 Obituary **2008**:4
Grove, Andrew S. 1936- **1995**:3
Grucci, Felix 1905- **1987**:1
Gucci, Maurizio
 Brief entry **1985**:4
Guccione, Bob 1930- **1986**:1
Gund, Agnes 1938- **1993**:2
Gutierrez, Carlos M. 1953- **2001**:4
Haas, Robert D. 1942- **1986**:4
Hahn, Carl H. 1926- **1986**:4
Hakuta, Ken
 Brief entry **1986**:1
Hamilton, Hamish 1900-1988
 Obituary **1988**:4
Hammer, Armand 1898-1990
 Obituary **1991**:3
Hammer, Bonnie 1950- **2011**:4
Handler, Ruth 1916-2002
 Obituary **2003**:3
Haney, Chris
 Brief entry **1985**:1

Harbert, Ted 1955- **2007**:2
Hart, Carey 1975- **2006**:4
Haseltine, William A. 1944- **1999**:2
Hassenfeld, Stephen 1942- **1987**:4
Hastings, Reed 1961(?)- **2006**:2
Hawkins, Jeff and Donna Dubinsky
 2000:2
Hearst, Randolph A. 1915-2000
 Obituary **2001**:3
Heatherwick, Thomas 1970- **2012**:1
Heckert, Richard E.
 Brief entry **1987**:3
Hefner, Christie 1952- **1985**:1
Heineken, Alfred 1923-2002
 Obituary **2003**:1
Heinricher, Jackie 1961- **2010**:1
Heinz, H.J. 1908-1987
 Obituary **1987**:2
Helayel, Daniella 1972- **2012**:2
Held, Abbe 1966- **2011**:1
Helmsley, Leona 1920- **1988**:1
Hemming, Nikki 1967- **2009**:1
Henderson, Tom **2011**:2
Hernandez, Lazaro and Jack
 McCollough **2008**:4
Herrera, Carolina 1939- **1997**:1
Hershberger, Sally 1961(?)- **2006**:4
Herzog, Doug 1960(?)- **2002**:4
Hesse, Dan 1954- **2011**:4
Heyer, Steven J. 1952- **2007**:1
Hilbert, Stephen C. 1946- **1997**:4
Hilfiger, Tommy 1952- **1993**:3
Hill, Graham 1971- **2010**:3
Hillegass, Clifton Keith 1918- **1989**:4
Hindmarch, Anya 1969- **2008**:2
Hirshberg, Gary 1954(?)- **2007**:2
Holbrooke, Richard 1941(?)- **1996**:2
Holden, Betsy 1955- **2003**:2
Hollander, Joel 1956(?)- **2006**:4
Holliday, Chad 1948- **2006**:4
Honda, Soichiro 1906-1991
 Obituary **1986**:1
Horrigan, Edward, Jr. 1929- **1989**:1
Horvath, David and Sun-Min Kim
 2008:4
Housenbold, Jeffrey 1969- **2009**:2
Houser, Sam 1972(?)- **2004**:4
Hudson, Dawn 1957- **2008**:1
Hughes, Cathy 1947- **1999**:1
Hughes, Mark 1956- **1985**:3
Huh, Ben 1978- **2012**:3
Huizenga, Wayne 1938(?)- **1992**:1
Hurd, Mark 1957- **2010**:4
Hyatt, Joel 1950- **1985**:3
Iacocca, Lee 1924- **1993**:1
Iger, Bob 1951- **2006**:1
Ilitch, Mike 1929- **1993**:4
Iman 1955- **2001**:3
Immelt, Jeffrey R. 1956- **2001**:2
Inatome, Rick 1953- **1985**:4
Ingersoll, Ralph II 1946- **1988**:2
Iovine, Jimmy 1953- **2006**:3
Isaacson, Portia
 Brief entry **1986**:1
Ive, Jonathan 1967- **2009**:2
Jacuzzi, Candido 1903-1986
 Obituary **1987**:1
Jagger, Jade 1971- **2005**:1
James, Jesse 1969- **2004**:4
Janklow, Morton 1930- **1989**:3
Jay-Z 1970- **2006**:1
Jobs, Steve 1955- **2000**:1

Thomas, Michel 1911(?)- **1987**:4
Thomas-Graham, Pamela 1963- **2007**:1
Thompson, John W. 1949- **2005**:1
Tilberis, Elizabeth 1947(?)- **1994**:3
Tillman, Robert L. 1944(?)- **2004**:1
Timberlake, Justin 1981- **2008**:4
Tisch, Laurence A. 1923- **1988**:2
Tompkins, Susie
  Brief entry **1987**:2
Touitou, Jean 1952(?)- **2008**:4
Toyoda, Akio 1956- **2011**:1
Toyoda, Eiji 1913- **1985**:2
Trask, Amy 1961- **2003**:3
Traub, Marvin
  Brief entry **1987**:3
Treybig, James G. 1940- **1988**:3
Trotman, Alex 1933- **1995**:4
Trotter, Charlie 1960- **2000**:4
Troutt, Kenny A. 1948- **1998**:1
Trump, Donald 1946- **1989**:2
Trump, Ivana 1949- **1995**:2
Turlington, Christy 1969(?)- **2001**:4
Turner, Ted 1938- **1989**:1
Tyler, Richard 1948(?)- **1995**:3
Tyson, Don 1930- **1995**:3
Unz, Ron 1962(?)- **1999**:1
Upshaw, Gene 1945- **1988**:1
Vagelos, P. Roy 1929- **1989**:4
Valli, Giambattista 1966- **2008**:3
Van Andel, Jay 1924-2004
  Obituary **2006**:1
Varvatos, John 1956(?)- **2006**:2
Vasella, Daniel 1953- **2005**:3
Veeck, Bill 1914-1986
  Obituary **1986**:1
Versace, Donatella 1955- **1999**:1
Versace, Gianni 1946-1997
  Brief entry **1988**:1
  Obituary **1998**:2
Vigdor, Ron 1970- **2011**:4
Vinton, Will
  Brief entry **1988**:1
Vischer, Phil 1966- **2002**:2
Von D, Kat 1982- **2008**:3
von Furstenberg, Diane 1946- **1994**:2
Wachner, Linda 1946- **1988**:3
Waitt, Ted 1963(?)- **1997**:4
Waldron, Hicks B. 1923- **1987**:3
Walgreen, Charles III
  Brief entry **1987**:4
Walker, Jay 1955- **2004**:2
Walton, Sam 1918-1992 **1986**:2
  Obituary **1993**:1
Wang, Alexander 1984- **2011**:4
Wang, An 1920-1990 **1986**:1
  Obituary **1990**:3
Ware, Lancelot 1915-2000
  Obituary **2001**:1
Waters, Alice 1944- **2006**:3
Watkins, Sherron 1959- **2003**:1
Weill, Sandy 1933- **1990**:4
Weinstein, Bob and Harvey **2000**:4
Weintraub, Jerry 1937- **1986**:1
Welch, Jack 1935- **1993**:3
Weldon, William 1948- **2007**:4
Westwood, Vivienne 1941- **1998**:3
Whiting, Susan 1956- **2007**:4
Whitman, Meg 1957- **2000**:3
Whittle, Christopher 1947- **1989**:3
Williams, Edward Bennett 1920-1988
  Obituary **1988**:4

Williams, Lynn 1924- **1986**:4
Wilson, Jerry
  Brief entry **1986**:2
Wilson, Peter C. 1913-1984
  Obituary **1985**:2
Wintour, Anna 1949- **1990**:4
Woertz, Patricia A. 1953- **2007**:3
Wolf, Stephen M. 1941- **1989**:3
Wong, Andrea 1966- **2009**:1
Woodcock, Leonard 1911-2001
  Obituary **2001**:4
Woodruff, Robert Winship 1889-1985
  Obituary **1985**:1
Wren, John 1952(?)- **2007**:2
Wrigley, William, Jr. 1964(?)- **2002**:2
Wu, Jason 1983- **2010**:3
Wynn, Stephen A. 1942- **1994**:3
Yamamoto, Kenichi 1922- **1989**:1
Yetnikoff, Walter 1933- **1988**:1
Yunus, Muhammad 1940- **2007**:3
Zagat, Tim and Nina **2004**:3
Zamboni, Frank J.
  Brief entry **1986**:4
Zanker, Bill
  Brief entry **1987**:3
Zetcher, Arnold B. 1940- **2002**:1
Zetsche, Dieter 1953- **2002**:3
Ziff, William B., Jr. 1930- **1986**:4
Zoe, Rachel 1971- **2010**:2
Zuckerman, Mortimer 1937- **1986**:3

DANCE

Abdul, Paula 1962- **1990**:3
Acosta, Carlos 1973(?)- **1997**:4
Ailey, Alvin 1931-1989 **1989**:2
  Obituary **1990**:2
Allen, Debbie 1950- **1998**:2
Astaire, Fred 1899-1987
  Obituary **1987**:4
Baryshnikov, Mikhail Nikolaevich
  1948- **1997**:3
Bausch, Pina 1940-2009
  Obituary **2010**:4
Bejart, Maurice 1927-2007
  Obituary **2009**:2
Bennett, Michael 1943-1987
  Obituary **1988**:1
Bissell, Patrick 1958-1987
  Obituary **1988**:2
Bocca, Julio 1967- **1995**:3
Bujones, Fernando 1955-2005
  Obituary **2007**:1
Campbell, Neve 1973- **1998**:2
Charisse, Cyd 1922-2008
  Obituary **2009**:3
Cunningham, Merce 1919- **1998**:1
Davis, Sammy, Jr. 1925-1990
  Obituary **1990**:4
Dean, Laura 1945- **1989**:4
de Mille, Agnes 1905-1993
  Obituary **1994**:2
de Valois, Dame Ninette 1898-2001
  Obituary **2002**:1
Dudley, Jane 1912-2001
  Obituary **2002**:4
Dunham, Katherine 1909-2006
  Obituary **2007**:2
Englund, Richard 1932(?)-1991
  Obituary **1991**:3
Fagan, Garth 1940- **2000**:1
Farrell, Suzanne 1945- **1996**:3
Feld, Eliot 1942- **1996**:1

Fenley, Molissa 1954- **1988**:3
Ferri, Alessandra 1963- **1987**:2
Flatley, Michael 1958- **1997**:3
Fonteyn, Margot 1919-1991
  Obituary **1991**:3
Forsythe, William 1949- **1993**:2
Fosse, Bob 1927-1987
  Obituary **1988**:1
Garr, Teri 1949- **1988**:4
Glover, Savion 1973- **1997**:1
Godunov, Alexander 1949-1995
  Obituary **1995**:4
Graham, Martha 1894-1991
  Obituary **1991**:4
Gregory, Cynthia 1946- **1990**:2
Guillem, Sylvie 1965(?)- **1988**:2
Herrera, Paloma 1975- **1996**:2
Hewitt, Jennifer Love 1979- **1999**:2
Hines, Gregory 1946- **1992**:4
Jackson, Janet 1966(?)- **1990**:4
Jamison, Judith 1944- **1990**:3
Joffrey, Robert 1930-1988
  Obituary **1988**:3
Jones, Bill T. **1991**:4
Kaye, Nora 1920-1987
  Obituary **1987**:4
Keeler, Ruby 1910-1993
  Obituary **1993**:4
Kelly, Gene 1912-1996
  Obituary **1996**:3
Kidd, Michael 1915-2007
  Obituary **2009**:1
Kistler, Darci 1964- **1993**:1
Lander, Toni 1931-1985
  Obituary **1985**:4
Lewitzky, Bella 1916-2004
  Obituary **2005**:3
Lythgoe, Nigel 1949- **2010**:4
MacMillan, Kenneth 1929-1992
  Obituary **1993**:2
Madonna 1958- **1985**:2
Marshall, Susan 1958- **2000**:4
Millepied, Benjamin 1977(?)- **2006**:4
Miller, Ann 1923-2004
  Obituary **2005**:2
Miller, Bebe 1950- **2000**:2
Mitchell, Arthur 1934- **1995**:1
Moiseyev, Igor 1906-2007
  Obituary **2009**:1
Moore, Rachel 1965- **2008**:2
Morris, Mark 1956- **1991**:1
Murray, Arthur 1895-1991
  Obituary **1991**:3
North, Alex 1910- **1986**:3
Nureyev, Rudolf 1938-1993
  Obituary **1993**:2
Parker, Sarah Jessica 1965- **1999**:2
Parsons, David 1959- **1993**:4
Perez, Rosie **1994**:2
Prowse, Juliet 1937-1996
  Obituary **1997**:1
Rauschenberg, Robert 1925- **1991**:2
Renvall, Johan
  Brief entry **1987**:4
Robbins, Jerome 1918-1998
  Obituary **1999**:1
Rogers, Ginger 1911(?)-1995
  Obituary **1995**:4
Stroman, Susan **2000**:4
Swayze, Patrick 1952-2009
  Obituary **2011**:1
Takei, Kei 1946- **1990**:2

Taylor, Paul 1930- **1992**:3
Tharp, Twyla 1942- **1992**:4
Tudor, Antony 1908(?)-1987
    Obituary **1987**:4
Tune, Tommy 1939- **1994**:2
Varone, Doug 1956- **2001**:2
Verdi-Fletcher, Mary 1955- **1998**:2
Verdon, Gwen 1925-2000
    Obituary **2001**:2
Whelan, Wendy 1967(?)- **1999**:3

EDUCATION

Abramson, Lyn 1950- **1986**:3
Alexander, Lamar 1940- **1991**:2
Ayala, Francisco 1906-2009
    Obituary **2011**:3
Bakker, Robert T. 1950(?)- **1991**:3
Bayley, Corrine
    Brief entry **1986**:4
Billington, James 1929- **1990**:3
Bollinger, Lee C. 1946- **2003**:2
Botstein, Leon 1946- **1985**:3
Bush, Millie 1987- **1992**:1
Campbell, Bebe Moore 1950- **1996**:2
Cartwright, Carol Ann 1941- **2009**:4
Casper, Gerhard 1937- **1993**:1
Cavazos, Lauro F. 1927- **1989**:2
Cheek, James Edward
    Brief entry **1987**:1
Cheney, Lynne V. 1941- **1990**:4
Clements, George 1932- **1985**:1
Cole, Johnetta B. 1936- **1994**:3
Coleman, Mary Sue 1943- **2010**:1
Coles, Robert 1929(?)- **1995**:1
Commager, Henry Steele 1902-1998
    Obituary **1998**:3
Condie, Ally 1978- **2012**:2
Cowen, Scott 1946- **2011**:2
Crow, Michael 1956- **2011**:3
Curran, Charles E. 1934- **1989**:2
Davis, Angela 1944- **1998**:3
Delany, Sarah 1889-1999
    Obituary **1999**:3
Deming, W. Edwards 1900-1993
    1992:2
    Obituary **1994**:2
Dershowitz, Alan 1938(?)- **1992**:1
Dove, Rita 1952- **1994**:3
Drucker, Peter F. 1909- **1992**:3
Duncan, Arne 1964- **2011**:3
Eberhart, Richard 1904-2005
    Obituary **2006**:3
Edelman, Jonah 1970- **2012**:4
Edelman, Marian Wright 1939- **1990**
    :4
Edwards, Harry 1942- **1989**:4
Escalante, Jaime 1930-2010
    Obituary **2012**:3
Etzioni, Amitai 1929- **1994**:3
Faust, Drew Gilpin 1947- **2008**:1
Feldman, Sandra 1939- **1987**:3
Ferguson, Niall 1964- **2006**:1
Fernandez, Joseph 1935- **1991**:3
Folkman, Judah 1933- **1999**:1
Fox, Matthew 1940- **1992**:2
Friedman, Milton 1912-2006
    Obituary **2008**:1
Fulbright, J. William 1905-1995
    Obituary **1995**:3
Futrell, Mary Hatwood 1940- **1986**:1
Futter, Ellen V. 1949- **1995**:1
Garcia, Juliet 1949- **2011**:1

Gee, E. 1944- **2011**:3
Ghali, Boutros Boutros 1922- **1992**:3
Giamatti, A. Bartlett 1938-1989 **1988**
    :4
    Obituary **1990**:1
Goldhaber, Fred
    Brief entry **1986**:3
Gordon, Mary 1947- **2011**:4
Gray, Hanna 1930- **1992**:4
Green, Richard R. 1936- **1988**:3
Greenberg, Moshe 1928-2010
    Obituary **2012**:4
Gregorian, Vartan 1934- **1990**:3
Groves, Robert 1949- **2011**:3
Gund, Agnes 1938- **1993**:2
Gutmann, Amy 1949- **2008**:4
Hackney, Sheldon 1933- **1995**:1
Hair, Jay D. 1945- **1994**:3
Harker, Patrick T. 1958- **2001**:2
Hayakawa, Samuel Ichiye 1906-1992
    Obituary **1992**:3
Healy, Bernadine 1944- **1993**:1
Healy, Timothy S. 1923- **1990**:2
Heaney, Seamus 1939- **1996**:2
Heller, Walter 1915-1987
    Obituary **1987**:4
Hennessy, John L. 1952- **2002**:2
Hill, Anita 1956- **1994**:1
Hill, J. Edward 1938- **2006**:2
Hillegass, Clifton Keith 1918- **1989**:4
Hockfield, Susan 1951- **2009**:2
Horwich, Frances 1908-2001
    Obituary **2002**:3
Hrabowski, Freeman 1950- **2012**:1
Hunter, Madeline 1916(?)- **1991**:2
Jablonski, Nina G. 1953- **2009**:3
Janzen, Daniel H. 1939- **1988**:4
Jin, Ha 1956- **2011**:3
Jones, Edward P. 1950- **2005**:1
Jordan, King 1943(?)- **1990**:1
Justiz, Manuel J. 1948- **1986**:4
Kandel, Eric 1929- **2005**:2
Kellerman, Jonathan 1949- **2009**:1
Kemp, Jan 1949- **1987**:2
Kerr, Clark 1911-2003
    Obituary **2005**:1
King, Mary-Claire 1946- **1998**:3
Kopp, Wendy **1993**:3
Kozol, Jonathan 1936- **1992**:1
Lagasse, Emeril 1959- **1998**:3
Lamb, Wally 1950- **1999**:1
Lang, Eugene M. 1919- **1990**:3
Langston, J. William
    Brief entry **1986**:2
Lawrence, Frederick 1955- **2012**:2
Lawrence, Ruth
    Brief entry **1986**:3
Laybourne, Geraldine 1947- **1997**:1
Leach, Penelope 1937- **1992**:4
Lee, Chang-Rae 1965- **2005**:1
Lerner, Michael 1943- **1994**:2
Levine, Arnold 1939- **2002**:3
Liebowitz, Ronald 1957- **2011**:1
MacKinnon, Catharine 1946- **1993**:2
Malloy, Edward Monk 1941- **1989**:4
Manson, JoAnn E. 1953- **2008**:3
Marier, Rebecca 1974- **1995**:4
McAuliffe, Christa 1948-1986
    Obituary **1985**:4
McCall Smith, Alexander 1948- **2005**
    :2
McMillan, Terry 1951- **1993**:2

Melton, Douglas 1954- **2008**:3
Morrison, Toni 1931- **1998**:1
Mumford, Lewis 1895-1990
    Obituary **1990**:2
Murano, Elsa 1959- **2009**:1
Nemerov, Howard 1920-1991
    Obituary **1992**:1
Nocera, Fred 1957- **2010**:3
Nye, Bill 1955- **1997**:2
O'Keefe, Sean 1956- **2005**:2
Owens, Delia and Mark **1993**:3
Padron, Eduardo 1946- **2011**:2
Pagels, Elaine 1943- **1997**:1
Paglia, Camille 1947- **1992**:3
Paige, Rod 1933- **2003**:2
Parizeau, Jacques 1930- **1995**:1
Pausch, Randy 1960-2008
    Obituary **2009**:3
Peter, Valentine J. 1934- **1988**:2
Rhee, Michelle 1969- **2012**:3
Riley, Richard W. 1933- **1996**:3
Rodin, Judith 1945(?)- **1994**:4
Rosendahl, Bruce R.
    Brief entry **1986**:4
Rowland, Pleasant **1992**:3
Samuelson, Paul 1915-2009
    Obituary **2011**:4
Scheck, Barry 1949- **2000**:4
Schuman, Patricia Glass 1943- **1993**
    :2
Sexton, John 1942- **2011**:4
Shalala, Donna 1941- **1992**:3
Sherman, Russell 1930- **1987**:4
Silber, Joan 1945- **2009**:4
Silber, John 1926- **1990**:1
Simmons, Adele Smith 1941- **1988**:4
Simmons, Ruth 1945- **1995**:2
Simon, Lou Anna K. 1947- **2005**:4
Singer, Margaret Thaler 1921-2003
    Obituary **2005**:1
Sizer, Theodore 1932-2009
    Obituary **2011**:2
Smoot, George F. 1945- **1993**:3
Sowell, Thomas 1930- **1998**:3
Spellings, Margaret 1957- **2005**:4
Spock, Benjamin 1903-1998 **1995**:2
    Obituary **1998**:3
Steele, Shelby 1946- **1991**:2
Strout, Elizabeth 1956- **2009**:1
Swanson, Mary Catherine 1944-
    2002:2
Tannen, Deborah 1945- **1995**:1
Thiebaud, Wayne 1920- **1991**:1
Thomas, Michel 1911(?)- **1987**:4
Tilghman, Shirley M. 1946- **2002**:1
Tohe, Laura 1953- **2009**:2
Tretheway, Natasha 1966- **2008**:3
Tribe, Laurence H. 1941- **1988**:1
Tyson, Laura D'Andrea 1947- **1994**:1
Unz, Ron 1962(?)- **1999**:1
Van Duyn, Mona 1921- **1993**:2
Vickrey, William S. 1914-1996
    Obituary **1997**:2
Warren, Elizabeth 1949- **2010**:2
Warren, Robert Penn 1905-1989
    Obituary **1990**:1
West, Cornel 1953- **1994**:2
Wexler, Nancy S. 1945- **1992**:3
Whitney, Patrick 1952(?)- **2006**:1
Wiesel, Elie 1928- **1998**:1
Wigand, Jeffrey 1943(?)- **2000**:4
Wiles, Andrew 1953(?)- **1994**:1

Wilson, Edward O. 1929- **1994**:4
Wilson, William Julius 1935- **1997**:1
Wolff, Tobias 1945- **2005**:1
Wu, Harry 1937- **1996**:1
Yudof, Mark 1944- **2009**:4
Zanker, Bill
  Brief entry **1987**:3
Zigler, Edward 1930- **1994**:1

FILM

Abbott, George 1887-1995
  Obituary **1995**:3
Abrams, J. J. 1966- **2007**:3
Adams, Amy 1974- **2008**:4
Adjani, Isabelle 1955- **1991**:1
Affleck, Ben 1972- **1999**:1
Aiello, Danny 1933- **1990**:4
Albert, Eddie 1906-2005
  Obituary **2006**:3
Alda, Robert 1914-1986
  Obituary **1986**:3
Alexander, Jane 1939- **1994**:2
Alexander, Jason 1962(?)- **1993**:3
Allen, Debbie 1950- **1998**:2
Allen, Dede 1923-2010
  Obituary **2012**:3
Allen, Joan 1956- **1998**:1
Allen, Woody 1935- **1994**:1
Alley, Kirstie 1955- **1990**:3
Allyson, June 1917-2006
  Obituary **2007**:3
Almodovar, Pedro 1951- **2000**:3
Altman, Robert 1925- **1993**:2
Ameche, Don 1908-1993
  Obituary **1994**:2
Anderson, Judith 1899(?)-1992
  Obituary **1992**:3
Andrews, Julie 1935- **1996**:1
Aniston, Jennifer 1969- **2000**:3
Apatow, Judd 1967- **2006**:3
Applegate, Christina 1972- **2000**:4
Arad, Avi 1948- **2003**:2
Arden, Eve 1912(?)-1990
  Obituary **1991**:2
Arkin, Alan 1934- **2007**:4
Arkoff, Samuel Z. 1918-2001
  Obituary **2002**:4
Arlen, Harold 1905-1986
  Obituary **1986**:3
Arnaz, Desi 1917-1986
  Obituary **1987**:1
Arnold, Tom 1959- **1993**:2
Arquette, Patricia 1968- **2001**:3
Arquette, Rosanna 1959- **1985**:2
Arthur, Jean 1901(?)-1991
  Obituary **1992**:1
Ashcroft, Peggy 1907-1991
  Obituary **1992**:1
Astaire, Fred 1899-1987
  Obituary **1987**:4
Astin, Sean 1971- **2005**:1
Astor, Mary 1906-1987
  Obituary **1988**:1
Atkinson, Rowan 1955- **2004**:3
Autry, Gene 1907-1998
  Obituary **1999**:1
Aykroyd, Dan 1952- **1989**:3
Bacall, Lauren 1924- **1997**:3
Backus, Jim 1913-1989
  Obituary **1990**:1
Bacon, Kevin 1958- **1995**:3
Baddeley, Hermione 1906(?)-1986

  Obituary **1986**:4
Bailey, Pearl 1918-1990
  Obituary **1991**:1
Bakula, Scott 1954- **2003**:1
Baldwin, Alec 1958- **2002**:2
Bale, Christian 1974- **2001**:3
Ball, Alan 1957- **2005**:1
Ball, Lucille 1911-1989
  Obituary **1989**:3
Bancroft, Anne 1931-2005
  Obituary **2006**:3
Banderas, Antonio 1960- **1996**:2
Banks, Elizabeth 1974- **2012**:2
Banks, Tyra 1973- **1996**:3
Bardem, Javier 1969- **2008**:4
Barker, Clive 1952- **2003**:3
Barkin, Ellen 1955- **1987**:3
Baron Cohen, Sacha 1971- **2007**:3
Barr, Roseanne 1953(?)- **1989**:1
Barry, Gene 1919-2009
  Obituary **2011**:4
Barrymore, Drew 1975- **1995**:3
Baryshnikov, Mikhail Nikolaevich
  1948- **1997**:3
Basinger, Kim 1953- **1987**:2
Bassett, Angela 1959(?)- **1994**:4
Bateman, Jason 1969- **2005**:3
Bateman, Justine 1966- **1988**:4
Bates, Alan 1934-2003
  Obituary **2005**:1
Bates, Kathy 1949(?)- **1991**:4
Baxter, Anne 1923-1985
  Obituary **1986**:1
Beals, Jennifer 1963- **2005**:2
Beatty, Warren 1937- **2000**:1
Belushi, Jim 1954- **1986**:2
Benigni, Roberto 1952- **1999**:2
Bening, Annette 1958(?)- **1992**:1
Bennett, Joan 1910-1990
  Obituary **1991**:2
Bergen, Candice 1946- **1990**:1
Bergeron, Tom 1955- **2010**:1
Bergman, Ingmar 1918- **1999**:4
Berman, Gail 1957(?)- **2006**:1
Bernardi, Herschel 1923-1986
  Obituary **1986**:4
Bernhard, Sandra 1955(?)- **1989**:4
Bernsen, Corbin 1955- **1990**:2
Berry, Halle 1968- **1996**:2
Beyonce 1981- **2009**:3
Bialik, Mayim 1975- **1993**:3
Bigelow, Kathryn 1951- **2011**:1
Bigelow, Kathryn 1952(?)- **1990**:4
Binoche, Juliette 1965- **2001**:3
Birch, Thora 1982- **2002**:4
Bird, Brad 1956(?)- **2005**:4
Bishop, Joey 1918-2007
  Obituary **2008**:4
Black, Jack 1969- **2002**:3
Blades, Ruben 1948- **1998**:2
Blanc, Mel 1908-1989
  Obituary **1989**:4
Blanchett, Cate 1969- **1999**:3
Bloom, Orlando 1977- **2004**:2
Bogosian, Eric 1953- **1990**:4
Bolger, Ray 1904-1987
  Obituary **1987**:2
Bonet, Lisa 1967- **1989**:2
Bonham Carter, Helena 1966- **1998**:4
Booth, Shirley 1898-1992
  Obituary **1993**:2
Boreanaz, David 1969- **2012**:2

Bosworth, Kate 1983- **2006**:3
Bowen, Julie 1970- **2007**:1
Bowie, David 1947- **1998**:2
Boyle, Danny 1956- **2009**:4
Boyle, Lara Flynn 1970- **2003**:4
Boyle, Peter 1935- **2002**:3
Braff, Zach 1975- **2005**:2
Branagh, Kenneth 1960- **1992**:2
Brand, Russell 1975- **2010**:2
Brandauer, Klaus Maria 1944- **1987**:3
Brando, Marlon 1924-2004
  Obituary **2005**:3
Bratt, Benjamin 1963- **2009**:3
Bridges, Jeff 1949- **2011**:1
Bridges, Lloyd 1913-1998
  Obituary **1998**:3
Brillstein, Bernie 1931-2008
  Obituary **2009**:4
Broadbent, Jim 1949- **2008**:4
Brody, Adrien 1973- **2006**:3
Bronson, Charles 1921-2003
  Obituary **2004**:4
Brooks, Albert 1948(?)- **1991**:4
Brooks, Mel 1926- **2003**:1
Brosnan, Pierce 1952- **2000**:3
Brown, James 1928(?)- **1991**:4
Brown, Jim 1936- **1993**:2
Brown, Ruth 1928-2006
  Obituary **2008**:1
Bruckheimer, Jerry 1945- **2007**:2
Brynner, Yul 1920(?)-1985
  Obituary **1985**:4
Buckley, Betty 1947- **1996**:2
Bullock, Sandra 1967- **1995**:4
Burnett, Carol 1933- **2000**:3
Burns, Edward 1968- **1997**:1
Burns, George 1896-1996
  Obituary **1996**:3
Burns, Ken 1953- **1995**:2
Burr, Raymond 1917-1993
  Obituary **1994**:1
Burstyn, Ellen 1932- **2001**:4
Burton, Tim 1959- **1993**:1
Burum, Stephen H.
  Brief entry **1987**:2
Buscemi, Steve 1957- **1997**:4
Butler, Gerard 1969- **2011**:2
Buttons, Red 1919-2006
  Obituary **2007**:3
Butz, Norbert Leo 1967- **2012**:3
Bynes, Amanda 1986- **2005**:1
Byrne, Gabriel 1950- **1997**:4
Caan, James 1939- **2004**:4
Caesar, Adolph 1934-1986
  Obituary **1986**:3
Cage, Nicolas 1964- **1991**:1
Cagney, James 1899-1986
  Obituary **1986**:2
Caine, Michael 1933- **2000**:4
Calhoun, Rory 1922-1999
  Obituary **1999**:4
Campbell, Naomi 1970- **2000**:2
Campbell, Neve 1973- **1998**:2
Campion, Jane **1991**:4
Candy, John 1950-1994 **1988**:2
  Obituary **1994**:3
Cannon, Nick 1980- **2006**:4
Capra, Frank 1897-1991
  Obituary **1992**:2
Carell, Steve 1963- **2006**:4
Carey, Drew 1958- **1997**:4
Carlin, George 1937- **1996**:3

Carney, Art 1918-2003
Obituary **2005**:1
Carradine, David 1936-2009
Obituary **2010**:3
Carradine, John 1906-1988
Obituary **1989**:2
Carrey, Jim 1962- **1995**:1
Carson, Lisa Nicole 1969- **1999**:3
Carter, Dixie 1939-2010
Obituary **2012**:3
Caruso, David 1956(?)- **1994**:3
Carvey, Dana 1955- **1994**:1
Cassavetes, John 1929-1989
Obituary **1989**:2
Castellucci, Cecil 1969- **2008**:3
Castle-Hughes, Keisha 1990- **2004**:4
Cattrall, Kim 1956- **2003**:3
Caulfield, Joan 1922(?)-1991
Obituary **1992**:1
Cavanagh, Tom 1968- **2003**:1
Caviezel, Jim 1968- **2005**:3
Cera, Michael 1988- **2012**:1
Chahine, Youssef 1926-2008
Obituary **2009**:3
Chan, Jackie 1954- **1996**:1
Chandler, Kyle 1965- **2010**:4
Channing, Stockard 1946- **1991**:3
Chappelle, Dave 1973- **2005**:3
Charisse, Cyd 1922-2008
Obituary **2009**:3
Chase, Chevy 1943- **1990**:1
Chase, Debra Martin 1956- **2009**:1
Cheadle, Don 1964- **2002**:1
Chen, Joan 1961- **2000**:2
Cher 1946- **1993**:1
Chiklis, Michael 1963- **2003**:3
Chow, Stephen 1962- **2006**:1
Chow Yun-fat 1955- **1999**:4
Christensen, Hayden 1981- **2003**:3
Christie, Julie 1941- **2008**:4
Clarkson, Patricia 1959- **2005**:3
Clay, Andrew Dice 1958- **1991**:1
Cleese, John 1939- **1989**:2
Close, Glenn 1947- **1988**:3
Coburn, James 1928-2002
Obituary **2004**:1
Coco, James 1929(?)-1987
Obituary **1987**:2
Cody, Diablo 1978- **2009**:1
Coen, Joel and Ethan **1992**:1
Colbert, Claudette 1903-1996
Obituary **1997**:1
Colbert, Stephen 1964- **2007**:4
Coleman, Dabney 1932- **1988**:3
Collette, Toni 1972- **2009**:4
Condon, Bill 1955- **2007**:3
Connelly, Jennifer 1970- **2002**:4
Connery, Sean 1930- **1990**:4
Connick, Harry, Jr. 1967- **1991**:1
Cooper, Bradley 1975- **2012**:3
Cooper, Chris 1951- **2004**:1
Coppola, Carmine 1910-1991
Obituary **1991**:4
Coppola, Francis Ford 1939- **1989**:4
Coppola, Sofia 1971- **2004**:3
Corbett, John 1962- **2004**:1
Cosby, Bill 1937- **1999**:2
Cosgrove, Miranda 1993- **2011**:4
Costner, Kevin 1955- **1989**:4
Cotillard, Marion 1975- **2009**:1
Cox, Courteney 1964- **1996**:2
Craig, Daniel 1968- **2008**:1

Cranston, Bryan 1956- **2010**:1
Craven, Wes 1939- **1997**:3
Crawford, Broderick 1911-1986
Obituary **1986**:3
Crenna, Richard 1926-2003
Obituary **2004**:1
Crichton, Michael 1942- **1995**:3
Cronenberg, David 1943- **1992**:3
Cronyn, Hume 1911-2003
Obituary **2004**:3
Crothers, Scatman 1910-1986
Obituary **1987**:1
Crowe, Cameron 1957- **2001**:2
Crowe, Russell 1964- **2000**:4
Cruise, Tom 1962(?)- **1985**:4
Cruz, Penelope 1974- **2001**:4
Cryer, Jon 1965- **2010**:4
Crystal, Billy 1947- **1985**:3
Cuaron, Alfonso 1961- **2008**:2
Culkin, Macaulay 1980(?)- **1991**:3
Curtis, Jamie Lee 1958- **1995**:1
Cusack, John 1966- **1999**:3
Cushing, Peter 1913-1994
Obituary **1995**:1
Dafoe, Willem 1955- **1988**:1
Dalton, Timothy 1946- **1988**:4
Damon, Matt 1970- **1999**:1
Dancy, Hugh 1975- **2010**:3
Danes, Claire 1979- **1999**:4
Dangerfield, Rodney 1921-2004
Obituary **2006**:1
Daniels, Jeff 1955- **1989**:4
Danza, Tony 1951- **1989**:1
David, Larry 1948- **2003**:4
Davis, Bette 1908-1989
Obituary **1990**:1
Davis, Geena 1957- **1992**:1
Davis, Ossie 1917-2005
Obituary **2006**:1
Davis, Sammy, Jr. 1925-1990
Obituary **1990**:4
Davis, Viola 1965- **2011**:4
Dawson, Rosario 1979- **2007**:2
Day, Dennis 1917-1988
Obituary **1988**:4
Day-Lewis, Daniel 1957- **1989**:4
De Cordova, Frederick 1910- **1985**:2
Dee, Sandra 1942-2005
Obituary **2006**:2
DeGeneres, Ellen **1995**:3
Delany, Dana 1956- **2008**:4
Del Toro, Benicio 1967- **2001**:4
Del Toro, Guillermo 1964- **2010**:3
DeLuise, Dom 1933-2009
Obituary **2010**:2
De Matteo, Drea 1973- **2005**:2
Demme, Jonathan 1944- **1992**:4
Dempsey, Patrick 1966- **2006**:1
Dench, Judi 1934- **1999**:4
Deneuve, Catherine 1943- **2003**:2
De Niro, Robert 1943- **1999**:1
Dennehy, Brian 1938- **2002**:1
Dennis, Sandy 1937-1992
Obituary **1992**:4
De Palma, Brian 1940- **2007**:3
Depardieu, Gerard 1948- **1991**:2
Depp, Johnny 1963(?)- **1991**:3
Dern, Laura 1967- **1992**:3
Deschanel, Zooey 1980- **2010**:4
De Vito, Danny 1944- **1987**:1
Diamond, I.A.L. 1920-1988
Obituary **1988**:3

Diamond, Selma 1921(?)-1985
Obituary **1985**:2
Diaz, Cameron 1972- **1999**:1
DiCaprio, Leonardo Wilhelm 1974-
1997:2
Diesel, Vin 1967- **2004**:1
Dietrich, Marlene 1901-1992
Obituary **1992**:4
Diggs, Taye 1971- **2000**:1
Diller, Barry 1942- **1991**:1
Dillon, Matt 1964- **1992**:2
Disney, Roy E. 1930- **1986**:3
Divine 1946-1988
Obituary **1988**:3
Doherty, Shannen 1971(?)- **1994**:2
Donahue, Troy 1936-2001
Obituary **2002**:4
Donovan, Jeffrey 1968- **2012**:1
Douglas, Michael 1944- **1986**:2
Downey, Robert, Jr. 1965- **2007**:1
Drescher, Fran 1957(?)- **1995**:3
Dreyfuss, Richard 1947- **1996**:3
Driver, Minnie 1971- **2000**:1
Duchovny, David 1960- **1998**:3
Duff, Hilary 1987- **2004**:4
Duffy, Karen 1962- **1998**:1
Dukakis, Olympia 1931- **1996**:4
Dunagan, Deanna 1940- **2009**:2
Dunst, Kirsten 1982- **2001**:4
Duvall, Robert 1931- **1999**:3
Eastwood, Clint 1930- **1993**:3
Ebersole, Christine 1953- **2007**:2
Ebsen, Buddy 1908-2003
Obituary **2004**:3
Eckhart, Aaron 1968- **2009**:2
Efron, Zac 1987- **2008**:2
Egoyan, Atom 1960- **2000**:2
Eisner, Michael 1942- **1989**:2
Elliott, Denholm 1922-1992
Obituary **1993**:2
Engvall, Bill 1957- **2010**:1
Ephron, Henry 1912-1992
Obituary **1993**:2
Ephron, Nora 1941- **1992**:3
Epps, Omar 1973- **2000**:4
Estevez, Emilio 1962- **1985**:4
Evans, Robert 1930- **2004**:1
Eve 1978- **2004**:3
Everett, Rupert 1959- **2003**:1
Fairbanks, Douglas, Jr. 1909-2000
Obituary **2000**:4
Falco, Edie 1963- **2010**:2
Fallon, Jimmy 1974- **2003**:1
Fanning, Dakota 1994- **2005**:2
Faris, Anna 1976- **2010**:3
Farley, Chris 1964-1997 **1998**:2
Farrell, Colin 1976- **2004**:1
Farrow, Mia 1945- **1998**:3
Favreau, Jon 1966- **2002**:3
Fawcett, Farrah 1947- **1998**:4
Feldshuh, Tovah 1952- **2005**:3
Felix, Maria 1914-2002
Obituary **2003**:2
Fell, Norman 1924-1998
Obituary **1999**:2
Fellini, Federico 1920-1993
Obituary **1994**:2
Ferguson, Craig 1962- **2005**:4
Ferrell, Will 1968- **2004**:4
Ferrer, Jose 1912-1992
Obituary **1992**:3
Ferrera, America 1984- **2006**:2

Fetchit, Stepin 1892(?)-1985
 Obituary **1986**:1
Feuerstein, Mark 1971- **2012**:2
Fey, Tina 1970- **2005**:3
Fforde, Jasper 1961- **2006**:3
Field, Sally 1946- **1995**:3
Fiennes, Ralph 1962- **1996**:2
Fierstein, Harvey 1954- **2004**:2
Fillion, Nathan 1971- **2011**:3
Finneran, Katie 1971- **2012**:1
Finney, Albert 1936- **2003**:3
Firth, Colin 1960- **2012**:3
Fishburne, Laurence 1961(?)- **1995**:3
Fisher, Carrie 1956- **1991**:1
Flanders, Ed 1934-1995
 Obituary **1995**:3
Fleiss, Mike 1964- **2003**:4
Fleming, Art 1925(?)-1995
 Obituary **1995**:4
Flockhart, Calista 1964- **1998**:4
Fonda, Bridget 1964- **1995**:1
Foote, Horton 1916-2009
 Obituary **2010**:2
Ford, Faith 1964- **2005**:3
Ford, Glenn 1916-2006
 Obituary **2007**:4
Ford, Harrison 1942- **1990**:2
Fosse, Bob 1927-1987
 Obituary **1988**:1
Foster, Jodie 1962- **1989**:2
Fox, Michael J. 1961- **1986**:1
Fox, Vivica 1964- **1999**:1
Franciscus, James 1934-1991
 Obituary **1992**:1
Franco, James 1978- **2012**:1
Frank, Robert 1924- **1995**:2
Frankenheimer, John 1930-2002
 Obituary **2003**:4
Franz, Dennis 1944- **1995**:2
Fraser, Brendan 1967- **2000**:1
Freeman, Morgan 1937- **1990**:4
Freleng, Friz 1906(?)-1995
 Obituary **1995**:4
Fugard, Athol 1932- **1992**:3
Gabor, Eva 1921(?)-1995
 Obituary **1996**:1
Gaiman, Neil 1960- **2010**:1
Gallagher, Peter 1955- **2004**:3
Garbo, Greta 1905-1990
 Obituary **1990**:3
Garcia, Andy 1956- **1999**:3
Gardenia, Vincent 1922-1992
 Obituary **1993**:2
Gardner, Ava Lavinia 1922-1990
 Obituary **1990**:2
Garfield, Andrew 1983- **2012**:4
Garner, Jennifer 1972- **2003**:1
Garofalo, Janeane 1964- **1996**:4
Garr, Teri 1949- **1988**:4
Garson, Greer 1903-1996
 Obituary **1996**:4
Gassman, Vittorio 1922-2000
 Obituary **2001**:1
Geffen, David 1943- **1985**:3
Gelbart, Larry 1928-2009
 Obituary **2011**:1
Gellar, Sarah Michelle 1977- **1999**:3
Gere, Richard 1949- **1994**:3
Getty, Estelle 1923-2008
 Obituary **2009**:3
Giamatti, Paul 1967- **2009**:4
Gibson, Mel 1956- **1990**:1

Gielgud, John 1904-2000
 Obituary **2000**:4
Gift, Roland 1960(?)- **1990**:2
Gilford, Jack 1907-1990
 Obituary **1990**:4
Gish, Lillian 1893-1993
 Obituary **1993**:4
Gleason, Jackie 1916-1987
 Obituary **1987**:4
Gless, Sharon 1944- **1989**:3
Glover, Danny 1947- **1998**:4
Gobel, George 1920(?)-1991
 Obituary **1991**:4
Godard, Jean-Luc 1930- **1998**:1
Godunov, Alexander 1949-1995
 Obituary **1995**:4
Goldberg, Leonard 1934- **1988**:4
Goldberg, Whoopi 1955- **1993**:3
Goldblum, Jeff 1952- **1988**:1
Gong Li 1965- **1998**:4
Gooding, Cuba, Jr. 1968- **1997**:3
Goodman, John 1952- **1990**:3
Gordon, Dexter 1923-1990 **1987**:1
Gordon, Gale 1906-1995
 Obituary **1996**:1
Gossett, Louis, Jr. 1936- **1989**:3
Goulet, Robert 1933-2007
 Obituary **2008**:4
Grace, Topher 1978- **2005**:4
Graham, Heather 1970- **2000**:1
Graham, Lauren 1967- **2003**:4
Grant, Cary 1904-1986
 Obituary **1987**:1
Grant, Hugh 1960- **1995**:3
Grant, Rodney A. **1992**:1
Gray, Spalding 1941-2004
 Obituary **2005**:2
Grazer, Brian 1951- **2006**:4
Green, Seth 1974- **2010**:1
Greene, Graham 1952- **1997**:2
Greene, Lorne 1915-1987
 Obituary **1988**:1
Grier, Pam 1949- **1998**:3
Griffin, Kathy 1961- **2010**:4
Griffith, Melanie 1957- **1989**:2
Grodin, Charles 1935- **1997**:3
Grusin, Dave
 Brief entry **1987**:2
Guest, Christopher 1948- **2004**:2
Guggenheim, Charles 1924-2002
 Obituary **2003**:4
Guinness, Alec 1914-2000
 Obituary **2001**:1
Gyllenhaal, Jake 1980- **2005**:3
Gyllenhaal, Maggie 1977- **2009**:2
Hackett, Buddy 1924-2003
 Obituary **2004**:3
Hackman, Gene 1931- **1989**:3
Hagen, Uta 1919-2004
 Obituary **2005**:2
Haggis, Paul 1953- **2006**:4
Haim, Corey 1971-2010
 Obituary **2012**:2
Hall, Anthony Michael 1968- **1986**:3
Hall, Arsenio 1955- **1990**:2
Hall, Michael 1971- **2011**:1
Hallstrom, Lasse 1946- **2002**:3
Hamilton, Margaret 1902-1985
 Obituary **1985**:3
Hamm, Jon 1971- **2009**:2
Hammer, Jan 1948- **1987**:3
Hanks, Tom 1956- **1989**:2

Hannah, Daryl 1961- **1987**:4
Hannigan, Alyson 1974- **2007**:3
Harden, Marcia Gay 1959- **2002**:4
Hargitay, Mariska 1964- **2006**:2
Harmon, Mark 1951- **1987**:1
Harrelson, Woody 1961- **2011**:1
Harris, Ed 1950- **2002**:2
Harris, Neil Patrick 1973- **2012**:3
Harris, Richard 1930-2002
 Obituary **2004**:1
Harrison, Rex 1908-1990
 Obituary **1990**:4
Harry, Deborah 1945- **1990**:1
Hart, Kitty Carlisle 1910-2007
 Obituary **2008**:2
Hartman, Phil 1948-1998 **1996**:2
 Obituary **1998**:4
Harvey, Steve 1956- **2010**:1
Harwell, Ernie 1918- **1997**:3
Hatcher, Teri 1964- **2005**:4
Hathaway, Anne 1982- **2007**:2
Hawke, Ethan 1971(?)- **1995**:4
Hawkins, Sally 1976- **2009**:4
Hawn, Goldie Jeanne 1945- **1997**:2
Hayek, Salma 1968- **1999**:1
Hayes, Helen 1900-1993
 Obituary **1993**:4
Hayes, Isaac 1942- **1998**:4
Haysbert, Dennis 1954- **2007**:1
Hayworth, Rita 1918-1987
 Obituary **1987**:3
Heche, Anne 1969- **1999**:1
Heckerling, Amy 1954- **1987**:2
Heigl, Katharine 1978- **2008**:3
Hemingway, Margaux 1955-1996
 Obituary **1997**:1
Hennessy, Jill 1969- **2003**:2
Henson, Brian 1964(?)- **1992**:1
Henson, Jim 1936-1990 **1989**:1
 Obituary **1990**:4
Hepburn, Audrey 1929-1993
 Obituary **1993**:2
Hepburn, Katharine 1909- **1991**:2
Hershey, Barbara 1948- **1989**:1
Heston, Charlton 1924- **1999**:4
Hewitt, Jennifer Love 1979- **1999**:2
Hickey, John Benjamin 1963- **2012**:3
Hill, George Roy 1921-2002
 Obituary **2004**:1
Hill, Lauryn 1975- **1999**:3
Hines, Gregory 1946- **1992**:4
Hodge, Douglas 1960- **2012**:4
Hoffman, Dustin 1937- **2005**:4
Hoffman, Philip Seymour 1967-
 2006:3
Holmes, John C. 1945-1988
 Obituary **1988**:3
Hope, Bob 1903-2003
 Obituary **2004**:4
Hopkins, Anthony 1937- **1992**:4
Hopper, Dennis 1936-2010
 Obituary **2012**:4
Horne, Lena 1917- **1998**:4
Hoskins, Bob 1942- **1989**:1
Hou Hsiao-hsien 1947- **2000**:2
Houseman, John 1902-1988
 Obituary **1989**:1
Howard, Ken 1944- **2010**:4
Howard, Ron **1997**:2
Howard, Trevor 1916-1988
 Obituary **1988**:2
Hudson, Jennifer 1981- **2008**:1

Hudson, Kate 1979- **2001**:2
Hudson, Rock 1925-1985
  Obituary **1985**:4
Huffman, Felicity 1962- **2006**:2
Hughes, John 1950-2009
  Obituary **2010**:4
Humphries, Barry 1934- **1993**:1
Hunt, Helen 1963- **1994**:4
Hunter, Holly 1958- **1989**:4
Hurley, Elizabeth **1999**:2
Hurt, William 1950- **1986**:1
Huston, Anjelica 1952(?)- **1989**:3
Huston, John 1906-1987
  Obituary **1988**:1
Hutton, Timothy 1960- **1986**:3
Ice Cube 1969- **1999**:2
Ice-T **1992**:3
Ireland, Jill 1936-1990
  Obituary **1990**:4
Irons, Jeremy 1948- **1991**:4
Irving, John 1942- **2006**:2
Itami, Juzo 1933-1997 **1998**:2
Ives, Burl 1909-1995
  Obituary **1995**:4
Izzard, Eddie 1963- **2008**:1
Jackman, Hugh 1968- **2004**:4
Jackson, Peter 1961- **2004**:4
Jackson, Samuel L. 1949(?)- **1995**:4
Jacobson, Nina 1965- **2009**:2
James, Nikki M. 1981- **2012**:3
Jane, Thomas 1969- **2010**:3
Janney, Allison 1959- **2003**:3
Jarmusch, Jim 1953- **1998**:3
Jay, Ricky 1949(?)- **1995**:1
Jillian, Ann 1951- **1986**:4
Johansson, Scarlett 1984- **2005**:4
Johnson, Beverly 1952- **2005**:2
Johnson, Don 1949- **1986**:1
Johnson, Van 1916-2008
  Obituary **2010**:1
Jolie, Angelina 1975- **2000**:2
Jones, Cherry 1956- **1999**:3
Jones, Jennifer 1919-2009
  Obituary **2011**:4
Jones, Tommy Lee 1947(?)- **1994**:2
Jonze, Spike 1961(?)- **2000**:3
Jordan, Neil 1950(?)- **1993**:3
Jovovich, Milla 1975- **2002**:1
Joyce, William 1957- **2006**:1
Judd, Ashley 1968- **1998**:1
Julia, Raul 1940-1994
  Obituary **1995**:1
Kahn, Madeline 1942-1999
  Obituary **2000**:2
Kanakaredes, Melina 1967- **2007**:1
Kasem, Casey 1933(?)- **1987**:1
Katzenberg, Jeffrey 1950- **1995**:3
Kaufman, Charlie 1958- **2005**:1
Kavner, Julie 1951- **1992**:3
Kaye, Danny 1913-1987
  Obituary **1987**:2
Kazan, Elia 1909-2003
  Obituary **2004**:4
Keaton, Diane 1946- **1997**:1
Keaton, Michael 1951- **1989**:4
Keeler, Ruby 1910-1993
  Obituary **1993**:4
Keitel, Harvey 1939- **1994**:3
Keith, Brian 1921-1997
  Obituary **1997**:4
Kelly, Gene 1912-1996
  Obituary **1996**:3

Kendrick, Anna 1985- **2011**:2
Kerr, Deborah 1921-2007
  Obituary **2008**:4
Kidman, Nicole 1967- **1992**:4
Kilmer, Val **1991**:4
Kimmel, Jimmy 1967- **2009**:2
King, Alan 1927-2004
  Obituary **2005**:3
King, Stephen 1947- **1998**:1
Kinski, Klaus 1926-1991 **1987**:2
  Obituary **1992**:2
Kitt, Eartha 1927-2008
  Obituary **2010**:1
Kline, Kevin 1947- **2000**:1
Knight, Wayne 1956- **1997**:1
Knightley, Keira 1985- **2005**:2
Knotts, Don 1924-2006
  Obituary **2007**:1
Kramer, Larry 1935- **1991**:2
Kramer, Stanley 1913-2001
  Obituary **2002**:1
Krause, Peter 1965- **2009**:2
Kubrick, Stanley 1928-1999
  Obituary **1999**:3
Kulp, Nancy 1921-1991
  Obituary **1991**:3
Kurosawa, Akira 1910-1998 **1991**:1
  Obituary **1999**:1
Kutcher, Ashton 1978- **2003**:4
LaBeouf, Shia 1986- **2008**:1
Lahti, Christine 1950- **1988**:2
Lake, Ricki 1968(?)- **1994**:4
Lamarr, Hedy 1913-2000
  Obituary **2000**:3
Lamour, Dorothy 1914-1996
  Obituary **1997**:1
Lancaster, Burt 1913-1994
  Obituary **1995**:1
Lane, Diane 1965- **2006**:2
Lane, Nathan 1956- **1996**:4
Lange, Jessica 1949- **1995**:4
Langella, Frank 1940- **2008**:3
Lansbury, Angela 1925- **1993**:1
Lansing, Sherry 1944- **1995**:4
LaPaglia, Anthony 1959- **2004**:4
Lardner Jr., Ring 1915-2000
  Obituary **2001**:2
Larroquette, John 1947- **1986**:2
Lasseter, John 1957- **2007**:2
Lathan, Sanaa 1971- **2012**:4
Laurie, Hugh 1959- **2007**:2
Law, Jude 1971- **2000**:3
Lawless, Lucy 1968- **1997**:4
Lawrence, Jennifer 1990- **2012**:4
Lawrence, Martin 1966(?)- **1993**:4
Leary, Denis 1958- **1993**:3
LeBlanc, Matt 1967- **2005**:4
Ledger, Heath 1979- **2006**:3
Lee, Ang 1954- **1996**:3
Lee, Brandon 1965(?)-1993
  Obituary **1993**:4
Lee, Jason 1970- **2006**:4
Lee, Pamela 1967(?)- **1996**:4
Lee, Spike 1957- **1988**:4
Leguizamo, John 1965- **1999**:1
Leigh, Janet 1927-2004
  Obituary **2005**:4
Leigh, Jennifer Jason 1962- **1995**:2
Lemmon, Jack 1925- **1998**:4
  Obituary **2002**:3
Leno, Jay 1950- **1987**:1
Leone, Sergio 1929-1989

  Obituary **1989**:4
Levi, Zachary 1980- **2009**:4
Levinson, Barry 1932- **1989**:3
Levy, Eugene 1946- **2004**:3
Lewis, Juliette 1973- **1999**:3
Lewis, Richard 1948(?)- **1992**:1
Li, Jet 1963- **2005**:3
Liberace 1919-1987
  Obituary **1987**:2
Liman, Doug 1965- **2007**:1
Ling, Bai 1970- **2000**:3
Linklater, Richard 1960- **2007**:2
Linney, Laura 1964- **2009**:4
Lithgow, John 1945- **1985**:2
Little, Cleavon 1939-1992
  Obituary **1993**:2
Liu, Lucy 1968- **2000**:4
Lively, Blake 1987- **2009**:1
Livingston, Ron 1968- **2007**:2
LL Cool J 1968- **1998**:2
Lloyd Webber, Andrew 1948- **1989**:1
Locklear, Heather 1961- **1994**:3
Loewe, Frederick 1901-1988
  Obituary **1988**:2
Logan, Joshua 1908-1988
  Obituary **1988**:4
Lohan, Lindsay 1986- **2005**:3
Long, Nia 1970- **2001**:3
Long, Shelley 1950(?)- **1985**:1
Lopez, Jennifer 1970- **1998**:4
Lord, Jack 1920-1998 **1998**:2
Lords, Traci 1968- **1995**:4
Louis-Dreyfus, Julia 1961(?)- **1994**:1
Lovett, Lyle 1958(?)- **1994**:1
Lowe, Rob 1964(?)- **1990**:4
Loy, Myrna 1905-1993
  Obituary **1994**:2
Lucas, George 1944- **1999**:4
Ludacris 1977- **2007**:4
Luhrmann, Baz 1962- **2002**:3
Lupino, Ida 1918(?)-1995
  Obituary **1996**:1
LuPone, Patti 1949- **2009**:2
Lynch, David 1946- **1990**:4
Lynch, Jane 1960- **2011**:2
Lyne, Adrian 1941- **1997**:2
Mac, Bernie 1957- **2003**:1
MacDonald, Laurie and Walter
  Parkes **2004**:1
MacDowell, Andie 1958(?)- **1993**:4
MacMurray, Fred 1908-1991
  Obituary **1992**:2
MacRae, Gordon 1921-1986
  Obituary **1986**:2
Macy, William H. **1999**:3
Madonna 1958- **1985**:2
Maggie Q 1979- **2012**:4
Maguire, Tobey 1975- **2002**:2
Maher, Bill 1956- **1996**:2
Mako 1933-2006
  Obituary **2007**:3
Malden, Karl 1912-2009
  Obituary **2010**:4
Malkovich, John 1953- **1988**:2
Malle, Louis 1932-1995
  Obituary **1996**:2
Mamet, David 1947- **1998**:4
Mancini, Henry 1924-1994
  Obituary **1994**:4
Mandel, Howie 1955- **1989**:1
Mantegna, Joe 1947- **1992**:1
Marber, Patrick 1964- **2007**:4

Margulies, Julianna 1966- **2011**:1
Marin, Cheech 1946- **2000**:1
Markle, C. Wilson 1938- **1988**:1
Marsalis, Branford 1960- **1988**:3
Marshall, Penny 1942- **1991**:3
Martin, Dean 1917-1995
  Obituary **1996**:2
Martin, Dean Paul 1952(?)-1987
  Obituary **1987**:3
Martin, Steve 1945- **1992**:2
Marvin, Lee 1924-1987
  Obituary **1988**:1
Masina, Giulietta 1920-1994
  Obituary **1994**:3
Mastroianni, Marcello 1914-1996
  Obituary **1997**:2
Matlin, Marlee 1965- **1992**:2
Matthau, Walter 1920- **2000**:3
Matuszak, John 1951(?)-1989
  Obituary **1989**:4
McCarthy, Melissa 1970- **2012**:4
McConaughey, Matthew David
  1969- **1997**:1
McCrea, Joel 1905-1990
  Obituary **1991**:1
McDonagh, Martin 1970- **2007**:3
McDonnell, Mary 1952- **2008**:2
McDormand, Frances 1957- **1997**:3
McDowall, Roddy 1928-1998
  Obituary **1999**:1
McGillis, Kelly 1957- **1989**:3
McGinley, Ted 1958- **2004**:4
McGoohan, Patrick 1928-2009
  Obituary **2010**:1
McGregor, Ewan 1971(?)- **1998**:2
McGuire, Dorothy 1918-2001
  Obituary **2002**:4
McHale, Joel 1971- **2010**:4
McKee, Lonette 1952(?)- **1996**:1
McKellen, Ian 1939- **1994**:1
McLaren, Norman 1914-1987
  Obituary **1987**:2
McMahon, Julian 1968- **2006**:1
Meadows, Audrey 1925-1996
  Obituary **1996**:3
Melnick, Daniel 1932-2009
  Obituary **2011**:2
Merchant, Ismail 1936-2005
  Obituary **2006**:3
Meredith, Burgess 1909-1997
  Obituary **1998**:1
Merkerson, S. Epatha 1952- **2006**:4
Messing, Debra 1968- **2004**:4
Meyers, Nancy 1949- **2006**:1
Midler, Bette 1945- **1989**:4
Milano, Alyssa 1972- **2002**:3
Milland, Ray 1908(?)-1986
  Obituary **1986**:2
Miller, Ann 1923-2004
  Obituary **2005**:2
Miller, Frank 1957- **2008**:2
Milligan, Spike 1918-2002
  Obituary **2003**:2
Minghella, Anthony 1954- **2004**:3
Minogue, Kylie 1968- **2003**:4
Mirren, Helen 1945- **2005**:1
Mitchell, Elizabeth 1970- **2011**:4
Mitchum, Robert 1917-1997
  Obituary **1997**:4
Miyazaki, Hayao 1941- **2006**:2
Molina, Alfred 1953- **2005**:3
Mo'Nique 1967- **2008**:1

Montalban, Ricardo 1920-2009
  Obituary **2010**:1
Montand, Yves 1921-1991
  Obituary **1992**:2
Montgomery, Elizabeth 1933-1995
  Obituary **1995**:4
Moore, Clayton 1914-1999
  Obituary **2000**:3
Moore, Demi 1963(?)- **1991**:4
Moore, Dudley 1935-2002
  Obituary **2003**:2
Moore, Julianne 1960- **1998**:1
Moore, Mandy 1984- **2004**:2
Moore, Mary Tyler 1936- **1996**:2
Moore, Michael 1954(?)- **1990**:3
Morgan, Tracy 1968- **2009**:3
Morita, Noriyuki Pat 1932- **1987**:3
Morris, Kathryn 1969- **2006**:4
Morrow, Rob 1962- **2006**:4
Mortensen, Viggo 1958- **2003**:3
Mos Def 1973- **2005**:4
Moss, Carrie-Anne 1967- **2004**:3
Murphy, Brittany 1977- **2005**:1
Murphy, Eddie 1961- **1989**:2
Murray, Bill 1950- **2002**:4
Myers, Mike 1964(?)- **1992**:3
Nair, Mira 1957- **2007**:4
Nance, Jack 1943(?)-1996
  Obituary **1997**:3
Neal, Patricia 1926-2010
  Obituary **2012**:4
Neeson, Liam 1952- **1993**:4
Nelson, Harriet 1909(?)-1994
  Obituary **1995**:1
Nelson, Rick 1940-1985
  Obituary **1986**:1
Nelson, Willie 1933- **1993**:4
Newman, Paul 1925- **1995**:3
Newton-John, Olivia 1948- **1998**:4
Nichols, Mike 1931- **1994**:4
Nicholson, Jack 1937- **1989**:2
Nixon, Bob 1954(?)- **2006**:4
Nolan, Christopher 1970(?)- **2006**:3
Nolan, Lloyd 1902-1985
  Obituary **1985**:4
Nolte, Nick 1941- **1992**:4
North, Alex 1910- **1986**:3
Northam, Jeremy 1961- **2003**:2
Norton, Edward 1969- **2000**:2
O'Connor, Donald 1925-2003
  Obituary **2004**:4
O'Donnell, Chris 1970- **2011**:4
O'Donnell, Rosie 1962- **1994**:3
O'Hara, Catherine 1954- **2007**:4
Oldman, Gary 1958- **1998**:1
Olin, Ken 1955(?)- **1992**:3
Olin, Lena 1956- **1991**:2
Olivier, Laurence 1907-1989
  Obituary **1989**:4
Olmos, Edward James 1947- **1990**:1
O'Neill, Ed 1946- **2010**:4
O'Sullivan, Maureen 1911-1998
  Obituary **1998**:4
Ovitz, Michael 1946- **1990**:1
Owen, Clive 1964- **2006**:2
Paar, Jack 1918-2004
  Obituary **2005**:2
Pacino, Al 1940- **1993**:4
Page, Geraldine 1924-1987
  Obituary **1987**:4
Pakula, Alan 1928-1998
  Obituary **1999**:2

Palance, Jack 1919-2006
  Obituary **2008**:1
Paltrow, Gwyneth 1972- **1997**:1
Panettiere, Hayden 1989- **2008**:4
Panjabi, Archie 1972- **2012**:3
Pantoliano, Joe 1951- **2002**:3
Paquin, Anna 1982- **2009**:4
Park, Nick 1958- **1997**:3
Parker, Mary-Louise 1964- **2002**:2
Parker, Sarah Jessica 1965- **1999**:2
Parker, Trey and Matt Stone **1998**:2
Parks, Bert 1914-1992
  Obituary **1992**:3
Parks, Gordon 1912-2006
  Obituary **2006**:2
Parsons, Jim 1973- **2012**:3
Pascal, Amy 1958- **2003**:3
Patrick, Robert 1959- **2002**:1
Pattinson, Robert 1986- **2010**:1
Paxton, Bill 1955- **1999**:3
Payne, Alexander 1961- **2005**:4
Peck, Gregory 1916-2003
  Obituary **2004**:3
Peete, Holly Robinson 1964- **2005**:2
Pegg, Simon 1970- **2009**:1
Penn, Kal 1977- **2009**:1
Penn, Sean 1960- **1987**:2
Perez, Rosie **1994**:2
Perkins, Anthony 1932-1992
  Obituary **1993**:2
Perlman, Ron 1950- **2012**:4
Perry, Luke 1966(?)- **1992**:3
Perry, Matthew 1969- **1997**:2
Perry, Tyler 1969- **2006**:1
Pesci, Joe 1943- **1992**:4
Peters, Bernadette 1948- **2000**:1
Peterson, Cassandra 1951- **1988**:1
Pfeiffer, Michelle 1957- **1990**:2
Phifer, Mekhi 1975- **2004**:1
Phillips, Julia 1944- **1992**:1
Phoenix, Joaquin 1974- **2000**:4
Phoenix, River 1970-1993 **1990**:2
  Obituary **1994**:2
Picasso, Paloma 1949- **1991**:1
Pinchot, Bronson 1959(?)- **1987**:4
Pinkett Smith, Jada 1971- **1998**:3
Pitt, Brad 1964- **1995**:2
Piven, Jeremy 1965- **2007**:3
Pleasence, Donald 1919-1995
  Obituary **1995**:3
Pleshette, Suzanne 1937-2008
  Obituary **2009**:2
Plimpton, George 1927-2003
  Obituary **2004**:4
Poehler, Amy 1971- **2009**:1
Poitier, Sidney 1927- **1990**:3
Pollack, Sydney 1934-2008
  Obituary **2009**:2
Ponti, Carlo 1912-2007
  Obituary **2008**:2
Portman, Natalie 1981- **2000**:3
Potts, Annie 1952- **1994**:1
Preminger, Otto 1906-1986
  Obituary **1986**:3
Presley, Pricilla 1945- **2001**:1
Preston, Robert 1918-1987
  Obituary **1987**:3
Price, Vincent 1911-1993
  Obituary **1994**:2
Prince 1958- **1995**:3
Prinze, Freddie, Jr. 1976- **1999**:3
Probst, Jeff 1962- **2011**:2

Prowse, Juliet 1937-1996
  Obituary **1997**:1
Pryor, Richard **1999**:3
Puzo, Mario 1920-1999
  Obituary **2000**:1
Quaid, Dennis 1954- **1989**:4
Queen Latifah 1970(?)- **1992**:2
Quinn, Anthony 1915-2001
  Obituary **2002**:2
Radcliffe, Daniel 1989- **2007**:4
Radner, Gilda 1946-1989
  Obituary **1989**:4
Raimi, Sam 1959- **1999**:2
Randall, Tony 1920-2004
  Obituary **2005**:3
Raven 1985- **2005**:1
Rawls, Lou 1933-2006
  Obituary **2007**:1
Raye, Martha 1916-1994
  Obituary **1995**:1
Reagan, Ronald 1911-2004
  Obituary **2005**:3
Redford, Robert 1937- **1993**:2
Redgrave, Lynn 1943- **1999**:3
Redgrave, Vanessa 1937- **1989**:2
Reed, Donna 1921-1986
  Obituary **1986**:1
Reese, Della 1931- **1999**:2
Reeve, Christopher 1952- **1997**:2
Reeves, Keanu 1964- **1992**:1
Reeves, Steve 1926-2000
  Obituary **2000**:4
Reid, Frances 1914-2010
  Obituary **2012**:2
Reilly, John C. 1965- **2003**:4
Reiner, Rob 1947- **1991**:2
Reiser, Paul 1957- **1995**:2
Reisz, Karel 1926-2002
  Obituary **2004**:1
Reitman, Ivan 1946- **1986**:3
Reitman, Jason 1977- **2011**:3
Remick, Lee 1936(?)-1991
  Obituary **1992**:1
Reuben, Gloria 1964- **1999**:4
Reubens, Paul 1952- **1987**:2
Reynolds, Ryan 1976- **2012**:1
Rhone, Trevor 1940-2009
  Obituary **2011**:1
Rhys Meyers, Jonathan 1977- **2007**:1
Ricci, Christina 1980- **1999**:1
Rice, Peter 1967(?)- **2007**:2
Richards, Michael 1949(?)- **1993**:4
Richardson, Natasha 1963-2009
  Obituary **2010**:2
Riddle, Nelson 1921-1985
  Obituary **1985**:4
Ringwald, Molly 1968- **1985**:4
Ritchie, Guy 1968- **2001**:3
Ritter, John 1948- **2003**:4
Robards, Jason 1922-2000
  Obituary **2001**:3
Robbins, Jerome 1918-1998
  Obituary **1999**:1
Robbins, Tim 1959- **1993**:1
Roberts, Doris 1930- **2003**:4
Roberts, Julia 1967- **1991**:3
Roberts, Pernell 1928-2010
  Obituary **2012**:1
Rock, Chris 1967(?)- **1998**:1
Rodriguez, Robert 1968- **2005**:1
Rogen, Seth 1982- **2009**:3
Rogers, Ginger 1911(?)-1995

Obituary **1995**:4
Rogers, Roy 1911-1998
  Obituary **1998**:4
Rohmer, Eric 1920-2010
  Obituary **2012**:1
Roker, Roxie 1929(?)-1995
  Obituary **1996**:2
Rolle, Esther 1922-1998
  Obituary **1999**:2
Rollins, Henry 1961- **2007**:3
Rollins, Howard E., Jr. 1950- **1986**:1
Romijn, Rebecca 1972- **2007**:1
Ross, Herbert 1927-2001
  Obituary **2002**:4
Roth, Tim 1961- **1998**:2
Rourke, Mickey 1956- **1988**:4
Rowan, Dan 1922-1987
  Obituary **1988**:1
Rudd, Paul 1969- **2009**:4
Rudner, Rita 1956- **1993**:2
Rudnick, Paul 1957(?)- **1994**:3
Ruehl, Mercedes 1948(?)- **1992**:4
Ruffalo, Mark 1967- **2011**:4
RuPaul 1961(?)- **1996**:1
Rush, Geoffrey 1951- **2002**:1
Russell, Kurt 1951- **2007**:4
Russell, Nipsey 1924-2005
  Obituary **2007**:1
Russo, Rene 1954- **2000**:2
Ryan, Meg 1962(?)- **1994**:1
Ryder, Winona 1971- **1991**:2
Sagal, Katey 1954- **2005**:2
Saldana, Zoe 1978- **2010**:1
Salonga, Lea 1971- **2003**:3
Sandler, Adam 1966- **1999**:2
Sarandon, Susan 1946- **1995**:3
Savage, Fred 1976- **1990**:1
Savalas, Telly 1924-1994
  Obituary **1994**:3
Scheider, Roy 1932-2008
  Obituary **2009**:2
Schlesinger, John 1926-2003
  Obituary **2004**:3
Schneider, Rob 1965- **1997**:4
Schreiber, Liev 1967- **2007**:2
Schroeder, Barbet 1941- **1996**:1
Schumacher, Joel 1929- **2004**:3
Schwarzenegger, Arnold 1947- **1991**:1
Schwimmer, David 1966(?)- **1996**:2
Scorsese, Martin 1942- **1989**:1
Scott, George C. 1927-1999
  Obituary **2000**:2
Scott, Jill 1972- **2010**:1
Scott, Randolph 1898(?)-1987
  Obituary **1987**:2
Scott, Ridley 1937- **2001**:1
Scott Thomas, Kristin 1960- **2010**:2
Sedaris, Amy 1961- **2009**:3
Sedgwick, Kyra 1965- **2006**:2
Seidelman, Susan 1953(?)- **1985**:4
Sevigny, Chloe 1974- **2001**:4
Seyfried, Amanda 1985- **2009**:3
Seymour, Jane 1951- **1994**:4
Shaffer, Paul 1949- **1987**:1
Shanley, John Patrick 1950- **2006**:1
Sharkey, Ray 1953-1993
  Obituary **1994**:1
Shawn, Dick 1924(?)-1987
  Obituary **1987**:3
Sheedy, Ally 1962- **1989**:1
Sheen, Martin 1940- **2002**:1

Sheldon, Sidney 1917-2007
  Obituary **2008**:2
Shepard, Sam 1943- **1996**:4
Shields, Brooke 1965- **1996**:3
Shore, Dinah 1917-1994
  Obituary **1994**:3
Short, Martin 1950- **1986**:1
Shue, Andrew 1964- **1994**:4
Shyamalan, M. Night 1970- **2003**:2
Silverman, Jonathan 1966- **1997**:2
Silverman, Sarah 1970- **2008**:1
Silvers, Phil 1912-1985
  Obituary **1985**:4
Silverstone, Alicia 1976- **1997**:4
Simmons, Jean 1929-2010
  Obituary **2012**:1
Sinatra, Frank 1915-1998
  Obituary **1998**:4
Singer, Bryan 1965- **2007**:3
Singleton, John 1968- **1994**:3
Sinise, Gary 1955(?)- **1996**:1
Siskel, Gene 1946-1999
  Obituary **1999**:3
Slater, Christian 1969- **1994**:1
Smirnoff, Yakov 1951- **1987**:2
Smith, Kevin 1970- **2000**:4
Smith, Will 1968- **1997**:2
Smits, Jimmy 1956- **1990**:1
Snipes, Wesley 1962- **1993**:1
Sobieski, Leelee 1982- **2002**:3
Soderbergh, Steven 1963- **2001**:4
Somerhalder, Ian 1978- **2012**:1
Sondheim, Stephen 1930- **1994**:4
Sorkin, Aaron 1961- **2003**:2
Sorvino, Mira 1970(?)- **1996**:3
Sothern, Ann 1909-2001
  Obituary **2002**:1
Southern, Terry 1926-1995
  Obituary **1996**:2
Spacek, Sissy 1949- **2003**:1
Spacey, Kevin 1959- **1996**:4
Spade, David 1965- **1999**:2
Spader, James 1960- **1991**:2
Spelling, Tori 1973- **2008**:3
Spheeris, Penelope 1945(?)- **1989**:2
Spielberg, Steven 1947- **1993**:4
Stack, Robert 1919-2003
  Obituary **2004**:2
Staller, Ilona 1951- **1988**:3
Stallone, Sylvester 1946- **1994**:2
Stamos, John 1963- **2008**:1
Stapleton, Maureen 1925-2006
  Obituary **2007**:2
Statham, Jason 1972- **2012**:2
Steel, Dawn 1946-1997 **1990**:1
  Obituary **1998**:2
Stefani, Gwen 1969- **2005**:4
Steiger, Rod 1925-2002
  Obituary **2003**:4
Stevenson, McLean 1929-1996
  Obituary **1996**:3
Stewart, Jimmy 1908-1997
  Obituary **1997**:4
Stewart, Kristen 1990- **2012**:1
Stewart, Patrick 1940- **1996**:1
Stiles, Julia 1981- **2002**:3
Stiller, Ben 1965- **1999**:1
Sting 1951- **1991**:4
Stone, Oliver 1946- **1990**:4
Stone, Sharon 1958- **1993**:4
Stoppard, Tom 1937- **1995**:4
Storm, Gale 1922-2009

Obituary **2010**:4
Streep, Meryl 1949- **1990**:2
Streisand, Barbra 1942- **1992**:2
Strummer, Joe 1952-2002
    Obituary **2004**:1
Studi, Wes 1944(?)- **1994**:3
Styler, Trudie 1954- **2009**:1
Styne, Jule 1905-1994
    Obituary **1995**:1
Susskind, David 1920-1987
    Obituary **1987**:2
Sutherland, Kiefer 1966- **2002**:4
Swank, Hilary 1974- **2000**:3
Swayze, Patrick 1952-2009
    Obituary **2011**:1
Swinton, Tilda 1960- **2008**:4
Sykes, Wanda 1964- **2007**:4
Tanaka, Tomoyuki 1910-1997
    Obituary **1997**:3
Tandy, Jessica 1901-1994 **1990**:4
    Obituary **1995**:1
Tarantino, Quentin 1963(?)- **1995**:1
Tatum, Channing 1980- **2011**:3
Tautou, Audrey 1978- **2004**:2
Taylor, Elizabeth 1932- **1993**:3
Taylor, Lili 1967- **2000**:2
Theron, Charlize 1975- **2001**:4
Thiebaud, Wayne 1920- **1991**:1
Thomas, Betty 1948- **2011**:4
Thompson, Emma 1959- **1993**:2
Thompson, Fred 1942- **1998**:2
Thornton, Billy Bob 1956(?)- **1997**:4
Thurman, Uma 1970- **1994**:2
Tilly, Jennifer 1958(?)- **1997**:2
Timberlake, Justin 1981- **2008**:4
Tomei, Marisa 1964- **1995**:2
Travolta, John 1954- **1995**:2
Tucci, Stanley 1960- **2003**:2
Tucker, Chris 1973(?)- **1999**:1
Tucker, Forrest 1919-1986
    Obituary **1987**:1
Turner, Janine 1962- **1993**:2
Turner, Kathleen 1954(?)- **1985**:3
Turner, Lana 1921-1995
    Obituary **1996**:1
Turturro, John 1957- **2002**:2
Tyler, Liv 1978- **1997**:2
Ullman, Tracey 1961- **1988**:3
Umeki, Miyoshi 1929-2007
    Obituary **2008**:4
Union, Gabrielle 1972- **2004**:2
Urich, Robert 1947- **1988**:1
    Obituary **2003**:3
Usher 1979- **2005**:1
Ustinov, Peter 1921-2004
    Obituary **2005**:3
Valenti, Jack 1921-2007
    Obituary **2008**:3
Vanilla Ice 1967(?)- **1991**:3
Van Sant, Gus 1952- **1992**:2
Vardalos, Nia 1962- **2003**:4
Varney, Jim 1949-2000
    Brief entry **1985**:4
    Obituary **2000**:3
Vaughn, Vince 1970- **1999**:2
Ventura, Jesse 1951- **1999**:2
Vidal, Gore 1925- **1996**:2
Vidov, Oleg 194- **1987**:4
Villechaize, Herve 1943(?)-1993
    Obituary **1994**:1
Vincent, Fay 1938- **1990**:2
Voight, Jon 1938- **2002**:3

Walker, Nancy 1922-1992
    Obituary **1992**:3
Wallis, Hal 1898(?)-1986
    Obituary **1987**:1
Waltz, Christoph 1956- **2011**:1
Warden, Jack 1920-2006
    Obituary **2007**:3
Warhol, Andy 1927(?)-1987
    Obituary **1987**:2
Washington, Denzel 1954- **1993**:2
Wasserman, Lew 1913-2002
    Obituary **2003**:3
Waters, John 1946- **1988**:3
Waterston, Sam 1940- **2006**:1
Watson, Emily 1967- **2001**:1
Watts, Naomi 1968- **2006**:1
Wayans, Damon 1960- **1998**:4
Wayans, Keenen Ivory 1958(?)- **1991**
    :1
Wayne, David 1914-1995
    Obituary **1995**:3
Weaver, Sigourney 1949- **1988**:3
Wegman, William 1942(?)- **1991**:1
Weinstein, Bob and Harvey **2000**:4
Weintraub, Jerry 1937- **1986**:1
Weisz, Rachel 1971- **2006**:4
Whedon, Joss 1964- **2006**:3
Whitaker, Forest 1961- **1996**:2
White, Betty 1922- **2012**:1
White, Julie 1961- **2008**:2
Wiest, Dianne 1948- **1995**:2
Wiig, Kristen 1973- **2012**:3
Wilder, Billy 1906-2002
    Obituary **2003**:2
Wilkinson, Tom 1948- **2003**:2
Williams, Robin 1952- **1988**:4
Williams, Treat 1951- **2004**:3
Williams, Vanessa L. 1963- **1999**:2
Willis, Bruce 1955- **1986**:4
Wilson, Owen 1968- **2002**:3
Winfield, Paul 1941-2004
    Obituary **2005**:2
Winfrey, Oprah 1954- **1986**:4
Winger, Debra 1955- **1994**:3
Winokur, Marissa Jaret 1973- **2005**:1
Winslet, Kate 1975- **2002**:4
Winters, Shelley 1920-2006
    Obituary **2007**:1
Wise, Robert 1914-2005
    Obituary **2006**:4
Wiseman, Len 1973- **2008**:2
Witherspoon, Reese 1976- **2002**:1
Wolfman Jack 1938-1995
    Obituary **1996**:1
Wong, B.D. 1962- **1998**:1
Woo, John 1945(?)- **1994**:2
Wood, Elijah 1981- **2002**:4
Woods, James 1947- **1988**:3
Woodward, Edward 1930-2009
    Obituary **2011**:3
Worthington, Sam 1976- **2012**:1
Wright, Joe 1972- **2009**:1
Wright, Robin 1966- **2011**:3
Wyle, Noah 1971- **1997**:3
Wyman, Jane 1917-2007
    Obituary **2008**:4
Wynn, Keenan 1916-1986
    Obituary **1987**:1
Xzibit 1974- **2005**:4
Yeoh, Michelle 1962- **2003**:2
Young, Loretta 1913-2000
    Obituary **2001**:1

Young, Robert 1907-1998
    Obituary **1999**:1
Zanuck, Lili Fini 1954- **1994**:2
Zeffirelli, Franco 1923- **1991**:3
Zellweger, Renee 1969- **2001**:1
Zemeckis, Robert 1952- **2002**:1
Zeta-Jones, Catherine 1969- **1999**:4
Zhang, Ziyi 1979- **2006**:2
Ziskin, Laura 1950- **2008**:2
Zucker, Jerry 1950- **2002**:2

LAW

Abzug, Bella 1920-1998 **1998**:2
Achtenberg, Roberta **1993**:4
Allred, Gloria 1941- **1985**:2
Andrews, Lori B. 1952- **2005**:3
Angelos, Peter 1930- **1995**:4
Archer, Dennis 1942- **1994**:4
Astorga, Nora 1949(?)-1988 **1988**:2
Babbitt, Bruce 1938- **1994**:1
Bailey, F. Lee 1933- **1995**:4
Baker, James A. III 1930- **1991**:2
Bikoff, James L.
    Brief entry **1986**:2
Blackmun, Harry A. 1908-1999
    Obituary **1999**:3
Boies, David 1941- **2002**:1
Bradley, Tom 1917-1998
    Obituary **1999**:1
Brennan, William 1906-1997
    Obituary **1997**:4
Breyer, Stephen Gerald 1938- **1994**:4
Brown, Willie 1934- **1996**:4
Brown, Willie L. 1934- **1985**:2
Burger, Warren E. 1907-1995
    Obituary **1995**:4
Burnison, Chantal Simone 1950(?)-
    1988:3
Campbell, Kim 1947- **1993**:4
Cantrell, Ed
    Brief entry **1985**:3
Carter, Stephen L. **2008**:2
Casey, William 1913-1987
    Obituary **1987**:3
Casper, Gerhard 1937- **1993**:1
Chase, Debra Martin 1956- **2009**:1
Clark, Marcia 1954(?)- **1995**:1
Clinton, Bill 1946- **1992**:1
Clinton, Hillary Rodham 1947- **1993**
    :2
Cochran, Johnnie 1937- **1996**:1
Colby, William E. 1920-1996
    Obituary **1996**:4
Counter, Nick 1940-2009
    Obituary **2011**:3
Crist, Charlie 1956- **2012**:1
Cuomo, Mario 1932- **1992**:2
Darden, Christopher 1957(?)- **1996**:4
Dees, Morris 1936- **1992**:1
del Ponte, Carla 1947- **2001**:1
Dershowitz, Alan 1938(?)- **1992**:1
Deutch, John 1938- **1996**:4
Dole, Elizabeth Hanford 1936- **1990**
    :1
Dukakis, Michael 1933- **1988**:3
Eagleson, Alan 1933- **1987**:4
Ehrlichman, John 1925-1999
    Obituary **1999**:3
Ervin, Sam 1896-1985
    Obituary **1985**:2
Estrich, Susan 1953- **1989**:1
Fairstein, Linda 1948(?)- **1991**:1

Fehr, Donald 1948- **1987**:2
Fieger, Geoffrey 1950- **2001**:3
Fitzgerald, Patrick 1960- **2006**:4
Florio, James J. 1937- **1991**:2
Foster, Vincent 1945(?)-1993
  Obituary **1994**:1
France, Johnny
  Brief entry **1987**:1
Freeh, Louis J. 1950- **1994**:2
Fulbright, J. William 1905-1995
  Obituary **1995**:3
Furman, Rosemary
  Brief entry **1986**:4
Garrison, Jim 1922-1992
  Obituary **1993**:2
Ginsburg, Ruth Bader 1933- **1993**:4
Giuliani, Rudolph 1944- **1994**:2
Glasser, Ira 1938- **1989**:1
Gore, Albert, Sr. 1907-1998
  Obituary **1999**:2
Grace, Nancy 1959- **2012**:4
Grisham, John 1955- **1994**:4
Harvard, Beverly 1950- **1995**:2
Hayes, Robert M. 1952- **1986**:3
Hill, Anita 1956- **1994**:1
Hills, Carla 1934- **1990**:3
Hirschhorn, Joel
  Brief entry **1986**:1
Hoffa, Jim, Jr. 1941- **1999**:2
Hyatt, Joel 1950- **1985**:3
Ireland, Patricia 1946(?)- **1992**:2
Ito, Lance 1950(?)- **1995**:3
Janklow, Morton 1930- **1989**:3
Kennedy, John F., Jr. 1960-1999 **1990**
:1
  Obituary **1999**:4
Kennedy, Weldon 1938- **1997**:3
Kunstler, William 1919-1995
  Obituary **1996**:1
Kunstler, William 1920(?)- **1992**:3
Kurzban, Ira 1949- **1987**:2
Lee, Henry C. 1938- **1997**:1
Lee, Martin 1938- **1998**:2
Lewis, Loida Nicolas 1942- **1998**:3
Lewis, Reginald F. 1942-1993 **1988**:4
  Obituary **1993**:3
Lightner, Candy 1946- **1985**:1
Liman, Arthur 1932- **1989**:4
Lipsig, Harry H. 1901- **1985**:1
Lipton, Martin 1931- **1987**:3
MacKinnon, Catharine 1946- **1993**:2
Marshall, Thurgood 1908-1993
  Obituary **1993**:3
McCloskey, James 1944(?)- **1993**:1
Mitchell, George J. 1933- **1989**:3
Mitchell, John 1913-1988
  Obituary **1989**:2
Mitchelson, Marvin 1928- **1989**:2
Morrison, Trudi
  Brief entry **1986**:2
Nader, Ralph 1934- **1989**:4
Napolitano, Janet 1957- **1997**:1
Neal, James Foster 1929- **1986**:2
O'Connor, Sandra Day 1930- **1991**:1
O'Leary, Hazel 1937- **1993**:4
O'Steen, Van
  Brief entry **1986**:3
Panetta, Leon 1938- **1995**:1
Pirro, Jeanine 1951- **1998**:2
Powell, Lewis F. 1907-1998
  Obituary **1999**:1
Puccio, Thomas P. 1944- **1986**:4

Quayle, Dan 1947- **1989**:2
Raines, Franklin 1949- **1997**:4
Ramaphosa, Cyril 1953- **1988**:2
Ramo, Roberta Cooper 1942- **1996**:1
Rehnquist, William H. 1924- **2001**:2
Reno, Janet 1938- **1993**:3
Rothwax, Harold 1930- **1996**:3
Scalia, Antonin 1936- **1988**:2
Scheck, Barry 1949- **2000**:4
Schily, Otto
  Brief entry **1987**:4
Sheehan, Daniel P. 1945(?)- **1989**:1
Sheindlin, Judith 1942(?)- **1999**:1
Sirica, John 1904-1992
  Obituary **1993**:2
Skinner, Sam 1938- **1992**:3
Slater, Rodney E. 1955- **1997**:4
Slotnick, Barry
  Brief entry **1987**:4
Souter, David 1939- **1991**:3
Spitzer, Eliot 1959- **2007**:2
Spitzer, Silda Wall 1957- **2010**:2
Starr, Kenneth 1946- **1998**:3
Steinberg, Leigh 1949- **1987**:3
Stern, David 1942- **1991**:4
Stewart, Potter 1915-1985
  Obituary **1986**:1
Strauss, Robert 1918- **1991**:4
Tagliabue, Paul 1940- **1990**:2
Thomas, Clarence 1948- **1992**:2
Thompson, Fred 1942- **1998**:2
Tribe, Laurence H. 1941- **1988**:1
Udall, Stewart 1920-2010
  Obituary **2012**:3
Vincent, Fay 1938- **1990**:2
Violet, Arlene 1943- **1985**:3
Wapner, Joseph A. 1919- **1987**:1
Watson, Elizabeth 1949- **1991**:2
White, Byron 1917-2002
  Obituary **2003**:3
Williams, Edward Bennett 1920-1988
  Obituary **1988**:4
Williams, Willie L. 1944(?)- **1993**:1
Wilson, Bertha
  Brief entry **1986**:1
Yudof, Mark 1944- **2009**:4

MUSIC

Aaliyah 1979-2001 **2001**:3
Abdul, Paula 1962- **1990**:3
AC/DC Grammy Awards- **2011**:2
Ackerman, Will 1949- **1987**:4
Acuff, Roy 1903-1992
  Obituary **1993**:2
Adams, Yolanda 1961- **2008**:2
Adele 1988- **2009**:4
Adkins, Trace 1962- **2012**:1
AFI **2007**:3
Aguilera, Christina 1980- **2000**:4
Akon 1973- **2012**:1
Albert, Stephen 1941- **1986**:1
Allen, Peter 1944-1992
  Obituary **1993**:1
Alsop, Marin 1956- **2008**:3
Ames, Roger 1950(?)- **2005**:2
Amos, Tori 1963- **1995**:1
Anderson, Marion 1897-1993
  Obituary **1993**:4
Andrews, Julie 1935- **1996**:1
Andrews, Maxene 1916-1995
  Obituary **1996**:2
Anthony, Marc 1969- **2000**:3

Apple, Fiona 1977- **2006**:3
Arcade Fire 1982- **2012**:2
Arlen, Harold 1905-1986
  Obituary **1986**:3
Arnaz, Desi 1917-1986
  Obituary **1987**:1
Arnold, Eddy 1918-2008
  Obituary **2009**:2
Arrau, Claudio 1903-1991
  Obituary **1992**:1
Arrested Development **1994**:2
Ashanti 1980- **2004**:1
Asheton, Ron 1948-2009
  Obituary **2010**:1
Astaire, Fred 1899-1987
  Obituary **1987**:4
Auerbach, Dan 1979-. See The Black
  Keys
Autry, Gene 1907-1998
  Obituary **1999**:1
Backstreet Boys **2001**:3
Badu, Erykah 1971- **2000**:4
Baez, Joan 1941- **1998**:3
Bailey, Pearl 1918-1990
  Obituary **1991**:1
Baker, Anita 1958- **1987**:4
Barenboim, Daniel 1942- **2001**:1
Barrett, Syd 1946-2006
  Obituary **2007**:3
Bartoli, Cecilia 1966- **1994**:1
Basie, Count 1904(?)-1984
  Obituary **1985**:1
Battle, Kathleen 1948- **1998**:1
Beastie Boys, The **1999**:1
Becaud, Gilbert 1927-2001
  Obituary **2003**:1
Beck 1970- **2000**:2
Beck, Jeff 1944- **2011**:4
Bee Gees, The **1997**:4
Benatar, Pat 1953- **1986**:1
Bennett, Tony 1926- **1994**:4
Bentley, Dierks 1975- **2007**:3
Berio, Luciano 1925-2003
  Obituary **2004**:2
Berlin, Irving 1888-1989
  Obituary **1990**:1
Bernhard, Sandra 1955(?)- **1989**:4
Bernstein, Elmer 1922-2004
  Obituary **2005**:4
Bernstein, Leonard 1918-1990
  Obituary **1991**:1
Berry, Chuck 1926- **2001**:2
Beyonce 1981- **2009**:3
Bieber, Justin 1994- **2012**:2
Bjork 1965- **1996**:1
Black Eyed Peas **2006**:2
The Black Keys **2012**:4
Blades, Ruben 1948- **1998**:2
Blakey, Art 1919-1990
  Obituary **1991**:1
Blige, Mary J. 1971- **1995**:3
Bogle, Bob 1934-2009
  Obituary **2010**:3
Bolton, Michael 1953(?)- **1993**:2
Bon Jovi, Jon 1962- **1987**:4
Bono 1960- **1988**:4
Bono, Sonny 1935-1998 **1992**:2
  Obituary **1998**:2
Borge, Victor 1909-2000
  Obituary **2001**:3
Botstein, Leon 1946- **1985**:3
Bowie, David 1947- **1998**:2

Bandaranaike, Sirimavo 1916-2000
Obituary **2001**:2
Barak, Ehud 1942- **1999**:4
Barbie, Klaus 1913-1991
Obituary **1992**:2
Basescu, Traian 1951- **2006**:2
Begin, Menachem 1913-1992
Obituary **1992**:3
Berger, Oscar 1946- **2004**:4
Berlusconi, Silvio 1936(?)- **1994**:4
Berri, Nabih 1939(?)- **1985**:2
Betancourt, Ingrid 1961- **2012**:1
Bhutto, Benazir 1953- **1989**:4
Biya, Paul 1933- **2006**:1
Blair, Tony 1953- **1996**:3
Bolkiah, Sultan Muda Hassanal
1946- **1985**:4
Botha, P. W. 1916-2006
Obituary **2008**:1
Bouchard, Lucien 1938- **1999**:2
Bourassa, Robert 1933-1996
Obituary **1997**:1
Bouteflika, Abdelaziz 1937- **2010**:2
Bozize, Francois 1946- **2006**:3
Brandt, Willy 1913-1992
Obituary **1993**:2
Brown, Gordon 1951- **2008**:3
Brundtland, Gro Harlem 1939- **2000**
:1
Buthelezi, Mangosuthu Gatsha
1928- **1989**:3
Caldera, Rafael 1916-2009
Obituary **2011**:4
Calderon, Felipe 1962- **2012**:2
Cameron, David 1966- **2012**:1
Campbell, Kim 1947- **1993**:4
Cardoso, Fernando Henrique 1931-
1996:4
Castro, Fidel 1926- **1991**:4
Castro, Raúl 1931- **2010**:2
Catherine, Duchess of Cambridge
1982- **2012**:2
Cavaco Silva, Anibal 1939- **2011**:3
Ceausescu, Nicolae 1918-1989
Obituary **1990**:2
Cedras, Raoul 1950- **1994**:4
Chaing Kai-Shek, Madame
1898-2003
Obituary **2005**:1
Chambas, Mohammed ibn 1950-
2003:3
Chavez, Hugo 1954- **2010**:4
Chen Shui-bian 1950(?)- **2001**:2
Chernenko, Konstantin 1911-1985
Obituary **1985**:1
Chiluba, Frederick 1943- **1992**:3
Chinchilla, Laura 1959- **2012**:2
Chirac, Jacques 1932- **1995**:4
Chissano, Joaquim 1939- **1987**:4
Chretien, Jean 1934- **1990**:4
Ciampi, Carlo Azeglio 1920- **2004**:3
Collor de Mello, Fernando 1949-
1992:4
Colosio, Luis Donaldo 1950-1994
1994:3
Copps, Sheila 1952- **1986**:4
Correa, Rafael 1963- **2008**:1
Cresson, Edith 1934- **1992**:1
Cruz, Arturo 1923- **1985**:1
Dalai Lama 1935- **1989**:1
Deby, Idriss 1952- **2002**:2
de Hoop Scheffer, Jaap 1948- **2005**:1

de Klerk, F.W. 1936- **1990**:1
Delors, Jacques 1925- **1990**:2
Deng Xiaoping 1904-1997 **1995**:1
Obituary **1997**:3
de Pinies, Jamie
Brief entry **1986**:3
Devi, Phoolan 1955(?)- **1986**:1
Obituary **2002**:3
Dhlakama, Afonso 1953- **1993**:3
Doe, Samuel 1952-1990
Obituary **1991**:1
Doi, Takako
Brief entry **1987**:4
Dong, Pham Van 1906-2000
Obituary **2000**:4
Duarte, Jose Napoleon 1925-1990
Obituary **1990**:3
Dubinin, Yuri 1930- **1987**:4
Duhalde, Eduardo 1941- **2003**:3
Ecevit, Bulent 1925-2006
Obituary **2008**:1
Enkhbayar, Nambaryn 1958- **2007**:1
Erdogan, Recep Tayyip 1954- **2012**:3
Fahd, King of Saudi Arabia
1923(?)-2005
Obituary **2006**:4
Ferguson, Sarah 1959- **1990**:3
Fernández, Leonel 1953- **2009**:2
Fernández de Kirchner, Cristina
1953- **2009**:1
Finnbogadoaattir, Vigdiaas
Brief entry **1986**:2
Fischer, Joschka 1948- **2005**:2
Fox, Vicente 1942- **2001**:1
Freij, Elias 1920- **1986**:4
Fujimori, Alberto 1938- **1992**:4
Galvin, Martin
Brief entry **1985**:3
Gandhi, Indira 1917-1984
Obituary **1985**:1
Gandhi, Rajiv 1944-1991
Obituary **1991**:4
Gandhi, Sonia 1947- **2000**:2
Garcia, Alan 1949- **2007**:4
Garcia, Amalia 1951- **2005**:3
Garneau, Marc 1949- **1985**:1
Gbagbo, Laurent 1945- **2003**:2
Ghali, Boutros Boutros 1922- **1992**:3
Gillard, Julia 1961- **2011**:4
Gorbachev, Mikhail 1931- **1985**:2
Gorbachev, Raisa 1932-1999
Obituary **2000**:2
Gowda, H. D. Deve 1933- **1997**:1
Gromyko, Andrei 1909-1989
Obituary **1990**:2
Guebuza, Armando 1943- **2008**:4
Guelleh, Ismail Omar 1947- **2006**:2
Gul, Abdullah 1950- **2009**:4
Habash, George 1925(?)- **1986**:1
Habibie, Bacharuddin Jusuf 1936-
1999:3
Halonen, Tarja 1943- **2006**:4
Hani, Chris 1942-1993
Obituary **1993**:4
Harper, Stephen J. 1959- **2007**:3
Harriman, Pamela 1920- **1994**:4
Harris, Michael Deane 1945- **1997**:2
Havel, Vaclav 1936- **1990**:3
Herzog, Chaim 1918-1997
Obituary **1997**:3
Hess, Rudolph 1894-1987
Obituary **1988**:1

Hillery, Patrick 1923-2008
Obituary **2009**:2
Hirohito, Emperor of Japan
1901-1989
Obituary **1989**:2
Honecker, Erich 1912-1994
Obituary **1994**:4
Hosokawa, Morihiro 1938- **1994**:1
Hua Guofeng 1921-2008
Obituary **2009**:4
Hu Jintao 1942- **2004**:1
Hume, John 1938- **1987**:1
Hussein, Saddam 1937- **1991**:1
Husseini, Faisal 1940- **1998**:4
Hussein I, King 1935-1999 **1997**:3
Obituary **1999**:3
Hu Yaobang 1915-1989
Obituary **1989**:4
Ilves, Toomas Hendrik 1953- **2007**:4
Izetbegovic, Alija 1925- **1996**:4
Jagdeo, Bharrat 1964- **2008**:1
Jenkins, Roy Harris 1920-2003
Obituary **2004**:1
Jiang Quing 1914-1991
Obituary **1992**:1
Jiang Zemin 1926- **1996**:1
Johnson, Pierre Marc 1946- **1985**:4
Juan Carlos I 1938- **1993**:1
Juliana 1909-2004
Obituary **2005**:3
Jumblatt, Walid 1949(?)- **1987**:4
Juneau, Pierre 1922- **1988**:3
Kabila, Joseph 1971- **2003**:2
Kabila, Laurent 1939- **1998**:1
Obituary **2001**:3
Kaczynski, Lech 1949- **2007**:2
Kagame, Paul 1957- **2001**:4
Kamel, Hussein 1954- **1996**:1
Karadzic, Radovan 1945- **1995**:3
Karamanlis, Costas 1956- **2009**:1
Karimov, Islam 1938- **2006**:3
Karzai, Hamid 1955(?)- **2002**:3
Kasyanov, Mikhail 1957- **2001**:1
Kekkonen, Urho 1900-1986
Obituary **1986**:4
Key, John 1961- **2012**:3
Khatami, Mohammed 1943- **1997**:4
Khomeini, Ayatollah Ruhollah
1900(?)-1989
Obituary **1989**:4
Kibaki, Mwai 1931- **2003**:4
Kim Dae Jung 1925- **1998**:3
Kim Il Sung 1912-1994
Obituary **1994**:4
Kim Jong Il 1942- **1995**:2
King Hassan II 1929-1999
Obituary **2000**:1
Kohl, Helmut 1930- **1994**:1
Koizumi, Junichiro 1942- **2002**:1
Kostunica, Vojislav 1944- **2001**:1
Kouchner, Bernard 1939- **2005**:3
Kufuor, John Agyekum 1938- **2005**:4
Kyprianou, Spyros 1932-2002
Obituary **2003**:2
Lagarde, Christine 1956- **2012**:4
Lagos, Ricardo 1938- **2005**:3
Lalonde, Marc 1929- **1985**:1
Landsbergis, Vytautas 1932- **1991**:3
Lebed, Alexander 1950- **1997**:1
Le Duan 1908(?)-1986
Obituary **1986**:4
Le Duc Tho 1911-1990

Yanukovych, Viktor 1950- **2011**:4
Yar'Adua, Umaru 1951- **2008**:3
Ye Jianying 1897-1986
  Obituary **1987**:1
Yeltsin, Boris 1931- **1991**:1
Yudhoyono, Susilo 1949- **2009**:4
Yushchenko, Viktor 1954- **2006**:1
Zedillo, Ernesto 1951- **1995**:1
Zeroual, Liamine 1951- **1996**:2
Zhao Ziyang 1919- **1989**:1
Zhirinovsky, Vladimir 1946- **1994**:2
Zia ul-Haq, Mohammad 1924-1988
  Obituary **1988**:4
Zuma, Jacob 1942- **2012**:1

POLITICS AND GOVERNMENT--U.S.
Abraham, Spencer 1952- **1991**:4
Abrams, Elliott 1948- **1987**:1
Abzug, Bella 1920-1998 **1998**:2
Achtenberg, Roberta **1993**:4
Agnew, Spiro Theodore 1918-1996
  Obituary **1997**:1
Ailes, Roger 1940- **1989**:3
Albright, Madeleine 1937- **1994**:3
Alexander, Lamar 1940- **1991**:2
Alioto, Joseph L. 1916-1998
  Obituary **1998**:3
Allen Jr., Ivan 1911-2003
  Obituary **2004**:3
Allison, Jr., Herbert M. 1943- **2010**:2
Alvarez, Aida **1999**:2
Archer, Dennis 1942- **1994**:4
Armstrong, Anne 1927-2008
  Obituary **2009**:4
Ashcroft, John 1942- **2002**:4
Aspin, Les 1938-1995
  Obituary **1996**:1
Atwater, Lee 1951-1991 **1989**:4
  Obituary **1991**:4
Babbitt, Bruce 1938- **1994**:1
Bair, Sheila 1954- **2011**:4
Baker, James A. III 1930- **1991**:2
Baldrige, Malcolm 1922-1987
  Obituary **1988**:1
Banks, Dennis J. 1932(?)- **1986**:4
Barnes, Melody 1964- **2011**:1
Barry, Marion 1936- **1991**:1
Barshefsky, Charlene 1951(?)- **2000**:4
Bass, Karen 1953- **2009**:3
Beame, Abraham 1906-2001
  Obituary **2001**:4
Begaye, Kelsey 1950(?)- **1999**:3
Benjamin, Regina 1956- **2011**:2
Bennett, William 1943- **1990**:1
Benson, Ezra Taft 1899-1994
  Obituary **1994**:4
Bentsen, Lloyd 1921- **1993**:3
Berger, Sandy 1945- **2000**:1
Berle, Peter A.A.
  Brief entry **1987**:3
Bernanke, Ben 1953- **2008**:3
Biden, Joe 1942- **1986**:3
Boehner, John A. 1949- **2006**:4
Bonner, Robert 1942(?)- **2003**:4
Bono, Sonny 1935-1998 **1992**:2
  Obituary **1998**:2
Boxer, Barbara 1940- **1995**:1
Boyington, Gregory Pappy
  1912-1988
  Obituary **1988**:2
Bradley, Bill 1943- **2000**:2
Bradley, Tom 1917-1998

Obituary **1999**:1
Brady, Sarah and James S. **1991**:4
Braun, Carol Moseley 1947- **1993**:1
Brazile, Donna 1959- **2001**:1
Bremer, L. Paul 1941- **2004**:2
Brennan, William 1906-1997
  Obituary **1997**:4
Brewer, Jan 1944- **2011**:4
Brown, Edmund G., Sr. 1905-1996
  Obituary **1996**:3
Brown, Jerry 1938- **1992**:4
Brown, Ron 1941- **1990**:3
Brown, Ron 1941-1996
  Obituary **1996**:4
Brown, Scott 1959- **2011**:3
Brown, Willie 1934- **1996**:4
Brown, Willie L. 1934- **1985**:2
Browner, Carol M. 1955- **1994**:1
Buchanan, Pat 1938- **1996**:3
Bundy, McGeorge 1919-1996
  Obituary **1997**:1
Bundy, William P. 1917-2000
  Obituary **2001**:2
Bush, Barbara 1925- **1989**:3
Bush, George W., Jr. 1946- **1996**:4
Bush, Jeb 1953- **2003**:1
Butts, Cassandra 1965- **2011**:2
Byrd, Robert C. 1917-2010
  Obituary **2012**:4
Caliguiri, Richard S. 1931-1988
  Obituary **1988**:3
Campbell, Ben Nighthorse 1933-
  1998:1
Campbell, Bill **1997**:1
Card, Andrew H., Jr. 1947- **2003**:2
Carey, Ron 1936- **1993**:3
Carmona, Richard 1949- **2003**:2
Carnahan, Jean 1933- **2001**:2
Carnahan, Mel 1934-2000
  Obituary **2001**:2
Carter, Billy 1937-1988
  Obituary **1989**:1
Carter, Jimmy 1924- **1995**:1
Casey, William 1913-1987
  Obituary **1987**:3
Cavazos, Lauro F. 1927- **1989**:2
Chamberlin, Wendy 1948- **2002**:4
Chao, Elaine L. 1953- **2007**:3
Chavez, Linda 1947- **1999**:3
Chavez-Thompson, Linda 1944-
  1999:1
Cheney, Dick 1941- **1991**:3
Cheney, Lynne V. 1941- **1990**:4
Chisholm, Shirley 1924-2005
  Obituary **2006**:1
Christie, Chris 1962- **2011**:1
Christopher, Warren 1925- **1996**:3
Chu, Steven 1948- **2010**:3
Cisneros, Henry 1947- **1987**:2
Clark, J. E.
  Brief entry **1986**:1
Clinton, Bill 1946- **1992**:1
Clinton, Hillary Rodham 1947- **1993**
  :2
Clyburn, James 1940- **1999**:4
Cohen, William S. 1940- **1998**:1
Collins, Cardiss 1931- **1995**:3
Connally, John 1917-1993
  Obituary **1994**:1
Conyers, John, Jr. 1929- **1999**:1
Cornum, Rhonda 1954- **2006**:3
Cuomo, Andrew 1957- **2011**:1

Cuomo, Mario 1932- **1992**:2
D'Amato, Al 1937- **1996**:1
Daschle, Tom 1947- **2002**:3
Dayton, Mark 1947- **2012**:3
Dean, Howard 1948- **2005**:4
DeLay, Tom 1947- **2000**:1
Dinkins, David N. 1927- **1990**:2
Dolan, Terry 1950-1986 **1985**:2
Dole, Bob 1923- **1994**:2
Dole, Elizabeth Hanford 1936- **1990**
  :1
Donovan, Shaun 1966- **2010**:4
Dukakis, Michael 1933- **1988**:3
Duke, David 1951(?)- **1990**:2
Duncan, Arne 1964- **2011**:3
Dunwoody, Ann 1953- **2009**:2
Ehrlichman, John 1925-1999
  Obituary **1999**:3
Elders, Joycelyn 1933- **1994**:1
Emanuel, Rahm 1959- **2011**:2
Engler, John 1948- **1996**:3
Ervin, Sam 1896-1985
  Obituary **1985**:2
Estrich, Susan 1953- **1989**:1
Falkenberg, Nanette 1951- **1985**:2
Farmer, James 1920-1999
  Obituary **2000**:1
Farrakhan, Louis 1933- **1990**:4
Faubus, Orval 1910-1994
  Obituary **1995**:2
Feinstein, Dianne 1933- **1993**:3
Felt, W. Mark 1913-2008
  Obituary **2010**:1
Fenwick, Millicent H.
  Obituary **1993**:2
Ferraro, Geraldine 1935- **1998**:3
Fish, Hamilton 1888-1991
  Obituary **1991**:3
Fitzgerald, A. Ernest 1926- **1986**:2
Fleischer, Ari 1960- **2003**:1
Florio, James J. 1937- **1991**:2
Flynn, Ray 1939- **1989**:1
Foley, Thomas S. 1929- **1990**:1
Forbes, Steve 1947- **1996**:2
Ford, Gerald R. 1913-2007
  Obituary **2008**:2
Foster, Vincent 1945(?)-1993
  Obituary **1994**:1
Frank, Anthony M. 1931(?)- **1992**:1
Frank, Barney 1940- **1989**:2
Franks, Tommy 1945- **2004**:1
Frist, Bill 1952- **2003**:4
Fulbright, J. William 1905-1995
  Obituary **1995**:3
Galvin, John R. 1929- **1990**:1
Garrison, Jim 1922-1992
  Obituary **1993**:2
Gates, Robert M. 1943- **1992**:2
Gebbie, Kristine 1944(?)- **1994**:2
Geithner, Timothy F. 1961- **2009**:4
Gephardt, Richard 1941- **1987**:3
Gergen, David 1942- **1994**:1
Giffords, Gabrielle 1970- **2012**:3
Gingrich, Newt 1943- **1991**:1
Giuliani, Rudolph 1944- **1994**:2
Glenn, John 1921- **1998**:3
Goldwater, Barry 1909-1998
  Obituary **1998**:4
Gore, Albert, Jr. 1948(?)- **1993**:2
Gore, Albert, Sr. 1907-1998
  Obituary **1999**:2
Gramm, Phil 1942- **1995**:2

Roosevelt, Franklin D., Jr. 1914-1988
  Obituary **1989**:1
Ros-Lehtinen, Ileana 1952- **2000**:2
Roth, William Victor, Jr. 1921-2003
  Obituary **2005**:1
Rotherham, Andrew 1971- **2012**:4
Rove, Karl 1950- **2006**:2
Roybal-Allard, Lucille 1941- **1999**:4
Rumsfeld, Donald 1932- **2004**:1
Rusk, Dean 1909-1994
  Obituary **1995**:2
Salazar, Ken 1955- **2011**:4
Sanchez, Loretta 1960- **2000**:3
Sanders, Bernie 1941(?)- **1991**:4
Satcher, David 1941- **2001**:4
Scalia, Antonin 1936- **1988**:2
Schaefer, William Donald 1921- **1988**
:1
Schapiro, Mary 1955- **2012**:1
Schiavo, Mary 1955- **1998**:2
Schwarzenegger, Arnold 1947- **1991**
:1
Schwarzkopf, Norman 1934- **1991**:3
Sebelius, Kathleen 1948- **2008**:4
Senghor, Leopold 1906-2001
  Obituary **2003**:1
Shalikashvili, John 1936- **1994**:2
Sheehan, Daniel P. 1945(?)- **1989**:1
Sidney, Ivan
  Brief entry **1987**:2
Sigmund, Barbara Boggs 1939-1990
  Obituary **1991**:1
Simon, Paul 1928-2003
  Obituary **2005**:1
Simpson, Alan 1931- **2012**:4
Skinner, Sam 1938- **1992**:3
Slater, Rodney E. 1955- **1997**:4
Snow, John W. 1939- **2006**:2
Snow, Tony 1955-2008
  Obituary **2009**:3
Snowe, Olympia 1947- **1995**:3
Solis, Hilda 1957- **2010**:1
Sotomayor, Sonia 1954- **2010**:4
Spellings, Margaret 1957- **2005**:4
Spitzer, Eliot 1959- **2007**:2
Starr, Kenneth 1946- **1998**:3
Steele, Michael 1958- **2010**:2
Stephanopoulos, George 1961- **1994**
:3
Stevens, Ted 1923-2010
  Obituary **2012**:4
Stewart, Potter 1915-1985
  Obituary **1986**:1
Stokes, Carl 1927-1996
  Obituary **1996**:4
Strauss, Robert 1918- **1991**:4
Suarez, Xavier
  Brief entry **1986**:2
Sullivan, Louis 1933- **1990**:4
Sununu, John 1939- **1989**:2
Sutphen, Mona 1967- **2010**:4
Sutton, Percy 1920-2009
  Obituary **2011**:4
Swift, Jane 1965(?)- **2002**:1
Taylor, Maxwell 1901-1987
  Obituary **1987**:3
Tenet, George 1953- **2000**:3
Thomas, Clarence 1948- **1992**:2
Thomas, Edmond J. 1943(?)- **2005**:1
Thomas, Helen 1920- **1988**:4
Thompson, Fred 1942- **1998**:2
Thurmond, Strom 1902-2003

  Obituary **2004**:3
Tower, John 1926-1991
  Obituary **1991**:4
Townsend, Kathleen Kennedy 1951-
2001:3
Tsongas, Paul Efthemios 1941-1997
  Obituary **1997**:2
Tutwiler, Margaret 1950- **1992**:4
Tyson, Laura D'Andrea 1947- **1994**:1
Udall, Mo 1922-1998
  Obituary **1999**:2
Udall, Stewart 1920-2010
  Obituary **2012**:3
Ventura, Jesse 1951- **1999**:2
Vilsack, Tom 1950- **2011**:1
Violet, Arlene 1943- **1985**:3
Walker, Scott 1967- **2012**:2
Wallace, George 1919-1998
  Obituary **1999**:1
Washington, Harold 1922-1987
  Obituary **1988**:1
Waters, Maxine 1938- **1998**:4
Watts, J.C. 1957- **1999**:2
Webb, Wellington E. 1941- **2000**:3
Weicker, Lowell P., Jr. 1931- **1993**:1
Weinberger, Caspar 1917-2006
  Obituary **2007**:2
Wellstone, Paul 1944-2002
  Obituary **2004**:1
Westmoreland, William C. 1914-2005
  Obituary **2006**:4
Whitman, Christine Todd 1947(?)-
1994:3
Whitmire, Kathy 1946- **1988**:2
Wilder, L. Douglas 1931- **1990**:3
Williams, Anthony 1952- **2000**:4
Williams, G. Mennen 1911-1988
  Obituary **1988**:2
Wilson, Pete 1933- **1992**:3
Yard, Molly **1991**:4
Young, Coleman A. 1918-1997
  Obituary **1998**:1
Zech, Lando W.
  Brief entry **1987**:4
Zerhouni, Elias A. 1951- **2004**:3
Zinni, Anthony 1943- **2003**:1

RADIO

Adams, Yolanda 1961- **2008**:2
Albert, Marv 1943- **1994**:3
Albom, Mitch 1958- **1999**:3
Ameche, Don 1908-1993
  Obituary **1994**:2
Autry, Gene 1907-1998
  Obituary **1999**:1
Backus, Jim 1913-1989
  Obituary **1990**:1
Barber, Red 1908-1992
  Obituary **1993**:2
Becker, Brian 1957(?)- **2004**:4
Bell, Art 1945- **2000**:1
Bergeron, Tom 1955- **2010**:1
Blanc, Mel 1908-1989
  Obituary **1989**:4
Campbell, Bebe Moore 1950- **1996**:2
Caray, Harry 1914(?)-1998 **1988**:3
  Obituary **1998**:3
Carson, Johnny 1925-2005
  Obituary **2006**:1
Cherry, Don 1934- **1993**:4
Codrescu, Andreaa 1946- **1997**:3
Cosell, Howard 1918-1995

  Obituary **1995**:4
Costas, Bob 1952- **1986**:4
Crenna, Richard 1926-2003
  Obituary **2004**:1
Day, Dennis 1917-1988
  Obituary **1988**:4
Denver, Bob 1935-2005
  Obituary **2006**:4
Donnellan, Nanci **1995**:2
Douglas, Mike 1925-2006
  Obituary **2007**:4
Dr. Demento 1941- **1986**:1
Durrell, Gerald 1925-1995
  Obituary **1995**:3
Edwards, Bob 1947- **1993**:2
Fleming, Art 1925(?)-1995
  Obituary **1995**:4
Ford, Tennessee Ernie 1919-1991
  Obituary **1992**:2
Glass, Ira 1959- **2008**:2
Gobel, George 1920(?)-1991
  Obituary **1991**:4
Goodman, Benny 1909-1986
  Obituary **1986**:3
Gordon, Gale 1906-1995
  Obituary **1996**:1
Graham, Billy 1918- **1992**:1
Granato, Cammi 1971- **1999**:3
Grange, Red 1903-1991
  Obituary **1991**:3
Greene, Lorne 1915-1987
  Obituary **1988**:1
Griffin, Merv 1925-2008
  Obituary **2008**:4
Gross, Terry 1951- **1998**:3
Harmon, Tom 1919-1990
  Obituary **1990**:3
Harvey, Paul 1918- **1995**:3
Harvey, Steve 1956- **2010**:1
Harwell, Ernie 1918- **1997**:3
Hill, George Roy 1921-2002
  Obituary **2004**:1
Hollander, Joel 1956(?)- **2006**:4
Hope, Bob 1903-2003
  Obituary **2004**:4
Houseman, John 1902-1988
  Obituary **1989**:1
Hughes, Cathy 1947- **1999**:1
Imus, Don 1940- **1997**:1
Ives, Burl 1909-1995
  Obituary **1995**:4
Karmazin, Mel 1943- **2006**:1
Kasem, Casey 1933(?)- **1987**:1
Keillor, Garrison 1942- **2011**:2
Keyes, Alan 1950- **1996**:2
Kimmel, Jimmy 1967- **2009**:2
King, Larry 1933- **1993**:1
Kyser, Kay 1906(?)-1985
  Obituary **1985**:3
Leaavesque, Reneaa
  Obituary **1988**:1
Limbaugh, Rush **1991**:3
Linkletter, Art 1912-2010
  Obituary **2012**:4
Magliozzi, Tom and Ray **1991**:4
Milligan, Spike 1918-2002
  Obituary **2003**:2
Nelson, Harriet 1909(?)-1994
  Obituary **1995**:1
Olbermann, Keith 1959- **2010**:3
Olson, Johnny 1910(?)-1985
  Obituary **1985**:4

Osgood, Charles 1933- **1996**:2
Paar, Jack 1918-2004
  Obituary **2005**:2
Paley, William S. 1901-1990
  Obituary **1991**:2
Parks, Bert 1914-1992
  Obituary **1992**:3
Parsons, Gary 1950(?)- **2006**:2
Pinsky, Drew 1958- **2012**:2
Porter, Sylvia 1913-1991
  Obituary **1991**:4
Quivers, Robin 1953(?)- **1995**:4
Raphael, Sally Jessy 1943- **1992**:4
Raye, Martha 1916-1994
  Obituary **1995**:1
Reagan, Ronald 1911-2004
  Obituary **2005**:3
Riddle, Nelson 1921-1985
  Obituary **1985**:4
Roberts, Cokie 1943- **1993**:4
Rollins, Henry 1961- **2007**:3
Sales, Soupy 1926-2009
  Obituary **2011**:2
Saralegui, Cristina 1948- **1999**:2
Schlessinger, Laura 1947(?)- **1996**:3
Seacrest, Ryan 1976- **2004**:4
Sedaris, David 1956- **2005**:3
Sevareid, Eric 1912-1992
  Obituary **1993**:1
Shore, Dinah 1917-1994
  Obituary **1994**:3
Smith, Buffalo Bob 1917-1998
  Obituary **1999**:1
Smith, Kate 1907(?)-1986
  Obituary **1986**:3
Stern, Howard 1954- **1988**:2
Swayze, John Cameron 1906-1995
  Obituary **1996**:1
Terkel, Studs 1912-2008
  Obituary **2010**:1
Toguri, Iva 1916-2006
  Obituary **2007**:4
Tom and Ray Magliozzi **1991**:4
Totenberg, Nina 1944- **1992**:2
Westergren, Tim 1965- **2012**:2
White, Betty 1922- **2012**:1
Wolfman Jack 1938-1995
  Obituary **1996**:1
Young, Robert 1907-1998
  Obituary **1999**:1

RELIGION
Abernathy, Ralph 1926-1990
  Obituary **1990**:3
Altea, Rosemary 1946- **1996**:3
Applewhite, Marshall Herff
  1931-1997
  Obituary **1997**:3
Aristide, Jean-Bertrand 1953- **1991**:3
Beckett, Wendy (Sister) 1930- **1998**:3
Benson, Ezra Taft 1899-1994
  Obituary **1994**:4
Bernardin, Cardinal Joseph
  1928-1996 **1997**:2
Berri, Nabih 1939(?)- **1985**:2
Browning, Edmond
  Brief entry **1986**:2
Burns, Charles R.
  Brief entry **1988**:1
Carey, George 1935- **1992**:3
Chavis, Benjamin 1948- **1993**:4
Chittister, Joan D. 1936- **2002**:2

Chopra, Deepak 1947- **1996**:3
Clements, George 1932- **1985**:1
Cleveland, James 1932(?)-1991
  Obituary **1991**:3
Coffin, William Sloane, Jr. 1924- **1990**
  :3
Cunningham, Reverend William
  1930-1997
  Obituary **1997**:4
Curran, Charles E. 1934- **1989**:2
Daily, Bishop Thomas V. 1927- **1990**
  :4
Dalai Lama 1935- **1989**:1
Daly, Mary 1928-2010
  Obituary **2012**:1
Dearden, John Cardinal 1907-1988
  Obituary **1988**:4
Dorsey, Thomas A. 1899-1993
  Obituary **1993**:3
Eilberg, Amy
  Brief entry **1985**:3
Falwell, Jerry 1933-2007
  Obituary **2008**:3
Farrakhan, Louis 1933- **1990**:4
Fox, Matthew 1940- **1992**:2
Fulghum, Robert 1937- **1996**:1
Gottschalk, Alfred 1930-2009
  Obituary **2011**:1
Graham, Billy 1918- **1992**:1
Grant, Amy 1961(?)- **1985**:4
Hahn, Jessica 1960- **1989**:4
Harris, Barbara **1996**:3
Harris, Barbara 1930- **1989**:3
Healy, Timothy S. 1923- **1990**:2
Henry, Carl F.H. 1913-2003
  Obituary **2005**:1
Huffington, Arianna 1950- **1996**:2
Hume, Basil Cardinal 1923-1999
  Obituary **2000**:1
Hunter, Howard 1907- **1994**:4
Hybels, Bill 1951- **2011**:1
Irwin, James 1930-1991
  Obituary **1992**:1
Jackson, Jesse 1941- **1996**:1
Jefferts Schori, Katharine 1954- **2007**
  :2
John Paul II, Pope 1920- **1995**:3
Jumblatt, Walid 1949(?)- **1987**:4
Kahane, Meir 1932-1990
  Obituary **1991**:2
Khomeini, Ayatollah Ruhollah
  1900(?)-1989
  Obituary **1989**:4
Kissling, Frances 1943- **1989**:2
Koresh, David 1960(?)-1993
  Obituary **1993**:4
Krol, John 1910-1996
  Obituary **1996**:3
Lefebvre, Marcel 1905- **1988**:4
Levinger, Moshe 1935- **1992**:1
Macquarrie, John 1919-2007
  Obituary **2008**:3
Mahesh Yogi, Maharishi 1911(?)-
  1991:3
Mahony, Roger M. 1936- **1988**:2
Maida, Adam Cardinal 1930- **1998**:2
Malloy, Edward Monk 1941- **1989**:4
McCloskey, James 1944(?)- **1993**:1
Morris, Henry M. 1918-2006
  Obituary **2007**:2
Mother Teresa 1910-1997 **1993**:1
  Obituary **1998**:1

Muller, Jim 1943- **2011**:3
Obando, Miguel 1926- **1986**:4
O'Connor, Cardinal John 1920- **1990**
  :3
O'Connor, John 1920-2000
  Obituary **2000**:4
Osteen, Joel 1963- **2006**:2
Patriarch Pavle 1914-2009
  Obituary **2011**:3
Perry, Harold A. 1917(?)-1991
  Obituary **1992**:1
Peter, Valentine J. 1934- **1988**:2
Rafsanjani, Ali Akbar Hashemi
  1934(?)- **1987**:3
Rahman, Sheik Omar Abdel- 1938-
  1993:3
Rajneesh, Bhagwan Shree 1931-1990
  Obituary **1990**:2
Reed, Ralph 1961(?)- **1995**:1
Reese, Della 1931- **1999**:2
Reverend Ike 1935-2009
  Obituary **2010**:4
Roberts, Oral 1918-2009
  Obituary **2011**:4
Robertson, Pat 1930- **1988**:2
Robinson, V. Gene 1947- **2004**:4
Rogers, Adrian 1931- **1987**:4
Rosen, Moishe 1932-2010
  Obituary **2012**:4
Runcie, Robert 1921-2000 **1989**:4
  Obituary **2001**:1
Schneerson, Menachem Mendel
  1902-1994 **1992**:4
  Obituary **1994**:4
Scott, Gene
  Brief entry **1986**:1
Sentamu, John 1949- **2006**:2
Sharpton, Al 1954- **1991**:2
Shaw, William 1934(?)- **2000**:3
Sin, Jaime 1928-2005
  Obituary **2006**:3
Smith, Jeff 1939(?)- **1991**:4
Spong, John 1931- **1991**:3
Stallings, George A., Jr. 1948- **1990**:1
Swaggart, Jimmy 1935- **1987**:3
Taylor, Graham 1958(?)- **2005**:3
Turabi, Hassan 1932(?)- **1995**:4
Violet, Arlene 1943- **1985**:3
Warren, Rick 1954- **2010**:3
Wildmon, Donald 1938- **1988**:4
Williamson, Marianne 1953(?)- **1991**
  :4
Youngblood, Johnny Ray 1948- **1994**
  :1

SCIENCE
Abramson, Lyn 1950- **1986**:3
Adams, Patch 1945(?)- **1999**:2
Adamson, George 1906-1989
  Obituary **1990**:2
Agatston, Arthur 1947- **2005**:1
Allen, John 1930- **1992**:1
Altman, Sidney 1939- **1997**:2
Aronson, Jane 1951- **2009**:3
Atkins, Robert C. 1930-2003
  Obituary **2004**:2
Axelrod, Julius 1912-2004
  Obituary **2006**:1
Bahcall, John N. 1934-2005
  Obituary **2006**:4
Bakker, Robert T. 1950(?)- **1991**:3
Ballard, Robert D. 1942- **1998**:4

SOCIAL ISSUES

Lang, Eugene M. 1919- **1990**:3
Leary, Timothy 1920-1996
    Obituary **1996**:4
Lerner, Sandy 1955(?)- **2005**:1
LeVay, Simon 1943- **1992**:2
Lightner, Candy 1946- **1985**:1
Lines, Ray 1960(?)- **2004**:1
Lipkis, Andy
    Brief entry **1985**:3
Lodge, Henry Cabot 1902-1985
    Obituary **1985**:1
Lord, Bette Bao 1938- **1994**:1
Louv, Richard 1949- **2006**:2
Lowry, Adam and Eric Ryan **2008**:1
Lum, Olivia 1961- **2009**:1
Maathai, Wangari 1940- **2005**:3
Mackey, John 1953- **2008**:2
MacKinnon, Catharine 1946- **1993**:2
Mahony, Roger M. 1936- **1988**:2
Makeba, Miriam 1934- **1989**:2
Mandela, Nelson 1918- **1990**:3
Mandela, Winnie 1934- **1989**:3
Maniscalco, Chuck 1953- **2010**:3
Mankiller, Wilma P.
    Brief entry **1986**:2
Maraldo, Pamela J. 1948(?)- **1993**:4
Marier, Rebecca 1974- **1995**:4
Martinez, Bob 1934- **1992**:1
Mathews, Dan 1965- **1998**:3
Matlovich, Leonard P. 1944(?)-1988
    Obituary **1988**:4
Mauldin, Bill 1921-2003
    Obituary **2004**:2
McCall, Nathan 1955- **1994**:4
McCartney, Bill 1940- **1995**:3
McCloskey, J. Michael 1934- **1988**:2
McDonnell, Patrick 1956- **2009**:4
McGuinness, Martin 1950(?)- **1985**:4
McKinnell, Henry 1943(?)- **2002**:3
McSally, Martha 1966(?)- **2002**:4
McTaggart, David 1932(?)- **1989**:4
McVeigh, Timothy 1968-2001
    Obituary **2002**:2
Menchu, Rigoberta 1960(?)- **1993**:2
Mengele, Josef 1911-1979
    Obituary **1985**:2
Menninger, Karl 1893-1990
    Obituary **1991**:1
Merritt, Justine
    Brief entry **1985**:3
Michelman, Kate 1942- **1998**:4
Monroe, Rose Will 1920-1997
    Obituary **1997**:4
Monsiváis, Carlos 1938-2010
    Obituary **2012**:4
Moose, Charles 1953(?)- **2003**:4
Morgentaler, Henry 1923- **1986**:3
Mortenson, Greg 1957- **2011**:1
Mother Teresa 1910-1997 **1993**:1
    Obituary **1998**:1
Mott, William Penn, Jr. 1909- **1986**:1
Muller, Jim 1943- **2011**:3
Mumford, Lewis 1895-1990
    Obituary **1990**:2
Munter, Leilani 1976- **2010**:4
Mycoskie, Blake 1976- **2012**:4
Nader, Ralph 1934- **1989**:4
Nasrin, Taslima 1962- **1995**:1
Newkirk, Ingrid 1949- **1992**:3
Ngau, Harrison **1991**:3
Nidal, Abu 1937- **1987**:1
Nixon, Bob 1954(?)- **2006**:4

Onysko, Joshua 1978- **2012**:2
Pacelle, Wayne 1965- **2009**:4
Parks, Rosa 1913-2005
    Obituary **2007**:1
Paton, Alan 1903-1988
    Obituary **1988**:3
Peebles, R. Donahue 1960- **2003**:2
Peltier, Leonard 1944- **1995**:1
Pendleton, Clarence M. 1930-1988
    Obituary **1988**:4
Politkovskaya, Anna 1958-2006
    Obituary **2007**:4
Power, Samantha 1970- **2005**:4
Pritzker, A.N. 1896-1986
    Obituary **1986**:2
Puleston, Dennis 1905-2001
    Obituary **2002**:2
Quill, Timothy E. 1949- **1997**:3
Quinlan, Karen Ann 1954-1985
    Obituary **1985**:2
Radecki, Thomas
    Brief entry **1986**:2
Ramaphosa, Cyril 1953- **1988**:2
Redmond, Tim 1947- **2008**:1
Reeve, Christopher 1952- **1997**:2
Rhee, Michelle 1969- **2012**:3
Ross, Percy
    Brief entry **1986**:2
Rothstein, Ruth **1988**:2
Rowley, Coleen 1955(?)- **2004**:2
Rubin, Jerry 1938-1994
    Obituary **1995**:2
Ruppe, Loret Miller 1936- **1986**:2
Sachs, Jeffrey D. 1954- **2004**:4
Sakharov, Andrei Dmitrievich
    1921-1989
    Obituary **1990**:2
Salbi, Zainab 1969(?)- **2008**:3
Sample, Bill
    Brief entry **1986**:2
Sams, Craig 1944- **2007**:3
Saro-Wiwa, Ken 1941-1995
    Obituary **1996**:2
Sasakawa, Ryoichi
    Brief entry **1988**:1
Saul, Betsy 1968- **2009**:2
Savage, Dan 1964- **2012**:3
Schiavo, Mary 1955- **1998**:2
Sendler, Irena 1910-2008
    Obituary **2009**:2
Seo, Danny 1977- **2008**:3
Shabazz, Betty 1936-1997
    Obituary **1997**:4
Sharma, Nisha 1982(?)- **2004**:2
Sharpton, Al 1954- **1991**:2
Shcharansky, Anatoly 1948- **1986**:2
Shilts, Randy 1951-1994 **1993**:4
    Obituary **1994**:3
Shocked, Michelle 1963(?)- **1989**:4
Shriver, Eunice 1921-2009
    Obituary **2011**:1
Sidney, Ivan
    Brief entry **1987**:2
Sinclair, Mary 1918- **1985**:2
Singer, Margaret Thaler 1921-2003
    Obituary **2005**:1
Slotnick, Barry
    Brief entry **1987**:4
Slovo, Joe 1926- **1989**:2
Smith, Samantha 1972-1985
    Obituary **1985**:3
Snyder, Mitch 1944(?)-1990

Obituary **1991**:1
Sonnenfeldt, Richard 1923-2009
    Obituary **2011**:2
Sontag, Susan 1933-2004
    Obituary **2006**:1
Spitzer, Silda Wall 1957- **2010**:2
Spong, John 1931- **1991**:3
Steele, Shelby 1946- **1991**:2
Steinem, Gloria 1934- **1996**:2
Stephens, Arran and Ratana **2008**:4
Steptoe, Patrick 1913-1988
    Obituary **1988**:3
Stevens, Eileen 1939- **1987**:3
Stevens, James
    Brief entry **1988**:1
Strong, Maurice 1929- **1993**:1
Strummer, Joe 1952-2002
    Obituary **2004**:1
Suckling, Kierán 1964- **2009**:2
Sullivan, Leon 1922-2001
    Obituary **2002**:2
Sullivan, Louis 1933- **1990**:4
Summers, Anne 1945- **1990**:2
Suu Kyi, Aung San 1945(?)- **1996**:2
Sweeney, John J. 1934- **2000**:3
Szent-Gyoergyi, Albert 1893-1986
    Obituary **1987**:2
Tafel, Richard 1962- **2000**:4
Tambo, Oliver 1917- **1991**:3
Tannen, Deborah 1945- **1995**:1
Terry, Randall **1991**:4
Thomas, Clarence 1948- **1992**:2
Tillion, Germaine 1907-2008
    Obituary **2009**:2
Tischler, Joyce 1956- **2011**:3
Travers, Mary 1936-2009
    Obituary **2011**:1
Ture, Kwame 1941-1998
    Obituary **1999**:2
Udall, Stewart 1920-2010
    Obituary **2012**:3
Unz, Ron 1962(?)- **1999**:1
Verdi-Fletcher, Mary 1955- **1998**:2
Vigdor, Ron 1970- **2011**:4
Vitousek, Peter 1949- **2003**:1
Waddell, Thomas F. 1937-1987
    Obituary **1988**:2
Waters, Alice 1944- **2006**:3
Wattleton, Faye 1943- **1989**:1
Wayburn, Edgar 1906-2010
    Obituary **2012**:2
Wei Jingsheng 1950- **1998**:2
Wells, Sharlene
    Brief entry **1985**:1
West, Cornel 1953- **1994**:2
Whelan, Tensie 1960- **2007**:1
White, Ryan 1972(?)-1990
    Obituary **1990**:3
Whitestone, Heather 1973(?)- **1995**:1
Wiesenthal, Simon 1908-2005
    Obituary **2006**:4
Wigand, Jeffrey 1943(?)- **2000**:4
Wildmon, Donald 1938- **1988**:4
Williams, Hosea 1926-2000
    Obituary **2001**:2
Williamson, Marianne 1953(?)- **1991**:4
Willson, S. Brian 1942(?)- **1989**:3
Wilmut, Ian 1944- **1997**:3
Wilson, William Julius 1935- **1997**:1
Wolf, Naomi 1963(?)- **1994**:3
Woodruff, Robert Winship 1889-1985

Obituary **1985**:1
Wu, Harry 1937- **1996**:1
Yard, Molly **1991**:4
Yeang, Ken 1948- **2008**:3
Yokich, Stephen P. 1935- **1995**:4
Youngblood, Johnny Ray 1948- **1994**:1
Yunus, Muhammad 1940- **2007**:3
Zamora, Pedro 1972-1994
Obituary **1995**:2
Zech, Lando W.
Brief entry **1987**:4
Zigler, Edward 1930- **1994**:1
Zinn, Howard 1922-2010
Obituary **2012**:1

SPORTS

Abbott, Jim 1967- **1988**:3
Abercrombie, Josephine 1925- **1987**:2
Adu, Freddy 1989- **2005**:3
Agassi, Andre 1970- **1990**:2
Agee, Tommie 1942-2001
Obituary **2001**:4
Aikman, Troy 1966- **1994**:2
Ainge, Danny 1959- **1987**:1
Akers, Michelle 1966- **1996**:1
Albert, Marv 1943- **1994**:3
Albom, Mitch 1958- **1999**:3
Ali, Laila 1977- **2001**:2
Ali, Muhammad 1942- **1997**:2
Allen, Mel 1913-1996
Obituary **1996**:4
Allen, Ray 1975- **2002**:1
Allenby, Robert 1971- **2007**:1
Allgaier, Justin 1986- **2011**:3
Alter, Hobie
Brief entry **1985**:1
Andersen, Chris 1978- **2010**:2
Angelos, Peter 1930- **1995**:4
Anthony, Carmelo 1984- **2012**:2
Anthony, Earl 1938-2001
Obituary **2002**:3
Aoki, Rocky 1940- **1990**:2
Arakawa, Shizuka 1981- **2006**:4
Armstrong, Henry 1912-1988
Obituary **1989**:1
Armstrong, Lance 1971- **2000**:1
Artest, Ron 1979- **2011**:1
Ashe, Arthur 1943-1993
Obituary **1993**:3
Auerbach, Red 1911-2006
Obituary **2008**:1
Austin, Stone Cold Steve 1964- **2001**:3
Axthelm, Pete 1943(?)-1991
Obituary **1991**:3
Azinger, Paul 1960- **1995**:2
Babilonia, Tai 1959- **1997**:2
Baiul, Oksana 1977- **1995**:3
Baker, Kathy
Brief entry **1986**:1
Barber, Tiki 1975- **2007**:1
Barkley, Charles 1963- **1988**:2
Barnes, Ernie 1938- **1997**:4
Baumgartner, Bruce
Brief entry **1987**:3
Bautista, José 1980- **2012**:4
Bayne, Trevor 1991- **2012**:2
Becker, Boris
Brief entry **1985**:3
Beckham, David 1975- **2003**:1
Bell, Ricky 1955-1984

Obituary **1985**:1
Belle, Albert 1966- **1996**:4
Benoit, Joan 1957- **1986**:3
Best, George 1946-2005
Obituary **2007**:1
Bias, Len 1964(?)-1986
Obituary **1986**:3
Bird, Larry 1956- **1990**:3
Blair, Bonnie 1964- **1992**:3
Bledsoe, Drew 1972- **1995**:1
Boggs, Wade 1958- **1989**:3
Boitano, Brian 1963- **1988**:3
Bol, Manute 1962-2010
Obituary **2012**:4
Bolt, Usain 1986- **2009**:2
Bonds, Barry 1964- **1993**:3
Bonilla, Bobby 1963- **1992**:2
Borel, Calvin 1966- **2010**:1
Bosworth, Brian 1965- **1989**:1
Boudreau, Louis 1917-2001
Obituary **2002**:3
Bourque, Raymond Jean 1960- **1997**:3
Bowe, Riddick 1967(?)- **1993**:2
Bowman, Scotty 1933- **1998**:4
Bradley, Keegan 1986- **2012**:4
Bradman, Sir Donald 1908-2001
Obituary **2002**:1
Brady, Tom 1977- **2002**:4
Brees, Drew 1979- **2011**:2
Bremen, Barry 1947- **1987**:3
Bright, Torah 1986- **2010**:2
Brown, Jim 1936- **1993**:2
Brown, Paul 1908-1991
Obituary **1992**:1
Bryant, Kobe 1978- **1998**:3
Burton, Jake 1954- **2007**:1
Busch, August Anheuser, Jr. 1899-1989
Obituary **1990**:2
Busch, Kurt 1978- **2006**:1
Busch, Kyle 1985- **2011**:4
Buss, Jerry 1933- **1989**:3
Butcher, Susan 1954- **1991**:1
Callaway, Ely 1919-2001
Obituary **2002**:3
Campanella, Roy 1921-1993
Obituary **1994**:1
Canseco, Jose 1964- **1990**:2
Capriati, Jennifer 1976- **1991**:1
Caray, Harry 1914(?)-1998 **1988**:3
Obituary **1998**:3
Carlsen, Magnus 1990- **2011**:3
Carter, Gary 1954- **1987**:1
Carter, Joe 1960- **1994**:2
Carter, Rubin 1937- **2000**:3
Carter, Vince 1977- **2001**:4
Castroneves, Helio 1975- **2010**:1
Chamberlain, Joba 1985- **2008**:3
Chamberlain, Wilt 1936-1999
Obituary **2000**:2
Chaney, John 1932- **1989**:1
Chastain, Brandi 1968- **2001**:3
Chen, T.C.
Brief entry **1987**:3
Cherry, Don 1934- **1993**:4
Chyna 1970- **2001**:4
Clemens, Roger 1962- **1991**:4
Clijsters, Kim 1983- **2006**:3
Coffey, Paul 1961- **1985**:4
Collins, Kerry 1972- **2002**:3
Conigliaro, Tony 1945-1990

Obituary **1990**:3
Conner, Dennis 1943- **1987**:2
Cooper, Cynthia **1999**:1
Copeland, Al 1944(?)- **1988**:3
Cosell, Howard 1918-1995
Obituary **1995**:4
Costas, Bob 1952- **1986**:4
Couples, Fred 1959- **1994**:4
Courier, Jim 1970- **1993**:2
Creamer, Paula 1986- **2006**:2
Crosby, Sidney 1987- **2006**:3
Cunningham, Randall 1963- **1990**:1
Curren, Tommy
Brief entry **1987**:4
Curtis, Ben 1977- **2004**:2
Daly, Chuck 1930-2009
Obituary **2010**:3
Damon, Johnny 1973- **2005**:4
Danza, Tony 1951- **1989**:1
Davenport, Lindsay 1976- **1999**:2
Davis, Eric 1962- **1987**:4
Davis, Terrell 1972- **1998**:2
Day, Pat 1953- **1995**:2
DeBartolo, Edward J., Jr. 1946- **1989**:3
De La Hoya, Oscar 1973- **1998**:2
Desormeaux, Kent 1970- **1990**:2
DiBello, Paul
Brief entry **1986**:4
DiMaggio, Dom 1917-2009
Obituary **2010**:2
DiMaggio, Joe 1914-1999
Obituary **1999**:3
Djokovic, Novak 1987- **2008**:4
Dolan, Tom 1975- **2001**:2
Donnellan, Nanci **1995**:2
Donovan, Landon 1982- **2011**:4
Doubleday, Nelson, Jr. 1933- **1987**:1
Douglas, Buster 1960(?)- **1990**:4
Dravecky, Dave 1956- **1992**:1
Draves, Victoria Manolo 1924-2010
Obituary **2012**:3
Drexler, Clyde 1962- **1992**:4
Drysdale, Don 1936-1993
Obituary **1994**:1
Duncan, Tim 1976- **2000**:1
Durocher, Leo 1905-1991
Obituary **1992**:2
Duval, David 1971- **2000**:3
Duvall, Camille
Brief entry **1988**:1
Dykstra, Lenny 1963- **1993**:4
Eagleson, Alan 1933- **1987**:4
Earnhardt, Dale 1951-2001
Obituary **2001**:4
Earnhardt, Dale, Jr. 1974- **2004**:4
Ederle, Gertrude 1905-2003
Obituary **2005**:1
Edwards, Carl 1979- **2012**:3
Edwards, Harry 1942- **1989**:4
Elway, John 1960- **1990**:3
Epstein, Theo 1973- **2003**:4
Esiason, Boomer 1961- **1991**:1
Evans, Janet 1971- **1989**:1
Ewing, Patrick 1962- **1985**:3
Fabris, Enrico 1981- **2006**:4
Faldo, Nick 1957- **1993**:3
Favre, Brett Lorenzo 1969- **1997**:2
Federer, Roger 1981- **2004**:2
Federov, Sergei 1969- **1995**:1
Fehr, Donald 1948- **1987**:2
Ferrari, Enzo 1898-1988 **1988**:4

Obituary **2000**:2
Newman, Joseph 1936- **1987**:1
Noyce, Robert N. 1927- **1985**:4
Ollila, Jorma 1950- **2003**:4
Otellini, Paul 1950- **2012**:3
Pack, Ellen 1963(?)- **2001**:2
Palmisano, Samuel J. 1952(?)- **2003**:1
Parsons, Richard 1949- **2002**:4
Peluso, Michelle 1971(?)- **2007**:4
Perlman, Steve 1961(?)- **1998**:2
Perry, William 1927- **1994**:4
Pfeiffer, Eckhard 1941- **1998**:4
Pincus, Mark 1966- **2011**:1
Probst, Larry 1951(?)- **2005**:1
Ramsay, Mike 1950(?)- **2002**:1
Raskin, Jef 1943(?)- **1997**:4
Rifkin, Jeremy 1945- **1990**:3
Rigopulos, Alex 1970- **2009**:4
Ritchie, Dennis and Kenneth
  Thompson **2000**:1
Roberts, Brian L. 1959- **2002**:4
Roberts, Steven K. 1952(?)- **1992**:1
Rosedale, Philip 1968- **2011**:3
Rutan, Burt 1943- **1987**:2
Schank, Roger 1946- **1989**:2
Schmidt, Eric 1955- **2002**:4
Scholz, Tom 1949- **1987**:2
Schroeder, William J. 1932-1986
  Obituary **1986**:4
Sculley, John 1939- **1989**:4
Seidenberg, Ivan 1946- **2004**:1
Semel, Terry 1943- **2002**:2
Shirley, Donna 1941- **1999**:1
Sinclair, Mary 1918- **1985**:2
Taylor, Jeff 1960- **2001**:3
Thomas, Edmond J. 1943(?)- **2005**:1
Thompson, John W. 1949- **2005**:1
Tito, Dennis 1940(?)- **2002**:1
Titov, Gherman 1935-2000
  Obituary **2001**:3
Tom and Ray Magliozzi **1991**:4
Toomer, Ron 1930- **1990**:1
Torvalds, Linus 1970(?)- **1999**:3
Treybig, James G. 1940- **1988**:3
Walker, Jay 1955- **2004**:2
Wang, An 1920-1990 **1986**:1
  Obituary **1990**:3
Westergren, Tim 1965- **2012**:2
Wright, Will 1960- **2003**:4
Yamamoto, Kenichi 1922- **1989**:1
Zuckerberg, Mark 1984- **2008**:2

TELEVISION

Abrams, J. J. 1966- **2007**:3
Adams, Amy 1974- **2008**:4
Adams, Don 1923-2005
  Obituary **2007**:1
Affleck, Ben 1972- **1999**:1
Alba, Jessica 1981- **2001**:2
Albert, Eddie 1906-2005
  Obituary **2006**:3
Albert, Marv 1943- **1994**:3
Albom, Mitch 1958- **1999**:3
Albrecht, Chris 1952(?)- **2005**:4
Alda, Robert 1914-1986
  Obituary **1986**:3
Alexander, Jane 1939- **1994**:2
Alexander, Jason 1962(?)- **1993**:3
Allen, Debbie 1950- **1998**:2
Allen, Steve 1921-2000
  Obituary **2001**:2
Allen, Tim 1953- **1993**:1

Alley, Kirstie 1955- **1990**:3
Allyson, June 1917-2006
  Obituary **2007**:3
Altman, Robert 1925- **1993**:2
Amanpour, Christiane 1958- **1997**:2
Ameche, Don 1908-1993
  Obituary **1994**:2
Amsterdam, Morey 1912-1996
  Obituary **1997**:1
Ancier, Garth 1957- **1989**:1
Anderson, Gillian 1968- **1997**:1
Anderson, Harry 1951(?)- **1988**:2
Anderson, Judith 1899(?)-1992
  Obituary **1992**:3
Anderson, Sunny 1975- **2012**:4
Andrews, Julie 1935- **1996**:1
Angelou, Maya 1928- **1993**:4
Aniston, Jennifer 1969- **2000**:3
Apatow, Judd 1967- **2006**:3
Applegate, Christina 1972- **2000**:4
Arden, Eve 1912(?)-1990
  Obituary **1991**:2
Arkin, Alan 1934- **2007**:4
Arledge, Roone 1931- **1992**:2
Arlen, Harold 1905-1986
  Obituary **1986**:3
Arnaz, Desi 1917-1986
  Obituary **1987**:1
Arnold, Tom 1959- **1993**:2
Arquette, Rosanna 1959- **1985**:2
Arthur, Bea 1922-2009
  Obituary **2010**:2
Astin, Sean 1971- **2005**:1
Atkinson, Rowan 1955- **2004**:3
Autry, Gene 1907-1998
  Obituary **1999**:1
Axthelm, Pete 1943(?)-1991
  Obituary **1991**:3
Aykroyd, Dan 1952- **1989**:3
Azaria, Hank 1964- **2001**:3
Bacall, Lauren 1924- **1997**:3
Backus, Jim 1913-1989
  Obituary **1990**:1
Bacon, Kevin 1958- **1995**:3
Baddeley, Hermione 1906(?)-1986
  Obituary **1986**:4
Bailey, Ben 1970- **2011**:4
Bailey, Pearl 1918-1990
  Obituary **1991**:1
Baker, Simon 1969- **2009**:4
Bakula, Scott 1954- **2003**:1
Ball, Alan 1957- **2005**:1
Ball, Lucille 1911-1989
  Obituary **1989**:3
Banks, Elizabeth 1974- **2012**:2
Baranski, Christine 1952- **2001**:2
Barbera, Joseph 1911- **1988**:2
Bardem, Javier 1969- **2008**:4
Barkin, Ellen 1955- **1987**:3
Barney **1993**:4
Baron Cohen, Sacha 1971- **2007**:3
Barr, Roseanne 1953(?)- **1989**:1
Barry, Gene 1919-2009
  Obituary **2011**:4
Barrymore, Drew 1975- **1995**:3
Basinger, Kim 1953- **1987**:2
Bassett, Angela 1959(?)- **1994**:4
Batali, Mario 1960- **2010**:4
Bateman, Jason 1969- **2005**:3
Bateman, Justine 1966- **1988**:4
Baxter, Anne 1923-1985
  Obituary **1986**:1

Beals, Jennifer 1963- **2005**:2
Beatty, Warren 1937- **2000**:1
Belushi, Jim 1954- **1986**:2
Belzer, Richard 1944- **1985**:3
Bergen, Candice 1946- **1990**:1
Bergeron, Tom 1955- **2010**:1
Berle, Milton 1908-2002
  Obituary **2003**:2
Berman, Gail 1957(?)- **2006**:1
Bernardi, Herschel 1923-1986
  Obituary **1986**:4
Bernsen, Corbin 1955- **1990**:2
Bernstein, Leonard 1918-1990
  Obituary **1991**:1
Berry, Halle 1968- **1996**:2
Bialik, Mayim 1975- **1993**:3
Bigelow, Kathryn 1951- **2011**:1
Bird, Brad 1956(?)- **2005**:4
Bishop, Joey 1918-2007
  Obituary **2008**:4
Bixby, Bill 1934-1993
  Obituary **1994**:2
Black, Carole 1945- **2003**:1
Blades, Ruben 1948- **1998**:2
Blaine, David 1973- **2003**:3
Blanc, Mel 1908-1989
  Obituary **1989**:4
Blanchett, Cate 1969- **1999**:3
Bloodworth-Thomason, Linda 1947-
  1994:1
Bloom, Orlando 1977- **2004**:2
Bochco, Steven 1943- **1989**:1
Bolger, Ray 1904-1987
  Obituary **1987**:2
Bonet, Lisa 1967- **1989**:2
Bono, Sonny 1935-1998 **1992**:2
  Obituary **1998**:2
Booth, Shirley 1898-1992
  Obituary **1993**:2
Boreanaz, David 1969- **2012**:2
Bourdain, Anthony 1956- **2008**:3
Bowen, Julie 1970- **2007**:1
Boyle, Lara Flynn 1970- **2003**:4
Boyle, Peter 1935- **2002**:3
Bradley, Ed 1941-2006
  Obituary **2008**:1
Bradshaw, John 1933- **1992**:1
Brady, Wayne 1972- **2008**:3
Braff, Zach 1975- **2005**:2
Brand, Russell 1975- **2010**:2
Brandy 1979- **1996**:4
Bratt, Benjamin 1963- **2009**:3
Brenneman, Amy 1964- **2002**:1
Bridges, Jeff 1949- **2011**:1
Bridges, Lloyd 1913-1998
  Obituary **1998**:3
Brinkley, David 1920-2003
  Obituary **2004**:3
Broadbent, Jim 1949- **2008**:4
Brokaw, Tom 1940- **2000**:3
Bromstad, David 1973- **2012**:2
Bronson, Charles 1921-2003
  Obituary **2004**:4
Brooks, Mel 1926- **2003**:1
Brosnan, Pierce 1952- **2000**:3
Brown, Alton 1962- **2011**:1
Brown, Les 1945- **1994**:3
Brown, Ruth 1928-2006
  Obituary **2008**:1
Brown, Samantha 1969- **2011**:3
Bruckheimer, Jerry 1945- **2007**:2
Buckley, Betty 1947- **1996**:2

Swinton, Tilda 1960- **2008**:4
Sykes, Wanda 1964- **2007**:4
Tandy, Jessica 1901-1994 **1990**:4
    Obituary **1995**:1
Tartakovsky, Genndy 1970- **2004**:4
Tartikoff, Brandon 1949-1997 **1985**:2
    Obituary **1998**:1
Tautou, Audrey 1978- **2004**:2
Taylor, Elizabeth 1932- **1993**:3
Tellem, Nancy 1953(?)- **2004**:4
Terkel, Studs 1912-2008
    Obituary **2010**:1
Tesh, John 1952- **1996**:3
Thomas, Betty 1948- **2011**:4
Thomas, Danny 1914-1991
    Obituary **1991**:3
Thompson, Emma 1959- **1993**:2
Thornton, Billy Bob 1956(?)- **1997**:4
Tillstrom, Burr 1917-1985
    Obituary **1986**:1
Tilly, Jennifer 1958(?)- **1997**:2
Timberlake, Justin 1981- **2008**:4
Tisch, Laurence A. 1923- **1988**:2
Tomei, Marisa 1964- **1995**:2
Totenberg, Nina 1944- **1992**:2
Travolta, John 1954- **1995**:2
Trebek, Alex 1940- **2010**:4
Trotter, Charlie 1960- **2000**:4
Trudeau, Garry 1948- **1991**:2
Tucci, Stanley 1960- **2003**:2
Tucker, Chris 1973(?)- **1999**:1
Tucker, Forrest 1919-1986
    Obituary **1987**:1
Turner, Janine 1962- **1993**:2
Turner, Lana 1921-1995
    Obituary **1996**:1
Turner, Ted 1938- **1989**:1
Tyler, Steven 1948- **2012**:3
Ullman, Tracey 1961- **1988**:3
Umeki, Miyoshi 1929-2007
    Obituary **2008**:4
Underwood, Carrie 1983- **2008**:1
Urich, Robert 1947- **1988**:1
    Obituary **2003**:3
Usher 1979- **2005**:1
Ustinov, Peter 1921-2004
    Obituary **2005**:3
Valastro, Buddy 1977- **2011**:4
Vanilla Ice 1967(?)- **1991**:3
Vardalos, Nia 1962- **2003**:4
Varney, Jim 1949-2000
    Brief entry **1985**:4
    Obituary **2000**:3
Vaughn, Vince 1970- **1999**:2
Ventura, Jesse 1951- **1999**:2
Vidal, Gore 1925- **1996**:2
Vieira, Meredith 1953- **2001**:3
Villechaize, Herve 1943(?)-1993
    Obituary **1994**:1
Vitale, Dick 1939- **1988**:4
Von D, Kat 1982- **2008**:3
Wagoner, Porter 1927-2007
    Obituary **2008**:4
Walker, Nancy 1922-1992
    Obituary **1992**:3
Walters, Barbara 1931- **1998**:3
Waltz, Christoph 1956- **2011**:1
Wapner, Joseph A. 1919- **1987**:1
Ward, Sela 1956- **2001**:3
Warden, Jack 1920-2006
    Obituary **2007**:3
Washington, Denzel 1954- **1993**:2

Wasserman, Lew 1913-2002
    Obituary **2003**:3
Waterston, Sam 1940- **2006**:1
Wayans, Damon 1960- **1998**:4
Wayans, Keenen Ivory 1958(?)- **1991**
    :1
Wayne, David 1914-1995
    Obituary **1995**:3
Weisz, Rachel 1971- **2006**:4
Weitz, Bruce 1943- **1985**:4
Whedon, Joss 1964- **2006**:3
Whitaker, Forest 1961- **1996**:2
White, Betty 1922- **2012**:1
White, Jaleel 1976- **1992**:3
White, Julie 1961- **2008**:2
Whiting, Susan 1956- **2007**:4
Whitmore, James 1921-2009
    Obituary **2010**:1
Whittle, Christopher 1947- **1989**:3
Wiig, Kristen 1973- **2012**:3
Wilkinson, Tom 1948- **2003**:2
Williams, Brian 1959- **2009**:4
Williams, Robin 1952- **1988**:4
Williams, Treat 1951- **2004**:3
Williams, Vanessa L. 1963- **1999**:2
Willis, Bruce 1955- **1986**:4
Wilson, Flip 1933-1998
    Obituary **1999**:2
Winfield, Paul 1941-2004
    Obituary **2005**:2
Winfrey, Oprah 1954- **1986**:4
Winger, Debra 1955- **1994**:3
Winokur, Marissa Jaret 1973- **2005**:1
Wolfman Jack 1938-1995
    Obituary **1996**:1
Wong, Andrea 1966- **2009**:1
Wong, B.D. 1962- **1998**:1
Woods, James 1947- **1988**:3
Woodward, Edward 1930-2009
    Obituary **2011**:3
Worthington, Sam 1976- **2012**:1
Wright, Steven 1955- **1986**:3
Wyatt, Jane 1910-2006
    Obituary **2008**:1
Wyle, Noah 1971- **1997**:3
Wyman, Jane 1917-2007
    Obituary **2008**:4
Wynn, Keenan 1916-1986
    Obituary **1987**:1
Xuxa 1963(?)- **1994**:2
Xzibit 1974- **2005**:4
Yetnikoff, Walter 1933- **1988**:1
York, Dick 1923-1992
    Obituary **1992**:4
Young, Robert 1907-1998
    Obituary **1999**:1
Youngman, Henny 1906(?)-1998
    Obituary **1998**:3
Zahn, Paula 1956(?)- **1992**:3
Zamora, Pedro 1972-1994
    Obituary **1995**:2
Zeta-Jones, Catherine 1969- **1999**:4
Zoe, Rachel 1971- **2010**:2
Zucker, Jeff 1965(?)- **1993**:3

THEATER

Abbott, George 1887-1995
    Obituary **1995**:3
Adjani, Isabelle 1955- **1991**:1
Albee, Edward 1928- **1997**:1
Albert, Eddie 1906-2005
    Obituary **2006**:3

Alda, Robert 1914-1986
    Obituary **1986**:3
Alexander, Jane 1939- **1994**:2
Alexander, Jason 1962(?)- **1993**:3
Allen, Joan 1956- **1998**:1
Allen, Peter 1944-1992
    Obituary **1993**:1
Ameche, Don 1908-1993
    Obituary **1994**:2
Andrews, Julie 1935- **1996**:1
Angelou, Maya 1928- **1993**:4
Arden, Eve 1912(?)-1990
    Obituary **1991**:2
Arkin, Alan 1934- **2007**:4
Arthur, Bea 1922-2009
    Obituary **2010**:2
Ashcroft, Peggy 1907-1991
    Obituary **1992**:1
Atkinson, Rowan 1955- **2004**:3
Aykroyd, Dan 1952- **1989**:3
Bacall, Lauren 1924- **1997**:3
Bacon, Kevin 1958- **1995**:3
Baddeley, Hermione 1906(?)-1986
    Obituary **1986**:4
Bailey, Pearl 1918-1990
    Obituary **1991**:1
Ball, Alan 1957- **2005**:1
Bancroft, Anne 1931-2005
    Obituary **2006**:3
Barkin, Ellen 1955- **1987**:3
Barry, Gene 1919-2009
    Obituary **2011**:4
Barry, Lynda 1956(?)- **1992**:1
Bassett, Angela 1959(?)- **1994**:4
Bates, Alan 1934-2003
    Obituary **2005**:1
Bates, Kathy 1949(?)- **1991**:4
Becker, Brian 1957(?)- **2004**:4
Beckett, Samuel Barclay 1906-1989
    Obituary **1990**:2
Belushi, Jim 1954- **1986**:2
Bening, Annette 1958(?)- **1992**:1
Bennett, Joan 1910-1990
    Obituary **1991**:2
Bennett, Michael 1943-1987
    Obituary **1988**:1
Bernardi, Herschel 1923-1986
    Obituary **1986**:4
Bernhard, Sandra 1955(?)- **1989**:4
Bernstein, Leonard 1918-1990
    Obituary **1991**:1
Bishop, Andre 1948- **2000**:1
Bishop, Joey 1918-2007
    Obituary **2008**:4
Blackstone, Harry Jr. 1934-1997
    Obituary **1997**:4
Blanchett, Cate 1969- **1999**:3
Bloch, Ivan 1940- **1986**:3
Bloom, Orlando 1977- **2004**:2
Bogosian, Eric 1953- **1990**:4
Bolger, Ray 1904-1987
    Obituary **1987**:2
Bonham Carter, Helena 1966- **1998**:4
Booth, Shirley 1898-1992
    Obituary **1993**:2
Bowen, Julie 1970- **2007**:1
Bowie, David 1947- **1998**:2
Brady, Wayne 1972- **2008**:3
Branagh, Kenneth 1960- **1992**:2
Brandauer, Klaus Maria 1944- **1987**:3
Brando, Marlon 1924-2004
    Obituary **2005**:3

Richards, Michael 1949(?)- **1993**:4
Richardson, Natasha 1963-2009
　Obituary **2010**:2
Ritter, John 1948- **2003**:4
Robbins, Jerome 1918-1998
　Obituary **1999**:1
Roberts, Doris 1930- **2003**:4
Roberts, Pernell 1928-2010
　Obituary **2012**:1
Roker, Roxie 1929(?)-1995
　Obituary **1996**:2
Rolle, Esther 1922-1998
　Obituary **1999**:2
Rowe, Mike 1962- **2010**:2
Rudd, Paul 1969- **2009**:4
Rudner, Rita 1956- **1993**:2
Rudnick, Paul 1957(?) **1994**:3
Ruehl, Mercedes 1948(?)- **1992**:4
Ruffalo, Mark 1967- **2011**:4
Rylance, Mark 1960- **2009**:3
Salonga, Lea 1971- **2003**:3
Sarandon, Susan 1946- **1995**:3
Schoenfeld, Gerald 1924- **1986**:2
Schreiber, Liev 1967- **2007**:2
Schwimmer, David 1966(?)- **1996**:2
Scott, George C. 1927-1999
　Obituary **2000**:2
Scott Thomas, Kristin 1960- **2010**:2
Seymour, Jane 1951- **1994**:4
Shaffer, Paul 1949- **1987**:1
Shanley, John Patrick 1950- **2006**:1
Shawn, Dick 1924(?)-1987
　Obituary **1987**:3
Sheldon, Sidney 1917-2007
　Obituary **2008**:2
Shepard, Sam 1943- **1996**:4
Short, Martin 1950- **1986**:1
Silvers, Phil 1912-1985
　Obituary **1985**:4
Sinise, Gary 1955(?)- **1996**:1
Slater, Christian 1969- **1994**:1
Smith, Anna Deavere 1950- **2002**:2
Snipes, Wesley 1962- **1993**:1
Sondheim, Stephen 1930- **1994**:4
Spacey, Kevin 1959- **1996**:4
Stamos, John 1963- **2008**:1
Stapleton, Maureen 1925-2006
　Obituary **2007**:2
Steiger, Rod 1925-2002
　Obituary **2003**:4
Stewart, Jimmy 1908-1997
　Obituary **1997**:4
Stewart, Patrick 1940- **1996**:1
Stiller, Ben 1965- **1999**:1
Sting 1951- **1991**:4
Stoppard, Tom 1937- **1995**:4
Streep, Meryl 1949- **1990**:2
Streisand, Barbra 1942- **1992**:2
Stritch, Elaine 1925- **2002**:4
Styne, Jule 1905-1994
　Obituary **1995**:1
Susskind, David 1920-1987
　Obituary **1987**:2
Swinton, Tilda 1960- **2008**:4
Szot, Paulo 1969- **2009**:3
Tandy, Jessica 1901-1994 **1990**:4
　Obituary **1995**:1
Taylor, Elizabeth 1932- **1993**:3
Taylor, Lili 1967- **2000**:2
Thompson, Emma 1959- **1993**:2
Tomei, Marisa 1964- **1995**:2
Tucci, Stanley 1960- **2003**:2

Tune, Tommy 1939- **1994**:2
Ullman, Tracey 1961- **1988**:3
Umeki, Miyoshi 1929-2007
　Obituary **2008**:4
Urich, Robert 1947- **1988**:1
　Obituary **2003**:3
Ustinov, Peter 1921-2004
　Obituary **2005**:3
Vardalos, Nia 1962- **2003**:4
Vogel, Paula 1951- **1999**:2
Walker, Nancy 1922-1992
　Obituary **1992**:3
Washington, Denzel 1954- **1993**:2
Wasserstein, Wendy 1950- **1991**:3
Waterston, Sam 1940- **2006**:1
Watts, Naomi 1968- **2006**:1
Wayne, David 1914-1995
　Obituary **1995**:3
Weaver, Sigourney 1949- **1988**:3
Weisz, Rachel 1971- **2006**:4
Weitz, Bruce 1943- **1985**:4
Wences, Senor 1896-1999
　Obituary **1999**:4
Whitaker, Forest 1961- **1996**:2
White, Betty 1922- **2012**:1
White, Julie 1961- **2008**:2
Whitehead, Robert 1916-2002
　Obituary **2003**:3
Whitmore, James 1921-2009
　Obituary **2010**:1
Wiest, Dianne 1948- **1995**:2
Wilkinson, Tom 1948- **2003**:2
Williams, Treat 1951- **2004**:3
Willis, Bruce 1955- **1986**:4
Winfield, Paul 1941-2004
　Obituary **2005**:2
Winokur, Marissa Jaret 1973- **2005**:1
Wong, B.D. 1962- **1998**:1
Woods, James 1947- **1988**:3
Worth, Irene 1916-2002
　Obituary **2003**:2
Wyatt, Jane 1910-2006
　Obituary **2008**:1
Wyle, Noah 1971- **1997**:3
Youngman, Henny 1906(?)-1998
　Obituary **1998**:3
Zeffirelli, Franco 1923- **1991**:3

WRITING
Adams, Douglas 1952-2001
　Obituary **2002**:2
Adams, Scott 1957- **1996**:4
Adiga, Aravind 1974- **2010**:3
Ahern, Cecelia 1981- **2008**:4
Albom, Mitch 1958- **1999**:3
Alexie, Sherman 1966- **1998**:4
Ali, Monica 1967- **2007**:4
Amanpour, Christiane 1958- **1997**:2
Ambler, Eric 1909-1998
　Obituary **1999**:2
Ambrose, Stephen 1936- **2002**:3
Amis, Kingsley 1922-1995
　Obituary **1996**:2
Amis, Martin 1949- **2008**:3
Amory, Cleveland 1917-1998
　Obituary **1999**:2
Anderson, Poul 1926-2001
　Obituary **2002**:3
Angelou, Maya 1928- **1993**:4
Angier, Natalie 1958- **2000**:3
Asimov, Isaac 1920-1992
　Obituary **1992**:3

Atkins, Robert C. 1930-2003
　Obituary **2004**:2
Atkinson, Kate 1951- **2012**:1
Atwood, Margaret 1939- **2001**:2
Axthelm, Pete 1943(?)-1991
　Obituary **1991**:3
Ayala, Francisco 1906-2009
　Obituary **2011**:3
Bacall, Lauren 1924- **1997**:3
Bakker, Robert T. 1950(?)- **1991**:3
Baldwin, James 1924-1987
　Obituary **1988**:2
Ball, Edward 1959- **1999**:2
Banks, Russell 1940- **2009**:2
Baraka, Amiri 1934- **2000**:3
Barber, Red 1908-1992
　Obituary **1993**:2
Barker, Clive 1952- **2003**:3
Barker, Pat 1943- **2009**:1
Barry, Dave 1947(?)- **1991**:2
Barry, Lynda 1956(?)- **1992**:1
Bass, Rick 1958- **2012**:4
Batali, Mario 1960- **2010**:4
Bechdel, Alison 1960- **2007**:3
Beckett, Samuel Barclay 1906-1989
　Obituary **1990**:2
Bedford, Deborah 1958- **2006**:3
Bell, Gabrielle 1975(?)- **2007**:4
Bellow, Saul 1915-2005
　Obituary **2006**:2
Benchley, Peter 1940-2006
　Obituary **2007**:1
Berg, Elizabeth 1948- **2012**:1
Betancourt, Ingrid 1961- **2012**:1
Binchy, Maeve 1940- **2010**:2
Bloodworth-Thomason, Linda 1947-
　1994:1
Bloom, Amy 1953- **2011**:3
Blume, Judy 1936- **1998**:4
Bly, Robert 1926- **1992**:4
Blyth, Myrna 1939- **2002**:4
Bombeck, Erma 1927-1996
　Obituary **1996**:4
Bourdain, Anthony 1956- **2008**:3
Bowles, Paul 1910-1999
　Obituary **2000**:3
Boyle, T. C. 1948- **2007**:2
Boynton, Sandra 1953- **2004**:1
Bradford, Barbara Taylor 1933- **2002**
　:4
Bradley, Alan 1938- **2012**:1
Bradshaw, John 1933- **1992**:1
Branagh, Kenneth 1960- **1992**:2
Bray, Libba 1964- **2011**:1
Breathed, Berkeley 1957- **2005**:3
Brite, Poppy Z. 1967- **2005**:1
Brodsky, Joseph 1940-1996
　Obituary **1996**:3
Brokaw, Tom 1940- **2000**:3
Brooks, Gwendolyn 1917-2000 **1998**
　:1
　Obituary **2001**:2
Brown, Alton 1962- **2011**:1
Brown, Dan 1964- **2004**:4
Brown, Dee 1908-2002
　Obituary **2004**:1
Brown, Tina 1953- **1992**:1
Brutus, Dennis 1924-2009
　Obituary **2011**:4
Buchwald, Art 1925-2007
　Obituary **2008**:2
Buffett, Jimmy 1946- **1999**:3

Martin, Judith 1938- **2000**:3
Mayes, Frances 1940(?)- **2004**:3
Maynard, Joyce 1953- **1999**:4
McCall, Nathan 1955- **1994**:4
McCall Smith, Alexander 1948- **2005** :2
McCarthy, Cormac 1933- **2008**:1
McCourt, Frank 1930- **1997**:4
McDermott, Alice 1953- **1999**:2
McDonell, Nick 1984- **2011**:2
McDonnell, Patrick 1956- **2009**:4
McEwan, Ian 1948- **2004**:2
McFadden, Cynthia 1956- **2012**:2
McGahern, John 1934-2006
  Obituary **2007**:2
McGraw, Phil 1950- **2005**:2
McKenna, Terence **1993**:3
McMillan, Terry 1951- **1993**:2
McMurtry, Larry 1936- **2006**:4
McNamara, Robert S. 1916- **1995**:4
Melendez, Bill 1916-2008
  Obituary **2009**:4
Meltzer, Brad 1970- **2005**:4
Menchu, Rigoberta 1960(?)- **1993**:2
Menninger, Karl 1893-1990
  Obituary **1991**:1
Merrill, James 1926-1995
  Obituary **1995**:3
Meyer, Stephenie 1973- **2009**:1
Michener, James A. 1907-1997
  Obituary **1998**:1
Millan, Cesar 1969- **2007**:4
Miller, Arthur 1915- **1999**:4
Miller, Frank 1957- **2008**:2
Miller, Sue 1943- **1999**:3
Milne, Christopher Robin 1920-1996
  Obituary **1996**:4
Milosz, Czeslaw 1911-2004
  Obituary **2005**:4
Mina, Denise 1966- **2006**:1
Mitchard, Jacquelyn 1956- **2010**:4
Mo'Nique 1967- **2008**:1
Monsiváis, Carlos 1938-2010
  Obituary **2012**:4
Montagu, Ashley 1905-1999
  Obituary **2000**:2
Moody, Rick 1961- **2002**:2
Moore, Michael 1954(?)- **1990**:3
Morgan, Piers 1965- **2012**:2
Morgan, Robin 1941- **1991**:1
Morris, Henry M. 1918-2006
  Obituary **2007**:2
Morrison, Toni 1931- **1998**:1
Mortensen, Viggo 1958- **2003**:3
Mortenson, Greg 1957- **2011**:1
Mosley, Walter 1952- **2003**:4
Moyers, Bill 1934- **1991**:4
Munro, Alice 1931- **1997**:1
Murakami, Haruki 1949- **2008**:3
Murdoch, Iris 1919-1999
  Obituary **1999**:4
Murkoff, Heidi 1958- **2009**:3
Narayan, R.K. 1906-2001
  Obituary **2002**:2
Nasrin, Taslima 1962- **1995**:1
Nelson, Jack 1929-2009
  Obituary **2011**:2
Nemerov, Howard 1920-1991
  Obituary **1992**:1
Newkirk, Ingrid 1949- **1992**:3
Niezabitowska, Malgorzata 1949(?)-
  1991:3

Nissel, Angela 1974- **2006**:4
Noonan, Peggy 1950- **1990**:3
Northrop, Peggy 1954- **2009**:2
Norton, Andre 1912-2005
  Obituary **2006**:2
Nottage, Lynn 1964- **2010**:1
Novak, Robert 1931-2009
  Obituary **2010**:4
Oates, Joyce Carol 1938- **2000**:1
Obama, Barack 1961- **2007**:4
Obreht, Tea 1985- **2012**:3
O'Brien, Conan 1963(?)- **1994**:1
Oe, Kenzaburo 1935- **1997**:1
Onassis, Jacqueline Kennedy
  1929-1994
  Obituary **1994**:4
Ondaatje, Philip Michael 1943- **1997** :3
Ornish, Dean 1953- **2004**:2
Osborne, John 1929-1994
  Obituary **1995**:2
Osteen, Joel 1963- **2006**:2
Owens, Delia and Mark **1993**:3
Oz, Mehmet 1960- **2007**:2
Pagels, Elaine 1943- **1997**:1
Paglia, Camille 1947- **1992**:3
Palahniuk, Chuck 1962- **2004**:1
Pamuk, Orhan 1952- **2007**:3
Paretsky, Sara 1947- **2002**:4
Parker, Brant 1920-2007
  Obituary **2008**:2
Parks, Suzan-Lori 1964- **2003**:2
Patchett, Ann 1963- **2003**:2
Patterson, Richard North 1947- **2001** :4
Paz, Octavio 1914- **1991**:2
Pekar, Harvey 1939-2010
  Obituary **2012**:4
Penny, Louise 1958- **2011**:1
Percy, Walker 1916-1990
  Obituary **1990**:4
Peters, Tom 1942- **1998**:1
Phillips, Julia 1944- **1992**:1
Picoult, Jodi 1966- **2008**:1
Pilkey, Dav 1966- **2001**:1
Pipher, Mary 1948(?)- **1996**:4
Plimpton, George 1927-2003
  Obituary **2004**:4
Politkovskaya, Anna 1958-2006
  Obituary **2007**:4
Pollan, Michael 1955- **2011**:3
Porter, Sylvia 1913-1991
  Obituary **1991**:4
Post, Peggy 1940(?)- **2001**:4
Potok, Chaim 1929-2002
  Obituary **2003**:4
Pouillon, Nora 1943- **2005**:1
Powter, Susan 1957(?)- **1994**:3
Pratt, Jane 1963(?)- **1999**:1
Proulx, E. Annie 1935- **1996**:1
Pullman, Philip 1946- **2003**:2
Pynchon, Thomas 1937- **1997**:4
Quindlen, Anna 1952- **1993**:1
Quinn, Jane Bryant 1939(?)- **1993**:4
Ramsay, Gordon 1966- **2008**:2
Rankin, Ian 1960- **2010**:3
Redfield, James 1952- **1995**:2
Reichs, Kathleen J. 1948- **2007**:3
Rendell, Ruth 1930- **2007**:2
Rey, Margret E. 1906-1996
  Obituary **1997**:2
Reza, Yasmina 1959(?)- **1999**:2

Rhone, Trevor 1940-2009
  Obituary **2011**:1
Rice, Anne 1941- **1995**:1
Riggs, Ransom 1979- **2012**:4
Ringgold, Faith 1930- **2000**:3
Roach, Mary 1959- **2012**:2
Robbins, Harold 1916-1997
  Obituary **1998**:1
Roberts, Cokie 1943- **1993**:4
Roberts, Nora 1950- **2010**:3
Roberts, Steven K. 1952(?)- **1992**:1
Robertson, Nan 1926-2009
  Obituary **2011**:2
Robinson, Peter 1950- **2007**:4
Roddenberry, Gene 1921-1991
  Obituary **1992**:2
Rodgers, Carolyn M. 1940-2010
  Obituary **2012**:3
Roizen, Michael 1946- **2007**:4
Rosenzweig, Ilene 1965(?)- **2004**:1
Rossner, Judith 1935-2005
  Obituary **2006**:4
Rosten, Leo 1908-1997
  Obituary **1997**:3
Roth, Philip 1933- **1999**:1
Rowan, Carl 1925-2000
  Obituary **2001**:2
Rowland, Pleasant **1992**:3
Rowling, J.K. 1965- **2000**:1
Royko, Mike 1932-1997
  Obituary **1997**:4
Rudnick, Paul 1957(?)- **1994**:3
Rushdie, Salman 1947- **1994**:1
Russell, Mary 1950- **2009**:2
Russo, Richard 1949- **2002**:3
Sacks, Oliver 1933- **1995**:4
Safire, William 1929- **2000**:3
Salinger, J. D. 1919-2010
  Obituary **2012**:1
Salk, Jonas 1914-1995 **1994**:4
  Obituary **1995**:4
Salzman, Mark 1959- **2002**:1
Sapphire 1951(?)- **1996**:4
Saramago, Jose 1922- **1999**:1
Saro-Wiwa, Ken 1941-1995
  Obituary **1996**:2
Sarraute, Nathalie 1900-1999
  Obituary **2000**:2
Satrapi, Marjane 1969- **2006**:3
Savage, Dan 1964- **2012**:3
Schaap, Dick 1934-2001
  Obituary **2003**:1
Schroeder, Barbet 1941- **1996**:1
Schulberg, Budd 1914-2009
  Obituary **2010**:4
Schulz, Charles M. 1922- **1998**:1
Sears, Barry 1947- **2004**:2
Sebold, Alice 1963(?)- **2005**:4
Sedaris, Amy 1961- **2009**:3
Sedaris, David 1956- **2005**:3
See, Lisa 1955- **2010**:4
Segal, Erich 1937-2010
  Obituary **2012**:1
Senghor, Leopold 1906-2001
  Obituary **2003**:1
Serros, Michele 1967(?)- **2008**:2
Sethi, Simran 1971(?)- **2008**:1
Sevareid, Eric 1912-1992
  Obituary **1993**:1
Shanley, John Patrick 1950- **2006**:1
Shawn, William 1907-1992
  Obituary **1993**:3

2012 Subject Index

This index lists all newsmakers by subjects, company names, products, organizations, issues, awards, and professional specialties. Indexes in softbound issues allow access to the current year's entries; indexes in annual hardbound volumes are cumulative, covering the entire *Newsmakers* series.

Listee names are followed by a year and issue number; thus **1996**:3 indicates that an entry on that individual appears in both 1996, Issue 3, and the 1996 cumulation. For access to newsmakers appearing earlier than the current softbound issue, see the previous year's cumulation.

Schroeder, William J. 1932-1986
Obituary **1986**:4

Artificial intelligence
Minsky, Marvin 1927- **1994**:3

Association of Southeast Asian Nations
Bolkiah, Sultan Muda Hassanal
1946- **1985**:4

Astronautics
Bean, Alan L. 1932- **1986**:2
Collins, Eileen 1956- **1995**:3
Conrad, Pete 1930-1999
Obituary **2000**:1
Dzhanibekov, Vladimir 1942- **1988**:1
Garneau, Marc 1949- **1985**:1
Glenn, John 1921- **1998**:3
Lucid, Shannon 1943- **1997**:1
McAuliffe, Christa 1948-1986
Obituary **1985**:4
Whitson, Peggy 1960- **2003**:3

Astronomy
Bahcall, John N. 1934-2005
Obituary **2006**:4
Bopp, Thomas 1949- **1997**:3
Geller, Margaret Joan 1947- **1998**:2
Hale, Alan 1957- **1997**:3
Hawking, Stephen W. 1942- **1990**:1
Hoyle, Sir Fred 1915-2001
Obituary **2002**:4
Marsden, Brian 1937- **2004**:4
Smoot, George F. 1945- **1993**:3

AT&T
Allen, Bob 1935- **1992**:4
Armstrong, C. Michael 1938- **2002**:1

Atari
Bushnell, Nolan 1943- **1985**:1
Kingsborough, Donald
Brief entry **1986**:2
Perlman, Steve 1961(?)- **1998**:2

Atlanta Braves baseball team
Lofton, Kenny 1967- **1998**:1
Maddux, Greg 1966- **1996**:2
Sanders, Deion 1967- **1992**:4
Smoltz, John 1967- **2010**:3
Spahn, Warren 1921-2003
Obituary **2005**:1
Turner, Ted 1938- **1989**:1

Atlanta Falcons football team
Sanders, Deion 1967- **1992**:4

Atlanta Hawks basketball team
Maravich, Pete 1948-1988
Obituary **1988**:2
McMillen, Tom 1952- **1988**:4
Turner, Ted 1938- **1989**:1
Wilkens, Lenny 1937- **1995**:2

Atlantic Records
Ertegun, Ahmet 1923- **1986**:3
Greenwald, Julie 1970- **2008**:1

Automobile racing
Allgaier, Justin 1986- **2011**:3
Bayne, Trevor 1991- **2012**:2
Busch, Kurt 1978- **2006**:1

Busch, Kyle 1985- **2011**:4
Castroneves, Helio 1975- **2010**:1
Earnhardt, Dale, Jr. 1974- **2004**:4
Edwards, Carl 1979- **2012**:3
Ferrari, Enzo 1898-1988 **1988**:4
Fittipaldi, Emerson 1946- **1994**:2
Franchitti, Dario 1973- **2008**:1
Gordon, Jeff 1971- **1996**:1
Johnson, Jimmie 1975- **2007**:2
Muldowney, Shirley 1940- **1986**:1
Munter, Leilani 1976- **2010**:4
Newman, Paul 1925- **1995**:3
Newman, Ryan 1977- **2005**:1
Penske, Roger 1937- **1988**:3
Porsche, Ferdinand 1909-1998
Obituary **1998**:4
Prost, Alain 1955- **1988**:1
Schumacher, Michael 1969- **2005**:2
Senna, Ayrton 1960(?)-1994 **1991**:4
Obituary **1994**:4
St. James, Lyn 1947- **1993**:2
Villeneuve, Jacques 1971- **1997**:1
Zanardi, Alex 1966- **1998**:2

Aviation
Burr, Donald Calvin 1941- **1985**:3
Dubrof, Jessica 1989-1996
Obituary **1996**:4
Fossett, Steve 1944- **2007**:2
Lindbergh, Anne Morrow 1906-2001
Obituary **2001**:4
MacCready, Paul 1925- **1986**:4
Martin, Dean Paul 1952(?)-1987
Obituary **1987**:3
Moody, John 1943- **1985**:3
Rutan, Burt 1943- **1987**:2
Schiavo, Mary 1955- **1998**:2
Wolf, Stephen M. 1941- **1989**:3
Yeager, Chuck 1923- **1998**:1

Avis Rent A Car
Rand, A. Barry 1944- **2000**:3

Avon Products, Inc.
Gold, Christina A. 1947- **2008**:1
Jung, Andrea **2000**:2
Waldron, Hicks B. 1923- **1987**:3

Bad Boy Records
Combs, Sean Puffy 1970- **1998**:4

Ballet West
Lander, Toni 1931-1985
Obituary **1985**:4

Ballooning
Aoki, Rocky 1940- **1990**:2

Baltimore, Md., city government
Schaefer, William Donald 1921- **1988**:1

Baltimore Orioles baseball team
Angelos, Peter 1930- **1995**:4
Palmeiro, Rafael 1964- **2005**:1
Palmer, Jim 1945- **1991**:2
Ripken, Cal, Jr. 1960- **1986**:2
Ripken, Cal, Sr. 1936(?)-1999
Obituary **1999**:4
Robinson, Frank 1935- **1990**:2

Williams, Edward Bennett 1920-1988
Obituary **1988**:4

Band Aid
Geldof, Bob 1954(?)- **1985**:3

Bard College
Botstein, Leon 1946- **1985**:3

Barnes & Noble, Inc.
Riggio, Leonard S. 1941- **1999**:4

Baseball
Abbott, Jim 1967- **1988**:3
Ainge, Danny 1959- **1987**:1
Barber, Red 1908-1992
Obituary **1993**:2
Bautista, José 1980- **2012**:4
Boggs, Wade 1958- **1989**:3
Bonds, Barry 1964- **1993**:3
Campanella, Roy 1921-1993
Obituary **1994**:1
Canseco, Jose 1964- **1990**:2
Caray, Harry 1914(?)-1998 **1988**:3
Obituary **1998**:3
Carter, Gary 1954- **1987**:1
Carter, Joe 1960- **1994**:2
Chamberlain, Joba 1985- **2008**:3
Clemens, Roger 1962- **1991**:4
Damon, Johnny 1973- **2005**:4
Davis, Eric 1962- **1987**:4
DiMaggio, Dom 1917-2009
Obituary **2010**:2
DiMaggio, Joe 1914-1999
Obituary **1999**:3
Doubleday, Nelson, Jr. 1933- **1987**:1
Dravecky, Dave 1956- **1992**:1
Drysdale, Don 1936-1993
Obituary **1994**:1
Durocher, Leo 1905-1991
Obituary **1992**:2
Dykstra, Lenny 1963- **1993**:4
Edwards, Harry 1942- **1989**:4
Fehr, Donald 1948- **1987**:2
Fidrych, Mark 1954-2009
Obituary **2010**:2
Fielder, Cecil 1963- **1993**:2
Giamatti, A. Bartlett 1938-1989 **1988**:4
Obituary **1990**:1
Gibson, Kirk 1957- **1985**:2
Glaus, Troy 1976- **2003**:3
Gomez, Lefty 1909-1989
Obituary **1989**:3
Gooden, Dwight 1964- **1985**:2
Greenberg, Hank 1911-1986
Obituary **1986**:4
Griffey, Ken Jr. 1969- **1994**:1
Gwynn, Tony 1960- **1995**:1
Hamels, Cole 1983- **2009**:4
Helton, Todd 1973- **2001**:1
Henrich, Tommy 1913-2009
Obituary **2011**:4
Hernandez, Felix 1986- **2008**:2
Hernandez, Willie 1954- **1985**:1
Howser, Dick 1936-1987
Obituary **1987**:4
Hunter, Catfish 1946-1999
Obituary **2000**:1
Jackson, Bo 1962- **1986**:3
Johnson, Randy 1963- **1996**:2

Djerassi, Carl 1923- **2000**:4
Falkenberg, Nanette 1951- **1985**:2
Morgentaler, Henry 1923- **1986**:3
Rock, John
Obituary **1985**:1
Wattleton, Faye 1943- **1989**:1

Black Panther Party
Cleaver, Eldridge 1935-1998
Obituary **1998**:4
Newton, Huey 1942-1989
Obituary **1990**:1
Ture, Kwame 1941-1998
Obituary **1999**:2

Black Sash
Duncan, Sheena
Brief entry **1987**:1

Blockbuster Video
Huizenga, Wayne 1938(?)- **1992**:1
Keyes, James 1955- **2011**:3

Bloomingdale's
Campeau, Robert 1923- **1990**:1
Traub, Marvin
Brief entry **1987**:3

Boat racing
Aoki, Rocky 1940- **1990**:2
Conner, Dennis 1943- **1987**:2
Copeland, Al 1944(?)- **1988**:3
Hanauer, Chip 1954- **1986**:2
Turner, Ted 1938- **1989**:1

Bodybuilding
Powter, Susan 1957(?)- **1994**:3
Reeves, Steve 1926-2000
Obituary **2000**:4
Schwarzenegger, Arnold 1947- **1991**
:1

Body Shops International
Roddick, Anita 1943(?)- **1989**:4

Bose Corp.
Bose, Amar
Brief entry **1986**:4

Boston, Mass., city government
Flynn, Ray 1939- **1989**:1
Frank, Barney 1940- **1989**:2

Boston Bruins hockey team
Bourque, Raymond Jean 1960- **1997**
:3

Boston Celtics basketball team
Ainge, Danny 1959- **1987**:1
Auerbach, Red 1911-2006
Obituary **2008**:1
Bird, Larry 1956- **1990**:3
Lewis, Reggie 1966(?)-1993
Obituary **1994**:1
Maravich, Pete 1948-1988
Obituary **1988**:2
Pierce, Paul 1977- **2009**:2

Boston Properties Co.
Zuckerman, Mortimer 1937- **1986**:3

Boston Red Sox baseball team
Boggs, Wade 1958- **1989**:3
Clemens, Roger 1962- **1991**:4
Conigliaro, Tony 1945-1990
Obituary **1990**:3
Damon, Johnny 1973- **2005**:4
DiMaggio, Dom 1917-2009
Obituary **2010**:2
Epstein, Theo 1973- **2003**:4
Henderson, Rickey 1958- **2002**:3
Ramirez, Manny 1972- **2005**:4
Vaughn, Mo 1967- **1999**:2
Williams, Ted 1918-2002
Obituary **2003**:4

Boston University
Silber, John 1926- **1990**:1

Bowling
Anthony, Earl 1938-2001
Obituary **2002**:3
Weber, Pete 1962- **1986**:3

Boxing
Abercrombie, Josephine 1925- **1987**:2
Ali, Laila 1977- **2001**:2
Armstrong, Henry 1912-1988
Obituary **1989**:1
Bowe, Riddick 1967(?)- **1993**:2
Carter, Rubin 1937- **2000**:3
Danza, Tony 1951- **1989**:1
De La Hoya, Oscar 1973- **1998**:2
Douglas, Buster 1960(?)- **1990**:4
Foreman, George 1949- **2004**:2
Graziano, Rocky 1922-1990
Obituary **1990**:4
Hagler, Marvelous Marvin 1954-
1985:2
Holyfield, Evander 1962- **1991**:3
Kallen, Jackie 1946(?)- **1994**:1
King, Don 1931- **1989**:1
Leonard, Sugar Ray 1956- **1989**:4
Lewis, Lennox 1965- **2000**:2
Moore, Archie 1913-1998
Obituary **1999**:2
Pep, Willie 1922-2006
Obituary **2008**:1
Robinson, Sugar Ray 1921-1989
Obituary **1989**:3
Trinidad, Felix 1973- **2000**:4
Tyson, Mike 1966- **1986**:4

Boys Town
Peter, Valentine J. 1934- **1988**:2

BrainReserve
Popcorn, Faith
Brief entry **1988**:1

Branch Davidians religious sect
Koresh, David 1960(?)-1993
Obituary **1993**:4

Brewing
Busch, August A. III 1937- **1988**:2
Coors, William K.
Brief entry **1985**:1
Stroh, Peter W. 1927- **1985**:2

Bridge
Goren, Charles H. 1901-1991
Obituary **1991**:4

British Columbia provincial government
Vander Zalm, William 1934- **1987**:3

British royal family
Catherine, Duchess of Cambridge 1982- **2012**:2
Charles, Prince of Wales 1948- **1995**
:3
Diana, Princess of Wales 1961-1997
1993:1
Obituary **1997**:4
Ferguson, Sarah 1959- **1990**:3
Princess Margaret, Countess of Snowdon 1930-2002
Obituary **2003**:2
Queen Elizabeth the Queen Mother 1900-2002
Obituary **2003**:2
William, Prince of Wales 1982- **2001**
:3

Broadcasting
Albert, Marv 1943- **1994**:3
Allen, Mel 1913-1996
Obituary **1996**:4
Ancier, Garth 1957- **1989**:1
Barber, Red 1908-1992
Obituary **1993**:2
Bell, Art 1945- **2000**:1
Brown, James 1928(?)- **1991**:4
Caray, Harry 1914(?)-1998 **1988**:3
Obituary **1998**:3
Cherry, Don 1934- **1993**:4
Chung, Connie 1946- **1988**:4
Cosell, Howard 1918-1995
Obituary **1995**:4
Costas, Bob 1952- **1986**:4
Couric, Katherine 1957- **1991**:4
Daniels, Faith 1958- **1993**:3
Dickerson, Nancy H. 1927-1997 **1998**
:2
Donnellan, Nanci **1995**:2
Dr. Demento 1941- **1986**:1
Drysdale, Don 1936-1993
Obituary **1994**:1
Edwards, Bob 1947- **1993**:2
Ellerbee, Linda 1944- **1993**:3
Firestone, Roy 1953- **1988**:2
Gillett, George 1938- **1988**:1
Goldberg, Leonard 1934- **1988**:4
Grange, Red 1903-1991
Obituary **1991**:3
Gumbel, Bryant 1948- **1990**:2
Gunn, Hartford N., Jr. 1926-1986
Obituary **1986**:2
Harvey, Paul 1918- **1995**:3
Hollander, Joel 1956(?)- **2006**:4
Imus, Don 1940- **1997**:1
Jones, Jenny 1946- **1998**:2
Kasem, Casey 1933(?)- **1987**:1
Kent, Arthur 1954- **1991**:4
King, Larry 1933- **1993**:1
Kluge, John 1914- **1991**:1
Koppel, Ted 1940- **1989**:1
Kuralt, Charles 1934-1997
Obituary **1998**:3
Madden, John 1936- **1995**:1
Moyers, Bill 1934- **1991**:4
Murdoch, Rupert 1931- **1988**:4
Musburger, Brent 1939- **1985**:1
Norville, Deborah 1958- **1990**:3

Obituary **2003**:3
de la Renta, Oscar 1932- **2005**:4
Ellis, Perry 1940-1986
  Obituary **1986**:3
Halston 1932-1990
  Obituary **1990**:3
Johnson, Betsey 1942- **1996**:2
Kamali, Norma 1945- **1989**:1
Karan, Donna 1948- **1988**:1
Klein, Calvin 1942- **1996**:2
Lauren, Ralph 1939- **1990**:1
Morris, Robert 1947- **2010**:3
Smith, Willi 1948-1987
  Obituary **1987**:3

Council of Economic Advisers
Tyson, Laura D'Andrea 1947- **1994**:1

Counseling
Bradshaw, John 1933- **1992**:1
Gray, John 1952(?)- **1995**:3

Counterfeiting
Bikoff, James L.
  Brief entry **1986**:2

Country Music Awards
Bentley, Dierks 1975- **2007**:3
Brooks, Garth 1962- **1992**:1
Carpenter, Mary-Chapin 1958(?)-
  1994:1
Chesney, Kenny 1968- **2008**:2
Harris, Emmylou 1947- **1991**:3
Hill, Faith 1967- **2000**:1
Jackson, Alan 1958- **2003**:1
Lady Antebellum 1982- **2011**:2
Lambert, Miranda 1983- **2012**:2
Loveless, Patty 1957- **1998**:2
McBride, Martina 1966- **2010**:1
McEntire, Reba 1954- **1987**:3
McGraw, Tim 1966- **2000**:3
Nelson, Willie 1933- **1993**:4
Newton-John, Olivia 1948- **1998**:4
Paisley, Brad 1972- **2008**:3
Parton, Dolly 1946- **1999**:4
Pride, Charley 1938(?)- **1998**:1
Rascal Flatts **2007**:1
Shelton, Blake 1976- **2012**:3
Spacek, Sissy 1949- **2003**:1
Strait, George 1952- **1998**:3
Sugarland 1970- **2009**:2
Travis, Randy 1959- **1988**:4
Twitty, Conway 1933-1993
  Obituary **1994**:1
Underwood, Carrie 1983- **2008**:1
Urban, Keith 1967- **2006**:3
Wagoner, Porter 1927-2007
  Obituary **2008**:4
Wilson, Gretchen 1970- **2006**:3
Womack, Lee Ann 1966- **2002**:1
Wynette, Tammy 1942-1998
  Obituary **1998**:3
Wynonna 1964- **1993**:3
Yearwood, Trisha 1964- **1999**:1

Creation Spirituality
Altea, Rosemary 1946- **1996**:3
Fox, Matthew 1940- **1992**:2

Creative Artists Agency
Ovitz, Michael 1946- **1990**:1

Cy Young Award
Clemens, Roger 1962- **1991**:4
Hernandez, Willie 1954- **1985**:1
Hershiser, Orel 1958- **1989**:2
Johnson, Randy 1963- **1996**:2
Maddux, Greg 1966- **1996**:2
Palmer, Jim 1945- **1991**:2
Saberhagen, Bret 1964- **1986**:1
Santana, Johan 1979- **2008**:1
Smoltz, John 1967- **2010**:3
Verlander, Justin 1983- **2012**:4

Daimler-Benz AG [Mercedes-Benz]
Breitschwerdt, Werner 1927- **1988**:4

DaimlerChrysler Corp.
Schrempp, Juergen 1944- **2000**:2
Zetsche, Dieter 1953- **2002**:3

Dallas Cowboys football team
Aikman, Troy 1966- **1994**:2
Irvin, Michael 1966- **1996**:3
Johnson, Jimmy 1943- **1993**:3
Jones, Jerry 1942- **1994**:4
Landry, Tom 1924-2000
  Obituary **2000**:3
Romo, Tony 1980- **2008**:3
Smith, Emmitt **1994**:1

Dance Theatre of Harlem
Fagan, Garth 1940- **2000**:1
Mitchell, Arthur 1934- **1995**:1

Dell Computer Corp.
Dell, Michael 1965- **1996**:2

Democratic National Committee [DNC]
Brown, Ron 1941- **1990**:3
Brown, Ron 1941-1996
  Obituary **1996**:4
Dean, Howard 1948- **2005**:4
Waters, Maxine 1938- **1998**:4

Denver Broncos football team
Barnes, Ernie 1938- **1997**:4
Davis, Terrell 1972- **1998**:2
Elway, John 1960- **1990**:3

Department of Commerce
Baldrige, Malcolm 1922-1987
  Obituary **1988**:1
Brown, Ron 1941-1996
  Obituary **1996**:4

Department of Defense
Cohen, William S. 1940- **1998**:1
Perry, William 1927- **1994**:4

Department of Education
Cavazos, Lauro F. 1927- **1989**:2
Riley, Richard W. 1933- **1996**:3

Department of Energy
O'Leary, Hazel 1937- **1993**:4

Department of Health, Education, and Welfare [HEW]
Harris, Patricia Roberts 1924-1985
  Obituary **1985**:2
Ribicoff, Abraham 1910-1998
  Obituary **1998**:3

Department of Health and Human Services [HHR]
Kessler, David 1951- **1992**:1
Sullivan, Louis 1933- **1990**:4

Department of Housing and Urban Development [HUD]
Achtenberg, Roberta **1993**:4
Donovan, Shaun 1966- **2010**:4
Harris, Patricia Roberts 1924-1985
  Obituary **1985**:2
Kemp, Jack 1935- **1990**:4
Morrison, Trudi
  Brief entry **1986**:2

Department of Labor
Dole, Elizabeth Hanford 1936- **1990**
  :1
Martin, Lynn 1939- **1991**:4

Department of State
Christopher, Warren 1925- **1996**:3
Muskie, Edmund S. 1914-1996
  Obituary **1996**:3

Department of the Interior
Babbitt, Bruce 1938- **1994**:1

Department of Transportation
Dole, Elizabeth Hanford 1936- **1990**
  :1
Schiavo, Mary 1955- **1998**:2

Depression
Abramson, Lyn 1950- **1986**:3

Desilu Productions
Arnaz, Desi 1917-1986
  Obituary **1987**:1
Ball, Lucille 1911-1989
  Obituary **1989**:3

Detroit city government
Archer, Dennis 1942- **1994**:4
Maida, Adam Cardinal 1930- **1998**:2
Young, Coleman A. 1918-1997
  Obituary **1998**:1

Detroit Lions football team
Ford, William Clay, Jr. 1957- **1999**:1
Sanders, Barry 1968- **1992**:1
White, Byron 1917-2002
  Obituary **2003**:3

Detroit Pistons basketball team
Daly, Chuck 1930-2009
  Obituary **2010**:3
Hill, Grant 1972- **1995**:3
Laimbeer, Bill 1957- **2004**:3
Rodman, Dennis 1961- **1991**:3
Thomas, Isiah 1961- **1989**:2
Vitale, Dick 1939- **1988**:4
Wallace, Ben 1974- **2004**:3

Detroit Red Wings hockey team
Bowman, Scotty 1933- **1998**:4
Federov, Sergei 1969- **1995**:1
Ilitch, Mike 1929- **1993**:4

Golden Globe Awards

Abrams, J. J. 1966- **2007**:3
Affleck, Ben 1972- **1999**:1
Arkin, Alan 1934- **2007**:4
Bacall, Lauren 1924- **1997**:3
Bakula, Scott 1954- **2003**:1
Bardem, Javier 1969- **2008**:4
Baron Cohen, Sacha 1971- **2007**:3
Bateman, Jason 1969- **2005**:3
Beatty, Warren 1937- **2000**:1
Bernstein, Elmer 1922-2004
    Obituary **2005**:4
Blanchett, Cate 1969- **1999**:3
Boyle, Danny 1956- **2009**:4
Bridges, Jeff 1949- **2011**:1
Broadbent, Jim 1949- **2008**:4
Bronson, Charles 1921-2003
    Obituary **2004**:4
Burnett, Carol 1933- **2000**:3
Caine, Michael 1933- **2000**:4
Carell, Steve 1963- **2006**:4
Carter, Chris 1956- **2000**:1
Cattrall, Kim 1956- **2003**:3
Cheadle, Don 1964- **2002**:1
Cher 1946- **1993**:1
Chiklis, Michael 1963- **2003**:3
Christie, Julie 1941- **2008**:4
Colfer, Chris 1990- **2012**:2
Connelly, Jennifer 1970- **2002**:4
Cooper, Chris 1951- **2004**:1
Coppola, Sofia 1971- **2004**:3
Cosby, Bill 1937- **1999**:2
Curtis, Jamie Lee 1958- **1995**:1
Damon, Matt 1970- **1999**:1
Danes, Claire 1979- **1999**:4
Dench, Judi 1934- **1999**:4
De Niro, Robert 1943- **1999**:1
Dennehy, Brian 1938- **2002**:1
Depardieu, Gerard 1948- **1991**:2
Downey, Robert, Jr. 1965- **2007**:1
Duvall, Robert 1931- **1999**:3
Elfman, Jenna 1971- **1999**:4
Falco, Edie 1963- **2010**:2
Farrow, Mia 1945- **1998**:3
Fell, Norman 1924-1998
    Obituary **1999**:2
Fiennes, Ralph 1962- **1996**:2
Finney, Albert 1936- **2003**:3
Firth, Colin 1960- **2012**:3
Flockhart, Calista 1964- **1998**:4
Ford, Glenn 1916-2006
    Obituary **2007**:4
Franco, James 1978- **2012**:1
Garner, Jennifer 1972- **2003**:1
Getty, Estelle 1923-2008
    Obituary **2009**:3
Giamatti, Paul 1967- **2009**:4
Goldberg, Whoopi 1955- **1993**:3
Hall, Michael 1971- **2011**:1
Hallstrom, Lasse 1946- **2002**:3
Hamm, Jon 1971- **2009**:2
Hanks, Tom 1956- **1989**:2
Hargitay, Mariska 1964- **2006**:2
Harris, Ed 1950- **2002**:2
Hatcher, Teri 1964- **2005**:4
Hawkins, Sally 1976- **2009**:4
Heston, Charlton 1924- **1999**:4
Hoffman, Dustin 1937- **2005**:4
Hoffman, Philip Seymour 1967-
    2006:3
Hudson, Jennifer 1981- **2008**:1
Huffman, Felicity 1962- **2006**:2

Irons, Jeremy 1948- **1991**:4
Jackson, Peter 1961- **2004**:4
Jarre, Maurice 1924-2009
    Obituary **2010**:2
Johnson, Don 1949- **1986**:1
Jolie, Angelina 1975- **2000**:2
Keaton, Diane 1946- **1997**:1
Lansbury, Angela 1925- **1993**:1
Laurie, Hugh 1959- **2007**:2
Leigh, Janet 1927-2004
    Obituary **2005**:4
Lemmon, Jack 1925- **1998**:4
    Obituary **2002**:3
Linney, Laura 1964- **2009**:4
Lucas, George 1944- **1999**:4
Luhrmann, Baz 1962- **2002**:3
Margulies, Julianna 1966- **2011**:1
Matlin, Marlee 1965- **1992**:2
Matthau, Walter 1920- **2000**:3
Merkerson, S. Epatha 1952- **2006**:4
Minghella, Anthony 1954- **2004**:3
Moore, Dudley 1935-2002
    Obituary **2003**:2
Moore, Mary Tyler 1936- **1996**:2
Norton, Edward 1969- **2000**:2
O'Connor, Donald 1925-2003
    Obituary **2004**:4
Owen, Clive 1964- **2006**:2
Pakula, Alan 1928-1998
    Obituary **1999**:2
Paquin, Anna 1982- **2009**:4
Parsons, Jim 1973- **2012**:3
Payne, Alexander 1961- **2005**:4
Perlman, Ron 1950- **2012**:4
Peters, Bernadette 1948- **2000**:1
Redgrave, Lynn 1943- **1999**:3
Reitman, Jason 1977- **2011**:3
Rhys Meyers, Jonathan 1977- **2007**:1
Ritter, John 1948- **2003**:4
Roberts, Julia 1967- **1991**:3
Russell, Keri 1976- **2000**:1
Sheen, Martin 1940- **2002**:1
Spacek, Sissy 1949- **2003**:1
Springsteen, Bruce 1949- **2011**:1
Streisand, Barbra 1942- **1992**:2
Sutherland, Kiefer 1966- **2002**:4
Swank, Hilary 1974- **2000**:3
Taylor, Lili 1967- **2000**:2
Thompson, Emma 1959- **1993**:2
Ullman, Tracey 1961- **1988**:3
Waltz, Christoph 1956- **2011**:1
Washington, Denzel 1954- **1993**:2
Waterston, Sam 1940- **2006**:1
Weisz, Rachel 1971- **2006**:4
Woodward, Edward 1930-2009
    Obituary **2011**:3

Golden State Warriors basketball team

Bol, Manute 1962-2010
    Obituary **2012**:4
Sprewell, Latrell 1970- **1999**:4
Webber, Chris 1973- **1994**:1

Golf

Allenby, Robert 1971- **2007**:1
Azinger, Paul 1960- **1995**:2
Baker, Kathy
    Brief entry **1986**:1
Bradley, Keegan 1986- **2012**:4
Callaway, Ely 1919-2001
    Obituary **2002**:3
Chen, T.C.

Brief entry **1987**:3
Couples, Fred 1959- **1994**:4
Creamer, Paula 1986- **2006**:2
Curtis, Ben 1977- **2004**:2
Duval, David 1971- **2000**:3
Faldo, Nick 1957- **1993**:3
Furyk, Jim 1970- **2004**:2
Hogan, Ben 1912-1997
    Obituary **1997**:4
Irwin, Hale 1945- **2005**:2
Kerr, Cristie 1977- **2008**:2
Kite, Tom 1949- **1990**:3
Lopez, Nancy 1957- **1989**:3
Martin, Casey 1972- **2002**:1
McIlroy, Rory 1989- **2012**:3
Mickelson, Phil 1970- **2004**:4
Nelson, Byron 1912-2006
    Obituary **2007**:4
Norman, Greg 1955- **1988**:3
Ochoa, Lorena 1981- **2007**:4
Pak, Se Ri 1977- **1999**:4
Pavin, Corey 1959- **1996**:4
Peete, Calvin 1943- **1985**:4
Sarazen, Gene 1902-1999
    Obituary **1999**:4
Singh, Vijay 1963- **2000**:4
Snead, Sam 1912-2002
    Obituary **2003**:3
Strange, Curtis 1955- **1988**:4
Webb, Karrie 1974- **2000**:4
Weir, Mike 1970- **2004**:1
Whaley, Suzy 1966- **2003**:4
Woods, Tiger 1975- **1995**:4

Gorillas

Fossey, Dian 1932-1985
    Obituary **1986**:1

Gospel music

Adams, Yolanda 1961- **2008**:2
Dorsey, Thomas A. 1899-1993
    Obituary **1993**:3
Franklin, Aretha 1942- **1998**:3
Franklin, Kirk 1970- **2010**:2
Houston, Cissy 1933- **1999**:3
Reese, Della 1931- **1999**:2
Staples, Roebuck Pops 1915-2000
    Obituary **2001**:3

Grammy Awards

Adams, Yolanda 1961- **2008**:2
Adele 1988- **2009**:4
Aguilera, Christina 1980- **2000**:4
Anderson, Marion 1897-1993
    Obituary **1993**:4
Anthony, Marc 1969- **2000**:3
Apple, Fiona 1977- **2006**:3
Arcade Fire 1982- **2012**:2
Arrested Development **1994**:2
Ashanti 1980- **2004**:1
Auerbach, Dan 1979-
(See The Black Keys)
Badu, Erykah 1971- **2000**:4
Baker, Anita 1958- **1987**:4
Battle, Kathleen 1948- **1998**:1
Beck 1970- **2000**:2
Beck, Jeff 1944- **2011**:4
Bee Gees, The **1997**:4
Benatar, Pat 1953- **1986**:1
Bennett, Tony 1926- **1994**:4
Berry, Chuck 1926- **2001**:2
Beyonce 1981- **2009**:3

The Black Keys **2012**:4
Blades, Ruben 1948- **1998**:2
Bolton, Michael 1953(?)- **1993**:2
Bono 1960- **1988**:4
Boyz II Men **1995**:1
Brandy 1979- **1996**:4
Braxton, Toni 1967- **1994**:3
Brown, James 1928(?)- **1991**:4
Brown, Ruth 1928-2006
    Obituary **2008**:1
Buble, Michael 1975- **2010**:4
Carey, Mariah 1970(?)- **1991**:3
Carney, Patrick 1979-
(See The Black Keys)
Carpenter, Mary-Chapin 1958(?)-
    1994:1
Carter, Benny 1907-2003
    Obituary **2004**:3
Cash, Johnny 1932- **1995**:3
Cash, June Carter 1929-2003
    Obituary **2004**:2
Chapman, Tracy 1964- **1989**:2
Charles, Ray 1930-2004
    Obituary **2005**:3
Clapton, Eric 1945- **1993**:3
Cleveland, James 1932(?)-1991
    Obituary **1991**:3
Coldplay **2004**:4
Cole, Natalie 1950- **1992**:4
Collins, Albert 1932-1993
    Obituary **1994**:2
Corea, Chick 1941- **1986**:3
Cosby, Bill 1937- **1999**:2
Cray, Robert 1953- **1988**:2
Crosby, David 1941- **2000**:4
Crow, Sheryl 1964- **1995**:2
Cruz, Celia 1925-2003
    Obituary **2004**:3
Daft Punk 1975- **2009**:4
Dangerfield, Rodney 1921-2004
    Obituary **2006**:1
de Larrocha, Alicia 1923-2009
    Obituary **2011**:1
Destiny's Child **2001**:3
Diddley, Bo 1928-2008
    Obituary **2009**:3
Di Meola, Al 1954- **1986**:4
Dion, Celine 1970(?)- **1995**:3
Dixie Chicks **2001**:2
Duran Duran **2005**:3
Dylan, Bob 1941- **1998**:1
Earle, Steve 1955- **2011**:2
Edmonds, Kenneth Babyface
    1958(?)- **1995**:3
Elliott, Missy 1971- **2003**:4
Eminem 1974- **2001**:2
Ertegun, Ahmet 1923- **1986**:3
Etheridge, Melissa 1961(?)- **1995**:4
Eve 1978- **2004**:3
Fantasia 1984- **2012**:1
Farrell, Perry 1960- **1992**:2
Fleck, Bela 1958- **2011**:3
Foo Fighters **2006**:2
Ford, Tennessee Ernie 1919-1991
    Obituary **1992**:2
Foster, David 1950(?)- **1988**:2
Franklin, Aretha 1942- **1998**:3
Franklin, Kirk 1970- **2010**:2
Franklin, Melvin 1942-1995
    Obituary **1995**:3
Furtado, Nelly 1978- **2007**:2
Getz, Stan 1927-1991

Obituary **1991**:4
Gill, Vince 1957- **1995**:2
Goldberg, Whoopi 1955- **1993**:3
Goodman, Benny 1909-1986
    Obituary **1986**:3
Goulet, Robert 1933-2007
    Obituary **2008**:4
Grant, Amy 1961(?)- **1985**:4
Gray, Macy 1970(?)- **2002**:1
Green, Cee Lo 1975- **2012**:3
Green Day **1995**:4
Hammer, Jan 1948- **1987**:3
Hammer, M. C. **1991**:2
Hancock, Herbie 1940- **1985**:1
Harris, Emmylou 1947- **1991**:3
Harrison, George 1943-2001
    Obituary **2003**:1
Hayes, Isaac 1942- **1998**:4
Headley, Heather 1974- **2011**:1
Hill, Lauryn 1975- **1999**:3
Hirt, Al 1922-1999
    Obituary **1999**:4
Hooker, John Lee 1917- **1998**:1
    Obituary **2002**:3
Horne, Lena 1917- **1998**:4
Hornsby, Bruce 1954(?)- **1989**:3
Houston, Cissy 1933- **1999**:3
Houston, Whitney 1963- **1986**:3
Hubbard, Freddie 1938- **1988**:4
Iglesias, Enrique 1975- **2000**:1
Indigo Girls **1994**:4
Jackson, Michael 1958- **1996**:2
James, Rick 1948-2004
    Obituary **2005**:4
Jarre, Maurice 1924-2009
    Obituary **2010**:2
Jay-Z 1970- **2006**:1
Jennings, Waylon 1937-2002
    Obituary **2003**:2
Joel, Billy 1949- **1994**:3
John, Elton 1947- **1995**:4
Jones, Norah 1979- **2004**:1
Judas Priest 1951- **2011**:3
Keillor, Garrison 1942- **2011**:2
Kenny G 1957(?)- **1994**:4
Keys, Alicia 1981- **2006**:1
Kings of Leon 1982- **2010**:3
Knopfler, Mark 1949- **1986**:2
Kronos Quartet **1993**:1
Lady Antebellum 1982- **2011**:2
Lady Gaga **2011**:1
Lambert, Miranda 1983- **2012**:2
Lauper, Cyndi 1953- **1985**:1
Lee, Peggy 1920-2002
    Obituary **2003**:1
Legend, John 1978- **2007**:1
Levy, Eugene 1946- **2004**:3
Lil Wayne 1982- **2009**:3
Linkletter, Art 1912-2010
    Obituary **2012**:4
Living Colour **1993**:3
LL Cool J 1968- **1998**:2
Ludacris 1977- **2007**:4
Lynn, Loretta 1935(?)- **2001**:1
Marin, Cheech 1946- **2000**:1
Maroon 5 **2008**:1
Mars, Bruno 1985- **2012**:4
Marsalis, Wynton 1961- **1997**:4
Martin, Ricky 1971- **1999**:4
Martin, Steve 1945- **1992**:2
Mary Mary 1972- **2009**:4
Mayer, John 1977- **2007**:4

McBride, Martina 1966- **2010**:1
McCartney, Paul 1942- **2002**:4
McEntire, Reba 1954- **1987**:3
McFerrin, Bobby 1950- **1989**:1
McLachlan, Sarah 1968- **1998**:4
Menuhin, Yehudi 1916-1999
    Obituary **1999**:3
Metallica **2004**:2
Midler, Bette 1945- **1989**:4
Miller, Roger 1936-1992
    Obituary **1993**:2
Mitchell, Joni 1943- **1991**:4
Monica 1980- **2004**:2
Moog, Robert 1934-2005
    Obituary **2006**:4
Morissette, Alanis 1974- **1996**:2
Murphy, Eddie 1961- **1989**:2
Muse 1978- **2012**:3
Ne-Yo 1982- **2009**:4
Nelson, Willie 1933- **1993**:4
Newton-John, Olivia 1948- **1998**:4
Orbison, Roy 1936-1988
    Obituary **1989**:2
Osbournes, The **2003**:4
OutKast **2004**:4
Paisley, Brad 1972- **2008**:3
Palmer, Robert 1949-2003
    Obituary **2004**:4
Parton, Dolly 1946- **1999**:4
Pass, Joe 1929-1994
    Obituary **1994**:4
Paul, Les 1915-2009
    Obituary **2010**:4
Peterson, Oscar 1925-2007
    Obituary **2009**:1
Phoenix **2011**:1
Pink 1979- **2004**:3
Pride, Charley 1938(?)- **1998**:1
Prince 1958- **1995**:3
Pryor, Richard **1999**:3
Puente, Tito 1923-2000
    Obituary **2000**:4
Radiohead **2009**:3
Raitt, Bonnie 1949- **1990**:2
Rascal Flatts **2007**:1
Rattle, Simon 1955- **1989**:4
Rawls, Lou 1933-2006
    Obituary **2007**:1
Reitman, Jason 1977- **2011**:3
Reznor, Trent 1965- **2000**:2
Riddle, Nelson 1921-1985
    Obituary **1985**:4
Rihanna 1988- **2008**:4
Rimes, LeeAnn 1982- **1997**:4
Rollins, Henry 1961- **2007**:3
Sade 1959- **1993**:2
Santana, Carlos 1947- **2000**:2
Sanz, Alejandro 1968- **2011**:3
Scott, Jill 1972- **2010**:1
Selena 1971-1995
    Obituary **1995**:4
Shakira 1977- **2002**:3
Silverstein, Shel 1932-1999
    Obituary **1999**:4
Simon, Paul 1942(?)- **1992**:2
Sinatra, Frank 1915-1998
    Obituary **1998**:4
Smith, Will 1968- **1997**:2
Solti, Georg 1912-1997
    Obituary **1998**:1
Sondheim, Stephen 1930- **1994**:4
Spalding, Esperanza 1984- **2012**:2

Springsteen, Bruce 1949- **2011**:1
Stafford, Jo 1917-2008
    Obituary **2009**:3
Stefani, Gwen 1969- **2005**:4
Stewart, Rod 1945- **2007**:1
Sting 1951- **1991**:4
Streisand, Barbra 1942- **1992**:2
System of a Down **2006**:4
T. I. 1980- **2008**:1
Taylor, Koko 1928-2009
    Obituary **2010**:3
Third Day 1976- **2011**:2
Timbaland 1971- **2007**:4
Timberlake, Justin 1981- **2008**:4
Torme, Mel 1925-1999
    Obituary **1999**:4
Tosh, Peter 1944-1987
    Obituary **1988**:2
Travers, Mary 1936-2009
    Obituary **2011**:1
Travis, Randy 1959- **1988**:4
Turner, Ike 1931-2007
    Obituary **2009**:1
Turner, Tina 1939- **2000**:3
Twain, Shania 1965- **1996**:3
Tyler, Steven 1948- **2012**:3
U2 **2002**:4
Underwood, Carrie 1983- **2008**:1
Urban, Keith 1967- **2006**:3
Usher 1979- **2005**:1
Vandross, Luther 1951-2005
    Obituary **2006**:3
Vaughan, Stevie Ray 1956(?)-1990
    Obituary **1991**:1
Wagoner, Porter 1927-2007
    Obituary **2008**:4
Washington, Grover, Jr. 1943- **1989**:1
West, Kanye 1977- **2006**:1
White, Barry 1944-2003
    Obituary **2004**:3
White Stripes, The **2006**:1
Wild, Earl 1915-2010
    Obituary **2012**:1
Williams, Joe 1918-1999
    Obituary **1999**:4
Williams, Pharrell 1973- **2005**:3
Williams, Robin 1952- **1988**:4
Wilson, Flip 1933-1998
    Obituary **1999**:2
Wilson, Gretchen 1970- **2006**:3
Winans, CeCe 1964- **2000**:1
Wynonna 1964- **1993**:3
Yankovic, Frank 1915-1998
    Obituary **1999**:2
Yearwood, Trisha 1964- **1999**:1
Zevon, Warren 1947-2003
    Obituary **2004**:4

Grand Ole Opry
    Bentley, Dierks 1975- **2007**:3
    McBride, Martina 1966- **2010**:1
    Snow, Hank 1914-1999
        Obituary **2000**:3
    Wagoner, Porter 1927-2007
        Obituary **2008**:4

Grand Prix racing
    Prost, Alain 1955- **1988**:1

Green Bay Packers football team
    Favre, Brett Lorenzo 1969- **1997**:2
    Howard, Desmond Kevin 1970-
        1997:2

Rodgers, Aaron 1983- **2012**:2
Sharpe, Sterling 1965- **1994**:3
White, Reggie 1961- **1993**:4

Greenpeace International
    McTaggart, David 1932(?)- **1989**:4

Greens party (West Germany)
    Schily, Otto
        Brief entry **1987**:4

GRP Records, Inc.
    Grusin, Dave
        Brief entry **1987**:2

Gucci
    Ford, Tom 1962- **1999**:3

Gucci Shops, Inc.
    Gucci, Maurizio
        Brief entry **1985**:4
    Mello, Dawn 1938(?)- **1992**:2

Gulf + Western
    Diller, Barry 1942- **1991**:1

Gun control
    Brady, Sarah and James S. **1991**:4

Gymnastics
    Hamm, Paul 1982- **2005**:1
    Johnson, Shawn 1992- **2009**:2
    Retton, Mary Lou 1968- **1985**:2
    Strug, Kerri 1977- **1997**:3

H & R Block, Inc.
    Bloch, Henry 1922- **1988**:4

Hampshire College
    Simmons, Adele Smith 1941- **1988**:4

Handicap rights
    Brady, Sarah and James S. **1991**:4
    Dickinson, Brian 1937- **1998**:2

Hanna-Barbera Productions
    Barbera, Joseph 1911- **1988**:2
    Hanna, William 1910-2001
        Obituary **2002**:1

Hard Candy
    Mohajer, Dineh 1972- **1997**:3

Harlem Globetrotters basketball team
    Woodard, Lynette 1959(?)- **1986**:2

Harley-Davidson Motor Co., Inc.
    Beals, Vaughn 1928- **1988**:2

Hartford, Conn., city government
    Perry, Carrie Saxon 1932(?)- **1989**:2

Hasbro, Inc.
    Hassenfeld, Stephen 1942- **1987**:4

Hasidism
    Schneerson, Menachem Mendel
    1902-1994 **1992**:4
        Obituary **1994**:4

Hasty Pudding Theatricals
    Beatty, Warren 1937- **2000**:1
    Burnett, Carol 1933- **2000**:3
    Hanks, Tom 1956- **1989**:2
    Peters, Bernadette 1948- **2000**:1

Hearst Magazines
    Black, Cathleen 1944- **1998**:4
    Ganzi, Victor 1947- **2003**:3

Heisman Trophy
    Flutie, Doug 1962- **1999**:2
    Howard, Desmond Kevin 1970-
        1997:2
    Jackson, Bo 1962- **1986**:3
    Testaverde, Vinny 1962- **1987**:2
    Williams, Ricky 1977- **2000**:2

Helmsley Hotels, Inc.
    Helmsley, Leona 1920- **1988**:1

Hemlock Society
    Humphry, Derek 1931(?)- **1992**:2

Herbalife International
    Hughes, Mark 1956- **1985**:3

Hereditary Disease Foundation
    Wexler, Nancy S. 1945- **1992**:3

Herut Party (Israel)
    Levy, David 1938- **1987**:2

Hewlett-Packard
    Fiorina, Carleton S. 1954- **2000**:1
    Hewlett, William 1913-2001
        Obituary **2001**:4
    Hurd, Mark 1957- **2010**:4
    Packard, David 1912-1996
        Obituary **1996**:3

High Flight Foundation
    Irwin, James 1930-1991
        Obituary **1992**:1

Hitchhiking
    Heid, Bill
        Brief entry **1987**:2

Hobie Cat
    Alter, Hobie
        Brief entry **1985**:1
    Hasek, Dominik 1965- **1998**:3

Hockey
    Bourque, Raymond Jean 1960- **1997**:3
    Cherry, Don 1934- **1993**:4
    Coffey, Paul 1961- **1985**:4
    Crosby, Sidney 1987- **2006**:3
    Eagleson, Alan 1933- **1987**:4
    Federov, Sergei 1969- **1995**:1
    Fuhr, Grant 1962- **1997**:3
    Giguere, Jean-Sebastien 1977- **2004**:2
    Gilmour, Doug 1963- **1994**:3
    Granato, Cammi 1971- **1999**:3
    Gretzky, Wayne 1961- **1989**:2
    Hextall, Ron 1964- **1988**:2

Miss Manners
Martin, Judith 1938- **2000**:3

Mister Rogers
Rogers, Fred 1928- **2000**:4

Modeling
Brando, Cheyenne 1970-1995
Obituary **1995**:4
Bruni, Carla 1967- **2009**:3
Campbell, Naomi 1970- **2000**:2
Crawford, Cindy 1966- **1993**:3
Diaz, Cameron 1972- **1999**:1
Dickinson, Janice 1953- **2005**:2
Fabio 1961(?)- **1993**:4
Fawcett, Farrah 1947- **1998**:4
Hurley, Elizabeth **1999**:2
Johnson, Beverly 1952- **2005**:2
Klum, Heidi 1973- **2006**:3
Leigh, Dorian 1917-2008
Obituary **2009**:3
Leslie, Lisa 1972- **1997**:4
MacDowell, Andie 1958(?)- **1993**:4
Marky Mark 1971- **1993**:3
McCarthy, Jenny 1972- **1997**:4
McCord, Catherine 1974- **2012**:2
Moss, Kate 1974- **1995**:3
Page, Bettie 1923-2008
Obituary **2010**:1
Parker, Suzy 1932-2003
Obituary **2004**:2
Romijn, Rebecca 1972- **2007**:1
Smith, Anna Nicole 1967-2007
Obituary **2008**:2
Tatum, Channing 1980- **2011**:3

Molecular biology
Blackburn, Elizabeth 1948- **2010**:1
Gilbert, Walter 1932- **1988**:3
Kornberg, Arthur 1918(?)- **1992**:1
Levinson, Arthur D. 1950- **2008**:3
Melton, Douglas 1954- **2008**:3
Mullis, Kary 1944- **1995**:3
Sidransky, David 1960- **2002**:4

Montreal Canadiens hockey team
Lemieux, Claude 1965- **1996**:1
Richard, Maurice 1921-2000
Obituary **2000**:4
Roy, Patrick 1965- **1994**:2

Monty Python
Cleese, John 1939- **1989**:2
Milligan, Spike 1918-2002
Obituary **2003**:2

Mormon Church
Benson, Ezra Taft 1899-1994
Obituary **1994**:4
Hunter, Howard 1907- **1994**:4

Mothers Against Drunk Driving [MADD]
Lightner, Candy 1946- **1985**:1
Potts, Annie 1952- **1994**:1

Motivational speakers
Brown, Les 1945- **1994**:3
Peters, Tom 1942- **1998**:1

Motorcycles
Beals, Vaughn 1928- **1988**:2
Hart, Carey 1975- **2006**:4
James, Jesse 1969- **2004**:4
Knievel, Robbie 1963- **1990**:1

Motown Records
de Passe, Suzanne 1946(?)- **1990**:4
Franklin, Melvin 1942-1995
Obituary **1995**:3
Kendricks, Eddie 1939-1992
Obituary **1993**:2
Payton, Lawrence 1938(?)-1997
Obituary **1997**:4
Ruffin, David 1941-1991
Obituary **1991**:4
Wells, Mary 1943-1992
Obituary **1993**:1

Mountain climbing
Grylls, Bear 1974- **2010**:2
Wood, Sharon
Brief entry **1988**:1

Moving Earth (dance company)
Takei, Kei 1946- **1990**:2

Mozambique Liberation Front [FRELIMO]
Chissano, Joaquim 1939- **1987**:4
Machel, Samora 1933-1986
Obituary **1987**:1

Mrs. Fields Cookies, Inc.
Fields, Debbi 1956- **1987**:3

Ms. magazine
Gillespie, Marcia 1944- **1999**:4
Morgan, Robin 1941- **1991**:1
Steinem, Gloria 1934- **1996**:2
Summers, Anne 1945- **1990**:2

MTV Networks, Inc.
Daly, Carson 1973- **2002**:4
Duffy, Karen 1962- **1998**:1
Duran Duran **2005**:3
Graden, Brian 1963- **2004**:2
Kutcher, Ashton 1978- **2003**:4
Laybourne, Geraldine 1947- **1997**:1
McGrath, Judy 1953- **2006**:1
Osbournes, The **2003**:4
Pinsky, Drew 1958- **2012**:2
Pittman, Robert W. 1953- **1985**:1
Quinn, Martha 1959- **1986**:4
Roedy, Bill 1949(?)- **2003**:2
Sethi, Simran 1971(?)- **2008**:1

Multiple birth research
Keith, Louis 1935- **1988**:2

Muppets
Henson, Brian 1964(?)- **1992**:1
Henson, Jim 1936-1990 **1989**:1
Obituary **1990**:4

Museum of Modern Art (New York City)
Gund, Agnes 1938- **1993**:2
Taniguchi, Yoshio 1937- **2005**:4

National Abortion Rights Action League [NARAL]
Falkenberg, Nanette 1951- **1985**:2
Michelman, Kate 1942- **1998**:4

National Academy of Science
Djerassi, Carl 1923- **2000**:4
Van Allen, James 1914-2006
Obituary **2007**:4

National Aeronautics and Space Administration [NASA]
Bean, Alan L. 1932- **1986**:2
Collins, Eileen 1956- **1995**:3
Conrad, Pete 1930-1999
Obituary **2000**:1
Garneau, Marc 1949- **1985**:1
Glenn, John 1921- **1998**:3
Jemison, Mae C. 1956- **1993**:1
Lucid, Shannon 1943- **1997**:1
McAuliffe, Christa 1948-1986
Obituary **1985**:4
O'Keefe, Sean 1956- **2005**:2
Schirra, Wally 1923-2007
Obituary **2008**:3
Shepard, Alan 1923-1998
Obituary **1999**:1

National Association for the Advancement of Colored People [NAACP]
Adams, Yolanda 1961- **2008**:2
Chavis, Benjamin 1948- **1993**:4
Evers-Williams, Myrlie 1933- **1995**:4
Johnson, Robert L. 1946- **2000**:4
LL Cool J 1968- **1998**:2
Mfume, Kweisi 1948- **1996**:3
Parks, Rosa 1913-2005
Obituary **2007**:1

National Audubon Society
Berle, Peter A.A.
Brief entry **1987**:3

National Baptist Convention
Shaw, William 1934(?)- **2000**:3

National Basketball Association [NBA]
Auerbach, Red 1911-2006
Obituary **2008**:1
Bryant, Kobe 1978- **1998**:3
Duncan, Tim 1976- **2000**:1
Garnett, Kevin 1976- **2000**:3
Laimbeer, Bill 1957- **2004**:3
Malone, Karl 1963- **1990**:1
Mikan, George 1924-2005
Obituary **2006**:3
O'Malley, Susan 1962(?)- **1995**:2
Parker, Tony 1982- **2008**:1
Stockton, John Houston 1962- **1997**:3
Wallace, Ben 1974- **2004**:3
Yao Ming 1980- **2004**:1

National Cancer Institute
DeVita, Vincent T., Jr. 1935- **1987**:3
King, Mary-Claire 1946- **1998**:3
Rosenberg, Steven 1940- **1989**:1

National Center for Atmospheric Research
Thompson, Starley
Brief entry **1987**:3

National Coalition for the Homeless
Hayes, Robert M. 1952- **1986**:3

National Coalition on Television Violence [NCTV]
Radecki, Thomas
Brief entry **1986**:2

Menchu, Rigoberta 1960(?)- **1993**:2
Milosz, Czeslaw 1911-2004
   Obituary **2005**:4
Morrison, Toni 1931- **1998**:1
Mother Teresa 1910-1997 **1993**:1
   Obituary **1998**:1
Muller, Jim 1943- **2011**:3
Mullis, Kary 1944- **1995**:3
Nirenberg, Marshall Warren
   1927-2010
   Obituary **2012**:1
Nuesslein-Volhard, Christiane 1942-
   1998:1
Oe, Kenzaburo 1935- **1997**:1
Pamuk, Orhan 1952- **2007**:3
Pauling, Linus 1901-1994
   Obituary **1995**:1
Paz, Octavio 1914- **1991**:2
Perutz, Max 1914-2002
   Obituary **2003**:2
Pople, John 1925-2004
   Obituary **2005**:2
Porter, George 1920-2002
   Obituary **2003**:4
Prusiner, Stanley 1942- **1998**:2
Sakharov, Andrei Dmitrievich
   1921-1989
   Obituary **1990**:2
Saramago, Jose 1922- **1999**:1
Singer, Isaac Bashevis 1904-1991
   Obituary **1992**:1
Suu Kyi, Aung San 1945(?)- **1996**:2
Szent-Gyoergyi, Albert 1893-1986
   Obituary **1987**:2
Trimble, David 1944- **1999**:1
Walesa, Lech 1943- **1991**:2
Wiesel, Elie 1928- **1998**:1
Yunus, Muhammad 1940- **2007**:3

No Limit (record label)
   Master P 1970- **1999**:4

North Atlantic Treaty Organization
[NATO]
   de Hoop Scheffer, Jaap 1948- **2005**:1
   Galvin, John R. 1929- **1990**:1

NPR
   Tom and Ray Magliozzi **1991**:4

Nuclear energy
   Gale, Robert Peter 1945- **1986**:4
   Hagelstein, Peter
     Brief entry **1986**:3
   Lederman, Leon Max 1922- **1989**:4
   Maglich, Bogdan C. 1928- **1990**:1
   Merritt, Justine
     Brief entry **1985**:3
   Nader, Ralph 1934- **1989**:4
   Palme, Olof 1927-1986
     Obituary **1986**:2
   Rickover, Hyman 1900-1986
     Obituary **1986**:4
   Sinclair, Mary 1918- **1985**:2
   Smith, Samantha 1972-1985
     Obituary **1985**:3
   Zech, Lando W.
     Brief entry **1987**:4

Nuclear Regulatory Commission [NRC]
   Zech, Lando W.
     Brief entry **1987**:4

Oakland A's baseball team
   Canseco, Jose 1964- **1990**:2
   Caray, Harry 1914(?)-1998 **1988**:3
     Obituary **1998**:3
   Stewart, Dave 1957- **1991**:1
   Welch, Bob 1956- **1991**:3
   Zito, Barry 1978- **2003**:3

Oakland Raiders football team
   Matuszak, John 1951(?)-1989
     Obituary **1989**:4
   Trask, Amy 1961- **2003**:3
   Upshaw, Gene 1945- **1988**:1

Obie Awards
   Albee, Edward 1928- **1997**:1
   Arkin, Alan 1934- **2007**:4
   Baldwin, Alec 1958- **2002**:2
   Bergman, Ingmar 1918- **1999**:4
   Close, Glenn 1947- **1988**:3
   Coco, James 1929(?)-1987
     Obituary **1987**:2
   Daniels, Jeff 1955- **1989**:4
   Dewhurst, Colleen 1924-1991
     Obituary **1992**:2
   Diller, Elizabeth and Ricardo
     Scofidio **2004**:3
   Dukakis, Olympia 1931- **1996**:4
   Duvall, Robert 1931- **1999**:3
   Ebersole, Christine 1953- **2007**:2
   Ensler, Eve 1954(?)- **2002**:4
   Fierstein, Harvey 1954- **2004**:2
   Fo, Dario 1926- **1998**:1
   Fugard, Athol 1932- **1992**:3
   Gray, Spalding 1941-2004
     Obituary **2005**:2
   Hickey, John Benjamin 1963- **2012**:3
   Hoffman, Dustin 1937- **2005**:4
   Hurt, William 1950- **1986**:1
   Hwang, David Henry 1957- **1999**:1
   Irwin, Bill **1988**:3
   Kline, Kevin 1947- **2000**:1
   Langella, Frank 1940- **2008**:3
   Leguizamo, John 1965- **1999**:1
   McDonagh, Martin 1970- **2007**:3
   McDonnell, Mary 1952- **2008**:2
   Merkerson, S. Epatha 1952- **2006**:4
   Miller, Arthur 1915- **1999**:4
   Pacino, Al 1940- **1993**:4
   Parks, Suzan-Lori 1964- **2003**:2
   Schreiber, Liev 1967- **2007**:2
   Sedaris, Amy 1961- **2009**:3
   Shanley, John Patrick 1950- **2006**:1
   Shepard, Sam 1943- **1996**:4
   Streep, Meryl 1949- **1990**:2
   Tune, Tommy 1939- **1994**:2
   Turturro, John 1957- **2002**:2
   Vogel, Paula 1951- **1999**:2
   Washington, Denzel 1954- **1993**:2
   Waterston, Sam 1940- **2006**:1
   White, Julie 1961- **2008**:2
   Woods, James 1947- **1988**:3

Occidental Petroleum Corp.
   Hammer, Armand 1898-1990
     Obituary **1991**:3

Oceanography
   Cousteau, Jacques-Yves 1910-1997
     1998:2
   Cousteau, Jean-Michel 1938- **1988**:2
   Fisher, Mel 1922(?)- **1985**:4

Office of National Drug Control Policy
   Bennett, William 1943- **1990**:1
   Martinez, Bob 1934- **1992**:1

Ogilvy & Mather Advertising
   Lazarus, Shelly 1947- **1998**:3

Ohio State University football team
   Hayes, Woody 1913-1987
     Obituary **1987**:2

Oil
   Adair, Red 1915- **1987**:3
   Aurre, Laura
     Brief entry **1986**:3
   Hammer, Armand 1898-1990
     Obituary **1991**:3
   Jones, Jerry 1942- **1994**:4

Olympic games
   Abbott, Jim 1967- **1988**:3
   Ali, Muhammad 1942- **1997**:2
   Anthony, Carmelo 1984- **2012**:2
   Arakawa, Shizuka 1981- **2006**:4
   Armstrong, Lance 1971- **2000**:1
   Baiul, Oksana 1977- **1995**:3
   Baumgartner, Bruce
     Brief entry **1987**:3
   Benoit, Joan 1957- **1986**:3
   Blair, Bonnie 1964- **1992**:3
   Boitano, Brian 1963- **1988**:3
   Bolt, Usain 1986- **2009**:2
   Bradley, Bill 1943- **2000**:2
   Brutus, Dennis 1924-2009
     Obituary **2011**:4
   Conner, Dennis 1943- **1987**:2
   Daly, Chuck 1930-2009
     Obituary **2010**:3
   Davenport, Lindsay 1976- **1999**:2
   De La Hoya, Oscar 1973- **1998**:2
   DiBello, Paul
     Brief entry **1986**:4
   Dolan, Tom 1975- **2001**:2
   Draves, Victoria Manolo 1924-2010
     Obituary **2012**:3
   Drexler, Clyde 1962- **1992**:4
   Eagleson, Alan 1933- **1987**:4
   Edwards, Harry 1942- **1989**:4
   Evans, Janet 1971- **1989**:1
   Ewing, Patrick 1962- **1985**:3
   Fabris, Enrico 1981- **2006**:4
   Freeman, Cathy 1973- **2001**:3
   Gault, Willie 1960- **1991**:2
   Graf, Steffi 1969- **1987**:4
   Granato, Cammi 1971- **1999**:3
   Grinkov, Sergei 1967-1995
     Obituary **1996**:2
   Guo Jingjing 1981- **2009**:2
   Hamilton, Scott 1958- **1998**:2
   Hamm, Mia 1972- **2000**:1
   Hamm, Paul 1982- **2005**:1
   Holcomb, Steven 1980- **2011**:2
   Holyfield, Evander 1962- **1991**:3
   Hughes, Sarah 1985- **2002**:4
   Johnson, Michael **2000**:1
   Johnson, Shawn 1992- **2009**:2
   Jordan, Michael 1963- **1987**:2
   Joyner, Florence Griffith 1959-1998
     1989:2

Obituary **1999**:1
Joyner-Kersee, Jackie 1962- **1993**:1
Kane, Patrick 1988- **2011**:4
Kerrigan, Nancy 1969- **1994**:3
Kim, Yu-Na 1990- **2011**:2
Kiraly, Karch
  Brief entry **1987**:1
Knight, Bobby 1940- **1985**:3
Laettner, Christian 1969- **1993**:1
LaFontaine, Pat 1965- **1985**:1
Lalas, Alexi 1970- **1995**:1
Leonard, Sugar Ray 1956- **1989**:4
Leslie, Lisa 1972- **1997**:4
Lewis, Lennox 1965- **2000**:2
Lindbergh, Pelle 1959-1985
  Obituary **1985**:4
Lipinski, Tara 1982- **1998**:3
Louganis, Greg 1960- **1995**:3
Lysacek, Evan 1985- **2011**:2
Mathias, Bob 1930-2006
  Obituary **2007**:4
Milbrett, Tiffeny 1972- **2001**:1
Milburn, Rodney Jr. 1950-1997 **1998**:2
Miller, Bode 1977- **2002**:4
Mulkey-Robertson, Kim 1962- **2006**:1
Phelps, Michael 1985- **2009**:2
Retton, Mary Lou 1968- **1985**:2
Rudolph, Wilma 1940-1994
  Obituary **1995**:2
Runyan, Marla 1969- **2001**:1
Samaranch, Juan Antonio 1920- **1986**:2
Scott Moir and Tessa Virtue 1987- **2011**:2
Shea, Jim, Jr. 1968- **2002**:4
Street, Picabo 1971- **1999**:3
Strobl, Fritz 1972- **2003**:3
Strug, Kerri 1977- **1997**:3
Summitt, Pat 1952- **2004**:1
Svindal, Aksel 1982- **2011**:2
Swoopes, Sheryl 1971- **1998**:2
Teter, Hannah 1987- **2006**:4
Thomas, Debi 1967- **1987**:2
Thompson, John 1941- **1988**:3
Tisdale, Wayman 1964-2009
  Obituary **2010**:3
Tomba, Alberto 1966- **1992**:3
Torres, Dara 1967- **2009**:1
Van Dyken, Amy 1973- **1997**:1
Vonn, Lindsey 1984- **2011**:2
Waddell, Thomas F. 1937-1987
  Obituary **1988**:2
Wariner, Jeremy 1984- **2006**:3
Wescott, Seth 1976- **2006**:4
White, Shaun 1986- **2011**:2
Witt, Katarina 1966(?)- **1991**:3
Woodard, Lynette 1959(?)- **1986**:2
Yamaguchi, Kristi 1971- **1992**:3

Ontario provincial government
  Peterson, David 1943- **1987**:1

ON Technology
  Kapor, Mitch 1950- **1990**:3

Opera
  Anderson, Marion 1897-1993
    Obituary **1993**:4
  Bartoli, Cecilia 1966- **1994**:1
  Battle, Kathleen 1948- **1998**:1

Berio, Luciano 1925-2003
  Obituary **2004**:2
Carreras, Jose 1946- **1995**:2
Domingo, Placido 1941- **1993**:2
Fleming, Renee **2001**:4
Grayson, Kathryn 1922-2010
  Obituary **2012**:2
Nilsson, Birgit 1918-2005
  Obituary **2007**:1
Pavarotti, Luciano 1935- **1997**:4
Potts, Paul 1970- **2009**:1
Schwarzkopf, Elisabeth 1915-2006
  Obituary **2007**:3
Siepi, Cesare 1923-2010
  Obituary **2012**:4
Soderstrom, Elisabeth 1927-2009
  Obituary **2011**:3
Upshaw, Dawn 1960- **1991**:2
Zeffirelli, Franco 1923- **1991**:3

Operation Rescue
  Terry, Randall **1991**:4

Orlando Magic basketball team
  Daly, Chuck 1930-2009
    Obituary **2010**:3
  Hardaway, Anfernee 1971- **1996**:2
  Howard, Dwight 1985- **2010**:1

Painting
  Appel, Karel 1921-2006
    Obituary **2007**:2
  Arikha, Avigdor 1929-2010
    Obituary **2012**:3
  Banksy 1975(?)- **2007**:2
  Bean, Alan L. 1932- **1986**:2
  Botero, Fernando 1932- **1994**:3
  Chagall, Marc 1887-1985
    Obituary **1985**:2
  Chatham, Russell 1939- **1990**:1
  Chia, Sandro 1946- **1987**:2
  Colescott, Robert 1925-2009
    Obituary **2010**:3
  Conner, Bruce 1933-2008
    Obituary **2009**:3
  Dali, Salvador 1904-1989
    Obituary **1989**:2
  de Kooning, Willem 1904-1997 **1994**:4
    Obituary **1997**:3
  Diebenkorn, Richard 1922-1993
    Obituary **1993**:4
  Dubuffet, Jean 1901-1985
    Obituary **1985**:4
  Ellis, David 1971- **2009**:4
  Emin, Tracey 1963- **2009**:2
  Frankenthaler, Helen 1928- **1990**:1
  Frazetta, Frank 1928-2010
    Obituary **2012**:4
  Freud, Lucian 1922- **2000**:4
  Graves, Nancy 1940- **1989**:3
  Haring, Keith 1958-1990
    Obituary **1990**:3
  Held, Al 1928-2005
    Obituary **2006**:4
  Hockney, David 1937- **1988**:3
  Kahlo, Frida 1907-1954 **1991**:3
  Katz, Alex 1927- **1990**:3
  Kelly, Ellsworth 1923- **1992**:1
  Kiefer, Anselm 1945- **1990**:2
  Kitaj, R. B. 1932-2007
    Obituary **2008**:4

Kostabi, Mark 1960- **1989**:4
Lichtenstein, Roy 1923-1997 **1994**:1
  Obituary **1998**:1
Longo, Robert 1953(?)- **1990**:4
Mardin, Brice 1938- **2007**:4
Martin, Agnes 1912-2004
  Obituary **2006**:1
Miro, Joan 1893-1983
  Obituary **1985**:1
Motherwell, Robert 1915-1991
  Obituary **1992**:1
Murakami, Takashi 1962- **2004**:2
Nechita, Alexandra 1985- **1996**:4
Neiman, LeRoy 1927- **1993**:3
Noland, Kenneth Clifton 1924-2010
  Obituary **2012**:1
Ono, Yoko 1933- **1989**:2
Peyton, Elizabeth 1965- **2007**:1
Polke, Sigmar 1941- **1999**:4
Pozzi, Lucio 1935- **1990**:2
Pratt, Christopher 1935- **1985**:3
Rauschenberg, Robert 1925- **1991**:2
Rothenberg, Susan 1945- **1995**:3
Schnabel, Julian 1951- **1997**:1
Stella, Frank 1936- **1996**:2
Tamayo, Rufino 1899-1991
  Obituary **1992**:1
Thiebaud, Wayne 1920- **1991**:1
Twombley, Cy 1928(?)- **1995**:1
Von Hellermann, Sophie 1975- **2006**:3
Warhol, Andy 1927(?)-1987
  Obituary **1987**:2
Wegman, William 1942(?)- **1991**:1
Wyeth, Andrew 1917-2009
  Obituary **2010**:1
Wyland, Robert 1956- **2009**:3

Pakistan People's Party
  Bhutto, Benazir 1953- **1989**:4

Paleontology
  Bakker, Robert T. 1950(?)- **1991**:3
  Gould, Stephen Jay 1941-2002
    Obituary **2003**:3
  Horner, Jack 1946- **1985**:2

Palestine Liberation Organization [PLO]
  Abbas, Mahmoud 1935- **2008**:4
  Arafat, Yasser 1929- **1989**:3
  Darwish, Mahmud 1942-2008
    Obituary **2009**:4
  Habash, George 1925(?)- **1986**:1
  Husseini, Faisal 1940- **1998**:4
  Hussein I, King 1935-1999 **1997**:3
    Obituary **1999**:3
  Redgrave, Vanessa 1937- **1989**:2
  Terzi, Zehdi Labib 1924- **1985**:3

Palimony
  Marvin, Lee 1924-1987
    Obituary **1988**:1
  Mitchelson, Marvin 1928- **1989**:2

Palm Computing
  Hawkins, Jeff and Donna Dubinsky **2000**:2

Paralegals
  Furman, Rosemary
    Brief entry **1986**:4

Paramount Pictures
Diller, Barry 1942- **1991**:1
Lansing, Sherry 1944- **1995**:4
Steel, Dawn 1946-1997 **1990**:1
Obituary **1998**:2

Parents' Music Resource Center [PMRC]
Gore, Tipper 1948- **1985**:4
Snider, Dee 1955- **1986**:1

Parents of Murdered Children
Hullinger, Charlotte
Brief entry **1985**:1

Paris Opera Ballet Company
Guillem, Sylvie 1965(?)- **1988**:2

Parkinson's disease
Ali, Muhammad 1942- **1997**:2
Langston, J. William
Brief entry **1986**:2

Parks
Mott, William Penn, Jr. 1909- **1986**:1

Parsons Dance Company
Parsons, David 1959- **1993**:4

Parti Quebecois
Johnson, Pierre Marc 1946- **1985**:4
Leaavesque, Reneaa
Obituary **1988**:1
Parizeau, Jacques 1930- **1995**:1

Paul Taylor Dance Company
Taylor, Paul 1930- **1992**:3

Peabody Awards
Child, Julia 1912- **1999**:4
Duncan, Todd 1903-1998
Obituary **1998**:3
Gross, Terry 1951- **1998**:3
Herbert, Don 1917-2007
Obituary **2008**:3
Keeshan, Bob 1927-2004
Obituary **2005**:2
Kuralt, Charles 1934-1997
Obituary **1998**:3
Melendez, Bill 1916-2008
Obituary **2009**:4
Miller, Arthur 1915- **1999**:4
O'Connor, Donald 1925-2003
Obituary **2004**:4
Osgood, Charles 1933- **1996**:2
Schulz, Charles M. 1922- **1998**:1
Terkel, Studs 1912-2008
Obituary **2010**:1

Peace Corps
Ruppe, Loret Miller 1936- **1986**:2

Pennsylvania State University
Paterno, Joe 1926- **1995**:4

Penthouse International Ltd.
Guccione, Bob 1930- **1986**:1

People Express Airlines
Burr, Donald Calvin 1941- **1985**:3

People for the Ethical Treatment of Animals [PETA]
Mathews, Dan 1965- **1998**:3
McCartney, Linda 1942-1998
Obituary **1998**:4
Newkirk, Ingrid 1949- **1992**:3

People Organized and Working for Economic Rebirth [POWER]
Farrakhan, Louis 1933- **1990**:4

People's Choice Awards
Almodovar, Pedro 1951- **2000**:3
Applegate, Christina 1972- **2000**:4
Burnett, Carol 1933- **2000**:3
Harris, Neil Patrick 1973- **2012**:3
Perry, Katy 1984- **2012**:1
Rihanna 1988- **2008**:4
Somers, Suzanne 1946- **2000**:1
Stewart, Kristen 1990- **2012**:1
Timberlake, Justin 1981- **2008**:4

Pepsico, Inc.
Calloway, D. Wayne 1935- **1987**:3
Chidsey, John 1962- **2010**:4
Nooyi, Indra 1955- **2004**:3
Sculley, John 1939- **1989**:4

Performance art
Beuys, Joseph 1921-1986
Obituary **1986**:3
Bogosian, Eric 1953- **1990**:4
Ellis, David 1971- **2009**:4
Finley, Karen 1956- **1992**:4
Irwin, Bill **1988**:3
Ono, Yoko 1933- **1989**:2
Penn & Teller **1992**:1
Pozzi, Lucio 1935- **1990**:2

Perry Ellis Award
Cameron, David
Brief entry **1988**:1
Chung, Doo-Ri 1973- **2011**:3
Hernandez, Lazaro and Jack McCollough **2008**:4
Kim, Eugenia 1974(?)- **2006**:1
Lam, Derek 1966- **2009**:2
Posen, Zac 1980- **2009**:3
Rowley, Cynthia 1958- **2002**:1
Spade, Kate 1962- **2003**:1
Varvatos, John 1956(?)- **2006**:2

Persian Gulf War
Amanpour, Christiane 1958- **1997**:2
Hussein I, King 1935-1999 **1997**:3
Obituary **1999**:3
Kent, Arthur 1954- **1991**:4
Powell, Colin 1937- **1990**:1
Schwarzkopf, Norman 1934- **1991**:3

Philadelphia Eagles football team
Cunningham, Randall 1963- **1990**:1

Philadelphia 76ers basketball team
Barkley, Charles 1963- **1988**:2
Bol, Manute 1962-2010
Obituary **2012**:4
Chamberlain, Wilt 1936-1999
Obituary **2000**:2
Iverson, Allen 1975- **2001**:4

Philadelphia Flyers hockey team
Hextall, Ron 1964- **1988**:2
Lindbergh, Pelle 1959-1985
Obituary **1985**:4

Philadelphia Phillies baseball team
Dykstra, Lenny 1963- **1993**:4
Hamels, Cole 1983- **2009**:4
Kruk, John 1961- **1994**:4
McGraw, Tug 1944-2004
Obituary **2005**:1
Roberts, Robin 1926-2010
Obituary **2012**:3
Schmidt, Mike 1949- **1988**:3
Utley, Chase 1978- **2010**:4
Williams, Ricky 1977- **2000**:2

Philanthropy
Annenberg, Walter 1908- **1992**:3
Astor, Brooke 1902-2007
Obituary **2008**:4
Bolkiah, Sultan Muda Hassanal 1946- **1985**:4
Duke, Doris 1912-1993
Obituary **1994**:2
Ferrell, Trevor
Brief entry **1985**:2
Gates, Melinda 1964- **2010**:4
Haas, Robert D. 1942- **1986**:4
Hammer, Armand 1898-1990
Obituary **1991**:3
Heinz, H.J. 1908-1987
Obituary **1987**:2
Hero, Peter 1942- **2001**:2
Judkins, Reba
Brief entry **1987**:3
Kaye, Danny 1913-1987
Obituary **1987**:2
Lang, Eugene M. 1919- **1990**:3
Lerner, Sandy 1955(?)- **2005**:1
Marriott, J. Willard 1900-1985
Obituary **1985**:4
Mellon, Paul 1907-1999
Obituary **1999**:3
Menuhin, Yehudi 1916-1999
Obituary **1999**:3
Mortenson, Greg 1957- **2011**:1
Pritzker, A.N. 1896-1986
Obituary **1986**:2
Ross, Percy
Brief entry **1986**:2
Sasakawa, Ryoichi
Brief entry **1988**:1
Stevens, James
Brief entry **1988**:1
Thomas, Danny 1914-1991
Obituary **1991**:3

Philip Morris Companies, Inc.
Maxwell, Hamish 1926- **1989**:4
Wigand, Jeffrey 1943(?)- **2000**:4

Phoenix Suns basketball team
Johnson, Kevin 1966(?)- **1991**:1
Majerle, Dan 1965- **1993**:4
Tisdale, Wayman 1964-2009
Obituary **2010**:3

Photography
al-Ani, Jananne 1966- **2008**:4
Alvarez Bravo, Manuel 1902-2002
Obituary **2004**:1

Avedon, Richard 1923- **1993**:4
Butterfield, Stewart and Caterina
    Fake **2007**:3
Cartier-Bresson, Henri 1908-2004
    Obituary **2005**:4
DeCarava, Roy 1919- **1996**:3
Dith Pran 1942-2008
    Obituary **2009**:2
Doubilet, Anne 1948- **2011**:1
Eisenstaedt, Alfred 1898-1995
    Obituary **1996**:1
Frank, Robert 1924- **1995**:2
Gottlieb, William 1917-2006
    Obituary **2007**:2
Hockney, David 1937- **1988**:3
Karsh, Yousuf 1908-2002
    Obituary **2003**:4
Land, Edwin H. 1909-1991
    Obituary **1991**:3
Leibovitz, Annie 1949- **1988**:4
Levitt, Helen 1913-2009
    Obituary **2010**:2
Mann, Sally 1951- **2001**:2
Mapplethorpe, Robert 1946-1989
    Obituary **1989**:3
Mark, Mary Ellen 1940- **2006**:2
Matadin, Vinoodh and Inez van
    Lamsweerde **2007**:4
McCartney, Linda 1942-1998
    Obituary **1998**:4
McDowall, Roddy 1928-1998
    Obituary **1999**:1
Meisel, Steven 1954- **2002**:4
Misrach, Richard 1949- **1991**:2
Mydans, Carl 1907-2004
    Obituary **2005**:4
Nars, Francois 1959- **2003**:1
Newman, Arnold 1918- **1993**:1
Newton, Helmut 1920- **2002**:1
Parks, Gordon 1912-2006
    Obituary **2006**:2
Penn, Irving 1917-2009
    Obituary **2011**:2
Ritts, Herb 1954(?)- **1992**:4
Ronis, Willy 1910-2009
    Obituary **2011**:1
Rosenthal, Joseph 1911-2006
    Obituary **2007**:4
Salgado, Sebastiao 1944- **1994**:2
Scavullo, Francesco 1921-2004
    Obituary **2005**:1
Sherman, Cindy 1954- **1992**:3
Shulman, Julius 1910-2009
    Obituary **2010**:4
Simmons, Laurie 1949- **2010**:1
Simpson, Lorna 1960- **2008**:1
Testino, Mario 1954- **2002**:1
Tillmans, Wolfgang 1968- **2001**:4
Tunick, Spencer 1967- **2008**:1
Wegman, William 1942(?)- **1991**:1
Witkin, Joel-Peter 1939- **1996**:1

Physical fitness
    Hughes, Mark 1956- **1985**:3
    Jones, Arthur A. 1924(?)- **1985**:3
    Michaels, Jillian 1974- **2011**:4
    Powter, Susan 1957(?)- **1994**:3
    Schwarzenegger, Arnold 1947- **1991**
        :1
    Tanny, Vic 1912(?)-1985
        Obituary **1985**:3
    Wilson, Jerry
        Brief entry **1986**:2

Physics
    Bethe, Hans 1906-2005
        Obituary **2006**:2
    Bohr, Aage 1922-2009
        Obituary **2011**:1
    Chaudhari, Praveen 1937- **1989**:4
    Chu, Paul C.W. 1941- **1988**:2
    Chu, Steven 1948- **2010**:3
    Crewe, Albert 1927-2009
        Obituary **2011**:3
    Davis, Raymond, Jr. 1914-2006
        Obituary **2007**:3
    Fang Lizhi 1937- **1988**:1
    Fano, Ugo 1912-2001
        Obituary **2001**:4
    Ginzburg, Vitaly 1916-2009
        Obituary **2011**:3
    Hau, Lene Vestergaard 1959- **2006**:4
    Hawking, Stephen W. 1942- **1990**:1
    Horowitz, Paul 1942- **1988**:2
    Lederman, Leon Max 1922- **1989**:4
    Maglich, Bogdan C. 1928- **1990**:1
    Maiman, Theodore 1927-2007
        Obituary **2008**:3
    Panofsky, Wolfgang 1919-2007
        Obituary **2008**:4
    Penrose, Roger 1931- **1991**:4
    Randall, Lisa 1962- **2009**:2
    Sakharov, Andrei Dmitrievich
        1921-1989
        Obituary **1990**:2
    Witten, Edward 1951- **2006**:2

PhytoFarms
    Davis, Noel **1990**:3

Pittsburgh, Pa., city government
    Caliguiri, Richard S. 1931-1988
        Obituary **1988**:3

Pittsburgh Penguins hockey team
    Jagr, Jaromir 1972- **1995**:4
    Lemieux, Mario 1965- **1986**:4

Pittsburgh Pirates baseball team
    Leyland, Jim 1944- **1998**:2
    Stargell, Willie 1940-2001
        Obituary **2002**:1

Pittsburgh Steelers football team
    Parker, Willie 1980- **2009**:3
    Rooney, Art 1901-1988
        Obituary **1989**:1
    White, Byron 1917-2002
        Obituary **2003**:3
    Woodson, Ron 1965- **1996**:4

Pixar Animation Studios
    Jobs, Steve 1955- **2000**:1
    Varney, Jim 1949-2000
        Brief entry **1985**:4
        Obituary **2000**:3

Pixillation
    McLaren, Norman 1914-1987
        Obituary **1987**:2

Pizza Kwik, Ltd.
    Paulucci, Jeno
        Brief entry **1986**:3

Pizza Time Theatres, Inc.
    Bushnell, Nolan 1943- **1985**:1

**Planned Parenthood Federation of
America**
    Maraldo, Pamela J. 1948(?)- **1993**:4
    Wattleton, Faye 1943- **1989**:1

Playboy Enterprises
    Hefner, Christie 1952- **1985**:1
    Ingersoll, Ralph II 1946- **1988**:2
    Melman, Richard
        Brief entry **1986**:1

Pleasant Company
    Rowland, Pleasant **1992**:3

Poetry
    Angelou, Maya 1928- **1993**:4
    Bly, Robert 1926- **1992**:4
    Brooks, Gwendolyn 1917-2000 **1998**
        :1
        Obituary **2001**:2
    Brutus, Dennis 1924-2009
        Obituary **2011**:4
    Burroughs, William S. 1914-1997
        Obituary **1997**:4
    Carroll, Jim 1949-2009
        Obituary **2011**:1
    Clifton, Lucille 1936-2010
        Obituary **2012**:2
    Codrescu, Andreaa 1946- **1997**:3
    Collins, Billy 1941- **2002**:2
    Darwish, Mahmud 1942-2008
        Obituary **2009**:4
    Dickey, James 1923-1997 **1998**:2
    Dove, Rita 1952- **1994**:3
    Dylan, Bob 1941- **1998**:1
    Eberhart, Richard 1904-2005
        Obituary **2006**:3
    Ginsberg, Allen 1926-1997
        Obituary **1997**:3
    Gioia, Dana 1950- **2008**:4
    Heaney, Seamus 1939- **1996**:2
    Hughes, Ted 1930-1998
        Obituary **1999**:2
    Jewel 1974- **1999**:2
    Jones, Sarah 1974(?)- **2005**:2
    Karr, Mary 1955- **2011**:2
    Kunitz, Stanley J. 1905- **2001**:2
    Milligan, Spike 1918-2002
        Obituary **2003**:2
    Milosz, Czeslaw 1911-2004
        Obituary **2005**:4
    Mortensen, Viggo 1958- **2003**:3
    Nemerov, Howard 1920-1991
        Obituary **1992**:1
    Paz, Octavio 1914- **1991**:2
    Rodgers, Carolyn M. 1940-2010
        Obituary **2012**:3
    Sapphire 1951(?)- **1996**:4
    Senghor, Leopold 1906-2001
        Obituary **2003**:1
    Tohe, Laura 1953- **2009**:2
    Tretheway, Natasha 1966- **2008**:3
    Van Duyn, Mona 1921- **1993**:2
    Walker, Alice 1944- **1999**:1

Polaroid Corp.
    Land, Edwin H. 1909-1991
        Obituary **1991**:3

Obituary **1988**:4
Hefner, Christie 1952- **1985**:1
Hillegass, Clifton Keith 1918- **1989**:4
Ingersoll, Ralph II 1946- **1988**:2
Kennedy, John F., Jr. 1960-1999 **1990**
:1
  Obituary **1999**:4
Lear, Frances 1923- **1988**:3
Levin, Gerald 1939- **1995**:2
Lewis, Edward T. 1940- **1999**:4
Macmillan, Harold 1894-1986
  Obituary **1987**:2
Maxwell, Robert 1923- **1990**:1
Maxwell, Robert 1923-1991
  Obituary **1992**:2
Morgan, Dodge 1932(?)- **1987**:1
Morgan, Robin 1941- **1991**:1
Murdoch, Rupert 1931- **1988**:4
Neuharth, Allen H. 1924- **1986**:1
Newhouse, Samuel I., Jr. 1927- **1997**
:1
Onassis, Jacqueline Kennedy
  1929-1994
  Obituary **1994**:4
Pope, Generoso 1927-1988 **1988**:4
Pratt, Jane 1963(?)- **1999**:1
Regan, Judith 1953- **2003**:1
Rowland, Pleasant **1992**:3
Steinem, Gloria 1934- **1996**:2
Sullivan, Andrew 1964(?)- **1996**:1
Summers, Anne 1945- **1990**:2
Tilberis, Elizabeth 1947(?)- **1994**:3
Wenner, Jann 1946- **1993**:1
Whittle, Christopher 1947- **1989**:3
Wintour, Anna 1949- **1990**:4
Ziff, William B., Jr. 1930- **1986**:4
Zuckerman, Mortimer 1937- **1986**:3
Zwilich, Ellen 1939- **1990**:1

Pulitzer Prize
Abbott, George 1887-1995
  Obituary **1995**:3
Albee, Edward 1928- **1997**:1
Albert, Stephen 1941- **1986**:1
Angier, Natalie 1958- **2000**:3
Barry, Dave 1947(?)- **1991**:2
Bellow, Saul 1915-2005
  Obituary **2006**:2
Bennett, Michael 1943-1987
  Obituary **1988**:1
Block, Herbert 1909-2001
  Obituary **2002**:4
Breathed, Berkeley 1957- **2005**:3
Brooks, Gwendolyn 1917-2000 **1998**
:1
  Obituary **2001**:2
Buchwald, Art 1925-2007
  Obituary **2008**:2
Caen, Herb 1916-1997
  Obituary **1997**:4
Chabon, Michael 1963- **2002**:1
Coles, Robert 1929(?)- **1995**:1
Copland, Aaron 1900-1990
  Obituary **1991**:2
Cruz, Nilo 1961(?)- **2004**:4
Cunningham, Michael 1952- **2003**:4
Dove, Rita 1952- **1994**:3
Eberhart, Richard 1904-2005
  Obituary **2006**:3
Ebert, Roger 1942- **1998**:3
Faludi, Susan 1959- **1992**:4
Foote, Horton 1916-2009
  Obituary **2010**:2

Geisel, Theodor 1904-1991
  Obituary **1992**:2
Halberstam, David 1934-2007
  Obituary **2008**:3
Haley, Alex 1924-1992
  Obituary **1992**:3
Jones, Edward P. 1950- **2005**:1
Kennan, George 1904-2005
  Obituary **2006**:2
Kirchner, Leon 1919-2009
  Obituary **2011**:1
Kushner, Tony 1956- **1995**:2
Lahiri, Jhumpa 1967- **2001**:3
Lelyveld, Joseph S. 1937- **1994**:4
Lindsay-Abaire, David 1970(?)- **2008**
:2
Logan, Joshua 1908-1988
  Obituary **1988**:4
Mailer, Norman 1923- **1998**:1
Mamet, David 1947- **1998**:4
Marsalis, Wynton 1961- **1997**:4
Mauldin, Bill 1921-2003
  Obituary **2004**:2
McCarthy, Cormac 1933- **2008**:1
McCourt, Frank 1930- **1997**:4
McMurtry, Larry 1936- **2006**:4
Merrill, James 1926-1995
  Obituary **1995**:3
Michener, James A. 1907-1997
  Obituary **1998**:1
Miller, Arthur 1915- **1999**:4
Morrison, Toni 1931- **1998**:1
Nelson, Jack 1929-2009
  Obituary **2011**:2
Nottage, Lynn 1964- **2010**:1
Papp, Joseph 1921-1991
  Obituary **1992**:2
Parks, Suzan-Lori 1964- **2003**:2
Power, Samantha 1970- **2005**:4
Proulx, E. Annie 1935- **1996**:1
Quindlen, Anna 1952- **1993**:1
Robertson, Nan 1926-2009
  Obituary **2011**:2
Rosenthal, Joseph 1911-2006
  Obituary **2007**:4
Roth, Philip 1933- **1999**:1
Royko, Mike 1932-1997
  Obituary **1997**:4
Safire, William 1929- **2000**:3
Shanley, John Patrick 1950- **2006**:1
Shepard, Sam 1943- **1996**:4
Shields, Carol 1935-2003
  Obituary **2004**:3
Smiley, Jane 1949- **1995**:4
Sondheim, Stephen 1930- **1994**:4
Styron, William 1925-2006
  Obituary **2008**:1
Terkel, Studs 1912-2008
  Obituary **2010**:1
Tretheway, Natasha 1966- **2008**:3
Trudeau, Garry 1948- **1991**:2
Tyler, Anne 1941- **1995**:4
Updike, John 1932- **2001**:2
Van Duyn, Mona 1921- **1993**:2
Vogel, Paula 1951- **1999**:2
Walker, Alice 1944- **1999**:1
Wasserstein, Wendy 1950- **1991**:3
Welty, Eudora 1909-2001
  Obituary **2002**:3
Wilkerson, Isabel 1961- **2012**:3
Wilson, August 1945- **2002**:2
Wilson, Edward O. 1929- **1994**:4

Quebec provincial government
Bouchard, Lucien 1938- **1999**:2
Johnson, Pierre Marc 1946- **1985**:4
Leaavesque, Reneaa
  Obituary **1988**:1

Radical Party (Italy)
Staller, Ilona 1951- **1988**:3

Radio One, Inc.
Hughes, Cathy 1947- **1999**:1

Random House publishers
Evans, Joni 1942- **1991**:4

RCA Corp.
Engstrom, Elmer W. 1901-1984
  Obituary **1985**:2

Real estate
Bartlett, Arthur 1933-2009
  Obituary **2011**:4
Bloch, Ivan 1940- **1986**:3
Buss, Jerry 1933- **1989**:3
Campeau, Robert 1923- **1990**:1
Portman, John 1924- **1988**:2
Trump, Donald 1946- **1989**:2

Reebok U.S.A. Ltd., Inc.
Fireman, Paul
  Brief entry **1987**:2

Renaissance Motion Pictures
Raimi, Sam 1959- **1999**:2

RENAMO [Resistanica Nacional Mocambican]
Dhlakama, Afonso 1953- **1993**:3

Renault, Inc.
Besse, Georges 1927-1986
  Obituary **1987**:1
Ghosn, Carlos 1954- **2008**:3

Republican National Committee
Abraham, Spencer 1952- **1991**:4
Atwater, Lee 1951-1991 **1989**:4
  Obituary **1991**:4
Molinari, Susan 1958- **1996**:4
Steele, Michael 1958- **2010**:2

Restaurants
Aoki, Rocky 1940- **1990**:2
Aretsky, Ken 1941- **1988**:1
Beisler, Gary J. 1956- **2010**:3
Bushnell, Nolan 1943- **1985**:1
Copeland, Al 1944(?)- **1988**:3
Ells, Steve 1965- **2010**:1
Fertel, Ruth 1927- **2000**:2
Fieri, Guy 1968- **2010**:3
Kaufman, Elaine **1989**:4
Kerrey, Bob 1943- **1986**:1
Kroc, Ray 1902-1984
  Obituary **1985**:1
Lagasse, Emeril 1959- **1998**:3
Melman, Richard
  Brief entry **1986**:1
Petrossian, Christian

Obituary **1985**:1
Sheffield, Gary 1968- **1998**:1

SANE/FREEZE
Coffin, William Sloane, Jr. 1924- **1990**
:3

San Francisco city government
Alioto, Joseph L. 1916-1998
Obituary **1998**:3
Brown, Willie 1934- **1996**:4

San Francisco 49ers football team
DeBartolo, Edward J., Jr. 1946- **1989**
:3
Montana, Joe 1956- **1989**:2
Rice, Jerry 1962- **1990**:4
Walsh, Bill 1931- **1987**:4
Young, Steve 1961- **1995**:2

San Francisco Giants baseball team
Bonds, Barry 1964- **1993**:3
Dravecky, Dave 1956- **1992**:1

Save the Children Federation
Guyer, David
Brief entry **1988**:1

Schottco Corp.
Schott, Marge 1928- **1985**:4

Schwinn Bicycle Co.
Schwinn, Edward R., Jr.
Brief entry **1985**:4

Science fiction
Anderson, Poul 1926-2001
Obituary **2002**:3
Asimov, Isaac 1920-1992
Obituary **1992**:3
Butler, Octavia E. 1947- **1999**:3
Clarke, Arthur C. 1917-2008
Obituary **2009**:2
Farmer, Philip José 1918-2009
Obituary **2010**:2
Hand, Elizabeth 1957- **2007**:2
Kelley, DeForest 1929-1999
Obituary **2000**:1
Lucas, George 1944- **1999**:4
Norton, Andre 1912-2005
Obituary **2006**:2
Sterling, Bruce 1954- **1995**:4

Sculpture
Appel, Karel 1921-2006
Obituary **2007**:2
Beuys, Joseph 1921-1986
Obituary **1986**:3
Bontecou, Lee 1931- **2004**:4
Borofsky, Jonathan 1942- **2006**:4
Botero, Fernando 1932- **1994**:3
Bourgeois, Louise 1911- **1994**:1
Chia, Sandro 1946- **1987**:2
Chillida, Eduardo 1924-2002
Obituary **2003**:4
Christo 1935- **1992**:3
Conner, Bruce 1933-2008
Obituary **2009**:3
Denevan, Jim 1961- **2012**:4

Dougherty, Patrick 1945- **2012**:2
Dubuffet, Jean 1901-1985
Obituary **1985**:4
Dunham, Carroll 1949- **2003**:4
Ellis, David 1971- **2009**:4
Gober, Robert 1954- **1996**:3
Goldsworthy, Andy 1956- **2007**:2
Graham, Robert 1938- **1993**:4
Graves, Nancy 1940- **1989**:3
Heatherwick, Thomas 1970- **2012**:1
Kaskey, Ray
Brief entry **1987**:2
Kelly, Ellsworth 1923- **1992**:1
Kiefer, Anselm 1945- **1990**:2
Lin, Maya 1960(?)- **1990**:3
Moore, Henry 1898-1986
Obituary **1986**:4
Mueck, Ron 1958- **2008**:3
Murakami, Takashi 1962- **2004**:2
Nevelson, Louise 1900-1988
Obituary **1988**:3
Ono, Yoko 1933- **1989**:2
Paolozzi, Eduardo 1924-2005
Obituary **2006**:3
Puryear, Martin 1941- **2002**:4
Raimondi, John
Brief entry **1987**:4
Rauschenberg, Robert 1925- **1991**:2
Rosenberg, Evelyn 1942- **1988**:2
Serra, Richard 1939- **2009**:1
Tamayo, Rufino 1899-1991
Obituary **1992**:1
Truitt, Anne 1921- **1993**:1

Seagram Co.
Bronfman, Edgar, Jr. 1955- **1994**:4

Sears, Roebuck & Co.
Brennan, Edward A. 1934- **1989**:1

Seattle Mariners baseball team
Griffey, Ken Jr. 1969- **1994**:1
Hernandez, Felix 1986- **2008**:2
Johnson, Randy 1963- **1996**:2
Suzuki, Ichiro 1973- **2002**:2

Seattle Seahawks football team
Bosworth, Brian 1965- **1989**:1

Seattle Supersonics basketball team
Kemp, Shawn 1969- **1995**:1
Wilkens, Lenny 1937- **1995**:2

Second City comedy troupe
Aykroyd, Dan 1952- **1989**:3
Belushi, Jim 1954- **1986**:2
Candy, John 1950-1994 **1988**:2
Obituary **1994**:3
Fey, Tina 1970- **2005**:3
Levy, Eugene 1946- **2004**:3
Radner, Gilda 1946-1989
Obituary **1989**:4
Short, Martin 1950- **1986**:1

Sedelmaier Film Productions
Sedelmaier, Joe 1933- **1985**:3

Seismology
Richter, Charles Francis 1900-1985
Obituary **1985**:4

Senate Armed Services Committee
Cohen, William S. 1940- **1998**:1
Goldwater, Barry 1909-1998
Obituary **1998**:4
McCain, John S. 1936- **1998**:4
Nunn, Sam 1938- **1990**:2
Tower, John 1926-1991
Obituary **1991**:4

Sharper Image, The
Thalheimer, Richard 1948-
Brief entry **1988**:3

Shiites
Berri, Nabih 1939(?)- **1985**:2
Khomeini, Ayatollah Ruhollah
1900(?)-1989
Obituary **1989**:4
Rafsanjani, Ali Akbar Hashemi
1934(?)- **1987**:3

ShoWest Awards
Cuaron, Alfonso 1961- **2008**:2
Driver, Minnie 1971- **2000**:1
LaBeouf, Shia 1986- **2008**:1
Lane, Diane 1965- **2006**:2
Ledger, Heath 1979- **2006**:3
Meyers, Nancy 1949- **2006**:1
Rogen, Seth 1982- **2009**:3
Swank, Hilary 1974- **2000**:3
Yeoh, Michelle 1962- **2003**:2

Shubert Organization
Schoenfeld, Gerald 1924- **1986**:2

Sierra Club
Bass, Rick 1958- **2012**:4
McCloskey, J. Michael 1934- **1988**:2

Sinn Fein
Adams, Gerald 1948- **1994**:1
McGuinness, Martin 1950(?)- **1985**:4

Skiing
DiBello, Paul
Brief entry **1986**:4
Miller, Bode 1977- **2002**:4
Street, Picabo 1971- **1999**:3
Strobl, Fritz 1972- **2003**:3
Svindal, Aksel 1982- **2011**:2
Tomba, Alberto 1966- **1992**:3
Vonn, Lindsey 1984- **2011**:2

Sled dog racing
Butcher, Susan 1954- **1991**:1

Small Business Administration [SBA]
Alvarez, Aida **1999**:2

Smith College
Simmons, Ruth 1945- **1995**:2

Smoking
Horrigan, Edward, Jr. 1929- **1989**:1
Maxwell, Hamish 1926- **1989**:4

Soccer
Adu, Freddy 1989- **2005**:3
Akers, Michelle 1966- **1996**:1
Beckham, David 1975- **2003**:1

Obituary **2011**:4
Robertson, Pat 1930- **1988**:2
Rogers, Adrian 1931- **1987**:4
Swaggart, Jimmy 1935- **1987**:3

Temple University basketball team
Chaney, John 1932- **1989**:1

Tennis
Agassi, Andre 1970- **1990**:2
Ashe, Arthur 1943-1993
  Obituary **1993**:3
Becker, Boris
  Brief entry **1985**:3
Capriati, Jennifer 1976- **1991**:1
Clijsters, Kim 1983- **2006**:3
Courier, Jim 1970- **1993**:2
Davenport, Lindsay 1976- **1999**:2
Djokovic, Novak 1987- **2008**:4
Federer, Roger 1981- **2004**:2
Gerulaitis, Vitas 1954-1994
  Obituary **1995**:1
Gibson, Althea 1927-2003
  Obituary **2004**:4
Graf, Steffi 1969- **1987**:4
Henin-Hardenne, Justine 1982- **2004**:4
Hewitt, Lleyton 1981- **2002**:2
Hingis, Martina 1980- **1999**:1
Ivanisevic, Goran 1971- **2002**:1
Kournikova, Anna 1981- **2000**:3
Kramer, Jack 1921-2009
  Obituary **2011**:1
Mauresmo, Amelie 1979- **2007**:2
Navratilova, Martina 1956- **1989**:1
Pierce, Mary 1975- **1994**:4
Querrey, Sam 1987- **2010**:3
Riggs, Bobby 1918-1995
  Obituary **1996**:2
Roddick, Andy 1982- **2004**:3
Sabatini, Gabriela
  Brief entry **1985**:4
Safin, Marat 1980- **2001**:3
Sampras, Pete 1971- **1994**:1
Seles, Monica 1974(?)- **1991**:3
Sharapova, Maria 1987- **2005**:2
Williams, Serena 1981- **1999**:4
Williams, Venus 1980- **1998**:2
Wozniacki, Caroline 1990- **2012**:2

Test tube babies
Steptoe, Patrick 1913-1988
  Obituary **1988**:3

Texas Rangers baseball team
Rodriguez, Alex 1975- **2001**:2
Ryan, Nolan 1947- **1989**:4

Texas State Government
Bush, George W., Jr. 1946- **1996**:4
Richards, Ann 1933- **1991**:2

Therapeutic Recreation Systems
Radocy, Robert
  Brief entry **1986**:3

Timberline Reclamations
McIntyre, Richard
  Brief entry **1986**:2

Time Warner Inc.
Ho, David 1952- **1997**:2
Levin, Gerald 1939- **1995**:2
Ross, Steven J. 1927-1992
  Obituary **1993**:3

TLC Beatrice International
Lewis, Loida Nicolas 1942- **1998**:3

TLC Group L.P.
Lewis, Reginald F. 1942-1993 **1988**:4
  Obituary **1993**:3

Today Show
Couric, Katherine 1957- **1991**:4
Gumbel, Bryant 1948- **1990**:2
Norville, Deborah 1958- **1990**:3

Tony Awards
Abbott, George 1887-1995
  Obituary **1995**:3
Alda, Robert 1914-1986
  Obituary **1986**:3
Alexander, Jane 1939- **1994**:2
Alexander, Jason 1962(?)- **1993**:3
Allen, Debbie 1950- **1998**:2
Allen, Joan 1956- **1998**:1
Arkin, Alan 1934- **2007**:4
Arthur, Bea 1922-2009
  Obituary **2010**:2
Bacall, Lauren 1924- **1997**:3
Bailey, Pearl 1918-1990
  Obituary **1991**:1
Bancroft, Anne 1931-2005
  Obituary **2006**:3
Bates, Alan 1934-2003
  Obituary **2005**:1
Bennett, Michael 1943-1987
  Obituary **1988**:1
Bloch, Ivan 1940- **1986**:3
Booth, Shirley 1898-1992
  Obituary **1993**:2
Brooks, Mel 1926- **2003**:1
Brown, Ruth 1928-2006
  Obituary **2008**:1
Brynner, Yul 1920(?)-1985
  Obituary **1985**:4
Buckley, Betty 1947- **1996**:2
Burnett, Carol 1933- **2000**:3
Butz, Norbert Leo 1967- **2012**:3
Carter, Nell 1948-2003
  Obituary **2004**:2
Channing, Stockard 1946- **1991**:3
Chenoweth, Kristin 1968- **2010**:4
Close, Glenn 1947- **1988**:3
Crawford, Cheryl 1902-1986
  Obituary **1987**:1
Crawford, Michael 1942- **1994**:2
Cronyn, Hume 1911-2003
  Obituary **2004**:3
Davis, Viola 1965- **2011**:4
Dench, Judi 1934- **1999**:4
Dennis, Sandy 1937-1992
  Obituary **1992**:4
Dewhurst, Colleen 1924-1991
  Obituary **1992**:2
Dunagan, Deanna 1940- **2009**:2
Ebersole, Christine 1953- **2007**:2
Fagan, Garth 1940- **2000**:1
Ferrer, Jose 1912-1992
  Obituary **1992**:3
Fiennes, Ralph 1962- **1996**:2
Fierstein, Harvey 1954- **2004**:2
Finneran, Katie 1971- **2012**:1
Fishburne, Laurence 1961(?)- **1995**:3
Flanders, Ed 1934-1995
  Obituary **1995**:3
Fosse, Bob 1927-1987

Obituary **1988**:1
Foster, Sutton 1975- **2003**:2
Gelbart, Larry 1928-2009
  Obituary **2011**:1
Gleason, Jackie 1916-1987
  Obituary **1987**:4
Glover, Savion 1973- **1997**:1
Goulet, Robert 1933-2007
  Obituary **2008**:4
Hagen, Uta 1919-2004
  Obituary **2005**:2
Harrison, Rex 1908-1990
  Obituary **1990**:4
Headley, Heather 1974- **2011**:1
Hepburn, Katharine 1909- **1991**:2
Hickey, John Benjamin 1963- **2012**:3
Hines, Gregory 1946- **1992**:4
Hodge, Douglas 1960- **2012**:4
Hoffman, Dustin 1937- **2005**:4
Howard, Ken 1944- **2010**:4
Hwang, David Henry 1957- **1999**:1
Irons, Jeremy 1948- **1991**:4
Jackman, Hugh 1968- **2004**:4
James, Nikki M. 1981- **2012**:3
Kahn, Madeline 1942-1999
  Obituary **2000**:2
Keaton, Diane 1946- **1997**:1
Kline, Kevin 1947- **2000**:1
Kushner, Tony 1956- **1995**:2
Lane, Nathan 1956- **1996**:4
Langella, Frank 1940- **2008**:3
Lansbury, Angela 1925- **1993**:1
LaPaglia, Anthony 1959- **2004**:2
Lithgow, John 1945- **1985**:2
LuPone, Patti 1949- **2009**:2
Mantegna, Joe 1947- **1992**:1
Matthau, Walter 1920- **2000**:3
McKellen, Ian 1939- **1994**:1
Merrick, David 1912-2000
  Obituary **2000**:4
Midler, Bette 1945- **1989**:4
Miller, Arthur 1915- **1999**:4
Moore, Dudley 1935-2002
  Obituary **2003**:2
Nichols, Mike 1931- **1994**:4
Nunn, Trevor 1940- **2000**:2
Orbach, Jerry 1935-2004
  Obituary **2006**:1
Pacino, Al 1940- **1993**:4
Papp, Joseph 1921-1991
  Obituary **1992**:2
Parker, Mary-Louise 1964- **2002**:2
Peters, Bernadette 1948- **2000**:1
Preston, Robert 1918-1987
  Obituary **1987**:3
Prince, Faith 1959(?)- **1993**:2
Reilly, Charles Nelson
  Obituary **2008**:3
Reza, Yasmina 1959(?)- **1999**:2
Richards, Lloyd 1919-2006
  Obituary **2007**:3
Richardson, Natasha 1963-2009
  Obituary **2010**:2
Robbins, Jerome 1918-1998
  Obituary **1999**:1
Ruehl, Mercedes 1948(?)- **1992**:4
Rylance, Mark 1960- **2009**:3
Salonga, Lea 1971- **2003**:3
Schreiber, Liev 1967- **2007**:2

Cumulative Newsmakers Index

This index lists all newsmakers included in the entire *Newsmakers* series.

Listee names are followed by a year and issue number; thus **1996**:3 indicates that an entry on that individual appears in both 1996, Issue 3, and the 1996 cumulation.

McEwan, Ian 1948- **2004**:2
McFadden, Cynthia 1956- **2012**:2
McFarlane, Todd 1961- **1999**:1
McFerrin, Bobby 1950- **1989**:1
McGahern, John 1934-2006
  Obituary **2007**:2
McGillis, Kelly 1957- **1989**:3
McGinley, Ryan 1977- **2009**:1
McGinley, Ted 1958- **2004**:4
McGoohan, Patrick 1928-2009
  Obituary **2010**:1
McGowan, William 1927- **1985**:2
McGowan, William G. 1927-1992
  Obituary **1993**:1
McGrath, Judy 1953- **2006**:1
McGraw, Phil 1950- **2005**:2
McGraw, Tim 1966- **2000**:3
McGraw, Tug 1944-2004
  Obituary **2005**:1
McGreevey, James 1957- **2005**:2
McGregor, Ewan 1971(?)- **1998**:2
McGruder, Aaron 1974- **2005**:4
McGuigan, Paul
  See Oasis
McGuinness, Martin 1950(?)- **1985**:4
McGuire, Dorothy 1918-2001
  Obituary **2002**:4
McGwire, Mark 1963- **1999**:1
McHale, Joel 1971- **2010**:4
McIlroy, Rory 1989- **2012**:3
McIntyre, Joseph
  See New Kids on the Block
McIntyre, Richard
  Brief entry **1986**:2
McKee, Lonette 1952(?)- **1996**:1
McKellen, Ian 1939- **1994**:1
McKenna, Terence **1993**:3
McKinnell, Henry 1943(?)- **2002**:3
McKinney, Cynthia A. 1955- **1997**:1
McKinney, Stewart B. 1931-1987
  Obituary **1987**:4
McLachlan, Sarah 1968- **1998**:4
McLaren, Malcolm 1946-2010
  Obituary **2012**:3
McLaren, Norman 1914-1987
  Obituary **1987**:2
McLaughlin, Audrey 1936- **1990**:3
McLaughlin, Betsy 1962(?)- **2004**:3
McMahon, Ed 1923-2009
  Obituary **2010**:3
McMahon, James Robert
  See McMahon, Jim
McMahon, Jim 1959- **1985**:4
McMahon, Julian 1968- **2006**:1
McMahon, Vince, Jr. 1945(?)- **1985**:4
McManus, Declan
  See Costello, Elvis
McMillan, Terry 1951- **1993**:2
McMillen, Tom 1952- **1988**:4
McMurtry, James 1962- **1990**:2
McMurtry, Larry 1936- **2006**:4
McNamara, Robert S. 1916- **1995**:4
McNealy, Scott 1954- **2009**:3
McNerney, W. James 1949- **2006**:3
McQueen, Alexander 1969-2010
  Obituary **2012**:2
McRae, Carmen 1920(?)-1994
  Obituary **1995**:2
McSally, Martha 1966(?)- **2002**:4
McTaggart, David 1932(?)- **1989**:4
McVeigh, Timothy 1968-2001
  Obituary **2002**:2

Meadows, Audrey 1925-1996
  Obituary **1996**:3
Medvedev, Dmitry 1965- **2009**:4
Megawati Sukarnoputri 1947- **2000**:1
Mehta, Zubin 1938(?)- **1994**:3
Meier, Richard 1934- **2001**:4
Meisel, Steven 1954- **2002**:4
Melendez, Bill 1916-2008
  Obituary **2009**:4
Mellinger, Frederick 1924(?)-1990
  Obituary **1990**:4
Mello, Dawn 1938(?)- **1992**:2
Mellon, Paul 1907-1999
  Obituary **1999**:3
Melman, Richard
  Brief entry **1986**:1
Melnick, Daniel 1932-2009
  Obituary **2011**:2
Melton, Douglas 1954- **2008**:3
Meltzer, Brad 1970- **2005**:4
Menchu, Rigoberta 1960(?)- **1993**:2
Mendoza, Lydia 1916-2007
  Obituary **2009**:1
Meneghel, Maria da Graca
  See Xuxa
Mengele, Josef 1911-1979
  Obituary **1985**:2
Mengers, Sue 1938- **1985**:3
Menninger, Karl 1893-1990
  Obituary **1991**:1
Menuhin, Yehudi 1916-1999
  Obituary **1999**:3
Merchant, Ismail 1936-2005
  Obituary **2006**:3
Merchant, Natalie 1963- **1996**:3
Mercier, Laura 1959(?)- **2002**:2
Mercury, Freddie 1946-1991
  Obituary **1992**:2
Meredith, Burgess 1909-1997
  Obituary **1998**:1
Merkel, Angela 1954- **2010**:2
Merkerson, S. Epatha 1952- **2006**:4
Merrick, David 1912-2000
  Obituary **2000**:4
Merrill, James 1926-1995
  Obituary **1995**:3
Merritt, Justine
  Brief entry **1985**:3
Mesic, Stipe 1934- **2005**:4
Messick, Dale 1906-2005
  Obituary **2006**:2
Messier, Mark 1961- **1993**:1
Messing, Debra 1968- **2004**:4
Metallica **2004**:2
Meyer, Stephenie 1973- **2009**:1
Meyers, Nancy 1949- **2006**:1
Mfume, Kweisi 1948- **1996**:3
Michael, George 1963- **1989**:2
Michaels, Bret 1963- **2011**:4
Michaels, Jillian 1974- **2011**:4
Michelangeli, Arturo Benedetti 1920- **1988**:2
Michelman, Kate 1942- **1998**:4
Michener, James A. 1907-1997
  Obituary **1998**:1
Mickelson, Phil 1970- **2004**:4
Midler, Bette 1945- **1989**:4
Mikan, George 1924-2005
  Obituary **2006**:3
Mikulski, Barbara 1936- **1992**:4
Milano, Alyssa 1972- **2002**:3
Milbrett, Tiffeny 1972- **2001**:1

Milburn, Rodney Jr. 1950-1997 ...... **1998**:2
Millan, Cesar 1969- **2007**:4
Milland, Ray 1908(?)-1986
  Obituary **1986**:2
Millard, Barbara J.
  Brief entry **1985**:3
Millepied, Benjamin 1977(?)- **2006**:4
Miller, Andre 1976- **2003**:3
Miller, Ann 1923-2004
  Obituary **2005**:2
Miller, Arthur 1915- **1999**:4
Miller, Bebe 1950- **2000**:2
Miller, Bode 1977- **2002**:4
Miller, Dennis 1953- **1992**:4
Miller, Frank 1957- **2008**:2
Miller, Merton H. 1923-2000
  Obituary **2001**:1
Miller, Nicole 1951(?)- **1995**:4
Miller, Percy
  See Master P
Miller, Rand 1959(?)- **1995**:4
Miller, Reggie 1965- **1994**:4
Miller, Robyn 1966?)-
  See Miller, Rand
Miller, Roger 1936-1992
  Obituary **1993**:2
Miller, Sue 1943- **1999**:3
Milligan, Spike 1918-2002
  Obituary **2003**:2
Mills, Malia 1966- **2003**:1
Mills, Wilbur 1909-1992
  Obituary **1992**:4
Milne, Christopher Robin 1920-1996
  Obituary **1996**:4
Milosevic, Slobodan 1941- **1993**:2
Milosz, Czeslaw 1911-2004
  Obituary **2005**:4
Milstead, Harris Glenn
  See Divine
Mina, Denise 1966- **2006**:1
Mindell, Jodi 1962- **2010**:4
Minghella, Anthony 1954- **2004**:3
Minkoff, Rebecca 1981- **2011**:3
Minner, Ruth Ann 1935- **2002**:2
Minnesota Fats 1900(?)-1996
  Obituary **1996**:3
Minogue, Kylie 1968- **2003**:4
Minsky, Marvin 1927- **1994**:3
Mintz, Shlomo 1957- **1986**:2
Miro, Joan 1893-1983
  Obituary **1985**:1
Mirren, Helen 1945- **2005**:1
Misrach, Richard 1949- **1991**:2
Mitarai, Fujio 1935- **2002**:4
Mitchard, Jacquelyn 1956- **2010**:4
Mitchell, Arthur 1934- **1995**:1
Mitchell, Elizabeth 1970- **2011**:4
Mitchell, George J. 1933- **1989**:3
Mitchell, John 1913-1988
  Obituary **1989**:2
Mitchell, Joni 1943- **1991**:4
Mitchell, Joseph 1909-1996
  Obituary **1997**:1
Mitchelson, Marvin 1928- **1989**:2
Mitchum, Robert 1917-1997
  Obituary **1997**:4
Mitnick, Kevin 1965- **2012**:4
Mittal, Lakshmi 1950- **2007**:2
Mitterrand, Francois 1916-1996
  Obituary **1996**:2
Mixon, Oscar G.
  See Walker, Junior